PIMLICO

842

ENLIGHTENING

Isaiah Berlin was born in Riga, now capital of Latvia, in 1909. When he was six, his family moved to Russia, and in 1917, in Petrograd, Berlin witnessed both Revolutions – Social Democratic and Bolshevik. In 1921 the family emigrated to England, and Berlin was educated at St Paul's School and Corpus Christi College, Oxford. Apart from his war service in New York, Washington and Moscow, he remained at Oxford thereafter – as a Fellow of All Souls, a Fellow of New College, Professor of Social and Political Theory and founding President of Wolfson College. He also held the Presidency of the British Academy. His published work includes *Karl Marx*, *Russian Thinkers*, *Concepts and Categories*, *Against the Current*, *Personal Impressions*, *The Crooked Timber of Humanity*, *The Sense of Reality*, *The Proper Study of Mankind*, *The Roots of Romanticism*, *The Power of Ideas*, *Three Critics of the Enlightenment*, *Freedom and Its Betrayal*, *Liberty*, *The Soviet Mind* and *Political Ideas in the Romantic Age*. As an exponent of the history of ideas he was awarded the Erasmus, Lippincott and Agnelli Prizes; he also received the Jerusalem Prize for his lifelong defence of civil liberties. He died in 1997.

Henry Hardy, a Fellow of Wolfson College, Oxford, is one of Isaiah Berlin's Literary Trustees. He has edited a number of other books by Berlin – including this volume's predecessor, *Flourishing: Letters 1928–1946* – and other authors, and is also the editor of *The Book of Isaiah: Personal Impressions of Isaiah Berlin* (2009).

Jennifer Holmes, a graduate of St Anne's College, Oxford, is a researcher and genealogist. She was a major contributor to the editorial apparatus in *Flourishing*, and with Henry Hardy co-edited Maurice Bowra's satirical poems on his contemporaries, *New Bats in Old Belfries* (2005).

For more information about Isaiah Berlin visit
http://berlin.wolf.ox.ac.uk/

Also by Isaiah Berlin

Karl Marx
The Hedgehog and the Fox
The Age of Enlightenment
The First and the Last

Edited by Henry Hardy and Aileen Kelly
Russian Thinkers

Edited by Henry Hardy
Concepts and Categories
Against the Current
Personal Impressions
The Crooked Timber of Humanity
The Sense of Reality
The Roots of Romanticism
The Power of Ideas
Three Critics of the Enlightenment
Freedom and Its Betrayal
Liberty
The Soviet Mind
Political Ideas in the Romantic Age

Uniform with this volume
Flourishing: Letters 1928–1946

Edited by Henry Hardy and Roger Hausheer
The Proper Study of Mankind

With Beata Polanowska-Sygulska
Unfinished Dialogue

ENLIGHTENING

Letters 1946–1960

ISAIAH BERLIN

Edited by Henry Hardy and Jennifer Holmes
with the assistance of Serena Moore

Additional research · Brigid Allen, James Chappel,
Jason Ferrell, Steffen Groß, Eleonora Paganini
Archival research · Michael Hughes
Transcription · Betty Colquhoun, Esther Johnson

Leastwise, if a man does anything all through life with a deal of
bother, and likewise of some benefit to others, the details of
such bother and benefit may as well be known accurately as the
contrary.

> Edward Lear, letter of *c.*1866 to Chichester Fortescue
> (Lord Carlingford), in Lear's *Nonsense Songs and Stories*,
> 6th ed. (London and New York, 1888), 5

If finance permits they should be given real competent hacks –
industrious and methodical ladies if possible – who could act as
research assistants, card indexers etc., to whom no hope of
necessary promotion need be held out.

> IB to Walter Eytan, April 1951

PIMLICO

Published by Pimlico 2011

2 4 6 8 10 9 7 5 3 1

First published in Great Britain in 2009 by Chatto & Windus

Pimlico
Random House, 20 Vauxhall Bridge Road,
London SW1V 2SA

www.rbooks.co.uk

Addresses for companies within The Random House Group Limited can be found at:
www.randomhouse.co.uk/offices.htm

The Random House Group Limited Reg. No. 954009

A CIP catalogue record for this book
is available from the British Library

ISBN 9781844138340

The Random House Group Limited supports The Forest Stewardship Council (FSC),
the leading international forest certification organisation. All our titles that are printed on
Greenpeace approved FSC certified paper carry the FSC logo. Our paper procurement policy
can be found at www.rbooks.co.uk/environment

Mixed Sources
Product group from well-managed
forests and other controlled sources
www.fsc.org Cert no. TT-COC-2139
© 1996 Forest Stewardship Council
FSC

Designed in the Department of Typography & Graphic Communication, University of Reading
Typeset by Deltatype Ltd, Birkenhead, Merseyside

Printed and bound in Great Britain by
Clays Ltd, St Ives PLC

For Aline Berlin

The values of the Enlightenment, what people like Voltaire, Helvétius, Holbach, Condorcet preached, are deeply sympathetic to me. Maybe they were too narrow, and often wrong about the facts of human experience, but these people were great liberators. They liberated people from horrors, obscurantism, fanaticism, monstrous views. They were against cruelty, they were against oppression, they fought the good fight against superstition and ignorance and against a great many things which ruined people's lives. So I am on their side.[1]

1 Isaiah *Berlin (hereafter IB), CIB 70 (for conventions and abbreviations see xxiii–xxvii). Cf. the conclusion of IB's introduction to *The Age of Enlightenment* (New York, 1956): 'The intellectual power, honesty, lucidity, courage and disinterested love of the truth of the most gifted thinkers of the eighteenth century remain to this day without parallel. Their age is one of the best and most hopeful episodes in the life of mankind.' POI 52.

CONTENTS

ILLUSTRATIONS

The subject is IB where not otherwise stated

CREDITS

Images from the Isaiah Berlin Papers, Oxford, Bodleian Library, © The Isaiah Berlin
Literary Trust 2009, are referenced by shelfmark and folio, thus: MSB 123/456 (i.e.
MS. Berlin 123, fo. 456). Otherwise credits name as many as are known to the editors
of the following: photographer/photographer's employer/collection/agent or
owner. Inconsistencies in the style and/or positioning of credits are due to requirements imposed by copyright owners.

Illustrations in the text (listed by page)

Plates (listed by Plate No)

PREFACE

He adores the complications of life and likes things to be as difficult as possible.[1]

AT THE END of the first volume of his letters, in April 1946, Isaiah Berlin was about to sail back to England from the United States, where he had spent most of the war. As this second volume opens he returns to life as an Oxford don, resuming the academic career that the war had interrupted.

Although his period of war service in the United States had not been free from worry about his parents in England, and guilt about escaping from physical danger, Berlin's living conditions there were comfortable. Post-war Britain was not. The country was on the verge of bankruptcy, widespread rationing was in force, mass starvation was a real possibility, and even the weather became more than usually hostile. Oxford University was soon bursting with students anxious to catch up on their deferred education, and their needs could be met only by a production-line approach very far from the leisurely pre-war style of teaching. For Berlin this was particularly frustrating, as it meant he had to defer his move from philosophy to the subject which had become his real passion – the history of ideas.

The early letters of this volume chart an uneasy combination of unremitting teaching in Oxford (mainly for New College) and a full social life both in London and in the country houses of friends and acquaintances. His ebullient, life-enhancing company was sought from all directions, and his wry observation of social quirks and quiddities is plentifully displayed in his letters. Out of term, Berlin visited Palestine at a crucial time as it moved towards independence, and played a minor but important role in setting up the Marshall Plan scheme that rescued the economies of Europe. His six-month visit to Harvard in 1949, the first of several, was intellectually rewarding, but on his return to Britain he faced criticism from all sides for the articles his visit had inspired. This made the beginning of the new decade a low point of severe self-doubt, but it was also a turning-point. His return to All Souls in 1950 as a Research Fellow in the history of ideas opened the flood-gates, and the letters record his rapid rise to the status of an intellectual celebrity featured in gossip columns and glossy magazines. His next trip to America – to Harvard and Bryn Mawr – led to the series of radio broadcasts of late 1952 which brought him national fame. He stood for the Wardenship of All Souls in 1951, but withdrew before the final vote; he was offered, but after much agonising declined, the Wardenship of Nuffield College in 1953.

1 Maurice Bowra to Alice James, 9 September 1954 [Wadham College Archives, Oxford].

His love for and knowledge of opera brought him Directorships of the Royal Opera House and Sadler's Wells. His Professorship followed in 1957, as did a knighthood (accepted reluctantly and soon regretted).

Berlin published widely: a translation of Turgenev's *First Love* in 1950, *The Hedgehog and the Fox* in 1953, *Historical Inevitability* in 1954, *The Age of Enlightenment* in 1956, and *Two Concepts of Liberty* in 1958, together with 'A Marvellous Decade' in 1955–6 and numerous other significant articles and reviews. The letters chart the often tortuous progress of Berlin's writings to publication and his mixed reactions to the acclaim (and criticism) he received.

But these public aspects of Berlin's life are only part of the story. The 1950s were for him years of emotional turmoil, and his sexual coming of age. His father's death in 1953 hit him hard and precipitated his pursuit of the unhappily married Aline Halban, who became his wife in 1956. At that point his life changed overnight from that of a bachelor don living in College to that of a married man with his own home, and three stepsons. This sea-change was certainly one of the main contributors to the growing maturity of the later letters in this volume.

The range of Berlin's correspondents in this period is even wider than in the first volume, as is the variety of subject-matter. There is a marked increase in intellectual content as the years pass, and many letters provide explanation or amplification of his published work. Others offer acute and often acid commentary on books, music, places and, above all, people. Berlin's travels in Europe and the United States, his visits to Palestine/Israel, and his trip to the Soviet Union with his new wife in 1956 showed him the changing post-war world far beyond the confines of Oxford, and the letters record his impressions. His contacts within the political establishments of several countries give an inside view of the personalities at the heart of major political events – the creation of the State of Israel, the Suez Crisis, the Cold War. In short, his letters provide a well-informed and idiosyncratically perceptive view of the era in which they were written, as well as a window on his own intellectual development.

THE EDITORIAL CHALLENGE

> Forgive me if I do not write a proper letter in answer to your splendid, spontaneous, disinterested, excellent, enjoyable, admirable one (the list of adjectives is like a parody of my own unfortunate style – there was a parody of my book in *Punch* recently – not very good but still, I suppose, taught me something – the sentences never ended at all, and that is the first basis of any parody of me).[1]

There is a marked stylistic development in Berlin's letters as he matures.

---

1 To Morton White, 15 March 1954.

Irony begins to oust the juvenile sparkle of the earlier period. Later in this volume, too, there are some remarkable sustained set pieces untypical of his earlier style. But certain characteristics – convoluted sentences and a profusion of adjectives – remain unchanged. One significant development is his discovery in 1949 of the Dictaphone; from then on, the majority of his letters are dictated and increasingly take on the somewhat loose and baggy characteristics of his conversation. Concision did not come naturally to him, and many of his letters are of extraordinary length, covering a broad range of subjects, mingling gossip and intellectual analysis. It has been part of the editorial task to preserve this characteristic flavour as far as possible within the unavoidable process of selection.

Selection

> [I]t seems to me (as it always does to authors in their delusion) that it is all indispensable and cannot be eliminated without grave loss to the sense.[1]

> I am sure that we all have far more to gain than to lose by the publication of even indiscreet documents, which always emerge one day and then do more harm than if they were published openly, candidly and quickly.[2]

The vast number of surviving post-war letters, and their length, have led us to be far more selective for this volume than for its predecessor (and further volumes will need to follow the same pattern).[3] This is regrettable in one way, but offers the compensatory advantage that we have been forced to concentrate on the most interesting material. The first volume contained most of the available letters until March 1946, but the amount of material amassed for the period covered here would fill four or five volumes of the same length. Reluctantly, we have abandoned the policy followed in the first volume of printing letters in their entirety, as the resulting cost in letters omitted would have been too great: many letters have instead been pruned to retain what seem to us their most interesting or important features.

Some of the excisions were straightforward: Berlin's complex travel arrangements, endlessly made, remade, and often abandoned, are of little continuing importance, and most of the purely domestic communications with his parents have been omitted. On the many occasions when the same information was provided, or opinion expressed, to several people, we have normally reduced the duplication by choosing the fullest or most entertaining version. Nevertheless the final choice of letters or parts of letters has

---

1 To Hamilton Fish Armstrong, c.21 November 1951.
2 To Boris Guriel, 1 January 1957.
3 Nevertheless, we welcome information about, copies of, or the opportunity to make copies from, letters not yet known to us. Please write to Henry Hardy at Wolfson College, OXFORD, OX2 6UD, UK, or *henry.hardy@wolfson.ox.ac.uk*.

been far from easy. We have aimed for a fair representation of the range of Berlin's correspondence, while not disguising the fact that certain pre-occupations, such as his own perceived lack of achievement, recur (though selection exaggerates the proportion of introspection). Portraying Berlin in a good (or bad) light has not influenced us; we have been guided purely by the intrinsic interest of the material. In the (relatively few) cases where we initially differed in our choice, discussion has led to agreement, compromise or surrender. What interests one person may be less absorbing to another, but we hope that the combination of Henry Hardy's enthusiasm for Berlin's ideas and Jennifer Holmes's interest in the letters as social and political history has produced a selection with wide appeal.[1]

Omissions, then, are almost all on the grounds of interest, with two exceptions. Very occasionally a letter or passage has been omitted out of consideration for the living. More important is the omission (as their recipient wished) of the large number of letters Berlin wrote to his wife Aline, mostly during 1954 and 1955, before their marriage. These show a passionate side of his nature not often on display elsewhere. We are grateful to Lady Berlin for allowing us to quote a few of their less personal passages in our editorial commentary and notes.

In a few cases items not included in the book have been posted in the Isaiah Berlin Virtual Library (the website of the Isaiah Berlin Literary Trust, hereafter 'IBVL'): URLs are provided in the relevant notes. It is hoped to add considerably to the material available online in due course, so that the website will supplement the published volumes substantially.

As before, letters received by Berlin normally feature only in brief quotations, if at all. However, at the suggestion of Valerie Eliot, we have included both sides of a crucial correspondence between Berlin and T. S. Eliot about the latter's alleged anti-Semitism.

---

1 *Note by HH*: Jennifer joined the team during the preparation of the previous volume, and I recounted in my preface there how crucial her contribution became. It is even more central to this volume, which is in many ways more hers than mine: readers should not be misled by my merely alphabetical precedence on the title page. Although I had already gathered the bulk of the raw material, we made the selection jointly, and Jennifer undertook almost all the research for the connective tissue, notes, chronology and biographical glossary, all of which she drafted. This kind of research requires exceptional reserves of persistence, as well as knowledge of where to look; and the drafting needs firm judgement about what to include, and considerable care in wording. In the continuous struggle to keep the volume within bounds, her common sense, realism and decisiveness have repeatedly reined in my self-indulgence and reluctance to cut. She has withstood my often pedantic and I dare say superfluous observations on her draft material, talked me out of some of my more obsessive editorial traits, and stamped on lapses of taste and judgement. I am incalculably in her debt; without her the volume would not have been completed when it was, or to the same standard, or perhaps at all.

Dating the letters

> [M]y sense of time is weak.[1]

Dating the letters has not been straightforward. Berlin was notably inexact about chronology. Many letters are undated or have incomplete dates; some dates are an inconsistent combination of day of the week and date (letters written, as so many of Berlin's were, in the early hours of the morning are particularly frequent offenders); a reference to 'last week' may mean several weeks earlier, while 'tomorrow' or even 'in half an hour' may mean days later. From 1949 another complication emerges: because of Berlin's increasing reliance on dictation into a machine, the date on typed letters may be the date of dictation, the date of typing, or (apparently the most common) the date of expected signature. When abroad he sent Dictabelts back to Oxford for typing, and his secretary would type them on previously signed blank sheets of paper. Precise dating of many letters (no matter what date they bear) is therefore a chimera, and this uncertainty makes it even more difficult to establish the dates of the past or future events referred to in the letters. We have done our best.

Reading Berlin's mind

> He notices several sentences [...] have been reduced to illiteracy by punctuation, quasi misprints for which his own handwriting may well be responsible, but which more careful sub-editing would perhaps have prevented.[2]

The top copies of many typed letters are a sometimes barely legible mixture of typescript and manuscript, since Berlin tended to add further thoughts to the letter presented to him for signature (when he read it through at all, which he often admitted he didn't), sometimes as a continuation, but often as insertions into the typed text (see, e.g., 142, 536). In addition, Berlin's frequently incomprehensible elocution could prove too much for his secretaries: typed letters are in places pitted with gaps where the typist has failed to understand the dictation. Some meaningless or amusing phrases are clearly desperate conjectures by a puzzled typist; on occasion Berlin noticed these omissions or inaccuracies and corrected them by hand on the top copy, but he could not always remember what he had dictated, so the imperfect typing may be accompanied by a manuscript commentary on its peculiarities rather than a correction. Here is one of the more intelligible products of the guessing game that Berlin's typists had to play:

---

1 To Morton White, 9 April 1957.
2 Hilary Chadwick Brooks, IB's secretary, to the *Partisan Review*, 12 July 1950.

> I arrived after an uneventful journey on the *Queen Elizabeth*, who had
> trouble with the running seas ⟨This strange & beautiful sentence springs
> from the unconscious of my stenographer: I said "in the company of
> Giles Constable & the Ronnie Trees"⟩[1]

Manuscript letters are transcribed as Berlin wrote them, warts and all. The
recipients of Berlin's letters must have had to devote some time to making
sense of them, and the occasional letter in this volume will require a certain
mental agility in the reader.

Other editorial points

The preliminary matter in the first volume served to some extent for the
whole series, and readers seeking a fuller background are recommended to
consult it (as well as Michael Ignatieff's biography of Berlin).[2] The broad
lines of editorial policy, which have remained almost entirely unchanged for
this volume, are also there described in detail. But the scheme of publication tentatively sketched at L1 xvi has had to be substantially revised. The
amount of irresistible material for what was to be the period covered by
the second volume, 1946 to 1966 (or even 1975), was much greater than we
estimated, which is why this volume finishes in 1960, and is longer, even so,
than the first volume. We hope to reach at least 1975 in a third volume.

In an undertaking of this scope and complexity, errors are unfortunately
inevitable. We welcome notification of those in this volume, and corrections
will be posted in the IBVL (under Texts, Published work), where a list of corrections to the first volume is already to be found, together with a selection
of letters from the period it covers (1928–46) that came to light too late for
inclusion in the book.

ACKNOWLEDGEMENTS

Pride of place under this heading should be given to Serena Moore, who has
now worked with Henry Hardy on what, in internal Wolfson College documents, is called 'The Berlin Papers Project' for nearly a decade. Although
she is formally known as Henry Hardy's Assistant, both editors are the daily
beneficiaries of her care, courtesy, discretion, reliability, hard work, generosity and imagination; and her role has been much wider than her job title
might imply. To start at the most humdrum level: the amount of paper that
has built up in Henry Hardy's office as the years go by has reached alarming
proportions, and his ability to keep track of it unaided has declined correspondingly. The task of keeping everything in order, and providing signposts

---

1 To William and Alice James, 1 October 1953.
2 Michael Ignatieff, *Isaiah Berlin: a Life* (London and New York, 1998). Once again, thanks are due
   to Michael Ignatieff for his largesse in allowing us to draw on his recordings and working papers:
   see L1 xxxi.

that enable specific items to be retrieved, requires meticulous organisation and record-keeping. Serena has created a variety of systems for this purpose, entirely on her own initiative, and has maintained them punctiliously. The importance of this sometimes mind-numbingly tedious work is hard to exaggerate: such efficiency as we achieve is entirely dependent on it. Serena has, moreover, taken over the task of following up new clues that point to further caches of Berlin's sprawling correspondence; she also researches many of the illustrations, maintains a detailed chronology of Berlin's movements and activities (on which the chronology in this volume draws), and helps in numerous other ways as the need arises. She spots opportunities that have escaped us, and exploits them successfully. Her dedication to the project has been of inestimable value.[1]

Next, we once again thank the many correspondents, or their heirs and representatives, who have supplied (copies of) letters in their possession, and sometimes help in interpreting them that no one else could have provided; without their co-operation this book would not exist in its present form. Since their names appear in the index of correspondents, they are not listed again here. We are grateful to them all: even when letters do not appear in this volume, the information they contain has often been vital. Many letters are now in institutional archives, and we also record our indebtedness to the archivists who have enabled us to publish letters in their care. In this context we ought perhaps to record that we have not been able to include letters to the officers of All Souls (with the exception of John Sparrow, whose letters from IB were kept among his personal papers) because access to the College's personal files is restricted under a 100-year rule.

Ever since this project began, in the early 1970s, it has been staffed serendipitously. No advertisement has ever been required to fill a position (including those of the present editors). Someone has always emerged when needed, and so (thus far) has the necessary remuneration, thanks to the generosity of our benefactors, to whom we are inexpressibly grateful. This providential provision may in part be a testimony to Berlin's power to inspire his readers, but it also seems to partake of the miraculous.

The names of the main collaborators who have worked alongside us are listed at the beginning of this volume. 'Additional research' refers mainly to the reading, summarising and selective copying of the mass of letters and other documents in the Isaiah Berlin Papers in the Bodleian Library in Oxford, as a basis for our selection, commentary and annotation. It is hard to exaggerate the importance of this time-consuming and sometimes enervating work: if we had had to do it all ourselves, this volume would

---

1 *Note by HH:* I should like to add that Serena has also offered me constant personal support, in life and work, in bad times as well as good, and that it is a measure of the self-effacing way in which she does this that I sometimes appear to take her for granted. But appearances can be deceptive – at least in this case, I hope.

have taken far longer to edit. James Chappel was the first, and extremely welcome, labourer in this vineyard: he set the standard that others have followed, and his intelligence and wit have enriched us. Brigid Allen joined him to excellent effect later, and between them they managed to keep ahead of us. Steffen Groß has most generously worked for us during part of his hard-earned breaks in Oxford from Cottbus University, and most recently Eleonora Paganini has joined in with infectious enthusiasm.

Michael Hughes's detailed catalogue of the very extensive Berlin Papers, completed in time for work on this volume, has naturally been an indispensable tool. Michael has also answered a steady stream of questions, and organised copies of items we needed to see, saving us significant time and trouble. We are most grateful to him.

Much of the material in this volume was transcribed by Betty Colquhoun in past years, when it first became available. More recently most of the transcription has been done by Esther Johnson. Transcribing Berlin's letters accurately, especially when they are handwritten, is very skilled work, and we are indebted to these two expert cryptographers, as we are to Myra Jones, who double-checked the transcripts against the original documents with painstaking care.

The publication of such a complex book involves numerous experts of various kinds, on whose skill and advice we have necessarily and gratefully relied. Our thanks go to them all, especially to Will Sulkin, Rowena Skelton-Wallace, Mary Gibson and their colleagues at Chatto & Windus; to Paul Luna of the Department of Typography & Graphic Communication at the University of Reading; to Peter Boswell and his staff at Deltatype Ltd; and to the indexer, Vicki Robinson.

We have received help from many other quarters, often well beyond the call of duty. We thank all those in the following list most warmly, regretting that there is not room to specify their contributions, and apologise to anyone whose assistance we have failed to record: the staff of the Bodleian Library, especially Colin Harris; the archivists of many Oxford Colleges, including Liz Baird, Judith Curthoys, Robin Darwall-Smith, Jennifer Thorp; Marcia Allentuck, Shlomo Avineri, Casey Babcock, Simon Bailey, Clare Baker, Philippa Bassett, Denison Beach, Charlotte Berry, Björn Biester, Jason Bigelow, Jo Blackadder, Rachel Bowles, Lelia Brodersen, Breda Brosnahan, Isabella Burrell, Margaret Burri, Marc Carlson, Justin Cartwright, Joshua Cherniss, Jennifer Cole, Julia Creed, Richard Davenport-Hines, Cliff Davies, Cressida Dick, Craig Dickson, Sue Donnelly, Arie Dubnov, Robert Dugdale, Clarissa Eden, Desmond FitzGerald, Jean Floud, Francesca Franchi, Tuvia Friling, Julia Gardner, John Geddes, Ruth Gibson, Susie Gilbert, Georgy Glotov, Jane Goodnight, Simon Green, Peter Halban, Colin Harris, Jenifer Hart, Jon Heal, Hanni Hermolin, Robin Hessman, Camilla Hornby, Margaret Hugh-Jones, Michael Ignatieff, Magda Jean-Louis, Carole Jones, Diane Kaplan, Ellen

Kastel, Clare Kavanagh, Sharon Kelly, Meredith Kirkpatrick, Jane Knowles, Yuka Kobayashi, Marina Kozyreva, Barbara Kraft, Nicola Lacey, Thomas Lannon, Carol Leadenham, Jenny Lee, William Lorimer, Hannah Lowery, Gavin McGuffie, Patricia McGuire, Sheila Mackenzie, Ruth MacLeod, Edna Margalit, Sandra Marsh, Elizabeth Martin, Martin Maw, Giordana Mecagni, Barry Moreno, Halyna Myroniuk, Dominique Nabokov, Barbara Natanson, Penelope Newsome, Cynthia Ostroff, Sara Palmor, James Peters, David M. Phillips, Elliot Phillips, Isabella Phillips, Stephen Plotkin, Tatiana Podznyakova, Jane Potter, Amy Purdon, Wang Qian, Helen Rappaport, Lily Richards, Timothy Robbins, Dean Rogers, Dean Ryan, Joanna Ryan, Geraldine Santoro, Rabbi Jacob J. Schacter, Taran Schindler, Natalia Sciarini, Caroline Seebohm, Merav Segal, Ellen Shea, Joseph Sherman, Adam Sisman, Judy Skelton, Norman Solomon, Linda Stahnke, Jon Stallworthy, William Stingone, Clare Stoneman, Geoffrey Strachan, Cathy Strain, Andrew Strauss, Michel Strauss, Fiorella Superbi, the Swedish Academy, Peter Thompson, Dag Einar Thörsen, Sidney Tibbetts, Penelope Tree, Verena Onken von Trott, Levin von Trott, Patricia Utechin, Natalie Walters, Leon Wieseltier, Richard Wiley, Martin Wood, Blair Worden, Marie-Claire Wyatt, Mary Yoe. Our gratitude survives those who have died while the book was in preparation.

HENRY HARDY
JENNIFER HOLMES

CONVENTIONS AND ABBREVIATIONS

The format of the names, addresses and dates in the letter-headings has been standardised, and the most common addresses abbreviated according to the following list:

New College	New College, Oxford
All Souls	All Souls College, Oxford
Hollycroft Avenue	49 Hollycroft Avenue, London NW3
Headington House	Headington House, Old High Street, Headington, Oxford

All Oxford colleges except New College (and Christ Church, which is not known as 'Christ Church College') are referred to in the notes without the word 'College'. Information in the form 'Balliol classics 1929–33' indicates that the person concerned was an undergraduate reading that subject at that Oxford college during that period. Page references are not introduced with 'p.' or 'pp.' when the context makes it obvious that that is what they are. Cross references of the form '(256/6)' mean 'see page 256, note 6'.

Originals are typed unless said to be in manuscript or retrieved from Dictabelts. The location of originals is provided as part of the index of correspondents.

People and other subjects requiring a gloss are in general footnoted when they are first referred to, but not otherwise. The index will quickly locate this introductory note if it is needed in connection with a later reference. Recipients of letters are referred to by their initials in notes to letters received by them.

Listed below are the people most frequently referred to. The incomplete versions of their names in the left-hand column are not annotated except on first occurrence; rather, these names can be assumed to refer to the individuals in the right-hand column unless otherwise stated. Many but not all of these individuals, together with other important or frequently mentioned people, are subjects of the entries in the biographical glossary that precedes the indexes. These people are glossed only briefly on their first occurrence, and on that occasion an asterisk before the surname indicates that an entry is to be found in the glossary, thus: 'Cecil Maurice *Bowra'.

Adam	Adam von Trott
Alice	Alice James
Aline	Aline Halban, later Berlin
Alix	Alix de Rothschild
Arthur	Arthur M. Schlesinger, Jr
Ava	Lady Waverley
Avis	Avis Bohlen
B.B.	Bernard Berenson
Ben	Benjamin V. Cohen
B.G.	David Ben-Gurion

Billy	William James
Bubbles	Jasper Ridley
Chaim	Chaim Weizmann
Chip	Charles Bohlen
Clarissa	Clarissa Churchill, later Eden
Clyde	Clyde Kluckhohn
Cyril	Cyril Connolly
David	Lord David Cecil
Diana	Lady Diana Cooper
Duff	Duff Cooper
Ed(ward)	Edward Fretwell Prichard, Jr
Eddy	Edward Sackville-West
Edgar	Edgar Wind
Edmund	Edmund Wilson
Emerald	Lady Cunard
Ernie	Ernest Bevin
Felix, F.F.	Felix Frankfurter
Freddie	A. J. Ayer
Fretwell	Edward Fretwell Prichard, Jr
Gladwyn	Gladwyn Jebb, later Lord Gladwyn
Goronwy	Goronwy Rees
Guy	Guy de Rothschild
Hants	Stuart Hampshire
Henry	Lord Anglesey
Herbert	H. L. A. Hart
Hubert	Hubert Henderson
Ida	Ida Samunov
Ike	Dwight D. Eisenhower
James	James Joll
Jenifer	Jenifer Hart
Joe	Joseph Alsop
John	John Sparrow
Josef	Josef Cohn
the Judge/Justice	Felix Frankfurter
Judy	Judy Montagu
Junior	Edward Fretwell Prichard, Jr
Kay	Katharine Graham
Liz	Elizabeth von Hofmannsthal
Marcus	Marcus Dick
Marian	Marian Schlesinger
Marietta	Marietta Tree
Marion	Marion Frankfurter
Mark	Mark Bonham Carter
Maurice	Maurice Bowra

Meyer	Meyer Schapiro
Michel	Michel Strauss
Moore	Moore Crosthwaite
Morton	Morton White
Moura	Moura Budberg
Myron	Myron Gilmore
Nicky	Nicky Mariano
Nicolas	Nicolas Nabokov
Noel	Noel Annan
Oliver	Oliver Franks
Olivia	Olivia Constable
Patricia	Patricia de Bendern
Phil	Philip Graham
Prich	Edward Fretwell Prichard, Jr
Rachel	Rachel Cecil
Rai(mund)	Raimund von Hofmannsthal
Richard	Richard Wollheim
Ronnie	Ronald Tree
Rowland	Rowland Burdon-Muller
Roy	Roy Harrod
Sam	S. N. Behrman
Shiela	Shiela Newsome, later Sokolov Grant
Shirley	Shirley Morgan, later Lady Anglesey
Sibyl	Lady Colefax
Stephen	Stephen Spender
Stuart	Stuart Hampshire
Susan Mary	Susan Mary Patten
Toynbee	Arnold Toynbee
Victor	Victor Rothschild
Yitzhak, Yitz(c)hok	Yitzhak Samunov

Other abbreviations used follow. For publication details of books listed see http://berlin.wolf.ox.ac.uk/lists/books/index.html.

⟨ ⟩	encloses manuscript addition to typed item
{ }	encloses matter mistakenly present in manuscript
[?]	uncertain transcription (follows doubtful word without a space)/illegible word
[…]	text omitted by editors; where a postscript has been omitted this symbol is printed to the right of the signature
AC	IB, *Against the Current*
b.	born
BL	British Library

CC	IB, *Concepts and Categories*
CCC	Corpus Christi College, Oxford
CCNY	The City College of New York
Ch. Ch.	Christ Church (Oxford College)
CIB	Ramin Jahanbegloo, *Conversations with Isaiah Berlin*
CTH	IB, *The Crooked Timber of Humanity*
d.	died
FDR	(US President) Franklin Delano Roosevelt
FO	Foreign Office (London)
FORD	Foreign Office Research Department (London)
FRPS	Foreign Research and Press Service (based in Balliol)
Greats	Literae Humaniores, the second part of the Classics course at Oxford, comprising (in the relevant period) Philosophy and Ancient History
IB	Isaiah Berlin
the IBVL	The Isaiah Berlin Virtual Library, website at http://berlin.wolf.ox.ac.uk/
KM	IB, *Karl Marx*
L	IB, *Liberty*
L1	The first volume (1928–46) of this edition of IB's letters
L1 supp.	Online supplement to L1, http://berlin.wolf.ox.ac.uk/published _works/f/l1supp.pdf
LMH	Lady Margaret Hall (Oxford College)
LOC	Library of Congress
LSE	London School of Economics (and Political Science)
MIT	Massachusetts Institute of Technology
MI Tape	recording of interview by Michael Ignatieff (interviews conducted 1988–97)
MP	Member of Parliament
MSB	Oxford, Bodleian Library, MS. Berlin, followed by specific shelfmark and folio(s), e.g. MSB 232/1–3 = MS. Berlin 232, folios 1–3
NA	National Archives, Kew, London (followed by the reference under which the cited document is catalogued, e.g. NA, FO 953/144)
n.p.	no place (i.e. no address given)
NY	New York
ODNB	*Oxford Dictionary of National Biography*
OUP	Oxford University Press
PAS	*Proceedings of the Aristotelian Society*
PASS	*Proceedings of the Aristotelian Society (supplementary volume)*
PhD	Philosophiae Doctor (Doctor of Philosophy)
PI; PI2	IB, *Personal Impressions*; 2nd edition
PIRA	IB, *Political Ideas in the Romantic Age*

POI	IB, *The Power of Ideas*
PPE	Philosophy, Politics and Economics (Oxford undergraduate course)
PSM	IB, *The Proper Study of Mankind*
RIIA	Royal Institute of International Affairs (Chatham House)
ROH	Royal Opera House, Covent Garden, London
RT	IB, *Russian Thinkers*
SM	IB, *The Soviet Mind*
SR	IB, *The Sense of Reality*
SSEES	School of Slavonic and East European Studies (London)
TCE	IB, *Three Critics of the Enlightenment*
TLS	*The Times Literary Supplement*
UCL	University College London
Univ.	University College, Oxford
UNO	United Nations Organization
UNRRA	United Nations Relief and Rehabilitation Administration

THE LETTERS

I romanticize every place I come to, I find: Moscow, Oxford, Ditchley, Harvard, Washington: each is a kind of legendary world framed within its own conventions in which the characters, suffused with unnatural brightness, perform with terrific responsiveness [...][1]

[...] my quest for gaiety & cosiness is a perpetual defence against the extreme sense of the abyss by which I have been affected ever since I can remember myself [...][2]

I am no letter writer & write as I talk, in an undisciplined, confused, almost irresponsible fashion [...][3]

1 To Marietta Tree, 7 July 1949.
2 To Marion Frankfurter, 23 February 1952.
3 To Violet Bonham Carter, 23 January 1954.

ENTR'ACTE

The war years had been a watershed for Isaiah Berlin. His life as an Oxford don had been replaced by a key role representing the British Government in the United States; his dispatches home on the state of American opinion had attracted the attention and admiration of men of power and influence; and he had become a prestigious if unreliable catch for the society hostesses of Washington and New York. The end of the war had allowed him to revisit Russia, where he had spent part of his childhood, and to establish contact with the oppressed but still active literary world there. Forced by the post-war pressure of undergraduate numbers to delay his planned change of subject from philosophy to the history of ideas, he sailed back to England in April 1946 to resume his academic career.

TO MEYER SCHAPIRO[1]

Tuesday [9 April 1946, *manuscript*]

[*Queen Mary,*] Cunard White Star [line]

Dear Meyer,

I made the most persistent & desperate efforts to get in touch with you & see you before I finally left. I arrived in N.Y. on the 2ᵈ April & the ship left in the early morning of the 7ᵗʰ – I telephoned literally every day & got no reply at all. I did have lunch with Edm. Wilson[2] who told me how ill he thought of the English & French, how well of Russians & Americans. I expect in an obscure way that is why I like his writings so much, the serious 19ᵗʰ century moral approach, the heavy quality of feeling, the absence of polish, elegance, & innate traditional manners & taste. Anyhow I found him very well worth talking with: shy & full of half articulated sentences gurgling upwards – he was stone sober which probably made him slightly stiff at first – later he thawed & bubbled away very agreeably – & said a lot of things. Now: when are you coming to Europe in general & Oxford in particular? I would really much rather, much *much* rather see you in Oxford than in N.Y. or London – you obviously must come fairly soon if only to have a look at what is left, & who is living – let me know a day or two in advance if you cannot sooner – & stay with me in Oxford as long as you like. You will find Freddie[3] too there (in Wadham) & other people (here) who may interest you. I really am exceedingly sorry not to have said a proper farewell. The two last impressions I have from, rather than of, America, are Wilson's

---

1 Meyer *Schapiro (1904–96), art historian and artist.
2 Edmund *Wilson (1895–1972), journalist and literary critic.
3 Alfred Jules ('Freddie') *Ayer (1910–89), philosopher.

approval of Auden's[1] anglophobia – terrific piece[2] – & the fact that the real name of Borodin[3] – the Soviet agent in China whom I met in Moscow – is Gruzenberg. I am incapable of seriousness now for at least 6 months, since I am so terribly intellectually pauperized.

    Yrs

      Isaiah   [...]

1 Wystan Hugh Auden (1907–73), English poet, critic, essayist and playwright, who moved to the US in 1939 and became an American citizen in 1946.

2 Presumably IB had seen an early draft of Wilson's review in the *New Yorker* (28 September 1946, 85–6) of Henry James's *The American Scene*, edited with an introduction by Auden (New York, 1946); on 23 February Wilson had written to Mamaine Paget mentioning this introduction, in which Auden was 'awfully interesting about Europe and America [...] He thinks that the United States is the only place where it is possible at present to be truly international, and I have felt this very strongly since I have been back. The intellectual and artistic vacuum that was created over here by the war is beginning to be filled now, and things are becoming more interesting' ('Edmund Wilson On Writers and Writing', *New York Review of Books*, 17 March 1977, 14). The introduction rather than Wilson's review may well be IB's 'terrific piece', as Auden not only provides a lively and insightful commentary on James's travelogue, but goes on to argue for the necessary though painful priority of liberty over values such as equality.

3 Mikhail Markovich Gruzenberg (1884–1951), alias Borodin, from Riga like IB, Comintern agent who built up a strong Bolshevik power base in China during the 1920s until Soviet plans to dominate China collapsed in 1928; in 1949 he fell victim to Stalin's anti-Jewish purge, dying in a Siberian prison-camp.

1946–1948

NEW COLLEGE

I am gloomily contemplating a life of grinding hackery for the next thirty years or so.[1]

[Philosophy] is a dreadfully punishing fatal subject to bear a secret hatred to – & gnaws at the vitals of those whose hearts have moved elsewhere in the most destructive way.[2]

1 To Philip Graham, 14 November 1946.
2 To Shirley Anglesey, 6 December 1948.

IB's visit to Russia in 1945 had intensified his interest in Russian thought and literature. Knowing of his enthusiasm for the works of Turgenev[1] in particular, the publisher Hamish Hamilton[2] suggested that IB should translate some of this writer's shorter pieces for publication. IB's continuing unrequited passion for Patricia de Bendern[3] inspired his first selection.

TO HAMISH HAMILTON

[Mid-May 1946, *manuscript*]

New College

Dear Hamish (or do you prefer Jamie?)

[...] What I shd love to do, if it at all recommended itself to you was to translate for you, afresh & from no previous text, Turgenev's *First Love*,[4] a wonderful long short story which you must know, about 150 pp. long (as I dimly recollect) & Turgenev's best, most moving most lyrical & obviously autobiographical book. Perhaps D. Cecil[5] might write an introduction to it for you – but of that I haven't spoken to him. All I know is that he & I at intervals rave about it. Mrs Garnett[6] did do it but not well. If you [think] that at all possible let me know, & I'll become serious about it. [...]

Isaiah

1 Ivan Sergeevich Turgenev (1818–83), Russian novelist, short-story writer and dramatist. IB valued his lack of dogmatism, his 'clear, finely discriminating, slightly ironical vision' and 'his power of minute and careful observation, his fascination with the varieties of character and situation as such, his detachment, his inveterate habit of doing justice to the full complexity and diversity of goals, attitudes, beliefs', and saw Turgenev, like many of his characters, as a 'well-meaning, troubled, self-questioning liberal, witness to the complex truth' (RT2 338, 348).

2 Hamish ('Jamie') Hamilton (1900–88); half-Scottish, half-American; medical student (briefly) then modern linguist and lawyer at Gonville and Caius College, Cambridge, subsequently called to the bar; founder of the publishers that bore his name (Chairman 1931–81, Managing Director 1931–72); accomplished sportsman and theatre-lover; known for his dynamism and competitiveness, capable of great friendships and equally fierce hatreds. With his second wife, Countess Yvonne Pallavicino (68/1), a notable literary host.

3 Lady Patricia Sybil de *Bendern (1918–91), née Douglas, daughter of the 11th Marquess of Queensberry.

4 Turgenev's semi-autobiographical short novel, published in 1860, tells the story of a boy whose unrequited adolescent passion for a seemingly heartless beauty gives way to a deeper understanding of the mysteries of adult love.

5 Lord (Edward Christian) David (Gascoyne) *Cecil (1902–86), Fellow of New College 1939–69, Goldsmiths' Professor of English Literature, Oxford, 1948–69.

6 Constance Clara Garnett (1861–1946), née Black, translator of many Russian classics. Although IB paid tribute to Mrs Garnett for making Russian literature available to English readers, he was dismissive of her 'plodding prose' and damned with faint praise her insensitivity to the poetry in Russian literature and to the naturalness of Turgenev's dialogue: 'Her prose, for all its old-fashioned clumsiness, is sober, honest, direct, seldom inaccurate, and occasionally achieves felicities of its own. [...] Mrs Garnett tends to miss the point and remains remorselessly flat and monotonous. [...] Nevertheless, if Mrs Garnett had been exposed to the fears and indecisions which a more sensitive insight would inevitably have brought with it, she might never have performed the Herculean labour upon which she was engaged throughout her long, blameless, competent, admirable working life.' 'On Translating Turgenev', review of I. S. Turgenev, *Smoke, On the Eve, Virgin Soil, Fathers and Children* and *A House of Gentle Folk*, trans. Constance Garnett, *Observer*, 11 November 1951, 7.

*IB had been a long-standing supporter of the Zionist cause in general and of
the policies of diplomacy and non-violence advocated by Chaim Weizmann[1]
in particular. But Zionist hopes of favourable treatment by the post-war
Labour government were dashed by the sympathy to the Arab cause shown
by the Foreign Secretary, Ernest Bevin,[2] and in particular his refusal to relax
restrictions on the immigration of European Jews into Palestine. Jewish
frustration at this policy led to anti-British attacks, escalating violence and, on
16–17 June, widespread sabotage by the Palmach[3] of the transport infrastructure
of Palestine. The (British) Palestine Government responded on 29 June ('Black
Saturday') by arresting 3,000 Jews, including all the most important members of
the Jewish Agency[4] except Weizmann and the absent Ben-Gurion.[5]*

IB poured out his views in a letter to The Times *but hesitated to send it
without Weizmann's approval.*

TO THE EDITOR OF *THE TIMES*

10 July 1946 [*typescript draft corrected in manuscript*]

[n.p.]

Sir,

The arrest by the Government of Palestine of several members of the
executive of the Jewish Agency for suspected complicity in acts of violence,
and the raid upon its offices by armed troops, create a new and critical
situation in that country for which old remedies will scarcely avail. Without
attempting to trace the unhappy course of events or to fix the responsibility
for them, this much seems worth recording.

The Jews of Palestine, unreasonably as later became clear, expected Allied
victory and the accession to power of a Labour Government in Britain,

---

1 Chaim *Weizmann (1874–1952), chemist and statesman; President of the Provisional Council of
the State of Israel 1948–9; first President of Israel 1949–52.

2 Ernest Bevin (1881–1951), General Secretary of the Transport and General Workers' Union 1921–
1940; Labour MP 1940–50; Minister of Labour and National Service 1940–5; Secretary of State for
Foreign Affairs 1945–51; Lord Privy Seal 1951; strongly opposed to increased Jewish immigration
into Palestine and to the Zionist aim of a Jewish State.

3 An elite fighting force set up in 1941, with British help, by the Haganah, the main Jewish paramilitary organisation in Palestine, to counter the Nazi threat there. When British support was
withdrawn after the Allied victory in North Africa, the Palmach became a left-wing underground
organisation, based in the kibbutzim.

4 Under the British Mandate (9/2) the Jewish Agency was a quasi-governmental organisation
which officially represented the Jewish community in Palestine, ran schools and hospitals, and
organised land purchase from Arabs; unofficially it set up the Haganah (previous note) and (from
1938) encouraged illegal immigration to Palestine. Originally including non-Zionist Jews, it had
by 1946 become virtually identical with the Executive of the Zionist Organization. On the proclamation of statehood in 1948 the Jewish Agency became the government of Israel.

5 David Ben-Gurion (1886–1973), né Grün, Polish-born Zionist military and political leader;
Chairman, Jewish Agency for Palestine, 1935–48; Israeli Prime Minister and Minister of Defence
1948–53 and 1955–63, largely responsible for the creation of the State of Israel, whose existence he
proclaimed on 14 May 1948.

committed to a maximum Zionist programme, to bring some measure of relief from what appeared to them a systematic frustration of those political hopes encouragement of which by the Balfour Declaration[1] and the League Mandate[2] had originally brought the majority of them or of their fathers to Palestine. When it became plain that no sign of any such new deal was to be looked for, despair led the extremer elements among them to intensify the methods of lawlessness & violence some of which they had learnt from Arab rebellions in Palestine, others from [the] Russ[ian] Rev[olution and] European resistance movements in the ranks of which individuals among them had fought & died during the war.

Terrorism & murder are weapons too vicious to invite comment and they have done the Zionist cause irreparable harm; but if they cannot be justified or condoned, use of them by Jews can certainly in part be explained by the spectacle of substantial concessions wrung out of earlier British governments by means of just such tactics of ruthless violence when employed by the Arab terrorists & assassins and the bitterness induced in even moderate Zionists by the growing contrast between the friendly tone of statements addressed to the Arabs and the harsh warnings latterly issued to the Jews by Government spokesmen in London and the Middle East.

When, following acts of isolated terrorism, the Anglo-American Commission[3] was set up last year, this may well have been interpreted by some Zionist hotheads as final proof that Dr Weizmann's temperate pleas had indeed fallen upon deaf ears, that only by violent methods could enough attention ever be drawn to Jewish grievances to yield tangible results. The findings of the Commission were received by HM Government with obvious distaste; Mr Bevin thundered against American friends of Zionism: bitterness and violence in Jewish Palestine increased once more. The Government struck against it and a new situation arose.

Relations between the British Government and the Jewish Agency have

1 In a letter dated 2 November 1917 the then Foreign Secretary Arthur Balfour conveyed to Lord (Walter) Rothschild, for onward transmission to the Zionist Federation, the Cabinet's declaration of sympathy with Zionist aspirations: 'His Majesty's Government view with favour the establishment in Palestine of a national home for the Jewish people, and will use their best endeavours to facilitate the achievement of this object, it being clearly understood that nothing shall be done which may prejudice the civil and religious rights of existing non-Jewish communities in Palestine, or the rights and political status enjoyed by Jews in any other country' [BL Add. MS 41178 A. (2) f. 3–4].

2 In 1922 the League of Nations drew up an official document, the Palestine Mandate, which closely followed the Balfour Declaration (see previous note) in defining Britain's powers and responsibilities in the former Ottoman territory of Palestine, which Britain had occupied since 1917 (from 1919 under the terms of the Versailles Peace Conference).

3 Composed of six American and six British members, from a variety of backgrounds, the Anglo-American Committee of Inquiry was set up in 1945 to attempt to reconcile the increasingly divergent views on Palestine of the US, who favoured allowing large numbers of displaced Jewish refugees in Europe to settle there, and Britain, who feared the Arab reaction to this. In April 1946 the Committee unanimously recommended that 100,000 displaced persons should be allowed immediate entry to Palestine. The British Government rejected the recommendation.

from the beginning presupposed, despite frequent stresses and strains, that minimum of elementary mutual courtesy which is the formal if precarious framework of all official dealings. Breaking point, which sometimes seemed dangerously near, had never actually been reached. The arrest of Mr Shertok[1] and the vast majority of his colleagues has probably destroyed this frame, inasmuch as the above humiliation of the Jewish Agency, be the basis of the legal charges preferred against it never so solid, renders further official relations with it to some degree unreal. Moreover Dr Weizmann's hitherto unshakeable policy of steady co-operation with HM Government, unpalatable to his extremer followers, has by this act been undermined, since what may have been sanctioned as an unavoidable disciplinary measure by the Palestine Government reestablishing order is in effect a political move tantamount to causing relations with the Agency to be broken off. This fact must make a difference.

This grim & bitter mood was fed by memories of the Struma & Patria incidents,[2] which the Jews of Palestine cd scarcely be expected to forget; & by increasingly gloomy accounts of the grisly conditions still prevailing in refugee camps in Europe, inflaming popular sentiment in favour of illegal immigration until even so conscientious an anti-nationalist as Dr Magnes[3] found he could not honourably condemn it. Against this atmosphere moderate Zionists, even so great a figure as Dr Weizmann, found they cd do little, particularly as they had seemed unable to temper, let alone stop, the icy winds which blew so steadily from Westminster & Whitehall to blight all Zionist hopes.

The creation of a Jewish political entity, recommended by the Peel

---

1 Moshe Shertok (1894–1965), Ukrainian-born Zionist leader who Hebraised his name to Sharett in 1948, Head of the Jewish Agency's political department 1933–48; Foreign Minister of Israel 1948–56, also Prime Minister 1954–5; a moderate who favoured diplomatic solutions, often at odds with the more extreme Ben-Gurion.

2 The desperate desire of many European Jews to reach Palestine and the reluctance of other countries, particularly Britain, to allow this led to a number of marine disasters. In November 1940, 3,600 East European Jews reached Haifa in three ships, only to find that the British classed them as illegal immigrants and proposed to deport them to Mauritius on board the *Patria*. While the refugees were being transferred between ships, Haganah agents (led by IB's cousin Yitzhak Sadeh, 29/5) mined the *Patria* in an attempt to disable it. The explosion was more powerful than intended: of the nearly 270 dead, over 200 were refugees. Initially the Irgun (12/5) were suspected and the Haganah's role was revealed only years later. The *Struma* was an unseaworthy ship chartered in 1941 by Revisionist Zionists in Romania to carry nearly 800 illegal Jewish immigrants to Palestine. The ship broke down in the Black Sea but managed to reach Istanbul. Weeks of argument between Turkey and Britain followed about whether, and if so how, any passengers would be allowed into Palestine; meanwhile almost all remained aboard. On 23 February 1942 Turkey towed the still-helpless ship back into the Black Sea. The next day the ship exploded, leaving one survivor. Later information suggests it was torpedoed by a Soviet submarine acting under orders to sink all neutral shipping in the Black Sea to prevent goods reaching Germany.

3 Judah Leon Magnes (1877–1948), American-born rabbi and Zionist leader; Chancellor (1925–35) and first President (1935–48) of the Hebrew University, Jerusalem; committed to the cause of Jewish–Arab harmony and to the concept of a single bi-national State in Palestine rather than partition.

Commission,[1] has always been a counsel of despair – despair of establishing peaceful co-operation between Arabs and Jews in a single State. This last act of the Palestine Government, seeming to underline the difference between its present attitude to Jewish and Arab leaders, increases, if it is possible, the gulf between them, and so renders the creation of some kind of separate Jewish establishment in Palestine, whatever its constitutional form & degree of independence, the only certain method of preventing a violent conflict between Britain and the Jewish colonists of Palestine, a prospect which no sane person, & certainly no sane Jew, even [?] of Zionism, can begin to contemplate without indescribable horror and stupefaction. It is difficult to see how any argument against this course can now outweigh the fact that it is far too late in the day for those milder alternatives which seemed to sensible men less enlightened and too impracticable in the past. At least such a scheme of partition, provided that it does not prescribe a collection of scattered microscopic cantons, or some metaphysical union deprived of a territorial basis, may well secure effective economic support both from Jews & Arabs from the USA; & it would have the vast merit of reducing the problem to its proper local proportions, and so remove it from the perilous sphere of international politics.

Thus far, the main group of American Zionists have shown conspicuous wisdom and self-restraint in publicly supporting the Loan to Britain[2] against their own zealots & despite their equally deep disapproval of British policy in Palestine; but no wisdom is proof against indefinite delays; Jews and Arabs alike can point to all too many occasions where, in their dealings with Britain, force has paid and patience, reason & goodwill have not; indeed Mr Attlee[3] honourably recognises that this is so: and that only a clear and immediate final decision imposed by HM Government and countersigned by that of the United States, providing territories & economic conditions within which both Jews & Arabs cd live & grow, would restore the tottering prestige of the Western Powers in the Middle East and above all end the long, intolerably painful story of broken hopes and pitifully ineffectual remedies.

1 The Royal Commission of Inquiry to Palestine, headed by Lord (Robert) Peel (1867–1937), appointed by the British Government to investigate clashes between Palestinian Arabs and Jews, in 1937 recommended temporarily reducing Jewish immigration, to assuage Arab fears, and partitioning Palestine to form a Jewish and an Arab State, with an exchange of population to effect this; a small area including Jerusalem, with access to the coast just south of Tel Aviv, would remain under the British Mandate. The British Government and the Arabs rejected the idea of partition; the Twentieth Zionist Congress accepted the principle but rejected as too small the specific area of land allocated to the Jews.

2 A loan by the US to Britain of $3.75 billion, finally authorised on 15 July 1946 after a year of difficult negotiations, to replace the Lend-Lease agreement, abruptly terminated by President Truman in August 1945, which had kept Britain economically afloat during the war.

3 Clement Richard Attlee (1883–1967), 1st Earl Attlee 1955, Labour politician, Deputy Prime Minister 1942–5, Prime Minister 1945–51, Leader of the Opposition 1951–5.

TO CHAIM WEIZMANN

[17 July 1946, *manuscript*]

The Dorchester Hotel, London[1]

Dear Dr Weizmann

I am very glad & excited to hear that you are returning. I have written a long letter to the 'Times' about Palestine which, I am told, might have an effect; I detest making a public exhibition of myself but I feel that there are moments when to be silent is shameful – 'Не могу молчать'.[2] But I do not want to send it before reading it to you, & if you think it wrong or unnecessary will only too gladly suppress it. I have gone about everywhere expressing passionate views, which I am sure you will not disapprove. *Please* let me know (at Hampstead 0912)[3] where I shall be sitting waiting when I may see you if only for a few moments – also if I could be of any possible help.

Much love to both of you.

Isaiah

IB discussed the letter to The Times *with Weizmann soon after he reached London on 18 July. The copious manuscript amendments to the typed draft (incorporated in the version printed here) may reflect Weizmann's comments. However, the letter was not published and was perhaps never sent. Since a draft also exists of a substantially longer piece[4] by IB on the same topic, apparently not a letter, Weizmann may have suggested that IB produce an article instead of a letter. If so, that too was soon overtaken by events. On 22 July the Irgun[5] blew up a wing of the King David Hotel in Jerusalem, killing 91 people and changing the political landscape again.*

In early August IB set off for a working holiday in Switzerland, breaking his journey in Paris.

TO MENDEL AND MARIE BERLIN[6]

Tuesday [13? August 1946, *manuscript*]

Pension de l'Athénée, Geneva

Dear Pa & Ma,

I had a splendid time in Paris. The evening of arrival I dined with John

---

1 Where the Weizmanns stayed when in London.
2 'Ne mogu molchat'' ('I cannot remain silent').
3 The telephone number of IB's family home, 49 Hollycroft Avenue, Hampstead, London NW3.
4 Posted in the IBVL at http://berlin.wolf.ox.ac.uk/lists/nachlass/palestine1946.pdf.
5 Group of Zionist militants, founded in 1931 as a right-wing offshoot from the Haganah, in favour of violence to defend Jewish interests in Palestine and bring about a Jewish State; also responsible for helping many European Jews to reach Palestine. The attack on the British military, police and civil headquarters housed in the King David Hotel was carried out by the Irgun at a time when it was working in collaboration with the Haganah and the Stern gang (Lehi, 21/2).
6 Mendel *Berlin (1884–1953) and his wife Marie *Berlin (c.1880–1974), IB's parents.

Foster[1] & Alsop[2] – & later saw Bohlen[3] & some other UNNRA [sc. UNRRA][4] Americans. Next day I lunched with more Americans – de Benderns[5] present, & relations peaceful & public & stable & non-existent – remarkable how little a wound feels when healed – then the Russian bookshop – intimate talk with Bohlen – dinner à l'Ambassade.[6] Guest of Honour, Mr A. V. Alexander,[7] First Lord, the leader of the delegation while Attlee & Bevin are away. A lot of interesting things about Munich – reminiscences of Duff C.[8] + Alexander, & irritation with Reb Yoshe,[9] who indeed is behaving very tiresomely. Denunciating Winston for what was thought irresponsible invitation to clear out of א.י.[10] We stayed up talking till 3 a.m. [...]. Diana[11] pressed me to spend day in Chantilly,[12] but I did not want to offend Ben Cohen,[13] George Backer[14] & the rest of the Minyan,[15] so I declined. Terrible complaints. Why can't I first have a *little pleasure*? however I stuck to guns, saw Ben, Loudon[16]

1 John Galway Foster (1904–82), lawyer, Fellow of All Souls 1924–82; Conservative MP 1945–74; a friend and colleague of IB in Oxford and the US.
2 Joseph Wright *Alsop (1910–89), US journalist.
3 Charles Eustis ('Chip') *Bohlen (1904–74), US diplomat and Soviet specialist.
4 United Nations Relief and Rehabilitation Administration.
5 IB's parents disapproved of his love for Lady Patricia de Bendern, currently living in Paris with her husband Count John Gerard de Bendern (1907–97), Duff Cooper's Private Secretary, hence IB's pretence that it had ended. However, when A. J. Ayer, who had started an affair with Patricia earlier that year at the same time as one with her best friend Penelope Felkin (37/3), and had been found out when the two compared notes, blamed IB for betraying him, IB denied responsibility, while relishing the end of Patricia's affair: 'I was in fact innocent, but I was not displeased since I was still in love with her' (MI Tape 12).
6 'At the Embassy'.
7 Albert Victor Alexander (1885–1965), 1st Earl Alexander of Hillsborough 1963, Labour (Co-operative) politician and Baptist lay preacher; First Lord of the Admiralty 1940–6; Minister of Defence 1947–50; Chancellor of the Duchy of Lancaster 1950–1; member (and acting leader) of the UK delegation to the Paris Peace Conference July–October 1946.
8 (Alfred) Duff *Cooper (1890–1954), 1st Viscount Norwich 1952; Conservative politician, diplomat and writer; Ambassador to France 1944–7.
9 Possibly Rabbi Joseph Dov Soloveitchik (1903–93), influential Polish-born Orthodox Jewish scholar and teacher from a leading rabbinical dynasty; Professor of Talmud and head of the rabbinical school, Yeshiva University, New York, 1941–85; honorary president, Religious Zionists of America (Mizrachi), from 1946.
10 'Aleph-Yod', the abbreviation by which 'Eretz Yisrael' ('The Land of Israel') was officially known. In the Parliamentary debate on Palestine on 1 August, the Conservative leader, Winston Churchill, recommended that the Government should consider resigning its Mandate in Palestine and letting the United Nations take on the thankless task currently borne by Britain alone.
11 Lady Diana Olivia Winifred Maud *Cooper (1893–1986), née Manners; former actress and socialite; a notable hostess at the British Embassy in Paris while her husband was Ambassador.
12 The Château de St Firmin, the Coopers' country home near Chantilly.
13 Benjamin Victor Cohen (1894–1983), lawyer and presidential adviser, key figure in the FDR and Truman administrations; Counsellor, State Department, 1945–7; US delegate to UN 1948–52; committed Zionist.
14 George Backer (1903–74), US Democratic politician, activist in many Jewish organisations, theatrical sponsor and writer; publisher and editor, New York Post, 1939–42.
15 A quorum at certain Jewish religious observances.
16 Possibly Alexander Loudon (1892–1953), Dutch diplomat, Minister then Ambassador to the US 1938–47; member, Council of State, 1947–51; Secretary-General, Permanent Court of Arbitration, The Hague, 1951–3. His second wife was Béatrice Candler Williams, née Cobb (b. 1911).

etc. all of whom I enjoyed seeing for different reasons. Loudon is really a v. nice man & most kind. I like him more than his wife & he is a very decent public spirited person with a sensitive heart about things which matter. Ben gloomy as usual & particularly impotent somehow. Donald Hall[1] ran in & out of my room. I avoided all other British & U.S. conferees & finally got off to Geneva at 8 p.m. At Bellegarde (7 a.m.) all passengers have to get off for *French* Customs. Very tiresome. Arrived Geneva 9. a.m. & met by Felkin[2] at the station. Conducted to his house or rather large flat (Rothschilds[3] come next week to hotel) where a small room assigned. A little noisy & hot I thought. So, tactfully, I suggested that instead of eating their rations I might move uphill (as mother wd say 'hill up') cooler & easier to work. They found me a v. nice Pension, on a hill overlooking the Lac de Léman,[4] peace, quiet, above all solitude, I know nobody here, nothing to do *but* work: when in need of company I take a tram (1 mile) or walk down, & see Felkins & their friends. I am sure that is how Plekhanov[5] lived in 1900. The cleanliness, politeness, good food need not be described. [...] How German Switzerland still is: how Wiesbaden–Marienbadlike is the Pension; what delicious Berliner Pfannkuchen;[6] wonderful croissants: prices are high but not impossible: St. Moritz pension is probably 15–20 Fr. a day maximum i.e. £1–£1·5·0, which is not so terrible. Am v. well. All my love & write & cable.

Shaya

On his homeward journey IB stayed as a guest at the British Embassy in Paris.

TO ELLIOTT FELKIN

15 September 1946 [*manuscript*]

British Embassy, Paris

Dear Elliott,

I cannot begin to describe to you what an immense contrast life in Paris presents: after the genuine peace & quiet in Geneva – in which all sensations are therefore a little heightened & one's general receptivity is made both

---

1 Donald John Hall (1903–84), civil servant and novelist; a wartime colleague of IB's.
2 (Arthur) Elliott *Felkin (1892–1968), international civil servant who spent most of his career in Geneva; Secretary, Permanent Central Opium Board, 1938–53.
3 Presumably (Nathaniel Mayer) Victor Rothschild (1910–90), 3rd Baron Rothschild, zoologist (Director, BOAC, 1946–58; Chairman, Agricultural Research Council, 1948–58; Assistant Director of Research, Dept of Zoology, Cambridge, 1950–70) and his second wife, the former Teresa Georgina ('Tess') Mayor (1915–96). They married on 15 August, so this would have been their honeymoon.
4 Properly 'Lac Léman': Lake Geneva.
5 Georgy Valentinovich Plekhanov (1856–1918), founder of Russian Marxism, who spent many years in exile in Geneva.
6 'Berlin pancakes', doughnuts traditionally eaten in Germany during the festivities leading up to Ash Wednesday.

greater & more sensitive – there is this hell. Hell it really is. If it were not for my old friends – Patricia, Nabokov,[1] Elizabeth Bowen[2] whom I enjoy seeing, life in the Embassy wd be literally intolerable. Diana Cooper has a picaresque & even tragic point & a power of self illusion which dramatizes life at any rate in her presence: but Duff merely puffs and heaves along in a semi-tipsy fashion: the chi chi of M. Bérard,[3] Comtesse Palffy,[4] is thin & beastly: I have all the proper outraged feelings of a XIXth century Scythian[5] plunged into fin de siècle decay: & I long for the bleak charms of Oxford. Lady Cunard,[6] Lord Rothschild (whose Ben Hurish[7] flamboyant looks Patricia finds splendid) & the rest all day & all night discuss each others' & other people's intimate affairs. The basic pattern is familiar & monotonous: & the changes rung are too few. Mutual tension of the young–middle aged is a very boring & at times drearily obscene entertainment: once again I privately ride high moral horses inside myself: this is felt & obscurely resented: Patricia too, I note, is felt to be a potential traitor to this very inferior Petit Trianon.[8] I know now exactly what Mr H. A. L. Fisher[9] & Mr Morley[10] felt, when, after being made to walk on a lawn, in Mid January, strewn 3 inches high with cut roses by their host Mr Alfred de Rothschild[11] (Alfred J. Ayer's godfather) they repaired (immediately) to Limehouse & walked in the slums expressing liberal indignation to each other as they were purified. I *hate* this bogus Carthage in

1 Nicolas *Nabokov (1903–78), né Nikolay Dmitrievich, Russian-born composer, teacher, writer and cultural administrator; cousin of the novelist Vladimir Nabokov.

2 Elizabeth Dorothea Cole Bowen (Mrs Alan Cameron) (1889–1973), novelist; one of IB's closest friends before the war.

3 Christian Bérard ('Bébé') (1902–49), openly homosexual French artist and theatre-designer; a 'scraggle-bearded, sack-bodied man who wore his jackets soiled and kept up his trousers with string' (*Time*, 9 May 1949, 28).

4 Louise Levêque de Vilmorin (1902–69), French novelist, poet and journalist whose brief second marriage was to Count Paul Pálffy ab Erdöd; Duff Cooper's long-time mistress and a close friend of Diana Cooper.

5 The name of the nomadic warriors who controlled southern Russia between the seventh and third centuries BC came to be applied to the nineteenth- and early twentieth-century Russian thinkers and writers who mistrusted the West and saw Russia as an elemental force, perpetuating Scythian independence and ferocity. As IB had expressed it in a lecture at the Royal Institute of International Affairs (Chatham House) on 27 June: 'There is a permanent neurosis resulting from this uneasy position which Russia feels she occupied – "Scythians" belonging neither to West nor East' (SM 90).

6 Lady (Emerald) Cunard (1872–1948), née Maud Alice Burke, American-born London society hostess. IB had been introduced to her by Clarissa Churchill (71/1) and became one of her regular guests, though as he later commented: 'If I'd known that Lady Cunard had been a friend of Ribbentrop I think I might not have' (MI Tape 12).

7 In the 1925 silent film of Lew Wallace's 1880 novel *Ben-Hur* the hero had been played by Ramon Novarro.

8 The building at Versailles where Queen Marie-Antoinette held court.

9 Herbert Albert Laurens Fisher (1865–1940), historian and statesman; Warden of New College 1925–40; greatly admired by IB.

10 Presumably John Morley (1838–1923), 1st Viscount Morley 1908, journalist, author, Liberal MP and statesman.

11 Alfred Charles de Rothschild (1842–1918), banker, who built Halton House purely as a venue for entertaining.

which Bérard & Girardoux[1] are thought the peaks of contemporary genius: I wish Herbert Hart[2] were here, embarrassed but intellectually strenuous (dry & resilient). I leave tomorrow & am really brimful of gratitude to you. Every moment in Geneva, every glass of yoghourt, every quill cigar, shines with a fine & noble light – a sort of cosiness raised to the height of moral principle – in this marsh. If there were a Robespierre come to pull this down I should assist him: the trouble about the Russians is that they are too prone to this themselves now given half a chance: unlike Mr Forster[3] I feel we must be unkind: otherwise the morass will swallow us all. This is an incoherent letter: I boil with bitter feeling: Patricia is in bed with a cold & so is John: I am well & glad to return to our starving shores [. . .]

My love
    Isaiah.

The busy social life IB had led in the US continued in England. As IB later recalled: 'I had a real social season between 1944 and 1953. [. . .] I used to dine a lot in London with smart persons. [. . .] I was an eligible bachelor [. . .] an extra man.'[4] Lady Colefax was one of London's leading hostesses and IB was often among her guests. But the ease with which he could combine academic commitments in Oxford with social events in London and weekends in country houses was under threat: unfamiliar pressures were placed on university dons as young men released from the armed forces sought to complete their interrupted education.

TO SIBYL COLEFAX[5]

9 November 1946 [*manuscript*]

New College

Dear Sybil,
    I cannot find words with which to apologize for my failure to write for so long – I heard steady news of your recovery[6] from a thousand sources – even Oxford is not the social desert it is sometimes described as being by would be proud disdainful local anchorites – which put my mind at rest. And I can only beg you to try & imagine the conditions under which I live at present – enjoying alas none of the benefits of heads of Colleges or practitioners of

1 Jean Girardoux (1882–1944), French playwright and novelist.
2 Herbert Lionel Adolphus *Hart (1907–92), Fellow and Tutor in Philosophy, New College, 1945–52; Professor of Jurisprudence, Oxford, 1952–68.
3 (Edward) Morgan Forster (1879–1970), novelist, critic and essayist, advocated 'Tolerance, good temper and sympathy': 'What I Believe', *Nation*, 16 July 1938, reprinted in Forster's *Two Cheers for Democracy* (London, 1951), 77.
4 MI Tape 12.
5 Lady (Sibyl Sophie Julia) Colefax (1874–1950), née Halsey, society hostess and interior designer.
6 From a broken hip.

sparsely cultivated subjects – with pupils, dull & polite & spiritless with too much humane army life – scores & scores of them cluttering up every available chink of time & space, morning & afternoon & evening, & all this immediately on top of the remoteness & leisure & tranquillity of my Swiss summer – from October, when I returned, until now, in an unending stream, at once tedious & hectic, remorseless and shapeless & limp – I hope I am conveying the repellent image of my present form of life. No doubt all this is the penalty of winning two great world wars, & must be taken in a humble & ironical spirit. I cannot do it. If the young men back from the war were a querulous neurotic demanding tiresome rude insolent lot, one would at least experience some sense of the role of the patient martyr of the humanities, trying to civilize rough & dangerous barbarians. Nothing is less true. The young men are very civil, modest, respectful, anxious to learn, decently ambitious and touchingly considerate. All they lack is life, & there is no moral or intellectual substitute which can begin to make that tolerable. They are so well trained that they not merely do not show boredom ever – they do not recognize it when they feel it. Or possibly they do not feel it at all. I am sure I am exaggerating: but, believe me, in the right direction. If one were only so dessicated oneself that mere courtesy was enough to keep one going, one might be delighted by these polite, easy & industrious sheep. Alas I do not feel dead enough to do them justice. With the result that one loses – after teaching 20 or so a week as I am obliged to during the present vast numbers – all sense of endeavour, one cannot write or talk or devote oneself to those personal relations, which according to Cambridge & to Bloomsbury, are the most sacred of all the ends of life. Hence I do not reply to letters which accumulate in disordered heaps everywhere – & then more come – from Washington, Moscow, – & those are the ones which really expect answers being concrete, & full of requests & questions – the smaller the prospect of dealing with any. At least the All Souls examination[1] is now over & done – even into that college to which I feel most devoted, grey nonentities & hacks are creeping – & the Warden of Wadham[2] keeps an enormous bold flag flying. But apart from that, tedium & death. You must not forgive me for inflicting this unprovoked jeremiad upon you – you have done nothing to deserve so dreary an outpouring, & it is in the course of thinking how sad the hospital must have been that I was suddenly stirred – in an access of sudden exaggerated self pity – to try & elicit a little sympathy for the poor don's sorry plight. There are the brighter aspects. One lives a private & not a public life & that is never enough to be thanked for.

1 The annual examination to select new Fellows for All Souls College. IB had himself been success-ful in this examination in 1932 although he had resigned his prestigious Fellowship there a year early in 1938 to return to New College.
2 (Cecil) Maurice *Bowra (1898–1971), classicist; Warden, Wadham, 1938–70; Professor of Poetry (1946–51) and Vice-Chancellor (1951–4), Oxford.

Agreeable, delightful & sympathetic faces from the outer world occasionally appear. The 3ᵈ programme,[1] oddly enough, is a great improvement of life. The nameless grey horde of undergraduates will one day subside & flow back. The appearance of Oxford is still most comforting & occasionally phenomenal & stunning. But while term is flowing on all thought of pleasure & creative work is equally futile. The delicious meals in Geneva & 10 happy days in the Embassy in Paris are fearfully far away. For the first time in my life I look forward to Christmas & a little time to oneself. Perhaps I might be allowed to see you then – who are now, I do hope, completely recovered & well & as happy as may be. I do again apologize for not writing earlier & then, having done so, not written well or even sensibly.

Yours ever
Isaiah Berlin

I did have regular news of you via Sir O. Sargent[2] & that assuaged one greatly.

TO PHILIP GRAHAM[3]

14 November 1946

New College

Dear Phil,

[...] I have no words in which to convey my feelings on reaching Paris. You do not deserve a letter I suddenly say but I cannot now not go on. There I was in an excessively uncomfortable French train, having started out twenty-four hours before the fixed date, as a result of desperate and fatally successful efforts, coughing and sneezing and wheezing with a cold, only to find you had left twenty-four hours before I arrived. Ben, with I fear a certain relish, said: 'So you didn't hear that Phil had left today? I thought he had been quite anxious to see you', etc. etc. Be that as it may, and overlooking your rapprochement with Chip Bohlen over my slandered body – not but that I think that an excellent thing in itself, and long overdue as you know, but deprecate the method – overlooking all this, I say, I cannot deny that I have a great desire to see you and Kay.[4] It seems to me absurd that in your slavish imitation of Mr Lippmann[5] you should have avoided the U.K. so carefully,

1 On 26 September 1946, the BBC's third national radio network, the Third Programme, had begun broadcasting classical music, talks and drama between 7 p.m. and midnight.

2 Sir Orme Garton Sargent (1884–1962), diplomat, Permanent Under-Secretary of State, FO, 1946–9.

3 Philip Leslie *Graham (1915–63), lawyer (former pupil of Felix Frankfurter), journalist, and publisher from 1946 of the Washington Post.

4 Katharine ('Kay') *Graham (1917–2001), née Meyer, Phil Graham's wife, who published the Washington Post after his death in 1963.

5 Walter Lippmann (1889–1974), political journalist and author, who wrote a nationally syndicated column, 'Today and Tomorrow', for the New York Herald Tribune, 1931–62; liberal early, more pragmatic later.

leaving Joe as the sole expert on that small but rich political field, not but what ('Not but what what' you wd at this moment interject.) he really did manage to get around in a tremendous fashion while he was here, and in consequence undoubtedly knows a thing or two. I should like to see you and Kay very much; I do not deny that I should not mind seeing our old Kentucky friend[1] either; my thoughts stray to him quite often, but I have not heard from him for so long, and my last memories of him in Washington are so confused with persons wholly irrelevant to him (and for that matter … but I should not go on) that you must tell him that he must make the first move. Of course I know that he is putting on weight again; and this is genuinely worrying. Perhaps I should almost come over for the sole purpose of arresting this process. But best of all if he comes to Europe, particularly to England. If he comes this Summer I promise to look after him in every sort of way. The normal diet of the British Isles will do its work far, far better than anything else could or will. Why don't you all three appear? There is, as you all know, no reason save of initial inertia. I shall write to the Judge[2] and set those tiny but persistent wheels in motion.

Of my own life and times there is little to relate. I work all day and I work all night at tasks not really worth fulfilling. The undergraduate population has more than doubled – Stakhanovite methods[3] are being employed – the statistics are splendid, we overproduced our quota by thousands of per cent. The young men are earnest and spiritless, and get one down to an uncommon degree. Tentative offers are made to me to leave my ancient subject and become a Russian historian, an occupation at once better paid and involving less physical and intellectual effort than philosophy. I am delighted to be wooed, but display at the moment a noble austerity of character, saying I could not leave my college in the lurch at its most critical moment, and merely seek my own pleasure; this I hope is producing a profound impression all round, and I shall ultimately be forced to do what I would like to do. At present however my protestations appear to be received on their face value, and I am gloomily contemplating a life of grinding hackery for the next thirty years or so.

America and Russia have really receded below the horizon, and I am back in 1937, with an uncontrollable feeling that something is not quite right, and that I should be doing something quite different, and that I never shall. But clearly if I go on in this way, this will turn into a tremendous piece of Alsopism, images of a longer and longer nose, more and more rigid cheeks, 2 a.m. and a terrible desire to get away. […]

1 Ed(ward) Fretwell *Prichard, Jr ('Prich') (1915–84), US lawyer (from Kentucky) of huge girth; briefly shared a house with IB in Washington during the summer of 1943.

2 Felix *Frankfurter (1882–1965), Associate Justice of the US Supreme Court, 1939–62.

3 Aleksey Grigor'evich Stakhanov (1906–77), a Russian miner who in 1935 allegedly achieved 14 times his work quota, gave his name to a movement designed to achieve greatly increased productivity throughout Russian industry

I have now acquired a set of political views as one does a suit of clothes, and peddle them everywhere. I know exactly what I should do if I were Mr Bevin. I also know what I should do if I were Mr Byrnes.[1] I am not quite clear as to what I should do if I were Mr Truman,[2] but I find that, oddly enough, more difficult to imagine. I have clear views on Russia, France and Palestine.

Thank you ever so much for my parcels, which are the greatest possible help, materially and morally. It will be wonderful now that parcels may be bigger to receive the famous ham, not necessarily from Twenty One.[3] What is not needed is tea or soup or soap. What are quite splendid are things like chocolates and sweets and salami and cake and pastry (please reimburse yourself for these) of every description. But I am not down to starvation level, and even luxuries occasionally occur.

Shaya

PS As for [Nicolas] Nabokov, he is a very gifted and delightful man, but I did not know he wanted to stay in the U.S. If he does, I should certainly recommend him warmly. He is not a very good composer, but understands far more than anybody, and in conversation at least talks about it with great magnificence and articulateness. I hope you like him. He is the most obsolete of all types – a Russian bourgeois Liberal of 1910, of which there will be no more ever again. Not for nothing did Zhdanov[4] condemn the period

1 James Francis Byrnes (1879–1972), influential US lawyer and Democratic politician; Secretary of State 1945–7; Governor of South Carolina 1951–5.
2 Harry S. Truman (1884–1972), US President 1945–53.
3 The prestigious New York restaurant named from its location at 21 West 52nd Street.
4 Andrey Aleksandrovich Zhdanov (1896–1948), Soviet government and Communist Party official (responsible for the defence of Leningrad during the war); proponent of socialist realism in the arts from 1934 but particularly in 1946–8, when, as Stalin's controller of culture, Zhdanov instigated the persecution of artists not following the official line (the 'Zhdanovshchina'). On 14 August 1946 the Central Committee of the Communist Party resolved that 'any preaching, which lacks ideas, and is apolitical, such as "art for art's sake", is alien to Soviet literature, is harmful to the interests of the Soviet people and the State' ('On the Journals *Zvezda* and *Leningrad*: From the Decree of the Central Committee of the All-Russia Communist Party', *Kul'tura i zhizn'*, 20 August 1946, 1, trans. Felicity Ashbee and Irina Tidmarsh in *The Central Committee Resolution and Zhdanov's Speech on the Journals* Zvezda *and* Leningrad, bilingual edition [Royal Oak, Michigan, 1978]), and singled out Anna Akhmatova (25/1) for particular vilification. In a speech delivered on 15 August to the Leningrad Communist Party and the next day to the Leningrad branch of the Union of Soviet Writers, Zhdanov continued his attack: 'after the 1905 Revolution, a great many of the intellectuals spurned the revolution and slid down into a morass of pornography and reactionary mysticism [...]. Anna Akhmatova is one of the representatives of this idea-less reactionary morass in literature. [...] she is one of the standard-bearers of the meaningless, empty-headed, aristocratic-salon school of poetry, which has no place whatever in Soviet literature. [...] Akhmatova's subject-matter is individualistic to the core. The range of her poetry is sadly limited; it is the poetry of a spoilt woman-aristocrat, frenziedly vacillating between boudoir and chapel. [...] It would be hard to say whether she is a nun or a fallen woman [*bludnitsa*]; better perhaps say she is a bit of each, her desires and her prayers intertwined. [...] This mood of solitude and hopelessness, which is foreign to the spirit of Soviet literature, runs through the whole of Akhmatova's work. [...] Akhmatova's work is a matter of the distant past; it is foreign to Soviet life and cannot be tolerated in the pages of our journals. [...] These works can sow nothing but gloom, low spirits, pessimism, a desire to escape the vital problems of social

1907–1917 as the worst in Russian art and history. It was in fact a moment of real Renaissance and full of major works of genuine value, at any rate in poetry and music. Now that my particular friends have been cracked on the head so brutally in Moscow and Leningrad, I find it difficult not to blow up in public. The only reason for their punishment is excessive popularity. Zhdanov's speech on the subject is well worth reading in full – I don't mean the one to the Politburo on the anniversary of the Revolution, but the one on Literature in Leningrad in August or September. It is a really radical pronouncement on the whole attitude to art and education, and worth a serious commentary. I cannot do it for the old reason that anything I do may get my friends into further trouble, the risk is too great, and Washington too leaky. But if someone else would sign them I might at least provide some notes if you thought that worth while. But perhaps I feel too hotly on the basis of messages from people which have reached me to be allowed to set pen to paper. What is happening is really unspeakably sordid and detestable – the slow humiliation of poets and musicians is more awful in a way than outright shooting. But I must not go on. Have Bevin and the Judge met yet? And are relations with the Embassy as warm as ever? I must write and ask direct. Meanwhile you will be pleased to hear that I was telephoned to by his Aunt and asked to look after 'a scholarly young man at Balliol' College, whom it was thought I would greatly like. His name is Nicholas Mosley,[1] and he is the son of Sir Oswald. ⟨I have oddly enough done nothing.

On Europe I think (our) Mr B[evin] wrong because what the noncommunists need is a political lead + help to all régimes of a social democratic nature, & not social cum economic good sense, which worthy as it may be, & vitally wanted in 1919, is not the magnetic force for Europeans at present. As for Palestine, my govt. seems equally terrified of Jews & Arabs: the Stern gang,[2] despite Koestler's[3] readable & in a way necessary but detestable & vulgar novel, are really ruining the Jews. What shd be done is Partition: with

---

life and activity into a narrow little world of personal experiences. [...] From Soviet writers the Soviet people expect reliable ideological armament, spiritual food to further the fulfilment of construction and rehabilitation plans and to promote the development of our country's national economy.' *Pravda*, 21 September 1946, trans. in A. A. Zhdanov, *On Literature, Music and Philosophy* (London, 1950), 25–6, 29–30, 41.

1 Nicholas Mosley (b. 1923), 3rd Baron Ravensdale 1966, Balliol 1946–7, novelist; son of Sir Oswald Ernald Mosley (1896–1980), politician and founder of the British Union of Fascists, and his first wife, the former Lady Cynthia Curzon. After the death of his mother in 1933, Nicholas Mosley was brought up by her unmarried elder sister, Lady (Mary) Irene Ravensdale (1896–1966), 2nd Baroness Ravensdale 1925, Baroness Ravensdale of Kedleston 1958, a devotee of music, foxhunting and alcohol (and one of Sir Oswald Mosley's many conquests).

2 In 1940 Avraham Stern rejected the Irgun's suspension of hostilities towards the British during the early part of the Second World War and set up 'Fighters for the Freedom of Israel' (known by its Hebrew acronym, Lehi), a small militant group committed to the use of terrorism to expel the British from Palestine. In 1944 they had murdered Churchill's friend Lord Moyne in Cairo.

3 Arthur Koestler (1905–83), novelist, journalist and writer on scientific and social topics; born in Hungary of Jewish descent; British subject 1945; supporter of Zionism. His novel *Thieves in the Night* (London, 1946) was based on his experiences of living on a kibbutz during the 1920s.

Peel-like frontiers:[1] & the Arab bit given outright, with no strings, to the Arab state of Iraq + Transjordan: giving a solid area of 4½ million Arabs unthrea[te]nable by even 2 million Jews. The Egyptians, Saudians & Iraqis wd take this: Oriental Jews cd be exchanged against the Arabs caught in the Jewish territory: & my God the thing wd be localized & cease to infuriate Jews, Arabs, British & Americans, & act as an irresistible temptation of a semi-sincere character to Soviet anti-imperialists. If plugged hard enough this wd go through: there is insufficient resistance in the Foreign Office & Parliament to it: all the people I talk to seem to accept it as the least evil: partition of Pal[estine] into 2 tiny states which is obviously foolish in a way is to some degree overcome if the Arab bit becomes part of a wider territory (Iraq & Transjordan) & the Jewish bit is tied down by UNO etc. to a not fully sovereign state but put on a sort of indefinite probation + right to self-immigration. [...]

Yrs

    Shaya⟩

IB's undertaking to translate Turgenev's First Love, *together with a further novel,* Rudin, *marked his return to the role of a published author, which had begun with the appearance in 1939 of* Karl Marx: His Life and Environment *but had been interrupted by the war. His contract for KM had specified completion within three years; in the event he took half as long again, not an unusual overrun in the academic world. But with* First Love *IB became (and remained) a publisher's nightmare: against the quality of what he produced had to be set the difficulty of extracting it from him as delay followed delay and publishing deadlines fell by the wayside. Hamish Hamilton was the first of many publishers to suffer in this way.*

TO HAMISH HAMILTON

14 December 1946 [*manuscript*]

New College

Dear Jamie,

    I fear that Roger Machell[2] treated my frivolous speeches too seriously, although alas there was only too much substance behind them – in the sense that I am being driven from pillar to post by this college & university. However your claims are very real & I must do something: so I have cancelled my trip to Brussels this month to deliver a lecture, & have got out

1 See 11/1.
2 Roger Victor Machell (1908–84), originally a journalist, became Hamilton's business partner after being seriously injured during the war; he was described in his obituary as 'one of the last of the old-style publishers' editors' who 'deployed superb reserves of tact, patience, intellectual discrimination and command of detail, but perhaps above all whole-hearted involvement with his authors and their books and lives' (*The Times*, 14 February 1984, 16).

of every other academic engagement until term starts when once more a million pupils settle like locust[s] & eat up the weeks: & I shall do any rate *one* of the T. stories before the end of January. The other I hope before the end of April.[1] If I can do it faster I will. My university lectures are the only superior priority: the rest of what I have to do in order not to be expelled will have to wait. And I understand your distressed impatience & will do my best.

Yrs

   IB

The leaders of the Jewish community in Palestine frequently put pressure on IB to play a more active role in the Zionist movement, and in particular to move to Palestine. IB's Oxford commitments provided an excuse for resisting offers of a post within the Jewish Agency made in early 1947; but the personal claims made by his old friends Chaim and Vera Weizmann[2] were harder to avoid.

TO CHAIM WEIZMANN

20 March 1947 [*manuscript*]

New College

Dear Dr Weizmann,

Thank you very much for your letter,[3] which arrived a week or so ago. Since then I have been trying to see if there was any method of joining you at Easter, for פסח[4] I mean. My chief difficulty is this: I am at the moment in bed with a temperature of about 101% [*sic*], not indeed v. bad or dangerous, ordinary 'flu I daresay, but the result of the combination of the Flood, the Ice Age[5] & the Hungry Forties[6] which, perhaps justly, have fallen on us like the plagues of Egypt. There is no fire, little food, & I am not expecting to recover enough to move about for at least a week: this brings us to the 27–28: & on the 17th I have to be back to examine here: & If I am to avoid a fiasco next term with my lectures, I have to have a week of solid work if only to set out the headings & accumulate a bibliography. So that the journey wd be a fearful panic stricken dash to & fro with my poor parents wringing their hands about my feeble health etc. etc. – I am sure that nature in Palestine must be most magnificent

1 IB eventually reneged on his agreement to translate two Turgenev stories, and his translation of *First Love* was published (in 1950) with Alex Brown's translation of *Rudin*.
2 Vera *Weizmann (1881–1966), née Chatzman, Russian-born paediatrician, married to Chaim Weizmann.
3 Dated 6 March, pressing IB to visit during his Easter vacation.
4 'Pesach' ('Passover').
5 The winter of 1946/7 was one of the harshest ever recorded in England. From late January to mid-March temperatures barely rose above freezing, constant snowfalls caused major disruption to transport, which exacerbated post-war fuel and food shortages, and there was almost no sunshine; in mid-March the thaw and gales caused widespread severe flooding.
6 The decade 1840–50 was so named because legislative changes and crop failure meant that the poor were in constant danger of starvation throughout the UK.

just now: even Mr B[evin] cannot alter that. His speech[1] was apparently a spontaneous performance, completely off & away from the prepared F.O. brief which was a less committal & more judicious exposition, & pro tanto wiser & less brutal. At present literally nobody seems to know what will happen next, at UNO or anywhere. As for what shd be done in the future, not immediately, but some day when things look brighter all round, may I come & discuss it with you in June? or will it be too hot in ארץ[2] & will you be back here? if so I shall wait in England. I have had an offer from Harvard[3] to come to them for a year, at something like 4 times my Oxford salary & with about 1/10 of the work, + the prospect of a permanent job. Needless to say the latter is out of the question, but even a short visit which is not unattractive I shall have to turn down, since Oxford is going through a fearful crisis & one must retain some shred of decency – I have a great love for it really & cannot bear the thought of repaying its kindness with inconsiderate behaviour at a difficult moment. But what distresses me far more is my inability to come to you at this moment: perhaps, if I recover sooner than I hope, & shake off the endless germs which have laid me low all through the term (I must have spent 4 or 5 weeks in bed by now half sick & half teaching) I might be able to fly, but on my present form it seems unlikely. Although I have not had pneumonia I am in somewhat the state I was in when you looked after me so nobly & unforgettably in the Catskills in 1942:[4] & for the moment I feel that I shall never travel again. If there is any chance, I shall, if I may, wire you. But if not, please forgive me: I have had to ask forgiveness all through the month for my broken engagements. I'll write again anyway.

My love to Mrs Weizmann & to Bergmann.[5]

Isaiah

1 Presumably Bevin's notably forthright speech in the Parliamentary debate on Palestine on 25 February, which followed the announcement on 14 February that Britain was to refer the problem of Palestine to the United Nations. Bevin had attacked with equal vigour the terms of the original mandate, the intransigence of the Jewish Agency, and the unhelpful interference of the US Government, whose pressure for increased Jewish immigration into Palestine had, he claimed, been influenced by domestic political considerations.

2 'Eretz Israel' (Palestine, 13/10).

3 On being advised by Felix Frankfurter, whose views he had sought, that IB had 'learning without pedantry, wisdom without heaviness, wit without flippancy, and critical judgment of a high order' (Felix Frankfurter to Donald McKay, 18 February 1947 [MSB 253/38]), McKay (89/2), of Harvard University, had written on 1 March inviting IB to teach on the USSR for the academic year 1947–8. IB replied on 14 March suggesting 1948–9 instead. But even this would be difficult: 'both New College & the university have separately & jointly forbidden me to go to Harvard for a year even if I were prepared to do so in 1947–8: & are not anxious to let me go even in 1948 or 1949': to Chaim Weizmann, 15 September 1947.

4 In November 1942 IB had spent some time with the Weizmanns in the Catskill Mountains, New York State, convalescing after a bout of pneumonia.

5 Ernst David Bergmann (1903–75), German-born organic chemist; Scientific Director, Daniel Sieff Research Institute (incorporated into the new Weizmann Institute of Science in 1949) 1934–9, 1946–51; Head of Scientific Department, Israel Defense Forces, 1948–66; Professor of Organic Chemistry, Hebrew University, Jerusalem, 1952–66; founding Chairman, Israel Atomic Energy Commission, 1952–66. Towards the end of the 1940s his allegiance shifted from Weizmann,

*Despite his protestations IB's illnesses did not prevent him taking a holiday in
Italy and France during his Easter vacation.*

*IB's visit to the poet Anna Akhmatova[1] in Leningrad in November 1945 had
been one of the most significant experiences of his life. But this and their further
meeting in January 1946 had led to an immediate increase in Soviet surveillance
of her. After Akhmatova's poetry was condemned by Zhdanov,[2] the few
privileges she had were reduced and her writings once again effectively banned.
An encouraging report from Gennady Rakhlin,[3] 'Tell our friend that Akhmatova
is well and living happily and quietly in her flat on a State pension of 600R.
a month', reached IB via Brenda Tripp,[4] who concluded 'it is not as bad as we
thought it was and of course you are not in any way guilty, as I do not really see
how your visits could have been responsible – so don't worry – Rachlin seemed
very reassuring about her though terrified out of his wits about himself'. But
Boris Nicolaevsky[5] was less sanguine.*

TO BORIS NICOLAEVSKY

10 May 1947

New College

Dear Mr Nicolaevsky,

[...] As for Anna A[ndreevna], so far as I know the facts are these: according to [Rakhlin][6] she still receives a pension of 600 roubles a month, which
is not much, but something. Of course this may not be true. Anyway, she is
obviously finished while things are as they are. I met her son L[ev] G[umilev][7]

whose protégé he had been in the 1930s, to Ben-Gurion, whose scientific adviser at the Ministry
of Defense he became in 1951.

1 Anna Akhmatova (1889–1966), pen-name of Anna Andreevna Gorenko; poet particularly associated with the Acmeist movement before the Revolution and with expressing the sufferings of
the Russian people after it. Her work was condemned by the State for its lack of social realism
and effectively banned from 1925 to 1952, with some slight relaxation during the war, when she
became a national figurehead.

2 See 20/4.

3 Gedali (Gennady) Moiseevich Rakhlin, bookseller and (unknown to IB) almost certainly an agent
of the security services. One of his State bookshops in Leningrad was used as an unofficial
literary salon. IB had bought books from him during his 1945 visit and later (via Brenda Tripp).
Rakhlin spent about eight years in the Gulag from c.1949. See L1, 604–7.

4 Brenda Muriel Howard Tripp (1906–2004), British Council representative in the Soviet Union
(formally FO cultural attaché with diplomatic status), who had accompanied IB on his memorable 1945 trip to Leningrad. Her letter is dated 12 February 1947.

5 Boris Ivanovich Nicolaevsky (1887–1966), Menshevik political activist who became a historian
and archivist of the Russian revolutionary movement; US-based from 1940. He had correctly
reported that AA had lost her writers' union card (and hence her ration card), but wrongly
thought she had also lost her apartment and was now living in servants' lodgings near Leningrad
(letter to IB of 20 March 1947).

6 Gap left by typist.

7 Lev Nikolaevich Gumilev (1912–92), historian, son of Anna Akhmatova and her first husband,
the pre-Revolutionary poet Nikolay Gumilev (executed in 1921); sentenced in 1938 to ten years in
the Gulag, he was released to fight in the Soviet Army during the war but re-imprisoned 1949–56.
Akhmatova blamed this re-arrest on his brief 1945 encounter with IB in her flat.

in 1945 – but please do not publish this or talk about it, otherwise the poor
young man may suffer. He was then back from Berlin, where he had been
an anti-aircraft gunner, and was certainly at liberty in January 1946. He is
a very competent Central Asiatic historian, and a pupil of Tarle.[1] By now
anything may have happened to him, of course. He was exceptionally well
educated, imaginative, charming, and devoted to his mother. I do not know
his poem,[2] but if you have it I should be very grateful to you for a copy.
Nor do I know the poem by his mother[3] of which you give the last line, for
which also I should be immensely grateful. The last poems by her I have seen
are those in the banned number of *Leningrad*.[4] She obviously cannot recant.
As for Zoshchenko,[5] he was recently declared to be writing a novel about
the Leningrad partisans, and is obviously trying to crawl back into favour.
I cannot feel very strongly about him, since he seems to be a man of little
talent or integrity, although I suppose that should not prejudice humanitar-
ian feeling. [...]
    Yours sincerely,
        Isaiah Berlin

*Now the Weizmanns expected him to fulfil his reluctant promise to visit them
later, despite the danger of anti-British terrorism. IB resorted to devious tactics:*

Weizmann asked me to go and see him. I knew that when I arrived, if I arrived,
he would have no idea why I had come. It was part of great men to behave
like that, they summon you and then they totally forget, but you go all the
same because they are who they are. Well I didn't terribly want to go. [...] You
certainly couldn't get into Palestine without a visa, quite difficult, there was
a kind of temporary wartime situation. And so then I wrote a letter to the
Foreign Office on a not very clean piece of paper saying 'Dear Sir, I would like
to spend a holiday in Palestine. Can I have a visa? Yours sincerely', then in a

---

1 Evgeny Viktorovich Tarle (1875–1955), leading Soviet historian.
2 'The Death of Prince Dzhamuga', a dramatic poem set in the time of Genghis Khan, not published at this time. Two versions are included in L. N. Gumilev, *Dar slov mne byl obeshchan ot
  prirody: literaturnoe nasledie: stikhi, dramy, perevody, proza*, ed. M. G. Kozyreva and V. N. Voronovich
  (St Petersburg, 2004), 75–80, 81–159.
3 *Requiem*, II. BN quotes (in the original Russian) the last couplet, 'Husband in the grave, son in
  prison, / Say a prayer for me', quoted here from *The Complete Poems of Anna Akhmatova*, trans.
  Judith Hemschemeyer, ed. Roberta Reeder, 2nd ed. (Boston, Massachusetts/Edinburgh, 1992),
  387. Written mainly during 1938–40 after the arrest of Lev Gumilev, *Requiem* is a memorial to the
  suffering of Stalin's victims; the complete text, first published in Munich in 1963, did not appear
  in the Soviet Union until 1987.
4 IB is probably referring to *Leningrad* 1946 Nos 1–2 (of which he owned a copy), page 13 of which
  is devoted to eight poems by Akhmatova under the heading 'Stikhi raznykh let' ('Poems from
  various years'), accompanied by a photograph of the poet. Her cycle *Cinque*, based on her meetings with IB, appeared in the next issue, Nos 3–4. These were the issues that prompted Zhdanov's
  suppression of *Leningrad* and, together with the work Akhmatova published in *Zvezda*, his vilification of Akhmatova in August 1946 (20/4).
5 Mikhail Mikhailovich Zoshchenko (1895–1958), satiric writer whose work was criticised for lack
  of social realism in the 1930s and damned by Zhdanov in 1946, an attack which destroyed him.

kind of tweeny hand, 'I. Berlin.' I knew what I'd get, I had not written on New College paper, you see, and naturally I got a printed little notice saying nobody was allowed into Palestine now, would I give up all ideas of that, which is what I wanted. I then wrote to Weizmann saying, 'Well, I've applied for a visa, and they haven't [given me one], and the idea of trying to wheedle one because I've been a British Official is rather embarrassing' – which it would have been if I'd had to do that, this is the truth.[1]

TO CHAIM WEIZMANN

11 June 1947 [*manuscript telegram as received, with part torn off*]

Oxford

Visa refused have consulted relevant official who made clear that would be quite useless and merely embarrassing to press journey present mom[ent] and saw no altern[ative] to postponment stop feel totally discouraged and embarassed and would value your advice love
Isaiah

But IB had underestimated Weizmann's talent for string-pulling: 'Then a telegram arrived from the High Commissioner[2] *saying "You are invited to Palestine, come whenever you like." That cut off my retreat.'*[3]

TO PHILIP GRAHAM

21 June 1947

All Souls

My dear Phil,
I am now in a condition to talk with a more certain voice. I am prepared, yes, and more than prepared, to wait for you in England until 2 September. After that I find myself committed to go to Southern Italy, where I should welcome you among the wild shepherds of Calabria, among whom I propose to spend September, a very cold month in England made no warmer by lack of permission to use any known form of fuel. If you are going to Oxford then I advise a fur coat and sealskin cap with ear flaps. [. . .] Mr Wallace[4]

---

1 MI Tape 19.
2 General Sir Alan Gordon Cunningham (1887–1983), High Commissioner and C.-in-C. for Palestine 1945–8.
3 MI Tape 19.
4 Henry Agard Wallace (1888–1965), agricultural scientist and left-wing Democratic politician, Vice-President 1940–5 but dropped by FDR in favour of Truman, Secretary for Commerce 1945–6, sacked by Truman for perceived Communist sympathies; editor, *New Republic*, 1946–8; founded Progressive Party and stood as candidate in 1948 presidential election, campaigning on a peace programme but unhelpfully endorsed by the US Communist Party; remained embittered by his treatment by liberals opposed to Communism. In April 1946 he visited Britain at the start of a speaking tour of Europe; his public speeches controversially criticised US policy towards the

painted a grisly picture of his political enemies to shuddering audiences here. The most remarkable statement he made, and I present this to you rather than to Herbert Elliston,[1] who does not like Fretwell, was that the person most responsible for his (Wallace's) downfall was none other than myself. He regards me as not merely dangerous, but the most deeply sinister agent ever sent from the United Kingdom to the United States. According to him, I wormed my way into the confidence of various United States Liberals, such as Fretwell and Arthur Schlesinger, Jr[2] (whom I met once), and by selling them the terrible slogan of the non-Communist Left, caused an inner split in the American progressive movement which led to a chain reaction of successive left-wing fission. If it were not for this carefully planted bomb, the American progressive movement might have effected a united front. As it is, it is nearly in ruins, destroyed single-handedly by me, with my dupes and stooges; among whom, I regret to say, you too are to be found, though a less hopeless case than some. All this was poured out to such faithful Marxists as Harold Butler[3] and Lord Pakenham[4] – the latter believed it all, and called on me hotfoot, virtually to offer the congratulations of the Roman Church for a very Christian piece of work. I find all this exhilarating but embarrassing. I feel that Gardner Jackson[5] ought to be told what a viper he has been nursing in his bosom; and what will Marion's[6] reactions be? I can just hear her say, 'Well, I expect he was rather sinister at times. He was very close to the Halifaxes,[7] you know. But then, so was Felix, of course.' It really does seem an unbelievable atmosphere from here.

[...] I wish I were coming to Harvard, but I cannot blame my College for being adamant. America has become a synonym for luxury and ease, and

Soviet Union, but his attack on IB (who always regarded Wallace as having 'a screw loose': MI Tape 7) presumably took place on a private occasion.

1 Herbert Berridge Elliston (1895–1957), British-born editor of the *Washington Post* 1940–53.
2 Arthur Meier *Schlesinger, Jr (1917–2007), US historian and liberal political activist.
3 Sir Harold Beresford Butler (1883–1951), Director, International Labour Office, 1932–8; Warden, Nuffield, 1939–43; Minister and Head of British Information Services at the British Embassy, Washington, 1942–6, where IB had been on his staff.
4 Francis Aungier ('Frank') Pakenham (1905–2001), Baron Pakenham 1945, 7th Earl of Longford 1961; socialist reformer and devout Roman Catholic; Student in Politics, Christ Church, 1934–46, 1952–64; Parliamentary Under-Secretary of State, War Office, 1946–7; Chancellor of the Duchy of Lancaster 1947–8; Minister of Civil Aviation 1948–51; First Lord of the Admiralty 1951; later (1964–8) a Labour Cabinet Minister.
5 Gardner 'Pat' Jackson (1896–1965), journalist and political activist best known for his earlier involvement in the unsuccessful campaign to prevent the execution in 1927 of the anarchists Nicola Sacco and Bartolomeo Vanzetti, whose letters he and Marion Frankfurter (next note) edited; influenced by Communists in the 1930s, he became a leading anti-Communist liberal (and lost his left eye when mugged in 1944 by Communist-dominated trade unionists).
6 Marion A. *Frankfurter (1890–1975), née Denman, wife of Felix Frankfurter.
7 Edward Frederick Lindley Wood (1881–1959), 1st Earl of Halifax, British Ambassador, Washington, 1941–6 (and thus the signatory of the political reports IB drafted in Washington 1942–6), and his wife Dorothy Evelyn Augusta (née Onslow), Countess of Halifax (1885–1976). The professional association between Halifax and IB was no doubt strengthened by their Oxford connections: Halifax was at the time a Fellow of All Souls and Chancellor of the University.

there is a powerful puritanical instinct against allowing people to go there. Anyhow, I am caught between two fires: so long as the Truman tyranny[1] continues, I suppose I am reasonably safe, but that can't last long; on the left Mr Wallace is baying savagely; on the right, Mrs Garrett,[2] through whom, according to D. Maclean,[3] I have caused a wave of Anglophobia to spread to Washington, has armed the forces of the right. We are not long for this world, Felix and I. I wish you would write at greater length. You must learn from Joe, my only friend in the US. Or perhaps Kay is too, but she gives no sign.

Yrs

Isaiah

⟨It is now certain that in 3 days I go to Jerusalem. God knows why, because the Old Boy – Weizmann – is clamouring for me. I *detest* the idea of going & nobody thinks really well of it but I cannot find out how not to go. So go I will by a Greek tramp steamer of 2000 tons across 10 days of Mediterranean heat into the arms of the Irgun as a blatant traitor. Pray for me: but also tell the Felixes – I hope it moves them to write.

IB.⟩

Accompanied by his father,[4] IB embarked at Marseilles on a boat which meandered slowly around the Mediterranean; during a two-day stop in Athens they were entertained by friends at the British Embassy. The ship eventually reached Haifa at a time of increasing anti-British terrorism. IB spent some days with the Weizmanns, meeting the High Commissioner and British officials who came to call on Britain's greatest ally in the Zionist camp. But he also saw another side of Palestine. Among the relatives he re-encountered there, the most memorable was Yitzhak Sadeh,[5] a Palmach commander and Chief

1 Revelations of Communist infiltration of government departments led President Truman to announce in March 1947 the introduction of 'loyalty boards' to monitor the actions and beliefs of State employees; any employee whose affiliations were considered suspect could be dismissed, though in practice few were.

2 Alice Warder Garrett (1877–1952), wealthy doyenne of the cultural life of Baltimore, widow of a former US Ambassador, John Work Garrett; 'a mad old lady' according to IB (MI Tape 7), who had stayed with her at Evergreen, her vast house full of artistic treasures, before they quarrelled for some reason.

3 Donald Maclean (1913–83), a wartime colleague of IB at the British Embassy in Washington, later revealed as one of the Cambridge spy-ring working for the USSR. Maclean had provoked a row at a Washington dinner party in 1944 by criticising IB's tolerance of people with right-wing views; but when IB fell out with Alice Warder Garrett, 'Maclean complained about me, said I was making a bad name for England by being not very nice to this old lady' (MI Tape 7).

4 The visit to Palestine at such a time by the normally cautious Mendel Berlin is surprising, and seems most probably to relate to a possible purchase of land there that he and Marie had been considering.

5 Yitzhak Sadeh (1890–1952), né Isaac Landoberg; Mendel Berlin's first cousin, who had married (and abandoned) Mendel's sister Evgenia; a hero in the Russian Army during the First World War; settled in Palestine in 1920, becoming a Haganah commander (and chief commander of

of the Haganah's general staff, whom he met clandestinely in Tel Aviv. A tour
of exploration[1] allowed him to see how much Palestine had changed since his
previous visit in 1934.

TO MARIE BERLIN[2]

14 July 1947 [*manuscript*]

Mines House, Mt Canaan

I have no more to say now than this morning when, at 7.30 a.m. we left on
our tour. Palestine has grown *incredibly* in the last 13 years – particularly Tel
Aviv & Jerusalem: but such a hotel[3] as the one we are staying in now was not
conceivable 13 years ago when I was here last [. . .]

My host is *far* better – physically – than in London, & truly enjoys his
Palazzo[4] & position.[5] Lady W. is also v. seigneurial. They were both charming to father. Towards the UNO Commission[6] he takes the attitude – it is the
19th commission since 1918 – "we have survived 18 & we shall live through
this too."

Love

Shaya

By the time IB left Palestine in late July the political situation had deteriorated
still further.[7] Two British sergeants were kidnapped on 12 July (and were later

the Palmach 1941–5); co-ordinated military operations against the British; played a major part in
the Arab–Israeli war of 1948. He is the subject of a memoir in PI2. IB valued his good humour
and vitality: 'I had about three hours with him – the most agreeable talk, which my family would
have disapproved of most strongly. [. . .] He was generous by nature, nothing mean or small. [. . .]
What he liked was the excitement [. . .]. He wasn't a serious Zionist, he was just a jolly figure; if
there was a fight, he liked getting into it; a sort of Irish character, fundamentally – frivolous' (MI
Tape 18).

1 IB, his father and his mother's sister Ida spent two days exploring the northern part of Palestine
   in a chauffeur-driven car provided by Chaim Weizmann.
2 Written on the back of a letter from Mendel to Marie [MSB 806/25r].
3 The Mines House Pension-Hotel on Mount Canaan in northern Galilee, near Safad, was 'a large
   european hotel with baths, douches, nice clean rooms, large halls & verandas': Mendel to Marie,
   14 July 1947 [ibid.].
4 The house which the Weizmanns had built for themselves at Rehovot.
5 Although Weizmann's pro-British stance and opposition to violence had lost him the Presidency
   of the Zionist Organization at the 22nd Zionist Congress in Basle in December 1946 (his speech
   there contained a paragraph drafted by IB rejecting Zionist terrorism), he still acted as the senior
   statesman of the movement, and addressed UNSCOP (next note) on 8 July.
6 The United Nations Special Committee on Palestine (UNSCOP) was appointed on 14 May 1947,
   and as part of its investigations visited Palestine from 16 June to 24 July, taking evidence in public
   hearings (held in the Jerusalem YMCA) which the Arab leaders boycotted. After discussions elsewhere and visits to displaced persons' camps in Europe, the Committee reported on 31 August;
   although India, Iran and Yugoslavia submitted a minority report favouring a federated Jewish–
   Arab State (and Australia abstained), the majority supported partition of Palestine into separate
   Jewish and Arab States. Although the 11 delegates came from countries without involvement in
   Palestine, their own national preoccupations inevitably contributed to their input.
7 IB wrote to Elliott Felkin on 17 July: 'I must attend the opening of a colony [i.e. a settlement] if

murdered by the Irgun in retaliation for the execution on 29 July of three Jewish terrorists). On 18 July the Haganah ship Exodus 1947, carrying some 4,500 illegal immigrants to Palestine, was rammed by British destroyers and taken to Haifa, where, in the sight of some of the UNSCOP delegates, the passengers were forced on to ships designed to return them to France, whence they had sailed. As the Haganah had anticipated, this event and the subsequent sufferings of the passengers, who were eventually returned to camps in Germany, had a major impact on world opinion.

IB returned via Geneva and Paris to teach in Oxford's Summer School for Graduates.[1]

TO PATRICK REILLY[2]
[British Embassy, Athens]
3 August 1947 [manuscript]

New College

Dear Patrick,

I ought to have written to you long ago to thank you & your wife[3] for your kindness, & hospitality, & general (I can't spell) acceuil[4] (is that right?) – you can't imagine how agreeable such a thing can be after a journey & before unknown, unknowable & frightening prospects. The rest of the journey was uneventful enough: in Haifa the entire British fleet appeared poised to swoop on our handful of legal immigrants, but before anything horrifying happened, Lord Oxford,[5] Asst. District Commissioner of Haifa, solemnly & with much dignity stepped aboard & bore me off before a gaping crowd of commonplace queued up passengers, who had previously treated me with the disdain proper to humble, boring, academic types. However, it was a moment of golden glory: I enjoyed every instant of it. As for the Holy Land itself, the top soldiers seemed to me more intelligent & certainly far better informed than the civilian authorities. It is a ludicrous thing when 80·000 or so troops – a greater number than ever were in India surely – are held at bay by 4000 terrorists. The only way to root out terrorists is by doing what Russians or Germans would do, i.e. shoot guilty & innocent alike in large numbers. This is not v. practicable in Palestine. Consequently someone else

the terrorists do not get me first. I am sure I am on one or two of the inferior lists of victims.'
1 The topic of the School was 'European Civilisation in the Twentieth Century'.
2 (D'Arcy) Patrick Reilly (1909–99), diplomat, Fellow of All Souls 1932–9, Counsellor at Athens 1947–8; Imperial Defence College 1949; Assistant Under-Secretary of State, FO 1950–3; Minister in Paris 1953–6; Ambassador to the USSR 1957–60. Later (1965–8) Ambassador to France.
3 Rachel Mary Reilly, née Sykes (1911–84).
4 sc. accueil, 'welcome'.
5 Julian Edward George Asquith (b. 1916), 2nd Earl of Oxford and Asquith, Balliol Classics 1934–8, Assistant District Commissioner, Palestine, 1942–8. It was from him that IB learned of the epigram by Archilochus that gave The Hedgehog and the Fox (245/3) its title.

must be got to do it, both for Jews & for Arabs (the Mufti's[1] men go on quietly bumping off "quislings" who are suspected of selling land to Jews & nothing said): presumably Jews & Arabs respectively. Hence I still see no alternative to partition of some kind: there is not a soldier in Palestine who doesn't agree: particularly the H[igh] Commissioner who seems to me a very fearless, honest, & reputable man, not fearfully clever, but then why be clever? it is a much overrated attribute. Your office is certainly blamed by all the unhappy soldiers for the state of affairs: not altogether without justice: since the soldiers insist with a degree of passion you should see to believe it that Arab resistance to partition would be far weaker & less convinced than our Bagdad & Damascus diplomatic missions report: whereas the Jews would go on guerillaing forever, until the Soviets swallow all. However that may be the UNSCOP Commission was a v. funny affair. The serious people were the Canadian, who is really wise & good, Judge Rand,[2] unknown to me. The Swedish chairman,[3] wonderfully Swedish: bland, fair, non-committal, full of pacifying bromides, seeking for signs of amiability in all. The Dutchman,[4] a colonial gov., equally balanced, moderate etc. Then came the comedy: the Persian[5] who kept repeating that he was *entirely uncommitted:* had *no instructions:*[6] could think anything he pleased: was totally independent: & gave one enormous significant oeillades:[7] nobody could make out what this meant: whether he had something to sell: what: & for how much. Dr [Garcia] Salazar[8] of Peru represented the Holy See but would have no time to stay for & sign any report & so took little interest. Dr [Garcia] Granados[9] of Guatemala was clear that since the dispute about the British Honduras

1 Mohammad Amin al-Husseini (*c.*1895–1974), Grand Mufti of Jerusalem (appointed in 1922 by the British High Commissioner Herbert Samuel to the post traditionally held by the al-Husseini family); Arab (and then Palestinian) nationalist, fervent anti-Zionist, wartime ally of the Nazis, and allegedly an instigator of the plan to exterminate European Jews.

2 Ivan Cleveland Rand (1884–1969), Canadian lawyer; Justice, Supreme Court of Canada, 1943–59. IB's favourable judgement was not shared by Ralph Bunche (33/9), who considered Rand unhelpfully verbose.

3 (Alfred) Emil F. Sandström (1886–1962), former justice of the Swedish Supreme Court; President of the Swedish Red Cross after the death of Count Folke Bernadotte in 1948; Chairman, League of Red Cross Societies, 1950–9.

4 Nicolaas Selhorst Blom (1899–1972), former colonial civil servant (and on several occasions Acting Lieutenant Governor-General) in the Dutch East Indies.

5 Nasrollah Entezam (1900–80), Iranian politician and diplomat; Minister of Foreign Affairs 1944–5; Permanent Representative to UN 1946–50; President of the 5th UN General Assembly 1950–1; Ambassador to US 1950–2, 1953–5, to France 1958–62.

6 The delegates had been appointed as independent individuals rather than national representatives: only the Dutch and Australian delegates took instructions from their governments.

7 'Meaningful glances'.

8 Arturo Garcia Salazar (b. 1886), Peruvian politician and diplomat, former Foreign Minister and ambassador (at one time to the Vatican); a devout Catholic whose main concern was to safeguard the role of the Catholic Church in relation to the holy sites in Jerusalem.

9 Jorge Garcia Granados (1900–61), Guatemalan diplomat and politician; from 1945 President, Guatemalan Congress, and Ambassador to the US and UN; subsequently wrote a book about his experiences on UNSCOP and became his country's first ambassador to Israel.

Frontier,[1] Britain had been hideously wrong & madly oppressive everywhere & thought the Jewish State should extend to the Euphrates: Dr [Rodriguez] Fabregat[2] of Uruguay had been insulted by the Foreign Office at sometime & thought the J. State could reasonably stop after swallowing Transjordan. The Slav representatives, Dr{s} Lisicky[3] of Prague & Dr Simič[4] of Beograd thought all would be well as soon as British troops cleared off & the Colonial office was liquidated. Sir Abdur Rahman[5] persecuted the Jews fiercely until told to stop doing so by Nehru[6] in a telegram (published everywhere). Hood[7] (Australia) was never sober & wandered about arm in arm with 2 enormous, hideous Jewish strumpets, uttering unprintable words. Not a v. good man. The Secretariat consisted of old friends: Dr Victor Hoo[8] (a jolly fellow: not overgiven to principle) my old friend Dr Bunche,[9] a negro from Washington, a good nigger, a sort of black Zimmern[10] who thinks goodwill etc. & various pupils of mine from New College who cd not be more affable or informative. At time of leaving the Commission, having been boycotted by Arabs & semi-boycotted by the government, left in a pro-partition, semi-pro-Zionist mood.

1 The century-old dispute between Guatemala and Britain over the Guatemalan claim to a signifi-cant portion of British Honduras (Belize) had flared up again in 1940 when Guatemala repudiated the 1859 treaty establishing the border. In 1945 a new constitution in Guatemala incorporated a claim to British Honduras.

2 Professor Enrique Rodriguez Fabregat (1885–1976), university teacher of Spanish literature, journalist, broadcaster, politician and diplomat; former Minister of Education. In 1997 Uruguay issued a stamp commemorating his participation in UNSCOP.

3 Karel Lisicky (1893–1966), Czechoslovak diplomat; Ambassador in London 1936–45; member of Czechoslovak delegation to UN 1945–8; Chairman, UN Palestine Commission 1948, appointed to oversee the partition of Palestine resulting from the UNSCOP report; close ally of pro-Zionist Foreign Minister Jan Masaryk; found asylum in England after the Communist takeover in 1948.

4 Vladimir Konstantin Simić (b. 1897), non-Communist Yugoslav lawyer, President of the Yugoslav National Assembly 1945–53; his brother was the Yugoslav Foreign Minister and chief delegate to the UN. Beograd is Belgrade.

5 Sir Muhammad Abdur Rahman (1888–1962), High Court judge, Lahore; a Muslim strongly opposed to religious nationalism in general and the partition of India in particular; a fierce inter-rogator of the Zionist witnesses to the Commission.

6 Shri Jawaharlal Nehru (1889–1964) was at the time Minister for External Affairs and Cultural Relations, and Vice-President of the Interim Government of India; on 15 August, on India's parti-tion from Pakistan and independence, he became Prime Minister.

7 John Douglas Lloyd Hood (1904–91), Australian diplomat; former Rhodes Scholar at Magdalen; on editorial staff of *The Times* 1929–36; from 1936 held various posts in the Australian Department of External Affairs, mainly in Europe; Ambassador to Indonesia 1950–52, West Germany 1952–6, the UN 1958–63, Israel 1963–5.

8 Victor Hoo (1894–1972), Chinese lawyer and diplomat, Vice-Minister for Foreign Affairs 1942–5; UN official 1946–72 (from 1946 assistant Secretary-General for trusteeship).

9 Ralph Johnson Bunche (1904–71), political and social scientist and international mediator; US civil servant during the Second World War, then permanent member of the UN Secretariat (Principal Director, Dept of Trusteeship, 1947–54); acting UN mediator in Palestine after Count Folke Bernadotte (59/6), whom he had been assisting, was murdered in 1948. For his almost single-handed brokering of the peace agreements between Israel and the Arab States in 1949, Bunche received the 1950 Nobel Peace Prize.

10 Sir Alfred (Eckhard) Zimmern (1879–1957), first Montague Burton Professor of International Relations, Oxford, 1930–44; Secretary-General, Constituent Conference, UNESCO, 1945; a firm believer in the furtherance of international understanding through personal contacts.

As for my own "mission" it worked almost too well. My host delivered a most passionately pro-British oration,[1] earning hisses from his more zealous ex-followers: I asked him why he had gone so much further than ever I had wanted him to go, he said "everyone in this country goes too far. I didn't see why I shouldn't". Nevertheless he's a great man & the Arabs now have begun to think so too: very odd, this last. The J[ewish] Agency struck me as a little scared: not personally – they all hope for exile as a means of acquiring glory in lieu of bankruptcy in political effectiveness – but anxious to start negotiating again on something like the basis of the Morrison plan.[2] I feel fanatically convinced that Partition – even one rejected by Jews & imposed upon them – would cost least blood in the end, provoke tho' it wd 2 civil wars among Jews & Arabs respectively. But I may be wrong. I flew back via Geneva & met Gilbert Murray[3] at lunch in Chantilly. Mr Cooper sang your praises to a degree seldom heard by anyone: since I am in a flower strewing mood, did you know that Wade Gery,[4] than whom there is no man more like a genius in Oxford, has preserved your Gk. History paper in Greats, illegally, to this day, & doesn't wish to have it known? there. I talked to him about the Daphni(?) Chapel (Church?)[5] but he detests Byzantine art & was outraged by my transports. But I really did enjoy myself fearfully: & am most grateful: & shall give your messages to Cox[6] who seems to be about: All Souls is half dead, one has long evenings of golden talk with Dr Jacob[7] respectfully listened to – or perhaps suffered in exasperated silence, by the junior Fellows, a job lot, but in patches quite good I say, patronisingly. Please tell your wife that I am most thankful to her for delicious supper

1 In his testimony to UNSCOP Weizmann declared: 'I should like to begin my statement – and I do so from [the] bottom of my heart – by expressing in the presence of you gentlemen and of the public sitting here my sincerest gratitude to the Mandatory Power, to Great Britain, for having inaugurated this policy [the Balfour Declaration] and for having, throughout many years, tried to go along with us in the implementation of this policy. There is no question, whatever may be the position today, that if we see today a great and interesting and thriving community in Palestine, it would not have been possible without first of all the conquest of Palestine by the British Army and the rule of Great Britain in this country.' UNISPAL (United Nations Information System on the Question of Palestine) website, A/364/Add. 2 PV. 21, 8 July 1947 (accessed 16 May 2008).

2 Herbert Stanley Morrison (1888–1965), Baron Morrison of Lambeth 1959, Labour Deputy Prime Minister, Lord President of the Council and Leader of the House of Commons 1945–51. In July 1946 an Anglo-American Conference in London led by Morrison and Henry F. Grady, head of Truman's Cabinet committee on Palestine, had produced a federal plan for Palestine under which the country would become a British trusteeship divided into four areas: a Jewish province, an Arab province and the districts of Jerusalem and the Negev. Both Arabs and Jews rejected the proposals.

3 (George) Gilbert Aimé Murray (1866–1957), Regius Professor of Greek, Oxford, 1908–36.

4 Henry Theodore Wade-Gery (1888–1972), Fellow of New College and Wykeham Professor of Ancient History, Oxford, 1939–53; Fellow of Merton 1953–8.

5 The church of the Daphni Monastery west of Athens is decorated internally with unique 11th-century mosaics.

6 Christopher William Machell Cox (1899–1982), Fellow of New College 1926–70; Educational Adviser to the Secretary of State for the Colonies 1940–61.

7 Ernest Fraser Jacob (1894–1971), Fellow of All Souls 1920–71 (Librarian 1960–70); Chichele Professor of Modern History, Oxford, 1950–61.

party: that I thought the company far better than any to be obtained in these shores at the moment – that I enormously look forward to being asked for a week-end when she is Ambassadress in Paris, an event which is inevitable anyhow but which we must all set ourselves to compass in as brief a space of time as possible. I asked Duff C. what he felt about that: he agreed that you would be far better than the list of persons he enunciated through clenched teeth as those who even now were casting greedy eyes upon his post.[1] Lady Diana agreed. When you are here do not forget the hermit of New College:

yrs
    Isaiah B.   [...]

IB's return to Oxford was followed by two attempts to extract him.

I was sitting very quietly talking with David Cecil in my room in Oxford. Telephone bell rang, then it said, 'This is Moshe Sharett' [...] and he said, 'We wish to offer you a post. Would you like to take charge of the whole of Eastern and Central Europe for the Jewish Agency?' [...] So I said, 'No, no, no thank you, no' – immediately. So then he said, 'But why not? It carries a very good pension.' So I said, 'No, no, that is not what I'm afraid of.' (I had no money – I was in debt.) I said, 'No I can't, I'm really terribly sorry.' [...] I knew then that it was absurd, I didn't want a job in any possible government there because I thought I would be torn to pieces, because I minded what people said and what people thought, I was too thin-skinned; and given the very tense and extremely quarrelsome atmosphere – it wasn't exactly peaceful: Jews versus Jews, Jews versus English, English versus the Arabs, Jews versus everybody – that I couldn't survive in an atmosphere of that kind, couldn't function; and I needed solid institutions to preserve me from being idle and feckless.[2]

The next approach was from Sir Oliver Franks,[3] the Chairman of the Committee of European Economic Cooperation (CEEC), which had been working since mid-July in the Grand Palais,[4] Paris, on the European response to the Marshall Plan[5] for European reconstruction. At very short notice IB joined the UK delegation on 18 August, nominally as an economic adviser: as he later

1 On 3 September Duff Cooper heard that he was to be replaced at the end of 1947, but Reilly was not his immediate successor.
2 MI Tape 18.
3 Sir Oliver Shewell *Franks (1905–92), philosopher and public servant.
4 This large hall, notable for its glass-domed ceiling, was built for the 1900 World Fair.
5 In a speech at Harvard University on 5 June 1947, General George Catlett Marshall (1880–1959), US Secretary of State, recognised that one of the major problems facing Europe was the economic disintegration brought about by the war: after a brief recovery in 1946 matters were now becoming far worse. In order to avert any risk of a Communist takeover, he offered US help if the countries of Europe could jointly draw up a programme for economic recovery: the Paris Conference, which first met on 12 July, undertook this task. Although the Soviet Union was originally invited, it rejected the terms of the invitation and ensured that Eastern European countries such as Czechoslovakia and Poland did not attend.

explained, 'having made a fuss about going to Palestine earlier I cd hardly, with
decency, refuse to perform odd jobs for the F.O. particularly as I believe in the
purpose of the Paris operation'.[1]

TO ELLIOTT FELKIN

Weds. 20 August 1947 [*manuscript*]

As from (a) Hotel de Crillon, Paris
(b) UK Delegation to Committee of European Economic Cooperation,
British Embassy

Too odd, my life. I was sitting peacefully in Oxford when I was bullied into
coming here by an appeal to my loyalty to Mr Bevin made by the Provost
of Queen[']s College who presides over this entire conference.[2] The atmosphere is odd. The French are very intelligent, of course, but work not v.
hard. The U.K. delegates are not stupid – vide Sir O. Franks, Sir D. Waley,[3] &
co-respondent Hampshire[4] – & madly industrious. God only knows what *I*
am doing in this galère, who know nothing about & *detest* economic items:
it is a middlebrow view which is responsible, whereby hacks do the work,
then a don appears, & by use of special Oxford black magic transforms it all
into deathless academic prose.[5] How shocked Sir A. Salter[6] – the breath of
whose nostrils this conference enormously is – wd have been – will be – to

---

1 To Chaim Weizmann, 15 September 1947.
2 'I felt I was being summoned by God. I could not refuse, though I knew it was a mistake. When
   the prophet Jonah was summoned by God, he refused. Everybody realised in a day or two I was
   hopeless.' IB quoted in Nicholas Henderson, 'The Franks Way – Then and Now', *The Times*, 17
   January 1983, 8.
3 Sir (Sigismund) David Waley (1887–1962), né Schloss, Third Secretary, Treasury, 1946–7; European
   Recovery Dept, FO, 1948.
4 Stuart Newton *Hampshire (1914–2004), philosopher, and (immediately after the war) civil
   servant in the FO and the Ministry of Food. Named in 1942 as co-respondent in A. J. Ayer's
   divorce from his wife Renée.
5 Otto Clarke (40/3) had earlier stressed the importance, urgency and difficulty of finding a suitable report-writer, and the high priority Franks placed on this. 'We need a document, in popular
   English, which sums up the whole thing in 5–7,000 words (i.e. can be printed in full in the *New
   York Times*). There can be masses of statistics and appendices, but what will count is the report.
   [...] This must be conceived by one writer, who must have the power of conception, presentation and writing skill, and must also be able to negotiate this concept through the shifting sands
   of Paris. [...] Our writer will have to throw his weight about.' Familiarity with American thinking (though not American nationality), fluent French, social skills and a lively writing style were
   all desirable, and the early candidates were all economists. Clarke (who admitted to 'atrocious'
   French) was tempted to do it himself but could not be spared from running the London end of
   the discussions for the three to four weeks required. Minute to Sir Edward Bridges, 31 July 1947,
   NA, T 325/22.
6 Sir (James) Arthur Salter (1881–1975), 1st Baron Salter of Kidlington 1953, public servant;
   Gladstone Professor of Political Theory and Institutions and Fellow of All Souls 1934–44 (thereafter Distinguished Fellow); Senior Deputy Director-General, UNRRA, 1944; MP (Independent)
   for Oxford University 1937–50; particularly knowledgeable on transport.

discover that *I* am here – who truly have no business with serious earnest things – wherever he is, as Mr James[1] wd say – tremendously – in ever so large, and irrevocably, irretrievably growing a sense – *not* here, not anywhere near, extruded, as it were, by the very degree, the overwhelming degree, of his aptness for, his relevance to, his passion for such things. But to come down: It is as hot as hell:[2] I cannot go to Penelope's wedding;[3] Paris is peaceful: Mr Cooper is away; so is Patricia: I am bored. I am a sq. peg in a r. hole: & if you *are* passing through, for God's sake give me a buzz, call me up, give me a tinkle at the Crillon, room 536[4] or the Brit Embassy, 'Conference' extn. 117. It is possible here to eat not too terribly badly.

Isaiah.

TO MARIE AND MENDEL BERLIN

Friday [22 August 1947, *manuscript*]

Hotel de Crillon, Paris

My dears

I am very well, really well. My task is a kind [of] rédaction générale[5] of the text which implies rewriting & tactful conciliation of contradictory suggestions by eminent civil servants & general drudgery.[6] The Coopers very

---

1 Presumably the novelist Henry James.
2 Paris was suffering the hottest summer then on record (not surpassed until 2003). To make matters worse, 'The Marshall planners [...] are working in the Grand Palais, one of the hottest buildings in town because of the immense amounts of glass. [...] the sense of urgency is great and they don't even seem to mind their hours, 9 a.m. to midnight.' Susan Mary Alsop, *To Marietta from Paris, 1945–1960* (New York, 1975), 115.
3 Penelope Joyce Felkin (1926–2002), Elliott Felkin's daughter, married the sociologist Dr James Douglas on 30 August.
4 Of the almost 250 members of the UK delegation, IB was one of the very few top officials allocated a suite. However, conditions at the Crillon provoked many complaints, and the delegation organisers resolved to use the Hotel Bristol in future.
5 'Overall drafting'.
6 The official papers confirm this description. IB, a notoriously late riser, regularly attended the 9 a.m. meetings of the UK delegation: the minutes for 22 August record that 'departmental comments on reports dealing with Food and Agriculture, Fuel and Power, and Maritime Transport should be sent to Mr Berlin' [NA, CAB 133/42], and by 29 August a draft of several chapters of the final report, drafted or compiled by IB, was in circulation. The Foreword, wholly or partly drafted by IB but not included in the published CEEC report, begins: 'Europe is today threatened by a great economic disaster', and concludes: 'The representatives of sixteen peoples, diverse in language, in national tradition and in history, have [...] worked together as a single body in a spirit of friendship and mutual understanding. [...] At every stage of this Conference they have been deeply conscious of the crucial importance of their work at this turning-point in European history; for they see two and only two possibilities before their peoples: either an opportunity with initial and immediate help to achieve recovery and stable prosperity by their own strenuous and concerted efforts; or else the decline of Europe into a condition of misery and violence which in due course may undermine the foundations of the entire civilised world' [NA, CAB 133/68].

affable, she likes me genuinely, & he not really very much.[1] Miss Beloff[2] is
the Observer correspondent & much feared as she obtains too much secret
stuff & is liked by no one. To morrow she visits me. I still find no difficulty
in telling her nothing. The work is somehow slightly futile – an enormous
begging letter pretending to be dignified & even proud – I shall at least, like
Mr Attlee, 'dehydrate it'.[3] [...] It is really not *too* hot – I sleep well & eat
well as my sterling cheques are cashed (1200 (not 1500) fr. fr. pays for barely
2 meals and nothing left for laundry bills – but I can't ask for *salary*!) – my
colleagues look at me as Sir O. Franks' private eminence grise & the other
Fifteen Nations don't know yet that I am to formulate their thoughts. A
Dutchman represents Benelux:[4] a Norwegian all 3 Scandinavias. How sensible. I am trying to get Bohlen[5] here: тогда штурмом воз[ь]мем.[6] So far there
is no objection to your coming to Paris – I wd enjoy it – my social life is dull,
all being away, but it is a bit empty, boring, hot – still say the word & I'll get a
room. There is not much traffic & one sleeps well. Good night.

Shaya

*In his speech General Marshall had offered 'friendly aid' to the Europeans in
drawing up their proposals, but, by late August, US representatives in Europe
were increasingly laying down the law about what was needed to ensure that the
final report met US requirements: there was a real prospect that without major
changes Congress would reject the whole plan. George Kennan[7] came to Paris to
find a way through the apparent impasse. Between his official meetings he had a
private conversation with IB, who next morning conveyed the key points to the
UK delegation:*

[...] no assistance would be made available to Europe after 1951 [...] the US
would look on participating countries as candidates for an examination, and
would allocate marks accordingly [...]. It seemed to [Kennan] that the [State]
Department did not really want a Customs Union to be set on foot in the

---

1 Duff Cooper noted in his diary on 25 August: 'Isaiah Berlin came to see me at 3 and showed me
   what he had so far written of the Marshall Conference report. I thought it very good.' *The Duff
   Cooper Diaries*, ed. John Julius Norwich (London, 2005), 447.
2 (Leah) Nora Beloff (1919–97; from 1977 Mrs Clifford Makins), journalist and author; reporter,
   Reuters News Agency, 1945–6; Paris correspondent, *The Economist*, 1946–8; foreign correspondent, *Observer*, 1948–78 (*pace* IB), political correspondent 1964–76.
3 According to a leading article in *The Economist* (9 August 1947, 225), 'That any speech of Mr
   Attlee's would be arid and uninspiring is, unfortunately, to be taken for granted; he touches
   nothing that he does not dehydrate.'
4 The customs union formed by Belgium, the Netherlands and Luxembourg came into effect in
   1947.
5 Chip Bohlen had drafted Marshall's Harvard speech.
6 'Togda shturmom voz'mem' ('then we take by storm').
7 George Frost *Kennan (1904–2005), US diplomat, historian and Soviet expert; at this time (1947–9)
   Director of Policy Planning, State Department. He saw the Marshall Plan as an important part of
   the containment of the Soviet Union that he had already advocated in an article on 'The Sources
   of Soviet Conduct' published under the pseudonym 'X' in *Foreign Affairs* in July 1947.

immediate future, but wished that the participating countries should react favourably to the idea of some eventual union. [...] there was a new set of men in Washington, with simple, honest minds. Subtlety on our part must at all costs be avoided, and we should send simple, honest men to represent us.[1]

For his part Kennan conveyed much-needed realism in his report to Washington, arguing that 'we must not look to the people in Paris to accomplish the impossible',[2] and suggesting practical approaches for resolving the deadlock.

The drafting and redrafting continued, but IB's lack of economic expertise made him reluctant to tackle the technical sections of the Marshall Plan report. After three weeks in Paris he extricated himself and joined his holiday companions in Italy.

TO MENDEL AND MARIE BERLIN

12 September 1947 [*manuscript*]

[Santa Caterina]

Dear Pa & Ma,

I cannot describe the peace, quiet, rest, sun, sea etc. The weather is not at all too hot. Cool in the morning, warm in the afternoon (cooler than Paris) when one rests – at first I slept, now I find I no longer fall asleep & work a little – then cool at night. The routine is: up by about 10–10.30 a.m., breakfast (toast, coffee, figs: grapes, pears, egg if I want it) then down to a piaggia (plage)[3] to Amalfi to bathe in the sea, an hour or so on the sand, back to Santa Caterina (by Chilver's[4] car, 2 minutes) through the tunnel, wash, rest, letters till 1 p.m., lunch, rest from 2.30 till 6 p.m. then a glass of lemonade, talk, dinner at 7.30, then if there is a festa[5] in Amalfi or Ravello go there, if not, bed by 10 p.m., reading or work, asleep by 11.30. It is absolutely idyllic: the food is good, better than in 1932, Gambardella[6] deaf, pathetic but из кожи лезет он[7] to please, my companions Bowra + Chilvers most tranquil, cosy, familiar, no strain, no strangers, no social life. I have already written a lecture for Oxford on Russ. revolution of 1905,[8] & am preparing an article

1 Minutes of UK delegation meeting, 30 August 1947 [NA, CAB/133/42].

2 George Kennan, 'Situation with Respect to European Recovery Programme' (4 September 1947), *Foreign Relations of the United States 1947*, vol. 3, *The British Commonwealth; Europe* (Washington, 1972), 398.

3 'Beach'.

4 Guy Edward Farquhar Chilver (1910–82), Fellow and Praelector in Ancient History, Queen's, 1934–63 (Senior Tutor 1948–63); later (1964–76) Professor of Classical Studies, Kent. His wife (who was accompanying him) was Sylvia Chloe, née Littell.

5 'Festival'.

6 Crescenzo Gambardella, whose family have owned and run the luxurious Albergo Santa Caterina, where IB was staying, since 1880.

7 'Iz kozhi lezet on' (literally 'he creeps out of his skin', i.e. 'he busts a gut').

8 Probably a contribution by IB to 'Crises in European History, 1867–1914', a course of lectures by various speakers organised by Alan Bullock (62/3) in New College in Michaelmas Term 1947.

for *Mind*.[1] As for Paris, I could not really stay when I had announced that I cd not write the purely technical sections of the Report – а вдруг скажу идиотство наобум[2] – only the general sections, & a high official in the Treasury, one Otto Clarke,[3] offered to do it all in 3 days. I cd only *fight* to be allowed to do it all myself – & why should I – when I did not feel it to be мой конёк[4] – & worked unwillingly & unsurely. They were all very impressed by the dignity & lack of recrimination & intrigue with which I behaved & told me how valuable it all was – & now I see by the paper that Bevin told Franks that the Report won't do & must be rewritten – i.e. in substance not style – & I certainly cannot cover up with *words* what the officials failed to do in facts, & had no authority to bully 16 nations about the substance.[5] So I am *delighted* not to be associated with what now looks inevitably like a ½ failure: a low thought perhaps, but between the quarrels of the Nations an unhappy draftsman – who had no authority to alter the substance – would be completely destroyed. So don't think that I left in the middle because of Bowra or anybody: the position was somewhat fake from the beginning: they were all embarrassed vis a vis me all the time & one of my colleagues congratulated me on the "fantastic dignity" & "incredible good humour" which I displayed. I am afraid that Franks will lose a little face over this now, maybe he'll recover it later in Washington.[6] Meanwhile I am very happy[7] – the incredibly real faces, the military band playing Traviata[8] in the Piazza at 11 p.m. by candlelight, the light, the air, the salt water the sun [...].

Love

Shaya

1 Presumably his review of Bertrand Russell, *A History of Western Philosophy*, Mind 56 (1947), 151–66.

2 'A vdrug skazhu idiotstvo naobum' ('and suddenly I say something idiotic without thinking').

3 Richard William Barnes ('Otto') Clarke (1910–75), financial journalist (and deviser of the *Financial Times* index), then civil servant, first at the Treasury, Assistant Secretary 1945–7, Under-Secretary 1947–55, Third Secretary 1955–62; later (1966–70) Permanent Secretary, Ministry of Technology. Clarke (father of Labour politician Charles Clarke) was famous for his fast, incisive drafting. His obituary recorded that 'after many false starts, with the aid of specially summoned outside "writers", it was Otto who wrote the triumphant, short, succinct, yet comprehensive report which was the European response to the Marshall speech'. *The Times*, 23 June 1975, 14.

4 'Moi konek [pronounced "konyok"]' (literally 'my little (hobby-)horse', i.e. 'my *métier*').

5 Soon after IB left Paris, discussions between the CEEC and the US representatives broke down completely. After a few days of frantic activity, Kennan's proposals led to a solution: the report would be considered as the first stage in a continuing process, the US retained the right to decide how much aid should be offered, and a preamble to the report, drafted by Otto Clarke, made all the right noises for American ears. Ministers reconvened in Paris on 22 September to sign the finally agreed CEEC report.

6 Where Franks was to join the propaganda drive to ensure the Plan's acceptance by Congress.

7 To Chaim Weizmann he admitted: 'At present I am recovering from all kinds of Job-like afflictions which the Paris Conference – the conditions of work were unbelievably awful – unbelievably – induced (but *please not a word about this to my parents* who think I am in an condition of rude & blooming heath – so I assure them –)'. Letter of 15 September 1947.

8 Giuseppe Verdi's 1853 opera *La traviata*.

IB's protestations to his parents of unalloyed happiness were, as often, a smokescreen concealing his real emotions.

TO PATRICIA DE BENDERN

[October 1947, *written on a postcard from P de B; not sent*]

[New College]

I have no desire to keep this waspish-mosquitoish little sting.[1] If you had deigned to tell me where to go at any moment before the 26th Sept. – you cd have telephoned to Santa Caterina – I shd have come & spent a week. As it was I merely got on Dr Bowra's nerves with my endless sighings after you, since I missed you alas more than ever you me. But you were perversely silent & Dr Weizmann was sick & pathetic & so were my family. I don't understand about 'public pleasure' except that Diana is one. All I know is Mrs Patten's[2] account of Mr Graves's daughter[3] & the gay company in Portofino while I sat cross alone but enchanted in Rome. Indeed I am cross, betrayed & 'dashed'. But I am miserable because I have not seen you. All my love.

I *always* long to see you. But if you so behave I shall try & learn to unlong.

I suddenly see about public pleasure. How horrible! as if to hold Dr W.'s hand was a pleasure at all: or the rain at Oxford when I might have been in Venice: & yet I might have acted like a cad, & indeed I would & have come to see you, & John[4] too – I lived on day dreams of Verona & Vicenza – & maddened my companions with recitals of how happy I should shortly be – if only you had taken a little trouble. And yet, all my love.[5]

I am now resigned to the thought that I shall always love you more than anyone in the world. That if I deny myself the right to see you (as I shall do again & again) I am punishing in the first place myself: that you

1 A reference to the (undated) postcard on which he is writing, sent to him at New College. The card reads: 'Sorry you left so soon [IB annotates: '? 27! Sept?'] Portofino was lovely, abandoned by Diana & Co, though I wonder you didn't think it your duty to give her a few days too, they seem to be so numerous now Isaiah dear and you should hesitate another time before calling *anyone else* [IB annotates both underlined words with a question mark] a "public pleasure" – Never mind I did genuinely miss you & hope one day you will be able to come with us – we drove here through the most beautiful towns very slowly I love Italy – much love.'

2 Susan Mary Patten (1918–2004), née Jay, wife of William Patten (115/6); from a cosmopolitan diplomatic background, she used her social skills and looks to overcome the limitations of her husband's modest post in the US Embassy (and consequent relative poverty) and become a leading socialite in post-war Paris, a close friend of Diana Cooper, and one of Duff Cooper's mistresses. Widowed in 1960, she was married 1961–73 to Joe Alsop, a family friend, subsequently became a writer, and edited her letters to Marietta Tree (72/1), *To Marietta from Paris* (37/2).

3 Presumably Jenny Pyrdie Nicholson (1918–64), eldest daughter of the poet Robert Graves (1895–1985).

4 John de Bendern.

5 IB continues on a scrap of card. He also addressed an envelope to P de B in Paris, but it is unstamped.

may not mind: that you may misinterpret it, but that it is not that but the pain of self denial that I shall mind most. That I shall, whatever you do, go about the world singing your praise, as I did in Italy, like an absurd Don Quixote, until they acknowledge your merit. And you can reply or not.[1]

IB's health problems[2] continued during the term, but he was sufficiently well to be invested with the CBE[3] at Buckingham Palace and to lunch with Winston Churchill, who sought, and received, IB's advice on the first volume of his memoirs.[4]

TO WINSTON CHURCHILL

14 February 1948 [⟨*draft manuscript*⟩ *and transcript made for Churchill*]

New College

⟨Dear Mr Churchill

I must apologize for taking so long to acknowledge your letter from Marrakesh,[5] but as Bill Deakin[6] could testify the monstrous overpopulation of post-war Oxford – & in particular of my College – has at any rate for the present, destroyed the civilized habits of a more leisurely time, with the result that one does what one can when one can.⟩ I have read the latest batch of proofs with close attention and greatly welcome the result – particularly such changes and re-arrangements as I have noticed. [...] In general, the architecture of the whole of Book I now strikes me as being far

1 Although this message was not sent, it seems likely that some such riposte was, since Patricia sent this telegram from Lausanne on 21 October 1947: 'DARLING HAVE JUST RECEIVED ALL YOUR LETTER[S] TERRIBLE MISUNDERSTANDING PLEASE FORGIVE ME DISAGREABLE POST CARD HAVE BEEN ANGRY AND MISERABLE WRITING AND WILL TELEPHONE FRIDAY MORNING UNLESS HEAR INCONVENIENT LOVE FROM BATH [sc. both] = PATRICIA'.

2 'I was on my back with tonsilitis and I had to retire to a Nursing Home to have a wisdom tooth out, then complications followed, and I am only now beginning to recover.' To Clyde Kluckhohn, 17 December 1947.

3 IB had been awarded a CBE in the 1946 New Year's Honours List for his contribution towards Anglo-American understanding during the war, though his own theory was that 'Halifax fixed it as a kind of reward for an appalling insult' (MI Tape 28) to make up for his exclusion by Anthony Eden (43/2) from the Potsdam conference (see L1 582–3).

4 *The Gathering Storm*, the opening volume of *The Second World War* (London, 1948–54). After the lunch IB read the draft text of the book and wrote about it at length to Churchill in letters that we have not been able to trace in the Churchill Papers.

5 Dated 25 December 1947. Churchill thanked IB for his work, sent him a revised version of the first six chapters, and asked him for his frank opinion. Martin Gilbert, '*Never Despair': Winston S. Churchill 1945–1965* (London, 1988), 383, citing a letter from the Churchill Papers [4/67] which we have not been able to trace.

6 (Frederick) William Dampier ('Bill') Deakin (1913–2005), historian, Fellow and Tutor, Wadham, 1936–49; wartime service as a Yugoslav expert in the Special Operations Executive (SOE) included a dangerous and successful mission to Tito (177/1) and his partisans in 1943; First Secretary, UK Embassy in Belgrade, 1945–6; Warden, St Antony's, 1950–68; formerly Churchill's research assistant, Deakin became prominent in the team helping Churchill prepare his war memoirs.

more symmetrical and impressive: the opening chapters particularly, which before seemed to me (I hope you did not mind my telling you that – you did, I recollect, order me to be quite candid) to get off to a slow start,[1] now set the tempo and the rhythm for the entire work: the awful descent to the abyss, liberated from technical digressions, is a magnificently cumulative rapid and continuous narrative. I admired the earlier version greatly and I now more than ever think it a literary and political masterpiece. I long for the rejoinders which you were kind enough to say that you might send – but I have no doubt that you are immensely busy and shall not repine. While I accept your verdict on disputed – or at least disputable – passages as your considered judgement, and, as such, final, there are two points which I venture to bring up again. The first is this: the story told, I imagine, for the first time in print of the events behind Mr Eden's[2] resignation in 1938[3] reminded me of an account I had heard of this during the War, and I remember being told by someone at the Foreign Office that after Mr Eden came back post haste from Grasse he forced through a formal reversal of the Cabinet decision rather in the teeth of Neville Chamberlain – although by that time it was all too late, the President felt he had been snubbed and bad consequences followed. If this is true, and I expect you will have had the benefit of Mr Eden's advice on this incident, the details of what occurred in the Cabinet may be worth greater detail and emphasis. But perhaps my memory has played me false, or the facts are confidential, and in any case I should not wish to make too much of this suggestion. The second point is the information given by Benes[4] to Stalin about the conversations between

1 In his comments on the previous draft IB had written that two or more of the early chapters were 'too episodic and insubstantial to act as an adequate scaffolding to the more tremendous story of the Rise of Hitler, with which the book really gets into a wonderful stride'. Gilbert, op. cit. (42/5), 393 (citing Churchill Papers 4/141; we have not found these comments either).

2 (Robert) Anthony Eden (1897–1977), 1st Earl of Avon 1961, Conservative MP; Foreign Secretary 1935–8, 1951–5; Prime Minister 1955–7.

3 Although Eden's resignation in February 1938 was nominally over appeasement of Italy, the major breach between him and the Prime Minister, (Arthur) Neville Chamberlain (1869–1940), had occurred earlier. In early January 1938 President Franklin Delano Roosevelt (1882–1945) had secretly proposed convening an international conference of the US, Britain, France, Germany and Italy in an attempt to alleviate the worsening international situation. In Eden's absence on holiday in the South of France, Chamberlain replied suggesting deferral of the US plan until the completion of British negotiations with Italy. Roosevelt agreed not to go ahead but expressed alarm at the possibility of Britain's accepting the Italian occupation of Abyssinia. Summoned back from France by his officials and horrified at the damage being done to his work on building up Anglo-American relations, Eden secured in Cabinet discussions a softening of the British position; mollifying messages were sent to Roosevelt, but the US proposal was effectively dead.

4 Edvard Beneš (1884–1948); President of Czechoslovakia 1935–8, 1945–8. Churchill recounts that in 1936 Beneš had heard of a conspiracy between the military and old-guard Communists in the Soviet Union to overthrow Stalin and establish a pro-German regime, and had immediately reported this to Stalin, who launched a merciless purge of the Soviet Army. IB's attempt to water down the relevant footnote (apparently based on information he had provided) seems to have failed, since in the published text it reads: 'There is however some evidence that Beneš's information had previously been imparted to the Czech police by the Ogpu, who wished it to reach Stalin from a friendly foreign source.' The Gathering Storm (42/4), 225.

the Soviet soldiers and the Germans in the middle thirties: the footnote in the text which notes the conjecture about the part played by the GPU[1] to which I drew your attention originally suggests that it is a well substantiated hypothesis. Perhaps I overstated the case in my account of it, and if so I must plead guilty: while I believe that the story is very plausible, the evidence for it rests on gossip and information collected by anti-Soviet Russian émigrés, and is therefore easily challenged. Hence it will perhaps be best to say no more than something like 'there are those who hold that' rather than 'there is some evidence that', otherwise the Czechs may make a fuss as well as the Russians. I think that I drew Deakin's attention to this and he probably has already offered a suitable emendation. ⟨It only remains for me to say again how grateful I am to have been allowed to see this work in progress, and how great an honour and a fascination it has been to me. I sincerely hope that you are now completely recovered & that I may one day be allowed to see you again.

Yours very sincerely
    Isaiah Berlin⟩

Post-war turmoil in Europe had, for many, enhanced the attractions of Communism, and there was a growing possibility that several countries in Western Europe might turn Communist. The FO set up a Working Party on the Spiritual Aspects of the Western Union to identify intellectual weapons for the expected battle of ideas. On its behalf Alan Dudley[2] had sought enlightenment from IB.[3]

TO ALAN DUDLEY

[Received 17 March 1948, *manuscript*]

New College

My dear Alan,

I doubt if I am competent to answer your question: in the realm of what one wd call technical philosophy – & that is the only kind that ever was

---

1 Gosudarstvennoe politicheskoe upravlenie (State Political Directorate), which replaced the Cheka as the Soviet political police force in 1922 and soon became the OGPU (Joint State Political Directorate), was renamed again as the GUGB (Main Directorate for State Security) when it became part of the NKVD (People's Commissariat for Internal Affairs) of the Soviet Union in 1934; it later evolved into the KGB.

2 Alan Alves Dudley (1907–71), diplomat; Director, British Press Service and British Information Service, New York, 1940–2 (hence a colleague of IB's); Head of Information Policy Department, FO, 1946–9.

3 'What we want to do is to put down briefly on paper the common factors in terms of attitudes towards a great variety of things (and ideas) ranging from art to social services, and also to make clear in what respects a contrast can be drawn with the attitudes typical of Communist thought. Behind all this, I think, must lie the fundamentals of philosophy, and we have no one here who feels competent to put down briefly what philosophical ideas there are which are common to the West.' Alan Dudley to IB, 9 March 1948.

worthy of the name – there are no ideas – at least I can think of none – which belong to the West as against the Marxist East, any more than in chemistry or mathematics. But you do not, of course, mean that. You mean to refer to general ideas, attitudes to this or that activity or form of life etc. & there, I am sure, you are right in suspecting that it wd be unwise to refer to Hegel:[1] no doubt Marxism is Hegelian: but so was the dominant English philosophy from, say, 1870 to say 1920: & liberal imperialism was not merely Hegelian but, say in the case of Cecil Rhodes[2] & his followers, qualified by a moderate racialism as well. So the less said about that the better. No doubt Mill[3] or B. Russell[4] didn't like this: but they weren't dominant, & admired only by members of one or other opposition. As the Soviets cd, if they chose, point out. Nor is it any good saying that we stand for scientific objectivity, pursuit of truth by disinterested means etc. – this might have done to distinguish Russia from Western Europe in the 19th century – mysticism, a religious view of life, communalism, absolutism, irrationalism versus positivism, liberalism, rationalism etc. but Marxists claim to be scientific, empirical, positivist, etc. etc. & it takes too long to explain how & why we think they aren't, & are telling fibs on the subject to themselves & others. So that I feel – but this theory may not be believed by others – that on a purely intellectual plane nothing very clear, simple, & obviously true can be said, without enfeebling qualifications. What our real differences seem to me to boil down to is conflicting views of social life. And to boil this down further – it revolves round two points:

(1) Civil Liberties. That we believe, if not in Natural Rights, 'self-evident propositions' about life, liberty & the pursuit of happiness, at any rate in the proposition that life is not worth living – or any ends worth pursuing, unless individuals have the right to a certain area of private life, & personal relations uninvaded by the state or any institution, at any rate, by forcible means; & that within this area people have the right to work out their own salvation – or damnation – in their own way: to go to the dogs in their own way, without interference by a state however benevolently intentioned. Unless this is guaranteed men may enjoy security & prosperity but not liberty: & there is no Eastern Democracy, as opposed to Western, any more

1 Dudley had written 'I did think of trying [...] to raise questions about Hegel and his influence; but on the whole I think that I have said enough to let you see what we are after.' ibid.
2 Cecil John Rhodes (1853–1902), imperialist whose aim was to extend British rule over much of Africa; businessman who developed the diamond industry in South Africa; Prime Minister, Cape Colony 1890–6. Rhodesia (now Zimbabwe) was named after him.
3 John Stuart Mill (1806–73), philosopher and political thinker who, while admitting that 'It is right to learn what Hegel is', concluded that 'conversancy with him tends to deprave one's intellect'. Letter to Alexander Bain, Collected Works of John Stuart Mill, ed. J. M. Robson and others (Toronto/London, 1963–91), vol. 16, 132.
4 Bertrand Arthur William Russell (1872–1970), 3rd Earl Russell, mathematician, philosopher, author and anti-nuclear campaigner; Fellow of Trinity College, Cambridge, 1895–1901, 1944–70; Nobel Prize for Literature 1950. A visit to Russia in 1920 left him deeply anti-Communist.

than there is Eastern Liberty, Eastern Equality or Eastern Truth. The former term is as silly as the latter – we pass 'Eastern Democracy' because the word 'Democracy' has had other suffixes – 'Social-D.', 'Liberal-D.' etc – but if 'Eastern Liberty' is silly so is the notion that Democracy can be of totally different brands. In a state of emergency certain liberties – of speech, or choice of a career, etc. may be suspended – but this must be felt to be a passing evil – if the emergency is permanent or lasts too long – the difference between normal & abnormal conditions is obliterated & the notion of civil liberty stultified. You can if you like say that this means that we believe that unless certain rights – or areas of freedom from interference – are guaranteed, no social good, even if it cd be shown to result from such coercion, would be worth having. And as a rider, that we do not believe that men below a certain economic level are as helpless & unable to use their freedoms as people coerced by totalitarian states. No doubt unofficial oppression & blackmail – e.g. by economic pressure, is very bad, & maims people & leads to injustice & inequality of opportunity: & we believe in the right to struggle against these evils: but so long as a tradition of political i.e. official liberty (e.g. the rule of law & not of individuals, reduction of laws to a minimum etc.) exists in a society, there is at least [a] publicly acknowledged ideal in the name of which these evils are fought. When this disappears, the notions of justice & liberty are themselves destroyed. Anyone who says that political liberty or civil liberty is impossible without some minimum of economic strength on the part of the individual is obscuring the issue, or lying (even if he is Prof. Laski)[1] – economic slaves in a political democracy can in principle organize & liberate themselves. Political slaves are done for, because their society has perverted the meaning of the words 'liberty' & 'law'. The gap between laws, however bad, & the rule of an individual however good, is absolute to the West, a matter of optimum means to Marxists.

(2) We believe, & the Marxists do not, that the value & truth of a man's opinions & activities does not wholly, or even decisively, depend on his place in the economic or social structure. We believe & the Marxists do not, that diversity of interests between individuals or groups or classes in some respects does not prevent them from having identical interests or ideals in others: nor do we believe, as Marxists do, that all ideals are open or disguised material interests; hence we believe that cooperation is possible & the class struggle not inevitable; and that such concepts as truth, goodness, justice, kindness, compromise etc. are not disguised forms of class interests, but genuinely common to different classes, individuals & societies. We judge

---

1 Harold Joseph Laski (1893–1950), Marxist-influenced political theorist; Professor of Political Science, London (LSE), 1926–50; member, Executive Committee, Labour Party, 1936–49, Chairman 1945–6.

each case on its merits & not in accordance with an a priori preconception to which no factual discoveries can in principle make any difference: hence we do not claim, while the Marxists do claim, to know in advance whether a man's views are correct or worth following simply by finding out his social or economic background or condition. The Marxist view about this – because it claims the irrefutability of its own theory – departs from the rationalist tradition of Europe which Marx either misunderstood or consciously betrayed. And so on.

I think all this – revolving round civil liberties & Jan Masaryk's[1] remark about the tramcar & the right to say he didn't 'think much of the government'[2] is much more central than the roots of our tradition in Christianity & Greece etc. which Marxists can – & wd – either equally claim or oppose with a materialist theory which in some measure we accept too.

I have gone on much too long & demonstrated, if this was needed, how unsuitable my dry exposition is to your purposes which must to some degree, & v. properly, be propagandist. If you have a large committee brooding about Western values – à la Toynbee[3] or Prof. Northrop's[4] immense & boring but clear book on Western v. Marxist (& v. every other) ideology ("The Meeting of East & West") – I honestly think it would be far better to dispense with it and instruct a professional eloquent liberal to write you a clear & unwoolly manifesto. If you don't want B. Russell I shd suggest Tawney,[5] unless he is gaga – or Leonard Woolf[6] who wd be very very good on this – or Gilbert Murray who is sharper than one thinks, or & don't scorn the thought – Salvador Madariaga[7] who is full of thoughts about the West &

1 Jan Garrigue Masaryk (1886–1948), son of the first Czechoslovak President, Tomáš Garrigue Masaryk; Minister of Foreign Affairs 1940–8. He had been killed mysteriously by a fall from his fourth-floor apartment in the Foreign Ministry on 10 March, a few weeks after a Communist government had taken control in Prague.
2 'I want to be able at any time I like to ride in a tramcar down the Wenceslas Square in Prague and say, "I don't think much of our present government."' Quoted in 'Masaryk the Man', The Times, 11 March 1948, 4.
3 Arnold Joseph Toynbee (1889–1975), historian and internationalist; Professor of International History, London, 1925–55, Research Professor from 1928; Director of Studies, RIIA, 1926–55; Director, FORD, 1943–6.
4 Filmer Stuart Cuckow Northrop (1893–1992), philosopher, Professor, Yale, 1932–47; Sterling Professor of Philosophy and Law, Yale 1947–62. In his major work The Meeting of East and West: An Inquiry Concerning World Understanding (New York, 1946) he surveyed the major cultures of the world and proposed greater integration between them.
5 Richard Henry Tawney (1880–1962), economic historian and social reformer, Professor of Economic History, London (LSE).
6 Leonard Sidney Woolf (1880–1969), author and political theorist; founder of the Hogarth Press with his wife Virginia; joint editor, Political Quarterly, 1931–59.
7 Salvador de Madariaga (1886–1978), engineer, linguist, journalist, novelist, literary and historical scholar and academic, diplomat, liberal internationalist; an opponent of Franco, hence an exile from Spain for many years, during which time he was based mainly in Oxford.

writes very well. What is no good for this is Lindsay[1] or Livingstone[2] or any of the professional philosophers or humanists. Dixi et salvavi etc.[3]

yrs ever

Isaiah Berlin.   [...]

The recipients of IB's analysis were in general admiring, but dubious about its practical usefulness.[4]

TO WINSTON CHURCHILL

26 April 1948 [*manuscript*]

New College

Dear Mr Churchill,

I am most grateful to you for your letter and covered with embarrassment by your generosity[5] which is out of proportion, I feel, to any help I may have been able to render. It was a great honour and a great pleasure to be associated even in so minor a fashion with the achievement of so handsome an edifice – it is a noble & beautiful ship that is about to set forth on its maiden voyage and I appreciate deeply the privilege of having been allowed to be present at its launching.

With my best wishes

Yours very sincerely

Isaiah Berlin

The UN debate of 29 November 1947 on the UNSCOP recommendations, and the resulting vote for the partition of Palestine, had led to violence between the Jewish and Arab communities there, initially sporadic but leading over the next few months to what was war in all but name.[6] *With the end of the Mandate*

1 Alexander Dunlop Lindsay (1879–1952), 1st Baron Lindsay of Birker, Master of Balliol 1924–49; socialist political philosopher; Principal of University College of North Staffordshire (later Keele University) 1949–52.

2 Sir Richard Winn Livingstone (1880–1960), classicist and educationalist; President of Corpus Christi 1933–50; Vice-Chancellor, Oxford, 1944–7.

3 'Dixi et salvavi animam meam' ('I have spoken out and saved my soul'). This religious formula was quoted ironically by Karl Marx at the end of a set of 'marginal notes' sent in 1875 to one of the social democratic movements in Germany, commenting critically on their programme for social change, and now known as *Critique of the Gotha Programme*. The document sets out Marx's thinking for the organisation of the post-revolutionary world. See Karl Marx and Frederick Engels, *Collected Works* (London, 1975–2004), vol. 24, 99.

4 One official commented ruefully that 'there are large numbers of people in Europe, by no means necessarily unintelligent, who as a result of economic and intellectual stress and turmoil have turned to the dogmas of Marxism because they provide a plausible and authoritative creed unquestioned by their adherents [...] These people do not want intellectual freedom.' Geoffrey Aldington, minute of 16 June 1948 [NA, FO 953/144].

5 Churchill had sent IB an honorarium of 200 guineas.

6 IB commented: 'Palestine – first & last – I can see no help for it but partition now + an international force. I am sure the F. Office are waiting for the situation so to deteriorate – civil war &

in sight, the British forces in Palestine largely refrained from intervening, and started to withdraw; in areas of Jewish military success much of the Arab population fled or was evacuated to neighbouring Arab countries, where they waited for Arab troops to defeat the Jews and allow the refugees to return to Palestine. On 14 May, the day before the Mandate was to expire, as the last of the British forces pulled out, David Ben-Gurion declared the existence of the State of Israel, though without defining its boundaries. The US recognised the new State at once, but Britain refused to do so. Attempts to place Jerusalem under UN control were unsuccessful. The armies of the five Arab countries that surrounded Israel (Egypt, Iraq, Transjordan, Syria and Lebanon) immediately launched assaults on Israeli-held territory, including the Jewish areas of Jerusalem. Within days the Jewish Quarter of the Old City of Jerusalem had surrendered to the Arab Legion[1] and a massacre of the Jewish inhabitants of the city seemed to be a real possibility.

TO LEO AMERY[2]

27 May 1948 [*manuscript*]

New College

Dear Amery

Thank you very much for your letter and for the steps you have taken.[3] I am afraid that you are only too deeply right in supposing that Bevin will prove almost immoveable. The State Dept. have Britain where they want her: they sympathize with the F.O. policy, have arranged for it to be executed by Bevin, so that he takes all the blame: every time Truman reports State Dept. policies Bevin merely grows more antisemitic. In the end he will probably have to climb down & recognize Israel;[4] but after blood & humiliating reluctances. Meanwhile it is difficult to acquit him of having almost inspired a war, & of fomenting it by might & main. I feel that a speech or interview by Cunningham – who has been very fair & wise & good – might illuminate the benighted but nothing else much. I shall be seeing Salisbury[5] myself next week, & if it isn't too late, I'll try to talk to him. My rich Arab ex-pupil from

mutual exhaustion – that a new Morrison plan– now too little & too late – can then be imposed by a bored, disgusted, relieved world'; Weizmann 'sits in the Dorchester & is the only person worth listening to on Palestine': [late January/early February 1948] to Phil Graham.

1 The army of Transjordan, the most effective of the Arab armies at the time. Its commander, Lieutenant-General Glubb ('Glubb Pasha', 51/6), and many of its officers were British, and some of its equipment had been supplied by Britain.
2 Leopold Charles Maurice Stennett Amery (1873–1955), Conservative politician, journalist, historian, indefatigable supporter of the British Empire; Fellow of All Souls (for the second time) 1939–55; a long-standing Zionist of part-Jewish descent who had drafted the Balfour Declaration.
3 Amery had written to Churchill (as IB had urged) and to Lord Salisbury (note 5 below) about the threat to the Jews of Jerusalem.
4 Britain did not accord Israel full de jure recognition until April 1950.
5 Robert Arthur James ('Bobbety') Gascoyne-Cecil (1893–1972), 5th Marquess of Salisbury from April 1947 (previously Lord Cranborne), Conservative politician; Leader of the Opposition in the

Palestine[1] now here is mild about the Jews, but murderous about the Mufti and Bevin in the same breath. He trusts Abdullah.[2]

Yours

Isaiah Berlin

TO CHAIM WEIZMANN

6 June 1948 [*manuscript*]

New College

Dear Dr Weizmann,

I feel very guilty about not having cabled you about the Presidency,[3] but I couldn't: I really couldn't: the office is so over-deserved, so onerous & difficult now, comes at so critical and heartrending (& yet marvellous) a moment, that simply to congratulate you – as others have so rightly done – seemed to me a semi-public act conveying no personal & private emotion. I remember talking to Coupland[4] about it. He said he would have done it if he had had the heart: but he thought that for an Englishman, who ought to hang his head in shame, to cable you wd be an insult to you: & Amery thought the same. Amery I have corresponded with hoping to make him talk to Winston which he has done: not altogether without effect: & he wrote to me to say that nothing short of [the] prospect of [a] really serious rift with America wd stop Bevin from his suicidal course. But Coupland's fear of offending you I understood: & he has been very brave in saying what he thought. And even Jimmy Rothschild[5] has taken courage & publicly denounced the government. It is a fantastic & monstrous situation: never in the course of recorded history – not even during the Boer War – has the entire press of the entire world so unanimously condemned British policy: there are plenty of anti-Jewish & pro-Arab countries & papers: but without exception pro & anti-Jewish, pro & anti communist or fascist or whatever – all have joined in

(Conservative-dominated) House of Lords 1945–51; Leader of the House of Lords 1951–7; Lord President of the Council 1952–7.

1 Abdul Majid Taji Farouki (1912–86), son of a wealthy Palestinian landowner; New College PPE 1932–5 (L1 102/11).

2 Abdullah of Transjordan (1882–1951), Emir of Transjordan (under the British Mandate) 1921–46; King Abdullah I of Jordan 1949–51; rival of the Grand Mufti for the leadership of the Palestinian Arabs; close ally of Britain and the most moderate of the Arab leaders, who in 1947 had indicated to the Jewish leaders that he wanted peace. However, pressure from other members of the Arab League (possibly coupled with Abdullah's own territorial ambitions) led Transjordan to join the Arab attack on Israel in May 1948. The Palestinian Arabs nevertheless remained suspicious of his intentions and Abdullah was assassinated in Jerusalem in 1951.

3 Weizmann (in France at the time of this letter) had been named President of the Provisional State Council of Israel on 16 May.

4 Sir Reginald Coupland (1884–1952), Beit Professor of the History of the British Empire, Oxford, and Fellow of All Souls 1920–48; Member of Palestine Royal Commission 1936–7 (11/1).

5 James Armand Edmond de Rothschild (1878–1957), Liberal MP 1929–45; born in France but became one of the leaders of the Jewish community in Britain; strongly Zionist.

damning British policy. But the press of this country has totally suppressed this fact & h[as] behaved with an injured vanity, an unworthy sense of pique, all save the Manchester Guardian, the New Statesman & the Tribune – which in previous periods only the Germans cd sink to. In Oxford my colleagues are very tactful: & some are pro-Jewish & like Coupland & Amery, ashamed. But by & large they behave like Chamberlainites at Munich: & still their doubts & stifle their consciences & think about two serjeants[1] or the King David.[2] Bevin's last antisemitic outburst – about there being no Arabs in the House of Commons – did embarrass the M.P.s of all parties, & several told me so. But that is merely a question of taste & style & articulating what many feel but are too well brought up to say. As for the Foreign Office I know nothing from any official source: but if I had to guess I shd say that of course their problem is how to prevent a Jewish State from occurring – which they have, I think, genuinely persuaded themselves wd be bound to fall within the Soviet orbit ideologically & politically. The State Dept has played its cards with great ability: au fond[3] they agree with Mr Bevin, Mr Wright[4] & Mr Beeley.[5] The deal with the British is that they should do the political & military tinkering in the Middle East: ergo: all the odium for an obviously anti-Jewish policy falls on the Foreign Office; the State Dept is virtuously neutral & unmentioned; & every time Truman makes a pro-Jewish move Bevin merely becomes more antisemitic since the London U.S. Embassy hint that they are as indignant as he about Truman's outrageous behaviour, but that politics, Jews, votes etc. are a form of political pitch which they cannot touch & are impotent before & betrayed by. It is, leaving Jewish considerations out of it, crass blindness & stupidity on Bevin & Attlee's part to allow themselves to drift into the position of international villains at once hypocritical & savage: & all I cd do was to try & persuade various people that if there is even a minor massacre of Jews in Jerusalem – which could perhaps still happen – it wd, if British Glubbs[6] etc. were anywhere about, kill all memory of Jewish terrorism & be the most unforgotten of all historic blots on the British record – Amritsar[7]

1 See 30–1.
2 See 12.
3 'Basically'.
4 Michael Robert Wright (1901–76), diplomat; British Embassy, Washington, 1943–6; Assistant Under-Secretary of State, FO, 1947–50; Ambassador to Norway 1951–4, to Iraq 1954–8.
5 Harold Beeley (1909–2001), academic and diplomat; Junior Research Fellow and Lecturer in History, Queen's, 1935–8; member of Foreign Research and Press Service of the RIIA and its successor, FORD, 1939–45; British Secretary to Anglo-American Committee of Inquiry on Palestine 1946; FO 1946–69 (Counsellor, Baghdad, 1950–3; Ambassador to Saudi Arabia 1955, to United Arab Republic 1961–4); Bevin's closest adviser at the end of the Mandate.
6 Lieutenant-General John Bagot Glubb ('Glubb Pasha') (1897–1986), commander of the Arab Legion 1939–56 and responsible for its transformation into the best-trained Arab army. At the time of the assault on Jerusalem, nearly 40 of the Legion's officers were British, over half on secondment from the British Army.
7 In 1919, when martial law had been imposed in the Punjab city of Amritsar after a number of

& the Indian Mutiny[1] & Black & Tans[2] wd fade into insignificance beside it. How far this has sunk in I cannot tell: but as an ad hoc point – & I cannot help feeling that this tragedy is both possible & still avertable – it [is] the only concrete proposition which it seems possible to try & make people realize. Otherwise there really is a mood of national resentment & wilful self right-eousness – the facing of facts which wd expose British policy for what it is wd be too morally painful to these au fond uncynical people – covers every-thing, and brave good letters in the Times – like ones by a Mr Connell[3] from Palestine accusing Bevin of wanton destruction and precipitating a war – of which he is surely guilty – get no real response. Yet I also have a funny feeling that even the Foreign Office believe that Israel has come to stay – that *some* sort of State *will* survive, & that the situation had better be stabilized quickly, before the Russians can take a hand. Certainly in his talks with Douglas[4] about the U.S. resolution before UNO[5] Bevin & Co must, I think, have taken the line that to declare the Arab States to be acting unlawfully & expose them to legitimate invasion by e.g. Russia wd be resisted by Britain at the cost even of a break with America; hence the American retreat & the adop-tion of Cadogan's resolution;[6] but this is a card they cannot play too often, & in the end some kind of de facto compromise is, I am sure, contemplated between Abdulla & the Jews, as soon as the Arabs say they are tired of war, or the Russians start to rumble, if ever they do. Certainly nobody here really has any idea of how black their acts look to the outside world: all the foreign correspondents of British dailies & weeklies softpedal foreign criticism: there is a national solidarity behind Bevin to resist horrible importations

violent incidents, British troops under Brigadier-General Reginald Dyer fired on an unarmed crowd celebrating a religious festival; hundreds were killed.

1 The revolt of Indian soldiers ('sepoys') in the army of the British East India Company led to widespread rebellion against the British in India during 1857–8; numerous atrocities were com-mitted by all concerned, including the eventually victorious British.

2 Additional recruits to the Royal Irish Constabulary over the period 1920–2 (named from the piecemeal uniform with which they were initially issued) gained a reputation for brutality in their treatment of the Irish during and after the Irish War of Independence.

3 In his letter John Connell refers to his observation of 'looting, hate, chaos, and destruction [...] a beautiful city being murdered' and the ruin of 'the constructive and creative work of 30 years', ruin 'willed by His Majesty's Government' since 'lack of decision becomes tragically decisive when it produces such results'. However, two other letters published alongside Connell's reflect different attitudes: that from E. L. Spears (Major-General Sir Edward Spears) concludes that 'Zionism is proving to be a fearful calamity for mankind', while the noted Arabist H. St J. B. Philby argues that Britain 'might have done otherwise than she did in 1917; but what else could she do today than what she has done?' (*The Times*, 20 May 1948, 5).

4 Lewis Williams Douglas (1894–1974), US Ambassador to London 1947–51.

5 On 17 May the US moved a resolution in the Security Council defining Arab military action in Palestine as a breach of the peace according to Article 39 of the UN Charter, and calling for a ceasefire within 36 hours, subject to UN enforcement; the resolution was not adopted.

6 Sir Alexander George Montagu Cadogan (1884–1968), diplomat; Permanent Under-Secretary, FO, 1938–46; UK Permanent Representative to UN 1946–50; Chairman of the Board of Governors, BBC, 1952–7. A resolution proposed by Britain calling for a ceasefire without invoking Article 39 was adopted on 22 May (Resolution 49); a further British resolution, calling for a four-week truce, was passed with amendments on 29 May (Resolution 50).

from abroad; & yet in their heart of hearts they all feel that the Palestine policy is a squalid failure, that so much self-justification denotes frightful sense of guilt: & that a new policy will have to be adopted soon. Even the A.J.A.[1] sends bleats of protest to the Foreign Office: & pro Arab speeches in Parliament have fallen off lately: the Times keeps advocating recognition of Israel, which is a straw – & altogether the anti-Jewish war, real though it may be in Palestine & the F.O., is half-hearted & riddled with moral doubts & a sense of failure on the part of public opinion – which *because* it is troubled and uncertain & dislikes Umkreisung[2] by foreign criticism, is correspondingly antisemitic. In the end Winston & only he can turn the tide: & I shall do my best to get the facts – the deductions he can well make for himself [–] he is still a clear headed British patriot – to him: But if there is something in particular which I cd do, please tell me – & I'll do my best about it. Goodness how often I have thought of you & Mrs Weizmann going through the ups & downs of this crisis – It is a terrible thing to say but somehow I feel that the heroism & the fighting are necessary if ever we are to have a State with memories & traditions & purehearted martyrs & political ideals for which men are ready to die – [. . .] I have been through so much with you in London & New York, & it has been so much the most honourable & genuine thing in my life, that I find myself isolated & on a desert island now. If I can be of any use please let me know. To day is my birthday & it has been its greatest pleasure to write to you and offer you both, as always, all my love & devotion and faith and everything whatever.

yrs
    Isaiah

In July IB needed treatment for two duodenal ulcers, which reduced his participation in Oxford's Summer School for Graduates.[3] Nevertheless, in August he set off for his first post-war visit to the Salzburg Music Festival, writing an article for the Observer,[4] *and commenting to his father: 'I despise the natives but their charm & endless courtesy is not at all disagreeable.'[5] Then followed relaxation on Venice Lido and near Lake Garda, and a stay in the French spa of Aix-les-Bains with his parents. Chaim Weizmann had been having eye treatment in Geneva, and IB took this opportunity to visit him and his wife shortly before they left for their new life as President and First Lady of Israel. In the face of Weizmann's pressure on IB to work for him in Israel, and*

1 The Anglo-Jewish Association, according to IB 'full of respectable British Jews, no Zionists at all' (MI Tape 16).
2 'Being surrounded'.
3 The School's topic was, as in 1947, 'European Civilisation in the Twentieth Century'. This time IB was (nominally) Director of Studies for Philosophy.
4 The article which IB submitted was considered too long for publication in its entirety, but an extract appeared as 'Karajan: A Study', *Observer*, 19 September 1948, 2.
5 Postcard of 26 August 1948.

his contempt for 'the withdrawal from life on the part of those to whom their
personal integrity, or peace of mind, or purity of ideal, mattered more than the
work upon which they were engaged and to which they were committed',[1] *IB*
responded with a mixture of guilt and determination.

TO CHAIM WEIZMANN

16 September 1948 [*transcript of missing manuscript*]

Aix les Bains

Dear Dr. Weizmann,

I cannot go back to England without saying, however briefly and inadequately, with what deep pleasure I saw you and Mrs. Weizmann yesterday,
due both to the greatly improved state of health in which I was delighted to
find you both – relieved and delighted – and to the moral happiness which
every occasion on which you allow me to see you always creates in me. I
should like to say that I am terribly well aware of my own insufficiencies, –
that I ought to collect such little resources as I have into a concentrated
whole, and direct them to some single end pursued with one's whole heart
and mind and soul, as you yourself have so memorably done. Whereas I tend
to disperse, and fritter and squander and so achieve little or nothing. And I
hoped you believed me when I said both to you and to Mrs. Weizmann that it
is this very guilty conscience that forces me to try and sit down and do some
serious work for the next few years – for otherwise I should become worthless in my own eyes and of no use to anyone in any serious capacity. And I
realise only too sharply that to do this in an hour of crisis for our own people
may seem unpardonable egoism and even a kind of levity. But I am sure that
you will understand when I say that unless one can stabilize one's own life,
one does more harm than good by trying to attach it to some public work.
But I could not dream of ever turning my back on Israel and its life. And the
only way I know of serving it is by serving you, for reasons which you will
not want me to put into banal words. For this reason I shall certainly get in
touch as we agreed, with the people you spoke of, to see if one could do
something worthy and constructive, and to see to it that you never lack for
worthy people at your side. And I will, of course, try and keep in touch with
you as often and as much and as fully as possible. My association with you
has been in all my life the thing in which I felt more pride and moral satisfaction than anything else whatever – not to speak of the personal pleasure and
the sense of justification for one's existence which it provided and provides.
I must apologize for suddenly pouring out before you this flood of feelings,
which spoken or unspoken, must have been experienced by many – only that
our last meeting seemed to bring home with peculiar intensity all that I owe

1 PI2 53–4.

you and all that I feel towards you. And now I must stop. And only add that I am sure that no constitution-mongering and no paper rules will make the slightest difference to the powerful and *assainissant*[1] influence which you are bound to have on the future of Israel. And to send you & Mrs. W. all my love and all my devotion & to say how warmly I look forward to seeing you again in Rechovoth or in Europe in spring or summer or autumn, and to wish you the realization of every wish and hope and prayer.

Yours

Isaiah.

By 23 September IB was able to report to Hamish Hamilton, with some incredulity, 'I scarcely know how to say it: but so far as I am concerned I can do no more to "First Love" – in short my text is complete. Now comes the rub. Slightly over a half is in the hands of Miss S. Morgan,[2] preoccupied, I fear, by her forthcoming nuptials to Ld Anglesey.'[3] Over the next few weeks preparations for the wedding seem to have taken precedence over the production of a legible text.

TO SHIRLEY MORGAN

3 October [1948, *manuscript*]

New College

Dearest Shirley,

What wd you like as a wedding present? a silver flute? the engraved MSS of F[irst] Love? I long to give you gramophone records[4] – but I expect you will have them all – or a new Grove[5] – but you will have that too, I expect; but do say: I am sure you dislike to decide, and in a matter so delicate as something which shd proceed spontaneously from the donor you will be particularly, and justifiably, inhibited. Nevertheless we have always been sensible above all things – a course I approve, & so do you though at the same time you also tend to repudiate any manifestation of this quality in yourself with fierce indignation – What then shall I do?! tell me if you have a moment: I shall do as you say.

---

1 'Purifying'.

2 (Elizabeth) Shirley Vaughan *Morgan (b. 1924), daughter of the novelists Charles Morgan (57/7) and Hilda Vaughan; IB's assistant in preparing the translation of *First Love* for publication.

3 (George Charles) Henry Victor Paget, 7th Marquess of Anglesey (b. 1922).

4 In the end IB gave them a recording of Mozart's *The Marriage of Figaro*.

5 *The Dictionary of Music and Musicians*, originally edited by Sir George Grove (1820–1900), a standard reference work first published in four volumes between 1878 and 1889. It would have been an appropriate present from IB to the Angleseys, who shared his love of music, since George Grove had in his youth worked as an engineer with Robert Stephenson on the Britannia Bridge across the Menai Strait to Anglesey, and in later life became an expert on the topography of Palestine.

Richard[1] & Marcus[2] seem to me to wander about Oxford in a melancholy unmarried way – I have never seen unmarriedness so bleak and lowering & corrosive – as for me I live in hideous chaos,[3] changing my mind about shelves, switches, chests, every six hours or so, waited on by deputations of exasperated electricians and builders, mixed with normal visitors, undergraduates, scouts, messengers – a kind of ludicrous mill of sometimes v. funny characters circulating in a second hand furniture shop after a pogrom. I can find nothing – & must stop.

Love
    Isaiah

TO SHIRLEY ANGLESEY

[Late October 1948, *manuscript*]

New College

Dearest Marchioness,

I only want to send this hurriedly to say how delightful & charming I found your entire wedding.[4] I enjoyed David's robust Christianity: the Lord's Prayer spoken in a tremendous voice & very loud amens, while Marcus refrained altogether: your father's exquisite appearance & sense of pace when leading you up – & every circumstance & detail including the Vichyssois sermon (famille: patrie: travail[5] – no joys for you, only hard labour & burdens: for keeps. This is partly, but not entirely G. Weidenfeld's[6] joke. He said Demo-Christian.[7] But Vichyssois is more accurate & wittier); I enjoyed everything: your appearance & Henry's:[8] my conversations with Violet B.C.[9] with a

1 Richard Arthur Wollheim (1923–2003), Balliol history 1941–2, 1945–6, PPE 1947–8 (tutored by Marcus Dick); Assistant Lecturer in Philosophy, University College London, 1949–51, Lecturer 1951–60, Reader 1960–3; later (1963–82) Grote Professor of Philosophy of Mind and Logic, London.
2 Marcus William Dick (1920–71), Fellow and Tutor in Philosophy and Politics, Balliol, 1947–63; later (1963–71) Professor of Philosophy, East Anglia.
3 IB had moved to new rooms in New College's Garden Quad.
4 On 16 October at Chiswick Parish Church, with a reception afterwards at Walpole House, Chiswick Mall, the home of the groom's aunt, Lady Violet Benson. The bride wore a white velvet dress, carried a bouquet of orchids from Bodnant, Lord Aberconway's garden, and had seven attendants.
5 'Family: homeland: work', one of the slogans of the wartime Vichy regime in France.
6 (Arthur) George Weidenfeld (b. 1919), Baron Weidenfeld of Chelsea 1976, of Viennese origin; publisher; joint founder (and Chairman) of Weidenfeld & Nicolson 1948; acted as Chaim Weizmann's political adviser and *chef de cabinet* (and senior counsellor, Israeli Foreign Ministry) 1949–50.
7 Christian Democrat. The centre-right Demo-Christian Party was in power in Italy at the time of this letter.
8 The groom.
9 Lady (Helen) Violet *Bonham Carter (1887–1969), Baroness Asquith of Yarnbury 1964, daughter of the Liberal Prime Minister Herbert Asquith (from 1925 1st Earl of Oxford and Asquith); married to Sir Maurice Bonham Carter (57/12); leading member of the Liberal Party and public figure.

slight air of a wicked fairy at the Christening: with Diana: with Duff: with Rose Macaulay[1] to whom every one kept reintroducing me (I have known her not well for 10 or 15 years) with Charles Parker[2] who is not allowed to reveal the name of the commercial enterprise with which he is connected: with – yes even Charlotte Bonham Carter[3] who is now a Beerbohm[4] carica-ture of all that she in fact is – with Mark[5] who must be up to something; with Caroline[6] – oh bliss I was kissed once more & heard how touched Q. Mary was by your father's elegant & gallant mode of address:[7] with Diana again who said she was above all afraid of boring people: with Gladwyn,[8] who, when I kept saying things about the French kept hissing pushing & rolling his eye, all because I would not notice M. Massigli[9] who was walking by his side – till I said 'why do you push' etc. & only left, with Mme Hofmannsthal mère[10] & Octavian[11] when the Fascists & Marcus had established themselves near what was left of drinks & the tone began to fall too rapidly. I am glad Bongy[12] is to give you 2 vols of Schnabel.[13] And I'd love to go to Anglesey &

1 (Emilie) Rose Macaulay (1881–1958), novelist.
2 Presumably Charles George Archibald Parker (1924–2004), New College Russian 1946–8; Times Publishing Co. 1949–56; Charringtons 1956–61.
3 Lady (Charlotte Helen) Bonham Carter (1893–1989), née Ogilvy, wife of Sir Edgar Bonham Carter.
4 Sir (Henry) Max(imilian) Beerbohm (1872–1956), caricaturist, essayist, novelist, drama critic and parodist, whose main targets were pretentiousness and affectation.
5 Mark Raymond Bonham Carter (1922–94), Baron Bonham Carter of Yarnbury 1986, son of Sir Maurice (note 12 below) and Lady Violet Bonham Carter.
6 The groom's sister, Lady (Alexandra Mary) Caroline Cecilia Paget (1913–73), daughter of the 6th Marquess of Anglesey. IB described her as a 'femme fatale' (to Maurice Bowra, New Year [1937], L1 supp.); loved by the artist Rex Whistler among others, she married Sir Michael Duff (65/4) in 1949.
7 Queen Mary (692/5), the groom's godmother, was among the guests. The exact compliment paid her is unknown, but the bride's father, Charles Langbridge Morgan (1894–1958), novelist, playwright and drama critic, was an accomplished, if solemn, wordsmith. His works had been fashionable in the 1930s but his metaphysical preoccupations later lost their appeal. He was vio-lently critical of humour, which he defined as 'talent's sneer at genius [...] mediocrity's hatred of the Spirit of Man', and claimed that many great men – including Shakespeare and Jesus – lacked a sense of humour ('On Singleness of Mind', published with The Flashing Stream, London, 1938). Stella Gibbons mercilessly caricatured him as Gerard Challis in her 1946 novel Westwood.
8 (Hubert Miles) Gladwyn Jebb (1900–96), 1st Baron Gladwyn 1960, diplomat; UK Permanent Representative to UN 1950–4; Ambassador to France 1954–60. Shirley Morgan had been his Personal Secretary at the FO.
9 René Massigli (1888–1988), French diplomat; Ambassador to UK 1944–55.
10 Gertrud ('Gerty') von Hofmannsthal (1880–1959), née Schlesinger, widow of Hugo von Hofmannsthal, lived in Oxford from 1939 and became a British citizen in 1947.
11 Octavian Charles Hugo von Hofmannsthal (b. 1946), son of Raimund and Elizabeth von Hofmannsthal (65/3), nephew of the groom and grandson of Hugo von Hofmannsthal, with whom Richard Strauss collaborated on the libretto of his opera Der Rosenkavalier (in which a central character is called Octavian). He and his six-year-old sister Arabella were among the bride's attendants.
12 The nickname of Sir Maurice Bonham Carter (1880–1960).
13 Artur Schnabel (1882–1951), pianist, born in Lipnik, Poland; settled in the US 1938; celebrated especially for his performances of the sonatas of Beethoven and Schubert. His recording (on some 200 sides of 78 rpm records) of the complete piano sonatas of Beethoven is probably what is referred to here.

stay a week-end but when, that is most difficult. This is only to tell you how gay & without blemish it all was – including the music – & how affectionate I feel to you both.

Isaiah

TO SHIELA NEWSOME[1]

21 October 1948 [*manuscript*]

New College

Dearest Shiela,

Your letter which pursued me madly across N. Italy & France arrived in Aix les Bains, & I put it with other sacred objects & they all, in some wallet or parcel, are buried in the unsightly heaps of shapeless stuff (how you wd dislike the sight) which clutter the floors of my rooms, still in chaos, with beautiful views but 1500 books on the floor, a ghastly lunar Berlin-like sight, while I helplessly (you cd imagine) flounder among them. The wallpapers are up & are very pretty (I have moved, you understand) but not the shelves, still I am in [a] shortlived mood of gaiety induced I can't think by what. Heart-freeness I daresay. Correspondence (the substitute you offer, I dimly remember from your truly charming letter) will not really do: as you know too I am sure. And the telephone is so expensive, & in my rooms now goes through the lodge (2225 just in case you receive a windfall: & what better cause, what more delightful pleasure though it's me that says so) so that even total privacy is prevented. But it is more that I cannot write systematically or often: because one's too quickly exhausted, one writes too much professionally to leave one energy for private exercises, because I am too sporadic a writer, & the emotional rapport so established is too precarious and undependable and frustrating. Only seeing is really any good: at worst talking. Writing is a peaceful pleasure for emotionally unengaged old age, & unless called for by some shock & impulse or agony or violent gust is not a steady or satisfying medium. In short I wish to see you. When, therefore will you come? even if it means staying with X. Hill.[2] (who when I see him at public lectures – e.g. of the enemy Toynbee – directs hard ironical looks at me as if to say that *he* knows all about me: how I know good from evil & open eyed choose evil, & belong potentially to the elect, & can be talked to, but

---

1 Shiela *Newsome (1913–2004), née Grant Duff, at this time married to Noel Newsome (see 796); Sokolov Grant from 1952, when she married Micheal Sokolov; journalist and writer, who had argued for the defence of Czechoslovakia before the war and remained deeply committed to the country and its people (Jan Masaryk was her eldest child's godfather); one of IB's closest friends.

2 (John Edward) Christopher Hill (1912–2003), Marxist-inclined historian; Fellow and Tutor in History, Balliol, 1938–65; later (1965–78) Master. IB had 'a total rift' with Hill 'because, in his book on Lenin, he said things he knew not to be true, and whatever the justification of such things in the Cold War, it makes personal relations, for me at any rate, intolerable'. Letter to Norman O. Brown, 28 October 1959.

have through perversity or weakness deliberately embraced the enemy, or sold myself, or chosen to live in chains, & so must be the first to be burnt, & mustn't pretend I don't know why or how deeply deserved) – or Thingmajig[1] in New College Lane (which I could fix, I daresay, only say the word) & if you came in the week (Monday to Weds) I cd produce Humphry[2] too: so there. I shan't be in London alas, nor can get any further, not for a month at least: whereas you certainly should & must & can get away from the horrid exile into which you have, so fearfully blundering, thrust yourself, all because of a blind faith in theory & puritanical resistance to spontaneous impulses & suppression of your quite sufficiently clear eyed view of what is bright, happy making & naturally good in favour of a dramatic dream & a very impressive but costly pride.[3] There now that is the whole of my sermon: but I long to see you if only because I am *never* happier than with you (I blush as I say it) & there is much to say.

Love, much love

Shaya

Frau von Trott[4] has not been round, after I formally accorded an audience via Diana.[5]

P.S. Or even for an afternoon one rainless (or rainy day – oh do.)

The Arab–Israeli war continued, interrupted at the UN's behest by truces of varying duration and on 17 September by the murder in Jerusalem of the UN mediator, Count Folke Bernadotte,[6] by a member of the Stern gang. But Israeli military successes made it increasingly unlikely that the new State would be overrun. As IB prepared for a six-month visit to Harvard he was able to write to the Israeli President with new confidence that Zionist aims were being fulfilled.

1 Jenifer Hart (186/1). On a visit to Herbert Hart in hospital, Shiela forgot Jenifer's name and called her 'thingmajig', which Herbert immediately repeated to Jenifer and others.
2 (Arthur) Humphry House (1908–55), Chaplain-Fellow and English Lecturer, Wadham, and Deacon in the Church of England 1931–2 (resigned after a crisis of faith); Director of Studies in English, Peterhouse, Cambridge, 1947–9; Senior University Lecturer in English Literature, Oxford, 1948–55; Fellow of Wadham 1950–5; Clark Lecturer, Trinity College, Cambridge, 1951–2; specialist in Dickens and Gerard Manley Hopkins, and long-standing friend of IB's.
3 Presumably a reference to SN's marriage (1942–52) to Noel Newsome, which she describes as 'a blunder but not caused by "blind faith in theory & puritanical resistance to ...", though there was a "dramatic dream" that he and I might achieve something in the post-war world. I made him stand in 1945 for Parliament (which cost him his position in the BBC: Hugh Carleton Greene, who had worked with him in the European Service, saw to it that he never set foot in the BBC again).' Note by Shiela Sokolov Grant on copy of letter.
4 Clarita von Trott (b. 1917), née Tiefenbacher, widow of Adam von Trott zu Solz (207/2).
5 Diana Mary Hopkinson (1912–2007), née Hubback, a close friend and lifelong admirer and defender of Adam von Trott.
6 Count Folke Bernadotte (1895–1948), diplomat, grandson of King Oscar II of Sweden; President, Swedish Red Cross Association, 1946–8; UN mediator in Palestine 1948.

TO DR CHAIM WEIZMANN

1 December 1948 [*manuscript*]

New College

Dear Dr Weizmann,

I was very proud and very happy to receive your letter – even our papers cannot conceal altogether what is going on and even they cannot deny that it must be a source of pleasure and passionate pride to Jews everywhere – the result is very evident already. There is, as you know, an enquiry[1] going on into the commercial practices of various shady characters vis a vis Labour ministers – the shady characters are mostly Jews, the antisemitism all this is creating is considerable – yet yet apart from a certain disgust & shame, the Jewish community is not in the old, hopeless, helpless, desperate, cowering condition – shrinking from slanders it cannot avoid – almost pinning them on to itself – the old Dreyfus–Beilis–Stavisky[2] condition. No, the people who suffer, beyond those concerned, are the Order of Trembling Israelites[3] & the decent Goyim[4] (are there any? you will ask: but there are) who dislike antisemitism violently. But not the Jews. Their eyes look elsewhere. The sense of overflowing happiness & security which comes from the abatement of agony & a painful desire which has finally culminated & come to rest in its object, is vast even here. Even if the State is overwhelmed – which seems beautifully remote – the mere fact that it existed is unexpungeable & makes a terrific difference. I can imagine what it must feel like in Tel Aviv or Rehovoth. Or rather I cannot – & ought to come & look. But my ship sails to America on the 27th December & my labours here last till the 17 or 18th – there is hardly time & I must see my parents before leaving them for so long. I really long to come – & who doesn't – to see it all come true. And even more I long to see & talk with you & Mrs Weizmann – every word I said in my letter to Geneva was literally & permanently true. I wish I wish I cd

---

1 During November and December 1948 a tribunal of inquiry chaired by a High Court judge, Sir George Lynskey, investigated allegations of corruption made against a junior minister in the Board of Trade and several senior civil servants in relation to the treatment of a football pools firm. The tribunal reported in January 1949, dismissing the most serious allegations of bribery, but criticising the conduct of a director of the Bank of England, George Gibson, and of the minister, John Belcher, whose parliamentary career the case destroyed.

2 Alfred Dreyfus (1859–1935), a captain (the highest-ranking Jew) in the French Army when he was falsely convicted of espionage in 1894; the resulting long-lasting political scandal split France. Menachem Mendel Beilis (1873–1934) was tried (and acquitted) in Kiev in 1913 for the kidnap and murder of a Ukrainian boy; the prosecution's allegations of blood libel and ritual murder provoked worldwide criticism of Russian anti-Semitism. Serge Alexandre Stavisky (1888–1934), a Ukrainian Jew living in France, a major financial fraudster, was shot in 1934, either by his own hand or by the police who were searching for him. Because his sales of false bonds had involved a number of officials, his death led to a major political crisis, including the resignation of the French Prime Minister.

3 A term applied by Lewis Namier (236/2) to Jews uncomfortable with their Jewishness. IB renamed it the Order of Trembling Amateur Gentiles (OTAG).

4 'Gentiles'.

come – but I must preserve a discipline else I go to pieces & become useless all round & for all purposes. I know that you appreciate my reason for this last: & I am bitterly frustrated about being unable to come before September or so. Then of course I will if you are still prepared to have me. How queer it is always with the Jews: when the world was going through an economic slump Palestine, you remember, in 1932–4 was going through a boom: when all other news is gloomy or semi-gloomy, our eyes look for, & light up at only one item. And it is an excellent thing about Truman. And I am sure that the wiser & better people here will realize the fearful blunder – from the point of view of British interests – of the present half hearted, pathetic efforts to perpetrate a wrong. It is a page of British folly, but they are a great people & will regain their vision & their moral standards. My love to Mrs W. & to Bergmann, & I shall write you from Harvard.

    yrs

      Isaiah   [. . .]

TO THE BOARD OF THE FACULTY OF LITERAE HUMANIORES

4 December 1948 [*manuscript*]

New College

Dear Sir,

In reply to your request for a report on my fulfilment of my duties as a University Lecturer I beg to enclose a statement dealing with the points at issue in the order in which you set them out. I regret that I possess no facilities for getting the statement typewritten.

    Yours sincerely.

      Isaiah Berlin

1. I have delivered, since the Michaelmas Term of 1946, four courses of public lectures. On three of the topics covered I have neither lectured nor written at any previous time; the fourth was largely based on the first, but did not closely resemble it either in form or in matter. They were:

(a) Political and Social Thought in the 19th century (M.T.[1] 1946)
(b) The philosophy of Berkeley (H.T. 1947)[2]
(c) Problems in the Theory of Knowledge (H.T. 1948)
and European political thought in the 19th century (T.T. 1948)

Besides this I have conducted university classes for Graduate Students

---

1 Michaelmas Term (MT) at Oxford runs from October to December, Hilary Term (HT) from January to March, Trinity Term (TT) from April to June.

2 A version of these lectures on Bishop George Berkeley (1685–1753), entitled 'Berkeley's Theory of the External World', is among Berlin's papers: a transcript is posted in the IBVL at http://berlin.wolf.ox.ac.uk/lists/nachlass/berkeley.pdf.

with my colleagues: Mr J. L. Austin[1] (M.T. 1946) with Dr F. Waismann[2] (T.T. 1948) and with Mr A. L. C. Bullock[3] of New College (M.T. 1948) and have delivered two or three isolated lectures in organized series of lectures on political philosophy.

2. I have during the period under review published a long critical notice of Lord Russell's *History of Western Philosophy* in *Mind* (1947),[4] and an article of some 14000 words on Socialist Theories in *Chambers's Encyclopaedia* (I believe still in proof).[5] And I propose to submit for publication within the next two months two contributions on philosophical topics. The first, on 'Phenomenalism'[6] I have read in various forms as papers to the Philosophical Society in Oxford and the Moral Sciences Club in Cambridge as well as at University College, London. The second, on 'Ostensive Definitions and Incorrigibility'[7] is to be read in March at Princeton University.

3. I am also engaged on preparing a volume on the philosophy of Berkeley[8] for a series edited by Prof. A. J. Ayer, which is to be ready for the press in 1951–2: my lectures on Berkeley mentioned above are to some degree a preliminary sketch for this more thorough and complete treatment of Berkeley's thought. I also have in preparation an essay on 'The Fallacy of Reducibility'[9] – a topic in logic and the theory of knowledge which I propose to submit for publication in the fairly near future in a philosophical periodical; this partly derives

---

1 John Langshaw Austin (1911–60), Fellow and Tutor in Philosophy, Magdalen, 1935–52; White's Professor of Moral Philosophy, Oxford, and Fellow of Corpus Christi 1952–60; the leader of the Oxford school of linguistic philosophy and a close friend of IB, who described him as the 'cleverest man I ever knew, apart from Keynes' (MI Tape 6); subject of a study in PI. The class was on 'Things'.

2 Friedrich Waismann (1896–1959), Austrian philosopher, mathematician and physicist, and a leading member of the Vienna Circle; New College from 1942; Lecturer in the Philosophy of Science and of Mathematics, Oxford, 1946–50, Reader in the Philosophy of Mathematics 1950–55, in Philosophy of Science 1955–9. The class IB mentions was possibly that on 'The Logical Force of Expressions' listed in the *Oxford University Gazette* as given by Waismann and Gilbert Ryle; perhaps IB participated.

3 Alan Louis Charles Bullock (1914–2004), Baron Bullock of Leafield 1976, Fellow and Tutor in Modern History, New College, 1945–52; Censor (i.e. head), St Catherine's Society (for non-collegiate students), 1952–62; Founding Master, St Catherine's, 1960–80. The class was entitled 'Concepts and Categories in History'.

4 See 40/1.

5 'Socialism and Socialist Theories', *Chambers's Encyclopaedia* (London/New York, 1950); reprinted in SR.

6 This appears to be 'The Refutation of Phenomenalism', an unpublished item posted in the IBVL at http://berlin.wolf.ox.ac.uk/lists/nachlass/phenomenalism.pdf. It is also related to IB's published article 'Empirical Propositions and Hypothetical Statements', *Mind* 59 (1950), reprinted in CC.

7 Apparently never published and not known to survive in this form; an unpublished paper on 'Synthetic a priori Propositions' read by IB at the Bryn Mawr Meeting of the American Philosophical Association in December 1951 (posted in the IBVL at http://berlin.wolf.ox.ac.uk/lists/nachlass/syntheti.pdf) may be based on it.

8 Yet more wishful thinking, though a contract was signed.

9 Published as 'Logical Translation', *Proceedings of the Aristotelian Society* 50 (1949–50); reprinted in CC.

from material used by me in my lectures on the Theory of Knowledge, but is a more technical treatment of the topics in question.

I am also proposing to embark on a wider study of social, political and scientific thought in Europe in [the] first half of the 19th Century in preparation for a volume on this subject which I have agreed to produce for the Oxford University Press.[1] My lectures on political thought in this period, principally in France and Germany, are directly related to this larger study.

4. (a) I have taught an average of 15-1 hours[2] a week during the period in question (beginning with 18 hours & stabilized at 15 since H.T. 1948) not counting supervision of advanced students.

(b) I have examined in Sections Ph 2 & 3 in the Michaelmas Term 1947 and Hilary 1948, and also one D. Phil thesis (with Prof. H. J. Paton).[3]

(c) I have performed the function of the Dean of Arts (i.e. of Degrees etc.) of my College since H.T. 1948 and of a Moral Tutor within it.

(d) I have not acted as a member of any seriously time or labour consuming committee in the University.

(e) I should, if only for the sake of completeness also add that I have, at the request of the Professor [of] Russian,[4] conducted a class for advanced students on Western Influence on Russian Thought in the 19th Century (T.T. 1947)[5] and delivered single lectures on related topics.

Some of my time was also taken up on researches into the origins of Russian revolutionary thought on which I am due to lecture at Harvard University next term: there are no authoritative works, in any language, on any but very restricted aspects and periods of this topic. I hope to publish something on this, if time allows, and have contributed an opusculum 'Russia in 1848',[6] which has appeared in the *Slavonic Review*; this I originally read as a paper to the Stubbs Society in this University. I feel I should also add that I delivered three lectures to the Summer School for Foreign Students held under the auspices of the Delegacy for Extra-Mural Studies in Oxford in July

---

1 This volume never materialised, but the preparatory work for it provided the basis for his Mary Flexner Lectures at Bryn Mawr College, Pennsylvania, in spring 1952 (see 774–5), and his Third Programme broadcasts of effectively the same material in late 1952, published posthumously as *Freedom and its Betrayal* (London, 2002). What survives of a book-length text he drafted in preparation for these lectures has been published as *Political Ideas in the Romantic Age: Their Rise and Influence on Modern Thought* (London/Princeton, 2006).

2 i.e. 15 tutorials, each of one hour.

3 Herbert James Paton (1887–1969), Fellow of Corpus Christi and White's Professor of Moral Philosophy, Oxford, 1937–52.

4 Sergey Konovalov (1899–1982), Professor of Russian, Oxford, 1945–67.

5 The four classes, beginning on 5 May, were formally entitled 'Radical Intelligentsia 1825–1881: Western Ideas'.

6 'Russia and 1848', *Slavonic Review* 26 (1948); reprinted in RT.

1947, & acted as director of its philosophical section in the summer of 1948, although, owing to my protracted illness during that time, the main burden of actual supervision fell on the shoulders of my Deputy Mr J. O. Urmson[1] of Christchurch. I do not think it necessary to add casual broadcasts and reviews on the history of ideas and the like as these fall outside my academic duties and involved little expenditure of time or labour.

I. Berlin

TO HAMILTON FISH ARMSTRONG[2]

6 December 1948 [manuscript]

New College

Dear Ham,

I wish I could! But I can't, I can't! can't, I mean, write a meditation, à la Tocqueville,[3] about the glories & miseries of Marxism, at least not yet: I've no collected or collectable (colligible?) thoughts on this truly desperate subject: while at Harvard I'll try & think about the general virtues & vices of sociology – which doesn't exist in England really & can be studied in its natural state virtually only in the United States – & try & tie Marxism on to these reflections. But I must be allowed to see how the 'scientific study of society' is carried on by its practitioners first, before bursting out against [it] with all the violent scepticism of it which at present, perhaps irrationally, I find I feel. And even then there is a long and ghastly chasm between stray thoughts which bubble easily (perhaps too easily) to my surface in talk, & a coherent, decently articulate, intellectually respectable written thesis. I am sure you know these fears & torments well, even though you are incomparably better at doing this not only than I – who am obscure, prolix, discontinuous – but than anyone at present writing about such topics (& I really do mean this most sincerely & firmly). It will be ever so nice to see you again: and your wife[4] whom I ought to have, & never have, thanked for sending me

1 James Opie Urmson (b. 1915), Student, Christ Church, 1946–55; Professor of Philosophy, Queen's College, Dundee (University of St Andrews), 1955–9; Fellow and Tutor in Philosophy, Corpus Christi, 1959–78.
2 Hamilton Fish Armstrong (1893–1973), editor 1928–72 of *Foreign Affairs*, the journal of the (American) Council on Foreign Relations, and author. When Armstrong died, IB wrote of his 'shining integrity, purity of heart and motive, political insight, kindness, public spirit, courage and [. . .] moral charm' and commented that 'his utter lack of pomp and solemnity, [his] spontaneity, candour, humanity and eager interest in people and ideas melted resistance on the part of those [. . .] who began by thinking of him as a pillar of the American "establishment"'. *The Times*, 28 April 1973, 16.
3 Alexis Charles Henri Clérel de Tocqueville (1805–59), French politician, author and liberal political thinker, committed to human freedom; his classic work *De la démocratie en Amérique* (Paris, 1835) analyses the implications of the American experience for the likely movement in Europe from aristocratic control to social equality and democracy.
4 Carman Dee Barnes (b. 1912), novelist.

her delightful book:[1] I shall be at Lowell House in Harvard from about Jan. 15: & most grateful to you if you cd sometime at your pleasure get in touch with me there.

yrs ever.

Isaiah Berlin

TO SHIRLEY ANGLESEY

Monday 6 December [1948, *manuscript*]

Reform Club

Dearest Shirley

I always seem to write to you from this gloomy club: like Paddington Station, but not so associated with the complicated hopes & fears & joys & miseries of journeys to & from Oxford: (I still, tho' more & more faintly, feel the original violent feelings with which as an undergraduate I used to travel up & down, the appalling crises & risks & excitement of getting to know people and wanting to know them & also not wanting to know them etc.) – I *couldn't* reply before, if you knew my life in the last few weeks, with not a scintilla of pleasure or personal relations of any kind, but merely legions of pupils, examination papers, journeys to Winchester to stay with a nervous & over-welcoming headmaster's wife[2] & odd social encounters with masters & their wives in the unfamiliar, & for me grotesque guise of the examiner from New College. If anyone with real powers, adequate instruments of social & moral & emotional analysis would apply himself to school life in a public school from the point of view of a master, a masterpiece of horror could be created unlike anything in existence. But how are you? very happy, I hear, & I am very glad: I am sure that marriage is excellent in itself and yours in particular: and that I shall go on believing unless brought face to face with contrary facts, & probably even then. But I long to hear about this from you personally. I sail, I suppose on the 29th December, or the 30th. Where are you? I am in Oxford on & off until the 15th Dec. & then (or on the 16th) in London. I went to the von Hoff's[3] at 6 p.m. one day last week in hopes of seeing you & Henry but saw only an unknown American miss and Sir someone Duff[4] your neighbour, who was very affable & breezy & funny but not sufficient. Where are you? I ask again. I suppose I cd ask George Weidenfeld who acts as

1 Presumably *Time Lay Asleep* (New York, 1946).

2 The Headmaster of Winchester College 1946–54 was Walter Fraser Oakeshott (1903–87); his wife was Noël Rose, née Moon (1903–76).

3 Raimund von *Hofmannsthal (1906–74), son of the Austrian poet, playwright and librettist Hugo von Hofmannsthal (1874–1929); for many years London correspondent of *Time* magazine; and his wife Lady Elizabeth Hester Mary von *Hofmannsthal (1916–80), née Paget, second daughter of the 6th Marquess of Anglesey, niece of Lady Diana Cooper, sister of Lady Caroline Paget; Shirley Anglesey's sister-in-law.

4 Sir (Charles) Michael Robert Vivian Duff (1907–80), owner of Vaynol Park, Bangor, just across the Menai Strait from Plas Newydd (67/1).

a kind of benevolent point of general contact – an infinitely well informed, stop-press-news bureau about everyone so far as I can see. Or Mark B.-C. whom I saw in conditions of excessive smartness two days ago at Dytchley:[1] but I should prefer to know directly from you. I am in London until the 9th & then at Oxford till the 15th & then back in Hampstead till I sail: so please let me know, & soon indeed instantly instantly instantly. Otherwise I shall telephone from Oxford: from the chaos & squalor but curiously exciting chaos of my new rooms: about which I think constantly during tutorials with my pupils, about what red goes with what blue, about whether eau de nil is right for the anti-macassars, always without real effect, always in a frustrated fashion leading to endless requests for advice & others to decide for me, as you can imagine (& sympathise too, let me add, ungrammatically). My thoughts automatically move to Lady Colefax: & oddly enough to Marcus.

I am now clear that Marcus cannot long continue at Oxford: his intellect is unimpaired but his life is obviously too pointless and ill adjusted. If one visits his room, his mild, dazed aspect, the opened bottles, velvet jacket, Byronic open shirt, air of endless hangover & liability to support himself with picks-me up before dinner & subsequent sad collapses – all this clearly means loss of interest in philosophy. He teaches it perfectly competently but it is a dreadfully punishing fatal subject to bear a secret hatred to – & gnaws at the vitals of those whose hearts have moved elsewhere[2] in the most destructive way. So he must leave, & administer some State controlled enterprise & make money if possible. His character continues to be excellent and he is, I am sure, much embarrassed by such thoughts on his friends' part. Mark & Richard – particularly the latter, gloat a little in a manner you can easily guess. So, to go on, I have activated Lady Colefax into asking him to dinner (I hope) to meet likely employers (I expect she'll forget her commission & ask the wrong parties – agreeable or famous or glamorous but useless for this purpose. And in this case I feel acutely that action is called for: at least he must be brought to the water, put in the saddle etc., & then he can ride, drink etc.). What do you think? I feel a sort of curious malaise about the whole of that generation, whose sense of pleasure is too self conscious & unspontaneous, & who are curiously tired – I suppose because of the war – & in Richard's case, doomed to turn things to ashes. The only successful young dons are the crude, functional, tone deaf, robotlike mechanics; which is intolerable: I feel the party is somehow being let down: that *some* imaginative, sensitive, intellectually lively, morally sympathetic, fastidious, scrupulous, life giving individual is on top of *his* academic subject. Otherwise the grey philistine ranks will close in. But do say where you will be in the immediate future: I

---

1 The eighteenth-century mansion at Ditchley Park, north of Oxford, owned by Ronald Tree (72/1) between 1933 and 1949, restored by him and his first wife (later Nancy Lancaster) (602/5); a venue for social and political gatherings and a country retreat for Churchill during the War.
2 Among whom IB himself was numbered.

have terrible doubts about being able to come to Plas Newydd:[1] but I cannot go to America without seeing you: & wd do much to achieve this: my goodness I am suddenly aghast at the idea of going to America: 6 months is too long: too [*intervening sheet/card missing: continues on a card*] my bonds thinned if not broken: impossibility of & horror of being uprooted & the awful torment of having to start afresh on return: it looked well enough at the time, but now I'd almost be relieved if something or someone let me off this journey – the mere thought of having to adapt myself to new Americans – I wish I were one of those dignified rocks who don't adapt & cause all that is pliable & ivy like to bend & twine round them: but it is no use: endless ups & downs of feeling is what my stolid exterior will, I suppose, always contain: & I mustn't go on so: here I am physically quite well: in movement: longing to see you: anxious to talk to Henry about possible musical festivals (I wish to spend *all* next summer & my gains in Harvard on carefully chosen musical events in Europe). Oh do do write: & forgive my silence:

    much love

      Isaiah

Can you ever read through your letters? I can't. But I am always ashamed of them, a little.

TO HAMISH HAMILTON

    [Mid- to late December 1948, *manuscript*]

                                      n.p.

Dear Jamie

    Merry Christmas. Happy New Year. Mille Belle Cose.[2] I am in bed with flu & sail on the 31st, & forgive you entirely for being a publisher even as you must forgive me for being a translator. I shall be in Lowell House, Harvard University Cambridge Mass till end of June, whither, if you would, proofs might be airmailed & I shan't sit on them at all. I haven't read David's introduction but I gather you are pleased with it, & I am sure it is very good & true & beautiful, & I bullied him daily for a fortnight to get it. As for the Translator's Note I haven't much to say in it save that 'my thanks are due to Lady Anglesey first & foremost, and to Lord David Cecil and to Mr M. W. Dick. & I shd like to dedicate it to 'P. de B.' (whose identity, transparent enough to some, I leave you to arrive at) so as not to make it appear that Turgenev was dedicating it to the same initials too. I don't know if David has said so in his essay but I feel it fairly important to say somewhere that (a) the story is autobiographical & known to be (b) that it is so good & suffers so

1 The Marquess of Anglesey's eighteenth-century mansion (now a National Trust property), which looks across the Menai Strait to Snowdonia.
2 'A thousand beautiful things'.

little from the weaknesses usually attributed to T. that even the harshest left wing critics & nationalistic Russian critics of his time did not, respectively, have anything to say against it, almost alone of his works. And that it throws more light on his view of men & women in later life than any other pieces of writing by him. But if there is no obvious way of bringing this in (I shan't be seeing David at all soon) I waive it all, & leave it unsaid, & anyway leave it all to you, having given enough trouble already. My love to Yvonne.[1]

Isaiah.

TO SHIELA NEWSOME

28 December 1948 [*manuscript*]

New College

Dearest Shiela,

Alas! too late! I received your letter just as I was about to go to Winchester to examine (my God what a horrible school), then, of course, as a result of rigours of life there, I fell duly ill: until it was time to return to Oxford to attend a very neurotic committee to elect or not elect Humphry House as D. Cecil's successor as English don at New College: & now I am in a hustle, & after a second spell, shorter, bout, of flu, to go to America, a step I find detestable & fatal now that it is inevitable. I am sure that I am right about your suppression of a large degree of love of life in favour of an ideal which you systematically misidentify with persons & institutions: more than this the Sibyl doesn't at present utter: if you write to Lowell House, Harvard University, Cambridge, Mass., U.S.A, I shall reply & reply with all the warmth which in fact I feel most steadily & unalterably. But dearest S., letters are very good but it is a deception to think them a relation.

Love

Shaya

I am really (now that I am warmed up) terribly sorry not to have seen you. But we are each displaying middle-aged rational egoism. Very horrible. I at least, apologize.

1 Countess Yvonne Pallavicino (1907–93), Hamilton's Italian second wife.

1949

HARVARD

I have a general notion that [. . .] teaching people how to do things, how to adjust themselves psychologically, how to arrange their own lives or those of other people, is driving out all forms of disinterested knowledge for its own sake in a sinister way, both here and in Europe.[1]

1 To A. H. Smith, 23 February 1949.

On 1 January IB set off from Southampton on the Queen Mary *bound via
Cherbourg for New York and his six-month attachment to Harvard University.
His shipmates included a number of friends and acquaintances, and the
journey proved socially rewarding. It began eventfully.*

TO CLARISSA CHURCHILL[1]

1 January 1949 [*manuscript*]

R.M.S. *Queen Mary*

Dearest Clarissa,

This is only to say how finely I have searched & re-searched my heart &
memory & how unnaturally – priggishly – spotless I have found them so
far as this monstrous charge against me is concerned. But I expect you don't
really believe it now even faintly. And I can well understand the sad condition
of your wildly flailing friend,[2] whom I neither like nor dislike, save that
circumstances have made it impossible for us to have relations of any kind,
even those, as Mr Froude once said of Prof. Freeman (q.v. D.N.B.)[3] of hostility.
Previously he only said disagreeable things about me to old private faces in
Geneva: & I minded that too. And tho' I in a sense forgive anyone unhappily
in love for outrageous behaviour, it is a nuisance. And there let us leave it.
But write to me to Lowell House, Harvard University, Cambridge, Mass, or I
shall worry. Life on this ship, which is just about to roar into a gale,[4] is quite
peaceful. I suppose I shall not succeed in not meeting Miss O. Lynn,[5] protected tho' I am by Dr Katkov,[6] desperately inventing disguises to reach me
from the second class in the face of very snubbing stewards. Peter Watson[7]

1 (Anne) Clarissa *Churchill (b. 1920), daughter of Winston Churchill's younger brother John
   ('Jack') Spencer-Churchill; a former pupil, and close friend, of IB's.
2 Alastair ('Ali') Forbes (1918–2005), US-born journalist and socialite, had apparently accused IB of
   a derogatory comment about CC. He and IB were linked by their love for Patricia de Bendern,
   whom Forbes had planned to marry until she abruptly abandoned him for Herman Hornak,
   who became her second husband.
3 Edward Augustus Freeman (1823–92), Regius Professor of Modern History, Oxford, 1884–92,
   used the *Saturday Review* to conduct a 20-year campaign against fellow-historian James Anthony
   Froude (1818–94), later his successor as Regius Professor, whom he accused of inaccuracy.
4 This severe gale caused major damage along the south coast of England, blew a bus full of
   passengers from a bridge into the river below and produced a 1,500-foot-high waterspout near
   Beachy Head.
5 Olga Lynn, née Loewenthal (c.1882–1957), former operatic soprano, concert-singer and singing
   teacher; indefatigable arranger of charitable events and ubiquitous socialite.
6 George Katkov (1903–85), Russian-born; Research Lecturer in Philosophy, Oxford, 1947–50; BBC
   Russian Service, 1950–9; Fellow, St Antony's, and University Lecturer in Soviet Institutions and
   Economics 1959–71.
7 Victor William H. ('Peter') Watson (1907–56), rich art patron (whose family's money came from
   margarine); co-founder with Cyril Connolly (86/3) and Stephen Spender (94/1) of *Horizon* magazine (268/4) 1939; one of four co-founders in 1947 of the Institute of Contemporary Art. Already
   depressed, he spent the journey shocked at the recent early death of a former (male) lover. His
   own death was mysterious.

is here whom I like: & the Trees[1] & Judy M.[2] whom I also like. And Sir A. Cadogan whom I like less well since he has just cut me dead in front of a banker called Warburg[3] to whom I had been boasting of his acquaintance. I wish you an extraordinarily happy New Year: very rich in events of the highest interest: full of very dark men & uncounted wealth and embarrassingly overflowing love & admiration.

But write.

Isaiah.

TO MARIE AND MENDEL BERLIN

Sunday. midnight [2 January 1949, *manuscript*]

[RMS *Queen Mary*]

My dear Parents

this is only a brief note to say that on board this ship *nothing* has happenned. Life is terribly gay & agreeable: breakfast in bed with every kind of delicious juices & eggs: then promenades with Mrs Halban,[4] the Trees, Miss Montague, Alain de Rothschild[5] (Mr Warburg alone & envious. Sometimes I throw him a kind word) – lunch with some friends: rest in bed 2–3 hours: a film: a little work: dinner 8.30 полный парад:[6] wonderful life in a luxury hotel with plenty of agreeable friends. Apparently we scratched our bottom in Cherbourg Harbour: altho' some say that not even that: but that Lloyds insist on looking. At the moment we are sitting off the Isle of Wight being looked at by divers: if all is well we go from Southampton at 1 p.m. on Monday: if not, dry dock & either we go 5 days later & transshipment to Caronia[7] or I don't know what. Meanwhile a holiday mood prevails. I imagine with what feelings you listen to the wireless. You can always find out by telephoning

---

1 (Arthur) Ronald Lambert Field *Tree (1897–1976), Anglo-American, Conservative MP 1933–45, at this time owner of Ditchley Park, north of Oxford, and his second wife Mary Endicott ('Marietta') *Tree (1917–91), née Peabody, US socialite and liberal political activist.

2 Judith Venetia ('Judy') Montagu (1923–72), daughter of Hon. Edwin Montagu and Venetia Stanley; later (1962) married Milton Gendel.

3 Presumably Siegmund George Warburg (1902–82), great-great-grandson of one of the founders of the German banking company M. M. Warburg & Co.; he established the London investment bank S. G. Warburg & Co. in 1946.

4 Aline Elisabeth Yvonne *Halban (b. 1915), daughter of Russian-born Paris banker Baron Pierre de Gunzbourg and his French wife; she had married her second husband Hans Halban (331/4) after early widowhood. IB had met her in the US during the War, and got to know her better after the Halbans moved to Oxford. He suggested that she join the crowd of friends travelling together, so she boarded the ship in Cherbourg en route from Paris to visit her mother in the US.

5 Baron (James Gustave Jules) Alain de Rothschild (1910–82), French banker and philanthropist, part owner of the wine-making estate of Chateau Lafite-Rothschild.

6 'Polnyi parad' ('dress parade', 'full fig').

7 About to leave for New York on her maiden voyage.

the Cunard Office: or at worst, at vast expense, me (IYI49) by radio. If books arrive from Blackwell *please* bring them all to America[1] (4 books).

I.B.

The damage to the Queen Mary *had been caused in Cherbourg harbour when the gale drove the stern end of the ship onto a sandbank, grounding her for 12 hours. After the forced return to Southampton, reinforcement of the keel with concrete to contain the damage took several days and the ship did not sail for New York until 5 January. Although most passengers stayed on board, IB and Aline Halban returned to Oxford until the ship was ready. On 10 January the* Queen Mary *docked in New York. IB went on to Harvard to take up his role as Visiting Lecturer on Regional Studies and Research Associate in the Russian Research Center,[2] and to re-establish contact with his many American friends.*

TO KAY GRAHAM

[Mid-January 1949, *manuscript*]

Lowell House

Dearest Kay,

Too much, too much pleasure, I *must* contract myself into the severe local framework, with a vision of Marion perpetually floating before me as a kind of call to fasting & prayer. Goodness how much I enjoyed myself in Washington! – I shall never, I am quite sure, forget bowls of sour cream as a symbol of a particularly delicious kind of late night reminiscence – I don't believe, I say sadly, that anything will ever replace 1941–1945 as an enormous last oasis as far as I am concerned after which youth is finally over & ordinary life begins, one more moment & I shall really begin to gush & I must clearly stop. This is written in the train – I apologise for the illegibility, I have no pen. I used to have a very bad one which scarcely wrote, but I have fortunately left it in your upper rooms somewhere, & there let it stay – I am really terrified of Cambridge & propose to plunge headlong into whatever is going on there & expel all thoughts of Franks & Acheson[3] & Israel & behave like a serious academic figure, meanwhile I cannot keep out of my head the image of Phil & Fretwell in their 2 beds, Fretwell's terrible small eye always only

---

1 Mendel Berlin was to visit New York on a business trip in late January.

2 The Russian Research Center, established at Harvard in February 1948, represented a fusion of academic, governmental, intelligence, military and business interests. Funded by the Carnegie Corporation (85/1), with the encouragement of the State Department and the Central Intelligence Group (the forerunner of the CIA), the Center undertook multi-disciplinary studies which were seen by the US Government as a vital source of information for fighting the Cold War (and any hotter war which might result). One of its first areas of study was Russian morale, since the US Air Force hoped to identify promising bombing targets through studies of the psychological make-up of different parts of the Soviet Union.

3 Dean Gooderham Acheson (1893–1971), US lawyer and public servant; Secretary of State 1949–53.

half closed – 'I am sure you will make her happier than I' etc. goodness! how much I enjoyed both those evenings. And I adored Mr Philip Graham's reasoned words on station WINX[1] in the newspaper next morning. New York is horrible after it.

love

Shaya

TO SHIRLEY ANGLESEY

21 January 1949 [*manuscript*]

Lowell House, Harvard

Dearest Shirley,

My solitude is absolute for the first time in my life to such a degree. I have been left tremendously to my own devices by this University in a bleak room overheated (so far good) but hideous to a degree. My only visitor so far, Mr Auden, not enough. The contrast to my delicious week in Washington is too acute. I am prepared to work furiously – but one human face a day wd surely not be too much. Perhaps I shall get used to this trappism, at present it is too gloomy even for work. Now, business: a *very* tiresome note from Capt. Hamilton to say (1) no money or space for a little prefatory note expressing thanks to you, David C. etc. (2) no money or space for a dedication to P. de B. which I am set on as this was the original impulse to the translation. He says will I trust you with the correction of proofs? Of course, yes, but only if (a) you really don't mind (b) I am allowed to thank you. On (a) your feelings matter, on (b) mine. I leave it to you to say to him, please, that not to be allowed to thank is unheard of: that you will not proof correct unless I am allowed to dedicate (this in case the thanking part of it is embarrassing to you to insist on) & generally that he mustn't behave like a monster (I may, being the "artist". But he has done nothing creative in his life). If I weren't so depressed I should ring up Mrs Constable.[2] But I can't. I can only work, very dourly. V. good for me, no doubt, but too dreary. Dr Bowra[3] is away, even. My love to Henry & do bully Hamish H (I'll write myself) – he is behaving horribly.

IB

Please come to Boston! You can't imagine with what pent up affection I shd greet you! my friend Nabokov is prepared to write an Opera on First Love:[4]

---

1 The WINX local radio station was owned by the *Washington Post* at the time.
2 Olivia Constable (1901–87), née Roberts, wife of the curator of paintings at the Boston Museum of Fine Arts, W. G. Constable (578/2); both were English.
3 Maurice Bowra was the visiting Charles Eliot Norton Professor of Poetry at Harvard 1948–9.
4 Which never materialised.

we cd both help: he is writing v. beautifully at the moment, his songs are enchantingly beautiful.

TO HAMISH HAMILTON

22 January 1948 [sc. 1949; *manuscript*]

Lowell House, Harvard

Dear Jamie,

Please melt. I have surely atoned for my (not in your clients so unusual) procrastination by gingering up David to splendid effect & furnishing you with a scrupulously good translation (altho' I really despair of the task. But it really is far better than Mrs G) – dedications by translators are not at all uncommon, from Le Motteux[1] to Scott Moncrieff[2] (who even wrote a poem) & the early Turgenev translations – not Mrs Garnett, obviously, but then not for nothing did Max Beerbohm call her Mr & Mrs Pegaway.[3] And how can you expect Shirley to look with a fine eye if I am not allowed to acknowledge her very real services? She refused money: worked really hard until the Marquis occurred: & it would be the lowest form of ingratitude to pass her by. So pray don't take me at my last sad words before leaving England for this waste of desolation – I am in a sad state & hard heartedness from you will complete my total collapse into despair: you have successfully withstood my other (doubtless idiotic) suggestions: & this last is both reasonable & very small. A few words on the left hand page – the obverse of the indispensable title page even if there is no fly leaf, would do it. My friend N. Nabokov, whose music is both beautiful & successfully played here at the moment, desires to turn F. Love into the libretto of his opera: there, now, are you not tempted? I leave Shirley to settle this. Certainly let her do the proofs & have her just reward, beside her abundant & attractive virtue.

love

Isaiah.

---

1 Pierre-Antoine ('Peter') le Motteux (1660–1718), French-born translator into English of Cervantes's *Don Quixote*.

2 Charles Kenneth Scott-Moncrieff (1889–1930), who translated into English (as *Remembrance of Things Past*) *À la recherche du temps perdu* ('In Search of Lost Time', 1913–27) by Marcel Proust (211/8).

3 Max Beerbohm's essay 'Kolniyatsch' (1913) mocks both the vogue for lionising foreign authors of dubious merit and the laborious efforts of some translators: 'Far be it from me to belittle the devoted labours of Mr and Mrs Pegaway, whose monumental translation of the Master's complete works is now drawing to its splendid close. [...] But Mr and Mrs Pegaway would be the first to admit that their renderings of the prose and verse they love so well are a wretched substitute for the real thing.' *And Even Now* (London, 1920), 53–4.

TO MARIE BERLIN

2 February 1949 [*manuscript*]

Lowell House, Harvard

Dearest Ma,

[...] I have just returned from addressing the local Foreign Policy Association, a Boston (not Harvard) body, on Russia, I only hope the press will not misreport it. I *hate* these public addresses but in America they are very insulted if you don't do them. My life is even. After my delicious week in Washington I calmed down here, where I have one or two old friends I find (it seems I have them almost everywhere). My "social life" repays itself sometimes! I rise at 9·30 a.m. & since breakfast in bed is not possible I dress & either breakfast in Hall with the boys (cafeteria) or go to a real cafeteria, buy 3 newspapers (delicious news about Israel.[1] Felix has written to ask do I not think Ernie a ממזר[2] which he spells "Mamsher".) & breakfast slowly, off eggs, coffee, doughnuts, orange juice, buttermilk etc. etc. till 11 a.m. then I go to the Widener Library where I have my own table next to the Russian shelves, perfect peace & comfort, & work till lunch, & after, till 6 p.m. My classes begin on the 8th Feb. but even with them I see that my life will be in this marvellous library from which one can borrow books home: I shall certainly write a book[3] here in some form. I don't see many people[4] & it is *much* better so. [...]

Love

Shaya

As well as contacting old friends, IB made new ones.

TO ALICE JAMES[5]

9 p.m., 19 February 1949 [*manuscript*]

Lowell House, Harvard

Dear Mrs James,

My last act before leaving for New York yesterday was to write to you to convey my very genuine gratitude for my delightful evening – the nicest I have spent in Cambridge yet. On return, a quarter of an hour ago I discovered the

---

1 On 25 January Israel held its first elections, as a result of which the Israeli Labour Party headed by Ben-Gurion remained in power. On 29 January Britain and several other countries accorded de facto (though not yet de jure) recognition to Israel.

2 'Mamzer' ('bastard').

3 On Russian radical thinkers of the mid-nineteenth century, based on his Harvard lectures (see letter of 19 August 1949 to Paul Brooks).

4 By 4 March he was admitting to his parents 'Invitations pour in. I refuse half.'

5 Alice Rutherford *James (c.1887–1957), née Runnells, wife of William ('Billy') James (95/1); a Cambridge society hostess.

hamper: Dear Mrs James what am I to say? that I am touched, moved, and very pleased: grateful and shocked that you shd have taken all this trouble: but I cannot & will not deny that it *does* alter the quality of my daily life: that I shd never have done it for myself, at least not soon, not wholly, not efficiently: it is almost humiliating – the degree, I mean, to which one's entire mood & work and feeling about the universe is altered by details of physical comfort: having come in a little melancholy after seeing off my father to his ship[1] – I really do feel that a parting is a small death – I am now comforted & beginning to grow gay: thank you ever ever so much for your great concern for me – I shall return the basket to its sender & establish an order of goods to be sent me: your kind act has awoken my dormant conscience: & I set off on Monday to send off food parcels to all my foodless Oxford colleagues' wives. Again thank you very much.

Yours

Isaiah Berlin

TO THE PRESIDENT OF ISRAEL, REHOVOT, ISRAEL[2]

20 February 1949 [*manuscript telegram as received*]

New York

May God bless you and Mrs Weizmann with many many years of unclouded happiness in reward for the overwhelming joy and pride and admiration and gratitude with which our entire people today looks upon you stop my father now here joins in this feeling stop with my warmest love to you both

Isaiah

TO ALAN BULLOCK

23 February 1949 [*carbon*]

Lowell House, Harvard

My dear Alan,

Talk of sociology! Far, far more terrible things are going on here than whatever we dreamed of at our celebrated class.[3] I shall curdle your blood with the stories of social sciences and their effect on academic life one of these days. The students, at least in my Russian classes, are surprisingly alert and intelligent, more so than they would be in that particular subject at Oxford, which I daresay is accounted for by their very diversified origins. But you will be glad to hear that Professor Sorokin,[4] a very cynical and intelligent

1 Mendel was about to return to Britain on the *Queen Elizabeth*.
2 The telegram is so addressed. Chaim Weizmann had been elected President by the new Israeli Constituent Assembly and sworn in on 17 February.
3 See 62/3.
4 Pitirim Aleksandrovich Sorokin (1889–1968), Russian-born sociologist; founding Professor of Sociology, Harvard, 1930–55.

impostor, has just secured for Harvard University $125,000 to research into the nature of altruism, which it is thought would, if formulated and applied, stop wars. I think this sum of money is to examine one thousand good neighbours and the lives of the Saints. Dr Bowra is making himself unpopular by spreading the view that wars are not produced by egoism but by excessive altruism and bring out the least egoistic qualities of man. This is not well received and leads to a dropping in the attendance at his poetry lectures. However, there is too much to tell you in a letter. How is the English Fellowship[1] getting on? Is the Warden[2] doing toboggans?[3] Can't there be a compromise on Robson[4] if House is not possible? [...]

Yours ever,
        Isaiah Berlin

TO URSULA NIEBUHR[5]

5 March 1949

Lowell House, Harvard

Dear Ursula:

[...] Here I began life in extreme squalor as Auden, who saw me in it, could describe to you, but have since been better favoured. (If you see Wystan A., do tell him that he didn't leave any kind of fur cap in any room inhabited by me or, so far as his host, Prof. Levin,[6] remembers or anyone else – I owe him a letter but I cannot write one containing merely this negative piece of information. If you should not happen to see him, alternatively forget to tell him even if you do, it couldn't matter less. I like him very much now, although I used not to. I wonder if the change is entirely in me.) I am glad you liked Dr Bowra. He is a great success here personally, even more than academically, and is a stout

---

1 David Cecil's election in 1948 as Goldsmiths' Professor of English Literature at Oxford created a vacancy for an English literature Fellow at New College. Before leaving Oxford, IB had had a serious disagreement with Cecil about the choice of his successor, since Cecil disapproved of professionalism, 'wanted a purely aesthetic approach, which ultimately [...] means some kind of delicate tracing of the actual creative, literary process', and favoured John Buxton (80/1), who, he believed, 'had a natural taste for literature in an amateur sort of way' (MI Tape 15). Cecil caused widespread anger in New College by threatening to resign if Humphry House was elected.

2 Alic Halford Smith (1883–1958), Warden, New College, 1944–58; Vice-Chancellor, Oxford, 1954–7; supported Cecil's choice of Buxton.

3 Perhaps a reference to a bicycling stunt of this name, involving a rapid change of direction in mid-air.

4 (William) Wallace Robson (1923–93), English Lecturer, Lincoln, 1946–8, Fellow 1948–70; later (1972–90) Masson Professor of English Literature, Edinburgh; an obituary described him as 'one of the finest critics of his generation [...] never happier than as a college tutor' (The Times, 5 August 1993, 17).

5 Ursula Mary Niebuhr (1907–97), née Keppel-Compton, English-born theologian; wife of Reinhold Niebuhr (79/4); Professor, Department of Religion, Barnard College, 1946–65.

6 Harry Levin (1912–94), literary critic and author; Associate Professor, Harvard, 1944–8, Professor of English 1948–55, Professor of English and Comparative Literature 1955–60, Irving Babbitt Professor of Comparative Literature 1960–83.

defender of everything in England including the things he hates most of a very Churchillian kind. Stoutness is undoubtedly his middle name. There are a thousand things I should like to talk about during that excellent weekend when you will be here – do let me know when and how as soon as possible. I think I am free throughout or could adapt myself to almost anything.

I find that I adore Washington in an almost indecent way and that my nostalgia for the last days of my youth there is extraordinarily acute, particularly in Georgetown[1] on Sunday afternoons. It is exactly like an old battlefield with all the action over and the ancient inhabitants once again established in the towns and villages and the old commanders of regiments and battalions not far away, only too anxious to rake over the lurid past. I indulged in it shamelessly – I shall never be so happy or so partisan again, I am sure.

Crossman[2] really is a queer problem. He is not a good or admirable man, but he has been apparently both brave and right in the immediate past, how I am not sure; it is worthy of a first-rate psychological political novel, better than Koestler and not as good as Dostoevsky, about the level of Malraux[3] I should say. Marion and Felix are marvellously unaltered, the same wonderful, never failing to react to everything, the same cosy bickering and everything.

I must be done – it really will be most enjoyable and delightful to see you and Reinhold[4] the weekend after next. Do let me know about details.

Yours ever, with love
    Isaiah.

TO MARIE AND MENDEL BERLIN
    Saturday 12 March [1949, *manuscript*]

Lowell House, Harvard

My dear parents
    [...] To-day Harrod[5] called on me. Very gloomy, & tired. Bad marriage

---

1 The affluent district of Washington near the British Embassy, where IB had lived from 1943 to 1945.

2 Richard Howard Stafford Crossman (1907–74), academic, journalist and Labour politician; Fellow and Tutor in Philosophy, New College, 1930–7 (responsible for IB's first academic post); assistant editor, *New Statesman and Nation*, 1938–55; MP 1945–74 (including Cabinet posts). While a member of the Anglo-American Commission on Palestine in 1946, Crossman had become a committed Zionist; in January 1949 his savage attacks on Ernest Bevin's policy towards Israel, in the *Sunday Pictorial* and in parliamentary debate, broke the Labour–Conservative accord on Israel and led a few days later to Britain's de facto recognition of Israel. Nevertheless, IB continued to dislike him as an unprincipled bully.

3 André Malraux (1901–76), French novelist.

4 (Karl Paul) Reinhold Niebuhr (1892–1971), US theologian; Professor of Christian Ethics and Philosophy of Religion, Union Theological Seminary, New York, 1930–60, Dean 1950–60; Niebuhr's concentration on Christianity as it applied to social and political questions made him influential and controversial.

5 (Henry) Roy Forbes Harrod (1900–78), economist, Student of Christ Church 1924–67. His wife Billa (347/3) was happily conducting a secret affair (and confiding in IB about it).

worse than none. Yes, Buxton[1] is the man I *didn't* want & all my friends wrote me how badly Smith behaved, cheating etc. & David, who voted *for* Buxton wrote a kind of self-exculpating letter saying it was not *wholly* his fault etc. However I was away & that was that. It doesn't really matter very much. I don't envy you your shipmates:[2] Lord Reading[3] is a dreary figure, slightly 'Mayoffes',[4] she is a vulgarian, Lord Samuel[5] is stiff & dead, Lady S. is a vanishing quantity. And I don't believe that their reception will be so v. terrific: if it is it will be for Lady R: or else because Jews are snobs after all. I don't know why I have suddenly adopted this irritable tone: they have done me no harm: but I suffer from incurable contempt for both Samuel & Reading: & prefer their stupider but nicer children. I am *really* allright: the classes are a genuine success: & I am determined to stay here all March & not be tempted to Washington till mid-April. [...]

Love
   Shaya

TO MENDEL BERLIN
18 March 1949

Lowell House, Harvard

Dear Papa:
[...] Everything here is proceeding nicely. The lectures[6] seem successful. The Boston dowagers do not understand a word I say, in this respect comparing unfavourably with the lecture class which scribbles away furiously from

---

1 The successful candidate (Edward) John Mawby Buxton (1912–89), Lecturer in English Literature, New College, 1946, Fellow 1949, later (1972–80) Reader in English Literature; according to IB 'Buxton was a great failure – he was learned, he was hard-working, but the great thing is that he lived outside Oxford, he did a bit of shooting, he was a tremendous gent and old-fashioned conservative of a rigid kind' (MI Tape 15).

2 Mendel and Marie Berlin were soon to sail to Israel.

3 Gerald Rufus Isaacs (1880–1960), 2nd Marquess of Reading, lawyer and statesman. His wife was Eva Violet (1895–1973), daughter of Alfred Mond, 1st Lord Melchett; a social worker and public figure.

4 'Given to toadying to Gentiles'; a term derived from the song and dance parodies of a Sabbath hymn which the early 19th-century Polish gentry forced Jews to perform for their entertainment. (The performance and the associated humiliation became known as 'mayufes' from the Askenazic pronounciation of the first two words of the Sabbath song, 'mah yafit' – 'how beautiful'.)

5 Herbert Louis Samuel (1870–1963), 1st Viscount Samuel, Liberal politician, philosopher and reformer; active Zionist who had been High Commissioner of Palestine 1920–5; married Beatrice Miriam Franklin (1871–1959).

6 On 'The Development of Revolutionary Ideas in Russia'. This title was reported to the FBI by their secret informant in the Russian Research Center, a graduate student on the staff, with the implied suggestion that IB might be fomenting revolution himself. Sigmund Diamond, *Compromised Campus: The Collaboration of Universities with the Intelligence Community, 1945–1955* (New York, 1992), 57.

the moment I say Good Afternoon.[1] I certainly hope to have a typed script of a book in some shape or form before I leave. [...]

I am racked by anxiety about an after dinner speech[2] I have to give next Saturday – It'll all be over by the time you see this letter – I detest having to make light after dinner causeries to a public at once tipsy and fastidious. However, if I must, I must, and sooner or later it is bound to happen.

Yours,

Love

Shaya   [...]

TO MARIE AND MENDEL BERLIN

23 March 1949 [*manuscript card*]

H-32 Lowell House, Harvard, Cambridge, Mass.

So you see, I have cards of my own. My speech on last Saturday night, to a Club here called the Signet, which cost me sweat, tears & almost blood was apparently a v. great success: people still come up & 'pump my hand': so was a joint broadcast with 2 other men on 'Britain'[3] the following Monday. Altogether the lectures etc. are going well, I am held in more respect (*destroy* this!) than even Dr Maurice B[owra] & the whole thing, if Kharkhat(?חרחט)'s[4] instrument comes in time will be a great success. Write abt yr plans. Rau[5] has seen me & can report.

Love

Shaya

(my reputation is curiously growing. The pupils are *very* fond of me)

1 Maurice Bowra had gleefully reported to IB (on 23 October 1948) that in the Harvard programme 'Mr Berlin of Oxford University' (a notoriously late riser) was due to lecture 'on Mon. Wed. and Fri. at 9', but in the event the lecture classes seem to have mainly been on Tuesdays and Thursdays, and clearly not in the morning. Presumably IB had protested.

2 At the Signet Society, a Harvard University club founded in 1871 to promote discussion of intellectual and artistic matters. IB was elected as an Honorary Member a few days later; the usual grounds for membership were artistic and scholarly merit.

3 The Lowell Institute Cooperative Broadcasting Council, a pioneer in the use of radio for adult education, had invited IB to take part in a programme on 'England in a Two-Power World'.

4 This appears to have been an early form of dictating machine. The Hebrew ('Charchat', the 'ch' sounding as in 'Chaim') is presumably IB's indication of how he thinks the unidentified 'Kharkhat' is pronounced.

5 Frederick Solomon Rau (1906–56), businessman from London now living in the US; his mother was a close friend of Marie Berlin.

TO MARIE AND MENDEL BERLIN

30 March 1949 [*carbon*]

[Lowell House, Harvard]

My dear parents:

[…] I am very well and in a particularly gay condition since I have been offered a professorship here ($10,000, to be divided between philosophy and anything I please), which shows that my visit has not been a total failure. I do not intend to accept, as I do not feel like changing cultures and I am sure I should feel very cut off here. I dare not tell Smith about this, as he may wish me to accept this, as I opposed his candidate for the English fellowship at New College, but I propose to tell Sumner[1] – anyhow to tell Maurice to spread the news at Oxford, since it may help with All Souls. Anyhow, I shall try and work out an arrangement whereby I do not altogether lose contact with Harvard and can come here occasionally to refresh myself.

[…] Everything is flowing very smoothly and happily, and I have, fortunately, nothing to relate.

Yours,

Isaiah Berlin

TO MICHAEL STRAIGHT[2]

15 April 1949 [*carbon*]

[Lowell House, Harvard]

Dear Michael,

Thank you for your letter and suggestion that I write an article or two for the *New Republic*. I am in a very unhappy situation about this, and beg you to accept what I say quite literally and not attribute it to false modesty or any other concealed motive. I feel that on the situation of Western Europe in general my thoughts are really not worth setting down, publicly or privately. I am deeply, and I fear incurably, ignorant on economics both theoretical and applied, and whenever experts discuss this subject I feel not even like an intelligent layman but like an earnest schoolboy attempting to understand but finding that his thoughts are always straying to other things: whenever I try to make even the political aspect of these things clear to myself, I find myself formulating at best plausible platitudes, at worst a confused scrap-heap of odd thoughts and memories casually thrown together. So I do assure

1 (Benedict) Humphrey Sumner (1893–1951), historian, Warden of All Souls 1945–51. IB had been a Fellow of All Souls 1932–8 and hoped to secure a further Fellowship there to allow him more time for research and visits to Harvard.

2 Michael Whitney Straight (1916–2004), US economist, author, lecturer and committed supporter of liberal causes; editor 1941–3, 1948–56 of the *New Republic*, a liberal journal founded in 1914 by his parents. (His admission in 1963 of his links to the Cambridge spy ring led to the unmasking of Anthony Blunt.)

you that on things like the UNO, the North Atlantic Pact etc. I have nothing worth communicating.

I feel a little more confident about my views on Russia – I was very sorry about my inability to come to your conference on this topic – and what inhibits me about that is something quite different, namely the thought that anything I may write will automatically involve most of the people I met in Moscow in 1945 in immediate trouble, however cautious I may be and however disguised my identity, unless I offer fulsome praise, which I am far from ready to do, seeing no reason for perjury. For this reason I have never written a syllable on this to me more and more fascinating topic, feeling that the individual safety of my unfortunate acquaintances in the Soviet Union clearly outweighs the value of anything which I might have to contribute to the public discussion of the subject.

I am therefore largely caught between two horns of a dilemma: where I could talk freely I have nothing to say, where I have something to say I cannot talk freely. It is a sad situation, and I am sure you will see how it might have arisen and will appreciate my frustration. If, while I am still in this country, I suddenly feel that I have got something to say – even on so limited a topic as education at Harvard – I will, if I may, submit something to you about it. But for the moment I feel very uninteresting and infertile. Please forgive me and please believe me.

Yours ever,
Isaiah Berlin

TO MENDEL BERLIN

23 April 1949 [*manuscript postcard*]

Well: I am in a train en route for N. York where the dinner for the President[1] occurs to-night. I am very well: again I was asked about the Prof.ship yesterday: I am keeping the situation molten. Not easy. I have acquired a Charchat instrument,[2] but talk too fast into it. I shall improve, or my secretary will. But it is more a toy than serious. W. Churchill said to Boothby,[3] when B. pleaded with him for Zionism a year ago: after growling about being betrayed,

1 Almost certainly Weizmann, of whom IB wrote to his father on 30 May that he 'wanted me to join his personal entourage, whose purpose is to intrigue against the Govt. Not very attractive. I got out of it with honour'; just possibly President Conant of Harvard (84/2), who held a series of dinners with influential guests in New York to boost the Russian Research Center's public image.
2 This was soon discarded (and sold to the leading Boston Jesuit) in favour of a wire recorder, which IB took back to England. Dictation of his academic work and letters produced a marked increase in IB's productivity and a gradual change in his writing style, bringing it closer to his (more wordy) habits of speech.
3 Robert John Graham ('Bob') Boothby (1900–86), Baron Boothby of Buchan and Rattray Head 1958; Conservative politician.

terrorists etc. "after all I am a v. old friend of Zionism & I am not ready to desert it in its hour of triumph".

Love

S.

Shall write separately to dear Ida & Yitzchok.[1]

TO SHIRLEY ANGLESEY

9 May 1949 [manuscript]

Hotel Kimball, Springfield, Mass.
As from Lowell House, Harvard

Dearest Shirley

I ought to have replied to you long long ago. But there is an extraordinary absence of background in America – a sort of lack of a 3[d] dimension which prevents the usual accumulation of experience which makes letter writing possible. I have lived peacefully in two little rooms in Lowell House, & enjoyed my Russian class of strange largely non-American graduates really very much. For the first time I have learnt something myself in the process, quite a lot in fact – & cd bore you or anyone else about it indefinitely for the rest of my life. At first I felt a tremendous failure: & was, despite Olivia Constable's great kindness & cosiness, enormously miserable. Then I suddenly seemed to get on with people I cd talk to, & ceased flying off to Washington for comfort: then I was suddenly offered a job of a permanent & (by my standards) vastly paid kind: this altered my whole view of the universe: I might be a failure but I couldn't be an utter failure: I refused, needless to say, since the prospect of permanent migration is ridiculous. It was a delicious offer: little work, 5 times more than I get at Oxford – why can't Oxford see me with these eyes? I was then put on electoral committees for splendid 12·000 dollar jobs: & entered into marvellous grave conclaves with Mr Conant[2] & greybeards generally, & was treated with nervous respect which I adored: now that's over too & I am working by & for myself in the magnificent peerless Harvard Library & am quite content & amiable to all without that undue anxiety to please which embarrassed my earlier, wooing & being wooed, stage. The Boston dowagers are fantastic: they are shrewd, independent, self confident ladies of about 1890, with a mixture of grandeur & genuine repulsive grasping 19th century vulgarity & coarseness – & a mixture of Florentine sophistication with New England tough hardboiled

1 Marie Berlin's younger sister Ida Volshonok (1887–1985) was married to Yitzhak (or 'Yitzchok') Samunov (1886–1950), Mendel Berlin's business partner while the couple lived in London. After the Samunovs settled in Jerusalem in 1934, Yitzhak qualified as a lawyer. At the time of this letter IB's parents were setting out on their first visit to Israel.

2 James Bryant Conant (1893–1978), organic chemist and educationalist; President of Harvard 1933–53.

anti-poetical really coarse grained bourgeois repulsive naive climbing snobbery which I find, all in all, fascinating. I have manfully repelled such few
advances as have been made: & work virtuously. Cambridge itself is *not* self
confident but guilt ridden: learning is seen as a luxury to be atoned for by
very bogus forms of social work: the scholars and men of learning are being
hemmed in by the missionaries & charlatans whom the great Rockefeller &
Carnegies[1] support: there is a great battle in progress between the old good
disciplines like History, Classics, Literature & the like & Sociology, social
anthropology, psychology etc. in which one cannot but be on the side of the
former:[2] the latter are neurotic quacks for the most part who believe that
education consists in 'adjusting' people so well that they lose all desire to
ask interesting & tormenting questions. I feel really bitterly hostile to them:
it is all Xtian[3] science at an academic level: every second student trots off
to the psychoanalyst in search of a bogus religion, & my little talks on the
Russian intellectuals etc. are viewed as a revelation from heaven by these
poor muddled wretches when it can all be read in books I expect if only
they wd cease to make beelines for the psychoanalysts' sofas all day & all
night. The pupils are ill taught but infinitely moving: when I go to Women's
Colleges – all those earnest horn rimmed faces, the bobby sox mocassins
bluejeans, infinite touching idealism & faith – it is like Russia in the 90ies: if
a real spellbinder got amongst them they would, I am sure, hurl a bomb at
some wicked governor without a thought: I rather love it really: tiers upon
tiers of these humourless Florence Nightingaly faces, all waiting for the
truth so sweetly & trustfully, with so much moral energy & goodness &
all so blindly wasted & made ridiculous. Americans even at their worst are
morally moving: the absence of Wollheims among them, if you see what
I mean, doesn't make them less so. What about 1st Love? have you looked
through it? I keep having memories of passages: 'my heart went pit-a-pat'[4]
is Mr V. Nabokov's[5] suggestion, but it is surely worse than what we have.

1 The Rockefeller Foundation (established 1913) and the Carnegie Corporation (1911), major
   charitable organisations dispensing large sums of money world-wide to causes including public
   health, education, agricultural development, the arts and social studies. Both organisations have
   at times been involved in supporting US foreign policy.
2 To A. H. Smith he had written on 23 February: 'The combined pressure of half-baked, largely
   counterfeit subjects like sociology, and the pressure by businessmen to stress practical skills at
   the expense of learning, is doing great damage to the genuinely strong and impressive humane
   tradition in this university.'
3 Christian.
4 The literal meaning of Turgenev's phrase in chapter 7 of *First Love* is 'my heart rolled down'
   ('покатилось'); IB later remembered this word as being one of the most difficult to translate in
   the entire book. On 6 June he wrote to SA asking her to replace the version in the proof copy
   with 'my heart slipped its moorings', but in the published text the sentence reads 'my heart
   missed a beat'.
5 Vladimir Vladimirovich Nabokov (1889–1977), Russian-born novelist; moved to US 1940, naturalised 1945; Professor of Russian Literature, Cornell, 1948–59.

I leave it all to you but do be careful & look devotedly after every paragraph: the simpler the better. [...] I am neither happy nor not. Write.

Isaiah.

TO CLARISSA CHURCHILL

10 May 1949 [*manuscript*]

Hotel Kimball, Springfield, Mass.
As from Lowell House, Harvard

Dearest Clarissa

[...] I have been (I proudly say) offered a fine job & declined it instantly (Of course, you say, disdainfully. But it really was freedom from drudgery & an alluring sum of money. But it was as absurd as Lord Beaverbrook's wooing[1] which I enjoyed so enormously) – I still suffer from a feeling that I am expected to do turns, & so display an unwonted tacturnity: but the resultant frost & boredom is so great that I burst out, reluctantly & with acute shame then & later, simply in order to survive & breathe at all. The students are touchingly sincere, grateful for every crumb of European culture, & have a moral vitality which I envy & love & romanticize & think Russian of the 1880ies. A terrible thing:[2] my fat friend Prichard, I don't know if you've met him, heralded by telegrams from Joe Alsop & me, who dined with Cyril[3] & Sybil Colefax & God knows who, (I think I cabled Raimund or Liz too) has been accused of forging election returns in Bourbon County, Kentucky, & is out on bail of $5000. Dr Bowra whom I've accused of neglecting him unduly – & I love him dearly but he *may* be a kind of Boothby[4] – will never let me forget this I am sure. I suppose I think him innocent still: I don't know if to write him or not: imagine: an urn of votes, all forged,[5] discovered the night before the ballot. I return July 25 or so: will you be in London? how

1 (William) Max(well) Aitken (1879–1964), 1st Baron Beaverbrook, Canadian businessman, newspaper proprietor, former UK government minister and political power-broker. In 1945 Beaverbrook had offered IB a job writing a weekly political article for the *Evening Standard* and had been taken aback by his instant refusal.

2 IB's enormously fat friend and house-mate from his time in Washington, Ed Prichard, had returned to his Kentucky home in 1945 after his career in Washington had appeared to stall. (Unknown to him, his New Deal sympathies and close contacts with the press had attracted the hostile attention of the Director of the FBI, J. Edgar Hoover; the FBI had consequently tapped his phone and reported all indiscreet comments to the President and others in power.) In Kentucky, Prichard set up a law firm, married, and attempted unsuccessfully to run for political office. On 2 November 1948, forged ballots for the Senatorial election were discovered (a not unusual event in Kentucky) in the precinct for which Prichard was election officer. Hoover instigated a full FBI investigation. When Prichard returned from a trip to Europe in April 1949, for which IB had provided introductions to many of his own friends, he was indicted (on 4 May) for ballot-stuffing.

3 Cyril Vernon Connolly (1903–74), critic, author and journalist; founder co-editor, *Horizon* (268/4), 1939–50.

4 Boothby had been forced to resign from his ministerial post at the Ministry of Food in 1941 when a parliamentary inquiry found that he had acted improperly in a financial matter.

5 An exaggeration; 17 forged ballots were discovered initially, and a further 237 in later investigations.

are you? I am, as always here, not alive nor dead, & doesn't matter what one does it is not part of the life that counts or is remembered, a sort of gap in the calendar series. Nicolas is almost literally penniless but his mermaid wife[1] works hard.

love
    Isaiah

Tell Gerald[2] that Stravinsky[3] thinks Boston ought to be renamed Koussevitzk[4] & Harvard Nijny Koussevitzk[5] by a grateful government.

TO MAURICE BOWRA

    14 May 1949 [carbon]

Lowell House, Harvard

Dear Maurice:

    [...] Prich has been committed by the Federal Grand Jury for trial and is out on $5000 bail. The charge is that he forged ballots in Bourbon County, Kentucky, in the last election. Some prime busybody, lifting the ballot box the night before the election, found it not empty but unliftably heavy[6] with ballots all made out for Senator Virgil Chapman.[7] Other boxes were found in a similar condition. Prich's partner, also charged, has the unpromising name of Funk.[8] The consternation, both here and in Washington, you can imagine for yourself. Nobody knows the facts. Ben Cohen believes Prich to be innocent. I take the line I was for Dreyfus and am for Prich. But what with Hiss[9] and Prich, a very disagreeable piece in this week's *New York Times*

---

1 Patricia Page Blake (b. 1925), Nabokov's third wife (of five) 1948–52 (married Ronni Dugger 1982); copywriter, *Vogue*, 1946 (when she became one of the many girlfriends of Albert Camus); correspondent, *Life* magazine, New York, 1954–62 (Moscow 1955, 1959, 1962); later wrote on and translated Russian literature; associate editor, *Time* magazine, 1968–87; described by Nabokov as 'a thoroughbred intellectual, brilliantly intelligent and good-looking', in *Bagázh: Memoirs of a Russian Cosmopolitan* (London, 1975), 232. The Shetland folk-tale *The Mermaid Wife* tells of a (seal-) woman kept away from her native element, the sea, to which she longs to return despite her marriage on land.
2 Gerald Tyrwhitt-Wilson (1883–1950), 14th Baron Berners, composer, author and eccentric.
3 The Russian composer Igor Fedorovich Stravinsky (1882–1971), who had moved to the US in 1939, becoming naturalised in 1945.
4 Serge (né Sergey Aleksandrovich) Koussevitzky (1874–1951), Russian-born conductor, Director of the Boston Symphony Orchestra 1924–49, founding Director of the Berkshire Music Center, Tanglewood, Mass., 1940.
5 Presumably on the pattern of the Russian cities Novgorod and Nijny Novgorod.
6 Another exaggeration: a few ballots were heard moving when a box which should have been empty was lifted.
7 Virgil Munday Chapman (1895–1951), lawyer and politician; Democratic Representative for Kentucky 1925–9, 1931–49, Senator from 1949 until his death in a car accident. All but one of the forged ballots were in his favour when he was elected Senator.
8 Al(varado) Erwin Funk, Jr (b. c.1922), son of the Kentucky Attorney-General; Prichard's law partner and co-defendant.
9 Alger Hiss (1904–96), lawyer (protégé of Felix Frankfurter) and influential government official

about the latter, the foundations of F.F.'s universe are tottering. There is some speculation as to whether Marion will say that a year in jail will do him good and eliminate the coarser sides of his nature. Joe, who caused the spate of telegrams, causing me to fling them, is not too happy. It would perhaps be kinder not to say anything about this to Connolly, etc. yet, but I thought you might like to know too. Prich himself is behaving with dignity, and demands an early trial, proclaiming his innocence. Judge Wyzanski[1] is not too sure. Nor really is anyone else. There is a touch of Boothby about my friend, I fear. Felix is, for once, very unamused. [. . .]

    Yours,
      Isaiah

⟨Very funny event. A mathematics concentrator walked into the exam. on Kluckhohn's[2] course, took it having read no books or listened to lectures, & passed v. easily with C+ (A– on one question). It was all published in the *Crimson*[3] which is *very* sound on Social Relations + extracts from the man's paper which were madly funny: Clyde is genuinely furious & humiliated & Buck[4] is not best pleased. [. . .]⟩

TO E. H. CARR[5]

14 May 1949 [*carbon*]

Lowell House, Harvard

My dear Ted:

    I apologise humbly and deeply for not replying before, and shall have

who had advised FDR at Yalta and contributed to the founding of the UN; President, Carnegie Endowment for International Peace, 1946–9. In 1948 a witness before the House Committee on Un-American Activities, Whittaker Chambers (387/3), had identified Hiss as a Communist Party agent who passed secret documents to the Soviet Union during the 1930s; he later produced documentary evidence to support his claim. Hiss could not be tried for espionage because of the passage of time, but was indicted for perjury for denying the charges (which he continued to do for the rest of his life). His first trial (May–July 1949), at which Felix Frankfurter was one of the prestigious character-witnesses for Hiss, produced a hung jury, but after a second trial Hiss was convicted in January 1950 and sentenced to five years' imprisonment, of which he served 44 months. Debate about Hiss's guilt continues.

1 Charles Edward Wyzanski (1906–86), US District Judge, Mass., 1941–86; a friend of Hiss, on whose behalf he testified in both trials (but in whose guilt he later came to believe).

2 Clyde Kay Maben Kluckhohn (1905–60), anthropologist; Professor of Anthropology, Harvard, 1946–60; first Director of the Russian Research Center, Harvard, 1947–54. The course in question was 'Anthropology and Modern Life'.

3 The *Harvard Crimson*, the daily student newspaper. The article, 'Undergraduate Passes Examination' (22 April 1949, front page), reported that Edward Messner, who claimed that his answers were written 'from the point of view of the Harvard man who doesn't stoop to mere detail', achieved 18 out of 20 for his assessment of Geoffrey Gorer's *The American People*, which he had not read.

4 Paul Herman Buck (1899–1978), historian; Professor, Harvard, 1942–69, Dean of Faculty of Arts and Sciences 1942–53, Provost 1945–53.

5 Edward Hallett Carr (1892–1982), historian and international relations specialist whose main

many extraordinary tales to tell you about the Russian Research Center when I return. It spends its time in deducing unexciting conclusions from devious and suspect material, and refuses to do the things which I urge upon it, as being either (a) too dangerous (such as expeditions to talk to D.P.'s[1] about their little corners of Russia, from which a synthetic picture could be established, demonstrating the coefficient of falsehood in official Soviet accounts), or (b) too contemporary, such as the financing of translations of nineteenth-century revolutionaries' memoirs, texts, etc. The result is that life starts in 1918 and rarely in 1946, and the main purpose is prediction. I have made discreet enquiries of McKay[2] and Kluckhohn. (Is it his name or Fainsod's[3] which is not always what it is? Do tell me and I shall pursue the problem further.) And the former is very affably disposed towards you;[4] the latter, who generally will not show his hand about anyone, is polite, and both say that the budget for next year is closed. (A British psychopathologist is being brought over to psychoanalyse the Soviet Union, as a unit I gather. Words really do fail me about this and many things.) As for two years hence, they don't know, they can't tell, will the money be there, general Harvard policy, etc. [...]

Yours,

Caricature of IB by Saxe, Harvard Crimson, *23 May 1949*

interest was Soviet Russia; Wilson Professor of International Politics, Aberystwyth, 1946–7; assistant editor, *The Times,* 1941–6; politics Tutor, Balliol, 1953–5; Fellow, Trinity, Cambridge, 1955–82.
1 Displaced persons.
2 Donald Cope McKay (1902–59), Professor of History, Harvard, 1946–56 (with special responsibilities for international and regional studies 1946–53); Anson D. Moorse Professor of History, Amherst College, 1956–9.
3 Merle Fainsod (1907–72), Soviet specialist; Professor of Government, Harvard, 1946–64.
4 Carr was interested in the possibility of spending further time at Harvard.

TO NOEL ANNAN[1]

20 May 1949 [*carbon*]

Lowell House, Harvard

My dear Noel,

There is so much to tell you that I cannot begin to set it out systematically. In certain respects the highly flexible American educational system, while making hay of serious parts of serious subjects, makes provision for the kind of thing you and I are interested in to a splendid and gratifying degree – the kind of prostitution which is entailed by becoming a specialist in 'general education' or the 'core subjects' at Chicago would keep you and me happy and ashamed, if you see what I mean, with no more than our normal weekly reading as material for the rest of our natural lives. We would make much more money than our colleagues, and be much more famous. I wish I could think of a system which is directed at producing this result as altogether wrong. You must certainly come here. The returns are most gratifying, and the graduate students are as much better than ours as the undergraduate ones are worse. I must not go on.

[...] Next weekend I secretly see Mr Edmund Wilson, with whom (don't tell Maurice) my relations are becoming quite close. And there is something to be said even for the *Partisan Review*[2] – I miss ideologists in England, A. J. P. Taylor[3] not being quite enough. [...]

Yours,

Earlier that year Edward Weeks,[4] editor of the Atlantic Monthly,[5] *had asked IB to review the second volume of Churchill's war memoirs.*

TO EDWARD WEEKS

26 May 1949 [*carbon*]

[Lowell House, Harvard]

Dear Mr Weeks,

What you must think about me is probably not sayable, let alone printable, but I do assure you that I have not been altogether idle. I have completed the

1 Noel Gilroy Annan (1916–2000), Baron Annan (1965), historian (particularly of political ideas) and academic administrator; Fellow of King's, Cambridge, 1944–56, Provost 1956–66; later Provost of University College, London, and Vice-Chancellor, University of London.
2 An American quarterly political and literary magazine with Trotskyist sympathies at this time.
3 Alan John Percivale Taylor (1906–90), historian and journalist; history Tutor, Magdalen, 1938–63, Fellow 1938–76; University Lecturer in Modern History 1946–54, in International History 1953–63; a committed and outspoken socialist.
4 Edward Augustus ('Ted') Weeks (1898–1989), editor, *Atlantic Monthly*, 1938–66.
5 Literary and cultural magazine with a national and international readership, founded in Boston in 1857 and published there until 2005.

second draft of my piece,[1] which seems even to me a queer hodgepodge of reflections, quotations, generalisations, trammelled by few facts. However, such as it is, I do not suppose I can do much more to it. I shall get it to you next week as soon as Mrs Brown[2] has finished typing it.

But now there is another consideration, which I hope you will forgive me for submitting to you. I feel a certain nervousness about letting anything appear about the great man which might upset him in any way. Apart from his general sacredness, he has been extremely kind to me personally in a number of ways, and I should feel very badly if I thought that he minded or resented anything I wrote about him. I therefore would like to propose the following arrangement: that I send the typed script to one of his friends,[3] who is an old, intimate friend of mine, and ask this man to submit the thing to him and ask him if there is anything he objects to, and to hold up publication until he has replied. In the meanwhile I could send you my original version on the firm understanding that you would not print it until I had had my reply from the diplomatic intermediary. When this has been received, we could see what we can do. I feel completely confident that Mr C., whatever he feels, would be much too proud to want to alter, or at least seem to want to alter, anything much, and therefore I think the result will not be affected by this pre-censorship, which would set my mind at rest. I realise how irregular this proceeding is and how undesirable it would be if generalised. Indeed I should probably be the first to protest against it. But if one is not a professional writer (and perhaps even if one is) a special problem does arise about writing about people one knows or loves or admires, and I am clear that in my case personal considerations of this kind and the demands of private life outweigh the public interest, unless the latter is really very strong. I am sure that you will understand my feeling on this matter, and forgive me for springing this on you after all these weeks, for I am sure that you do not, any more than I, want to wound the Old Man (who, I somehow feel sure, has not so very much longer to live) because of a few unimportant trifles. It will be interesting to see what, if anything, he does object to, and this, of course, I will communicate to you as soon as I know myself. I propose to write my intermediary to tell him what I am doing without, however, telling him that you will have seen the original version, and so you will know how much, if anything, is being altered, since this may be something which Mr C. may not wish to be known; on the other hand, I feel that it is right you should know about this transaction in all its stages and details. What it comes to is that I cannot bring myself to do anything to distress Mr C., to whom I really

1 IB's review of Churchill's second volume of war memoirs, *Their Finest Hour* (London, 1949); eventually published as 'Mr Churchill' in the *Atlantic Monthly*, September 1949, and as 'Mr Churchill and FDR' in the *Cornhill Magazine*, Winter 1949/50; reprinted as *Mr Churchill in 1940* (London, Boston/Cambridge, [1964]), and as 'Winston Churchill in 1940' in PI.
2 Presumably his long-suffering secretary.
3 Bill Deakin.

feel a curiously powerful devotion. I feel certain that you will appreciate this sentiment and will forgive me.

I have told my agent to let me have Mr C.'s reactions by June 15 at the latest, which may, I fear, delay publication until August. For this I beg you once more to forgive me, as for all my other sins of omission.

Yours ever,

P.S. I must, of course, ask you not to show this letter to anybody else, for obvious reasons.

IB duly sent Bill Deakin a typescript of the review for Churchill to vet, since he did not wish to publish anything that would 'upset or annoy or even irritate the Old Man, for whom my reverence, I discover with some surprise, is without limit'.[1] On 27 June Deakin replied: 'I have just recovered the script from [the] Master, whose comment on the passages which he read in my presence was "It's too good to be true"!'

TO GEORGE KENNAN
30 May 1949

Lowell House, Harvard

Dear George,

[...] The Russian Research Center continues to go its own queer way, but Harvard in general I now find increasingly attractive and impressive and interesting. Although Mr Eliot is right, and one must stay where one belongs and live in one's own country and not be a rootless cosmopolitan and keep one's passport in order, and avoid kowtowing to the Wall str.–Arthur Schlesinger–Anna Louise Strong[2] group – and therefore I shall return to Oxford – Harvard is not without its powerful temptations. I shall interview the Provost of this university early next week, and although my reasons for returning are fundamentally not difficult to state, I shall be conscious of a desire to keep at least a fortochka[3] open to Harvard, which I shall be ashamed openly to propose. I should love to tell you about my complicated love affair with this university sometime. This is really only to say that I should love to see you in early July. As doubtless you are tremendously busy, please don't trouble to reply unless you have a moment – I can easily telephone when I do come.

Yours ever,
    Isaiah B.

---

1 To Bill Deakin, 30 May 1949.
2 Anna Louise Strong (1885–1970), US journalist and fellow-traveller, spent much of her life in the Soviet Union and China.
3 'Window'.

PS Have you read the story by Chekhov called *Skuchnaya istoriya?*[1] It is certainly a work of genius and describes some of my colleagues here in a most uncanny way.

TO ELENA WILSON[2]

Postmark 3 June 1949 [*manuscript*]

Lowell House, Harvard

Dear Mrs Wilson,

I have never written a Collins[3] (you are acquainted with the expression?) with greater pleasure or gratitude. As you may have observed I enjoyed myself, if anything, too much. I have occasional non-conformist moments when too much enjoyment is going on, that God cannot wish one to enjoy oneself so much. Like all Russians I like conversation better than anything else in the world – all the unspoken rules, all the strong & ubiquitous influences of England which gets its results by a kind of systematic pattern of inhibiting influences, hasn't destroyed this. I look on my talks with your husband as a great luxury – he is the most unsurrendering intellectual – the most unyielding keeper up of standards I have ever met – someone asked me whether he enjoyed writing; did he write for pleasure, or for, let us say, fame, or love, or money? I had to explain that the question was as misconceived as to ask whether Toscanini[4] conducted "for pleasure": he conducts because he wishes to conduct, as a Ding an sich,[5] and the notion of 'pleasure' as a deliberate coldly calculated motive is a hideous misconstruction of the state of mind & 'way of life' – no English translation of the Russian "Byt"[6] exists. But I mustn't run on so. I spent the entire week end in a slightly exalté[7] state, doubtless both cause & effect of the grippe[8] which struck me immediately on return – punctuated by moments when I felt general inadequacy – the kind of Drang[9] towards irrelevant frivolity which Tolstoy – & all – Russian novelists rightly condemn as neither cosy nor gay but empty. But I really must stop. [...]

Yrs ever

Isaiah Berlin

1 'A Boring Story'; a portrayal, both moving and amusing, of an ageing though still celebrated lecturer waiting for death.
2 Helene-Marthe ('Elena') Wilson (1906–79), née Mumm, became Wilson's fourth wife in 1946; daughter of a German father (of the Mumm Champagne dynasty) and Russian mother; assistant to editor, *Town and Country* magazine, during her earlier marriage to James Thornton.
3 A letter of thanks (from the character of Mr William Collins in Jane Austen's *Pride and Prejudice*).
4 Arturo Toscanini (1867–1957), Italian conductor; one of IB's heroes, both morally, because of his opposition to Nazism, and musically.
5 'Thing in itself'; Kant's term for 'noumenal' reality as contrasted with perceived phenomena.
6 'Form of life'.
7 'Uplifted'.
8 'Influenza'.
9 'Impulse'.

TO SHIELA NEWSOME

6 June 1909 [sc. 1949; *manuscript*]

Lowell House, Harvard

Dearest Shiela,

To-day is my birthday, I am 40, & frightfully gloomy. I don't quite know why but it is a dreadful hump to cross – nothing will ever be quite so gay again, more cosiness, less gaiety; & in general I cannot quite think of myself as on the side of authority, judgment etc. & I hear myself chatter & the only excuse for it is that one is full of unsifted ideas & too choc-a-bloc to have time to think, & too warmblooded to reckon the consequences & so on, & this is absurd when one is viewed as an old bachelor – you will say, (how emotional all this is! I shall feel nothing, perhaps, in an hour or so. And perhaps one's own contemporaries help one in a kind of sense of timelessness, a sort of life which moves in a time-medium but itself has no date, but I must stop this – all induced by seeing Stephen S[pender]¹ who is here & as young as ever any of us were with all the very nice solemnity of our past in the nice romantic thirties – for they were, weren't they) you or someone will say that I always looked about 40 anyhow – but I mustn't go on about my melancholy. I leave on July 15, & arrive in Cherbourg on 20, & then go & stay with a rich man at Aix en P.² & then visit a man in Lucerne³ & return circa Aug. 5 or 6, & then don't move much. I shd like to see you at once, indeed here & now. I still believe & always will (I remember the conversation perfectly) that you didn't, foolishly, follow your heart but an abstract image, & so wedded are you to ideals which alone justify so much of what you've done (& more, failed to do) that you won't face the truth quite even now, any more than Communists, Zionists, philosophy lecturers etc. Be that as it may – & your life is a great puzzle unless one realizes how obstinate about big things (very unusual) you are – with certain concessions & disarming deviations in little ones towards the facts, towards your friends – but when big things i.e. ends of life occur you push firmly on to the mirage – be that as it may if we are to meet – & we must – then not at Salzburg: not this year: but after seeing each other frequently everywhere in London, Oxford etc. we might go (improperly?) somewhere in very late September for 5 days. Italy even. What do you think? I shall be in London about Aug 5, at Hollycroft. Dearest Shiela, how are you? I do love you.

Shaya

---

1 Stephen Harold Spender (1909–95), the poet and critic; co-editor of *Encounter* 1953–67. He and IB had been undergraduates together and remained lifelong friends.
2 Rowland *Burdon-Muller (1891–1980), English-born art connoisseur who had settled in Boston.
3 Chaim Weizmann.

TO ELIZABETH VON HOFMANNSTHAL

10 June 1949 [*manuscript*]

Lowell House, Harvard

Dearest Liz,

I suddenly, now, at 2 a.m. have felt an overwhelming impulse to write you & ask: how are you? are you well? are you enjoying yourself? how is Raimund? is he enjoying himself? because I *am* enjoying myself & feel ashamed. The first days were misery. I was put in a garrett (is that how it is spelt?), knew nobody, thought I shd be a failure, everyone was very New Englandy & stiff, I kept on dashing off to N.Y. & Wash. where at least I knew some faces, & so on. Suddenly the ice broke with delicious warm water underneath. First the Russian scholars & the historians became affable. Then the Old Boston hostesses & their Cambridge dependencies. I was very haughty to the former, who are a formidable but to me unattractive crew, but adored the latter who preserve a distinguished blue stockingy quality. The nephew of Henry James[1] is particularly sweet, & speaks with a tortured expression on his face, unable to find the right, the wholly adequate, the exactly apposite, word, poised over a precipice like a very sensitive unhappy large bird, suddenly darting for a scarcely perceptible little fish – the proper Boston ladies are curiously coarse inside: very formidable sharp, well informed, heavily rich, but undelicate (not in- but un-) possessive, with Victorian rapacity & ungracefully bourgeois: but on the other hand full of an unexhausted vitality, inquisitive, savage and independent. *Not* civilized. All save Mrs Winthrop Chandler[2] who is 90 & quite wonderful, having lived in Rome & much better than anyone in England now; & her daughter Mrs Pickman,[3] very Catholic, very gay, very cultivated, very original – indeed in the county round about there lurk ancient untouched Edwardian originals of great splendour of personality. I have not, however, moved among them, but stuck to my colleagues & worked hard, for once. In due course I was offered a job here, declined, but felt I cdn't be an *utter* failure after that. I have an idea they feel the need of worldliness & I appeared to have that. Isn't it awful. I did my best to get them to invite Freddie (*don't* tell him, he wd mind dreadfully, & I feel & am priggish as I tell you – & no one else) but it was no go. They falsely think themselves superior to him, without a vestige of justice. My virtuous, smug self satisfaction knew no bounds when, after they carefully explained why they didn't want him, they praised my loyalty & said that he, on the contrary, had assured them that I had lost all interest in my subject

---

1 William ('Billy') *James (1882–1961), painter, art critic and arts administrator; son of the philosopher William James, whose younger brother was the novelist Henry James.

2 Margaret ('Daisy') Chanler (*sic*) (1862–1952), daughter of artist Luther Terry, widow of Winthrop Astor Chanler; novelist and convert to Catholicism.

3 Hester Marion Pickman (1893–1990), née Chanler, wife of Edward Pickman (264/2); a devout Catholic.

& had gone downhill. I displayed much moral grandeur & said that he was too absorbed in abstract thought to know much about what was going on in others & it was a price you had to pay for genius. All this was put down to my greatheartedness & revolting hypocrisy was exhibited by all sides. But *don't* tell him. Let him indulge his fury, as he is entitled: all because of the Marchioness[1] I fear: & how is she? I wrote & asked her in a postcard, to look after a particular passage in 'First Love' – if you see her do remind her. The translation is dedicated to Lady P. de B. which is surely right?[2] I hope she comes to Aix with me for 5–6 days. [...] The Hiss case, of which you mayn't have heard is fascinating & dreadful & has a Dreyfus like quality & if we were Americans we'd talk of little else – the characters (the question is what a State Dept. official called Alger Hiss was or was not – but Raimund knows all about it & so do you) have all been described in Greenwich Village novels[3] in the last ten years – literally I mean – under thinly disguised names, & the novels are part of the unofficial evidence. Everything Americans are petrified & fascinated by is in it: psycho-analysis, communism, what an uncle of mine once called 'sexual perversity', the New Deal, etc. – someone – Diana – cd write a masterpiece on it, it is so dramatic, like art, & the figures & acts full of fantasy. Duff wd adore it too as it involves love, honour, treachery etc. It is now 2·30 & I must stop. Next week I start going away & propose to visit the New York highbrow bohemia once: viz Nic. Nabokov with whose new wife I (& almost I alone) get on. I've met there a v. clever girl called Mary McCarthy,[4] v. Irish, a friend of Connolly, who was very full of malicious gossip about everyone, particularly Prof. Ayer – all the British lecturers go about saying the other ones are a terrible failure, arrogant, hostile to Americans, let down the side etc. but I can testify to the succès fou[5] of the Sitwells:[6] I went to the Boston Abend[7] – it all went off splendidly. My best moment was when Osbert was saying goodbye with a frozen but gracious smile on his fine features to gushing hostesses – 1200 bucks I may say they took for *Façade*[8] – when suddenly one particularly sweet looking lady

1 IB had warned Shirley Morgan against romantic involvement with Ayer.
2 The dedication was dropped when the translation was reprinted (with illustrations, but without *Rudin*) in 1956.
3 Lionel Trilling's 1947 novel *The Middle of the Journey* contains a character based on Whittaker Chambers, the main accuser of Hiss, and many readers assumed that other characters were based on Alger Hiss and his wife, though Trilling denied this.
4 Mary Therese McCarthy (1912–89), novelist, critic and liberal political activist, who had been Edmund Wilson's third wife.
5 'Wild success'.
6 The English poets Edith Louisa Sitwell (1887–1964) and her brother Sir (Francis) Osbert Sacheverell Sitwell (1892–1969) made a highly successful US tour between October 1948 and March 1949, giving lectures and poetry-readings.
7 'Evening'.
8 The highlight of the Sitwells' tour was a performance on 19 January of Edith Sitwell's entertainment with poems, *Façade*, with music by William Walton, at the Museum of Modern Art, New York, a sell-out at $35 a ticket.

said "Good-bye Sir Osbert. It really was very good of you to have liked so very many people so very much." I am now babbling on with no system & *must* stop. I was sorry Mrs Kahn[1] died, very. I liked her very much & it really stunned poor Nin.[2] Is she in London now? I did write, but I shd like to say to her how genuinely sorry I was. I liked the terrific independence & downrightness & undeceivable sense & imagination v. much.

Oh dear oh dear I must go to bed. But why – & I mean this au plus grand sérieux[3] – don't you & Rai come to Aix on July 23 or so? or a little later? it wd be v. delightful. The Marchioness I gather is expecting an heir[4] (we hope) – do remind her about Tourgueniev: do you ever see M. Dick? & you did see my fat friend Prichard – now also out on $5000·00 bail on a charge of ballot stuffing of which I believe him wholly innocent – I adore him, & so I gather, did Cyril – & you? & Raimund? I haven't seen him yet & now seems a difficult time for him, but he is much the gayest, cosiest, cleverest, most sympathetic American I know. Yet he has slight – v. slight – Boothbyish characteristics. But sophisticated as he is he, like Joe Alsop, was shocked by London Society, like H. James – shocked by the horrible things they told him about one another, the public knowledge of affairs & brutal mockery at parties etc – I don't know what he'd have thought of Emerald – funny, I don't feel it at home, much more at Harvard where all the brilliant men backbite like mad & are psychoanalysed all & every day, & go off to be done for an hour as to the dentist. Seems much worse to me – it is like Berlin v. Vienna. My love to Raimund & yr little ones. Where will you be in Aug? do write.

Isaiah.   [...]

IB's final weeks at Harvard had been spent examining. Recovered from his ulcers but suffering now from sciatica, he reflected 'the heat has come, the osteopath is at work, and I feel much better but fearfully exhausted after examining the extraordinary outpourings of my own students who return my own words to me in grotesque shape, a duly humbling experience, no doubt excellent for one's self-esteem, but severely shaking to one's general faith in the rationality of man'.[5]

1 Adelaide ('Addie') Kahn (1875–1949), née Wolff, widow of the wealthy financier and patron of the arts Otto Hermann Kahn, died on 15 May in London.
2 Margaret Dorothy ('Nin') Ryan (1901–95), née Kahn, wife of journalist John Barry Ryan; like her father, Otto, a patron of the arts, especially music. On her death IB wrote of her 'omnivorous curiosity' and described her as 'gentle, modest, deeply civilised, with a sharp sense of humour, a sweet nature and immense charm, and a gift for friendship which seemed to have no limits'. *Independent*, 10 February 1995, 16.
3 'Absolutely genuinely'.
4 The Angleseys had a daughter in July 1949; their second child was a son and heir.
5 To Rowland Burdon-Muller, 22 June.

TO ROWLAND BURDON-MULLER

24 June 1949 [*manuscript card*]

Lowell House, Harvard

Thank you for your excellent, reassuring, pleasure promising, detail-settling, peace-of-mind-inducing altogether admirable, tranquillizing at once pattern-of-life-creating & particular-to-brass-tack-down-getting letter. I have in short been reading modern American philosophy. I have had a curiously satisfying talk about it with Pres. Conant, who if somewhat nervous, is splendidly anti-uplift & clouds of counterfeit pseudoreligious glory. [...]

I.B.   [...]

One of IB's last engagements in the US was his speech on 'Democracy, Communism and the Individual' on 28 June at the second annual session of the Mount Holyoke College Institute on the United Nations, alongside speakers such as Eleanor Roosevelt,[1] Sir Alexander Cadogan and Abba Eban.[2] In agreeing to speak he had stressed the importance of discretion to protect his vulnerable informants in the Soviet Union: 'I must again beg you not permit any of this to appear in print under my name as the consequences to various persons in the U.S.S.R. would be very grave, & I should certainly decline to speak if I thought that there [was] any risk of my words appearing in print anywhere.'[3] But the Mount Holyoke contact to whom he had written in these terms, Elizabeth Green,[4] 'then explained that publicity was important for the purposes of the Institute, and made me feel that it would be altogether ungracious and wrong to refuse to have any dealings with the press, and after much hesitation on my part and persuasion by Miss Green, I consented to see the New York Times *correspondent'.[5] The consequences of a brief chat with a reporter in IB's room appeared in the next day's* New York Times *under the heading 'Study of Marxism Backed at Parley: UN Institute at Holyoke Told Russian Revolution Was Paramount Event':[6]*

1 (Anna) Eleanor Roosevelt (1884–1962), née Roosevelt, widow of FDR; active in the UN since its inception; US representative to UN 1945, 1949–52.

2 Abba Eban (1915–2002), né Aubrey Solomon in South Africa, Israeli diplomat and politician; political officer, Jewish Agency, 1946–7; Jewish Agency's liaison officer with UNSCOP 1947; Jewish Agency delegation to UN 1947; Israeli representative to UN 1948–59; Israeli Ambassador to US 1950–9; President, Weizmann Institute of Science, 1958–66; Member of Knesset from 1959; held various ministerial posts 1959–74; an outstanding linguist and orator.

3 To Elizabeth Green (next note), 22 June. As IB explained to George Kennan on 30 June, 'I refused to let the press quote my lecture, which was somewhat Fascist Beast in character, on how a modus vivendi wasn't really possible between any democracy and "them", etc., because I thought if I did, poor Pasternak etc. would finally be shot'.

4 Elizabeth Alden Green (1908–92), Director, Mount Holyoke College News Bureau, 1942–67; Professor of English, Mount Holyoke, 1948–74.

5 To Ruth Lawson, Associate Professor of Political Science at Mount Holyoke, 30 June.

6 The piece, which appeared in the City Edition on 29 June, 20, but not in later editions, was by John H. Fenton (1906–73), Boston correspondent of the *New York Times* 1947–70.

The Russian Revolution was described today by a member of Harvard University's Russian Research Center as 'about the most influential event of the twentieth century'.

Dr Isaiah Berlin, a research associate, held that its impact on present-day thinking was comparable to that of the French Revolution a century ago. He addressed a discussion meeting of the second Mount Holyoke College Institute on the United Nations. It is most important 'not only to the Russians, but also to the people who are against them,' said Dr Berlin, to examine the Communists' 'fanatical belief in Marxism' and to find out what they believed at the time of the Revolution and 'what they still believe in'.

The former First Secretary of the British Embassy in Moscow, who last came out of Russia in 1945, held that the Marxist theory had made a 'deep impact, even on people who are not Marxists'.

The 'very exaggerations and distortions' of the Marx theory, said Dr Berlin, had 'stirred people's imaginations', and to ban a study of it would be 'putting on the label of forbidden fruit'.

TO THE EDITOR OF THE *NEW YORK TIMES*[1]

30 June 1949

Cambridge, Mass.

In your issue of June 29 there appeared an item with the headline, 'Study of Marxism Backed at Parley', and a sub-headline, 'UN Institute at Holyoke Told Russian Revolution Was Paramount Event'. The account given of my remarks by your correspondent John H. Fenton conveys the clear impression that my principal purpose was to impress upon my audience the importance of studying Marxism, and specifically of not placing a ban upon such studies. I should like to point out that, in the first place, whatever remarks I made in connection with the subject were not made in any address delivered by me to the United Nations Institute, since this was not, at my request, given any publicity, in order not to compromise my informants, some of whom came from behind the Iron Curtain.

The remarks upon which your correspondent based his report were made by me in the course of a private interview with him at his request in answer to his questions: I was asked whether I favoured the study of Marxism in general. I replied that the October Revolution was clearly an important event if, in some respects, a disaster; that it was made by men steeped in Marxism; that like other semi-obsolete nineteenth-century doctrines which had had a large influence both on its adherents and its opponents, it deserved careful study; that Marx was more important as the father of economic history and the originator of a new approach to social history than as a revolutionary theorist; and that I saw no reason to forbid the study of his views, provided

---

1 'Attitude on Marxism Stated: Dr Berlin Amplifies his Remarks Made at Mount Holyoke', *New York Times*, 8 July 1949, 18.

that those responsible preserved an attitude sufficiently critical to take account of the errors and distortions in which Marxism abounds.

Above all I remember insisting that such students of the subject must remain detached and analytic and not on any account slip into the attitude of preachers; and that if Marxism were to be refuted, which I believed to be both possible and desirable, it must first be understood.

Your correspondent's report, as well as the headlines attached to it, clearly conveys the impression that my lecture to the United Nations Institute was mainly concerned with the advocacy of Marxist studies. As anyone who heard it can testify, my actual lecture stressed the incompatibility between any form of democratic belief and Marxist doctrine; while my replies to your correspondent's questions were intended mainly to stress the necessity for a sharply critical approach to doctrines which even today tend to be swallowed whole by the fanatical Marxist sectaries, both orthodox Communists and the heretics whom they have excommunicated. Since I feel that my position in this matter has not been correctly represented, I should be grateful if you would be so kind as to publish this letter.

Isaiah Berlin,
Fellow and Tutor of New College, Oxford, England

TO JOSEPH ALSOP

1 July 1949 [*manuscript card*]

Lowell House, Harvard

My dear Joseph –

I have plenty to say to you one way & another – our Fat Friend – the extreme delight of the week-end about which I must instantly write to your mother[1] – & the horrors of Holyoke: but I enclose some entertaining matter: it really is infuriating if, after weakly yielding to importunate female publicity directrices, & telling a N.Y.T. man that Marx is an important but semi-obsolete 19th century prophet more important as an economic & social historian than as a political leader – an article appears making one out a kind of knock-kneed feeble fellow straggler (as Cyril C. calls them) trying to hide his real inclinations behind a facâde of bogus objectivity! & one is described as 'last' emerging out of the U.S.S.R. cesspool in 1945 – having more or less lived in it ever since 1918 I suppose! I feel that the rest of my life will be spent in démentis[2] to people like the Provost of Harvard that I am an ambiguous snake of some sort. I've written a little note to Scottie R.[3] asking him to beat

1 101/1.
2 'Denials'.
3 James Barrett ('Scotty') Reston (1909–95), Scottish-born journalist; national correspondent, *New York Times*, 1945–8, diplomatic correspondent 1948–53, bureau chief and columnist 1953–64; later held various editorial positions and became a leading columnist.

someone on the head: & I shall tell George or Chip. I don't want to blow it up unnecessarily but I feel absolutely berserk at the moment. [...]

TO CORINNE ALSOP[1]

5 July 1949 [*carbon*]

Lowell House

Dear Mrs Alsop,

[...] disaster began to occur almost as soon as I left you. The drive to Holyoke with the Schlesingers was pleasant if uneventful except for slight tiffs between them about which was the quickest way, etc. Then came Mrs Roosevelt's address in the evening – she really is one of the greatest moral assets of which even this morally far from queer country can boast. Not that she said anything very new or very important, but the dignity and disarming quality of her rectitude and virtue are so great that all melts before it. I feel that she really did, almost single-handedly, make it possible for people here to be critical of the USSR and still not afraid of being condemned as Fascist Beasts – the opportunity for an anti-Soviet but 'progressive' attitude, which her quarrel with Vyshinsky[2] about civil liberties gave to hundreds of thousands of school mistresses and high-minded but muddled persons who might otherwise have been Wallacites, really does seem to me to be important and very satisfying.

At Mount Holyoke I was asked if the press might take down my remarks. I said no because I proposed to criticise the Soviet Union, and if my name appeared in print in connection with this, my innocent friends in Moscow who talked to me so freely would most certainly be shot. Were the journalists prepared to take that on their consciences? It appeared they were not. But publicity was important for Mount Holyoke, so would I see the *NY Times* man secretly, privately in my bedroom? This was odd but I said I would, whereupon an extraordinary interview occurred, in which I said that Marx, like other semi-obsolete Victorian doctrines of much influence, deserved careful study, that to drive it underground would merely make it too attractive as forbidden fruit, that students of it should be sharply critical and not preachers, who anyhow had no place in respectable academic institutions except as preachers, etc. All this came out in fantastic form the next day when I was represented as backing more and more Marxism in American universities and staunchly defending the Russian Revolution and all the other horrors. I have written an indignant letter to the *Times* – I do not

1 Joe Alsop's mother Corinne Douglas Alsop (1886–1971), née Robinson, later Cole, niece of former President Theodore Roosevelt, cousin of both Eleanor Roosevelt and Alice Longworth.

2 Andrey Yanuar'evich Vyshinsky (1883–1954), Soviet jurist (Chief Prosecutor in the Moscow show trials of the 1930s) and diplomat; permanent Soviet delegate to the UN 1947–54; Minister for Foreign Affairs 1949–53; Eleanor Roosevelt had clashed with him in the UN General Assembly and during her Chairmanship of the UN Human Rights Commission.

know whether they will print it – washing myself of these horrible stains.
I shall never feel the same about the *New York Times* again, like a place in a
room where the carpet suddenly slithered and one tripped. I saw this fearful
paragraph in Cincinnati,[1] where I was trying to comfort my about-to-be-
tried friend, and I was so filled with indignation at my own 'frame-up' that
I am afraid I was not able to be sympathetic enough about his really serious
predicament. In the end I lost my nice old London brown felt hat, and looked
for it and could not find it, and this somehow appeared as the final stroke
in the series of disasters – then the airplane did not fly and came down in
West Virginia with a damaged motor, my arrangements collapsed, endless
telegrams were sent which brought about their own complicated and unpredictable consequences, and in the end I fetched up in Boston at a fantastic
hour, tremendously bloody but in some mysterious way not wholly bowed.

But I must not go on inflicting all these sordid details of my life upon you.
Thank you again very much for my now remote-seeming bliss – I expect I
shall recover soon, but at the moment, having just had a tooth pulled out
(anything may happen – I hardly care) etc. etc., I am not too buoyant. But I
am never melancholy for long, alas, as I am not of a too profound nature, and
I should like to say again how delighted I was to see you and your husband
[...].

Yours ever,
    Isaiah Berlin

TO MARIETTA TREE

2.30 a.m., 7 July 1949 [*manuscript*]

Lowell House, Harvard

Dear Marietta,

Alas, all good things end. And I have enjoyed Harvard very much really,
there is a moral vitality despite the Brahmins, which has the effect of refuel-
ling me – I hate leaving places, & in spite of a slow & in some ways gloomy
start, I find it curiously a wrench to go. I never never thought it wd be. The
idea of staying here for good I don't entertain: but it is delicious being offered
things: & I am very well disposed towards the local authorities. Also it is nice
to meet Pres. Conant under the elms in the Yard at 12.30 – full moon, very
beautiful – after a farewell visit to Mrs Whitehead[2] – & to talk to him for

1 IB had flown to Cincinnati (presumably on 29 June) to dine with Ed Prichard before the start of
   his trial on 5 July.
2 Evelyn Ada Maud Rice Whitehead (1865–1950), née Wade, widow of Alfred North Whitehead
   (106/3), who paid tribute to her aesthetic sensitivity; of Irish descent but educated in France;
   Bertrand Russell fell in love with her while collaborating with her husband. IB met her – through
   Myron Gilmore (136/2), husband of her son's stepdaughter – when she was no longer mobile but
   retained her keen interest in people. IB later remembered long, fascinating conversations with
   her, and described her as a very strong personality who dominated her family, a 'predacious'

1½ hrs about the foundations of physics – & then try & induce him to take a milk shake at a Cafeteria – but alas in this I failed. The young men are less well treated than ours, fuzzier, more of a big buzzing blooming confusion, but more receptive, eager, wide open, less provincial, & more excitable by ideas & vistas & intellectual speculation. The thought of 16 hrs teaching a week is a little depressing. Still, I really like grooves, routine, harness etc. or I say I do: & although (isn't it awful) I haven't seen Dr A. Cohn,[1] the life of reason is no doubt the cosiest for me. I did enjoy your letter tremendously: it made me suddenly long to be back & see all the characters in these little plays which are going on – I suddenly thought, why shd Sir O. Franks (whom I like v. much) [not] meet them too? After all he adored meeting Duff & Diana. If you are entertaining at Ditchley at all in the last great glorious burst,[2] do get David Cecil who loves him to bring Sir O. Franks to something – young Tories or Young Anybody wd suit him v. well. He ought to be taken out a bit in our general interest. I wrote to Pamela Berry[3] to tell her to do so – but she probably won't as she doesn't know him etc. David might take him out a bit. He is a sort of great man I am beginning to think.

Goodness! my room is sordid with chaos & cigar ash & luggage & MSS. & obviously represents the disorder of my life which no analyst will ever be permitted to tidy: I romanticize every place I come to I find: Moscow, Oxford, Ditchley, Harvard, Washington: each is a kind of legendary world framed within its own conventions in which the characters, suffused with unnatural brightness, perform with terrific responsiveness & character. Am I a bemused provincial lady, almost Hokinson,[4] at times: I really think I am. [...] Alas, I can't come to Ditchley for what will be a terrific fin de la saison[5] I am sure. When are you & Ronnie leaving? not before I see you surely? do

hysteric who was nevertheless capable of great kindness and perceptiveness. 'She naturally heightened every friendship [...]. She would keep [I]B talking long into the night. She loved to have people dependent on her. She particularly went for the company of people who were unfortunate in one way or another: the poor, Jews, Negroes' (from notes by Victor Lowe, A. N. Whitehead's biographer, on a conversation with IB, 9 November 1965 [Johns Hopkins, Victor Lowe papers, MS 284, Box 2.8]). An admirer of generosity, gallantry and boldness, she had little time for the English, including her husband's family, and had more sympathy for men than for women, some of whom, including Marion Frankfurter, loathed her. As IB wrote to Lowe: 'I think that Mrs Whitehead on the whole did not like women, but she loved Felix Frankfurter, who was a great friend and favourite of Whitehead. I think that Mrs F. was always sceptical, detached, ironical, and exceedingly distinguished in her own right, and perhaps did not pay enough homage to Whitehead. I think that Marion Frankfurter thought of Mrs Whitehead as excessively vain, self-centred, possessive of Whitehead, acid, unkind, domineering etc. – all of which is partly to be said about herself' (letter of 23 December 1965; ibid.).

1 Alfred Einstein Cohn (1879–1957), pioneer cardiologist; friend of Felix Frankfurter, through whom IB had met him during the war.
2 The Trees were about to sell Ditchley Park and move to the US.
3 Lady Pamela Margaret Elizabeth Berry (1914–82), née Smith, daughter of 1st Earl of Birkenhead; wife of the newspaper editor Michael Berry (Baron Hartwell 1954); a famous society hostess.
4 The US cartoonist Helen Hokinson (1893–1949) specialised in portraying just such ladies; she died in an air crash over Washington, DC, a few months after this letter.
5 'End of the season'.

let me come in Aug. & say goodbye to you – I shall be reachable at New College after the 7ᵗʰ Aug – but perhaps you'll be in Paris before that, & I'll see you there in the course of returning? sometimes I think I am too silly & frivolous: because I wish to be, like Sibyl, in too many situations at once, & miss nothing, & communicate at all levels, & be in the stream of life like Mr Roosevelt. Mrs R. is terrific: she is the greatest moral asset of the U.S.A. I heard her at Mt. Holyoke explain with disingenuous pseudo simplisme how she kept Franco out of U.N.O. & it was both funny & moving: I do believe that she alone has made it possible for liberals in the U.S. to be anti-Soviet & it is a stupendous achievement. I've written a glowing article about Winston for the Atlantic & now feel I've overdone it but no matter. I stop, no paper. fondest love to you & Ronnie.

Is.

Do write – either to Q. Elizabeth or Hotel Roi René, Aix en Provence.

TO ALICE JAMES

    16 July 1949 [*manuscript*]

                        Cunard White Star, RMS *Queen Elizabeth*

Dear Alice,

    I must begin by saying how very happy I was to get your letter:[1] I meant to reply to it before but neither mood nor general circumstances were propitious: the general disorder & fuss in which I live my life have not escaped you: & the leaving was even more cluttered up than the coming. Goodness me! I suddenly realized all the undone things: the unwritten promised reviews: the lectures at points in New England: all the things I should never have consented to do but for an almost morbid inability to say no, plus a feeling that unless I obligate myself to do rather more than I can I shd never do anything at all, but just spend time happily in armchairs and talking with friends. But I really was tremendously pleased to receive your letter: I suspected for some time that neither you nor Billy found me altogether insufferable: but evidence of friendship is infinitely delightful: indeed I am grateful and shall assuredly write to you, if I may, from time to time from Oxford – I do hope you will come to England soon & that I shall be allowed to see you under my normal peaceful circumstances & not in the fantastic topsy turvydom in which my last weeks in America were spent. I went to Mt. Holyoke & delivered a lecture & gave an interview: this last was misquoted by the N.Y. Times which seemed to me to make me out a kind of half hearted fellow traveller, too timid or shifty to proclaim my adhesion to Marxism: so I wrote a letter to proclaim my non-Marxism: & then, when it appeared,

1 Dated 22 June.

felt ashamed of publicly avowing my solidarity with the safe majority: I am indeed anti-communist, but perhaps when heretics are being burnt right & left it is not the bravest thing in the world to declare one's loyalty to the burners, particularly when one disapproves of the Inquisition: the letter, which the Provost of Harvard[1] advised me to write (I told him how indignant etc. I was with the N.Y. Times) sounded apologetic. And when Harry Levin to whom I poured out all this pointed out in his remorseless fashion that in trying to avoid the charge of cowardice I had perhaps incurred it all the more, I thought he was quite right: but I wasn't grateful to him for rubbing it in. Elena[2] was rather embarrassed & was extra-affable & nice: but I brooded for days about my lack of stoutness. It was all very trivial: nobody had noticed the Times report nor my letter: I felt an awful fool. I shouldn't go on pouring out like this: let me tell you of two more episodes which marked my leaving: one charming, one comico-dreadful. The first occurred after I took leave for the last time of my beloved Mrs Whitehead with whom I made great friends – wonderful I think her to be. I left at the relatively (for her) early hour of 11·30 p.m. & was wandering home sentimentally through the Yard, gazing at the buildings in which I had felt genuinely happy (as you noticed) when I met President Conant. He was walking home in the opposite direction, stopped, & addressed some convenable remarks on my departure: we chatted agreeably for some minutes & then he asked me about some point in Russell's last book on philosophy,[3] which he had liked & I hadn't. I expounded some sort of thesis about physics: he argued back: we moved to logic & then to ethics & why one shouldn't murder people one didn't like. In this way, about 1¼ hours were spent. After which we parted affably & went, he to bed, I to do a night's packing. What was extraordinary & most touching was his still unexhausted curiosity about abstract problems: his lack of sense of importance, his not being eaten out by administration or a public personality. I do not know that it was a particularly remarkable conversation: the wonderful thing was that it shd have occurred at all: he was bleak, dry, not v. imaginative, & has an ugly Yankee peasant voice: but he was eager, terribly clear & honest, & touchingly interested and boyish & sweet. I thought I liked him very much & cd talk easily to him, & that the greatest danger to College Presidents – high minded Tartuffery,[4] lofty corruption, smoothness,

---

1 Paul Buck appears to have had close links with the intelligence community and perhaps suggested that the FBI might be suspicious of IB's alleged views; on 30 June IB wrote to George Kennan mentioning his fear of misconstrual by State Department or FBI staff, and on 18 July to his parents: 'the New York Times published my letter of démenti which some thought a little cowardly but in view of F.B.I. etc. I thought necessary'.

2 Elena Levin (1913–2006), née Zarudnaya, married to Harry Levin; teacher of Russian, critic and translator.

3 Presumably *Human Knowledge: Its Scope and Limits* (London, 1948).

4 In Molière's eponymous satiric comedy, first performed in 1664, Tartuffe is the embodiment of hypocrisy.

all things to all men fausse bonhomie,[1] had not touched him at all. Maurice had obviously not clicked particularly with him: Felix Frankfurter thinks him inferior to his old enemy Mr Lowell:[2] Harry Levin, when I told him of my nocturnal conversation, said it made him wish to pity Mr Conant: but I couldn't agree less with all this. He seemed a very truthful & direct man & I admired him greatly: he said he couldn't understand Whitehead[3] & William James[4] was far better & greater & so was Hume[5] & I agreed. I went away very touched & pleased & with a really charming memory of the Widener at midnight & this almost undergraduaty sincerity. After this I went off to Washington & said goodbye, much saddened by the fate of my friend Prichard who was condemned to 2 years in prison for election frauds,[6] which I am privately convinced is a great miscarriage of justice: then I went to New York, where Mrs K. Roosevelt[7] had most kindly invited me to stay: & I would have done so but for the comico-awful incident. 2 hours after my arrival I had my pocket picked – heaven knows where – & lost my pass-port, sailing permit, Cunard ticket, about £12, & a number of documents. The trauma really is terrific: for a minute one feels what the Soviets call a passportless vagabond: a rootless cosmopolitan. I had only 36 hours before the boat sailed. So in a daze, & with Mrs Roosevelt no longer – or indeed anyone else in mind, I raced off to the British Consulate, a British subject in distress, a well known most tiresome category of people. Fortunately the Consul General, one Sir F. Evans[8] knew me well: & so it was all fixed up, with calls to Washington, Consular officials scurrying to & fro in the sizzling weather, & I was got off somehow. I must explain to Mrs R.: I did send her a telegram regretting my truancy: it really was a nightmare while it lasted: the properties are still unfound: some international criminal is sure to use my passport & I shall probably be arrested in mistake for him quite soon. If you see an item saying I had been captured & lodged in Brixton jail you will know the true reason even if you can do little to liberate me. And now peace & tranquillity &, wonderful to relate, v. few acquaintances on this ship, & a nice

1 'False friendliness'.

2 (Abbott) Lawrence Lowell (1856–1943), President, Harvard, 1909–33.

3 Alfred North Whitehead (1861–1947), British mathematician and logician (Bertrand Russell's collaborator on *Principia Mathematica*) who later addressed broader philosophical questions, particularly after moving to the US; Professor of Philosophy, Harvard, 1924–37.

4 William James (1842–1910), elder brother of Henry James the novelist, and father of IB's friend William ('Billy') James; philosopher and psychologist, particularly associated with the philoso-phy of pragmatism.

5 David Hume (1711–76), the Scottish philosopher and historian on whom IB had once hoped to produce a book (L1 253/3).

6 Prichard was sentenced on 14 July, spent one night in custody, and was then released on bail pending his appeal.

7 Mary Lowe ('Polly') Roosevelt (b. c.1918), née Gaddis, wife of Kermit Bulloch ('Kim') Roosevelt (1916–2000), grandson of President Theodore Roosevelt and CIA agent.

8 Sir Francis Edward Evans (1897–1983), diplomat; Consul-General, New York, 1944–50; Ambassador to Israel 1952–4, to the Argentine 1954–7.

Catholic priest, German, very liberal, very left wing, from Cincinnati at my table. I shall write again & meanwhile thank you once again for befriending me – as you see I get into scrapes – when I knew nobody: & all affection to Billy & yourself
    Yours
        Isaiah Berlin

TO MARIETTA TREE

    16 July 1949 [*manuscript*]

Cunard White Star, RMS *Queen Elizabeth*

Dear Marietta,

I am filled with melancholy thoughts as I proceed in what is externally not unlike the Q. Mary, but oh how different socially! just as well, perhaps, rest, sleep, peace, one's frayed nerves and shaken health & advancing years … still it is a sad, sad contrast. Such persons as I know are, as you will see, not even neutral but horrible. I spend my time avoiding them. The first thing which happened after my final farewells at Cambridge Mass (which contains some splendid people) Washington [*sic*]: the Hiss affair, who may indeed be guilty (goodness how his friends hate one for even speculating about this) but who will be convicted on inadequate evidence, I feel. The nightmare of my poor friend Prichard who probably did stuff some votes in Bourbon County, Ky. but if he did it, did so only as schoolboys do, to show they are not prigs & New Deal hoity toity intellectuals: & when the judge says that this kind of thing undermines the very foundations of democracy, he is in a sense, absolutely right. Yet poor Prich has been destroyed over a trivial thing, & the real culprit[1] has gone scot free. I really am miserable about it, I fear suicide, altho' when I went down to see him (before the conviction) he swore he wdn't. He is one of the best people I ever knew: & the gayest, warmest, most imaginative, fearless and politically infallible: & even morally so, despite this idiotic schoolboy act (2 or 3 votes,[2] I believe, forged in a county where the result was a foregone conclusion). While we are on these sad things let me relieve it by a touch of farce. 24 hrs before sailing I lost, or had stolen, on a Madison Av. bus (avoid them like the plague! I mounted it out of a sudden mistaken sense of economy) a wallet containing my passport, Cunard ticket, sailing permit, £12, & papers & papers & papers. The trauma is appalling: worst thing since Mr Eden declined to take me to Potsdam. Grief & shock & despair! I rushed off to the Brit. Consulate: for 10 mins or so I was treated like a British subject in distress: was offered horrible bits of paper likely to take me, & very suspectly too, only to England: not to Aix en Provence as planned: then a familiar

---

1 IB means Funk, who was acquitted; Prichard later admitted that he, Funk and another man were all guilty.
2 254 forged ballots were found.

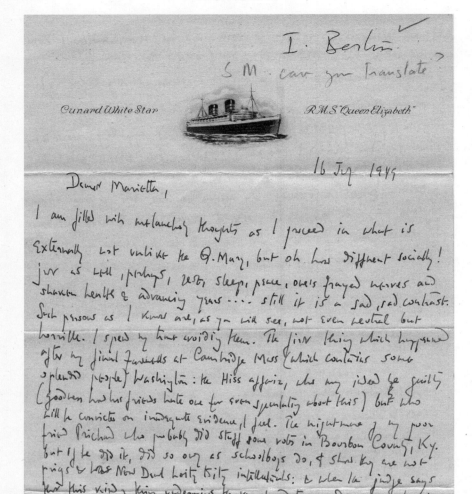

The first page of IB's letter to Marietta Tree, 16 July 1949

face appeared in the person of dear old Read Adam[1] (never mind the name) a Commercial consul, despised by my grander friends in H.M. Embassy in the old delicious 1943 days, but now a friend, an ally, above all a protector. I shed tears of relief & gratitude: the piece of paper gave way to a Passport valid for 1 year; & I was almost in order. Then sailed in the Consul General himself, Sir Francis Evans; he thought I had come [to pay] my respects; reminisced about the old days in the F.O. of various Jocks & Jacks & Derricks & John Russells:[2] the Consulate staff listened with awe & amazement & very deferentially: my true plight was revealed: my passport was extended to 5 years: all details were waived: I felt that Mr Stanley[3] was right: Contacts are all. Then the Embassy itself telephoned through: gloria in excelsis: man cd ask for no more: I was introduced all round like Mr Churchill: & left wearing a gracious but slightly distant smile as befits persons whom Lord Halifax & Sir O. Franks had dignified by personal acquaintance who had had occasion to make use of the services of the underworld of consular troglodytes. The rest was literally plain sailing: but no you & Ronnie, no Judy & Aline, no amiable Rothschilds, no Katz,[4] no Perkins[5] – & alas no Dr Katkov! but who is here? (a) Rabbi Silver[6] of Cleveland, a brazen voiced bull like Zionist demagogue of the most violent kind, a Republican, a foe of Dr Weizmann, virtually a terrorist, a dry eyed crocodile. Worse is to come: Johannes Steel,[7] a weak, slimy fellow travelling bit of German corruption, too impure even for a decently stout communist, who knew me: received information from me in 1941 when Ronnie & he fought on the same side: worse still (not really) Mr J. Mallik,[8] the Soviet Ambassador to Uno: at whose table I found

1 Randle Reid-Adam (sic) (1912–82), British Consul, New York, 1947–9, Consul-General (Commercial) 1949–52; IB had known him while Reid-Adam was on Ministry of Economic Warfare duties in Washington during the war.

2 These wartime colleagues of IB are probably the diplomats John ('Jock') Balfour (442/2); John ('Jack') Ogilvy Rennie (1914–81), later (1968) head of MI5; (Fre)derick Robert Hoyer Millar (1900–89), 1st Baron Inchyra 1961; and John Wriothesley Russell (1914–84).

3 Oliver Frederick George Stanley (1896–1950), son of 17th Earl of Derby, MP and senior member of the Conservative Party, who had held several Cabinet posts before Labour came to power.

4 Perhaps Milton Katz (445/3), at this time Professor of Law, Harvard, and Deputy US Special Representative in Europe with rank of Ambassador (dealing with the Marshall Plan).

5 Milo Randolph Perkins (1900–72), government administrator working for Henry Wallace during his time as Secretary of Agriculture and at the Board of Economic Warfare; subsequently a foreign investment consultant. With his wife, the former Tharon Kidd (1902–76), founded a noted azalea garden in Washington to commemorate their two sons, who had both died during the war.

6 Abba Hillel Silver (1893–1963), Lithuanian-born Reform Rabbi, leading Zionist; rabbi of Tifereth Israel congregation, Cleveland, 1917–63; President, Zionist Organization of America, 1945–7; as Chairman of the American section of the Jewish Agency, a major influence behind the UN vote for the partition of Palestine; eloquent orator and prolific writer.

7 The professional name of Herbert Johannes Steel (1908–88), US radio commentator on politics; American Labor Party Congressional candidate 1946 (supported by Henry Wallace and the Communist Party).

8 Jacob Aleksandrovich Malik (sic) (1906–80), Soviet diplomat and politician; Deputy Foreign Minister 1946–8; Ambassador to UN 1948–52; Ambassador to Britain 1953–60. He had been on board the Queen Mary on IB's outward journey too.

myself, a hearty jolly cad, whom I addressed boldly in Russian (grave error!) after which he & his wife disappeared & now consume their meals in their cabin: the Chief Steward cannot understand it & eyes me suspiciously. My other neighbours are charming: Mme Passy, obviously not her real name, (the Colonel's lady?)[1] a rich widow from Auteuil. A florist from Michigan, 78 yrs of age, on the rough side, makes dubious jokes which shock Mr & Mrs Roth, of Cleveland, Ohio, a business man, never been abroad before, comes from Colorado, wife *very* affable, introduces everyone to everyone else, a bit suspicious of me until Rabbi Silver gave her my 'background'. God help me! they are to do Europe in 3 weeks; the question is: shd they go to Belgium, Holland, Luxemburg (they don't know H.E. Mrs Mesta)[2] or Switzerland instead? are the Alps more scenic than the Rockies? Finally Msgr. Ratke[3] of Cincinnati. Very nice. Is to fetch 400 priests from Germany to the U.S.A. Knows Spellman[4] & finds travel more interesting than St. Thomas[5] (he said that as we walked, arm in arm, on the Prom. deck, which has frightened off J. Steel for good & all) – Mr Roth who hates Roosevelt & will vote for Taft[6] (I am to make no mistake about him, a very able man & a fine American) is not too pleased about this introduction of more refugees into America: though a member of Rabbi Silver's congregation he is bitterly anti-refugee: but is prepared to welcome 100 priests, Catholic or Prot. – his wife is nervous of his xenophobia & assures (1) me that they are pro-British, pro Israel, pro Truman etc. (2) the Monsignor that they think the Roman Church quite fine. In addition to this there is Dr Paul N. Rosenstein-Rodan[7] an inferior substitute for Katkov who assures me that Keynes[8] & Barbara Ward[9] both call him Rosie & is worried about the latter's sex life which [he] holds to be non-existent. Do you remember Mr Gombos?[10] Dr Rosenstein-Rodan is not dissimilar but nicer. He may even take my luggage to what he is, following

1   'Colonel Passy' was the wartime code-name of André Dewavrin, a leading member of the Free French military intelligence.
2   Perle Reid Mesta (1889–1975), née Skirvin, American political hostess, loyal supporter of Harry Truman, Ambassador to Luxembourg 1949–53. The central character in Irving Berlin's 1950 musical *Call Me Madam* is based on her.
3   Untraced (probably 'Rathke').
4   Francis Joseph Spellman (1889–1967), Catholic Archbishop of New York 1939–67; Cardinal 1946.
5   Presumably the Christian theologian St Thomas Aquinas (418/1).
6   Robert Alphonso Taft (1889–1953), lawyer; Senator from Ohio 1939–53; made unsuccessful attempts in 1940, 1948 and 1952 to be selected as Republican presidential candidate.
7   Paul Narcyz Rosenstein-Rodan (1902–85), Polish-born economist; moved to London 1930; taught at UCL and LSE until 1947; Assistant Director, Economics Department, World Bank, 1947–53; Visiting Professor, MIT, 1953–9, Professor 1959–68.
8   The economist John Maynard Keynes (1883–1946), 1st Baron Keynes of Tilton 1942.
9   Barbara Mary Ward (1914–81), married Robert Jackson 1950; Baroness Jackson of Lodsworth 1976; economist, journalist and author; assistant editor (then foreign editor), *The Economist*, 1939–50; Governor, BBC, 1946–50; Visiting Scholar, Harvard, 1957–68.
10 Possibly Gyula Gömbös de Jákfa (1886–1936), Fascist-inclined Prime Minister of Hungary 1932–6.

Mr Stanley's brother,[1] occasionally pleased to call the Old Country. When are you leaving it? not before I come to say good bye I hope: I shall be back, if my passport etc. remains unstolen, & if some crook does not use the old one in a way which lands me in Brixton gaol – about August 9: or 7: or 8. I shall telephone Ditchley: I shall ask to come: I long to tell you about Harvard, & my conversations with Dr Conant under the immemorial elms of the Yard at midnight (this was most touching & interesting) & now I must speak to the Baggage Master: my suitcases have split open: Rabbi Silver is approaching to ask me to play Gin Rummy: oh for the delicious Queen Mary: Judy is well: Joe's father is quite open abt what a fool Joe is not to marry the girl. Miss Judy Coplon[2] is a fool. The F.B.I. is too strong.

Love
Isaiah

TO ARTHUR SCHLESINGER

18 July 1949 [*manuscript*]

Cunard White Star, RMS *Queen Elizabeth*

Dear Arthur

Peace, tranquility, & on board, apart from the usual clever but not tremendously nice Hungarian economists who have met one in someone's rooms in Oxford in 1937, Miss Garbo;[3] & Mr Jacob Mallik of the U.S.S.R. to tantalize you, we take the second first: very blonde, huge, coarse, post-Litvinov.[4] Sat at my table & not too pleased when, in an insidious voice I turned from the Cleveland couple on the other side & informed him that I understood all he was saying to his wife & he had better realize it – a move apparently prompted by pure delicacy of feeling. He talked with great apparent affability about the dreadful pursuit of dollars in the U.S.A: compared the system of capitalist exploitation of Russia in the 19th century by the European powers with the analogous purposes of the Marshall plan: recommended though only as "interesting" the works of Johannes Steel also on board & clearly acquainted with us both (J. Steel, one of my clients in 1941 before his true colours flown. So far successfully avoided by me. But I expect we shall collide during the Bingo hour this evening). At the next meal, Malliks disappeared.

1 Presumably Edward Montagu Cavendish Stanley (1894–1938), son of the 17th Earl of Derby, brother of Oliver Stanley; Conservative politician; Dominions Secretary 1938 (joining his brother in the Cabinet).
2 Judith ('Judy') Coplon (b. 1922), later Socolov, Justice Department analyst and Soviet agent, was convicted of espionage in 1949 and of conspiracy in 1950, but both convictions were overturned on technicalities, partly because the FBI had carried out illegal wire-tapping.
3 Greta Garbo (née Greta Lovisa Gustafssohn) (1905–90), the Swedish film actress.
4 Maksim Maksimovich Litvinov (1876–1951), né Meer Genokh Moiseevich Wallakh-Finkelstein, sometimes known as Max Wallach, Soviet Minister of Foreign Affairs 1930–9, Deputy Minister 1941–3; Ambassador to US 1941–3; helped to bring the Soviet Union into the international community.

Obviously they decided the ship was really too unsafe: spies everywhere: crude British Intelligence Tactics: you might suggest to Chip to whom I shall not have the energy to write that he might enquire about me from Mr Malik when next he sees him. That will clinch it & a report to Moscow will certainly be despatched. I sleep, I eat, I brood about your kindness for which I haven't thanked you enough: not only in general but in particular: during the nightmare asymptomatic approach to the Q. Elizabeth. [...] As for Miss Garbo, goodness she is dumb. By a series of accidents I found myself at a party next to her: she is beautiful beyond belief & no less stupid: she painfully, slowly, terribly, tells stale anecdotes of 1925. Stories about Irishmen Scotsmen etc. something a little like Zuleika Dobson[1] without any oomph at all. Her White Russian escort Mr Schlee[2] tells the same sort of stories, but less proper, & drinks. I now know why (1) Miss Garbo uses lipstick (someone thought she should) (2) Miss Garbo prefers Chesterfields to Camels (or the other way) – she can't tell the difference but may be there is one – then a tinkling laugh – the words Oo la la – it is a nightmare. Mr J. Ringling North[3] of the Circus in my presence invites her to go to Paris in the special coach, otherwise reserved for elephants etc. very suitable too. Yet she is an object of religious veneration to my generation, I see that. Do write, & keep Buck up to the mark, do. Love to Marion[4]

Isaiah

V. silly letter. I apologize for it & for apologizing.

1 The eponymous heroine of Max Beerbohm's satirical 1911 novel, whose beauty drives a generation of Oxford undergraduates to suicide.
2 George Schlee (c.1901–64), entrepreneur; Garbo's frequent companion and business adviser over 20 years; his wife was the fashion designer Valentina Schlee.
3 John Ringling North (1903–85), nephew of the circus-owning Ringling brothers; President 1937–43 and 1947–56, Ringling Bros and Barnum & Bailey ('The Greatest Show on Earth').
4 Marian (sic) Schlesinger (b. 1912), née Cannon, painter and author, Arthur Schlesinger's first wife.

1949–1951

NEW COLLEGE AND ALL SOULS

I make too many promises, seek too many pleasures, am caught in too many conflicting currents of pleasure, duty, etc.[1]

To sag at 42 with nothing done is dreadful.[2]

1 To Hugh Trevor-Roper, 6 September 1950.
2 To Jenifer Hart, August 1951.

On reaching Cherbourg, IB spent two days in Paris before attending the Aix-en-Provence music festival,[1] where he and Patricia de Bendern were the guests of Rowland Burdon-Muller.

TO JOSEPH ALSOP

1 August 1949 [*manuscript*]

Aix en Provence

My dear Joe

Very well, now what? about Prich I mean? I long to write him but cannot without some knowledge of how it all stands. Is he hopelessly doomed? is he alive? is he fighting? please let me know [...] Paris was not hot & delightful. I saw Alix de Rothschild[2] who was going to Salzburg: I was tempted to follow but decided it was too Nazi & am doing my duty instead by going to stay for 3–4 days in Buergenstock near Lucerne auprès du[3] Pres. Weizmann, military A.D.C. & all, where I shall get nothing but headwashings & pinpricks from Mrs W. but somehow my duty seems clear: like the Walkers'[4] dinner. I lunched with Susan Mary[5] & Bill,[6] they were just about to fly to London, to Ditchley for the last, grandest of all, Tree farewell dance. As nobody dislikes the Trees & many have affection for them, it probably was v. splendid & terrific. My old love Lady P. de Bendern wasn't asked & wrote to complain. Susan Mary seemed sad to me: or am I wrong? sweet about Prich, & asked for news to convey to the Ambassadress.[7] Bill said that his Dept of Justice friends told him they had Funk sewn up[8] but little on Ed. So it was all Ardery?[9] God! I wish you'd tell me what to do. His late hours seemed to have got our London friends down somewhat: the moral for me is

1 Founded in 1948, the festival originally concentrated on Mozart operas. The initial centrepiece was *Cosi fan tutte*; the new production for 1949 was *Don Giovanni*, an opera which IB described as 'very real' and 'just like life at Oxford'. To Elliott Felkin, 8 July (sc. August) 1949.

2 Alix Hermine Jeannette de Rothschild (1911–82), née Schey de Koromla; first wife (1937–56) of Guy de Rothschild (172/4).

3 'Near'.

4 Presumably John Walker (1906–95), Chief Curator, National Gallery of Art, Washington, 1939–56, Director 1956–69, and his wife Lady Margaret (Gwendolen Mary) (1905–87), née Drummond, daughter of the 16th Earl of Perth.

5 Susan Mary was expecting her second child (the first was a son from her secret affair with Duff Cooper).

6 William S. Patten, Jr (1909–60), US Embassy, Paris, 1944–55; World Bank, Paris, 1955–8; a long-term sufferer from the emphysema that eventually killed him.

7 Presumably Evangeline Bruce (1914–95), née Bell, wife of David Bruce (145/3), the new US Ambassador; Ed Prichard had once been in love with her.

8 The handwriting evidence put forward by the FBI that Funk had forged most of the ballots was contested by the defence and did not convince the jury.

9 Philip Pendleton Ardery (b. 1914) had been Prichard's law partner before political and personal tensions ended the partnership; he volunteered significant information to the FBI against Prichard. But IB probably means Ardery's father, Judge William Breckenridge Ardery (1887–1967), to whom Prichard had confessed his guilt despite (or perhaps because of) Ardery's role in investigating the ballot-stuffing, and whose damaging evidence at the trial (after the dismissal of

obvious: but I must do something to restore his credit. Also there is a hideous rumour that Dr Bowra's lectures at Harvard were not all liked by everyone all the time: I shall stamp on that too. My intentions are 100% loyalty to the party, coûte que coûte,[1] & down with the enemy which is growing too strong. My goodness but some queer appointments seem to be being made in Washington? who is this Clark?[2] is he not a very ignorant sort of man? (this is Lady Cunard on Mr. Bevin. And I am beginning to sympathize with the point of view) the Herald Tribune[3] (surely nonsense about being sold? really Arthur must move in less irresponsible circles) was v. sound on that. The music here is splendid: my Harvard pupils are present in force: it is too warm to write: Mr Burdon Muller is reminiscing to the Comtesse de Pastré[4] about Montesquiou[5] (he started, I mean B.M., Chips Channon[6] on his awful path: by letting himself be spoken to in the Ritz in Paris in 1918, by Henry C., then unknown) & I must write letters of condolence to 3 wives of friends who have died. I enjoyed my last evening (with Judy) & regretted bitterly your business in Washington. Do write: I literally cannot communicate unincited: & need proof of interest. I did not, queer to say, for once waste too much time in Harvard: it is just too puritanical to let me fritter too much; so, oddly enough, a book may yet result. WRITE.

Isaiah   [...]

After an overnight train journey to Geneva, where he stayed with Elliott Felkin, IB addressed the Israeli Delegation to the Lausanne Conference,[7] then went on

the defence's claim that Prichard's conversation with him was privileged) was the crucial factor in Prichard's conviction.

1 'Whatever it costs'.
2 Thomas Campbell ('Tom') Clark (1899–1977), US Attorney-General 1945–9; Associate Justice of the Supreme Court 1949–67. Truman later came to agree with IB's assessment, calling Clark 'a dumb son of a bitch [...] about the dumbest man I think I've ever run across'. Merle Miller, *Plain Speaking* (New York, 1974), 226.
3 The fortunes of the Republican *New York Herald Tribune*, established in 1924, had started to decline after the death in 1947 of its publisher Ogden Mills Reid, but his family continued to publish the paper until its sale in 1958.
4 Countess Lili Pastré (1891–1974), née Double de Saint-Lambert, wealthy art patron, one of the festival's founders.
5 Count Robert de Montesquiou-Fezensac (1855–1921), French Symbolist poet, aesthete, socialite, critic and patron of the arts; allegedly Proust's inspiration for the baron de Charlus in *À la recherche du temps perdu*.
6 Henry ('Chips') Channon (1897–1958), American-born; right-wing Conservative MP 1935–58; enthusiastic appeaser with a passion for European aristocracy, famous for his posthumously published diaries.
7 Convened by the United Nations Conciliation Commission for Palestine (UNCCP) and comprising representatives of Israel, Egypt, Lebanon, Syria, Transjordan and the Palestinian refugees, this conference lasted from April to September 1949, and sought to resolve disputes outstanding from the 1948 Arab–Israeli war, principally concerning boundaries, the status of Jerusalem, the repatriation of refugees, the treatment of their land and property, and Israel's claims for compensation for war damage. It ended in failure.

to visit Chaim and Vera Weizmann at Bürgenstock, near Lucerne (where yet
another music festival was in progress).

TO ROWLAND BURDON-MULLER

Tuesday [8 August 1949, manuscript]

Bürgenstock-Hotels[1]

Dear Rowland,

Thank you for your letter which I much enjoyed: it reminded me of the whole Aix Dix Journées[2] which seem to me now – from the entourage of the Président d'Israel – idyllic. I meant to leave today: but the flesh is weak: I was bribed into staying till Thursday by the prospect of (a) a concert at which the to me fascinating pianist Edwin Fischer[3] is to play the 3ᵈ Beethoven Concerto (b) a rehearsal by the to me unknown but interesting Paul Klecki (Kletsky so to say),[4] a gifted Pole little heard in England. The President is a little unwell & so cannot anyhow go to the opening concert which is to be conducted by the not so very 'ex'-Nazi, Herr von Karajan:[5] which is just as well. Geneva was hot: & I do warn you against couchettes in French trains which are hard, dirty, soot swept, & involve the company of women & children & are really rather worse than sitting up; also against the bus to Marseilles which leaves one porterless on a blasted heath not too near the station. However I overcame these obstacles, like the prince in the *Magic Flute*, by patience, pathos, & stoicism: & arriving exhausted in Geneva didn't go on to Lausanne but stayed a night in Felkin's flat & listened to *Fidelio* on the wireless from Salzburg: Furtwängler[6] & Fröken Flagstad[7] made it into a terrifically elongated piece of Wagnerian india rubber, beautiful in a limp, Teutonic, non-romantic, humid sort of way, not what I like, not related to Mozart or Gluck or indeed Beethoven, but in the to me detestable Weber–Schumann–Wagner boneless tradition. On the next day I continued to Lausanne where I talked like an uncle to the diplomats from the Holy Land, who took it all quite well, & told them they were an ungentlemanly little State, formidable but unattractive, unless they practised civil liberties & decent methods. I there met the new American 'mediator', (the old one[8] retired sickened) Mr Paul

1 Bürgenstock was, and is, a luxurious resort on Lake Lucerne; IB stayed in the Palace Hotel.
2 'Ten days'; perhaps a reference to John Reed's eye-witness account of the Russian Revolution, *Ten Days That Shook the World*.
3 Edwin Fischer (1886–1960), Swiss pianist and conductor.
4 Paul Klecki (sometimes Kletzki) (1900–73), Polish violinist, conductor and composer.
5 Herbert von Karajan (1908–89), Austrian conductor compromised by his association with the Nazi Party from 1933; Music Director, Berlin Philharmonic, 1955–89.
6 Wilhelm Furtwängler (1886–1954), German conductor; Music Director, Berlin Philharmonic, 1922–34, 1952–4; regularly conducted *Fidelio* at post-war Salzburg Festivals.
7 Kirsten Målfrid Flagstad (1895–1962), Norwegian operatic soprano particularly known for Wagnerian roles. 'Froken' is Norwegian for 'Miss'.
8 Mark Foster Ethridge (1896–1981), newspaperman and government official; publisher of the

Porter,[1] an old New Deal ally of ours, whose affability to me raised my stock in the Israeli eyes. The trouble about the Israelis is not only their partly unconscious conviction born of experience that virtue always loses & only toughness pays, but a great provincialism & blindness to outside opinion, & a tendency to take the remarks of U.N. colleagues – who are as a rule cynical characters interested in day to day logrolling, for world opinion. I did my best & only got back an offer to become the Vansittart[2] of Tel Aviv, with splendid status & guaranteed immortality. I then went to Lucerne. Dr W[eizmann] was mainly preoccupied with fusses in his chemical institute:[3] but listened patiently to the Burdon-M. doctrine as expounded by me & agreed, so it seemed, wholeheartedly. The key word I found throughout was "ungentlemanly"!! That cuts them all to the quick. I think I have persuaded him to institute a new tradition, that of an annual address to his Parliament, a State of the Nation Speech, solemn, ceremonious & orbi et urbi,[4] in which the right things can be publicly trumpeted. I shall be after him in the relevant direction till I leave on Thursday evening. He is certainly most receptive: & agrees that the effects of post-Bernadotte cynicists were dreadful: how much of this will take, or get expressed, remains to be seen. [...] My regards to the Salems:[5] I find I am a great friend of Mme Halban who knows him well & says he is from Turkey.

    love

      I.B.

Courier-Journal of Louisville, Kentucky, 1936–63; the State Department's investigator of Balkan politics 1945–8; US representative on UNCCP 1949 (the other representatives were from France and Turkey); Trustee, Ford Foundation, 1954–67. He later recalled his brief involvement with UNCCP: 'somebody else had been designated to be the American representative and he had sense enough to see what the situation was, so he went on a binge. I was called in the last minute. [...] I kept demurring and finally Truman lost his temper and he said, "Listen, I can get a million sons of bitches to make war tomorrow, can't I get one son of a bitch to help me make peace?" I [...] got one day's briefing for each thousand years of Palestine history. [...] neither side was ready for peace [...] I finally had to ask to be released, and I suggested they designate Paul Porter [...]; but he couldn't get anywhere with it either. Nobody got anywhere with it.' Oral history interview with Mark F. Ethridge, Truman Presidential Museum and Library website, http://www.trumanlibrary.org/oralhist/ethridge.htm, accessed 10 January 2008.

1 Paul Aldermandt Porter (1904–75), journalist, lawyer and government official; US Economic Mission to Greece 1947; US representative on UNCCP 1949.

2 Robert Gilbert Vansittart (1881–1957), 1st Baron Vansittart of Denham; Permanent Secretary, FO, 1930–8; Chief Diplomatic Adviser to Foreign Secretary 1938–41.

3 The Daniel Sieff Research Institute, which Weizmann had founded in 1934, was being considerably expanded; it was rededicated as the Weizmann Institute of Science in November 1949.

4 'Urbi et orbi' ('to the city [of Rome] and to the world'), an ancient Roman formula now used in certain papal communications.

5 Raphael Salem (1898–1963), mathematician working mainly on Fourier series; born in Saloniki to a Sephardic Jewish family; studied in Paris, qualifying in law, science and engineering; took up a career in banking while pursuing mathematics as a hobby; doctorate in mathematics 1940; emigrated to US 1940; taught maths at MIT 1941–55 (Professor 1950–5), Professor of Mathematics, Caen, 1950–5 (dividing his time between the US and France), at the Sorbonne 1955–63. His wife was the former Adriana Gentili di Giuseppe (1903–76).

IB eventually arrived home to be reunited with his impatient parents and to
continue the academic work he had embarked on at Harvard. But his sciatica
was no better.

TO MARIETTA TREE

[Mid-August 1949, *manuscript*]

49 Hollycroft Avenue

Dearest Marietta,

Bob Boothby when he heard of it said "It will pass. But he will have
to change his life for the worse" – & indeed I feel like Cherubino[1] in the
Opera, that days of promiscuous delicious guzzling are over – but perhaps
not. What puzzles me more is: wd you say that I was a fear-ridden, maniac-
ally anxious, overworked, tremulous, gloomy, introspective paranoiac? If
not why am I suffering from this particular ailment? is there not something
undeserved & peculiar? or will you tell me that in my deepest subconscious
such monsters are lurking, such hideous & terrible visions as not the most
tolerant Freudian censor wd dream of passing? terrible thought. And all my
apparently innocently extrovert life, all a screen & a deception covering who
knows what horrors. Or can I really have been overworking? will anyone
believe it? anyhow thank you ever so much for asking me to Ditchley with
milk & a rusk or two: I shan't be back in Oxford till the 25th Aug. or so: but
then I shd be most grateful if I might come for a little while, provided the
Summer School I am supposed to supervise (sic indeed) doesn't turn on me
& hold me down. I shall, if I may, telephone when I get back. I am very
glad about Susan Mary: it will be a thinnish child I fear, either very very
sternly New Englandy or else a rip & a rake past bearing. I shall observe with
interest.

Love to Ronnie & thank you again.

Isaiah

TO PAUL BROOKS[2]

19 August 1949

New College [sc. 49 Hollycroft Avenue?]

Dear Mr Brooks,

Thank you very much for your cable which travelled for some time hither
and thither over the continent of Europe before finally reaching me. Arthur
Schlesinger's information to you is perfectly correct and it was very kind
of him – kind to me that is – to give it to you. I am planning a book based

---

1 A character in Mozart's opera *The Marriage of Figaro.*
2 Paul Brooks (1909–98), publisher, environmentalist and author; editor-in-chief, Houghton Mifflin
(135/2), 1943–67.

on my lectures delivered at Harvard in the spring and summer of this year, on a group of Russian Radical thinkers starting in 1825, when the abortive Decembrist rebellion[1] got the whole thing going and ending with the assassination of the Emperor, Alexander II[2] in 1881. The reason for choosing this period is that the interesting figures, who like many precursors of an event are usually more fascinating than the men of action, lived at this time; and I therefore propose to write a series of essays each dealing with a central figure – e.g. the critic Belinsky,[3] the great publicist, Alexander Herzen,[4] the revolutionary agitator, Michael Bakunin,[5] Lavrov,[6] Petrashevsky[7] and his friends in whose conspiracy Dostoevsky was involved, as well as such minor influences as Turgenev, the radical journalists Chernyshevsky[8] & Pisarev[9] etc. This is to be preceded by an introductory chapter on the radical tradition in Russia in the last [sc. late?] eighteenth and nineteenth Century and by a concluding chapter summing up the importance of these individuals and of their influence on the course of events that culminated in the Russian revolution. With the exception of E. H. Carr's *Bakunin*,[10] there is nothing adequate

1 A group mainly comprising Western-influenced, liberal-minded Army officers staged an unsuccessful revolt in St Petersburg on 14 December 1825, the first outbreak of revolutionary activity in Russia, with the aim of replacing Russia's autocratic system of government by (initially) a constitutional monarchy.

2 Alexander II (1818–81) succeeded his father Nicholas I as Tsar in 1855; in general a reformist, responsible for the emancipation of the serfs in 1861, he was assassinated by extreme revolutionaries.

3 Vissarion Grigor´evich Belinsky (1811–48), radical journalist, newspaper editor, essayist, literary critic, who saw literature of moral integrity as conducive to social reform, and whose 'Letter to Gogol' of 1847 was adopted as a manifesto of Russian liberalism (and therefore banned by the State).

4 Aleksandr Ivanovich Gertsen (the Russian transliteration of Herzen, the German name – from 'Herz', 'heart' – given by his mother to her illegitimate son) (1812–70), socialist thinker and writer who lived in Western Europe from 1847; publicist and publisher (in London) of influential exposés of the injustices perpetrated by the Russian Government; one of IB's intellectual heroes for his commitment to personal liberty and his clear-sighted and humane dislike of dogma and extremism, especially totalitarian violence inflicted in pursuit of distant Utopian goals.

5 Mikhail Aleksandrovich Bakunin (1814–76), charismatic revolutionary who spent much of his life outside Russia; ideological rival of Karl Marx; 'morally careless, intellectually irresponsible, a man who, in his love for humanity in the abstract, was prepared, like Robespierre, to wade through seas of blood' ('Herzen and Bakunin on Individual Liberty', RT2 129).

6 Petr Lavrovich Lavrov (1823–1900), alias Mirtov; friend of Karl Marx; mathematics teacher, writer of reviews and essays, who argued that the Russian intellectual élite had a moral duty to lead the struggle for social justice; important member of the Russian populist movement.

7 Mikhail Vasil´evich Butashevich-Petrashevsky (1821–66), civil servant, liberal (though perhaps not revolutionary) editor and author, host of a discussion group (including Dostoevsky) which explored socialist ideas and read banned literarure, for which in 1849 he was convicted, subjected to mock execution and exiled to Siberia.

8 Nikolay Gavrilovich Chernyshevsky (1828–89), editor, literary critic and author, leading radical in the mid-nineteenth century, who argued for revolution leading to a socialist society; his 1863 novel *What Is To Be Done?*, written in prison before he was sentenced to penal servitude followed by exile in Siberia, influenced many, including Lenin, whose identically titled revolutionary tract appeared in 1902 (see RT2 255–64).

9 Dmitry Ivanovich Pisarev (1840–68), radical social thinker and literary critic who influenced Lenin.

10 According to IB, a 'lively, informative, exceptionally readable account of the great revolutionary's

in English and scarcely anything in any other language on the forerunners of the Russian revolution, which is a queer fact, since the lives and writings of the figures I have mentioned seem to me far more interesting, even in themselves, and apart from their historical role than those of the European or American political writers of the same period. There has of course been a vast output of Soviet writing about these early heroes and martyrs but apart from bibliographical information it is largely official hagiography and almost worthless.

The book ought to be about eight or nine chapters in length and I am vaguely proposing not to make it more than 150,000 words in length, but of this I am not quite sure. I have thought of sending the first (introductory) chapter as a separate article to the *Atlantic Monthly*, and of offering some of the other chapters, e.g. the specific sketches of Belinsky, Herzen etc., either as contributions to various learned periodicals or as introductory essays in an anthology of translations from the Russian radicals,[1] a plan to issue which is at present under discussion by a group of scholars in the Russian field at Harvard and elsewhere. At any rate I ought to have something like the semblance of a book, to be entitled *Studies in Russian Radical Thought* or *Russian Radical Thinkers* or the like, by 1952. As the topic is an abiding interest with me I should like, if all goes well, to follow this up with a second volume on later Russian thinkers up to and perhaps beyond 1917. If the publication of such a volume were of interest to you I should be most interested and grateful if you would let me know your ideas on the subject.[2] [. . .]

Yours sincerely,
Isaiah Berlin.

life' ('The Father of Anarchism', review of E. H. Carr, *Michael Bakunin*, *Spectator*, 31 December 1937, 1186) and despite its faults 'a work of originality and importance [. . .] a genuine masterpiece' (to Richard Kahn, 12 December 1952).

1 This major project to translate (in seven large volumes) 'adequate amounts of the Russian political thinkers of the nineteenth century [. . .] with adequate introductions, notes etc. by competent scholars' (to N. V. Riasanovsky, 5 April 1949) had apparently been proposed by IB, who had sought the support of a range of scholars and institutions; the Harvard University Press was a potential publisher. The scheme was eventually judged commercially impracticable.

2 Houghton Mifflin's general sales manager, Hardwicke Moseley, commented to Brooks on 29 August, 'This letter from Isaiah Berlin scares the hell out of me. I don't see any sales at all and very little prestige in it. I think we ought to stay in bed and pull the sheet up over our heads' [Houghton Mifflin Company Correspondence, Houghton]. Brooks replied rather more diplomatically to IB on 8 September, recommending a continuous narrative, preferably continuing until 1917, rather than separate essays (which tended to fall into a 'commercial *oubliette*'). The book as a whole never materialised, though IB mined the topic for individual pieces, later gathered together in RT, which despite Moseley's pessimism has been continuously in print since its publication in 1978, has inspired Tom Stoppard's trilogy of plays *The Coast of Utopia* (London, 2002), and in 2008 appeared in Penguin Classics in a revised edition.

TO ALEXANDER SACHS[1]

19 August 1949 [carbon]

n.p.

Dear Alexander,

[...] I wish we could have met and talked about all these things[2] including the Rockefeller situation; I have not exactly had a misadventure with them, but the responses are all very vague and cloudy as one mounts the ladder of importance. What they ought to be encouraged to do is to promote a serious study of Russian history and Institutions at Harvard, Oxford, or wherever there are competent persons and not mind so much about the larger hope, humanism, and silly nonsense generally. If you could induce them to look into the translation scheme of the 19th-century Russian social thought which is very near my heart and which is now in the hands of Professors Karpovich[3] and Mosely[4] (of Harvard and Columbia respectively) that would indeed be a service. Also if I could come and organise the available Russian experts in Oxford – say Sumner or Obolensky,[5] Konovalov, Seton-Watson Jnr.,[6] even Beloff,[7] even myself – into some coherent scheme of publication of monographs – all that is needed is money to relieve us of our pupils and someone to egg on the sluggish to publish with date lines – carrots and all. That would be a real service since it would extract a lot of hidden learning, and it is not the nature of Oxford to ask for this themselves and indeed they would need to be slightly bullied into it. But all this will not be clear to you or convincing unless and until we can have a talk and that alas must wait until you come to

1 Alexander Sachs (1893–1973), né Sacks in Lithuania, economic adviser to commercial institutions and the US government.

2 The Prichard case and IB's letter to the *New York Times* about the report on his Mount Holyoke talk, an action which he recognises elsewhere in this letter as 'not too courageous' but on which he comments 'can it ever be wrong, when there is a babel [sc. Babel?] of confusion to say what one thinks as clearly as one can and put oneself on record unmistakably?'

3 Michael Karpovich (1888–1959), Russian-born Professor of History, Harvard, 1946–54; Curt Hugo Reisinger Professor of Slavic Languages and Literature, Harvard, 1954–7; according to IB 'a very learned and nice Russian of about 60, an ex-S[ocialist] R[evolutionary] of 1917 liberal variety, светлая личность ['a good soul'] etc.' (to his mother, 28 January 1949).

4 Philip Edward Mosely (1905–72), Professor of International Relations, Columbia, 1946–72; Professor of International Relations, Russian Institute, Columbia, 1946–55, Director 1951–5, Adjunct Professor 1955–63; President, East European Fund, 1952–61; Director of Studies, Council on Foreign Relations, 1955–63; later (1963–72) Adlai E. Stevenson Professor of International Relations, Columbia.

5 Dmitry Dmitrievich Obolensky (1918–2001), Russian-born historian; Fellow, Trinity, Cambridge, 1942–8, Lecturer in Slavonic Studies, Cambridge, 1946–8; Reader in Russian and Balkan Medieval History, Oxford, 1949–61, Student, Christ Church, 1950–85; later (1961–85) Professor of Russian and Balkan History, Oxford.

6 (George) Hugh Nicholas Seton-Watson (1916–84), son of Professor R. W. Seton-Watson; Fellow and Praelector in Politics, Univ., 1946–51; Professor of Russian History, SSEES, London, 1951–83.

7 Max Beloff (1913–99), Baron Beloff of Wolvercote 1981; Nuffield Reader in Comparative Study of Institutions, Oxford, 1946–56; Fellow, Nuffield, 1947–57; Gladstone Professor of Government and Public Administration, Oxford, 1957–74; Fellow, All Souls, 1957–74; later (1974–9) Principal, University College at Buckingham.

my abode or I to yours – surely it has been a very long time since you have been to Europe and it is time you came to Oxford? Let me know and I will arrange to welcome you as you deserve. And thank you for your letter, it will be a pleasure to hear from you on any topic.

Yours,

In early September IB took to his bed on medical advice.

TO ROWLAND BURDON-MULLER

5 September 1949

Hollycroft Avenue

My dear Rowland,

I was most delighted to get your charming letters which have solaced my sad predicament. For, I regret to tell you that on returning from Buergenstock, I fell into the hands of doctors, who have condemned me to spend a month in bed, stirring as little as possible, since my sciatica is alleged to be due to a herniated disc, whatever that may be, which only rest can cure, if I am to avoid an operation. I mind this almost less than anyone else I know. To be prone and in bed, and able to work and dictate I secretly like, and the tedium, after all the gadding about, is doubtless very good for me. But it *is* a little dull. I was therefore doubly delighted to get your letters.

My visit to Buergenstock, about which I think I wrote to you, was on the whole a success. My hosts are a gloomy couple now, and Dr W. has once more written to me, agreeing with all I said about the necessity of reaffirming moral standards but doubting whether his henchmen will let him do it, and full of despondency and woe. I may, indeed, conceive the pompous plan of telling them myself what I think they ought to do, and get nothing but abuse for my pains. As for Aix and *Don Giovanni*, I had a slight tiff with the *Observer*,[1] which proposed to publish something else by me, truncated and too late, and so I thought that perhaps it would be just as well to turn to the B.B.C. which is most amiable to me. They asked me to do something in the Third Programme, and so I have recorded two talks for them, both of which may be published in the *Listener*, one on *Don Giovanni*,[2] and one on the Anglo-American Predicament.[3] They pay far better than anybody else

1 'I was commissioned to do a piece by the *Observer*, who finally cancelled it because they had some other piece from somebody else – and here I was with my piece on Anglo-American relations and somebody at the BBC discovered about this and asked me if it could be broadcast; it was quite short.' MI Tape 21.
2 Recorded on 30 August. The original tape was accidentally destroyed so IB had to re-record the talk in a mobile van in Oxford on 26 January 1950, the day it was eventually broadcast (as 'Don Giovanni in Aix-en-Provence', on the Third Programme). A transcript is posted in the IBVL at http://berlin.wolf.ox.ac.uk/lists/nachlass/dongiovanni.pdf.
3 'The Anglo-American Predicament', broadcast on 21 September, then published in the *Listener*, 29 September 1949; included as an Appendix below, 743–8.

and the Third Programme is a miracle of civilised activity. Not only after America, but even France and Italy. It really is very good indeed, and tied to my bed as I am I listen to it with genuine avidity.

[...] My friend Clarissa Churchill wrote me a very gloomy letter about Salzburg, the atmosphere of which is half decayed Austrian aristocracy, half unrepentant Nazi, and newspapers vie with each other in printing semi-Nazi things. This doesn't surprise me, and I shall never go there again. The Ondine[1] is very much off the Coon,[2] who doesn't seem to have treated her too well, but you are not supposed to know anything of that. There is a good deal of gossip here about the very peculiar marriage of Caroline Paget to Michael Duff,[3] and of the even odder engagement of Michael Tree,[4] to Anne Cavendish.[5] [...]

Ronnie Tree is wonderfully depressed about going to America, and it is, I am sure, a stupid thing to do for anyone aged fifty or whatever he is, since one cannot, I am sure, readjust oneself at that age at all satisfactorily.

The government here did treat him rather badly[6] but he ought to be wiser than to want to spite his face by cutting off his nose.

And now I must apply myself to serious labours and use my three weeks for the purpose of some kind of intellectual import to compensate for the fearful pauperisation which I am continually aware is happening to me. This is obviously a time when people are reaching tremendous dead-ends, but I do not believe I shall ever get into the condition of Eddie Sackville-West,[7] who has just embraced Catholicism.

Harold Nicolson[8] professes to be very shocked. I wonder. But we shall discuss all this when I see you – the Ondine also says how eager she is to see you, she seems a little low. No doubt some knight on a white horse is urgently needed as she sits at her casement or leans against some weed-covered rock.

À bientôt,[9]
    Yours ever,
    Isaiah

1 The pregnant Patricia de Bendern. In German mythology, Ondine was a beautiful water-nymph whose immortality and happiness would be destroyed by bearing a mortal's child.
2 Patricia's Franco-Cuban lover Jacques (Jaime) Sanchez Abreu (1923–90); a student at MIT while Patricia was in Cambridge, Mass., during the war; grandson of Rosalia Abreu, who had built up a world-famous collection of monkeys and apes at her Havana estate.
3 Both were bisexual.
4 Michael Lambert Tree (1921–99), son of Ronnie Tree and his first wife Nancy Lancaster (602/5).
5 Anne Evelyn Beatrice Cavendish (b. 1927), daughter of the 10th Duke of Devonshire.
6 The Labour government had introduced punitive taxes on income from foreign trust funds, thus causing the financial difficulties which led Tree to sell Ditchley and move to the US.
7 Edward ('Eddy') Sackville-West (1901–65), 5th Baron Sackville 1962; musician, literary and music critic, translator and author; an Anglo-Catholic when young, he rejected religion for 25 years before converting to Roman Catholicism in 1949.
8 Harold George Nicolson (1886–1968), diplomat, author (particularly of biographies), columnist, broadcaster, politician, diarist.
9 'See you soon'; RB-M was planning a visit to Oxford.

TO FELIX FRANKFURTER

12 September 1949 [*manuscript*]

Hollycroft Avenue

Dear Felix,

Your note to hand: congratulations on your new colleague, poor Francis Biddle[1] if you see what I mean. And now I see poor Rutledge[2] is gone too – I suppose that Steelman[3] comes next? wd you rather have him or Morris Ernst?[4] or Dulles[5] himself? You must forgive all this impertinent wandering, but I am, and quite contentedly, in my most natural habitat, in bed. One look at my condition & I was pronounced to have a dislocated disc, all exercise was forbidden strictly & I was told that hard as it wd be on me, I must go to bed. For 4 weeks. I am delighted. Time, rest, books, the 3ᵈ programme from the B.B.C. very highbrow very good. Regular visits from Sylvester[6] who is charming: but reports that Prich, while here, was in a painfully heightened state, seldom sober, very odd & too much in a great spin like a monstrous top. Rather like what Mary Hand–Churchill–?[7] said to me, when I complained that that was move No 3 or so in a flirtation & not No 1 as she had assumed. To my bed of sickness rumours come vaguely floating – Judge Hand[8] had a good time with Lord Radcliffe[9] – at a dinner I cdn't attend, and Joe Rauh[10] is not as pessimistic about Edward's chances as others, I should have thought reasonably, are – what is happening in that dreadful story, like a play by Elmer Rice[11] save for its Judenfrei[12] atmosphere? as for me I forge on in my Fascist Beast Career: I have just recorded a broadcast in which I assert that one of the things which annoys Americans is the blithe British supposition

1 Francis Beverley Biddle (1886–1968), lawyer; US Attorney-General 1941–5; US member, International Military Tribunal (Nuremberg) 1945–6; National Chairman, Americans for Democratic Action, 1950–3. Biddle had earlier opposed the choice of Clark to succeed him as Attorney-General.
2 Wiley Blount Rutledge (1894–1949), US Associate Justice of the Supreme Court 1943–9.
3 John Roy Steelman (1900–99), Assistant to the President 1946–52.
4 Morris Leopold Ernst (1888–1976), lawyer (specialising in civil liberties) and author; active in the American Civil Liberties Union, which he helped to found.
5 John Foster Dulles (1888–1959), lawyer and active Republican; US delegate to UN, 1946, 1947, 1950; Secretary of State 1953–9.
6 Sylvester Govett Gates (1901–72), barrister and banker; an old friend of IB's who had worked with Frankfurter while studying at Harvard Law School.
7 Mary Dershon Hand (1905–2004), daughter of Learned Hand (next note), married first John Churchill, son of the American writer Winston Churchill, and secondly Norris Darrell, whose name clearly eluded IB.
8 (Billings) Learned Hand (1872–1961), US lawyer; judge, US Circuit Court, 1924–51.
9 Cyril John Radcliffe (1899–1977), Baron Radcliffe 1949, 1st Viscount Radcliffe 1962; barrister, judge and public servant; Lord of Appeal in Ordinary 1949–64.
10 Joseph Louis Rauh, Jr (1911–92), a former law clerk of Frankfurter's; liberal lawyer particularly committed to civil rights and liberties; co-founded, with Eleanor Roosevelt, Americans for Democratic Action 1947, Vice-Chairman 1952–5, Chairman 1955–7; counsel to United Auto Workers 1951–63, 1966–87; one of Prichard's main helpers in his appeal.
11 Elmer Leopold Rice (1892–1967), né Reizenstein, playwright, novelist and stage director.
12 'Jew-free'.

that they are in fact not indissolubly married to the U.S. – that they can & will run away, not return, go off with Western Europe, have an affair behind the curtain etc. etc. which is totally unreal & merely annoys great Realpolitiker[1] like Bill Elliott[2] & myself. It is a v. poor American 5th columny sort of talk, & will I fear, if they see it, annoy Messrs Laski & Eccles[3] equally, not to speak of Crowther,[4] Shinwell,[5] E. H. Carr, Lord Winterton,[6] Sir S. Cripps,[7] T. Balogh,[8] R. Crossman, Sir Nevile Butler,[9] Mr Pollitt[10] & other nationalists. Not that any of them will know about it, but they will have read a very able, smooth, typical letter by Eccles in this (12 Sept) morning's *Times*[11] to which I draw your attention. It is his great alibi for some later act of treachery to someone on the ground that England cd have saved herself when he told her how, but didn't choose to, so there, & that lets *him* out of obligations – & he a New College Wykehamist too!

And now for the answers to your questions:

[...] Israel. The trouble with them is that they are a somewhat ungentlemanly little state. Every other merit: brave, resourceful, efficient, formidable, but a little like Hungary in 1919[12] or Poland: fearless, but if touched, blows up: dangerous: respectworthy: but somehow not too nice. I don't say that it

1 'Advocates of practical politics'.
2 William Yandell Elliott (1896–1979), historian, poet and presidential adviser; Leroy B. Williams Professor of History and Government, Harvard, 1942–63; Director, Harvard Summer School, 1950–60; Assistant Director, Office of Defense Mobilization, 1951–3; Planning Board, National Security Council, 1953–7; State Department adviser 1958–63.
3 David McAdam Eccles (1904–99), 1st Viscount Eccles 1964, Conservative MP 1943–62; Minister of Works 1951–4, of Education 1954–7, 1959–62; President of the Board of Trade 1957–9.
4 Geoffrey Crowther (1907–72), Baron Crowther of Headingley 1968; editor, *The Economist*, 1938–56; Chairman, Central Advisory Council for Education (England), 1956–60.
5 Emanuel ('Manny') Shinwell (1884–1986), Baron Shinwell of Easington 1970; Labour politician; Minister of Fuel and Power 1945–7; Secretary of State for War 1947–50; Minister of Defence 1950–1.
6 Edward Turnour (1883–1962), 6th Earl of Winterton (an Irish title), Baron Turnour of Shillinglee 1952; Unionist politician and sometime Cabinet member; MP 1904–51.
7 Sir (Richard) Stafford Cripps (1889–1952), lawyer and Labour politician; Ambassador to Soviet Union 1940–2; Chancellor of the Exchequer 1947–50.
8 Thomas Balogh (1905–85), Baron Balogh of Hampstead (1968); Hungarian-born economist; Institute of Statistics, Oxford, 1940–55; Fellow, Balliol, 1945–73; Special Lecturer, Oxford, 1955–60; for many years economic adviser to the Labour Party in and out of government.
9 Sir Nevile Montagu Butler (1893–1973), diplomat; Minister at Washington Embassy 1940–1; Head, North American Dept, FO, 1941; Ambassador to Brazil 1947–51, to the Netherlands 1952–4.
10 Harry Pollitt (1890–1960), General Secretary, British Communist Party, 1929–60, Chairman 1956–60.
11 Eccles claimed that Britain faced a choice between economic integration with the US or with Western Europe; that those who 'favour the American solution, do not realise that if Britain withdraws from the Continent all Europe must soon be dominated either by the Russians or by the Germans. I think by the Germans'; and British separation from Europe would 'make certain the division of the world into Oceania and Eurasia, between whom a war for final mastery would appear inevitable'. *The Times*, 12 September 1949, 5.
12 A year of economic disintegration, political upheaval and bloodshed in which Hungary was governed successively by an alliance of parties dominated by the Social Democrats, the first Communist government outside the Soviet Union, and the right-wing government of Miklós Horthy.

cd have been otherwise: & it is very good as it is: but when Bernadotte was killed they didn't make enough fuss, however insincere: the attitude was, *we* mind because we don't want terrorists gnawing at our vitals, but really after 6 million slaughtered, one more Goy or one less doesn't make all *that* difference, & he a British stooge to boot. In a way one cannot wholly blame them. Whenever they behaved well they were punished for it promptly, as soon as they flouted, flaunted etc. they did well. But with a memory of where that led Germany they shd know where to stop. Ben G[urion] I am sure does. But I am not so sure about the younger people of any party. My parents came back very bezaubert.[1] As for me (your Q 4.) I saw the Dottore & Dottoressa[2] W. in Lucerne, & it is a sad business. He is a man all his life wedded to power stripped of it now most remorselessly. And he is very bitter. And now smells intrigues against himself in the Institute at Rehovoth, & behaves just like Stalin, Ivan the Terrible etc. & wd certainly hack off heads if he could: he has been treated badly: & he is in a ludicrous position: he is a man of action or nothing, not a Masaryk[3] or a Jefferson:[4] Winston at least has the Cons. party to play with: Chaim not even that: he hates the right & the left because they are right & left: the present government because it is not he; & the spectacle of a state which without him wd never have occurred, at least as it is now, gives him too little satisfaction: his health is much better though his eyes are dim & he walks like a man of 90, & his conversation still entrancing: but he alone in all that life & heat & bustle & really wonderful spring of hope & achievement is a huge bitter tragic ruin, not en rapport[5] with anyone much, childishly pleased by an hon. degree from Fribourg[6] or the visit of the Swiss Bundespräsident.[7] Mrs W. is much less ravaged, but she dreads Israel too: she is not very Jewish, she is a Russian, & has no friends there: she rightly, if snobbishly, creates the magic of distance between him & the followers which was indispensable to his position & work – but now pays for it with a great desolation & an unloved son:[8] there is a little grandchild[9] to delight them, but despite him, & the stalwart, uniformed Israel A.D.C., a 'real major', & the blue & white flag of de jure recognition & all it is a heartbreaking spectacle: two old people in a Swiss hotel, dreading the return to a theoretically glorious condition of peace with honour: like a sick old lion

1 'Bewitched'.
2 'Doctors' (male and female): Chaim Weizmann was a renowned chemist, Vera Weizmann a qualified paediatrician.
3 Tomáš Garrigue Masaryk (1850–1937), founding President of Czechoslovakia, philosopher and social thinker.
4 Thomas Jefferson (1743–1826), third US President; multi-talented political philosopher.
5 'In sympathy'.
6 Fribourg (or Freiburg) was the Swiss University where Weizmann had gained his PhD in 1899.
7 'Federal President'.
8 The Weizmanns' elder son, Benjamin (1907–80), had a more difficult relationship with them than their younger son, Michael (killed in action in 1942 while serving in the RAF).
9 David Weizmann (b. 1940), son of Benjamin and his wife Maidie.

he paces about & about. I tried to cheer them up – there being no obvious or mentionable cause of sadness: but in the end secretly succumbed myself, & left with shameful & unconfessable relief. [. . .]

Ernie. He is in a v. queer state. He seems foolishly happy like a man under gas in the dentist's chair. Our old friend Mr Eden for once ventured on almost an epigram. He goes about saying that the only people not worried about the crisis are the government – Attlee inspecting cruisers and air shows, Bevin with an idiot smile saying all is for the best, Cripps relishing the daily bitter pill administered to his colleagues etc: – the Israeli Minister, Dr Eliash,[1] maintains that Bevin wd like to end his career by suddenly doing a bon papa[2] and arranging things with Israel & forgiving & forgetting. Possibly. And no doubt it is statesmanship to suppress everything & negotiate & our old friends ought to do so. Funnily enough Helm,[3] who is a mamzer of the 1st water, spoke up for the Israelites at the F.O. Mid eastern Conference,[4] & must have helped to swing it to the Desmond Morton[5] point of view which is very good & sane. Whereas so relatively nice if colourless a man as poor Sir W. Strang[6] is hostile, particularly after the President of I. said to him at Rechoboth: 'Do you [know] Sir Villiam what you hav tried to do to os? to *morrder* us by prrroxy. Dats all.'

But your next query is stamping impatiently outside the door (you say how Buchstäblich[7] I can be)

– Mrs R. won over the Cardinal[8] hands down I thought – & the Vatican showed every sign of distress. How splendid she is – & how effective. I think Ben ought to take over Israel–Roman relations, I can conceive a Jerusalem–Vatican axis directed against the F.O. & the C. of E. very easily. As for All Souls, the delicacy of the situation is immense. I feel sure that Sumner will not make the first move, & neither shall I. elaborate strings stretching all the way to Harvard via Mr McKay will sooner or later be gently tugged at by me & an even softer, scarcely perceptible ripple will travel across the ocean and faintly ruffle the sensitized surface of Humphrey's American antenna – & still nothing will happen. And, I, like some Jane Austen heroine will sit still & continue to make nervous small talk waiting for my hand to be asked – the

1 Mordecai Eliash (1892–1950), lawyer; Israeli Ambassador to UK 1949–50.
2 'Playing the indulgent patriarch'.
3 (Alexander) Knox Helm (1893–1964), diplomat; Minister to Israel 1949–51; Ambassador to Turkey 1951–4; Governor-General of the Sudan 1955–6.
4 A gathering to exchange information between senior British diplomats based in the Middle East, held in London during July 1949.
5 Sir Desmond John Falkiner Morton (1891–1971), Personal Assistant to the Prime Minister 1940–46; Vice-Chairman, UN Economic Survey Mission for the Middle East, 1949.
6 Sir William Strang (1893–1978), 1st Baron Strang 1954, diplomat; Permanent Secretary, FO, 1949–53.
7 'Literal'.
8 In July 1949 Eleanor Roosevelt, who had little sympathy for the Roman Catholic Church, had used her syndicated newspaper column 'My Day' to criticise the State funding of some non-religious aspects of Catholic schools. Cardinal Spellman had responded with personal abuse.

proposal – but the suitor will not come up to scratch – & so I shall grow grey and spectre thin until my New College pension has matured. That is how I see it, & see no help, since no one can intervene, unless some impossible figure like Foster whom nobody would mind. Rowse[1] grows more & more impossible & awful daily. He now (a) writes letters to the Times[2] to say that education is bad for the poor, since most of them are incurably barbarous & do badly on a little knowledge, & he knows because he springs thence himself etc. & the money had better go to Oxford etc. & the opposite view is 'silly continental theory'. (b) is saying that he must vote against labour because they haven't made him a peer and also all he cares about is keeping his money & he doesn't mind saying so etc. It is all very mad & distressing, & Sumner keeps saying he ought to be Regius Professor because we must disseminate as well as create knowledge, & he does at least write books. I hesitate to repeat the opinion of him held by the Harvard history dept.

[...] There is a great flurry in Bloomsbury & King's because of the late Maynard's admission[3] that the early Bloomsbury faith is *not* valid, nice tho' it wd have been if it had been. This is thought selling oneself gracefully to the philistines, but still selling oneself – or perhaps justly peacefully surrendering – but anyhow appeasement. [...]

Love
     Shaya

When IB's views on Anglo-American relations were made known, they produced lively reactions. A column headed 'Mr Berlin' in the Evening Standard *of 5 October*[4] *was devoted to exposing the 'specious arguments' uttered by this 'acute don' whose talk had consisted of*

propaganda in favour of the immediate recognition by the British public that a state of marriage exists between Britain and America.

He pictured the American partner as resigned to the marriage, but frustrated and irritated by the failure of the British to recognise that the marriage lines had been spoken. So Mr Berlin spent the greater part of his 20 minutes trying to convince his listeners that the marriage was both desirable and inevitable.

Now why does Mr Berlin take such an interest in this marriage? He is a bachelor. Perhaps that is why his mind dwells on marriage.

1 (Alfred) Leslie ('A. L.') *Rowse (1903–97), historian and poet; for many years a colleague of IB's at All Souls.
2 'One colleague of mine, at a new university college, tells me that two-thirds of his students ought never to be at a university [...] They are not up to it, and money and resources spent on them are largely wasted. [...] quality and selection should be our guiding ideas all through our educational system, not the undiscriminating outpouring of money on the education of the hardly educable' (*The Times*, 16 August 1949, 9). Further letters from Rowse restating his arguments appeared in *The Times* on 6 and 16 September.
3 In John Maynard Keynes's 'My Early Beliefs' (1938), published posthumously in *Two Memoirs* (London, 1949): for this admission see 98 ff.
4 On p. 4.

While agreeing with IB's dismissal of alignment with Western Europe or the East, the writer deplored that IB

did not even mention the third alternative: that Britain should ride out the storm alone, placing her faith in the strength and the resources of the Empire.

Why is Mr Berlin so blind to the attractions of this simple creed? The answer is as simple. He is not an Empire man. His disdain for the Empire is as extensive as his ignorance of its glory. He cannot be expected to appreciate the value of the imperial tradition.

Mr Berlin is therefore trying to induce Britain to abandon a faith which he does not understand in favour of a condition of life which he has not experienced.

Other critics found different faults in IB's arguments.

TO THE EDITOR OF THE *LISTENER*[1]

Oxford

Sir,

I have, of course, no quarrel with the thesis of your correspondent, Mr R. H. Hilton,[2] that an increase in East–West trade is desirable. Indeed the American no less than the European planners of Marshall aid assumed the likelihood of such increase in formulating their requirements. This forecast may well turn out to have been much too optimistic, but it was firmly presupposed in predicting economic 'viability' by 1952; nor do I wish to maintain the absurd proposition, which Mr Hilton is at some pains to refute, that such increase of trade would injure the interests or threaten the liberties of Britain. But then this is not at all what an Eastern orientation is commonly held to mean. This phrase is usually held to connote the view and degree of general political sympathy (what the late Herr Hitler used to call 'loyalty', in which e.g. the Czechs proved so deficient in 1938) which was shown towards the USSR by, for instance, the Baltic Republics in 1938–9 or by Czechoslovakia in 1945–8 or by Finland today. And to maintain that such an attitude, whatever its intrinsic merits, on the part of a nation is compatible with the preservation of its full civil liberties is, in the face of recent history, scarcely plausible.

Mr Hilton shows greater fear of potential American 'economic penetration', because of 'many historical precedents', than of actual Soviet practice. Precedent for precedent Soviet acts speak louder than the most mischievous American words; the effects of Marshall aid to date can hardly be described as a threat to British democracy; it is not economic co-operation with the

1 'The Anglo-American Predicament', *Listener*, 20 October 1949, 681.
2 Rodney Howard Hilton (1916–2002), Lecturer and Reader in Medieval History, Birmingham, 1946–63; Professor of Medieval Social History, Birmingham, 1963–82. He had argued (*Listener*, 6 October) that trade with the Eastern bloc offered many potential benefits and was less likely to come with political strings attached than economic dependence on the US.

United States that threatens to undermine the social gains of British labour, but lack of resources due to economic causes too obvious to enumerate: nor is there anything in such co-operation, however close, which is incompatible with an expansion of East–West, or inter-imperial, or Western European trade, unless it is assumed that American capitalists are in full control of US policy and bent on converting Great Britain into a colonial dependency. And for this I see no adequate evidence.

Yours, etc.,
      Isaiah Berlin

TO JOSEPH ALSOP
    21 October 1949

New College
My dear Joe,

I wish you would respond to my little friendly messages which were meant to stimulate you to some sort of correspondence. There is almost nothing to report about myself.

I delivered a violently pro-American broadcast of which I ought to send you a copy, but which perhaps you might procure for yourself. It was in the *Listener* of 29 September. It was called 'The Anglo-American Predicament'. What it said was that America was married to England, did not necessarily enjoy the thought, but the marriage was indissoluble; that England did not consider herself married at all, at least not irrevocably, and that all her threats to run away and not come back merely irritated the realistic Americans, who realised that she would have to come back in the end, after knocking about in disreputable places in Eastern Europe, and that there would be a doctor's bill to settle as well. Or something of the sort, expressed in more pompous language. It produced not only angry correspondence by various local isolationists, but also a terrifying blast by Lord Beaverbrook[1] in the leading article in the *Evening Standard* of 5 October (I am sending you none of the documents, for I fear they may amuse you) with the horrifying headline, 'Mr Berlin', [which] does a sort of Westbrook Pegler[2] on me and reveals my unfitness for giving advice of this type to the British people. This in its turn produced a mass of sympathetic condolences, and I found myself in a most disagreeable limelight for some days. My colleagues were excited and horrified – rather as if one had been discovered to have a lurid political past as a favourite to a dissolute ruler – and my stock simultaneously went up and down, if you see

---

1 IB had commented to Alsop on 9 October: 'it is v. Hearstish, personal & below the belt. But does Lord B. know where the belt is?'
2 Westbrook James Pegler (1894–1969), US journalist and syndicated columnist; vehement right-wing critic of, among others, FDR and Eleanor Roosevelt.

what I mean. On the other hand, the article on Churchill[1] produced some unfavourable comment among my left-wing friends, so what with blasts from right and left I am in a queer position. After my articles on American vs. British students, to appear in *Time and Tide*[2] (I shall not forward a copy – I publish but am terrified of being read), my position in Oxford as well as my return to the United States would doubtless be still more severely shaken.

You really might send me a line and tell me what is going on. I deserve and need every comfort. My impression of our rulers is that they are like an acrobat on a tightrope with a large net cosily below them; they know that if they fall they will fall into the net (USA) and will suffer at worst loss of face but not of life. They realise subconsciously that they will never be allowed to sink utterly, if only from the most self-regarding motives. And this takes away from the acute sense of crisis which otherwise would drive them dotty. They are like the son who knows that his debts will ultimately be settled by his annoyed and angry parents, with much humiliation all around, but that he will not go to jail. Hence no pistols, and no talk of suicide, and no desperate remedies, and Attlee, Cripps etc. are in a relatively quiet frame of mind, excellent for conditions of business but not for spectacular heroism or ideas of genius. This view on my part is not well received in any quarter, and I keep it dark. I have sold out to the United States long ago in my own mind, and am now patiently waiting for events to catch up. I may be wrong, but I think not. The two axes of British foreign policy seem to be reluctance to surrender to the USA, accompanied by hot denials of it, plus assumptions that there will not be war with the Soviet Union. I am beginning to think that Communism in China[3] really is the beginning of some kind of very formidable end, but I am still incapable of thinking about that country and perhaps am thereby disqualified from having political opinions. Do tell me what you think, and settle the enclosed bill for me.

My private life is wonderfully uneventful. I teach, or I write on two books; I feel elderly and responsible, and every act against this is a kind of escapade unsuited to my years. I shall therefore not attend the Duchess of Devonshire's party to celebrate her daughter's engagement, shall not be meeting the new master of Ditchley,[4] who, I think, is a friend of Judy's, and generally shall behave in every way like a nice dim don.

When are you coming to Europe? You might come and spend a quiet

1   This had appeared in the US in the September issue of *Atlantic Monthly*; on 19 September Myron Gilmore had reported on the 'wonderful and deserved success your Churchill article is having. It is read and discussed everywhere.' The article was published in the British *Cornhill Magazine* in mid-December.

2   A political and literary magazine founded by Lady Rhondda, a committed feminist, in 1920. The magazine never had a large circulation, always lost money, and closed in 1977.

3   A Communist government had been declared in the new People's Republic of China on 1 October 1949 at the end of a long civil war.

4   Seymour William Arthur John Egerton (1921–99), 7th Earl of Wilton, whose tenure of Ditchley Park was brief: it was sold again in 1953.

week here far from the ladies Colefax and B. [sc. P.?] Berry, whom I shall see at rarer and rarer intervals. I have been in this mood successfully now for a month, and there is no reason why it should stop. London is very far away. It is all suspiciously like poor Prich, but I do not feel that I shall end up exposed for stuffing ballots in a New College election of the Professor of Russian.

How is Prich? I have not written to him yet. I must, I must.

Yours ever,

Isaiah   [...]

TO ARTHUR SCHLESINGER

21 October 1949

New College

My dear Arthur,

Thank you very much for your two splendid letters, which came almost simultaneously. After three weeks in bed – what a wonderful opportunity that gives of working solidly for once – if one cannot have a wife, one at least enjoys the stern protection of a conscientious mother – I suddenly found myself in a most horrible limelight. Overflowing as you know me to be with pro-American sentiment, I delivered a passionate address upon the third pro-gramme of [the] BBC, explaining how indissoluble the marriage between England and America was, implying that it was not merely inevitable, but desirable, etc. This brought down upon my head the terrible wrath of Lord Beaverbrook in person, who, ever since I refused his offer of Parliament in 1945, has regarded me with some resentment. The leading article in the *Evening Standard* entitled, hideously, 'Mr Berlin' blasted me from top to toe. I was described as a don, a raconteur, as 'not an Empire man', which I fear is a euphemism for something far far worse ⟨⟨which you can guess⟩⟩. ⟨I fear that your friend Mr Wintour[1] is the suspected author – that he is accused of every crime, from venality to antisemitism, & that after my heroic efforts to get him on to Sir O[liver] F[ranks]'s staff! You might reproach him?⟩ A correspondence in the *Listener* ensued. Simultaneously with this the article on Churchill percolated with consequent thunder from the left. So there I was, execrated from both sides as a kind of pro-American traitor moved by unintelligible motives. Something possesses me to go on publishing more and more ephemeral stuff about the Anglo-American situation, but I have now stopped, and am keeping myself to more serious tasks.

1 Charles Vere Wintour (1917–99), journalist (then political editor), *Evening Standard*, 1946–52, deputy editor 1954–7, editor 1959–76, 1978–80; assistant editor, *Sunday Express*, 1952–4, managing editor 1957–9. Taxed by Arthur Schlesinger with anti-Semitism, Wintour protested: 'The sug-gestion of anti-Semitism is of course absolutely ridiculous. The phrase "not an Empire man" is copyright by the Beaver, who dictated almost word by word large hunks of the leader, and it covers anyone who does not agree with his own peculiar Empire policies' [MSB 278/5, extract enclosed with Schlesinger's letter of 11 December to IB].

Your book[1] has arrived, but so far all I have seen in it is a passage pointed out to me where you make me responsible for a sinister movement called NCL.[2] I must say the footnote opens up a really terrifying picture of the secret movement inside the United States government operated by just such an agent as Mr Wallace imagines me to be. The research carried out on my 'influence' on, let us say, Harriman,[3] may turn up literally anything. Would you really say that the NCL was a movement in a sense in which the OTAG (Order of Trembling Amateur Gentiles) is not? I cannot believe, despite Charlie Thayer[4] and all the jokes Chip and I used to make about it, that the NCL was ever any more than a funny Washington phrase which Marquis Childs[5] took too seriously. ⟨on the other hand it might be maintained that words is exactly what creates entities, Logos,[6] a sociological hypothesis very akin to Sorokin's.⟩ But I must read the rest of your book now – is it possible that I was involved in the vast event as unaware of my own and other people's part in it as the English governess in the French Revolution who disliked the noise in the streets and the funny dirty red bonnets? Also I am trying to get Mr Viereck's book[7] about which I must say I agreed with Mac Bundy's[8] review in the *Reporter*[9] – considerably more to the point than his encomium of the to me still unintelligible work by dear Sam Beer.[10]

1 *The Vital Center: The Politics of Freedom* (Boston, 1949).
2 Non-Communist Left. The reference is to a footnote on p. 168: 'A full history of the NCL movement would have to include the key role of a brilliant Oxford don, Isaiah Berlin.'
3 (William) Averell Harriman (1891–1986), businessman, diplomat and Democratic politician; US Ambassador to the Soviet Union 1943–6, to the UK 1946; Secretary of Commerce 1946–8; US Coordinator, European Recovery Program, 1948–50; Special Assistant to the President 1950–2; Governor, State of New York, 1955–9.
4 Charles Wheeler Thayer (1910–69), writer and diplomat; head of international broadcasting at Voice of America 1947–9; brother of Avis Bohlen (176/4).
5 Marquis William Childs (1903–90), journalist and author; columnist, United Feature Syndicate, 1944–54; special correspondent, St Louis Post-Dispatch, 1954–62.
6 An allusion to the divine *logos*, the Word of God, incarnated (for Christians) in Jesus ('the Word was made flesh, and dwelt among us', John 1:14).
7 Peter Robert Edwin Viereck (1916–2006), poet, political thinker and specialist in Russian history; Professor of History, Smith College 1946–7, Mount Holyoke College 1948–87. His book was *Conservatism Revisited: The Revolt Against Revolt, 1815–1949* (New York, 1949).
8 McGeorge ('Mac') Bundy (1919–96), political analyst, Council on Foreign Relations, 1948–9; Visiting Lecturer, Harvard, 1949–51, Associate Professor of Government 1951–4, Professor 1954–61, Dean of Faculty of Arts and Sciences 1953–61; later (1961–66) Special Assistant to the President for National Security Affairs, and (1966–79) President of the Ford Foundation. In his review ('Return to Metternich', *Reporter*, 11 October 1949, 38) Bundy questioned Viereck's attempted rehabilitation of Metternich's political philosophy.
9 The *Reporter*, a US news magazine, liberal in outlook, edited and published by Max Ascoli (146/2), appeared fortnightly between 1949 and 1968.
10 Samuel Hutchison Beer (1911–2009), Assistant Professor, Harvard, 1946–8, Associate Professor 1948–53, Professor of Government 1953–71 (thereafter Eaton Professor of the Science of Government). In *The City of Reason* (Cambridge, Mass., 1949), Beer took A. N. Whitehead's system of metaphysics as the basis for a philosophy of liberalism. Bundy's review is '"City of Reason"', *Reporter*, 13 September 1949, 17–18.

Here all is wonderfully quiet and peaceful, and life consists of trying to explain to Dr Bowra why it is that he is still not regarded as a steady pillar of Conservative tradition by the permanent university officials, who are scared to death of his impending reign[1] over the University of Oxford, and choose me of all people to confide their fears to. I have to thank you for a thousand things: for putting me on with Messrs Houghton Mifflin,[2] with whom ultimately I shall try to do some business; for originally stimulating Dean Buck on my behalf; but of course principally and mainly for transforming my entire existence in Cambridge, Mass., which I now see as a delightful idyll, in contrast to Dr Bowra, who does not speak of it at all, and merely occasionally grinds his teeth when he thinks of the mind and face of Harry Levin; but I must not go on – otherwise this will become pure MacLeish.[3]

I am sending to see you a Miss Betty Ackroyd,[4] who is a kind of prodigy. I wonder if you will like her. She is tremendously English, brought up in Oxford, consumed with moral integrity and an organising passion, the Chairman of the OEEC Iron and Steel Committee, too severe for Sir O. Franks, rather like someone out of George Eliot. Quite unique, and I consider very nice. You should have seen her with sheer moral unswervingness reducing shifty French and Belgian industrialists to a terrible pulp in Paris in 1947. ⟨When Sir S. Cripps was not quite straight with the French she declined to speak to him for 3 days – Florence Nightingalish she is.⟩ She is certainly a woman of the future, and remarkably unlike Mary McCarthy. I am much interested in your lunch with Parsons;[5] I enjoyed your attack[6] forwarded by the faithful George Fischer,[7] and can only say – I can't say more – that I couldn't have put it better myself. What is the defence, I should like to know? Do tell me if it is something we have not thought of. [...]

I wrote a nice long critical letter to a man called Barrington Moore[8] about

1 Bowra was to be the Vice-Chancellor of Oxford University 1951–4.

2 A Boston publishing company specialising in educational texts.

3 Archibald MacLeish (1892–1982), poet and liberal political activist; Boylston Professor of Rhetoric and Oratory, Harvard, 1949–62.

4 (Dorothy) Elizabeth ('Betty') Ackroyd (1910–87), civil servant 1940–70; Commonwealth Fund Fellow 1949–50; Director, Steel and Power Division, Economic Commission for Europe, 1950–1; UK Delegation to High Authority of European Coal and Steel Community 1952–5.

5 Talcott Parsons (1902–79), Professor of Sociology, Harvard, 1944–73, Chairman, Department of Social Relations, 1946–56.

6 Schlesinger had attacked sociologists, including by implication Kluckhohn, in 'The Statistical Soldier', *Partisan Review* 16 No 8 (August 1949), 852–6, reviewing *The American Soldier*, the first two (of four) volumes comprising the series 'Studies in Social Psychology in World War II'.

7 George Uri Fischer (1923–2005), son of the journalist Louis Fischer; Associate, Russian Research Center, Harvard, 1947–61; Assistant Professor, Brandeis University, 1953–8, Associate Professor of History 1958–60; taught later at Cornell, Columbia and the City University of New York.

8 Barrington Moore, Jr (1913–2005), political sociologist; Russian Research Center, Harvard, 1948–79, senior research fellow from 1951; 'reclusive, sharp, and demanding in the classroom' (obituary by Benjamin L. Weintraub, *Harvard Crimson*, 28 October 2005, A10). He had sent IB a pre-publication copy of his *Soviet Politics: The Dilemma of Power* (Cambridge, Mass., 1950) for comment.

his book; I can't do right I fear: the poor man replied that he would be more troubled by my criticism if he were not told the opposite by others, and that I should not refer to his book as a thesis, since he had written that many years before. In the future I shall produce nothing but praise so fulsome that it will at once be seen through, but impossible to show up.

My own plans are moving very slowly; I should on the whole quite like to move to A[ll] S[ouls] and I am assured that it is indeed possible, and even probable, in about a year, in which case I could come back to Harvard from time to time. But a year is a long time, and Sumner is a very timid and tentative man. So I must try to crystallise things a little sooner. But in the meantime I cannot write anything definite to Dean Buck. However, I shall try to keep it gently simmering one way or another. ⟨Do remind him of me from time to time. Or perhaps better not.⟩

Is it true that Joe and Chip have really quarrelled? Or is it merely another of these tiresome collisions so boring to all our friends? What is the news of Prich? I haven't written to him yet, but only to Phil telling him to act as he suggested,[1] out of my possessions in his care rather than in yours. Can an appeal really yield anything?

Myron Gilmore[2] has written me a most magnificent letter which raises genuine issues of principle which I must think about before answering; and as is known, that is, for academic persons, an unwelcome prospect. However, I will very soon. I really have the greatest admiration for him. He has the effect on me of shaming me into a reexamination of the moral premises of both what I believe and how I behave, much in the way in which fifteen years ago (and not since) Stephen Spender used to. Don't tell him this, or he will think that I treat him like a clergyman or a moral confessor, which is not quite right. But although I am sure he regards himself as riddled with doubts and weaknesses, in fact he is mistaken; his wife[3] is right, and he is very rock-like; in the Revolution I should follow him unhesitatingly; there is nothing better I like than the feeling that there is someone to whom I can have that relationship. The more tentative his manner, the more inexorable the principles which are visible through it. Really he is a very splendid man. His task at present, however – before the Revolution, that is – is to rescue Stuart Hughes[4] – a full-time job –

1 To contribute on IB's behalf towards a fund set up to help Prichard, who was in serious financial difficulties, to pay the legal expenses of his appeal.
2 Myron Piper *Gilmore (1910–78), Renaissance scholar; Associate Professor of History, Harvard, 1942–54, Professor 1954–74; married to Sheila Dehn (next note).
3 Sheila Gilmore (1917–95), née Dehn; English stepdaughter of A. N. and Evelyn Whitehead's son North.
4 (Henry) Stuart Hughes (1916–99), cultural and intellectual historian; Associate Professor of History and Associate Director, Russian Research Center, Harvard, 1948–52, Professor 1957–75 (Gurney Professor of History and Political Science from 1969); Associate Professor, then

and to stop R. Wolff[1] from denigrations of Mosely. To that let him direct himself. [...]

Love to Mrs Roosevelt.

Yours ever,

Isaiah

⟨Forgive me this very silly letter: I shall try & be serious, informative & morally solider next time. The cold grey blanket of Oxford takes sometime to sink into – but I shall re-emerge by winter.⟩

TO THE EDITOR OF THE *LISTENER*[2]

Oxford

Sir,

Mr R. H. Hilton asserts[3] that it is impossible sincerely to advocate East–West trade without believing (*a*) that political pressure by the Soviet Union is seldom, if ever, a source of danger to societies attached to their civil liberties, and (*b*) that the policy of the United States does at present constitute precisely such a danger. I am to believe (*a*) because its opposite is too often used as camouflage for reactionary policies, and (*b*) because it is true. In my last rejoinder to Mr Hilton, I stated my reasons for believing (*a*) not to be the case; nor is the fact that true propositions are sometimes liable to misuse by propagandists for their own bad purposes a good reason for declaring them to be false or drawing false conclusions from them. I do not believe that East–West trade depends on the truth of (*a*); and for this I gave reasons which Mr Hilton does not discuss.

As for (*b*), one would not have guessed from Mr Hilton's letter that Mr Thomas Dewey[4] had in fact lost the United States elections in 1948; yet he did lose them; his friends are not in power; and if they try to exercise the kind of undesirable financial pressure feared by the French circles to which Mr Hilton refers, this kind of thing should, of course, be resisted, not without the help of that same United States administration whose political colour

---

Professor, of History, Stanford, 1952–7; his career at Harvard was damaged by his left-wing political activities, particularly his support for presidential candidate Henry Wallace in 1948.

1 Robert Lee Wolff (1915–80), Assistant (then Associate) Professor of History, Wisconsin, 1947–50; Associate Professor of History, Harvard, 1950–5, Professor 1955–65, later (1965–80) Coolidge Professor of History.

2 'The Anglo-American Predicament', *Listener*, 10 November 1949, 813. At the end of this letter the editor announced that the correspondence was now closed.

3 In his response (*Listener*, 29 October, 723), Hilton had outlined the dangers of economic colonisation, described as 'somewhat ingenuous' the claim that 'capitalists do not control US policy' and pointed to the restrictions being placed by the US on the civil liberties of Marxists and, in one instance, their lawyers.

4 Thomas Edmund Dewey (1902–71), Republican presidential candidate 1944 and 1948.

Mr Hilton so firmly chooses to ignore. As for the trial of the Communists in New York, I see no reason why this should affect the course of British justice; if it is wrong to condemn men for their opinions rather than their acts (the lawyers in the trial were condemned for an astonishing degree of contempt of court, and not for the reasons given by Mr Hilton) we are free to denounce and avoid such procedures in this country (as I hope we should), and although it is possible to do so in this country at the moment perhaps more effectively than in the United States, there is no comparison between either Britain or the United States and that half of Europe from which Mr Hilton indeed anticipates no danger to civil liberties, yet where such trials cannot be protested, nor could either Mr Hilton's letters or mine conceivably have been allowed to appear. Mr Hilton cannot seriously mean to maintain in this day and hour that civil liberties, as they are understood in this country, are in a more flourishing condition in eastern Europe than in the United States. Or to say more than that all is not well even in the comparatively free American democracy. With this last I should not disagree. Nor would the President of the United States.

Yours etc.

Isaiah Berlin

IB's disorganised lifestyle at this time concerned his friends on both sides of the Atlantic:

Isaiah seems to have recovered from his bad back and is on the straight for the moment. But he always gets ill. It comes from never going to bed and leading the lives of five men. In the end nature, who is quite tolerant really, complains and swipes him one. His rooms are too odd. Rather nice, with a good view of the New College garden, but covered with books in piles on the floor, gramophone records, cooking apparatus, parcels of food, unopened letters, telephones ... I wonder he can live in it, but it suits him. He has much too much teaching to do and seems to do a lot late at night. Perhaps a good time for him, but what about the poor victims?[1]

Music provided IB with distraction from his academic duties.

TO SHIRLEY ANGLESEY

3 December 1949 [*manuscript*]

New College

Dearest Shirley

I am glad that you are recovered: still more that you are heading South again this month: as for me I shan't get away from this now dank & morose marsh till the 15th or so: I don't think I could face Lohengrin: I really detest

1 Maurice Bowra to Alice James, 5 November 1949 [Wadham College Archives, Oxford].

the composer, more than people who have been through a Wagnerian phase
& out again: I suppose I cd listen to the Flying Dutchman if *very* well done:
or even Tannhäuser: but not Lohengrin, not now, if you see what I mean,
not after hearing bits of it here & there & being violently hostile to them.
Although I expect it is charming really, & all this is non-musical preconception of some kind. How long are you in London for? do write to me here
(before the 15th) or to 49 Hollycroft Av. or telephone, after. Meanwhile we
had a rather unexpectedly agreeable Iphigenia in Tauris here: the singers
cdn't act, nor the producers produce, but it was very beautiful all the same.
Gluck[1] is a divine composer & I can't think why Armide, for example, isn't
done more often: we were honoured by the arrival of Lord Harewood[2] who
was v. gracious, & I thought, very nice. The Countess, though agreeable
enough, seemed somewhat null to me: is that unjust? What other music are
you going to hear? I am v. musically starved: but what other starvation does
Dr Bowra protect me from?

   Love
      Isaiah

*IB's American friends soon had more to disturb them. His articles[3] on the
intellectual life of American universities appeared in the British periodical*
Time and Tide *in three weekly instalments from 12 November;* Time *magazine
then attempted to summarise them for its American readers.[4] Arthur Schlesinger
wrote at once in shock and reproof.[5]*

1 Christoph Willibald von Gluck (1714–87), German composer of, among other operas, *Armide*
   (1777) and *Iphigénie en Tauride* ('Iphigenia in Tauris', 1779). This production of Gluck's last
   major opera took place in Oxford Town Hall; the *Times* music critic commented: 'The Oxford
   University Opera Club did Gluck's other *Iphigenia* many years ago and it was a fitting choice
   to undertake its twin, since only amateurs will tackle them.' 'Oxford University Opera Club,
   "Iphigenia in Tauris"', *The Times*, 1 December 1949, 2.
2 George Henry Hubert Lascelles (b. 1923), 7th Earl of Harewood; editor, *Opera* magazine, 1950–3;
   Director, Royal Opera House, 1951–3, on staff 1953–60; many later positions in the worlds of
   music and football. On 29 September he had married Maria Donata ('Marion') Stein (b. 1926), née
   Theresa Pamplamousse Stein in Austria, concert pianist and opera singer, who after their divorce
   married Jeremy Thorpe.
3 'Notes on the Way' column, *Time and Tide*, 12, 19 and 26 November 1949. Included below as an
   Appendix, 'The Intellectual Life of American Universities', 749–60.
4 The purported summary, a selection of (mainly critical) quotations from IB's three articles,
   appeared in the issue of *Time* dated 12 December (but on sale earlier).
5 'I have only seen the first of your *Time and Tide* pieces. I very much regret to say that it sounded
   to me very much like the kind of pieces British travelers write about America; indeed, it sounded
   more sensible in *Time* than in the original. Your thesis about our preoccupation with the social
   consequences of learning does apply, I think, to many of the undergraduates; but surely not to
   the faculty.' Arthur Schlesinger to IB, 11 December 1949.

TO ARTHUR SCHLESINGER

21 December 1949

New College

My dear Arthur,

Thank you very much for your letter and valuable enclosures. I am easily moved to repentance, feel myself misunderstood and long to rush into print (as well you know) and explain myself at immense length in letters to the public, to my friends, etc. etc. But, taught by bitter experience, I desist. The *Time* article plunged me, of course, into the deepest dismay: you must remember that I suffer from the deepest contempt for everything I have ever written – no sooner does it appear in print that it seems hollow, false, vulgar, glib, clumsy, at once too smooth and too awkward, but above all it has long since ceased to convey anything I wish to say; and if I defend it, it is out of pure pique – it always seems to me that everything my detractors say is *always* profoundly true and unanswerable. This is what happened with my broadcast – immediately I felt I had overdone it, I had understated the British position, insulted my compatriots, over-praised America and, anyhow, failed to convey all the elaborate nuances upon which everything depends. Clearly, if that is how one is, one mustn't have political positions at all, except for purely private purposes, least of all rush into print. And with the articles in *Time and Tide* I now feel profoundly dissatisfied (not to say virtuously indignant): I don't think I said anything that is false, but clearly you detect some sort of shallow, superior, world-weary, patronising false tone which I myself vehemently denounce in the case of Connolly, Osbert Sitwell, even Stevens.[1] (the thought that I am not as far away from Gorer[2] is what really gets my goat – after my passionate denunciations of his revolting gibes about America etc.) I do certainly think that there is too much moral preoccupation, not merely on the part of the students, but on the part of persons who determine University policies in America, obviously less so at Harvard and I dare say Princeton and Yale, and possibly Columbia, than in the Middle West, but in the departments I came across – the Russian-Sociological, and, during the election of the Professor, the Philosophy ⟨not dept., but electors,⟩ – it stuck out rather, at least in comparison with Oxford and Cambridge, though we are leaning that way, too. But in fact, of course, I was talking mainly about the students and I dare say exaggerated their moralism, too, but *Time* seems to me to have lifted all the critical bits and to have left out all

1 Presumably the modernist American poet Wallace Stevens (1879–1955).
2 Geoffrey Edgar Gorer (1905–85), (amateur) British anthropologist and sociologist, student of Margaret Mead; spent several years working and travelling in America; wrote *The Americans: A Study in National Character* (London, 1948; as *The American People*, New York, 1948), and then (with John Rickman) *The People of Great Russia: A Psychological Study* (London, 1949), in which the swaddling of infants is identified as a major formative influence on the Russian character; in 1950 he returned to Britain and concentrated on analysing the English.

the profound ones, and gave me a sense of nightmare. I can see how all this emphasis on moral vitality plus inability to write coherently, etc. conjures up a picture of the virtuous Huron,[1] the stock figure who lacks the exquisite sensibilities and fastidiousness and balance and civilised approach and inner poise and all the rest of it which are supposed to make European life worth living, and if that is the picture I conveyed, I am really ashamed; but is it? Do I? What I wanted to say was that American students on the whole, quite apart from their splendid, and to me more sympathetic, 'Russian' characters, also actually had more to say and a vision which was more original ⟨& much larger & freer⟩ and an intellect which was tougher and more capable of producing great original critics like E. Wilson than our delicate culture, which produces Desmond MacCarthys[2] and my own dear friend David Cecil, whom intellectually speaking I would swap for Wilson and even the Harvard English faculty as it stands with all its persecutions any day (may Dr Bowra ⟨& my other colleagues⟩ never hear this, he really does loathe it rather ⟨– this is a blackmailing weapon in yr hands of an efficacy I cannot overstate.⟩). I suppose that I rode my thesis too hard – about the danger to scholarship and love of subjects from the wave of world-improving techniques – and perhaps I used American students too much as a medium for preaching, but, believe me, in comparison with Oxford the moral preoccupation of American higher education – and I do not mean Harvard especially ⟨although, of course it must have seemed so in the articles – & especially *Time*⟩ – is tremendous; I do not mean that the professors adulterate their subjects to meet moral criteria, ⟨⟨though I daresay some do: in the 'social' subjects such as govt. & philosophy too⟩⟩ but that people's political pasts seem too relevant to their present relationships – the Hugheses, the Levins, the Schorskes,[3] Wilson himself indeed, not to speak of MacLeish etc. and indeed even yourself, are so affected, as was I, by who was and who had not been a fellow-traveller, when and how, that this in itself confuses things and causes complications which on the whole we are free from, and certainly drearier and less interesting – again, believe me – as a result; and possibly happier, too. ⟨I don't mean that intellectuals pay too much attention to an intrinsically non essential characteristic – political affiliation; I mean that it *is* a central factor in the life of the US intelligentsia – & there is such a body more than anything here now – & stems from & partly causes an approach of dons as moral teachers, a responsible minority on whom, e.g. as by M[a]cLeish the decadence of the times can be plausibly blamed, or who, like

1 In his satire *Le Huron, ou L'ingénu* (1767) Voltaire mocks the religious and political systems in France through his portrayal of the misfortunes of a naïve visitor at a loss in a sophisticated country.
2 Desmond MacCarthy (1877–1952), critic and author; David Cecil's father-in-law.
3 Carl Emil Schorske (b. 1915), cultural historian and socialist; Assistant Professor of History, Wesleyan University 1946–50, Associate Professor 1950–5, Professor 1955–60; later Professor of History at Berkeley (1960–9) and Princeton (1969–80).

Levins, the Schorskes, Wilson himself indeed, not to speak

of McLeish, etc. and indeed even yourself, are so affected,

as was I, by who was and who ~~was~~ (had been) not, a fellow-traveller, when

and how, that this in itself confuses things and causes

complications which on the whole we are free from, and (certain) drearier

and less interesting - again, believe me - as a result; and

possibly happier, too. This kind of moral preoccupation I did

not mention in the articles and preferred the more commonplace,

noble young man concerned about the poor [model], but in the

end it comes to the same. But surely I said all this to you

hundreds of times in conversation and did you stop me? Or

or did I not? At any rate I feel as after the New York Times

headline - I wish that nothing had happened at all and I were

back in 1939 or thereabouts,

        Also, it was very well for me to preach devoted

scholarship and high academic standards when here I am frittering

away, writing and talking simultaneously about Communism and (Br Dell Smith)

Old Russia and (Churchill &) music and political theory and Anglo-American

relations and Prince Mirsky and epistemology and ~~India and~~

the logic of conditional sentences and God knows what else,

including the Encyclopaedia Britannica on Contemporary Culture,

indulging above all in journalism against academic journalism

like someone calling a public meeting to protest against the

unfortunate habit of holding public meetings. I feel like Joe

in one of his darker self-lacerating moods.

        Above all, I feel a cad. After all, nobody could

have enjoyed Harvard more than I did or liked individuals in

it better or made warmer friendships. Oxford descended on me

like a grey blanket after all that. I am genuinely sorry I

cannot come in 1950 (but my secret plan to return to All Souls -

and so be able to come back again to Harvard won't work unless

I give up 1950) and although I do not believe that Mackay or

Buck ~~or~~ Brinton or Donald Williams or any of those men will refuse

to have me back as a result of what they see in Time magazine,

yet I feel an ungrateful guest, almost a viper. And since Conant

Page 3 of IB's letter to Arthur Schlesinger, 21 December 1949

Dos Passos[1] can write political tracts in the sense in which say H. G. Wells[2] didn't quite. I don't mean that this kind of preoccupation is necessarily bad for splendid standards in writing & scholarship of all kinds – it is even good for it, provided the opposite is really obscurantist as in Russia in the 1870ies etc. – but not where the sides are confused, there is no single great brave liberal tradition with universally honoured martyrs and saints, but mainly a domestic squabble between persons moving forwards & backwards & sideways in all directions & sure neither of the goals nor of the value of trying to discover them by slow & costly methods.⟩ This kind of moral preoccupation I did not mention in the articles and preferred the more commonplace, noble young man concerned about the poor [model][3] ⟨what model? where? curious touch of Freudian Bohème – models aren't poor in the US – very odd.⟩, but in the end it comes to the same. But surely I said all this to you hundreds of times in conversation, and did you stop me? Or did I not? At any rate I feel as after the *New York Times* headline – I wish that nothing had happened at all and I were back in 1939 or thereabouts.

Also, it was very well for me to preach devoted scholarship and high academic standards when here I am frittering away, writing and talking simultaneously about Communism and Bedell Smith,[4] Old Russia ⟨& Churchill &⟩ music and political theory and Anglo-American relations and Prince Mirsky[5] and epistemology and the logic of conditional sentences and God knows what else, including the Encyclopaedia Britannica on Contemporary Culture,[6] indulging above all in journalism against academic journalism like someone calling a public meeting to protest against the unfortunate habit of holding public meetings. I feel like Joe in one of his darker, self-lacerating moods.

Above all, I feel a cad. After all, nobody could have enjoyed Harvard more than I did or liked individuals in it better or made warmer friendships. Oxford descended on me like a grey blanket after all that. I am genuinely sorry I cannot come in 1950 (my secret plan ⟨& it really is secret, at least from English ears, at the moment⟩ to return to All Souls – and so be able to come back again to Harvard – won't work unless I give up ⟨journeys in⟩ 1950)

1 John Roderigo Dos Passos (1896–1970), US novelist, poet, essayist and dramatist whose youthful socialism inspired his best work.
2 Herbert George Wells (1866–1946), English novelist and social thinker.
3 The square brackets are IB's. He must have meant 'the noble-young-man-concerned-about-the-poor model'.
4 General Walter Bedell Smith (1895–1961), US Ambassador to Soviet Union 1946–9; Director, CIA, 1950–3; Under-Secretary of State 1953–4. For what IB wrote about him, see 147/2.
5 Prince Dmitry Petrovich Svyatopolk-Mirsky (1890–1939), pen-name D. S. Mirsky, aristocratic Russian literary critic; taught at London University during the 1920s, then turned to Communism and returned to the Soviet Union, but was eventually sent to the Gulag. IB was working on 'Russian Literature: The Great Century', his review of Mirsky's classic *A History of Russian Literature* (*Nation*, 25 February 1950, 180–3, 207–8).
6 IB contributed 'The Trends of Culture' to 'The Year 1949 in Historical Perspective', in *1950 Britannica Book of the Year* (Chicago/Toronto/London, 1950), xxii–xxvii.

and although I do not believe that Mackay or Buck or Brinton[1] or Donald Williams[2] or any of those men will refuse to have me back as a result of what they see in *Time* magazine, yet I feel an ungrateful guest, almost a viper ⟨my father, normally a solid & indeed dapper business man was v. stern & quoted the Bible – Gen. [ ][3] about this. It is, alas, rather good.⟩ And since Conant and Buck etc. will surely have seen *Time* etc., I now feel I must write to them enclosing all three articles for better or for worse, since otherwise God knows what they will think I may have written. Dear me, am I making too much heavy weather again? I propose to write at least to Conant, Buck and Mackay and say that I love and respect Harvard, as indeed I do, and that I meant all I said in the articles and think they are not unfair. I feel I must say something ⟨or is this too sucking up? I shan't say I *love* Harvard – indeed I am not sure that I love any institution although All Souls comes nearest – nor that I respect it: only that I was very happy there. This is like a letter of a distraught governess in some E. M. Forster novel: 'Shall I say I love them? will that be a little *too* much? or say nothing at all? & just bow? it is always safe to bow isn't it? or just nod' that's what *I* feel like: I wish I were like Mary Perkins: sure footed: not socially nervous like poor Mrs W. James and Perk.⟩[4] This afternoon *Time and Tide* rang up and said that their *Alumni Bulletin* wanted to reprint the second of the two articles. I refused this, as I did not want to become the centre of a formal controversy about morality in education etc. in the United States. But I should be grateful to you if you could tell me whether people really are offended. I should be genuinely distressed if that were so, ⟨& shall do nothing about it⟩ but I might as well know. My Social-Democratic colleagues at Oxford are very worried about me: the article on Churchill did not sound pro-Labour; the Anglo-American broadcast infuriated ⟨not merely the Beaver but⟩ Crossman and some milder socialists as well; the *Time and Tide* articles are pronounced ⟨politically⟩ reactionary, and finally Mr Churchill does not think I can like him personally very much ⟨⟨although he sent me a telegram[5] & Xmas greetings – again compromising⟩⟩ and Randolph[6] is on my trail. Clearly to survive one wants to have crude, simple views and a thick skin. I have decided I have

1 (Clarence) Crane Brinton (1898–1968), pioneering intellectual historian; McLean Professor of Ancient and Modern History, Harvard, 1942–68.
2 Donald Cary Williams (1899–1983), Professor of Philosophy, Harvard, 1939–67; Chairman, Philosophy Department, 1947–54.
3 IB leaves a blank here for a reference, perhaps Genesis 44:4, 'Wherefore have ye rewarded evil for good?'
4 Elliott Perkins (1901–85) taught history at Harvard 1937–69; Master of Lowell House 1940–63. His English second wife Mary Frances (1904–94) was the daughter of Sir Philip Baker Wilbraham.
5 Dated 4 December 1949, it reads: 'I HAVE READ WITH SO MUCH PLEASURE WHAT YOU WROTE IN YOUR AMERICAN ARTICLE BEST WISHES FOR CHRISTMAS AND NEW YEAR WINSTON CHURCHILL'.
6 Randolph Frederick Edward Spencer Churchill (1911–68), author, journalist and Conservative politician; Winston Churchill's only son.

no views and no skin, and although I am prepared not to write *Time*, *Time and Tide*, the *Alumni Bulletin* etc., I feel I must do something somewhere if I am not to leave the impression of a sort of general superciliousness and indeed malicious chatter. Do advise me and do not spare me the facts.

[...] Lord Beaverbrook never offered me the editorship of anything, only a columnist's job which I must have rejected too quickly. ⟨i.e. without asking how much money I was being offered: what he said was 'leave those musty dons at Oxford; let me set you up in Claridge's; as much money, wine, women as you please; you can put up your friends in my house; it's a privilege reserved for very few'. So like a comic pantomime devil did he look, & so pleasing was the thought that I was being shown all the kingdoms of the earth from the roof of Arlington House[1] that I am afraid I giggled. Hence all these blasts. But I enjoyed the interview much too much. I had a similar contretemps once – which Chip can tell you of – with Luce:[2] yet I don't see myself as a tough little fellow taking on these giants: odd.⟩ Chip has been here and very nice too; he does not deny the substance of Joe's story; I see how, on paper, he and Bruce[3] and Harriman are right, but in fact I am sure that Kennan is: England cannot really enter into European Union – economically it halves the standard of living and nobody is ⟨or is really capable of being psychologically⟩ prepared for it at all – American opinion may be annoying but it is real; its influence may be resented, but it is allowed for, whereas the French and Italians hardly exist and mean nothing at all to the man in our street, who thinks he likes them better ⟨, but only⟩ because they are much much remoter. Chip seemed well, quite important, and obviously got on moderately well, but had not clicked with the Ambassadress in Paris.[4] We discussed the sources of your enthusiasm for her and agreed that it was entirely to your credit, or at least to that of your heart and senses. I am ashamed to say I have not yet read your book, which Chip says is a work of genius and timely, too. Apart from the burning footnote[5] which is at present the sole sentence in the book read by me, I am predisposed, powerfully, in favour of it, and shall read it ⟨⟨& doubtless let off some terrible public squib⟩⟩ at once. I have, I may add, read no other books either, including Morton White's[6] which I am to review for *Mind*. I am sure it is excellent. He is a very nice and clever man, and Levin's antipathy to him does him

1 The location of Beaverbrook's West End apartment.

2 Henry Robinson Luce (1898–1967), Republican editor and publisher; founder of magazines, including *Time* (1923, jointly with Briton Hadden) and *Life* (1936), and editor-in-chief of all his publications until 1964.

3 David Kirkpatrick Este Bruce (1898–1977), US diplomat and politician; Assistant Secretary of Commerce 1947–8; Ambassador to France 1949–52, to Germany 1957–9; Under-Secretary of State 1952–3; later (1961–9) Ambassador to UK.

4 Evangeline Bruce.

5 134/2.

6 Morton Gabriel *White (b. 1917), philosopher and historian of ideas; Assistant Professor of Philosophy, Harvard, 1948–50, Associate Professor 1950–3, Professor 1953–70. His book was

(White) credit. He (White) says that he (White) is the only person I haven't made slighting remarks about. Really! How unjust, how untrue. I am back to where we began, I am filled with affection, admiration, enthusiasm for you and everybody else. And yet my words appear to belie it. Life is too difficult. I see myself as a simple, gay chatterbox, ⟨an amiable rattle⟩ who dislikes only difficult, prickly, solemn or malicious individuals; can this be a deep illusion which nobody else perceives, like one's voice heard on the radio? In Oxford I have been described by Dr Bowra as an out-and-out American collaboration- ist, whereas he is a crypto-resister. He is very well, agreeably malicious and is writing many not-very-good books, of which I read excerpts aloud to his various friends, pretending they come from their own works, and obtaining suitably horrified ⟨& justly incredulous⟩ reactions. The experiment worked particularly well with the pompous Kenneth Clark.[1] Oh dear, somebody will now say that I am not being altogether fair or kind ⟨to my oldest friend & the Greatest Influence in my life – & he is, he is.⟩. I shall never get things right. And must now sit down and send off copies of *Time and Tide* to the President of Harvard and dear old Mackay. If you will reply at once, you may yet stop me. ⟨Too late! copies gone.⟩ But make haste, every word I write, whether printed or in manuscript, obviously gets me into further messes. I promise that 1950 shall be a quiet year. In my persecuted mood I fancy that even Joe, who is mysteriously silent, cannot forget my clumsy non-staying policy. ⟨Just in time, a parcel arrived. Dear Joe; not a word against him, & I shall stay with him *a lot*.⟩ I require building up, reassuring, much affec- tion and confidence-building emotions. But not at the expense of truth, so do tell me the naked facts. And when are you coming to Europe? I shall plan my life accordingly. If you don't stop me, I shall in an accession of guilt write an article for Ascoli[2] called 'Horae Harvardianae',[3] full of nostalgia and praise. This is a less frivolous ⟨threat⟩ than it sounds. My condition is deplorable. You must write at once. Even Perry Miller,[4] who has just failed to keep an appointment with me and was exposed by Laski telling ⟨huge white ('enough to ice a Xmas Cake' said Lady Oxford[5] once)⟩ lies about his health ⟨(curious reversal of roles)[6] has written to reproach me. Laski is very affable. I value even that now. You see how low I am. Write. ⟨Love to Marion [*sic*], to Elena Levin (Harry has sent me an offprint: about foreign reactions

---

   Social Thought in America: The Revolt against Formalism (New York, 1949). IB's review eventually appeared in *Mind* 61 (1952), 405–9.

1 Kenneth Mackenzie Clark (1903–83), Baron Clark 1969; art historian; Slade Professor of Fine Art, Oxford, 1946–50, 1961–2; Chairman, Arts Council, 1953–60.

2 Max Ascoli (1898–1978), Italian-born writer and editor; publisher and editor, the *Reporter*, 1949–68.

3 'Harvard Hours'.

4 Perry Gilbert Eddy Miller (1905–63), intellectual historian; Professor of American Literature, Harvard, 1946–63, Powell M. Cabot Professor of American Literature from 1960.

5 Anne Mary Celestine (1916–98), née Palairet, wife since 1947 of the 2nd Earl of Oxford and Asquith.

6 Laski was a well-known fantasist.

to Amer. Lit: very cautious: must I send him T & T too? No. no. no.) to the Whites[1] to whom I shall write. I am in a mood where, about to dedicate myself to the intellectual-moral history of the Russian revolutionary intelligentsia, I think that the contemporary US academic situation is more like the life of my heroes than anything anywhere, whereas the English don't see the point. Why then all this Gorerism on my part? I wish to sing a paean to the character of Mr Gilmore as nobler than anything in my vicinity: & even old Sam Beer is a familiar agrarian idealist of circa 1888: & why does the NYT man here think my NYT review of Bedell Smith[2] (in Sunday NYT any day) almost too pro-Soviet? write about that too for your poor harried Old World liberal friend. When *are* you coming?⟩

Isaiah

P.S. *And by the way.* Would you, in fact, consider a year in Oxford as Harmsworth Professor? if so, say; & I'll get Beloff to fix it. Do come.

TO MYRON GILMORE

Boxing Day, 26 December 1949 [*manuscript*]

New College

My dear Myron,

I have owed you a letter for I don't know how long: & feel, as I nearly always do, a feeling of obscure guilt, shame, inability to face moral & intellectual & personal obligations, obligations in some very ineradicable, non-formalizable, non rationally stateable, work-to-rule reducible kind: indeed I am beginning to wonder uneasily whether my perpetual protests against preoccupation with morality and the elimination of spontaneous pursuits of truth, pleasure etc. in favour of some puritan or sentimental or Hegelian pattern of social duty, doesn't spring from obsession with something wrong in the region within myself: I see a horrifying sort of picture which Mr Gorer or Mrs Mead[3] or even Clyde K. K. cd draw: I draw back: I wave it away, I exorcise the vision. But [it] does not, alas, wholly vanish.

Goodness me! I have done nothing but things which get me into trouble since return. I am sure my loss of my passport before sailing had a deep Freudian significance: I have written a breastbeating epistle to Arthur & I am in that mood still: I regret you will have to bear some of its consequences: it is the price of friendship which I cannot lift. Hear then my tale of woe: I came back & apart from a harmless & idyllic piece on Don Giovanni as per-

---

1 Morton White and his wife Lucia (1909–96), née Perry.
2 '"A Sense of Reality" about Russia', review of Walter Bedell Smith, *My Three Years in Moscow*, *New York Times Book Review*, 8 January 1950, 1, 25.
3 Margaret Samaira Mead (1901–78), American cultural anthropologist (known by her maiden name despite her three marriages).

formed at Aix discharged all my accumulated journalistic obligations at once:
I wrote a much too (I suppose) violently pro-U.S. piece which I spoke on the
radio, & got lammed both by Ld Beaverbrook & by some communists for it:
my trouble being that once in the grip of a metaphor capable of expansion
& development, particularly if slightly comical, I cannot resist temptation: I
ride ideas consciously too hard: the article on Churchill is full of exaggerated
patterns: once an analogy crops up, I cannot bear not [to] play games with
it, knowing this to be frivolous & possibly dangerous: & I feel guilt at once:
as of one playing about with some Crocean[1] superstructure (or Pareto[2]
or what you will) which is fascinating, amusing, coherent, has outlines, &
pushing away the boring, dreary but vitally important accumulation of facts
not capable of such symmetrical & gay treatment: provided this is done as a
quasi-jeu d'esprit, in articles in the popular press, perhaps it doesn't matter
so much: but I shall find the lesson hard to learn that the boring truths must
be stated too: all the things we superior persons take for granted – & above
all the socio-economic slag which no conveniently formalizable Zeitgeist has
troubled to penetrate & make amenable to neat formulae. Oh dear: you see
I am beating away: but let me go on; these metaphors really are fatal & cause
trouble: not just metaphors but models: in terms of which alone I think that
I think: & try & explain the world in terms of nearness to them, like teatast-
ing, if you see what I mean: not by deduction or induction or reasoning:
but by nearness to this, that & the other idealized arrangement. If one has
enough such standards knocking about in one's head, this method may be
quite fruitful: the sinister thing is if there are too few, & one goes riding off.
Thus: Europe v. America; XVIII v. XIXth centuries; actor's clothes as a means
of psychological transformation; statesmen with antennae, absorbing, &
statesmen without, hypnotizing; etc. etc. make the Churchill article jolly but
perhaps a trifle superficial. The Old Man himself is not quite sure what to
think of it: & is about ¾ pleased & has sent me a funny telegram for Xmas.
but my socialist friends – & they are my dearest – are properly shocked: &
yet can't quite find anything to denounce as false or wicked: but shocked
they are. From one model I go fatally travelling to others: the *Listener* article
which provoked Ld Beaverbrook's attack which Arthur showed you, was
obsessed by the idea of the indissoluble marriage: again I believe it to be true
but why it appealed to me, alas, was not so much its plausibility but its gaiety:
surely surely it is time one was serious: & argue sophistically as one will
seriousness & gaiety are not ultimately quite compatible: seriousness is not
the same as solemnity, dullness, etc. nor gaiety as frivolity, cynicism, etc. etc.
etc. nevertheless. And so it went on: no sooner did I let off the *Listener* squib
than I felt that something must be done against the painful self-involvements

1 Benedetto Croce (1866–1952), Italian idealist philospher and politician, whose writings dealt
   mainly with the philosophy of history and of aesthetics.
2 Vilfredo Federico Damaso Pareto (1848–1923), Italian economist and sociologist.

of U.S. academic life: which in one way reminds me of my spiritual home, the Russian self examining intelligentsia of the 19th Century – far more like that than the deeply, deeply philistine academic & intellectual life of England: & U.S. students are far less philistine than English ones too (why didn't I say that? because the pattern, the idealized entity, the Newtonian perfect sphere[1] rolling along an infinite plane, no doubt stopped me) but also it unnerved & persecuted me a little: the quantity of psychoanalysable matter seemed too great: perhaps it is a matter of media: Mrs Frankfurter, for example, whose antennae & appalling powers of insight no one has yet exceeded, found Oxford in 1934 & 1939 full of infinite involuted elaborate Louis XIV malice, overfinesse, complication, & was excited but done down by it: whereas I find Oxford shallower, easier, simpler, gayer, & less worthy, further from the moral heart of things, more nonchalant, more superficial, less penetrating, less directly concerned with what I care about most, than Harvard. Does this seem to you insane? even though you don't know Oxford? my other trouble is that I invariably find myself in the wrong company on the whole, i.e. approved from the wrong quarter. The Anglo-Am. Listener article, tho' approved by worthy Rhodes Scholars, only obtained praise from rich Conservatives & hisses from Labour (obviously). the Churchill article, you can imagine: I doubt if it will be used as election propaganda: but even so. The Time & Tide pieces, much approval from Learned Hand, & I daresay Grenville Clark:[2] but I see social democrats resentful: & clearly Arthur thinks me a deutero-Gorer: & there is literally nobody I despise more or wish to be like less, in any respect: & fulminate sincerely about his horrid travesty of the U.S.A., plainly my movement, as far as public issues is concerned, consists of moving from one false position to another: that's what a false position is: it consists not of lack of sincerity or even depth necessarily, but of failing to discount the objective relationships in the world, & one's own situation in it. The moral is what? to withdraw from the arena altogether, since to be in it at all is to have to adopt big, crude, non-nuancé[3] positions & lay about one with little concern for fine detail or private feeling: like Mr Churchill, & I daresay Justice Holmes[4] & all great men. This I accept, & will, on completion of present obligations, too late to retrieve without promise-breaking (observe old morality again, very anti-spontaneous self realization in the approved free world) relapse into contented, if somewhat arid, academicism. I feel sure this is right: & 1950 will be a quiet year with no publicity: the piece in *Time* magazine, sent me in many clippings by devoted friends, every day, + 3

1 The First Law of Motion formulated by Isaac Newton (1642–1727) states: 'Every object persists in its state of rest or uniform motion in a straight line unless it is compelled to change that state by forces impressed on it.'
2 Grenville Clark (1882–1967), US lawyer, active and influential in public affairs; on Harvard Corporation 1931–50.
3 'Without nuances'.
4 Oliver Wendell Holmes, Jr (1841–1935), Associate Justice, US Supreme Court, 1902–32.

letters from ex-students at Harvard commending my "courage" (for causing so many good people to wince) gave me horrible cold shivers. So, back into the private world, & an attempt to do justice even to sociology in mugging up the facts. Such is my New Year's resolution. My plans at present are to try & insert myself back into All Souls where I shall have few & dispensable pupils: which would enable me to return to U.S. if wanted from time to time, as originally hoped for: this is a most delicate negotiation & will take till end of 1950: so in 1951, new life begins. I should like to know (& have asked Arthur to tell me) have I hurt the feelings of anyone not deserving of it (I don't terribly mind e.g. about Clyde K., but I wd about, funnily enough, Inkeles[1] or Parsons)? if so there is nothing I can do. I don't mind about being ideologically unsatisfactory (as e.g. I expect Harry Levin thinks me: that is inevitable. I am so.) only about seeming ungrateful or vulgarly offensive (in any degree). I did, after all, enjoy myself at Harvard without end: & was tremendously renovated by it: & have made friendships: & have a feeling for it. But if there is resentment I am very sorry: I meant no harm.

About History being what Alcibiades (not Alexander as I stupidly let pass in the Atlantic) did & suffered (Aristotle on diff. between history & poetry).[2] I suppose I do believe that. The account of an economic situation or the political machinery of Rome or modern Albania, is pointless unless at some stage it is at least implied what the effect was on human beings, & again not a mass effect on a mass-individual, but on some vague model 'average' person, whose activities & feelings & thoughts alone give direction to the researches of even such pure specialists as historians of technology etc. – & as the research becomes more & more confined by impersonal categories – say the history of harvests & prices of agricultural produce involving no names of people, no accounts of individual fortunes, or feelings stirred, it gets to be less & less like history & more & more like geology or whatever science soci- ology or economic history is supposed to try to attain to the condition of. Of course I don't mean that the intentions of Napoleon or the effects of this or that on Metternich or Beethoven are in some sense the goal, & the analysis of average incomes of Austrian peasants in 1810 the background: but only that at bottom (horrible word) history is an analogical & not a behaviourist science: it tries to convey what 'a man' – ultimately I, the historian + you the reader, wd have felt like, & in what forces we shd have been caught up, had we lived then: & cannot dispense with motives, purposes, frustrations, ideal ends, miseries & splendours of vice & virtue & achievement & failure whereas the ideal sociology cd be written in a purely behaviouristic way, i.e.

1 Alex Inkeles (b. 1920), sociologist and Russian specialist; Lecturer in Social Relations, Harvard, 1948–57; Professor of Sociology, Harvard, 1957–71; later (1971–90) Professor of Sociology at Stanford University.
2 'Poetry tends to express the universal, history the particular. [...] The particular is – for example – what Alcibiades did or suffered.' Aristotle, *Poetics* 9. 4, 1451b11.

causally: when what happens, what else, on the whole happens: bad harvests, high prices; destructive wars: undernourishment: technological decline: etc. & wd be none the worse for it, & very good & useful too if it cd get around to discovering some decent general propositions to start off as hypotheses from. Whereas history is in principle not seeking to attain to the status of an if–then causal science: & you don't refuse the title of history to something containing vivid portraits of persons or predicaments, & demand evidence of an analogical kind – likeness to a model already present to your mind from personal experience – & not of an inductive statistical kind presupposing no reference to the way in which you 'understand' people's characters without reference to the laboratory. Is all this dreadfully obscure? again I fear I might find myself in the wrong company: with a lot of obscurantist "intuitionists" & metaphysicians against honest, scrupulous empirical scientific progressives: & of course I shd be indignant & have to explain that it is one thing to ignore or deny sources of the truth or their relevance, as discovered by empiricists (with whom I shd align myself) & another to maintain that there is a turnstile: that what isn't discovered or believed by the tested techniques of this or that science, isn't knowledge but mysticism or humbug (which I shd deny. All attempts to erect turnstiles however enlightened end in dogmatism & denying the facts. The only proof [of] the pudding is in the eating. And Aristotle made the profoundest of all observations ever uttered in the ancient world when, somewhere in the Nicomachean Ethics he said that 'in the observing is the judging'[1] i.e. you can only tell what is what, either in particular or in general, [by] looking at the actual situation & then indicating the truth without fear of disloyalty to principles. Once principles are applied rigorously absurdities follow from the non-generalizability of the situations which originally suggested the principles.) – but I mustn't go pouring out a great confused methodological essay on you like this. And I must end this great logorrhoea as Mr Joyce[2] once called loquacity, & Wyndham Lewis[3] accused Miss Stein[4] of it. I have dreadful guilt about Mrs Whitehead for whom my feelings are, if anything, stronger than when I used to call on her. She sent me that sweet & touching telegram[5] about my ailment, & I cd, of course, not follow her advice (& indeed my sciatica, after 8 months unbroken life, is better) but I ought to have replied at least by cable: but I was in bed & in a state of accidie, unable to think or will much: & once 3–4 days had

1 He says it twice: *Nicomachean Ethics* 2. 9 (109b23), 4. 5 (1126b4). The question at issue is: When has a person departed far enough from the right course to be worthy of blame? Aristotle observes: 'It is not easy to define the extent and gravity of error that deserves blame. Indeed nothing we perceive is easily definable: such questions depend on circumstances, and our judgement is based in the perception itself.'

2 James Augustine Aloysius Joyce (1882–1941), Irish novelist, short-story writer and poet.

3 Percy Wyndham Lewis (1882–1957), artist and author.

4 Gertrude Stein (1874–1946), American writer.

5 Dated 26 September: 'DEAR ISAIAH I AM SO SORRY TO HEAR OF YOUR ILLNESS DO HAVE THE OPERATION'.

passed, with me in this awful hebetude, it seemed absurd to wire. So I did nothing. I promised I wd write to her, & was told to inscribe gigantic letters on great sheets of paper: & will do so too, yet, if given time. I wd rather not have my letters read aloud, even the most trustworthy transmitter, either the most discreet & understanding, or the stupidest & least aware, still form obstacles & inhibit one. So wd you be very kind & tell her that I think of her continually, & miss our evenings more than any other single activity in the U.S. (which is true) & will write & apologize for leaving her perfectly sensible & infinitely thoughtful advice unacknowledged, but I thought a telegram would, if formal enough to be read to her, sound too dry: & I *shall* write: & shd be grateful to you for all news of her. [...]

I cannot end without, quite suddenly, remembering your dilemma about the Welfare State v. the freedom allowed by institutions, e.g. the Church into which one can escape from the best of all possible New Dealing paternal administrations. I don't know what the answer is: mainly, for me, in the need for less faith & more ad hoc empiricism. That is, one must judge each situation, so far as possible, on its own merits & not commit oneself to campaigns for general principles: only for liberation from specific wrongs & then for liberation from the defects of the remedy, & so on. I suspect this of being some kind of irresponsible late 19th cent. radicalism but it is, I think, what I believe in. The problem being, how can milk be supplied to children & poverty cured yet freedom for 'aristocratic' or "liberal" virtues & styles be kept? there can be no general solution. One must vote for minorities which wd be fatal if they became majorities. One must fight for the rights of 3 Communist professors & against 19. One obviously votes for Roosevelt & indeed Truman too: because above all one must avoid the thin end of the wedge argument: which as someone in some meeting here said, only means that you refuse to do what is right because you fear that you (or others) will not, when it is pushed too far, have enough moral courage (or strength) to stop it then. The great weakness & vanity is search for general principles of permanent reliability: even pragmatists do: whereas one shd have the courage, I suppose, to die for undemonstrated & unself-evident positions, not bolstered up by absolute faith. I wonder if this is too cosy a way out.

Much love
   yrs
      Isaiah B.

God what a letter! I do apologize 1000 times.

TO MORTON WHITE

29 December 1949

New College

Dear Morton,

[...] Being bored and in bed I indulged in a lot of reckless ephemeral journalism which came home to roost very rapidly. [...] While I suppose I still believe in the gist of the theses enunciated, the *Time* version and even perhaps the true version now seem to me much too glibly and gaily reeled off; also from Arthur's inevitable reaction I infer that it may, whether true or false, hurt the feelings of many good people to whom I owe genuine debts of gratitude and whom indeed I like or respect or both, in some cases moderately, in others very much indeed. Hence I was plunged into great agony of spirit, which I am capable of developing over tiny and even non-existent occasions. The first thing I felt I must do is draft a true version of my arguments to anyone who might wish to judge me on the *Time* caricature (as it seemed to me), so I sent off copies to Arthur, to the President, the Provost etc. with brief notes ostensibly about other subjects but about which I had to write to them, plus disingenuous little postscripts to say that as they may have seen the *Time* story they had better see the original – then feeling I must not grovel I declared with some firmness that I stood by my text, and only hoped it would not be misunderstood, but without any indication of what 'the true meaning' was supposed to be, there still remained an infinite possibility of misunderstanding. Then the *Alumni Bulletin* desired permission to reproduce the second article in the series; this was too much. The prospect of becoming the centre of controversy appalled me and I brusquely refused, no reason given. If there is any brou-ha-ha about all this do tell me – not that I shall do anything – but I invariably become appalled at any consequence of what I have done; the articles now seem to me to be a caricature, at least a foreign ⟨my typist is really too sharp: I meant to say 'fanciful'⟩ exaggeration of a tenable position but for the moment I don't fancy a public admission of this. Anyhow, it is all nothing at all. How awful that I shall be regarded by your friends as such a destroyer of reputations. In my own ears it only shows how different the words sound to the speaker and the recipient, like the shock of hearing one's own voice on the record and the realisation that this is what the external world hears and the image of oneself which one would construct from hearing such a voice from oneself. My view of course is that with certain notable exceptions, none of them philosophers, I thought every-one exceptionally nice and with a degree of intellectual candour and fidelity which influenced me, permanently, I now think. Do betray the source to me and I shall never give it away to him or to anyone; and if I like him as much as I expect I did, I shall take some opportunity of exhibiting my feelings. As it is, I suspect everyone, which is far worse, so do say, and liberate me from suspense. I must say this sort of thing which has been said to me before and which I obstinately believe false, like someone who refuses to accept public criteria for tables and supposes that the rest of the world is under a multiple illusion and only he and Bishop Berkeley have seen the truth. My late colleague Professor Prichard[1] held the extraordinary view that we think we see objects but don't, in fact, although they exist and are like what we think we see, but aren't what we see.

Which reminds me that I have now had a letter (for God's sake keep this under your hat) from your President about the Philosophy Department, once more canvassing my views, i.e. Carnap[2] as full professor v. Sellars[3] or Chisholm[4] as associates. I have read all the testimonials etc. and I gather you and the Department would still prefer Carnap but if he is rejected – and the opposition was very powerful last time – then S. rather than C. Nelson Goodman,[5] I gather, is out in any case. I ought to remember Sellars as he was at Oxford in 1936 and has often sent to me all his offprints, which I am ashamed to say I never acknowledged. I do not know about his great merits but he is obviously a more enlightened and intellectually candid figure than Chisholm, who I see is being pushed by Demos[6] and Wild[7] for what seemed to me obvious reasons. I cannot believe that anything more arid than a theory of vision along Moore–Broad–Price[8] lines, now discarded or abandoned by these persons themselves, can exist; nothing is more maddening than people who bark up the obsolete trees rather than use razors, Occam's, Russell's etc.,[9] and this alone apart from counterfactual metaphysics etc. set me somewhat against Chisholm. ⟨my typist's fondness for propositional functions is a new horror: God knows what I did say.⟩[10] Will you quickly tell me what to say and I shall think about it – *by air mail and at once if you would,*

1 Harold Arthur Prichard (1871–1947), White's Professor of Moral Philosophy, Oxford, 1928–37.
2 Rudolf Carnap (1891–1970), leading member of the Vienna Circle; Professor of Philosophy, Chicago, 1936–52; Professor of Philosophy, University of California at Los Angeles, 1954–62.
3 Wilfrid Stalker Sellars (1912–89), Assistant Professor of Philosophy, University of Minnesota, 1946–51, Professor 1951–9; Professor of Philosophy, Yale, 1959–63; University Professor of Philosophy and Research Professor of the Philosophy of Science, Pittsburgh, 1963–89.
4 Roderick Milton Chisholm (1916–99) taught philosophy at Brown University 1947–87 (as Andrew W. Mellon Professor of the Humanities from 1972).
5 Henry Nelson Goodman (1906–98), Associate Professor of Philosophy, University of Pennsylvania, 1946–51, Professor 1951–64; later (1968–77) Professor of Philosophy, Harvard.
6 Raphael Demos (1892–1968), Greek-born; Alford Professor of Natural Religion, Moral Philosophy and Civil Polity, Harvard, 1945–62.
7 John Daniel Wild (1902–72), Professor of Philosophy, Harvard, 1946–61.
8 George Edward Moore (1873–1958), Professor of Philosophy, Cambridge, 1925–39; Charlie Dunbar Broad (1887–1971), Knightbridge Professor of Moral Philosophy, Cambridge, 1933–53; Henry Habberley Price (1899–1984), Wykeham Professor of Logic, Oxford, 1935–59.
9 The recommendation of simplicity attributed to the English Franciscan friar and influential scholastic philosopher William of Occam (c.1285–c.1347), and known as Occam's razor, is usually expressed as 'Entities should not be multiplied beyond necessity.' Bertrand Russell developed this into a key feature of his philosophy.
10 At this point in the letter the typist left numerous blanks, which IB filled in by hand.

as I cannot keep Conant waiting long and must produce what is called a thoughtful letter. The thought that it is bound to be circulated terrifies me at once. As Conant was most affable and said nothing about the article in *Time*, and probably never saw them, I immediately began to regret my sending to him the *Time and Tide* originals, and generally making a thing. Oh dear! Why cannot one have an iron Lewis-like character,[1] unflutterable, monadic, calm and spreading calm, and not living in a universe filled with the putative reactions of other people which normally are completely imaginary but possess Meinongian reality[2] of a, to me, overwhelmingly powerful kind.

I have been reading Morris Cohen's[3] autobiography, which I have to review for an obscure periodical, with a horrible fascination. It is a really touching pathetic and not altogether ignoble but dreadfully embarrassing *reductio ad absurdum* of immigrant high-minded Liberalism. The naive emphasis and the passion for intellectual vested interest in philosophy is curiously moving and he inspires, at least in me, a sense of pathos. In philosophy he really does seem to have been a clear combination of quite good instincts and an embittered defence of obsolescent concepts which he defended with the over-compensated zeal of a foreign convert. Or am I wrong? I often think I am about everything, but then as Cohen would have brightly added, so is everyone else.

I must stop, but do reply quickly about Carnap etc. and all the other things. The thing which really troubles me about Carnap is that he is precisely wrong for this moment, since the fruitful direction seems to me to be in the direction of loosening rather than a tightening of discipline, and when he loosens he loosens too much because he depends on mechanical gears, and plays too little by ear, if you see what I mean. ⟨if not syntax, doesn't matter *what* you say – the deluge – & that might lead to too little tolerance in technique, & a rapid tolerance in real meanings:⟩ But again I may be wrong. I must now sit down and read your book and review it.

Mind you write at once.

    yrs ever

      Isaiah B.

---

1 Clarence Irving Lewis (1883–1964), pragmatic philosopher who taught at Harvard from 1920; Edgar Pierce Professor of Philosophy 1946–53.

2 Alexius Meinong (1853–1920), Austrian philosopher, author of a theory concerning the reality of thoughts about non-existent objects.

3 Morris Raphael Cohen (1880–1947), Russian-born logician and philosopher; Professor of Philosophy, City College of New York, 1912–38. His autobiography is *A Dreamer's Journey* (Boston, 1949). If the review was written, we have not traced it.

TO ROWLAND BURDON-MULLER

29 December 1949

New College

My dear Rowland,

I ought, of course, to have written to you long before to thank you for all your letters and kindnesses in connection with Mr Graham[1] etc., but I cannot describe to you what the end of Term was like, with all the unprepared lectures, unwritten papers, unthought-about talks, which I suddenly had to disgorge when the hour of payment came. Then a vast college intrigue began about my Warden's[2] desire to alter all our pretty Queen Anne and Regency windows in the front Quad – the library front which you may have noticed – into some sort of sham Gothic, just because the Bursar had discovered some ancient tracery behind the stone walls of the library and my sheep-like colleagues, while I was in America, voted him three or four hundred pounds to enable him to put in one specimen window,[3] which is now up and very hideous and vulgar and discreditable too. Suddenly my peaceful college, where all seemed to be friends of all, was converted into a madhouse of jangling nerves. The Warden, that nice, remote, but very strong character, suddenly emerged as a ruthless Napoleon, possessed, moreover, like all tyrants, with a passion to build and to leave a physical mark upon his world – from the ancient Greek tyrants to Hitler and Mussolini plus a touch of Ludwig II's[4] architectural madness, and I, as the sub-Warden, have to represent my colleagues, divided into implacably opposed camps, and reclaim the lost democratic rights of the Fellows of New College, usurped by the devouring despot. I am, you perceive, exaggerating somewhat, but quite genuinely the intrigues and counter intrigues nearly drove me off my head in the last weeks of term. And so I did not reply to your letters, which gave me a great deal of pleasure as always, and I enjoyed your stay a very great deal too, and so did John Sparrow,[5] who told me afterwards how much he had enjoyed meeting you. I asked him about the Turner – and his picture is by the celebrated William Turner of Oxford[6] and not, therefore, by your Turner, who is surely not William? He followed your advice about the Constables and his room is prettier than ever. I am seized with a deep

---

1 RB-M had apparently helped transfer IB's contribution to Prichard's appeal costs to Phil Graham (presumably in breach of exchange control regulations)

2 A. H. Smith.

3 The anomalous Gothic window remains, a reminder of the architectural ambitions to which Wardens are prone.

4 Ludwig Friedrich Wilhelm, King Ludwig II of Bavaria (1845–86), an enthusiastic builder of castles, including Neuschwanstein in Bavaria.

5 John Hanbury Angus *Sparrow (1906–92), classicist and barrister; Fellow of All Souls 1929–52, then (1952–77) Warden.

6 William Turner (1789–1862), painter of landscapes, mainly watercolours; dubbed 'of Oxford' to distinguish him from the more famous artist Joseph Malord William Turner (1775–1851).

nostalgia for All Souls, where I should have no undergraduates to teach and be able to travel a little more freely, and I think that the plan to restore me to its bosom is proceeding slowly but fairly promisingly. I shall lose money over the transaction but gain leisure and much peace of mind. As for returning to the United States, it is always nice to be asked to do things, and Harvard did ask me to come back, both in the Summer and the Autumn Terms. The Summer School[1] is, I suspect, anyhow, sheer hell, what with the heat and four days' lecturing a week and not even very many dollars; fortunately I have to examine in the Final Schools in Oxford in the Summer and could produce that as an excuse, at once graceful, serious and veracious, to my Harvard inviters; as for the autumn, that is when the crisis about All Souls may mature, in which case I had better not go away precisely when that happens. I wonder if I shall be asked in 1951 or 52? [...]

[...] Patricia seems well, although I have not seen her for some time – she has disappeared to some country house or other for Christmas and will doubtless give birth to her child there – it is expected in February. My mother is gradually becoming reconciled to her as she perceives the danger to have vanished – very comical it all is. We are moving forward towards the election, and goodness knows what will happen. I cannot somehow believe that the Conservatives will, in fact, get in. I went to a dinner party the other night given by Oliver Lyttelton,[2] and it turned out to be a kind of meeting of the Conservative shadow Cabinet – I don't quite know why I was asked, as I was not known well to anybody there and went because I was alone in London that day, my parents being away, and had nowhere in particular to go. There were there: Winston and Mrs C., Oliver Stanley, Oliver Lyttelton and his wife,[3] who were the hosts, Lord and Lady Salisbury,[4] Lady Pembroke,[5] a man called Andrew Scott and his wife,[6] and for some peculiar reason myself. Winston was splendid on the subject that what we need is greater multiplicity of choices – choices which may many of them be bad, but choices nevertheless. Lyttelton said that Lord Ancaster[7] had delivered a fine speech in his Home County, saying that there was to be 'no ⟨my secretary you perceive, too delicate minded, & left a gap: *damned*⟩ nonsense about policies or anything of that kind', whereupon

1 Founded in 1871, the Harvard Summer School provides intensive short courses for large numbers of US and international students of varying ages over eight weeks from June to August each year.
2 Oliver Lyttelton (1893–1972), 1st Viscount Chandos 1954, businessman; Conservative MP 1940–54; Secretary of State for Colonies 1951–4.
3 The former Lady Moira Godolphin Osborne (1892–1976), daughter of the 10th Duke of Leeds.
4 Elizabeth Vere Gascoyne-Cecil (1897–1982), Marchioness of Salisbury, daughter of Lord Richard Cavendish.
5 The Countess of Pembroke, wife of the 15th Earl, Beatrice Eleanor Herbert (1883–1973), daughter of Lord Alexander Paget.
6 Colonel (Claud) Andrew (Montagu-Douglas-)Scott (1906–71), Brigade of Guards, and the former Lady Victoria Doris Rachel Haig (1908–93), daughter of 1st Earl Haig (and sister of Hugh Trevor-Roper's future wife Xandra, 602/3).
7 Gilbert Heathcote-Drummond-Willoughby (1867–1951), 2nd Earl of Ancaster.

Winston remarked that Lord A. 'had the root of the matter in him' and generally carried on in a gay and remarkable manner. He obviously had not the
remotest notion of who I was but I identified myself to his wife, with the
result that some weeks later I received a Christmas telegram ⟨& an Xmas card
reproducing *his* painting of Mt{e} Ste. Victoire, whose crudity has to be seen
to be believed: but I must say, [a] very fearless thing to do: you wdn't know he
and Cézanne lived on the same earth⟩ from him thanking me for my article in
the *Atlantic*. I only hope it won't be used as election propaganda. I wish I could
wish Labour well, but they depress me too much because of the minor public
school morality which is the tone Mr Attlee adopts. No doubt he is a morally
better man than any who have ever been Prime Ministers of England, but the
effect is too flat. People like to have some picture of themselves idealised as a
goal for which to strive and the ideal citizen of the Labour Government is too
unattractive an individual. I have decided that I must not have political views
at all except in times of genuine crisis and must vote as my heart and not my
head tells me. [...] My Warden still speaks enthusiastically about your interest
in the Celadon bowl in our Treasury – if you have anything to tell him about
that sort of thing he would be terribly pleased. He is a very nice and original
and curious man but fundamentally frivolous and careless of the feelings of
others, and I feel at the moment that I alone stand between him and a mutiny
among his colleagues. I really ought to keep Oxford memoirs – so many funny
things happen between my colleagues, such odd persecutions, such peculiarly grotesque views of one another – still I do not see myself as the author
of a book called *From a College Window*. Perhaps one day. Do write.

Yours ever,
Isaiah.   [...]

TO JOSEPH ALSOP
29 December 1949

New College

My dear Joe,
[...] I have decided that everything I do is liked by the wrong people for
the wrong reasons and lands me in positions precisely opposite to those in
which I wish to be. The moral is that I must stop having opinions on public
issues and cease from all expression save in my own proper Oxford garden.
When I act as a shock absorber between my Warden and his colleagues and
try to persuade him that this is not the season to spend six thousand pounds
on putting up hideous mock Gothic windows in place of elegant existing
Queen Anne or Regency ones I feel in my proper element. Similarly when I
act as a bridge between various men of genius who might otherwise plunge
their fangs into one another (more bait) but not when I pronounce upon

world important topics. I must follow my heart and not my head and that is
how I shall vote in the next election.

I saw Chip, who seemed very well, and read your piece about him.[1] I have
no doubt that George Kennan and you were right and Chip and Harriman
wrong if your account is correct. I did not have the opportunity of talking
to Chip about it, but have a feeling that there exists a basis for a concrete
Anglo-American alliance with Scandinavia, whereas a Western union plus
the Atlantic Pact is an ad hoc somewhat ramshackle arrangement which may
serve its use but is too unreal to form a foundation for genuine European
development. I wish you would come here and we could talk about this.
[...] How is the Prichard case? I had a very sweet and touching letter from
him, to which I found it very difficult to reply. Do keep me posted about this.
About twice a month I suffer from acute nostalgia for America. At other
times not. It happens mainly when I have dealings with American pupils or
students who are morally superior to our own. That appeal, as you know, I
find irresistible. Hence my escape world in the Russian 19th century. I have
written a very queer article for *Foreign Affairs*,[2] bullied by Ham Armstrong,
who is of all men probably the best. He will probably reject it, and rightly,
as being too philosophical and misty about the political ideas of the 20th
century. If so I shall not know what to do with it and will in the end destroy
it. But I shall send you a copy in any case and accept your advice as to what
to do with it after it has been rejected. Write at once and say when you are
coming and which weekend will suit you best.

Yours ever,
Isaiah

⟨The Justice quite liked, he said, the articles in T. & T. but we all know how
reactionary *he* is.⟩

TO ALICE JAMES
31 December 1949

New College

Dear Alice,

I hope you will forgive me for not writing this by hand but I am not very
well again – I really do not know why I am being punished so. I am aware
of no special sins or offences – and find it painful to write propped up with
cushions.

---

1 Joseph and Stewart Alsop, 'Two Steps Back', in their 'Matter of Fact' column, *Washington Post*,
   7 December 1949, 15. The Alsops had supported George Kennan's proposal for a closer Anglo-
   American alliance, which had been fiercely opposed by the French Government, the senior US
   diplomats in Paris (David Bruce and Chip Bohlen) and Averell Harriman.
2 168/2.

I am most grateful to you both for your charming warm letters which brought back to me the atmosphere of affection and human kindness which, I suppose, like everyone else, I feel blissful in, and which too often is absent from the peaceful, solid, courteous but wonderfully unhurried life which everybody leads at Oxford. It has certain advantages; it allows a very large measure of personal freedom, but it has less social life than most small communities (less than at Harvard, for example) and to strongly individual and independent natures it provides a non-abrasive environment. But I would not send a helpless or weak person to live there, as very little help is given. You are allowed to do and live as you please, I think sometimes too much so; for all the others care you may be perishing of the most violent ills and although you are treated with genuine courtesy and politeness, everyone is terrified of knowing too much about the condition of everyone else. Those who have lived there for years and have established permanent forms of life and have made warm and lasting friendships are, of course, all right; my own life is placid and satisfactory, but I pity strangers who come; I wonder about Americans, for example (the French never last beyond one term or at most two, nor do the Italians. It is too cold and too dull for them) – I have a warm feeling for American students as I think has everyone else (and might have for the Russians if they were here, I have a suspicion). They come full of genuine moral enthusiasms, a tremendous desire to learn and to discover and to relate dissimilar things and are subjected to a gentle douche not exactly cold, but what can be worse, tepid, by their English instructors and a gentle irony which undermines them more than the kind of direct opposition which, say, the French offer when they rush to defend their own. I cannot bear to see this happen, and sometimes try to do something to help, but I have little time, pupils are many, the work is long and I can do very little indeed; but au fond I think they are more sympathetic, I like their naïve ardour, and their fanatical desire to discover the answer at all costs; they go on questioning people day and night until some conclusion is reached, God is proved or disproved, war is shown to be inevitable or a mere conspiracy, learning is shown to be the sole good or else destructive of all spontaneous impulses which make life delightful at all – I am more on the side of that⟨, perhaps because of some atavistic strain⟩ than on that of balance, scepticism, Olympian wisdom, gentle irony, and the civilised and fastidious values tinged with [a] certain world-weariness, with a great inner solidity and self-confidence which is still present at Oxford in general, where the worldly and the unworldly ⟨combine in a very queer way. But if you want to see me, of all people, identified with the languid sceptical denial of robust values you must look at the New Year's issue of *Time* Magazine where a *very* angry Rhodes Scholar at Balliol named Wiley,[1] not known to me, attacks me with terrible fury for views the

1 Richard Arthur Wiley (b. 1928), former student at Bowdoin College and Harvard Law School,

opposite of which I hold. But I cannot bring myself to answer, & will ask the author to tea sometime & he will become my greatest friend, I expect.⟩ [...]
With much love
    Isaiah B.

⟨[...] as you can see the typist understood not a word of what I said: & I might just as well have written it all in my own dreadful handwriting: I am sure my sentences in this letter are not what I said, or meant, or mean: but what she heard, or thinks she heard, or thinks it right for me to be saying. The problem of human communication is an agonising one still: as who knew better than your late uncle Henry J.: but the readiness to accept a typescript which one suspects to be different from one's original thought is a new kind of crux: something Mr Matthiessen[1] hasn't thought of: but I can see a very clever monograph by Harry Levin, can't you, on "Humpty Dumpty: or who is Master, you or the words:".[2] [...]
    I.B.⟩

TO RICHARD SCHWARTZ[3]
    31 December 1949 [*carbon*]

New College

Dear Mr Schwartz,
    Thank you very much for your letter to me stimulated by an excerpt in *Time* magazine which on the whole seemed to me an inadequate account of what I wrote. I have now asked for three copies of *Time and Tide* to be sent to you so that you can judge them for yourself. They were not intended in the first place to be about Harvard and I very much hope that people there did not take them as such although I fear that some of them at least must have

---

Rhodes Scholar, Balliol, 1949–51 (and subsequently US lawyer) had responded to *Time*'s selected extracts from IB's articles with a fierce letter (*Time*, 2 January 1950, 2) affirming American values as opposed to the 'all too prevalent Oxonian preciousness and desire to escape from the realities of our contemporary world'; however, another letter in the same edition expressed agreement with IB. The promised meeting over tea never happened.

1 Francis Otto Matthiessen (1902–50), literary critic and historian of literature; Professor of English, Harvard, 1942–50; socialist, Christian and homosexual, he jumped from a window to his death.

2 '"When *I* use a word," Humpty Dumpty said in rather a scornful tone, "it means just what I choose it to mean – neither more nor less." "The question is," said Alice, "whether you *can* make words mean so many different things." "The question is," said Humpty Dumpty, "which is to be master – that's all."' Lewis Carroll [Charles Lutwidge Dodgson], *Through the Looking-Glass, and What Alice Found There* (London, 1872), chapter 6, 'Humpty Dumpty', 124.

3 Richard S. Schwartz, writing on 9 December from Chicago to agree with IB's analysis as summarised in *Time*, had argued that the formative frontier way of life demanded that each member of a community perform useful practical work for the benefit of all and that this led to an 'absolute, implicit and profound' obligation on each person to care for others. 'On the frontier' curiosity with no practical issue in sight 'is a crime [...] Socrates would not have lasted a day on the frontier.' The descendants of the early settlers still embodied these values.

done so. I now think that perhaps what I said was too glib and superficial and sounded too much like the supercilious remarks of a casual European visitor criticising another area's culture by some frivolous standards, inapplicable even to his own, more discreditable to himself than to the object criticised.

I am most grateful to you for your letter because I am sure that what you say is true: the needs of life on the frontier of an inclement nature no doubt do create that grim utilitarian [*word(s) missing*], thus communities continuing as a combination of fanatical fear and disunity together with a great deal of warmth of sentiment within and a rich inner life and a concrete capacity for friendship and using social energy – cannot have the phenomena I was discussing. In a sense the passionate seriousness and genuine open-mindedness which I found among my students at Harvard seemed to be more valuable and potentially capable of discovering more truths and building more inspiring and aesthetic objects than all the fastidiousness and delicate sensibility of the sheltered university worlds of England or of France. At any rate it interested me immoderately and I made very warm and I hope abiding friendships among people there; at the moment there is a lot of crudity and muddling, largely because America as a whole has not yet reached that level of homogeneity – I do not mean racial but cultural – which alone creates the thick walls and the mental security with which alone it seems really arresting developments occur in the sphere of the humanities; science can flourish in a less established atmosphere. But this will come in America and will not again, I have a feeling, happen in the crowded cultivated areas, at any rate of north and west Europe. I doubt if our generation will live to see it but equally I have no doubt that it does not happen without the extreme appetite for life in all its forms, the insistence upon moral and intellectual truths which the social guilt tends to frustrate but which is not there, even to be frustrated, any longer in the more exhausted areas of old civilisations. The frontier mentality of which you speak so well will vanish and leave behind it squalls, which, however destructive from time to time, have an indestructible moral impulse behind them as the English had it in the seventeenth and nineteenth centuries – from which alone major works of genius flow. Thank you once more for your very illuminating letter, which has taught me something which I ought not to have been without when I wrote my three perhaps too carelessly dashed off articles and which I am most grateful to you for having written to me about.

Thank you also for your Christmas wishes. I wish you a thoroughly {and} satisfactory New Year. When the cigarette shortage here really reaches desperate straits I shall send you a pathetic SOS, but thank you for your kindly thought; I do smoke, I fear, like a chimney.

TO MARION FRANKFURTER

5 January 1950

New College

My dear Marion,

[...] I have been living with singular quietness so far as I myself am concerned but with great brickbats flying round my head, only occasionally grazing an excessively vulnerable surface as a result of the go of journalism in which I was suddenly impelled to indulge. [...] I can never actually stop myself from saying what I want to say either about or to people – if I do life immediately loses all possible savour and I see no point in carrying on at all; on the other hand I invariably cause a certain amount of discomfort not to say pain by these means, and for this I am only too anxious to make amends, all my anxiety to please leaps forward, reckless of any justification of what I may have said, and then some degree of pride and defence of the truth intervenes and I oscillate unhappily between the desire to retract what is wounding while not withdrawing what is true. This is plainly unmanageable and I therefore spin helplessly. I immediately shoot back into private life and pretend that I have done nothing at all and above all said nothing but the most innocuous and obvious things and sternly refuse offers of American periodicals – from New York weeklies to the *Harvard Alumni Bulletin* – to reprint articles which would then land me in a dreadful Laski-like storm centre – maintaining a little disingenuously that I had said nothing at all and nothing was worth preserving. ⟨The late, charming, Professor A. C. Clark of Oxford,[1] a Latinist of 80, when taxed with absurd observations wd say with a blandness I envy 'I do not recollect having said anything at all.'⟩

It is really a great satisfaction at such moments to sit in Oxford in the moist and the damp and the cold, among colleagues on the whole still sublimely unaware of the outside world, protected by the monastery to such a degree that one feels that these outside stirrings are public events not easily connected with oneself at all, which, if ignored long enough, will melt away, since they are happening on a stage, are kept in being only by the interest of the audience, and if ignored must automatically vanish. I really do not wish to wound feelings, but neither can I bear to walk on tiptoe and speak in a low voice for the sake of the unknowable reactions of too many incompatible persons and worlds. So plainly Oxford with its isolationist atmosphere is the place for me. America becomes dreadfully remote at once and so to a degree does London. ⟨Maurice is *very* pleased about my predicament: just as he told people how little either of us enjoyed Harvard – which loyally & very falsely I at least didn't deny very strenuously except a little behind his back: now he thinks we have *both* burnt our boats, bridges etc. at Harvard whereas I should *quite* like to return there in 1951 or so: I wonder if there really is annoyance:

1 Albert Curtis Clark (1859–1937), Corpus Christi Professor of Latin, Oxford, 1913–34.

or whether I just imagine that I cause violent passions in angry breasts, whereas in fact no one takes the slightest notice of what I say. [...] I feel in a frivolous mood, suddenly, & that nothing very bad is happenning anywhere, despite Hiss, Formosa,[1] Communists in China, Bevin etc. everything has suddenly lost its fateful & sinister significance. I expect to go to Israel in the spring, at the imperious behest of the figure whom Pres. Truman calls the Old Doctor & *that* will be comic & I shall be delighted by everything but no longer moved. I went to a party given by Frank Pakenham at Xmas and saw Father D'Arcy S.J.,[2] Victor Gollancz[3] & Lady V. Bonham Carter talking uncomfortably together & joined them at once & felt it was like early Evelyn Waugh[4] & realized that terrible as either a defeat or a victory of the Labour Govt. wd be, compared to 1932–1934–1936 etc., up to 1945 it didn't dreadfully matter: I *cannot* fear war; I think the U.S. government on the whole the best [in] the world; I am deeply unrevolté.[5] Surely you see the bone beneath the flesh somewhere? the crack? the Alsopian doom? do write & tell me & when oh when are you coming to Europe?

Shaya.   [...]⟩

TO MAX ASCOLI

5 January 1950 [*carbon*]

New College

My dear Ascoli,

Thank you very much for your letter which I much enjoyed reading. I wish I could accept your advice and turn my random thoughts into well-remembered *feuilletons* for the *Reporter*. But I feel several times bitten and therefore extremely shy. The repercussions to my recent ventures into journalism have been so sharp, and the notoriety thereby achieved so definite, that I am now in a state of rapid retreat into, at any rate, temporary trappism. If there is anything I have no wish to become it is a Laski *de nos jours*, and therefore must have a period of silence – I hope fruitful – but in any case,

---

1 In November 1949, in the wake of Communist success in the Chinese civil war and the declaration by Mao Tse-tung on 1 October of the People's Republic of China, the defeated General Chiang Kai-shek, leader of the Kuomintang Party (the Chinese Nationalist Government), named Taipei on the island of Formosa (Taiwan), to which his forces had withdrawn, as the temporary capital of the Republic of China. The Nationalists prepared for a counterattack on the mainland and for the expected Communist invasion of Formosa, which never materialised. Formal British recognition of the People's Republic of China on 6 January 1950 caused tension in Anglo-American relations: the US did not follow suit until 1979.

2 Martin Cyril D'Arcy (1888–1976), Master, Campion Hall, Oxford, 1932–45; Provincial, English Province, Society of Jesus, 1945–50.

3 Victor Gollancz (1893–1967), publisher; Governor, Hebrew University of Jerusalem, 1944–52.

4 (Arthur) Evelyn St John Waugh (1903–66), novelist. His first works satirised the upper echelons of English society; later ones were more serious, reflecting in particular his conversion to Catholicism.

5 sc. un*révolté*, 'unrebellious'.

silence, before venturing to offer any opinions to anyone or anything again. So you must think of me ensconced in the grey misty gloom of the island monastery of Oxford, absorbed in academic studies of the most minute and unworldly kind, while my more articulate contemporaries and betters make themselves heard. At any rate, this is my mood for the present and it will be a little time until it wears off.

Meanwhile I enjoy reading the *Reporter* more and more. It contains items of great freshness and unexpectedness and I am a genuine peruser of it. If there is any criticism I could venture it is this: in the last number in talking about European integration too little seemed to me said either by Flavius[1] or by Helen Hill Miller[2] about the reasons which have made England isolationist, as she certainly seems to be and about what precisely the benefits would be either (a) to the Continental countries through integrating and (b) what the loss is to England. I think both (a) and (b) are very large and they are worth setting out in full economic detail. Helen Hill Miller's parallel between the isolationism of the early New Deal and our present Government is well worth developing – along the lines that any body of planners must wish to reduce possible shocks from unpredictable outside acts to a minimum; therefore unless the plan is virtually a worldwide one it must take the form of insulation – Socialism in one country, à la Stalin. This connection between Socialism, planning and isolationist foreign policy seems to me a theme worth exploring.

The other thing is the precise assessment of whether in fact, as our Treasury obviously believes, the British standard of living would really be halved by economic integration of a serious kind with Europe. This also seems to be worth discussion. I do not feel competent to offer views on either subject but can you not put some politico-economic expert of real quality on to it? It is a very central 1950 issue, it seems to me, particularly the inner contradiction between the nationalism and internationalism on which Socialism as such seems to be impaled, so to speak. [...]

I wish you an excellent 1950.

Yours sincerely,

1 Flavius (perhaps a pseudonym for Ascoli himself), 'With or Without Britain', *Reporter*, 20 December 1949.
2 Helen Hill Miller (1899–1995), US journalist and author; Washington correspondent, *The Economist*, 1943–50, *Newsweek* 1950–2; contributing editor, *New Republic*, 1958–62. Her article was 'New Outpost of Isolationism', *Reporter*, 20 December 1949.

TO KAY GRAHAM

11 January 1950 [carbon]

New College

Dearest Kay,

I have been remiss, too. First of all, I cannot bear to conceal from you the acute pleasure which your gifts have brought me. Despite the fact that the *New Statesman* and other publications sternly forbid us to complain about the rigours of life and represent England as a derelict area, the arrival of your ham, with its extraordinary memories of that never-to-be-forgotten night in Twenty One, when the non-arrival of Edward marked the first lapse which has led to the present decline and fall, and the subsequent arrival of the other things, produced in me those humiliating but undoubtedly pleasurable feelings of mixed guilt and greed which I used to see, once more, in Edward when, after a slimming cure, he was presented with a steak and was not able to repress the terrible pleasure he felt. One really ought not to depend upon material conditions so much, but I have reached the time of life when in choosing rooms etc. – a prospect I may have to face again fairly soon here in Oxford – I behave like a confirmed old hypochondriac, consider the distance to the bathroom or whether the path between my room and the lecture hall is under cover, the possibilities of summoning servants, etc., counting, as I do, on being ill at least one day a week. I look forward to these illnesses with ungovernable delight. I have decided that I am happy only in bed. I remember Lord Halifax once informed me that he had never been happy in his life – but never, you understand – after 10 p.m. It is exactly what I feel about being on my feet at all. Sitting can be quite good. Standing or walking is an absolute hell, everywhere, always. In the end, I shan't stir, and become a real monster, worse than Joe (don't tell him!). [...]

Two things I have discovered about myself:

(*a*) that I never have time for anything at all. This is very mysterious. I have never yet in my life felt that I had time enough to do anything that I wanted to do. Whatever I do, I do under tremendous pressure because of all the other things which I cannot possibly discard or dismiss. I have never in my life been in the position where I can say that I had literally nothing to do for one, two, three days and how, therefore, best to set about enjoying oneself. Every holiday is poisoned by the work, real or imaginary, which one vaguely thinks one must do in the course of it. I have never completed anything, except in the most desperate urgency, anxious, distraught, and horrified by the result if it appears in print. I cannot quite make out why this is so; I seem to get very little done, and yet I have for the past 25 or so years led a purely pillar-to-post existence, never free from the lash for one instant. Hence my attribution of this uneasy feeling to other probably perfectly gay and heedless characters.

(*b*) I cannot bear the consequences of what I do do. I say what I imagine to be true; I never by any chance think of what reactions this will cause; as soon as such reactions occur, instead of loftily ignoring them I rush about with a tremendous pot of salve trying to assuage bruised feelings, thus completely destroying any force the original might have had, and making myself undignified and suspect. This is what happened about the *New York Times* and again about the *Time and Tide–Time* magazine articles on education. No doubt it all springs from an excessive anxiety to please.

At this point I must cease this Buchmanite[1] outpouring and enquire about your plans. When are you coming to Europe? Surely it is high time that your early Swiss pension, finishing school atmosphere was superseded by more contemporary impressions? Why cannot you come in the middle of the beautiful English summer, say late July or early August? After all, I shall not be entertaining the United States (and just as well, after all this spilt milk) in 1950 and to see you in Oxford would be a great pleasure and a rich, comical experience for both of us. I can promise you some astonishing characters. I see no reason for coming necessarily with the Ellistons,[2] but if you must, you must. On the other hand, you might come with the Judge and Marion, that would be wonderful in all kinds of ways which I could not begin to explain. Think about it seriously and let me know.

What is happening about the Hiss case? Is there anything fresh? Have people lost interest? And what about Junior? He wrote me a long and very nice letter, to which I cannot possibly reply without knowing how far off a striped suit he is. Do tip me off and I shall write to him.

Also I suffer from a perhaps unreasoning sense of admiration for US foreign policy at the moment, which seems to me to be holding the line quite well against wicked generals, industrialists etc., and be suffering neither from the acute isolationism of one part of our Government nor the straightforward imperialism of the other. Here the left identify all Americans with all other Americans and look on Truman as a kind of Dewey. My fine distinctions would go down well with Rhodes scholars (except the ones who write serious letters about me in *Time* following exactly the lines which I attributed to them in my unfortunate piece), but are regarded as pro-American pettifogging by everyone else. It obviously does not do to have a political position at all unless it is a good crude, simple thing, painted in bright colours. Nuances are merely a nuisance and cannot possibly be articulated and are treated as confusion or evasion or just specious preciosity of some sort, unworthy of the great critical moral questions, which ought to drive one into one lobby or the other. I shall never understand or believe this and ought, therefore,

---

1 According to Franklin Nathaniel Daniel Buchman (1878–1961), controversial Christian evangelist who founded the Moral Re-Armament movement, the public and private confession of sin was essential to moral goodness.
2 Herbert Elliston and his (second) wife, the former Joanne Shaw.

not to have views on such topics at all but go back to pre-1939 private Oxford life, and relax. Don't you think? Or is that not right, and should one not have relations with the enemy after all, as you and N. O. Brown[1] used to think?

Do come in summer.

TO HAMILTON FISH ARMSTRONG

1 February 1950

New College

Dear Ham,

You will wonder that I dare to write to you at all, so humble and guilty do I feel. Never can so much consideration and understanding have been expended upon a recipient so unworthy. And although my various minor ailments were genuine enough, my tendency to conceal from myself the unmanageable chaos of my life must have been an appalling nuisance to you, for which I apologise most deeply. And, as if this were not enough, I have many other crimes to atone; I have really done nothing right, as you will see. The article[2] is of a monstrous length, as I shall be the last to deny; its sentences are inelegant, its style turgid, its grammar uncertain. The treatment of the subject is not at all such as is rightly expected by you and your readers: it is all, you will justly complain, too abstract, large, vague, metaphysical. It does not deal with the events and views of the past 50 years either seriatim or in some lucid, coherent, detailed fashion, as behoves an expert sufficiently qualified to appear in your pages. It oscillates between the obvious and the obscure; in short it is a Carlylian[3] monstrosity which you have every moral right to reject; I beg you not to let any personal feeling restrain you from this obviously just and proper course. But this presupposes that you will detect some sort of intrinsic merits in my piece and will be deterred merely by such considerations as prolixity, clumsiness etc., and even this seems to be at present too high a claim. In short, as you will see, I am in a contrite and far from megalomaniac mood.

I have a more terrible thing to confess (this is becoming like a speech

1 Norman Oliver Brown (1913–2002), unorthodox Oxford-educated US philosopher and historian, a former pupil of IB's; taught classics, Wesleyan University, Connecticut, 1946–62 (Assistant Professor then Jane A. Seney Professor of Greek); later taught at the universities of Rochester and California (Santa Cruz); a Marxist when young, he was later more influenced by Freud.

2 Armstrong had suggested (letter of 31 August 1949) that IB should contribute an article tracing the development of political ideas in the first half of the 20th century for an issue of *Foreign Affairs* marking the century's halfway point: possible topics for exploration might include the social responsibilities of the State, the case for and against nationalism, and the concept of world organisation. IB missed the original November deadline, so that his article was delayed until the April 1950 issue. 'Political Ideas in the Twentieth Century', *Foreign Affairs* 28 No 3, later became the first of IB's famous *Four Essays on Liberty* (London, 1969), reprinted in L.

3 Thomas Carlyle (1795–1881), Scottish essayist and historian, famous for his distinctively tortuous writing style.

in a Russian trial in which the culprit never thinks the prosecutor goes far enough). I read your original letter with the greatest attention, and indeed agreed with all it said. And it is possible that you will find its leading ideas incorporated somewhere in the vast bulk of my white (or rather, by the colour of the sheets, pink) elephant, but towards the end I realised that, almost worthless as the piece undoubtedly was (though I believe it all), I could not alter it and would merely drive myself into a condition of melancholia and utter desperation if I tried {consequently}, so I sedulously avoided looking at the pages of your letter, although no sooner will the parcel begin its way, than I shall look again at your wise and excellent suggestions, and be stricken with more remorse than even before, though this scarcely seems possible.

How I should like to have had a very different character, to be grandly impervious to the pricks of either vanity or conscience, able to assess such passing anxieties as ephemeral ripples on the surface of a vast, complacent, self-interested, self-admiring surface, like that, say, of my revered ex-chief, Lord Halifax. But I do not resemble him at all, alas, and go through infinitely unnecessary agonies of which I don't know why you should become the innocent and courteous victim. In brief (though brevity is not the quality of which you will think when you think of me) this is a letter to beg forgiveness on all the counts. Whatever you do I shall accept not only without a murmur but convinced of its justness and rightness; if, for a moment, the thought of printing the MS does cross your mind, would it please you more if the first – historico-philosophical – section were omitted? Covering the last shreds of an author's amour propre, I think I would rather keep the elephant un-truncated, but if you want to chop, pray do, only I should like to know which limbs have been hacked off.

Perhaps, after all, you will forgive me for my document and come and see me this summer when you will surely not omit to come to Europe? There is no Ditchley any more, so to speak, so perhaps you would consider coming to stay, at least a night, in some discomfort here, and David Cecil and I will do our best to entertain you.

Meanwhile, I hope you are very well, and thank you again for your so dreadfully misplaced confidence.

yours ever,
Isaiah B.

TO ROWLAND BURDON-MULLER

2 March 1950

New College

My dear Rowland,

[...] Our election[1] has led to a very peculiar result as you will have seen; the new Labour Government, although it has kept its left wing, is in essence more right-wing than it was, and is not expected to last long. The lives of individual MPs will certainly be made unbearable by it. Six minutes is the longest period during which they can safely absent themselves from the House – it is the time during which the division bell is rung – otherwise they threaten a snap vote, and defeat by the other side. This means that no Conservative member can go away on any pretext unless he can take a Labour member away with him – such pairing may lead to very unexpected friendships. I cannot make up my mind about the parties; the Labour Party's foreign policy, because all planning presupposes some degree of isolationism in order to minimise the area within which one is vulnerable by unpredicted outside forces – seems to be unrealistic. On the other hand, it is difficult to maintain that the Conservatives are nice to the poor or other minorities, on the domestic front. What I long for is Mr Roosevelt and a New Deal to vote for – even Mr Truman – and that I am not being offered. So one takes refuge in private life.

Sir Thomas Beecham[2] has conducted a splendid concert[3] but accompanied with too much Edwardian chit chat, calculated for a Bradford audience, rather than my refined colleagues; Dr Bowra has been in splendid form, roaring away with great effect, at friend and foe alike; we were visited by my friend Alsop, who left us exhausted, himself worn out by his own social demands, by Professor Perry Miller of Harvard, who comes flying across from Holland and stays with Laski, and indeed every day has its curious visitor, to what I now realise must be one of the more intense forms of life in England now that London is at a relatively low ebb. Lady Colefax[4] is an unconscionable time a-dying in her bed surrounded by friends, with dinner parties in the dining room below which she is herself unable to attend; but the guests come up two by two and sit around the bedside in a slightly macabre atmosphere. I like her and I am prepared to pay this tribute to those indomitable social powers of which the Edwardian is obviously the

---

1 The constituencies for the election of 23 February 1950, the first after a full-term Labour government, had been substantially changed since 1945. The Labour majority was cut to five.
2 Sir Thomas Beecham (1879–1961), conductor.
3 Given by the Royal Philharmonic Orchestra in the Sheldonian Theatre on 9 February. The main works were Mozart's Prague Symphony and Haffner Serenade.
4 Dying of cancer but sustained by willpower, she never gave up attempting to continue her active social life; Beverley Nichols admired 'the sheer tenacity of this little shrivelled featherweight of a woman who refused to leave the ballroom of life until the last guests had gone'. Kirsty McLeod, *A Passion for Friendship: Sibyl Colefax and Her Circle* (London, 1991), 172.

last repository. There is something almost Winstonian in this extraordinary tenacity which refuses to retire under the most adverse blows of physical disease; it might have been indecent, this long published inability to die in peace, but it is not; it has a certain weird splendour, which Henry James would have appreciated.

I must stop and preside over dinner in Hall, and then read my article for Ham Armstrong to a collection of gaping undergraduates; the least intelligent in this College and therefore the fondest of being read aloud to. [...]

Yours ever,

Isaiah.

TO EDGAR WIND[1]

15 March 1950

New College

Dear Wind,

Forgive me for dictating this letter, but I am off tomorrow morning early to the Holy Land, whither I am summoned by the irresistible voice of the Old Monster, my friend and persecutor Dr Weizmann. He writes thirty letters about how old, ill and lonely he is, surrounded by inferiors on all sides. All this is doubtless true and at the time of writing he probably thinks he would quite like to see me. As in the case of all great men, by the time I arrive, he has forgotten everything and shows complete surprise. I am quite well treated and even spoken to sometimes, but on the whole the reason for my coming is considered obscure. If I don't come, the pathos changes into saeva indignatio[2] and there is a smell of oaths in the air. So go I must in tiny uncomfortable ships through equinoxial storms at vast expense and for no particular purpose at the beckoning of my daimon. Hence, everything at the last moment is in a fluster and a flurry and I can't put pen to paper.

How well I understand your feelings and desire for escape from that cage of weak and malleable gold[3] which discredits that noble metal. Here the situation is peculiar; there was at the time when I left Oxford to have been a Professorship of Fine Arts but it was for some reason stopped and has not been heard of for some time; doubtless because of the panic about expense which broke out in 1949. But there is also the Slade Professorship (forgive me for being so very concrete, but my wishes, if I may say so, regarding yourself are very concrete too) held by Kenneth Clark, who has resigned it for the surprisingly reputable reason that he has no more to say and does not wish to go on

1 Edgar Wind (1900–71), Professor of Art, Chicago, 1942–4, William Allan Neilson Research Professor, 1944–8; Professor of Philosophy and of Art, Smith College, 1948–55; Professor of History of Art, Oxford, 1955–67.

2 'Fierce indignation'.

3 Wind had admitted that, after six years, being surrounded by the young ladies of Smith College had lost its charms and he would welcome a post at Oxford.

giving lectures for no particular reason. It is not properly paid of course – and entails only weekly or fortnightly visits to Oxford – but is very full of prestige. It has to be applied for like all normal appointments and the committee of electors is really rather terrible – I think it is the President of Magdalen (the not unfamiliar Boase,[1] of whom it is originally said that it was difficult or even impossible to keep a second-rate man down) plus various nonentities who originally kept Roger Fry[2] out of this University. Nevertheless I think it would be an excellent thing if you could hold this post during your sabbatical year, while Seznec[3] is here; this would create not merely the appearance but the reality of a Renaissance, and perhaps lead to something very good. I shall ask the Warden of Wadham to supply you with the details. [...]

Yours,

Isaiah Berlin

IB spent his Easter vacation in Israel, visiting Chaim and Vera Weizmann. En route he visited friends in Paris before the slow sea journey from Marseilles to Haifa.

TO MARIE AND MENDEL BERLIN

[22? March 1950, *manuscript*]

[As from] New College

Dear Pa & Ma,

All very good. In Paris, usual round of pleasures. Not even too exhausting. Arrival: dinner with Bohlens, Harriman, Guy de Rothschilds,[4] Hayters (invites for me).[5] Lunch Sunday with Coopers & the monde (Sylvester Gates & Victor R. agreeable surprises). Dinner chez Guy de R: M & Mme de Guinzbourg,[6] Lord Hood[7] de l'Ambassade,[8] M. Boris Souvarine,[9] intellec-

---

1 Thomas Sherrer Ross Boase (1898–1974), Professor of History of Art, London, and Director, Courtauld Institute, 1937–47; President, Magdalen, 1947–68; Vice-Chancellor, Oxford, 1958–60; not highly regarded by IB and his friends.

2 Roger Eliot Fry (1866–1934), artist and art critic, member of the Bloomsbury group; in 1910 and 1927 he was passed over for the Slade Professorship at Oxford, which his ability as a lecturer merited.

3 Jean Joseph Seznec (1905–83), Smith Professor of the French and Spanish Languages, Harvard, 1947–50; Marshal Foch Professor of French Literature, Oxford, 1950–72.

4 Guy Edouard Alphonse Paul de Rothschild (1909–2007), French banker; IB had known him in the US during the war.

5 William Goodenough Hayter (1906–95), diplomat; Ambassador to the Soviet Union 1953–7; Warden of New College 1958–76. His wife was the former Iris Marie Hoare (1911–2004).

6 Possibly Victor de Guinzbourg (c.1906–76), son of the owner of the Russo-Asiatic Bank; Allied intelligence agent during the Second World War and interpreter with the UN after it; married to the former Edith Heinlein.

7 Samuel Hood (1910–81), 6th Viscount Hood, diplomat; Counsellor, British Embassy, Paris, 1948–51.

8 'Of the Embassy'.

9 The pseudonym of Boris Konstantinovich Livshitz (1895–1984), Ukrainian-born French

tuel russe,[1] Mme la Baronne Edouard de R.[2] All v. charming & nice. Monday, lunch at the Hayters with Sir O. & Lady Harvey.[3] Old friends of Weizmann. [...] Cabin on ship comfortable, & ship very new & pretty looking. Full of American Hinton Court'ites.[4] Yiddish prevalent either *immediately*, or after 3 official sentences in English: honoured by being put at Captain's table. My neighbours, the only other respectable people: a Danish family, Cohn,[5] he a high official of the Danish foreign office, most dignified & charming: his wife, very innocent & nice, a Bamberger from Nürnberg (or Fürth?) 2 pretty Danish looking daughters (too young alas! 13 & 14!) with Mogen Dovids[6] dangling like little crosses. All round us a roaring ghetto: we, a dignified & snobbish little island of "superior people" like "Anglo-Jews". The Captain, a Buda Pesth Jew who was a sailor under Franz Josef,[7] full of British decorations & Goyish outlook. Quite all right. I was approached by somebody, either a friend or relation of Mara[8] (at first I thought may be his wife! or sister in law! I *think* neither. I am v. nice to her. Left Russia in 1934. I suppose a relation of one of the wives. Perfectly nice Paris Jewish emigrée. At the moment she is dancing with a Salonika merchant, while the Danish family is seeing a film) so I have bowing acquaintances. I bow to the Purser with the hauteur of an Important Person & feel you wd enjoy me in this role. I make oblique references to Dr Weizmann which make a deep impression, & feel it is easy to be a Khlestakov.[9] All round a tremendous Sholom Aleikhem[10] world is going on: Jews are photographing each other & feel *excellent* ("Ich

political activist; a Bolshevik during the Russian Revolution and one of the founders of the French Communist Party, he soon became fiercely anti-Stalinist (as he remained) and later a moderate socialist.

1 'Russian intellectual'.
2 The former Germaine Alice Halphen (1884–1975), widow of Baron Edouard Alphonse James de Rothschild (1868–1949) and mother of Guy de Rothschild.
3 Sir Oliver Charles Harvey (1893–1968), 1st Baron Harvey of Tasburgh 1954, diplomat; British Ambassador, Paris, 1948–54; and his wife, the former Maud Annora Williams-Wynn (1893–1970).
4 The Berlin family had apparently stayed at the Hinton Court Private Jewish Pension in Grove Road, Bournemouth, and retained vivid memories of its clientele (see also L1 316).
5 Georg Arye Cohn (1887–1956), influential adviser on international law to the Danish Foreign Ministry; before the war, expounded the moral case for neutrality; Danish representative, 1948 Red Cross Conference (Stockholm) and 1949 Diplomatic Conference (Geneva), which approved final drafts of the Geneva Conventions. His wife (from a famous rabbinical family) was the former Elfriede Veilchen Bamberger (d. 1994), of Kitzingen, Bavaria; the daughters (their youngest) were Anne Margrethe and Emilie (who later settled in Israel).
6 The Yiddish form of Magen David ('shield of David'), the six-pointed star that symbolises Judaism.
7 Franz Josef (1830–1916), ruler of the Austro-Hungarian Empire 1867–1916.
8 Apparently an acquaintance of the Berlin family from Riga or Petrograd who had settled in France.
9 The central character of Nikolay Gogol's 1836 play *The Government Inspector*, who inflates his status by dishonest boasting.
10 Sholom Aleichem (*sic*) was the pen-name of Sholem Yakov Rabinovitz (1859–1916), writer from Ukraine who spent his last years in New York; famous for his tragi-comic stories in Yiddish about East European Jewish life.

hob gevelt nehmen a aeroplan, ober *Sie* muz fahren in a Iddische Schif: Sie Muz und sie muz, und jetzt is ir nit gut. A Meshugaas; Idischer schiff! finf teg und finf necht vet Sie krechtzen etc.'[1] That is who my company is like, but cosiness ohn a Sof.[2] Sir O. Harvey cd not fully savour the taste, & the Danish Jews are innocently wondering if all Israel talks Yiddish? the crew & officers speak Hebrew officially (like Lebanese speak French) & secretly German: the upper personnel is Yekish[3] & very efficient: the Captain refuses to speak German (his native tongue) to the Dane's wife & for my sake talks English. So we have 5 people talking broken English instead of one talking broken German, which wd please Mrs Berlin. The sea is like glass, not a ripple. To-morrow we stop 3 hrs in Naples, where I shall send this, in order to accept passengers & the coffin of a Jewish Hungarian heroine[4] who parachuted into Hungary was caught & executed in 1943 or 1944. We arrive on Sunday, where an official reception of the Coffin will precede embarkation: I am sure it will be dignified & moving. Mr Bohlen is in Rome (a conference) & promises me a sleeper if Pernikoff[5] fails: so I *should* be O.K. – I am looking *very* well already, after 2 days in the sun, & am, for want of anything better, actually working gently: i.e. reading philosophy for my last duties in the subject: The bed is soft, breakfast is served in bed by a Viennese stewardess who does not know the Hebrew for pillow: anyway there is only one: but the life belt under it provides maximum comfort for me. There is no nonsense about Boat Drill: Jews Unter Uns[6] don't indulge in nonsense. [. . .]

Love

Shaya

1 IB's Yiddish is somewhat approximate. Strictly: 'Ikh hob gevolt nemen an aeroplan, ober zi muz forn in a yidishe shif: zi muz un zi muz, un itst iz ir nit gut. A meshugas; yidishe shif! finf teg un finf nekht vet zi krekhtsn etc.' ('I wanted to go by plane, but *she* insisted that we take a Jewish ship. She went on and on about it, and now she is unwell. Such madness; a Jewish ship! Five days and five nights she will be complaining etc.')

2 'Without an end'.

3 The Yiddish 'Yekke' is a pejorative nickname for German Jewish immigrants to Israel, implying extreme formality, punctuality and politeness.

4 Hannah Szenes (1921–44), Hungarian Zionist and poet; settled in Israel 1939; joined the British Army 1943; volunteered to return to Hungary to establish contact with partisans; parachuted into Yugoslavia but was caught soon after crossing into Hungary; stayed silent under torture and was executed by firing squad. Her remains were re-interred on Mount Herzl.

5 (Ossip) Alexandre Joseph Pernikoff (1894–1952), Russian-born French citizen; author and tourism expert (who had helped Germans to escape from Nazi persecution); of dubious reputation, he had offered to make IB's travel arrangements.

6 Probably a reference to *Die Mörder sind unter uns* ('The murderers are among us'), the first postwar (1946) German film.

TO MARIE AND MENDEL BERLIN

[Early April 1950, *manuscript*]

Weizmann House, Rehovot, Israel

My dear parents

I don't believe for a moment that this will reach you in time: letters take a tremendous time to get out (I suspect, on account of the censorship which, I must say, I think Israel probably still badly needs. So I don't complain. But you will of course be worried – no letters etc. which will be ludicrous). There is too much to say: the country is remarkable in every way: some Schlamperei[1] there *is*, but considering the obstacles, remarkably little [...]. At Haifa I was met by Dr W's A.D.C., Major Arnon,[2] & whisked off to Rehovot. Warm welcome. But about the personalities here & at Tel-A. I have not time to write (Mr Weisgall's[3] auto – to take me round the Institute – is at the door – I must be off. When I return – after lunch with Akiba Persitz[4] in Tel-A. – I'll tell you about Yitz. & Ida) Very nice lunch. To-morrow I have to lunch with Nebi Samuel & Hadassah[5] – Mrs W. threatens to expel me if I do as she is not favourably disposed – However I think I must. Yitz. is really ill, poor man, he has cardiac asthma – a weakening of one of the muscles of the heart – & has been in bed for 5 months – & Ida has now let the nurses go (a) because she thinks she is better (b) because it costs £7 a day. The first is true: but it is also true that by going in every hour & asking Yitz. how he feels she introduces a tragic atmosphere bad for his nerves on which much depends, & lowers his resistance. He is worried, of course, about his job, his pension etc. [...] I think father might seriously consider a week's stay in Tel-Aviv or Jerus. – in a hotel – (a) to save Ida from going mad with pride about money (b) to talk to Max[6] about plans![7] I think the latter can all be made satisfactorily, the

1 'Negligence, sloppiness'.
2 Rav-Seren (Major) David Arnon (1912–68). According to George Weidenfeld, Arnon, whose wife-cum-secretary ran the Weizmanns' household, was 'deeply unpopular, not least because of his peacock-like vanity. But he had the backing of Mrs Weizmann', who demanded he be given a rank higher than that of Ben-Gurion's military aide. *Remembering My Good Friends* (London, 1995), 215.
3 Meyer Wolf Weisgal (*sic*) (1894–77), Polish-born US journalist, editor, impresario, active Zionist and fund-raiser of genius; Chaim Weizmann's personal representative in US 1940–9; played a leading role in planning and funding Weizmann Institute of Science 1944–9; Chairman, Executive Council, Weizmann Institute of Science, 1949–66, Acting Director 1952–9, President 1966–9, Chancellor 1970–7; one of the general editors of Weizmann's letters and papers.
4 Akiva Persitz (1912–83), Oxford-educated lawyer in Tel Aviv; long-standing friend of IB. 'Akiba' is an alternative transliteration of the Hebrew name.
5 Edwin Herbert ('Nebi') Samuel (1898–1978), 2nd Viscount Samuel 1963, formerly an administrator in the Palestine Government; Director of Broadcasting, Palestine, 1945–8; Senior Lecturer in British Institutions, Hebrew University, Jerusalem, 1954–69; his wife was the former Hadassah Grasovsky (1896–1986).
6 Max Cohn, IB's second cousin on his father's side, a Polish-born architect who had settled in Israel and become a close friend of the Samunovs.
7 The Samunovs and IB's parents appear to have been considering a joint project to build one or more rental properties in Israel.

house built with Yitz's money to pay itself off within 6–7 years completely. I suppose you will want to talk ab[ou]t it. – I really think you'll have to go again this year. Second impressions when we meet. [...]

On Tuesday I am to attend a party "in my honour" to which the crème de la crème has been asked. I saw Walter:[1] I think he has organized his ministry excellently but the Yékivth[2] is oppressively sterile: so there is a natural revolt by the imaginative, energetic, & restless. Had a good talk with B.G. & think the whole State a terrific success.

love

ישעיהו[3]

TO ARTHUR SCHLESINGER

20 April 1950

New College

Dear Arthur,

[...] I have just had an extraordinary tour of Israel followed by a happy week in Paris staying with Avis[4] who is an angel. About Israel I shall tell you by word of mouth – it is both touching and comical; I was myself received with a mixture of suspicion about the motives of my apparent unwillingness to stay plus offers of jobs, about which I was so indefinite, although indicating general respectful reluctance, that more than one person in the Ministry of Foreign Affairs wondered whose job I was after. I was thus treated with a mixture of flattery and obscure apprehension which could not have been funnier in view of the extreme innocence of my intentions. However, all that when I see you. But it is nevertheless an NCL State and so far as I can see the only genuine representative of the type. The nicest persons there are also the silliest, namely the pro-Soviet left-wing socialists who emerge out of a pre-1917 Russia entirely unaffected by all that happened after; a kind of maddening naivety and political purity which simultaneously discredits political philosophy as a subject – there is little wrong with the theories of these men – and increases one's liking, though not one's respect, for its exponents. [...]

I feel utterly exhausted after my perilous flight from Tel Aviv in a rickety Israeli machine out of which engines appeared to be dropping over the Mediterranean, flown by some man who smuggled these objects from the United States during the Arab wars, very brave, not very skilful. Goodness it

---

1   Walter George Eytan (1910–2001), né Ettinghausen in Germany; IB's contemporary at St Paul's School and Oxford; first Director-General of Israel's Foreign Ministry (1948–59).

2   'The German Jewish contingent' (see 174/3).

3   'Isaiah'.

4   Avis Howard *Bohlen (1912–81), née Thayer, wife of Chip Bohlen (at this time second in command of the US Embassy in Paris).

is an extraordinary country. Joe is returning here soon from behind the iron curtain; I should have given much to have been present at his interview with Tito.[1] I wonder which quailed first. I am now expecting your long letter, having carefully written nothing myself, in order to husband my resources for the reply.

Yours ever,

Isaiah   [...]

TO AVIS BOHLEN

24 April 1950 [*manuscript*]

As from New College

Dearest Avis,

I really am overwhelmed with mounting feelings of gratitude & reminiscences of pleasure. You really were angelic to let me stay so long; long suffering about being involved in my chaotic, time consuming, involved, endlessly complicated, Rube Goldberg[2] like arrangements whereby, as always in my life, the most difficult, roundabout, precarious, complex methods are employed to bring about the most obvious results; & life is spent in half-remorseful worries about the hypothetical reactions of various persons indirectly involved, or thought to be involved, in possible small debacles made likely by the assumption that everybody is terribly sensitive, omniscient, and that all one does, thinks, says, is known & resented by everyone, everywhere, all the time. Hence my life is almost entirely occupied by trying to wipe off entirely non-existent illusory droplets of bad blood allegedly occasioned by imaginary crimes on my part. Very exhausting and unnecessary. However you have seen me at my most tiresome & displayed an incredible patience, benevolence, even disposition to humour me like a child. For this I shall be endlessly grateful. [...]

I have had a letter[3] a) from Ben Cohen telling me in pretty severe language how poorly he thought of my gloomy article in *Foreign Affairs*: what about Holmes, Brandeis,[4] & after that some very third rate thinkers, he wanted to know? I believe him to be wrong & myself to be right (a very rare state of mind on the part of one so very liable to guilt) & shall reply with great

---

1 The name adopted by Josip Broz (1892–1980), wartime leader of the Communist partisans in Yugoslavia; Prime Minister of Yugoslavia 1945–53, President 1953–80.

2 Reuben Lucius ('Rube') Goldberg (1883–1970), US cartoonist whose most celebrated drawings, like those of W. Heath Robinson, featured complicated machines designed to perform simple tasks in a ludicrously roundabout way.

3 Protesting against the idea that 'political ideas in the 20th century are dominantly communist and Russian and that any other ideas like those of Roosevelt are essentially of the 19th century mold [...] and that there is no alternative between 19th century liberalism and 20th century totalitarianism' (7 April 1950).

4 Louis Dembitz Brandeis (1856–1941), Associate Justice, US Supreme Court, 1916–39.

magnificence & pomp, like Macaulay[1] or Lord Acton.[2] On the other hand I was quoted by Phil Graham, who wrote me a characteristically insulting set of compliments, to an audience of advertising executives. There is no doubt. My future is to be a darling of Babbitts[3] & reactionaries and an object of scorn to the left, who have a feeling that I ought to be like Laski, Lerner,[4] etc. & obviously am not. [...]

Isaiah   [...]

TO PHILIP GRAHAM

28 April 1950

New College

Dear Phil,

Thank you for your letter, the typography of which I admired almost more than the style and beauty of the contents. I am more than proud to have been advertised not by, but to the advertisers' convention in this fashion. This really does mean that I have arrived. So unassailable do I feel that I now have taken to writing letters to newspapers explaining why I don't propose to write not only for them, but to them (my private correspondence with the New York Times is at the moment even more interesting than the public one). This you will doubtless call a typical example of my opaqueness of style. But then I never did look upon you as the audience to which I wished to address myself, ever since your barbarian attitude to my earlier opus.[5] I direct your attention to the attitude of B.V.C[ohen], who while writing plaintively in words strangely reminiscent of the actual tone of his views about why I don't mention Keynes, Brandeis, Morris Cohen, and Northrop (!), concedes my style to be full of verve and vigour. So there. So now you know why I shall never never offer anything to the Washington Post again. The lofty gaiety of my writing is unsuited to the brisk thudding of its middle of the road clichés. I am very sorry about our poor friend;[6] I should like to hear as soon as possible about his fate. A not very nice (I thought) film financier

1 Thomas Babington Macaulay (1800–59), 1st Baron Macaulay, Whig politician, historian, essayist and poet; robust in the self-confidence of his judgements.

2 John Emerich Edward Dalberg-Acton (1834–1902), 1st Baron Acton, historian with a deep moral commitment to speaking the truth, liberal in politics and in his Catholic faith.

3 The eponymous hero of Sinclair Lewis's 1922 novel Babbitt was an archetypal blinkered, smug, middle-class materialist.

4 Maxwell Alan ('Max') Lerner (1902–92), Russian-born US journalist, editor and academic; editorial director, PM, 1943–8; syndicated columnist, New York Post, 1949–92; Professor of American Civilization, Brandeis University, 1949–73; at this time an influential left-wing liberal with an enthusiasm for Stalin.

5 Presumably the Washington Post had been offered and declined an earlier piece by IB.

6 Ed Prichard's appeal had failed on 4 April. He and his advisers decided on a further (and final) appeal to the Supreme Court. However so many of the Supreme Court Justices disqualified themselves because of their links with Prichard that a quorum could not be reached; the finding of the lower court in favour of his conviction therefore stood. On 14 July his appeal against

called Bienstock[1] whom I met in Paris began a long denunciation of him, Felix etc., and I was forced to intervene in the middle of a very stuffy dinner party – all the other diners being ignorant and bored – because I decided that disloyalty on the whole preys more on one's conscience than making unnecessary scenes.

Look after yourself, old boy; the toll of death is mounting dangerously. Laski, Matthiessen, Blum,[2] soon, there will be few left of us.

Yours,

Isaiah

TO HAMILTON FISH ARMSTRONG

27 May 1950

New College

My dear Ham,

[...] As for the article itself; I have had a curious reaction from Chip: he said he had talked most seriously with George Kennan about it, and they thought it was unfinished (!) and there should have been a long piece explaining why Communism cannot last and is contrary to human nature etc., and in effect formally refuting it and its claims to survive. But that would have necessitated another essay, and I can imagine your face if I had been struck by the same inspired idea, and sent you a long coda full of exorcisms against the devil. Moreover, I cannot believe that description and analysis need necessarily be propaganda even in the best and worthiest sense, and I thought I made my own position clear enough throughout. This is apparently not so for everyone, since Professor W. Y. Elliott of Harvard is actually reported to think that I have made totalitarianism not too unattractive, and my piece might seduce the weaker brothers into positive support for it. But Bill Elliott is not a very balanced judge of anything, and apart from [not?] particularly wishing to have a fracas with him and Harvard, his judgement does not impress me. That George Kennan should also half think this seems to me more serious. If you see him perhaps you would ask him what he really thinks. I meditated a letter, but then, as it is all hearsay, I decided I would wait until I saw him.[3] [...]

My fan mail has been curious: I had a reproachful letter from Ben Cohen complaining that I had not done justice to Messrs Holmes, Brandeis, Keynes,

sentence (in a Kentucky court) also failed and Prichard began his two-year prison sentence in the Federal Correctional Institution, Ashland, Kentucky (Plate 14).

1 Probably Abraham Lawrence Bienstock (1904–80), lawyer based in New York and closely involved in the film world.

2 Harold Laski died on 24 March and Matthiessen committed suicide on 1 April. Léon Blum (1872–1950), first socialist Prime Minister of France, died on 30 March.

3 Kennan wrote a long and thoughtful response to the article (letter dated 26 April but probably a secretarial error for 26 May) to which IB did not reply until 13 February 1951 (213–20).

and even Northrop, Morris Cohen and similar figures, and that my bugbear was exaggerated, and from Ascoli who thought I ought to have written the article for the *Reporter* (I like Ascoli but not, alas, the *Reporter*, but would you keep this from him) and did not attack America nearly enough for possessing Mr Luce. Imagine my guilt therefore when, by the very next post, the fan letter arrived from Mr Luce in person followed by one from Lord Brand;[1] I have begun to feel that my allies come from curiously unexpected directions, and wonder where I was and what I was doing. I can see now I shall never be a member of any party though I may continue to pay dues just in order to avoid the priggishness of neutrality. [...]

Yours

Isaiah B.

IB's translation of First Love *was eventually published in May 1950, but the* Foreign Affairs *article continued to dominate his correspondence. Henry Luce had written to offer his 'profound congratulations'; despite his disagreement with IB's concluding call for less faith and more scepticism, which he thought did not follow from the preceding analysis, Luce considered the article 'superlatively good'.[2] IB responded with a letter of profuse thanks for Luce's praise; only in the postscript did he return to the intellectual argument:*

Perhaps I ought to explain that I don't of course wish to plead for scepticism for its own sake – only for a greater degree of self-examination, less organised, precipitate, uncritical mass pursuit of things however intrinsically noble, in which too much is trampled under foot, too little is allowed for the gap between theories and the infinite complexity of individuals – a gap which is I am sure unbridgeable (and I should like to say fortunately so).[3]

The correspondence continued.

TO HENRY R LUCE

1 June 1950

New College

Dear Mr Luce,

Thank you very much for your letter of 20 May.[4] At the risk of being a terrible bore, I just wish to explain myself one degree further. I don't think that the nature of human beings is a mystery, if by mystery is meant something in principle not discoverable, i.e. which not merely does but must

1 Robert Henry Brand (1878–1963), 1st Baron Brand of Eydon, businessman, historian and public servant; Fellow of All Souls 1901–32, 1937–63.
2 Luce to IB, 26 April 1950.
3 IB to Luce, 4 May 1950.
4 Which concludes: 'Could we say that mystery is the unlimited invitation to the exercise of reason, yet it is only faith which discerns the nature of this invitation?'

for ever and in all cases elude the ordinary human understanding – which perhaps you do mean in a sense in which Pascal[1] or Dostoevsky or Mr T. S. Eliot mean it. I see no reason on the contrary for not thinking that sufficient care and patience and sensibility – and no doubt humility and not generalising, not jumping to conclusions etc., enables one to unravel the most complex of mysteries if one works hard enough and long enough and is endowed with sufficient natural gifts. Only I do believe that this can only be done ad hoc for a given person in a given context in a given way, and not for bodies of men or whole cultures as is so glibly assumed by some sociologists and persons who misapply scientific techniques valid and valuable in their own province. But I think the gifts required are natural and not supernatural.

I hope you will forgive me for going on like this, but I feel this is a crucial issue and one on which it is worth explaining oneself.

Please do not trouble to acknowledge this, and I do hope to see you whenever and wherever it may be possible to do so. I apologise again for chewing on this bit of string – it is a poor reward for your niceness in writing.

Yours sincerely,
Isaiah Berlin

TO VERA WEIZMANN
1 June 1950 [*manuscript*]

New College

Dear Mrs Weizmann

This time I write at once: I see that you think that I have not behaved well. Perhaps you are right: but I can, temperamentally, only live one life at a time: & after returning I duly fell ill with exhaustion (I do this six times a year) & then tried to catch up with the endless Oxford duties neglected in the spring & write an immortal paper on philosophy ordered by a Learned Society[2] (& produce ephemeral rubbish) & once absorbed I do things as Russians say Запоем,[3] I cannot plan, order, distribute my time neatly & sensibly between occupations, I am not a German, & not a Sharett, & doubtless suffer for it. Hence I don't answer letters (or answer them in a rush, too much & chaotically) & then suffer agonies & then go to bed again with ulcers or sciatica or other diseases brought on by an disorderly bachelor life. My mother's heart is really breaking about my mode of life: but it obviously cannot be helped. A secretary arrives now once a week & takes dictation: & if I were permitted to dictate letters to you, I cd have done so far far more often. But this last one I really cd not but write myself: & for that I scarcely have

---

1 Blaise Pascal (1623–62), French mathematician, physicist and religious thinker.
2 'Logical Translation', *Proceedings of the Aristotelian Society* 50 (1949–50), included in CC.
3 'Zapoem' ('non-stop').

physical energy enough at the end of teaching & examining 350 candidates.[1] Oh dear! I did not mean to make this a personal jeremiad. I am very sorry indeed that Dr Weizmann is not well: there are conflicting rumours here: I received a visit from the Gestetners[2] who are worried about where to send their son to school, & they gave an optimistic account. Of course if you are in Burgenstock I shall try to come to see you from Vevey to which I shall take my parents: but write I cannot. Either one writes at immense length & tells everything (& that is too frightening & I used to do it but haven't for a long time now) or it is all sticks & fragments. I am very very sorry that you are in a melancholy mood: I am in that condition now as soon as I am left alone in my rooms in New College, & I wait for the mice to start scratching as they do now every night – the cat I have imported is lazy & humane, like the judges of Israel – & plays with the mice peacefully & refuses to eat them. But I shall try to cheer you up if you are sad, in Switzerland: perhaps you cd ask the Major to let me know of where you will be when. I shall only come if you are really not too tired to see me – or otherwise occupied – in August – I shall wait indefinitely if you are, please treat me as you think I deserve; or better still as you please. I have devotion enough to Dr Weizmann & yourself to accomodate myself to almost anything.

With great love & affection,
Isaiah.

TO THE PRESIDENT, BRYN MAWR COLLEGE, PENNSYLVANIA[3]

13 June 1950

New College

Dear President,

I have now had time to co-ordinate my arrangements and shall, I think, be able gladly to accept your kind invitation to deliver the Mary Flexner lectures[4] in the winter of 1952, if that is a suitable date. I shall be at Harvard in the Fall term of 1951, i.e. from September to Christmas, and, if that were suitable, could come in January 1952, and stay until some time in March before sailing home.

As for the subject of my lectures; I was wondering whether you would find the political ideas of the late eighteenth and early nineteenth century a

---

1 Cf. (on examining) 'as a mixture of heavy responsibility, triviality, tedium, anxiety and stupefying physical labour it is unique' (to Edmund Wilson, 16 July 1950).

2 Sigmund Gestetner (1897–1956), Chairman and Managing Director of the duplicating firm founded by his father, and his Swiss-born wife Helen ('Henny'), née Lang. Both were prominent Zionists.

3 Bryn Mawr College, near Philadelphia, was founded in 1885 to offer women at least the same intellectual standard of higher education as was available to men. Katharine Elizabeth McBride (1904–76) was President 1942–70.

4 A series of six lectures extending over six weeks and accompanied by seminars, given by 'scholars of distinction in the humanities' (from Katharine McBride, 21 April).

suitable topic. What I should like to talk about is the different fundamental types of approach to social and political problems – e.g. the Utilitarian; that of the Enlightenment (rational and sentimental) from the Encyclopaedia[1] to the French Revolution; the Authoritarian-Reactionary (de Maistre[2] and his allies); the Romantic; the Technocratic-Scientific (Saint-Simon[3] and his followers), and perhaps the Marxist. These seem to me to be the prototypes from which our modern views in their great and colliding variety have developed (only stated, it appears to me, with much more clarity, vigour and dramatic force by the founders than by their modern epigoni). My lectures, while occupied with the history of ideas, would thus have a very direct bearing upon our present discontents. I don't know what I ought to call this subject – it is part of a work on the history of European ideas from 1789 to 1870 which, in any case, I must at some [time] write for the *Oxford History of Europe*, but perhaps the title could be thought of later. Perhaps something quite simple, 'Six (or however many) Types of Political Theory', or perhaps something a little more arresting. However, if this kind of subject is suitable I could set to work and prepare some lectures.

I need hardly say how profoundly I appreciate the compliment that you pay me in asking me to follow in the steps of so many notable masters of their subjects. I should of course have no objection to seminars and such informal instruction as may be part of the obligation of the Lecturer in this series. I hope you will have no hesitation in rejecting my suggested lectures if for some reason they are not what you desire, but I am preoccupied with the thought of the early nineteenth century and its antecedents, and should find it difficult to turn my attention to something very different; but that is no reason why you should allow this to be foisted upon you if some other plan would suit you better. If, on the other hand, my suggestion is acceptable to you, I have no doubt that I shall myself vastly profit by the experience.

Yours sincerely,
Isaiah Berlin

On 1 July IB's campaign to return to All Souls reached its successful conclusion with his appointment to a Robertson Research Fellowship there (initially for five years). Although allocated a room in All Souls, he opted for the time being

1 The *Encyclopédie, ou dictionnaire raisonné des sciences, des arts et des métiers* ['Encyclopaedia, or Systematic Dictionary of the Sciences, Arts and Crafts'] (Paris, 1751–80), planned as a comprehensive survey of human knowledge and containing contributions from many of the leading intellects of the time, was a manifesto of the Enlightenment, implicitly undermining traditional political and religious doctrines.
2 Joseph Marie, comte de Maistre (1753–1821), born in Savoy of French descent; lawyer, diplomat and influential counter-revolutionary who advocated the re-establishment of the supreme authority of monarch and Pope.
3 (Claude) Henri de Rouvroy, comte de Saint-Simon (1760–1825), impoverished French minor aristocrat who welcomed new technologies and argued for the meritocratic reform of (increasingly industrialised) society; amongst his followers, these ideas developed into socialism.

to continue living in his comfortable accommodation in New College, where he
would still have some (much reduced) teaching responsibilities.

TO E. R. DODDS[1]

27 July 1950

New College

Dear Professor Dodds,

As there have been certain changes in my status since my re-appointment as a C.U.F. Lecturer[2] at the instance of the Board of Literae Humaniores, I feel it is appropriate to report these changes to the Board in order to enable it to make whatever dispositions it may think proper. On 1 July of this year I was elected to a Research Fellowship at All Souls College and consequently ceased to be Fellow and Tutor of New College. All Souls College elected me to a Fellowship in order to enable me to pursue a course of research which is to include:

(a) The preparation of a volume on the history of human ideas from 1789 to 1870 to be published as part of the Oxford History of Europe by the Oxford University Press.

(b) An investigation of the antecedents of the Russian revolution which is to take the form [of] an extended study in three or four volumes of the ideas, personalities and social and cultural factors followed both in Russia and in Europe from the beginning of the nineteenth century until 1917, whose interplay culminated in the Russian Revolution.

(c) The preparation of a volume on the philosophy of Berkeley which I have undertaken to do for a series to be published under the editorship of Professor A. J. Ayer.

(d) The preparation of material enabling me to deliver lectures both on political philosophy and general philosophy in the sub-faculties of Politics and Philosophy of the kind which I have been engaged in delivering during the past four years; these to include a course of lectures which I have to deliver at Bryn Mawr College during my prospective stay in that American Institution (of six weeks' duration) in the spring of 1952 on 'Types of Political Theory' to be entitled the Mary Flexner Lectures and published by the Oxford University Press.

At the same time All Souls College has permitted me to take up to 8 hours

---

1 Eric Robertson Dodds (1893–1979), Regius Professor of Greek, Oxford, 1936–60.

2 A Common University Fund Lectureship at Oxford is funded partly by the University and partly by the College where the Lecturer holds a Fellowship; it involves a combination of college teaching, individual research and participation in University-wide activities such as lecturing and examining.

a week teaching in the University and I have consequently been made a Lecturer in Philosophy of New College with a maximum of five or six hours teaching a week, to continue to teach philosophy in the Schools of Literae Humaniores and PPE very much as before.

This naturally represents a considerable shift of interest in the field of my studies, in particular in the direction of the history of nineteenth-century ideas and the history of Russian ideas and practice. In the light of this it may be that my field of interest may now be considered to be more nearly within the scope of Social Studies than of Literae Humaniores; I am not myself wholly clear about this but I have had a letter from Mr D. Worswick[1] (Chairman of the Social Studies Board) saying that he was inclined to that view; and in view of the above considerations I am inclined to agree with him. I propose of course to be engaged to a considerable degree upon philosophical work; not merely political philosophy but logical theory of knowledge both in the form of tuition at New College and intercollegiate lectures and classes, and this traditionally falls within the field of Literae Humaniores. I have until now worked principally in this field both as a lecturer and teacher and have published papers on it in *Mind*[2] and the *Proceedings of the Aristotelian Society* during June and July of this year, and this type of work I do not intend to abandon. At the same time I have also published articles and long reviews on political philosophy and on cognate Russian topics both in British and in American specialist periodicals and this side of my work, with the aid of the Research Fellowship granted to me by All Souls College, I intend considerably to expand. My problem arises from the fact that although as a teacher and lecturer the subjects with which I shall deal will be those within the province of philosophy as that subject is understood in this University, i.e. logical theory of knowledge, political philosophy etc., much of the new leisure which the diminution in the number of my pupils will give me will be devoted to topics not normally included in this School. If, therefore, I am to be allowed to retain my existing CUF lectureship I do not myself know whether this should continue to be a Literae Humaniores Lectureship or a PPE Lectureship. Mr Worswick's suggestion seems to me very plausible but this is an administrative matter on which I feel that I have no expert knowledge.

I am in process of making tentative arrangements with Harvard to visit them occasionally there to give lectures both on philosophy proper and the history of Russian ideas but I shall certainly continue to reside and teach and lecture in this University in at any rate four terms out of every six and most often two terms out of every three, so that no arrangements which I

1 (George) David Norman Worswick (1916–2001), economist; Oxford University Institute of Statistics 1940–60; Fellow and Tutor in Economics, Magdalen, 1945–65, Senior Tutor 1955–7.
2 'Empirical Propositions and Hypothetical Statements', *Mind* 59 (1950), included in CC.

may make with Harvard would preclude me from performing to the full the duties of a CUF Lectureship.

I should therefore be most grateful if you could make whatever use of this information that you consider most proper, and convey this to the Board of Literae Humaniores if that seems to you the proper course and be so kind as to let me know your conclusion.

I have sent a copy of this letter to Mr Worswick in case he and the Social Studies Board wish to consider the matter.

Yours sincerely

I. Berlin

By now a dramatic change had occurred in IB's life: he had recently embarked on an affair (his first sexual relationship) with Jenifer Hart,[1] the wife of his friend and colleague Herbert Hart. IB initially found the affair all-consuming, so that the long-awaited visit in mid-July of Felix and Marion Frankfurter did not receive his full attention. His examining duties over, IB joined his parents for their holiday in Switzerland.

TO MARION FRANKFURTER

17 August 1950 [*manuscript*]

Le Grand Hotel, Vevey, Suisse,
but as from New College, Oxford & sent via Oxford
to save foreign currency. I am v. tightfisted & mean suddenly.

Dear Marion,

I have never, I think, had so frustrating an experience as *not* seeing you in Oxford. It is very well about my withdrawing myself from the world etc. but I had a feeling that I hadn't seen you at all: or as in a dream, clearly but thinly, so that the memory is of something unreal: my first tea party when, I mean, you came to tea, I loved: after that it was all agreeable enough, but turned to dust at once. I must say, I was living in a nightmare such [as] I've scarcely ever known before: I had been sick, I was examining which I'd never done before on such a scale, & which got me down absolutely: I was being injected with penicillin throughout your visit. I worked till 3 a.m. every morning & sat in the Schools from 9.30 till 5.30 every day: my meetings with you were indeed oases but it was a very exhausted traveller who reached them, and drained of all capacity for feeling. Goodness me! I've never known such a slow pointless nightmare as that month in Oxford: while you were with the Goodharts[2] I

1 Jenifer Margaret *Hart (1914–2005), née Williams; a close friend of IB from their first meeting in 1934. The affair started when IB was confined to bed with laryngitis in his New College rooms and JH came to visit him. Later IB and JH each claimed that the other had made the first move; both stressed the importance of the relationship in their lives.

2 Sir Arthur Lehman Goodhart (1891–1978), Professor of Jurisprudence, Oxford, 1931–51; Master, Univ., 1951–63; and his wife, the former Cecily Agnes Mackay Carter (1896–1985).

didn't really expect to see you: & while you were with Maurice I could not enjoy anything very much: I longed to see you together (with Felix I mean) then alone, then Felix alone, then together, then a good deal more alone: having by deliberate effort taught myself to endure solitude, & having reacquired the coccoon of private life, why was it not possible to sit & talk? or even look out of the window? all my sad little suggestions about going for walks were a figurative reference (I *hate* walking as you must know) to that – & unlike you, I do not assume that what is bad & frustrating is perhaps part of the unavoidable texture of existence, I retain an optimistic if childish belief in malleability, & ascribe disaster to specific causes against which it is possible to rage, or on which one can at least fix to concentrate one's gloom or anger. But in this case I cannot blame anyone or anything except Oxford University, & that's no use. Emotionally, too, I was, I suppose, in a perturbed state, tho' that, thank God, is a secret known literally to nobody save the persons concerned, & nobody knows, & for once I have achieved a secret life. Why then am I boasting about it now? because I am determined to set out in full the causes of what I feel to have been a frustrating experience: nothing tragical, nothing any of us can be blamed for, nothing irremediable (though I suspect you think nothing is remediable) but unusually, to me at least, maddening. I shd like to see you very much: I couldn't in London since I sat in New College till the last moment, & left London on the next day half dead & tended by my dear mother: & have, in this absurd country, really pre-1914, with nerves infinitely unshattered, full of such bourgeois bliss as you can't conceive, such heavenly dullness, such Edwardian massive vulgarity, such determined inescapable cosiness, everything so trivial, small, but self confident, in this splendid mediocre 19th century life which I madly regret and lament the passing of – I feel well again. I've seen nobody but my parents, I've read lots & lots of books & Swiss newspapers, I read Joe on Korea[1] with a sense of unreality & undeserved amusement (I do *not* believe in a general war this or next year. Even though Russia's tactic of slowly bleeding America is bad enough & dangerous enough) & when Duff Cooper said to me in Paris that Truman was his hero – & had never made a false decision on a crucial matter – I almost believed him, & in my Swiss mood, Mr Truman is thoroughly appropriate: & when I think of 2 worlds (not quite Jock Balfour's two worlds which Phil blew up about, do you remember, one evening in Joe's house in 1946) one full of tiny little benevolent vulgarians, Swiss officials, Trumans, Shertoks, Nileses,[2] Conants, Attlees, reputable limited

---

1 On 25 June the Communist state of North Korea had launched an invasion of South Korea. Truman sent US forces to assist South Korea (later supplemented by forces from several countries in response to a UN call for military aid to combat the aggression), but by August only a small part of South Korea was still holding out. Alsop had joined the many foreign journalists there.

2 David K. Niles (c.1890–1952), US political adviser; Presidential Administrative Assistant 1942–51; believed to have influenced Truman on behalf of the Zionist cause.

mediocrities, & on the other flashing swords & Winston, Tito, Ben Gurion, Uncle Joe [Stalin], Bullitt,[1] De Gaulle,[2] served by wonderful Leonardos & Vaubans & Schachts & Monnets,[3] & compare the flat 2 dimensional semi-literate prose of the first with the undoubted poetry of the second, I don't feel Nietzschean indignation! I know that I can't breathe among the former, & that they wd suspect dislike & liquidate disorderly gossips like me: yet I wd vote for them: I wd work for them: & I wd rather be done in – killed by attrition by them than struck down splendidly by the heroes. Why? because unscrupulous trampling seems to me worse than pettiness & mediocrity. Because the rights of individuals matter more than glorious achievements: because liberty & even a passive semi-toleration matter more than armies on the march to ends however magnificent. I do not believe you agree with this at all. You support the martyrs & the minorities, surely, because they stand for the impossible assertion of certain values in the world, which, allowed to triumph would destroy us all: I mean because you (like, I think, Maurice) hate the establishment as such: the big batallions because they are on top: the successful statesmen, soldiers etc. because they are successful, smart & applauded: & see no reason why there need be an order & an authority at all when all that is necessary is for people to be uninflated, genuine, have the feelings they have (& not some imaginary kind or an imaginary or real absence of them) & tell the truth. Whereas I believe (not altogether confidently but I think I do) in the need for some collective security, some establishment, some idées reçues, some accepted doctrines, hence some ideologists, theorizers, & therefore some degree of the falsification of individual experience, some degree of unreality in the public standards to which there is to be that minimum allegiance without which too many would go to the wall. Is all this obscure (& illegible) nonsense? these are Swiss thoughts, certainly, & I will stop boring you with them. I shd like to spend Xmas with you in 1951: will that be possible? & shall I be able to go to America at all? I can't go through 1940 again: even though nobody thinks I did anything wrong. But if there is nervousness in England by Sept 1951, but no war (as I believe) do I fulfil my Harvard contract ('Certainly' Felix may say 'you will be at the disposal of His Majesty's Govt. wherever you are. And Boston will be no *safer* than London, for once. And you can always, as in 1940, return;) but what do you say? but all this is too silly & hypothetical. Still if there is war I

1 William Christian Bullitt (1891–1967), US Ambassador to the Soviet Union 1933–6, to France 1936–41.
2 Charles André Joseph Marie de Gaulle (1890–1970), French general and leader of the Free French government in exile 1940–4; head of French Provisional Government 1944–6; Prime Minister of France 1958–9, President 1959–69.
3 Sébastien Le Prestre, Seigneur de Vauban and later Marquis de Vauban (1633–1707), brilliant military engineer under Louis XIV of France; expert in attacks on and defence of fortresses. Hjalmar Horace Greeley Schacht (1877–1970), pre-war President of the Reichsbank whose financial skills had funded German rearmament. Jean Omer Marie Gabriel Monnet (1888–1979), major driving force towards European unity.

have no personal problems – I *like* doing what I am told – but I should like to put my parents in a safe place. But all this is an unnecessary topic too. On Sunday I go auprès le Président d'Israël,[1] H.E. Dr Weizmann, in Berne: he is in a clinic, having had some sort of relapse in Lucerne. There I shall be told to work for Israel and abandon all the ludicrous efforts to teach little English boys unnecessary subjects. Dr W. is certainly my Headmaster: when I go there I go to the Head's study: & I prepare to face some sort of 'music'. He is said to be in a sad condition: more neglected than ever, not only now, politically, but by his chemical staff also, who, whenever he leaves Rehovot, cease writing, with obvious relief, as soon as the Old Boy's back is turned, to him about matters which they think he no longer comprehends. It is really too pathetic. At such moments I feel I must write his life one day, & vindicate this gigantic figure before the ungrateful pygmies into whom he & he alone breathes life. And *do* go to Israel with Felix. It is far more unlike anything than anything can convey: again my Swiss feelings: for the life there is a sort of 1910 life: the ideas, the fights, the purity of the socialist idealists, the embarrassments of the hemmed in capitalists, the Sacro Egoismo[2] of the fascist-like bands & 'leaders', the entire picture is something, which, with 19th century categories one can make out. And this is much more intelligible in American terms which also, despite Ben Cohen's indignation with me for thinking so, are 19th century. So do come: next year: at Easter & I'll come with [you] & you'll enjoy it and so will I & the Justice, enormously. Not necessarily via England – but straight, via Naples or Cherbourg: do – you won't you won't regret it. The pen drops from my nerveless hand. Good bye, I feel far closer than at Oxford. How silly I am being, & unSylvesterish.

Love

Shaya

On the way to his own holiday in Italy, IB went first to Berne to visit Chaim Weizmann. There he heard from his father of the death of Yitzhak Samunov.

TO MENDEL BERLIN

25 August [1950, *manuscript*]

Hotel Bellevue Palace, Berne

Dear Pa,

I've just read your letter about Yitzchok's end – just after I finished my own letter to you at 49 Hollycroft, so fortunately it was quite unartificial & genuine.

Now:

---

1 'To the President of Israel's side'.
2 'Sacred self-interest', the policy which led Italy to join the Allies in the First World War.

1) You shd. tell mother. She was expecting this for some time, & in the face of real crises is commendably firm & good – another matter if it had been Ida herself – but Yitz. also [sc. although] very much in the family was not attached by real ties, somehow, of blood – even love. So do tell her.

2) In such things speed is of the essence: I mean the *sooner* we do something for Ida the better. Not only she but all the Israeli eyes of our friends will be directed at *us* – to see exactly how kind or hard-hearted we are. It is a *very* provincial community & Ida is affected by public opinion. I agree that she shd be summoned most warmly to London at once. True we have no maid and it is difficult. At worst she will have to sleep in some neighbouring boarding house: but of course *they* – even Halevys[1] – will half expect one of us to go to Jerusalem at once to help: mother can plead her legs etc.,[2] you cannot leave mother: as for me, perhaps I *should* go: but actually, of course, it would be a mere sentimental gesture, there is nothing for me to do there at the moment.

What in my opinion should be done is that you shd *cable* Ida to come here *as soon as possible*: one cannot overestimate the importance of an *immediate* gesture.

3) You shd also cable Halevys to ask *them* to influence Ida to come to London at once.

4) Perhaps you should get an air company to present her with a paid voucher for a ticket to London to be used during the next fortnight or so. Above all you must act at once & with *an exaggerated warmth*. I assure you, vis a vis the Jerusalem mood of distant rich and grand relations, who don't take enough interest this is all important, if only this is not to become a permanent source of reproach against you, me, etc. forever, there. I'll cable of course & advise I. to go to London: but this is no good unless you support it: so I shan't know till say 28th (Monday) Cd you cable me to Athenée[3] (or even telephone from the office) & then I'll cable to Jerus. If you don't get this letter till Monday I'll expect *something* before midnight Monday or 8am Tuesday when I go to Milan: after that I am hors de communication[4] for a bit.

Meanwhile I know nothing yet: I don't want just to cable my sorrow: I am expected to make a concrete suggestion: to come: or tell Ida to come: and if I do the latter before you it will look as if I am being considerate whereas you, who alone matter, are not – I am generous in *your* place: which won't do. [...] Please do not think I am being too hasty or hysterical: you can't imagine how much they read into everything in Jerusalem: it is *very hot* there: & they are silly and petty, & so I want to coordinate our wires: you wire first from

1 Yitzhak Samunov's sister Rivka (1892–1971) and her husband Elazar Halevy (1897–1976).
2 Marie Berlin had injured her foot on holiday.
3 The pension where IB was to stay in Geneva.
4 'Incommunicado'.

London: tell me what: & I'll wire from Genf:[1] otherwise fine differences
will be perceived between "your" versus "my" alleged attitudes. So I know
nothing till Monday: I am unfindable in Europe: on Monday I re-emerge from
"the mountains" to wire. [...]
  Love
    Isaiah

TO VERA WEIZMANN

  29 August 1950 [*manuscript*]

                                    Hotel-Pension de L'Athénée, Geneva
Dearest Mrs Weizmann

Lausanne This is written in the train. So my handwriting, terrible enough
at normal times is likely – as soon as the train moves out of Lausanne – to
become more illegible – punishing to the innocent recipient – still. To thank
you as I have had so many occasions to do in the past, to say that I value my
days and hours more than I shall ever be able to describe – you know that
already; but it is our Russian conversations which I adore & look forward to
& think about and remember the longest. (The train is moving! slowly now,
but you will, alas, know by the writing when it gathers speed) I can never
talk so to anybody not to my parents because they are my parents – nor to
anybody in England (No! I cannot go on writing, – I wait till Vevey – then till
Montreux etc.)

Vevey (2 minutes d'arrêt)[2] – Russian to me is more imaginative, intimate
and poetical than any other – & I feel a curious transformation of personality
when I speak it – as if everything becomes easier to express, & the world
brighter and more charming in every way – and I retain the most grateful,
delightful recollections of our Russian gossip (the train is moving!) and shall
all my life be grateful to you for it. No more ink! but I go on. *Montreux* I
hope these talks which I enjoy so much are not a burden to you – I adore
staying with you & Dr Weizmann, of course, for every possible reason – but
I am always afraid (here people & luggage are coming on – interruption –)
that perhaps, at times, I may not be such a convenient guest – e.g. when Dr
Weizmann is not well – I do hope that I was not a nuisance & that if ever you
feel *the slightest* feeling that another time will be better you will not hesitate
to tell me – I shall feel this in itself to be a token of intimate friendship.
And I always hate leaving you & I wish Rehovot weren't so far & I bless
Switzerland – about which I feel sometimes as Maidie[3] does – no character,

---

1 The German name of Geneva. IB was going there 'to see again 2 aged Russian Revolutionaries,
   both 85 apiece, he bearded & holy, she moustached & like Mrs Webb & very pure & noble & 18th
   century'. Letter of 23 [August] to Jenifer Hart.
2 '2-minute stop'.
3 Maidie Weizmann (1913–2002), née Minnie Pomeranz, wife of the Weizmanns' son Benjamin.

no flowery, Germanized Frenchmen in Geneva, Germans without Hitler in Zurich – for being where it is. So again thank you very very very much.

St. Maurice George[1] mentioned Dr W's letters to me & your proposal that I shd write something.[2] I was excited, flattered, & appalled. My first thought was that I shd love to do it – in a way (& this is really what I think) my only chance of immortality. On the other hand, although perhaps presumptuously I feel I know you & the President very well, do I know enough – about the early years – the circumstances – the historical context – the moments – to dare say something before the terrible critical world – & worse Jewish – & worse Israel – eye, I who am still such a coward, who so hate & fear criticism, when I am *really* not an expert, an amateur? & can one, in general, ever write in public about human beings one loves & admires so much, & to whom one owes so much, without terrible self consciousness? But it is a thrilling idea; I'll try; I'll steal time from Oxford & Harvard: I may fail, if so I'll tell George & you – but I'd love to look at the letters – I *think* this is the *wrong* decision: but I want to risk it. I'd love to be associated with you in some [way]. I'll talk to you about this in Paris if I may & to Dr Weizmann: I hope my chatter did not bore him too much – (Martigny) & all my love & wishes, & I feel Dr W will be in blooming health on Sep. 25.[3]

Isaiah

TO MARIE AND MENDEL BERLIN

31 August 1950 [*manuscript*]

Grand Hotel Miramare, Santa Margherita Ligure

Dear Pa & Ma,

This is paradisaic. Not too hot: delicious sea breezes; I was brought here by the Hofmannsthals who leave for Paris tomorrow: we arrived last (Wed.) night, & stay till to-morrow (Friday). Then I go per treno[4] to Aulla. [...]

Now as for Ida. No doubt *there* "they" expect one of us to come at once as a gesture. It is not materially required of course: the Halevys, Jacob Samunovs[5] & a thousand gloomy Yekish[6] acquaintances more than fill the need for actual help: but with the suspiciousness, inferiority complexes etc. – rich Londoners v. poor Israelis etc. whatever we do or don't do will be treated as a symptom of *coldness*. I shall write, for example, from Italy:

---

1 George Weidenfeld, who in September 1949 had taken a year's leave of absence from his newly-established publishing firm to act as Weizmann's *chef de cabinet*.
2 Vera Weizmann was keen for IB to be her husband's biographer; on this occasion she appears to have suggested that IB should write a biographical introduction to an edition of Weizmann's letters.
3 When IB next planned to see Weizmann, in Paris (in the event he saw him a few days later).
4 'By train'.
5 Jacob Samunov was the brother of Yitzhak Samunov and Rivka Halevy.
6 See 174/3.

if I am in Italy – presumably enjoying myself – why cannot I fly over? for 24 hrs – just as a gesture – moral support – warmth, family feeling? & if I didn't think you wd tremble too much, possibly I wd – just for 1 day. But obviously you *would* tremble, & it is perfectly unnecessary: there is nothing particular to say. But if you want to go "anyhow" about the house, mid-September is a good time, & as I anyhow cd not be properly available in London till well after Oct 5 or so, perhaps you might both or one – papa – kill two birds? but just as you like. I *believe* in sudden decisions & swift action. Go by boat from Genoa & I'll come to see you. Curiously enough I did *not* have mother's feeling about a gap in one's life. Yitzchok somehow never occupied a place in it: & that wounded both him & Ida. Hence Ida's anxiety that I should show due respect for Yitzchok always – it corresponded to nothing: I didn't respect his judgment: his honesty, decency, etc. seemed to me, unlike Ida's, negative absences of temperament & not presence of active principle. I was surprised at my own coldness of reaction: for an hour or two I had a sinking feeling (the letter reached me in Berne): I told the Oisermans[1] that evening & they thought how much happier Ida wd in the end be: this was Zemach's thought, & curiously enough *not* the realistic Anna's. I minded much more about my friends Branch[2] & Ridley[3] or even Charles Henderson:[4] funny. Mother is right: blood is what, in our family, counts: if I heard that Leiba[5] in Moscow died I wd mind much more. I must write to Ida: yes, she will be obstinate to not move, & the flat etc. Can one telephone to Israel now? I think one can. If you don't go, do write & explain why: otherwise, I warn you, it will be grievance, unreasonably, but it will. Not that it is so important, but still: tell about mother's foot, about the empty office, about your objection to my flying etc. it all counts. But of course you must avoid giving the impression of qui s'excuse.[6] At least send another telegram – it acts differently from letters, urging her to come to London: even, as I suggested before, send her a voucher for a ticket via Peltours: believe me: one must not behave too sensibly.

love

Shaya

1 Zemach Oiserman, apparently a business connection of Mendel Berlin's, was married to Anna Schneerson, a distant cousin of the Berlins; they lived in London before emigrating to Israel.

2 Guy Rawstron Branch (1913–40), friend of IB at Oxford; killed in the Battle of Britain.

3 Jasper Maurice Alexander ('Bubbles') Ridley (1913–43), a close Oxford friend of IB's, killed in action in Italy; husband of Cressida Bonham Carter (315/8).

4 Charles Gordon Henderson (1900–33), Fellow and Tutor, CCC, 1929–33 while IB was an undergraduate there. They were close friends until Henderson's death from pleurisy while on honeymoon in Rome.

5 Leo Berlin (1897–1955), one of Mendel's younger brothers, Professor of Dietetics at Moscow University. IB had visited him clandestinely in 1945. For his later detention and death, see 357/2.

6 'Qui s'excuse, s'accuse' ('He who excuses himself accuses himself', i.e. excuses always suggest a guilty conscience).

Maurice Bowra had rented a sixteenth-century castle, the Fortezza della
Brunella[1] near Aulla, as the base for their Italian holiday.

TO ALICE JAMES

3 September 1950 [*manuscript*]

Castello della Brunella, Massa Carrera, Aulla, Italy

Dear Alice,

I meant to write to you a thousand times, but always something intervened: either work or sickness: never very serious (the sickness I mean) – I
was dreadfully sorry to hear that you had not been well – I cannot claim grave
distempers of any kind, but having had to examine this summer, & having
accepted an unnecessary lot of obligations to write short articles, reviews
etc. – I swore in June to cease from such things – they tax one enormously: I
sweat far more blood over tiny things of that kind than over ostensibly larger
things – & in the end it always looks at once dogmatic & over qualified, banal
and rhetorical, obscure & empty – however I must not go into all that – to
return: having had an overbusy term, I then had to examine, & began to be
visited by a succession of small & irritating diseases, sinusitises, laryngitises
etc. etc. & took to my bed & couldn't think or write anything to anybody.
Until my parents removed me to Vevey, peace & calm and Swiss dullness, &
a pre-1914 world, tidy, pedestrian, comfortable & secure. Others may sneer
at these unheroic virtues. After the nightmare of Oxford in July I adore it.
Then I went to Bern & Geneva to stay with friends & finally wound up here,
an earthly paradise, with three other dons[2] & Maurice Bowra. The Castello
belongs to a Mrs Waterfield[3] who lives in Florence & whom we don't know;
we are merely tenants. It is situated in the fabulous manner, above the village
of Aulla, which is about 15 miles from Lerici (where Shelley was drowned)
among the marble hills of Carrara. It is large, cool, & has admirable local
servants. One can bathe in the sea, walk in the hills, read, talk, even think occasionally. Our friends are young dons from Oxford, younger than Maurice & I,
gentle, sympathetic, industrious & gay. More one cannot ask for. Maurice is
in splendid form, swims about with energy, burns his skin in the sun with an
intensity & an enthusiasm from which no blisters or anything else can keep
him; his vitality is prodigious and he is the life & exuberant centre of the
party. Around this dazzling orb we rotate at our various speeds like planets
reflecting the central light in various degrees. It is a peaceful, fruitful and

---

1 This large fortress, in a dominating hilltop position with spectacular views, is now a natural
    history museum.
2 Marcus Dick, James Joll (203/3) and David Pears (501/2).
3 Lina Waterfield (1874–1964), née Duff Gordon, from a family of literary women; helped found
    British Institute, Florence, 1917; Italian correspondent, *Observer*, 1921–39; foreign correspondent,
    Kemsley Newspapers, 1946–50. She and her late husband Aubrey, a painter, had restored and lived
    in the Fortezza della Brunella before the war.

delightful form of life, with a regular rhythm very good for the nerves and one's general balance. I am the least enterprising of us: while my friends go for distant drives or walk on the battlements of Lucca, I tend to hang back & do all or part of the reading which Oxford makes utterly impossible: contrary to popular belief it takes much toughness to be a don.[1] Towards the end of the month I may try & call on Bernard Berenson[2] who has sent me several kind letters & whom I've never met.[3] He is to be in Vallombrosa:[4] Maurice won't hear of going & has virtually forbidden me to, since for some reason he has an animus against B.B.: but I may brave his displeasure, & go; if only as a tourist: I have a great desire to meet celebrities once: a single meeting always disappoints a little – one's hopes are so incredibly high pitched always – but I like to have the image of a face & a voice whenever the name occurs in later life: it enriches one's life enormously. Next term I am to leave New College (I was so very glad to hear, for Belle Roosevelt's[5] sake that Dirck[6] obtained a 2^d class in Final History Honours: it will set him up: & make things look up) & go to All Souls where I shall have very few pupils, but appalling obligations to write. I cannot tell you how this frightens me. I talk & talk, as you know, heedlessly & too much because, however falsely, one thinks that spoken words vanish, & no responsibility lingers, & one is freed from these embarrassing witnesses of one's momentary states – if ever I see a letter or any other handwriting of mine anywhere, I am possessed by a furious desire to destroy it – but to write – above all to write books, seems to me a terrible prospect. And lacking the means – the will power – to do it without an external sanction, I have had to contrive to place myself in a situation where I cannot escape this duty: & voluntarily, with eyes open, accepted the yoke of an All Souls research Fellowship (how ungrateful this sounds!) which obliges one to produce or be condemned by one's peers. It is like taking the vows of a monastery whose customs one has long admired but felt unequal to. At any rate the die is cast, & I am a slave by my own free choice. And yet, if one considers how my books[7] are praised by the review-

1 Cf. 'The truth is I have discovered the life of a don presupposes tremendous toughness and not the usual monastic properties. The output – the endless need to feed the intellectually hungry pupils – exhausts one far more rapidly than any form of settled activity in a civil service or a business office. Also the turnover of new humanity is too great. Nevertheless I feel committed to this form of life and it is too late to change.' 30 December 1949 to Vera Weizmann.

2 Bernard *Berenson (1865–1959), Lithuanian-born US art historian who settled in Italy; leading authority on the Italian Renaissance.

3 Both IB and Berenson appear to have forgotten their first meeting in a third-class carriage of an Oxford–London train in 1929, during which BB was 'delighted [...] by Isaiah's conversation, which lasted all the way to London'. Kenneth Clark, *Another Part of the Wood* (London 1974), 170.

4 Berenson's summer retreat, the Casa al Dono, was 20 miles south-east of Florence in a mountainous, forested area near the former Abbey of Vallombrosa (from the Latin for 'shady valley').

5 Belle Wyatt Roosevelt (1892–1968), née Willard, widow of President Theodore Roosevelt's son Kermit; her children included Kermit, Jr, and Dirck Roosevelt (next note).

6 Dirck Roosevelt (1925–53), New College history 1946–50; allegedly committed suicide.

7 At that point only his biography of Marx and his translation of Turgenev's *First Love*.

ers & fall into almost immediate oblivion – how this happens to one's most admired contemporaries – all this vanity and fuss seem remarkably unnecessary: this was the line taken by the President & Prime Minister of Israel when they conceived the flattering but absurd scheme whereby I might become a Near Eastern politician – they spoke of the millions of useless books poured out by the presses & enquired whether it was for this ridiculous purpose that I propose to "immure" myself in the remote & ineffectual city of Oxford. But Maurice is hurrying me: we must, he says, go to the Station to meet a friend & buy some postage stamps & anti-sunburn lotion. So I must swiftly end. According to present plans I shall be in Cambridge in the autumn of 1951 & at Bryn Mawr, to deliver the Mary Flexner lectures (to be printed! horror! the self imposed torment!) in Feb. 1952. I do not, somehow, believe at all in a general war, however many Asiatic ones there are, unless things fall out over Berlin: (& even that need not occur if a clear statement is made by Pres. Truman about the circumstances which he would & would not regard as Russian intervention): & remain "optimistic" in a, to many persons, infuriating way. If there are rumours of war by the autumn of 1951 will it be fainthearted to come to Cambridge or stay at Oxford? in any case I propose, as things are, to come [. . .].

Yours,

Isaiah B.

TO HUGH TREVOR-ROPER[1]

6 September 1950 [*manuscript*]

Castello della Brunella

Dear Hugh

I am an abominable manager of my own life, a fact which I try to disguise from myself but which humiliates me in recurrent, ever increasing, doses (doses of facts? there obviously *are* such.). Consider: for the moment all seems superficially well. My friends are in the sea. I am not, I am alone, I am well, I am at peace. But wait: I know obscurely that I have to be in Oxford at 10 a.m. on the 29th to attend an All Souls examiners' meeting. I am but just elected, I am suspected of insufficient attention to College discipline, I do not wish to be ignored, I must be there. More awful: I have given offence to my friend Mr Bohlen, an American in Paris. I am attached to him by many ties, I must placate him: I must also call on the ailing if not dying Dr Weizmann,

1 Hugh Redwald Trevor-Roper (1914–2003), later (1979) Baron Dacre of Glanton, historian; Student, Ch. Ch., 1946–57; Regius Professor of Modern History, Oxford, and Fellow of Oriel, 1957–80; later (1980–7) Master of Peterhouse, Cambridge. Trevor-Roper was a regular guest and correspondent of Bernard Berenson's: see *Letters from Oxford: Hugh Trevor-Roper to Bernard Berenson*, ed. Richard Davenport-Hines (London, 2006).

frustrated President de l'Etat d'Israel,[1] a Chaka-like[2] figure, now powerless, but an historical figure whose letters sooner or later I shall have to introduce: he leaves his Sanatorium on the 26th: I must be in Paris, therefore, not later than that date (this is all news: & I didn't know it when I thought of Rome) I have promised to attend the Siena performance[3] of works by the composers Jommelli & Zingarelli,[4] it may mean little to you, but a man is coming all the way from England to hear these with me, I cannot fail him: this occurs on the 20/22[d]: I have promised my friend Dick to drive with him to Paris, besides the convenience, undoubted, from my point of view, I cannot face the prospect of letting *him* down & letting him travel alone. I make too many promises, seek too many pleasures, am caught in too many conflicting currents of pleasure, duty, etc. How am I to reach Berenson at all, ever? and yet I should like to, very much indeed, & to do it with you. [...] But perhaps all this is too difficult, too unarrangeable: also I suffer from acute nerves about meeting Mr B.: I conceive a large company & brilliant general chit chat & nothing discomposes me more. I only really like tête à têtes, & not because as you will, I fear, be too quick to suggest, because then I can chat away myself: No! No! in this [sc. this has] a horrible plausibility but is deeply false. However all this may be, I apologize & grovel about being so very incompetent. So if you are writing paint me to the Vallombrosiani in dark colours as feckless & confused: but still ardently panting to see them: write me Miss X's[5] address: & perhaps at the last moment the sun will shine upon us & I shall turn up. But don't count on me: make your own arrangements as they suit you: forgive me. I am sorry Ireland was so horrible:[6] *why* will you choose the Brit. Isles in August? next summer I shall find you something nicer to do. But you won't now believe me.

Love,
Isaiah.   [...]

---

1 'Of the State of Israel'.
2 Chaka (1787–1828), autocratic Zulu ruler who by diplomacy, social change and military innovation made his previously insignificant nation the most powerful in southern Africa.
3 The Siena Musical Week was founded in 1939 to introduce to wider audiences undervalued composers of the past, starting with the then little-known Vivaldi. The 7th Week, 16–22 September 1950, concentrated on the 18th-century Neapolitan school of composers.
4 Niccolò Jommelli (1714–74), born near Naples; composer of opera and religious music. Niccolò Antonio Zingarelli (1752–1837), prolific Neapolitan composer of, first, operas, then mainly sacred music; choirmaster of the Sistine Chapel, Rome, 1804–11; Director of the Naples Conservatory 1813–6; choirmaster, Naples Cathedral, 1816–37.
5 IB had mislaid HT-R's letter with the name of Elizabetta ('Nicky') Mariano (1887–1968), who had joined Berenson as his librarian in 1919 and became an essential part of his life, liked and admired by all for her intellectual curiosity and accomplishments, efficiency, personal warmth and tolerance. She read books and letters aloud to Berenson, travelled with him, ran the household, and acted as hostess to Berenson's guests, especially after the death in 1945 of his wife Mary.
6 HT-R had written from a house in a Galway bog, where he was suffering from incessant wind, rain and 'the ancient, invariable intermingled smells of peat and popery'; to distract himself he was reading Jacobean comedies (letter of 13 August).

Despite the practical difficulties, IB succeeded in attending the music festival in Siena and then paying a visit to Bernard Berenson at Vallombrosa.

TO BERNARD BERENSON

24 September 1950 [*manuscript*]

Castello della Brunella

Dear Mr Berenson,

I don't know how to thank you sufficiently for the unbroken delight of my visit. From the moment of arrival, after the long, frightening drive in our feeble vehicle along a road which looked as if it might have no ending, in cold & gloom & in beautiful & terrifying surroundings – like some romantic experience by a minor German poet acidly analysed by Brandes[1] – from the moment of arrival till our most reluctant departure, I was in a haze of mounting pleasure; and went away, my head in a great whirl with all the ideas, images, glimpses of persons & relationships, forms of life which, if you will allow me to say so, you scatter with so prodigal & unreckoning a hand. I felt afterwards, & told my companions who did not trouble to deny it, that perhaps I talked too much: was too excited, & may have exhausted you (I have that effect on people & regret it, but, alas, don't notice it at the time) & if this is so I hope you will forgive me & not refuse me an opportunity of behaving in a more staid fashion. But I am afraid I enjoyed myself too much: & perhaps allowed my intoxication (it is the only kind I know) to overstimulate me. If so, once again, I must ask you to forgive me & ascribe it all to the relative isolation & provincialism of my daily Oxford life. Mme Mariano half suggested that I might perhaps be allowed to come again: there is nothing, literally, that I should like more: & if next Spring, on my way to my now annual visit to the Holy Land I might be allowed to come & see you, I should be very grateful. If Hugh Tr. Roper is with you my love to him.

   Yours sincerely
      Isaiah Berlin.

TO ROWLAND BURDON-MULLER

3 November 1950

New College

My dear Rowland,

   It was very agreeable to receive your last letter as indeed the former ones; you must forgive me for being an intermittent correspondent, but I live my

---

1 Georg Morris Cohen Brandes (1842–1927), influential Danish literary critic who argued for realism in literature; his *The Romantic School in Germany* (1873), English translation (London, 1902), vol. 2 of his *Main Currents in Nineteenth-Century Literature*, was a source for IB's 1965 lectures on romanticism.

A typically illegible (and misdated) postcard from IB: this one is to Avis Bohlen,
15 [September] 1950

life in fits, if not in bounds; at any rate I am glad that Mr Wollheim, now
married to his Merry Widow,[1] sent you a civil thanks for your Portuguese
advice.

After Vevey I went to Milan and from there for two horrible days to
Santa Margherita. I don't know why that went so wrong. I stayed with the
Hofmannsthals; the weather was not good, they were tired, I was tired;
Santa Margherita is ugly, vulgar, expensive, and without any charm or
attractiveness.[2] From there I went to the Castello for which you heard us
negotiating that evening. Dr Bowra was already in place and had taken over
the management of our enterprise. The castle itself is imposing enough in a
superb situation with splendid views of the hills of Carrara. The amount of
furniture within is somewhat exiguous; there were few lamps for the evening
and the hard chairs and half-broken arm chairs, illuminated by the dim light
of feeble bulbs, presented a somewhat melancholy spectacle. The plumbing
was appalling – running water which did not run, which if you know what I
mean is far worse than more primitive but reliable arrangements. The servants were most willing, the food adequate and the rooms themselves quite
large and well built. Certainly, we enjoyed ourselves. The immense vitality
of the Warden of Wadham lifted us on the wings of its blast across the dis-

1 Richard Wollheim had recently married Anne Barbara Denise Powell (1920–2004) after her
  divorce from Philip Toynbee (408/5).
2 Clearly not a permanent judgement. After his marriage in 1956 IB regularly spent his summer
  holidays in Portofino or Paraggi (where he and his wife built a house), both near Santa
  Margherita.

tance that separated us from the sea, and there was some vigorous bathing in which I participated half-heartedly, preferring to stay in the shade like an old lady watching the younger people gambol in the sunlight.

[...] I do not really like Siena; the sinister streets and excessive medievalism depress me too much. The most delightful town we saw was Lucca, where I should like to live one day. The walls are splendid, there are no tourists, the mixture of Romanesque and Marie Louise[1] is gay and delightful, and has a Stendhalian charm.[2] Pisa is very queer; the centre frighteningly ancient, the rest not very attractive. But the burnished doors on the Baptistery in Florence are really splendid. I could not resist curiosity and we went to call on Berenson at Vallombrosa. He is all that you think he is and his moral character is perhaps not above suspicion. But at 86 he is remarkable. His brain is very clear, his eye very sharp, his sentiments malicious. He reads everything, or has it read to him, and reminds one to talk to of no one so much as Freud[3] (whom he despises). To like him is difficult, perhaps even to respect him, but in a curious way one can be fascinated by so much controlled rational self-love. He feels himself to be a failure, as indeed in some sense he is; still, when he talks about contemporaries and about the past, there is something of Goethe's genuine hard-hearted irony and shrewdness about him. He is the toughest human being I have ever met, with the sentimentality which usually goes with that degree of real hardness; but when he says that he is descended from the Lithuanian Jewish aristocracy, that is a sad weakness on his part; it is as if one were to say the aristocracy of North Oxford, or of Notting Hill Gate – it is not a very real concept. His snobbery must have been devouring during the middle years, but it has somehow burnt out now, and at 86 he is prepared to assess the values of things as honestly as he can. I was horrified by such appalling, walled-in, windowless self-centredness by which everything – history, art, religion, politics – is related to himself. But when he told me that the people above all he liked to meet were persons immediately after defeat – defeated generals, fallen prime ministers, exposed crooks etc. – that was genuinely interesting – and when he talks about himself and his tastes he no longer poses, or falsifies I think. I went away with a slightly creepy feeling but not undisposed to see him again. After 80 a sort of emaciation occurs which reveals the bony structure and that is seldom dull even though it may be somewhat repellent at times. Has anyone ever liked him very much? Perhaps poor Lady Colefax[4] who died on the evening on which I dined with Berenson. For all her silliness, and fuss

1 Maria Luisa (1782–1824), Duchess of Lucca 1817–24, daughter of Charles IV of Spain, made major changes to the appearance of the town; but IB may be confusing her with Napoleon's widow, Marie-Louise, Duchess of Parma from 1814 until her death in 1847.
2 Marie-Henri Beyle (1783–1842), French novelist under the pseudonym Stendhal, spent much of his later life in Italy, about which he wrote with admiration.
3 IB had met the psychoanalyst Sigmund Freud (1856–1939) in 1938 (L1 67/7).
4 Sibyl Colefax, a friend and correspondent of Berenson's, died on the morning of 22 September.

and snobbery, she was kind and amiable by nature and I regretted her death genuinely.

I am settling down to my Russian labours now, and find this much easier and more satisfactory than philosophy. I am engaged at the moment in a major row with Viscount Simon,[1] the eminent ex-statesman, about the candidates for All Souls College. His power of inventing formulae which mean nine different things is prodigious and I see both the secret of his worldly success and the nature of English politics in the thirties. What a very waspish mood I seem to be in. I think I had better stop. [...]

I.B.

TO MORTON WHITE

[November 1950]

[Oxford]

Dear Morton,

[...] Dreben[2] is here and making, as you can imagine, a curious and interesting impression. He is full of innocent zeal, and regards himself as Quine's[3] prophet, if no longer a Baptist, gets up at all societies and classes and testifies hard. His line is that it is all very well for us to scorn the logical machine of the United States but we are much too ignorant to be able to despise it all, and need 'treading on' hard. All this he says with burning conviction and great naivety. He has converted his funny charmless manner into a kind of charm of its own, and is infinitely disarming at his best. His technique is to get up to his full 5 ft 2 ins and deliver a tirade interdispersed with reference to the fact that he is but a poor interpreter of Quine, and then ask 'Am I right?' or 'Am I right or not?' in a sweetly ingenuous and harsh manner. This is going down very well here so far as I can see, and even Ryle,[4] who is a vain man, does not seem to mind. On the whole I am sure that having come to scoff, Dreben will stay to praise, and this before the term is out. [...] [He] will probably in the next four weeks win all hearts, and the whole thing, I predict, will be a great success, cross-fertilisation etc.; by the time you come he ought to be a cactus in full flower.

What you say about synthetic/analytic, logical and non-logical, emotive and non-descriptive etc. is endlessly discussed here and is indeed the centre

1 John Allsebrook Simon (1873–1954), 1st Viscount Simon of Stackpole Elidor; barrister and Liberal politician; Lord Chancellor 1940–5; Fellow of All Souls 1897–1954.

2 Burton Spencer Dreben (1927–99), US philosopher; Fulbright Fellow, Magdalen, 1950–1 (studying under J. L. Austin); Junior Research Fellow, Harvard, 1952–5; Instructor, Chicago, 1955; Assistant Professor of Philosophy, Harvard, 1956–61; later (1981–90) Edgar Pierce Professor of Philosophy, Harvard.

3 Willard van Orman Quine (1908–2000), Associate Professor in Philosophy, Harvard, 1941–8, Professor 1948–56, Edgar Pierce Professor of Philosophy 1956–78.

4 Gilbert Ryle (1900–76), Waynflete Professor of Metaphysical Philosophy, Oxford, 1945–68; editor of Mind 1947–71.

of everybody's thinking. The effect of Wittgenstein has suddenly become very powerful, ⟨& the suspicion of *any* general statements, hatred of syntax, efforts to follow out the convolutions of individual sentences without sudden Procrustean impatience[1] etc.⟩ the need to spell everything out before classification occurs etc. is the most characteristic philosophical habit of my colleagues at present; you will find it all very congenial I am sure. The trouble is that these people will not publish nearly enough, although Strawson's[2] recent articles in *Mind* and the *PAS*[3] seem to be minor masterpieces. There is a clever, tied up, man called George Paul[4] who, seeking rest and quiet, is going to Bowdoin College in Maine in January – he was offered a post in CCNY but feels tired and wants peace; nevertheless, if you can get him to Harvard, not necessarily to read a paper (which I suspect he will not want to do) but just to talk to, you will find him a remarkable figure. He is full of Presbyterianism crossed with Wittgenstein, Wisdom[5] etc. and shares your views of [G. E.] Moore. He is an odd but very clever man, I wonder what you will think of him. I could not agree more strongly with you [about] the appalling difference between the sufficient but shallow waters of Geistesgeschichte[6] as against the deep dark wells of philosophy proper. Indeed, I feel a weakling and a poltroon for leaving the latter for the former. Philosophy is a fearfully difficult subject, more so with every advancing year. One needs, I am sure, a singular capacity for shutting out irrelevant interests and love of variety, with which I am sadly afflicted, and, believe me, you are a far more effective writer than I shall ever be; you seem to combine a capacity for phi and psi[7] with civilised subjects in a most enviable manner, and this I shall duly say some time in *Mind*.

I must dine with Dreben tonight (this brings me back to earth) and somehow convey to him that he must not buttonhole eminent philosophers in the street and require them there and then to say whether classes exist, and if so in what sense; I am fascinated by him, the provincial looks, which remind me of fanatics in Russian or Polish villages, and the sweetness, fervour, crudity, total lack of manners, etc., but I must go. ⟨also the fact that

---

1 An urgent desire to enforce compliance with a pre-existing, arbitrary standard. In Greek mythology Procrustes tortured and killed his victims by cutting or stretching them to fit his bed.

2 Peter Frederick Strawson (1919–2006), Fellow and Praelector in Philosophy, Univ., 1948–68, Domestic Bursar 1949–55; later (1968–87) Waynflete Professor of Metaphysical Philosophy, Oxford, and Fellow of Magdalen.

3 'On Referring' (*Mind* 59) and 'Truth' (*PASS* 24), both published in July 1950.

4 George Andrew Paul (1912–62), Fellow and Praelector in Philosophy, Univ., 1945–62, Domestic Bursar and Garden Master 1955–62; Visiting Professor, Bowdoin College, Maine, 1951; died after a sailing accident on Coniston Water.

5 (Arthur) John Terence Dibben Wisdom (1904–93), Lecturer in Moral Sciences, Cambridge, 1934–52, Professor of Philosophy 1952–68 (Fellow of Trinity College, Cambridge, from 1935); later (1968–72) Professor of Philosophy, Oregon.

6 Literally 'the history of the mind' – intellectual history.

7 φ and ψ, shorthand (being the initial letters of the Greek words) for philosophy and psychology.

he obviously *thinks* in Yiddish, & his whole manner is that of a ex-Talmud student turned socialist agitator in 1890.)

[...] I really am very glad that you are coming here at last – there is no doubt that you will see what is going on better than any American philosopher who has been here yet; there really is something worth sampling here and you will not be sorry to have done so.

Yours ever,

Isaiah B.

IB makes no mention in these letters of an event which rankled at the time and which he never forgot, but whose long-term effects were beneficial. The journalist Robert Kee[1] was writing a copiously illustrated article on Oxford for Picture Post,[2] *and James Joll[3] arranged for him to interview IB. The article[4] opened with a description of an unnamed but easily identifiable 'Very Important Don': 'Fat, animated, forty, swollen with sedentary delight at the miracles and absurdities of this persisting world [...] the best talker in Oxford.' To rub salt in the wound, the caption to the unflattering photo of IB made a similar reference to his conversational abilities, while the other dons pictured were credited with their publications. James Joll appears to have conveyed to Kee IB's horror at what he considered 'squalid and mendacious' behaviour.[5] And although IB's weight had not previously worried him, the idea that it might be affecting his health and productivity seems to have sprung from this incident: nevertheless it was several months before (on his doctor's insistence) he took remedial action.*

TO HARMAN GRISEWOOD[6]

25 November 1950 [*manuscript*]

New College

Dear Grisewood,

What a good friend Miss Kallin[7] is! But, alas, your most kind proposal is founded on a generous misapprehension. I cannot possibly talk about Wagner: I am bored stiff by his most eloquent moments: I detest him so

1 Robert Kee (b. 1919), journalist, author and broadcaster; *Picture Post* 1948–51; *Observer* 1956–7; BBC TV 1958–62.

2 Magazine (1938–1957) which pioneered photo-journalism in the UK.

3 James Bysse Joll (1918–94), Fellow and Tutor in Politics, New College, 1946–50; Fellow, St Antony's, 1951–67; Stevenson Professor of International History, London, 1967–81.

4 'Eternal Oxford', *Picture Post*, 25 November 1950, 13–21.

5 Robert Kee to IB, 24 November 1950.

6 Harman Joseph Gerard Grisewood (1906–97), Controller, Third Programme, BBC, 1948–52, Director of the Spoken Word 1952–5, Chief Assistant to Director-General 1955–64. Anna Kallin had suggested that IB might give a 'fascinating' talk about the ideas that Wagner used in his *Ring* operas; Grisewood hoped that IB would provide this 'very pleasant Christmas present to the Third Programme' (letter of 22 November 1950).

7 Anna ('Niouta') *Kallin (1896–1984), Russian-born radio producer, a driving force behind the BBC's Third Programme.

much that I have avoided knowing more than a minimum about his musical
& poetical practice: I really am remote from & hostile to everything to [do?]
with him & would have nothing – even of a worthless kind – to say about
him. All this is probably a sad commentary on my own vast deficiencies –
& I am far from feeling complacency about so odd a deaf spot in musical
feeling – but at any rate it does thoroughly disqualify me from speaking about
the *Ring*: but if you require a non-musician to talk about him – would not
Mr E. M. Forster do something? He once delivered a very amusing lecture
in America in which he said that Wagner was the Puccini of music[1] – in his
works there are references implying a passion for Wagner – he probably has
very imaginative & fascinating ideas about the ideas in the *Ring*; or someone
could rig[?] selections from the late G.B.S.:[2] there is more than enough about
Wagner even outside the "Perfect Wagnerite" – Furtwängler is certainly the
most marvellous Wagner conductor in the world, & La Scala orchestra probably the best (after Berlin) for this purpose: I wish I could feel the required
excitement at the prospect: now if it were Les Troyens[3] you were speaking
of ...

yrs ever
    Isaiah Berlin

TO THE PRIVATE SECRETARY TO THE PRIME MINISTER OF ISRAEL
[in the UK]

8 December 1950 [*manuscript*]

New College

יאדוני הנכבד,

תסלח לי אם אכתוב בלשון שהיא ביותר שגורה בפי מעברית.[4]

I only write this to say that I do not propose to be importunate. I am
sure that the Prime Minister wishes to be left undisturbed.[5] But if there is
anything he wants done in this city; anything or anyone he wants to see; any
meal or books or anything else, in private or public which he (or you) wd

---

1 'When our English humorist Beachcomber says, "Wagner is the Puccini of music", he means
   rather more than he says. Besides guying a well-worn formula, he pierces Grand Opera itself,
   and reveals Brünnhilde and Butterfly transfixed on the same mischievous pin': from Forster's
   lecture at a 1947 Harvard symposium on 'Music and Criticism', published as 'The *Raison d'Être* of
   Criticism' in *Horizon*, December 1948, and in *Two Cheers for Democracy* (London and New York,
   1951), 110. No use by Beachcomber (J. B. Morton) of the remark IB cites has been traced; rather
   it appears to have been coined by Gordon Beckles (*Daily Express*, 5 March 1929, 8).
2 (George) Bernard Shaw (1856–1950), Irish-born playwright, essayist, critic and socialist; his
   enthusiasm for Wagner's works appears in much of his music criticism, notably in *The Perfect
   Wagnerite: A Commentary on the Ring of the Nibelungs* (London, 1898).
3 Opera by Hector Berlioz based on Virgil's *Aeneid*, written and composed 1856–8, but not performed in its entirety until 1890; IB's enthusiasm was unusual at the time as the 1957 production
   at the Royal Opera House (during IB's Directorship) was the opera's first major success.
4 'Dear Sir, Forgive me if I write in a language that is more fluent on my tongue than Hebrew.'
5 Ben-Gurion had arrived in Britain on 4 December for a week's private visit.

like to be provided, you (or he) have but to say, & I shall do whatever is in my power. I shd be grateful, moreover, if you could convey to Mr Ben Gurion from me that I considered his visit to me the other night[1] as a unique honour & pleasure; that, if he does not mind my saying so, he is the only statesman I have ever met in my life who possesses a rich inner life, distinct from public achievements however heroic; and that this is something so rare, valuable and marvellous that I shd like to express here, sincere and profound homage to it. In short I shd be delighted to be of service and sad, but not surprised, if there is none I can render. And, of course, if there is anything I can do for you & your colleague, I hope you will not hesitate to let me know.

שלום וברכה

ישעיהו ברלין.[2]

TO FELIX FRANKFURTER

10 January 1951 [*manuscript*]

New College

Dear Felix

Very many thanks for delicious cigars – *most* welcome. Much news of earth shaking character here. Maurice's knighthood[3] I think a very good thing: it pleases him, is thoroughly suitable, & makes up for much. He is in a very good state, despite a really vicious & horrible attack in the Observer.[4] [...] He has taken it v. well, i.e. decided to ignore it. Don't know about it. I did not even condole with him, thinking even that a little malicious, but in Oxford sympathy is universal, & enemies are taking the opportunity of saying that *this* they couldn't approve. [...]

One of the pleasantest moments of my life was the 'secret' appearance of B.G., who called on me, refused to see the London notables, talked about Indian mysticism exclusively, particularly about the role of elephants in Indian fables, also a little about Plato, avoided all politics, when offered by me a glass of port asked 'what is port?' I explained it was a local variant or equivalent of Richon Le Zion,[5] & he drank tumblers of it, became excited, & denounced my mode of life with great charm: he is a proper peasant leader,

---

1 For a description of this, see next letter.
2 'Greetings and peacefulness, Isaiah Berlin.'
3 The 1951 New Year Honours included a knighthood for Bowra (conferred on 14 February).
4 In the 'Table Talk' gossip column written under the pseudonym Pendennis: 'A stout person, jocose, moody and clever, his conversation has seemed to convey to bright young men the dazzling possibility that malice might be a form of courage and gossip a form of art. [...] He has perhaps been at his weakest in judging the more serious problems of real life, such as those of an anti-Nazi German determined to resist Hitler; and at his strongest as a host producing his version of an eighteenth-century man of letters and bully-boy combined.' *Observer*, 7 January 1951, 5.
5 The vineyards of Richon-le-Zion (near Rehovot), established by Baron Edmond de Rothschild in 1882, produced mainly sweet fortified wines at the time of this letter.

& the only politician I've ever met with a real, rich, spontaneous inner life. The Israeli papers printed stories of how he came to see me, & I got Lord Salisbury, & we talked about bases. He wandered about bookshops followed by bodyguards, was followed also by Jewish undergraduates asking for 'messages', pretended deafness, was denounced by the Jewish press for standoffishness & flew to the Riviera having seen nobody. I was very delighted by it all. It is as always 3 a.m. & I must sleep & tomorrow go to the cinema with Hart & my mother who get on well. My love to Marion.

I.B.

TO ROWLAND BURDON-MULLER

18 January 1951

New College

My dear Rowland,

I must begin by thanking you for your most generous hamper containing ham, sugar, figs etc. that arrived this morning; they will make a greater difference than it is decent to admit. I have a dim recollection – it seems immodest and greedy to mention it – that you said something also about cigars; there is a mysterious parcel that did arrive at Christmas time on which there was a duty of about one pound to pay which I should willingly have done, but being away and the temporary porters of New College being terrible cretins, all knowledge of me was denied, the parcel taken away by the postman and lost I suppose for ever in the recesses of the British post office. It is a chagrin[ing] thought to me that a number of minor postal officials should sit smoking small but light and exquisite Boston cigars. I duly complained, they promised to enquire, but if you at your end sent a remonstrance it might help. It is maddening to be deprived of so delightful a present.

Here we sit vaguely expecting war[1] in a passive manner. Without hysteria, without initiative, and determined not to be involved in a war with China without quite knowing what to do if one occurs. It really is a most idiotic business. And even the Pentagon must by now be a little disillusioned in MacArthur.[2] Meanwhile the principal item of home news is the knighthood of the Warden of Wadham. Although on the whole affably dealt with,

1 UN military successes in Korea had taken the American-led forces through North Korea almost to the Chinese border and prompted Chinese fears of an invasion. The consequent entry of China, with limited assistance from the Soviet Union, into the Korean War in late 1950 led to a major retreat by the UN forces and the loss of Seoul to the advancing Chinese. General MacArthur urged the use of nuclear weapons against China. A major East–West nuclear conflict seemed a real possibility.
2 Douglas MacArthur (1880–1964), controversial US general; Supreme Commander Allied Powers in Japan 1945–51 (overseeing the post-war occupation); commander of UN forces in the Korean War 1950–1, during which he favoured taking the war into Chinese territory. MacArthur's disagreement with Truman on this, particularly his press campaign and an unauthorised ultimatum to China, led to his dismissal on 11 April 1951 for insubordination.

except by the *Manchester Guardian* which wondered a little why it should have occurred, and the *Observer* which printed the most offensive and vicious attack I have ever seen delivered on a human being by a British newspaper, accusing my jolly old friend of corrupting the youth by teaching them that malice was courage and gossip was art. It led off with the headline 'Clever fellow knighted', gave an offensive description of Dr Bowra's appearance and character, said that he was a mixture of eighteenth-century man of letters and a 'bully boy', whatever that may be. Said that on his first visit to the United States he was a great social success, stressing 'first' and 'social': that his books were stodgy and pedagogic and finally that he was at his worst in dealing with serious matters such as his attitude to anti-Nazi Germans engaged in opposing Hitler. Even if this were fair it was written more in Pegler's style than of any English newspaper. It breathed venom and babbled with real hatred and I wondered why David Astor[1] hated him so much.

The paragraph about Nazis made one think he was accused of frivolous lack of anti- Nazi sentiment, than which nothing is less true, since he used to thump the table with Laski in the old 1936 days here in Oxford in the most creditable manner. In fact this is all about a German Baron called von Trott,[2] who was indeed hanged by Hitler in 1944 for taking part in the famous plot, but was nevertheless a nationalist and an ambitious, handsome, complicated young man who played with fire and took large risks and lost, but was not a democrat or on our side all the same and this is all Dr Bowra said about him plus some good straight anti-German sentiment which we don't think

---

1 (Francis) David Langhorne Astor (1912–2001), son of 2nd Viscount Astor and his redoubtable American wife Nancy, the first woman to sit (1919–45) in the Commons; editor, *Observer*, 1948–75.
2 Adam von Trott zu Solz (1909–44), German lawyer who had been a close friend of IB while a Rhodes Scholar at Balliol in the early 1930s and was hanged by the Nazis for his role in the July 1944 plot to kill Hitler. While recognising that von Trott had no specifically Nazi sympathies, IB came to mistrust his intense patriotism and fell out with some of von Trott's English friends over this (see L1 717–19 and index s.v. Trott zu Solz, Adam von). IB later explained the background to the *Observer* attack: 'There was a meeting of the Institute of Pacific Affairs in New York [in late 1939]. America was neutral. Von Trott came as a German delegate. [...] he certainly went to the State Department [...] and saw a man called Messersmith, who was the expert on German Affairs. And what he said to Messersmith was, "We must have a peace of Amiens", that's to say a truce (this is after Poland and before the hot war) – the purpose of it being presumably to have a plot. [...] And Messersmith [...] said to Frankfurter, "Is he all right?" Frankfurter wrote to Maurice Bowra, who was his great friend in Oxford – fortunately not to me – and said, "Is he all right?" Maurice Bowra never liked him, although he pretended he did, and replied and said, "Well, some of us were a little doubtful about where he stands." This letter was intercepted by the British censorship – a wartime letter – it got on to the file. So when von Trott appeared in Sweden – I don't know when, '43 – and tried to get in touch with British intelligence – which he *did* try and do – the orders from the Foreign Office were not to touch him. And David Astor therefore attributes his subsequent death to Maurice Bowra, and regards him as a murderer, and more or less said words to that effect. Maurice Bowra in his autobiography says he was mistaken, and shouldn't have said whatever he did say, but [...] I don't think there was any reason why *he* should have suspected anything in particular. [...] Anyway, David Astor has never forgiven him: he says that if Maurice Bowra hadn't written that letter, all kinds of things might have been done.' MI Tape 10.

less of him for. But David Astor was Trott's greatest friend and is a neurotic, muddled, complicated, politically irresponsible, unhappy adventurer,
permanently resentful of somebody or something and a typical poor little
rich American boy surrounded by a court of dubious toadies which gives his
newspaper its queerly disoriented look. Perhaps he was not, when an undergraduate, a frequent guest at Dr Bowra's table. However this may be, it was a
most violent revenge, and upsetting even to Dr Bowra's numerous enemies.
The charges are all genuinely unfair and the tone detestably vulgar. However
he is enjoying his knighthood immensely and it has made up for many stings,
and I am genuinely glad he has it; if people long for knighthoods they shall
have them and nobody will be the poorer for it, but Cadogan's OM is a real
absurdity – whatever else the OM was, it was an order uniquely associated
with some kind of cultural distinction and was given only to superior and
intellectually awe-inspiring persons and should have gone to Keynes, but
why should a perfectly competent Foreign Office official who has done his
duty dully and solidly and uncomplainingly for years, put in charge of the
Foreign Office when Vansittart was considered too pro-German, why should
he be regarded as the equal of Russell or even Fisher? There is something
hopelessly and poignantly petit bourgeois about the present government
which nothing will cure them of.

My college, following the general trend, declined to elect the virtuous
Gaitskell,[1] the Chancellor of the Exchequer, to an honorary fellowship.
Rejected Duff Cooper by a huge vote and elected A. P. Herbert[2] by an equally
huge vote, so you see which way things are going.

What more am I to tell you? I spent Christmas in London and Brighton
where I received an indignant letter from Sparrow addressed to 'Sir Isaiah
Berlin'; he was seething with indignation about Dr Bowra's ennoblement
and said he was addressing everybody like that today. He proposed to write
to Dr Bowra congratulating him on his baronetcy (due to faulty intelligence),
explaining how much more distinguished this was than a paltry knighthood,
which nowadays went to every Tom, Dick and Harry. Or else to write saying
that 'I suppose they gave it you when you weren't looking, like an OBE, but
I thought about knighthoods they always asked.' But I doubt whether in the
end he did either.

As for me, here I sit with half my books in New College and half in All
Souls, trying to write about the sources of Tolstoy's queer theory of history
and French reactionary philosophers, and reviews of books about Russia,
and to brace myself to begin a serious book. In the end I suppose I shall do

1 Hugh Todd Naylor Gaitskell (1906–63), Minister of Fuel and Power 1947–50; Chancellor of the
   Exchequer 1950–1; Leader, Labour Party, 1955–63.
2 Sir Alan Patrick Herbert (1890–1971), barrister, author and writer for *Punch*; Independent MP,
   Oxford University, 1935–50 (promoter of the 1937 Matrimonial Causes Act).

it but the pain and the torture are as bad as described and I am already in agonies at the thought of the agonies which are still to come. [...]

Talking of the Holy Land: Evelyn Waugh and Christopher Sykes[1] have been commissioned by *Life*[2] to write about the holy places controversy, and if I know Evelyn Waugh at all, he will turn out a pompous Catholic anti-Dreyfusard, mordant, disreputable piece with horrible implications and hideous ironies, followed by a novel full of really devastating malice about the Jews, whose idealistic, kindly but vulgar, mannerless, ugly and secular establishment with some of the virtues and many of the vices of Russia, Poland and the Middle West, is wonderful grist for E.W.'s monstrous mill. The novel when it appears will cause general trouble here and in America and be prominently cited by the Russians and cause Harry Levin much pain. I don't say that this is inevitably bound to happen but Evelyn Waugh is a kind of Maurras[3] – a fanatical, angry, neurotic, violent writer, thoroughly un-English in most ways. Much more like the French fanatic than any kind of English reactionary and his snobbery is of the same curiously Continental sort full of dramatisation, social mistakes and vulgarities which, on the whole, impresses the English. [...]

I am to write about 1950 for the *Encyclopaedia Britannica*[4] but I find that no books of serious merit, no good plays, no very good music, no serious intellectual works, nothing but a good edition of Theocritus[5] has been published in that year. It was the worst year yet from the point of view of memora[bi]lity. On this melancholy note I close and beg you to write me about your health and thoughts.

Yours ever,
Isaiah.

⟨The cigars are here! the duty well worth it: Thank you very very much.⟩

1 Christopher Hugh Sykes (1907–86), author; BBC, Deputy Controller, Third Programme, 1948; Features Department 1949–68.

2 US magazine founded in 1883 and originally designed for light entertainment; from 1936 transformed by Henry Luce into a prestigious photographic news magazine, at its most popular in the decade after the end of the war.

3 Charles(-Marie-Photius) Maurras (1868–1952), French journalist, author and political activist; reactionary, monarchist, anti-democratic, strongly nationalist, anti-Semitic, agnostic supporter of all forms of authority (including the Catholic Church); sentenced to life imprisonment in 1944 for his support of General Pétain and collaboration with the occupying German forces.

4 'Nineteen Fifty: A Survey of Politico-Cultural Trends of the Year', in the 1951 *Britannica Book of the Year* (Chicago / Toronto / London, 1951).

5 Theocritus (*c.*310–*c.*250 BC), Greek pastoral poet. The edition was by A. S. F. Gow.

TO EDGAR WIND

[early February 1951?, *manuscript*]

New College

My dear Wind,

Indeed indeed I owe you an apology. Certainly I was in Italy. I was confined in a handsome & dreadfully uncomfortable castle with Sir Maurice (then plain Mr) Bowra & 4 others,[1] & gradually, as a result of discomfort & accidie, lost all desire for pleasure, life, movement, people. At last I tore myself from this queer melancholy & visited Florence, about 1½ hrs by motorcar, & then, exhausted, went home. Oh I meant to write, indeed I did, but did not precisely know where to. And the thought of a letter, however trivial, ill written, clumsy, obscure, wandering in strange hands & read by unknown eyes, froze me. So as soon as I returned I asked Seznec for your address. He gave it me, I am sure: I forgot it; I asked him again; again he gave it; but all the time I kept thinking that I could write nothing worthy of you, as well as labouring under a sense of distress at so muddling our summer arrangement – oh I am a very bad, very inefficient useless friend. So it went on from day to day, from midnight to midnight (it is 1 a.m. now; & I no longer care if all this *is* trivial, empty etc. – I have a determined desire to communicate: Besides your enclosed essay[2] is so elegant, so true, & so distinguished, original & infinitely superior to anything done by anyone of this kind – so genuinely classical & you must believe me I mean every syllable – that I am lifted by its vitality from the dreadful Oxford slough into activity) – that I finally could bear it no longer. How are you? you must be in full creative force since otherwise your perfect opuscule could not have been achieved. Whoever called Freddie 'the poor man's Russell'? believe me not I. Not that I am incapable of this sort of thing, but it is not, save in the literal sense (Principia Mathematica is very very expensive) true or fair – Joad[3] is much more the horrible entity so describable. But I see that ripples & oscillations travel easily through the social ether, even to the extent of misidentifying sources. I've said, I fear, more wounding things about my old friend than this – but not this particular jeu.[4] How are you, I repeat? Are you engaged in some magnum opus? I hope so: I mean to be, but some obvious inner frivolity keeps interposing smaller & more ephemeral things – reviews of Prof. E. H. Carr's most Hegelian opus

---

1 Four including Bowra.
2 Wind must have enclosed a recent essay of his, published with cuts in a short-lived critical quarterly by the University of Chicago: 'The Ark of Noah: A Study in the Symbolism of Michelangelo', *Measure* 1 No 4 (Fall 1950), reprinted in full (without the subtitle) in his *The Religious Symbolism of Michelangelo: The Sistine Ceiling*, ed. Elizabeth Sears (Oxford, 2000).
3 Cyril Edwin Mitchinson Joad (1891–1953), Head of Philosophy, Birkbeck College, London, 1930–53; well known as a popular broadcaster on philosophy.
4 'Witticism'.

on the Russian revolution[1] – which repels me but attracts Shurochka[2] who is growing very very realpolitisch & welthistorisch[3] – reviews of other books, little essays on De Maistre[4] & still more fascinating, the sources of Tolstoy's philosophy of history[5] – his queer interview with Proudhon[6] in Brussels in 1861; etc. etc.

I find that I admire Tolstoy more & more. His point of view is often dreadful; his conclusions paradoxical in the most absurd & offensive ways: but he is always very clever, he has a kind of grim high spirits, a sharp quality like a big bread knife which makes suitable nonsense of the absurd theorists of his time. His parody of [the] 19th century is very good: & his questions, to which the answers are always deliberately & sophisticatedly simpliste,[7] are always real: in the sense that while one rejects his answers as idiotic etc. one is not so sure what the true answer is. Someone called Dostoevsky a cruel genius. But au fond Tolstoy is far crueller: he does not force one to contemplate horrors or humiliate one by forcing open concealed & locked up skeletons – but far worse, he introduces a sense of silliness – robs of significance & dignity, the normal relied on processes to a most devastating degree. One can reject Dostoevsky or recover from him as from a nightmare; but Tolstoy's very flatness of tone, ruthless intelligent ironical tone, iron impregnability, superiority to his own emotions, unbelievable degree of control over the material – the sense he conveys of understanding & knowing everything without the exaggeration or violence which offers one the excuse for escape – ultimately undermines one more. All talk of his "humanity" or "deep feeling" seems to me nonsense. He is absolutely heartless, & maddeningly sane & methodical: and destroys the avenues of escape – which any dramatising or lovingly analytic writer – Dostoevsky, Proust,[8] always

1 'Soviet Beginnings', review of E. H. Carr, *A History of Soviet Russia*, vol. 1: *The Bolshevik Revolution 1917–1923, Sunday Times*, 10 December 1950, 3.

2 Alexander (of which 'Shurochka' is an affectionate diminutive) Yakovlevich Halpern (*c.*1879–1956), Russian-born lawyer whom IB had met in left-wing Russian émigré circles in New York during the war, where Halpern was working partly for British Intelligence. His wife Salome (1888–1982) had belonged to the literary and artistic worlds of pre-revolutionary St Petersburg and between-the-wars Paris. After the war the Halperns lived in London, where Anna Kallin, a close friend of Edgar Wind, was their lodger. See IB's 'Alexander and Salome Halpern', in Mikhail Parkhomovsky (ed.), *Jews in the Culture of Russia Abroad: Collected Articles, Publications, Memoirs and Essays*, vol. 1, *1919–1939* (Jerusalem, 1992) – as yet published only in Russian translation in this Russian collection.

3 'Realpolitik-ish and world-historical'.

4 See 646/1.

5 See 245/3.

6 Pierre-Joseph Proudhon (1809–65), French radical political thinker who called for non-violent economic and social reform. A self-styled anarchist, anti-Semite, racist and sexist, he opposed both capitalism and communism, and favoured a decentralised form of libertarian socialism. He influenced, among others, the young Karl Marx, Mikhail Bakunin and Tolstoy, whose mid-life embrace of Christian anarchism appears to have been encouraged by his March 1861 meeting with Proudhon, then living in exile in Brussels.

7 'Simplistic'.

8 (Valentin-Louis-Georges-Eugène-)Marcel Proust (1871–1922), French novelist.

leaves open – absolutely. Stendhal, you can at least say, paints no attractive characters. They are all âmes damnées.[1] Tolstoy avoids explicit diabolism & imports it into everything. The French called him a nihilist in the 8oies: the Russians protested, the English protested very violently – but wrongly. He leaves nothing standing & his Christianity is an act of bankruptcy. Hence I should like to know where all this comes from (what rosy idealists Marx & Lenin are by comparison! & how silly Lenin is about Tolstoy)[2] – but why am I boring you about Tolstoy (*there* was a real master of precise metaphor: goodness how impossible it is to translate him into Russellese: & if Russell likes to accuse him of indulging in a metaphysic of savages – unscientific – there is something to be said for savages) – I shall, I hope, be in Rome for a few days at the end of March or beginning of April: I am bound, as always at such seasons, for Israel; but promised the Foreign Office to deliver a lecture in Rome.[3] [...]

Yours ever
    Isaiah Berlin

George Kennan's letter of 26 [May][4] 1950 to IB commenting on 'Political Ideas in the Twentieth Century' still remained unanswered. In this, Kennan, remarking that IB's conclusion was 'laconic, and almost perfunctory', had written at length on 'the weakness and fallaciousness of modern totalitarianism', which took advantage of human vulnerability to manipulation, but was itself flawed by the human weaknesses of those operating the system: 'the one thing no man can do is to manipulate his own psychological nature'. As a result 'a society in which it is thought that problems have been caused to disappear in order that they may not have to be solved can be, in reality, only a fake'. In the long term, widespread commitment to totalitarian creeds and practices seemed likely to give way to a jaded habit of conformity: 'People acquiesce, but do not believe.' And, more hopeful than IB, Kennan believed that totalitarianism would eventually destroy itself.

    Alongside this intellectual conclusion, Kennan expressed his emotional revulsion from totalitarianism:

I really believe that this thing that the totalitarians have done – this taking

1 'Familiar demons'.
2 Lenin admired Tolstoy's literary genius and his recognition of the need for social change but crit-icised other aspects of his thinking (such as his pacifism and religious beliefs) in several articles, of which the best-known is 'Leo Tolstoy as a Mirror of the Russian Revolution', *Proletary*, 24 September 1908.
3 R. L. Speaight of the FO had requested on 28 June 1950 that IB should take part in a programme of visits to Italy by 'suitable people [...] to stimulate a sense of Western European solidarity, to shake faith in Communism and to clarify the issues in the struggle between democracy and totalitarianism' by talking to 'small hand-picked groups' or individuals. After the FO, with IB's agreement, set up a programme of meetings in several Italian cities, IB changed the dates of his trip; it seems likely that all or most of the meetings had to be abandoned.
4 See 179/3.

advantage of the helpless corner of man's psychic structure – is the original sin. It is this knowledge which men were not supposed to develop and exploit. It was this desecrating curiosity, I believe, which Milton really had in mind as his reason for the fall of man and his eviction from Paradise. For when a man's ultimate dignity is destroyed, he is killed, of course, as a man. This exploitation of his weakness is therefore only another form of taking human life arbitrarily and in cold blood, as a result of calculation and not of passion. [...] The success of civilisation seems somehow to depend on the willingness of men to recognise that by taking advantage of this Achilles' heel in man's moral composition, they shame themselves as well as others; on their readiness to refrain from doing so; and on their sticking to the rational appeal which assumes – perhaps in defiance of the evident – that in the long run each man can be taught to rise above himself. Perhaps this is the supreme make-believe. If so, I am persuaded that it is an indispensable one, and the inexorable price of human progress. In any case it is surely our reason for clinging to the belief that questions are important, are susceptible of solution by rational processes, and should be so approached and solved.

IB eventually responded.[1]

TO GEORGE KENNAN

13 February 1951 [carbon]

New College, Oxford

Dear George,

I have ill rewarded your wonderful letter by leaving it so long unanswered. I received it towards the end of term here when I was genuinely worn out by teaching and examining, and scarcely capable of taking anything in, but even then it moved me profoundly. I took it off with me to Italy and read it and re-read it, and kept putting off the day on which I would write an answer worthy of it, but no such day ever came. I began many letters but each seemed trivial, and what the Russians call 'suetlivo'[2] – full of hurrying sentences, scattered and moving in all directions at once, inappropriate either to the theme or to your words about it; but I cannot bear (if only because of the feelings which your letter excited in me) to say nothing merely because I am not sure how much I have to say. So you must forgive me if what I write is chaotic, not merely in form but in substance, and does little justice to your thesis. I shall simply go on and hope for the best, and beg you to pardon me if I am wasting your time.

I must begin by saying that you have put in words something which I believe not only to be the centre of the subject but something which, perhaps because of a certain reluctance to face the fundamental moral issue

---

1 His letter is also published in L.
2 'In a fussy or bustling manner'.

on which everything turns, I failed to say; but once forced to face it, I realise both that it is craven to sail round it as I have done, and moreover that it is, in fact, what I myself believe, and deeply believe, to be true; and more than this: that upon one's attitude to this issue which you have put very plainly, and very, if I may say so, poignantly, depends one's entire moral outlook, i.e. everything one believes.

Let me try and say what I think it is; you say (and I am not quoting) that every man possesses a point of weakness, an Achilles' heel, and by exploiting this a man may be made a hero or a martyr or a rag. Again, if I understand you correctly, you think that Western civilisation has rested upon the principle that, whatever else was permitted or forbidden, the one heinous act which would destroy the world was to do precisely this – the deliberate act of tampering with human beings so as to make them behave in a way which, if they knew what they were doing, or what its consequences were likely to be, would make them recoil with horror and disgust. The whole of the Kantian morality (and I don't know about Catholics, but Protestants, Jews, Muslims and high-minded atheists believe it) lies in this; the mysterious phrase about men being 'ends in themselves' to which much lip-service has been paid, with not much attempt to explain it, seems to lie in this: that every human being is assumed to possess the capacity to choose what to do, and what to be, however narrow the limits within which his choice may lie, however hemmed in by circumstances beyond his control; that all human love and respect rests upon the attribution of conscious motives in this sense; that all the categories, the concepts, in terms of which we think about and act towards one another – goodness, badness, integrity and lack of it, the attribution of dignity or honour to others which we must not insult or exploit, the entire cluster of ideas such as honesty, purity of motive, courage, sense of truth, sensibility, compassion, justice; and, on the other side, brutality, falseness, wickedness, ruthlessness, lack of scruple, corruption, lack of feelings, emptiness – all these notions in terms of which we think of others and ourselves, in terms of which conduct is assessed, purposes adopted – all this becomes meaningless unless we think of human beings as capable of pursuing ends for their own sakes by deliberate acts of choice – which alone makes nobility noble and sacrifices sacrifices.

The whole of that morality, which is most prominent in the nineteenth century, in particular in the romantic period, but implicit in both Christian and Jewish writings, and far less present in the pagan world, rests on the view that it is a marvellous thing in itself when a man pits himself against the world, and sacrifices himself to an idea without reckoning the consequences, even when we consider his ideal false and its consequences disastrous. We admire purity of motive as such, and think it a wonderful thing – or at any rate deeply impressive, perhaps to be fought but never despised – when somebody throws away material advantage, reputation etc. for the sake of bearing witness to something which he believes to be true, however mistaken and fanatical we may think him to be. I do not say that we worship passionate self-abandonment or automatically prefer a desperate fanaticism to moderation and enlightened self-interest. Of course not; yet nevertheless we do think such conduct deeply moving even when misdirected. We admire it *always* more than calculation; we at least understand the kind of aesthetic splendour which all defiance has for some people – Carlyle, Nietzsche, Leont'ev[1] and Fascists generally. We think that only those human beings are a credit to their kind who do not let themselves be pushed too far by the forces of nature or history, either passively or by glorying in their own impotence; and we idealise only those who have purposes for which they accept responsibility, on which they stake something, and at times everything; living consciously and bravely for whatever they think good, i.e. worth living and, in the last resort, dying for.

All this may seem an enormous platitude, but, if it is true, this is, of course, what ultimately refutes utilitarianism and what makes Hegel and Marx such monstrous traitors to our civilisation. When, in the famous passage,[2] Ivan Karamazov rejects the worlds upon worlds of happiness which may be bought at the price of the torture to death of one innocent child, what can utilitarians, even the most civilised and humane, say to him? After all, it is in a sense unreasonable to throw away so much human bliss purchased at so small a price as *one* – only one – innocent victim, done to death however horribly – what after all is one soul against the happiness of so many? Nevertheless, when Ivan says he would rather return the ticket, no reader of Dostoevsky thinks this cold-hearted or mad or irresponsible; and although a long course of Bentham[3] or Hegel might turn one into a supporter of the Grand Inquisitor,[4] qualms remain.

Ivan Karamazov cannot be totally exorcised; he speaks for us all, and this I take to be your point, and the foundation of your optimism. What I take you to say, and what I should have said myself if I had had the wit or the depth, is that the one thing which no utilitarian paradise, no promise of eternal harmony in the future within some vast organic whole will make us accept

---

1 Konstantin Leont'ev (1831–91), reactionary Russian philosopher who advocated closer ties with the East as a defence against Western liberalism.

2 Dostoevsky, *The Brothers Karamazov*, book 5, chapter 4: vol. 1, 287, in the Penguin Classics edition, trans. David Magarshack (Harmondsworth, 1958): 'too high a price has been placed on harmony. We cannot afford to pay so much for admission. And therefore I hasten to return my ticket of admission.'

3 Jeremy Bentham (1748–1832), British philosopher and social reformer who argued that social policy should conform to a principle of utility and hence promote 'the greatest happiness of the greatest number'.

4 The Grand Inquisitor, in a story by Ivan Karamazov, argues that most people cannot cope with freedom of choice, and that it is the role of the few who can do so to make decisions for the rest of humanity and enforce their obedience, sacrificing those who resist for the sake of the happiness of the majority.

is the use of human beings as mere means – the doctoring of them until they are made to do what they do, not for the sake of the purposes which are their purposes, fulfilment of hopes which however foolish or desperate are at least their own, but for reasons which only we, the manipulators, who freely twist them for our purposes, can understand. What horrifies one about Soviet or Nazi practice is not merely the suffering and the cruelty, since although that is bad enough, it is something which history has produced too often, and to ignore its apparent inevitability is perhaps real Utopianism – no; what turns one inside out, and is indescribable, is the spectacle of one set of persons who so tamper and 'get at' others that the others do their will without knowing what they are doing; and in this lose their status as free human beings, indeed as human beings at all.

When armies were slaughtered by other armies in the course of history, we might be appalled by the carnage and turn pacifist; but our horror acquires a new dimension when we read about children, or for that matter grown-up men and women, whom the Nazis loaded into trains bound for gas chambers, telling them that they were going to emigrate to some happier place. Why does this deception, which may in fact have diminished the anguish of the victims, arouse a really unutterable kind of horror in us? The spectacle, I mean, of the victims marching off in happy ignorance of their doom amid the smiling faces of their tormentors? Surely because we cannot bear the thought of human beings denied their last rights – of knowing the truth, of acting with at least the freedom of the condemned, of being able to face their destruction with fear or courage, according to their temperaments, but at least as human beings, armed with the power of choice. It is the denial to human beings of the possibility of choice, the getting them into one's power, the twisting them this way and that in accordance with one's whim, the destruction of their personality by creating unequal moral terms between the gaoler and the victim, whereby the gaoler knows what he is doing, and why, and plays upon the victim, i.e. treats him as a mere object and not as a subject whose motives, views, intentions have any intrinsic weight whatever – by destroying the very possibility of his having views, notions of a relevant kind – that is what cannot be borne at all.

What else horrifies us about unscrupulousness if not this? Why is the thought of someone twisting someone else round his little finger, even in innocent contexts, so beastly (for instance in Dostoevsky's *Dyadyushkin son*,[1] which the Moscow Arts Theatre used to act so well and so cruelly)? After all, the victim may prefer to have no responsibility; the slave be happier in his slavery. Certainly we do not detest this kind of destruction of liberty *merely* because it denies liberty of action; there is a far greater horror in depriving

---

[1] 'Uncle's Dream' (1859), a novella in which the central event is the manipulation of a muddled old man by the other characters.

men of the very capacity for freedom – that is the real sin against the Holy Ghost. Everything else is bearable so long as the possibility of goodness – of a state of affairs in which men freely choose, disinterestedly seek ends for their own sake – is still open, however much suffering they may have gone through. Their souls are destroyed only when this is no longer possible. It is when the desire for choice is broken that what men do thereby loses all moral value, and actions lose all significance (in terms of good and evil) in their own eyes; that is what is meant by destroying people's self-respect, by turning them, in your words, into rags. This is the ultimate horror because in such a situation there are no worthwhile motives left: nothing is worth doing or avoiding, the reasons for existing are gone. We admire Don Quixote, if we do, because he has a pure-hearted desire to do what is good, and he is pathetic because he is mad and his attempts are ludicrous.

For Hegel and for Marx (and possibly for Bentham, although he would have been horrified by the juxtaposition) Don Quixote is not merely absurd but immoral. Morality consists in doing what is good. Goodness is that which will satisfy one's nature. Only that will satisfy one's nature which is part of the historical stream along which one is carried willy-nilly, i.e. that which 'the future' in any case holds in store. In some ultimate sense, failure is proof of a misunderstanding of history, of having chosen what is doomed to destruction, in preference to that which is destined to succeed. But to choose the former is 'irrational', and since morality is rational choice, to seek that which will not come off is immoral. This doctrine that the moral and the good is the successful, and that failure is not only unfortunate but wicked, is at the heart of all that is most horrifying both in utilitarianism and in 'historicism' of the Hegelian, Marxist type. For if only that were best which made one happiest in the long run, or that which accorded with some mysterious plan of history, there really would be no reason to 'return the ticket'. Provided that there was a reasonable probability that the new Soviet man might either be happier, even in some very long run, than his predecessors, or that history would be bound sooner or later to produce someone like him whether we liked it or not, to protest against him would be mere silly romanticism, 'subjective', 'idealistic', ultimately irresponsible. At most we could argue that the Russians were factually wrong and the Soviet method not the best for producing this desirable or inevitable type of man. But of course what we violently reject is not these questions of fact, but the very idea that there are any circumstances in which one has a right to get at, and shape, the characters and souls of other men for purposes which these men, if they realised what we were doing, might reject.

We distinguish to this extent between factual and value judgement, that we deny the right to tamper with human beings to an unlimited extent, *whatever* the truth about the laws of history; we might go further and deny the notion that 'history' in some mysterious way 'confers' upon us 'rights' to do this or that; that some men or bodies of men can morally claim a right to our obedience because they, in some sense, carry out the behests of 'history', are its chosen instrument, its medicine or scourge or in some important sense 'welthistorisch'[1] – great, irresistible, riding the waves of the future, beyond our petty, subjective, not rationally bolsterable ideas of right and wrong. Many a German and I daresay many a Russian or Mongol or Chinese today feels that it is more adult to recognise the sheer immensity of the great events that shake the world, and play a part in history worthy of men by abandoning themselves to them, than by praising or damning and indulging in [ ][2] moralisings: the notion that history must be applauded as such is the horrible German way out of the burden of moral choice.

If pushed to the extreme, this doctrine would, of course, do away with all education, since when we send children to school or influence them in other ways without obtaining their approval for what we are doing, are we not 'tampering' with them, 'moulding' them like pieces of clay with no purpose of their own? Our answer has to be that certainly all 'moulding' is evil, and that if human beings at birth had the power of choice and the means of understanding the world, it would be criminal; since they have not, we temporarily enslave them, for fear that, otherwise, they will suffer worse misfortunes from nature and from men, and this 'temporary enslavement' is a necessary evil until such time as they are able to choose for themselves – the 'enslavement' having as its purpose not an inculcation of obedience but its contrary, the development of power of free judgement and choice; still, evil it remains even if necessary.

Communists and Fascists maintain that this kind of 'education' is needed not only for children but for entire nations for long periods, the slow withering away of the State corresponding to immaturity in the lives of individuals. The analogy is specious because peoples, nations are not individuals and still less children; moreover in promising maturity their practice belies their professions; that is to say, they are lying, and for the most part know that they are. From a necessary evil in the case of the education of helpless children, this kind of practice becomes an evil on a much larger scale, and quite gratuitous, based either on utilitarianism, which misrepresents our moral values, or again on metaphors which misdescribe both what we call good and bad, and the nature of the world, the facts themselves. For we, i.e. those who join with us, are more concerned with making people free than making them happy; we would rather that they chose badly than not at all; because we believe that unless they choose they cannot be either happy or unhappy in any sense in which these conditions are worth having; the very notion of 'worth having' presupposes the choice of ends, a system of free preferences;

1 'World-historical'.
2 Inaudible word omitted by the typist.

and an undermining of *them* is what strikes us with such cold terror, worse than the most unjust sufferings, which nevertheless leave the possibility of knowing them for what they are – of free judgement, which makes it possible to condemn them – still open.

You say that men who in this way undermine the lives of other men will end by undermining themselves, and the whole evil system is therefore doomed to collapse. In the long run I am sure you are right, because open-eyed cynicism, the exploitation of others by men who avoid being exploited themselves, is an attitude difficult for human beings to keep up for very long. It needs too much discipline and appalling strain in an atmosphere of such mutual hatred and distrust as cannot last because there is not enough moral intensity or general fanaticism to keep it going. But still the run can be very long before it is over, and I do not believe that the corrosive force from inside will work away at the rate which perhaps you, more hopefully, anticipate. I feel that we must avoid being inverted Marxists. Marx and Hegel observed the economic corrosion in their lifetime, and so the revolution seemed to be always round the corner. They died without seeing it, and perhaps it would have taken centuries if Lenin had not given history a sharp jolt. Without the jolt, are moral forces alone sufficient to bury the Soviet grave-diggers? I doubt it. But that in the end the worm would eat them I doubt no more than you; but whereas you say that is an isolated evil, a monstrous scourge sent to try us, not connected with what goes on elsewhere, I cannot help seeing it as an extreme and distorted but only too typical form of some general attitude of mind from which our own countries are not exempt.

For saying this, E. H. Carr has attacked me with some violence, in a leading article in *The Times Literary Supplement* last June.[1] This makes me believe I must be even more right than I thought, since his writings are among the more obvious symptoms of what I tried to analyse, and he rightly interprets my articles as an attack on all he stands for. All this comes out particularly in his last œuvre – on the Russian Revolution – in which the opposition and the victims are not allowed to testify – feeble flotsam adequately taken care of by history, which has swept them away as, being against the current, they, *eo ipso*,[2] deserve. Only the victors deserve to be heard; the rest – Pascal, Pierre Bezukhov,[3] all Chekhov's people, all the critics and casualties of *Deutschtum*[4] or White Man's Burdens,[5] or the American Century,[6] or the Common Man

1 'The New Scepticism' (unsigned), *The Times Literary Supplement*, 9 June 1950, 357.
2 'By that very fact'.
3 One of the central characters in Tolstoy's novel *War and Peace* (1865–9).
4 'Germanness', either cultural or racial.
5 'The White Man's Burden', the 1899 poem by Rudyard Kipling about the US conquest of the Philippines, gave its name to the theory that imperialism, specifically the spreading of Western values and a Western way of life in undeveloped countries, was an onerous but necessary duty for developed countries.
6 Henry Luce's term, first coined in 1941, alluding to US political and economic dominance in the 20th century.

on the March[1] – these are historical dust, *lishnye lyudi*,[2] those who have missed the bus of history, poor little rats inferior to Ibsenite rebels[3] who are all potential Catilines and dictators. Surely there never was a time when more homage was paid to bullies as such: and the weaker the victim the louder (and sincerer) his paeans – vide E. H. Carr, Koestler, Burnham,[4] Laski, *passim*? But I must not waste your time any further.

Once more I should like to say how deeply moved I was by your formulation of what it is that excites in us the unparalleled horror which we feel when we read of what goes on in Soviet territories, and my admiration and unbounded moral respect for the insight and scruple with which you set it forth. These qualities seem to me unique at present; more than this I cannot say.

Yours ever,

TO ARTHUR SCHLESINGER

[Between 18 and 24 February 1951]

[Oxford]

My dear Arthur,

It was a great pleasure to receive your letter – I must say I do feel a certain curious satisfaction in reflecting on our beautiful symmetrical positions vis-à-vis each other.[5] Neither of us sufficiently credited for our passion for each other's countries, which in our view, but in no one else's, gives us the right to wonderful freedom of criticism. About Acheson you are obviously quite right;[6] he has become an embarrassment to his own policy and to any other. All the curious weaknesses which his personally good character, tendency to lean over backwards etc. concealed, are now patent. It is sad to me to confess that Lippmann, who ought to know about this particular form of misery

---

1 In May 1942, in a fiercely anti-Nazi speech published in *The Century of the Common Man* (New York 1943), Henry Wallace had referred to 'the march of freedom for the common man' and called for victory in war to lead to 'the century of the common man'.

2 'Superfluous men'. The character-type of the 'superfluous man', common in 19th-century Russian literature, was given its familiar name by Turgenev in his 1850 novella *Dnevnik lishnego cheloveka* ('Diary of a superfluous man'): see entry for 23 March 1850. The term was also used as a catchphrase by Dostoevsky in *Zapiski iz podpol'ya* ('Notes from Underground', 1864).

3 The central characters in the plays of Henrik Ibsen (1828–1906) are often rebels against social conventions. His first play *Catalina* (1850) dramatised the life of the Roman noble Lucius Sergius Catilina (Catiline: *c.*110–62 BC), who attempted to overthrow the Roman Republic.

4 James Burnham (1905–87), US political theorist who moved from Trotskyite Communism in the 1930s to aggressive anti-Communism during the Cold War.

5 Some gloomy articles about Britain by Schlesinger in the *New York Post* had provoked 'bitter, hurt and resentful letters from English friends' (letter of 2 February).

6 Schlesinger had reported that attacks on Acheson during the recent election had destroyed him as 'an independent or wise foreign secretary'; in Lippmann's words, he had 'traded policy for time'. The Far Eastern policy he was following might well lead to war with China. ibid.

by his own long sad hours of self-contemplation, should be the instrument chosen by the world spirit to tell the truth.

The spirit in question has altogether been behaving very oddly; it suddenly chose G. D. H. Cole,[1] with whom I have a weekly class on Hegel and Marx, to be the trumpet of British isolationism. It is all very odd and sad. You ought to read the *New Statesman* of 3 February,[2] which contains his Credo. Cole is basically a very nice, sincere, kind, un-grown-up, boyish figure, who hates all forms of industrialism and materialism and suffers from a pathological hatred of America, where his daughter[3] lives married to someone in New York. He is by now an acute isolationist, says he hates the Russians but thinks they may produce something in 300 years time whereas the Americans never will; he is a ready follower of William Morris,[4] Cobbett,[5] nostalgic for a chiefly mediaeval world and sees himself uncalculated [*sic*], treated with mechanical courtesy in All Souls, regarded as a great man by no one. Still good-looking, still full of integrity, courage etc. but with his books treated not so much as contributions to any subject but as utilities – like directories or almanacks – by reviewers mechanically regarding their likeness or unlikeness to the last tedious overlong volume from the same pen. He feels a terrible back number, hates all foreigners particularly refugees and is really a type commoner today [in America?][6] than in England. His idealism is of the same type as President Hutchins's,[7] i.e. a little mad and psygenies [*sic*].[8] Now suddenly by writing to the *New Statesman* he has fame and a following and a vast fan mail and adores his position – alone in a minority of one espousing an unpopular cause etc. He spoke in Oxford in a manner which brought lumps to everyone's throats, quite genuine lumps; it is impossible to dislike him but it is difficult to take him seriously. In one sense he is so very childish: second-rate, vulgar and thin in every sense. There is always a deep pathos I

1 (George) Douglas Howard Cole (1889–1959), socialist theoretician and writer; IB's predecessor as Chichele Professor of Social and Political Theory, Oxford, and Fellow of All Souls, 1944–57; Chairman, Fabian Society, 1939–46, 1948–50, President 1952–9; Research Fellow, Nuffield, 1957–9.

2 In which Cole criticised US military action in Korea and declared: 'If Great Britain gets dragged into war with China by the Americans, I shall be on the side of China.' 'As a Socialist Sees It', *New Statesman and Nation*, 3 February 1951, 121.

3 Janet Elizabeth Margaret Cole (b. 1921) had married William Abraham, an economist in the US Army, in 1945, and settled in the US the following year.

4 William Morris (1834–96), designer, poet, translator, publisher, one of the founders of the Pre-Raphaelite Brotherhood and of the Arts and Crafts Movement, and one of the first British socialists.

5 William Cobbett (1763–1835), political radical and journalist; Cole had written a biography of him in 1924.

6 Gap left by typist.

7 Robert Maynard Hutchins (1899–1977), educational theorist; President, University of Chicago, 1929–45, Chancellor 1945–51; opposed to intellectual specialisation, job-related learning and the distractions of sport (he banned Chicago's participation in intercollegiate football), he saw the role of academic institutions as producing responsible citizens through broad liberal education, using the great books of the world as texts.

8 sc. *sui generis*?

suppose about people who belonged to some earlier nobler idealistic movement, outlive it, and then appear once again on the stage and move people
not by their argument [but] by the pathetic memory of a poorer day.

I have serious conversations with him in the course of which I asked
him how he differs from, let us say, M. Paul Faure,[1] who in 1938 declared
himself unable to go to war over an internal Czech issue in company with
the detested Chamberlain government, Col Beck[2] and other Feudal monsters. Cole says that if I think the Communists are to be equated with the
Nazis then I may be right but he does not. He obviously thinks, and his wife[3]
thinks, and his brother-in-law J. P. Postgate[4] thinks, that the Communists are
somehow on the left, SOBs on their own. I now am armed with a copy of
Questions of Philosophy[5] No 3 for 1951, in which he is flayed in a most horrific
manner together with the *New Statesman* – an enormous heap of refuse is
thrown at them. Kingsley Martin[6] will probably rather like this but Cole may
rebel. We shall see. He is very much our Matthiessen but less neurotic if just
as sweet and silly and doesn't get on at all well with, say, E. H. Carr. [...]

I reviewed the book myself in our own *Sunday Times*[7] and received a
queer letter from Carr thanking me and protesting at the same time. What
a strange man he is! In a sense he knows exactly what is wrong with his performance and doesn't trouble to defend himself – does it with a dedicated air
of someone who has decided once and for all on which side he is, sees all its
faults but hates its opponents too much to admit anything in public although
he enjoys admitting this in private to such as me. I found the same thing in
the case of Ralph Parker,[8] the London *Times* correspondent in Moscow in
my day, now representing the *Daily Worker* and some Egyptian papers, who
talked sensibly and critically to me and then published a book denouncing
the British Embassy man by man in a Bucar-like manner[9] (but omitting me),
this almost enough to compromise me, out of some sentimental memory

1 Paul Faure (1878–1960), French socialist politician associated with appeasement and the Vichy
   regime.
2 Colonel Józef Beck (1894–1944), Polish Foreign Minister 1932–9, who attempted to keep on good
   terms with both Nazi Germany and the Soviet Union.
3 Margaret Isabel Cole (1893–1980), daughter of Professor J. P. Postgate; socialist writer, biographer
   and political analyst, who collaborated with her husband on many books, including a series of
   detective stories embodying social comment.
4 IB presumably means Margaret Cole's brother Raymond William Postgate (1896–1971), author,
   socialist and wine expert; editor, *Good Food Guide*, 1951–71. John Percival Postgate (1853–1926),
   formerly Fellow of Trinity, Cambridge, and Professor of Latin, Liverpool, was their father.
5 i.e. *Voprosy filosofii*, a Moscow periodical.
6 (Basil) Kingsley Martin (1897–1969), editor, *New Statesman* (*New Statesman and Nation* 1931–57),
   1930–60.
7 See 211/1.
8 (Arthur) Ralph Parker (1907–64), journalist, author and Soviet apologist; Moscow correspondent
   for *The Times* and other newspapers and periodicals 1942–7.
9 Annabelle Bucar (c.1925–98), an official in the US Embassy in Moscow 1945–8, left her job after
   marrying a Russian opera singer, and subsequently produced a book, *The Truth about American
   Diplomats* (Moscow, 1949), alleging espionage by the Embassy.

of the last free conversation he could have had. Carr, who attacked me in the *Times Literary Supplement*, nevertheless gives every sign of not wishing to break with me. Writes letters of apology, visits me, shows affection, insists that he does not mind my not very friendly reviews, thanks those who, like Deutscher,[1] publicly defend him against me, and swears eternal friendship to me in the same breath. Evidently there is some affinity with characters out of Dostoevsky. But I must finish and get on with something genuinely disagreeable – work – a paper for a historical conference in London.

I have had a letter from [Elliott] Perkins inviting me back to Lowell House and assuring me of greater comfort, even in the matter of breakfast, written in his usual aggressive, defensive, nevertheless affably meant, fashion. I have also had a letter from Earle in Princeton[2] asking me to go there, madly tempting in as much as no teaching etc.; obviously this cannot be thought of in view of previous obligations so I shall turn up in autumn, September I expect, and you will find me on your doorstep as so often before. Your remarks about Washington policy corroborate what I have not dared to suspect. Acheson, but this is how my letter began, and if this is not to adopt a rondo form and begin again and say everything again – it is the sixth week of term and a well-known time for feeble-witted automatism – particularly for those who as at Oxford say the same things over and over again to the same unhappy pupils, forgetting who is who, what they are learning, when they are coming, or why they or anyone else or anything else is and are what they are. So, as you can see, being in no fit state to articulate, I end, with warmest wishes to Marian. [...]

Yours ever,

Isaiah   [...]

Maurice Bowra described to Alice James IB's life at this time:

Isaiah has gone off to Palestine for three weeks. He has a deep and touching devotion to old Dr Weizmann and goes at once when summoned. The old man feels very isolated and gets much comfort from Isaiah's presence – which does both of them much credit. In October Isaiah returns to the US; so you will see him then. He seems to be writing lectures day and night, or rather dictating them to handsome girl secretaries, who totter out gasping for breath after taking down that flow of words.[3]

---

1 Isaac Deutscher (1907–67), Polish-born author, lecturer and broadcaster; *Observer* 1942–7, *The Economist* 1942–9; intensely disliked by IB, partly for his Marxist opinions but even more for his personality: 'I suffer from profound, perhaps exaggerated antipathy to all his writings – I think him specious, dishonest, and in any case possessed of some quality which causes some kind of nausea within me.' To William Phillips, 8 October 1959.

2 Edward Mead Earle (1894–1954), historian of the role of the military in US foreign relations; Professor, Institute for Advanced Study, Princeton, 1934–54.

3 Maurice Bowra to Alice James, 31 March 1951 [Wadham College Archives, Oxford].

IB spent much of the Easter vacation in Israel, on this occasion staying only briefly with the Weizmanns: Chaim Weizmann's health was deteriorating and from about this time until his death he was bedridden. In Israel IB met current and future political leaders, including Ben-Gurion, as well as his own friends and relatives.

TO WALTER EYTAN

[10 April 1951?, *typed transcript of untraced manuscript*]¹

[Israel]

I sail in an hour and write this in some haste. I tried to get through to you on the telephone from Jerusalem yesterday (a) to bid you farewell (b) to ask whether it would be of any use sending you the suggestions going through in my head re your intelligence and research department. But you were not to be spoken to according to your secretary, then or at a later hour. So to salve my conscience I have no alternative but to inflict this on you now. It all arises out of my lecture No. 1 at Natanya,² and the questions asked when I talked to your Machlaka Medinit³ at their request, last Tuesday. I thought the young men both at Natanya and at the FO exceptionally intelligent and worth encouraging. I cannot think but that you are the proper person to whom to address all this in so far as you equal Sir W. Strang, say, to whom I would normally be writing this if I were still in 1946–7, say. If this is wrong forgive me. Anyhow all my proposals may have no use or relevance since I don't know the exact nature either of the 'set-up' nor of the circumstances. If so, throw it all into what Cecil Roth⁴ still calls the Wagger Pagger Bagger,⁵ or anyway ignore it. My one purpose is to try and hint at errors which cost the British F.O. very dear in the last ten years – and they are exceedingly avoidable. I start from the assumption which is not self-evident, but which I very strongly believe, that planners and executors of policy, and even researchers, should, as far as practicable, be identical. That planning bodies which do not consist of people who do day to day work at all are liable to be both mildly resented and largely ignored: and that researchers who sit insulated, researching only, lose all morale and play little part in decisions.

The F.O. (London) Research Department, growing out of the Library of the F.O. and Chatham House, live as a basement of slaves, despised, ignored,

1 At the foot of the transcript it is recorded that copies were sent to 'Sar Hachutz, Dr L. Kohn, Mr R. Shiloah, Mr A. Levavi', a normal distribution list: the Minister ('Sar Hachutz', at this time Moshe Sharett); Leo Kohn, his counsellor; Reuven Shiloah, then head of the Machlaka Medinit (note 3 below); and Aryeh Levavi, a senior official in the Ministry of Foreign Affairs.
2 IB had been invited by the Israeli Foreign Ministry to give several lectures, apparently to diplomats in training.
3 'Political Department', an intelligence unit forming part of the Mossad, which in March 1951 was being reorganised and transferred from the Foreign Ministry to the Prime Minister's Office.
4 Cecil Roth (1899–1970), Reader in Jewish Studies, Oxford, 1939–64.
5 'Waste paper basket' (Oxford slang).

and being kept from things, as being only semi-secure and far from pukka, become themselves more and more academic and remote. Some of the most staggering blunders of the F.O. vis-à-vis the Middle East generally in 1936–1950 (say) are partly traceable to failing to use their human resources. The diplomats are impertinent, prejudiced and ignorant, the researchers feel their stuff is ignored and their persons kept from going abroad to look at their subjects in the flesh, contact is bad and even so relatively clever a man as Beeley forms grotesque opinions because he was kept from visiting the Middle East years ago and not listened to unless he adjusted himself to the absurdities believed by the grander beings above him. I therefore think it would be a very good thing if

(1) Your researchers and F.O. intelligence people could *be sent abroad*, and work in legations and embassies, for not less than six months at a time, they could draft 'long term' reports in the embassies while there, and work with the junior members of the embassy staffs on regular diplomatic work. Above all they should *not* be confined to 'secret' work while abroad, but be normal embassy officials. This applies to friendly and neutral countries. As far as enemy countries are concerned, it is something to be allowed to sit geographically next door to them, if possible, and listen through closed doors. I could write you a little book on what a difference this policy made to British policy vis-à-vis USA in 1940–50 and still even now. Anglo-American relations are immeasurably better than ever before, despite popular sentiment etc.; as a result of closer contacts of officials, researchers, journalists, politicians etc. in Washington. It made a really gigantic difference and gained a lot for England.

That these same researchers and intelligence collectors be fairly freely interchanged with junior members of executive departments within the F.O. lest they feel – and be – relegated to a cave – the Research Dept. – for good. When this occurs, the 'regulars' look askance at them, they feel persecuted, and Cinderella-ish, their stuff becomes functionally academic and out of political focus, and they begin to acquire the vices – too much unweighted information – irrelevant speculation – divorce from day to day questions etc. – with which they are anyway normally charged. If finance permits they should be given real competent hacks – industrious and methodical ladies if possible – who could act as research assistants, card indexers etc., to whom no hope of necessary promotion need be held out. But the researchers themselves should be appointed to executive jobs from time to time, despite the bureaucratic dislocations, in order to create better esprit de corps, a better sense of reality, closer relations with their employers. And they should be allowed directly to feed the outgoing diplomats with whatever they feel urgently needed (perhaps this happened already. Remember, I really know nothing, and was careful not to ask organizational questions of this kind) and not [merely?][1] via channels.

1 Transcript omits illegible word(s).

The Library and Archives of a F.O. is a queerly specialized thing, which the F.O., State Dept., Quai d'Orsay etc. have brought to a high pitch of perfection. I am sure they would not mind being asked how they do it. Their organisation genuinely economises much effort both in long term policy and in day to day telegrams, by preserving continuity in policy or making discontinuity clearer: one wants to know, to be discontinuous, what one is being discontinuous with and how far; at least retrospectively one does. Historians also will bless you if archives are properly kept (perhaps they are? and this is all happening? I had a sense that not. But I may *easily* be wrong.) and don't underestimate their influence on opinion here and abroad – the diplomatic history of early Israel, besides being intrinsically very valuable, will provide material for friend and foe for years. And if Israeli sources are scattered, British and US sources will not be, and will be used.

All this really comes to is that your researchers should be allowed, indeed, forced to go abroad and do 'fixed work', should be mixed up systematically with executives in a regular and enroutinée[1] manner, and should be able to lean not on their own personal office files, but on a solid collection of easily accessible, sifted, stuff. I have of course (as you can imagine since you know me much too well) lots and lots more to say, and could go on and on and on ... but I feel that even this may be a very unwarranted butting in, and if so apologise in advance and beg you to ignore it all. [...]

Yours,

Shaya

IB and his widowed aunt Ida sailed from Haifa on 10 April to join IB's parents in Nice. Soon after IB's return to Oxford, the unexpected death of Humphrey Sumner (on 25 April, after a short illness) left All Souls in need of a new Warden.

TO MARIE AND MENDEL BERLIN

Sunday [29 April 1951, *manuscript*]

Titlarks Farm, Sunningdale, Berks.

Dear Ma & Pa

Here I am, in the palatial 'Farm'[2] of Sir Simon Marks.[3] Asked for the week-end, I evaded it by saying I wd come for one day + night: on Saturday

---

1 'Routine'.

2 According to Anthony Blond 'Titlarks was a very unfarmy farm, lacking even a cat or a dog, but it was long on Renoirs, gilt French furniture and central heating'. *Jew Made in England* (London, 2004), 54.

3 Sir Simon Marks (1888–1964), 1st Baron Marks 1961; Chairman, Marks & Spencer, 1916–64, and dedicated Zionist; 'a little man who reeked of power', with 'a wicked owly face with shiny brown eyes, from which the fire poured like a torrent', and 'to the Israeli ambassador [...] the most important man in England'. ibid., 56, 58.

I gave dinner to Conant; buried Sumner; had a talk with my old friends Lords Halifax & Brand; & later with Sir Maurice Bowra, Arthur Salter etc. Below a Knight I do not descend. All Souls is full of intrigue: Rowse?[1] (khas v'shalom)[2] Sparrow? Dr Jacob? I think even I could collect 5 or 6 votes, so scattered is the situation. The thing is like a conclave: cardinals are gathering in every corner. Now to-morrow I shall have a talk about this in the Reform Club: I wish it weren't so, but Sumners absence causes deep relief to me: I shout at dinner much more freely: he used to inhibit me, & I him. The election will be fierce: & much bad blood will flow (*some* people must remain unelected: Rees,[3] for example). [. . .]

　　Love
　　　Isaiah   [. . .]

TO EDWARD MEAD EARLE

6 May 1951

New College

Dear Earle,

　　You will by now, I fear, have heard, Humphrey Sumner died very suddenly in the Radcliffe Infirmary on 24 April,[4] which has plunged us all into genuine gloom. You know as well as anyone how delicate his health was and how mercilessly he spent it upon those endless chores which he performed with such endless conscientiousness. He really did spend himself in the service of the College and of Russian scholarship, for I have no doubt that the two books[5] which he recently published on that subject materially hastened the total exhaustion from which, in effect, he died. The actual proximate cause was lesion, apparently due to some kind of adhesion left over after his operation for appendicitis, and not connected with his ulcer. He was operated on urgently here and died a few days later. His last words were concerned with the welfare of two junior Fellows of the College for whom he was anxious to do certain specific things and to whom he sent messages to say that he had not forgotten about their needs. All this was very typical and his whole life and death most pathetic and moving and somehow a tragic story. I do not think he had much pleasure in his life, it was all too far consumed by duty. The obituary in *The Times*, mainly written by the Regius Professor

---

1　On a lecture-tour of the US at the time.

2　'Heaven forbid' (literally 'pity and peace').

3　(Morgan) Goronwy Rees (1909–79), journalist and author; Fellow of All Souls 1931–46 and (as Estates Bursar) 1951–4; Principal, University College of Wales, Aberystwyth, 1953–7. See also L1 713–14.

4　In fact 25 April.

5　*Peter the Great and the Ottoman Empire* (Oxford, 1949) and *Peter the Great and the Emergence of Russia* (London, 1950).

of History, Galbraith,[1] was moderately just, though it did not do credit; it did not pay enough homage to his unique distinction, and his aristocratic freedom from any form of meanness or capacity for the ordinary rough and tumble of even academic life. I cannot deny that I survey the future of the College with considerable apprehension. It is at present plunged, as you may imagine, in the preliminaries for the new election with no obvious candidate in sight.[2] In a way it is saddest of all for Beatrix Sumner[3] who is as you know an excellent person, a very good fellow indeed and whose life here she enjoyed more than her brother, is brought to a sudden bitter end. And as for me personally, I owed everything to the late Warden in the way of encouragement in my Russian studies, my return to All Souls would, I think, have been impossible without him. However, he is in his grave now and we must think about a worthy successor. [...]

Thank you again for asking me to the Institute.[4] [...] I should like to come very much and fully intend to do so, although I am still not quite clear whether January or March would suit me best. I think perhaps March would be better if only because I should then not be working on my Bryn Mawr lectures; so long as I have a task ahead of me I am acutely nervous, work in great spurts and fits and bounds and tend to be distrait and unsociable. Once this burden is off my shoulders I shall be only too delighted to come and do whatever you would wish me to do for a week or two. [...] I do not wish to add to my burdens by delivering lectures to the university as well [...]. I have too many things to do altogether while I am in America and do not wish to return to Europe as I did in 1949, so physically exhausted that I was sent to bed for five weeks.

President Conant has just been here with Mrs Conant[5] and very delightful their visit has been to us all. I saw something of him but his arrival coincided with Humphrey Sumner's death and there was a pall of sadness over All Souls where he was entertained during part of the time. I think he may have thought us all a little too snug, not personally I mean, but less aware of educational and social problems than they are in American Universities and more liable to see ourselves as an elite, polishing our fiddles for a few exquisite performances, ignoring the smell of smoke from the world burning at no great distance from us. In this he may have been partly right. At any rate, his great sincerity, and uprightness and sweetness of character made a great impression on those who met him. [...]

I had a fascinating conversation with Chip Bohlen in Paris about a

1 Vivian Hunter Galbraith (1889–1976), Regius Professor of Modern History, Oxford, 1947–57.
2 IB was already being considered as a possible candidate.
3 Beatrix Mary Sumner (1888–1972), Humphrey Sumner's sister, lived with him in the Warden's Lodgings and acted as his hostess.
4 IB was hoping to pay a brief visit to the Institute of Advanced Study, Princeton (the rough equivalent of All Souls in the US), in early 1952.
5 Grace Thayer ('Patty') Conant (1898–1985), née Richards.

fortnight ago. Your people are really far more penetrating and imaginative about Russia than ourselves. About China we seem to be about equally blind.

Yours ever,

Isaiah Berlin

After Wittgenstein's death on 29 April, the BBC invited Gilbert Ryle to give a talk about his philosophy; Anna Kallin wondered whether something about his character was also needed, perhaps from Elizabeth Anscombe.[1]

TO ANNA KALLIN

9 May 1951

New College

Dearest N.,

[...] The Wittgenstein intimates – Miss Anscombe, her husband Geach,[2] and others – were thinking of founding a colony in order to live, think, eat and be like Ludwig. Originally it was intended to invite L. himself, but now that he is dead they propose to establish it anyhow. A great deal of violent artificial neurosis, not washing etc., anyhow you can imagine – hideous stammering in place of articulate speech, perverted Catholicism and all the other delicious attributes. Anyhow I think that while Ryle is excellent for talking about the doctrine, it is not necessary that anyone else talk about W. as a person. He was known to very few, the whole subject is genuinely painful, nobody who knew him intimately can bring himself to talk in public and the whole thing threatens to degenerate into a piece of dreary bad taste. The best person probably would be his mad, one-armed pianist brother Paul.[3] The person who would like to do it best would, I should think, be Mrs Braithwaite,[4] but there will be colossal embarrassment and frissons if she does so. My advice is to do nothing. [...]

Yours ever,

Шая[5]

1 (Gertrude) Elizabeth Margaret Anscombe (Mrs Peter Geach) (1919–2001), philosopher; Research Fellow, Somerville, 1946–64, Fellow, 1964–70; later (1970–86) Professor of Philosophy, Cambridge; translator and editor of Wittgenstein's later works, in particular the *Philosophical Investigations*.

2 Peter Thomas Geach (b. 1916), philosopher; taught philosophy at Birmingham University, 1951–61, Reader in Logic 1961–6; later (1966–81) Professor of Logic, Leeds.

3 Paul Wittgenstein (1887–1961), concert pianist, the philosopher's elder brother, lost his right arm during the First World War, but continued playing specially composed pieces; he became a US citizen in 1946.

4 Margaret Mary Braithwaite (1910–86), née Masterman, wife of the Cambridge philosopher R. B. Braithwaite; writer, philosopher and former student of Wittgenstein who worked on developing a computational theory of meaning based on his ideas; Director of Research, Cambridge Language Research Unit, from 1956; later (1965–75) founding Vice-President, Lucy Cavendish Collegiate Society, Cambridge.

5 'Shaya'.

TO ARTHUR SCHLESINGER

18 May 1951

New College

Dear Arthur,

Thank you very much for your letter which I greatly enjoyed.

Professor White duly arrived[1] and I have an awful feeling that, although I see a certain amount of him, we are not doing quite what we can for him and that he is perhaps at times a little lonely. Despite liking him very much, and knowing him fairly well, I fear that there is a certain permanent reserve inside him which occasionally breaks down in small neurotic rushes but which on the whole is kept severely under lock and key. He is, I think, suitably impressed by the local philosophers and will undo the somewhat unfavourable impression of them which my poor friend Irving Singer,[2] who had a tormenting time here, will inevitably have brought back.

Everyone here is in splendid form at the moment, so I anticipate some dreadful debacle fairly soon.

Joe arrived, his nose longer than ever, full of the most terrific black gloom about Persia[3] which, alas, one cannot shrug off quite so easily this time. He has been pitching into various members of our Foreign Office. I don't say with good effect, but at any rate deservedly. He has a low opinion of Sir W. Strang, which, although he is a nice man, is probably just. He has been behaving somewhat like Dr Bowra at Harvard, i.e. fending off every attack on US policy, including MacArthur, with ferocious patriotism. I am as devoted to him as ever but I cannot deny that after six hours of black on black I begin to wilt, and even show signs of wishing to go to bed, which annoys Joe who presses anyone else who may be in the room to stay, pointing out that although they might get a present from me if they left, and although he knows he has outstayed his welcome etc. etc., yet to bed he cannot and will not go. I must say there is something prodigiously wrong-headed about him, particularly when he points out how much better it would be to have MacArthur as President in preference to Taft, as MacArthur is really quite

1 Morton White had arrived in Oxford on a Guggenheim Fellowship during IB's absence. On his return IB had given a lunch party in honour of the Conants in All Souls, at which White met 'Mrs Hart, the wife of a philosophy don at New College. Both of them are quite nice [...] and then there was a German refugee atomic physicist named Halban married to a woman who was described as a millionairess to me by Hart's wife, and the "representative of wealth in Oxford".' Letter of 26 April to his wife Lucia, quoted in *A Philosopher's Story* (University Park, Pennsylvania, 1999), 204.

2 Irving Singer (b. 1925) studied at Oxford 1949–50 immediately after graduating from Harvard; Instructor in Philosophy, Cornell, 1953–6; Assistant Professor of Philosophy, Michigan, 1956–9, MIT 1959–69 (Professor from 1969).

3 In March the Iranian Parliament had voted to nationalise the Anglo-Iranian Oil Company, in which British companies had a major stake, provoking an immediate incident (the Abadan crisis), a long-running dispute between Iran and Britain, and eventually, in 1953, the restoration of the Shah, engineered by the US and British intelligence services.

an intelligent man with a sensible policy that, in short, war if not desirable is not terribly undesirable either. However, I may be doing him an injustice under the influence of Chip's views (whom I saw in Paris) who is much more sensible as you would expect. Why one really likes Joe so much is that he is despite all a private face full of endearing personal miseries and not in the inhuman sense a journalist or public personality at all.

Meanwhile Sir Maurice is enormously happy and benevolent – strange how much so little can do – Evelyn Waugh also longs for a knighthood, with a terrible devouring passion and is thinking of presenting a horse to Sir Maurice as a mark of his admission to the equestrian order, to celebrate this partial triumph of the immoral front and to work off his personal neurosis on the subject. The jokes here, as you can imagine, are numerous. You will kindly be tactful and discreet if I tell you that it is only with the greatest difficulty that I prevented a dinner being held during a certain day in July or whenever it is to celebrate 'The shortest knight of the year', or frown when people say [sic] of 'The knight has a thousand eyes' (a work[1] the Knight himself has retranslated from the Russian into which it was rendered in the eighties, being thought then one of the most beautiful of English poems. The Knight was not altogether aware that he was translating a translation but it has been eliminated from his published works, the less said about it the better, and malice must have an end).

The combination of A. L. Rowse and Morison[2] must indeed have been remarkable. Rowse is hurrying back to survey the situation left by Sumner's sad death. All Souls is in a chaos and heaven knows what will result. To be very indiscreet: Rowse will have to face the fact that there is less support for him than he could imagine in his darkest nightmares – Lord Simon, our senior Fellow, is determined to break this to him before he gets off the *Queen Elizabeth* on Tuesday next. Simon hasn't enjoyed himself as much as this since the Manchurian crisis;[3] but what are we to do? My bet is on Sir E. Bridges,[4] son of the poet, head of our Civil Service, the most powerful man in England and the least resistance-creating. He is a cold fish, a dry stick, a ronde de cuir[5] etc., but he is very safe. Nobody would notice his election. All Souls would carry on as before. Sir A. Salter will vote for him. Lord Halifax

---

1 'The night has a thousand eyes', by the Victorian poet Francis William Bourdillon, in *Ailes d'alouette* (Oxford, 1890).

2 Samuel Eliot Morison (1887–1976), Jonathan Trumbull Professor of American History, Harvard, 1941–55; historian of the US Navy in the Second World War.

3 In September 1931 the blowing-up of part of a Japanese-owned railway in Manchuria (north-east China) supplied the pretext for a Japanese invasion, unresisted by the Chinese, and the internationally condemned establishment by Japan of the puppet State of Manchukuo; Japan left the League of Nations in 1933 because of its refusal to recognise Manchukuo.

4 Edward Ettingdene Bridges (1892–1969), 1st Baron Bridges 1957; son of the former Poet Laureate Robert Bridges; civil servant; Fellow of All Souls 1920–7, 1954–68; Permanent Secretary, Treasury, and Head of the Civil Service, 1945–56.

5 'Bureaucrat' (literally 'leather cushion').

will bless him. He is sixty – will last ten years; in short, if he wants it I think he can have it. The other candidates – Professor Jacob, a mordant literary barrister, and a very old friend of mine, John Sparrow, and one or two others, seem to me to have less chance. The newspapers are speculating busily, and so far have got things all wrong, which delights us all. I have joined a block consisting of a montenegro [*sic*] named Plamenatz,[1] a Roman lawyer named Jolowicz,[2] and the Indian Ambassador to Moscow, who is also Professor here in some astral sense, called Sir Sarvapalli Radhakrishnan,[3] who form the foreign-born pressure group, and have secured the support of Cole on the ground that support for one of us would swiftly destroy the College, which he would be delighted to see. However, so far nobody else seems to see the attractions of this policy.

Do reassure Donald McKay about Harvard. I never had the slightest intention of abandoning my liaison with it in favour of the Princeton Institute – it is only that I could not bear not to reveal its siren-like behaviour, doubtless from some obscure vanity on my part, a desire to raise my price. Indeed at this moment I am haggling with [Elliot] Perkins about the rent for my rooms (having been rent-free last time but demanding more luxury boldly now) – unless unforetold events occur, I shall be with you in September.

Nicolas arrives next week. That will, I suppose, as usual, churn up our lives and throw into chaos whatever Joe has left standing. I am looking forward to his visit more than I can say. The first two days are always a delight, after that we exhaust each other physically and spend the next fortnight in gay mutual recrimination. When that ceases, I shall know the old world is really done for at last.

I cannot believe that Old Fade-Away[4] represents any serious danger. If I am wrong do tell me.

⟨Much⟩ love to Marian.

    Yours ever,

      Isaiah

1 John Petrov Plamenatz (1912–75), Montenegrin by birth; Fellow of All Souls 1936–51, 1967–75; University Lecturer in Social and Political Theory, Oxford, 1950–67; Fellow, Nuffield, 1951–67; later (1967–75) IB's successor as Chichele Professor of Social and Political Theory; subject of a memoir in PI.

2 Herbert Felix Jolowicz (1890–1954), Fellow of All Souls 1948–54; Regius Professor of Civil Law, Oxford, 1948–54; specialist in Roman law.

3 Sir Sarvapalli Radhakrishnan (1888–1975), Fellow of All Souls 1939–52; Spalding Professor of Eastern Religions and Ethics, Oxford, 1936–52; Indian Ambassador to the Soviet Union 1949–52; Vice-President of India 1952–62, later (1962–7) President.

4 General MacArthur, whose farewell speech to Congress on 19 April 1951 included a quotation from an old barrack-room ballad: 'Old soldiers never die; they just fade away.' Despite MacArthur's promise to do the same, his public popularity was temporarily so great that he was thought a likely Republican candidate for the 1952 presidential election.

In All Souls the election of a Warden followed time-honoured processes. The election itself was expected to be unanimous, which meant that any battles had to be fought beforehand during official and unofficial exploratory meetings, which were interspersed with soundings-out of likely candidates, lobbying on behalf of declared ones, and the constant counting of votes promised to each contender. IB was among the possible candidates for the Wardenship from the start. During the first official exploratory meeting on or about 19 May IB received several votes, as did a number of others, including Sparrow, Jacob and Kenneth Wheare,[1] but it seemed likely that the final consensus would be for Edward Bridges. The younger dons who favoured IB, dubbed the 'sans-culottes' and led by Goronwy Rees and John Cooper,[2] nevertheless continued lobbying on his behalf. A few days later A. L. Rowse, the Sub-Warden, arrived back from his interrupted lecture-tour of the US, but did not stand as a candidate himself. When Bridges, unexpectedly facing a contested election, withdrew from the contest towards the end of May, Rowse proposed Sir Eric Beckett[3] as a suitable replacement; this candidacy split the electorate, IB being favoured by those unwilling to accept Beckett (widely seen as likely to allow Rowse to control the College). The 'sans-culottes' campaigned vigorously, and while IB never gained a majority of votes, his continued candidacy effectively blocked Beckett's election. Rowse was driven to call on IB in New College in an attempt, unsuccessful at the time, to persuade him to withdraw. Eventually, in the final weekend of negotiations (9–10 June), after stalemate had been reached several times, IB withdrew and a compromise candidate, Sir Hubert Henderson,[4] was elected.

TO CHRISTOPHER COX

Tuesday 12 June 1951 [*manuscript*]

New College

Dear Xtopher

Thank you **very**[5] much for your note – I can't deny that the last 3 weeks have been among the most disagreeable & difficult in my life, mainly because they precluded normal intercourse with other human beings, & placed me, so it seemed to me, in a thoroughly false position. I never, objectively, considered myself as a suitable candidate, & persuaded myself that I wasn't

---

1 Kenneth Clinton Wheare (1907–79), Australian; Fellow, All Souls, 1944–57 (and 1973–9), Nuffield 1944–58; Gladstone Professor of Government and Public Administration, Oxford, 1944–57; Rector, Exeter College, 1956–72; later (1972–9) Chancellor, Liverpool University.

2 John Phillips Cooper (1920–78), historian; Fellow of All Souls 1948–52; Fellow and Tutor, Trinity, 1952–78.

3 Sir (William) Eric Beckett (1896–1966), barrister; legal adviser to FO 1945–53 (when ill-health forced his resignation).

4 Sir Hubert Douglas Henderson (1890–1952), economist; Fellow of All Souls 1934–52; Drummond Professor of Political Economy, Oxford, 1945–51; subject of a memoir in PI.

5 Underlined twice.

doing anything, not applying, not moving, only being moved, letting others act, neither advising nor being advised.[1] I daresay that was only a delusion, which I half felt to be one throughout, to which I need not have given way if I had been tougher or honester with myself. The only time I ever did act – finally – was when, on my own, & against the generous but foolish advice of the good but not very wise young men who used to call on me, I withdrew and thereby helped to promote the good result finally obtained against what did seem to me a bad prospect, though most of the people on the other side were moved by very reputable motives. All except one. And I daresay I may be wrong about him too. I am glad, too, that from the very outset I wrote that I wd on no account 'stand' against Richard Pares[2] – I had a good correspondence with him: his claims were, on the whole, badly overlooked: perhaps if I had occupied myself with him solely he might have had a better run. Perhaps not. Apart from his physical debilities he had a fairly strong permanent opposition to him in any case. I am terribly relieved about it all, & so, to my surprise, totally undisappointed, that it is clear that I never did want the W. much: & others did, terribly, & more justifiably. So perhaps it *was* wrong to go on with it. Anyway I am most grateful to you for your letter: sometime I'd love to tell you something about it all.

Yrs

Shaya

TO ANNA KALLIN

27 July 1951 [*manuscript card*]

All Souls College

I shall telephone you on Monday, d.v. but don't have anything to do with Jaspers[3] – he talks dim rubbish & is a façade with an interior partly hollow, partly squalid, too bogus even for Continental metaphysicians. Jung[4] is only a charlatan & a Nazi, but Jaspers is not even that now, but *nothing* & very

---

1 IB had written to his mother on 5 May: 'my "candidature" is simply a piece of Goronwy nonsense: the question when to withdraw gracefully'.

2 Richard Pares (1902–58), Fellow, All Souls, 1924–45, 1954–8; Professor of History, Edinburgh, 1945–54; suffered for many years from progressive muscular atrophy; admitted to IB that although the Wardenship of All Souls had been the one position he would have wanted in Oxford, 'I can't believe the College would ever elect anyone in my condition unless it strongly desired to avoid electing somebody else', and considered that IB would make 'a most agreeable Warden' (letter of 24 May 1951); subject of a memoir in PI.

3 Karl Theodor Jaspers (1883–1969), German psychiatrist and existentialist philosopher; concerned about continuing Nazi attitudes in Germany, in 1948 he moved from Heidelberg to Basle University.

4 Carl Gustav Jung (1875–1961), Swiss psychiatrist and pioneer of analytical psychology; briefly a friend, then a rival, of Freud; his attitude to Nazism was debatable.

shaming: if you *must* have a sage Santayana[1] or E. R. Curtius[2] would be better.

    Yours

      I.B.

TO ROWLAND BURDON-MULLER

28 July 1951

All Souls

Dear Rowland,

    I must apologise for my long silence, which has been due mainly to the terrible ups and downs of the All Souls Wardenship campaign, which has exhausted all and sundry during the past two months. I cannot describe to you what a business it all was, and with what toil and trouble we finally chose a successor to poor Humphrey Sumner, who died so suddenly. Sparrow was one of the unsuccessful candidates, and begs me to send you his love.

    When I see you I hope to give you a full account of these dramatic events – believe me, they made things quite impossible while they were occurring, and totally eclipsed the larger events of the outside world going on at the same time. Burgess and Maclean[3] were forgotten in the intensity of feeling which surrounded our local issue. Wounds were inflicted, dreadful truths were discovered about one another's characters; the emotional strain was almost unbearable at times, but we have now gone through it all, and there is peace once again, at least on the surface. Our elected Warden immediately collapsed[4] and was taken off to a nursing home, which, with the stress and storm of the election, seemed intelligible enough at the time. He is thought to be recovering.

    Every move of the game was widely known[5] to almost every undergraduate of this University. Sir Maurice Bowra enjoyed himself over it all almost

---

1 George Santayana (1863–1952), né Jorge Agustín Nicolás Ruiz de Santayana, Spanish-American philosopher and author.

2 Ernst Robert Curtius (1886–1956), German scholar of European (particularly medieval) literature, who from 1929 taught in the University of Bonn.

3 In the middle of the All Souls Wardenship electioneering, IB attended a dinner party given by Lady Pamela Berry on 29 May. Among the other guests were John Betjeman and Lady Elizabeth Cavendish, whose first meeting that evening led to a lifelong relationship, and Anthony Blunt. One expected guest who did not appear was IB's friend Guy Francis de Moncy Burgess (1911–63), an unsuspected Soviet spy, who had, it later emerged, defected to the Soviet Union on 25 May with his fellow spy Donald Maclean.

4 During the Encaenia ceremony on 20 June Warden-elect Henderson, who had a history of heart trouble, had a further heart attack in the Sheldonian Theatre.

5 See for example Hugh Trevor-Roper's magnificently entertaining letter to Bernard Berenson in *Letters from Oxford* (196/1), 67–71. A. L. Rowse's later published account – far less informative than his almost contemporary unpublished version (Rowse Collection, University of Exeter) – is perhaps most notable for his description of IB, whom he does not identify, as 'a lightweight of a young academic'. *All Souls in My Time* (London, 1993), 157.

too much. I was left prone and exhausted on the ground. However, I am slowly recovering myself, having moved into new and, surprisingly enough, better rooms in All Souls, which, having fewer doors, are less like the set for a French farce and much more peaceful. There is no telephone yet, quite wonderful in itself. [...]

[...] My address is now All Souls, and my condition equable to sanguine. Peace is visibly breaking out in all directions, and for the next year or so, this will do well enough.

Yours ever,
    Isaiah

TO MYRON GILMORE
    10 August 1951

All Souls

Dear Myron,

Thank you very much for your letter. I cannot describe to you what a painful effort it is to me to cease any kind of life, however dreary and monotonous, in order to gear myself into any other kind of one, however delightful and stimulating. I therefore return to Harvard full of hope and terrors – which is practically the mood in which I anticipate any experience, however familiar, or almost any. My time seems taken up in nerving myself to do things, then doing them not very well, then resting after the great expenditure of emotion, not at all commensurate with the importance of it. But I must stop talking about myself.

Thank you very much for concerning yourself with my Lowell House quarters – I am sure that Dr Brüning's[1] rooms will do very well, and if I can have them I shall be more than content. I saw [Elliott] Perk[ins] for a second, flanked by Namier,[2] at the Anglo-American Historical Conference. To this body, I regret to inform you, I read at breakneck speed a paper I had written[3] on the views of de Maistre. The first time I read it was in Cambridge (England) when I was asked to read for 45 minutes, starting at 5.15, discussion to occur 6 to 6.30. 6.30 p.m. everyone, according to tradition, to scatter. I read for one hour and thirty-five minutes, and at the end people got up with hardly a polite word and rushed away in a frenzied manner. This time I thought that I would cut it down a little, and so read it much faster, the fastest you have ever heard, for an hour and ten minutes, presided over by

1 Heinrich Aloysius Maria Elisabeth Brüning (1885–1970), German economist and Centre Party politician; Chancellor 1930–2, Foreign Minister 1931–2; forced to resign by President Hindenburg because his attempts to rescue the German economy were unpopular; fled Germany 1934; Professor of Political Science, Harvard, 1939–52, Cologne 1952–5.

2 Lewis Bernstein Namier (1888–1960), Professor of Modern History, Manchester, 1931–53; subject of a memoir in PI.

3 See 211 and 646/1.

Brogan,[1] who had heard it already at Cambridge and was colossally bored and kept on shoving notes at me with the word 'time' written in larger and larger letters. This produced panic in me and I finished by reading about two sentences from each page with no obvious coherence – intelligible neither to myself nor to my audience. Namier afterwards complained of deafness. Others scarcely troubled to do that, but Perk can tell you about this dreary little debacle. [...] I agree about Malia.[2] He is gifted and attractive. I saw him in New York before I left in 1949, but having lost my passport on that day was slightly distraught; then again in Oxford, and arranged to go and see Herzen's daughter with him in Paris. She is Madame Gabriel Monod[3] and lives at Versailles. I can't deny that the most remarkable fact about her is that she is 101 years of age; but I fear it won't materialise – my visit I mean. Will Malia be in Harvard in the autumn? I gathered from him that he would. I wish him very well and he certainly ought to be kept by Harvard as a Russian expert, though he still has a certain amount to learn. I can't quite make out what exactly goes on inside him, though whatever it is I think I approve of it. But perhaps you will tell me.

Yours ever,
Isaiah

TO ALICE JAMES
14 August 1951

All Souls

Dear Alice,
I should have written before, I know, but was deterred by many causes. One was that I know how illegible my handwriting is and my clerical aid suddenly gave way. The thought of putting my friends either to the torment of trying to decipher my hieroglyphics or of resigning myself to having my letters not read is a grave inhibiting factor. Secondly, the election of the Warden at All Souls occasioned by the sudden very tragic death of our last Warden, the eminent historian, Humphrey Sumner, produced a crisis such as not even Trollope[4] ever conceived. Human passions, thinly disguised by the veneer of academical good manners, rose to a pitch of extraordinary violence; old friendships were severed, people could not bear to speak to one another or look at one another for three or four weeks; charges and

---

1 Denis William Brogan (1900–74), Professor of Political Science, Cambridge, 1939–68.
2 Martin Edward Malia (1924–2004), historian and Soviet specialist; taught at Harvard from 1951, Assistant Professor of History 1954–8; Assistant Professor of History, University of California, Berkeley, 1958–64, Professor of History 1964–91.
3 Olga Herzen (1850–1953), Alexander Herzen's youngest daughter, who had been legally adopted by Malvisa von Meysenbug and married the French historian Gabriel Monod (1844–1915) in 1873.
4 It was his 1855 novel The Warden that brought Anthony Trollope (1815–82) his first major literary success.

counter-charges darkened the sky. The most unlikely candidates secured the most improbable number of votes. Finally, after the dramatic defeat of several favourites (some of whom thought they could not fail to get the post), we elected a very nice, good, distinguished and worthy man, our Professor of Economics, Sir Hubert Henderson, the most modest of men, who was genuinely surprised to find himself in the position and will occupy it very well. Maurice composed three magnificent but unprintable[1] election poems for various factions involved. The whole University seemed to talk of nothing else. Even the undergraduates seemed to know, not merely how people had voted but how each individual meant to vote and what finally altered his mind and what was said about it afterwards. It was like a game of Consequences without secrets and very exhausting and disagreeable while it lasted. During that time it was quite impossible to write and I am very glad it is all over.

I have now moved from New College to All Souls into the nicest set of rooms I have ever occupied and I am slowly preparing to get myself on to the *Mauretania*, which should bring me to New York in early September. I saw Elliott Perkins briefly in London and he held out great hopes of comfort at Lowell House in Dr Brüning's rooms, at any rate after October. My present plan is to go from New York, not to Cambridge but into Maine to stay with Rowland Burdon-Muller for ten days or so before the Spartan discipline of Lowell House. I am genuinely anxious to live a retired and minimally social life this term, but even in Maine I shall have to take action if I am to avoid having to fulfil my obligations to Mrs Morrow[2] and the Frankfurters and Ronnie Tree and others who will be there then. There is something which must be deeply wrong in the whole conduct of my life and has been for two score years or more, since I never seem to get anything done quite in time: nothing that I do seems to be properly done; a little more time, a little more care, a little more patience and planning and it would have been so much better. I always have too much to do, I always go to bed too late: nothing ever lasts long enough before I must interrupt it in order to avoid some disaster, some breaking of the elaborate texture which seems to me at the time of supreme value and importance, and so I go careering from pillar to post like an American student perpetually harassed by examinations, perpetually judging and being judged, unable to achieve even a moment of the large calm, the minimum of tranquillity which all tolerable lives require. I am in consequence never faced with the prospect of genuine tedium – there is too much to do, not too little, I know nothing, I have written nothing, I have not

---

1 Now, however, published as 'Election Songs' in Maurice Bowra, *New Bats in Old Belfries, or Some Loose Tiles*, ed. Henry Hardy and Jennifer Holmes (Oxford, 2005).
2 Elizabeth Reeve Morrow (1873–1955) née Cutter, poet, mother-in-law of Charles Lindbergh and of IB's friend and former colleague Aubrey Morgan.

said what I wish to say, I no longer remember what it was I would wish to say. Presently someone will notice how empty my activity is, the bluff will be called, the game over. Then present needs obtrude themselves and I go spinning on until I bump into some perfectly avoidable obstacle, stopping only long enough to recover to enable me to spin away from it even faster. This is to some degree a caricature and I apologise for so suddenly inflicting it upon you, but it seems to me an exaggeration in a truthful direction. Next term, I say to myself during this quiet Oxford summer in which I am almost happy, I shall control and discipline myself into a decent, leisurely, orderly and properly planned existence. But I expect greater men than I – Tolstoy and all the poets – say this to themselves too, but to be endowed with their leisureliness without their talent seems a hard fate, and to enjoy it as much as I do positively shameful.

But I must not go on: this is only to wish you a complete recovery from what I am afraid must have been a trying period of poor health and to send both to you and Billy my fondest love. It is a great pleasure to me to think that I shall, as I hope, see you in September.

Yours ever,

Isaiah B.

TO HAMILTON FISH ARMSTRONG

16 August 1951 [*manuscript*]

All Souls

Dear Ham,

As I greatly doubt whether I shall be in New York for more than a few hurried hours before October – I arrive, indeed, in early September, but go to Maine & then Harvard, & being in constant terror of failing in any job I undertake, 'swot' away like a schoolboy & delay journeys to N.Y. until I seem to be riding my always dangerous seeming steed more or less confidently – as all this is so, I venture to enclose my 'piece'[1] in this envelope. The circumstances are these: months & months & months ago Ascoli wrote, not once but repeatedly, reproaching me for writing for you & for the N.Y. Times & for the Atlantic Monthly, but never for him. I have, I must admit, no great opinion of his 'Reporter', but him I like quite well. At any rate, bullied in this way, I sat down, wrote a piece, & sent it him, explaining that though it might be too long for him, I wd rather have it rejected & forever unpublished, than cut or edited (he criticized the piece in *Foreign Affairs* for being too long, filled with truisms which he cd have cut out, etc.). He replied eulogistically, sent

1 'Generalissimo Stalin and the Art of Government', *Foreign Affairs* 30 (1952), published under the pseudonym 'O. Utis'; reprinted in SM as 'The Artificial Dialectic' (IB's own title), with the *Foreign Affairs* title as a subtitle.

me a handsome turkey for Christmas, then fell ill & there was a long silence. I took (I am ashamed to say) the opportunity of the silence, & wrote (not altogether truthfully) that I wanted the piece back in order to lengthen it, which wd doubtless make it still more unsuitable for him. He returned it, I did add a line or two in ink (as in MS enclosed), & [he] asked me to give it back to him in October. This I am determined not to do whatever happens. I am not keen to appear in the *Reporter*; my obligation vis a vis Ascoli is now discharged; I wd rather always be printed by yourself, or if you don't want it, by the N.Y.T., or if they don't, by nobody. After doing nothing with the piece for 3 or 4 months (although he assured me it was scheduled for publication in August) Ascoli can have no claims.

The second point is more difficult: as I have (I hope still) relations in the U.S.S.R., & as I visited innocent littérateurs there, I have always followed the policy of publishing nothing about the Sov. Union directly under my own name, because that might easily lead to something frightful being done to people I talked to there. I needn't enlarge on that prospect. Hence if I am to publish anything about Uncle Joe [Stalin] it must be (a) anonymously or under a pseudonym (b) the identity of the author must be really, & not as in George Kennan's case,[1] only notionally secret. I invented the name of John O. Utis for the 'Artificial Dialectic'. OUTIS means 'nobody' in Greek & you will recall elaborate puns about this in the Odyssey where Odysseus deceives the one-eyed ogre by this means. Also it sounds vaguely like a name which a Lithuanian D.P., let us say, or a Czech or Slovene cd have: & so, plausible for the author of such a piece. Ascoli & possibly a confidential typist may know the secret. Nobody else; & he will certainly be honourable & lock it in his breast, whatever his feelings about where & how the piece is published. Do you ever publish anonymous pieces? if not, I shall, of course, fully understand: since lives depend upon it, I wd obviously rather suppress altogether than compromise on this – I really have no choice. There is only one other person to whom I showed it – Nicholas Nabokov – who has begged it for his "Preuves'[2] – some Paris anti-Soviet institution. If you do want it, I shd be grateful if you cd give me permission to have it translated, after U.S. publication, into German (Der Monat) & French etc.: I shall, of course, never read it aloud myself to anybody: my authorship must remain a secret from as many as possible: but I may let Nabokov have a copy, provided he promises formally not to have it published anywhere (until you reply) but only uses it

1 'The Sources of Soviet Conduct' had been published in *Foreign Affairs* in July 1947 under the pseudonym 'X' (following normal practice for this journal), but it soon emerged that the author was George Kennan and that the article, which argued for 'containment' of the Soviet Union, was a development of his influential 'Long Telegram' to the State Department of 22 February 1946.
2 'Evidence', anti-Communist journal founded in Paris in March 1951 by François Bondy and closely allied to the (covertly CIA-funded) Congress for Cultural Freedom, of which Nicolas Nabokov was Secretary-General.

for informal discussion as a letter from an unknown source, offering various loose ideas. I apologize for this rigmarole – these queer conditions – the recital of the past etc. I hope you'll like it, but I've no opinion, as you know, of anything I write: & if you'd rather have nothing to do with the piece, pray forget this letter. [...]

yrs ever
   Isaiah Berlin

TO JENIFER HART

   [August 1951, *manuscript*]

[All Souls]

[...] It is absolutely quiet here, few servants, scarcely any Fellows. My parents have just left, they are really very nice, & their very idiosyncracies seem cosy to me. But they cling wonderfully, most of all when they try not to: & their departure leaves me with a sense of pathos mixed with relief: but I view their demise one day with real horror. I daresay too much about me altogether is to be explained by this. Now & then Wheare passes under my windows, looking suddenly very Australian, full of elaborate defences against the sophisticated world: when he & Dunbabin[1] walk up & down the lawn, I am glad not to be as they are: & Rowse's absence is a source of happiness too. Sparrow walked in on my parents who thought him more than delightful. And I like wandering in the late hours, in empty flood lit space, & suddenly the unmistakeable figure of Roniger,[2] crouching in a Bodleian doorway, at midnight: he pounces on me, explains he is to present himself for an interview to a translator's board somewhere, he *has* a suit, he *has* a shirt, but his *shoes* are *impossible*. What size are mine? all *his* friends wear 9 at least: & all have only *one* pair of shoes, it seems. I have more than one, but they are 11 (*his* are 7). *What* is he to do? I give him 8/3$^{\rm d}$ & walk away. He goes on shouting at me 'I know I am like Marx. But I won't produce even one volume of Kapital. And you are not Engels: can you shave? do you know of a cheap or charitable barber? shall I shave off my entire beard? or leave a small bit à la Richelieu?' it is obvious that I live in an Oxford very different from other people's. I am trying to starve in order to lose a portion of my belly.[3] One chin of my three or four has visibly diminished: secretly from my parents I take a London quack's pills which are doubtless bad for the heart, but I am in a most desperate mood: if I am to do my work I cannot slump about with an enormous stomach in a perpetual condition of semi-lethargy. These

---

1 Thomas James Dunbabin (1911–55), Fellow, All Souls, 1937–55, Domestic Bursar 1950–55; Reader in Classical Archaeology, Oxford, 1945–55; like Wheare, an Australian.
2 A tramp-like lapsed intellectual.
3 Cf. 'I have been told by the doctors that I must cut down my fat if I am not to perish miserably.' Letter of 23 August to Rowland Burdon-Muller.

headaches, piles, sudden wearinesses, ulcers, sciaticas, wd do for someone who had achieved something & was wearily paying a price. To sag at 42 with nothing done is dreadful. Hence this unusual mood of physical self improve-ment & wilfulness in execution. [...]

1951–1952

HARVARD AND BRYN MAWR

I seem to myself to be screaming meaningless phrases to a vaguely
discernible, half darkened, audience; & feel terrified before, hysterical
during & ashamed afterwards.[1]

1 To Marion Frankfurter, 23 February 1952.

On 28 August IB sailed for New York on the Mauretania.

TO EDMUND WILSON

1 September 1951 [*manuscript*]

RMS *Mauretania*

Dear Wilson,

I write to you full of guilt – not that it takes much to induce it in me; I seem to myself to spend more time in balancing alternative courses of action intended to meet the imagined feelings of others than in any other single activity: this is probably a Central European more than a Russian characteristic: it is no less futile a form of being a Lishni Chelovek,[1] but a different one (Russians think they know about the difference of good & evil so clearly that they have no need of elaborate psychological speculation of that kind.) You wrote to me; you sent me a sympathetic and delightful Christmas Card; you sent your stepson[2] to New College (heaven knows what *he* thought; he dined with me in odd company: there was a tipsy archaeologist – a real eccentrical dipsomaniac scholar full of romantic chauvinism and nonsense of an ultimately tedious kind – there was also David Cecil, who whatever his literary shortcomings is a great smoother-over – I don't know what he could have thought of us all: I shouldn't blame him if he thought us all deranged – however perhaps one day I'll be told) you did all these things & I did not reply. Not but what I began to do so quite often. But I felt it was no good unless I had something to say: & I never had; I suffered the torments of some terrible Russian student about to write a letter to Count L. Tolstoy: (Tolstoy meeting the 9000th delegation of students is a kind of Beerbohm cartoon to me) & this went on & on until every time I sat down to reply (slightly comforted by the thought that Sylvester, too, that far surer footed man who knows what he wants with a French directness & clarity, also wanted badly to write you & hadn't) the ludicrous image of the letter to Tolstoy which mustn't be empty chatter used inevitably to crop up. Until finally I began to think about Tolstoy & re-read the end of *War & Peace*, the famous 'dreary' epilogue about history, & so far from finding it dreary, thought it all surprisingly good sense, better than anyone else, & wrote a long piece on that instead,[3] which I am having printed in an obscure series of which so far only one number appeared – the Oxford Slavonic Papers or Studies: & will send you a copy of it, if I may, when it appears even though you may think that chatter too: but certainly when I wrote it I thought I had something to say,

---

1 'Superfluous person': see 220/2.
2 Henry H. M. Thornton (b. 1932), banker.
3 'Lev Tolstoy's Historical Scepticism', *Oxford Slavonic Papers* 2 (1951), reprinted with additions (one of which was the dedication to Jasper Ridley) as *The Hedgehog and the Fox: An Essay on Tolstoy's View of History* (London and New York, 1953) and in RT and PSM. IB later claimed to have dictated the original version in two days (MI Tape 24).

& think so still I suppose. The central theme derives from the proposition by Archilochus[1] – an isolated fragment – which I think I quoted to you on Cape Cod where he says 'the fox knows many things; but the hedgehog one big thing'. Which means, I daresay, no more than that the fox has many tricks but the hedgehog, one worth all of that & can't be captured. But perhaps it isn't too improper to divide writers into foxes (Shakespeare: Goethe: Aristotle & other seers of many things:) hedgehogs who see only one big usually incomplete thing (Plato, Pascal, Proust, Dostoevsky, Henry James etc.) anyway it is no worse than naïve v. sentimental & other such categories & dichotomies. Tolstoy I maintain was by nature & gifts a fox who terribly believed in hedgehogs & wished to vivisect himself into one. Hence the crack inside him which everyone knows. This I tried to work out in terms, partly, not of Stendhal or Rousseau, his official inspirers, but Joseph de Maistre who is a far more interesting Nietzschian pseudo-Catholic sort of man than anyone thinks. However I won't go on now. I arrive at Lowell House, Harvard, on about the 17th of this month: I have lost your address: & leave it at Christmas: & if there is a chance of seeing you I'd be ever so grateful. I shd like to ask you e.g. about Spender's autobiography[2] which I (apparently alone) don't think bad, only not v. attractive: & about the astonishing behaviour of all the English poets the 'pylon boys' as Connolly once called them, in re Burgess & Maclean.[3] Please forgive me for this illegible mess.

Yrs ever
    Isaiah Berlin

Sylvester v. anxious to send you his love, his respect, more than he ever expresses for anyone else. A very un-English & very admirable man, I think.

TO MARIE AND MENDEL BERLIN

4 September 1951 [*manuscript*]

RMS *Mauretania*

Dear Pa & Ma.

It is remarkable what a few days of good food & sunshine can do. I am sunburnt to a high degree (no longer 'red' but 'brown'. As an old *malade imaginaire*[4] I have to add that unless one is v. well one doesn't get brown.)

---

1 Greek poet (*c*.680–*c*.645 BC).
2 *World Within World* (London, 1951).
3 Just before his defection Burgess had attempted to telephone W. H. Auden while he was staying with Stephen Spender; Auden, who had left for his holiday home in Italy a few days after the defection, initially denied having heard about the call, and eventually returned to the US without entering the UK (where MI6 were anxious to interview him). Spender's poem 'The Pylons' in *Poems* (London, 1933) had led Cyril Connolly to refer to the Auden school of poets as the 'pylon boys'.
4 'Hypochondriac'.

The food on this ship is *delicious*, & so is the service. Let me state at once that (a) because the Ship is not too big the service is better (b) that this ship is five times *steadier* than either Q. Mary or Elizabeth. Those who know say it is steadier than Caronia. We ran into a violent wind – I don't say a storm yesterday, & one felt nothing. Consequently whenever possible I propose to go by this ship & not Q. Mary (also fewer friends. More rest). It takes a day longer but the mere quality of the food makes that worth it. I have done a lot of work, & have absolutely nothing to complain of: I must have eaten 2 lb. of beef a day: sat for 30 hrs in the sun: had a haircut: written my last English reviews. [...]

Love
   Shaya

IB went to stay with Rowland Burdon-Muller at his country home on the coast of Maine before reporting for duty at Harvard, where he was to spend the rest of the year as Visiting Professor, lecturing once again on Russian intellectual and social history.

TO MARIE AND MENDEL BERLIN

7 September 1951 [*manuscript*]

                c/o R. Burdon-Muller, Cedar Ledge, Camden, Maine

Dear Pa & Ma.

All is well. The voyage as you know was pleasant & uneventful. I arrived in N.Y. 4.30 p.m., landed, & the first to greet me was my friend George Fischer; it is *always* nice to be met; gives one a general sense of confidence in foreign lands & even at home: to be seen off is always a little sad: to be met always agreeable. For a long time my luggage was incomplete (father will explain how the suitcases come slowly off an escalator: *you* have to go about collecting them: when you have them all, you stand in a queue to acquire a Customs Inspector; all this took hours: one trunk took ½ hour to come after the others etc. Finally, with the last trunk came Josef,[1] late as usual, but apologetic. Finally came the Inspector. Here trouble began: one of the keys (of the book-trunk) no longer worked (why?) so it was forced open: i.e. a man appeared: unscrewed the lock in 10 seconds: & *riveted* everything with *iron* straps in 5 seconds: brutal opening & equally quick & efficient reclosing: both v. unlike England. Were the books dutiable? Was I a religious institution? No? Was I an educational institution? no? then 50 dollars duty. I demanded an official. I argued for 25 minutes & finally was let off; in what languages were my books? foreign? I said French, German, etc. What was

---

1 Josef Cohn (1904–86), German-born scientist who acted as Chaim Weizmann's personal assistant and US representative for Sieff Institute affairs for many years; Executive Vice-President, European Committee, Weizmann Institute, from 1955.

"etc."? a great nuisance. Apart from the forcing of the lock all ended peace-fully. And I've written Cunard in London that *they* will have to pay for the new lock since in *their* ship the lock got out of use. Oovidim.[1] [...] this is a *wonderful* holiday, cool, food deliciously cooked by French chef (my weight, alas, *same* as in London – 13½ stone, I shall return to my mild diet only at Harvard where temptations less strong. But no bread & sugar, otherwise I eat everything. I am very happy here indeed & shall the day after to-morrow write you a glossary of obscure words in Kobers article about Pa Gross[2] in New Yorker of Aug 30 ("Moom pickches: moving pictures: words like Fortune-Teller-keh" etc.)

Love
    Isaiah   [...]

TO ROWLAND BURDON-MULLER

Tuesday 9 p.m. [postmark 19 September 1951, *manuscript*]
                            The Preacher's Room, Lowell House, Harvard
Dear Rowland,

I thought, in the first place, that the above address would please you. I am not to be the Preacher for long: although my black Homburg does make the few undergraduates who wander about whisper reverently about me, & make room for me more respectfully, perhaps, than they would otherwise do. I travelled safely and comfortably, sustained by apples & my precious figs (of which a great consignment is to arrive presently – I derive exotic pleasure from chewing them, like some oriental traveller alone in a barbar-ous land, segregated from the outside world by his ancient customs – an atavistic feeling, doubtless) although a tipsy soldier kept my fellow travellers in an uproar with his jests from Portland on; he was crippled; he was a hero; he was very young; but I have a horror of drunkenness, & sank more & more deeply into my book, in fact unable to read out of sheer embarrass-ment. I thought as the train began nearing Boston, the soldier sang, jeered, stumbled & tumbled over himself & giggling girls, & denounced Europe, how precious one's world was; how dependent one was on manners and the affections; & felt infinitely grateful to you for the small circle of gentle light – I can't breathe in any other atmosphere – which you provided, and resolved with much fervour to wave the flag of civilised values & personal relationships as bravely as I dare in an environment which, on the whole, believes in the opposite. You compromise, in this country, less than anyone I

1 'We'll see.'
2 Bella Gross and her parents, Ma and Pa Gross, were the central characters in many stories, infused with the life and idiom of the Bronx, by Arthur Kober (1900–75), playwright and humor-ist. In 'Reconciliation in the Bronx', *New Yorker*, 1 September 1951, 25–8, the expressions that caught IB's attention are 'moom-pickchehs' and 'Miss Futchin-Tellekeh'; '-keh' is a feminine suffix in Yiddish.

know: & deserve a V.C. Beside having been made happy, comfortable, well, I was morally much set up: & am duly *reconnaissant*:[1] (14 hrs later) your mode of living – I don't know what further epithets I was about to lavish: I was in a mood last night (it is now Wed., 11 a.m.) of almost uncritical adulation of all you did & were: partly due to a view of you I still hold: partly to the ubiquity of the barbarians suddenly all round me. However a very nice barbarian came in to see if I was comfortable: & then, tediously, sat down to tell me about the troubles & intrigues in his laboratory: I nodded sagely but understood about as much as Masetto[2] about the Trinity (your letter just arrived. Thank you for Beilage[3] & Dr Joyner:[4] & I am sorry about the pump[5] etc.) he left me at 1.40 a.m. & I collapsed wearily to bed. I was telephoned to by Mr E. Wilson who is coming to dinner & by Joe Alsop. The latter is behaving with much courage. Poor Prof. Fairbank,[6] a respectable liberal – middle of the road like me & your Senatrice[7] – if ever there was one, has been denounced as a member of the Communist Party by its ex-member Mr Louis Budenz,[8] before the Un-American Committee.[9] Joe A., who having been a Chiangist was bitterly opposed to Fairbank & his School of anti-Chiangery, wrote in his column that he believed this charge to be groundless: implying that Budenz etc. were lying: & generally defending the accused anti-Chiangists: (I have not read the columns: but this is what I am told by neutral & disinterested parties) thereupon the *Herald-Tribune* – your friend Mr Heckscher's[10] 'bosses' – wrote an *editorial* disowning Alsop's intemperate attack on the McCarran[11] Committee & its Counsel: & beating its breast so violently in its anti-communist terror, as to denounce poor Joe for his raising

1 'Grateful'.
2 Another of RB-M's guests.
3 'Enclosure'; a letter which IB had accidentally left behind at Cedar Ledge.
4 Dr (James) Craig Joyner (1893–1978), a New York surgeon, whose address IB had asked for, perhaps in relation to the problems which had caused his sciatica.
5 IB's over-enthusiastic flushing of the toilet on departure had caused the house's water pump to run uninterruptedly for hours.
6 John King Fairbank (1907–91), historian and pioneering China specialist; Professor of History, Harvard, 1946–59; Francis Lee Higginson Professor of History 1959–77; Director, East Asian Research Center, 1955–73. His wife Wilma was the sister of Marian Cannon Schlesinger, first wife of Arthur Schlesinger, Jr.
7 Margaret Madeline Chase Smith (1897–1995), moderate Republican Congresswoman 1940–9; Senator for Maine 1949–73; the first woman to be elected to both Houses of Congress. Her June 1950 'Declaration of Conscience' speech was one of the first public expressions of opposition to the tactics of Senator McCarthy.
8 Louis Francis Budenz (1891–1972), US journalist and author; former Communist activist and Soviet spy who became anti-Communist in 1945, assisted the FBI, and acted as an expert witness on Communism in many investigations; Professor of Economics, Fordham University, 1946–56.
9 The House Committee on Un-American Activities, a committee of the House of Representatives with investigative powers, established in 1938, made a standing committee in 1946, and renamed the Committee on Internal Security in 1969.
10 August Heckscher (1913–97), *New York Herald Tribune* 1948–56; Director, Twentieth Century Fund, 1956–67; later (1962–4) special consultant on the arts to President Kennedy.
11 Patrick Anthony ('Pat') McCarran (1876–1954), strongly anti-Communist Democratic Senator for Nevada 1933–54; Chairman, Senate Judiciary Committee (1949–53), and (1950–3) Senate Internal

a voice against Budenz: Senator Lehmann[1] thereupon attempted to 'read' the Alsop piece into the Congressional Record: but was (I've never heard of such a thing before, have you?) prevented by a group of Senators who voted this suggestion down as implying disrespect to McCarran; & not one single voice rose in Lehmann's support. Am I exciting you too much? have I caught your own mood too closely? Oh dear. But now there really is something for you to write to Mr Heckscher about: if only to ask him *what*, if anything, his newspaper attacked Alsop for: & to your Senator to ask why a column from a Republican paper by a respectable, almost right wing journalist, was refused the Congressional Record? all very distressing I find, & much worse than 1949. I wish I were still in Oxford or in Maine, unexposed to these raw realities. Certainly I'd love to dine on the 6th Oct. at 7 p.m. but, on the whole would rather not go to the concert,[2] even to criticise: but, virtuously, back to my books, like an unworldly scholar, which I long to, but alas shall never, be. I have not really seen anyone here yet. Only the Bullingdon Boy[3] & the Frankfurters & they're not part of the establishment. Mrs F. is very unbarbarous: but my friend Philip Graham, publisher of the *Washington Post*, made a speech here to some advertising businessmen, very much in the spirit of the times: but I must say did beg me with tears in his eyes & genuine concern not to come to hear it & collapsed into very un-Big Businesslike petulance & pathos when I threatened to come all the same. I must stop: I must behave like a real man: I must go to the Coop: lunch in the Faculty Club: say "grand to see yah' I must I must I must but I won't. And thank you once again for your oasis & – perhaps when I praise "cosiness & gaiety," I mean 'charm & gaiety'? – everything else. I am very glad Lord Amulree[4] thinks you are secure: & I admired the cascades[5] but could not bear the vulgarity of D. Thompson[6] whom I met here in 1941.

Yrs ever
Isaiah

Security Subcommittee (SISS; 'the McCarran Committee'), which had been granted extensive powers to investigate alleged subversive activities in the US.

1 Herbert Henry Lehman (*sic*) (1878–1963), leading liberal politician; Director, UNRRA, 1943–6; Democratic Senator for New York 1949–57.

2 On 6 October the Boston Symphony Orchestra, conducted by Charles Munch, was to perform a concert in memory of Serge Koussevitzky, who had died in June. IB had been dismissive about the programme: Mozart's *Mauerische Trauermusik*, Strauss's *Tod und Verklärung* and Tchaikovsky's 6th Symphony.

3 A Bullingdon Boy is a member of the Bullingdon Club, a (largely Etonian) drinking society at Oxford; here it means Marcus Dick, a heavy-drinking Wykehamist, who had married Cecilia Rachel Buxton (1927–95) in July 1951 and spent 1951–2 as a Commonwealth Fellow at Harvard.

4 Basil William Sholto Mackenzie (1900–83), 2nd Baron Amulree, RB-M's next guest after IB, a geriatrician who was optimistic about RB-M's health prospects.

5 Presumably the waterfalls of Vermont. RB-M was about to visit the Louis de Rothschilds, who lived there, but was threatened with a compulsory call on Dorothy Thompson.

6 Dorothy Thompson (1894–1961), journalist and broadcaster; syndicated political commentator and columnist 1941–58.

TO MARIE AND MENDEL BERLIN

Thursday [postmark 21 September 1951, *manuscript*]

Lowell House, J11, Cambridge, Mass.

Dear Pa & Ma

I am at last safely installé[1] in Lowell House. Staircase J. no 11 (address as above). All is entirely well. The Maine holiday was really very charming: delicious food, peace, rest, work etc. Now the whirl again, but not too much I am determined. I have called on all the people I had to see; the arrangements are complete. I have seen some of my friends: to-night I dine with the Frankfurters. To-morrow I instal a radio: & so on. Everyone is, of course, most friendly: I am met like an old friend. I think that having been through the social ice-breaking of 1949 I can now afford *not* to allow people to waste my time, contract my social life & work. [...] My new rooms are much larger than the ones father saw in 1949 – about double the size, & contain enough furniture – sofa, armchair, 3 wooden armchairs etc. for a decent life. It is possible that when ex-Reichskanzler[2] Brüning, der Alte Fuchs[3] – a thoroughly sinister figure I feel – goes back to Cologne in October I shall move into his palatial quarters. But even so, Dayenu.[4] I am eating very well: & a *great* exception is to be made for me – I am to be given breakfast in my rooms. It really makes a gigantic difference. The Jewish Chronicle proofs[5] have arrived: Frankfurter has skimmed over them: & says they are all right. Also the proofs of the *Foreign Affairs* (anonymous) article: that needs a little more work as the editor wants a positive "message". Oovidim.[6] [...] What more to tell you? I am in a mood for work: not tired, not fat, not sluggish, longing to read & write. What cd be better? I feel like that too rarely. But if I felt I had to *stay* here for life I wd despair & stop. [...]

Au revoir with much love

Shaya

---

1 'Settled in'.
2 'Chancellor of the Reich', i.e. head of the German Government.
3 'The Old Fox'.
4 'It is enough', the title of a Passover song of gratefulness for gifts received.
5 Of 'Jewish Slavery and Emancipation' (*Jewish Chronicle*, 21 and 28 September, 5 and 12 October 1951), written after IB's 1951 visit to Israel. The essay was commissioned for a volume published to mark the silver jubilee of the Hebrew University of Jerusalem: Norman Bentwich (ed.), *Hebrew University Garland: A Silver Jubilee Symposium* (London, 1952). It was not reprinted again until after IB's death, in POI.
6 'We'll see.'

TO RALPH E. TURNER[1]

12 October 1951 [*carbon*]

Lowell House

Dear Professor Turner,

[...] And now about 'meta-history': I was a little surprised – and I suppose should have felt flattered – when I found this expression attributed to myself and my colleague, Alan Bullock, in an article[2] where I expect you saw it. I raised the matter sharply and he assured me that I had used it in a seminar with him at Oxford. Possibly so; the word ought, I suppose, to be 'methistory',[3] but my Greek scholarship is never good and I certainly no longer remember precisely what I could have meant by it. So far as I recollect, what we were discussing in the seminar was whether there are any concepts or categories particular to history, as there are to, say, physics, theology or common sense; and we tried to examine the use of the central words 'because' and 'therefore' as used by historians, and the differences between ways in which such words are used by historians and, e.g., by mathematicians, inductive scientists, metaphysicians etc. I do not remember what conclusions we reached, except that I think I maintained that historians use such words in much the same way as ordinary men – in other words, that the only assumptions made by historians were those of normal common sense about the behaviour of persons and objects – and differently from the specialised senses in which analogous terms are used by physicists, psychologists etc. Given that anything properly called a science uses such key words (or concepts and categories, which in the end come to the same thing – in this case causal ones, but this would apply equally to such concepts as 'evidence', 'probability', 'truth' etc.) in strictly delimited ways, history, if I was right, was not a science; and the questions then arose (*a*) what was meant by calling some sorts of history 'scientific' as opposed to 'unscientific' – did this apply only to the degree to which natural sciences entered into the accumulation of evidence – palaeographical, archaeological etc. – or in some other senses as well? and (*b*) whether special kinds of history – e.g. economic, legal, etc. – made use of narrower and more natural-science-like concepts by excluding the rich mixture which ordinary history and common sense alike semi-consciously employ. Moreover, there were, of course, the more ordinary questions such as whether historians employed merely such general propositions as all talk and thought inevitably embody, or 'presupposed' special generalisations, akin to sociological laws, of however hazy and unsubstantiated a kind as might be analogous to those found in more

1 Ralph Edmund Turner (1893–1964), US cultural historian; Professor of History, Yale, 1944–61.
2 Alan Bullock, 'The Historian's Purpose: History and Metahistory', *History Today* 1 No 2 (February 1951), 5.
3 Because in Greek 'meta-' becomes 'meth-' before an aspirated vowel, as 'met[a]' + 'hod[os]' yields 'meth-od'.

precise sciences, and whether such general 'conceptual schemas' as those which dominated entire ages, say, teleology versus mechanical causation, or evolutionary attitudes as opposed to the view of things as relatively static or chaotic – something resembling that which Collingwood[1] called 'absolute presuppositions' – where such generalisations played a different role and deserved another and probably grander title ... and so on and so forth. You see the kind of thing.

Well, all this discussion of the conscious and unconscious methods of historians is what I suppose, in an unfortunate moment, I must have called 'meta-history'. In the philosophy of history, which historically implies a cut and dried schema of how historical events fit in with each other – patterns etc. – by the humbler, though ultimately more far-reaching business of the task of analysing the way in which one historical proposition is supposed to follow or not to follow from another in the thought and writings of actual working historians, and what constitute criteria of truth and validity when one historian argues with another, and how different this is from the weapons used by, e.g., experimental psychologists, palaeographers or organic chemists. You see what you have brought on yourself; practically a lecture. I apologise to you, I really do.

As for the scepticism of our historians about 'causes' in history, I agree with you. There is no need to commit oneself to the sometimes stimulating but ultimately not very serious imaginative constructions of Toynbee, but it is pedantic and sterile and no less frivolous to deny that causal schemas are in fact present, whether they know it or not, in all historical 'proof'. Namier once observed to me that 'historical sense' is a knowledge of how things could not have happened; this seems to me a good observation and presupposes a conceptual framework (to use a pompous phrase) which automatically eliminates some suggested historical sequences as being 'impossible', and that for reasons which historians, not being meta-historians, are not obliged to give, but which nevertheless can and should be brought out and examined by persons interested in how men think and how they think they should think about subjects of abiding interest.

I hope I have been reasonably lucid. If not, I apologise again. This is a subject which has always interested me deeply and on which Anglo-Saxon philosophers have had singularly little of interest to say, and only blame themselves if a great many metaphysical Germans have rushed in where the English fear to tread, and have thrown up so much dust that men complain they cannot see, and suspect all such discussions of being fuzzy, unscientific and with an element of charlatanism. It need not be so. And philosophers know far more about history, which even they occasionally read, than about

1 Robin George Collingwood (1889–1943), philosopher and Roman historian. For 'absolute presuppositions' see *An Essay on Metaphysics* (Oxford, 1940), *passim*, esp. chapter 5.

physics or mathematics, which they usually know very little about. They would be far more usefully engaged in discussing the former. [...]

Yours ever,
    Isaiah Berlin

TO MARIE AND MENDEL BERLIN
    21 October 1951 [*manuscript*]

Lowell House, Harvard

Dear Pa & Ma

Forgive me if I don't write at length: I am really working v. hard, & long letters with 'Bytovyye Zapiski'[1] are impossible for me: but *of course* I shall write from time to time. I am *very* well: that is (a) not the faintest trace of my *piles*: I attribute this to better blood circulation due to less rich food, & my reduced weight (I am 178 lb. I think I stop here and begin to eat more or less normally.) – this makes me feel far better than I've felt for ten years. I now realize that the heavy lunches and dinners – whether at home or elsewhere are fatal for me: make me ill, stop my work, make me sleepy in the morning etc: here I feel far better. I must obviously eat no bread, potatoes, or sweets. My life is very normal: to bed at midnight, breakfast 9 a.m.: nothing to report: no *new* friends, but avoidance of some old ones, otherwise no time for work: delivering my four lectures per week + composing ones for Bryn Mawr takes *all* my time. I treat Harvard like a monastery & sit in the library whenever possible. [...] My *lectures* are being taken down by my own secretary, so *should* be a record. I am refusing to address societies etc. & feel happier about my own work: as soon as my Bryn Mawr book is ready, I sit down to vol 1 of the Big Book (Belinsky etc.) on which I am accumulating material here. [...]

Love,
    Shaya

TO HAMILTON FISH ARMSTRONG
    30 October 1951

Lowell House, Harvard

Dear Ham,

Do forgive me for my long delay, but Mr Utis has been far from well and overworked. He will be in New York next Saturday, but too briefly – for a mere 4 to 5 hours – to be of use to anyone. But he will, under my firm pressure, complete his task, I think, within the next fortnight and you shall have the result as soon as possible. He is displaying a curious aversion to social

---

1 'Everyday jottings'.

life at present, but it is hoped that the completion of some, at any rate, of his labours will restore his taste for pleasure, at any rate by mid-December. I shall certainly keep you posted about the movement of this highly unsatis- factory figure.

All this was composed before your telegram[1] – the technique of your communication has by now, I perceive, been established in a firm and not unfamiliar pattern of the patient, long-suffering, but understanding editor dealing with an exceptionally irritating and unbusinesslike author who does, nevertheless, in the end respond, apologize, and produce, although after delays both maddening and unnecessary, which only the most great-hearted editor would forgive. [...]

Yours ever,

Isaiah

TO HAMILTON FISH ARMSTRONG

20 November 1951

Lowell House, Harvard

Dear Ham,

Thank you very much for your very nice letter. I see that a somewhat different analysis of U[ncle] J[oe Stalin] is presented by Mr A. J. P. Taylor in the *New York Times* this last Sunday,[2] but Mr Utis sticks to his views. I think the signature had better remain as arranged. All things leak in time and there are at least a dozen persons in the world now who know the truth. Nevertheless, the difference from the point of view of possible victims in the country under review seems to me genuine; and so long as the real name is not flaunted, and room for doubt exists, their lives (so I like to think) are not (or less) jeopardised. More thought on these lines would make me suppress the whole thing altogether on the ground that you must not take the least risk with anyone placed in so frightful a situation. (Never have so many taken so much for so long from so few. You may count yourself fortunate that this sentence is not a part of Mr Utis's manuscript.) So, I drive the thought away and Mr Utis is my thin screen from reality behind which I so unconvincingly conceal my all too recognizable features.

Only one thing has occurred to Mr Utis since his last letter to you; and that is whether some added point might not be given to the bits scrawled in manuscript concerning the chances of survival of the artificial dialectic.

1 Dated 1 November, it began: 'DELIGHTED YOU ARE GOING TO EXERCISE FIRM PRESSURE ON DR UTIS SO THAT WE SHALL RECEIVE HIS MUCH DESIRED MANUSCRIPT IN FINAL FORM IN MIDDLE OF NOVEMBER. MANY THANKS TO YOU FOR YOUR WELCOME AND EFFECTIVE INTERVENTION.'

2 'Stalin as Statesman: A Look at the Record', *New York Times Magazine*, 18 November 1951, 9, 53–7, 59–60. The subsidiary headline proclaimed that 'Close study of Russian diplomacy reveals him to be tough and nervy but without real skill.'

Perhaps something might be said about how very like a permanent mobilisation – army life – the whole thing is for the average Soviet citizen and that considering what people do take when they are in armies – particularly Russians and Germans – provided that things really are *kept* militarised and no breath of civilian ease is allowed to break the tension, there is no occasion for surprise that this has lasted for so long, nor yet for supposing that its intrinsic wickedness must bring it down (as our friend Mr X[1] seems to me too obstinately to believe). I was much impressed by what someone told me the other day about a conversation with one of the two Soviet fliers[2] – the one who did not go back. He was asked why his colleague who returned did so (I cannot remember the names, one was called, I think, Pigorov, but I do not know whether this is the man who stayed or the man who returned). He replied that after they had been taken for a jaunt around Virginia, they were dumped in an apartment in New York, provided with an adequate sum of money, but given nothing very specific to do. The flier who ultimately returned found that this was more intolerable than a labour camp in the Soviet Union. This may be exaggerated, but obviously contains a very large grain of truth. Apparently the people here who were dealing with some of the 'defectors' found the same problem – how to organize them in a sufficiently mechanical, rigid and time-consuming manner, to prevent the problem of leisure from ever arising.

If you think well of the military life analogy, could I ask you – you who now know Mr Utis and his dreadful style and grammar* so intimately – to draft a sentence or two, to be included in the proof in the relevant place, saying something to the effect that the question of how long the lives either of executive officials or the masses they control can stand the strain of a system at once so taut and so liable to unpredictable zigzags is perhaps wrongly posed; once the conditions of army life and army discipline have been imposed, human beings appear to endure them for what seems to the more comfort-loving nations a fantastic length of time; provided they are not actually being killed or wounded, peasant populations show little tendency to revolt against either regimentation or arbitrary disposal of their lives; the decades of service in the army which Russian peasants in the eighteenth or nineteenth centuries had to endure led to no serious rebellions and the emancipation of the serfs less than a century ago had less psychological

---

1 George Kennan (see 38/7).

2 In October 1948 two pilots in the Soviet Air Force, Anatoly Barsov (b. *c.*1917) and Petr Afanasevich Pirogov (1920–87), flew their plane to a US base in Austria, criticising the Soviet regime and declaring that they wanted to go to America. In due course the somewhat embarrassed US Government took them there. Pirogov wrote a book about his escape and eventually settled permanently in Virginia (whose attractions the pilots had heard described by the Voice of America), but within a few months Barsov regretted his flight and was in touch with the Russian Embassy about a possible return to the Soviet Union. Warned by Pirogov, the US promptly deported Barsov to Austria for visa violations and allowed him to choose whether to return to the Soviet Union from there, which he did in August 1949.

effect than is commonly assumed, or civilised persons hoped it would have. The possibility of cracking under the strain is smaller in a system where everything obeys a dead routine, however inefficient and costly in lives and property, than one in which ultimate responsibility rests in nervous or fumbling fingers; hence, the prospect of upheavals and revolt, etc. when M. Stalin (I hope you will keep the 'M.') is succeeded is greater than during his years of power, however oppressive, arbitrary, and brutal. But perhaps I have said this already in the article. If so, I apologise for repeating myself this way.

I long to see you and propose to appear for a weekend on about 10 December, if I can get away, and perhaps stay with Nin Ryan. I shall certainly let you know beforehand and would much rather come to dinner by myself, or nearly so, monomaniacal as this may seem. I am all for cosiness and private life, and the fewer and the less of everything, the better.

Yours ever,
    Isaiah Berlin

* Did you know that 'grammar' is the same word as 'glamour'? It proceeds via 'grimoire'. If further explanation is needed, I shall provide it when I see you.

TO MRS SAMUEL H. PAUL[1]
    20 November 1951

Lowell House, Harvard

Dear Mrs Paul,

Thank you for your letter of November 12. I am not sure what the best title of my lectures would be, perhaps 'Political Ideas in the Romantic Age' would be best, and you can put in '1760–1830' if you think well of that. I have been looking for some title denoting what I really want to talk about; i.e. the particular period during which modern political and social beliefs really came to be formulated and the controversies acquired their classical expression in the sense that present-day arguments still deal in concepts and even terminology which crystallised during those years. What I wanted to avoid was a term like 'origins' or 'foundations' since this would commit me to talking about people like Machiavelli, Hobbes, Locke etc. who may be the fathers of all these things, but are definitely felt to be predecessors and precursors, and certainly as far as mode of expression is concerned, altogether obsolete. ⟨I had therefore thought I had an alternative title 'The rise and crystallisation of modern political ideas'.⟩ If you can think of something more elegant than either I should be grateful. ⟨Perhaps the first might be the title, the second a subtitle. I leave that to you.⟩

1 Assistant to the President of Bryn Mawr, Katharine McBride.

As for the individual lectures, I should like to suggest the following: (1) 'The Concept of Nature and the Science of Politics' (Helvetius and Holbach);[1] (2) 'Political Liberty and the Ethical Imperative' (Kant and Rousseau); (3) 'Liberalism and the Romantic Movement' (Fichte[2] and J. S. Mill); (4) 'Individual Freedom and the March of History' (Herder[3] and Hegel); (5) 'The Organisation of Society and the Golden Age' (St Simon and his successors); (6) 'The Counter-Revolution' (Maistre and Görres).[4]

I hope this will do. If there is anything you would like to alter or amend particularly if general titles strike you as too pale, I could try and mend it.

Thank you so much for making provision for my mother should she wish to come, but her arrival in this country seems to be somewhat uncertain.

Yours sincerely,

Isaiah Berlin

TO CLARISSA CHURCHILL

[? November 1951, *manuscript*]

Lowell House, Harvard

Dearest Clarissa

I never see you, & then I suffer from acute moments of nostalgia for some sort of golden past and a great desire to see you: how are you? what are you doing? are you reasonably contented? I am in a state between depression & numbness, induced by work & fasting in order to fulfil medical threats which can always terrorize me. The second visit to Harvard is in a way flatter than the first – same faces, same affability, same touching students with their earnest truth seeking faces, yet also the same dehydration, dryness, lack of inside, inability to have or give life, – I cd not live here if I did not think of return all the time, & cannot write either, because of a kind of centrally-heated grimly unaltering temperature which dries up all the sources of imagination & feeling. Hence the aridity of all this: having decided to go to a monastery, to a monastery I went; & declined to go to Washington even once; & to New York only to hear Toscanini. Now he *is* the greatest figure, to me, in the world: now in his last phase, all the rich circus master Italian eloquence gone, & a wonderful transcendental bare-bones quality left, like poets in their last absolutely taut contrapuntal phase, when the skeleton is bared & a kind of X-ray lucidity is achieved & a sense of ultimate truth,

1 Claude Adrien Helvétius (1715–71), French utilitarian philosopher, and Paul Henri Thiry, baron d'Holbach (1723–89), strongly anti-religious philosopher, German-born but brought up in France; both contributed to the *Encyclopédie* (183/1).
2 Johann Gottlieb Fichte (1762–1814), German idealist philosopher and nationalist.
3 Johann Gottfried Herder (1744–1803), German romantic philosopher, poet, critic and peaceable nationalist.
4 Johann Joseph von Görres (1776–1848), German writer and political activist who moved from republicanism to liberal nationalism; fiercely opposed to Napoleon.

objectivity without the self-intrusion of the artist. His performances now are like the march of nature or of history as conceived by mythological historians: an inexorable procession of inevitable phases which silences all criticism & completely subjugates one's senses & inclinations & demands on how things should be: I mustn't go on rhapsodizing so. *Do* write me. I am too solitary for me: & suffer from cut offness: G. Weidenfeld is, I hear, to ally himself to the Sieffs:[1] there is a terrible fitness about it. If you tell me he is in love I shan't believe or care – it is all a cosy central European comedy whatever happens. Judy Montagu also is said to be engaged to a roughish American.[2] I didn't take to him much on first & only meeting. My continued singleness is thought *very* suspect here: Burgess-like almost.[3] Are you well? have you new friends? does the new govt. excite you? [. . .] do you really love Miss Garbo whom I found so self conscious & impossible & quite nice & all right but epicene & trivial? am I mistaken? do do write. I need encouragement & letters.

    yours with great love
      Isaiah

TO ANNA KALLIN

  11 December 1951[4]

Lowell House, Harvard

Dear N,

    This is a hurried, quasi-official note to reply to your latest *cri de coeur* about the date of the talks;[5] the position is this. It is indeed true, I am even now in process of hysterical dictation of the rough draft for these lectures, and it is quite clear that there will not be anything like a finished text by the time I have to start delivering them on 11 February. I do not, of course, need to submit a manuscript for publication immediately after the lectures are over in late March, and although I may have enough material – with the help of God and the good will of the lady who will type this letter – I rely

1 George Weidenfeld married Jane Sieff (b. 1931), daughter of Teddy Sieff (whose brother Israel was Joint Managing Director, with Simon Marks, of Marks & Spencer), in January 1952 after a brief courtship; the marriage foundered in 1954.

2 Ray Livingston Murphy (1923–53), writer and art collector. After his early death 'his mother, crazed with grief, moved into his house in New York, the last private house on Park Avenue, nestling among the tower blocks, and lived as a recluse', surrounded by her son's rapidly appreciating art collection (*The Times*, 6 November 1985, 16).

3 Marietta Tree may have been among the doubters, suspecting one friend of homosexuality because 'the only girl he has ever been interested in is a wildly promiscuous type'; she would have known of IB's feelings for Patricia de Bendern, but not that he had transferred his affections to Jenifer Hart. Caroline Seebohm, *No Regrets* (New York, 1997), 318.

4 AK annotated: 'Mr. Grisewood / I think you should see this (*with* the P.S.) NK'.

5 IB had agreed to repeat the Mary Flexner lectures he was to give at Bryn Mawr as talks for the Third Programme (and for these talks to be published in the *Listener*); the original intention was that this should happen soon after IB's return from the US.

on the latter rather more than the former – to make the delivering of the
actual lectures possible, this material will be in a dreadful state, without all
the historical references which alone will not merely corroborate the wild
generalisations contained, but, in fact, check their truth so far as I myself
am concerned. You will easily perceive how it is one thing to say a lot of
things in a general fashion to an audience and a very different one to commit
words to cold print even though it may be only the *Listener*. I shall arrive
in England only in very late April. With me I shall have (*a*) the rough draft
of the lectures, partly in typescript, partly in my own fantastic handwriting; (*b*) possibly a wire recording transcript of the lectures themselves;[1] (*c*)
an inchoate collection of odd references picked up here and there which
may or may not tally with the text and which will need to be supplemented
by quite a lot of Blunt-like research[2] before anything like an approach to
a dependable truth can be achieved. Therefore, before I can deliver a text
in the hands of the Oxford Press, I shall need to do at least three months'
work on all those original sources (what the subjects of my lectures actually
said as opposed to what they ought to have said to support my theses about
them) and this cannot be ready, if I get to work in May, before, say, August, if
then. I certainly do not propose to send a text to the press here (in the USA)
before 1953, though I may be able to achieve this in, say, November 1952.
On the other hand, I ought to have an adequate text, if I work properly, by
August or early September and from this text condensation for broadcasting
will, of course, be feasible. I realise that you perform miracles of cutting,
condensing, crystallising etc., but I do not believe that I shall have written-
out lectures to deliver even into your magical hands in late April, which,
anyhow, will be a little too late. Nor would you or the BBC wish to print
in the *Listener* statements for whose accuracy I shall certainly not be able
to vouch on topics of which a good deal of exact knowledge exists on the
part of benevolent scholars let alone captious rivals. You may reasonably ask
why I had not thought of all this before when suggesting May. To which the
answer is – as it always must be – error, sheer error on my part, miscalcula-
tion of the time it takes to write a book and guarantee reasonable accuracy
of the statements which it contains. I do not deny that I should be able to
produce impromptu lectures of a somewhat speculative kind by May – but
that would certainly be unprintable in the *Listener*,[3] which is surely undesirable. So on these grounds – mainly, that is, of the probable absence of a
condensable version of my lectures by the beginning of May – I must, with

1 This has not been found – if it ever existed.
2 A reference to the intensive and extensive research undertaken by Anthony Frederick Blunt
   (1907–83), art historian, authority on Poussin, former Communist spy; Surveyor of the King's
   Pictures 1945–52; Director of the Courtauld Institute of Art 1947–74; Surveyor of the Queen's
   Pictures 1952–72.
3 The broadcast lectures were not printed in the *Listener* (or indeed elsewhere at the time); the
   editor of the *Listener* ruled that they were too long.

great guilt and a sense of my incorruptibly Oblomovian[1] nature, beg to be postponed until October or November and promise sacredly to deliver an elastic text into your hands by September. It really is better so; the text will be much better if propped up with solid 'research', even though this may not find its way into the text; I should be terribly ashamed and you would not be pleased to have a rough and chaotic sketch when you can have the finished article, however poor, however dull. In any case, I cannot be home before the end of April and how much time will that leave for the preparation of the text? Imagine the frantic hurry of those last hours, the mistakes made, the apologies subsequently required, instead of which, tranquillity, detachment, harmony, culture and rest in September. Please convey my humblest apologies to Harman Grisewood etc. – I realise that this is an alibi which one is allowed to use only when in the throes of genuine despair.

In this unhappy state I greet you with the last remnant of my failing powers.

Yours ever

Shaya

PS ⟨to be cut off if you want to show the rest of the letter to anyone⟩ On the subject of Wind,[2] I shall write to Kahn[3] saying how nice I think him, how sweet and delightful as a human being quite apart from his genius, but I am informed that Rylands[4] and the Provost[5] will have been influenced decisively against him by Blunt and possibly Boase. Is this so? I shall also write to Noel. Is there anything else I can do? I really feel passionate on the subject. Kings will cover themselves with shame if they give it to anyone else of those mentioned so far.

Once he had finished his Harvard lectures, IB relaxed in Washington and New York. But alarming news reached him from All Souls.

1 The central character in Ivan Goncharov's eponymous novel *Oblomov* (1859) is a well-meaning day-dreamer who spends most of his life in his room, clad in a dressing-gown or in bed; he loses any capacity for decisions or action and achieves nothing.

2 Edgar Wind was a candidate for a research post at King's College, Cambridge; IB had been lobbying on his behalf.

3 Richard Ferdinand Kahn (1905–89), later (1965) Baron Kahn; Fellow of King's College, Cambridge, 1930–89, First Bursar 1946–51; Professor of Economics, Cambridge, 1951–72.

4 George Humphrey Wolferstan ('Dadie') Rylands (1902–99), literary scholar, theatre director and actor; Fellow of King's College, Cambridge, 1927–99; University Lecturer in English Literature, Cambridge, 1935–62.

5 Sir John Tresidder Sheppard (1881–1968), classicist; Provost, King's College, Cambridge, 1933–54.

TO MARIE AND MENDEL BERLIN

2 January 1952 [*manuscript*]

Lowell House, Harvard

Dear Ma & Pa,

I am actually in New York, in Sam Behrman's[1] flat. My holiday is coming to an end. I worked *very* hard in Cambridge till December 24: finished my lectures: [. . .] went to Bryn Mawr to read a paper on philosophy[2] (back to the old circus) which achieved an unexpected success & which therefore I shall publish sometime (my collected opuscula will outweigh my longer 'master-pieces', I expect) From there to Washington (in the train met Kollek:[3] & then Tosco Fyvel:[4] they told me, not without amusement that Weidenfeld has capitulated & is marrying Teddy Sieff's[5] daughter. Money, I fear, is money, even in sterling) to stay with Felix. That was *charming*: both send their love: stole off secretly to visit Visson[6] (I am a little ashamed of *that* acquaintance) who also + wife send love: he is fatter than ever, envies my "slimness"[7] (I'll try to get photograph) & was *very* welcoming, delicious Russian food, not good for my jealously guarded & daily weighed figure. Saw Bohlens, & met Acheson who is a nice man but too like you & me:[8] I always expect states-men to have inner confidence like Winston or Weizmann or even Bevin who believed in their own inner *machine* – & so can lead: but Acheson, though honourable, gentlemanly, high minded, intelligent, civilized etc. etc. is just a nice educated lawyer with an English background – & needs propping

1 Sam(uel) Nathan *Behrman, (1893–1973), US playwright.
2 'Synthetic A Priori Propositions', a reply to Wilfrid Sellars in a symposium, chaired by Morton White, during the meeting of the American Philosophical Association held at Bryn Mawr College 27–9 December 1951. See 62/7.
3 Theodor ('Teddy') *Kollek (1911–2007), worked for the Haganah and the Jewish Agency before independence and for the Israeli Foreign Ministry after; Director-General, Prime Minister's office, 1952–65.
4 Tosco Raphael Fyvel (1907–85), né Raphael Joseph Feiwel, son of the committed Zionist (and friend of Chaim Weizmann) Berthold Feiwel; journalist, broadcaster, author, editor and sociolo-gist; literary editor, *Tribune*, 1945–50, succeeding his close friend George Orwell; member of the Congress for Cultural Freedom; helped found *Encounter* in 1953.
5 (Joseph) Edward ('Teddy') Sieff (1905–82), Assistant Managing Director, Marks & Spencer, 1946–63, later (1963–72) Joint Managing Director and (1967–72) Chairman, succeeding his brother Israel.
6 André Visson (c.1899–1971), Russian-born naturalised American; author, international corre-spondent for the *Washington Post* and *Reader's Digest*. His wife was Assia (1911–83), née Rubinstein, for many years the executive editor of the *Gazette des beaux-arts*.
7 By the time IB returned to Oxford he was 'terrifyingly thin', according to the somewhat stout Maurice Bowra. Letter of 27 April 1952 to Alice James [Wadham College Archives, Oxford].
8 Cf. 'I feel that Stevenson like Eden, is too nice, although much nicer than Eden, and that what one needs in politics is people who love them, who love the rough and tumble, who have the very qualities which make them uninteresting in private life and marvellously reliable and expert in public affairs. I cannot believe that either Stevenson or Eden enjoy politics, and if one doesn't enjoy them one doesn't do it well. Whereas Roosevelt, Truman, Churchill, even McCarthy and Mussolini, whatever else they did, enjoyed doing what they did, with horrible or beneficent results as the case might be, but always effective ones.' Letter of 2 May 1955 to Henry Brandon.

himself: Truman is the prop – for all his provincialism he *has* an inner quiet & more confidence in his own values – but they were all *terrified* of Winston's approach[1] – like chickens before an aged eagle – all holding their pockets in case the old boy stole or wheedled something out of them while they were dazzled by the glory & the brilliance. Very funny. Saw Franks, – nervous but rather nice – & the Morgans[2] – both very nice, she absolutely true & sweet – & Mrs Graham. Then returned to New York (saw Prichard also poor man: ex-jailbird:[3] pathetic & nice to all his friends, Frankfurter etc. anxious to be extra nice to him) tonight I go to the opera. [...]

[...] a letter from Sparrow about All Souls, hinting that Henderson will *not* take it, owing to bad heart: so we are back in the mess: hinting that I should return to take part in the brouhaha which has not begun yet. I replied that I do *not* propose to offer my candidature as last time – I really don't wish to be Warden – it would be an insane burden on me – the Flexner lectures here *cannot* be suddenly abandoned: & that if there is a *terrible* crisis I would like to be told, & if I *must* hurry back I would consider it: but not if it can possibly be avoided. Now I *really* don't want to go through the nightmare again: the only thing is to avoid some awful idiot or enemy: to avoid *that* I *might* return a little earlier: but hope it won't be necessary: nothing is public yet & Rowse is probably plotting in great secrecy: I would rather be left out of the scandals to come. Still I don't suppose I shall be let. [...]

Love,
Shaya

TO DAVID CECIL

3 January 1952 [*manuscript*]

Lowell House, Harvard

Dear David,

I meant & meant & meant to write to you & couldn't because, as I used to tell you this country dehydrates one: removes the third dimension in which alone the Stuff for anything, even so trivial a composition as a letter is possible: I can occasionally make myself do a brief machine-gun like collection of jokes & gossip for Maurice because he will feel wounded if I don't: & get an amusing letter in return: very nice too: but familiar rather than

---

1 The general election on 25 October 1951 had returned a Conservative government, and Winston Churchill was once more Prime Minister. He arrived in the US on 5 January 1952 for discussions there and in Canada.

2 Aubrey Niel Morgan (1904–85), Welsh-born Deputy Director-General of British Information Services 1942–5, Personal Assistant to UK Ambassador in Washington (Sir Oliver Franks) 1948–52; and his wife Constance Cutter Morgan (1913–95), daughter of Dwight Morrow, former US Ambassador to Moscow. Both had been wartime colleagues of IB's.

3 In December 1950 President Truman had commuted Ed Prichard's sentence to time served and he had been released from prison. Since then he had struggled to find ways of making a living.

intimate. Privacy is really difficult here: I stayed in Harvard for 4 months: first a fortnight with my pansy friend Mr Burdon Muller, gentle, sweet & agreeably tedious: stories about minor German royalty & rich young men of 1908. Then Harvard. Not as nice this time as last, possibly because it *is* the second time, possibly because I had too much work to do: the lectures for Harvard + the coming ones for Bryn Mawr: everyone very kind, very sweet, but everything stuffier than at Oxford: the hates & loves deeper, as in Cambridge, England: the hostesses just as welcoming but the Dickensy-Martin Chuzzlewit comedy[1] of it all no longer as exhilarating as in 1949. On the other hand a lot of work done: & adequate monastic conditions. One couple – the Pickmans – you really *would* like: she – Hester Pickman – aged about 60 – as good as any civilised & agreeable lady anywhere: & her husband[2] very rich & very nice. Otherwise I think you'd find a desert more than Maurice did. The *douceur de vivre*[3] is too lacking in the Perry Millers[4] & I rest[?]: it is a very good place for work: & like a gap in one's experience. I made only one new friend: a Frenchman called Raphael Salem – from Salonika in the end I imagine – who ½ the year is a banker in Paris & a patron of music: & half a professor of mathematics at the Massachusetts Institute of Technology (beautiful name): he & his Italian wife are a great refuge – dry, French, hyper-civilized, art-collecting & agreeably cynical, they were in the sharpest possible contrast with the dough-like environment. I felt much more exiled than before. And worked away with real ferocity & produced 2 articles & six lectures which will be the centre of a book on political thought. I left Cambridge before Xmas for New York & at once found myself in a world again. Judy's fiancé was the first touch of reality: a hulking brute named Murphy: the author of works on Lear (Edward) & Mountbatten: a collector of Beckfordiana: neurotic, embarrassed, difficult, possibly quite nice, but too much trouble, I thought, loud meaningless laughter, obviously well read, very rich, a handful: a great awkward lump of violent contradictions – "tied up" as they say: not my cup of tea: & I should have supposed not hers either. We shall see. It is better that she marry & leave him than not marry at all, from her point of view: or live in sin if need be: Joe is at once relieved & angry: & says terrible things about the poor young man. I have been thinking about Joe & now feel this (I wonder if I am right) that he is a) very high minded b) fearless c) splendid in Dreyfus cases etc. d) all too human e) understands nothing at all about people f) understands nothing about politics. He denounces public vices splendidly: but his political analyses are highbrow, industrious, grandiloquent & plumb wrong: Ronnie Tree

---

1 Charles Dickens's novel *Martin Chuzzlewit* (1843–4) includes a section set in America satirising American attitudes and behaviour.
2 Edward Motley Pickman (1886–1959), lawyer, historian and music patron.
3 'Sweetness of life'.
4 Perry Miller's wife was Elizabeth, née Williams.

understands more. Talking of whom: he is *not* happy in New York: he would *much* rather have lived in England: he is miserable with a Tory govt & he not there: he is like Lord Beauchamp[1] in Australia, not quite so bad; but cannot get over all his cronies in power & he just a rich man without a function. Marietta says *country* life in England is better than anything: but loves it here more: & is learning Greek from a Frenchman in French (I cannot tell how comical the sounds of the lessons are on both sides) & I stayed with them & very nice it was, for two days at Xmas. Ronnie suspects your sister in law[2] of not liking Americans all *that much*, rightly I think: he is not wholly deceivable. He likes Judy's young man because he is awkward, rich, a collector of pictures, & not up to Judy's rapid intelligence, if you see what I mean. I haven't seen Auden but only Isherwood[3] who is very gentle, polite & improper: & has all E. M. Forster's gooey sentimentality & spinsterish malicious eye. Which reminds me: I fear David Garnett[4] was *very* angry with my kind patronising words[5] about his mother, & his letter in the *Observer*,[6] if you saw it, was a model of courteous fury. Did they print my reply?[7] They didn't say. Last night I saw John Foster – very unaltered – I don't know why I assume that old faces in new places will seem different – & Enid Jones[8] who is, as they say, not quite first rate ("my new friend Lady Jones," Diana calls her still) who thought the *private life* of your father in law,[9] as opposed to his conversation & writing, was *a great mystery*, known to nobody. [...] Acheson has had a row with Eden in Paris, when E. said if America had backed us up at points x, y, z, we shouldn't now be facing ruin: while Ach.'s line is that he is listening now to the same damn silly officials as led us down the garden in Persia[10] & how *could* he back such idiots etc. meanwhile the great American people *adore* Winston: his is the only really cosmic voice, almost divine, which will enunciate some great solution to the present problems: he is certainly more

1 William Lygon (1872–1938), 7th Earl Beauchamp, Governor of New South Wales 1899–1901, a competent administrator resented by the local population and frustrated by the limitations of his role; subsequently a Liberal politician; bisexual like Ronnie Tree (though IB may not have intended to refer to, or known of, this similarity).
2 Presumably Lady Salisbury.
3 Christopher William (Bradshaw-)Isherwood (1904–86), British novelist and playwright who had settled in the US.
4 David Garnett (1892–1981), author and member of the Bloomsbury group.
5 In 'On Translating Turgenev', review of I. S. Turgenev, *Smoke, On the Eve, Virgin Soil, Fathers and Children* and *A House of Gentle Folk*, trans. Constance Garnett, *Observer*, 11 November 1951, 7; see 7/6.
6 In which David Garnett questioned some of IB's generalisations about his mother's approach to translation (*Observer*, 25 November 1951, 9).
7 They didn't: it had been lost in the *Observer*'s office. See IB's letter of 27 January 1955 to David Astor (473–6).
8 Lady (Enid Algerine) Jones (1889–1981), the novelist and playwright Enid Bagnold, married to Sir Roderick Jones of Reuters.
9 Desmond MacCarthy.
10 During the 1951 Abadan crisis (230/3), the US initially saw the retention of Iran as an anti-Communist ally as more important than the defence of British interests.

influential here, with the masses, than any other human being: hence terror
in Washington. Winston has refused to produce an agenda & that keeps
them in suspense too: what *communiqué* will be issued to the journals? It
really is comical to see a sort of Tolstoy parody in actual life: Statesman –
Acheson – who is a nice honourable private face, wringing his hands & being
weak, in despair, lost, exactly as the "important" people are in Tolstoy: now
that Bevin's immemorial peasant wisdom has been withdrawn. I suppose
Winston is Napoleon & Truman is Kutuzov.[1] My God how Tolstoy would
have hated Roosevelt. It was rather 'fun' I must say, to go to Washington for
2 days & see the ferment & bad temper & worry & nonsense behind the
coulisses:[2] I felt very like Mme Lieven[3] & very gay. Joe is prophesying the
worst: so you may be sure it will all end well: he really is an ass politically: the
noblest, most high minded & bravest of asses, but an ass. A far worse ass is
Archie M[a]cLeish: empty to a degree – the last silver trumpet of democracy.
E. Wilson I saw & he is in a baddish state – drunk & so on – but about, he
says, to write something on Malraux. He thinks there are two T. S. Eliots: the
one one meets & inside a *scoundrel*, that is the term used, whom the respectable Eliot rather admires. I don't quite understand but dimly perceive something. [. . .] Sparrow has written me a secret letter about All Souls prophesying
that Sir Hubert will not reign or rule, & finding some pretty good evidence
of Rowse's machinations to get an agreed candidate quickly before it is
known that Henderson cannot survive. He therefore wants me to come
home "whether as rival or friend or observer". I am clear that unless there is
a totally unlikely popular movement of "Imperator, Imperator"[4] I am *not* a
candidate: & cannot leave my Bryn Mawr lectures, which are fearfully
pompous & grand (to Bryn Mawr I mean) suddenly to go & plot for anybody:
& am far better off out of the way. Maurice's advice I cannot take too seriously about this sort of thing, I fear: he will want me to come back just
because it is not necessary to be in America anyway: "what is he doing there,
wasting his time etc." will be the line. I dread the smudged letters of my sans
culotte friends piteously "begging" me to "stand". What should be my line?
I think silence & remoteness. Let them do as they will. Rowse if he cannot

---

1 Field Marshal Prince Mikhail Illarionovich Golenishchev-Kutuzov (1745–1813), commander-in-
  chief of the Russian Army during Napoleon's attempted invasion of Russia, who appears in
  Tolstoy's *War and Peace*.
2 'Stage scenery'.
3 Dorothea Lieven (1785–1857), née de Benckendorff, wife of Count (later Prince) Christopher
  Lieven, Russian Ambassador in London 1812–34; through her role in London society, and her
  close personal relations with many political leaders throughout Europe, she herself acquired a
  major diplomatic role both in London and later in Paris, and had inside knowledge of European
  diplomacy for 45 years.
4 Under the Roman Republic, a victorious general could be acclaimed as 'imperator' (only 'commander' at that time) by his troops, thus achieving one of the qualifications for a ceremonial
  triumph.

get Bridges will turn to *anybody* but Sparrow – Hodson[1] – any old hack & try
& lobby them in. But for him I would not mind what happens – the fellows
of A.S. are otherwise dreary but not too lunatic – but A.L.R. brings in a note
of paranoiac madness + thirst for revenge, & in that mass of putty may do
harm. I wish you could sound matters out a little – via some sensible source,
not Rowse or Dummett[2] but some respectable mediocrity – & tell me if I
really must hysterically fly back for 3 days through snow & wind – surely I
can behave sanely & remain here peacefully working? or can't I? I met Mrs
Eden[3] this afternoon. Much nicer than A.

I must finish & quickly, because of the opera. Apart from All Souls & the
tensions about the lack of knowledge & the water in my lectures, I am really
rather well: 30 lb. lighter in weight & feeling altogether nicer & younger.
I am about to write a piece for the Encyclopaedia Britannica about 1951 &
religion seems to me the prevalent tone: all the most talked about things in
the year are Robsonian.[4] The kind of Eliot–Auden–Butterfield[5]–Maurice–
Graham Greene[6]–Evelyn W.–Niebuhr etc. mood is what is fashionable, & it
has made of a literarified religion the latest means of presenting unpleasant
facts – which used to be the monopoly of Marxists or Psycho-Analysis users:
the thing now is to say either a) the hideous things are hideous because men
do not understand God: but this which is traditional, & in a sense true, is
rare: more frequent is b) the hideous, chaotic, tragic, is *true*: & religion is the
mode of apprehending it: what is repellent to normal morality or aesthetic
sense *is* the divine order: the uglier & bleaker & less intelligible the more
necessary – a kind of Augustinian Calvinism, a quia absurdum[7] doctrine,
a mystique whereby on the other side of the horrible & painful is always a
radiance & a salvation which is (to me) a very shallow translation of Marxism
or psycho-analytic romanticism into religious terms. Am I mistaken? I expect
I am. I saw Elizabeth[8] here before she flew away & she was sane, charming,
delightful as ever. She adores this country – which seems to her a source of

---

1 Henry Vincent ('Harry') Hodson (1906–99), Fellow of All Souls 1928–35; assistant editor, *Sunday Times*, 1946–50, editor 1950–61; later (1961–71) Provost of Ditchley.
2 Michael Anthony Eardley Dummett (b. 1925), philosopher; Fellow of All Souls 1950–79; later (1979–92) Wykeham Professor of Logic, Oxford.
3 Beatrice Helen Eden (1905–57), née Beckett, Anthony Eden's first wife, who had left him to live in New York in 1946.
4 Does IB mean Robinsonian? John Arthur Thomas Robinson (1919–83; Fellow and Dean, Clare College, Cambridge 1951–9; Assistant Lecturer in Divinity, Cambridge, 1953–4, Lecturer 1954–9) did not produce his controversial *Honest to God* until 1963 but his first book, *In the End God*, had been published in 1950.
5 Herbert Butterfield (1900–79), Professor of Modern History, Cambridge, 1944–63 (Regius Professor 1963–8; Master of Peterhouse 1955–68; his much-discussed *Christianity and History* had been published in 1949.
6 (Henry) Graham Greene (1904–91), novelist whose Catholicism greatly influenced his works.
7 From the Latin 'Credo quia absurdum est' ('I believe because it is absurd'), a saying often used to ridicule the reliance on faith in defiance of reason of some types of religious belief.
8 Presumably Elizabeth Bowen.

life while Europe is a heap of cinders: I see what she means & disagree. And she will never abandon this: starved of something in her youth she will *never* have enough [of] it (like Judy Montagu) & only New York & Hollywood (no I cross out Hollywood) has enough of it – an imaginary Balzac[1] sort of tough glitter & life – to quench the thirst. Greta Garbo said how nice it had been to be with you: did you see her much? I find her embarrassingly dull but have never been with her for more than ¼ hour. Has Mr Eden proposed again to Clarissa? & how is she? Was she in love with Garbo too? she told me she wishes to return to Oxford to see you & me. One last point. There is a clever, vulgarly beautiful, malicious writer here called Mary McCarthy (*nobody* more different from your m. in law[2] could be *conceived*) who wishes to lecture in Oxford on the 19th century European novel, paid by Fulbright.[3] She writes stories for the *New Yorker*, very clever & lethal to the N.Y. intellectuals she enjoys killing, & was Edm. Wilson's 3rd wife. She is very amusing & clever & tough & worth talking to about literature, somewhat malignant & might put us all in a novel: & would probably have an affair or two. I am in favour of such a flutter for a term: does your sub-faculty have to apply for her? She says yes. From Oxford she would go to Greece, Do let's have her. Her account of repulsing Freddie & Koestler simultaneously is very funny. Could you tell me about her? *Horizon*[4] printed a story by her I think: & we would not have to pay: & there is no limit on such persons so Trilling[5] could come as well. Do write please *please*. Love to Rachel.[6]

Isaiah

TO MARION FRANKFURTER

3 January 1952 [*manuscript*]

As from Lowell House, Harvard

Dear Marion,

I have never enjoyed staying in your or any house as much as during these four days. Partly for reasons which you wd not wish me to set forth at length & explicitly: & partly, no doubt, because I was in some curious way starved – this year much more than last time – at Cambridge & came

---

1 Honoré de Balzac (1799–1850), novelist and playwright, who portrayed French society with satiric realism.

2 Mary Josepha ('Molly') MacCarthy (1882–1953), née Warre-Cornish, writer; wife of Desmond MacCarthy and mother of Rachel Cecil (note 6 below).

3 The Fulbright award scheme, established in 1948, provides funding for, inter alia, US academics to lecture, study and undertake research in the UK.

4 Influential monthly literary magazine founded in 1939 by Cyril Connolly – editor throughout its publication (January 1940 to December 1949) – Stephen Spender and Peter Watson.

5 Lionel Trilling (1905–75), US literary critic; taught English at Columbia University from 1932, (full) Professor 1948–74 (George Edward Woodberry Professor of Literature and Criticism 1965–70, University Professor 1970–4), Visiting Professor, All Souls, 1971–2.

6 David Cecil's wife, née Rachel Mary Veronica MacCarthy (1909–82), daughter of Desmond MacCarthy.

to my meal with an enormous appetite. I found both you & Felix very well, very much in possession of that inner tranquillity the lack of which strikes me so painfully in the good Mr Acheson; I saw only the people I wanted to see: I enjoyed every moment: I enjoyed enormously my evening with you alone even though my blindness to Mrs Whitehead's true character makes you think of me as gazing through a telescope at remote, dimly distinguishable, dwarves round whom I construct mythologies which sometimes fit & sometimes don't but always smother the subjects: I do that a little: I like rounded vignettes: & I cling to my hypotheses: it is the only sense I attach to understanding about people as opposed to moment-to-moment reactions to, or impressions of, them; I like a three dimensional model & am v. bad at immediate perceptions of the flow of life: but I am prepared endlessly to modify the models in the face of facts: but it is the long run, not the short which fascinates me: character not moods: doesn't it you? at any rate we did well with the M[a]c.L[eish]s: & I'll swap Mrs Whitehead for D. Astor if need be: & we shall have, I expect, to compromise about Foster. I'll accept Barbara Ward if you concede Arthur Schlesinger: & so on: but I cannot bring myself to believe that I am making fundamental mistakes: about the Grahams, or the Morgans, or the Walkers or the Frankses: or is it really hopeless to cling to the firm clay models which cannot in principle reflect the minute particles of lives & characters? if so I am certainly doomed & you are deeply right. But until some catastrophe proves [this] to me I'll persist in my coherent fantasy. I wish Prich weren't there at the moment of parting, either in Dumb[arton] Av[enue] or at the Station: he doesn't mean to intervene, but does: he is half-aware of the need not to be there, but sheer physical grossness prevents him from any sort of tact, & so he stands about like a peasant, uneasy, bursting to 'connect' as Mr E. M. Forster wd say,[1] but unable & preventing others from it. For once I felt genuine emotion: but he blocked all possibility of even the most conventional expression of it. I'll call upon you in Feb. if I may.

Shaya

I spoke to Judy M. on the telephone to-day. No symptom of anything; nor did I press. If there is anything wrong I am not to be told casually anyway: rightly perhaps.

TO MENDEL BERLIN
4 January [1952, *manuscript*]

Lowell House, Harvard

Dear Pa,
[...] If Henderson is really resigning All Souls I shall be *ordered* to return

1 'Only connect the prose and the passion, and both will be exalted, and human love will be seen at its height.' E. M. Forster, *Howards End* (London, 1910), chapter 22, 227.

by *my* party, not so much to succeed him, which is not probable and anyway I *really* don't want it; but to keep out some nominee of Rowse: I alone being a possible anti-Rowse party leader. But how *can* I betray Bryn Mawr (to which, by the way, I move on February 5. Till then here.) with their pompous official lectures? but I know I shall be persecuted from All Souls with cables telling me to return quickly: & shall be called a coward if I do not. So the whole holiday may be impossible. Still: let us proceed on the assumption that all goes peacefully. I am *very* well: still 170 lb: still very happy (if only All Souls didn't *nag* like a toothache) & am about to reply to an indignant letter from T. S. Eliot[1] who says I accused him falsely in my J[ewish] C[hronicle] articles which "somebody" sent him. I really am working *so* hard again, I simply cannot write often. And your worries are absurd.

Love
    Isaiah

TO DAVID CECIL

5 January 1952 [*manuscript*]

Lowell House, Harvard

Dear David,
    You are right, a thousand times, but how could I write you when really at the end of the day I felt always, after a lecture + 6 hours of dictation, so limp so dead that I could only go on mechanically dictating, but not write even a fragment of the kind of thing one writes to friends. So I *dictated* [a] letter to Maurice – one has a very stylised sort of correspondence with him – familiar & indiscreet but like wireless bulletins – harsh little "news flashes" – & to Tony[2] etc. but not to Stuart & not to you for the same intimate reason. Then, really half mad with Harvard work & the extreme stuffiness of life I tore away to New York & Washington which I adored as never before. And now this awful All Souls cloud: I am *sure* that even if I could tear myself from my official lectures it would not have the right effect. Stuart has written severely to me: sympathising, saying, quite correctly, that my first instinct would be to make myself as remote as possible from the situation & announce that I am not playing: but that it was my *duty* to resist Rowse etc. Now he *is* right, monomaniacal though this sounds, when he says that I can, & no one else today can, rally *some* of the sans-culottes & other odds & ends into a *bloc*, capable of resisting at least the worst excesses into which A.L.R.'s desire to preserve his *amour propre* & have a spectacular *revanche*[3] as well, may lead him. But *not* if I appear unnaturally early, breaking my engagement

1 See 277–8.
2 Presumably Antony Andrewes (1910–90), Fellow, Pembroke, 1933–46; New College, 1946–77; Wykeham Professor of Ancient History, Oxford, 1953–77.
3 'Revenge'.

here (which I don't think possible anyway) & therefore obviously arrive to be a candidate or do some intrigue. Hence I pray & hope they'll persuade Hubert to *delay*: to resign only in April or June, when I am back. do talk to Stuart: he is quite shrewd about All Souls: & see if you cannot suggest something which does not indeed save me from the need to take *some* part in the hurly-burly, but does free me from having to come dramatically, breaking sacred oaths, & all, I am sure, for nothing. One can achieve some sane result by plodding common sense: but [sc. by] opposing to Rowse's faith in blitz tactics, dull & honest virtue: but I cannot do this if I come scurrying home for a week or so (which, if someone lent me some money I could do) or gave no valid excuse here & suddenly left them all in the most horrible lurch (my lectures are something like Ford lectures:[1] one *couldn't* suddenly say one would not come, 3 weeks before, with the excuse that one has to go home to do some indispensable intrigue) – only if it was all put off till April. Do tell me what to do. I am sure it isn't right to break the engagement here: & best to stop thinking about what one cannot help: but the reproachful voices of the young men will haunt me.

Isaiah

TO MENDEL BERLIN

15 January 1952

[Lowell House, Harvard]

Dear Pa,

[...] As for Eliot, what he minds about is a passage in which I couple him with Koestler[2] and speak of souls filled with terror and clinging to dogma; also in which I say that however unattractive, tactless, aggressive, certain persons may be, neither Eliot nor Plato have any right to put them beyond the bounds of the city. I have now discovered a very aggressive passage on this subject in his own writings and shall write him a very polite letter forgiving him for all this. [...]

Yours, with love

Shaya

---

1 Richard Pares regarded the invitation to deliver the Ford Lectures in English History as 'the highest honour [...] which an English historian can receive'. *King George III and the Politicians: The Ford Lectures Delivered in the University of Oxford 1951–52* (Oxford, 1953), v (Preface).

2 See 278.

TO DAVID CECIL

Postmark [1]9 January 1952 [*manuscript*]

Lowell House, Harvard

Dear David,

I am rather in a stew. The All Souls predicament keeps me awake at nights. Do I *want* to be Warden? no: I would not *mind*: but I would be very glad not to: it is not my thing: if offered it, I would accept: but I would not fight: & anyway it is not likely. But far more than any personal wishes, is the real nausea at the thought of e.g. Rowse enthroned: I really should have to resign I think: & I *don't* dislike him at all: but not at all: but it would be a nuisance & a monstrosity. And with that College – 46 electors are always sheep & geese – one never knows: Curtis[1] & Salter & Falls[2] & Rowse all screeching away: in an open Sparrow–Rowse duel I am, of course, a hot Sparrovian: & anyway I feel it is romantically necessary that Sparrow should have his go: & his Jacobite follower, Lionel Butler,[3] burning bright on the deck of that old fashioned handsome little ship: so let *that* happen. After that, Wheare or Faber[4] perhaps. Stuart thinks I ought to return & prevent disaster: as, without boasting, I suppose I did to some degree in the last phase of the anti-Becket[t] war. Maurice thinks I ought to be pro-Sparrow so long as he is seriously in, & I agree: & have written him so. If they delay, on the 19th Jan, by giving Henderson a leave of absence instead of listening to Rowse in accepting his resignation & proceeding to an immediate election, I'll be back in April & May & say my word for Sparrow: who will be a difficult, irritating, unjust but conceivable Warden. I should not mind Bridges: or Franks. Maurice is madly anti-Franks of course, but *don't* tell him or *anyone* that I've told you so: his views on this are not too relevant: & I should be happy under Oliver: I would be writing so to Brand, who wants him, straightaway only that that would be disloyal to Sparrow with whom I've no wish to quarrel. Of course I should *like* to be left out of all this – my Flexner lectures still in a chaotic state – & more to do – & the torment of intrigue while living in a building with the adversary – but I should burn eternally if I thought my absence helped him into power. [...]

Meanwhile Judy Montagu failed to turn up to lunch with me today: & is said to be disengaged from the hulking brute, her fiancé. I shall find out more about this on Sunday when Joe comes to stay with me. Joe is splendid: article after article through which the fine booming voice is audible. Singing

---

1 Lionel George Curtis (1872–1955), public servant and historian; Fellow of All Souls 1921–55.
2 Cyril Bentham Falls (1888–1971), military correspondent, *The Times*, 1939–53; Chichele Professor of the History of War, Oxford, and Fellow of All Souls 1946–53.
3 Lionel Harry Butler (1923–81), Fellow of All Souls 1946–57; Professor of Medieval History, University of St Andrews, 1955–73; later (1973–81) Principal, Royal Holloway College, London.
4 Geoffrey Cust Faber (1889–1961), barrister and publisher; Fellow of All Souls 1919–61, Estates Bursar 1923–51.

paeans to the great Old Boy, Winston, & damning Acheson & Truman for the hideous squalor of not getting closer to him & making an 'organic' alliance with us & carrying us over all the swamps & mountains: the photographs of Winston + Franks are ludicrous: I look forward to staying with the Frankses in February: he looks on me as a licensed expert in the forbidden fields of personal relations: & almost sees me as a 90ish decadent: I like that: & could live in his vicinity quite gaily. And now I say to you: WRITE.

Isaiah

When All Souls accepted Warden Henderson's resignation, A. L. Rowse became a candidate in the forthcoming election and started canvassing for support; even IB did not escape.

TO A. L. ROWSE

20 January 1952 [*manuscript*]

Lowell House, Harvard

Dear Leslie,

Thank you ever so much for your sweet, candid and altogether good and wholly fair-minded letter: I had heard disquieting rumours, of course, about poor Hubert's health: but it is a terrible business for the College to have to go through again – & for you too – & I hope it will not be so tense as last time. Let me begin by saying that I understand your position well & realize what a heavy, thankless task it was that came down on you from a clear sky; every one knows that what you want to be doing is to *write*: & nobody admires your attitude & practice in this matter more than I do. Indeed I am even now in the throes of the most awful agony of writing lectures for Bryn Mawr to be given in February & then printed, I suppose next year: you are *terribly* right (as dear Lightfoot[1] would say) about the duty to *produce*: & I am really grateful to you both for the passion with which you spoke to me about the proper ends of All Souls & your own part in returning me to the College: I do not suppose that without your generous urgency Humphrey wd have plumped: nor do I forget our conversation that evening in my rooms in New College: we did not convince each other about who shd be Warden: but when I spoke of our own personal relationship I spoke from the heart: I was deeply moved by the occasion and I meant every syllable: whatever happens I shall always be genuinely & deeply fond of you, & happy about your affection for me in which I believe: goodness me! One cannot live for twenty years on & off with someone as wonderful & unique as, if you'll let me say so, you are & not develop a strong & permanent bond. You imply that there

---

1 Revd Robert Henry Lightfoot (1883–1953), Fellow of New College 1921–50; Ireland Professor of Exegesis of Holy Scripture, Oxford, 1934–49.

are those who seek to disrupt this: in a College full of talkers (& inevitably & perhaps usefully so) things are bound to be said & distorted & magnified & invented: if I listened to all that people said I shd have little confidence in human relations in which I believe even more deeply & passionately than even you I think: & All Souls means more to me than any other human institution, & you are an indissoluble part of its image & concept, as you are, I think, to most of us. Of course if you are elected Warden I shall unite loyalty to my affection: so will, I think almost everybody else. All Souls has, I think, a really fantastic hold over the life & being of us all: & in my case private feeling for you is joined to this. I am thoroughly glad to have had the opportunity of saying all this: & that your carrying of the burden during this interim has been a great model of efficient, devoted, selfless service to the College: whatever happens you are a great part of its past & present & future.

Now to the matter in hand: of course I understand about the pressure upon you & your motives for 'standing': you were a very natural candidate last time – more so than I – & your support of Beckett – though I could not follow you – was a great tribute to your desire to realize the College's General Will.[1] And certainly I have no wish to put my name forward this time: Il Collegio [h]a sempre ragione[2] – we must assume that else life is intolerable – there *must* be a unanimous Chapel election & we must accept the College's judgment, & I admired you for being there when Henderson was elected & wd have marched in myself, as I told you, if the College had chosen Beckett: I really do accept the College's judgment absolutely.

I am relieved to be buried in writing here (how wonderful the Widener Library is!) & yet I hate not being in All Souls now; I loathe the hurly burly, the tension, the looks, yet when a crisis is on one ought to be where life is intensest & not stay out & let things roll off one: but of course I shall stay here now: & I'll write to Simon as you propose when I have been told the dates i.e. when it is clear that I cannot be there to vote. What *will* the College do? will it again seek peace and the tertius gaudens?[3] both you & John are so intolerant of fools & mediocrities: he niggles & you demand so much from life, bold colours & flashing swords and see no reason for putting up with tiresome sans culottes or grey hacks or suffer inferiors – does the College want a heroic Warden: or will it again seek security & compromise. I am secretly glad to be out of it all: I really do think you have behaved most beautifully since the election & I send you all my warmest personal blessings.

Love,

Isaiah

---

1 The General Will as formulated by Rousseau represents a unanimous (and correct) decision about the common good reached by a body politic blessed with perfect knowledge, powers of reasoning and public spirit.

2 'The College is always right'.

3 'Rejoicing third'; a term normally attributed to the sociologist Georg Simmel, denoting a third party who exploits competition between two others.

PS I still remember with pleasure your epigram about Wheare as the 'Adams[1] de nos jours' & I look on W. Adams, as you do I think, with real love & respect: and I am v. fond of Wheare & think him a wise man.

TO DAVID CECIL

29 January [1952, *manuscript*]

As from Bryn Mawr College

Dear David,

I cannot tell you how much moved, how deeply & permanently moved, I was by your letter. I read it once & then not again because I was, for once, too ému[2] (as Rowse wd say) by its sentiments & ideas, & despite the great, & as I knew, sincere compliments which it contained, I believed every word. And do still. You are perfectly right about me, more so than anyone else I've ever known & I am convinced that your advice is utterly right & shall follow it. I don't mean your estimate of my capacities: even allowing for friendship, kindness, your feeling about my vulnerability at the moment, your overestimate is vast: I wish I cd attain to Pater's[3] intellectual or Moore's[4] moral knee if you know what I mean. However you are right about my being what a schoolmaster of mine once called an opsimate: I *am* a late developer: slow to start, difficult to uproot. And I *am* in a critical phase: & it *is* now or never: you are quite right. And here I am trying to write this book on political ideas, & it is coming out all awry – sentimental, vague, clumsy, soft, unscholarly, a mass of verbiage & dough unseasoned, no sharp points, only occasionally little gleams of what I thought I said, what I thought I wanted to say. However I persist. I don't know what the lectures will sound like, but there *will*, unless I fall ill or die, be a book. Not very good, less so than I can do on the Russians. But I must get the circulation of blood going: I accepted the lectures because I knew that would lay the foundation of a book – & having dictated 150.000 words, I suppose there is: I shd rather like Cole's professorship at Oxford: perhaps the book will help with that: I am being quite frank. About All Souls: of course I do not, really not, want to be Warden, quite apart from its impossibility. I am not being unduly modest: I think I wd do not much worse than some of them: but I wd really rather not: if I were offered it I might be vain enough to take it: but it wd be a mistake, I am sure, in the quite short run, at least for me (how monomaniac & absurd I am being!) – what frightens me is one thing only & that is if Rowse is appointed. I do not think it impossible: he has flattered them so long, so heavily, so

---

1 (William) George Stewart Adams (1874–1966), Gladstone Professor of Political Theory and Institutions, Oxford, 1912–33; Warden, All Souls, 1933–45 (L1 703).

2 'Affected'.

3 Walter Horatio Pater (1839–1894), critic of literature and art, essayist and novelist.

4 G. E. Moore was the philosopher of the Bloomsbury group.

obviously; it works. Sparrow some of them really fear & hate quite absurdly, but they do, and since he is dreadfully obstinate & of no judgment where his own affairs are concerned, he may drive them into Rowse's arms. Wheare I wd accept with relief (Sparrow of course) & *anybody* else: I agree it doesn't matter all that much: dim or good, the College will go on, I shall try & write something & live a life. But can I go on there under Rowse? Can I? Will it not be too maddening for him in the first place, & then for me? he doesn't *hate* me, I am sure, but I *am* a thorn: I *cannot* make myself cosy with him, not cosy as he likes it, not the giggly, silly – old Oxford crumpets & Jacob & English glories & all the rest of it. And this is *all* that frightens me. Quinton[1] wrote me that the Jun. Fellows wd see to it that nothing of this sort wd happen: that his campaign is absurd; that his lies wd be exploded swiftly, etc. but they are very innocent & not at all politically shrewd. He did really quite well with the dreadfully unpromising Beckett last time, & (it sounds maniacal again) if I hadn't intervened, B. wd have been elected. I almost regret my interference now. Beckett is null & so therefore preferable to Leslie. If I knew *that* was impossible I'd forget all about events at All Souls & get on with my work fiercely. As it is, by huge efforts of will, I do for 3 or 4 hours at a time, & then start worrying. Stuart Hampshire, dear goosey Stuart writes me alarmist letters which I do not believe to be without substance: he is a good observer & a poor politician (he thinks he is a wonderful one) so I get fearfully fussed & send off wires to Goronwy etc. & then feel a fool. And go to New York for 1 evening & dine between Laelia Westminster[2] & Barbara Agar[3] & opposite Cecil Beaton[4] & Baba Metcalfe[5] & feel a little better. This must sound genuinely foolish to you. You say you've written me a Roy like letter – I am really *enormously* grateful: for as I said, I accept every word: & I am promising to follow it – no one has ever been so disinterested (you see my meaning, I don't mean detached) or right about me: one always knows when the bell rings sharply & at once: in return I am saying to you what I haven't said to anyone, about the ups & downs of my foolish moods. If I felt secure about Rowse *not* being Warden, a vast load would roll from me & I should be free & happy. As it is I don't know what to do. If I came home suddenly I *think* I could prevent his election & put in Wheare, tho' not, I think, Sparrow. (I think he is too hated by those who really hate him: no one else in the last election was

---

1 Anthony Meredith Quinton (b. 1925), later (1982) Baron Quinton, philosopher; Fellow of All Souls 1949–55, of New College 1955–78; later (1978–87) President, Trinity.
2 Loelia (*sic*) Mary Grosvenor (1902–93), daughter of 1st Baron Sysonby, wife 1930–47 of the 2nd Duke of Westminster; later (1969) married Sir Martin Lindsay.
3 Barbara Agar (1898–1981), daughter of Sir Edwin Lutyens and formerly stepmother of IB's Oxford friend David Wallace (killed in action in Greece in 1944), had married the US-born newspaper editor, historian and writer Herbert Sebastian Agar (1897–1980) in 1945.
4 Cecil Walter Hardy Beaton (1904–80), photographer and designer.
5 Lady Alexandra Naldera ('Baba') Metcalfe (1904–95), daughter of the 1st Marquess Curzon of Kedleston, wife 1925–55 of Major Edward Dudley ('Fruity') Metcalfe; sister-in-law and former mistress of Sir Oswald Mosley.

openly called worthless, cruel etc.) – yet, of course, I *shan't* come back: if I were a genuine man of action, on a large unself-conscious scale, I should. But it is too late for me to do so: I feel like Dr Brüning faced with Hitler:[1] I cannot do a Blücher[2] to change the image. Anything to set my mind at rest about the one contingency I shd be touchingly grateful for. So do enquire. And if the news is "bad" – make someone – Hants or Goronwy *telephone* me at Harvard (tho' I leave it for Bryn Mawr on the 8th Feb. But I'll give them my Bryn M. address & telephone: they'll forward everything) I think I might be able to advise *ad hoc*, & in an eleventh hour situation, anything helps. They all – my A. Souls friends, seem made of cardboard & paper to me, & collapse at the slightest breath of wind. I don't think myself all that tough & strong, but I don't crumple as easily as they seem to – particularly the operatic figure of Goronwy – Papageno[3] – frightened by Monostatos Rowse. Am I making fantastically heavy weather? Not in my scale of values, really, you know. But I must stop. I've written Faber & Brand what I think about ALR[owse], moderately but firmly. I have written in reply to a canvassing letter from himself – imagine it! – extolling our splendid private relationship, with very few words about his ambitions – but he knows I am not for him. And he wd take Wheare: or Wilberforce:[4] or anybody but Sparrow (or I think me). If there is a real danger of him, they, my allies, must drop out & go for a safe mediocrity *at once*. Do they realise this? or are they waffling & divided & unable to speak & gentlemanly? One real person – you, I, Hubert, – not born for College politics – let alone those who are, would make a gigantic difference. That's all that is my wish now. And in 10 days I shall lunch with Auden, who is dotty to a degree. But you see why you must write.

Much love
Isaiah

I really am most infinitely & unforgettingly grateful to you for your letter & shall remember it forever.

IB's articles on 'Jewish Slavery and Emancipation' in the Jewish Chronicle *had prompted the following letter of protest from T. S. Eliot:*

I have read with much interest and respect four articles in the *Jewish Chronicle* which were sent to me, whether at your suggestion or not I do not know. Beyond thanking you my only reason for writing is in relation to the fourth

1 Brüning's attempts to prevent Hitler seizing power largely involved constructing political coalitions.
2 Wipert von Blücher (1883–1963), German Ambassador to Finland 1935–44, for several years successfully persuaded the Finns that as an ally Germany was preferable to the Soviet Union.
3 The comic bird-catcher in Mozart's opera *The Magic Flute*, whose bizarre appearance puts to flight the brutal Monostatos, thereby saving the heroine Pamina from his unwelcome attentions.
4 Richard Orme Wilberforce (1907–2003), later (1964) Baron Wilberforce, barrister; later (1961–4) High Court Judge and (1964–82) Lord of Appeal; Fellow of All Souls 1932–1990.

article. Whether you are right in general in associating me here with Arthur Koestler, I do not know, but it seems to me that you have drawn inferences about my views which do not seem to me to follow from my few words here and there in connection with this subject. I am certainly not an advocate of the emigration of all Jews from everywhere to Israel, and I certainly should not take that view even if there was room in that country for everybody. I think it would be a great pity if the Jewish community of Western Europe and America were parted from those countries. Where you seem to me particularly to have read into my words something I am surprised to find is in your remarks at the head of the fourth column of your article on page 8 of the issue for 12 October. Your sentence would appear to suggest that I have either made explicitly these derogatory criticisms or that they can be reasonably inferred from something which I have said. This is highly misleading and I certainly have had no awareness of wishing to place anybody, even if I held these views, 'beyond the borders of the city'.

What seems to be easily overlooked is that for me the Jewish problem is not a racial problem at all but a religious problem. This is a very different problem and I do not know whether there is any solution for it.[1]

IB held his ground:

TO T. S. ELIOT

30 January 1952 [*manuscript*]

As from Bryn Mawr College

Dear Eliot,

[...] And now to the substance of the articles. I have not a copy of them here, in this splendid Northampton wilderness,[2] for I only received one: & mislaid it. But I think I remember sufficiently what I said in them. And I must continue to apologize (but not for long) – I think I spoke both of Arthur Koestler & of yourself as 'minds filled with terror & attached to dogma' or something of the sort. This seems to me now very unwarranted & arrogant: I do not know how truth in such matters is ever discovered: and to attribute states of mind or heart or spirit to other human beings in this rough & ready fashion seems to me offensive & irresponsible: when the articles appear (as they were originally meant to) as a connected single essay in a volume to be published for the University of Jerusalem, I shall certainly try to delete this passage: & remove all proper names;[3] you have been kind enough not

1 Letter of 28 November 1951.
2 He was staying at Edgar Wind's home in Northampton, Massachusetts.
3 Square brackets in the following extract from the *Jewish Chronicle* indicate the cuts which IB made for publication in *Hebrew University Garland*: 'Fearful thinkers, with minds seeking salvation in religious or political dogma, souls filled with terror, [like T. S. Eliot and Arthur Koestler,] may wish to eliminate such ambiguous elements in favour of a more clear-cut structure, and they are, in this respect, true children of the new age which, with its totalitarian systems, has tried to institute just such an order among human beings, and sort them out neatly, each to his own category,

to rub this point in: but I can plead only haste and carelessness on my part; published statements are fair objects of comment & inference: but in the passage which associates your name with that of Arthur Koestler I seem to myself now to have perpetrated an aspersion. This I shall attempt to remedy: indeed if you would wish me to do so, I shd be ready and not unhappy to write to the Jewish Chronicle[1] & make public the view I have tried to state.

With the real substance of your rejoinder I do not, however, think that I agree. When I gave a list of annoying characteristics which the Jews have, I think, been thought to possess, & which indeed some of them may in fact have, I did not, of course, wish to imply that you had ever so spoken of them: & if I conveyed that impression I must correct that too: I thought that in associating your name, this time with Plato's, I had avoided that danger:[2] after all Plato could not have wished to segregate or displace Jews: although I cannot think that he would have got on with either St. Paul or Spinoza; but that is, I fear, beside the point. And now I ought to explain how I came to have an impression of your attitude to the "Jewish problem". Besides what you speak of, in your letter, as your "few words here and there', both in prose and in verse, the passage which lingered in my mind was, as I expect you will have guessed, that which is to be found (on p. 20 of the 1934 American edition) of your Virginia University Lectures – "After Strange Gods". You are there discussing, if I remember the text correctly (I have copied out the reference, but have not the text here) the virtues of a traditional society, and you think it should not be too heterogeneous or mixed and you say "reasons of race and religion make any large number of free-thinking Jews undesirable' – if, that is, the kind of society to which you are favourable is to be maintained. Now it seemed fairly plain to me that you were, on this occasion at least, thinking of the Jews as a race & not solely as a religious community: for one of the reasons against "any large number" is explicitly stated to be "racial" as well as religious; moreover 'free-thinking' can

and has suppressed civil liberties in varying degrees in order to achieve this purpose, which is sometimes defended on ultra-rationalist, scientific grounds. [Doubtless Eliot and Koestler would protest at being associated with each other or with the *Zeitgeist* in this way. Eliot particularly abhors societies organised on a rationalistic or scientific basis; Koestler is foremost among the enemies of totalitarianism. And yet,] to protest about a section of the population merely because it is felt to be an uncosy element in society, to order it to alter its outlook or get out – while the psychological explanation of this tone may be obvious enough (particularly when the accuser is himself prey to doubts and suffering) – is nevertheless a kind of petty tyranny, and derives ultimately from the conviction that human beings have no right to behave foolishly or inconsistently or vulgarly, and that society has the right to try and rid itself by humane means, but rid itself nevertheless, of such persons, although they are neither criminals nor lunatics nor in any sense a danger to the lives or liberties of their fellows.' Towards the end of his life IB concluded that he had been 'excessively polite – almost obsequious – to Eliot' (note to Henry Hardy, March 1996) and requested the reinstatement of the cut passages should the essay be reprinted.

1 He appears not to have done so.

2 For the *Jewish Chronicle* version see 283/2. For *Hebrew University Garland* IB replaced Eliot with Maurras; Eliot is restored alongside Maurras in POI.

scarcely be applied to a religious community. After all "Free-thinking Roman Catholics' or "Free-thinking Baptists' or 'F.-T. Moslems' seems to me an almost meaningless phrase (you must forgive this lapse into philosophical 'Sprache-analyse'[1] – to a cobbler there's nothing like leather – I seem to have to continue to apologize, alas –) whereas 'Free-thinking Frenchman' or 'Free-thinking Negro' seems quite natural. This made me think that 'Jew' was a term more analogous to 'Frenchman' than to 'Catholic' in your usage. This seems to me quite natural and proper, for I certainly think the Jews to be other than only a religious community, though what they are, & how to be described, I should find it very difficult, perhaps impossible to say at all clearly. But since you say in your letter that the 'Jewish problem is not' for you 'a racial problem at all, but a religious problem' I infer, I hope correctly, that whether or not you think the Jews to be a race in fact, it is only as a religious group that they constitute a problem. But in the early 'thirties, the Jews found themselves ill treated by Hitler and his followers, and outside Germany too, for 'reasons of race' rather than religion: the topic began to be more widely discussed than ever before; the question of whether the Jews were a race, and whether, if so, it was right to expel, imprison, torture them etc. became, to say the least, a central issue over which there was acute disagreement in Europe and beyond. And since this was the time at which you spoke of 'reasons of race', what could I think but that you were using those words in the way in which it was most common to use them at that time? and that you thought it undesirable for large numbers of Jews to be found in the midst of relatively homogeneous Christian societies (I do not know if you thought this about groups of Moslems too e.g. in Yugoslavia) if they were 'free-thinking'. Of course I did not, & do not think that you were or are advocating methods of barbarism in any circumstances, or used against anyone; and of course I believe you without question, when you say in your letter that you do not favour the mass emigration of Jews from Western Europe, or America to Israel; but am I profoundly mistaken if I think that, at any rate in 1934, you thought it a pity that large groups of 'free-thinking Jews' should complicate the lives of otherwise fairly homogeneous Anglo-Saxon Christian communities? and that it were better otherwise? and that if this could be done by humane means, and persuasion and without coercion, it would be better for such communities if their Jewish neighbours, or a sufficiently large proportion of them, were put 'beyond the borders of the city'? If my interpretation of your views as held then is erroneous I am very sorry; and if you said that it was so, I shd be very ready to make public (or private) amends; and if my interpretation is not incorrect in substance, but you have altered your views: or in some way modified them, I shd be grateful to be put right: and suitably contrite if told that I should not make rash inferences

1 'Speech analysis'.

from your views of 1934 to your attitude to-day. And when the articles come
to be reprinted as a chapter of a composite book, I should of course be only
too anxious to emend the text accordingly. But have I been unperceptive,
unfair, slapdash, stupid? perhaps. Certainly I should never have published
that sentence about Koestler & yourself: & I shall eliminate it.

I hope that you will forgive me for writing at such length in reply to your
charming and courteous letter which is more than I deserved. But in addition to the intrinsic fascination (and importance) which the topic has always
held for me, I am genuinely anxious not to misrepresent anyone, least of
all someone for whom, for all my disagreement with this or that political
opinion, I feel the greatest admiration, respect, and if you will forgive me
(this is my last attempt at apology) for saying so, personal liking.

yrs v. sincerely

Isaiah Berlin

P.S. I apologize for the length & repetitiveness of this screed. I have not read
it: for I do not think that if I did, I should be able to improve it – I wish I
wrote better, or at least more briefly. I.B.

Eliot replied at length:

[...] The only thing that really distressed me, in the last of your four articles,
was a paragraph which listed some of the grossest prejudices against Jews, in
such a context as (it seemed to me) to lead the reader to infer either that I had
been guilty of enunciating them somewhere, or that my acceptance of them
could legitimately be deduced from my writings. I could not believe that you
thought that I held these views; but I was afraid that your readers might make
this assumption. I think I have the copy of the *Chronicle* at my office; and if I
find it I will send you the passage in question so that you may judge for yourself
whether I was justified in this apprehension. I am however glad that I did not
write a letter to the Editor: when I know and respect the author of a misleading
statement I prefer to take the question up with him.

As for any parallel between my views and Koestler's, I have no first-hand
knowledge of Koestler's views on this subject, and so was simply surprised
to find myself bracketed with him, and felt that there must have been some
misunderstanding.

What makes your letter useful to me, however, is that you do make a very
cogent point about one sentence of mine which occurs in the Virginia Lectures
which were published under the title of *After Strange Gods*. This is, in fact, an
essay with which I was never much pleased; and some years ago I instructed my
firm to let it go out of print. In particular, I felt that what I had written about
Hardy and Lawrence (as well as my treatment of some of my friends) was
much too harsh and violent – it approximated to invective rather than criticism.
(I am not wholly repentant about Hardy, but I have felt it my business to make
some amends to Lawrence.) I say this not apologetically but contritely, and it

has no direct bearing on the sentence in question. Except that it goes to explain my putting something I believed to be true, in the manner most likely to invite misunderstanding. It is not a good thing to trail one's coat, or to invite attack by deliberately saying what will be misunderstood.

The sentence of which you complain (with justice) would of course never have appeared at all at that time, if I had been aware of what was going to happen, indeed had already begun, in Germany. Or, if I had wished to say the same thing, I would have been careful to say it at such length that there could be no possible doubt as to what I meant. I still do not understand why the word 'race' occurs in the sentence, because my emphasis was on the adjective *free-thinking*.

'Race' seems to me a biological concept: the sociological concept is 'culture'. The latter is what interests me. Whether 'the Jews' are a race is disputable: but undoubtedly Judaism means a culture. I do not think that the term 'race' is altogether meaningless, and I am not convinced by biologists who maintain that because blood-groups are distributed irrespective of race, race is of no importance. There appear to be 'inferior races' (black-fellows, veddahs, todas etc. and some Dravidian tribes) but a great deal of what is called 'racial inferiority' or 'racial superiority' seems to me a question of *which type is most successful under the conditions prevailing*. There was a time when the Irish were more civilised than the English. This has nothing to do with the Jews. But crude minds tend to turn sociological realities into biological fictions, as the Nazis did. And I suspect that the assertion of *racial* superiority will follow from the belief amongst Russians that Communism, because it has first been realised (in the way in which it has been realised) in Russia, implies the superiority of the Muscovite (even when his leaders come from alien provinces of Russia) over everybody else.

Now my thesis in *Notes Towards the Definition of Culture* is that the proper sociological concept is not 'race' but 'culture'; and that a 'culture' is developed with a particular religion, and cannot justify its continuance apart from that religion. Can the Jewish Faith survive? From a Christian point of view, the Jewish Faith is finished because it finds its continuation in the Catholic Faith. Theoretically, the only proper consummation is that all Jews should become Catholic Christians. The trouble is, that this ought to have happened long ago: partly because of the stiffneckedness of your people, and largely* because of the misbehaviour of those who called themselves Christians, this did not happen. The present situation is difficult, not only because this did not happen. It is difficult, because large numbers of Jews, in Europe and America, have ceased to be Jews in faith, without becoming Christians. But those who lose their faith, remain attached to their culture, because the culture is the body and the faith the soul, and (as Aldous Huxley once said) we needs must love the lower when we see it.

Not that the Jewish culture is something that we should gladly give up. Its disappearance would be a loss to the world. What should have happened was an integration of Jew and Gentile in Christianity, in which each contributed from his culture to make a new culture common to both.

It is much easier to lose our faith than our culture. One is in our mind and heart, the other in our marrow. There is an illusion of meeting when both Gentiles and Jews abandon their faith. But this abandonment is more deadly for the Jew. For the Gentile is still in a world which retains some connection with the faith which it has, piece by piece, abandoned: the Jew, in this abandoned Gentile World, is more completely cut off from the source of his 'culture' than is the Gentile who is still in his own world, however degraded. This is what my adjective 'free-thinking' implies.

The reconciliation of Gentile and Jew in a world in which both repudiated their antecedents is a possibility, but means, I think, a reconciliation on a lower plane of culture: the common culture will be an inferior culture. The only possibilities are: that Jews should maintain their own culture by maintaining their own religion (and I do not see why there should not be Jewish communities in a Western civilisation) or else that they should be assimilated completely – affirming that the only real assimilation would be by acceptance of Christianity.

Perhaps this is enough for the moment. But I should be glad to continue this conversation, at such intervals as our respective engagements impose. [. . .]

* perhaps chiefly! The apportionment is not immediately relevant.[1]

IB did not respond, despite a follow-up letter from Eliot:

I don't want to be tiresome, but having found the article in question, I want to send you the relevant passage.[2] It doesn't seem to me that I gain any benefit from the company of Plato! who was not concerned with this particular problem; and I do think that the reader might very naturally infer, as I said, either that I had uttered these censures at one time or another, or else that it could be taken for granted that I endorsed them. The next sentence might be construed in two ways, as meaning either that I object to Jews because they behave like apes and parrots, or that I object to them because they don't.

There are of course two distinct questions:

1. whether you have interpreted me correctly, and

2. whether you give the impression of saying something different from what you meant.[3]

---

1 Letter of 9 February 1952.
2 'An American wit once declared that the Jews were a peculiar people only because they are just like everybody else, only more so. There is a bitter truth in this remark. Doubtless no one likes to be aped, to see their characteristics exaggerated to the point, sometimes, of caricature. But to use force to prevent people from doing so, however irritating their behaviour, is nevertheless an infringement of minimal human liberties. To be over-sceptical or over-critical or insensitive or over-sensitive; to lack dignity, or practise vulgar ostentation; to be obsequious or neurotically aggressive, or lack a sense of moral or aesthetic measure or certain forms of spiritual tact, is doubtless unattractive and thoroughly regrettable, but it is not a crime, and neither Plato nor Eliot, nor any of their followers, have a right to place men, for this alone, beyond the borders of the city. If the Jews are to continue to suffer for failing to please their neighbours by behaving like apes and parrots, they will at least do so individually.' *Jewish Chronicle*, 12 October 1951, 8; cf. POI 183–4.
3 Letter of 2 March 1952.

TO ANNA KALLIN

3 February 1952

Lowell House, Harvard

Dear N,

This is but a hurried note – I am in a state of chaos, despondency, gloom, terror not on account of All Souls, which after going rather badly for a bit is suddenly going better, but on account of having to move with lightning speed from the handsome suite which belongs to Dr Brüning who suddenly returned from Cologne and is moving in on me very much as he was moved in on himself by Von Papen[1] exactly twenty years ago (you will remember when the Prussian Premier on the telephone said to Von Papen, 'I consider that I can only yield to force' and Von Papen answered, 'I should be only too pleased to oblige you in this regard.') So, I am packing my things in a panic, the Bryn Mawr lectures are in a worse mess than ever, the world is dark, there is little hope. Your *Podorozhnik*[2] is like a golden shower in the midst of all this and I am most grateful to you for it, most touched, on the point of tears. Yet I cannot review Kennan's book[3] for I have not read it, I shall not read it for a month or two, I do not know about American foreign policy in the last seven years, I can do nothing until summer and that, I am sure, will be far too late (I hope). As for Utis, do anything you like with it, read it aloud, get Michael Tippett[4] to set it to slow, gloomy, 'inward' music, get Mr Heller[5] to meditate about it as a phenomenon of the discord of our time – in short, anything you please except reveal my identity (the consequences in Moscow really would be tragic) – or get Carr to attack it. But even the last I would not severely mind except that I do not really want controversy to which I cannot reply. You had better negotiate about copyright etc. with *Foreign Affairs* yourself and ask the editor formally to ask the author's permission without revealing that you know who he is. And that even though at least 100 persons in this country must know the facts. And now I must set off for what the Vice Chancellor of Oxford calls the 'girls' school' and say those golden words which I hope to get recorded for your benefit. [...]

I stayed a splendid week with the divine, never-enough-to-be-thanked, Edgar Wind, who gave me his own study for eight days and protected me beautifully and sweetly while I worked on the first two lectures. There is nothing I would not do to get him his Cambridge job. I have written to

1 Franz Joseph Hermann Michael Maria von Papen (1879–1969), German army officer, diplomat and politician who briefly succeeded Brüning as Chancellor in 1932 (and was later influential in bringing Hitler to power).
2 *Plantain*, a book of poems published in 1921 by Anna Akhmatova.
3 *American Diplomacy 1900–1950* (Chicago, 1951).
4 Michael Kemp Tippett (1905–98), composer.
5 Erich Heller (1911–90), scholar of German literature and philosophy, born in the Sudetenland, naturalised British, moved to US; Professor of German, University of Wales (Swansea), 1950–9, Northwestern University 1960–7.

[Richard] Kahn and I know he is to stay with Noel in the summer – what else can I do?

Yours ever,

Шая[1]

TO EDGAR WIND

[Early February 1952, *manuscript*]

Bryn Mawr College

Dear Edgar,

Even you, with all your courtesy and good will, must have wondered how I, not by nature very rude or very dead to feeling, could have borne not to have written to you to thank you for one of the greatest services which one human being can confer on another. I can only plead the 'natural' chaos of my life. I went to New York: I spoke: I returned to Cambridge: all was disorder: Dr Brüning was unexpectedly returning: I was unexpectedly turned out of his rooms: in the attic in which I found myself there was no paper, no ink, & I am easily discouraged: I could think neither of Herder nor not think of him: I had to wind up my Harvard affairs: complete the examination: say good bye to my associates: & all this in an atmosphere of six swords of Damocles, in the form of lectures, not merely threatening to fall, but actually certain to; so I did nothing but pack, unpack, repack, & spin in an endless squirrel-like purposeless circle. I have not done a stroke of real work since I left you: that is I have read books, reread what I did in your house, etc. but some peculiar sense of general insecurity – of inability to begin when one does not know how long one will have – has stopped me from all else. I feel like a Tolstoy character: why am I? are any of the things I do worth doing? why do people who *know* that they are not nevertheless pretend that they are? Yet are there *other* 'really' important things? Why should I stand on a platform & pronounce in an indistinct & nervous voice words which persons present have no wish to hear except either (a) out of routine (b) to kill an evening (c) malicious hope that one will not do well (d) as an acte gratuit?[2] etc. etc. etc. all this has much increased since coming here. Nahm[3] is quite kind in a very believable manner: Mrs Manning (née Taft)[4] patronising: (at this moment Prof. Nahm came in. I went to the reception in my "honour". It was very like what such things are. But Miss McBride is a female Conant: good, unpretentious American timber: the best material

---

1 'Shaya'.

2 'Impulsive, unreasoning act'.

3 Milton Charles Nahm (1903–91), Professor of Philosophy (and Chairman of the Department of Philosophy), Bryn Mawr College, 1946–72.

4 Helen Herron Manning (1891–1987), daughter of US President William Howard Taft; Dean, Bryn Mawr College, 1917–44 (Acting President 1919–20, 1929–30), Professor of History 1941–57.

this country provides: for use, not enjoyment; but like wood or leather: not a noble metal, but not plastic either.) [...]

yrs
    Isaiah

TO ANNA KALLIN
    13 February 1952

                                        Bryn Mawr College
Dear Nyuta,
    I am installed at Bryn Mawr College in 'dignity and peace' (as M. Daladier[1] once promised the Italians on the Riviera that they would live if they resisted Mussolini in 1939. They didn't; about dignity they do not care, as for peace they do not regard war as identical with peace). [...]
    And now something else: I have delivered my first lecture[2] in the Flexner series here – it was a monstrosity which lasted for sixty-five minutes and did not correspond to either my text or the scattered notes which in their turn had little to do with the text. I thought it dreadful but there were those who courteously disagreed (they are all much too kind and very impressionable). [...] ⟨But it really is very nice here – a kind of aseptic Swiss atmosphere, away from everything whatever with neutral looking plastic ladies in cellophane cooing gently over library desks. I see the point of an abbé in a convent. [...]⟩
    IB

The impression created by IB's lectures at Bryn Mawr was vividly recorded by one of his secretaries there, Lelia Brodersen,[3] in a letter to a friend:

At the end of last week Mrs Manning called me & boomingly inquired whether I could assist international relations to the extent of helping Isaiah Berlin with his correspondence. [...] she thought the most important thing was to be able to understand him [...]. The previous incumbent, she said casually, had broken down & never returned. I said I would try. Shortly thereafter he called. He has an Oxford accent, a lisp, an inability to say r, & the most inconceivably rapid "delivery" that I have ever heard outside of a patter song. [...] we arranged that I was to appear at 11 Tuesday morning, Monday evening I went to his lecture on Fichte & was appalled. He bowed hastily, established himself behind the lectern, fixed his eyes on a point slightly to his right & over the heads of the audience, & began as if a plug had been pulled out. For precisely an hour, with scarcely a second's pause & with really frightful speed, he poured forth what was evidently a brilliant lecture from the little I could catch of it. He never shifted the direction of his gaze once. Without a pause he swayed back & forth, so far

1 Édouard Daladier (1884–1970), Prime Minister of France 1933, 1934 and 1938–40.
2 'Nature and the Science of Politics', on 11 February.
3 Lelia Brodersen (1912–2006), at this time a graduate supplementing her income by secretarial work; later chief clinical psychologist of the child guidance clinic at Bryn Mawr College.

that each time one was sure that he was going to topple over, either forward or backward. His right hand he held palm up in the palm of his left hand, & for the whole hour shook both hands violently up & down as if he were trying to dislodge something from them. It was scarcely to be believed. And all the time this furious stream of words, in beautifully finished sentences but without pauses except for certain weird signals of transition such as " ... & so it is evident that Kant's idea of freedom was in some ways very dissimilar to the idea of freedom which Fichte held, WELL!" I was exhausted at the end, & yet I am sure that if ever I saw & heard anyone in a true state of inspiration it was then. It is really a tragedy that communication is almost impossible.[1]

"WELL!" On Tuesday, typewriter in hand & despair in heart, I arrived at the Deanery, where he is staying. The rest is anticlimactic. I took his letters directly on the typewriter, which forced him to make pauses, since the noise of the machine forced itself upon him; he is happy to have things struck over, x'ed out, etc., & will sign literally anything; his letters are charming & occasionally pathetic; & he is movingly shy, polite, helpless, & apologetic. And – on Thursday, when I went again, & he was shortly called to the telephone, I started to read a reprint which he had lying on his desk – "Lev Tolstoy's Historical Scepticism." I was at once caught up into it; & when he came back I asked him if he could spare it for a few days. "Oh, take it, take it," he said, fumbling madly among his papers. "I have them to send to people – take it – keep it." So I did, & when I had finished it I settled once & for all into the impression that here was a near-great, if not a really great man.[2]

TO HERBERT HART

15 February 1952 [*manuscript card*]

Bryn Mawr College

Oh I *am* glad!*[3] it is the first good thing – good really without qualification, like the G. Will,[4] – that has happened in Oxford since God knows when: I feel like Mrs Fisher,[5] hugging myself with the repulsive gesture & dancing like Hitler at the news of the surrender of Paris: these are the ungainly A.

---

1 IB described the lectures to Anna Kallin: 'these are improvised performances, with no notes of any kind to help me, since if I look at notes the propellor ceases to revolve and the machine crashes immediately – delivered at the rate of 243 words per minute, and at total variance both with the typescript, first draft, of the book, and the ad hoc notes which I do not in fact use' (26 February 1952). To his biographer he later explained: 'I fixate myself on some still point and then just emit. [...] my lectures always take the same form. I make fifty pages of notes, which I throw away [...]. These I boil down to about ten pages. The ten pages I boil down to a page and a half, mainly of headings, [...] in case I am struck with aphasia, and then I don't look, and wind myself up like a clockwork clock, and proceed to the end. The relief of its being over is enormous.' MI Tape 6.
2 To Sheema Z. Buehne, postmarked 2 March 1952 [Lelia Brodersen].
3 Herbert Hart had just been elected Professor of Jurisprudence at Oxford.
4 Kant's Good Will, mentioned in the first sentence of the main text of *The Groundwork of the Metaphysic of Morals*.
5 Lettice Fisher (1875–1956), née Ilbert, historian and economist; wife of H. A. L. Fisher.

Huxley[1] images I have; but the ghost in the machine[2] is rejoicing in a nobler & sublimer fashion. Your first task will have to be to review the remains of Prof Isaac Husik,[3] edited by *Nahm* (who is a pompous ass, pedantic, v. stupid, & ludicrous but has a heart of gold & is a perfectly nice man) for *Mind*: subjects: Aristotle: Gersonides (at last!) & Kelsen + Stammler: I have a lot to ask you about the last. love to Jenifer.

Isaiah

* your inaugural? 'From Austin to Austin?'[4] oh I see the Univ. School so clearly: 'Taxonomists & Analysts: all Cupboards Swept & Garnered'. Still I wish I were there.

TO KARL POPPER[5]

19 February 1952

Bryn Mawr College

My dear Karl,

I am most grateful to you for your letter and invitation[6] and I feel genuinely honoured by being asked to deliver the first of a series of new lectures which you have established. I wish I could feel more enthusiasm about the epony-mous hero[7] who presides over this activity – there is something genuinely repellent about that cold, yet sometimes embarrassingly and touchingly yet grotesquely passionate, little man, so jealous, so pedantic, so monomaniacal, so full of insights, so learned and so blind; but above all irredeemably absurd, more absurd even than Spencer[8] at a time when there was no need to be

---

1 Aldous Leonard Huxley (1894–1963), novelist and essayist, whose 'squalid & nauseating' images were not to IB's taste (L1 172).

2 The (dismissive) term used by Gilbert Ryle in his *Concept of Mind* (London, 1949) for the mind as seen in Descartes' theory of mind–body dualism.

3 Isaac Husik (1876–1939), philosopher, translator and Jewish historian; Professor of Philosophy, University of Pennsylvania, 1922–39. His posthumous *Philosophical Essays: Ancient, Mediaeval and Modern*, edited by Milton Nahm and Leo Strauss (Oxford 1952), includes articles on Aristotle, on Gersonides (Levi ben Gershon, 1288–1344), Jewish philosopher and mathematician born in France, and on the legal philosophies of Hans Kelsen (1881–1973), Austrian jurist, Professor of Political Science, University of California, Berkeley, 1945–52, and of the German neo-Kantian legal philosopher Rudolf Stammler (1856–1938).

4 John Austin (1790–1859), British jurist, and J. L. Austin, linguistic philosopher and Hart's Oxford colleague, were both major influences on Hart's work.

5 Karl Raimund Popper (1902–94), Austrian-born philosopher; Professor of Logic and Scientific Method, London (LSE), 1949–69.

6 To give the first Auguste Comte Memorial Trust Lecture in 1953.

7 (Isidore Marie) Auguste François Xavier Comte (1798–1857), French positivist philosopher; pioneer of sociology and founder of a 'religion of humanity'.

8 Herbert Spencer (1820–1903), philosopher and liberal political thinker, proponent of a theory of social evolution, and originator of the term 'survival of the fittest'.

absurd in order to be heard – when Marx and Taine[1] and Michelet[2] and Mill and Renan[3] and Herzen and Schopenhauer[4] – not to speak of the scientists or novelists – were saying things far more interesting and to a very attentive public. However, all this is frivolous and not to the point, to which I come at once if I may.

I feel, as I say, deeply honoured by this invitation and should like to accept it. [...]

Yours ever,
    Isaiah B.

TO MARIE AND MENDEL BERLIN

    21 February 1951 [sc. 1952; *manuscript*]

                                    Bryn Mawr College

Dear Pa & Ma
    [...] all well here: 2 lectures delivered:[5] 4 more to go: *Philadelphia* hostesses very affable: it is a wonderfully 19th century Riga-ish life. At All Souls everything is I think all right. I wrote a letter, as I had to, supporting *Sparrow* with whom I still quarrel from time to time but who is an old friend of mine & grateful to me for supporting him: & he will be elected more easily than people think over Rowse who will become *impossible* under defeat & make life hell for a little while. Still, that cannot be helped: & he would have been a dreadful Warden. Henderson, I am afraid, is dying or dead;[6] I should never have been elected & should have hated the job if I had been: I realise that now: & I *have* written the first draft of a *book*. Which is an event. It will take about another 6–8 months to polish but should appear, in U.S., in 1953.[7] [...]

    Love
        Isaiah

1 Hippolyte Adolphe Taine (1828–93), French literary and artistic critic, historian and positivist social thinker, contextual and historicist in approach, influential in the development of French naturalism.
2 Jules Michelet (1798–1874), French historian.
3 Ernest Renan (1823–92), French historian (mainly of religion). His 1882 lecture 'What Is a Nation?' is directly relevant to IB's correspondence with T. S. Eliot on race and religion.
4 Arthur Schopenhauer (1788–1860), German philosopher.
5 The second, on 18 February, was on 'Political Liberty and the Ethical Imperative: Kant and Rousseau'.
6 Henderson died on 22 February.
7 The surviving chapters (corresponding to the first four lectures) were eventually published as PIRA in 2006.

TO ALICE JAMES

22 February 1952 [*manuscript*]

Bryn Mawr College

Dear Alice

[...] I cannot tell [you] how well Bryn Mawr is treating me: peace, quiet, civilised persons. I am being allowed to do what I like – work in peace – waste my time in peace – it is an oasis of tranquillity and sweetness – & I, who consider myself a hater of solitude & an almost neurotic avoider of it – am enjoying this blessed peace more than I can say. Apart from the weekly agony of the Lecture – & it is *agonising* in a huge Hall etc – I am really happy. Harvard is in every way more splendid but this time – probably because I had a little too much work to do because of these lectures – I was exhausted by it. I shall be everlastingly grateful to the local ladies for restoring me as they have. They are kindness and courtesy itself & I must tell them all so sometime. My bedroom is too wonderful: two huge bronze beds, imported from India, it seems, circa 1900, by Miss Carey Thomas,[1] wonderful Oriental fantasies of the Vanderbilt–Gould[2] period everywhere – a kind of high minded Newport[3] – & a heating system not under control, which, as T. S. Eliot said from whom I had a curious letter & who remembered staying in my present rooms – "blows a hot sirocco wind during the night, all night".[4] But I love it all. [...]

love

Isaiah   [...]

TO MARION FRANKFURTER

23 February [1952, *manuscript*]

Bryn Mawr College

Dear M.F.

Thank you for your note. I am glad you like Annan – who hasn't much substance but a certain amount of sensibility & is the Bloomsbury (official) dauphin &, they hope, commemorator (which Roy has so signally failed to be. Roy was not elected to the economics professorship vacated by poor Hubert Henderson who is dying this week, or perhaps dead; the Wardenship

1 (Martha) Carey Thomas (1857–1935), pioneer in women's education; Founding Dean, Bryn Mawr College, 1885–94, President and Professor of English 1894–1922. The Deanery, a much-enlarged Victorian house, was her home, its design and decoration the subject of detailed consideration and no little expenditure; oriental crafts were a particular interest of Lockwood de Forest, the designer most involved in the Deanery's furnishing.

2 Cornelius Vanderbilt (1794–1877) and Jay(son) Gould (1836–92), rival railroad magnates in the 1860s and 1870s.

3 The resort on Rhode Island favoured in the late 19th and early 20th centuries by the wealthiest families in the US, who built many luxurious mansions there.

4 In a PS to his letter of 9 February: 'blew a hot sirocco wind all night'.

killed him I am afraid; he was too good-natured to refuse it. It really is sad.) –
Bryn Mawr is a great success. Peace, & civilized relationships. I am left alone
for hours & days & adore every instant of my solitude as I never thought I
could. The lectures are an agony, of course, I seem to myself to be screaming
meaningless phrases to a vaguely discernible, half darkened, audience; &
feel terrified before, hysterical during & ashamed afterwards. But the other
days are divine: I work, read, go for small walks alone, very occasionally
consume meals with the Faculty, mostly by myself, in the clean, hygienic,
swept & garnered, somewhat prissy feminist atmosphere of this establishment: served by tremulous young students, anxious to please, & liable to chat
about the subject of the lectures, given a tenth part of a chance. I adore it all:
I have made no friends, & am grateful to be left alone. No, Harvard wasn't
a failure this time: it all went off perfectly well: but I had too much work to
do, & got tired & depressed; [...] I did think Harvard very tense this time,
the hatreds even deeper, & the young men less eager & exhilarating than
in 1949 when the war veterans added a half-adult half perplexed & rather
moving contingent which I liked very much. Also I was not so sure how I
had done – whether my lectures had done any good to anybody – whether
I was any use; but I was very melancholy the last time too: being away from
home for more than 3 weeks produces that almost automatically: my quest
for gaiety & cosiness is a perpetual defence against the extreme sense of the
abyss by which I have been affected ever since I can remember myself: &
that is why these days in Bryn Mawr – solitude without sense of utter inadequacy – are so pleasing to me: evidently I've learned some minimal degree
of self subsistence. [...] Barbara Ward I cannot regard as a person of either
much value or interest: she is a public face: quite sincere, good, & capable,
but surely a public face: [...] I am affable to her when we meet as I am to
some official person with whom personal relations do not begin to be even
conceivable. She does a good job on the Economist; she writes on Freedom
& Democracy; Democracy & Liberty; The Western Tradition & the Human
Spirit; the Values we Cherish and the freedoms of Man; Democracy and
Freedom; The Challenge of the East; The Destiny of the West; the Unity
of the Free; the freedom of the united; & so on for the N.Y. Times, which I
suppose is none the poorer for it; she has an infectious schoolgirl freshness,
& claps her hands, & is sure-footed, & a good fellow and a bright purveyor
of the higher values. Of a human being – I suppose there is one there, somewhere – I see no trace. Perhaps when the glossiness and the streamlined jolly
smile wear off – & the twinkle which is the surest sign of the absence of any
genuine humour – when this is gone, *something* may emerge. I don't dislike
her, but only as one has no objection to the cellophane which covers objects:
it is too tasteless & neutral to mind, unless one really believes in principles,
or has a Bloomsbury passion for the genuine article: in which case, I suppose,
one wd dislike her. Do *you* see her as a someone? a Catholic? a woman? an

intelligent observer even? am I being too violent? but I cannot *bear* the upper middle brow: & there is a dreadful Miniverishness[1] in your protegée; but Dr Cohn[2] *might* like her – pretty – not poor – not demanding – & as Catholics go, liberal. [...]

Love

I.B.

TO ALICE JAMES

13 March 1952 [*manuscript*]

Princeton, New Jersey

Dear Alice,

[...] John Sparrow was elected Warden of All Souls by a vast majority. Now the problem is how to live with the embittered Mr Rowse who will *never* forget or forgive, I fear. Oh dear, life is too full of difficulties of an unnecessary kind. And I am, alas, incapable of shuffling off even what is obviously trivial, & always find myself entangled in superfluous webs. A bientot,[3] & love to Billy.

Isaiah

Lelia Brodersen had mixed feelings about IB's departure from Bryn Mawr:

On Monday I cope with Isaiah for the last time [...] Last time was remarkable. He dictated for an hour & a half & stood squarely in front of me for the whole time, which certainly made the understanding much easier. Somehow, in the middle of a letter, he became aware that the huge window-pane beside him had a hole at the top & a crack running down from it the whole length of the window. He made noises of interest & ran his finger along the crack. I muttered something about somebody's having been shooting at him, & he looked at me with an absolute gleam in the face, saying, "Yes, exactly! It does look exactly like a bullet hole, doesn't it?" After a moment spent in silent & joyful contemplation of this fact he went on dictating, & I, of course, went on typing. Suddenly I heard him say, "Oh, good heavens!" I looked up, & saw him helplessly affixed to the window by his sleeve. He had leaned against the pane, the crack had nipped up a length of his sleeve, & there he was, unable to reach the situation with either hand. I rose up to rescue him, he assuring me repeatedly, as I worked, that "Such a thing never happened before – absolutely never happened before!" Eventually I pried him out, exhorting him the while to hold still & not cut the cloth, & being exhorted with equal vehemence not to cut my fingers. Cloth,

1 Mrs Miniver, an upper-middle-class Englishwoman, was a fictional character in Jan Struther's columns in *The Times* 1937–9 (subsequently published in book form); films starring Greer Garson as Mrs Miniver appeared in 1942 and 1950, the first helping transform US attitudes towards joining the war.

2 Dr A. E. Cohn.

3 sc. *à bientôt*, 'see you soon'.

1 In the cloisters, New College, 1950

2 Mendel and Marie Berlin

3 Chaim Weizmann

4 Vera Weizmann, 1957

5 George Kennan

6 Oliver Franks at the Marshall Plan
Conference, summer 1947

7 With junior members of Harvard's Department of Government, 1949:
in front, Sam Beer, IB, Adam Ulam; *behind*, Roy Macridis, Louis Hartz, Robert McCloskey

8 Aline Halban, late 1940s

9 Anna Kallin

10 Maurice Bowra, 1951

11 Stuart Hampshire, 1940s

12 Joseph Alsop, 1947

13 Katharine ('Kay') and Philip Graham, c.1948

14 Edward F. Prichard, Jr (*centre*; *left and behind*, Deputy US Marshals Charles Webb and Charles Dudley; *right*, Julian Elliott, a relative of Prichard's wife Lucy), leaving the Federal courthouse in Lexington, Kentucky, for Ashland Federal Correctional Institution after final confirmation of Prichard's sentence of two years' imprisonment, 14 July 1950

15 'Oh felicitous evening!' Dining with Ronnie and Marietta Tree on the *Queen Elizabeth*, September 1953 (the description is Marietta Tree's, written on the back of the photograph)

LARGE COURTYARD OF LOWELL HOUSE, HARVARD UNIVERSITY, CAMBRIDGE, MASS

16 Postcard of Lowell House, Harvard, sent in 1953

17 Jenifer and Herbert Hart, mid-1950s

18 Nicky Mariano and Bernard Berenson
at I Tatti, 1954

19 Clarissa and Anthony Eden, April 1954

20 One of some 70 photographs of IB taken by Cecil Beaton in July 1955. When Beaton's secretary sent proof prints to IB, he responded: 'I was torn by horror at my own features and admiration for his devastating art. […] I genuinely think that he is the best photographer who has ever lived.' Letter to Eileen Hose, 23 September 1955.

fingers, & personnel survived. It is, somehow, in spite of his protestations, just the sort of thing one would expect to happen to him.

I have grown curiously fond of him. I won't be sorry to conclude the secretarial part of it, but I will be sorry to see him go. There is a peculiar sweetness & charm there which grows upon one half-imperceptibly. It has really been quite an experience altogether.[1]

1 Letter to Sheema Z. Buehne, postmarked 17 March 1952 [Lelia Brodersen].

1952–1953

ALL SOULS

I cannot remember who it was who once described research as a condition of resentful inactivity.[1]

A great guy, and I don't see how he missed. I mean, stuck there in All Souls.[2]

1 To Katharine McBride, 22 January 1953.
2 Mike Todd of Todd-AO, *New Yorker*, 15 January 1955, 'The Talk of the Town', 20.

After leaving Bryn Mawr IB embarked on a rapid circuit of social visits. He was
due to sail on the Queen Mary *on 29 March but a Toscanini concert in New*
York that day proved an irresistible temptation. Concealing his late change of
plan from his parents (who were convinced that any plane with their son aboard
would crash), IB flew to Paris, where he was to meet them before a family
holiday in Nice and Italy.

TO ALICE JAMES

2 April 1952 [*manuscript*]

Paris

Dear Alice,

You must forgive me for not writing to you before about how deeply I enjoyed my stay with you and Billy in Cambridge: despite the whirl in which I lived, it was a sweet & tranquil oasis in what, despite all my beliefs, intentions, doctrines, seems to me my feckless, pillar to post, over-hurrying, ill managed, exhausting yet not sufficiently productive life. I always mean to settle down to months & months of solid uninterrupted steady labour. Perhaps, when I return to Oxford this time, I really shall. At any rate I'll try. You know I have this low opinion of all I do: & assume that others must see as clearly as I do the heap of inadequacies of which I am compounded ("You must not think about *yourself* so *much*" I hear Rowland sharply observing) & therefore your & Billy's kindness to & about me sets me up, & is valued by me more than I should care to try & state in words. I don't doubt you know that there is nobody to whose house I love to come more, or in which I feel better: & that it is one of the bright images in my head when I have to begin to think about coming & not coming to Harvard. I adored my few days: I am sorry in a way that I did not part from you alone, with the charming but irrelevant figure of the eccentric polymath Jakobson[1] interjecting at the last moment; but then I really mismanage things. Toscanini was wonderfully well worth waiting for: the programme[2] to which perhaps you listened was

1 Roman Jakobson (1896–1982), Russian-born linguist and literary historian; S. H. Cross Professor of Slavic Languages and Literatures, Harvard, 1949–67 (and of Linguistics 1960–7).

2 On 29 March, four days after his 85th birthday, Toscanini had conducted the NBC Orchestra in Beethoven's 1st and 9th Symphonies in a broadcast concert at Carnegie Hall. IB provided a more detailed account to Ramy Alexander: 'he conducted the Ninth Symphony in the new "serene" style, not thrilling but exceedingly noble, broad and moving – in fact the best performance of that work which I have ever heard. Toscanini himself was apparently furious. The work was recorded because he was, rightly, not pleased with the earlier recording. I went to the rehearsals and realised at the performance that the particular punctuation which he had introduced with much sweat and blood during the rehearsals [was] blurred by the orchestra during the performance. This, which only those who attended the rehearsals would have noticed, apparently ruined the performance for the conductor; at the age of 85 he doesn't anticipate being able to record it again, I suppose; to leave his ideal imperfectly realised is maddening for him. But from the point of view of the uninitiated audience it was a flawless and magnificent performance. [...] I was glad to be in time to hear the last dying voice of the Risorgimento.' Letter of 11 April.

of unique nobility breadth & depth: yet the old man was apparently not pleased: details went wrong though nobody but he could have known this: I am glad I waited: it was the climax of his life, & in a sense of my own too. Really of vast symbolic importance. [...] All my love to Billy & you & do write me to All Souls.

yrs ever
    Isaiah

The planned visit to Nice and Italy never happened: disaster struck IB's parents and their fears about the risks of flying proved justified.

TO VERA WEIZMANN
    10 April [1952], Passover [*manuscript*]

As from All Souls

Dear Mrs Weizmann,

It is a terrible thing to write from *America*. Something comes over one to make it altogether impossible: in England, in Europe, in Israel even, one accumulates experience which one does not immediately export: it forms a kind of inner sediment which evolves inside one's mind (and heart) and makes some kind of creative activity possible. In America one is like an open pipe, a corridor: nothing stays, everything rushes & gushes past, at the end of every evening one is exhausted physically & spiritually, one gives out, & takes in nothing. Hence I *cannot* write from there except on business or the emptiest family platitudes to my family. As soon as one returns to the Old World human beings once again have faces & not just knees: one slowly begins to react again & to think & to become capable of some degree of feeling: I worked in Harvard as never before: all day & part of every night: I had too much work to do, & I *hate* work & so did not enjoy myself: work one *can* in America: nothing distracts one as the people have little sense of real pleasure, only of activity. I was terribly distressed to hear of Dr Weizmann's low condition in the early winter: & thought of writing but also realized that you wd be snowed under with telegrams & messages & letters & that it wd be a horrible nuisance to have to reply to them all & so desisted: short of telephoning to New York every day to find out how things were, I did nothing. Then Josef came back & reported. Poor Josef: he lives as a bridge, as a connecting link between others: we all do to some degree, but he especially has no other life: he seems non-existent when one is not there oneself: when one is, he is, to me at least, a sad sweet sympathetic face from a less mechanical world: certainly he [is] a symbol of melancholy Schlamperei:[1] but I feel old at present & prefer the decrepit old world to the streamlined new one full

---

1 'Negligence, sloppiness'.

of gadgets in which I am required to live. In short I left America with *relief*. There is absolutely nothing to tell about that country: I feel sympathetic to Americans as to boys of 17: but their ailments & their remedies seem equally crude & childish to me: I *could* not live there. In Paris in 4 days I had an acuter sense of humanity than in America in 7 months (America has libraries with books I need & pays for my subsistence & pleasures. C'est tout)[1] I met first the Harveys who inquired *most* tenderly about you & the President (despite the timorous withdrawal of which you once spoke to me) & then met Raymond Aron,[2] the outstanding French political journalist, a most intelligent, sad, shrewd, sympathetic realistic disillusioned Jew: 100% Jew + 100% French, detached as only Jews can be, & with a hard, subtle, quiet intellect, the most impressive political observer (right wing – almost Gaullist – yet Gaulle is surely *bound* to attract antisemites in to his party?) I've ever met. I saw Teddy Kollek there & persuaded him to take the Air France plane with me to London. I intended to go to Nice & thence – who knows? – to skip over to Rehovot for a second & visit you – but suddenly received news that my mother slipped on the floor of our house & dislocated her shoulder; my father developed a congested lung with a high temperature; I was told to take "no notice" but in fact realized that I must fly to London at once with a supply of aueromycine.[3] So Teddy K. & I entered our Air France Languedoc aeroplane which ½ hr later, while attempting to rise, caught fire. [...] We all jumped out: the ladies were a little hysterical: I remembered breaking a mirror in New York & that the number of my pieces of luggage was 13: we were given champagne: I refused to drink, preferring to be angry. Having deceived my dear parents, both in bed, about flying I now had to telephone to say I wd be late: lied clumsily: took nobody in: & arrived in London 1½ hrs late in another plane. And exhausted after 7 months in the Sahara went to bed myself. Nothing is more cheerless than to be ill in America; the solitude grows greater than ever: I spent my time there too in a kind of bachelor-ish physical malaise, partly imaginaire, partly real (another reason for not writing. Every time I sat down to write I felt absolutely *empty*: nothing but nothing to say. And I am *ashamed* to write *absolute* rubbish. In Europe it comes more easily. Please forgive me) – In Paris I also met Nicolas Nabokov, my friend the Russian composer whom I hope you will soon see. He is a *delightful* man – the last voice of the old liberal intelligentsia, bohemian, easy going, *very* intelligent, with heart & soul & mind & a Judenknecht[4] all his life. Do ask him to tea: & Tête a Tête: you will {his} enjoy his society: he is cosy, gay, clever & sympathetic & full of life: he is the one who sent you

1 'That's all'.
2 Raymond Aron (1905–83), French sociologist, philosopher, political scientist, author and journal- ist; columnist, *Le Figaro*, 1947–83; Professor of Sociology, Sorbonne, 1956–68.
3 Aureomycine (*sic*), an antibiotic.
4 'Servant of the Jews'.

his book. Now I must return to my duties as male nurse to both my parents (round whom my life is still hopelessly – & satisfactorily – wrapped) but I shall write you again v. soon. If it is at all possible I shall try to invite myself, if only for 1 day this summer: my endless love to you & Dr Weizmann: to know you is still the largest single factor in my life.

Isaiah.

P.S. I met Einstein:[1] a genius but surely a foolish one, with the inhumanity of a child [...]

TO SAM BEHRMAN

11 April 1952

All Souls

Dearest Sam,

I have an infinitely melancholy tale to tell you – all due to illicit relations with Mr Garson Kanin[2] and Ruth Gordon;[3] why I am not allowed to see them and have dealings with them has never been made clear to me, but I realise that it is wrong, wicked and somehow forbidden. That, plus the deception practised on my poor, trusting parents, to whom I said that I would be coming by the *Queen Mary* when in fact, as you know, I was having a thoroughly distraught lunch with you and Wilson – that is what must have sealed my doom. Providence invariably lulls one into insensibility before raining down the cruellest blows. Consequently my initial flight to Paris was superficially tranquil and without incidents. Even the stop at Gander, Newfoundland, was not disagreeable, although it is not an attractive country for a lengthy stay. I am surprised that the Western world does not use it for the purpose of exiling political culprits. It has precisely the right attributes, remote, [ ]-looking,[4] repellently healthy climatically, with natives to occupy the attention of the more serious minded among the exiles, and every inducement to escape. I see Miss Lillian Hellman[5] writing some splendid memoirs in the best 19th-century Russian Revolutionary style; some letters of genius from Prichard, and George Backer sending parcels of increasing

1 Albert Einstein (1879–1955), physicist. IB met Einstein during a three-day visit to the Institute for Advanced Study at Princeton, where Einstein had been a Professor; neither man was impressed by the other. In response to Felix Frankfurter's letter introducing IB, Einstein commented: 'The man is really highly intelligent and a kind of spectator in God's big but mostly not very attractive theatre.' Letter of 12 March 1952 forwarded to IB by Frankfurter together with a copy of his letter of introduction [MSB 253/87].

2 Garson Kanin (1912–99), US playwright, scriptwriter and director.

3 The stage name of Ruth Gordon Jones (1896–1985), US actress, author, playwright and scriptwriter; married Garson Kanin 1942.

4 The brackets indicate an inaudible word omitted by the typist.

5 Lillian Florence Hellman (1905–84), US playwright of left-wing sympathies.

value, against Evie's[1] protests, to all the noble Radicals there confined. But let me continue.

I was met in Paris by Nabokov, conducted to my respectable dwelling, and all went well for a while. Lady Diana was away, which, generally devoted though I am to her, was a source of great relief in that it enlarged my liberty of action. I had lunch with the Backers, who were perfectly OK and going to Madrid, not without some qualms on the part of the tender-minded, politically sensitive, not wholly self-confident George. I met the extremely intelligent M. Raymond Aron, a clever, melancholy, fearfully sharp little man who rightly objects to being described as the Lippmann of France as an unmerited insult. Unlike Mr Trilling, whom he resembles in some obvious respects, he did not discuss liturgical questions with me but merely gave me his secret telephone number and said that, although, to all appearances, he seemed to be a supporter of General de Gaulle, when the crisis came he would no more be so than I or you (this is beginning to resemble the paragraphs at the opening of the *New Yorker*; I must take myself in hand and revert to my natural style). At the end of all that, just as I was preparing for a cosy family journey to Nice, I received a telephone call from my papa (who seldom spends money in so idle a fashion) and was told (*a*) that my mother had dislocated her shoulder while packing my books, if you please, (*b*) that my father, while driving her to hospital to have the bone set, developed a fever of many degrees and looked to me to fetch some antibiotics swiftly. This really was a hideous blow. I immediately obtained control of a small store of aureomycine, informed my parents that I would return to them the next day by the Golden Arrow,[2] cancelled everything, by this time deeply steeped in my career of deception, bought a ticket on the Air France plane for the Monday and spent a sleepless night, with images of my uncared-for parents, each suffering in his own fashion, floating before my eyes. On the next day I stepped briskly into the plane, which, after a great deal of ineffective taxiing, gathered speed, whizzed along the ground, skidded, nearly turned over and burst into flames. This was so unreal a spectacle, so unlike any form of life as lived by me that I felt no anxiety whatever, only acute surprise that I should be in the middle of so theatrical and unreal (I apologise for juxtaposing these words) a situation. Everyone got up simultaneously and adjured everyone else not to panic. One or two women showed signs of obvious hysteria. I am entirely ignorant about aeroplanes and was only later informed that as the petrol tanks were so many inches away from the blazing propeller the chances of our exploding for good and all were quite high, and the hysteria was therefore perfectly justified. However, this I did not know,

---

1 George Backer's second wife Evelyn ('Evie') (1905–71), née Weil.
2 The part-Pullman train which at that time ran once a day in each direction between London and the cross-Channel ferry at Dover; the equivalent connection between Calais and Paris was the similarly named *Flèche d'Or*.

and therefore looked blandly on this scene, which was becoming more and more like fiction. I concluded that the flames would take at least five minutes to reach me, personally, and that therefore there would be plenty of time, not only to walk off in a dignified manner, but also to save my valuable new American overcoat, on which all my thoughts were centred. I therefore presented the picture of beautiful British sangfroid, founded on utter ignorance and stupidity. In fact there were no casualties. My fellow passengers were distinctly shaken, particularly an American Negro, who shook and quaked until he was filled with champagne, when he became inexcusably jolly and became the life and soul of the party in the most embarrassing fashion possible. The airport authorities offered us bad champagne, but I preferred to remain coldly enraged. By this time I was naturally afraid that my parents would begin to be worried as to the cause of my delay in returning, and I telephoned them a greatly distorted version of the truth which could not have taken a cat in. I arrived in London later that day, carrying my valuable medicines, and found my parents a great deal better than I had feared. However, the journey to Nice and Florence was plainly impracticable, and so now here I sit, mainly concerned to prevent them from tending to me – they think I look pale and not as well as I might. And all my efforts to act as a trained nurse are firmly frustrated by my mother's uncontrollable energy and my father's immovable common sense and grasp of reality. In their presence I continue not merely to be treated as, but to feel, about seventeen years old, and a very irresponsible, callow, undeveloped, gullible seventeen at that. The sooner I return to Oxford the better.

I am glad to say that Mr Rowse, though furious with everyone else, regards me as too innocent and out of this world to be concerned at all in the realities of politics – the general view of me as an ineffectual angel is new to me, but I am more than ready to settle for it here and now. Will you not come to London and Oxford instead of Nice and Florence? True it is not the same thing. Nevertheless it will distract you. It may even rest you a little, particularly if you do not stay under the same roof with me (my friends the Jameses report from Cambridge that they sleep more now that I have left them); do come, if only to look after me in Oxford, to prevent me from committing those daily and hourly blunders which my parents are convinced that I perpetrate with perverse gusto on account of my sheltered education – a form of dissipation which only marriage can cure. I must hurry now and eat a special, healthful food which is to cure my pallor. I have no time for letters or anything else, but only to be looked after by my ailing parents, a wholetime occupation, I assure you. Goodbye. And do come. [...]

Yishayohu Hanovi[1]

---

1 'Isaiah the Prophet'.

TO WILLIAM JAMES

14 April 1952 [*manuscript postcard*]

As from All Souls

Dear Billy,

I was very glad to get your letter & to hear Alice has recovered from my ravages: being alone I, too, sleep. I agree: it was fortunate for your uncle Henry,[1] though not for me, that we never met: or would I have remained silent out of some vast deposit of humility & terror with which you may easily not credit me, or credit me sufficiently? 'Impossible' you say. But in the presence of men of genius I am dreadfully frightened & cooped up. I don't believe in soft v. hard: the alleged hard i.e. fact gatherers & rigorous verifiers are more easily taken in outside the realm of the measurable & weighable than many an apparent woolly headed richly tropical luxuriant soft-head. I stick to dry v. wet: was Tolstoy hard or soft? his methods were apparently flintlike, yet his doctrines were v. v. soft: but what *is* surely (when one says 'surely' one means to bully a little: since it is anything but sure in such cases) *indubitable* (i.e. open to doubt but not to the speaker) that he was dry: clear: & not at all factual in the dull sense. Hence my suspicion of hard v. soft as inadequate. I am living v. drily: my parents suddenly both fell ill after I arrived in Paris: so I cancelled Nice & Florence & flew home. The aeroplane caught fire: very picturesque & interesting but I must admit 'superfluous' – very terrifying. Air France is too dry: & I prefer a softer & wetter passage in future.

love

Isaiah

IB continued to suffer mishaps: an illicit rendezvous with Jenifer Hart in his parents' house during their absence on a rearranged holiday (Bournemouth replacing Nice) was disturbed by neighbours suspecting burglars. And on his return to Oxford, IB was distressed to find that he had been deprived of the private telephone line on which he relied.

TO DOUGLAS VEALE[2]

[Received 23 April 1952, *manuscript*]

All Souls

Dear Veale

I hope you will forgive me if, as on past occasions, I appeal to you on a personal matter. It concerns my telephone which, trivial as it may seem, plays an essential part in my existence. For nearly twenty years I have used

---

1 William James had commented: 'Do you understand how, if you and the dear old uncle had only been acquainted, you would *never* have gone to bed?' (letter of 7 April).
2 Douglas Veale (1891–1973), Registrar of Oxford University 1930–58.

a private telephone – first at All Souls and then at New College. When I moved back to All Souls I applied for its transfer to my rooms in All Souls, thinking it, I am afraid, on the basis of my 1938 & 1948 experiences, a semi-routine matter. Upon my return from America this April I was dismayed to discover that the telephone had been cut off altogether, with little hope of early restoration. Quite apart from the amenities of ordinary life, & the fact that in All Souls one is far more cut off from the world (on the 4th floor) than at most Colleges – which has its compensations but becomes grim if one wants a doctor (as I do too frequently) & finds oneself very distant from the nearest instrument – I am singularly dependent on a telephone. As a result mainly of my wartime activities I find that I am in constant communication with all kinds of persons, official & private, in London & abroad, some of whom provide me with the extra income without which, as I made it clear to the late Sumner, I could not afford to return to All Souls; & some of whom (like the B.B.C., or the Encyclopaedia Britannica in Chicago, or our representatives in the Paris & Washington Embassies & editors in Boston & New York) have developed a tendency to consult me on all kinds of odd matters – I wish this did not sound ridiculously self-important or irrelevant to my academic work: but in fact, in view of the relative scarcity of e.g. Russian material in this country, these international contacts are essential to me if I am to find legitimate ways of going abroad even for purely research purposes. At present I find myself altogether without a telephone, & have to be fetched great distances by porters when they are ready to take the many steps up to my rooms: after 10 p.m. the Lodge closes, & I cannot expect it to remain alert for the sake of messages to me; so that even if an extension from the lodge is put in – which now takes three weeks I gather – I should be unreachable by e.g. Americans who, extravagant as it undoubtedly is, insist on ringing one up less seldom than one would think likely. After about 20 years of a life organised in terms of easy access by telephone it really is a grave inconvenience (apart from its effect on one's income) to be suddenly insulated: & while I am well aware, (from Mr Forsyth of Telephone Exchange who has talked to me) of how tight the position about telephones is, surely the transfer of an existing subscriber's line cannot be so dreadfully difficult? I have been told (by my local authorities) & warned not to know it, that an unused line exists; & that the difficulty is one of principle & not of material feasibility; & Forsyth tells me that it is to you I am to speak, & that he too will do so. I told the Vice-Chancellor whom I saw yesterday about my despair: & he kindly agreed to furnish me with a testimonium paupertatis,[1] which Forsyth said "would help": but I have not pressed him to do this before placing my case before you: I am sure that if it were necessary, institutions like the B.B.C., & the Foreign Office, & even the Bank of England (in the

---

1 'Testimony of poverty'.

interests of my dollar income) would support my application if this became required. But I am most reluctant to pull strings of this kind unless you think it advisable – in the meanwhile I do beg you not to think me unduly importunate: it cannot be so very difficult to continue an existing service, even in England today; & in my case it makes – for better or for worse, but, alas, it is too late to alter one's habits now – a crucial difference to my way of life. And I have done my best to feel no sense of injustice: & to ascribe the situation to the hardships of life & their psychological consequences. I hope you are very well: & apologise for troubling you. I should never have dreamt of doing so if the matter were not of such importance to me.

Yours ever

Isaiah Berlin

A further month – and action at the highest level – was needed to resolve this major crisis:

Isaiah moved Heaven and Earth, and in the end the Postmaster-General, Kitty Giles' father, Lord de la Warr,[1] in order to have a telephone installed in his rooms at All Souls, so that his friends might be able to communicate with him; but he then defeated the whole purpose of the operation by having a highly complicated machine attached to the telephone to prevent it ever ringing, as he finds that the noise disturbs his social meditations![2]

TO IRVING SINGER

16 May 1952

All Souls

Dear Irving,

[...] Forgive me for being brief, for I really am drowning, as so often. This time my troubles have been added to by having no telephone which, so far from leaving me free and untroubled in beautiful monastic seclusion, merely means that all my visitors come in at the wrong times, come in on top of one another, that I keep fulfilling non-existent appointments and failing to keep others, and all sorts of other horrors which you can imagine. I am physically very well and working peacefully quite well and quite happily, but the mere effort of reading a book is painful and self-conscious to a degree, and I keep reinforcing myself in order to delay the need to use it.

The Vice-Chancellor is in literally roaring form and very happy and powerful and all-wise. He looks enormous in his robes as he majestically strides through Oxford – his happiness is very infectious. This college, having

---

1 Herbrand Edward Dundonald Brassey Sackville (1900–76), 9th Earl de la Warr, Postmaster-General 1951–5. His daughter Lady Katharine Pamela ('Kitty') Sackville (b. 1926) was married to the *Times* journalist Frank Giles.

2 Hugh Trevor-Roper to Bernard Berenson, 5 February 1953, *Letters from Oxford* (196/1).

changed Wardens, seems at last set on a firm path and altogether we are going through a flowering which will doubtless prove all too brief and end in some fearful disaster. On the other hand it may not.

After escaping from a burning aeroplane on the way from Paris I believe my quota of misfortunes to be temporarily filled and I am preparing myself for a benign old age, maturing gently and mouldering nicely within ancient walls. As such you must conceive me and as such you must come and visit me.

I am glad you liked Mrs Whitehead. I do not think I like anyone better or admire anyone more or am happier in anyone's presence. I wish she were here. I wish you were here too. I wish there were no gaps in spaces [sc. space?]. My love to Jo.[1]

Yours,

Isaiah

TO SAM BEHRMAN

4 June 1952

All Souls

Dear Sam,

[...] Now that the terrible storms and tempests of the great All Souls election are over, now that what is called the time of troubles is at last at an end, a curious golden peace has descended upon this place. The late Warden, Mr Sumner, had an unsettling effect upon my junior colleagues. Full of agreeable and conscientious aims, he would for ever test the abilities of his junior colleagues, in order to discover whether they were in fact doing their work with the required degree of industry. Not that he really wanted to know, or that he really suspected them of indolence or sabotage, but his natural nervousness was so great that work was the only subject about which he found it easiest to talk: with the result that, without knowing it himself, he established a kind of mild continuous reign of terror among these unfortunate beings. Now, under good Warden Sparrow, who by nature belongs to an Oxford circle no less than the members of it whom you mention, the junior Fellows can scarcely believe their good fortune. They are like people suddenly let out into the light of day from a dark dungeon. They are like people testing the ground which had hitherto been marshy and uncertain, delighted, but even more astonished to find that the earth is firm and wholesome. You must imagine a collection of released persons blinking delightedly in the light, scarcely believing that the new reign, the new regime is established [...] that freedom is apparently to reign for ever. [...]

Yours, with much love

Isaiah

1 Irving Singer's wife Josephine (b. 1928), née Fisk.

Mendel Berlin had continuing health problems which preoccupied IB for much
of the summer. But in late July IB managed to spend a week at the Aix-en-
Provence music festival, to which Aline Halban drove him in her car. It was
during this week that their friendship started to develop into a more intense
emotional relationship.

TO ALICE JAMES

7 August 1952 [*manuscript*]

All Souls

Dear Alice

You must forgive me for not writing for so long: but I have had a troubled
summer. And I don't really like sending postcards, although I do that to
Rowland, who, unless one does, feels forgotten & abandoned & old & dull
etc. etc. & tells one so in no unmeasured or obscure terms. My troubles are
entirely to do with my poor father who has been ill now for some months &
whom I have, in effect, had to look after from my departure from America
till now. As you know I left the U.S. early in April, after the Toscanini concert:
it was a splendid & moving & unique occasion and I am not sorry to have
stayed for it; next day I flew to Paris quite comfortably. There I received news
that my father was not too well, was loaded with anti-biotics & flew to
London. En route the aeroplane caught fire and scenes of extraordinary
panic occurred. It was an Air France – Air Chance is a better name – aeroplane, & there was no pretence about women & children. We came down
rapidly. We alighted. Fiery notices ordered us to "regagner vos places".[1] No
one obeyed. I saw a thin flame crawling up the side of my window & decided
that it would take at least 10 minutes to reach me & there was, therefore, no
reason for haste. I was, however, mistaken in this: the French keep their spare
gasoline behind the propeller: the propeller, it is true, had broken off some
minutes before & was peacefully blazing some yards off; the aeroplane was
emptied amid screaming etc. I thought of little save how to save (a) my
Abercrombie & Fitch new overcoat to which I felt devotion (b) a particularly
neat small wireless set which I was bringing as a present to my parents. I
therefore behaved with a false calm & as I imagined some detached dix
huitième[2] observer of life might have behaved. But no sooner was I out &
contemplating the burning wreck in a Gibbonian manner[3] than I was
screamed at by a loud speaker: told not to be mad: the machine might blow
up at any moment: & to run fast. It was only then that I observed that the
other passengers were as specks in the distance & that I was alone in my

---

1 'Return to your seats.'
2 sc. *dix-huitième*, '18th[-century]'.
3 It was while contemplating the ruins of the Capitol that Gibbon first considered writing the
history of the Roman Empire's decline and fall.

distinguished detachment. I ran, feeling absolutely ridiculous, by myself, across the intervening ½ mile or so it seemed to me. The aeroplane did not, in the end, blow up, so I felt sillier still. However I had my overcoat & my little radio. We were offered disgusting champagne at the airport. I coldly refused, preferring to nurse my fury. An hour later we all flew off, really scared this time, in another plane: everybody kept a stiff upper lip though it twitched a little at times [...]. On arrival in London I found my father recovering from mild pleurisy: but then this caused various swellings here & there: & so he was put in a clinic. I lived a vagrant life between London & Oxford, but June was warm & delightful: the new Warden of All Souls is a great success & most capable, just & amusing all at the same time: his defeated rival is behaving idiotically: like Malvolio:[1] & won't speak to those who actually voted against him: he is immensely civil to me: & violently rude to most of my colleagues: I don't know which to mind the more. Poor Seznec is not spoken to by him: but he calls on me & coos at me & tells me how I alone understand his dark & troubled soul: I try, as always, to produce a détente (I really hate personal rows not over principles but due to wounded vanity) by representing himself to himself as a farouche & solitary genius, part Heathcliff[2] part Carlyle, not heeding the suffrages of the milling bourgeoisie which cannot grasp the bleak sublimity of his lonely flights: but he thinks he is at least Pericles[3] or Marlowe[4] or a mixture of the two; so my diplomacy is dashed against real megalomania about which there is nothing to be done. I encourage him to visit me, though this gets me cross looks from my colleagues who by now would like to expel this poor frustrated would be King Stork, like a fiery Latin American General whose *coup* has failed. But I think that if [he] has nobody to talk to he will go literally mad & assassinate someone. So, with my compromise-loving, accommodating, all too unromantical, *juste milieu*,[5] soul, I try to soothe him down. But it is a tedious & often ludicrous occupation: I *wish* someone gave him some small throne somewhere: nothing is more exhausting than being the self-appointed shock absorber to a monomaniac. In due course Philip Hofer[6] appeared: then Edgar Wind; & through a series of mischances I missed the Learned Hands. I went to a Slavic Committee meeting in Brussels,[7] & had a long

---

1 When Malvolio, in Shakespeare's *Twelfth Night*, discovers that he has been tricked, he threatens 'I'll be revenged on the whole pack of you' (v. i. 384).
2 The brooding, tormented hero of Emily Brontë's 1847 novel, *Wuthering Heights*.
3 Pericles (*c.*495–429 BC), Athenian general, statesman and orator who led the city for over 30 years.
4 Christopher Marlowe (1564–?93), poet and dramatist; probably homosexual, as was Rowse.
5 'Happy medium'.
6 Philip Hofer (1898–1984), librarian; founder and curator, Department of Printing and Graphic Arts, Harvard Library, 1938–67.
7 In mid-June, organised by the Institut d'Études Slaves of the University of Paris; described as 'useless but wonderfully funny' by IB (14 June 1952 to Rowland Burdqn-Muller). In *Revue des études slaves* 29 (1952), 299, 'Irving Berlin' is listed as a British representative to the conference.

evening with Spaak,[1] who, I thought (with Gladwyn Jebb), talked more sense about European politics than anybody I had met: whatever their public utterances they both wish to keep Germany divided & not rearm her in a hurry. But both are desperately anxious that this be not imputed to them: & anyway it is only my impression of what they said. Then my father grew somewhat worse again: & I hurried back to London: & came 2 very anxious weeks during which I virtually lived in his clinic. He pulled through, but the treatment was only a partial success: & I am afraid that he may have to be 'done' again. The surgeons & doctors claim to have made mistakes: & there is nothing mortal or fatal about my father's ailments. But my ordinary life is at a standstill. During a lull I got away to Aix en Provence: the company was delightful: old friends & my hostess, Mme Guy de Rothschild, a very nice, pensive, civilised, Frankfurt-born grande dame with whom I talk about the past & feel well: the music was very poor: the French always succumb to their mania for economy in the end: & the 4th rate German singers & 5th rate German orchestra, not eked out by violently garish décors, in *Figaro*, by fashionable pupils of Picasso[2] who mingled the master's savage primitivism with a kind of tired salon sentimentality, produced absurd effects. The local (& Paris) critics talked about the unsurpassable perfection of all this. France is the only country where critics lie boldly, openly, and shamelessly:[3] where everyone knows that their motives are not artistic or moral but social; & where music at least is governed by what seems to me a very worthless kind of smart set, genuinely unconnected with any kind of artistic sensibility. I suppose that the arts are, for financial reasons, bound to be connected with fashion: & that in socialist or communist societies the fashion instead of being that of a set of rich persons or snobbish arbiters of taste is that of the bureaucracy which can be even worse, less corrupt but immovably philistine & far more permanent & difficult to fight against: & that the tribulations of say, Mozart or Hugo Wolf[4] led to richer artistic results than those of Shostakovich;[5] & anyway led to a reaction which made it possible for e.g. Schubert or Beethoven to do what they wanted instead of crushing all possibility of freedom: yet it is melancholy to what degree the triviality and

1 Paul-Henri Spaak (1899–1972), Belgian socialist politician and one of the prime movers towards greater European integration; Prime Minister of Belgium four times between 1938 and 1949; President, Consultative Assembly, Council of Europe, 1949–51; Chairman, International Council of the European Movement, 1950–5; Secretary-General, NATO, 1957–61.

2 Pablo Diego José Francisco de Paula Juan Nepomuceno María de los Remedios Crispín Crispiniano de la Santísima Trinidad Ruiz y Picasso (1881–1973), Spanish painter and sculptor who with Georges Braque developed Cubism.

3 The *Times* music critic had no such inhibitions: '*Figaro* was totally misconceived [...]. Herr Rosbaud is not an inspiring conductor [...] rather wooden singing'. *The Times*, 4 August 1952, 9.

4 Hugo Wolf (1860–1903), Austrian composer, mainly of lieder.

5 Dmitry Dmitrievich Shostakovich (1906–75), Russian composer; performances of his music were sporadically banned by the Soviet Government under Stalin.

dreary mondanity & superficiality & heartlessness of Paris (you must not tell
Rowland this; but somehow this is what the méchante[1] Mme de Becker,[2] his
great friend, irresistibly conveys to me) empties French art of content at the
moment: Poulenc is quite a good composer, so is Milhaud: but the younger
set are terrible: & if there is to be no inspiration I would rather have the
laboured seriousness of the younger Americans – Copland & Sessions &
their disciples – uninspired but honourable & at least not spurious – or the
dull lyricism – the quiet dull talk of the younger English – Lennox Berkeley,
Rawsthorne[3] – imitative, thin blooded, ungifted but not repellent – than the
gifted and skilful but disgusting *pourriture*[4] of the Parisians. Dear me! is it
thus that the sillier & heavier Russians of the late 19th century might have
spoken of Debussy or Ravel or Fauré?[5] I hope not. Yet I cannot avoid a kind
of moral approach. I prefer the dreadful German soul, with all her cruelties
& ponderosities to the French powder puffs & mascara & appalling quality
of falseness & spuriousness & manufacture. I apologise for pouring all this
out at you. In Literature Malraux is still a wonderful writer: & Sartre[6] & Co
are very gifted, very interesting but politically & personally repulsive. I
wonder what Harry Levin will think of it all: he is liable, I think, to be carried
away by virtuosity as such: like any clever, serious, manqué creative persons,
he overestimates the value of *all* creative & imaginative art & prefers a breath
of life, however thin & even counterfeit, to criticism and intellectualism
however genuine. It is sweet & touching in him, that; but it falsifies his vision.
Enough, I feel, of all that. I was delighted to hear that your son was better in
Washington. No one, now particularly, knows better than I the clouds which
sickness in one's family can bring: I am in the midst of it now: & to try &
write a book, while on a kind of string to a beloved patient, is a peculiar
experience. However I am really very tough: through lack of imagination or
whatever quality, I suffer intensely at the time from every imaginary cause:
yet no visible scars remain: & it is almost pleasant to me to linger in memory
over past disasters, even past humiliations: it all acquires a kind of impersonal & natural quality – the landscape through which one has been now
purified of the hopes & fears it inspired at the time, seen at last simply as

1 'Naughty'.
2 Renée de Becker-Remy (1899–1987), née Lambert, lived partly in the US after her 1938 divorce
  from Paul de Becker-Remy; daughter of a Belgian banker and one of the French de Rothschilds;
  sister-in-law of Hansi Lambert (384/1).
3 The composers IB lists are: Francis Jean Marcel Poulenc (1899–1963); Darius Milhaud (1892–1974);
  Aaron Copland (1900–90); Roger Huntington Sessions (1896–1985); Lennox Randal Francis
  Berkeley (1903–89); and Alan Rawsthorne (1905–71).
4 'Rottenness'.
5 An earlier generation of French composers: (Achille-)Claude Debussy (1862–1918); (Joseph-)
  Maurice Ravel (1875–1937); and Gabriel Urbain Fauré (1845–1924).
6 Jean-Paul Charles Aymard Sartre (1905–80), French philosopher (who developed the theory of
  existentialism), playwright, novelist, critic and Communist sympathiser.

what occurred: I do not know how it is with you or with Billy: are there bits of the past you cannot touch? windows which you may not open knowing, and not knowing quite, what you will find behind them? Nothing like this (funnily enough. For I am the worst coward you know, believe me, but not about this) in my life: I am delighted to look at *anything* provided it is past, frozen immovably into some vast 'given' natural stuff of which life in general – the external world – & what is internal now or in the future, gradually grows external simply as a result of time & distance – like memories once so private, now mere data of history. Is this unnatural & queer? I've no idea.

Meanwhile Oxford flows on. Maurice is off to Amalfi with two friends of mine: I am in London in August when "nobody is in London". As Dr Weizmann once said to me: "nobody" means that instead of 10 million inhabitants London contains only 9.900.000 persons: this is what is meant by saying "London is empty in August." It is raining and I have just bought tickets for Toscanini here in September: the Dicks will return soon I suppose. He is an honest fellow, a little crude, matter of fact, direct, capable & prosy with a queer streak of long hair & velvet jackets which makes him interesting. She – I don't know. She is what all central Europeans are attracted by in any English women: cool, firm, obstinate, dogmatic, isolationist, intolerant, & in the end, very neurotic. I can't quite take to it. She is too unwriteable about by Tolstoy: she is too middle class in the cold not warm sense of the word: too clear, too terre a terre[1] & not like a Frenchwoman who knows how to live & make use of everything but a little insular, self centred & rapacious. Is this unfair? untrue? I'll report to you in a year or so. I hardly know her: but I am not cosy in her presence: some thin chill draught, tiny, pencil like, seems to me forever blowing. If I am wrong I shall own it to you: & I've told this to nobody else. As soon as my papa recovers & I am free once more I'll write again. My fondest love to Billy & to you & please forgive this rambling, unreadable, absurd letter.

Yours
    Isaiah

TO ROWLAND BURDON-MULLER

8 August 1952 [*manuscript*]

All Souls

Dear Rowland,

Thank you for your most welcome letters. I have had a peculiarly trying time on account of my poor papa: to whom I am devoted. You remember my projected tour of Italy came to naught because he suddenly was stricken

---

1 sc. *terre à terre*, 'earth-bound, matter-of-fact'.

with some pulmonary disease & I had to rush home with "anti-biotics": he recovered from this, duly, but began in a general way, to ail. He then had a "fissure" – a concave complication of the distemper of which you so sharply warned – with your customary candour – the German princess of your childhood. After much to-ing and fro-ing, it was decided to operate: an easy, regular, routine operation etc. This was done by a celebrated surgeon[1] who specialises in such activities. My poor father then found he could not pass water: for 9 agonising days he was gratuitously informed that this was due to some peculiar psychological resistance on his part. Then, when near giving up the ghost, he was operated on again, for prostate. This time by an even more eminent surgeon,[2] whose wife, however, was dying & whose hand had, to that degree, faltered in its cunning: water passed again; & has now ceased: now he can easily regulate its flow. Forgive me for inflicting all this upon you: it gives some concreteness to the flitting to & from the nursing home – the horrible London Clinic – which I have had to do, unable to work or really think or do anything much: my mother is very heroic & devoted but not [a] great help. The end is not yet; I think he will have to be operated on again; he is 70, quite strong, but still; he has a childlike nature, is a good deal younger than I mentally, I have to rally him, try & stop his panic defeats, his Caporettos[3] each time a mischance occurs. The doctors openly declare they mishandled his case: blame their own stupidity + fate. I got away for a week to Aix during a lull in all this, & very nice it was. A great celebration of h–intern.[4] Benjamin Britten + Peter Pears,[5] an obvious ménage,[6] appeared & he sang with a degree of sentimentality, deeply & sincerely in love with his own unbeautiful voice, which was embarrassing. The Don Giovanni was much worse than in 1949: the voices less good, Herr Rosbaud[7] more grotesque; Figaro was worse still: hideous Wagnerian ladies from Vienna; an obscure little creature[8] from die Wiesbadener Opera to sing Cherubino; and

1 Possibly Stephen Eisenhammer (1907–95), a specialist in treating anal fissures, at this time based in St Mark's Hospital, London.
2 Almost certainly Eric William Riches (1897–1987), urologist; later (1961–2) Vice-President, Royal College of Surgeons.
3 Caporetto in Slovenia was in 1917 the site of a battle in which the Italian Army was decisively defeated by Austro-German forces.
4 'Homintern', a term coined by Bowra by analogy with 'Comintern', to describe homosexuals.
5 (Edward) Benjamin Britten (1913–76), later (1976) Baron Britten of Aldeburgh, composer. Peter Neville Luard Pears (1910–86), tenor.
6 'Household', i.e. couple.
7 Hans Rosbaud (1895–1962), Austrian conductor; principal conductor, Munich Philharmonic, 1945–8, Southwest German Radio Symphony Orchestra 1948–62. He conducted both *Don Giovanni* and *The Marriage of Figaro* at Aix-en-Provence in 1952. Leonie Rysanek sang Donna Elvira and the Countess respectively, Heinz Rehfuss Don Giovanni and the Count; in *Figaro* Graziella Sciutti was Susanna and Michel Roux took the title role.
8 Gisela Litz (b. 1922), German mezzo-soprano.

décors by M. Clavé,[1] a Spanish Picasso + chichi-painter: conceive to yourself two huge Aztec idols, hideous & terrifying, in the 3ᵈ act of Figaro to flank the Countess's beautiful arias: Don Giovanni, no longer our romantic Italian[2] (now singing badly under the corrupting Herr Bing[3] at the Metropolitan) but a huge Swiss clod,[4] with quite a good voice, but Swiss movements. All excellent people, but unsuited to interpreting Don Giovanni. I was asked to write about it for the Manchester Guardian, but think it kinder not to. It was brave to put on Iphigénie en Tauride by Gluck:[5] & the ménage of Orestes & Pylades with no distracting female romancer moved the Tanti Quanti[6] gathered here to tears: but it was very dully done: & Miss Neway[7] who sang earnestly, had little dix huitième about her. The archéveché[8] looked charming; the weather was good, Alix de Rothschild was charming & agreeable & Marschallin-like;[9] I saw the Salems & enjoyed their society – particularly his – but hers too – very much: their villa really is exquisite & the views marvellous; no Patricia this year, no coon; but dear Agnes Mongan[10] whom Alix de R. & Mme Halban of Oxford, who duly appeared too, liked, rightly, very much. She is a very nice woman, & followed your instructions dutifully. Please give her my love when you see her. The orchestral playing – the Stuttgart Germans, some very like S.S. & S.A.[11] men: playing Petrouchka they were grotesque: a meaningless German bit by bit gallop over – to them – totally unintelligible music. I shan't say much about [it] for Ted Weeks – I don't know when that will appear.[12] I must stop & tend to my father. I also have too much work to do as always. You are 1000 times right about the Germans & Europe:[13] it is a very grave blunder, & an American one, to have summoned up this dreadful

1 Antoni Clavé (1913–2005), Catalan artist who settled in France after the Spanish Civil War; the publicity based on his designs for this production gave a major boost to his career.
2 Renato Cappechi (1923–98), baritone, who at the beginning of his successful stage career had sung Don Giovanni in the 1949 production at Aix.
3 Rudolf Franz Joseph Bing (1902–97), Austrian-born (though naturalised British) General Manager, Metropolitan Opera, New York, 1950–72.
4 Heinz Julius Rehfuss (1917–88), German-born bass-baritone, naturalised Swiss, later naturalised American; Zurich Opera 1940–52; the Figaro and Don Giovanni at Aix in 1952.
5 Carlo Maria Giulini conducted this production of Iphigénie en Tauride.
6 i.e. homosexuals.
7 Patricia Neway (b. 1919), the US soprano who played Iphigénie; New York City Opera 1951–66; Mother Abbess in the original Broadway production of The Sound of Music (1959–63).
8 sc. archevêché, 'archbishop's palace'.
9 A reference to the heroine of Richard Strauss's 1911 opera Der Rosenkavalier.
10 Agnes Mongan (1905–96), curator of drawings, Fogg Art Museum, Harvard, 1947–75 (assistant director 1951–64; associate director 1964–68; director 1969–71).
11 The Schutzstaffel ('protective squadron'), the Nazi Party's security and military organisation, and the Sturmabteilung ('storm division'; stormtroopers), brown-shirted paramilitary group within the Nazi Party.
12 Never.
13 RB-M had written on 15 September: 'I think Dulles is a menace: how can he expect Poland and Czechoslovakia to revolt to please us when we do not even recognize their frontiers with Germany whom we are arming and who would gladly attack them? Please answer me that.'

force again which will crash duly over our heads. Eisenhower v Stevenson.[1]
Surely it might have been worse? but Nixon![2]

Yrs

    Isaiah

P.S. I saw Gladwyn at the club to which our Clubs, shut in August, sent us: he
was well, most agreeable, intelligent &, I think, right on all points. Morally &
Politically he is *much* the best person in the F.O. & I like him greatly besides.
[. . .]

> *IB's friend Clarissa Churchill had told him some time previously that Anthony*
> *Eden wished to marry her. The message she sent on 8 August that she had*
> *accepted Eden's proposal and was about to be married nevertheless came as a*
> *surprise. The official announcement of the engagement was made on 12 August:*
> *the wedding followed two days later.*

TO CLARISSA CHURCHILL

Tuesday [postmark 12 August 1952, *manuscript*]

                                          49 Hollycroft Avenue

Dearest Clarissa,

I waited until I collected my thoughts (more or less) and now let me say
that I think it is, all ways considered, a magnificent act. I have always (despite
occasional moments of fright & dismay[3] – but these are all long past &
incapable of returning) loved you most deeply, & therefore I wish you a vast
& unending happiness – full of gaiety and glory and splendours of every kind,
like the Tintoretto Paradise[4] – and I see no reason why you should not have it:
and besides love I have an ardent & jealous sense of your objective attributes
particularly your noble & unbending pride and disdain for the minutest kind
of cheating & compromise – hence my sense of personal humiliation as
well as sense of unfitness in the universe when you spoke of friends – even

---

1 Dwight David Eisenhower (1890–1969), Supreme Commander, Allied Powers, Europe, 1950–2;
   US President 1953–61; at the time of this letter the Republican presidential candidate. Adlai Ewing
   Stevenson (1900–65), US lawyer and Democratic politician; Governor of Illinois 1949–53; presidential candidate 1952, 1956.
2 Richard Milhous Nixon (1913–94), Republican Representative 1947–51, Senator 1951–3, at the time
   of this letter Eisenhower's running-mate, then Vice-President 1953–61; later (1969–74) President.
3 In 1945 their friendship had been temporarily threatened. According to IB, 'she wrote me a letter
   [. . .] when I was in Moscow, saying: "When I first knew you, you were an innocent and pure don,
   extremely nice; now your head's been turned by society you're not at all the same – you mustn't
   continue; this is not your world, you'll perish in it; this is all right for people like us, no good for
   people like you"' (MI Tape 12). IB reacted with fury.
4 The massive, figure-filled painting of *Paradise* (1587–90) is one of the greatest achievements of
   the Venetian Renaissance painter Tintoretto, the name adopted by Jacopo Comin (1518–94), and
   dominates the Great Council Hall in the Doge's Palace, Venice.

acquaintances – Prof Z.[1] is the most comical instance – whom I revolted against as unworthy of you (in a queer sense you used to have an inkling of the same objective view of me: hence your reproaches when I seemed to you to betray some clear standard of integrity or even manners) – & your marriage will surely help to create the golden world for which you were created. I never saw you as often as I wanted to, perhaps because, at times, I was too ashamed to see you when I felt in a sordid mood, & dared not reveal my endless inadequacies: & now, I am afraid, you will inevitably (do what we may) sail out of my life in a very princessy & swan-like way. I feel like Schubert in *Lilac Time*,[2] a musical comedy you can scarcely have seen. But do let us, now & then, go for little reminiscent walks in St. James's Park; almost too like the Queen Mother & Sir Jasper Ridley.[3] So much the better; but don't put yourself out; you are to go, I hear, to Portugal which is a divinely romantic country, ½ pastoral ½ 18th century & the gothic made exotic & agreeably unserious by African influences. After this you will have to take time to instal yourself; to find a house in the country (I regret more bitterly than I can say that I never stayed in your cottage[4] while the staying was good) – so you will be busy. I shall, without any doubt feel twinges, duly, of this and that when, duly, I hear that other, remoter people have seen you when I have not; but I shall swallow them: the twinges, I mean. All marriages inevitably involve elimination: more by the course of events than deliberate design. But still, you must not abandon me utterly, and relationships only survive if nursed actively & continuously. I feel enormously sentimental: like a horribly bogus Evelyn Waugh nanny:[5] & remember the occasion when I first saw you, at Mells,[6] in 1937 or 8, Ben,[7] boomerangs & your extreme shyness & hostility to the liberal culture produced aggressively & imaginatively in spurts by Bubbles and relentlessly & gravely & nervously by Cressida;[8] I remember

1 Robert Charles ('Robin') Zaehner (1913–74), Spalding Professor of Eastern Religions and Ethics, Oxford, 1952–74; he had been a Research Lecturer at Christ Church when CC was studying philosophy at Oxford in 1940.
2 The English title of a Viennese operetta about the purported love-life of the Austrian composer Franz Schubert (1797–1828), using his music, which opened in London in 1922 and remained popular. At its conclusion Schubert remains alone with his music while his friends and the girl he loves marry others.
3 Sir Jasper Nicholas Ridley (1887–1951), banker, father of IB's friend Jasper Ridley; adviser on her art collection to his close friend Queen Elizabeth (born Elizabeth Angela Marguerite Bowes-Lyon 1900, Duchess of York 1923–36, Queen 1936–52 during the reign of her husband King George VI, Queen Mother 1952–2002).
4 At Broad Chalk, in Wiltshire.
5 In Waugh's *Brideshead Revisited* Nanny Hawkins is a comforting figure of stability for the other characters.
6 Mells Manor House in Somerset, owned by the Horner family since the mid-sixteenth century.
7 Presumably (Lionel) Ben(edict) Nicolson (1914–78), son of Harold Nicolson and Vita Sackville-West and, as a Balliol undergraduate 1933–6, one of IB's close friends; art historian; Deputy Surveyor of the King's Pictures 1939–47; editor, *Burlington Magazine*, 1947–78.
8 (Helen Laura) Cressida Ridley (1917–98), daughter of Sir Maurice and Lady Violet Bonham Carter, married to Jasper Ridley from 1939 until his death in 1944; later an archaeologist.

being a failure with Lady Horner[1] & a conversation with your mother[2] about walks; then the astonishing *petite saison*[3] at Oxford; then I stop. I can't continue: I can only again & again wish you an Elysian life, like an Empress in a very *ancien régime* ballet, but they don't move much, & so you must have more cosiness and gaiety with your grandeur (I insist on the inevitability of grandeur: not opulence, but grandeur) & I wish the Emperor very well too (my little hatchet[4] is long buried: & he knows little enough about it. Just as well) & you must not be ironical about my 'magnanimity'; & don't grudge his great very great good luck. This note will come mingled with & modified by many others – let it vanish with them & don't ever reply to it. And do let's go for our walk quite soon: I'll say many intensely agreeable & overdone things & you'll return to tea or dinner in an unbelievably good temper. God bless you & grant all your wishes.

Much love
    Isaiah.

TO S. H. BERGMAN[5]

27 August 1952 [*typed transcript*]

All Souls

Dear Professor Bergman,

[...] And now I must embark on something infinitely more painful and embarrassing to myself, namely your own very kind and generous letter enquiring whether I should myself contemplate a post in the University as teacher of philosophy. You must believe me when I say that I have given this question much anxious and, at times, tormenting thought. I have been a Zionist all my life, that is I believe that the only corporate future which the Jewish people can possibly have lies in Israel and there alone. I have, moreover, a personal sense not merely of duty but of homecoming every time I visit Israel. Morally and perhaps spiritually I should, I think, feel happy in Jerusalem, the responsiveness of students, and the moral satisfaction which any lecturer in Jerusalem must derive from a sense of identification with the unique process of helping, however humbly, to create his own nation,

---

1 Lady (Frances Jane) Horner (1854–1940), née Graham, maternal grandmother of IB's friend Lord Oxford (Violet Bonham Carter's brother Raymond Asquith had been her son-in-law).
2 Lady Gwendeline Theresa Mary ('Goonie') (Spencer-)Churchill (1885–1941), née Bertie, daughter of the 7th Earl of Abingdon.
3 'Little season'; CC spent a short time studying philosophy at Oxford at the beginning of the war.
4 Eden had incurred IB's displeasure by refusing to let him attend the 1945 Potsdam Conference as an interpreter.
5 Samuel Hugo Bergman (1883–1975), Czech-born philosopher, prolific author and translator; founding member and mainstay of the philosophy department, Hebrew University, Jerusalem, 1928–55, Professor from 1935; first Rector, 1935–8. He had written to IB on 11 May, in Hebrew, mentioning Leon Roth's resignation and his own forthcoming retirement, to suggest that IB take up a post at the Hebrew University.

and above all the irreplaceable sentiment of solidarity with Jews at a unique moment of creative endeavour ... all this makes an appeal to me which I ought not even [to] try to resist. But there are even graver considerations on the other side. I have, in effect, ceased to be [a] teacher of philosophy in Oxford, and become a Research Fellow of All Souls in order to try to do something about the social and intellectual antecedents of the Russian Revolution. This is what I now lecture about at Harvard, and to do this work I need libraries with Russian books, not obtainable outside London, Paris and the United States (in effect). Until and unless I have produced, or at least done my best to produce, the work on which I am now engaged, I shall feel useless and a drone in the social hive. Without the research facilities – having books and periodicals – and the peculiar tranquil conditions obtaining in Oxford I cannot, alas, do my work. And if I now ceased from it and came, in response to your generous invitation – by which I am most genuinely and deeply moved, and which has created a kind of moral crisis for me – I think, knowing my own character, that I should feel too much guilt about work not done, to be of any use. It is for this and no other reason that I must regretfully and sadly decline your invitation. That you should have thought of me in itself fills me with joy and shame: joy which I feel for any contact with the Israel community for which I shall live [sic] – and be proud – to do whatever I feel that I can; and shame at being in a situation which precludes me from direct participation in the work of the builders. I am sure you will appreciate my difficulties and the reason for my hardly come by decision. I should like, in conclusion, to thank you personally for your letter and to beg you to convey to your colleagues – whomever this concerns – my sense of gratitude at the honour which they conceived it possible to offer me, and my profound sorrow that at this juncture I feel obliged to decline it. If there is anything I can do for the University short of physically joining it, I shall be delighted to be given the chance of doing it.

Sincerely yours,
Isaiah Berlin

TO MAURICE BOWRA

27 August [1952, *manuscript*]

The Reform Club, Pall Mall, SW1

Dear Maurice

Immediately after your telephone call I went to look for Heroic P.[1] – but No 48, Hollycroft Av. doesn't exist. I communicated with the Post Office. They were vague. I therefore loyally bought a copy. The original arrived some days later. But even the uninscribed copy revealed the dedication. I

1 Bowra's most recent book, *Heroic Poetry* (London, 1952), was dedicated 'To Isaiah Berlin'.

was, & am, most deeply moved and childishly grateful. As you know I take a low view of myself & all I do & friendship means more to me – and always has – than anything else at all; any evidence of it props me for a little: and this great and handsome gift is like a vast inheritance with immense guarantees of security which, I suppose, is of all things what I lack the most. I really am moved beyond words: as you know it is not merely love and admiration for you that I feel, though these emotions are genuine enough; but [I] owe you a transformation of my entire mode of life and attitude towards it. It is a trite way of putting it perhaps, but you did 'liberate' me. Whether you had any such purpose – whether I shd have been less of a nuisance in chains – is something else. At any rate I am very clear that what is free, generous, life- and pleasure loving, warmhearted and intellectually anti-the prig front, anti-Eliot, anti-solemn, anti-Balliol, everything which makes one not merely a *de facto* but a conscious and devoted member of the immoral front, all or most of that I owe to the *seisachtheia*[1] which your influence brought about. And to say that I am grateful for that, is a ludicrous understatement. Having arrived in England with Russian sentiments & habits, & had a firm, narrow, tidy English uniform clapped on all this, I should, I think, have grown into a ludicrous caricature of English attributes but for this great act of rescue. I do not for a moment suppose that you were aware of the strength and eman-cipating power of your mere presence but if I am anything to anybody – if I am not altogether like Kahn or Prof. Pinto,[2] the responsibility is largely yours. I owe a debt to Stephen Spender too, and to no one else I think. I have always longed to say some of this to you, but direct statement is impos-sible, although I have tried to convey it to other people; & even now I don't begin to say all that I want & ought, but probably shall never be able, to say. [...] I feel honoured, delighted, publicly congratulated, proud, and in that special elevated & happy state in which one is nicer, abler, better, & capable of writing oneself. I wish I cd convey what I feel, but all the words are like sticks: I can't go on: when do you return? I shd like to tell you about Mrs Eden. My love to Bob B[oothby.] And thank you again.

Isaiah

P.S. And I shd like to talk to you about Heroic & romantic poets, if you could bear it.

---

1 Greek for 'shaking off the burdens'; an emancipatory law forbidding the mortgaging of land, passed under Solon in Athens in the early 6th century BC.
2 Vivian de Sola Pinto (1895–1969), Professor of English, Nottingham, 1938–61.

TO JOSEPH ALSOP

4 October 1952

All Souls

Dear Joe,

Thank you very much for your splendid letter, which I enjoyed a very great deal. And you must forgive me for not replying to it worthily. Indeed the whole notion of only writing letters when one feels that one has something to say and is in a mood to say it is thoroughly wrong and leads to conscious effort and formal correspondence of the kind of which the Laski–Holmes letters[1] – or what I read of them in the Atlantic – are such an embarrassing example.

I have had a miserable summer what with my father's illness and a job to do for the BBC and am only just about beginning to see vague daylight, but I am surrounded by All Souls examination papers, doctors' theses etc., still I would rather read than write, coward I am and coward I remain. My book is due in early spring. Toscanini's visit[2] has moved me profoundly, particularly his joy at meeting Charlie Chaplin[3] in the Savoy, he treated him like a toy which had mysteriously acquired reality, and he gave a wonderful account of why his meeting with President Truman was not a success. His concerts were a unique triumph, like Voltaire's[4] return to Paris, everyone stood up, the atmosphere was tense and filled with pathos and veneration, until the terrible moment when some boys, probably hired by Sir T[homas] Beecham, let off some crackers in the roof of the concert hall during the last movement of Brahms' 4th symphony. The orchestra almost stopped playing, but Toscanini apparently did not hear it. Meanwhile Charlie Chaplin will certainly become the focus of all the latent and patent anti-American sentiment here. I do not doubt that we shall give him an honorary degree etc. Do you really think that Stevenson will be elected? His jokes are so good, so genuinely funny, that surely a large number of persons in the United States will vote against anyone who pleases people like you and me. It is interest-

---

1 *Holmes–Laski Letters: The Correspondence of Mr Justice Holmes and Harold J. Laski, 1916–1935*, ed. Mark De Wolfe Howe (Cambridge, Mass., 1953).

2 Toscanini conducted two concerts in the Festival Hall in London on this visit. The programme on 29 September was Brahms's *Tragic Overture* and his first two symphonies; Brahms's 3rd and 4th symphonies and his *Variations on a Theme by Haydn* formed the second concert on 1 October. The *Times* critic echoed IB in concluding that Toscanini 'belongs to the world of heroes rather than of ordinary men' (2 October 1952, 9).

3 Charles Spencer ('Charlie') Chaplin (1889–1977), actor and film producer. He arrived in London on 23 September (his first visit in 21 years) in preparation for the London première of his latest film *Limelight* on 16 October (to which IB was invited); although he had lived in the US from 1914, his left-wing political views prevented his return there and he subsequently settled in Switzerland.

4 The pen name of François-Marie Arouet (1694–1778), French Enlightenment thinker and writer, whose radical political and religious views kept him in exile from Paris for many years. He returned there in 1778, shortly before his death, to great popular acclaim.

ing to see the attitude of those who regard him and Ike as of equal and indistinguishable merit (Lew Douglas is wonderfully on the fence, so are a good many others). I may be wrong, but I think Ike to be a good deal more reactionary and stupider, however kind and sincere, than most others think him. However, I expect I am wrong.

Mrs Eden I have not seen, and indeed will not until I have sent her wedding present. I have had kind messages from her, but think that on the whole I have lost rather than gained a friend. Not but what I shall go for little walks with her now and then. It was a strange act, even though one can explain it all and indeed I shall explain it all when you come here, if you wish to hear. Mr E. is only relaxed and happy with about half a dozen people, Jim Thomas[1] and Lew Douglas among them, and not with you or me, but I shall tell you all about that when I see you.

I dined last night with our old friend Lady Pamela Berry, there were there the Vice Chancellor and Brigadier Head.[2] Such rudeness as those two developed towards each other I have not heard for over ten years ⟨worse than Randolph, much.⟩, I shall not quote and if you repeat shall not embellish to you when I do see you. So contain yourself in patience and ask me when you come (when do you come by the way? You had better come straight to Oxford as before, it would give me intense pleasure). Lady P. kept kicking me under the table and begging me in a loud voice to stop the dreadful duel – both sides being very brutal and violent – but whenever I attempted to do so and was beginning to succeed she would empty another bucket of oil into the flames. Ultimately it is what she likes best, the old F. E. Smith gypsy blood[3] and a frustrated longing for White's Club.[4] But it was the most disagreeable evening I have spent for a long time. The V.C. certainly won on points and gave better than he got, he did not lose his temper and was altogether admirable. The Brigadier went on boiling after Sir Maurice left the room, and was told by me that he had gratuitously insulted the greatest humanist in the world; if this is not strictly accurate, it was necessary to penetrate that, whatever you may say, thickish hide, and yet I like the Brigadier, as you do, but mum's the word until we meet. [...]

Yours ever,
Isaiah

1 James Purdon Lewes Thomas (1903–60), 1st Viscount Cilcennin 1955, Conservative MP; Vice-Chairman, Conservative Party, 1945–51; First Lord of the Admiralty 1951–6.
2 Antony Henry Head (1906–83), 1st Viscount Head 1960, Conservative MP; Secretary of State for War 1951–6.
3 Pamela Berry's father was Frederick Edwin Smith (1872–1930), 1st Earl of Birkenhead, grandson of a gypsy, a brilliant, glamorous and hedonistic barrister, Unionist MP and Attorney-General, who relished combat.
4 A long-established and exclusive London club with traditions of gambling, self-indulgence and Conservatism.

TO MORTON WHITE

4 October 1952

All Souls

Dear Morton,

Thank you for your letter – I have had a sad summer, my father has been ill and I have had to record six hour-long talks for the BBC,[1] why they should want them like that God knows, I shall be blamed, not them, when my chaotic babblings stupefy the listener. Unlike you I have plunged into the mud of German romanticism etc., I do not say with enthusiasm, but with no nostalgia for either the thin clear streams of genuine logic or the heavy water of Wittgenstein. [...]

[...] I think we could produce a book on the philosophy of history and I think what we ought to do is to write letters to each other on the subject, and I am not sure that a correspondence between us on the subject might not make a better book? It could at any rate be tried. Certainly no such thing has ever been done before, novels have been written in the form of letters and philosophers have answered 1st and 2nd Objections, but a formal correspondence on a selected topic entitled, say 'Letters on the Philosophy of History' or the like has never been perpetrated to my knowledge, only imaginary ones like Lowes Dickinson's[2] *Letters to John Chinaman*, and things by Diderot and the like. I really do not see why not, do say what you think. I would be prepared to start early in the spring.

[...] About Sir M. Bowra's book:[3] I do not begin to defend it, I have not read it, and now that he has dedicated his last book to me I am in no position to criticise. All that you say is true, but it is quite hopeless. I would rather not commit my thoughts to paper on this topic. I like him very much and feel personally gratefully devoted to him, but he himself is aware of a certain attitude of disparagement about his works which I do not so much feel as evidently convey. When I see you I shall tell you all about all that.

Yours ever,

Isaiah

---

1 'I did two sittings of three and a half hours each: three lectures in one go, the other three lectures in the second [...]. I started at two and ended at half past five each day, talking continuously.' MI Tape 23.

2 Goldsworthy Lowes Dickinson (1862–1932), historian and pacifist. His *Letters from John Chinaman* (1901) is an unfavourable critique of Western political institutions supposedly written by a Chinese.

3 *The Romantic Imagination* (London, 1950), whose opening chapter MW had comprehensively damned for philosophical flabbiness.

TO ROWLAND BURDON-MULLER

7 October 1952

All Souls

Dear Rowland,

I see a little more daylight now. I have returned to Oxford, where the college is running beautifully under its new Warden, although not without some internal ructions. I was much amused by your delightful account of the visit to the Jameses and in particular Alice's musical talk, and this brings me straight to the subject of the great comble[1] of our season, namely the two concerts of Toscanini. He really is the greatest man in the world and there is no one for whom I have a greater admiration. His manager arrived and through him I was able to procure tickets for at any rate the second concert, where I observed Sir A. Cadogan sitting next to Lord Tedder[2] in the box immediately above me. It was the one concert which really did recapture to some small degree the magnificence of old-world social occasions, like the first night of an opera. No doubt a great many of those present were pure snobs and quite deaf and indeed anti-musical, nevertheless unless persons of this sort are attracted, the kind of panache they give to large costly events like these concerts, without which they cannot be given at all, becomes important, and therefore ultimately I approve. He conducted all the four Brahms symphonies in two concerts and although I do not really like Brahms very much, it was the most magnificent musical occasion, almost, that I attended, almost better than the concerts I went to in New York. Beethoven and Mozart to some extent play themselves, that is to say one is so charmed and delighted by the music itself that conductors, while they make an immense difference, nevertheless make it over and above the intrinsic pleasure which almost any performance of these works automatically produces. In the case of Brahms, to extract sounds of such lucidity and beauty out of material intrinsically so very unpromising is the property only of men of genius. There is something infinitely touching about his appearance, enhanced by the fact that he never uses a mirror by which to shave, because he so hates his own features and is seen swinging his legs on his bed with a Gillette razor – ridiculous and pathetic. Anyhow the concerts were a great triumph. I had Alix de Rothschild over for it from Paris, she looked to me rather melancholy, which perhaps is not surprising since her husband is really rather difficult to live with. [...] Toscanini was very pleased with the London orchestra and the whole thing went off in great style. He is as you know, 86, and he does not want to go off with a whimper but with a bang, and therefore he intends, if still alive and well, to bring the entire NBC orchestra over for a triumphal tour of Europe

1 'Summit, high-point'.
2 Arthur William Tedder (1890–1967), 1st Baron Tedder, Marshal of the Royal Air Force; Chancellor of Cambridge University 1950–67.

next spring and summer. I really feel one ought to get a caravan and follow him from town to town in a kind of final farewell to the greatest humanist, the greatest survival from the kind of nineteenth-century Europe which I love and admire. He says he is willing to go to any country which pays – he does not like France, he does not greatly like England, but if they pay he will come. The only countries he is not prepared to visit are Spain and Germany. Again what can one do but approve most warmly?

My father is better and I was able to leave him in London in fairly optimistic frame of mind and come to Oxford in order to read the papers of candidates for All Souls, and my goodness, it is a boring task. It is extraordinary how even brilliant people can become flat and almost nauseatingly platitudinous under examination conditions. [. . .]

Meanwhile I am still looking for a wedding present for my old friend Mrs Eden. That is a queer marriage about which I must write to you some time. In a way suitable, in a way enormously not. She once told me, the bride I mean, that she had no objections to Mr Eden's talking to his dogs and cats, all Englishmen do that, but that she was a trifle embarrassed when he addressed his strawberries and raspberries which grew in his garden as 'my darlings' and 'my dears' and enquired when it was that they would be appearing above the surface of the soil. I was therefore slightly surprised when she wrote to me secretly that she was engaged. He is, as you know, quite a nice man, very dull and genuinely conscientious, and, as again she once told me, almost dehumanised by patriotism. But you must not repeat these things, at least not as coming from that particular source. She is a curious girl, very independent, very first-hand, full of a kind of general independent Churchill personality, who lived in a flat by herself for almost too long on what resources I do not know. I doubt if she is in love with him, as for him I think he simply said to himself that he would marry the first girl he fell in love with. She loves him I think without being in love with him, if you know what I mean, pities him, regards him as pathetically inadequate in obvious social respects, and is determined to help him so far as she is able.

I should not be writing a letter of this kind to you, who are after all an American citizen – it is highly improper – and you know what happens in cases of this sort. I know that you and many others are afraid that Ike will simply be a prisoner of Taft and the right-wing Republican Party. I take a grimmer view of him than that and always have. I may be wrong, but I think he is very reactionary on his own account, I think there is no need to bring in sinister right-wing influences, I have a feeling that he is like all generals, unless one knows something to the contrary, liable to certain simple-minded, even high-minded, retrogradeness.

But I must go to bed, it is 2.15 a.m. and I shall not fall asleep before 3.00 because working in the evening which I have been doing before dictating this letter to my dictaphone is something which keeps me awake all night.

I had a terrible time recording enormous lectures of 50 minutes each at the BBC – I did not do it from scripts because I thought the scripts if read aloud would sound very dull – with the result that I simply roared hysterically into the machine, said a number of things I did not mean to say, for 8 hours on end – if they are put end to end – and will spend the whole of November and December in fear and trembling lest my colleagues and, alas, many others listen to me for 2 hours a week, if you please. Not Pericles, not Demosthenes,[1] not Cicero,[2] not Winston, could really hold people for that length of time. However, that is the BBC's business, and I blush as I think of it. The BBC is in a condition of great uproar. They have no Director-General, and no Director of the Third Programme, and the last is really the most civilised institution in Europe. The head of affairs is Cadogan, who is the Chairman of the Board of Governors, and is alleged to be insisting on some kind of censorship of talks. This may be a libel, but at any rate they are all at sixes and sevens at the BBC and, like a lot of rather amiable but highly neurotic ladies, keep rushing into each other's rooms reporting the latest news about appointments, dismissals, promises, pious resolutions etc. It is worse than Oxford, worse even it seems than the election at All Souls, the atmosphere is wonderfully electric, and I am very glad that at least one belongs to one institution and not to two. Our crisis is over and nicely over.

When I come back from London next week I shall write you a proper letter in long hand. Meanwhile keep yourself well, do not over-tire yourself, do not give yourself up to melancholy brooding about the future of the world, which although no doubt disastrous, is never quite so disastrous in the sense which one imagines it is going to be. And I do beg you to give my love to Alice B,[3] who has written me a very nice letter to which I have not yet replied.

It would be a great kindness if you could send me some delicious dried figs, but it is not at all necessary. Neither Fortnums, nor anyone else seems to have any until late December.

With all my love,

Yours ever,

Isaiah

As the broadcasts based on IB's Bryn Mawr lectures approached, the Radio Times *tried to interest potential listeners: it was most unusual for talks on 'such a difficult theme' not to be delivered from a script, but 'Mr Berlin [. . .]*

---

1 Demosthenes (384–322 BC), Athenian statesman and celebrated orator.

2 Marcus Tullius Cicero (106–43 BC), Roman lawyer, statesman and philosopher, famed for his oratory.

3 Almost certainly Alice Ethel Bitter (c.1885–1958), née Richardson, English wife of Francis Bitter, Professor of Physics at MIT; previously married to the Anglo-Sinhalese art historian and philosopher Ananda K. Coomaraswamy (and mistress of the occultist Aleister Crowley); under the name of Ratan Devi, a popular singer of Indian songs.

*is renowned for his fluent and witty expositions of abstract ideas. He has a
reputation as a conversationalist which extends far beyond Oxford.'*[1] *Mr Berlin
was not amused.*

TO ANNA KALLIN

Sunday [26 October 1952, *manuscript*]

All Souls

Dear Niouta

I must say that the note on me on p. 1. of the Radio Times did strike me as
revolting: and I cannot pretend that the errors & vulgarities about my philosophers (Helvétius was *not* of Swiss origin: & I say so in my talk: nobody ever
called Hegel Georg: etc.) touch me more deeply than the vignette of myself:
I expect it is all too true – the most belittling parts of it – like everything
that is disagreeable it too often turns out to be just – but one does not like
any the better. I cannot understand why it was allowed to appear: after all
the R.T. wd not or at least has not said things like that about Alan Pryce
Jones[2] or Eddie Sackville West or David Cecil or Cecil Day Lewis[3] or Stephen
Spender: & although I may be a mere jolly & garrulous *vulgarisiteur*[4] this is
not the capacity in which I thought I was being employed: certainly if I had
for a moment thought that anything like this could happen I shd never never
have agreed to broadcast. And now I do beg you to liquidate whatever can
be liquidated: don't repeat me more than is absolutely necessary: don't press
the *Listener*: they are quite right on the basis of this note to put me out of all
their thoughts: the *Listener* ought to occupy itself with more serious people.
You must not think that I am making heavy weather but, since I am treated
like a subject for *Picture Post,* I can at least refuse to collaborate. And I shd
like to make it clear that I wish to have nothing to do with broadcasting &
its affiliates so long as the present system prevails & people like you have no
control over what appears in the R.T.

One thing I do want to make quite quite clear & that is that I do not blame
you or H[arman] G[risewood] or anybody I know personally for anything:
& I have given you much too much trouble as it is, & have not always been
as considerate as I might have been, & shall always be most grateful to you
for all your infinite patience & encouragement & help. And everyone else at
the B.B.C. have always treated me with infinite courtesy and benevolence.
But, alas, I cannot now look my colleagues in the face: & so, I must cut my
losses and divorce myself from the B.B.C. – (I speak as if I was endlessly

1 *Radio Times,* 24 October 1952, 1. Anna Kallin apologised for the 'incredibly vulgar' wording over
   which she had no control (postcard postmarked 23 October).
2 Alan Payan Pryce-Jones (1908–2000), literary and theatre critic, author and journalist; editor, *The
   Times Literary Supplement,* 1948–59.
3 Cecil Day Lewis (1904–72), poet.
4 sc. *vulgarisateur,* 'populariser'.

employed by it. If this sounds pompous I apologise). Your first instinct will be to assuage my feelings. I do beg you, this time, not to. What is done is done & the sense of injury which I don't deny I feel may seem unjustified & silly in view of the apparent smallness of the cause. Still, I shall feel it.

One more thing: the Fichte & Hegel may need repairing – there seem some literally meaningless passages there – if so, I'll let you know v. soon – on Tuesday, say, & a van[1] may have to be sent: I wd rather not visit the hallowed portals just at the moment. And again I do send you my warmest gratitude for your part. Next time we shall talk about private matters. My little wound will heal: but I shall not again venture to expose myself so.

yrs ever
Isaiah

Don't distress yourself about this letter. I cannot help writing it: but you have done nothing to deserve it. So I apologise in advance.

On 29 October the schedule of broadcasts for the Third Programme included, at 9.30 p.m., sandwiched between 'Historical America in Song' and 'Beethoven', an item listed as 'Isaiah Berlin on Freedom and Its Betrayal'. IB's six talks, pre-recorded and broadcast at weekly intervals, soon became required listening for many. But IB himself remained unsure how they would be received.

TO URSULA NIEBUHR
30 October 1952

All Souls

Dear Ursula,

[...] Philosophy at Oxford is in a wonderfully flourishing condition – I don't know how long it will continue in that state, but the young men are very keen, new and important truths are discovered every hour, rigours of old-fashioned mechanistic positivism have been banished for ever by the imaginative romanticism of the followers of Wittgenstein. Philosophy and literature appear to be drawing together again in mysterious ways, altogether a tiny renaissance appears to be taking place, soon, soon, I expect to give way to an equally minute recession.

I am a little worried about what my dear old friend Stephen Spender ought to do. It seems to me that he has not written any very good poetry now for a very long time. He writes reviews, he attends conferences, he animates, he dashes about. He offers food for acid reflections by neo-Gothic reactionary writers. He is also becoming poorer. He wanted to be a Byron Professor in Athens, but that was given to somebody else. So now he has been invited to

1 An Outside Broadcast van in which parts of the talks could be re-recorded.

Cincinnati,[1] which I daresay was a good idea, for six months or longer. There is a kind of general tide against him for the moment, which he had better sit out somewhere else. And yet the atmosphere created by Mary McCarthy's *Groves of Academe*,[2] which I am sure is only too dreadfully accurate, as I think she has not much imaginative but an enormous analytical gift, is too depressing to set my mind at rest as to what will happen to dear Stephen. Do you know? Despite his complicated relations with Wystan, who I am sure is more than embarrassed about him, he is a very nice and noble character with a sort of devastating and ironical simplicity which makes conversation with him – to me at any rate – always marvellously repaying, so if you don't know him do get hold of him and Reinhold is bound to like him too, but perhaps you detest him already. Anyway I shall ask him and if it is all right I shall tell him to get in touch with you somehow when he goes to New York quite soon.

Meanwhile I am going through the agonies of having recorded for the BBC *hour-long* lectures on the model of the Bryn Mawr ones, which by a noble lie that maintains that the splendid spontaneity which listeners demand cannot be secured by script, have been poured out extemporarily. This is all very well, but no one can wish to listen to these talks of an hour each by anybody or on anything – not Demosthenes, not Winston, not Ike himself could or should hold an audience for that length of time. Moreover I have now looked at the script, the sentences are barbarous, ungrammatical, sentimental, not to say [ir]rational, and the whole effect hideously embarrassing. I shall not listen to them, but I expect angry remonstrances from all quarters, to which I propose to be too proud to reply. At least I shall not print them, and prevent the *Listener* from doing so. So you can I am sure detect that I am in a somewhat fluttery state and envy those who produce firm works of moral and political argument like Reinhold, either because they genuinely know their own mind or to what degree they do know them. I do neither the one nor the other.

Meanwhile I hear there is a conference in New York subsidised by Rockefeller[3] for legal and political thinkers to consider what means can be taken to stimulate new ideas etc. There is surely something wonderfully comical about a large number of solemn persons, well thought of in the public or academical worlds, sitting down absolutely soberly to consider ways and means to stimulate shy genius into self-expression. The attenders of the conference are not as bogus as they might have been, I hear, – apart

1 As the Elliston Professor of Poetry, University of Cincinnati, for 1953.
2 Mary McCarthy's satire on university campus life, *The Groves of Academe*, was published in 1952.
3 The 'First Conference on Legal and Political Philosophy' convened by the Rockefeller Foundation at Arden House, Harriman, New York, from 31 October to 2 November 1952 was intended to provide a philosophical and sociological input into the legal system so as to equip lawyers to provide political leadership.

from the lawyers I don't [know] who those will be – there will be Mabbott[1] who is dull, but I suppose 'sound', a good old Oxford tutor of what I might call 'our day'; Herbert Hart, who has become Professor of Jurisprudence, do you know him? He was a contemporary of 'ours' and was a favourite pupil of Joseph.[2] [...] He is a very nice and serious and altogether good man, much the best of our delegates; and finally Michael Oakeshott,[3] Laski's successor in London, deeply suspected of being a deliberate gesture to the right by an institution too long suspected of radical leanings, who I cannot for my part make out at all, some kind of neo-Burkean aestheticising essayist, very smooth and eloquent, with a good deal of charm and even fascination for all uses, but for the life of me I cannot reduce what he says to any kind of brass tacks. However I may be wrong and brought up in too wooden a tradition, and perhaps that is how metaphysical physicists used to talk and perhaps it is all about something after all.

I have been reading, I regret to inform you, Hegel, and he is a very disagreeable and in most respects terribly bogus writer, but a man of genius all the same and I suppose invented the notion of the development of thought. But I won't bore you with all that. I have decided – but I expect I decided that a long time ago – that the only man I really admire is Toscanini, who combines discipline and spontaneity and is generally a kind of embodied categorical imperative to a greater degree than anyone else now about. It gives me pleasure to think that when some woman went up to him in Milan and said, 'Maestro, you are great', he virtually spat at her with genuine fury and said that no conductors could be great, only composers could be that and that although he was 'perhaps a little better' than the others, nevertheless what was that and strutted angrily away. All this is genuine and not mere histrionic exhibitionism. In short I wish I lived in the nineteenth century and there were large and simple causes like Italian liberty or Russian peasants to mobilise all one's proper emotions on one side, instead of the confusing black and white pattern of the present. But then all Reinhold's works are designed to show that this is an illusion. I am sure it is and yet I cannot quite bring myself to believe him, and suffer from an acute nostalgia for a Victorian age.

I must not babble on like this. Do write and tell me anything you like. I shall be most grateful.

With much love to you and Reinhold,

Yours ever,

Isaiah

---

1 John David Mabbott (1898–1988), philosopher; Fellow, St John's, 1924–63, Tutor 1930–56, Senior Tutor 1956–63, later (1963–9) President.

2 Horace William Brindley Joseph (1867–1943), philosopher, Fellow of New College 1891–1932, Supernumerary Fellow 1932–43.

3 Michael Joseph Oakeshott (1901–90), Fellow, Nuffield, 1949–50; Professor of Political Science, London (LSE), 1951–69.

Chaim Weizmann had been gradually slipping towards death for many months.
The end came on 9 November.

TO ELIAHU ELATH[1]

12 November 1952 [*typed transcript of untraced original*]

All Souls

Dear Eliahu,

I really do not know what to say. You know what my personal relations
were to the late President, and I know what you think of him, too. To me
he seems a superhuman figure likely to grow larger rather than smaller with
time, as much as any gracious historical figure whom we now see as a fabulous or legendary one. Bigger than Lloyd George,[2] bigger than Roosevelt,
perhaps not to me bigger than Winston, but at least of that size, and of the
size of Henry of Navarre[3] or Cromwell,[4] or something of that kind. All his
faults, which both you and I knew so well, will recede into oblivion, of that
I am sure. The number of persons who have been able to make nations and
their memories are much brighter than those of other perhaps more morally
deserving but smaller personalities. He really was what the German romantic philosophers liked to call 'world-historical individuals'. But I must not go
on like this. I wrote in the moment induced by the first shock of the news
a quick note to the London *Times* because I did not think that anyone else
(unworthy thought) would contribute anything sufficiently worthy – not
that I thought I could say anything very much myself. I then saw the official
obituary notice,[5] which was exceedingly thin, and a letter from Brodetsky,[6]
which I thought thinner still. *The Times* telephoned this morning and said
that my note was a little too long, but that if I liked to cut it they would print
it.[7] So I shall do this as soon as I get it from them. I then immediately had the
feeling that I ought to go out and see Vera, and then as immediately thought
that this was a really very unnecessary thing to do. She will be surrounded
by all the Markses and Lord Nathan[8] and all the rest of it and would not
need me. So I shall write her a letter. In *The Times* I do not really say all that I

1 Eliahu Elath (1903–90), né Epstein, diplomat; Director, Political Department, Jewish Agency for
  Palestine, Washington, 1945–8; Israeli Ambassador to US 1948–50, to UK 1952–9.
2 David Lloyd George (1863–1945), 1st Earl Lloyd George 1945, Liberal politician and social reformer;
  Prime Minister 1916–22.
3 Henri IV (1553–1610), King of Navarre 1572–1610 and of France 1589–1610, promoter of religious
  toleration and social welfare.
4 Oliver Cromwell (1599–1658), leader of the victorious Parliamentary forces in the English Civil
  War; Lord Protector 1653–8.
5 *The Times*, 10 November, 5; the product of several hands.
6 *The Times*, 11 November, 8. Selig Brodetsky (1888–1954), Professor of Mathematics, Leeds, 1924–
  1948; President of the Board of Deputies of British Jews 1939–49; President of the Hebrew
  University of Jerusalem 1949–51.
7 IB's supplementary obituary was published in *The Times* on 17 November, 8.
8 Harry Louis Nathan (1889–1963), 1st Baron Nathan; solicitor; Minister of Civil Aviation 1946–8.

thought; I once promised an article for the *Atlantic Monthly*, which I suppose I shall now have to write, though I have really wonderfully little time, even for me. It is due, no doubt, to sheer inefficiency and chaos, but you know what my life is like. I feel like Maimonides[1] without his genius or justification, in the famous letter written to the Yemenites.

But I must not go on about my own trivial obligations in the shadow of this event. I did wonder too who would write, and the best letter, I am sure, written by an Englishman would have been written by Coupland; sad that poor Coupland is dead too,[2] and I have this very day to go to a memorial service[3] for him, and as it appears that he had no relations at all, I shall probably have to go to the crematorium too, as one of the very few people here who genuinely knew and liked him – very few is perhaps an exaggeration, but not as many as you might think. He really would have written a very noble piece about our late friend. I really feel very flat about the thing at the moment, and shall no doubt soon start collecting those fragments of reminiscences, those odd legends and sayings and aphorisms of the Master, which will then gradually accumulate into a kind of penumbra of myth. I am sure I shall be blamed for not attending the funeral, but that I am prepared to face. I think I can do more by commemorating his memory in some other way.

In the meanwhile, I shall be grateful to you for a favour: there will no doubt be a memorial service in London and I would like to go to it. So would my parents. As there is likely to be a huge influx of people, it would really be a very great kindness, if there are tickets, if I could be supplied with three of these. Apart from official persons – and there will no doubt be far too many – I suppose that I really am among the not so very many people who really did know him intimately, and who have some kind of moral claim, otherwise I would not burden you with this request. [...] You did promise to come and see me in Oxford this Term, but perhaps you are too overburdened at the moment. If not, I should like to hold you to your promise – [...] or would you rather wait until all this is over? Though I do not quite see why you need, when mourning is over it is over, and one is free to live again. There is no one of particular importance to meet here (I should think), but the town is still beautiful, and it really is a change and a quiet and tranquil place of refuge from daily routine. The late President always refused to come on the grounds that the place was 'too churchy'. I have ceased to feel that – if ever I felt it a long time ago. So do come.

Yours ever,

Isaiah.

---

1 Maimonides (*c.*1138–1204), influential rabbi, philosopher and physician, based mainly in Egypt, who codified Jewish law; when approached by the Jews of Yemen he advised them how to cope with Muslim persecution.
2 Coupland had died on 6 November.
3 It was the funeral that was held at All Souls on 12 November. The memorial service was held on 18 November at St John's Wood synagogue, with IB again in attendance.

In the US presidential election on 4 November, Eisenhower had convincingly defeated Stevenson. Liberals feared the worst.

TO ARTHUR SCHLESINGER

25 November 1952 [*manuscript*]

As from All Souls

Dear Arthur,

How wonderfully wrong Joe is about everything. First he predicted Stevenson (heavily) then he voted for Eisenhower, then, he swore J. F. Dulles wd *not* be secretary of state. And so on. Yet he continues to be listened to like an oracle. One loves him for himself: he spent a week-end with me: hummed & said ah-h-h-h-h a great deal between words and spoke of the "maaass of Russian power" & the like & ultimately endeared himself as always. I *am* gloomy about your election. Dulles is very like a Munichite: I've thought so ever since his welcome to Westrick[1] in 1940 which struck my imagination most powerfully. No worse than the Chamberlainites: but no better: & that in 1952 is bad enough (& was so in 1932, 1942 etc.) – quiet dry rot you think. I think so too. I have just had lunch with R. Makins:[2] make his acquaintance, do. He longs to, & I've told him he could get hold of you easily via Phil or Chip or anybody in Washington. He is not fascinating; but a cow exuding common sense like milk; & an old buddy of Ike's from Algiers. Right of centre: but immensely sane, sage, safe, & understanding all one says. Perfectly genuine, businesslike & less austerity-utility than Sir O[liver Franks]; but utility enough: pre-war utility so to speak, when luxury was more common, but utility more luxurious. He inquired sympathetically after Prich (*tell him!*) which is something. Oxford flows on: cold war between the factions at All Souls with Rowse more Malvolio-like than ever. I am glad that R. B. Muller has at last found a responsive correspondent. I do my best but what is that? Man[?] is (only morally) stouter.

And now I must consult you on a series of thorny questions.

1) Dear Mary Jane Benton.[3] I owe her a sum of money: for typing out my lectures & sending them. [...] I don't suppose you can pay her this without lending me: my friend Mrs Halban, whose husband[4] you met with me in Oxford, & who is *much* nicer (& prettier) than he, & is now at the Carlyle

---

1 Gerhard Alois Westrick (1889–1957), German Commercial Counsellor, corporate lawyer, high-ranking Nazi and commercial spy in the US during 1940, until his activities were exposed.

2 Sir Roger Mellor Makins (1904–96), later (1964) 1st Baron Sherfield, diplomat; British Ambassador to US (where he succeeded Oliver Franks) 1953–6; Joint Permanent Secretary of the Treasury 1956–9.

3 One of IB's secretaries in the US.

4 Hans Heinrich *Halban (1908–64), né von Halban, Austrian-born (naturalised French) nuclear physicist who had played a major role in the development of nuclear fission; based at the Clarendon Laboratory, Oxford, 1946–55.

Hotel in N. York, would pay you: & so do anyhow call her up & invite yourself to tea: you'll find her charming & very soignée: or if not very, yet very
agreeable anyhow [...].

2) What am I to do about Harvard: I shall have written Bobby Wolff a
gigantic muddled letter about all this. I don't much want to stay away, this
time, more than the statutory 4 months or so: Oppenheimer[1] has kindly
invited me to the Institute for 1 year; I wd [not] come for a year anyway, but
4 months of leisure, books, no classes, & more money than Harvard pays
(1000 a month) is certainly tempting: but yet I don't want (a) to break off
my Harvard connection (b) behave like a cad (c) be away for more than 4–5
months because of my aged parents whom it does plunge into gloom. (d)
leave England in 1953 at all, since, having finished the politics – Bryn Mawr
book – I want to get properly into the Russian one. [...]

I'd be most grateful for help & advice. In England, politically, literarily,
artistically, intellectually, we are not retrogressing, but marking time. I feel
guilty about not going to Israel to Ch. Weizmann's funeral: ominous cold
silence from the widow. I wrote a sentimental but sincere piece in the *Times*
(better than F.F.'s[2] though I say so) & feel obliged, but not eager, to write
what Nicholas N. calls a necrology (he wanted me to produce one for *Preuves*:
but I cannot ladle these out like a new industry belabouring & exploiting
my friend & master's corpse) for the Atlantic: but I cannot, somehow, "do"
Winston, & not Weizmann. I feel like Fontenelle, Bossuet, Condorcet[3] – professional éloge-producers – & I can imagine H. T. Levin's comments on this
my megalomania. I am trying to get him asked to Oxford for a lecture. For
me – pure pleasure, as Time wd say.

Much love to Marian

Isaiah   [...]

*Although John Sparrow was settling comfortably into his role as Warden of All
Souls, IB was anxious to prevent complacency taking hold.*

1 (Julius) Robert Oppenheimer (1904–67), physicist; Director, Los Alamos Scientific Laboratory,
1943–5; Director and Professor of Physics, Institute for Advanced Study, Princeton, 1947–66.
2 Frankfurter's letter about Weizmann had appeared in the *New York Times* on 12 November.
3 Frenchmen noted for their eulogies to the deceased: Bernard de Bovier de Fontenelle (1657–1757),
philosopher, writer and scientist; Jacques-Bénigne Bossuet (1627–1704), bishop, theologian and
orator; Marie Jean Antoine Nicolas Caritat (1743–94), Marquis de Condorcet, philosopher and
mathematician.

TO JOHN SPARROW

26 November 1952 [*carbon*]

All Souls

My dear Warden,

This is not a letter intended to be communicated as it stands to the College, either to a committee or the entire sovereign assembly. All I have done is to put down some reflections about what seem to me to be certain needs of the College. As we are presently constituted, we have among our forty-nine fellows twelve professors, five senior research fellows and three researchers in the first seven-year category, with perhaps two to follow among those elected this year. So far as professors are concerned, I think we are doing our duty, and more than our duty, to the University. On the other hand, I feel that we ought to do rather more for learning, unconnected with University teaching, than we are doing.

The importance of academic research seems to me to have grown vastly during the last quarter of a century. When I first came up, although it was of course respected, the main duty of college research was thought to be to teach; some thought, like Dundas[1] or Masterman,[2] that this was sufficient; others, like Roy Harrod or Beazley,[3] thought research was more important – this battle was fought for years at Christ Church. Certainly college tutors and even professors were not made to feel that research was the principal, or indeed a very important part, of their function. Since then, all this has changed; I think for good, but whether or not this is so, the change is very great indeed. The claims of research are now treated by every college with the utmost seriousness and tutors are more or less despised unless they show evidence of it. Every college with the means for it, with the notable exception of New College, tries to endow research fellows. I think this is all to the good, and that the kind of dreary and useless academic production, which some people feared, has not in fact resulted. It therefore seems to me that with this new emphasis, we ought to do our part, and are not doing perhaps quite enough, towards the advancement of learning. The same obligation seems to fall on the other colleges devoted to learning, Nuffield and St Antony's for example. And sometime, even though this may be thought forward of me, I propose to talk to the heads of these colleges on this topic.

I should like to propose: (1) That we enquire into the material means for electing additional research fellows, not necessarily from among our own examination fellows, but from the outside world, as was done in the case of Warden Henderson, and McCarthy,[4] Plamenatz and Dunbabin. I have

1 Robert Hamilton Dundas (1884–1960), classicist; Student and Tutor, Christ Church, 1910–57.
2 John Cecil Masterman (1891–1977), historian; Student, Christ Church, 1919–46; Provost, Worcester, 1946–61; Vice-Chancellor, Oxford, 1957–8.
3 John Davidson Beazley (1885–1970), Professor of Classical Archaeology and Art, Oxford, 1925–56.
4 A typing error for Carlile Aylmer Macartney (1895–1978), Research Fellow, All Souls, 1936–65;

several names in mind, but perhaps these need not be mentioned at this stage. As for the classes of fellowships into which such candidates may be fitted, that obviously depends on their age, standing and needs. I have in mind, during the next five years, the election of four or five additional fellows into this category, so far as compatible with the statutory limitations upon the various classes of research fellowships. (2) Another way in which we might promote learning would be to offer facilities for research to existing members of the University, notably fellows of colleges in humane subjects. Several sub-faculties and faculties have recorded the fact that they feel there is an acute need for sabbatical years and the like for college teachers who have begun on a book or some other considerable learned enterprise, and who are debarred from continuing or finishing it by demands of college teaching. Some among the richer colleges can of course afford to give their members such an occasional year, but many are too poor. It would, I think, be a real service to learning to assist other colleges in the following way: if we decided that a man was worthy of such aid, we could propose that he could retain his existing fellowship, supply a grant (for one year, renewable for a second, and in exceptional cases for a third, sufficient to pay for the teaching of the man's relevant number of pupils), offer the scholar in question membership of Common Room and other facilities as he may need and we possess, e.g. rooms, free dinners, etc., and on occasions even small sums to enable him to go abroad if this is plainly required by his work, with the clear understanding that he would leave us after the 'sabbatical' period had expired. I believe strongly that this would go a long way towards satisfying a mounting need, introduce interesting and stimulating persons into our midst and be very well received by the University at large. And I think that St Antony's and Nuffield might be well advised to do the same. Perhaps a concerted scheme could be devised for directing scholars to the most appropriate environments. I have talked about this with the Vice-Chancellor and the Registrar, and they adduced additional arguments in support of this, which they would be only too glad to let you have. I do not think we need to extend this principle beyond this University, since Cambridge provides for its own, and the provinces allow tutors far more time for their own work than the average Oxford tutor. No doubt it would be nice for provincial professors to live in Oxford without teaching or lecturing duties, for the completion of some piece of work, but this seems to me to be a luxury, whereas my scheme is only intended to cover necessities or near necessities.

My main motive in suggesting all this is the advancement of learning and the improvement of the academic quality of the College, which seems to me to be in some need of care; but I cannot deny that the goodwill which such a step would, I am sure, secure in the sight of the University and academic

Montagu Burton Professor of International Relations, Edinburgh, 1951–7.

circles generally, including the University Grants Committee, does not seem to me to be unwelcome. Of course, there may be other proposals for increasing the numbers of the College and other ways of spending its income, e.g. on the accommodation of other classes of fellows, the election of distinguished statesmen or other public persons, and no doubt this proposal has to be weighed against the rest. I merely send it to you for what it is worth. I should be grateful if you would turn it over in your mind, and perhaps speak to one or two of the persons whom you think suitable. I have spoken to very few of my colleagues as yet.

Yours ever,

TO ROWLAND BURDON-MULLER
2 December 1952

All Souls

My dear Rowland,

Well, you have done it now, you have elected your President and the fruits are gradually appearing on the tree one by one. Am I right to be gloomy? I don't know. Joe Alsop has certainly been here and though he is genuinely high-minded and brave, his political prophecies are not always correct, he was sure that Stevenson would win. He wrote me a letter saying that I was to put on any loose money that I might find wandering about Oxford on Stevenson for him. Even after Eisenhower was elected (for whom I think Joe voted, though he was a little embarrassed about admitting it, although courage played its part and he stood up to the situation like a man and confessed everything like somebody in a Prague trial) he still thought that it was impossible for Dulles to be made Secretary of State. He prophesied the opposite virtually the night before Dulles was appointed, and so I know now what to think of the prophecies of qualified political forecasters. What will Winthrop Aldrich[1] be like as Ambassador to London? I have never met him but only heard glancing references to him. The general impression which was conveyed to me was that he was an averagely stupid, averagely conservative, relatively unoffending figure, quite nice, rather dim-witted, high-minded, earnest but no great shakes. Is this true? I am sure you know him. Do tell me.

Thank you very much indeed for the figs. The parcel arrived about three days ago, after wandering about an unconscionably long time. I did not like to say to your previous enquiries that it had not arrived because I was sure that in the end it would and it seemed ungrateful and ungraceful to emphasise its absence. However they are here now and very delicious too. Quite different from the ones I consumed in such quantities and with such enthusiasm

---

1 Winthrop Williams Aldrich (1885–1974), US lawyer and banker, Ambassador to Britain 1953–7.

during the unforgettable days in 1951. And of a kind not obtainable here. Thank you very much for them.

So you have been having Mrs Halban to stay. I like her very much. She is beautifully bred and altogether charming: and lives in a curiously detached and half [awake?] way in Oxford, to which she does not belong in any sense and which she reacts to in a half sleepwalking fashion. But her house[1] is charmingly appointed and very agreeable to get away to from the formally functioning, occasionally dreary functioning of our ordinary lives here. Her husband is another story and I won't write to you about him here and now. When we meet I should love to tell you about him, it is all like a German nouvelle[2] of the late 1920s by Thomas Mann[3] or someone of that kind.

All Souls is functioning fairly peacefully, the Warden is wonderfully frivolous – and that has its advantages and disadvantages – advantages when proposals come up to which one is hostile oneself and which he manages to laugh out of court with extreme irony and skill. Disadvantages when one is seriously concerned about some proposal and one finds exactly the same treatment meted out to that too. But he is a very superior person and I am very glad that we have him. [...] I am in great hesitations, difficulties, doubts etc. about whether and when to return to Harvard. I think they expect me at the end of about 1953, and meanwhile I have had a letter from Oppenheimer from Princeton asking me to go there for a year. Well of course in a way Princeton is more attractive because they pay me as much as they do at Harvard and there is no work to do at all, one is allowed in short to get on with one's own book, and although it is physically nearer New York, yet somehow it is much more remote and withdrawn. But on the other hand I have a quasi-official gentleman's agreement to go to Harvard once in two or three years and although they will see only too well what the advantages of Princeton are, yet it will inevitably annoy them and I don't really wish to break my connection, in short I don't want to go too far, behave too badly, be too self-regarding. And yet, when I think of what happens to me at Harvard, I feel that I enjoy my lectures and do quite a lot of work as far as Harvard is concerned, and am indeed generously and well paid for it, but that it leaves me relatively too little time for my own work, perhaps I have only my own social nature to blame, but I think that must be taken as a datum, I really do not think I can re-educate myself now too abruptly or too dramatically. Certainly I can refuse more engagements than I do, sit in my room more continuously than I do and work harder. That was always possible in my life, yet it is no real solution to my problems. I am not a regular worker. I cannot do any work if I only have say an hour to do it in,

1 Hill Top House in Headington, so named because it stands at the top of the hill east of Oxford that links the main city to Headington; bought by Sir Oliver Franks when the Halbans moved to Headington House in 1953.
2 'Novella', '(long) short story'.
3 (Paul) Thomas Mann (1875–1955), German novelist and social critic.

after which there is some inevitable interruption. I can only seriously work in enormous spurts of 6 or 7 hours at a time, for 2, 3, 4, 5 or 6 weeks, after which there is a long period of idleness. I am in short a slow starter and difficult to uproot, and under these conditions regular teaching work, for [sc. or?] delivering lectures about which I take, being a nervous and insecure speaker, almost more trouble than they are worth, plus pupils coming in at odd hours, break up that continuity which I require for the purpose of getting anything done at all. Hence long empty days in Princeton are really something; whereas half teaching, half one's own work in Harvard is relatively less good. However I enjoy going there, I do not wish to stop it, and I do not wish to irritate them too much, so I have tumbled out all these arguments and hesitations and doubts to the man who deals with these things, i.e. Prof. Wolff at Harvard and asked him what he thinks, now I am awaiting his reply. Really I do not want to get away in 1953 at all. My first book should be ready by about March and I want six or seven months to get into my bigger one before going abroad. Ideally I should not like to leave England in 1953 at all except for short journeys in Europe for pure pleasure. Perhaps I could go to Harvard in the autumn term and perhaps go on to Princeton in the spring as I did with Bryn Mawr, but then my poor parents are getting old and they miss me very much and I really cannot stay away from them for about 7 months without plunging them into the most pathetic melancholia. Consequently I think I should have to bring them over to New York at Christmas or something of that sort. Then there is the problem of how they could be paid for. I am not sure that Harvard pays me quite enough to enable me to do that. If they would pay me a little more this year I think the whole thing would be more feasible. However, I do not know why I should burden you with all this. Cast it out of your mind and let us think of other things. I shall continue my dreary correspondence on the subject and settle it somehow. If no problems were graver then this life would be very happy indeed.

[...] Meanwhile my dear old friend the President of Israel died and I wrote a little letter about him to *The Times*, because I thought that nobody else would, nobody else did in effect. They misprinted the end of it – I wrote it in my own illegible hand and said that he was the noblest and wisest man I had ever known. They said that he was the noblest and best man I had ever known. Well of course he was not in a sense a good man at all, not as goodness is normally spoken of. He was vindictive, he was too ambitious, too political, too public a figure altogether to be either altogether nice or altogether good. What he was was a great man, which is a very different thing, and I compared him to Cavour[1] and I daresay could compare him to Parnell,[2] certainly Parnell's attitude to his own followers, their admiration

1 Count Camillo Benso di Cavour (1810–61), reforming journalist and politician, Prime Minister of Piedmont, then of the new Kingdom of Italy which he had helped to create.
2 Charles Stewart Parnell (1846–91), Irish political leader, whose commitment to the cause of Irish Home Rule transformed the political scene at Westminster.

and hatred of him, his indispensability and at the same time half-maddening hauteur, were very similar to Weizmann's complicated and hostile relations to his immediate lieutenants. And yet I do not feel like writing a little note to *The Times* to correct the error. Imagine what it would have been like for *The Times* to print a little note say in the personal column saying, 'Mr I. Berlin wishes it known that Dr Weizmann was not the best man he had ever known.' So I let it stand.

I had a charming letter from Salem, in which he speaks of coming here in the spring. I very much hope he does, I should be delighted to see him here or indeed anywhere.

The Prague trials[1] are too awful: as you know it is not the kind of thing which I did not expect, it seems to me a routine matter, and yet the particular list of defendants is the most grotesque that was ever drawn up. The lists the Russians drew up in 1936, 1937, 1938 may in their way have been just as absurd, but one did not know it at the time, because one did not know the personalities involved, but the splendid collection of criminals associated with each other in this particular catalogue is too wonderful to be true. A list consisting of John Foster Dulles, Alexander Werth,[2] who is virtually a Communist correspondent of the *New Statesman*; Noel Coward,[3] the character referred to throughout as 'the spy Jebb', Zilliacus,[4] and Crossman under orders from Allen Dulles,[5] arm in arm with the pro-Communist members of the Israel Left Socialist groups: all these persons engaged in subverting the freedom of Czechoslovakia together with Tito, and I daresay Elsa Maxwell,[6] Ronnie Tree, Billy James and you and me as well. Zilliacus made a splendid statement saying that he had in his day visited both Stalin and Molotov[7] and sincerely hoped that they would not get into trouble through associating

1 On 20 November in Prague the trials began of Rudolf Slansky, formerly Secretary-General of the Czech Communist Party, and 13 other prominent individuals, accused of being 'Trotskyist-Titoist-Zionist bourgeois-nationalist traitors, and enemies of the Czechoslovak people' (*The Times*, 22 November 1952, 5) and of collaborating with Western secret services (whose agents allegedly included some most surprising individuals); 11 of the 14 accused were Jews. All pleaded guilty and comprehensively damned their own actions. Slansky and 10 others were executed, the remaining three sentenced to life imprisonment. The Western press ridiculed the charges and pointed to anti-Semitism and the desire to impress Moscow as motivating factors in the trials.
2 Alexander Werth (1901–69), journalist and author; correspondent, *Sunday Times* and BBC, Moscow, 1941–6; *Manchester Guardian*, Moscow, 1946–8; *New Statesman*, Paris, 1949–53; *New York Nation*, Paris, 1949–53, 1957–69. One of the Prague defendants confessed to contact with him in 1947.
3 Noel Peirce Coward (1899–1973), actor, playwright, writer and composer of popular songs, worked for the intelligence services during the war.
4 Konni Zilliacus (1894–1967), of mixed Finnish, Swedish, Scottish and American parentage; left-wing Labour MP 1945–50, 1955–67; a supporter of Tito against Stalin. Several of the Prague accused were alleged to have had contacts with him.
5 Allen Welsh Dulles (1893–1969), brother of John Foster Dulles; US lawyer; Deputy Director CIA 1951–3, Director 1953–61.
6 Elsa Maxwell (1883–1963), leading US party-giver known as 'the hostess with the mostest'.
7 Vyacheslav Mikhailovich Molotov (1890–1986), leading Soviet politician and diplomat, regarded as Stalin's deputy; Foreign Minister 1939–49 and 1953–6.

with him. I am very sorry about the poor Jews of Czechoslovakia and the other popular democracies who are going to be the innocent victims of this particular purge, but I see [that] in a State which is determined to crush all thought and all ideology and rule everybody in an absolutely wooden and iron way, the particular sort of political liveliness and love of argument and desire to talk which the Jews certainly possess, there is no room for them. I tremble a little for the fate of the ones I know in Moscow. [...]

What can I tell you of England? My friend, the new Mrs Eden, received an extremely violent letter from Evelyn Waugh,[1] in which he told her that she was in effect an adulterous renegade (from the Roman Church in which she was educated) for marrying poor Mr Eden. This letter she received on the morning of her wedding, and although she knows Evelyn Waugh is mad and although he is not a great friend of hers, yet I must say I think it would be a shock to one on one's wedding day to receive a bitter lunatic denunciation by a well-known person. Nothing happened about it. She did not reply, but her entire family was naturally incensed and in due course Randolph, waiting for an opportunity when White's Club was full of the peerage and other persons whom Evelyn Waugh naturally admires and respects and wishes to be well thought of by – approached him with apparent innocence at the bar (they are old friends still from the days when they both served as Commandos in Yugoslavia) and said something like – 'It is interesting to observe that while the premier Catholic families of England received my cousin Clarissa's marriage with every mark of approval and sympathy, it took a lower middle-class Catholic convert of recent date and dubious morals to defend the position of the Church', or something on those lines and apparently genuinely routed him in the sense that poor Evelyn fled or so at least the anti-Evelyn gossips relate. [...] I heard *Norma* in Covent Garden most beautifully sung by Madame Callas,[2] and Signora Stignani.[3] Madame C.'s gestures were somewhat Levantine when, as the [*word(s) omitted*] she reproached the virtu-

1 IB's account is rather misleading. Evelyn Waugh, a fervent Catholic convert, wrote to Clarissa Churchill (with whom he was avowedly in love) on 13 August, the day between the announcement of her engagement and the wedding: 'I mourn the loss of a greatly loved friend & wish I had been gentler at our last meeting [...]. Can I have Mass said for your marriage, or is that impossible? Yours, with my love, Evelyn'. Immediately after the encounter with Randolph Churchill, himself no admirer of Eden, in White's Club on 2 September, Waugh (with a 'fuddled nut', as he admitted on 6 September) wrote again to explain that the purpose of his previous letter was to ask whether she had left the Catholic Church, or whether Eden's previous marriage might have been secretly annulled; now accepting that she was no longer a Catholic, Waugh lamented: 'Did you never think how you were contributing to the loneliness of Calvary by your desertion?' But he nevertheless ended: 'My love to you always'. *The Letters of Evelyn Waugh*, ed. Mark Amory (London, 1980), 378, 382, 381.

2 Maria Meneghini Callas (1923–77), née Maria Anna Sofia Cecilia Kalogeropolous, US-born Greek operatic soprano, who made her London début in five performances of *Norma* at the Royal Opera House between 8 and 20 November (not long before her dramatic mid-career weight loss).

3 Ebe Stignani (1904–74), Italian mezzo-soprano, who played Adalgisa.

ous Roman Consul for leaving her, her gestures were rather like those of an Athenian landlady casting out a drunken lodger. She sang in a harsh but splendid voice, and the music is absolutely golden. I heard the opera once in the Metropolitan and it is far better done here. He is a wonderful composer, Bellini,[1] and I wish more works by him were performed. The miserable Mr Howes[2] of *The Times* talked about outdated opera and the dreary rumtitums of pre-Wagnerian Italian bel canto. It is exactly as if one complained about the dreary inaptitudes of Shakespeare's absurd characters in comparison with the splendours of Alexander Dumas[3] or Alexander Sautre.[4] Still I must not run on, I must do some work, I must get on with it all. There is no one that loves work less than I, and no one needs to do it more.

　　With great affection,

　　　　Yours ever,

　　　　　　⟨with much love⟩

　　　　　　Isaiah

TO ALICE JAMES

9 December 1952

All Souls

On the whole it is better that my letters be typewritten; I cannot believe that the intimacy and directness of handwriting compensates for the appalling torments which it inflicts upon my friends. And now that I have a dicta-phone, this toy absorbs me entirely, and every childish instinct I have is set in play by its attractiveness as a 'gadget'. In one sense, I detest our time and look back even on the 1930s with acute nostalgia. I would much have pre-ferred to have been born a hundred years before I was, to have been once present at an evening in Paris given by George Sand[5] (smoking a cigar) – at which Chopin, Merimée, Musset, Heine, Proudhon, Delacroix, Turgenev, Bellini, Nerval, Hugo, and the young Flaubert, the ageing Sainte-Beuve and

1　Vincenzo Salvatore Carmelo Francesco Bellini (1801–35), Italian composer of bel canto operas.

2　Frank Stewart Howes (1891–1974), lecturer, Royal College of Music, 1938–71; music critic, *The Times*, 1943–60. His review of *Norma* praised the singers (who included Joan Sutherland in a minor role) but damned the 'tedious opera' as 'an object lesson in musical vapidity' for 'the pizzicato bass, the rum-tum wind chords, the scrubbed string accompaniment, and the eternal arpeggia [...] which Wagner made for ever out of date', and summed up Bellini's work as 'an opera of the type that did for perhaps half a century make the form a byword for absurdity' (*The Times*, 10 November 1952, 2).

3　Alexandre Dumas (1802–70), né Alexandre Dumas Davy de la Pailleterie, French novelist and playwright, famous for *The Three Musketeers* (1844) and *The Count of Monte Cristo* (1845–6).

4　This apparently unknown gentleman is likely to be an invention of IB's typist, struggling with a dictation system capable of repeating and distorting words; Sir Walter Scott seems a likely candidate for the missing author.

5　The pen-name of the French novelist Baroness Dudevant (1804–76), née Amantine-Lucile-Aurore Dupin.

Paganini,[1] were all talking like mad – not to speak of all the other Russian, German, Italian, Hungarian etc. revolutionaries, and, alas, no Englishman at all. On the other hand, modern gadgets, talking machines, unbreakable thermometers, inextinguishable lighters, buttons which convert rooms, rotate houses, and simultaneously play the Seventh Symphony and tell one the news, fascinate me enormously, and this too is perhaps rather like typical early nineteenth-century preoccupation with scientific schemes and Utopias – like mad Russian squires who used to invent carriages which, once set in motion, played military marches, ground coffee and did something else as well, like unrolling the map of Australasia – except that these carriages never worked, and always broke down almost at once. And yet I feel (I hope you do not mind this absurd rambling of mine) that Dr Wiener[2] and cybernetics really does mark an important and sinister stage in our development, and that Toynbee is extremely wrong in supposing that it is atomic energy which marks the 'third industrial revolution'. The atom bomb is very, very powerful, but that is all. Two hundred kinds of bombs could have been already doing that kind of damage. Atomic energy may replace coal and that will transform things a bit; but all this is rather like what was going on already, only more so. But if clerical workers and civil servants are replaced by mechanical memories and brains – and if there is another war, they certainly will, and perhaps even if there is not (I cannot think there will be war at all soon, despite everything) – that will upheave our lives totally, and change everybody's occupations and cause people to need a quite different education and to feel and to think quite differently. That is what marks a real change, and all the talk about the 'atomic age' is a kind of short-sighted vulgarity. [. . .]

All Souls also is gradually growing peaceful. The wounds have not entirely healed, but new skin seems to be growing over them. The conditions of cold war still somewhat persist. Seznec is enjoying it all very much. [. . .]

Life goes away in the pursuit of small pleasures and the avoidance of small pains, the performance of small tasks, etc. I have had the hideous experience of recording six lectures on the wireless, of no less than an hour each, which involved me in a kind of agonised bawling into a machine with no script and no notes and what seemed to me a hysterical fever, with notations stretched in front of me in chaotic heaps, dropped with the noise of a thunderclap,

---

1 Those of IB's chosen fellow-guests not so far annotated are Frédéric François (né Fryderyk Franciszek) Chopin (1810–49), Polish pianist and composer; Prosper Merimée (1803–70), French archaeologist, playwright and short-story writer; Alfred Louis Charles de Musset (1810–57), French playwright, novelist and poet; Christian Johann Heinrich (né Chaim Harry) Heine (1797–1856), German lyric poet, journalist and essayist; Ferdinand Victor Eugène Delacroix (1798–1863), French romantic painter; Gérard de Nerval, pen name of Gérard Labrunie (1808–55), French romantic poet; Victor-Marie Hugo (1802–85), French novelist, playwright and poet; Gustave Flaubert (1821–80), French novelist; Charles Augustin Sainte-Beuve (1804–69), French literary critic; and Niccolò Paganini (1782–1840), Italian violinist and composer.

2 Norbert Wiener (1894–1964), American mathematician who founded the science of cybernetics.

lest I read them over again in my agony and confusion. I felt exactly like someone walking over Niagara looking neither right nor left, only hoping to get across, perhaps more like a parachutist reading my notes feverishly and knowing that as one tugged the string, the world might come to an end and anything might happen. However, all that is over now. The absurd fan mail and all. One wonderful letter from Lydia Keynes[1] saying in Russian, 'Your stammerings and stutterings are cosy and appropriate.' One of my correspondences with T. S. Eliot. Little controversies with colleagues, the usual touching nonsense from social credit cranks, and some splendid letters of this kind: 'I AM A THIRSTY STUDENT OF THE PHILOSOPHICAL AND THE HIGHER SCIENCES. I WILL TELL THE TRUTH THOUGH IT MAY HURT. YOUR BUBBLES AND STOPS ARE TOO MUCH FOR ME. YOU ARE THE MOST EXCITED SPEAKER I HAVE EVER HEARD. YOU MUST GO SLOWER AND FASTER. NO OFFENCE.' The other letters I enjoy most, those and the kind which begin, 'I have a manuscript of fifteen hundred pages which I am sure you will be ...' One kind lady sent me a pair of red socks knitted personally, which she thought I would need sitting by the light of a guttering candle in an old college, painfully working over my script. [...]

Social life continues to make its embarrassing demands, but I am very good about this this term and have actually brought myself to decline to dine with august personages in London (very genteel paper games after dinner, and everyone very rigid and respectable and the air stiff with good will and people wondering what next), and dined instead with my good friend, Elizabeth Bowen, the novelist. She is a really wonderful woman. I admire her writing, but her charm and courtesy and general style are almost more impressive. I have known her for many years and am very devoted to her – I see no vices in her at all. She has great wit and cleverness and imagination and charm, and, although she is far from beautiful, has looks like a very distinguished and intelligent horse, which I admire very much indeed, and find it more delightful than formal beauty. [...] She is at once distinguished, exhilarating, and cosy if you know what I mean. [...]

[...] So you see, our lives are in tiny Trollope-like units, but I expect all lives are, and there is nothing big in the world but is composed of tiny molecules, each of which is an intelligent fragment of experience in itself, and there are no large lives, but only collections of small worlds and combinations of isolable parts of living, each of which is all important in itself as it occurs; and one should not pursue distant goals and ask for the ultimate reason for anything – as the Russian revolutionary Herzen once said, 'What is the purpose of the song the singer sings? It is the song.'[2] If you ask for the

1 Lady Keynes (1892–1981), née Lydia Lopokhova, Russian ballerina and actress; widow of John Maynard Keynes.
2 Herzen's (implied) answer to his own question is in fact that the purpose of the song is the listener's pleasure in it: see IB's translation of Herzen's *From the Other Shore* (408/1), 35.

ultimate reason, it is because you have not heard the song, or do not like singing. 'What is the end of life? Why, you and I.'[1] And so on. It is a marvellous little piece, *From the Other Shore*, and somebody at Harvard is translating it into English.[2] [...]

I.B.

IB's broadcasts attracted widespread public attention, including an unprecedented Times *leader[3] on 6 December. Describing IB's argument that 'the tyrannies of the twentieth century find their intellectual origin in the eighteenth-century passion for unlimited liberty' as 'one of those healthy shocks against which the public ought not to be protected', the article concluded, 'The need of the twentieth century is not so much for a new political faith (it has had too many) as for a firm foundation for political doubt.' The topic was taken up in the correspondence columns of the paper.*

TO THE EDITOR OF *THE TIMES*[4]

Reform Club, London SW1

Sir,

Mr E. W. Jones,[5] in his letter in your issue of 12 December, reproves us all – yourself, Professor Cammaerts,[6] the modern scholars to whom you refer, and me – for misrepresenting Rousseau's view of liberty. And I am in addition accused of doing violence to the ideas of Rousseau and his contemporaries by means of a 'Hegelian straitjacket'. I cannot be sure at what point of my (unpublished) talk I am thought to have committed this grave offence: but I must own to having (if that is possible) even less confidence in Mr Jones's capacity to understand Rousseau than he appears to have in mine. For in Mr Jones's version Rousseau emerges as a mild and tolerant democrat, all for accommodation and compromise, in agreement with yourself, and me and Mr McKie,[7] scarcely distinguishable from a good English liberal. Surely anyone who can believe this of Rousseau can believe almost anything. Rousseau said many things and some of them were incompatible; and

1 This too somewhat distorts Herzen's text. For Herzen life is 'an end attained' rather than 'a means to something else'; and this end is partly 'you and [I]', partly 'the present state of everything existing'. See ibid., 36.

2 George Siegel (407/3).

3 'The Fate of Liberty' (6 December 1952, 7).

4 'The Fate of Liberty', *The Times*, 16 December 1952, 9.

5 A letter from Edgar W. Jones (12 December 1952, 9) proclaimed that Rousseau was really 'a good democrat' and criticised IB for 'an attempt to compress eighteenth-century thinking into a kind of Hegelian straitjacket'.

6 Émile Leon Cammaerts (1878–1953), Belgian poet, translator and critic; Professor of Belgian Studies and Institutions, London, 1931–47; wrote in support of the leading article (9 December, 9).

7 James Ivor McKie (1900–60), Fellow and Tutor in Philosophy, Brasenose, 1938–60, Vice-Principal, 1956–60; his comments had also been published (9 December, 9).

almost every social and political movement in the two centuries that followed, bitterly opposed to each other as they were, could claim descent from him with equal justice. They all 'did violence' to him, some of them without benefit of Hegel. There is the Rousseau of Robespierre[1] and the Rousseau of Fichte; the Rousseau of Bonald[2] and the Rousseau of Proudhon and of Tolstoy; the Rousseau of Professor Babbitt[3] and the Rousseau of Professors T. H. Green[4] and Bosanquet.[5] And in our own day Professor G. D. H. Cole says one thing and M. de Jouvenel[6] and Mr Plamenatz quite others.

And yet, in spite of so much lucidity and sympathy and penetration, the full context of Rousseau's thought and the secret of his unparalleled influence still elude us. It took 200 years and your correspondent Mr Jones to reduce it all to an innocuous liberal platitude. But then he claims to know what Rousseau 'really meant' and not merely what he said. Your readers are too well informed to need texts to support this thesis.

Yours faithfully,
    Isaiah Berlin

Edgar W. Jones's further letter, protesting that IB had misinterpreted him as well as Rousseau, was published on 18 December; IB did not respond.

TO ROWLAND BURDON-MULLER
25 December 1952 [*manuscript*]

All Souls

Dear Rowland
    Merry Christmas. Happy New Year. I hope you are well; better than I who am not. But that is another story. Thank you ever so much for offering to help with my parents should I come to America next year: it is very kind of you, & does credit to your very good heart, if that were required (it has credit enough already: you ought to let portions of it to people whose hearts are congealed or by nature too small & hard and concealed) but I could not dream of it, I fear; nor would my parents consent to come on such terms. This may be foolish but it is so. I'll have to manage in some other way. You are unjust to poor Mrs Weizmann to whom I spoke on the telephone to Paris, & who is totally broken and behaving well: & went to N. York *a contre*

---

1 Maximilien François Marie Isidore de Robespierre (1758–94), lawyer who played a leading role in the French Revolution and the subsequent Reign of Terror; devoted admirer of Rousseau's philosophy.
2 Louis Gabriel Amboise (1754–1840), vicomte de Bonald, French social and political philosopher and counter-revolutionary.
3 Irving Babbitt (1865–1933), Professor of French Literature, Harvard, 1912–33.
4 Thomas Hill Green (1836–82), idealist philosopher.
5 Bernard Bosanquet (1848–1923), neo-Hegelian philosopher and political thinker.
6 Bertrand de Jouvenel (1903–87), French philosopher and political economist.

coeur,[1] because she promised my poor old friend that she would – it was originally fixed to celebrate his birthday – to collect money for his research institute. Palm Beach was never remotely possible; her *snobbisme*[2] is of a very different kind. As for Mrs Ryan: snob she certainly is (as who, save the saints & the mechanical & dead, is not? if snobbery, as Proust maintained, is a matter of presentability to someone?) but with me alone, candid and not at all false about people; also she has a kind heart & does kindness by stealth: as I happen to have discovered. I am glad to see Momo[3] (or Mau-mau) from time to time because she is a Loch Ness Monster: a charcoal profile, no human semblance: & this is remarkable & exhilarating, in occasional doses, by itself. Mrs R. is a human being: she is unaccountably in love with her dreadful husband, whose tastes & views are appalling: & McArthur no doubt comes from an excess of this: but her virtues, to me, much outweigh her vices: our tastes differ: & why not indeed? there is a splendid old Hebrew prayer congratulating God on introducing variety among his creatures. As for me & Prof. Wolff & my unmanliness,[4] I think (with all respect as public speakers say at banquets) you are deeply mistaken. I don't in the least mind being, or being thought to be, as unmanly as anyone wishes to think me: masculinity is not a quality I like. [...] I must next "clear" this with Sir M. Bowra who hates anyone to go to the U.S.A. ever for any purpose: & Sparrow to whom I am devoted, but who will be frivolous, difficult & a little waspish all at the same time. But unmanly I am & unmanly I shall remain: I do my best to live up to your stern ideals, but it is not easy: you have a fierce black & white vision of right & wrong, especially in public life, you are the Calvin[5] of the beau monde: & I am aware that you have had to extend indulgence to my fallings short & am duly grateful. The severer you grow in your condemnations & anathemata, the more dubious I grow about who I am for, & who against: unmanly again, I fear. But I expect you are right, & I wrong: I always assume that about myself: having no confidence in anything I do or am, & resting my dogmatism of speech on endless doubt, hesitancy, & an all devouring self distrust: I preach the virtues of liberty, choice, action, and flee from them myself, & always always shall. My love to your servants.

yrs affectionately

Isaiah   [...]

1 sc. *à contre-coeur*, 'reluctantly'.
2 sc. *snobisme*, 'snobbery'.
3 Maud Emily ('Momo') Marriott (1897–1960), née Kahn, Nin Ryan's sister; married to Major-General Sir John Charles Oakes Marriott (1895–1978).
4 RB-M had berated IB (letter of 17 December) for 'unmanliness' in being indecisive about his arrangements with Harvard and Princeton.
5 John Calvin (1509–64), né Jean Chauvin, rigorous French Protestant theologian.

TO MYRON GILMORE

27 December 1952 [*manuscript, unfinished and unsent*]

All Souls

Dear Myron,

I should, of course, have written you long ago. And now that I do you won't be able to read it. I did mean to, very often: & I kept enquiring & re-enquiring about your address in the spring from Sheila:[1] all to no purpose. Then you wrote to me, about Tolstoy etc. (did you really mean all that? but I can't deny it: it is delicious to receive & read such words) then the unsteady ship of state at All Souls, under its new Captain, with new sailing orders, began slowly to heave out to sea. Some swells, some queer hands on board: A. L. Rowse like Malvolio, speaking to none that spoke against him, honey-sweet to me, but muttering in the best stage whisper "I never forgive & I never forget; never, never, NEVER!" "these fools, dolts, imbeciles, 9th & 10th & 11th rate creatures who cannot *abide* true gifts among them – ha! I shall not speak to them: they must work their passage back, ha!" etc. etc. all cross gartered[2] poor man. Curious. In *a way* better than the stiff English upper lip, & stoicism, hypocrisy, & inner rages: I have sympathy with people who let their emotions flow however disagreeable the spectacle & embarrassing the consequences. But in this case it is like a classical case of foiled ambition, & villains hissing at good men, & all the old world melodrama black & white: Rowse twirls his moustachioes so villainously & hisses so frequently that one cannot believe it is all real. Yet it is. He wrote the second volume of his memoirs & it was too libellous – about Oxford – to publish.[3] So we go on.

TO MARION FRANKFURTER

28 December 1952 [*manuscript*]

All Souls

Dear Marion,

Happy New Year! Joe always writes to *me*, when explaining why no letters, by talking of the moral & intellectual *effort* required to produce a letter likely to pass *my* criteria; & I am not sure that I am altogether pleased: I believe in haphazard spontaneity with all the chaff that goes with it: & this pernickety picking out of such available grain as may be in hand is cold and, in the result, unsatisfactory. *I* have this feeling when, for instance, I telephone Sir Maurice, ostensibly for a chat. And a chat it is, but one must be ready with the agenda: 'What *news*?' you are sharply asked; & you *must* have prepared an agenda: otherwise no good. *And* go through it pretty sharply too: this happened even

---

1 MG's wife, Sheila Gilmore.
2 Another reference to Malvolio, who is tricked into so dressing, and ridiculed for his pains.
3 *A Cornishman at Oxford* was not published until 1965.

now, after his awful accident.[1] He went to Greece to lecture, saying he felt jaded etc, Athens heavenly town, jolly poets, he is adored there etc., While driven in Charles Peake's[2] car a huge lorry crashed into him: windscreen into his face: he fainted (I think) & heard his companions assume him dead: his last thoughts being (apparently) that *if* he died, A. H. Smith could still be Vice-Chancellor: so Oxfordy is he now, so utterly. We were 'all' genuinely worried: I felt v. anxious & unwell until a familiar voice boomed through to London from Oxford (after my poor mama was surprised to hear him say he was not well, showing a shameful remoteness from the daily & Sunday press which featured 'accident to Vice-Chancellor Bowra' very prominently) & reported that he had just returned: with three holes in his head, & a nose very queerly shaped (you must send your imagination spinning) and general sense of doom. However both then & in the morning when he felt better (& is quite all right now, I *think*: but he has a phobia of doctors which is very deep & which I am far from sharing) his thoughts were not very godly: & he gossiped gaily & the vitality bounced through & in a three quarter dead condition he has more life than anyone I know. He really is recovering I think: without benefit of science. And I? I am as always, ashamed. Ashamed of broadcasting too much, too popularly. Ashamed of not writing enough – too much rubbish, & avoiding the real sour apple. Ashamed of inability to choose between Harvard & Princeton, both of which have kindly invited me for roughly the same season, the former with obligation to teach the other not: automatically I try to devolve this on to others (having no pride: only anxiety to accomodate: not even to please, just to get by): result: fuss. Nobody at either place knows where I am going to: like 2 dinner parties, both semi-accepted, embarrassment, social conflict, nonsense, apologies all round, absence of savoir vivre, undignified behaviour for everyone more or less. I *think* I shall come to Harvard for the autumn months, & subside into Princeton (Dr Oppenheimer: God what an eerie man: madly uncosy, madly ungay as we shd have said in the twenties: 'not quite absolute bliss' is what the smart set say now, I am told) for the spring. I shall be quite glad to return: but it is a little too soon: pillar to post (Billa[3] to Post[4] – you see material for one of the Vice-Chancellor's jokes, do you not?)

What is it? Why do I forever long for, expect, feel guilt about work not quite done, books not quite read, libraries not sufficiently plumbed etc., knowing well, in a sense, that the possibilities of sitting down, solidly, protected, & working, not frantically, not desperately, but steadily, coolly & solidly, like the scholars & writers one reads of, – indeed the whole purpose

1 For an account of this see Francis King's 'Pray You, Undo This Button' in *Maurice Bowra: A Celebration*, ed. Hugh Lloyd-Jones (London, 1974).
2 Charles Brinsley Pemberton Peake (1897–1958), diplomat; British Ambassador, Athens, 1951–7.
3 Wilhelmine ('Billa') Harrod (1911–2005), wife of Roy Harrod.
4 Presumably a reference to Emily Post (1873–1960), née Price, US author and columnist, arbiter of etiquette and good taste.

of my retirement to the All Souls monastic cell. But if one *is* in this perpetual condition of bits & pieces & hither & thither, & in fragments & unable to slough anything off, bits of dust & gay tiny precious stones too – if one cannot coagulate & acquire enough specific gravity, then, if one is a genius, one is a tragic poet like Chopin or my friend the Russian writer Pasternak[1] or Musset – never the best sort of genius, for which great ruthlessness at the centre is obviously needed, but still somebody. If one is even a talent one is like Nicholas Nabokov. But what is the use of all this to an Oxford don & a lecturer of Bryn Mawr? & so by insensible steps, in a condition of shameful self pity I arrive at my promise to write an éloge of Dr Weizmann for Ted Weeks. I liked him so much because he possessed all the qualities I lack & admire. Yet when I think of him now, & having written my little piece in the *Times*, I suddenly only think of his vices. Isn't it awful? they stand out in bold black relief. His terrible ruthlessness: lack of scruple: his crass cynicism: his total lack of interest in the arts: his attitude to human beings purely from the point of view of their potential usefulness, true, not to himself, but still; his blindness about individuals whose feelings he misunderstood & his belief in the corruptibility of almost everyone. This is outweighed, of course, by his nobility, genius, monolithic properties, sheer size – 'rich & old & wise' attributes. Still, I shd like to tell the truth: I leant over backwards a little, perhaps, over Winston, I suppose because he is alive: & no doubt I shd do so all the more for W. who is dead. I absolutely adored him: & always left his company in a condition of pleasure: heightened: & all objects seemed larger & more worth while. His book[2] was pretty terrible: but he was much – far & away the greatest man I ever knew well – & really did create a nation: a pretty unbelievable thing to have done: & hated & loved his fellows exactly like Moses: & wanted them dead as often as Moses: & lived out the last year in a kind of desert of his own making, embittered, & turning everything angrily to dust: all except his wife. And that was a queer relation too. However one cannot publish all this before the public. Ordinary miseries – the Proustian tragedies – the small but appallingly painful trivialities – the results of hitches in personal relationships, the persecutions, guilts, the utter ruin due to small – minute – maladjustments he had no idea of, at all. [. . .]

Isaiah.

1 Boris Leonidovich *Pasternak (1890–1960), Russian poet, novelist and translator, Jewish by birth; IB had met him in 1945 in the writers' village of Peredelkino and in Moscow and had been entrusted with an early draft of part of his novel *Dr Zhivago*.

2 Weizmann's 1949 autobiography *Trial and Error*.

TO HERBERT ELLISTON

30 December 1952 [*carbon*]

n.p.

Dear Herbert,

[...] The *Times* piece,[1] which I cannot complain of in general, was written, I am told, by a blind member of the staff called Utley,[2] a pious, high-church neo-Conservative, who helped Talmon[3] with the writing of his book and, I suppose, half consciously brought me into line with Talmon. I have much respect for Talmon's book but I think it erroneous in one or two ways, although in general constructed along very much the right lines. Anyhow, I do not subscribe to the sentence about 'firm foundation for political doubt', although I endorse the first half of the sentence about the 'too many political faiths'. Certainly I do not think that the answer to Communism is a counter faith, equally fervent, militant, etc., because one must fight the devil with the devil's weapons. To begin with, nothing is less likely to create a 'faith' than perpetual reiteration of the fact that we are looking for one, must find one, are lost without one, etc. I am reminded of a particularly silly article which I read in 1940 or '41 by Mortimer Adler,[4] saying that American youth was floundering without faith or certainty and that what was needed was a set of axioms about conduct, very firm, very true, from which rules of behaviour could be deduced by simple logic, like Jesuit casuistry. It is no good saying to a drowning man: 'Don't flounder – hang on to something – dry land is better than the bottomless ocean to people in your condition.' If you actually possess something relatively dry or firm, such as a spar, or raft or piece of dry land, you must somehow try to attract the drowning man's attention to it. If you have a truth you must certainly teach it or testify to it, but not say: 'There must be a truth somewhere; what we need is irrefutable principles; what we need is something stronger than what the other side has.' If we have it we shall use it; and either we or they will win. If we haven't we haven't, and it is then no use looking round at the available models – Catholic, Protestant, Democratic, Socialist, Liberal, and Existentialists etc. to see which is the most effective antidote to corrosive doubt or destructive totalitarianism. If you really don't believe in anything very much then I daresay we probably shall lose the battle – certainly doubt by itself is no solution and nothing to live

1 343/3.

2 Thomas Edwin ('Peter') Utley (1921–88), journalist and Conservative theorist; *The Times* 1948–54.

3 Jacob Leib Talmon (1916–80), Polish-born Israeli historian; secretary to Palestine Committee, Board of Deputies to British Jews, 1944–7; Lecturer, Hebrew University, Jerusalem, 1949–60, Professor of Modern History 1960–80. His book *The Origins of Totalitarian Democracy* had recently been published.

4 Mortimer Jerome Adler (1902–2001), anti-pragmatist philosopher and educator; Associate Professor in Philosophy of Law, Chicago, 1932–42, Professor 1942–52; founder, Institute for Philosophical Research, 1952; popularised the idea he shared with Robert Hutchins of Chicago, that enduring truths were to be found in the world's Great Books.

by, but then very few people have ever been in that precise condition – the number of genuine sceptics and cynics is very small and I daresay always has been. Even your Chinese must have had a very firm set of secular beliefs – a way of life – even if it was not religious or fanatical. But then, both my article in *Foreign Affairs*[1] and the undercurrent of these lectures, which have merely tried to trace contemporary influences to their more or less innocent sources in the past, did not preach systematic doubt as such – although I was attacked for it in the *Times Literary Supplement* by E. H. Carr in 1950, and duly praised for it by Mr Utley in another section of the same journal in 1952, but rather more a kind of cautious empiricism, something not unlike the doctrine with which Popper's book on *The Open Society and Its Enemies*[2] ends; I even find myself in some sympathy with the wicked Hayek,[3] although I think he is quite wrong in assuming that political liberty is indissolubly tied to economic private enterprise. I think that what I am pleading for is really what used to be called Liberalism, i.e. a society in which the largest number of persons are allowed to pursue the largest number of ends as freely as possible, in which these ends are themselves criticised as little as possible and the fervour with which such ends are held is not required to be bolstered up by some bogus rational or supernatural argument to prove the universal validity of the end. Everyone does, in fact, have purposes and values for which they live and for which they are occasionally prepared to die. In times of crisis, when a large number of people appear to be living and dying for ends which we find repellent, it is desirable to make explicit what it is that we are prepared to fight for, but I think nothing is gained by pretending that because the other side all want one and the same thing, tidily summed up in Communist slogans, therefore we must, although in fact we don't, and that because the other side pretend that their purpose is scientifically demonstrable, although this turns out to be a meaningless phrase – therefore ours must be one, binding on all, and with the quasi-mathematical validity as firm and certain and demonstrable as theirs. Ends are not demonstrable, they just are held and in a healthy society there are a great many of them, occasionally colliding with each other, and this needs a machinery of conciliation etc. but not bogus arguments for identifying the unidentifiable. I do not believe in general principles myself, because they bear down too cruelly upon actual human beings in actual situations too often; I believe, on the whole, in each case on its merits as far as possible, but I do not see why it is not possible to believe in the various ends in which we do believe with as much fervour and self-dedication as Communists believe theirs; and in a social framework

1 168/2.
2 London, 1945.
3 Friedrich August von Hayek (1899–1992), Austrian-born economist and social philosopher; Tooke Professor of Economic Science and Statistics, London (LSE), 1931–50; Professor of Social and Moral Sciences, Chicago, 1950–62.

which allows this vast variety of [in]compatible beliefs as strongly as, say, the Swiss or the English have believed in those basic principles which have allowed of such mutual admiration and encouraged differences and eccentricities. One loses something, no doubt, in the energy and drive which all monolithic – one country, one faith – establishments have, but one gains enormously in flexibility, enterprise and, of course, happiness, and one loses these in proportion as one is hypnotised by the blood-curdling threats of the enemy into a frame of mind similar to his own – either hypnotised or infuriated into it – as people here think is happening in America, what with McCarran Acts[1] etc., although I keep trying to persuade them that this is not so.

Forgive me for pouring out these platitudes before you – I only did so in order to disassociate myself from The Times's attitude, which is something to do with a curious mixture of tough realism and Christian scepticism about the powers and rewards and values of this world. I prefer this to beloved [sic] – but it savours too much of the Vatican for me – expediency as the only instrument in a sin-corrupted world where everything crumbles away all the time – what I believe, I think, is all that J. S. Mill said in his essay on liberty, and the Russian revolutionary, Herzen, in a work called From the Other Shore, a society in which liberty is more important even than happiness, people are forced to choose, though they do not necessarily like it, people do not accept supernatural or scientific sanctions for their ultimate ends but are content with the fact that they are ultimate for them individually (which is all that is ever true) – a society in which people are wary of (a) remote ends, distant goals which justify you in slaughtering thousands that millions may be happy, and where all that happens is that the thousands (or millions) are duly slaughtered while the beneficiaries reap nothing; (b) all ends which are [not] relatively near and attainable and ad hoc; and where general principles are avoided, lest human beings are sacrificed to some general rule which has lost any validity which it may ever have had, and, finally, (c) in which things are done in the light of common sense, and people do not do violence to their own instincts because they become spellbound by doctrines or fanatics or vivisect themselves morally in order to acquire enough inner power, dynamism etc. to do down the other side. We all do this in wartime to some degree, but with clear memories and hopes of peace. I see no purpose in defeating the other side if our beliefs at the end of the war are simply the inverse of theirs, just as irrational, despotic etc. But this never happens and it

---

1 The Internal Security Act (1950) required Communist organisations to register with the Attorney-General, provided for the investigation of those allegedly engaged in 'un-American' activities, and introduced stringent powers against aliens and subversives. The 1952 Immigration and Nationality Act strengthened controls on immigration into the US. Senator McCarran had been a sponsor of both bills; in each instance Congress over-ruled Truman's veto.

is usually only a slogan adopted by pacifists and is invariably a vast exaggeration of some genuine but not very urgent or present peril.

I may well be in America next September and certainly in the spring of '54, and I shall hope to see you. Destroy this letter. It is terribly confused and dictated while I am in a muzzy condition consequent upon Christmas and fog and all that.

Yours ever,

TO DENIS PAUL[1]

30 December 1952 [*carbon*]

n.p.

My dear Paul,

[...] Your point about my lectures interested me a good deal and I plead guilty, (*a*) to not saying enough of what I myself thought was right and wrong, and it is not a sufficient answer to this to say that I don't know; for certainly, if one talks in public, modesty and diffidence may be mere excuses for cowardice or indolence (how disagreeably moralistic all this sounds); and (*b*) to ending the whole thing irrelevantly with de Maistre, who was not even a pretended friend of freedom but an open enemy, and had no excuse for being in that *galère* except that I was interested in him and was determined to drag him in. No doubt it should all have ended with Marx. But perhaps it was better to leave the great monster looming on the horizon rather than inside the zoo. Now, as to your point: you say that I left the impression that Communism and Fascism were wicked, but that this is not enough and leaves people complacent – and what about our own discontents? I think the cap fits, and perhaps I should have said something. But what about? For example, should I have said that economic planning was in itself a threat to political freedom? Or that it was not? I did try and make it clear that the notion of freedom which I approved of was what the English and French Liberals and Radicals were preaching in the early 19th century as opposed to the German brand, that it was a negative concept, that it was what you call elbow-room freedom, that it meant largely non-interference, that it was not the sole end to be sought after, that ultimate needs clash and that when the desire for non-interference collides with other purposes – security, happiness, desire for fixed patterns of life, equality, fraternity, self-expression, order etc., there is no clear solution and that it is all a matter for compromise and balance and adjustment and empirical Popperism etc., and, in short, that the truth, when found, is not dramatic but possibly rather dreary. What are the threats

1 Denis Eric Paul (1925–2006), New College PPE 1948–51 (hence presumably a pupil of IB's); in 1951–2 working with Elizabeth Anscombe on the translation of Wittgenstein's *Philosophical Investigations*; statistician with the Coal Board 1952–5; thereafter taught science and maths in secondary schools, Nottingham College of Education and privately.

to freedom in a country like ours? There are obviously a good many but they all seem to be weaker versions of that whose caricature is to be found in Communism and Fascism, which for that reason are words hurled at each other with little justification by the various sides in our milder local conflicts. Is there some native form of danger, specially threatening us, or the French, or the Italians, or even the Americans, which is not a subaltern tense [sic] of what happened in Germany, Russia, China etc.? What should I have said? That not enough people have the material means for living minimally satisfactory lives? That there is much social injustice? That the notion of freedom depends upon what form of activity you most value and are in greatest fear of losing or having curtailed? All this seemed to be relatively irrelevant to my main theme, which was to distinguish a group of thinkers who were neither open enemies of freedom – the official reactionaries – nor the true friends of it in a sense in which I understood the word, e.g. Tom Paine,[1] Godwin,[2] Constant,[3] Tocqueville, J. S. Mill, etc., but the false friends, the ostensible champions of it – people who thought perhaps that they were defending it but enunciated doctrines which had too many seeds of the opposite. Some of these doctrines are of a kind which people still hold today without realising what the consequences are – surely as I expounded the doctrines it must have been reasonably clear that Rousseau, Helvétius, Saint-Simon etc. were not themselves Fascists or Communists – but they said things which mild liberals think that they accept now, and yet the consequences of these things have been terrible, and that if people still want to go on believing the premisses they must somehow see to it that they are so modified as not to lead to these consequences, or else accept different premisses; but I did not think it my duty to tell people what premisses or beliefs they should hold. However, how else should I have disturbed them? I was principally concerned to tell the story of ideas still strong amongst us and what happened to them in other contexts, and let that particular seed quicken. But I daresay I really avoided crucial issues and should have said something else. I wish you would tell me what.

I hope the Logical U.[4] will soon come out. Don't ask Miss Anscombe for permission to show me your translation. You must not misunderstand me but I would rather not have her asked for favours on my behalf. She has always seemed to me too arrogant and fanatical for even that minimum of

1 Thomas Paine (1737–1809), political radical, social thinker, deist, supporter of revolutions in America (to which he had emigrated) and France, whose writings in favour of liberalism played a major role in the establishment of the US.
2 William Godwin (1756–1836), radical political thinker, journalist and novelist, whose arguments for the freedom of the individual tend towards anarchism.
3 Henri-Benjamin Constant de Rebecque (1767–1830), Swiss-born liberal political thinker; member of the French National Assembly.
4 i.e. Wittgenstein's *Philosophische Untersuchungen*, published in 1953 as *Philosophical Investigations*.

personal consideration which makes for this [*sic*] relationship in which it is possible for people to try and discover the truth by some degree of indelible good will between them. And so I would rather you left her alone so far as I am concerned. I shall read it with great eagerness if and when it is published. If it is not I should like to be shown it secretly, or if that is against your principles, as no doubt it should be, then not at all.

Yours ever,

TO JACOB TALMON

30 December 1952 [*carbon*]

n.p.

Dear Dr Talmon,

[. . .] Now I must sit down to the hideous task of writing a book. God knows, the awful shadow of Marx broods over the entire thing, and I do not know whether to put him in or keep him out, and I still feel terribly obscure and muddled about Rousseau. You and I think that he is the father of totalitarianism in a sense. Why do we think this? Because of the despotism of the general will. What does he, in fact, say? He talks about (*a*) the necessity to keep out selfish and sectional interests, so that each man shall ask himself what is it right to do from the point of view of the community in general; this assumes that there is such a thing as a general interest or some courses of action which are better for entire societies than others, and this, although none too clear, obviously is in some sense valid; so far so good. One may raise questions about how one ever knows which course is best and then one may reasonably answer that Rousseau's recommendations about eliminating selfish and sectional interests, as practical tips, have a certain value, at least in some situations, and that the difference between what is traditionally considered to be the right frame of mind for members of the English Parliament as against, say, American Senators, who quite openly represent territorial or economic interests, is a case in point. Again so far so good. Furthermore, everyone in the Assembly has the right to express his views as he pleases. Any suppression automatically breaks the social contract and destroys the general will, the Sovereign etc., so that liberty seems to be guaranteed. But once the decision has been reached the dissidence must form and this, I suppose, is the ordinary practice of all democratic assemblies, from Quaker meetings to Lenin's Regional Central Committee and Politbureau. What then do we complain of? Simply, (*a*) that Rousseau thinks that an absolutely objectively true answer can be reached about political questions; that there is a guaranteed method of doing so; that his method is the right one; and that to act against such a truth is to be wrong, at worst mad, and therefore properly to be ignored, and that all these propositions are false? (*b*) the mystique of the *soi commun*[1] and the organic metaphor which runs away with him and leads to mythology, whether of the State, the Church, or whatever. Is this all? or is there more to complain of? I don't feel sure. The muddle is so great. The precise transition from absolute freedom to absolute necessity is still not very clear to me – it is in Hegel but not in myself. I suppose I must read him again, but if you have thoughts I wish you would tell me. [...]

[...] *The New Statesman* is behaving very comically, as two members of its staff have been accused of plotting for John Foster Dulles and all the Fascist beasts. Their position is odd and they are denouncing the Prague trials in a three-quarter-hearted way, while trying to balance this, as usual, by saying how awful the Americans are too. But I feel that, as a result of the obvious hatred and contempt for fellow-travellers which Communists, from time to time, display, they are a little shaken. I fear that in the end they will clutch at the next straw and, if given the smallest opportunity, will rally back to the pro-Soviet banner; but for the moment they will, I think, be prepared to publish a critical article, since they guard themselves against charges of bias, printing letters from Communists who are suddenly oppressed by doubts about Moscow and counter-denunciations by Mr Gallagher[2] of such weaker brethren. So do send them your piece about how difficult yet possible it is to follow a leader after he has put on the tarbush and how very very millennial Western Communists are, particularly of the idealistic *New Statesman* type. In France, people like Sartre are much more like Such,[3] with a straight tough line that Totalitarianism is bound to win, and it is frivolous not to identify oneself with the Hegelian march of history, which is always 'unpleasant'. I am sure that the Prague trials are simply stimulated by the desire to have simple, straightforward, practical, reliable men who take orders, and out with all dabblers in ideas, intellectuals, people who look up texts, potential Westerners etc., and that anti-Semitism is an incidental by-product of this, although its popularity in Central Europe is so great that this has an added advantage and tipped the scale if there was ever any doubt. The subjective and objective dialectic is really fascinating (so is mechanistic dialectic, etc.). How deeply this must appeal to everything that is Talmudic in human beings. Might it not be that Mr Churchill or John Foster Dulles, who are subjectively against the Soviet Union, are objectively its warm champions? Why not? One ought to be able to construct a very effective parody along these lines. [...]

Yours ever,

---

1 'Communal self'.
2 William Gallagher (1881–1965), former Clydeside docker, Communist MP 1935–50.
3 *Sic*. Probably another dictating glitch: a repetition of 'Sartre', heard as 'such', obliterating the intended name (perhaps Croce).

TO JOAN ROBINSON[1]

7 January 1953

All Souls

Dear Joan,

I ought to have returned your delightful *jeux d'esprit*[2] to you before but I have been ill in bed, neither seriously nor interestingly. They really did delight me, and of course puzzled me too. [...] I am in matters of economics far, far stupider than anyone has a right to be, certainly any don or anyone who opens his mouth on any topics in public ought to be, but I really am: this is not false modesty. I feel when presented with the simplest economic argument, more or less what I imagine a football tough must feel on looking at a page of Kant. It has always been so and I have always been ashamed of it and it is almost a complex, so I am the last person to be able to judge the intrinsic merit of the Marx–Keynes–Marshall pattern[3] – but it all seemed very amusing and stimulating to me – how much more then to those who know what is what. [...]

I suspect you underestimate my feelings about pukka Marxists: I think by now that the genuine ones, those who really do cite texts and excommunicate, are either dotty or rogues, or both. I think that the old boy really did pour a lot of light on dark places up to about 1910 say, and that after that it was sheer ideological devotion and a desire to blow up the old world that made people wish to find in him authority for what other people, or they themselves, said much more clearly, and which he, on the whole, said either very obscurely or not at all. His economics I don't presume to judge. The rest has surely done its work, entered all our systems, changed everybody's views and style, and in so far as he is faithfully adhered to, leads to clouds of darkness, puffed at almost every easy and difficult subject; the temptation to stick to him, therefore, being due to either (*a*) being rotted by him beyond recall, (*b*) desire for political discipline – never mind what we say provided we say it all the time; (*c*) love of ingenious sticks with which to beat various intolerable opponents in a manner they are likely to object to most; (*d*) a mixture of ingenuity and loyalty to the political ideals of one's youth, whereby one likes to say what one says in language in which one has invested so very much; (*e*) the commonest and most frightful – escape into a wild and impenetrable jungle where nothing is anything else and nobody can get at you at all and you can shout and snap to your heart's content; (*f*)

1 Joan Violet Robinson (1903–83), née Maurice, economist; Reader in Economics, Cambridge, 1949–65, later (1965–71) Professor.

2 A draft of three essays light-hearted in style but on serious topics, 'Would You Believe It?', 'A Lecture Delivered at Oxford by a Cambridge Economist' (on equilibrium and time) and 'An Open Letter from a Keynesian to a Marxist'; these were eventually published as *On Re-Reading Marx* (Cambridge, 1953).

3 The first essay identified similarities between certain economic assumptions held by Marx, Keynes and the Cambridge economist Alfred Marshall (1842–1924).

stupidity; (*g*) ignorance; (*h*) an *a priori* belief that the truth must be unpleasant and harshly expressed, and automatic alliance with the enemies of one's enemies, particularly when they look as formidable as the Marxists, without intrinsic love or respect for them as such, except for their practical effectiveness; (*i*) a mixture of all or any of these. Having said all this I naturally apologise. I think your essays should certainly be published, even if there is no possible way of inducing you not to be so generous to Marxists. [...]

Yours ever,
    Isaiah Berlin

TO BURTON DREBEN

    22 January 1953

All Souls

Dear Burton,

    [...] There is a curious book[1] I am reading now by Hayek who is accounted reactionary by everybody and indeed to some extent is and yet the strictures he has to pass on the indiscriminate application of scientific analogies beyond their proper sphere seem to me to be exaggerated but just, that is say just in principle, exaggerated in his particular application of it. Hayek and Popper are the two, as it were, reactionary liberals who have somehow put on sheep's clothing. I have an inveterate sympathy for traitors in both camps, crypto-reactionary progressives and crypto-progressive reactionaries. I like both these sides [sc. sorts?] of persons more than I like the official standard-bearers of either side. And this I think may occasionally irritate you and people like you who, I daresay rightly, believe in a straight line, the right, the free, the good, as against the convolutions in which I perpetually find myself. [...]

    [...] Were you shocked by the Soviet news about the Jews?[2] I was not very, I more or less expected it. That is just the sort of thing that people occasionally have against me, that I ought to have believed in the Russians more when I did not and should not now be saying it with quite the degree

---

1 Von Hayek's *The Counter-Revolution of Science: Studies on the Abuse of Reason* (Glencoe, Illinois, 1952).

2 On 14 January *The Times* had reported Soviet accusations that a number of (mainly Jewish) doctors had murdered Zhdanov and another Soviet leader, and, in league with Western intelligence organisations, were plotting to kill many more leading Soviet officials. Those accused had allegedly 'confessed'. IB's uncle, Leo Berlin, Professor of Dietetics at Moscow University, had been sent to a Siberian prison-camp in 1952 for alleged Jewish nationalism, but in December he was brought back to Moscow, accused of belonging to a British spy-ring which supposedly included IB and Mendel, and tortured to the point of attempted suicide to extract a false confession; IB did not know this at the time. Stalin's death on 5 March produced a dramatic reversal: on 6 April the new regime proclaimed the innocence of the doctors and accused members of the security services of fabricating evidence. Leo Berlin was not released until February 1954; he died the following year of a heart attack on seeing his torturer in the street.

of complacency, that nothing less could have been expected, and yet I did and do. But it really is terrifying: it only shows at what enormous price the truth is bought, what a tremendous amount of delusion and illusion has to be pricked and penetrated and at what an enormous cost in suffering before the facts – which we speak about so glibly when we talk about the philosophy of science – are acutely apprehended by a human being. [...]

Yours ever,
    Isaiah B.

TO KATHARINE MCBRIDE

22 January 1953

All Souls

Dear Miss McBride,

[...] In the great mists of England in which we are living at present – tonight most of my colleagues with cars and families came back miserably to college because every 100 yards they gently collided with other cars in front of them, and they all came back to the grim little bedrooms that they occupy here in case of such emergencies, preferring the acutest discomfort to the terrors of the great English Fog[1] – wrapped in these mists, I have returned to my normal somewhat torpid condition (I cannot remember who it was who once described research as a condition of resentful inactivity). I have thought of Bryn Mawr often when I delivered lectures substantially identical with those given under the auspices of Mary Flexner, over the radio in London, when instead of being faced with 100 faces, I looked at a neat functional table and cork-lined walls – and I fear preferred that on the whole, so terrified am I. These lectures have brought in the most astonishing volume of correspondence from the most extraordinary persons who appear to listen to such things and seem to be filled with inarticulate feelings and thought on the subject of history and politics which have come bursting out in the most surprising fashion, and to all of which I suppose I now have the duty of sending some kind of answer. [...]

Now let me thank you again for your gift[2] and your kind thought and for existing at all, both individually and corporately. ⟨And I send my love to the entire institution.⟩

Yours sincerely,
    Isaiah Berlin

1 This was one of the worst weeks in a particularly foggy winter; most of England was affected, with visibility at or below five yards in many areas.
2 A Christmas cake.

TO SHIRLEY ANGLESEY

23 January 1953 [*manuscript*]

All Souls

Dearest Shirley

Alas! I always seem to be doomed to contemplating great pleasures, living in the thought of them, building castles, only to have them dashed – & by what? not even the serious claims of work, or College business, or other respectable obstacles to happiness: but by twinges of old old men's diseases. In London I was laid low with gout – painful, honourable & in my case absolutely ludicrously unmerited: where is my life of pleasure, my dissipations, my long bibulous nights & fuddled mornings? & now by some curious racking disease – called locally fibrocitis – more like pleurisy or the ague: a long piercing thrilling ache, from my heart to the ribs in the back – thin, stiff, & clear: not a vague unlocated discomfort or a spreading pain, but absolutely sharp, continuous, & constant, like a high flutey sound. But I must not go on so about my symptoms – though they are what I most acutely feel at the moment – the centre of my world. So, having received a visit from Sir O. Franks, who is in the remarkable condition of being plied with more handsome offers of employment[1] than anyone in England, is like a beauty, unable to reject or accept any one of her suitors (a condition surely more familiar to you than, say, to me) seeks advice. He was to have dined with me to-night: but I had to put him off, on account of being in bed, whence I am writing. He is a very strange man, cold, yet touching & v. human: very clever, very solid, very thorough, like a perfect machine etc. yet shy, modest even, full of sentiment, ancient feeling, with few friends (else how cd he come to me?) but underneath a thin icy crust flowing with a kind of stream of feeling: not warm & not cold, not passionate but not insipid: like a good, well trained, religiously brought up, efficient, simple, earnest young American from some Middle-Western manse perhaps? he really does fascinate me a little: I cannot really do anything for him: but he {he} thinks I can: & I have long, touching conversations with him, & like him, whom nobody likes much, a great deal. [...]

Much love to Henry. As to you.

Isaiah.

---

1 Possibilities mooted included the Chairmanship of British Railways and of British Petroleum, the editorship of *The Times*, a senior position in the Treasury, the Headmastership of Harrow School, the Director-Generalship of the BBC and the Chairmanship of Lloyds Bank (which Franks accepted).

TO JOAN ROBINSON

23 January 1953

All Souls

Dear Joan,

Thank you for your letter. Yes, indeed do write to George Weidenfeld
[...]. He is a pretty shrewd publisher, I don't know if you have a literary
agent but I think it may help to put the essay through him, but I think he is
fundamentally honest – I like him very much. Some people think he is too
slick and Central European altogether, but oddly enough in his case I rather
like these qualities, he is full of life, full of imagination and even though he
seems to me to have an incorrigible taste for the bogus, I prefer that to the
virtues of solidity and solemnity which seem to me somehow overdone at
the moment. At any rate I am always made to feel gayer by him, he is a gay,
cosy, perhaps none too reliable, but fundamentally sympathetic individual.
However, you will feel about him as you will feel.

If Marxism is the opium of Marxists,[1] I suppose that liberalism is the opium
of liberals, that logical positivism is the [opium] of logical positivists and so on.
How is one to stop this? Certainly not by some bogus Tory mystique, according to which the beauty of the Conservative Party is that it is not a party of the
British system, that it is not a system etc. I suppose the most original words
about this sort of thing spoken in our time were spoken by Wittgenstein in
Cambridge,[2] but then nothing is more terrible than religious Wittgensteinism
as you must know better than I. How is one to avoid the emotional consequence of intellectual conversion? Or is conversion intellectual? It is a very fascinating problem, I think, that of conversion, how and in what circumstances
and with what results a general shift of focus occurs, the replacement of one
model by another in which all the facts remain the same, at the same time the
relationships alter not so much between the objects within the system as in
some occult analogy which the system as a whole possesses to something else
which may not be very clearly apprehended in connection with it. I should
love to discuss this subject with you – I mean how one alters not so much one's
specific faiths, as one's general outlook, how things become clearer and how
things become obscurer (it is a very odd thing that many things which one
found so clear in one's youth, say the philosophy of Bradley[3] or something of
the sort, now seem opaque and unintelligible, why does one grow denser as
one grows older, I should like to know?) [...]

Yours ever,

Isaiah B.

1 The epigraph of *On Re-Reading Marx*.
2 Presumably 'Wovon man nicht sprechen kann, darüber muß man schweigen' ('Whereof one
  cannot speak, thereof one must be silent'): Ludwig Wittgenstein, *Tractatus Logico-Philosophicus*
  (London, 1922), proposition 7 (the last sentence of the book).
3 Francis Herbert Bradley (1846–1924), philosopher influenced by Hegel; Fellow of Merton
  1870–1924.

TO ROWLAND BURDON-MULLER

12 February 1953

All Souls

Dear Rowland,

[...] The wife of a professor of Italian, Comtesse d'Entrèves,[1] has just imported an Italian cook and her mother: they cannot be induced to leave their room since the newspapers declare that we shall all be swept away by an almost total flood on the 14th,[2] they have only three days in which to prepare themselves for the last trump and they prefer to be with their own Italian friends rather than in this strange and horrible country full of people who seem callously unconcerned about their own souls and the judgement to come. Perhaps we shall be swept away, in which case we need an ark, the Vice-Chancellor, Sir Maurice Bowra, would make an excellent Noah with his stentorian voice ordering us to enter, two Fellows from each college, two ladies from North Oxford, two representatives of each nationality, religion and social and personal habits on a cross section of our wonderful society; he would enjoy herding us I am sure. I can see exactly which professors he would hurl into the flood with the greatest satisfaction. You might ask yourself one day when you are depressed and bored how you would select from Cambridge and Harvard on these principles. [...]

How is Harvard going to stand up to the meditated attack by McCarthy[3] etc? I do see that it is very tiresome for them to be abandoned by Conant[4] at this moment and captains ought not to leap off their bridges quite so nimbly. I can see myself in the red-hot subject being investigated ferociously by some not very friendly characters. I am at my worst in answering questions and making statements which are at once sufficiently true and sufficiently courageous. I think nothing true without endless qualifications, and get into a flap and take it back and talk nonsense and get into a worse flap and leave covered with confusion. I wish I were one of those monolithic characters with a clear conception of right and wrong and went steadily forward regardless of things, persons and ever-present possibilities of error,

---

1 Contessa Giuseppina ('Nina') Passerin d'Entrèves (b. c.1906), née Ferrari d'Orsara, wife of Conte Alessandro (Alexander) Passerin d'Entrèves (1902–85), Serena Professor of Italian Studies, Oxford, 1946–57.

2 During the night of 31 January high tides and fierce northerly gales had breached the sea defences along much of the east coast of England, causing widespread flooding. Over 250 people died and 30,000 had to leave their homes. An even higher spring tide was due on Friday 13 February. In the event the weather was calmer and the hastily reconstructed sea defences held; Oxford was never in danger.

3 Robert Gorham Davis (393/2), who taught English at Smith College, had recently admitted to the House Committee on Un-American Activities (HCUA) that he had belonged to a Communist cell at Harvard while teaching there in the late 1930s; as not all those he named had left Harvard, an investigation by HCUA or by the Senate committees chaired by McCarthy seemed inevitable.

4 Conant had been appointed US High Commissioner to West Germany.

like Toscanini. That is why he is to me such a hero – total unlikeness has great attractions. [...]

Yours ever,
    With much affection
        Isaiah.

TO MORTON WHITE

4 March 1953

All Souls

Dear Morton,

[...] I have received a simply splendid invitation from a man most appropriately called Dr Faust,[1] summoning me to a Ford Foundation Conference in London[2] with marvellously black characters – T. S. Eliot, Toynbee, Karl Barth,[3] Jaspers, as well as Heisenberg,[4] Bohr,[5] Tawney, C. S. Lewis,[6] Sir Arthur Keith[7] (I am sure he is dead), and we are to discuss (if I accept, but how can I possibly do?) the philosophy of education, but before we get to the philosophy of education we must discuss the nature of the purposes of education, that is to say, the good life, that is to say, the nature of man, that is to say, the nature of the universe in which men are situated, in short vent our subject. [...] I cannot see how I can avoid investigation when I arrive at Harvard. My subject seems to be plumb in the middle of the field of investigation and everything about me simply asks for Senator McCarthy's probe. [...]

As for Bronowski,[8] I have never met him but all you say about him is obviously perfectly true, he does these things rather better than his American counterparts, nevertheless it all comes to obviously nothing as far as I know,

1 Clarence Henry Faust (1901–75), minister in Evangelical Church; Professor of English, Chicago, 1941–7 (Dean, 1941–6); Dean of Humanities and Sciences, Stanford, 1948–5; President, Fund for the Advancement of Education, 1951–7; Vice-President, Ford Foundation, 1957–75.
2 Not an official Ford Foundation event, but a semi-private initiative by Robert Hutchins, at this time one of the Foundation's Associate Directors, who had organised a similar gathering in Princeton. The London conference in early May, held under the auspices of the Fund for the Advancement of Education (an independent agency established in 1951 and funded by the Ford Foundation), was to discuss 'the problems of education in relation to the philosophical diversity of our times' (letter of 9 April 1953 from Faust).
3 Karl Barth (1886–1968), Swiss theologian; Professor of Theology, University of Basle, 1935–62.
4 Werner Heisenberg (1901–76), German physicist, Professor and Director of Max Planck Institute for Physics, Göttingen, 1946–58.
5 Niels Henrik David Bohr (1885–1962), Danish physicist; Professor in Theoretical Physics, University of Copenhagen, 1916–62. (The meeting in 1941 between Bohr and his former student Heisenberg is the subject of Michael Frayn's 1998 play Copenhagen.)
6 Clive Staples Lewis (1898–1963), author, critic and Christian apologist; Fellow and Tutor of Magdalen 1925–54; Professor of Medieval and Renaissance English, Cambridge, 1954–63.
7 Sir Arthur Keith (1866–1955), physiologist and anthropologist; Fullerian Professor of Physiology, Royal Institution, 1917–23; Rector, University of Aberdeen, 1930–3.
8 Jacob Bronowski (1908–74), Polish-born mathematician, scientist, broadcaster and popular writer on literature and science; Director of Coal Research Establishment, National Coal Board, 1950–9.

I don't know why, but listening to him on the wireless, reading his articles in the *Observer*, I feel that he is a kind of public sophist, better than Joad, but still a sophist, ready to discuss anything with anybody in any market-place. I should not think he does any harm however, but he is not really a credit to any profession, at least not sufficiently a one. Perhaps one is being too malicious about one's fellow dilettanti, but I feel that it is very easy to discredit the kind of thing one really likes and admires very much and he just does manage to do it. I therefore do not feel enthusiastic about him, he was caught young I am sure by Santillana,[1] who is in some respects another such, though much cleverer, and as a human being more interesting. He was a Cambridge man and an exact contemporary of mine, perhaps that is why I feel so strongly, rather like oneself in some disagreeable and close respects.

As for the young Oxonian I shall think about that. I will certainly send you a few names though they had better not come from me, otherwise it might be thought I am trying to drive them out. You might consider (a) Quinton, Anthony Quinton, about whom dear old Dreben can tell you. He was a friend of his. He is extremely hardworking, industrious, married now to a Bryn Mawr American wife,[2] an excellent tutor and a solid, businesslike philosopher who has read all the Finns, all the Poles, all the Germans and Austrians, Americans, Englishmen and Israelis etc. [...]

We have an exceedingly clever man, a Catholic logician called McGuinness[3] who is rather narrow in scope but a philosopher [...], is extremely meticulous and minute and hardworking and knows his stuff exceedingly well. [...]

⟨*Much* the best I've now decided.⟩ There is a very sweet man also called Lucas[4] who you may prefer to the others in some ways: he is from Winchester College and Balliol, and was trained as a mathematician, learned Greek beautifully and perfectly in something like 6 months, is a considerable scholar as far as Plato and Aristotle are concerned, Waismann thinks very highly of him, so do I in a way. He is [a] slightly muddled, bright, interesting, deeply sincere, imaginative, exceedingly sweet man with large streaks of dilettantism, something Aikenish[5] about him, but he is much sweeter and nicer than the others and has a richer background of Anglican culture if you know what I mean; also his mathematics come in usefully. [...]

There is of course an American here better than all these I should think,

---

1 Giorgio Diaz de Santillana (1902–74), Italian historian and philosopher of science; Assistant Professor of the History of Science, MIT, 1942–8, Associate Professor of the History and Philosophy of Science 1948–54, Professor 1954–67.

2 Anthony Quinton had recently married Marcelle Wegier (b. 1930), Bryn Mawr graduate, translator and sculptor.

3 Bernard Francis ('Brian') McGuinness (b. 1927), Junior Research Fellow, Queen's, 1953–4, Fellow and Tutor in Philosophy 1954–88.

4 John Randolph Lucas (b. 1929), philosopher; Junior Research Fellow, Merton, 1953–6, Fellow and Tutor 1960–96; Fellow and Assistant Tutor, Corpus Christi College, Cambridge, 1956–9.

5 A reference to Henry David Aiken (1912–82), Associate Professor of Philosophy, Harvard, 1946–54, Professor 1954–65.

called Rawls,[1] but I imagine he has been bespoken by Cornell, from whence
he comes. [...]
> yrs
>   Isaiah

*During the Easter vacation IB spent time with his parents in Monte Carlo
and Nice, then continued via Florence to join Maurice Bowra in Rome before
returning home.*

> *On 12 May IB delivered the inaugural Auguste Comte Memorial Lecture
at the LSE, on 'History as an Alibi'.[2] Unfortunately Michael Oakeshott, who
introduced him, was not one of his admirers:[3]*

He introduced me in the most ironical, hostile manner imaginable. He said,
'Here we have the Paganini of the lecture platform' – that sort of thing; went
on in this style, I mean mocking me, a lot of irony, for something like twelve
minutes, a real revenge. This rather rattled me: I was nervous anyway. I had
forty pages, I couldn't begin to get through them, and half way I got myself
into a total tizzy, I saw Popper, Robbins,[4] all kinds of people, Hayek – all these
persons sitting there, and began reading one sentence from each page, and the
whole thing ended in total disaster.[5]

TO KARL POPPER

13 [May 1953, *manuscript*]

All Souls

Dear Karl,

[...] I feel somewhat ashamed of my lecture; one should either talk or
read: in the middle I tried to do both (& read odd sentences from each page
which failed to connect, I fear) & got into a mess. The MS., such as it is, did
contain much more argument than I gave impression of: but I shall try to
mend it further for publication: e.g. by explaining how big abstractions have

---

1 John Bordley Rawls (1921–2002), political philosopher; studied at Princeton (not Cornell, *pace* IB);
taught philosophy at Princeton (1950–2) and Cornell (1953–9); Fulbright Fellow, Christ Church,
Oxford, 1952–3; Professor of Philosophy, MIT, 1960–2; later John Cowles Professor of Philosophy,
Harvard, 1975–9, James Bryant Conant University Professor 1979–91. Rawls seems to have
attended (and been impressed by) the seminar given by IB and Stuart Hampshire in January–
March 1953 on 'Moral Presuppositions of Liberalism (Condorcet, Kant, Mill, Moore)', which
ranged more widely than the gazetted title announced, also dealing with Rousseau, Herzen and
Keynes: Thomas Pogge, *John Rawls: His Life and Theory of Justice* (Oxford, 2007), 16.

2 Published as *Historical Inevitability* (London, 1954), reprinted in *Four Essays on Liberty* (168/2) and
L. A shorter version of the lecture was recorded and broadcast on the Third Programme on 15
July 1953.

3 Not without reason: Oakeshott had been Jenifer Hart's lover before IB.

4 Lionel Charles Robbins (1898–1984), Baron Robbins 1959; Professor of Economics, London
(LSE), 1929–61.

5 MI Tape 23. The handwritten text on which Oakeshott based his introduction survives. Though
much shorter than IB's recollection of the speech itself, it confirms the tone: 'Listening to him
you may be tempted to think that you are in the presence of one of the great intellectual *virtuosos*
of our time, a Paganini of ideas' [LSE Archives, Oakeshott 1/3].

London School of Economics & Political Science

(University of London)

The Auguste Comte Memorial Trust

The English Positivist Committee

have pleasure in announcing that

The Inaugural Auguste Comte Memorial Lecture

entitled

HISTORY AS AN ALIBI

will be given by

ISAIAH BERLIN, C.B.E., M.A.,

Fellow of All Souls College, Oxford,

on Tuesday, 12th May, 1953, at 5 p.m.,

at

The London School of Economics & Political Science

HOUGHTON STREET, ALDWYCH, LONDON, W.C.2.

ADMISSION FREE, WITHOUT TICKET.

All who are interested in Positivism, Sociology, or Humanism, and the pioneer work of Auguste Comte in these fields are invited to attend.

(See over)

Flyer announcing the lecture that became Historical Inevitability

to be used in history & sociology & yet must be prevented from being reified & used as alibis by individuals. I do apologize if I compromised you – since I feel sure that you were responsible for getting me asked. And I shall write to Ginsberg[1] & send him the MS. so that I say nothing too grossly unfair about sociology, much as I dislike it. I went away covered with genuine guilt: I don't feel very Paganini-ish: do you remember Heine's description of him?[2]

    Yrs
        Isaiah B.

TO MORTON WHITE

17 May 1953 [*manuscript*]

                                                                All Souls

Dear Morton
    Forgive hurry – as usual I am unnecessarily harried – this time because of the consequences of a lecture I unwisely delivered to the L. S. of Economics under the somewhat curious title – at once cryptic & illiterate – of 'History as an Alibi'. It raised a hornets' nest of sociologists: I see that I am viewed as a supercilious Oxford obscurantist, who hurls a few silly, disdainful broadsides at the patient, decent, industrious empirical workers on the dull but useful edifice of sociological progress. No matter. [...] the Wittg. Book[3] is of course the latest sensation. Ryle vaguely wants me to review it + one or two other reviews. We'll see. Freddie A. breathes slaughter against it & the whole worship & cénacle[4] of the faithful. Miss Anscombe publicly lacerates herself for her mistranslations ('I ought to be *shot* I ought to be *beaten*, for rendering x as y' etc.) [...]
    yours
        Isaiah

TO ARTHUR SCHLESINGER

30 May 1953

                                                                All Souls

Dear Arthur,
    There really is incredibly little to write about. Everything here is even more so than everything at Cambridge Mass. The Vice-Chancellor still continues his glorious Periclean reign with magnificence ⟨& satisfaction⟩ to himself and others. The trip to Rome was a great success. I arrived a week

---

1 Morris Ginsberg (1889–1970), Martin White Professor of Sociology, London (LSE), 1929–54.
2 Heine included an imaginative evocation of Paganini and his playing in his *Florentinische Nächte* ('Florentine Nights', 1836).
3 Elizabeth Anscombe's translation of Wittgenstein's *Philosophical Investigations* (Oxford, 1953), which had just been published alongside the original German text.
4 'Literary circle'.

after to find him with my friend Stuart Hampshire wandering about Rome in a state of extreme satisfaction, and that peculiar freedom of behaviour and expression which only occurs when he leaves the precincts of Oxford. It is a queer thing: his importance on the whole decreases as he leaves the centre of power, i.e. Oxford; his satisfaction and general satisfactoriness as a human being, gaiety, happiness, general enhancement of life increases as he goes further and further, at any rate south. I saw old Berenson in Florence, and I must say I am continually impressed. I know all that is said against him as an old, cunning, foxy humbug, his snobbery, his artificiality, his heartlessness etc. On the other hand, he is a man of extreme intelligence, of enormous intellectual liveliness, who really does stimulate one and make one think about subjects one by one with great rapidity and brightness, which a great many younger persons of equal or greater fame do not seem to me to be able to do. In his presence one appears to oneself to be talking better and more profitably than in the presence of most people. No doubt it is this flattering capacity which is partly responsible for his great reputation. I enjoyed myself a great deal there. I received a typical letter from him after I left saying that he detected in me a certain tendency to assume a disparity in our ages, personally he felt himself my contemporary, as to what I should be at his age was indeed a peculiar speculation.

[...] we have had Harry Levin here to deliver a lecture.[1] [...] About Harvard he was very sober and perfectly intelligent and expressed great fears that you would appoint some terrible businessman who would sell you to the Philistines or worse – and he deplored the absence of some splendid Civil Liberties Republican who would save you from a fate worse than death.

The American scene really does look terrible from here. I daresay that it does not all seem so very terrible at home – except that McCarthy obviously must – but Dulles does seem to be a horrifying mixture of Simon and Hoare,[2] except that he is I daresay even weaker than they are, even more pointlessly cunning, even more personally unattractive. Meanwhile everyone has been behaving in character – Lord Jowitt[3] has written an obviously bad book on Hiss,[4] the motive of which cannot have been money, but I think more his feeling that an English lawyer ought to try and condemn anything in America as miscarriages of British justice. Rebecca West[5] did really write a rather competent review

---

1 On which IB comments later in this letter: 'It was about the social novel of the 19th century and all I remember of it is an amusing reference to persons who indulged in unctuous pessimism.'

2 Sir Samuel John Gurney Hoare (1880–1959), 1st Viscount Templewood 1944, Conservative politician; Foreign Secretary in 1935 when Italy invaded Abyssinia (Ethiopia), but resigned in the wake of public outrage at the pact he reached with French Prime Minister Pierre Laval, which was favourable to Italy; Ambassador to Spain 1940–4.

3 William Allen Jowitt (1885–1957), 1st Earl Jowitt 1951, barrister and Labour politician; Lord Chancellor 1945–51.

4 The Strange Case of Alger Hiss (London, 1953). The first edition had to be withdrawn because of major factual errors; the author's naivety about Communism was widely ridiculed.

5 Rebecca West, the name (borrowed from an Ibsen heroine) used professionally and often

of it, although she is undoubtedly a dreadful woman. She came to see me on some ostensible excuse or other and talked absolute drivel about Schine and Cohn.[1] I think she sincerely believes that there are Communists under every bed and every chair, and that we ought to be on our guard everywhere and all the time. I can't help thinking that this has something to do with Wells's last romance[2] with the somewhat left-wing Baroness Budberg,[3] for whom Miss West must have been abandoned. I told her what I thought of her article in the *Sunday Times*,[4] but she would none of it, and although she remains polite to me personally, is obviously sick and mad. But then Mary McCarthy wrote something not altogether dissimilar in the *Listener*,[5] which she broadcast – much abler, much wittier, much more elegant, much more ironical about both sides, nevertheless the total effect of it a little sad I think. [...]

Meanwhile I had a fantastic time with a body of men organised by the Ford Foundation which sat in Grosvenor House for the purpose of discussing how their millions might be spent on the betterment of man. You know my views on these topics, yet I thought somehow that one was not allowed to go about criticising such enterprises without at least attending a meeting or two if one was specially summoned, and saying what one thought to the members concerned, to their faces as well as their backs. I must say it really was an astonishing nightmare. There were gathered together Sir

personally by Cicily Isabel Andrews (1892–1983), née Fairfield, author, critic and journalist, whose early socialism developed into fierce anti-Communism.

1 Roy Marcus Cohn (1927–86), lawyer; Senator McCarthy's chief counsel in hearings of the Permanent Subcommittee on Investigations, known for his aggressive interrogation of witnesses, and his close friend, and possibly lover, (Gerard) David Schine (1927–96), an unpaid consultant on McCarthy's staff. In April 1953 they conducted a whistle-stop 17-day tour of nine European cities, allegedly (though no one, including the main protagonists, seemed entirely sure) on the trail of pro-Communist literature in the libraries of the US International Information Administration, but also seizing any opportunity to harass suspected Communist sympathisers. Their 'grotesque voyage' (*The Times*, 29 April 1953, 7) was enthusiastically ridiculed by the European press.

2 H. G. Wells had numerous extra-marital relationships; that with Rebecca West, by whom he had a son, lasted for ten years from 1913, but Moura Budberg was not her immediate successor.

3 Baroness Maria Ignatievna ('Moura') Budberg (1892–1974), née Zakrevskaya; married first to Ivan Benckendorff; famous for her relationships with Robert Bruce Lockhart, Maxim Gorky and H. G. Wells (whose companion she was for 13 years until his death); translator, indefatigable creator of myths about herself, and inveterate survivor (to which end, perhaps an occasional spy).

4 The *Sunday Times* published Rebecca West's 'Facts Behind the Witch-Hunts', a series of four long articles on aspects of the Communist threat in the US: (i) 'Hiss Case Hid Graver Issue: US Civil Servants Betrayed War Secrets' (22 March 1953, 4); (ii) 'The Surprising Mr Kaplan: US Official's Reticence Gave Cause for Alarm' (29 March 1953, 4); (iii) 'The Terrified Teachers' (5 April 1953, 2); and (iv) 'McCarthy the Demagogue: But America's Gravest Danger Lies Elsewhere' (12 April 1953, 4). A typical comment from the last article is: 'Nobody has ever accused [McCarthy] of maiming and murder. But the American Communist Party is guilty of all these offences.' Her views attracted liberal criticism, but when the articles were reprinted in the *US News and World Report*, the response was largely favourable.

5 'The Menace to Free Journalism in America' (*Listener*, 14 May 1953, 791–2), in which Mary McCarthy criticised the lack of independent thinking and the formulaic repetition of stock attitudes in the US press: 'the greatest menace to free journalism in America today is not Senator McCarthy [...]. It is the conceptualised picture of the reader that governs our present-day journalism', a 'hypothetical dolt' patronised and propitiated by editors.

Arthur Keith, who is 89 rising 90, who talked in a quavering voice about the greatness of Charles Darwin, and who is a dear old boy and an eminent biologist with really nothing wrong except advanced years. Next to him sat Sir Richard Livingstone, the last silver-tongued orator of classical scholarship and Victorian democracy. He talked as usual silvery nonsense. Then came Professor Polanyi,[1] who was once a good physical chemist and is now a general dabbler in ideas, an intelligent, muddled, curious sort of man, no fool, but frightfully anxious to get on with powerful persons, who is a professional anti-Communist of extreme violence who was refused a visa to the United States on the grounds of associating with Reds. It is a great comedy – not that he thinks it that – and on the whole he was the most intelligent as well as the least reliable person there. Next to him sat Professor Niels Bohr – who is a saint and a most morally imposing figure and a great man and a genius and a physicist of splendid achievement, who talked the most unutterable bosh throughout the proceedings in a low gentle disarming sweet voice. He is one of the nicest men I have ever met and kept on in the most disarming way apologising for repeating himself, but if there had been even one proposition however platitudinous which he was repeating it would have been better than nothing. But a row of noughts adds to nought, and in fact he has got into a state of senility and logorrhoea, which it is pathetic to listen to. He thought that what we ought to talk about were such small and concrete subjects as Truth, Ideas and Man. Next to him sat Professor Heisenberg, who nearly produced the atom bomb for the Germans and is a very bright intelligent amusing man, obviously ready to serve any master, who did not talk nonsense at all, but adapted himself to the general tone by saying that the truths of poetry were more important than the truths of science. [...] Next to him was Ortega y Gasset,[2] the sage from Spain who came from Lisbon, who thought that he must have a large staff for the purpose of investigating Moslem Puritanism, which was an important development of the last fifty years, and generally that a huge history book should be written by himself with support from the Ford Foundation. Nobody had anything against that but it did not seem to 'jibe' with the rest. Then there was Goodhart who thought that the whole thing was rather nonsense, but feebly acquiesced with everything. Then there was Butterfield, who is very sweet and very nice and who was not sure how far the whole thing was all right for him to go to at all, and felt roughly the same worries as I did, except that he thought that some good for Christianity might come from it all. Then there was Colin Clark,[3] a statistician who had been to Australia and is now back in

1 Michael Polanyi (1891–1976), born in Budapest, chemist and philosopher of science; Professor of Physical Chemistry, Manchester, 1933–48, of Social Studies 1948–58.

2 José Ortega y Gasset (1883–1955), Spanish philosopher and essayist whose thinking had something in common with that of Heidegger and Sartre.

3 Colin Grant Clark (1905–89), economist and statistician; adviser to the government of Queensland, 1938–52; Director of the Institute for Research in Agricultural Economics, Oxford,

Oxford – he is a fervent Catholic and what he wanted was not scholarship or learning or discussion but propaganda not to hundreds of thousands but to hundreds of millions, and what he wanted was schools and wireless stations and enormous newspapers and a large organisation for the purpose of blasting forth ideas which we already had and had had for over two thousand years with every means of public communication possible. He pressed for that with immense violence and great eloquence and sincerity, and Hutchins obviously rather liked the idea. Tawney, who was also present, made the best remark of the session when he said 'When propaganda comes in through the door, truth flies through the window, she breaks her neck, and she is seldom, seldom missed.' Next to him sat Mortimer Adler, who really is the most frightful man I have seen yet. Hutchins in a sort of funny way I can see one might like, he has charm, he has wit, he is possessed, he is independent, he is somebody. Whatever his views. But Adler is a minor figure of extreme horror, who combines with his fanaticism and nonsense a kind of *bassesse*,[1] a horrible slimy cunning, and [the] general looks and behaviour of a shyster philosopher, a kind of philosophical spiv which I had never encountered before. (Really you had better destroy this letter.) For five mornings they sat and I did not attend them all and at the end they decided that it would be a good thing to set up an Institute, not in America because of the McCarran Act, to collect sages for three or four months in the year for the purpose of discussing ideas of Man, Truth etc. with the help of a powerful secretariat, – like the Communist Party – which would process ideas dialectically. I tried to insinuate that if you got any men, however wise, however good, and gave them no specific job to do – they would soon lose all respect for themselves and each other and collapse into a sort of hideous degradation. This point of view however was not accepted and Hutchins later told me that the idea of getting hold of people who had their own work to do and might do it, was the basis of his Institute of Human Relations at Yale, where he got a good physiologist and physicist and historian of art and architect and metaphysician, and philosopher and theologian and what not, and did these men talk to each other? – they did not – did they produce any books? damn all they produced, he was not going to do that again. I went away with a real feeling of unctuous pessimism.[2] [...]

　　With much love,

　　　　Yours ever,

　　　　　Isaiah

1953–69; later (1964–6) lay member of the papal commission on population which led to the encyclical *Humanae Vitae*.

1 'Baseness'.

2 To Alice James he added: 'Very strange and queer the atmosphere of it all was, rather like talking to early Victorian Utopians who believe that everything can be cured by beetroot or that the number 3,742 is what we must all cling to for ever.' 6 June 1953.

⟨PS [...] Clarissa Eden. She arrives in Boston about 10th I shd think. For ten days she will be, she says, incommunicado on account of A. but after that, do see her. Do you know her? She is a large, blond, somewhat formidable girl, with a strong personality, handsome, uncompromising, & downright in an upper class way. At least I think this. I like her, as you know, v. much. She is not much approved of in Conservative Party circles, because she seems sour and proud to them; she is v. genuine & first hand; with an acute and somewhat intolerant humour; she liked and then disliked Nick Nabokov; she is in love with her husband (*I* think) and is thought revolté[1] and difficult by her aunt Clementine.[2] She is Winston's favourite, because his only, niece. I don't know how she will get on with such Boston society as will try & get hold of her inevitably. [...]

Isaiah⟩

TO MORTON WHITE
30 May 1953

All Souls

Dear Morton,

Thank you very much for your letter of 24 May. I shall reply to it briefly for I am, as always, in a violent hurry due to general disorganisation. I feel that what one has too little of is time. People are intent on producing more gold, more steel, more atomic energy etc., what they ought to concentrate on producing is more time, it is particularly scarce in this University, where little fragments of it cannot be collected even as conveniently as at Harvard. Somebody ought to write an essay on the economics of producing and distributing time. [...]

On Nelson Goodman I shall report to you as soon as his Oxford season is over. I know that he is better than the finite extensional system – the curious universe in which every antidote [sc. attribute] is labelled and no general terms can be used – may indicate him to be. It is a wonderful world which he produces like a kind of Flatland[3] – and it is no excuse to say that he is not trying to legislate for the whole world, only for a modest portion of it, that is what behaviourists and people like La Mettrie[4] used to say. And it did not help them.

I shall write again soon.

Yours ever,

I. Berlin p.p.

1 sc. *révoltée*, 'rebellious'.
2 Winston Churchill's wife, Clementine Ogilvy (Spencer-)Churchill (1885–1977), née Hozier, Baroness Spencer-Churchill 1965.
3 *Flatland: A Romance of Many Dimensions*, an 1884 novella by 'A. Square' (Edwin Abbott Abbott), satirises Victorian social structure through its depiction of a two-dimensional world.
4 Julien Offray de La Mettrie (1709–51), physician and philosopher of the French Enlightenment; a materialist who viewed men as mere machines and advocated atheism and the sensual pleasures from which he died.

TO VIOLET BONHAM CARTER

3 June 1953 [*manuscript*]

All Souls

Dear Violet,

I know that honours are supposed to be vain baubles & that personal relations are more important; nevertheless they must be, however obviously deserved, however inadequate, however overdue, be a pleasure: & I congratulate you most warmly.[1] I have a general feeling, perhaps absurdly pessimistic and groundless – that we are slowly but surely, being overtaken by a kind of early-Victorian philistinism, full of dull virtue and militantly anti-highbrow sentiment; certainly this is the colouring of all the worthy but to me somewhat depressing new young colleagues here: and if you'll forgive me for saying this – but it is easier in writing than in spoken words – all that you are & do & represent is a continual, noble, effective protest against this, a great resistance to the lowering of standards both here (and in America) & I should like to pay my deep & genuine homage to it. I am embarrassed by the depth of my own feeling & must not go on for fear of going on & on: but I seize this opportunity for saying, however badly, what I feel. On no account should you think of acknowledging this, for I am sure you will be buried under worthier tributes: & you will, I hope, forgive me for these confused few words.

I do hope I may see you very soon.

Yours ever
Isaiah.

P.S. I propose to dedicate a short book on Tolstoy to Bubbles.[2] Cressida[3] does not seem to think ill of this.

TO ALICE JAMES

6 June 1953

All Souls

Dear Alice,

I ought to have written to you months and months ago, and really ought to have done so, but I have had a comparatively difficult and full time. Not merely the normal wear and tear and chaos of my existence – that has been somewhat smaller than before – but the poor health, first of my father, then of my mother, then of my father again. He is a very nice man, much younger than I am mentally and emotionally, but quite helpless when struck

---

1 VBC had been just been made a Dame of the British Empire.
2 *The Hedgehog and the Fox* is dedicated 'To the memory of Jasper Ridley'.
3 VBC's daughter, Cressida Ridley.

by illness. He had a bad time in the summer when he was operated upon twice, and although this particular sickness did not recur, yet he has been in fairly poor health ever since and has had to be propped and looked after in all kinds of ways. In the spring I went to Monte Carlo with my parents and then to Nice. And then for a week to Rome by myself, where I found Maurice in tremendous form [...]. I had a week with him there, in the course of which I went to tea with a charming lady, the Marchesa Origo,[1] whom at first one takes to be simply a literary lady of amateur attainments, but after one has read her book on Byron, suddenly realises to be almost a major critic. She was very nice to me and so were various other people. I found that the Princess Caetani,[2] Mrs Biddle's sister, who edits a literary periodical which I expect you know called *Botteghe oscure*, was much disapproved of by smart Roman society (which is genuinely frightful, I have never seen an aristocracy to equal that of Rome in genuine baseness, worthlessness and idleness); but when I went to tea I found her absolutely charming, I may be wrong, but I enjoyed her society for the hour or two during which I was in it, a great deal. I thought she was perhaps a tiny little [bit] bogus and a tiny little bit bluestocking, but this is compensated for by genuine warmth of personality, desire to help young writers – which I cannot think bad – and obviously a great many good deeds done in that connection which obviously made her happy, as it did the young writers, and a general atmosphere of gaiety, spontaneity and benevolence in the Palazzo. When I see books and periodicals scattered anywhere in a manner to suggest that they are opened and read by people, I feel well at once. It is tidiness, and spicness and spanness which depress me.

After Maurice had left, I was alone for an entirely blissful week, in the course of which I wandered about the city in a state of total contentment. I think I like Rome almost better than any town in the world. Florence seems to me a 19th-century city with trams, with things that are wonderful inside, but not so very handsome seen from within itself. I did call on B.B. there and, I must say, his sparkle and animation, the number of ideas which he generates, the tremendous unabated intellectual vitality which still goes on is something to marvel at. He said that he approved of industry but did not believe in work between meals. Again he went over his extraordinary childhood in New York and again he attacked the bullies and oppressors of that

1 Iris Margaret Origo (1902–88), née Cutting, Anglo-American wife of Marchese Antonio Origo; writer and biographer. Her book on Byron (about his relationship with Countess Teresa Giuccioli) was *The Last Attachment* (London and New York, 1949).

2 Marguerite Caetani (1880–1963), née Chapin, American literary publisher, wife of the Italian composer Prince Roffredo Caetani; half-sister of Katherine Garrison Biddle (1890–1977), née Chapin, poet. The Palazzo Caetani in Rome stands in the via delle Botteghe Oscure ('Street of the Dark Shops'), which suggested the name for the international original-language literary review which Princess Caetani funded and edited biannually from 1948 to 1960; her particular enthusiasm was discovering new young authors.

remote age. I have had a letter from him asking me to go and stay a fortnight with him in the summer, but I do not think that will be possible. I must say that in spite of the propaganda against him, in spite of Rowland's view of him as a conscienceless old humbug, a charlatan etc. etc., I like and admire him. And his company is genuinely, in his own phrase, life-enhancing.

After Italy I came back slowly through Paris, saw Rowland, came to England and found the American Embassies both in Paris and in London enormously demoralised by the McCarthy persecutions.[1] You have to go to Europe to realise what effect upon conservative Americans all this has, and how wrong are those rich persons who see in him a protector of their security, whereas in fact he is really a kind of radical of the Rasputin[2] type. And a genuine menace to them as much as to unregenerate radicals and respectable men generally. In England I found my parents much improved, although shortly after I arrived my father again fell ill and had to be nursed back to health, which I must say my mother does exceedingly well, although it wears her out. I really do not know what to do about departing from them. They take it badly, and my original idea was that my mother might come to stay with me at Christmas if I go to Harvard for the autumn term and then go on to Princeton for the spring. But it seems clear to me now that my father cannot be left alone in England and that they must either both come or neither, and if neither I must fly back to wherever they are in Europe, the Riviera I expect, for Christmas, and if I must do that I shall. [...]

I came back to Oxford slightly depressed to be given a sudden sharp jolt by the arrival of Harry and Elena Levin. After immense intrigue and negotiations I got him invited to deliver something called the Deneke Lecture[3] – he does not know that I was virtually the only person responsible for his invitation, and had better not. I think it would somewhat diminish his pleasure in what was undoubtedly something of a personal triumph. Not very many people came to the lecture, but among them distinguished persons. David Cecil presided and the lecture was an absolute masterpiece of exquisite little polished precious stones set with wonderful Swiss watchmaker's care to dovetail into each other with perfect precision and marvellous contiguity. The lecture lasted exactly for one hour, and the last dying cadences of

1 As Chairman of the Senate's Committee on Government Operations and its Permanent Subcommittee on Investigations, McCarthy was at the height of his power during 1953. His anti-Communist witch-hunt was conducted through an intensive programme of closed and open hearings, and involved the bullying of witnesses and the threat that anyone refusing to name possible Communist sympathisers would risk imprisonment. But the low morale amongst US diplomats in Europe seems to have sprung in particular from the humiliating antics of Schine and Cohn.

2 Grigory Efimovich Rasputin (1869–1916), Russian mystic and alleged healer whose influence over Tsar Nicholas II and (especially) Tsarina Alexandra led to his assassination and played a part in the discrediting of the Romanov dynasty, thus facilitating the Russian Revolution.

3 The prestigious Philip Maurice Deneke Lecture was at the time given annually at LMH; earlier speakers had included Einstein and Albert Schweitzer.

Harry's voice coincided with the third stroke of the clock as it struck 4.00. During the final stroke he bowed elaborately. The lecture was courteous and old-fashioned with such expressions as 'by your leave' and 'if you please', which he doubtless thought especially suitable to our atmosphere. It was a most brilliant display of the most exquisite fireworks, such as no one else that I know could have done. After it we were indeed plunged in darkness, which, as Seznec pointed out, is the inevitable effect of all fireworks. Nevertheless it was a masterpiece and I greatly admired it, the subject was 'The Social Novel in the 19th Century'. I wish I could lecture as well or make so much with so little. Elena was as ever charming, Harry I admire and respect and am prepared to do things for, defend, feel a certain solidarity with, but cannot altogether like. Elena I like very much and always shall. She is like Lady Keynes, to some degree a child of nature, to some degree a flirt, who uses her very simplicity and naivety as weapons and I like both qualities almost equally.

After the Levins, the Coronation. Despite the disapproval of my more radical friends and colleagues I went up to London and placed myself in the window of the *Daily Telegraph* office in Piccadilly whence the returning procession could be seen. The rest could be seen on television. It really was very impressive. The skill with which all the extraordinary dances and counter-dances in which the figures involved in the Coronation were executed was something to be admired. Lord Salisbury, whom I really like very much indeed, really was transported with a religious emotion of an obviously genuine kind, as he stood rigidly to attention with his naked sword looking genuinely medieval and dedicated. And the Queen carried the whole thing through with a kind of curious slow trance, wearing the heavy Byzantine robes not at all like an actress on the stage, nor like someone intent and serious, but in a kind of curious religious mist – I am sure that her religious mother and general upbringing in her home have made of her something genuinely early Victorian. The whole Coronation was obviously something much more like that of Victoria than it can have been that of Elizabeth. It is not a neo-Elizabethan but at most a neo-Victorian age on which we are embarking. Morally this certainly is so, and I am sometimes made to feel like the old rakes of the Regency among the serious, earnest, sober, high-minded young men and women of the new age. The Queen of Tonga[1] was really everything she is painted to be in the press, large, brown and jolly, she sat upright with a small Union Jack in her hair and waving two twigs. Opposite her looking rather annoyed was the Sultan of somewhere, I think

1 Queen Salote Tupou (1900–65), the imposing (over 6 feet 3 inches) hereditary ruler of Tonga since 1918. 'Her braving of the rain during the Coronation procession in her carriage, which she insisted on keeping open, endeared her to the London crowds; and this episode, together with a majestic personality radiating friendliness, made her the outstanding overseas figure at the celebrations. Such was the popularity she won in Britain that June babies were christened Charlotte in her honour, a race-horse was named after her, and she was the subject of popular songs.' *The Times*, 16 December 1965, 12.

Brunei,[1] he obviously did not enjoy sharing a carriage with this commanding figure. Maurice who went to the Abbey as Vice-Chancellor was photo-
graphed in a still more commanding attitude in a large *Times* picture of the
scene. The degree of devotion which was displayed really was very startling
to the English themselves. As for foreigners, the French came back genuinely impressed by the fact that even in the poorer districts where normally
there would be Communism and discontent, the number of Union Jacks
was perhaps greater than among the rich and the powerful. The number
of persons who secretly enjoyed the Coronation after promising themselves
that they would not do so either because it was childish or because they
nursed secret Republican radical sentiments, was also very large. The most
enjoyable moment of all to me was when Winston appeared in a carriage
with huge fat fingers stuck out in a V sign blessing the populace in a gracious manner, when suddenly he caught sight of my host Michael Berry,[2]
the son of Lord Camrose, to whom the *Daily Telegraph* building belongs,
and immediately the happy grin of public jollity was succeeded by a scowl
of private recognition, very much as one is suddenly checked in the middle
of some public activity by suddenly seeing a quizzical private face glaring at
one from some unexpected corner. He withdrew back into his carriage like
a snail, took back his hand, growled at his wife, buried his head sulkily in his
shoulders, and continued in this fashion for another five minutes, after which
he stuck out his head again, the fingers came out again and all was radiance
once more. A thing that always surprises one, nobody would quite have
thought that this sober, unimaginative and essentially prosy country could
rise to such a pitch of national excitement over this dark mystical Byzantine
ceremony, which seems in a sense so out of keeping with the reticent, moderate, good taste-seeking undemonstrative English character.

Just before the Coronation I went and had dinner with my friend Mrs
Eden, who is shortly going to Boston. I wonder if perhaps something could
be done about her when she is there. For the first 10 days after her arrival
there, she does not wish to be disturbed, after that I think she would like to
go out a little. Let me tell you about her: I have known her since the age of
about 16, when she was a very shy Catholic heiress, when I met her at Mells,
when she was thought a 'possible' for the very very pious and Catholic young
Lord Oxford. However this did not come about and she gradually relapsed
from her faith and became a very *revoltée* young woman and displeased her

1 IB muddles two of the seven Sultans in the procession. The Sultan of Brunei, Sir Omar Ali
   Saifuddin Saadul Khairi Waddien (1914–86), was in a later carriage; Queen Salote shared a carriage
   with the Sultan of Kelantan, Ibrahim Petra ibni Almarhum Sultan Muhammad IV (1897–1960).
2 (William) Michael Berry (1911–2001), Baron Hartwell 1968, 3rd Viscount Camrose (disclaimed)
   1995; newspaperman; Chairman and editor-in-chief, *Daily Telegraph*, 1954–87. His father was
   William Ewart Berry (1879–1954), 1st Viscount Camrose 1941, editor-in-chief, *Daily Telegraph*,
   1928–54.

charming, gentle and curious mother, Lady Gwendoline Cecil[1] (she was
the Catholic in the family, Jack Churchill[2] her father, being I suppose, an
ordinary Anglican). Then her mother died rather tragically and she blamed
herself a great deal for embittering her last hours, I think unjustly, but quite
understandably. Then during the war she did a certain amount of war work,
and then fell ill with some mysterious sickness and spent two years in bed,
in the course of which I visited her at least once when I was on leave from
America in 1942, very romantic she was, very handsome in bed, pining to
get away from this mysterious sickness which the doctors could not diagnose, then suddenly, as suddenly as she sickened, she arose to her feet and
got a job from Sir A. Korda,[3] who is a benefactor to all the needy members
of the Churchill family. She lived a curious lonely life in a flat by herself,
somewhat déclassé, since the British upper classes do not like that degree
of independence. I do not mean she was a hermit, she went out a little, but
obviously had a life of her own, and not being rich had to work for her living.
Then Mr Eden proposed to her, and after a long period of cogitation and
secrecy she accepted him, and still went out a little without telling anyone
she was engaged, and like some mysterious Caliph[4] used to learn people's
true opinion of her husband when they spoke freely in front of her before
they knew that he was about to marry her. It was not fair, but from her point
of view amusing. I am genuinely fond of her and have [been] for many years.
She is not easy, she is a large, blonde, handsome girl, who would have done
very well as an Edwardian hostess in a very different, richer and grander, and
I suppose heavier atmosphere. The tempo of modern life does not suit her
at all. She is very genuine, very authentic, very first-hand, she says what she
thinks, she is far from empty, her temper rather difficult, and I think in some
sense is rather charmless. I like her a very great deal, but always find that
when I go to see her, I have to make the running somewhat and after I have
been with her for an hour or two, although it has been a great pleasure, since
she is interesting to talk to and what she says has an absolutely unique and
first-hand quality of its own, yet it is also rather exhausting when she does
not, as they say, 'give' much. Whether she was in love with Mr Eden when
she married him I don't know; I doubt it. That she is so now seems quite
clear. She has been an exceedingly good wife to him, she has been through
a great deal – and his illnesses[5] really have taken it out of her. Whether you

1 IB confuses Lady Gwendeline Bertie with Lady Gwendolen (Gascoyne-)Cecil (1860–1945), the
   biographer of her father, the Conservative statesman Lord Salisbury.
2 John Strange ('Jack') (Spencer-)Churchill (1880–1947), Winston Churchill's younger brother (or
   half-brother: their mother, Jennie Jerome, had many extra-marital relationships).
3 Sir Alexander Korda (1893–1956), né Sándor László Kellner in Hungary, film producer; settled in
   England, founded London Films in 1932, and revived the moribund British film industry.
4 Stories in *The Book of One Thousand and One Nights* describe Caliph Harun al Rashid wandering
   the streets of Baghdad in disguise.
5 Eden had had two operations in London in April 1953 for a gall-bladder problem, and one in
   Boston in June to remedy the life-threatening damage which the earlier operations had caused.

will entirely like her I am not sure. I am devoted to her, and so is David Cecil, and Maurice likes her quite I think. She is not frightfully easy to go on with, she dislikes company naturally, fashion, and cleaves a kind of imperious way of her own through them all without exactly attaching herself to them. Men on the whole tend to like her, women rather less. But if it is not a great nuisance to you, perhaps you would ring her up if you are in Boston. [...]

As for myself, I must go and get my American visa. In a way I tremble before going this time (I sail on 10 September). The news about American politics is so very disturbing as one reads it here and I cannot disbelieve it all. I think it really is frightful about McCarthy. I do not for a moment believe in the doctrine of giving him enough rope – enough rope and he will hang everybody else. I may have been unduly affected by the tales of Marietta Tree, but I do not believe that she is alone in saying this kind of thing. Will the President ever act? I don't doubt everyone, all decent persons are asking themselves that in America, that he is a good person I have no doubt and I never have had; decent, anxious to do good, but surely, surely, limited and slow. Dulles I really do think is a kind of compound of our own Simon and Hoare or am I wrong? You could not say anything to me that was much worse than that, but they have their admirers in this country still. [...]

And now it is, as it always seems to be in my life, well after 2.00 a.m. in the morning, and I must go to bed. I have an appalling day tomorrow, but then every day is appalling. Do give all my fondest love to Billy and pray accept it for yourself.

Yours ever, with much affection

Isaiah   [...]

TO LINCOLN SCHUSTER[1]

13 June 1953 [*typed transcript of untraced original*]

All Souls

Dear Mr Lincoln Schuster,

[...] I am naturally delighted that you should think so highly of *The Hedgehog and the Fox* and hope that it will not prove financially disastrous to you. In the meanwhile I have added two further sections to the original which appeared in the Oxford volume of *Slavonic Studies*, I hope they will not spoil the rest too much. They deal with what Tolstoy and de Maistre meant by such concepts as 'inexorable' and 'inevitable' and move de Maistre a little more into the picture which earns him that place in the subtitle which other-wise seemed a little odd. Is there anyone else in the world besides yourself and me who does *not* think that Tolstoy's long epilogues and philosophical

---

1 Max Lincoln Schuster (1897–1970), Austrian-born co-founder (with Richard Simon) of the pub-lishing firm Simon & Schuster (IB's US publisher for *The Hedgehog and the Fox*).

excursuses are not tedious interruptions of the story? Typical Russian amateur home-made bits of eccentric philosophy? As for me, I am becoming worse and worse. Indeed, I think I am almost a disciple of Tolstoy as far as history is concerned and am meditating a separate essay which I propose to deliver in the form of a lecture at Smith College[1] some time in October or November of this year [...], on what is meant by inexorable and inevitable by people who perhaps rightly feel that a great deal in their lives is in fact not alterable by any conscious decision on their part. When people think that there are various non-malleable factors in their lives or environments, this usually stems from a certain dim recognition on their part of the fact that there are no laws governing these portions of experience, or that if there are, they do not or cannot know them, rather than the opposite assumption – made strongly by Hegel and Marx and more weakly by say Toynbee – that what they mean by speaking of the inevitable [is] that there are laws in a sense in which there are laws in the natural sciences. My argument is directed to showing that the analogy is false, not merely in its conscious forms where people actually try and construct a philosophy of history on 'scientific' principles, but even to analyse such principles as having something common to similar-sounding but very different notions when they are applied to the sciences. In this respect I see that I follow in the reactionary wake of Tolstoy and perhaps even the dread figure of Hayek rather than what is called the progressive or scientific thought of our time. But I cannot help that, it seems to me to be true and I should like to write it down somewhere even if it emerges in a confused and unplausible form. But I will not bore you with all that, although you will perhaps allow me to send you an offprint of the lecture, if it ever appears, when the time is ripe. [...]

I saw B.B. in Florence this last spring and I must say the experience was most magnificent and stimulating. His 88 or 89 years sit upon him far more lightly than my 43 years – alas I ought to say 44 since a few days ago – sit upon me. [...] To my great delight I discovered that he too detested schemata in history and used a quotation from his *Rumour and Reflection*[2] as an opening in a somewhat empty scientific lecture which I delivered to the London School of Economics on a cognate topic. He speaks of the notion of historical inevitability as a kind of Moloch which makes people think that to resist history is both useless and in some way immoral. I suppose I do in fact think that this kind of historicism – the notion that it is adult as well as expeditious

1 'The Sense of Reality', the first Elizabeth Cutter Morrow Lecture, Smith College, 9 October 1953; the title essay in SR.

2 *Historical Inevitability* opens with a reference to Berenson's words about the 'Accidental View of History', on which his thoughts 'led me far from the doctrine, lapped up in my youth, about the inevitability of events and the Moloch still devouring us today, "historical inevitability". I believe less and less in these more than doubtful and certainly dangerous dogmas, which tend to make us accept whatever happens as irresistible and foolhardy to oppose.' Bernard Berenson, *Rumour and Reflection: 1941:1944* (London, 1952), 116 (entry dated 11 January 1943), cited at L 94.

to yield to the forces of our time – is both intellectually and morally the most deplorable doctrine abroad. But again do not let me bore you with my private fads. [...]

Yours sincerely,

Isaiah Berlin

TO DENIS GOACHER[1]

16 June 1953

All Souls

Dear Mr Goacher,

Thank you for your letter of 14 June and the kind remarks contained in it about at any rate the first portion of my talk on de Maistre. I am sorry if I seem to you to be unfair to Ezra Pound[2] in it – no doubt the works of so unusual a writer are subject to many interpretations and my references may have struck you as not doing justice to something which you yourself found in them. I can only plead that I am not a great student of his works but I have read one or two social or economic treatise[s], such as came my way in New York when I was there during the war years, and I did actually look at some transcripts or broadcasts of his during the war for which he was subsequently condemned in the United States. No doubt one's conception of him will differ from that of a great many writers or thinkers, but it did strike me very forcibly that the Italian system which Mr Pound defended, his attacks on liberals, nationalists, Jews &c. (those persons who profess what Trotsky[3] once described as 'Kantian, liberal, Quaker, vegetarian nonsense'), did entail as strongly as any words can that he rejected the kind of liberal principles which were declared before and after the French Revolution by persons who believe in very strictly defining individual rights and objected to interference with these by anyone, whether State or Church or any other agency, save for very special and exceptional reasons – and entail acceptance of something like the Maistrian opposite. Msr Maurras has said that we cannot ask him questions, but I feel reasonably sure that whether he did say so or not he would, if he had been asked, have admitted and indeed claimed a great deal in common with Ezra Pound, at any rate during the period of which I speak, namely after 1930. I should not like to volunteer anything about his views before that time. Nor did his acts – his visits to Germany

1 Denis John Goacher (1925–98), British actor and poet; became Ezra Pound's secretary in 1953; played a major role in the campaign for Pound's release from a mental institution.

2 Ezra Weston Loomis Pound (1885–1972), US modernist poet and critic, who spent much of his life in Europe; editor of T. S. Eliot's *The Waste Land*; anti-Semitic Axis propagandist and admirer of Mussolini; brought to the US on charges of treason, he pleaded insanity and was confined in a mental institution 1946–58.

3 453/4. In *Terrorism and Communism* (Petrograd, 1920) – p. 63 in the English translation *The Defence of Terrorism* (London, 1920) – Trotsky writes: 'As for us, we were never concerned with Kantian-priestly, vegetarian-Quaker chatter about "the sanctity of human life".'

despite his quarrels with the Nazis etc. – provide concrete evidence of any enthusiasm for the kind of individual freedom which the citizens of democracies, despite their financial systems, do retain in a sense clearly distinguishable from that in which totalitarian countries fail to provide such freedom. Pound's anti-Semitism, which I should have thought no one could possibly deny, is perhaps not relevant, one is obviously entitled to detest individuals or whole sets of individuals or communities of them as much as one wishes, provided one does not deduce from this the need of depriving them of certain basic rights. As to whether Pound wishes to do that with regard to the Jews I do not know and I must admit do not greatly care. At any rate the mere existence as one of the ingredients of his thought would certainly not entail the kind of conclusion which I still believe to be just with regard to his general social and political views. Whether he was technically a traitor to the United States or not is not I think directly relevant; what is relevant is the fact that he should have chosen openly to defend a totalitarian system against a democracy during a war between them on whatever grounds. He was entitled to do it of course, but one cannot have one's cake and eat it, and he cannot be regarded as defending such minimum of liberal values as his own native democracy retains and at the same time attack it for the benefit of a totalitarian system which confessedly contains none. That is my case. I fear I have expressed it very inadequately and if you really wish me to change my opinion about Mr Pound's views (not I am afraid that my views are of any importance in this matter or that I am worth troubling about in this connection) I should be grateful if you could send me some concrete evidence in support of your interpretation of his views and behaviour. If I have done Mr Pound an injustice I shall of course be extremely contrite, and shall freely confess it. At present I cannot see that I have.

Yours sincerely,
    Isaiah Berlin

TO SAM BEHRMAN

16 July 1953 [*manuscript*]

All Souls

Dearest Sam,

I have earache, headache, my right forefinger is rac[k]ed with arthritis but I am not in misery. I am in that absurd hectic condition in which one is when trying to write something – endless crossings & recrossings out – but haven't reached the stage of actual publication, which for me at least, is nothing but one long night of shame, remorse, desire to be dead & undo the entire past, my own, and everybody else's. I hear from your admirable brother in law[1]

---

1 The Lithuanian-born violinist Jascha Heifetz (1901–87), whose sister Elza was Behrman's wife.

[...] that Mr Schuster of the firm of the Inner Sanctum[1] has mimeographed my reply to his grotesquely fulsome letter to me about my little opusculum on Tolstoy (which he is to publish, I am sure in a horrible jolly jacket) & sent it to his 4000 most intimate friends. I am sure my reply (of which I remember not a word) was insincerely fulsome too – & probably hideously facetious too. Oh God. Perhaps nothing said or printed in America matters too much – the grain is so very lost in the billions [of] other grains which form the desert of human intercourse. [...] Mrs Luce[2] I cannot stomach even the thought of: I don't know why, quite: I know Henry L. slightly & don't much like him, but wd, faced with him, talk to him with some interest. His papers I now genuinely hate. *Life* I never read: *Time* I read weekly with horror & fascination like a terrible drug I cannot break myself of the habit of. But Mrs Luce – with a photograph in her bedroom from Bishop Sheen[3] "To darling Claire [*sic*], a golden arrow shot from the bow of God, yours in Christ, Fulton J.S." is too much. It is the sugariness of her entire personality – the combination of saccharine, sincerity, political streamlined vulgarity, humourless ruthlessness, commercialisation of spiritual inadequacies that I cannot stomach. The looks, is I think, what I find nauseating. But don't pass this on: for I must restrain my critical faculty, my parents keep telling me. Where will you be on the 16th Sept or so?

    love

      Isaiah.

TO CLARISSA EDEN

    Postmark 16 July 1953 [*manuscript*]

                                      All Souls

Dearest Clarissa,

    Thank you very much for your letter. I also had one from your hosts – some of them. Mrs James went on for 12 pages about how wonderful you were – how you bore your predicament etc. – she is what is called a dear creature: I did not, I admit, expect you to like any of the Cambridge figures *much*: the Schlesingers I like; him as well as her; but for you he is too much a bright young journalist and untidy: & has no taste at all. She *is* much more intelligent & a better man in all ways. I am fond of Arthur & respond to his golden heart, affection gaiety etc. but only wrote him because his adored

1 Schuster's office stationery was headed 'The Inner Sanctum of Simon and Schuster', an allusion to the 'Inner Sanctum' series of mystery novels published by his firm, on which a famous radio series was based.

2 (Ann) Clare Boothe Luce (1903–87), wife of Henry Luce; editor, playwright, politician, journalist, diplomat; Republican Congresswoman 1943–7; US Ambassador to Italy 1953–6; Catholic convert 1946.

3 Fulton John Sheen (1895–1979), television preacher; Auxiliary Bishop of New York 1951–65; later (1966–9) Bishop of Rochester; credited with converting Clare Boothe Luce to Catholicism.

Marietta thought it right: he falls in love with any pretty face – the more insipid & humourless the better – e.g. Mrs David Bruce[1] who is a v. mild affair: John Julius[2] dissolved in water and with touches of Victorian flirtatiousness is what suits Americans best. He, of course, thought you were splendid but sphinx-like & enigmatical: had you enjoyed yourself? he was not quite sure. But thought, I am glad to report, in the end, that you did. Mrs James is a kindly & comical snobbish lady – Mrs Leo Hunter out of Dickens[3] – who assembles lions in her parlour & then doesn't know what to do with them; they jostle each other in a gloomy way & she loses her nerve very quickly.

[...] Here we've had the Clore Ball.[4] Very grand, I am told, & those who went are divided into (a) those who really know them: e.g. John Foster; Sir Simon Marks; Mrs Halban; rich stockbrokers, relations of Paris Rothschilds, etc. who went by right (b) the upper class who appeared *en bloc* & in great force, & were ashamed the next day & explained that it really was difficult to draw lines – that once one started drawing where did one stop etc. but felt "bad" because unlike Hultons' parties[5] they *were* formally introduced to the hostess (whom I've never met but who said about Freddie Ayer + Bill Deakin "ces petits intellectuels ne me déplaisent pas")[6] & were invited to further social relationships – unbargained for – unwelcome – unlike the Hultons who didn't know who came & who didn't & could be cut with impunity & security later. Loelia[7] arranged everything, & had some trouble in beating off shameless enquirers who wanted to be told how much she had been paid; I witnessed all this the next night, when under some slight pressure from Raimund I went to the Austrian Embassy & was meant to keep company

1 Evangeline Bruce.
2 John Julius Cooper (b. 1929), 2nd Viscount Norwich 1954, son of Duff and Diana Cooper, author and broadcaster.
3 In *The Pickwick Papers* (1837) Charles Dickens satirises social lion-hunting in the person and name of Mrs Leo Hunter (author of 'Ode to an Expiring Frog').
4 The hosts of the dance on 8 July (for which guests were informed in *The Times* on 6 July that 'Decorations will be worn') were Charles Clore (1904–79), business tycoon, who in 1953 enjoyed his first major success as a pioneer of the 'takeover bid' (in private life a philanthropist and collector of art and antique furniture) and his (French-born) wife, the former Francine Rachel Halphen (c.1920–93).
5 On 9 June IB had written to Rowland Burdon-Muller: 'I have to go to dinner [...] and am afraid that they may have invited the awful owners of *Picture Post*, the Hultons. I swore to myself that I would not, if I possibly could avoid it, meet them, or if I met them, talk to them. I wonder if I shall be able to keep to my resolution. They keep inviting me to their grand parties and I cannot go anywhere if the hosts are people I should be ashamed to have in my own room. And this is what I feel about this particular couple.' Edward George Warris Hulton (1906–88), founder of *Picture Post*, proprietor 1938–57, and his Russian-born wife, formerly Princess Nika Yourievitch (b. 1916).
6 'I don't dislike these little intellectuals.'
7 Loelia, Duchess of Westminster.

to M–lle Lambert (Hansi L's daughter)[1] who hates dancing, loves music & is thought very like me. There I sat firmly like a huge cactus, & talked to Loelia & Fred Warner[2] all night & was thought not to have done well. Loelia when I asked if the Clores were now "made", thought not yet: 3 more parties at least needed; like a doctor in a watering place who tells a rich patient that the treatment has done him good already but 3 more visits are needed else it is all a great waste. Most enjoyable: & a great Edwardian piece of vulgar & comical parvenu-hood. She complained that Mrs Clore did not ask all the suggested guests & crossed Lady Marriott off because she had been snubbed by her in Paris. I don't know why I go on to you like this, except that the spectacle of people avid for pleasure & yet under some vague necessity to explain their conduct in moral terms – or at least in terms of some sort of rules – is a Proustian spectacle.[3] I've decided that I am M. Swann:[4] & if I ever called on David & Rachel & said that I was dying they wd behave with some sort of mixture of genuine concern & necessity to go to dinner at the Duc & Duchesse de Guermantes. Is this not so? [...]

love

  Isaiah

Marie Berlin had been told in April of the diagnosis reached by Mendel's doctors. Now she confided in IB, who learned that his misgivings over his father's continuing ill-health were fully justified.

TO ROWLAND BURDON-MULLER

26 August 1953 [*manuscript*]

Brooks's, St James's Street, London sw1

Dear Rowland,

Thank you for your letter. All is settled, I sail on the 10th etc. & send my books by separate cover to avoid painful scenes in the N.Y. customs despite

1 Lucie Lambert (b. 1933; married Alain Capeilleres 1965) was the daughter of Baroness Johanna ('Hansi') Lambert (1899–1960), née von Reininghaus, Austrian-born widow of the Belgian banker Baron Henri Lambert. IB had met Hansi Lambert in the US during the war, after which she returned to Brussels.

2 Frederick Archibald ('Fred') Warner (1918–95), diplomat (Moscow 1950–1) whose career was at this time temporarily blighted by his earlier friendship with Guy Burgess; later (1972–5) Ambassador to Japan.

3 To Rowland Burdon-Muller IB added: 'The first appearance of the nouveau riche is always comic in this way and I adore hearing about the Balzacian details of it, all more Balzac than Proust I must say. Mr Clore offered Mrs Clore £3000 not to have the party because that was costing less in the long run and because he was terrified of failure, and when at 4 o'clock in the morning she drank a great toast to him in champagne saying that the party had been a success after all – the Duchess of Kent and members of the nobility being there – he was most sincere and said: "But there are no Rothschilds."' Letter of 28 July 1953.

4 In Marcel Proust's novel *À la recherche du temps perdu*, the duc and duchesse de Guermantes, hurrying to dine out, take little notice of Charles Swann's admission that he is dying.

the protection of Moore's[1] minion sent to meet me. My father – I wish I could think his doctor wrong – probably has leukaemia. This is a dead secret from him, of course: but I know; my mother knows; & the whole thing is a dreadful nightmare. His doctor now is a competent man called Harman[2] in Harley Street who sees no use in a blood specialist since the symptoms, he says, afford of no doubt. He will I suppose decline steadily & without knowing that he has this fatal malady. I won't go on about it – but I shall sit in Harvard expecting a wire daily to call me back. Not to go (for me) would worry him more, of course. So go I must: otherwise perhaps I should have broken my "gentleman's agreement' with Harvard. The *New Republic* has printed a false account[3] of something I said, in an ill hour, to the detestable Michael Straight about the poetess Akhmatova. [...] Why must rich neurotic Americans behave *so* much worse than their worst European equivalents? I apologise for packing this letter so full of irritation & gloom: why do people who ought to know better go to Bayreuth & see Winifred Wagner,[4] Hitler's early devoted friend? I repent *my* journey to Salzburg in 1947: but Bayreuth 1953 is surely much worse? on this note of gloom & self righteous indignation I end. Much love & I shall see you soon: on the 19th wd you like me? or the 26th?

   Love

     Isaiah

The vulgarity[5] of Michael Straight's article, and the possible threat it posed to Akhmatova, drove IB to a furious round of letter-writing.

---

1 IB's friend (Ponsonby) Moore Crosthwaite (1907–89), diplomat, Deputy UK Representative to UN 1952–8; Ambassador to the Lebanon 1958–63, Sweden 1963–6.

2 John Bishop Harman (1907–94), consultant physician, St Thomas' Hospital 1938–72, Royal Marsden Hospital 1947–72; father of the Labour politician Harriet Harman.

3 'To Our Readers', signed 'M.S.', *New Republic*, 24 August 1953, 23.

4 Winifred Wagner (1897–1980), English-born widow of Richard Wagner's son Siegfried, had run the Bayreuth Festival 1930–45 until she was banned because of her close friendship with Hitler (whereupon her sons took over).

5 Straight's fictitious account of IB's visit to Akhmatova read in part: 'The light was poor, the walls were dingy, the furnishings were ancient and ugly. But in the midst of all this, he saw with astonishment on one wall a masterpiece of post-Impressionist painting, a magnificent portrait by Modigliani of a young woman. "What a nice picture!" he remarked as they drank tea. "Who is it of?" "It's of me!" the old woman sighed happily, "done when I was a girl in Europe before the war." "Who did it?" he asked innocently. She smiled: "Such a nice boy! He was handsome, with curly black hair. He had only one old sweater to wear – he was terribly poor! When he finished the picture he gave it to me for a loaf of bread and a bottle of wine. I never saw him again. Modi..., Modi..., Modigliani was his name," mused Akhmatova. "Amadeo [sic] Modigliani! I always wondered what happened to that poor boy!"' loc. cit. (note 3 above).

TO ARTHUR SCHLESINGER

27 August 1953

All Souls

Dear Arthur,

The Michael Straight thing really is serious. The Princess Margaret affair[1] was, after all, only a successful practical joke, for which the New York Times have not ceased apologising (to date four letters, unstimulated by me, each explaining how humiliated they feel by being made the plaything of high-spirited British upper-class young men); but the thing on the Russian poetess is very bad. I met Michael Straight at Dartington Hall (which his mother[2] pays for) when delivering a lecture on, of all things, a musical topic.[3] I have never liked him, and knew that he spread the stories you referred to about me, and have always regarded him as a kind of junior Archie McL[eish], only I suppose more dishonest. He declared he had specially come down in order to have a quarter of an hour with me, and we dined together after my lecture – which was unavoidable – and he talked of his experiences in the Soviet Union and I of mine, and I reminded him of his intimate friendship with Burgess, which he didn't like much. The Stalin story[4] was a popular Moscow anecdote in my time, which of course I told him as such; the incredible vulgarities about Modigliani's[5] curly black hair, bottles of wine etc. are a pure Straight invention of the most ghastly sort (his name really is the best known example to me of a *lucus a non lucendo*[6] – straight his name but not his nature). The whole thing is quite horrible – and for anyone who knows her makes me out an unspeakable cad and liar, which I deserve richly (I say, beating myself on the breast in the Russian manner) for talking to our friend Michael. He and David Astor both represent a kind of neurotic, twisted, poor-little-rich-boy character of whom pre-Nazi Germany was full, and who

1 When Mark Bonham Carter, the regular butt of jokes about his intimacy with the Royal family, was approached by the New York Times for information about Princess Margaret (Princess Margaret Rose, 1930–2002, younger daughter of King George VI), he kept his name out of the piece by offering those of his own friends. The article therefore suggested that IB ('a political philosopher who suffers from being known as "the cleverest man in the world"'), who had barely met the Princess, belonged to her inner circle. Charles Hussey, 'The Limelighted Princess Margaret', New York Times Magazine, 2 August 1953, 13 and 30, at 13.

2 Dorothy Payne Whitney (1887–1968), wealthy US philanthropist and social activist, whose first husband, who died in 1918, was Willard Straight; with her British second husband Leonard Elmhirst she transformed Dartington Hall in Devon into an educational and artistic centre.

3 IB lectured to the Dartington International Summer School on 2 August on 'The Beginnings of Russian Music'.

4 Straight had alleged that Akhmatova had been rehabilitated after the war because Stalin's daughter had found some of her poems, liked them, and asked her father what had become of her.

5 Amedeo Clemente Modigliani (1884–1920), Italian-born artist who first met Akhmatova while she was in Paris soon after her marriage to Nikolay Gumilev in 1910; in 1911 he produced a number of drawings of her, some of them nudes.

6 '[Called] *lucus* from its not being lucent'; not fully translatable since it plays on the Latin words 'lucus', 'a dark grove', and 'lucere', 'to shine'; it offers a paradoxical 'etymology' for a name that appears to suggest the opposite of its bearer's actual nature.

at present flourish most richly in New York. Why is it (do not be angry with me) that such things happen only in America? Even the lowest journalist would not print such a story here. However, that is not the point – what Madame A. will feel after the kind of interview I had with her in Leningrad – certainly one of the most moving experiences of my life – if ever she sees this nauseating rubbish, I do not like to think. But what matters, of course, is her physical security. So I have written to Michael Straight (I enclose a copy) asking him to print a brief *démenti*. Do you think this is a good idea? I see all the advantages of not blowing the thing up further, but as I feel sure the Russian émigré press will carry the story somewhere, it is surely best to kill it if I can. If he doesn't print it should I send it to the *New Leader*?[1] Or where? When I come to Cambridge I shall boldly associate with W. H. Chamberlin[2] and firmly join the Association of Fascist beasts. My transformation into a Whittaker Chambers,[3] an intimate of Miss Rebecca West, etc. seems now certain. I shall send my letter to Michael Straight by the same post as you receive this. If you think badly of it send me a wire to London, Hampstead 0912, and I shall re-instruct him. Why do I get into such needless hot water in the United States? You do see, don't you, my motives for reluctance to reach your blessed shores? However, there is nothing like dauntless courage. I arrive in New York on the 15th. I am sending my books to Cambridge under separate cover. A repetition of the scene at the Customs in New York in 1951 would be too much for me. I have had a letter from Kay, who is coming here with Phil, but I shall be gone when they arrive. Just as well, I expect. I am glad to know you and Chip and Felix and nobody else.

Yours ever,
Isaiah

⟨No doubt I shall cool down about this as about everything. But at present I feel it is the most horrible thing that has happened.⟩

TO MICHAEL STRAIGHT

27 August 1953 [*carbon sent to Arthur Schlesinger*]

All Souls

My dear Michael,

I have just received a clipping from the *New Republic* of 24 August, in which

---

1 The *New Leader* was a liberal political and cultural magazine, published 1924–2006 (thereafter online only).

2 W(illiam) H(enry) Chamberlin (1897–1969), historian and Soviet specialist; contributing editor, *New Leader*, 1940–69; his early sympathy for the Soviet Union gave way to fierce criticism.

3 Whittaker (né Jay Vivian) Chambers (1901–61), US writer, editor and former Communist agent who turned equally strongly anti-Communist; *Time* 1939–48. His testimony to the House Committee on Un-American Activities in 1948, in which he named those he had known as Communist spies, led eventually to Alger Hiss's downfall.

there is a report over your initials of a story about the Russian poetess Anna Akhmatova, purporting to come from me. I scarcely recognise the story; and I do not quite know how to begin to tell you what the consequences of your act are likely to be.

First, as to the facts. I did, in an ill-starred moment, at Dartington, at the beginning of this month, tell you that I had met Madame A. in the Soviet Union (not in Moscow, as you state), and I told you of an anecdote about how Stalin's daughter etc. helped to rehabilitate Madame A. – this appears in a somewhat garbled form in your version, but the principal point is that I told it to you, not as a true story, for which I had solid evidence, but as a current anecdote. I did also tell you that I saw a painting of Madame A. by Modigliani, hanging upon the wall of her room; and added that she did not seem to know that the painter had become famous since she had seen him in Paris before 1914. She said no more about him than this, to my knowledge, and so far as I remember I said no more to you. Where do black, curly hair, the jersey – the bottle of wine and loaf of bread – and all the rest of your scenario come from?

I have several points to make and the last of these is the most painful and ominous, but the others are bad enough.

1. I thought I knew enough about American journalism after my long and, on the whole, exceedingly happy acquaintance with journalists of every sort and character to think that a private conversation which occurred under such private circumstances would not be reported, even in an accurate form, with the source named, without seeking the source's permission in the normal manner; especially as we were talking as old acquaintances and not as an interviewer and his copy. It has never happened to me before, nor to anyone I know, in the form which it took on this occasion. Do you know of any other instance?

2. There are still people alive who know Madame A. well, and if they read your account of my conversation with her they will believe me to be a liar and a vulgarian, and an unspeakably nasty cad, and rightly so. If they insult me with this to my face, I should have nothing with which to answer them except that I did not say what I am reported as having said; but I could scarcely hope to be believed. People believe in the printed word a great deal more than they should. The thought that Madame A. herself might one day be given these words to read is something which I find too unbearable to conceive. Madame A., besides being a poetess of genius, is an exceedingly distinguished woman of great sensibility whose life has been a martyrdom for many years; I should of course never have talked about my meeting with her to you or anyone, for fear that something like this should happen: and I must say that of the people I have spoken to, American journalists among them, everyone understood the situation and refrained, on human grounds, from giving it publicity. Your account bears as much relation to the kind of

thing Madame A. would be likely to say as if the late Mrs Woolf[1] had been made to talk like a gangster's moll. I cannot describe to you how ashamed I am to occur by name in the course of the same paragraphs. All this is painful and distressing enough, but the main point is somewhat different, and on a different plane altogether.

3. You must know better than most people that in the Soviet Union all contact with foreigners (especially British or U.S. officials ("spies & saboteurs")) on the part of Soviet citizens, especially those suspected of unorthodoxies or dubious adherence to Communism, is exceedingly danger-ous. An account in a foreign newspaper of a meeting, particularly in order to emphasise an anti-Soviet point (perfectly justified though, of course, it is), seems to be almost certain to endanger the safety of the Soviet personality concerned. Madame A., as you know, has had enough trouble already – after her brief rehabilitation she was publicly condemned by none other than the late Zhdanov. Her position must be even more precarious than it was. Your story makes things worse. And the blood seems to me on both our hands. I do not deny my own responsibility, although of course I never dreamed that what I said to you would be printed. Still, I should, I suppose, have known better, and I have no excuse for what I did. But I do appeal to you as someone who understands the nature of Communism and how things are run in the Soviet Union – I appeal to you as a human being, and not as a journalist – to do what you can to minimise the effects of what has been done. Believe me, I am not exaggerating the situation. Perhaps one has to have been in the Soviet Union to realise what the consequences of casual pieces of this kind in the Western press can be to Soviet citizens. Your story is likely to be cabled to Russia direct by some Soviet informant in the USA, and is likely, anyhow, to be reprinted by the Russian emigré press, and so get to Moscow in the end. Of course I mind about the position in which it puts me – I feel terribly humiliated by what has occurred – but I hope you will believe me when I say that Madame A's safety concerns me much more than this; if a human life has been put in danger, however inadvertently, one must do anything to remedy the consequences of one's act. I do not know quite what to do: but I should say the best thing to do would be for you to print a letter in your next issue, which I enclose on a separate sheet. [...]

I do hope that I have brought home to you the gravity of the issue and the fact that we both have direct responsibility in the matter.

Yours sincerely

---

1 (Adeline) Virginia Woolf (1882–1941), née Stephen, novelist, short-story writer, essayist and liter-ary critic.

TO THE EDITOR OF THE *NEW REPUBLIC*[1]

[27 August 1953]

Oxford

In your issue of 24 August you tell a story about the Russian poetess, Madame Anna Akhmatova, which you attribute to me. I do not recognise the facts in the form in which you state them. I have heard the story of Madame Akhmatova and Stalin, but only as a piece of casual gossip; I understand Madame Akhmatova to possess a portrait by Modigliani, but the statements you report as having been made about him by her were never communicated to me. I am not concerned with the reliability of the story, but merely to make clear that I am not its source, and that the greater portion of it is as new to me as it must be to the majority of your readers.

Isaiah Berlin

---

1 'Madame Akhmatova', *New Republic*, 14 September 1953, 22–3.

1953

HARVARD

I do not know what strange fate it is which plunges me in personal crises every time I leave England to come to this hospitable but maddening city.[1]

1 To John Sparrow, 21 November 1953.

In September IB left London for the US, travelling on the Queen Elizabeth *in the company of Ronnie and Marietta Tree; his third session as Visiting Lecturer at Harvard was to be followed by a working visit to Princeton. One of IB's first commitments was the lecture on 9 October at Smith College,¹ where his friend Edgar Wind was deep in academic controversy.*

TO ANNA KALLIN

15 October 1953

Lowell House, Harvard

Dear N,

[...] I have just been to Smith College. There there is an undeclared war between the government, which wants people to testify before committees, and Edgar who is a very effective, subtle and formidable leader of the opposition. I stayed with the government ex-officio, and was forced to behave as a kind of Swiss neutral perpetually visiting people on the other side of the curtain.

[...] There was much agitation at Smith about a Professor of English, named Gorham Davis,² who was apparently once a Communist – he looks like a neurotic casualty of some kind – he testified before McCarthy, and got various people into trouble – you could imagine that his horrible conduct caused a terrific controversy between those who thought he should have talked, and those who thought he shouldn't, and what one should and shouldn't do, etc., etc.; some said he did it by collusion with the people he named; some that he did not, etc. However, I could not help remembering the story of the 1890s, told to me by my friend Roman Jakobson (who also ought to go to England). In the 1890s the Russian police arrested a secretary of the well-known revolutionary, Dragomanov,³ who lived in Switzerland; he would not implicate his accomplices, so they sent for his father – a monarchist black village priest – and told him that his son was threatened with execution; which was in fact not true; and begged him to use his influence with the son. The priest said he would try if left alone with the son. Left face to face with him he advanced upon him and said in a sepulchral voice, 'My son, you have, I know, committed horrors and abominations of every kind

---

1 On which IB reported to his parents: 'I have been to Smith College & delivered my lecture (400 bucks) & was well received. A huge dinner party was given for me, I knew at the end of it, inevitably, I would be put in an armchair, all the other guests would be drawn up in a C-shaped manner, & I would be put through a kind of press conference. If one must, one does: so I talked for 3 hours about England, Russia, myself, etc. etc.' Letter of 13 October 1953.

2 Robert Gorham Davis (1908–98), literary critic, who had taught English at Harvard for many years and was now doing so at Smith College; Professor of English, Columbia University, 1957–76.

3 Mikhail Petrovich Dragomanov (1841–95), Ukrainian scholar, historian and supporter of Ukrainian independence, formerly a professor at Kiev University, forced to live in exile in Geneva and later in Bulgaria because of his political activities.

in the accursed West. For this God will punish you as you deserve; you will be hanged & justly. But if you add to your sins that of a Judas and a traitor & betray your friends you will indubitably go to Hell, and I shall curse you publicly from my pulpit.' Saying these words he left. When they asked him afterwards whether he had had any success he said, 'I did my best: he was obdurate.'

The moral of this story I leave to you – it moved me a great deal and also somewhat impressed the President of Smith[1] – Edgar was hysterically delighted with it, and made me promise to tell the head of the opposite faction at Smith – which with courage unusual for me, and the aid of memories of Mr E. M. Forster,[2] I bravely carried out. [...]

Yours ever,
Isaiah

TO MAURICE BOWRA
16 October 1953 [*carbon*]

Lowell House, Harvard

My dear Maurice,

Let me begin with the budget of local news.

Levin is back, theoretically mellowed but, in fact, hissing violently against the new administration. Extremely polite to me. Almost warm. Refers to my poor friend, Nabokov, as quite a 'shady international operator'; to the new President[3] as 'Red Kellogg's[4] God-hopping friend'.

The new President dined here last Monday – I did not speak to him, but observed him closely. He looks like a touched up photograph of an idealised Rhodes Scholar, kept in cellophane in an icebox. He is like an earnest, Victorian, young Bishop of the 90's, who has returned after a slum parish and great work in the mission field to some vigorous churchmanship. He is humourless – very religious – and filled with a sense of mission. He is quite a nice man, simple hearted, and I should think all right on civil liberties and the like; not at all clever; his provincialism is splendid and enormous.[5] His wife

1 Benjamin Fletcher Wright (1900–76), Professor of Government, Harvard, 1945–9; President of Smith College 1949–59.
2 '[I]f I had to choose between betraying my country and betraying my friend, I hope I should have the guts to betray my country.' E. M. Forster, 'What I Believe' (16/3), 78.
3 Nathan Marsh Pusey (1907–2001), President, Lawrence College, 1944–53; President, Harvard, 1953–71; a firm opponent of Senator McCarthy (whose power base in Wisconsin surrounded Lawrence College), who commented on Pusey's appointment to Harvard that 'Harvard's loss is Wisconsin's gain' (*Time*, 13 July 1953, 15). His wife was the former Anne Woodward (1914–2004).
4 Revd Frederic Brainerd ('Red') Kellogg (1909–58), Episcopalian Chaplain at Harvard and Radcliffe 1940–58.
5 To Morton White IB commented that Pusey would 'probably remove the stigma of dangerous thought from Harvard, but in the course of it gently lower the standards also, but the decline will be very slow and very gradual – for a decade no difference will be felt – by that time he will probably go to wider fields'. Letter of 21 October 1953.

like a sprightly vicar's wife. He did not belong with Mary Perkins. Young Arthur is breathing slaughter and thundering against him everywhere. He believes in teaching – dislikes research – and believes in direct relations between the King and his people; i.e., the student across the heads of the Faculty bureaucracy. Bundy is crazy about him. There will be much trouble this year.

Billy James does not see why he should not insult the memory of dear old President Eliot[1] for his impious views – others have done so and got away with it; Alice, although she approves of virtue and piety, thinks he brings in God a little too much, and without elegance of phrase. Perry Miller, who is at Princeton, has sent him all his books, received a polite note of acknowledgement which he has shown to everyone, I am told. Levin will get on better as he loves mediocrities. Finley[2] believes he is badly distressed and rather sweet. He led off by saying that what this University needed was a Philip Sidney,[3] and what it got was a Tom Sawyer.[4] He apparently called his colleagues at Eliot House to ask their views on how to act when he became President. The election of Pusey springs from the same corners as that of Keir[5] and Ike. Finley does not realise yet about Hawkes[6] – the heavier qualities – thinks he is very unlike yourself. He did an amusing and wistful turn to me about how the Harvard Presidents alternate between Huckleberry Finn (Eliot and Conant) and Tom Sawyer (Lowell and Pusey). Altogether I like him much better this term, misery goes well with him and sits well upon him, and has made him milder and more interesting. [...]

Wind is most anxious to leave America, and has applied formally to King's, giving Seznec and two Art Historians as his referees. I wish they would take him, but I doubt if they will – he is an absolutely charming man outside, and no bother at all, and I have written Noel so if you see him, or write to him, do please quote me to that effect. If and when Pares becomes incapable All Souls might well do worse than to take him. [...]

I saw Jakobson, who is much upset at the local situation, and says that if you or I named him to Oxford, he would have accepted the job. This I do not believe. He says that even if now something is invented for him he would

1 Charles William Eliot (1834–1926), President of Harvard 1869–1909, who dramatically improved the University and its status.
2 John Huston Finley (1904–95), Eliot Professor of Greek Literature and Master of Eliot House, Harvard, 1942–76; a pioneer of general education at Harvard.
3 (Sir) Philip Sidney (1554–86), soldier, scholar, courtier (to Elizabeth I) and poet.
4 In Mark Twain's novels *The Adventures of Tom Sawyer* (1876) and *Adventures of Huckleberry Finn* (1884), Tom Sawyer, a small-town boy in the Deep South, is the conventional follower of society's rules, his friend Huckleberry Finn the questioning rebel.
5 Sir David Lindsay Keir (1895–1973), Vice-Chancellor, Queen's University, Belfast, 1939–49; Master of Balliol 1949–65.
6 John Clendennin Burne Hawkes, Jr (1925–98), postmodern novelist and poet; Harvard University Press 1949–55; taught English at Harvard 1956–8, at Brown University 1958–88 (Professor 1967–88, T. B. Stowell University Professor 1973–88).

come – e.g. – a part-time Research fellowship, say of £600, – perhaps Jesus or All Souls? He could spend one term here and two at Oxford, and says he will be more than delighted to do that – he would go on being paid handsomely here where they are terrified that he may leave.

Konovalov apparently wrote to him a letter during the election activities, telling him that the pay was low – facilities non-existent – work enormous – that he must not think of coming as it would be not at all nice for him at Oxford. He and Wind would both be great acquisitions, and Joy, who would make an admirable Research Fellow, as, unlike Wind, he has devoted disciples all over Europe. Karpovich will retire in two years time, whatever happens, as he dislikes being here now too much, he says. [. . .]

Mrs James is much worried about the poor impression made in Boston by Mrs Eden, who was found very ungracious.

I haven't been to New York or Washington, and don't intend to go until the last moment. I am comfortably lodged, for once, in a six room flat in Lowell House[1] – see few people – and work at Widener very happily with a lot of splendid Russian books, not to be found anywhere else.

When I don't think about my father I am quite contented – it is just like the exile of the Russian radicals in the early 19th century of Perm or Wyatka,[2] and has its compensations.

Love to everybody.

Yours as ever,

---

1 '[A]part from an embryo in a bottle which I cannot look at, and a few stuffed monkeys, my five rooms are very commodious, and much better than anything I have ever had before.' 21 October to Morton White.

2 Perm′ and Wyatka (or Vjatka; now Kirov), cities near the Ural mountains, often used for internal exile. Alexander Herzen was exiled to Wyatka in 1835.

*IB had been associated with Nuffield College as a Faculty Fellow since 1952.[1]
But a letter[2] from the Senior Fellow there came as a surprise: 'a very large
majority' of the College's Executive Committee wanted him to stand for the
Wardenship that was to fall vacant in October 1954.*

TO MARGERY PERHAM[3]

7 November 1953[4] [*typed transcript*]

Lowell House

Dear Miss Perham,

I must begin by apologising for not replying earlier: but I was away, lecturing in New England, when your letter arrived and I saw it only three days
later. I was, as you may imagine, moved most deeply by its contents. Such
an expression of confidence on the part of my colleagues at Nuffield, which
I have done so little to earn, is something for which I can only express my
profound, astonished but lasting gratitude.

The news of the proposal which the Executive Committee would wish
to put before the Warden and Fellows came to me as a bolt from the blue,
and I have not collected my thoughts sufficiently to be able to reach a clear
decision. After recovering from the first shock which the possibility of this
great honour and responsibility gave me, I began to weigh your words about
the critical decade which the College is about to enter – the need in particular to raise funds for building the Library, Dining Hall, Tower etc., and
came to the conclusion that I was, perhaps, less well fitted for such a task
than any other Fellow of the College. I wondered, too, whether I could, in
all decency, leave All Souls so soon after my readmission for a very specific

1 'Nuffield College in its beginnings had proper Fellows and also Faculty Fellows – which meant
   you were a Fellow of another College but you were allowed to be a kind of external Fellow –
   while they were being nurtured. And I was one of these because I was a friend of Cole.' MI Tape
   28.
2 2 November 1953 from Margery Perham, enclosing details of the Warden's remuneration, and
   assuring IB of 'the great goodwill and warm welcome' awaiting him in the College.
3 Margery Perham (1895–1982), Official Fellow, Nuffield, 1939–63; Reader in Colonial Administration,
   Oxford, 1939–48. In IB's opinion 'a hysterical old idiot': 28 November [1953] to Maurice Bowra.
4 Two versions of the letter were typed with this date. The discarded first version (of which a
   carbon survives), though largely similar to its successor, is notably more negative: 'I wish I could
   promise, on due reflection, to send a definite reply by the date which you mention, but I fear I
   may not be able to do this. [...] I should not, above all, wish to let my name go forth as candidate
   for this post if there were any rival candidates with any degree of support set against me [...] I
   could say no, of course, and am strongly tempted to do so and remain free and unfettered at All
   Souls, and put this preferment from my thoughts, but this I think I am stopped from [...] doing,
   and think perhaps the Fellows at Nuffield are wiser than I, and [one] ought not to avert one's gaze
   so readily from such an honour and opportunities and responsibilities. [...] my administrative
   experience is really infinitesimal. [...] my own interests are more historical and ideological than
   related to the contemporary or social obligations. [...] I might find little favour in the eyes of the
   Lord Nuffield [400/2], even though politically I should not perhaps shock him. [...] I should want
   to go off from time to time to look up Russian books in the libraries of Paris and sometimes in
   the United States.'

research purpose; whether the duties of the Wardenship would leave me
time to write those books which, by now, I feel a decisive moral obligation
to try to produce; all this apart from my general fitness for the post, which
may well be clearer to others than to me – but I will not burden you with the
tale of my doubts and hesitations. What did seem to me a crucial consideration was the question of what this post entailed. For I do not, I must admit,
feel clear about the duties and problems of a Warden of Nuffield – about
the area of his responsibility, or the degree of freedom possessed by the
College to dispose of its resources or institute changes. I do not mean that
I have specific schemes in mind and am asking how feasible they are; but
more generally how rigid the statutes are – how far in theory or practice
the College is dependent on Council, or the Nuffield Trustees,[1] how far its
endowment is earmarked for specific purposes, etc. I am deeply ashamed
to admit my ignorance of all this – I ought to know the relevant facts, even
separated from all papers. But I fear I am ignorant about these very essential
factors. I do not feel that I could be effectively enlightened by correspondence – nor that I should feel justified in placing such a burden on your own
shoulders or any other Fellows – the burden, I mean, of conducting a correspondence course designed to teach me the rudiments of the government
of Nuffield. But equally I feel that I cannot make up my mind, or even try
to still my numerous doubts, until I grasp those facts more clearly. And this,
I feel sure, can only be done properly in personal discussion. Unfortunately
I am obliged to stay here until nearly the end of December, and am due in
Princeton in early spring. But if you and the College thought this a useful
thing to do, I could come to Oxford in the first or second week of the Hilary
Term next year – and talk about the matter then. I can understand only too
well that you would prefer to have a clear reply from me in time for the next
meeting of the Warden and Fellows; I wish I could provide it; but I cannot.
And if you would prefer not to postpone matters till January and decide to
settle them by Christmas, I should, of course, understand and appreciate
your reasons. But the more I reflect on it the surer I become that I could
not possibly accept such opportunities and responsibilities without knowing
more clearly what they are – and that for that purpose a personal visit seems
to me indispensable. If, in the meanwhile, you feel that it would be proper or
helpful to bring up my name before the Warden and Fellows, on a tentative
basis, committing neither the College nor myself, to test opinion, I should
have no objection. I only hope that what I am asking for is not to involve too
grave an inconvenience for the College – if it does, I should feel it right to
withdraw at this stage. If not, I should arrange to stay in Oxford during the
second half of January; and could remind you of my various shortcomings

1 Nuffield was the first Oxford College not to be fully autonomous at its foundation, and began life
   under the direction of the University's Hebdomadal Council.

then. But one thing I ought to say at this stage – and beg you to be so good as to convey it to the other members of the Executive Committee and any one else concerned – namely, that whatever the outcome, their action has filled me with more pride and happiness than any other event in my life. For this, I shall always be infinitely grateful to them all.

Yours sincerely,
Isaiah Berlin

TO MARIE AND MENDEL BERLIN

Friday [postmark 8 November 1953, *manuscript*]

Lowell House, Harvard

Dear Pa & Ma.

What *about* Nuffield? salary £1800 + £400.0.0 non (taxed) *expenses*: Income after tax: about £1400? Starting in autumn 1954. a house: no rates or taxes: retirement age: 65: duties: to be in Oxford six weeks of each term; (one *can* go away for 7 weeks or so at a time: even to U.S.)

Advantages: 1) status. Quite decent: my predecessors: Sir Harold Butler, Sir Henry Clay,[1] Mr Loveday.[2] administration & bureaucracy: I don't mind & do quite well; contact with politicians & businessmen: not fatal. The buildings are between the road which leads from station to Carfax & Worcester: one gate into where Bus No 1 passes between Carfax & Station: other door into George Street near the electric shops there: I wd import Italian couple to look after me, if I could.

2) no more moral obligation to lay golden eggs

3) a clear function in life.

Disadvantages: loss of freedom: loss of beautiful rooms, All Souls, charming life, isolation of the throne, even a humble one: Professorship will produce same money: status about same, even a little lower perhaps: & obligated to lecture for 20 years: which might drive one mad:

Colleagues at Nuffield: bleak: dull: stiff: but *real* – economists, experts on local government, люди в футляре,[3] & want *me* to humanise & civilise them:

I shall write a temporising letter: saying I'll come & see them *end of January*: (Xmas no good: nobody there) i.e. en route home from *Nice*. [...]

Isaiah.

I shall ask advice from: David, Hampshire, & [A. H.] Smith (which I shall respect) Bowra, Sparrow, Hart (less respect: Maurice will be slightly jealous;

1 Sir Henry Clay (1883–1954), economist; Warden of Nuffield 1944–9.
2 Alexander Loveday (1888–1962), economist; Fellow of Nuffield 1946–9, Warden 1950–4.
3 'Lyudi v phutlyare' ('people in a shell', i.e. withdrawn beneath a defensive carapace), a reference to Chekhov's short story 'The Man in a Shell'.

Sparrow genuinely displeased to lose me because I give prestige to All Souls;
Hart too narrow).

Don't you think this is correct analysis? whom else should I ask? enough.

*IB duly dispatched a shoal of letters to those likely to have helpful advice to offer
on his dilemma (and some less likely). With at least some of these he enclosed
the following analysis of the advantages and disadvantages of becoming
Warden of Nuffield.*[1]

ARGUMENTS FOR

1. I secretly quite like administrative and bureaucratic routine, and am not quite
   as bad at it as I obviously appear.
2. One might hope to stimulate genuine work in better and more interesting
   fields than are now being pursued, and suppress some bogus research.
3. Adequate salary, house etc., making journeys to Harvard etc. unnecessary.
4. Freedom from moral obligation to lay, if not golden, then at any rate decent
   copper, eggs, at regular intervals.
5. Time free for research about the same as now if other academic obligations –
   i.e. teaching, lecturing – removed.
6. Anyway I am determined to carry out my programme promised to All Souls
   wherever I am.
7. Subjects pursued at Nuffield may be bleak, but they are for the most part
   genuine; so are the people. A certain honesty and decency of atmosphere.
8. I should like to try to organise and build something sometime in my life, and
   have a certain suppressed and secret desire to do good, to which this would
   give an outlet.

ARGUMENTS AGAINST

1. Awful colleagues, not likely to alter much at all soon.
2. Need to gather money for new library, dining hall etc.; at which I should be no
   good at all.
3. Relations with embarrassing personalities like Lord Nuffield,[2] and various
   businessmen and politicians; who will not like me at all.
4. Unattractive physical environment.
5. Being tied down to Oxford – impossibility of being off to look up books in the
   USA for more than four or five weeks at a time during vacations. General loss
   of liberty.
6. Unreal authority over an unreal college full of absurd appendages in the form
   of Faculty Fellows, businessmen and other patrons, making sovereignty and
   freedom of action probably impossible to achieve.
7. One would be wrong to leave All Souls.

1 IB also identified some key questions about the governance of Nuffield. His notes on these conclude: 'I have an idea that most people would instinctively consider this to be a totally unsuitable
   thing for me to do. This strongly inclines me towards it' [MSB 317/113].
2 William Richard Morris (1877–1963), 1st Viscount Nuffield, car manufacturer and philanthropist;
   Chairman of Morris Motors Ltd 1919–52. The College which bears his name was originally
   funded by him and built on land he owned.

8. Foolishness of losing a free and comfortable existence in exquisite surroundings for the rest of one's life – for what?

TO DAVID CECIL

8 November 1953 [*carbon*]

Lowell House, Harvard

Dear David,

Forgive me for typing this, but it will be more legible, and thank you ever
so much for your letters – I found them so comforting at moments when I
most needed comfort. I really do not know why I keep coming here when
gloom falls upon me almost immediately, and persists until I return. I can see
the Halbans' house[1] very vividly before me, and poor Aline not quite sure
what is wrong, or whether anything is, in the midst of styles and everything.

There are many other things which I long to write about – the effects
of Elizabeth here[2] – the approaching Violet Bonham Carter festival,[3] and
the reactions of hostesses here to it; all splendidly Victorian and well worth
describing. It is the last hope of genuinely provincial sentiment and morals,
and really enormously unlike our lives, but I must write you about the crisis
which always seems to burst over my head as soon as I come to these shores.

I don't know if the gossip has reached you, but Nuffield has suddenly
decided to offer itself to me – it has to go through the Council there, but if
they put forth only one name I suppose I should get it if I said 'yes'. At first it
seemed lunatical, but I enclose a list of pros and cons, which I shall also send
to Stuart and possibly Maurice.

Before you speak, let me say this – All Souls has grown terribly dull and
bleak. The need to have long neurotic arguments with Sparrow on every
small piece of college policy can be enormously exhausting and dreary. I
should like to live in a house and not a room – have a couple to look after
me – and be able to entertain weekends – the salary is £1800, plus £400 for
entertainment; it is not much but one can jog along.

I secretly am rather embarrassed at being such a Fellow and having a

1 The Halbans had recently moved to Headington House, an imposing eighteenth-century
mansion with extensive grounds in Old Headington, on the outskirts of Oxford. David Cecil had
written to IB that what had been 'a dyed-in-the-wool 18 century English house' was now 'Munich
1925 – all brown naked "Volk" woodwork + a few Cezanne scrawls on the walls. Not very nice.
However poor Aline is aware something is wrong & looks at one nervously & one lies & says it
is delightful. Meanwhile the Franks family have got into the Halbans old house & – lo & behold
it is turned from Munich into Edwardian English Middle-Middle Class.' Undated letter.
2 Widowed in 1952, Elizabeth Bowen undertook regular lecture tours and stints as writer-in-
residence at universities in the US in an attempt (ultimately unsuccessful) to maintain her home
in Ireland, Bowen's Court.
3 'I am wearing myself to the bone, butchering myself to make a holiday for Lady Violet – I have
organised a liberal festival week – Lady Violet Bonham Carter festival – in Cambridge, Mass' (to
George Weidenfeld, 17 November 1953). IB and Raymond Bonham Carter also organised a large
party for Lady Violet on 16 November.

moral obligation to lay golden eggs, or even copper ones, and believe that
the amount of time one wastes is approximately the same wherever one
lives. I do not dislike administrative and paper work, but rather secretly enjoy
it; possibly as an escape from more painful tasks – e.g. writing – and did not
do too badly at it in Washington during the war.

I moved to New College in '38 really in order not to have the obligation
to write as I would have done at All Souls, and wrote neither more nor less
there than later at All Souls, and shall certainly produce all the books which
I promised to produce wherever I am – that I should be terribly ashamed not
to do, and a change of job would not stop me. On the other hand Nuffield is
the child of Lindsay and Cole – is bleak and a bogus imitation of some social
Council in London – everything that I find grotesque and unsympathetic.
And I fear that they want me because they feel too bleak themselves and
would like to be Oxfordised and generally humanised. The place is rather
like a women's college, etc. I need not go on. I don't know how much I
could send it spinning in any one direction, but, somehow, I should rather
like to try, or is it absurd to give up my pretty room in All Souls and my very
powerful life for that?

Suppose I were offered St Antony's[1] instead, with Bill Deakin retiring. In a
way I should prefer Nuffield because St Antony's seems to me (for God's sake
don't tell anyone that) something like a club of dear friends, and I should
be terribly afraid that the thing was becoming too cosy and too bogus, but,
again, the very bleakness and reality of the grim atmosphere of Nuffield
would give one a certain sense of seriousness and justification; therefore
please write and tell me what you think.

I thought of writing to Smith – I dare not write to Sparrow until the last
moment; he will be very outraged, and if I do accept will never understand
my motives. It is a little like your Cambridge Chair.

On the assumption that I shall not marry soon I am not sure that I want
to go on living in a college room for ever.

I propose to write to them and delay matters and say I will come in
January and talk it over – even that I feel to be somewhat more committal
than I want it to be. I could refuse the post; probably if informed that I had
been formally appointed, or decisively rejected, I should feel equal measures
of relief; choosing is hell; yet I shall choose in the end, and suffer no qualms. I
am far less certain that I want to be a Professor and lecture on political theory
for twenty years, even if it were promised me virtually, so write swiftly, and I
shall be most grateful. Forgive me for writing and sending this off as quickly
as I can – I must reply within the next week, so do send your answer by air
mail – however brief.

---

1 At that time All Souls, Nuffield and St Antony's were the only Oxford colleges without
undergraduates.

I apologise ten thousand times for putting this upon you, and yet you know me better than anyone else and your judgement will be by far the most valuable, the wisest, and the best. I say this because I have always found it so in the past. I shall ask Stuart but he is full of ideology; Maurice will be prompted by peculiar sentiments. Of Sparrow there is no need to speak (anyway I haven't written to him yet), and who else is there left for me to ask? James will be horror stricken – I may ask Bill Deakin; perhaps Wheare; but I repeat I will trust you a great deal more than anybody else, and a little more than myself because, as you often said, our attitudes are utterly similar, and the scales of value, too, and because I feel greater confidence in your emotions and conclusions than in those of anyone else I have ever known.

As ever,

Advice began to arrive from Oxford.

TO MAURICE BOWRA
19 November 1953

Lowell House, Harvard

Dear Maurice,

I am most grateful for your letter.[1] It more than any other single factor, including my own instincts, has helped me to make up my mind about Nuffield. I am sure you are quite right on all grounds, and your judgement is really final.

I write this in an extreme haste, but shall write more tomorrow; meanwhile, I have written to Miss Perham saying that I could not say 'yes' or 'no', but would come and talk to them about it in January, and then wrote her a second letter, which I shall send off by this post, saying that if the facts and resources are as I think they are I should like to accept,[2] but still think before clinching it I should have a talk with them, so at their next meeting, which I think is 25 November, they could regard me as favourable but not yet decided, and almost certain to accept but not quite. I hope this is good.

Meanwhile I must bite into the sour apple and write to Sparrow to whom I have written a frivolous postcard but nothing else. He is the only man I know who is capable of making a scene in a letter; one of the reasons for which

1 Bowra had written on 11 November when he heard of the offer on the Oxford grapevine, and again the next day after receiving a letter from IB. After a crisp, perceptive analysis of the situation, forthright comments on the personalities involved and self-deprecation about his own skilful handling of Lord Nuffield, he strongly urged IB to accept.
2 'I [. . .] have reached the conclusion that I should like to accept the proposal of the Executive Committee, but am still unable to do so outright because I really am profoundly and shamefully ignorant of the functional powers of the College and of the Warden; that is why I should be grateful if my proposal were accepted and I were allowed to come and talk to members of the College about it towards the end of January.' To Margery Perham, 16 November 1953.

I want to leave All Souls is the perpetual possibility of the particular rows of which he is such a master. I agree with you that us against his enemies is absolutely right, and I am very sorry to see the triumph of Monteith[1] and Company. I am sure to be accused by John of treachery etc. but as it was I more than anyone else, in the beginning and the end (after havering in the middle), who helped put him in, he cannot complain too much, and if he does I should be grateful if you would point this out to him some day.

I shall certainly require your help with Lord Nuffield; the others I feel sure are quite manageable; Smith has not written yet, but I am glad he is favour-able – do tell him to write at once. Stuart began by disapproving – then came round. Quinton, who has discovered all this from somewhere, has written pathetically begging me not to go. In the end he will have to be taken into Nuffield, too, I expect. He is a wonderful teacher, and might turn himself into a political specialist. He seems to me to be naturally a Nuffield soul.

Yours,

Isaiah   [. . .]

TO JOHN SPARROW

21 November 1953 [*manuscript*]

Lowell House, Harvard

My dear old friend![2]

Again, alas, the time has come for this mode of address: I do not know what strange fate it is which plunges me in personal crises every time I leave England to come to this hospitable but maddening city. In 1949 it was the New College Fellowship in English which put what is called "a severe strain" on my friendship with David C. In 1951, All Souls, which ended so much more happily and honourably & creditably to all concerned. And now this sudden invitation to me from Nuffield College to be their Warden, contained in a letter from the Senior Fellow, Miss Perham, declaring that it was their nem. con. & "almost" unanimous wish to recommend me to the Hebdomadal Council for this exalted state. I received the letter about a fortnight ago, & since then have gone through many sets of thoughts. My natural instinct was to reject it firmly & think no more. *Prima facie* what cd possibly tempt me? a bleak Institute near the Station, dedicated to local government, Public Administration, Black men, the eccentric home of Plamenatz, administra-tive chores, a College which feels itself an academic slum, a cross between an inferior London School of Economics & Sheffield University, of which not a (male) Fellow but would prefer to be a Fellow of somewhere else, a

---

1 Charles Montgomery Monteith (1921–95), barrister and publisher; Fellow of All Souls 1948–88; joined Faber and Faber in 1953, made a director 1954, later (1977–80) Chairman.

2 As IB admitted to Sparrow in a letter of 21 June 1962, 'This mode of address always indicates a crisis.'

"College" barnacled with business men, bankers, Herbert Morrisons, Civil Servants, grim graduates from the Dominions & the Schools of Commerce, fumed oak,[1] Dunlopillo rubber cushions, looked down on by the rest of the University, hated by its own Founder as a bunch of reds,[2] likely to lock me from daily intercourse with whom I am pleased to think of as my equals, depriving me of freedom, delightful rooms, independence, Status, – this against all the very genuine sentiments which I have for my "old College" as I once sincerely called it – why should I even think of it? And yet, in a sober mood on the next day, I thought: if this robbed me of so much leisure that I shd not write the books I promised to All Souls, then I need not think of accepting, & that's the end of that. But would it? all kinds of considerations swam up to the surface: none decisive: but cumulatively strong.

(a) The embarrassment, which I feel acutely at being a goose expected to lay if not a golden at least leaden or copper eggs. I know that if my magnum opus is not ready by 1955 & any two other books appear etc. I am not too likely to be expelled, but I am dreadfully sensitive – much too much – to opinion, & mere expectancy, attached to any Research Fellow, petrifies me: I went to N. College in 1948 [sc. 1938] to avoid just this (though I had written a book & articles in learned journals) & wd not have returned if my new interests had been compatible with an ordinary teaching Fellowship at New College. It does not oppress me so much that I cannot live, work, enjoy myself: but I *mind* it greatly. And also the *need* to lecture & teach which is both moral & legal. Without the need, I wd, now & then.

(b) I don't have to go on all my days in a College room, with the door too open, as is inevitable, given my character etc. I am unlikely to marry. And I shd like a front door & ability to have guests to stay, & not be bottled up with them in a room.

(c) I have a hidden desire to improve mankind, though I denounce it vigorously in others. As to promoting learning. If I *can* reform Nuffield – cast out the dead wood – raise the level – extend the terms of "Social Study" to include history, & history of all kinds – science, art, Russia etc. (that's a typical zeugma; typical of what, of whom? I leave you to establish that) I'd like to try.

(d) I am not, curiously enough, a hopeless bureaucrat: & it steadies the nerves – for me – as against the agonies of writing & all I have to set against writing now is social life & that merely increases my guilt.

(e) All Souls with its numbers & its clashes is a little too *emotional* for me: I *mind* the Monteithery etc. too much to be useful – so much more, so very

---

1 Oak darkened (to simulate ageing) by exposure to ammonia fumes; popular for furniture in the early twentieth century; for Noel Coward in his eponymous short play of 1935 a symbol of stifling respectability, but for IB perhaps associated with the spartan Utility furniture of the 1940s.

2 Lord Nuffield, a social conservative, had hoped to found a college for engineering, but the University preferred a centre for social studies, with which he had little sympathy. Nuffield College nevertheless inherited the bulk of its founder's substantial fortune.

much more, I think, than you do, who know your own mind better & are commendably, enviably, independent & strong willed (which is indeed why you are, justly & rightly, Warden).

All this left me not quite decided: I thought *if* there is not time to write books (as e.g. Wheare thinks) or *if* the power & finance of Nuffield & its Warden are not such that the minimally desirable reforms are feasible, then *No*. So I can't decide unless I know the facts. If these threats are overcomable, then perhaps, & despite all the dullness & the smoked oak & the absurdity of the place, why, possibly, yes. So I wrote to Miss Perham: expressed apprecia-tion: & said I wd return to Oxford in mid-January & as the Americans so beautifully say, "Case the joint" or explore the facts in personal conversa-tion. I am uncommitted: to the man who promoted my case – Honest Jack Butterworth[1] – I wrote more warmly. Then I received a letter from our wise old Vice-Chancellor: a model of good sense & sympathy, which on such occasions, as you know, he displays so admirably. Accept, he said, accept accept accept. And then another letter – the next day, saying the same, more strongly & warmly & sweetly. Then a letter from David Cecil saying the same in more moderate terms with more cautions: and Stuart: first no, then yes: with only *Quinton* against (who'd heard of it). Something prevented me from writing to you in the first week – because I misjudged the date of the elections & thought to leave you in peace while Morse[2] & Holloway[3] were raging on: & also, more strongly & deeply perhaps, because (although I may be flattering myself much too much) because I thought you might be too set against: & induce too much shame & distress in me too early before I had pondered & weighed & considered: but I *must* bite into the sour apple: & I long for your views as a devoted friend, as a sober & wise judge, & as Warden. If [I] *were* Warden of Nuff. cd I, theoretically, constitutionally, become a Fifty Pounder?[4] be like Brook[5] when he was Censor? I am not sure that not: how I shd love that! despite the emotionné[6] elections (but I feel I am speaking like Faber. Stop.) I wd, I *think*, rather have Nuffield, than a Chair: I'll return in January anyway to negotiate: I told Nuffield that if they could not wait they must elect someone else & I'd be relieved.

1 John Blackstock ('Jack') Butterworth (1918–2003), later (1985) Baron Butterworth; Fellow of New College 1946–63 (Bursar 1956–63); Faculty Fellow, Nuffield, 1953–8; later (1963–85) Founding Vice-Chancellor, University of Warwick.

2 (Christopher) Jeremy Morse (b. 1928), banker; elected Prize Fellow of All Souls 1953 (Fellow 1953–68 and from 1983); later (1977–93) Chairman, Lloyds Bank. (Colin Dexter's fictional detective was named after him; coincidentally the other Prize Fellow elected with Morse was P. S. Lewis.)

3 John Holloway (1920–90), philosopher turned literary critic and poet; Fellow of All Souls 1946–60; Lecturer in English, University of Aberdeen, 1949–54, Cambridge, 1954–66; Fellow of Queens' College, Cambridge, 1955–82; later (1972–82) Professor of Modern English, Cambridge. His (unsuccessful) application for a Research Fellowship had provoked dissension in All Souls.

4 A Fellowship worth £50 per annum available to certain former Fellows of All Souls.

5 Victor John Knight Brook (1887–1974), Fellow of All Souls 1938–59 (Chaplain from 1935); Censor (i.e. head), St Catherine's Society (previously Non-Collegiate Students), Oxford, 1930–52.

6 sc. *émotionné*, 'overexcited'.

What are your views? the most surprising thing to me about myself is not ambition to be a Warden – Nuffield is a grotesque one after all, with less status than what I have at present – but the secret strain of crusading zeal which I had little idea I had in me. Dear me: I don't know what I really want: & never shall. I wd even seek to be Professor so as not to *have* to write books: which, then, (as Karl Marx) I shall write. Do write to me [. . .].

  yrs affectionately
  Isaiah

TO RICHARD WOLLHEIM

  3 December 1953

Lowell House, Harvard

Dear Richard,

  Forgive me if I am brief, but it is very late at night and I am utterly exhausted, but I feel you ought to have a rapid answer to your letter about Herzen.[1]

  I wish I knew what to say: I realise that Moura's version[2] is terrible – I have gone over about the first twenty or twenty-five pages with her, and those are not now so bad – but I seriously under-estimated the time it would take me to correct the whole thing. I am afraid that mere corrections of style and idiom would not be enough, as there are some terrible horrors in the first twenty-five pages, and no doubt many more in the succeeding ones – I do not believe that she did this herself, but obviously lent it out to some kind of awful syndicate of parasites.

  Now there is a man here called George Siegel[3] who has produced a much more tolerable version of it, free of crude mistakes, and needing some correction of style and idiom only. He would I think let us have it for no payment at all. Do you think that one could, quite cynically, ignore Moura's version and regard the money paid to her as lost, and print Mr Siegel with no further reference to anything or anybody? It is a bold manoeuvre, would distress Moura and her friends but in these circumstances unless we are to wait until I have time to go through the whole thing, which will certainly not be until into April or May, I think the other course more suitable. Is it too unscrupulous? Poor Siegel, who has produced a version for some kind of

---

  1 In his undated but clearly recent letter Wollheim described as 'unreadable' Moura Budberg's translation (for Weidenfeld & Nicolson's 'Library of Ideas' series, edited by IB, Stuart Hampshire and Wollheim) of Alexander Herzen's *From the Other Shore*. Wollheim was willing to remove the stylistic defects if IB could assure him that the translation was accurate.
  2 Moura Budberg did not have a high reputation as a translator: according to her biographer, 'there is a certain insecurity in her translations, something amateur and haphazard about them'. Nina Berberova, *Moura: The Dangerous Life of the Baroness Budberg* (New York, 2005), 285. Many of her attempts required further attention by another translator.
  3 George Siegel (1924–2000) taught Russian literature at Harvard; later at Brandeis University and University of Massachusetts.

doctorate thesis, does not know what to do with it. It is infinitely better than the other, though vulgar and imperfect in places.[1]

Tell me what you think. I wish I knew what was happening about the *Hedgehog*.[2] I gather that Noel Annan was kind about it, but have seen no script. The *TLS* leading article, although benevolent and well meaning, is really too unperceptive and has Joad-like finesse; very funny about the Weldon[3] and Woolf, but what has he said about me in his new book?[4] It is terrible to be so cut off from one. One is forced to become egocentric by the extraordinary flatness of the surrounding scenery here. And what about Nuffield? Of which you must have heard. I propose to be in England in the second part of January and to see you then (could I stay when in London?).

Philip[5] writes me that his father is to review my book in the *Observer*.[6] Oh God, I really have ceased minding. It is nice to think that Mr T. S. Eliot should have taken a fancy to a book on the Conservative mind by a man called Kirk[7] (I should think Oakeshott will love it too). It is one of the cheapest and most bogus books I have read on almost any subject lately – smart, smug, empty, and ill intentioned. Faber and Faber are fools to produce it. It is the beginning, I suppose, of the new Monteith regime.

Yours ever,
Isaiah

1 In the event Wollheim concluded that Siegel's version would itself require too much revision to justify its substitution for Moura Budberg's translation. IB therefore revised the latter, eventually commenting ruefully to Martin Malia (30 April 1955): 'As for *From the Other Shore*, I have finally completed what is in fact my own translation of that. I long to put on the book cover "translated from Russian by Baroness Budberg and into English by Mr I. Berlin", but dare not.' IB's Introduction to the translation of Alexander Herzen's *From the Other Shore* credited to Moura Budberg and Richard Wollheim's translation of *The Russian People and Socialism* (London, 1956) appears in POI.

2 IB's short book *The Hedgehog and the Fox* had been published in London in November (US publication was to be in March 1954). Most reviews, including Annan's 17 November broadcast on the Third Programme ('The Hedgehog and the Fox', *Listener*, 3 December 1953, 943–4), were enthusiastic. IB wrongly assumed that the leading article in *The Times Literary Supplement*, 20 November, 743 ('Fox and Hedgehog') was by the editor, Alan Pryce-Jones: the author was E. H. Carr.

3 Thomas Dewar ('Harry') Weldon (1896–1958), Fellow and Tutor in Philosophy, Magdalen, 1923–58; his book *The Vocabulary of Politics* (London, 1953) was scathingly reviewed by Leonard Woolf ('Words and Politics', *New Statesman and Nation*, 26 September 1953, 351). Wollheim had complained to IB that, although the book was indeed 'indescribably bad' (undated letter), Woolf had selected the few sound points in it for criticism.

4 *Principia Politica: A Study of Communal Psychology* (London, 1953), the third volume of *After the Deluge*, in which (243–4) LW quotes approvingly from IB's 'Political Ideas in the Twentieth Century'.

5 (Theodore) Philip Toynbee (1916–81), son of Arnold Toynbee; novelist, critic and journalist; *Observer*, 1950–81; his former wife Anne was now married to Wollheim.

6 Wholly favourably: Arnold Toynbee, 'Men and Supermen', *Observer*, 6 December 1953, 8.

7 Russell Kirk (1918–94), US conservative political thinker, social theorist and writer of supernatural fiction; his (influential) book, based on his doctoral dissertation for the University of St Andrews, was *The Conservative Mind: From Burke to Santayana* (Chicago, 1953).

TO ANTHONY QUINTON

7 December 1953 [*carbon*]

Lowell House, Harvard

My dear Tony,

[. . .] the local Philosophy Department is much madder than most kinds of [asylum, more?] schizophrenic than anything conceivable at the moment at Oxford. Imagine cautious luncheons between on the one hand Prof. Demos, a gentle, slightly bogus Platonist, who hasn't had an idea for many years; is quite nice, and immensely unanxious to have any thoughts, who invariably talks to me about Churchill and English politics.

Next to him is Prof. Donald C. Williams, the Chairman of the department, who is quite bright, quite astute, makes mistakes, has been got down by severe contempt which the grander positives feel for him; is in conviction a 19th-century materialist; has eccentric views due to general maladjustment, and the fact that he belongs anywhere but Harvard in general atmosphere; writes letters to the newspapers supporting McCarthy, but nevertheless cannot be boycotted, even by the most left-wing and indignant among his colleagues on account of a certain touching beauty of character, which evidences itself in his personal relations and appears to have no connection with his lunatic political views.

After that we have Prof. Henry Aiken, an intelligent, confused, sentimental, tipsy, kindly, not unshrewd man; rather like me in the sense of knowing what is right and wrong in philosophy rather more clearly than able either to state it or demonstrate it; infinitely prolific in pouring out monographs on ethics etc. (Morton White is away this term at Princeton.)

Then you must imagine Prof. John Wild, who has been through Hegel, Fichte, Kierkegaard,[1] Heidegger,[2] Plato, Aristotle, Christian Philosophy and is now grappling with Dialectical Materialism. Opinions vary between considering him somewhat touched and a charlatan; I incline to the former view – I think he is a nice confused man, of no value, by now, except for a certain sweetness of character (he has also written a book on Berkeley – that, by the way).

Sheffer[3] is no longer functioning, but is to be found at the top of the Widener Library; in the cellar of which dwells Wolfson,[4] who arrives at 7.30 a.m. every morning by special arrangement with the Janitor, and works until luncheon; then from 2.00 till 7.00; then after dinner, and then he goes to a

---

1 Søren Aabye Kierkegaard (1813–55), Danish philosopher and theologian.

2 Martin Heidegger (1889–1976), German philosopher interested mainly in the nature of being.

3 Henry Maurice Sheffer (1883–1964), Ukrainian-born logician; Professor of Philosophy, Harvard, 1938–52 (thereafter emeritus).

4 Harry Austryn Wolfson (1887–1974), Lithuanian-born scholar (particularly known for his work on the early Jewish philosopher Philo); Nathan Littauer Professor of Hebrew Literature and Philosophy, Harvard, 1925–74.

cinema where he falls asleep within the first quarter of an hour. He has completed several volumes of Philonic Philosophy in which Augustine has been
utterly destroyed; not a sentence has been left standing and have all been
proved to have been lifted from somebody else. The nature of the activity is
to lead up to Spinoza,[1] which he already has, as you know, written – what he
is doing now is gradually leading up to him from all avenues which converge
into that splendid ocean, which is the culmination of human thought. He is
a nice man, and anxious to share his intellectual discoveries with one at any
hour of the day or night; it is not wise to urge him to stay as he always wants
to awaken up, without aid of the alarm clock, at 5.00 a.m., which taxes the
hospitality of some hosts. Upon being woken up (he wakes with difficulty)
he opens the book which is reposing on his stomach, and continues reading
until 9.00.

Who else have we here? Prof. Firth[2] just arrived, the world's leading
Epistemologist. Quite a nice man, not too good, a very decent, honourable
figure of about thirty years ago, whom Price would like.

Also Prof. McLendon,[3] a hearty, enthusiastic Bullock of the subject.

Who else? Stevenson[4] is here – 'Steve' to me; a good fellow; less bright
than his books, but very, very nice personally. (I mean book.)

Also Hempel,[5] who is absolutely sweet; one of the nicest men in the
world, and the most creditable exponent of Carnap to be found anywhere.

This is about it – you will see that it is not exactly intellectually harmonious, nor do the discussions between these persons lead to much light.
Even we are better, is all I can say.

About the general education specialists I say nothing – (do you know the
great philosophers Rhinelander[6] and Bugbee?[7] they are men of genius).

There is also Olafson.[8] There has been some attempt to include Sir

---

1 Baruch de Spinoza (1632–77), Dutch rationalist philosopher (and lens-grinder).
2 Roderick Firth (1917–87), taught philosophy, Swarthmore College, 1945–53; Associate Professor of
   Philosophy, Harvard, 1953–8, Professor 1958–87.
3 Hiram James McLendon (1919–2000), a former student of Bertrand Russell, taught philosophy at
   the University of California (Berkeley) from 1947 and was then Assistant Professor of Philosophy,
   Harvard, during the 1950s.
4 Charles Leslie Stevenson (1908–79), philosopher best known for his emotivist theory of meaning;
   Associate Professor, then Professor, of Philosophy, Michigan, 1946–77; Visiting Lecturer, Harvard,
   1953–4. The book IB refers to is *Ethics and Language* (New Haven / London, 1945).
5 Carl Gustav ('Peter') Hempel (1905–97), German-born philosopher of science, for much of his
   career a logical positivist; Assistant Professor of Philosophy, Queens College, New York, 1940–8;
   Associate Professor of Philosophy, Yale, 1948–55; Visiting Lecturer, Harvard, 1953–4; Stuart
   Professor of Philosophy, Princeton, 1955–73.
6 Philip Hamilton Rhinelander (1908–87), taught philosophy and general education, Harvard,
   1952–5; Dean, School of Humanities and Sciences, Stanford, 1956–61.
7 Henry Bugbee (1915–99), philosopher and educationist who stressed the importance of experience of the natural world and of great literature in philosophical thought; taught at Harvard
   1948–54, at Montana 1957–77.
8 Frederick Arlan Olafson (b. 1924), Canadian-born philosopher; taught at Princeton 1950–1,
   Harvard 1952–4, Vassar 1954–60; later (1960–4) Associate Professor of Philosophy, Johns Hopkins

Herbert Read[1] on the ground that he is a philosopher, but he has become, very wisely, eschewed company. On the other hand there is an admirable man called Ziff[2] who saw Wittgenstein plain[3] when he was at Cornell with Malcolm.[4] He is far the brightest young man here, and you would enjoy talking to him very much. He thinks poorly of Stuart's philosophy as being a prisoner of narrow concepts and obsolete words. Such is the fate of all men over thirty. Did not the Russian revolutionary Tkachev[5] once say that all persons over twenty-five years of age should be put to death; otherwise no good world would ever ensue? Something in that.

But what about Nuffield? – I am in fearful agony.

Yours ever,

TO JENIFER HART

10 December 1953 [carbon]

Lowell House, Harvard

Dear Jenifer,

I don't know what to think about Nuffield. Every time I think of accepting it I draw back. On the one hand the horror of being in the same old room at All Souls for another twenty years is very considerable to me – All Souls is too emotional and I am really rather off it at the moment; yet Sparrow is quite right: if it is near the station I want to be, the prison is even nearer the station than Nuffield, and why don't I apply for the Governorship of that?

If I get Cole's Professorship,[6] which perhaps I would do, do I really want to lecture on political theory for years and years? I like intellectual history; I like the history of ideas, and in particular I like the personalities associated with ideas, and the particular flavour which they give to them and in terms of which they exchange them with one another, but political theory and philosophy in the proper sense – in the sense in which there is the delusion

University, (1964–71) Professor of Education and Philosophy, Harvard, (1971–91) Professor of Philosophy, University of California (San Diego).

1 Sir Herbert Edward Read (1893–1968), poet and writer on art, literature, culture and politics; co-founder (with Roland Penrose) of the Institute of Contemporary Arts 1947; Charles Eliot Norton Professor of Poetry, Harvard, 1953–4.

2 (Robert) Paul Ziff (1920–2003), artist and philosopher; studied at Cornell; taught philosophy at Harvard 1953–9 (Assistant Professor 1954–9); Assistant (then Associate) Professor, Pennsylvania, 1959–64; later held Professorships at Wisconsin, Illinois and North Carolina.

3 Cf. 'Ah, did you once see Shelley plain, / And did he stop and speak to you [. . .]?' Robert Browning, 'Memorabilia', in Men and Women (London, 1855).

4 Norman Adrian Malcolm (1911–90), US philosopher, former student and friend of Wittgenstein; taught philosophy at Cornell University 1947–78 (Susan Linn Sage Professor of Philosophy 1964–78).

5 Petr Nikitich Tkachev (1844–86), Russian journalist and radical, whose view that the revolution needed dedicated revolutionaries to spur on the peasantry influenced Lenin.

6 G. D. H. Cole was currently the (first) Chichele Professor of Social and Political Theory at Oxford.

that there is a subject there, with arguments for and against, as say Plamenatz or Herbert think of it, I think, about that I am not so sure. At the same time if I do accept the Wardenship I am sure I shall be able to raise no money for the place, and the whole thing will be a terrible flop.

You say I must not accept a flat or maisonette, I think Butterworth calls it, inside the place because the physical surroundings are too ghastly, but you don't recommend North Oxford either, do you? So what on earth am I to do? Take it. Not take it. I have a letter from Ian Little,[1] telling me it is my duty to take it; almost the same from Maurice; the only one dead against it is James and a lot of people here.[2] Wheare, who originally wrote and told me not to take it, because it was a whole time job and a waste, now as a result of a letter from me explaining that I am far more persecuted by people at All Souls than I should be at Nuffield, has reversed himself, says that Chester[3] would not have been given it anyway, and will prove a very loyal and free colleague. So what am I to do? [...]

Yours ever,   [...]

IB's deliberations about Nuffield were interrupted by the news he had been dreading.

TO ROWLAND BURDON-MULLER
11 December 1953 [*telegram*]

Boston, Mass.

SERIOUS NEWS ABOUT MY FATHER CONSEQUENTLY FLYING LONDON TOMORROW ISAIAH

---

1 Ian Malcolm David Little (b. 1918), economist; Fellow of All Souls 1948–50, of Trinity 1950–2, of Nuffield 1952–76; Deputy Director, Economic Section, Treasury, 1953–5; later (1971–6) Professor of Economics of Underdeveloped Countries, Oxford.
2 Aline Halban had also written opposing the idea.
3 (Daniel) Norman Chester (1907–86), specialist in public administration; Fellow of Nuffield 1945–54, Warden 1954–78.

1953–1955

ALL SOULS

Clearly nothing will ever be the same again.[1]

---

1 To Sam Behrman, 26 December 1953.

IB flew home, arriving early on Sunday 13 December, and spent 'two quite cheerful days'[1] with his father in hospital. They discussed the Nuffield offer, about which Mendel Berlin was quite firm: '"No, no, no, on no account, don't take it, it's not right for you at all."'[2] They 'parted very normally and peacefully at 9 p.m. on Monday evening'[3] for the last time.

TO ROWLAND BURDON-MULLER

15 December 1953 [*telegram*]

London

MY FATHER PASSED AWAY PEACEFULLY TODAY ISAIAH

The week after Mendel's death was a period of mourning, in accordance with Jewish tradition. Then IB tried to come to terms with the altered landscape of his life.

TO WILLIAM AND ALICE JAMES

23 December 1953 [postmark 1 January 1954, *manuscript*]

[As from] All Souls

Dear Billy & Alice,

Thank you ever so much for your telegram & Billy's letter. I arrived on a Sunday morning & found my father not only conscious but quite alert & not in great pain: He had no idea that his disease was fatal: he knew he was very ill – he did not clearly know what of: & he contemplated the idea of leaving the world much as a child looks on Father Christmas: he believed it & he did not, both, and seriatim. I had two very good days with him: he died in his sleep on Tuesday morning, the 15th. Although I knew before that this was inevitable sometime soon, the effect is not lessened: you are quite quite right: a large part of oneself, a root which was there ever since one remembers anything at all, is gone. Too much affection, intimacy, devotion is always, I suppose, paid for; at present I am somewhat numbed: nothing produces much reaction in me: I go about settling financial matters, looking after my mother, etc. glad to have a routine & mechanical tasks to perform.[4] The immediate future is uncertain: possibly I'll return in the Spring with

1 To Anna Kallin, 13 January 1954.
2 MI Tape 28.
3 To Shirley Anglesey, 3 January 1954.
4 To Sam Behrman he wrote: 'my father died very suddenly (unexpected to the doctors) &, I am told, peacefully, in his sleep at 6 a.m. on the morning of the 15th. My mother has taken it all as well as possible: the funeral was large & the friends all rallied round in a most touching fashion. My feelings are queer: very numb: nothing seems to me to matter much, if war were declared to-morrow I shd not react strongly: no doubt it will be all be worse when I recover full consciousness. Clearly nothing will ever be the same again.' 26 December 1953.

my mother: or without; or not: it depends on too many factors which I shan't touch till the New Year. Meanwhile I wish to say how very much your affection means to me – & always will wherever & whatever. I suppose I shall recover – people do. At present his handwriting is what bothers me most; but it will pass.

Much love
Isaiah.

TO LEONARD WOOLF

29 December 1953

[As from] All Souls

Dear Mr Woolf,

Thank you ever so much for your word to me about my brief little contribution to the *Sunday Times*.[1] I do indeed remember coming to your house in Tavistock Square before the war – or just at the beginning of it – and, indeed, receiving an invitation to come again when I was already in America on government service – and I was, of course, very glad of this opportunity of paying a tribute – although it seemed to me terribly inadequate – to the genius of Mrs Woolf. I met her three times in all,[2] and have never had any experience to compare with it – I thought her the most beautiful and the most divinely endowed human being I had ever met in my life, and I think so still. And while, of course, I never knew her, these meetings did, in fact, alter my ideas about things and persons for good. But I expect many must have felt the same, and you are probably tired of hearing such confessions.

Thank you also for your kind word about my few chaotic writings – thank you very much for sending me your book, which I shall read with the greatest interest, as I imagine that your ideas about liberty and servitude will be extremely sympathetic to me – everything which you write is. If you come to London at all it would be a great pleasure and a privilege to me to meet you. I am here on and off until the end of January, when either I return to Oxford or go to America again for two or three months – my father died about a fortnight ago and I am kept here by various duties which arise as a consequence. Please do not put yourself out in any way.

Yours sincerely,
Isaiah Berlin

---

1 IB's contribution on Virginia Woolf's *A Writer's Diary* to 'Books of the Year', *Sunday Times*, 20 December 1953, 6.

2 Perhaps four: at various times IB mentioned encounters with VW at dinners in New College in 1933 (L1, 68–71), at Elizabeth Bowen's house in 1934 (L1, 85), and at the Woolfs' home as well as at a gathering in Ben Nicolson's Bloomsbury flat (the last two probably in 1938; MI Tape 9).

TO MORTON WHITE

5 January 1954

All Souls

Dear Morton,

I did not leave a moment too early, for my father died peacefully in his sleep two days after I arrived. I will not go over the details for you – it was all rather terrible, and since my family is excessively close-knit, the effects are totally incalculable. At the moment all I can do is look after my mother and make some business arrangements to deal with my father's estate, which will not ruin us all immediately. I find myself a director of a company whose business I do not understand and whose assets seem to me to be dubious, or at any rate not easily predictable. So long as probate and similar details go on I cannot really leave, nor can I leave my mother alone. I could, no doubt, induce her to go and stay with her sister in Jerusalem, but I think I had better stay with her for the time being, as there are no other children or relations to speak of (I mean relations to speak of, not a null class of children to speak of).

Nor have I decided about Nuffield. In a way it still tempts me, but all my thoughts are set at the moment somewhat against it, on the grounds: 1) that it would take up too much time and leave me no room to write any books at all; 2) that the centre of their interests, which is, after all, semi-practical applied politico-economic – is not only too distant from but too unsympathetic to me, and that to twist them out of their proper goal, set for them by their pious founder and the people who originally created them, although intrinsically desirable, and indeed rather wished for by them, requires somebody much tougher, much more energetic and much more passionate about ruling and guiding a foundation than I am ever likely to be. I regard myself as somewhat thin-skinned and susceptible to minding criticism; if one is that, perhaps one should not rule or govern anyone very much, quite apart from the general bore of bureaucracy and administration, which actually I do not mind and secretly rather like. So perhaps I had better wait for the Professorship in Oxford, although it is perfectly possible that I shall not get it,[1] as the electoral committee is exceedingly queer. [. . .]

I really cannot make up my mind about Nuffield and am waiting for some mysterious precipitation of thoughts and feelings, so that one fine morning I wake up and realise that I have decided – I am told that these mysterious, irrational processes happen, and as, according to some reviewers of my recent little book, I am, in fact, on the side of these dark forces myself, perhaps it is in them that I ought to put my trust. At the moment,

---

1 IB had, however, confided to his parents that the Chair held by G. D. H. Cole had been 'virtually promised' to him (30 November 1953).

I am still negotiating with Nuffield, anti-Nuffield and everyone else in a very distracted manner, and dash up to the City and look at the totally unintelligible ledgers in between times. I wonder if my life will ever settle down again into its accustomed channels. It is an extraordinary moment when one is promoted from the ranks of those who are looked after into those who are lookers after. I do not enjoy the transition a bit.

My love to Lucia, and do write quickly.

Yours ever,

Isaiah

TO MEYER SCHAPIRO

5 January 1953 [sc. 1954]

All Souls

Dear Meyer,

[...] Now, as to the fox etc., I expect you are right. I expect I did exaggerate the merits of both Tolstoy and Maistre. I think they are very acute indeed, acuter than you think, but perhaps less scrupulous than I make out. And you are quite right if you detect in me a certain excessive tendency to parade dry, mordant, 'tough' qualities as against woolly idealism and general sentimentality and sweetness, which I detest much more than intellectual or even moral wickedness, since I think that it destroys standards and smothers issues – I would rather have Jesuits, who may hold evil views but at least keep the weapons polished bright and make the issue worth fighting about and do not derogate from intellectual standards, than compromisers of the softer kind who sink the entire enterprise into a morass and swamp everything so that one has no capacity for saying or thinking anything. On points of detail, the irony of Tolstoy is very like that of de Maistre; the shafts sent at the liberal intellectuals, the contemptuous sweeping out of hopes and optimism, unbolstered by empirical observation or rational argument, and an open declaration of non-rational faith. I do not think you are quite right in thinking that de Maistre did not believe in great men. I think he did believe in great medieval figures, as well as Moses and the Fathers of the Church etc., and in this respect he is not so much like as unlike Tolstoy – no doubt there are organic laws but they are the expressions of them rather in the way Hegel talked. What I do not believe in is de Maistre's rationalism. He does, of course, talk about 'science', but to him science means what St Thomas[1] taught. He compares St Thomas to Newton[2] (if I remember

---

1 St Thomas Aquinas (1225–74), Italian Dominican friar, scholastic philosopher and theologian.
2 Sir Isaac Newton (1642–1727), mathematician, physicist and natural philosopher, often regarded as the founder of modern science.

rightly)[1] and says one is to the other as an eagle to Montgolfier's balloon.[2] Whilst officially he quotes St Thomas and the Aristotelians this seems to me largely eye-wash – he is really an Augustinian[3] – and does not believe in rational theology so much as in mystical inspiration, the Divine Spirit, Old Testament heroes, blood etc., and when he speaks of physical sciences as being applicable to history, this is merely a gibe against those who prefer abstract principles, like the French rationalists or Rousseau. Certainly God shows himself to him in zoology and not in Cartesian logic, but what it shows is the chaos and murderous battlefield of the world and not an intelligible system – hence the violent onslaughts on Bacon, to whom, as you know, he devoted a special work.[4] Of course Tolstoy would have rejected Maistre's explanation of the French Revolution, but then his own account of what happened is very like Maistre's fun over Condillac.[5] It was not meant to be taken too seriously. It was a conscious parody, but makes his point. ⟨The use of 'science', 'physics' etc. shd not take anyone in: Maistre's advice to Alexander I[6] is to retard sciences & expel scientists as subversives & political morons. Science for him is theology + any second causes authorised by the Church. No more.⟩ The thing about Tolstoy to me is that, of course, his views are often perverse and false, but it is both difficult to see what makes them false and what a truer answer to his very pointed questions would be. And therein lies the superiority of his intellect to that of the scientific patter of his time. You speak of Michelet. The quotation is very fascinating and I am most grateful to you for it, but of course Tolstoy would have rejected this, as you suggest, not merely as a romantic account of the people but at a deeper level, because Michelet wants to make out that the people (or 'man') is for ever fighting nature in a heroic way, imposing its forms upon blind necessity, struggling for truth, emancipation, human values etc., all of

---

1 IB's recollection is faulty. Discussing the Asiatic taste for the marvellous rather than the scientific, Maistre observes that 'primitive science' was 'an era of *intuition*. Does an eagle in fetters ask for a *mongolfière* so that it can rise into the air? No, it asks only that its bonds be broken.' *St Petersburg Dialogues* (1821), 2nd Dialogue: *Œuvres complètes de J. de Maistre* (Lyons/Paris, 1884–7), iv 78–9.

2 The Montgolfier brothers, Joseph Michel (1740–1810) and (Jacques-)Étienne (1745–99), demonstrated their hot-air balloon in 1783.

3 A reference to St Augustine of Hippo (354–430), Christian theologian and philosopher.

4 Francis Bacon (1561–1626), Viscount St Albans, lawyer, statesman, essayist and natural philosopher who developed scientific methodology; studied by de Maistre in his *Examen de la philosophie de Bacon* ('Examination of the Philosophy of Bacon', published posthumously in 1836).

5 'Maistre enjoys himself a great deal at the expense of eighteenth-century speculations about the origins of language: Rousseau, he declares, is puzzled about how men first began to use words, but the omniscient Condillac knows the answer to this and to all other questions: language clearly came about as a result of the division of labour. Thus one generation of men said BA, another added BE; Assyrians invented the nominative, and the Medes invented the genitive.' CTH 141, citing *Œuvres complètes* (note 1 above) iv 88.

6 'A great political step in this country would be to retard the reign of science, and use the authority of the Church as a powerful ally of the sovereign, until such time as science may safely be allowed to penetrate society.' *Quatre chapitres sur la Russie* (1811), *Œuvres complètes* (note 1 above) viii 344.

which, I suppose, comes from the Germans. Tolstoy certainly rejected this – for him the hero is not a Prometheus – whether individual or social – but the sage who in his humility does not oppose his own reason or will to the mysterious process – which is almost, if not quite, divine, in war and peace, and becomes openly Christian later – but understands it in some non-calculating, non-analytical fashion, and I suppose, identifies himself with it. The whole element of proud opposition to inanimate nature and the bold assertion of human values, democracy, patriotism etc. in Michelet (which is much more like Herzen) is still liberal twaddle for Tolstoy, and indicates the fallacy of thinking that the desires of men, or the people taken as a whole, contain the criterion of right and wrong superior to some impersonal process – or personal if you bring in God – which it needs great humility, a moment of revelation to apprehend. Tolstoy oscillates between this straightforwardly anti-rationalist view and the hypothesis that an omniscient rational being could integrate all the infinity of small causes – what he rejects in either case is heroism, the pointed assertion of will, individual or collective, which is the heart of Michelet's doctrine, certainly. Still, I may be exaggerating and you may be right. Anyway, I am sure you have a case, although I should be, as you can see, disposed to dispute it. What I think really offends you is a certain enthusiasm which you perceive in me for debunking scientific rationalism as applied to human affairs. To that I admit. I really think that sociology is in principle impossible, a mad dream founded on a false analogy. On that I propose to write an essay which I shall send you before I publish it, if I may. I think there may be some genuine disagreement between us here. But I should value your views more than anyone else's on this topic – I delivered this 'essay' as a lecture at Smith where I don't think anybody understood it particularly, or liked it. Do let me send it to you some time.

Where will you be in March? In Europe already? Please let me know.

Yours ever, with much love

Isaiah

TO MARY FISHER[1]

13 January 1954 [*manuscript*]

Reform Club, Pall Mall, London sw1
As from All Souls, to which I've returned

Dear Mary

I did, of course, know that my father had leukemia: which is both incurable & always fatal. No cure having thus far been discovered, that was that. The doctor detected it in the Spring: told my mother in April: & she told me

1 Mary Letitia Somerville Fisher (1913–2005), daughter of H. A. L. and Lettice Fisher, and a long-standing friend of IB's; married John Bennett 1955; Colonial Office 1945–56; later (1965–80) Principal, St Hilda's.

in June. The months from June till Sept you can imagine: I persuaded my father to go [to] a specialist by bribing his not v. good ordinary doctor to tell him he had anaemia, a harmless word, & symptoms v. similar. The specialist (whom I did not terribly like – a golf-playing brother of Lady Pakenham[1] he turned out to be) said he might, it being chronic, live for some years. I wd not have gone to America, but thought, I think still rightly, that as it had been arranged years ago, he wd have [been] frightened if I did not. I left in acute distress but with shameful relief at not facing the deception – & my father's obvious progressive decline – for 2–3 months. Then came a telegram written in my mother's transparently "non-worrying" style, I flew back & found my father uncomfortable – ill in hospital – not in great pain, but obviously wondering whether he wd survive: but clearly not aware of the fatal quality of his illness. He died, I was told, & hope truthfully, in his sleep. And that was that. I liked him excessively, & nothing will ever be the same (do forgive me for going on so: but you knew the over-intimate quality of my domestic life better than almost anybody) – I find it most difficult to readjust myself. I felt curiously protective about him – he was so very innocent, young, elegant in habits of mind, fastidiously dressed, & knew neither what life nor dying was like. Now I am surrounded by lawyers, accountants, business managers, go to the City out of politeness, look at stock lists & account books, & think about very irrelevant facts. [...] Will you be in Oxford? I shd be truly grateful if you wd tell me & come to see me.

　　With much love,
　　　Isaiah.

TO NOEL ANNAN

　13 January 1954 [*manuscript*]

　　　　　　　　　　　　　　　　　　　　　　　As from All Souls
Dear Noel,
　　This ought to be a letter of uninterrupted gratitude, not merely for what you have done, but for being there to be able to do it. What I shd like is to see you. How? When? you can come to Oxford whenever you please: I shall, perforce, live quietly this term: & shd welcome you whenever you choose to come. Wd you say? any day when I am not in London (towards the ends of weeks). I *am* miserable. I was extremely attached to my father and he was a very innocent, youthful, elegant, agreeable, civilized, mild and entirely honest & pure hearted man, whose society I loved, & whom I find I looked on as a kind of younger brother. He had no friends, needed none, lived entirely knit into his small family, did not understand life in any ordinary practical sense, was timid, clear headed & guileless. He had no notion

---

1 Lady (Elizabeth) Pakenham (1906–2002), née Harman, Countess of Longford 1961.

there was a disease called leukaemia, & died in no great pain, in discomfort
& ignorance. The pathos of the whole thing was unique: & I shall never
wholly recover from it, nor will anything ever be the same. It has shifted me
into some queer front line, in which reluctantly I shall now stay. But I shan't
go [on] to you about that. I go to the City from time to time, & like Pierre
B[ezukhov], understand nothing. Unlike him, no revelation will occur. All
you said about the Hedgehog[1] was infinitely wonderful for me: I shall never
cease from mentioning you in my prayers. Never mind Postan[2] & Balogh: the
latter is remote from anything to do with truth or disinterestedness, & judges
in Sicilian Camorra[3] terms: with the gang: against it: & I like him genuinely.
Postan is a hopeless old Marxist intellectual, despite all, & is a clever & malicious survival from the 1790ies who served Napoleon, & remained unperse-
cuted under the Restoration: but still finds it agreeable to conceive himself as
superior to the confusion of contemporary ideas & words by applying some
"tough" materialist criterion, disillusioned, cynical & no longer optimistic
& revolutionary, as alone capable of sifting the real – "scientifically" treat-
able grain, from the foolish impalpable chaff. But progress *has* occurred: old
fashioned 'scientism' *is* invalid, as Mill's [methods][4] were in say 1890, even
though the later empiricism of the 1930ies was better than the degenerate
idealism in which the older empiricism got drowned. He is a clever ill intentioned man: & the desire to do down & triumph mars his intellectual virtues:
like Carr: like all the professional tough men who are playing a part & not
speaking spontaneously either from the heart or from the intellect. Your
praise seemed to me (but I am obviously hideously biassed) discriminating:
you were quite right about me, for better & for worse: I do try to paint the
anschauung[5] of these men: & delight in the colours themselves: & try to find
out & say what their worlds looked like to them, & underrate the importance of whether the actual arguments are valid or not, because political or
cultural attitudes & beliefs don't seem logical systems to me, but more like
works of art. This is obscurantist or romantic or Oakeshottian only if one
assumes that everyone is talking about much the same thing & that valid
argument is what leads one to the truth in these matters. But this seems to
me mere blindness: 18th century dogmatic misrepresentation: & what leads
virtuous men to kill other virtuous [men] for the sake [of] principles which
in practice come to very little: like the sentences produced by schoolboys in

1 Annan described *The Hedgehog and the Fox* as 'the most important study of Tolstoy's thought
   written in English for a long time' and its author as having 'the gift beyond all other historians of
   thought to make ideas exciting' ('The Hedgehog and the Fox', Third Programme, 17 November
   1953; *Listener*, 3 December 1953, 943–4).
2 Michael Moissey Postan (1899–1981), born in Bessarabia (at that time Russian); Professor of
   Economic History, Cambridge, 1938–65.
3 IB seems to confuse the Camorra (based in Naples and Campania) with the Mafia of Sicily, which
   it closely resembles.
4 Hole punched: restoration conjectural.
5 'Outlook'.

debates: when in fact what they mean is something somewhat, if not quite, different: & what *that* something is, one can only gather as one gathers any-thing, [by] listening to what people say, looking at their faces, lives, gestures, & trying to make out & understand: why is this obscurantist? if human rela-tionships were mathematically deducible or describable it wd be: but nobody, literally nobody, believes that to-day. I was sorry that my awful title misled reviewers (almost all but you) into taking the myth – the jeu d'esprit about the animals – so seriously. Taylor's review[1] I did not much mind: he knew no better & it was his equivalent of White's Club rough chaff – a roll thrown across the table – he is like an urchin with a catapult, a banana skin etc, & not in any sense serious at all, least of all when he sets up as a noble outraged radical who can keep silence no longer. Carr tried to be polite[2] but is too philistine & cheaply political to understand much anyhow: I like him but he is a hopelessly mediocre vulgarian all the same: Rex Warner wrote I thought a very entertaining piece[3] which, had it been about someone else, I shd have greatly enjoyed: & quite penetrating: disrespectful: frivolous & rather good. I simply detested it: & wondered unworthily whether if Barbara[4] weren't so deeply (& vocally) offended with me for never inviting her to anything (I *cannot*. Too much sex for me. too choc-a bloc. Stuart adores it & is hideously embarrassed when this is pointed out) he wd have written it. Of course what one wants is nothing but undiluted praise, & not one breath of criticism of any kind: only the highest praise will do; and the torments & agonies of either criticism or fun at one's expense, or even stupid compliments is to me exceptionally and unnecessarily agonizing. Still, it is all over, at least in this country. And my moral debt to you will never be repaid. Apart from yourself no one had anything to say which I cd profitably remember (this sounds arrogant, & perhaps is) – & so I must turn my thoughts to Nuffield. I don't know what to do. I think I am being asked somewhat as Mr & Mrs Clore hired, or were said to hire, the dear Duchess of Westminster to do their party for them: I am expected to introduce douceur de vivre[5] & 'culture' & bring them into the heart of old civilized Oxford etc. etc. – it seems to me more

1 A. J. P. Taylor commended IB's 'convincing explanation' of Tolstoy's contradictory approach to history, but his review was not without barbs: the book is 'an intellectual firework display' and at its conclusion 'The sentences get longer and longer, the thought soars higher and higher, and what had begun as an essay in literary criticism ends as an utterance of the Delphic Apollo' ('Thoughts on Tolstoy', *New Statesman*, 12 December 1953, 768).
2 Carr described *The Hedgehog and the Fox* (mistakenly referred to as *The Fox and the Hedgehog*) as a 'brilliant essay' and a 'searching and profound analysis' before going on to question some of IB's classifications ('Fox and Hedgehog', *The Times Literary Supplement*, 20 November 1953, 743).
3 Rex Ernest Warner (1905–86), poet, novelist, translator and critic; his generally favourable review of *The Hedgehog and the Fox* characterised IB's wordy style as 'innumerable and vigorous prod-dings, all in the right direction' ('Tolstoy and History', *Spectator*, 1 January 1954, 20).
4 Rex Warner had married Lady (Barbara Judith) Rothschild (1911–89), née Hutchinson, the former wife of Victor Rothschild, in 1949; after their divorce the sexually magnetic Barbara then married Niko Ghika.
5 'Sweetness of life'.

probable that they will corrugate me. I respect them & even their purposes:
but since they are professionally interested in contemporary affairs – remote
& repulsive to me – can it be a good idea to preside over their fortunes?
they are all manqué civil servants or politicians: yet, *cd* one do something
with such an instrument? I am havering & dithering between the Napoleonic
Vice-Chancellor & the Iron Warden of All Souls & God knows what the
solution – modified by the advices of Cole & all the rest will be. [. . .]

   love
      Isaiah

*IB had replied to many of the letters of condolence he had received, but not to
all.*

TO VIOLET BONHAM CARTER
23 January 1954 [*manuscript*]

                                                                    All Souls

Dearest Violet,
   Your last letter,[1] as you can imagine, caused me the very deepest distress
and I answer it at once (it lay unforwarded in London for 5 days & I came
upon it among my mother's letters into which in our general chaos it had
strayed during my few hours here today) because I cannot bear not to. I did
not communicate because I could not, & if I did not realise that you were
being frozen by my conduct, could not now. Let me explain: the news about
my father was of course not unexpected: I flew home in a kind of daze;
it was a very rough flight & the rougher the less I minded, since one pain
nullifies another: indeed the clash of the two is in a sense a relief. After my
father's death, which the doctors had not expected to occur when it did,
despite all possible psychological preparation on my part, I felt absolutely
numb & unable to think or act normally. For two or three hours at a time
I managed to go through necessary routines, then I used to feel paralysed
with a feeling I had never known before – much worse – & duller than – the
loss of something – the oldest root – which one remembered ever since one
remembered anything. For a week I literally did not communicate with the
outside world: did not speak on the telephone to friends or relations, did
not go into the street, behaved in a to me astonishingly Oriental fashion of
blank passivity. Then I came to life: & found I could endure only the most
frivolous, lightest, emptiest, hollowest sort of social intercourse: I went
once or twice to Brooks's[2] & chattered gaily, saw a few people, plunged into

---

1 VBC had written on 18 December in condolence and later (in a letter which appears not to
   survive) in fear that, as she described it in her next letter, 'you had felt me intrusively trying to
   share your very private suffering' (25 January 1954).
2 A private London club, founded in 1764, the Whig equivalent of the Tory-dominated White's; IB
   had been a member since 1950.

my Oxford crisis (I have been offered Nuffield College which I don't think
I *can* accept. For ultimately snobbish reasons, to put it most woundingly
to myself. I cannot breathe among those good, virtuous, salt of the earth
people – but that is another & far less painful story) dictated a million formal
acknowledgements of letters of condolence: performed religious rites, inter-
viewed all the Fellows of Nuffield one by one for hours; dined at All Souls
(where nobody seemed to know about my condition & nobody did more
than murmur woodenly about it – & *that* not much) & lived in an agony of
fear of having to talk seriously about myself to someone or hearing something which would touch the seared portions of my consciousness. It was
(& is) very queer: I heard Diana Cooper[1] criticised for wanting endless jokes
and anecdotes told her, & no serious sad words. I never reached that stage of
suppressed hysteria, but I sympathised: I saw how it could be: & marvelled at
my own neurotic reaction – mine, when I had always thought myself placid,
well balanced, stolid, normal, lacking in the sensibilities which drive to art or
religion or lunacy. If I saved myself from nervous collapse it was by desperately swimming at a superficial level, & as I said, chattering on in a frivolous,
slightly febrile way, & seeing only institutional persons – Fellows of All Souls,
Bob Brand, people in clubs – nobody in circumstances in which I had to talk
intimately or seriously. Whatever letters I could answer in swift quasi-formal
ways, I answered. The real ones not possibly – & I can't now. I received a
most moving one from Rachel Cecil whose mother died the day before she
wrote – & could not say a word to acknowledge it even. I recognised limits:
the thought of parties – like the drowning of sorrows in drink – was too
repellent; but I associated, or tried to, with the lightest & slightest – looked
for occasions in which nothing could remotely touch the abraded surface –
social persons – cynical friends – Americans – anybody but those where mere
presence would of itself give me a sense of reality, to whom I shall have to
talk properly (as I love to do) whose personalities were part of the real world.
I did not always succeed, but I did my best: your letters were absolutely
wonderful: your words about your relationship to your father – even though
mine was so very different, shy, remote, much younger than I, half alive, in
a sense – unrealised & touchingly innocent of almost everything – of little
interest to anyone but his family – your words were the only ones which possessed a solidity & a penetration which gave me an acute pang of reality – &
for the moment, owing to their very aptness, truth, excellence, imagination,
the depth of insight and the reality of the personal relationship which they
conveyed – made me shut my eyes & go on floating at a relatively painless
surface level. Do you see? it is not something I am pleased about, proud
of, anxious to describe; indeed, if anything, I despised myself, in my lucid
painful intervals of sorrow, for being able to bear so little, for such unmanli-

---

1 Whose husband Duff Cooper (Viscount Norwich) had died on 1 January.

ness, such inability to cope with anything but practical details of life (I went to the City daily, saw & see lawyers & accountants & bankers with zeal & enthusiasm – anything but what relates with inner life) but this is what it was. I longed to come & see you – telephone & ask if I might – but then I thought (surely with justice) that I should then be unable to carry on artificial light talk with a you I respected so deeply, in circumstances which are genuine, private, disposed to sincerity and real aveux.[1] I sought for frivolity, Sparrow, College business, flotsam & jetsam, & am only now rising to the surface again. I cannot believe that it is I – so matter of fact – flat & unpoetical & full of sense & foursquare – I who should have been so broken by an event, which however painful, was expected – but so it – I – was. American letters arrived – the dear Jameses – the dear Hofers[2] – full of kindness, sympathy, gossip – affection – but with a lack of three dimensionality – an inner hollowness – which made them unaffecting, tangential like balloons. I replied to them conventionally, truthfully, without more than physical effort. But your letters were very very different: & I kept putting off what I knew they deserved – which I should despise myself for being unable to do – a proper response, something worthy – at least in my intention – of you and your friendship. But I have behaved with inexcusable, if intelligible (I hope) selfishness – & displayed apparent negligence. I am terribly distressed to have caused you a second's doubt – or any misunderstanding. Even so I don't know whether these incoherent sentences – I am no letter writer & write as I talk, in an undisciplined, confused, almost irresponsible fashion – convey anything of what is in my still unsettled brain.

I *am* recovering: but I can't write or speak otherwise than in formal set phrases about my own condition. I shall return to London on Thursday (or Wednesday) – may I come to see you then? if on Wednesday, at 5.30 or so? if on Thursday after dinner – or better on Friday (I ought to spend evenings with my mama, who has taken it all rather "badly") to tea? The hours are dictated by my hours in the City & with lawyers – the 'estate' is confused – I *am* recovering: by the middle of the week when the Nuffield crisis is over I should be "all right"; & I shall apologise to you as best I can, in person. I feel I have not really explained: only gone on & on; that one should be stoical & English & contained; or like Natalie Ridley,[3] reduced to a kind of primary dignity, tragic & grand (it is an *experience* to meet her now) & simple & shaming to all the triviality of one's nature. But I cannot: I am too unprepared to push off the recommencement of stabilisation – life, friends, work, all that really means most to me, to the last moment. But I should love to

1 'Confessions'.
2 Philip Hofer and his wife, the former Frances Louise Heckscher (1908–78).
3 Lady (Nathalie Louise) Ridley (1887–1968), daughter of Count Alexander Konstantinovich Benckendorff, Russian Ambassador in London 1903–17, widow of Sir Jasper Ridley and the former mother-in-law of VBC's daughter Cressida.

come if I may: I shall understand it if you'd rather not: but be unhappy too (there is no limit to the amount of additional unhappiness one can suffer, I find, alas) so I shall await your message to Oxford. And I do beg you to forgive me.

yours

Isaiah (with much love & gratitude)

Violet Bonham Carter responded with a telegram:

THOUSAND THANKS LOVELY LETTER UNDERSTAND EVERYTHING [...][1]

After extensive discussions with various members of Nuffield, IB eventually reached a decision about the Wardenship.

TO MARGERY PERHAM

26 January 1954 [*typed transcript of untraced original*]

All Souls

Dear Miss Perham,

I have seldom, if ever, written a letter with such profound reluctance or after so much anxious thought, but I feel that to ask for more delay would be a mere abuse of the College's patience and goodwill which I have already stretched further than I meant to do, or should have done. I terribly regret to say it, but I am sure that I must decline. My reasons are those which I gave you when we last met. The first and greatest is that, being as I am, and my interests being what they are, I should always feel that I am insufficiently close to, or representative of, what I regard as the true and proper central purpose of Nuffield. The second, which seems to me hardly less fatal, is that I should not find enough leisure to do my own work: I am not immodest enough to put this reason first, but I cannot deny that it too counts decisively with me.[2] My decision has been made the more difficult by the kindness and consideration – the like of which I have never found anywhere – with which both the College as a whole, and its Fellows individually, have behaved towards me: which in itself naturally increased the temptation to accept until it almost overcame my scruples. But in the end, my scruples – and I hope you will believe me when I say that the final reasons were those of conscience – prevailed. I did try to explain them as clearly and exactly as I could

1 Dated 25 January. A letter followed the same day.
2 To Norman Chester (who became Nuffield's next Warden) IB had written 'the reasons I shall give her [...] will be the only true and & final ones: that I cannot sufficiently identify myself with what I regard as the proper ends of Nuffield to represent it honestly & fully: [...] my own central interests are just – perhaps only just – too remote from its centre to let me feel morally comfortable about accepting. And I wd like to do my own work – but am not immodest enough to put that first' (undated letter).

to the Fellows who were good enough to allow me to consult them, and to the Warden also. I realised in the course of these conversations that I could count on a degree both of wisdom and generosity scarce enough anywhere and certainly not often found in governing bodies of Colleges. This made it even harder to turn away the opportunity of working under such personally ideal conditions. Nevertheless I remain convinced that it would be wrong for me [to] accept. I do not wish to reiterate what I have said to you so often and so sincerely, both in writing and in speech – that this proposal has meant more to me than other in my life. It has been a source of the greatest pride and much agony to me, and I should like to thank you and the College once again for their confidence, and their forbearance. I regret my own decision exceedingly: I apologise for wasting so much of the College's time collectively and individually; I can only plead in extenuation that I arrived at my final answer by slow and painful stages; and that I should like to demonstrate my regard for the College and all it stands for by doing whatever I can to help in its activities, particularly with the work of the students, if that is thought useful by yourself or anyone else. I should like to thank you particularly for your last letter to me – I wish I could think that I began to deserve it.

Yours sincerely,
Isaiah Berlin

TO SAM BEHRMAN
29 January 1954

All Souls College

Dearest Sam,

I have myself in hand. I have refused Nuffield with the warmest protestations of affection, assuring them that I should like to be a brother to them, an uncle, anything short of a father or a husband. I cannot look after bloodless academics while the lure of the bristles[1] beckons me. You must come and help me share the millions which we shall undoubtedly make together. It is a romantic trade connected with the rolling steppes of Russia and the immense plains of China, where some very peculiar animals seem to roam – the only pigs I have ever seen in England or America seem to grow no bristles, only a gentle silken down, obviously useless for the tough commerce I am engaged in. What about hedgehogs? I intend to raise the possibilities with my advisers. I am delighted to know that you are coming here in mid-February or just before. I shall be available for you in London and in Oxford indefinitely. I am flattered by Sir Max Beerbohm's interest,[2] but the book is written in a style

1 Mendel Berlin had been a trader in timber and bristles.
2 SNB, whose biography of Beerbohm appeared in 1960, had been visiting him at Rapallo.

so tortuous, clumsy and bristling with dependent clauses that it must annoy that master of luminous and really beautiful prose.

As for B.B., I am sure he suffers from persecution mania, all due to having no heart, to which also, however, he owes his long life. [Edmund] Wilson was splendid here. He went to a number of parties in London and claimed to like them all. He was most mild and suppressed his Anglophobia most gallantly. In Oxford he was terrifically bored with the few intellectuals I scratched together for him. They were impressed deeply but he thought them quite awful, I am convinced – and had eyes only for my two most revolting colleagues – Mr A. J. P. Taylor, who wrote what is called a critical review of my book – which I probably deserved – and has spent his time since in apologising for it, which I do not care for. He is a very worthless man but Wilson loved him. My more revolting colleague is Dr C. Roth, the Hebrew scholar, whose full horror you would appreciate better than Wilson. I intend to introduce them both to you just to give you a taste of Wilson's splendid unworldliness. [...]

Yours ever, ⟨with much love, hope, & in a peculiar state –⟩

Isaiah

TO ARTHUR SCHLESINGER

29 January 1954

All Souls

Dear Arthur,

Thank you ever so much for your letter and will you please thank Marian for hers. I shall write to her separately almost immediately. This is only to tell you that I survive. The death of my father really did have a very shattering effect on me, I feel as if I am at the edge of a very deep precipice and in some fearful front line with no support behind or in front or at the sides. However, I shan't go on about that. ⟨The only personal problem is constituted by the solitude of my mother. That is not really soluble.⟩

At present my time is spent in trying to construct some kind of scheme enabling my mother to have a more or less reliable income – I do not understand a word about business, I am sure that my interest in philosophy was almost entirely due to horror at ever being associated with it – the only quality I inherit from my father in that respect is that I am just as reluctant to write books as he was to make money – I do not understand double bookkeeping, I do not understand why debts to my father should go into the column marked debts by him or vice versa, I am told that unless this is done the account will not be balanced, but that seems just as unintelligible to me as it did before – however I am learning more and more about pigs' bristles – nevertheless the temptation to become a bristles king does not arise. My conflicts with lawyers and accountants are very strange and remarkable and you would enjoy them far too much, could you be present. ⟨The naiver I am, & the sillier my questions the more sinister & elaborate my behaviour seems.⟩ [...]

I feel very flat and exhausted and with nothing to write about, so I think I had better bring this letter to an end. I am not exactly melancholy, I tick over quite nicely and lead in a sense quite a normal life, and yet I feel that nothing will ever be quite the same again. My mother, who is a woman of enormous resource, took it all comparatively well, there is much to be said for the Jewish religion, which enjoins that for a week after the death of a close relation you sit at home and do not go out, and are visited by your friends rather in the manner of Job. This means that between you and life there is a week blocked, it is socially exhausting no doubt to be visited by people, but far better than having nothing to do and trying to arrange your emotions with no institutional framework to externalise the feelings which one has at such a moment. I cannot over-praise functionally organised religion in creating banisters which can be leant upon during the very first moment of such an event.

[...] Your friend Miss Bacall[1] sent me a telegram to the effect that she was coming, but I could not in the circumstances see her, and sent her a message on the telephone which may indeed not have been delivered to her. I was very pleased that she should remember me, but experience no great wish actually to see her. If our acquaintance can be kept warm and indeed close without any actual meeting I shall be delighted to support such an arrangement. [...]

Yours ever,
    Isaiah

PS [...] ⟨Wilson is off to Israel – he will like it if we all tell him he won't; anyway better than Trevor Roper who obviously could not bear it – no Dukes, Kings, large scale scoundrels, drab social democracy, & only a minor outrage or two to keep things going. Love to Miss Arendt.[2] I adore the very

1 Lauren Bacall, stage name of Betty Joan Perske (b. 1924), wife of Humphrey Bogart 1945–57; actress and committed Democrat.

2 Hannah Arendt (1906–75), German-born Jewish political theorist, in US from 1941; chief editor, Schocken Books, 1946–8; Executive Director, Jewish Cultural Reconstruction, 1949–52; visiting professor at various US universities. Her book *The Origins of Totalitarianism* had appeared in 1951. IB had met her during the war; she soon occupied a prominent position on his 'most hated' list. He later recalled 'when I first met her in 1942 her fanatical Jewish nationalism – which has now turned into its opposite – was, I remember, too much for me' (4 November [1963?] to Bernard Crick), and concluded: 'On the subject of the Jews she is a little touched' (19 July 1963 to Sam Behrman); and 'in her ideological works, she indulges in a kind of metaphysical free association which I am unable to follow except that the premises seem to me to be inaccurate and the conclusions unswallowable' (7 May 1963 to William Phillips).

thought of her; or of her + Borkenau[1] + Dr Lazersfeld[2] in a room. Bakunin was right to explain that for all his generous generalisation about what 'all men' desire, the Germans & they alone were to be expressly excluded.[3] [...]〉

TO ROWLAND BURDON-MULLER

Postmark 22 February 1954 [*manuscript*]

All Souls

Dear Rowland,

My life is slowly picking up again, but *very* slowly. The immediate impact of my father's death was to plunge me into a fanatical round of routine activities. His burial: the problem of re-establishing a regular routine for my mother: Oxford – Nuffield: my father's estate etc. I sat down & wrote 100 letters acknowledging notes of condolence: of course you are quite right: one can write semi-mechanical notes to acquaintances when one can[not] string two words together to friends. I sorted my letters out: formal ones: semi-formal ones: letters which could be dictated: letters which could not. I wrote to Alice James without difficulty: even to Olivia whose letter flowed with simple sincere feeling and needed no reflection to respond to. But I was absolutely incapable in those first weeks of writing a proper letter – about something – them, me, the different world in which I seem to live – if Arthur complains he is being a schoolboy. I answered him, but Marian wrote me a letter which is still unacknowledged: it was very very good. My father died without ever discovering that he had leukaemia or anything else: he may have suspected something: he told the (not very good) doctor that I had, in his view, arrived "in time" which sounded ominous. But I don't think he thought he wd die as quick as that; nor did the foolish doctors: who discovered Cortisone (which made him worse) and operations 8 hours before he died. He died alone, painlessly one hopes, in a coma, as I shd wish to do. My mother reverted at once to her religion – there is much to recommend Judaism for bereavement – it finds things to do for a whole week after the funeral. She was pleased by the number of persons who turned up, most of them totally unknown to me: by the letters (there are no flowers at Jewish funerals – did you know?) by the petites visites de condolléance.[4] But the

---

1 Franz Carolus Richard Borkenau (1900–57), Austrian-born writer; former Communist activist who became a fiercely anti-Communist Kremlinologist and authority on totalitarianism; Professor of History, University of Marburg, 1946–9; involved in the Congress for Cultural Freedom.

2 Presumably Paul Felix Lazarsfeld (1901–76), Austrian-born sociologist; Professor of Sociology, Columbia University, 1940–67.

3 Possibly a reference to the passage in Bakunin's *Statism and Anarchy* quoted at RT2 126 and inaccurately at 466 below, where Bakunin implies that all people desire freedom except Germans, who want to remain slaves. But similar remarks about Germans are to be found in many places in Bakunin's works (if 'all men' is a quotation from Bakunin, we have not found it).

4 sc. *condoléance*, 'little visits of condolence'.

centre of her life is gone. She bullied my father in his lifetime but now there is too little to do. Except to worry about my health & the estate: my solicitor is the admirable friend of Moore – one Dickie;[1] my father's two managers are by turns terrified & defiant: they wd like to buy the business from me but like the Dutch they offer too little: so the accountant says. But they feel that nobody else will rid me of my boxes of pigs' bristles (!) & so tend to black-mail me; but then they feel that if I protest too much my honest & innocent plight will attract attention & do them no good in the City: so then they suck up & appease; I don't understand much of what is said to me, & feel like a football hearty being taught the philosophy of Kant; there are plenty of sage advisers: but what I need is a man of action who will either bully my would be buyers for me into paying the normal price fixed by some outside disinterested agent, or buy me out himself. So I go on. Nuffield was absurd as soon as I returned to Oxford: why, I cannot tell you, but I felt it was *absurd*: these grim honourable social workers and manqué civil servants looked on me as a decayed gentlewoman who had lived in a house & knew something about "gracious living" & douceur de vivre.[2] I took one look & fled. There is a play by Gogol[3] called *Marriage* where the potential bridegroom escapes through the window a second before the marriage ceremony. And Nuffield now regard me in a quasi-insulted way: like a heartless flirt who escaped from in front of the altar: almost guilty of breach of promise. Meanwhile I must have compared Nuffield – its bleak but solid worth, its lower middle class but honest toilers – with St Antony's – a Corinth, and Ottocento[4] Court – to Brian Urquhart[5] who repeated it all to James Joll who was duly outraged & chided me for spreading lying malicious rumours about Pompeian luxury & Neronic evenings at his College. How indiscreet of Brian: & *Moore* was alleged to report the same: but I never *spoke* to Moore about Nuff. or St. A's, comparing their attractions. I refused Nuff. with *much* relief. All Souls seems nicer to me by comparison: Sparrow is marvellously frivolous about it all. I feel odd: while my father was alive I felt genuinely sheltered from the daily hardships of life: responsible for myself alone: vaguely part of the cared-for, not the carers: now I am in a front line – responsible for securing my mother's income – & the abnormality & bleakness of this position gets me down. I escape from it at Oxford to some degree: & propose, if I can afford it to acquire a flat in Oxford in which I can settle my mama for weeks at a time so as not to have to go to London & "face life". But we'll see. Nothing, I am sure, will be the same, more's the pity. My unconscious investment – much

1 (Alexander Hugh) Hamon Massy Dickie (1907–87), IB's solicitor at this time.

2 'Sweetness of life.'

3 Nikolay Vasil'evich Gogol (1809–52), Ukrainian-born Russian novelist, playwright and short-story writer; his second comedy, *Marriage*, was published in 1842.

4 'Eighteenth-century'.

5 Brian Edward Urquhart (b. 1919), with the UN from its inception; later (1974–86) Under-Secretary-General, UN.

as I grudged it often – in my family was too great. [...] I am really deeply miserable: but at some level which does not stop me from carrying on. Except that I enjoy nothing much at the moment: the thought of excitement about a meeting with someone, a piece of music, a book, a letter, now seems to me unintelligible. Perhaps I shall recover appetite. I'll telephone you on arrival, of course. Please greet Marian Schlesinger warmly for me. Arthur too.

   My love,

      Isaiah.   [...]

After one of his business trips to London, IB was driven back to Oxford by Aline Halban. He took the opportunity to express the depth of his feelings for her. Although she did not immediately reciprocate, they began to meet clandestinely.

The most important of IB's outstanding commitments in the US was a lecture[1] forming part of the bicentennial celebrations of Columbia University: 'I agreed to appear on 24 March, and I got a visa and I got vaccinated and I got a cabin in a ship and an alternative seat in a plane should the ship be unsuitable',[2] but in the end 'I suddenly realised about four days ago that it was quite impossible for me to go. And that's for several reasons: mainly the fact that my mother's condition is really too low. [...] When private distress such as my mother's – unrevealed until last week – she urged me to go and then suddenly broke down – comes into conflict with public obligations, I think the latter must yield to the former unless one really does cause great unhappiness by the latter.'[3] The business complications resulting from Mendel Berlin's death could also be cited publicly as a reason for cancelling the trip: his growing closeness to Aline could not.

TO ARTHUR SCHLESINGER

17 March 1954

All Souls

Dear Arthur,

   I am still under the curious weight of my father's death, which has somehow made my whole life instantly artificial – the house in London is rather like hired rooms and I can't get adjusted at all. Oxford is now rather more like home. [...] I shall not be coming to America this spring at all, I have to announce. And I feel frightful guilt about that. The reason is my mother's condition – she says she cannot come to America and see new people while in her present state of mind, and obviously cannot be left alone either. She urged me to go in a quixotic manner before and I made all arrangements and got my visa and was vaccinated and booked a cabin and made arrangements

1 On 'Philosophy and Government Repression' (eventually published in 1996 in SR).
2 15 March 1954 to Morton White.
3 16 March 1954 to Rowland Burdon-Muller.

to stay in New York, etc. etc., and then perceiving her hapless condition I realised that it really would be frightfully wrong to go and had to send a grovelling cable to Professor Gutmann[1] of the Philosophy Department at Columbia and explain to him that although he had deferred my pompous official lecture in honour of the Bicentenary twice, I should, in fact, not be coming to deliver it. I really felt terribly badly about this – you know how liable to guilt I am anyhow – and one certainly ought to keep promises, as Professor Beer has pointed out to me with some sharpness the other day. It was while we were dining at All Souls and M. André Maurois[2] suddenly appeared as Seznec's guest and I displayed moral indignation, remembered that Winston had said about him: 'We thought we had a friend and found we had only a customer.' This was in 1941 when he was attacking us in America in a very inelegant manner – do you remember how Henri Bernstein[3] struck him once on each cheek saying: 'Celle-ci comme français et celle-ci comme juif'?[4] Anyway, during this and while I was refusing to shake hands with Maurois and generally riding a high moral [horse] Beer pointed out that my not delivering a lecture at Columbia was of about the same order of depravity. I cannot altogether think that this is so. My mother really was in a rather low state, which has become lower in the last few weeks, partly owing to the fact that my father's estate is still unsettled, and I move in a dazed way in an odious world of bristle-brokers and merchants, bankers, accountants and financiers, solicitors, barristers, Swiss crooks who come from Geneva, where my father appears to have had a small company, and other terribly unattractive figures who are far worse than even the lowest portions, believe me, of either the academic or the political underworlds. They all assure me that I am being cheated on all sides and perhaps I am, but there is no way of avoiding this so far as I can see.

Wilson's prophecy that I shall certainly become a bristle king soon will certainly not be fulfilled. So, observing my mother's sad state and observing that her relief was absolutely enormous when I so much as suggested that I might not go back to America and that she would, in fact, not be left alone, my doubts were stilled and I sent Professor Gutmann my cable, also to Professor

1 James Gutmann (1897–1988) taught philosophy at Columbia University from 1920; Professor of Philosophy 1948–62.

2 André Maurois (1885–1967), né Émile Salomon Wilhelm Herzog, French biographer, novelist and man of letters. In the US in 1941 he had lectured, broadcast and written about the plight and enduring glory of France, becoming known as an apologist for Marshal Pétain, but also claimed a deep attachment to Britain; he later alleged that splits between different French factions, particularly a campaign waged by an unnamed enemy [Henri Bernstein], had led to his misrepresentation. André Maurois, *Memoirs 1885–1967* (1948), trans. Denver Lindley (London, 1970), 285.

3 Henri(-Léon-Gustave-Charles) Bernstein (1876–1953), French dramatist whose plays often dealt with (and had encountered) anti-Semitism. Bernstein conducted a long campaign against Maurois, whom he despised for abandoning his original Jewish name and for not condemning the Vichy Government and its anti-Jewish legislation.

4 'This one as a Frenchman, this one as a Jew'.

Simmons,[1] Professor Mosely, Miss Lawson at Mt Holyoke, various persons at Princeton etc. etc. I am prepared to use any amount of rancid butter to assuage the raging breasts of the Columbia authorities and have offered them a text, recording or anything, at once useless and presumptuous, I am afraid. I am thinking of taking my mother to Rome in April, but even that is fairly uncertain. I am going to write a long and proper letter to Marian. The real letters about real subjects, unlike this kind of patter which I can keep up indefinitely, are at once more difficult and infinitely more satisfactory to write. But I really cannot face serious issues very much at the moment and have to live on a kind of false bottom, if you know what I mean.

The lecture I wrote for Columbia, for which Ted Weeks has now asked, is really rather an odd affair, proving that philosophers are and must be subversive as such, and in a highbrow way placing ample weapons in the hands of the persecutors of intellectuals. It is so complicatedly written, however, the words are so long, the texture is so opaque that it could not be made much use of except by anti-intellectuals of the calibre of Harry Levin, if there were such; but there aren't. My thesis is that only first-class philosophers are worthy of existing at all, that whereas second, third, fourth, fifth, sixth-rate composers, poets, historians, scholars of all kinds are perfectly worthy characters and have a function to play, second, third and fourth-rate philosophers are an obstacle, a nuisance and a menace. I am not sure how Donald Williams will react to it. I feel a little like my good friend Archie MacLeish about the 'irresponsibles', and am trying to eliminate the element of priggishness from my thesis. But it is not easy: I am, as Philip Toynbee has observed in his last and not very good book,[2] a natural member of the 'Prigs' front', and alignment with anarchists has always been infinitely disagreeable to me, which is why I've always detested Bohemians and liked ordered persons even when they were slightly Philistine, slightly snobbish, slightly disreputable to know.

Meanwhile, I feel about McCarthy (merely to change the subject) that he is much more like a Beaverbrook or Northcliffe[3] than he is like Mussolini etc., that his end is not power and not glory and not money, but enjoyment of a peculiarly detestable kind; that he is really a sadist who enjoys tormenting the egg-heads who give him a sense of inferiority and that he does all these things for the sake of a kind of hideous enjoyment, keeping his head, remaining cool in battle, using all his wits and enjoying the mere spectacle of the destruction and besmirching of decency and respectable values as such;

1 Ernest Joseph Simmons (1903–72), Professor of Slavic Languages and Russian Literature, Columbia University, 1946–59; pioneer of Russian area studies in the US.
2 In which Toynbee recalled that IB and Jasper Ridley 'evolved the concept of the "Prig Front", a proud yet also a self-mocking picture of themselves and a few others kneeling together in a sort of Waterloo square to defend their meticulous way of life against immoral, undisciplined and ferocious assailants'. *Friends Apart: A Memoir of Esmond Romilly and Jasper Ridley in the Thirties* (London, 1954), 77.
3 Alfred Charles William Harmsworth (1865–1922), 1st Viscount Northcliffe, newspaper proprietor.

and this is something very different [from] an obsession by an idea, ruthless drive for power, etc., but is not something which has been understood, either by his friends or by his enemies; the Texas millionaires rightly support him because they feel him to be a proper representative against all forms of civilisation and gentility, a proper leader of the guttersnipe front in the sense in which Huey Long[1] never quite was because there was some primitive social ideology mixed up in his views. Yet McCarthy too has elements of perverted populism, in so far as he is genuinely against all stuffed shirts, highbrow culture etc. etc. I can see that he might even, to some people, and in private, appear jolly and almost cosy. [...]

Also you will be receiving about $200 from my Bank in settlement of my debt to you, and I daresay in the course of time something from the Harvard Co-operative Stores. On this sordid note I must end and go to Oxford with my accountant tomorrow and talk about whether it is really true that, owing to your terrible embargo on my Chinese goods, now succeeded by the still more dreadful ban on British brushes made of Chinese bristles (there is no subject I know more about at present, or feel far more deeply about, I may add) I am on what is called a losing market, circling down an irresistible, unstoppable escalator to my financial doom. On this terrible note I end.

Yours ever,
Isaiah

TO MORTON WHITE
22 March 1954

All Souls

Dear Morton,

I read your letter of 27 February again – when I last wrote I was so filled with my own guilt over my bad behaviour to Columbia, etc., that I did not take it in as I might have done. I am still riddled with terrible Angst and yet I don't see what else I could possibly have done. My mother is suffering from the effects of delayed reaction profoundly and there is literally no one else to look after her. Still – the ominous silence from all the aggrieved institutions does rather terrify me. I feel exactly like someone who has written a letter explaining why they can never see somebody again, and has received no reply. Very persecuting. I feel much the same about Nuffield, which I can hardly pass without inner embarrassment. I am beginning to feel like Director O[ppenheimer] (wonderful Kafka character) who can hardly pass through any corridor, or near any dwelling, because of either real or imaginary doors which he has shut against himself, or thinks he has.

1 Huey Pierce Long (1893–1935), US lawyer and Democratic politician; Governor of Louisiana 1928–32; Senator 1932–5; virtual dictator of Louisiana who used dubious methods to achieve radical social reform.

How well I understand your feeling about Mr Fergusson.[1] What it reminds one of is those, to me, best of all documents, the accounts of the lives and behaviour of the Russian critics in the 1840s where similar scenes were enacted. For example, my favourite, Belinsky, who was certainly nothing more than a slightly left-wing radical, when in the presence of a genuine reactionary, who suggested that those who write letters attacking the Russian regime should be at any rate restrained by mild censorship, would more or less lose his temper and ask why; upon being told that in a civilised country such insults to the public should not go with impunity, would blow up and say that in even more civilised countries persons who advocated views of this type were subjected to the guillotine. And so on and so on and so on; this is what is called the *pas devant eux*[2] principle, which does not apply to servants alone. I know very well the feeling you mean – here was I who really feel bitterly unsympathetic to Bolshevism, far more so than you do, with far more of a penchant of a 'disreputable' kind towards all kind of romantic views, but when faced with Adler and Hutchins during that notorious meeting of the Ford Foundation in London I developed a most tremendous, violent, fanatical defence of Bolshevist practices, which distressed everyone at the table but was, it seemed to me, the only thing to do. I feel myself to be on the extreme right-wing edge of the left-wing movement, both philosophically and politically, and rightly regarded with suspicion by the orthodox members of the left-wing movement; but when faced with people conspicuously outside it who wish to attack it as such, there is nothing to do but man the walls, behave as in war and adopt a hundred per cent position. We absolutely agree about that. To compromise then is ignoble, and is the suppression of the real truth in favour of some kind of formal, moral alibi. The notion of a united front has always appealed to me enormously, even though one knows that sooner or later it will be blown up by the real fanatics whom one detests already, even in the moment of forming the front. As for Director O. – I always feel he'll be all right in the end. He is an intelligent man who, however he may react to this or that and be drawn towards all kinds of pseudo-religious broodings and every form of soft intellectual sentimentality imaginable, in the end knows where the enemy is lacking, and although he may not be grateful to have this emphasised more harshly by people a good deal freer than himself, nevertheless, in the end is an ally and on the right side of the barricades. It is this that ultimately makes him tolerable at all – mere cleverness, even brilliance, allied to such a degree of Angst and neurosis would not by itself make it possible to talk to him, it seems to

---

1 Francis Fergusson (1904–86), literary critic; Professor of Comparative Literature, Rutgers University, 1952–73. MW had complained that at a dinner Fergusson 'had delivered an ill-tempered attack on logical positivism that made me furious in spite of my not being a positivist'. Morton White, *A Philosopher's Story* (230/1), 226.

2 'Not in front of them'.

me. There it is – he is a rather noble figure. I wrote him a letter about my not coming, etc., and I hope that he has forgiven me. I suggested I might invite myself for next year, although even that, I suppose, is really very uncertain.

And I am glad you like James Joll so much – he has a sweet, sensitive, loyal and easily amused disposition; his trouble is self-distrust and I think a certain degree of boredom with his chosen subject, which can undermine one deeply. Save for some degree of moral purification in solid disciplined work, what means have we of rescuing ourselves from the corruptions of the world, I suddenly ask solemnly? I really indulge in nostalgic pleasures in the Russian nineteenth century; but James has not that avenue – the German nineteenth century is from that point of view exceedingly awful; he funda- mentally hates philosophy – it is, as a world of thought, entirely unsympa- thetic to him – but he knows the difference between the genuine and the bogus and is, for that reason, an absolutely sound ally with almost a complex about being loyal under fire – in any of the conflicts which occur. And politi- cally also. I cannot tell you how sharp the lines are becoming between 'ours' and 'not ours' – I adore having relations with the enemy and crossing the lines – one always pays for this but I shall not at my time of life stop doing so. Nevertheless, the whole pleasure of doing even that derives from the fact that one does know where the lines are drawn and what one is doing. At least one tells oneself that.

Do tell me about your movements, and whether they really are furious at Columbia. Do tell, at any rate Nagel,[1] that I really would have come if I possibly could. [...]

Yours ever,
    Isaiah

TO JOHN SPARROW
23 March 1954

All Souls

My dear John,

The O.B.[2] Yes, of course. A qui vous le dites?[3] Why do I refuse the invita- tions of our pressing friend Lady P[amela] B[erry] when I know that our friend is to be there? Why does even our friend on the whole feel and indeed sometimes is good enough to express relief when I tell him that I shall, in fact, not take advantage of some kind invitation designed to make us meet? Because I cramp his style. And he knows it – and there is nothing I can do about that. Dear old Stuart, who has been instructed to admire vitality by you

1 Ernest Nagel (1901–85), born in Czechoslovakia; Professor of Philosophy, Columbia University, 1946–55, John Dewey Professor of Philosophy 1955–66, later (1967–70) University Professor.
2 'Old Boy', i.e. Maurice Bowra.
3 'You're telling me'.

know who,[1] is really better with him than you or I, acts as a foil, is sympathetic to his inner pathos. You experience shame before the Chancellor. How shall I ever forget my visit with the O.B. to the distinguished and exquisitely beautiful old Russian poet Vyacheslav Ivanov[2] in Rome, to whom I could have spoken in Russian about the great Blok[3] himself and about Mommsen,[4] whose pupil he had been, and a number of things about which, though I say it, I knew but the O.B. perhaps didn't. And there I sat while the O.B. went roaring in his terrible French about nothing – platitudes about Sophocles, about Russia, about Rome, about everything of a most shaming, appalling kind, which the distinguished, refined, infinitely sensitive, exquisitely fastidious old Roman Catholic poet obviously enjoyed enormously. What is the use, one asks oneself, of one's own carefully wrought, shy, *unerring* taste, if that is what one's admired friends really like? That is how he came to be where and what he is. Was it worth it? He dares not ask himself. But he knows that we do, & lies awake at nights. How much are you prepared to pander, and for how long? I am; quite a lot; for quite a long time. But why? Affection? Habit? Gratitude? Can you answer? Genuine relations are quite impossible, as Sylvester [Gates] has found; ⟨except here & there, now & then, in tantalizing glimpses, too quickly & angrily suppressed in favour of the new ungainly & shamelessly 'public faces' policy. The old Maurice, the one we (& more especially you) knew and were rightly dazzled & warmed by wd have been no use to S.N.H[ampshire] at all; & indeed the O.B. strenuously objected to my introducing him – Stuart – into his life; "nice boy, but dull; prig; lowering; philosopher; all right for you: can't *bear* him myself" was the original line. But he came in with the non-abrasive friends: & very nice too, but as in the case of Victor R[othschild], a symptom of general subsidence, self-amputation, surrender, security-before-self-expression & pleasure and general audacity: it astonished me that I, of all people, shd lament the passing of the grosser & bolder characteristics – τα φυσικώτερα[5] to some extent – but this Origen[6] like behaviour is a terrible surrender. Enough of all this.

Isaiah   [. . .]⟩

1 Presumably Renée Ayer (737/5), with whom Hampshire had a long-standing relationship (they eventually married).
2 Vyacheslav Ivanovich Ivanov (1866–1949), Russian poet and playwright, influential in the Symbolist and Acmeist movements; spent much of his life outside Russia, especially in Rome.
3 Aleksandr Blok (1880–1921), lyric poet, leader of the Russian Symbolist movement.
4 (Christian Matthias) Theodor Mommsen (1817–1903), German classicist, jurist and Roman historian.
5 The Greek 'ta phusikōtera' literally means 'the more natural things', i.e. the physical side of life.
6 Origen (185–c.284), Christian theologian, influenced by Plato's idealism, with a reputation for eschewing the material world.

TO ALAN PRYCE-JONES

1 April 1954

All Souls

Dear Alan,

[...] Have you read a book called *Lucky Jim*?[1] It lowers me more than I can say. No doubt it is a realistic and even gifted description of certain conditions of life, but I cannot bear the tone, the contents and the images which it forcibly brings up to me. Is this pure escapism? I dare say. The novel was vastly praised by everyone as a masterpiece, an equal to Evelyn's early novels. Anything and everything was said. I think it revolting and take it like medicine in fixed doses, so much every week, and have as a result become infinitely more reconciled to my life as it is lived, when I suddenly realise what the alternative to it might be. If anything is needed to cure one of a desire to be a socialist, it has had the same effect on me as a visit to Israel last year on dear James Joll.

Yours ever,

Isaiah

En route to a holiday in Nice, IB and his mother visited Geneva, where, as IB later recalled:

I had a long conversation with Aline, who was in Paris in her own house, for an hour, which is what we tended to do. By the time I arrived in Nice, I had received a letter from her in which she said that her husband had listened to this conversation on another telephone [...]; that he flew into the most terrible tantrum; that he then threatened – if she carried on – to divorce her and keep the children, threatened her in every possible way and said she was never to see me again, roughly; that unfortunately she was devoted to her children, she was after all married, and we must never see each other again. [...] I went to bed for two days after that in Nice, I've never felt so miserable in all my life – I really became debilitated.[2]

TO ALICE JAMES

21 April 1954 [*manuscript*]

Hotel Ruhl, Nice

Dear Alice,

I long to see you and Billy. I really could not write to you properly – it is difficult to describe how choc a bloc my life has been with the need to

---

1 *Lucky Jim* (London, 1954) was the award-winning first novel, set in a provincial university, by Kingsley William Amis (1922–95).

2 MI Tape 14. The children mentioned are Peter Francis Halban (b. 1946), later a publisher, and Philippe Alexandre Halban (b. 1950), later a cell biologist specialising in diabetes (Professor of Medicine, Geneva).

arrange my father's infinitely complicated affairs – to prop my mother – not that she lacks moral stamina and belief in life – and all the terrible odds & ends with which a break in one's life suddenly clutters one's world. Everyone was most kind, most helpful – but the business-banking-legal world is *odious* to me, far more than ever I thought it would be. I dreaded the solemn meetings in banker's offices, & the need to defend my mother's interests against various forces & influences, sometimes far from noble. The whole term was passed in a miserable fashion: then I felt I *must* take my mother away for Easter & we came here. My parents have been coming here for I don't know how long – as their parents & grandparents from Riga did since 1870 or so – & I wondered if this would be intolerable – all the memories – to my mother. On the contrary. It seems to give her comfort. The same hotel, restaurants, cafés, waiters, liftmen, the warmth, familiarity, all this helped. The thing I *was* ashamed of was not coming to Columbia etc. – but I *could* not leave my mother – I saw that even so, when I was away for as many as five or six days in All Souls, she looked a bit bleak when I returned: & a month or so's absence in America – to which she would not come with me, since it involved meeting people & affecting some cheerfulness – & this I understood – would have depressed her too deeply. So I wrote grovelling letters, begged everyone's pardon humbly, pleased only Maurice (but *don't* know this – only he has real scars from Harvard) & stayed in London. To my horror I kept getting newspaper clippings from Mt. Holyoke where I was supposed to give the "Purington Lectures" (I am not sure what they are) – or rather from local papers with a hideous photograph of me, looking like a negro Baptist preacher, with captions "Mr I.B. who will deliver the P. Lectures *tomorrow*" with reproachful scribbles by Arthur Schlesinger who sent them, saying "why don't you tell them?" but I did, I did! in letter & cable! What more could I do. So angry were they that no reply came from them, not even a sour one. I have a terrible amount of work to do: lectures, pupils, a book to finish, 200 unanswered letters of condolence, some from my dearest friends – I've written, in America, only recently to dear Rowland: because he writes once a week: lives on & by letters: has few sources of happiness save the conversations & messages of his friends – & seems to me to have a claim (although it often strains one's patience) on one's loyalty & time. I wrote him two or three times: & shall not now for 2 or 3 months: his own letters as always are a hotchpotch of political maxims & observations & social notes: Gladwyn, Renée etc: (I think he knows now that Renée de B[ecker] is a little too much for me) – "Gladwyn" I saw myself indeed: at a party given for the Edens by Lady Waverley[1] – whose husband is a rock

---

1 Viscountess Waverley (1896–1974), née Ava Bodley, political hostess, whose second husband, Sir John Anderson (1882–1958), 1st Viscount Waverley 1952, civil servant then independent politician, Chancellor of the Exchequer 1943–5 (after whom Anderson shelters were named), was Chairman of many organisations, including the Royal Opera House and the Royal Ballet.

of strength but pompous & boring beyond belief – & whose brother is the peculiar Mr Bodley of Boston[1] – where I rattled away to Mrs E. & made uncosy conversation with our future Prime Minister who is an admirable man I cannot bear (nor, I think he me; though Clarissa denies it; but these things are reciprocal) – he is a fine fellow Gladwyn but cold as ice. His predecessor, Harvey, is thought dimmish, but I like him & his wife much better: he is civilised, honest, anti-German, & his wife is a warm human being: which reminds me: the British Ambassador in Madrid is an enchanting friend of mine called Sir John Balfour:[2] civilised, eccentric & poetical: who used to be Minister (to Halifax & Inverchapel)[3] in Washington, then Ambassador in Buenos Aires: with a charming wife, Frances. I must write him anyway to thank him for writing to me about my father: would you tell me (to All Souls – I leave here on the 25th) *where* you will be in Madrid & *when* & I'll ask him to get in touch. He is absent minded – loses his shoes for instance, in his Foreign Office room – forgets his tie – knows much Russian (modern) poetry by heart – so you could send him a card perhaps: but if you tell me *when*, I'll apprise him. [...]

Love
  Isaiah.

TO ALICE JAMES
24 April 1954 [*manuscript*]

Hotel Ruhl, Nice

Dear Alice,
  Thank you ever so much for your Toscanini enclosures – I find it unbearable that the end of his musical life should have come like this[4] – as you know I admire him so terrifically – as the last proud, noble, unbending representative (with Salvemini)[5] of the Risorgimento & 19th century ideals of human liberty – I have just returned from visiting the cemetery in Nice, where there

1 Ronald Victor Courtenay Bodley (1892–1970), soldier and writer on the Arab world: 'Lady Waverley's brother is a very shady local character called Mr Bodley, whom nobody approves of; regarded with extreme disfavour by all, he has married a rich and innocent Bostonian who has all her life avoided fortune-hunters, only to fall into his clutches.' IB to David Cecil, 5 December 1953.
2 Sir John ('Jock') Balfour (1894–1983), diplomat; UK Minister, Moscow, 1943–5, Washington, 1945–8; Ambassador to the Argentine Republic 1948–51, to Spain 1951–4. Lady Balfour was Frances Hope Dorothy (1904–99), née van Millingen.
3 Archibald John Kerr Clark Kerr (1882–1951), 1st Baron Inverchapel 1946, eccentric, UK Ambassador to Moscow 1942–6, to Washington 1946–8.
4 Toscanini's final concert was on 4 April 1954 in the Carnegie Hall; the enclosures sent by Alice James were presumably press cuttings suggesting that he had been forced to retire or reporting that he had suffered a lapse of memory during the concert.
5 Gaetano Salvemini (1873–1957), anti-Fascist Italian historian and politician.

is a terrific memorial to Garibaldi[1] who was born here – "premier chevalier de l'humanité"[2] rhetorical but to me really moving: & I told the Editor of the *Times*[3] that when he publishes Toscanini's obituary, probably written by some hack musical critic, he *must* let me write just one opening or closing paragraph, to indicate that T. was not just a great conductor, but a symbol of discipline & spontaneity in one – the most morally dignified & inspiring hero of our time – more than Einstein, (to me) more than even the superhuman Winston. [...] Where will you stay in Lisbon? In the *Aviz*,[4] with the almost centenarian millionaire Gulbenkian[5] who has the marvellous pictures? I loved Lisbon in 1940 & 41; & Belem; & Coimbra: & the road from Estoril to Cintra in the early early morning (when I am scarcely awake) with gentle 18th century donkeys carrying panniers of flowers & fruit: Nice is full of lilac & carnations: my mother is relatively all right: & you must meet her in London or Oxford in June. [...]

All my love to Billy & yourself – Isaiah

TO LOUIS FINKELSTEIN[6]

28 April 1954

All Souls

Dear Dr Finkelstein,

Thank you for your letter of 8 April which reached me in France. Firstly let me thank you for your kind words about the review of my book etc., if it is the one I am thinking of I think it over-praised me grossly. However, there is no denying that when one writes books what one wants is not justice but praise, however unfair. So I am well content.

Now as to the real topic of your letter. I agree of course, as you know, with your general appraisal of the problem. The danger (perhaps particularly acute in America but by no means absent in this country) is that as a result of mass spoon-feeding by lectures, a standardised and mechanical generation of men will arise and that this can only be limited by some degree of personal

1 Giuseppe Garibaldi (1807–82), Italian revolutionary nationalist (born in Nice), played a major role in the unification of Italy.
2 'Mankind's leading knight'.
3 Sir William John Haley (1901–87), Director-General, BBC, 1944–52, editor, *The Times*, 1952–67.
4 One of Lisbon's leading hotels.
5 Calouste Sarkis Gulbenkian (1869–1955), immensely rich Armenian-born pioneer of the oil industry, art collector and philanthropist, who from 1942 lived in a suite in the Hotel Aviz.
6 Louis Finkelstein (1895–1991), Jewish scholar and leader of Conservative Judaism; Chancellor, Jewish Theological Seminary, New York, 1951–72. He had written to IB on 8 April with a proposal to counter the loss of 'the experience and wisdom of the ancients' in US mass education by establishing a summer session bringing together promising students and selected teaching staff to discuss 'some specific problem relating on the one hand to philosophical outlook and on the other to immediate social issues avoiding both pure theory and debate on specifics': IB would be the ideal director for the project.

contact with teachers of sufficient originality and temperament, who are themselves not likely to emerge out of the sinister process of mass-produced and mass-distributed information which is prevalent at the moment. Such a conference therefore as the one you adumbrate would be a very good thing. But with the best will in the world, and the greatest degree of sympathy for it and for the ends which it is intended to encompass, I cannot think myself a suitable person for the position which you so flatteringly offer me – an honour by which I am deeply moved. I am a bad chairman, not a good guider of discussion, either I talk too much myself or preserve a stony silence. I have done these things in the past with such a conspicuous lack of success that I assure you that it is not false modesty which makes me say these things, but mere fruit of experience, of which I am not ashamed. I do not think that the gift of intellectual hegemony of this kind is one which it is shameful not to possess – nevertheless they are the facts. [...]

Yours very sincerely,
    Isaiah Berlin

On his return to Oxford IB had reported to his mother the latest developments in his private life: 'I received a letter from my "anonymous" lady asking me not to be furious or sad or resentful, & could she see me etc. – stony silence on my part: as far as I am concerned, forever. I can be very hard when I am driven to it.'[1] *Then, IB recalled, he*

received a telephone call from Aline, who could hardly speak, a kind of strangled voice, explaining that Alan Pryce-Jones, who was then editor of *The Times Literary Supplement* and was a great friend of Aline's family, was coming to stay with them – and I'd asked them all for a drink before these things had happened – that they were bringing him to my drinks all the same because Hans Halban, her husband, thought that if it became known that we weren't on very good terms, his career in Oxford might be affected. [...] And so I gave the party: about ten people came to my room in All Souls. They appeared; she was like a sheep led to the slaughter, I've never seen anyone so white, so unhappy, so miserable. I didn't speak to her at all, nor she to me. I spoke to him, quite affably, I mean we got on and did a turn. I didn't mind, I chatted to him, I thought it was no fault of his, jealousy was a perfectly intelligible emotion. I didn't think that what he'd done was all that wrong – it was unfortunate from my point of view. Then nothing happened for a bit, I was terribly unhappy. Then she telephoned me and said, 'I can't go on, we must meet.' So we began seeing each other clandestinely again, the whole thing was restored.[2]

1 28 April 1954 to Marie Berlin in Israel.
2 MI Tape 14. By 2 May IB could report to Marie on his private life 'I am calm & happy.'

TO MORTON WHITE

3 June 1954

All Souls

Dear Morton,

Thank you very much for your letter about 'the project'.[1] Your suggestions seem to me wholly admirable, and I am sure that Mr Gilpatric[2] will do
much better for us than Mr Katz.[3] $5000 for each of us seems about right
to cover two years' work with two months for each of us in each country,
although it seems to me a little difficult to promise that I would spend two
months next year and the year after that in the States; however we can see
about that.

As for 'research assistants', I wonder whether we shall need them or not.
The only purpose for which they could be needed would be to dig into and
make some kind of précis and reports on some of the more voluminous
but nevertheless not unimportant German and French writers whom we are
likely to wonder about. I profess great admiration for, for example, Dilthey,
whom I have been reading, and even for Weber,[4] and there are various metaphysicians in the nineteenth century who might contain bits of matter of a
vaguely stimulating kind. I wonder whether we might profitably not get hold
of somebody who reads foreign languages simply in order to tell us what to
look for and what kind of things these people discuss in which chapters of
their enormous works. I do not think this would represent either much work
or much expense, nor really relieve us to an appreciable extent of having
to read the stuff ourselves, nevertheless I think some preliminary digging
might really be done by somebody else under our direction. Consequently
I think some money might be spent on that – this could be better done by
somebody in America than here.

I have been lecturing on the subject this term[5] and have some fairly strong
views which may be modified by discussing with you and by mysterious
processes of inner thought themselves. Anyway I should like to try it out.
My suggestion is that during the summer vacation I talk into my beautiful
London dictaphone which has got plastic discs which can be sent abroad. It is
an Ediphone Voice Master VP model and if you could acquire the equivalent

---

1 IB and MW were about to seek funding ($10,000) to spend some time together to write the book
   on the philosophy of history that they had been discussing for five years; their applications to the
   Rockefeller and Ford Foundations failed.
2 Chadbourne Gilpatric (1914–89), CIA 1947–9; Associate Director, Rockefeller Foundation, 1949–75.
3 Milton Katz (1907–95), US Ambassador and Special Representative in Europe for the Economic
   Co-operation Administration 1950–1; Associate Director, Ford Foundation, 1951–4; Director,
   International Legal Studies, and Henry L. Stimson Professor of Law, Harvard, 1954–78.
4 Wilhelm Dilthey (1833–1911), German epistemologist and cultural philosopher; Max(imilian) Carl
   Emil Weber (1864–1920), German sociologist and political economist. Both wrote on historicism
   and the methodology of history.
5 In Trinity Term 1954 IB lectured on 'Historicism'.

at your end – it is a very amusing and agreeable small elegant-looking toy –
we could really do a great deal that way, far easier certainly than dictating or
writing. The discs are pretty little things and fit into special envelopes which
are provided for them and you will find the VP model easy to procure in New
York, but it is rather expensive, about $350. Possibly it can be hired, I don't
know. Anyway I am prepared to send you a prospectus of the sort of things
I would like to discuss some time in July. Do you think that we would simply
write a book as others do, namely compounded chapters – in which you
would write a draft and I would go over it and I would write a draft and you
would go over it and so on, some chapters yours and some mine, like Messrs
Cohen and Nagel,[1] or do you think that our original idea of writing letters
to each other might not prove more rewarding? I do not think there would
be any need to make this into a series of real letters – starting 'Dear Morton'
and 'Dear Isaiah' I mean – but simply documents – theses that I would send
to you and then get objections and then write answers to objections and vice
versa rather in the manner of Descartes and his contemporaries, except that
there would be two Descartes instead of one. Some genuine spontaneity
really is obtained that way without any Edman-like[2] or Santayana-like airs
and graces. Anyway I am prepared to write you a draft prospectus in July
indicating the kind of questions to be dealt with and then we really might
set to and meet next year (unless you want to come here this autumn, which
I should welcome). [...]

I am off to lecture at this moment on the subject of why it is all right for
physicists to be doctrinaire (except that nobody would call them that) and
why it is not all right for historians or critics. I must be off.

Much love,
    Yours ever,
        Isaiah

IB's relationship with Aline Halban reached another crisis:

Then one day [...] we were going to have a meeting in a chemist's shop in the
High Street opposite All Souls College – [...] there we'd get into a car and go
somewhere. I had just finished a lecture that I'd delivered at ten o'clock. At
eleven o'clock I proceeded to go [...] and suddenly saw Professor Halban, as he
was by that time, and his wife talking to each other at the corner of the street
opposite which the chemist was. So, more dead than alive, I bowed, went into
the chemist's shop, bought objects which I didn't need, and returned, took off
my hat again, went back to All Souls without a word. I was then rung up by
Halban, who said: Would I mind coming round to the house, because he'd like
to have a talk with me? I agreed, so I took a taxi, went to the house in which

1 *An Introduction to Logic and Scientific Method* (New York, 1934) by Nagel and Morris Cohen.
2 Irwin Edman (1896–1954) taught philosophy at Columbia University from 1918 (Professor 1935–50,
   Johnsonian Professor of Philosophy 1950–4).

I live at present, which was then their house, [...] and I said to him, 'Look, I know that you're entirely right. You have justice on your side. She's married to you, you love her, there's nothing I can say. You have a perfect right over your wife and family.' [...] He said, 'Well, it's a difficult situation, let's talk about it.' I said, 'Well, look, I fully understand your position, you needn't expound it to me. There's only one thing I'd like to say to you. Let me give you a piece of advice: it's not entirely unbiased, as you'll see; I have a certain interest in saying it to you but I will say it to you. If you keep somebody in prison, the prisoner is more anxious to get out in the end than the jailer is to keep the prisoner there. In the end, this will not end well. If you stop her from seeing me, this will not go on indefinitely. Sooner or later it's bound to be broken, even if I do nothing at all. I don't think you'll succeed psychologically – you may realise that I have a motive for saying it, but it is true also, and therefore it would be easier if you lifted this ban, from the point of view of family life, for you.' [...] And then he began saying this and that, and we had a quite amiable conversation after that. He then said, 'Will you go for a walk with Aline in the garden? She has something to say to you.' So off I went for a walk with poor Aline, she was in a very bad state, she didn't know how long this would last, but she was sorry for him because he was in a state of utter misery about the whole thing, and after all 'He is quite a nice man really', and was rather attractive in some ways, she was not unfond of him, he was the father of her children and she didn't know what we ought to do. I told her what I'd said to him. He rushed into the garden with a note for me. The note said: 'I accept your proposal. You may see her once a week.' OK. After that, she came to tea at All Souls on Thursdays. We saw each other at other times as well, but still, it was more or less legitimised.[1]

TO ROWLAND BURDON-MULLER

21 June 1954

All Souls

Dear Rowland,

You must forgive me as always for not having written for so long and also now for writing you so depersonalised a letter in typescript. It is 1 a.m. and I am in my usual exhausted state. Why? I cannot say myself. I fritter my life in small acts. I have done some solid work today but every time I finish a job, for about three hours it seems to me to contain nothing worth doing and to be infinitely inferior to anything anyone else does on anything.

I have spent my term in the usual lecturing, teaching, and visits from such incompatible and curious visitors as the President of Notre Dame University[2] – a robust priest who however was very civil and considering

---

1 MI Tape 14.
2 Theodore Martin ('Ted') Hesburgh (b. 1917), Catholic priest, President, Notre Dame University, 1952–87; influential and outspoken educational and social reformer; Civil Rights Commission 1957–72 (Chairman 1969–72); later, vocal opponent of the Vietnam War.

everything exceedingly interesting – and Dr Placzek,[1] a dotty but agreeable scientist – physicist – from the Princeton Institute, who gave me the latest news of the Oppenheimer case.[2] I cannot see what is wrong in what the poor man has done except that he failed to turn over the people who asked him for information to the police in 1943, and told the investigating committee all about it in 1947 and when they asked him why he told them a cock and bull story said very simply and pathetically, 'I was an idiot.' I cannot feel that it is anybody's duty except in extreme circumstances to be a willing informer – though if you ask me whether there is a general principle applying, i.e. that one should never turn over one's friends to the police or alternatively that one always should if one thinks that they are being subversive against the order which one is pledged to support – I should answer that there is no general principle and one must follow one's conscience and do whatever seems right and just in the circumstances. Anyway I have written Oppenheimer a friendly letter expressing sympathy for his plight and put my name and address on the back of the envelope so that the letter need not be steamed open by the authorities to find out who had written it. I did not feel that Hiss was unjustly convicted – though he may have been – but I did not see that there was much evidence for him and I did think that his case looked pretty phoney; I feel the opposite about Oppenheimer.

The summer term has flown by without much dramatic incident. I went to Paris to see the Moscow Ballet, but on account of Dien Bien Phu[3] they did not dance, so I went to Longchamps instead with the Rothschilds, which was boring and peaceful. Lady Marriott was there with a special balcony over the Arc de Triomphe to see the Gaullist revolution[4] which was expected but nothing much happened since the police were there in great force. I wandered about too at about 5.00 p.m. and merely saw large truckloads of soldiers and policemen as in 1848. It was historic, menacing and peculiar. I do hate all persons in authority I must say. I did not have such sensations of

1 George Placzek (1905–55), Czech physicist who had previously worked with Hans Halban, Niels Bohr and on the Manhattan Project; Institute of Advanced Study, Princeton, 1948–55.
2 Oppenheimer's left-wing sympathies and Communist friends and colleagues were cited in 1953 as evidence that he was a security risk, and President Eisenhower asked for his resignation. Oppenheimer requested a formal hearing, pending which his security clearance (necessary for his work on the Atomic Energy Commission) was suspended. During the June 1954 hearing, despite the testimony of many top scientists, the powerful enemies Oppenheimer had made during his career (aided by his own inconsistent and erratic testimony) succeeded in obtaining permanent revocation of his security clearance.
3 On 7 May 1954 the decisive defeat at Dien Bien Phu of the French forces in Indochina, besieged for 56 days by a Vietnamese army (Viet Minh) of nationalists and Communists, marked the effective end of France's role as a colonial power in south-east Asia and led to the division of Vietnam.
4 General de Gaulle planned to lay a wreath at the tomb of the Unknown Soldier at the Arc de Triomphe on 9 May as his personal commemoration of the anniversary of the end of the war in Europe. Pro-Gaullist demonstrations were expected because of widespread anger in France at the fall of Dien Bien Phu.

brutal authority since I was in Moscow in 1945, it was not quite as bad as
there but began to resemble it. [...]

After the play,[1] which was more like a cocktail party than a theatrical performance, we went to a party given by Mrs Agar, where Princess Margaret
duly appeared and addressed me in lively but not very fascinating terms. I did
not enjoy it much and on the whole desired to get away from her, from which
I infer that I cannot really be very snobbish. On the next day she appeared in
Oxford to open something at St Hilda's and finding herself at table with the
Warden of Wadham and the Warden of New College, enquired if Oxford
was the university I came from; you can imagine how this story was spread
and how much incalculable damage it will have done me by the time you
get this letter. But how could I help it? All I wanted to do was to be nice to
Alix and faced with Royal personages I suppose it is discourteous to refuse
to exchange any conversation with them. And anyhow she is quite amusing
and gay and amiable. However, I do not think I am really made for frequent
contact with Royalty.

I also went to watch the Trooping of the Colour and there sat next to Miss
Fonteyn,[2] who was absolutely charming, very simple and very amiable; on
my other side I had Cecil Beaton and Alan Pryce-Jones and all that passed
off very pleasantly and very agreeably too. I then came back and worked
very hard for a fortnight to atone for my woeful tastes. Hampshire was very
shocked and thought it was terrible to meet persons of this kind in these
kinds of circumstances. I dearly enjoy teasing him about the joys of social
life and the terrible 'contamination' which they necessarily cause.

[...] [the Jameses] are coming here and I propose to have them for the
Encaenia Lunch, which is a grand affair in honour of all the persons who
have been given honorary degrees that day, and so they will meet an uncommon quantity of celebrated persons and will be in a spin of giddy happiness – at least dear Alice will – all day I hope. The Vice-Chancellor is having
them to stay, they will be given dinner by him once or twice and the whole
thing will I am sure be a roaring success. Rowse is bringing Lady Astor,[3] who
is surely the most detestable woman in England; boring, rude, and guilty
of interference in British politics which has brought nothing but disaster
for many years. Winston is very right to refuse to know her. My guests are
Elizabeth Bowen, the wife of my friend Anthony Rumbold,[4] who is now

1 An amateur performance for charity of Edgar Wallace's *The Frog* at the Scala Theatre, London,
  on 1 June, which IB had reluctantly attended with Alix de Rothschild.
2 Margot Fonteyn (1919–91), née Margaret ('Peggy') Hookham, the leading ballerina of the (then)
  Sadler's Wells Ballet; married Roberto de Arias in 1955.
3 Nancy Witcher Astor (1879–1964), née Langhorne, Viscountess Astor; sharp-tongued US-born
  widow of Waldorf Astor, 2nd Viscount Astor; Unionist MP 1919–45, the first woman to take her
  seat in the House of Commons.
4 Sir (Horace) Anthony Claude Rumbold (1911–83), diplomat; later Ambassador to Thailand
  (1965–7) and to Austria (1967–70). His (first) wife was Felicity Ann (1917–84), née Bailey.

Private Secretary to Mr Eden (and very amusing about him), the Cecils, the Halbans, and possibly Lady Harcourt,[1] to whom I thus repay many kind invitations. Her husband is going to be financial adviser and member of the World Bank etc. in Washington as from September and it is a good choice – he is a modest, sensible nice man, married to a Becky Sharp.[2]

Well, I shall stop now and write my next letter to you after the Jameses have departed, when I can describe their Oxford visit; I would much rather do that [than] anything else.

I wonder how long Mendès France[3] will last in Paris – he is a most intelligent man and although he says about me that one cannot understand a word I say and that any reputation I have is entirely due to the fact that nobody can understand a word and assumes that there may be something in it – I wish him well.

I received a letter yesterday from William Hayter in Moscow asking me to go and stay with him there. I do not think I can this summer because of my mother etc. I would love to otherwise, to see what has happened in the last seven years or so. I have a feeling that they may be relaxing their controls a little. Not so much because they feel any more liberal, as because it is a waste of time to crush so many literary persons so much of the time and that literature does not have all the effects that it is supposed to have. ⟨I wonder what Nancy Mitford[4] will have made of it all.⟩ [. . .]

Yours affectionately, with all possible wishes
    Isaiah

In early August IB spent a weekend with Guy and Alix de Rothschild at their stud-farm in Normandy, and met the Halbans, who were staying nearby, at Deauville casino.[5] The situation was taking its toll on all three: 'Dr Halban saw her reading a letter, sitting on the beach at Deauville, which she tore into little pieces and scattered on the sands, and the letter, he decided, was from me – indeed it was – and he then went to the shore and spent an hour piecing them together.'[6]

---

1 Elizabeth Sonia ('Betty') Harcourt (1910–59), Viscountess Harcourt, née Snagge, wife of William Edward Harcourt (1908–79), 2nd Viscount Harcourt, merchant banker; Minister (Economic), UK Embassy, Washington, and UK Executive Director, International Bank for Reconstruction and Development, and of International Monetary Fund, 1954–7.
2 The opportunistic social-climber heroine of William Thackeray's 1847–8 novel *Vanity Fair*.
3 Pierre Mendès France (1907–82), who became Prime Minister of France in June 1954 when the previous government fell in the wake of the Dien Bien Phu disaster. During his brief administration (until February 1955) he started on the demolition of France's colonial role in Indochina and North Africa.
4 Nancy (Freeman-)Mitford (1904–73), daughter of 2nd Baron Redesdale, novelist; based in Paris after the war, married to (but separated from) Peter Rodd.
5 IB later responded to his mother: 'No, Dr Halban did not eat me alive. He was not too pleased; but he concealed it.' 21 August 1954.
6 MI Tape 14.

13 August 1954 [*manuscript*]

Haras de Reux, Pont-l'Évêque

Dear Marion

I ought to have written to you before, of course, And what you say is much too true. Felix (to whom, also, very barbarously I did not reply) said the truest thing of all, that after one's father dies, nothing is ever quite the same. [...] Still, I am slowly climbing out of it now, my mother is, I think, going to be financially 'all right', my life can re-start. Yet it cannot. Hitherto I lived like an undergraduate (if I ever {I} write my autobiography – which I never shall – it wd be called 'Late Awakening') – terms in Oxford, vacations in London in my parents' house. Now I have to see my mother, obviously, a good deal more often. So I go up & down, & cannot bear it. She is too careful not to be a nuisance, not to interfere, & thereby does. She is behaving beautifully: I shd cope better if she were a little more selfish, irritated, dissatisfied. I suppose it *will* all stabilize. My heart is free, people are ever so kind, efforts to find me brides are made with ill concealed lack of skill by my 'social' friends. All this is comical & I don't mind it very much. This week-end, chez les Guy Rothschild, is real rancid butter, & I am proud to inform you, I cannot take it: I have, rudely but desperately, locked myself into my little bedroom, & read some Russian 19th century memoirs. I've decided that I neither write nor speak English, but Russian with English words: & that the only landscape I like is human beings, that I am a fancier of them as others of birds. Now I shall stop, & write again from Italy in a day or two.

I.B.

Aline drove IB to Paris, whence, after a round of social events, he went on to Italy by train. After a visit to Perugia he joined friends from Oxford for a week in Cortona, to which he responded with enthusiasm:

Cortona is tiny: has one small main street; 2 cafés; but if people are one's landscape, ideal. The flow of life is incredible: it is a cure for anxiety and too many dialoghi interni:[1] imagine a small, fabulous looking piazza, with a small caffè: all round, stalls, trade, life, beggars, ebullient black middle aged ladies, occasional operatic looking gipsies, wonderful looking girls of the most romantic exquisite appearance, priests sucking ice creams arm in arm in the street, children, etc. Even the ugly & the crippled are never subhuman, never brutish, always this play of life ('interplay' – interjeu) – at this moment a fantastic looking old figure with a long white beard & a pipe in rags, of extreme dignity & gaiety is approaching my café – & all round are persons with beady little eyes watching everything, discussing, picking to pieces, extracting everything possible from everything – surely this is it; to come into the least contact with it is to acquire

---

1 'Internal dialogues'.

juster proportions & stability: & the scattering of the sad & terrifying images
induced by our northern torpor. [...] It seems to me 1000 times more delightful
than life in Florence, Venice, Siena. Of course one can build one's own existence
in a socially thin milieu: if one is fanatically devoted to a cause, or insulated, –
carapace etc or sufficiently self absorbed & self intoxicated: but I find it easier
to exist in a medium filled with other persons filled with their own purposes,
bubbling with vitality, who never don't react & smile & frown perpetually
& don't sink under their own weight or get blown about because of lack of
it – like here. All Souls is the best I can find in England. But small unrepressed
communities are the thing.[1]

*IB then moved on via Urbino and Ravenna to Venice for a few days, breaking the
journey home with a weekend at the home of Raphael and Adriana Salem near
Aix-en-Provence.*

TO MORTON WHITE

4 October 1954 [*typed transcript of missing original*]

All Souls

Dear Morton,
    [...] you give a list of the topics it is hoped to discuss.[2] To this I should like
to add what is, in my mind, one of the most important of these, namely, the
nature of historical understanding – that is to say of what is meant when it is
said that historians understand a period well or badly, that they are good historians or poor, or profound or shallow, or that their accounts are plausible
or unconvincing. You partly cover this by your term 'historical explanation',
but not perhaps quite. I have been lecturing on this subject at Oxford, and
have had very interesting reactions to the view which I have expounded,
which is somewhat different to official positivist views, from historians who
have come to these lectures, and in particular from the eminent Professor of
Latin – just retired – Eduard Fraenkel,[3] who explained to me why it was that
he had declined to write the life of Mommsen when requested to do so by
Wilamowitz,[4] and taught me a great deal about German historicism in the
process. He came to all the lectures and generally took a great deal of lively
interest in the whole thing. The nature of the logic of the human studies, in
general, for example, the reconstruction of the classical past, the technique

1 24 August 1954 to Aline Halban.
2 MW had suggested 'the nature of historical knowledge, the relation between history and the
   social sciences, the role of value judgements in historical research, the nature of historical
   explanation and causation, the character of historical language, the similarities and differences
   between history and the natural sciences, the nature of an adequate historical description of a
   given culture, period or event'. Letter quoted in *A Philosopher's Story* (230/1), 228.
3 Eduard Fraenkel (1888–1970), German-born; Corpus Christi Professor of Latin, Oxford, 1935–53.
4 Enno Friedrich Wichard Ulrich von Wilamowitz-Moellendorff (1848–1931), German classical
   philologist; son-in-law of Mommsen.

of emendation of historical and literary texts, and the relationship of historical imagination to rigorous canons of inference, as used, for example, by palaeographers, seems to me to be highly relevant to our study. [...]

No English and no American writer seems to me to have been particularly illuminating on this subject – nor any Frenchman, not even Taine, or Marc Bloch.[1] But Dilthey – wrongly accused of being a metaphysical muddler and a Hegelian, whereas he is merely both empirical and imaginative and a practising historian, and a man of very great gifts – particularly in the matter of historical generalisation, superior not merely to Toynbee but to Whitehead – seems to me to have talked a great deal of highly luminous sense on the subject. However, all that we must discuss, if our scheme works, when finally we meet again.

Yours ever,

Isaiah B.

Soon after IB had delivered the Northcliffe Lectures[2] at UCL, he succumbed to bronchitis and spent over a week being cared for by his mother in Hampstead and reading romantic novels; he returned to Oxford only towards the end of term. IB's friends were used to the regular breakdowns of health caused by his erratic lifestyle: 'Isaiah had his usual collapse about a fortnight ago and has not been seen since. He never goes to bed, and in the end it catches him out.'[3]

TO ELENA LEVIN

30 November 1954

All Souls

Dear Elena,

[...] I should, of course, have written this letter to you months and months ago, from Italy, where I think I received yours about Trotsky.[4] I wrote quickly

---

1 Marc Léopold Benjamin Bloch (1886–1944), French medieval historian and historiographer, shot by the Nazis; his book *The Historian's Craft* was published posthumously in 1949.

2 IB delivered the four Northcliffe Lectures for 1954 weekly from 18 October, under the collective title 'A Marvellous Decade: Literature and Social Criticism in Russia 1838–48', at University College, London. The lectures were broadcast by the BBC Third Programme in early 1955, published in *Encounter* in 1955–6, and reprinted as 'A Remarkable Decade' in RT. The original recordings of the second and third lectures were used for the broadcast but IB had to re-record the first and fourth on 16 December 1954, and admitted to Aline (abroad on a skiing holiday at the time) that he irrelevantly inserted the anti-German sentiments of Herzen and Bakunin because he missed her and resented Hans Halban.

3 Maurice Bowra to Alice James, 11 December 1954 [Wadham College Archives, Oxford].

4 Leon Trotsky (1879–1940), né Lev Davidovich Bronstein, Ukraine-born Bolshevik revolutionary, at one point the likely heir to Lenin, eventually lost the power struggle with Stalin and his allies; expelled from the Soviet Union in 1929, he spent the rest of his life in exile in Turkey, France, Norway and Mexico, where he was assassinated. Elena Levin had asked IB to provide an introduction to her translation for the Harvard University Press of Trotsky's *Diary in Exile, 1935*, eventually published in 1958.

to Tom Wilson[1] because I thought he had to know at once, and meant to write to you on the very next day; and then fell ill and then began travelling about, and then began several times and wanted to write it in manuscript and in Russian, and I write in Russian very badly and all the letters go wrong. And then I came back and there was too much to do and I had to deliver some public lectures (on Russian literature) in London, which actually reduced me to complete hysteria and torpor at the same time and prevented anything else from being done – and so on and so on. But nevertheless I throw myself upon your mercy, for certainly I need it. Please forgive me. And now let me explain about Trotsky.

I was fascinated by the bits you quoted; nevertheless, Lev Davidovich is not for me. I do not like him for, I suppose, the obvious reasons: because he is too dry, too ⟨? что же я сказал ?⟩[2] and too obsessed. One of the great splendours of the Russians in the nineteenth century, it seems to me, is that, in spite of their fascination by foreign doctrines and their view that truth does exist, that it can be discovered, that one has to suffer for it, that one can then attain it and, having discovered it, one can then devote one's life to realising it on earth – in spite of all this, their emotions and imaginations are so active and their sense of individual experience is so concrete and sympathetic (as opposed to their sense of social or political or economic reality, which is feeble) that when it comes to the point they don't act like fanatical bulldozers, at least in the nineteenth century they did not advocate that in the manner of genuine Western doctrinaires. 'From the crooked timber of humanity no straight thing was ever made' said Kant,[3] and this seems to me to be the central motto of the whole of Russia after the nineteenth century. It applies to the non-Russian nationalities as much as to Russians, certainly to Georgians and Eastern Poles and Jews (Zionism, for instance, is a human Russian movement with specific Russian idealism, despite its Western origins and the attempts to formulate it in the style of nineteenth-century Western liberal nationalism). Herzen is the absolute epitome of all this intellectual fascination by Western ideas and emotional recoil from the vivisection of living human beings in the name of any abstractions – a theoretical adherence to all kinds of doctrines and propositions and theorems, plus an [in]ability not to see the truth and reality as they actually appear and not to say what he saw, in the most vivid and, if need be, the most pungent, sceptical and constructive language possible. This kind of ironical realisation, an [in]ability to suppress the truth in the interests of anything at

---

1 Thomas James Wilson (1902–69), Director of Harvard University Press 1947–67.
2 '? Chto zhe ya skazal ?' ('? but what did I say ?'), written in a gap left by the typist.
3 Immanuel Kant, 'Idee zu einer allgemeinen Geschichte in weltbürgerlicher Absicht' (1784), *Kant's gesammelte Schriften* (Berlin, 1900–), vol. 8, 23. When this quotation was used as an epigraph for CTH, IB added a more literal translation, of which the final recension runs: 'Out of timber so crooked as that from which man is made nothing entirely straight can be built.'

all – pandering to one's own particular conceptions and prejudices because it is, in fact, how one sees the world, however one ought to be seeing it – all this was rightly regarded as terrible self-indulgence by the more rigorous type of revolutionary, who thought that casual, individual facts ought to be suppressed in the interests of the over-mastering goal, and individual emotional facts etc. were in a certain sense trivial entities which could be regarded, if need be, as not existing at all. I do not want to begin a long lecture on doctrinaires and empiricists of the nineteenth century, but my point is that Trotsky seemed to me to be genuinely obsessed by a few fanatical Marxist notions; intelligent, lively, imaginative as he was, apply and deflate them as he did in his own individual fashion, he was nevertheless a dry biscuit; a fanatic like de Gaulle or Robespierre or Comte, who really did sacrifice their human qualities, whatever they had, upon the altar of some enormously oversimplifying principle. I see exactly what you mean when you compare Trotsky with Herzen – the history of the Revolution and bits of his autobiography certainly possess a kind of ironical humour, and of course brilliance and genius, compared to Herzen's; and yet they are very polar opposites: Trotsky was genuinely soulless and genuinely inhuman: his colossal power of oversimplifying the issues, which I suppose is one of the great gifts of revolutionary leaders of certain types, by which you cast a violent beam of light upon the centre path, which automatically blacks out everything else so that all your weaker and more cowardly followers derive strength from the sheer strength and simplicity of the central vision – is paid for by lack of interest in people, arrogant contempt for most of them and absence of genuine personal relations, which makes such people no good to me, so to speak, however objectively magnificent and great and important and serious they may be.

I think Lenin had some of this too, though not as much as Trotsky, although Edmund Wilson tries to make him into a human being out of affection and admiration – I think he does him far more than justice in this regard. Trotsky's failure to protect himself against Stalin partly derives from this terrific blindness to the smaller, more delicate elements of human social texture around him, to an almost Hitler-like dynamism, by which you simply blaze your way through the human blanket, ignore the medium until you get tangled up and destroyed (or win, as the case may be). I recently listened to a paper by Deutscher on Trotsky at Alma Ata.[1] Apart from hunting and the like – of which the more sedentary type of Social Democrats seem pathetically and snobbishly proud – there was a lot of correspondence with a lot of other people in Siberia about the fact that if, for example, Stalin were to move to the left against the wish of the Central Committee, then 'we would

---

1 Trotsky spent a year in internal exile in Alma Ata (now Almaty in Kazakhstan, formerly Vernyj) during 1928.

have to throw in our whole weight in the scale for him and not, as now, against him'. Deutscher took all this frightfully seriously, and yet the ghastly unreality of it was extraordinary: here was Trotsky sitting in Central Asia, with his letters being censored by the SKUD [sc. NKVD?], writing to other equally feeble and discredited Bolsheviks, still talking the language of 1910, in which this faction plus that faction could combine against some third trend inside the party, where it was still important what particular division a particular group might pursue for the next party congress, etc., and all this had become trivial nonsense before the [*words missing*] and Soviet Government. What was he talking about? And what do people like Deutscher, who think it was so important to know exactly what he was telling his followers on that date, think about the importance of it all? The whole thing seemed to me a kind of fantastic caricature of the earlier Marxist scholasticism – which was bad enough – now used as a kind of escape from the obvious facts – which Trotsky and his followers would not recognise – the subtleties of 1910 had ceased to play even a superficial role in all this – that they were living in the imaginary world of heresies and sub-heresies and fissions within the sub-heresies of the earlier Christian theologians – which no longer corresponded to anything that was anything in the 'real world'. And all this is a pathetic and repulsive spectacle, the kind of nemesis which comes on blind and heartless bigots when something goes wrong with the system and their particular carriage slips off the narrow railway lines along which alone they are capable of moving. But perhaps I am doing injustice to all this. I suspect I am and that is why I am not really fit to deal with Trotsky and his problems and his situation. I do hate conscientious, coherent, high-minded doctrinaire torturers of human beings into neat and tidy shapes, very much indeed. Trotsky is almost an exaggerated example of this type, and therefore I am not a suitable person to understand him or write about him. One is either a Dantonist or a Robespierrist and I am quite clear that I am the former and cannot really sit at the same table as the latter. All this, I need hardly say, I did not convey to Mr Wilson, but it does make me frightfully unsympathetic to all the effective and successful people in the politics of the twentieth century – from Lenin and Kemal[1] onwards. And I much prefer Churchill and Weizmann, who are clearly men of the nineteenth century who survived by some historical accident.

Have I made myself understood? I dare say not. I keep on reading and re-reading Herzen, who seems to me to have been right about almost everything, including personal relations. And I have read for the second time *Madame Bovary*, which seems to be an obsessed work of a maniac, in which the author takes sides to an almost hysterical degree. I keep being excited

1 Mustafa Kemal Atatürk (1881–1938), founder of the secular Turkish Republic, President of Turkey 1923–38.

by it and having to take deep draughts of the antidote in the form of *Anna Karenina*, to keep myself in balance.[1] So I dislike Flaubert in a sense for reasons not so very different to those which make Trotsky so unpalatable – fanaticism, obsession, a violent distortion into one mould.

But I really must stop. How are you? I wish I was coming to America soon, but I am not.

Yours ever,

Isaiah

Ах, если б[ы] я только мог писать по русски – все было бы лучше и более authentic –[2]

TO ROWLAND BURDON-MULLER

3 December 1954

All Souls

My dear Rowland,

I apologise for not writing for so long, but it was due to a whole set of causes. There was, as you rightly surmise, All Souls. What a neurosis that is, how much time it absorbs, the many meetings, the quarrels between old friends, the rereading and rereading of old papers by the same worthless hacks, and finally the climactic meetings at which in this case we decided to elect nobody[3] – you can imagine how painful that was to the candidates and their colleagues. Whenever anyone is elected, those who were not, if they are very nice, think that they were defeated by their betters. If they are not so nice, they attribute it to envy, intrigue, prejudice, incompetence etc., when no one is elected they cannot but think – what is indeed true – that the standard is considered not to have been attained, and that is extremely painful to all concerned. However, having embarked upon this brave decision, the admirable John Sparrow and the rest of our little band thundered at the College to such effect that they agreed to behave in a proud and negative manner.

After this I had my Russian lectures to deliver in London. That was fantastic, in an old anatomical theatre of University College in London amid ghastly yawning skeletons, I stood like a corpse about to be dissected under the arc lights whilst steeply rising rows of hard seats contained an extraordinary collection of casuals, students, mysterious old ladies who turn up to such things and are never seen anywhere else, one or two old friends, and at the last

---

1 *Madame Bovary* (1857) by the French novelist Gustave Flaubert (1821–80) and Tolstoy's *Anna Karenina* (1873–7), despite their differences, both describe the sad fate of errant wives.

2 'Akh, esli b[y] ya tol'ko mog pisat' po russki – vse bylo by luchshe i bolee authentic –' ('Oh, if only I could write in Russian – everything would have been better and more authentic –').

3 Most unusually, All Souls elected no Prize Fellows in 1954.

lecture of all Viscount and Viscountess Waverley – not really very welcome – just to give tone. She was very complimentary about it and employed exactly the same voice as her brother in Boston when they attended at a similar occasion. However, that is over too now, thank God, and apart from one or two little squibs in the Press I have escaped lightly. They are all to be given over the BBC next year, and then I expect heavier attacks.

After that I came back to Oxford and tried to make up for lost time but immediately began to feel fearfully ill and like a madman went and lectured in provincial Universities out of pure philanthropy, sleeping in unheated rooms in the squalid lodging-houses in which I was placed. I thereupon went to London to hear Heifetz[1] to console myself and on the next day went down with enormous bronchitis which kept me in London for more than a week. That I rather enjoyed, but I was forbidden all exertion as the result of a high fever obtaining, which the sulpha drugs which I took did very little to abate. I am now back here a little shaky, but recovering.

[...] An enormous amount of my time is still being wasted on 'business' details designed to produce a tolerable income for my mother, which is proving far less easy than it had at first seemed. My father's death has genuinely impoverished us both and the problem of making ends meet is by no means abstract. I cannot take it with due seriousness because I never have been able to think of money in very serious terms, having never wished to have any or needed it very much. Nevertheless at the moment I am as money-conscious as anyone; nevertheless I cannot face the prospect of going to Chicago in the spring in order to make $3000, and prefer modesty and poverty.

The Ballet arrived[2] and I gave a luncheon party for them (very expensive), but they were charming, not only Freddie Ashton,[3] whom you know, and Robert Irving,[4] who would not come to lunch but went to the races instead and won £350 – one cannot blame people as successful as that for anything – but Miss Fonteyn and Mlle Beriosova,[5] to whom I talked Russian with great pleasure, and Mrs Elvin,[6] to whom you remember I sent flowers in Boston, but who did not remember it. There was a tremendous row because two parties were being given simultaneously for the Ballet on the same evening and the poor dancers did not know which one to go to and had to be given

1 Jascha Heifetz played at the Festival Hall in London on 18 and 21 November; IB probably attended the first concert, conducted by Sir Thomas Beecham.
2 Sadler's Wells Ballet performed in Oxford while on tour in November 1954.
3 Frederick William Mallandaine Ashton (1904–88), principal choreographer, Royal Ballet, 1933–70, Director 1963–70.
4 Robert Augustine Irving (1913–91), conductor, Royal Ballet, 1949–58; Musical Director, New York City Ballet, 1958–89.
5 Svetlana Beriosova (1932–98), Lithuanian-born ballerina; Sadler's Wells Theatre Ballet 1950–2; Sadler's Wells Ballet 1952–75; married Masud Khan 1959.
6 Violetta Elvin (b. 1925), née Prokhorova, later Weinberger, then Savarese, Russian ballerina; Sadler's Wells Ballet 1946–56.

strict moral advice by David Cecil and myself – it was worthy of Cambridge, Mass. – the repercussions which followed it I mean.

At this point Sir Robert Mayer[1] – your old friend – came in to consult me about something or other and kept me for about an hour and a half. Then Aline came in to continue with the translation of *The Hedgehog and the Fox*,[2] on which she seems fanatically intent. This flatters me, but I wonder if any publisher is rash enough to publish it. [...]

I shall have a slightly gloomy Christmas with my mother, who is worried about her income – not unreasonably – and thinks she can never afford to go for a holiday abroad again. Endless new debts keep coming in which my father's business appears to have contracted, so that we shall really be left not nearly as well off as I had supposed even six months ago. I suppose I must start writing articles for Ted Weeks or something of the kind.

Last week I dined with Jimmy Rothschild at Aylesbury – not last week, about three weeks ago, before my illness – and there met Germaine [de Rothschild] dressed a little too young, with her son-in-law Piatigorsky.[3] He is an amusing man and a terrific liar, she seemed a little too worshipful towards him and herself madly anxious to acquire new culture; she is obviously enjoying life far more than when her husband was alive [...]

My friend Victor Rothschild's sister, Mrs Lane,[4] has now settled at Elsfield Manor, where John Buchan[5] used to live, which gives me great pleasure, as it gives me another house where I can have a room to work where I am not disturbed by telephone calls etc. The attic of the house at Stanton Harcourt[6] is not yet furnished, all that is there is the refectory table which you so kindly gave me with Aline, a carpet and some curtains kindly presented by Lady Goldsmid.[7] I feel too poor to purchase anything further for it now. [...]

Affectionately,

Isaiah

1 Sir Robert Mayer (1879–1985), German-born businessman, philanthropist and music patron; founder of the Robert Mayer Concerts for Children.
2 Aline Halban had volunteered to translate *The Hedgehog and the Fox* into French and had been coming to IB's room in All Souls every afternoon to work on it. Her translation was eventually published in the French edition of RT, *Les Penseurs russes* (Paris, 1984).
3 Gregor Piatigorsky (1903–76), Russian-born cellist; married Jacqueline, daughter of Baron Édouard de Rothschild.
4 Miriam Louisa Lane (1907–2005), née Rothschild, entomologist and conservationist.
5 John Buchan (1875–1940), 1st Baron Tweedsmuir, novelist and (Scottish Unionist) politician; Governor General of Canada 1935–40.
6 'I have rented two servants' bedrooms in a pretty country house near Oxford taken by John Foster – it is a property of All Souls, a seventeenth-century post-house, and my sub-tenancy is ill viewed by John Foster's female acquaintances, [...] and yet, since I need a peaceful haven (like London) from the busy distractions of Oxford, I propose to acquire these rooms notwithstanding.' 7 August 1953 to Felix Frankfurter.
7 Presumably Lady (Rosemary Margaret) d'Avigdor-Goldsmid (1910–97), wife of Sir Henry Joseph ('Harry') d'Avigdor-Goldsmid (1909–76), banker, bullion broker and Conservative politician (MP 1955–74).

TO E. H. CARR

3 December 1954 [*manuscript*]

All Souls

Dear Ted,

Thank you for letting me see the review.[1] I have no possible demurrers until p. 3: (naturally enough! for that is where your temperate criticism begins)

1. I do not, of course, deny causation in history: indeed on p. 30 of my opusculum I positively praise the persons who, by showing how limited the area of human freedom is, substitute humane social behaviour for blind persecution; my only point is that if there is nothing but causality – no area of choice at all, however small – then we cannot go on thinking & talking as we do; 'impersonal' factors alter the area of freedom i.e. the kinds of alternatives choosable; but if they block everything, & all choice is an illusion, we must think quite differently; & if, as is the case, we can't & won't, this means that to pretend to take determinism so seriously as some do, is self deception, sloppy thinking or hypocrisy; I don't dream of denying causes in history: or the need for cool judgment: only that all causes are 'impersonal' & morally neutral: & that individuals play little part: or do as they do because they cannot help it: whereas I think they are among the main causal initiators of change (or its absence) & responsible accordingly. All I want to do is to say that individual acts cannot be wholly analysed into impersonal influences: only to the extent of 90%, say.

2. It is true that I attack overweening 'historicists': but then so does e.g. Butterfield: & I object to his views too: one of the ways of declining moral responsibility is by the humility of relativism – we are all blind, weak, sinful, children: how can men be blamed, miserable straws that we are? this seems to me the other *alibi* which won't stand up. Wd you consider mentioning that?

3. Your last sentence: do I ever say that the best history is that which is primarily concerned to moralize? no no! only that to exclude moral judgments is as unnatural as to write tracts. History is not a branch of moral philosophy; but neither is it of a non-existent sociology. Am I niggling? your little note is really perfectly fair & generous, save the very last words.

yrs
    Isaiah.

1 A draft of Carr's review of *Historical Inevitability*, published (apparently with some of IB's comments incorporated) as 'History and Morals', *The Times Literary Supplement*, 17 December 1954, 821.

TO ALICE JAMES

7 December 1954

All Souls

Dearest Alice,

You must forgive me for using this mechanical means of communicating with you but I am so fascinated by my talking machine that I cannot refuse myself the pleasure of using it for any and every occasion. [...]

Thank God my Russian lectures in London are over; I hate all lectures, but particularly lectures delivered in these bleak conditions – I cannot say that I cared much for the paragraph in the *Sunday Times*,[1] which is the one which John Finley must have sent you – however I think it was kindly intended but seemed to me a trifle vulgar and uncalled-for, but that may be over-sensitiveness. At any rate, the editor of the *Sunday Times* was so upset by the thought that I had not entirely liked it, someone must have told him, that a very humble little review which I wrote of Adlai Stevenson's Godkin lectures[2] – which I like very much – was printed in a prominent place in the centre of the *Sunday Times* on 5 December with a tremendous headline which made me out to be 'Calling America to Greatness' – I have no objection to doing so but it seems not a role I am cast for. More suitable to Sir Winston Churchill. I do not think any statesman in Europe would disagree with a single sentiment of Mr Stevenson's, and it shows the lamentable distance between us that what are regarded almost as truisms here should be regarded as brave paradoxes in some sections of the United States, or am I wrong? Talking of Sir Winston Churchill, his speech made on accepting the remarkable – harsh but by no means unfair – portrait of him painted by Graham Sutherland[3] was one of the most entertaining things I have

1 '[...] this Farinelli of the lecture-room was accorded, after his final cadenza, an ovation more appropriate to the opera-house than to the Gower Street Anatomy Theatre, where the benches are penitentially hard and the visitor is greeted on arrival by a row of crouching skeletons. [...] the Northcliffe Lectures were recorded, on the spot, for retransmission by the BBC. Listeners will miss, of course, the peculiar fixity of Mr Berlin's gaze, as he re-creates with warm personal affection the predicaments of Herzen. Nor will they see him throw back his head, like a sea-lion in search of a high-thrown mackerel; but they will learn once again how it is possible to preserve, within a scrupulous academical framework, the wit and high courtesy of private conversation.' *Sunday Times*, 14 November 1954, 3 – in the Atticus column, at the time the preserve of Ian Fleming, but according to IB (12 January 1955 to Arthur Schlesinger) written on this occasion by John Russell (471/1).

2 'Calling America to Greatness', review (*Sunday Times*, 5 December 1954, 6) of Adlai Stevenson's *Call to Greatness* (New York, 1954), the published version of the three Edwin L. Godkin Lectures, on 'A Troubled World', which Stevenson had given at Harvard in March 1954.

3 For Churchill's 80th birthday on 30 November 1954, the Houses of Parliament commissioned (as a gift) a portrait by Graham Vivian Sutherland (1903–80), painter and designer. Churchill loathed the painting, which accurately showed his advancing age and declining energy (Lady Churchill later destroyed it). At the presentation ceremony Churchill's comments were ambiguous: 'The portrait is a remarkable example of modern art. It certainly combines force and candour.' [Speech broadcast on BBC Radio, Home Service, 30 November 1954; transcript at BBC Written Archives Centre.]

ever listened to. I listened to it on the wireless and the whole occasion was
extremely gay and agreeable. Nobody today enjoys life as much as people like
Sir Winston Churchill and Sir Thomas Beecham. When one listens to them
talking, even when they are talking nonsense, or rather when Sir Thomas
conducts and Sir Winston talks, it is like listening to the old prima donnas,
Caruso or Tetrazzini,[1] sing – there is no question but that their voices were
far far superior to any that one listens to now, however cracked and old the
record, there is absolutely no doubt of it, and from the same rich cornucopia
of temperament and passion flow the gifts of these 80-year-old virtuosi. My
love for the nineteenth century is really assuming alarming proportions –
I like almost everything that reminds me of it and almost nothing which
reminds me of our own times. This cannot be right, but I do not seem able
to help it.

To return to private life. Maurice is well, the Cecils are well, John Sparrow
is well, we are all in quite good condition. I have had bronchitis and been in
bed for about ten days, fortunately in London, for All Souls is no place to
have even the slightest of distempers; the scout visits one twice, otherwise
one is as abandoned as in the Sahara desert. On the other hand, to lie comfortably at home in London with no excessive pain seems to me a form of
bliss, I read books and even think a little. This is more than I normally do
at Oxford. [...] I wrote a vignette of Dr Weizmann for a Jerusalem paper[2]
and – since I can no longer avoid dichotomies – talked what I daresay is a lot
of rot about there being two kinds of statesmen in the world, the inhuman
over-simplified monolithic fanatical, slightly mythical ones like de Gaulle,
Garibaldi and Hitler – some good, some bad – as opposed to the subtle,
richly endowed, infinitely sensitive multiplex ones like Cavour,[3] the late Mr
Roosevelt, Lloyd George and my old friend Weizmann. I really must stop
writing articles and thinking fanciful thoughts and playing games and sit
down and write a book. So I shall proceed to London on 15 December and
remain there immured and guarded closely by my mother until 15 January,
by which time I shall have written quite a lot, since I always do everything in
starts. Having started I then go on frantically and fanatically in order to get it
over, like people walking very fast uphill, not because it is easy but in order
to make the agony last as little time as possible. I detest lecturing, I detest
writing, in fact I have decided that I detest all work and have to make myself
do it by the most appalling efforts. By nature I am indolent and could let
things drift past me without stirring a finger to alter them, merely uttering

1 Enrico Caruso (1873–1921), tenor, and Luisa Tetrazzini (1871–1940), soprano, world-famous Italian
  opera singers.
2 'Men Who Lead', *Jerusalem Post*, 2 November 1954, 5–6; reprinted as 'The Anatomy of Leadership'
  in *Jewish Frontier* 21 No 12 (December 1954), 13–17, and as 'Chaim Weizmann's Leadership' in POI.
3 Camillo Benso, conte di Cavour (1810–61), leading player in the unification of Italy; Prime
  Minister of Piedmont–Sardinia 1852–9, 1860–1.

a small cry of indignation now and then which I myself know will not stop events.

I have sent you, by way of proving that I do sometimes do a little work, a lecture – 70 or so pages long – which I honestly – not even I – cannot have delivered in one go at the London School of Economics in London, called *Historical Inevitability*. There is really no need to read it – as I say I only send it as a token of the fact that I am not altogether idle, partly to convince myself.

I am glad you like Hampshire – he is a serious and idealistic young man – who falsely believes himself to be very tough and realistic, and reminds me of nothing so much as the young Russian intellectual of the nineteenth century who believed that science and progress and the destruction of priests, kings, soldiers etc. would almost automatically regenerate the world.

As for Rowland, I know exactly what you mean. He gets me down no less than you; my lot is cast among such persons[1] in some ways much more than I care – and I have to forgive feelings which each month and year grow more pungent and antipathetic to that form of life and that kind of character. I am by nature a great appeaser and try and adjust myself to things I dislike almost unconsciously; nevertheless I find the quality of feeling – which I think is what we most dislike – is at times almost unbearable. Dear Rowland! I have letters from him which complain of solitude, which I think is very real; he is shrewd, kind, fearless and perverse; genuinely civilised, not a little snobbish and talks too much; when I stayed with him in Camden, that was almost too much for me, certainly after three days, and I shall never do it again. But I like him and respect and am exasperated with him and cannot be genuinely intimate with him for reasons which you will understand; he is loyal, affectionate, understanding and commendably independent, I vote for him: but Parker Poe[2] and Henry McIlhenny[3] are too much for me. Everything that I am and believe and admire goes against it; I try and understand, I try and conceive that one must be tolerant and sympathetic and enter into other values and other forms of life, but I cannot, I daresay it has something to do with heredity and upbringing and not having been to an English public school, and being as firmly grounded as I am in old nineteenth-century human values. [...]

I long to go to London and bury myself in my little room in the house you visited and get on with writing a book. Term is a terrible waste, one cannot settle down to anything, too many people come and go and even though I lead a much quieter life than I did in Cambridge, Mass., still it is full enough. In my mother's house I really can be locked away and she is a wonderful

1 Homosexuals.
2 Parker Barrington Poe (1914–91), who in 1949 had married the wealthy (and much older) horse-woman Elizabeth ('Pansy') Ireland (1897–1978), the owner of the Pebble Hill estate in Georgia.
3 Henry Plumer McIlhenny (1910–86), wealthy US art collector (his family's money came from his Irish grandfather's invention of the gas meter); Curator, Philadelphia Art Museum, 1939–64; a bachelor, noted for his hospitality in Philadelphia and at his castle in Donegal.

protector. My last social engagement will be tomorrow when I shall go to lunch to meet Anthony Head and his wife[1] (he is the Minister of War and she is charming), John Betjeman[2] and Elizabeth Cavendish[3] (David Cecil's niece, I doubt if you noticed her at Violet Bonham Carter's party) – after that I shall go to a party in the Italian Embassy – Brosio[4] is leaving London to go to Washington and is a charming man, a Turin lawyer, with good principles, of great modesty and intelligence, who spent four very profitable years in Moscow – and after that no more social life, and hard work. I really am capable not only of forming, but of keeping such resolutions. I was visited by somebody from the Rockefeller Trust[5] who asked me if I needed any money and I said no, not this year, I did not want to be taken away from here, I only wanted to be left alone. Unless I write at least two books in the course of the next two or three years I shall feel dreadfully ashamed. These are my New Year resolutions and with them I send my fondest love to you and to Billy and I am sure that if my mother was here she would do the same.

Yours, with much love
Isaiah

TO VIOLET BONHAM CARTER

[16 December 1954, *manuscript*]

All Souls[6]

Dearest Violet

I have procured a copy of the *N. Statesman* & read the piece[7] & it is truly infamous. Not that one ought to mind an attack from that particular quarter – it is nothing but bitter boiling class conscious spite by someone who plainly does not know you at all – there is a plain difference between informed & ignorant malignity – but uses your name & reputation to hang his (or her) accumulated *ressentiment*[8] – against distinction, charm, fastidiousness, every

---

1 Lady (Dorothea Louise, 'Dot') Head (1907–87), née Ashley-Cooper, daughter of the 9th Earl of Shaftesbury; Viscountess Head 1960.
2 John Betjeman (1906–84), poet and critic; later (1972–84) Poet Laureate.
3 Lady Elizabeth Georgiana Alice Cavendish (b. 1926), daughter of the 10th Duke of Devonshire; Extra Lady-in-Waiting to Princess Margaret 1951–2002.
4 Manlio Brosio (1897–1980), Italian lawyer, politician and diplomat; Ambassador to Soviet Union 1947–51, to UK 1952–4, to US 1955–61; later (1964–71) Secretary-General of NATO.
5 Perhaps a slightly fanciful account of the meeting: the Rockefeller Foundation had just turned down the request for funding made by IB and Morton White.
6 Probably sent from Hampstead.
7 The *New Statesman* had published a profile of VBC, complete with cartoon by Vicky, entitled 'Last Asquithian', in which VBC (referred to as 'Lady Vi') was gently mocked as a 'fully conscious member of the ruling class – without anyone to rule', who, 'exiled from her promised land, has remained indomitably determined to do good to those who do not know what is good for them' (*New Statesman and Nation*, 11 December 1954, 781). IB joined Harold Nicolson, Raymond Mortimer and Rose Macaulay in a letter of protest (*New Statesman and Nation*, 8 January 1955, 45).
8 'Resentment'.

kind of civilised quality – it is an old war – since Rousseau – between the civilised and superior and their enemies – not just barbarians, but corrupt and resentful victims & casualties of the social system – moral & emotional cripples of various kinds – sometimes brazen thunderers like Carlyle or D. H. Lawrence[1] or A. J. P. Taylor, sometimes stabbing from mean & squalid dark corners, anonymous poison pens (something similar was done in the N.S & N[2] to Gaitskell, & for much the same reasons – because he is tidy & decent Wykehamist etc) – when it happens to me – & it has again & again, always to my astonishment – I think myself so mild and harmless – I mind terribly – even when I know that it will soon be forgotten – & hasn't been read by the whole world (which one imagines it *must* be) & that one hasn't really been caught redhanded in some awful crime – that is why I felt such waves of relief & sympathy when I read in Virginia Woolf's diaries how much she minded the least little criticism – she who seemed so disdainful & aloof – how you feel, I do not know; I hope you are protected by enough proper contempt; if one carries any kind of banner high enough, & doesn't spend one's time in appeasing everyone all the time – like Hugh Walpole,[3] poor man – some mud is bound to be flung by guttersnipes: & guttersnipey is what the "profile" in the N. *Statesman* seemed to me to be. I am now particularly glad that I have never never contributed a syllable to this great radical journal. Nor ever shall, so long as it continues under its present management; I read it as I do *Time Magazine*: with an ashamed & horrified fascination – like inability to rid oneself of obsessive but disgusting tunes – but enough about this. As I do feel ashamed of not writing to you about your brother's death[4] – but I have an awful exaggerated fear of not being able to communicate when impalpable personal relationships are involved – like my inability to reply to your wonderful letter to me about my father – I feel petrified & no words come. Despite my advanced years I cannot really cope successfully with the invisible & the untouchable – perhaps one day I shall be able to; & so I am exposed & vulnerable beyond necessity. May I come in to see you one evening in early January? How is Cressida?

My love

Isaiah.

---

1 D(avid) H(erbert) Lawrence (1885–1930), novelist and poet.

2 The *New Statesman and Nation* (incorporating *The Weekend Review*) was the official title of the *New Statesman* 1934–57.

3 Sir Hugh Seymour Walpole (1884–1941), novelist; for IB's memorable description of him see L1 193–5.

4 VBC's brother, Lord (Cyril) Asquith of Bishopstone (1890–1954), Lord of Appeal in Ordinary since 1951, had died in August.

TO HAMILTON FISH ARMSTRONG

23 December 1954

All Souls

Dear Ham,

First my love and best wishes to you and Christa[1] for Christmas and otherwise, with much affection, and thank you for your letter. I am in bed with a variety of diseases, none individually fatal but accumulatively disagreeable. My mind is sluggish, my outlook melancholy. Yet it is not this that makes me, with deep reluctance, as always, close my ears to your siren call. For there is nothing I like so much as yielding – if only as an alibi for my 'proper' work in Oxford. But this time I really must not yield.

I believe in national character, certainly for the purposes of conversation, and my favourite Russian of the nineteenth century, Herzen (if you like I will write one day for you an article on his excellent 'Letters to an Old Comrade', which explain to his dear friend Bakunin why a violent revolution will ruin the bad old world but produce a worse one instead – or would this be too historical for you? It is the best essay on the future of socialism I know, written in 1868, and totally unread) – to return, dear old Herzen is always inveighing against the Germans with great wit and charm and unfairness; so does Bakunin – they are funny about the French too, and about the English, and, of course, about the Russians. And there is nothing I like better than entertaining and unforgettable caricatures of this kind. ('When an Englishman or an American says "I am an Englishman" or "I am an American", he means "I am a free man." When a German says "I am a German", he means "My Emperor is more powerful than all your kings, and the German officer who is strangling me now will soon strangle you all."[2] This, by Bakunin, is fairly typical.)

However, I have no idea what has happened in the Soviet Union – whether there is 'a new Soviet man', whether Turgenev's sympathetic, weak, introspective men and strong, ardent women do or do not survive. I don't know that the new Soviet man has been liquidated so entirely. He is still being plugged, more or less, not as intensely as before, because everything seems to have subsided a little, though Deutscher's articles in *The Times*[3] about the mellowing of the old regime seem to me clever rubbish. [...]

Yours ever,

Isaiah

---

1 Armstrong's German-born third wife, the former Christa von Tippelskirch (b. 1917), translator, writer and photographer.

2 From Bakunin's 'Gosudarstvennost´ i anarkhiya' (1873), in *Archives Bakounine*, ed. Arthur Lehning (Leiden, 1961–81), vol. 3, 159/358; Michael Bakunin, *Statism and Anarchy*, trans. and ed. Marshall S. Shatz (Cambridge, 1990), 192. See also RT2 126 and 431 above. IB here omits a key phrase: the explanation of what the German means should begin 'I am a slave, but my Emperor [...]'.

3 'Ferment of Ideas in Russia', *The Times*, 16, 17 and 18 November 1954.

By now the difficulties of communicating with Aline, abroad on a family skiing holiday, were causing IB acute emotional tension and his health was giving increasing cause for worry:

I went to the doctor yesterday, endless X-rays, blood tests etc. finally the Cardiograph: funny wobbly lines. He thinks I have a virus infection of the epicardis – the bag in which the heart is contained – that it will pass, is not chronic or coronary or anything – after 2 weeks of "complete rest" – then a further cardiogram – then if all right, permission to return to Oxford; if not, 2 more weeks etc. – The general line is that on ne badine pas avec le coeur[1] – have I had emotional 'tension' of any kind? No, of course not – well then it is just an unaccountable virus – like pneumonia – & one must wait for it to die out.[2]

The reading which occupied IB's time during his enforced rest, combined with reflections on his emotional commitment to Aline, led him to a philosophical revaluation:

I have been reading, of all people, the detestable Sartre. The novels are too slimy & dark, but he is a *very* clever man & his moral philosophy *is* what I think I ¾ believe. What a fool I was to be deceived by Freddie's articles in *Horizon*[3] at the end of the war which concentrated on Sartre's obscure logic & his attitudes to sex & 'proved' it all bogus. It is not. It is most imaginative & bold & important.[4] In effect it says that all theories of life & morals – scientific, metaphysical, theological – are human efforts to s'arranger[5] – to pretend that the chance & chaos of circumstances are "explainable" in some *tidy*, cosy, easy fashion – rationalistic *alibis* to justify one's own weaknesses, vices, misfortunes – to show that it must all be all right "in the end" & that we cannot help doing what we do – weak feathers in the wind – & must "sacrifice" & go against our instincts in the name of some vast abstraction – State, God, Humanity, Family,

1 'One mustn't play games with the heart.'
2 31 December 1954 to Aline Halban.
3 A. J. Ayer, 'Novelist-Philosophers: V – Jean-Paul Sartre', *Horizon* 12 No 67 (July 1945), 12–26, No 68 (August 1945), 101–10.
4 To Morton White IB commented 'And there is this to be said about Sartre and his friends, that such questions as the moral sanction for conduct – the justification for Communist atrocities, the notion of personal liberty as an autonomous being, as opposed to one obeying authority, or drifting along a stream not of one's seeking, etc., above all the notion that all theories and all rationalisations are vicious fallacies as such, alibis invented by human beings to save themselves from the necessity of responsibility for their choices – for which no reason can ever in principle be found – all this seems to me original and important, and certainly to be found in literature from the seventeenth [century] onwards and left comparatively alone by professional philosophers, who concentrated on the natural sciences and when they did talk about morals and the like, chose their examples from too trivial and philistine a world and analysed none of the problems which appeared central and agonising to sensitive and superior persons. Kant, however, did deal with problems that agonised his contemporaries – so did Hegel, so did Comte and J. S. Mill. But after 1880, even including William James and Dewey, I don't think anybody did in the sense in which Sartre at least tried to. And a mark ought to be given to him for that.' From comments, sent on 11 January 1955, on the manuscript of MW's *The Age of Analysis: Twentieth Century Philosophers* (New York, 1955).
5 'Come to terms with' (the way things are).

Duty, etc. etc. Whereas all this is illusion; the world is not morally directed anywhere; it is just what it is: neither good nor bad: just events & persons & things – we do what we can with them: we are, apart from physical weakness etc, free: if we plead passion as an excuse, it is not: we could control it: if we don't it is because we choose not to: if we go for advice to a priest or a friend, it is because we know in some sense what they are likely to say, & choose them ourselves for that reason, freely, ourselves. We are what we make ourselves: Marx, Freud, are all attempts to treat us as material objects played on by outside forces: we know that this is not so: we choose, we are responsible, we commit ourselves, & when we don't – when we let ourselves drift or be managed blindly by others, we know that we choose passivity, & we can if we like, but it is still we who are responsible & answerable if anybody asks why; we need not give reasons for our behaviour but we must not give false ones – such as psychological rot or conventional nonsense: or rather if we do, we are concealing something & deceiving ourselves or others: which again we can do if we like, but it is unworthy, undignified, squalid: or at least some people feel lies to be so. Surely this is true, largely: we are what we feel, do, intend, & want.[1]

TO ARTHUR SCHLESINGER

12 January 1955

[As from] All Souls

Dear Arthur,

Do write me a letter. I have been in bed now for three weeks with a peculiar amalgam of illnesses – some very normal and almost agreeable, like bronchitis, sinusitis, flu etc., which produce no great pain and keep one in a state of total immobility, which I adore. My doctor,[2] however, who believes in full use of all the instruments of modern technique, has now X-rayed me from all directions, applied every possible electric computing machine to me, and insists that there is a mysterious deviation on my cardiac chart, the electrocardiogram – which indicates an eccentric condition of something called the pericardium – the great specialist[3] to whom I was sent in London, however, thinks this is not so, and that the deviation is due to some abnormal workings of my eccentric organism, and that I am, in fact, a mild but firmly set monster. So that what would in other cases indicate grave disturbances, in my case indicate nothing at all. ⟨2nd specialist[4] is slightly more ominous: & says my *nerves* are in a terrible state & my heart an enigma – so Harvard is

1 3 January 1955 to Aline Halban.
2 Dr Jacob Snowman (1871?–1959), the Berlins' General Practitioner; a well-known family doctor in Hampstead.
3 Sir John Parkinson (1885–1976), cardiologist; long-term consultant physician, London Hospital and National Heart Hospital; President, British Cardiac Society, 1951–5.
4 Probably Dr Leo Rau (c.1905–64), who was involved in IB's treatment at about this time and on 18 March noted IB's subsequent recovery with surprise: 'I looked at your ECG again, and the change is remarkable [...]. There is no doubt that the earlier ones were pathological.'

lucky not to have me this year.) While the dispute is going on about me I am in bed, have been told to take 'a complete rest', which, as you can imagine, is extremely strenuous – I like immobility, but not rest. That is, I like talking on the telephone, dictating letters, reading books, and private polemics – what I don't like is people on tiptoes –while all this is going on I am the recipient of a certain amount of idle gossip. So, for example, I believe there is a genuine row going on in the offices of the *New Statesman*. The *Observer*, as you must have noticed, said that Kingsley Martin was going and then was forced to print a very prominent démenti[1] by the *New Statesman*, which shows that what they said must be absolutely true.[2] And so, apparently, it turns out to be. The story is that John Freeman[3] is to succeed him, but I don't know who Freeman is, only that he is a fanatical left-wing socialist – a Bevanite[4] – with violent and stupid views on almost everything – his integrity is not questioned but his judgement is apparently appalling and the reason for having to appoint him is that he is about to marry somebody's wife[5] in such circumstances as make his departure from politics advisable (for God's sake don't refer to me in this connection ever, it is obviously libellous, sueable, and probably perfectly false – I got it all from the *Spectator*, which is the hostile rival organ), and therefore will be left without money and therefore must get a job and therefore the *New Statesman* seems the best one. I shall be sorry to see old Kingsley Martin go because, although fuzzy and not very honest, he was a kindly, old-fashioned idiot journalist of an absurd, irresponsible, madly irritating, but in some sense human, sort, whereas Freeman, from all accounts, is a humourless monster, a dreary third-rate fanatic. I assume Crossman and company remain in their usual positions. [...] What an awful man J. B. Priestley[6] is – I fear it is partly because I have read a hearty, Philistine piece on James Joyce[7] by him in the *Observer* or the *Sunday Times* – I think the *Sunday Times* – in which he was mainly blamed for not writing like Priestley and in which a scathing reference is made to Harry Levin. It shows

1 'Denial'.
2 It wasn't. Kingsley Martin did not retire from the *New Statesman* until 1960.
3 John Horace Freeman (b. 1915), Labour politician, political journalist, editor and broadcaster; MP 1945–55; Parliamentary Secretary, Ministry of Supply, 1947–51 (resigned with Aneurin Bevan and Harold Wilson over proposed introduction of National Health Service charges); assistant editor, *New Statesman*, 1951–8, deputy editor 1958–60, editor 1961–5; interviewer for BBC TV's *Face to Face* 1959–62; later (1965–8) British High Commissioner in India and (1969–71) British Ambassador, Washington.
4 The group of left-wing Labour MPs who followed Aneurin 'Nye' Bevan (1897–1960), who had been responsible for setting up the National Health Service, in opposing the shift in government expenditure from social reforms to defence.
5 Freeman married four times, but his next marriage was not until several years after the death of his second wife in 1957.
6 John Boynton Priestley (1894–1984), prolific and popular journalist, novelist, playwright and essayist.
7 J. B. Priestley, 'gems choice in fuchsia yaws' (*sic*), review of James Joyce, *Dubliners*, *Sunday Times*, 2 January 1955, 5.

how much I must despise Priestley if I really mind on Harry's behalf, and I do. Partly my view of him is coloured by the suspicion that he is about to attack me in the *New Statesman* for my latest piece of obscurantism,[1] of which I sent you a copy – an awful LSE lecture. Or if he doesn't attack me Crossman will. I have decided that, although I have never read a line by him, I feel affinities with the late Lord Acton and shall ultimately develop into a hideous compound of Herzen and Acton, with dashes of radical positivism and existentialism loosely thrown in. Could anything sound more bogus – more pseudo-avant-garde – more awful in every way – oh, I forgot to add a dash of Niebuhr, which all right though it may be in itself, makes the cocktail even more depraved. Anyway I feel at the moment a cross between Joad and Philip Toynbee, so you see how low I have sunk, how depressed I feel. Stupid and awful as I think Philip Toynbee to be – fond as I am of him personally – still I think him superior in some vague way to his terrible father, who, again, is a very nice man, but whose latest work[2] is a monstrosity of monstrosities. I *want* Trevor-Roper to persecute him[3] by the vilest weapons in his armoury.

But enough of all this fierceness. Do write me a letter and comfort me. I enclose the usual enclosure,[4] the proceeds of which press to your bosom in eternal remembrance of me. My deepest love to Marian, to whom I still owe a letter. How is Archie?[5] Joe (who is responsible for the deepest rifts yet in our Conservative Party)?[6] You will be pleased to see that my puff for the ex-governor[7] produced a sale of 400 copies of his book the day after it appeared. After that sales declined again. So you might employ me in the next campaign.

Yours ever,

PS Your letter of January 3, just to hand, is a source of great delight. [. . .] It is true that the *Sunday Times* printed a gossip item about my solemn series of lectures in the Anatomical Theatre of University College by a horrible

---

1 *Historical Inevitability.*
2 Vols 7–10 of Arnold Toynbee's *A Study of History* were published by OUP in 1954.
3 In his review of vols 7–10 of *A Study of History* ('Testing the Toynbee System', *Sunday Times*, 17 October 1954, 5), Trevor-Roper had condemned Toynbee's 'terrible perversion of history', and to Bernard Berenson (8 September 1954; *Letters from Oxford*, 152) he had described Toynbee's pronouncements as 'the most arrant rubbish'. Trevor-Roper's later onslaught on Toynbee's work as 'the religion of Mish-Mash, of which he is the prophet and Messiah' ('Arnold Toynbee's Millennium', *Encounter* 8 No 6 (June 1957), 14–28, at 27) did major damage to Toynbee's reputation.
4 Probably financial: Schlesinger acted as IB's agent in many US transactions.
5 Archibald MacLeish.
6 Joe Alsop's reports from Formosa about the skirmishing between the rival Communist and Nationalist governments of China (which threatened wider conflict, and possible nuclear war between the US and the USSR) consistently stressed the need to resist the Communist threat. But the Conservative Party had also to consider the forthcoming UK General Election (held in May 1955).
7 See 461/2.

pseudo-aesthete, whom I know quite well, called John Russell,[1] who thought he was being very nice about me when he described my performances as those of a farinelli.[2] I did not exactly protest but my views became known to the Editor,[3] who is a late Fellow of my College, and the glorification of my humble review of Stevenson's book was, I think, in fact intended as compensation. At any rate that is my own version of what happened. There is no official sanction for it. As for the Yugoslav Ambassador,[4] that too, alas, is true. I was visited by a monster called Frank [sc. Mike] Todd[5] – I know nothing about him, and am much exhilarated to hear that he is a night-club impresario – who informed me that he was using sixty thousand Yugoslav troops for his *War and Peace* film, that Sherwood[6] is writing the script – he did not engage my services as historical adviser – indeed I have not seen him since – but he did hint that my fortune would be made, owing to the billions that this magnificent film, done by some hitherto unused method, would create – millions of buses of schoolchildren would be run towards it – all film stars would be delighted to take part in it, simply as a religious act of homage to the greatest of all writers and the greatest of all subjects, etc., etc. All he wanted from me was, in a few pages, to convey the 'message' of the immortal work. I demurred a little at this – I was much [*word(s) missing*] by the whole visit – he entered the room with a cad's camel-hair coat and a huge cigar – he really was the stage American of the 1920s – and told him that I was not sure whether the message would be suitable; for instance, Tolstoy was hotly anti-New Deal, did not care for official security – did not believe in the common man in the sense in which he, Todd, obviously believed in him etc., etc. This shook him a bit, but he nevertheless told me he would come back and bribe me with a Pactolus[7] of gold. I have since then had several affable telegrams, but no new Epiphany. I have not seen Hampshire and shall carefully enquire about your new news from him. If you are talking about mediocrity you should come *here*. You should come here in any case!

⟨My poor LSE Lecture is getting an appalling press[8] – gibes from the horrible

1 John Russell (1919–2008), art critic, *Sunday Times*, 1949–74.
2 Farinelli was the stage name of Carlo Broschi (1705–82), celebrated Italian castrato.
3 Harry Hodson.
4 Vladimir Velebit (1907–2004), Yugoslav Ambassador in London 1953–6.
5 Michael ('Mike') Todd (1907–58), né Avrom Hirsch Goldbogen, theatre and film producer involved in the development of a high-definition widescreen film format (Todd-A[merican] O[ptical]), for which he was seeking a suitable film. Candidates included *War and Peace, Moby Dick, The Man Who Would Be King* and *Richard III*; having failed to obtain Russian co-operation for *War and Peace*, Todd eventually filmed *Around the World in 80 Days*, a spectacular success.
6 Robert Emmet Sherwood (1896–1955), US playwright; his pre-war plays often depicted the futility of war, but he came to support US involvement in the Second World War, and worked as a speechwriter for FDR.
7 A river in Asia Minor (now in Turkey) from whose sands gold was washed.
8 The reviews of *Historical Inevitability* that IB (with characteristic over-sensitivity) recoils from are: Isaac Deutscher, 'Determinists All', *Observer*, 16 January, 1955, 8; E. H. Carr, 'History and Morals',

Deutscher in the *Observer* – cracks from Carr in *TLS* – vicious onslaught from the Christian neo-Burkeans in the *Spectator* – I am dead and buried.⟩

TO JOHN LEHMANN[1]

12 January 1955

[As from] All Souls

Dear John,

[...] I should love to print in your magazine, if we are both [alive] at the time, an account of a visit[2] which I paid to an eminent poetess in Leningrad in 1945, under marvellously romantic conditions – her conversations with me – and the whole scene, which is certainly unique in my experience and vivid in my memory. I shall write it down anyway, but would not like to publish it while she is still alive. She was 61[3] and suffering from heart trouble when I saw her in 1945, and cannot live very long, alas. Akhmatova is her name and when she dies we shall all know. If you hold me to *this* promise, I promise you to keep it; and no BBC or anything else shall win me from it. [Dan Davin?][4] would retain his right of reprinting it at some time in a volume of Russian essays. It really is a story worth having, not because of me, but because of the extraordinary circumstances which surrounded my visit, the fact that she is a poetess of some genius who had not seen anyone from the West since 1917, and because of her [literary] and personal opinions. I had thought of printing it in the *New Yorker*, which would certainly accept it. But if you want me to do it in the *London Magazine* I shall do so. [...]

TO ALAN PRYCE-JONES

20 January 1955

[As from] All Souls

Dear Alan,

[...] Condorcet,[5] as the father of all liberalism and all radicalism in Europe, should surely have a proper review done of his ideas – which seems to be a perfectly good peg for intelligent reflections. Me it moves to tears, others may

---

TLS, 17 December 1954, 821; and Henry Fairlie (511/1), 'Mr Berlin's Anti-Determinism', *Spectator*, 14 January 1955, 48.

1 John Frederick Lehmann (1907–87), literary editor; Managing Director, John Lehmann Ltd, 1946–52; founding editor, *London Magazine*, 1954–61; brother of the novelist Rosamond Lehmann.

2 Not written until 1980 as 'Meetings with Russian Writers in 1945 and 1956', in PI.

3 In fact 56.

4 Dan(iel) Marcus Davin (1913–90), New Zealander of Irish descent, academic publisher and author; OUP 1945–78. IB had corresponded with him about a volume of pieces on Russian topics.

5 IB was requesting a *TLS* review of Condorcet's *Sketch for a Historical Picture of the Progress of the Human Mind*, trans. June Barraclough, with an introduction by Stuart Hampshire (London, [1955]), the third volume in Weidenfeld & Nicolson's 'Library of Ideas', edited by Hampshire, Wollheim and IB.

think it rather outworn and not tough enough. Whom can I recommend to you as a possible reviewer? Stephen Spender (who shares C's ideas whether he knows it or not)? I think perhaps not. But a really good thing would be done for you by Professor A. Momigliano,[1] the Professor of Roman History in University College, London, who is an exceedingly interesting and remarkable man with thoughts on general history and historiography, as well as his own proper subject. It is true that the Warden of Wadham does not like him much but this ... If he refuses there is Venturi,[2] whom I suppose you would get at the University of Genoa. Failing these, somewhat on the lower scale, come Cole and, bottom, Cobban,[3] or someone you may think of yourself. At any rate, I implore and beg you that this splendid, touching figure of the eighteenth century be not entirely forgotten between the daggers of the Marxist left and the nets of the Burkeian right, both of whom are falling upon me at the moment with the utmost ferocity. Am I the only follower of John Stuart Mill left alive? Russell and I? Can you think of any others?

I do hope you are well, and really we might sometimes meet.

Yours ever,

Isaiah

⟨You aren't *really* leaving *T.L.S.*?[4] If you are I should like to beg you to think of J. Joll.⟩

TO DAVID ASTOR

27 January 1955 [*carbon*]

All Souls

My dear David,

You must forgive me for the letter that follows, and if you think it a waste of your time, as it may well be – throw it away, and think no more about the subject. It is concerned with my latest imbroglio with the *Observer*. There is curious ill luck which seems to dog my steps whenever I come into any relation with your admirable journal. Years ago, in 1948, you and William Clark[5] commissioned an article from me, and when I wrote it you would not print it and so it was printed in the *Listener* and involved me in a terrible row with Beaverbrook. I never did understand why it was not accepted

---

1 Arnaldo Dante Momigliano (1908–87), Italian-born Professor of Ancient History, London (UCL), 1951–75.
2 Franco Venturi (1914–94), Italian historian of the Enlightenment, of liberal and socialist ideas, and of Russian populism; cultural attaché, Moscow, 1947–50; Professor of History, Cagliari, 1951–4, Genoa 1955–8, Turin 1958–84.
3 Alfred Cobban (1901–68), Professor of French History, London (UCL), 1953–68.
4 Pryce-Jones stayed at the *TLS* until 1959.
5 William Donaldson Clark (1916–85), London editor, *Encyclopædia Britannica*, 1946–9; diplomatic correspondent, *Observer*, 1950–5; Public Relations Adviser to the Prime Minister 1955–6; a former wartime colleague of IB's in the US.

but did not worry myself about the matter. Two years later your Mr Rose[1] asked me to review the reprint of Mrs Garnett's translation of Turgenev's novels, which I did from America.[2] You then printed a furious but court-eously expressed letter by David Garnett, defending his mother's memory against what he (not altogether wrongly) took to be a somewhat patronising attitude on my part. I was rung up by Alastair Buchan[3] from Washington, who said he would cable my reply if I wished to say anything on the subject; so with considerable trouble and great (in my then not very affluent dollar circumstances) expense to myself, I did cable a reply, but this was neither printed in the *Observer* nor acknowledged – and I then received a very courte-ous letter from your Mr Kilmartin,[4] months later, explaining that it had been lost in the office and that they were very sorry etc., all of which I accepted in perfectly good part (and still do). I only quote these things in order to explain that the latest incident seems to follow the same fatal pattern set up by impersonal agencies of a sinister and malevolent sort, whose nature I cannot begin to fathom. Kilmartin, who has always treated me with most exquisite courtesy and is always trying to get me to review books which I always find unsuitable, telephoned to me about ten days ago and said that a review was about to appear of my latest pamphlet, on *Historical Inevitability*, by Isaac Deutscher, that it was 'very critical', and did I want to reply to it? I said that I thought it wrong in principle for authors to reply to reviewers; even when facts were misstated and views grossly misrepresented; that I assumed that Deutscher's article would be unfriendly, since the whole gist of my thesis was directly aimed at his own cherished beliefs. And added that if he wanted to stir up controversy – to which I had no possible objection – I did not wish to take part in it myself, but if he invited other persons, say Dr Popper, who would probably sympathise with me rather than Deutscher in this subject – he was perfectly welcome to do so as far as I was concerned, and suggested one or two other names. The review duly appeared and I must confess was nastier than I had conceived possible. I must own to you at once that I have the greatest contempt for Deutscher. I do not believe him to be a man honest even in terms in his own Marxist framework; I distrust him as a person and as a writer and think his book on Stalin[5] a deception, and his attitude towards the Soviet Union is too unsympathetic to me – he seems to me in his views of Russia rather like one of those Germans who

1 Eliot Joseph Benn ('Jim') Rose (1909–99), literary editor, *Observer*, 1948–51; Director, International Press Institute, Zurich, 1951–62; later (1973–80) Chairman, Penguin Books.

2 265/5.

3 Alastair Francis Buchan (1918–76), son of the novelist John Buchan (1st Baron Tweedsmuir); assistant editor, *The Economist*, 1948–51; Washington correspondent, *Observer*, 1951–5, diplomatic and defence correspondent 1955–8; later (1972–6) Montague Burton Professor of International Relations, Oxford.

4 Terence Kevin Kilmartin (1922–91), literary editor, *Observer*, 1952–86.

5 *Stalin: A Political Biography* (London, 1949).

thought Hitler was perfectly splendid until, say, 1938, and that he committed blunders by fighting the Russians, or the like, and so betrayed the Germans' future. This is what Deutscher's attitude towards the Bolsheviks seems to me to be; he is a diffident Bolshevik, and not a defender of any kind of liberal values at all – but also I think him cunning, dishonest and cheap by comparison with E. H. Carr, with whom I have had my rows – he is a sweet human being and a decent public personality. Be that as it may, the review appeared, and after a certain amount of specious praise, seemed to me to be nothing but a mockery and a travesty of my views and ascribed to me views which I certainly do not hold and which, so far as I know, no human being holds.[1] However, I stuck to my original resolve and preserved what is called a dignified silence. Authors publish books, reviewers publish reviews, and the authors must take them stoically, and that is that.

My friend, Richard Wollheim, however, decided to take up the cudgels on my behalf and 'rallied round'. He wrote a letter, which he did not show me, to the *Observer*, and had a letter from your Mr Davy,[2] explaining, (1) that it was rather long, (2) that Deutscher might wish to reply and this would be a bore, (3) that the readers would have to know something about Deutscher's review and about my pamphlet, which they might not have retained, 4) that it was a subject of small public interest. And consequently, he said he would not print the letter, though he offered to send it on to Deutscher, which would have been a perfectly useless thing to do, since Deutscher is interested in the truth less than in any other aspect of things whatsoever. (His articles on the Soviet Union today[3] have, I suppose, been more frequently falsified by events than those of any other Soviet expert. About that he is marvellously unblushing.) This is the bit which I cannot understand: if you print David Garnett when he attacks me, even though you don't print my reply, if you print Bill Empson[4] and other people who criticise reviews, if in general it is your practice to print letters by reputable persons – and Richard is a very respectable reviewer and philosopher – then why this protection of Deutscher? To say there is no space cannot be right, since Kilmartin solicited a rejoinder from me on the subject. On the whole, I am well content to let things be – the less said about Deutscher and me the better, and the tussle might have been unedifying, since there is nothing in Deutscher's review to

---

1 IB also damned Deutscher's review to Terence Kilmartin: 'he used the time-honoured method of Lenin [...] of attributing views to his opponent which he does not hold and then knocking [them] down with triumph. [...] he accuses me of one or two mis-statements of fact, but any second-class undergraduate in his second year of PPE in Oxford could quote chapter and verse to prove Deutscher an ignoramus.' Letter of 27 January.

2 Charles Bertram Davy (1897–1985), *Observer* 1944–73, at various times leader writer, letters editor and deputy editor (according to David Astor, 'Many Lives of Charles Davy', *Observer*, 26 May 1985, 6); film buff, critic of English and French poetry and committed follower of the anthroposophical movement founded by Rudolf Steiner.

3 466/3.

4 The literary critic and poet William Empson (1906–84).

get hold of, for it is mainly crude historical error (by which I mean ascription of views to, say, Spinoza and Tolstoy which are refutable with chapter and verse with the greatest possible ease) and abuse of the old-fashioned Marxist-Leninist type. So that I am only too pleased to let the whole thing die. But if you have a moment to spare I would be grateful to you if you could tell me whether this is due to some consistent policy or is just a series of accidents – I do not propose to alter my attitude towards your admirable journal, which I have always read and always admired and shall continue to read, and above all I don't wish to nurse petty grievances and minor resentments; if you think the whole thing had better be forgotten, so be it. If not I should be grateful if you could explain the thing to me – on the telephone if you like [...]. Or if you are too busy, do nothing at all, and I shall perfectly understand. I am not in a state of sizzling indignation, but I cannot deny that I am totally and utterly perplexed.

Yours sincerely,

IB's patience in waiting for Aline Halban to free herself from her marriage was eventually rewarded. When Hans Halban was offered a job in Paris, Aline refused to go with him: their marriage was at an end. 'Then one day, as I was standing in All Souls Lodge [...], the telephone rang; it was Aline, who said, "It's all over. He's gone. We've separated. It's finished. I couldn't bear it any longer. Would you like to come and see me?"'[1]

TO HAMILTON FISH ARMSTRONG

5 February 1955

[As from] All Souls

Dear Ham,

Thank you ever so much for your sweet letter of 11 January – how Utopian of you to think that I could have written a letter so cheerful and so gay from the appalling discomforts, the weird mixture of luxury and squalor of All Souls! I am comfortably tucked away in a bed in my mother's house in London, where I spend four to five days a week now until I recover. And until I do that, and that I fear will take some time, I cannot, alas, think thoughts, write words, or in other respects bore the heads off my friends as I am wont to. So everything becomes a little remote and I cast my eye again over the list of alluring possibilities which you outline with the to me always uncomfortable sense that some work must be done, some thought must be given, general propositions evolved which are at least half false and may turn round and collapse altogether like pricked balloons, leaving nothing but humiliating tatters, which seems to me true about everything I have ever said

1 MI Tape 14.

in the past, particularly those remarks which seemed to me particularly full of significance and depth at the time when I originally evolved them. [. . .]

I hope you and Christa are well and send you my warmest good wishes. I love being in bed and doing nothing. That is part of the Russian national character undoubtedly. Do you remember the wonderful beginning of Oblomov,[1] where the hero, with his arms under the blankets, cannot make up his mind whether it is or is not worth his while to try and test the temperature of the outer atmosphere by thrusting his arm from underneath the blanket for even a minute, or whether, on the whole, greater comfort and security is to be obtained by lying still? These are the kinds of problems which I deal in at present – you see how remote all this is from the eagle flights that you so ardently desire and so seldom obtain from this contributor.

With all my love again,

Yours ever,

Isaiah

TO MARY BYSE[2]

17 February 1955 [*carbon*]

All Souls

Dear Miss Byse,

Thank you ever so much for your letter of February 14 – I hope you were not too disappointed by my lecture on Herzen, which the BBC broadcast this evening – I am afraid it did go rather fast but that is the only way I know of speaking. I am, as the lecture must have shown, utterly devoted to the memory of Alexander Herzen *père* – and indeed think him one of the greatest as well as the nicest and noblest men in the nineteenth century. Indeed, there is no one, if I were given a choice, whom I would rather have met in the whole world. I admire his personality and delight in his works more, I should say, than any one now living, certainly in England. And since I propose to write a book dealing with the youth of Herzen and his friends in Russia, I hope to construct one day a monument worthy of him. Certainly no such monument, excepting his own work, exists as yet.

I hope the members of the Herzen family derived some satisfaction from my talk – but I fear the reception of the Third Programme and my own tempo probably proved too much for them. I did mean to go and visit Madame Natalie Herzen[3] near Paris, where she lived, but she died two years

1 261/1.

2 Marie ('Mary') Byse (1880–1971), the daughter of an Evangelical pastor in Lausanne, knew the Herzen family well, had notified them of the forthcoming broadcast of IB's Northcliffe lecture on Alexander Herzen, and had written to IB on 14 February to plead for some means of making IB's rapid delivery intelligible to overseas listeners. (In the event a power cut thwarted the attempt by the assembled Herzen descendants to hear the broadcast, but IB later sent them the text.)

3 IB muddles Herzen's daughters, referring to the eldest, unmarried, daughter, Natalia ('Tata')

ago and I never fulfilled my wish – was she 102 or 103? Something of the kind – and I admire that too. [...] I may go to Vevey myself this spring, in March, and if you think that the great-grandson – Monsieur Serge Herzen,[1] who you say works in Nestlés, would like it at all, I should be very glad to meet him and talk to him, not necessarily only about his great-grandfather. Any link with the Herzen family – and Mr E. H. Carr told me once about his dealings with the two surviving daughters, Mesdames Natalie and Tatiana [sc. Olga], in the 1920s – is a source of excitement and pleasure to me. It was therefore very good of you to have written to me.

Yours sincerely,

Isaiah Berlin.

IB's expectations about the quantity of his future output reflected the triumph of hope over experience.

TO THE WARDEN OF ALL SOULS

17 February 1955

[All Souls]

Dear Mr Warden,

I should like to apply for re-election for the quinquennium 1955–60 to a Research Fellowship of the same class – the 'Robertson' – as that to which I was elected in the summer of 1950. On that occasion I undertook to work in two fields: Russian social and intellectual history, and European political thought. In the first of these fields I have published two overlapping studies of the origins and contents of Tolstoy's view of history,[2] and a study of the political opinions of Herzen and Bakunin;[3] and have prepared for publication, in an English periodical (and later in book form), the substance of lectures I delivered for the Northcliffe Foundation[4] at University College, London (they were subsequently, in part, broadcast by the BBC), dealing with origins of Russian radical thought in the 30s and 40s of the last century. The articles are due to appear in the course of this year; the book, if it is worth publishing, in 1956. In addition to this I have prepared for the press an English edition and translation of *From the Other Shore*,[5] a book by A. I. Herzen; and have contributed notices and reviews to learned periodicals in

---

(1844–1936), when he means her younger sister Olga (Madame Gabriel Monod), who had died in 1953.

1 Serge Herzen (1913–2003), Swiss-Belgian food chemist and mountaineer; grandson of Natalia and Olga Herzen's brother Alexander ('Sasha').

2 245/3.

3 'Herzen and Bakunin on Individual Liberty', in Ernest J. Simmons (ed.), *Continuity and Change in Russian and Soviet Thought* (Cambridge, Mass., 1955), 473–99; reprinted in RT.

4 453/2.

5 408/1.

England and the United States, as well as articles for two encyclopaedias.[1] I have also in draft nine chapters of my book on the critic Belinsky[2] – the first volume of a projected history of the forerunners of the Russian Revolution; this last is to be ready in 1956–57. In my other field I have published an essay (Auguste Comte Memorial Lecture) on the inevitability of history,[3] under the auspices of the London School of Economics; and concluded the second draft of a book on *Political Ideas in the Romantic Age*,[4] arising out of lectures delivered at Bryn Mawr College and later broadcast by the BBC. I meant to finish this book at the end of last year, but bad health intervened. I hope to have it in the hands of the Oxford Press by June of this year. I have also completed for publication an article on historical method[5] (originally delivered as the first Elizabeth Morrow Lecture at Smith College in the USA), and almost completed one on the Russian writer Prince V. Odoevsky.[6]

Should the College re-elect me, I propose to devote myself during the next five years to the completion of the first, and work on, and I hope completion of, at least one other volume of my history of the Russian radicals and revolutionaries. As for the study of European political thought, I should propose to accumulate material for the volume on the history of European ideas from 1789 to 1848 for the Oxford History of Europe,[7] commissioned from me by the editors of this series, combined with general work in this and adjacent fields. I have carried out my duties as a University Lecturer, and Lecturer in Philosophy of New College, and I have examined in the College Fellowship Examinations thrice. I have also supervised a number of graduate theses, examined thrice in the B.Phil., once in the Final Examination of Literae Humaniores (I am to examine in the PPE Final School this summer) and examined PhD theses in London and Cambridge. I have, in accordance with my original proposal to the College, twice been away to teach and lecture at Harvard and other American Universities, but propose, if re-elected, to do so at less frequent intervals and for shorter periods of time; and also to curtail, so far as practicable, the work of examining, but not necessarily my other College and University tasks.

Yours sincerely,
Isaiah Berlin

1 For the first see 209/4; the second was 'Nineteen Fifty-One: A Survey of Cultural Trends of the Year', in *Britannica Book of the Year 1952* (Chicago/Toronto/London, 1952), xxii–xxxi.
2 If these chapters were indeed written, they have not survived. Certainly neither this book nor its intended successor volumes were ever completed, though IB did write various articles in this territory.
3 364/2.
4 63/1.
5 379/1.
6 Not published at this time, though IB presumably drew on the same material for his foreword to Neil Cornwell, *The Life, Times and Milieu of V. F. Odoyevsky 1804–1869* (London, 1986), ix–x.
7 The contract for this book had been signed in 1950. In 1959 IB recognised that he was almost certainly never going to write it and persuaded the OUP to release him from the contract.

In IB's Oxford University Diary for 1955, under 18 February, there occurs an entry that is most unusual for him: instead of being a note of a forthcoming appointment, it records events after they occurred (in the Oxford Botanical Garden). The entry runs as follows:

Midday. Very cold.
Proposed. 11.50
Accepted. *11.55*.

This revolution in IB's private life, in theory to be kept secret until Aline was free to remarry, required changes in his plans for the rest of the year. Using the convenient pretext of his state of health, IB immediately extricated himself from a proposed trip to Israel in the spring, and substituted a convalescent week in Switzerland with Marie, to be followed by a discreet holiday in Italy with Aline.[1]

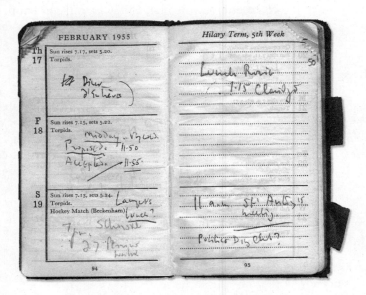

Diary entry recording proposal of marriage to Aline Halban, 18 February 1955

1 The President of the Hebrew University of Jerusalem, Benjamin Mazar (686/3), had on 23 January 1955 invited IB to give the Orde Wingate Memorial Lectures for that year – two or three lectures in English on a religious or philosophical subject. IB had accepted on 2 February, even though 'I am at present not too well and my doctors are a little dubious about this journey, but on the whole optimistic'; he offered either 'the lecture on *Two Concepts of Freedom*, which deals with a philosophical issue – the conflicting concepts of freedom in Europe at the beginning of the 19th century, which falls within the framework of the history of political ideas' or '*The Logic of History*, largely devoted to the question of how historians in fact infer from their data and what constitutes truth and reliability in history as opposed to the natural or social sciences'. But on 18 February he withdrew: 'on medical advice, I am not to be allowed to travel to Israel this spring. The doctors are quite categorical about this. They tell me that my illness is not "dangerous" but that I need a "complete rest", for which purpose I am being sent to Switzerland.'

TO SAM BEHRMAN

20 February 1955 [carbon]

All Souls

Darling Sam (that is what Lady Goldsmid calls you, and I do not see why I should not too – I regard her taste in such matters as impeccable) [...]

As for my illness, heaven knows what it is. Fibrositis, bronchitis, sinusitis, every kind of -itis, have invaded me simultaneously and left my poor old heart – a poor organ that I call by that name – in a sad condition. So I spend my time between Oxford and London, happily cancelling engagements and chatting to my mother occasionally, quietly, in the evenings. She doesn't believe in my disease at all but uses it as a pretext for lecturing me about my evil life in the past, present and future. The result of all this is that I shan't get to Israel in the spring, as intended, but instead to Switzerland, probably alone, to some miserably dull part of it – I detest the place – in order to 'relax', since I am regarded as being in a state of 'perpetual nervous tension'. My nerves are jangling, it is dangerous to talk to me, still more to cross me in any way.

[...] I love trunk calls and when you get to Rapallo you must ring up almost at once (charging it to Mr Todd, who seemed to prepare to undertake all expenses). His account to me of what it would be like for me to go to Hollywood to see his new process – the greatest discovery since print – likely to transform the universe in at least as great a way – was really worth listening to. The account in the *New Yorker*[1] did not tally with the facts. He did not stay with me until the afternoon, but only for forty minutes. On the other hand his entrance, flapping an enormous yellow cad's camel-hair coat, with a huge, outsize cigar, like an American producer on the comical stage, was something to be seen. The porters at All Souls were deeply moved. Nor did we have any concrete negotiations. Nor many laughs – when he told me about his mother and his grandfather, the rabbi, etc. etc., I forced a sickly smile, certainly nothing larger, like even a guffaw. It is curious that our financial relations never matured. Nothing was ever said about money and yet it somehow hovered everywhere in the background. The interview in the *New Yorker* as reproduced in the *Manchester Guardian* and the *Oxford Mail*,[2] has done me very little good. On the other hand, money is money, and I cannot tell you what a year in business has done for me. I now think of

1 'I went over to Oxford a couple of weeks ago to talk to the philosopher Isaiah Berlin, who wrote that book on Tolstoy – the hedgehog one. I told him my conception of the movie [of *War and Peace*], and he said it sounded wonderful. He'd been going to give me a few minutes at 11 a.m., and at 4 p.m. we were still jabbering away. What a lot of laughs! I told Berlin he was the showman, not me, and he told me I was the philosopher, not him. A great guy, and I don't see how he missed. I mean, stuck there in All Souls.' Mike Todd, quoted in 'The Talk of the Town', *New Yorker*, 15 January 1955, 20. A card to IB from Fred Rau dated 23 January 1955 comments: 'You should be more careful who you talk to & avoid Mr Todd in future.'

2 'Stuck There in All Souls', in unsigned 'Our London Correspondence' column, *Manchester*

little else – practically all dons think about nothing but money, it seems – and you and I might do a brisk business together by working up our respective principals, you the Italian,[1] me Mike Todd, to higher and higher competitive fees to yourself and me respectively. We should discuss this in Italy later, in a sinister hotel.

Do write me from Rapallo, or ring up Oxford or London. I long to talk to you – principally about money, of course.

Yours ever,

PS I may not be well but I am quite happy, whereas normally I am very well and not at all happy. How is it with you?

TO DENYS PAGE[2]

17 March 1955 [carbon]

All Souls

Confidential

Dear Denys,

[...] Now, as to E. H. Carr: I must own to you at once that I have had to do this once before, when King's were offering a very similar kind of Research Fellowship [...]. I don't think my opinion has altered about Carr since. It is, in brief, that he is a distinguished and interesting man with a somewhat *raté*[3] career. He suffered during his years in the Foreign Office, I think, from being intellectually superior and socially inferior to his milieu, which gave him all kinds of chips on his shoulder. In a mood of revolt, he resigned and set up as a publicist and writer on historical and political topics. He seems to me to write exceedingly well and be a man of first-rate scholarly attainments, and I say this to you advisedly, knowing what I am saying. His researches are original and scrupulous; he discovers new facts; he is a genuine authority on his subject of a unique kind. His early books on Dostoevsky and Karl Marx[4] are beta plus plus;[5] his first remarkable book was a life of Bakunin,[6] which became the standard biography. The interesting thing about it was that he

Guardian, 7 February 1955, 6; 'A Great Guy', in Radio and Television column by 'W', *Oxford Mail*, 11 February 1955, 5. These were not the only papers to pick up the story.

1 SNB had refused an offer from an Italian film company to contribute to a possible rival production of *War and Peace*.

2 Denys Lionel Page (1908–78), Student and Tutor, Christ Church, 1932–50; Regius Professor of Greek, Cambridge, 1950–73 (and Fellow of Trinity College, Cambridge, 1950–60); Master of Jesus College, Cambridge, 1959–73. Trinity were considering E. H. Carr for a Research Fellowship, and Page had sought IB's views.

3 'Failed'.

4 *Dostoevsky (1821–1881): A New Biography* (New York, 1931); *Karl Marx: A Study in Fanaticism* (London, 1934).

5 β++ is good second-rate (beta being the second letter of the Greek alphabet).

6 *Michael Bakunin* (London, 1937).

wrote it still from a kind of Foreign Office point of view: he wrote with supercilious irony (as he did in his amusing and very readable novel, *The Romantic Exiles*,[1] which can now be bought in a Penguin edition, about the personal troubles of the Russian revolutionary, Herzen), exactly indeed as a good Foreign Office official, asked to write a report on the doings of some obscure sect in Bulgaria, would do so, taking special care to be comprehensive and accurate but regarding himself as infinitely remote from the subject of investigation and writing about it with a patronising and somewhat supercilious air, for the amusement as well as the information of his colleagues at the office. After writing *The Twenty Years' Crisis*,[2] which was a powerful attack on Toynbee and Zimmern[3] and liberalism generally, and a tremendous blast in favour of power politics, and taking a tough line – predicting that Germany would win and that we must lump it – he wrote a book called *The Conditions of the Peace*,[4] which, in the later war years and immediately after the war, had a very great influence, and together with his leading articles in *The Times* and his lectures on *The Soviet Impact*,[5] he established his position as a tough-minded anti-anti-Communist; someone who took the line that whatever we may think of the Soviet Union – and it is a waste of time to indulge in moral sentiments, for things will happen as they do, whatever we may feel – we must allow for these realities and study them in a dispassionate manner. And his *History of the Russian Revolution*[6] is, in a sense, also a major achievement of scholarship, beautifully written, lucid, digesting and ordering an immense quantity of documentary evidence, acclaimed, in a sense rightly, by all the journals, as virtually the only major work of historical scholarship produced in England lately by anyone (this gave little pleasure to my colleague A. L. Rowse). The only thing wrong with this very important point of view is that it is less like a history and more like a superb Government report, based on official documents. This is not quite just because he uses Trotsky as well as orthodox Soviet evidence. But with that exception he resolutely refuses to look at the evidence offered by the opposition – whites and pinks of all kinds – on the ground that they were, after all, defeated, that history is history of what happened, not what might have happened, that history in that sense is a success story and that what one wanted to know are the intentions and acts of the victors. It is not at all unfair to say that the first volume is simply an extended and, in its own way, marvellously illuminated commentary on the work of Lenin; certainly the later volumes, dealing with

1 *The Romantic Exiles: A Nineteenth-Century Portrait Gallery* (London, 1933).
2 *The Twenty Years' Crisis, 1919–1939: An Introduction to the Study of International Relations* (London, 1939).
3 Zimmern, a liberal internationalist, had been an enthusiastic supporter of the League of Nations.
4 *Conditions of Peace* (London, 1942).
5 *The Soviet Impact on the Western World* (London, 1946).
6 *The Bolshevik Revolution, 1917–23* (London, 1950–3).

484   17 MARCH 1955

the Soviet foreign policy and economic development, depart widely from this. Nevertheless, his four volumes are like the very best kind of official report, extremely intelligent, extremely well written, based on an immense amount of work, and presenting a coherent picture from one single point of view. Carr is enough of a Hegelian or a Marxist to see history as an enormous *autostrada*[1] down which the main line of historical traffic is majestically moving, and he systematically ignores the little by-paths which take themselves to marshes and lead to no great cities. There is no doubt that the work is a masterpiece in the sense that anyone dealing with the subject will have to look upon it as the greatest monument thus far erected on his path; and there is further no doubt that, these strictures apart – I mean impartiality with regard to or excessive passion for the victors or the use of documents as if they were always an accurate description of what occurred, and the systematic ignoring of revolts and rebellions, and the evidence offered by victims (I dare say the same could be said about Livy)[2] – he deserves major support. He is far cleverer and more distinguished, if in some sense a more crotchety man, than most historians or politics specialists in our universities; and when he was living in Appleton near Oxford in a condition of considerable need, eking out a not very satisfactory life by writing reviews for *The Times Literary Supplement*, and longing to get on with his proper work, I felt that he was being badly treated, that the political school of economics [sc. the LSE?] was mistaken not to give him the Fellowship he applied for and that King's was mistaken not to give him their Fellowship; and tried to do everything possible on his behalf, and when he was finally given a lectureship at Balliol, where he now teaches, and which has made him financially more secure, it did seem a very belated and not wholly adequate act of justice. Any criticisms which may be made of him are, so to speak, on the highest level, of the kind of historian he is, the kind of political effect he has, the kind of use which he makes of evidence, etc. What, in fact, cannot be denied is that the whole thing amounts to a major phenomenon, and I feel rather like Moore when he was asked to look at Wittgenstein's *Tractatus* as a thesis for the Cambridge MA degree. He said: 'I consider this a work of genius, but even if I am mistaken in this, it seems to be fully up to the standard of the Master of Arts degree in Cambridge University.' I feel approximately that about Carr. I disagree with all his views, I abhor his historical approach, I attack him in print and in lectures, I hold classes with him, but I have a great admiration and indeed affection for him. I think, in fact, you will do well to give him the Research Fellowship in question if he really needs it. But do get hold of my original document from Noel Annan if you can. I don't think

1 'Motorway'.
2 Titus Livius (59 BC–AD 17), whose history of Rome extends from the founding of the city to the reign of the Emperor Augustus.

it will contradict any of this. I shall be amused if it does, and I shall let you know next time in Cambridge.

Yours ever,

In the end even IB's plans to spend a token few days with his mother in Lugano before joining Aline in Italy were abandoned. Instead IB and Aline spent a happy few weeks together in the South of France, their holiday ending with a memorable encounter:

I have had a splendid time in Nice, Grasse and places of that kind, and went to a party near Avignon where I met simultaneously Picasso and Cocteau.[1] The first is splendid, despite the Communism and the nonsense; he makes an immediate impression of genius. The calm, the happiness, the strength and the general nobility are overwhelming. Cocteau on the other hand is simply the greatest cocotte of our age, with all the charm and the gifts and the influence and the capacity for creating atmospheres and movements which such ladies have (don't you find, in your experience?), but small and embarrassing in the presence of the painter. Picasso was quite funny about how it was that every time he was invited to Moscow he suggested that he might open an exhibition of his own works there, and how this always brought the invitation to an abrupt end. He is perfectly independent, his Communism is not really relevant to anything, and it is a pleasure to be in his society. He belongs ultimately to the same type of humanity as Casals,[2] Toscanini and, despite his silliness, Einstein.[3]

TO MORTON WHITE

2 May 1955

All Souls [in fact, 49 Hollycroft Avenue]

Dear Morton,

Forgive me if my letter is rather briefer than usual. This is due (*a*) to the fact that I have just come back from abroad this day[4] and have found about 900 letters waiting for me, some of which are purely business ones dealing with my mother's income etc., and have to be dealt with for three or four hours; (*b*) to the fact that I am trying to finish off my volume for our slave-driver,[5] and am doing so in a great hurry – Marcus Dick has done a lot of the work, which has, oddly enough, increased rather than decreased the amount

---

1 Jean Maurice Eugène Clément Cocteau (1889–1963), avant-garde French poet, playwright, designer and film-maker.

2 Pau Carles Salvador ('Pablo') Casals i Defilló (1876–1973), Spanish cellist, conductor and composer; voluntarily exiled himself from Spain during Franco's regime.

3 2 May 1955 to Arthur Schlesinger.

4 IB had in fact been back in England for a week or more, though probably not in Hampstead.

5 Victor Weybright (1903–78), editor-in-chief of the New American Library of World Literature 1945–66, for whom IB and MW were each producing a volume in the 'Mentor Philosophers' series. IB's was *The Age of Enlightenment: The Eighteenth-Century Philosophers* (Boston and New York, 1956) and MW's *The Age of Analysis* (467/4).

I have to do – I thought comfortably that I would let him do the donkey work and not have very much to do myself; of course the opposite has turned out and I have crossed out every one of the sentences, and even so it will have a very odd appearance; (*c*) I feel rather feeble, as always after a holiday, and shall therefore not go on with a lot of personal details. I am not sure about *Reunion in Philosophy*[1] – it seems to me a little smart. I do not believe titles with special significance wear well and should myself be inclined to recommend something frightfully simple (Austin, oddly enough, has a taste for epigrams in such matters, as when he lectured on 'Sense and Sensibility',[2] or something of the sort, in Oxford, of which I disapproved rather priggishly, I'm afraid). I should call it *Essays in Philosophy*, or something frightfully flat like that, despite all publisher's advice. I am very sorry to have called my own book *The Hedgehog and the Fox*. I wish I hadn't now.[3]

"*They say, 'The fox knows many things, but the hedgehog knows one great thing.' Want to hear it?*"

Cartoon from the New Yorker, 9 November 1998, by Charles Barsotti[4]

I have not given up the thought of our book at all. Far from it. And I propose to meet with you in August. [...]

About James, Arthur, Stuart, Sidney Hook[5] etc. – I do not propose to trouble – I think this will settle itself. I do not believe that either James or

1 MW eventually called this book *Toward Reunion in Philosophy* (Cambridge, 1956).
2 'Sense and Sensibilia'.
3 This may be sincere, but both the commercial success and the intellectual influence of the book have surely been significantly enhanced by its felicitous title. 'Lev Tolstoy's Historical Scepticism', the title under which the essay was first published, is somewhat less memorable.
4 © The New Yorker Collection 1998 Charles Barsotti from cartoonbank.com. All rights reserved.
5 MW had reported that Arthur Schlesinger had not taken to Stuart Hampshire, and that his initial enthusiasm for James Joll had cooled on hearing from Mary McCarthy that Joll had criticised AS as a reactionary. MW believed that Joll's criticism had in fact been of Sidney Hook (1902–89), Professor of Philosophy, New York, 1939–72, a former Marxist turned fervent anti-Communist. Letter of 7 April 1955.

Stuart will ever become warm friends of Arthur's, about whom my sentiments coincide entirely with yours.[1] He does say silly things but (and he was
dreadfully embarrassed to read this in some letter to me once) he is a very
good character and is very good and very nice and very noble-hearted, and is
the most reliable foul-weather friend I can think of. I don't know about being
mature but I agree that it is always a pleasure to be with him, and altogether
I have the fondest feelings and the warmest friendship for him. It is all to do
with having one's heart in the right place and perhaps in the first place with
having a heart at all. I really am only going to Chicago[2] because it is a month
and not longer, and if Harvard were willing to have me for a month and not
longer I would much rather come to it. So if you think it is a relevant thing
to say to anyone do tell them so.

Forgive me for this very dry and empty letter. I have no thoughts in my
head beyond further thoughts on history which I shall communicate to you
when, or perhaps before, we meet. And blast all Foundations.[3]

I now ask myself two questions: (1) Is the belief in historic forces mainly
caused by the desire to have one's own inner longings, as it were, justified,
confirmed and pushed into existence by forces so strong that, despite all dis-
couragement, they and you must win, and not for any of the reasons stated
in my lecture?[4] and (2) Is the proposition that every individual in the world
has free will and can choose between at least two possibilities in all situations
(e.g. to do or not to do something) logically compatible with the proposition (whether true or false does not matter) that however individuals act,
the behaviour of sufficiently large quantities of persons is always, within a
certain margin of error, predictable – so that, however individuals act, it is
always possible to say that, say, more than 70 per cent within a given group of
persons will act thus or thus, however this 70 per cent may be composed, and
whatever the effects of the 'free' acts of its members are upon each other? If
the latter proposition is true,[5] then obviously Marxism and other forms of
strict determinism are compatible with the strictest forms of metaphysical
free will, and there is no issue, so that the question of right and wrong in
responsibility remains unaffected by the question of how nations or other
groups are likely to behave in specifiable circumstances – the fields of interest become quite different and there is neither relevance nor clash.

I do not believe in all this myself. I am merely asking. It is like saying that
I do not know who or how many persons will stop this particular lunatic
from trying to gouge out this particular lady's eye, but I can guarantee that

1 MW had written: 'Arthur is a mature, sensible, satisfied man, and it's always a pleasure to be with
  him – even when he talks Niebuhrian rot.' ibid.
2 In November 1955, as an Alexander White Visiting Professor.
3 MW and IB had failed to get financial support from a foundation for their plan to write a joint
  work on the philosophy of history.
4 *Historical Inevitability*.
5 sc. if the answer to the second question is affirmative.

no fewer than three persons, given there are more than twenty present, will try and do so – is this compatible with total free will on the part of all the twenty? not to speak of the lunatic?

    Yours ever,
      Isaiah

TO FRANK WISNER[1]
4 May 1955 [carbon]

                                        All Souls

Dear Frank,

    [...] I have, of course, no views. I wish I could maintain to you now that when so rashly I spoke about the warm friendship between Malenkov[2] and Beria,[3] which was obviously out of date at the time, this was still true and that Malenkov was simply a prisoner of those who could not get rid of Beria without at least his tacit support and meant to get rid of Malenkov next. But all this is mythologised speculation for which there is not the faintest [scintilla?] of real evidence and is only the kind of thing which would be said by Crankshaw[4] or Deutscher. The former is a hard-working journalist busy making bricks without straw every week, and my sympathies go out to him, for he really has no information and it is quite impossible for him to know what to do. The latter is a full-sized charlatan and not a word he says, it seems to me, is to be believed. No man has made a larger number of false predictions in the last three years, and how he dares pose as an expert at all it is difficult to conceive, or rather not so much difficult as shocking. However, I must stop moralising. The one method, therefore, which I think it is useless to adopt is that of Deutscher – just to speculate about the political 'directions' various persons are taking and try to deduce the political direction of X from the fact that he opposes Y who opposes Z, whose political 'direction' one already knew. I think this did make sense in the 1920s, when D. was a member of the Comintern and when often deviations to the left and to the right really meant something and indeed a great deal, and there was a

1 Frank Gardiner Wisner (1910–65), CIA 1947–62 (Head of the Directorate of Plans, responsible for covert anti-Communist operations worldwide 1952–8); a member of the Georgetown set in Washington, close to many of IB's friends; suffered a major mental breakdown in 1956 and eventually committed suicide.

2 Georgy Maksimilianovich Malenkov (1902–88), Stalin's close collaborator and heir apparent after Zhdanov's death; Chairman of the Council of Ministers (i.e. Prime Minister) 1953–5; replaced in February 1955 by Marshal Bulganin, a supporter of Khrushchev.

3 Lavrenty Pavlovich Beria (1899–1953), ruthless Georgian head of the NKVD 1938–46; one of Stalin's closest supporters; a Deputy Prime Minister 1941–53; successfully allied with Malenkov against Zhdanov and his followers but later damaged by growing anti-Semitism (many of his supporters were Jewish) and the ambitions of Khrushchev, which led to his downfall and execution for alleged conspiracy.

4 Edward Crankshaw (1909–1984), correspondent on Soviet affairs, Observer, 1947–68.

great deal of Talmudical casuistry to which great attention was paid, both in Russia and in Communist circles abroad, so that the degree by which you had deviated from Radek[1] or gravitated back towards Preobrazhensky[2] really mattered; all this ceased to be real in about 1932, and the attempt to apply this particular technique to the cracking of contemporary problems seems to me to lead to nothing but nonsense. Consequently the theory that Beria was 'liberal', therefore Malenkov liquidated him, was 'anti-liberal', therefore those who liquidate Malenkov must be liberal again, or any such form of reasoning, seems to me mere gibberish. Starting from this then I think the facts of this matter are: (a) economic and military; (b) personal rivalries, but this we knew already.

I still hold to my ancient view that all disagreements inside the Politburo, or whatever the Commune body now may be, are never genuinely ideological, and not even primarily personal, but always and explicitly strategical and tactical. I think there is something in the view that after Stalin's death, when Malenkov did try some kind of 'softer' policy with regard to consumer goods and fair words to foreign countries – that this did produce at least an internal crisis or aggravated it; but his belief that, say, the French would fail to ratify the rearmament of the Germans in some guise under the combined pressure of their own Communists and Russian 'mildness', coupled with threats, did not mature; and that those who maintained throughout that it was unnecessary to 'appease' the West or make life easier for their own citizens, either on the ground that the opposite policy would prove intolerable and crack, or on the ground that the policy that mildness would pay enormous returns in the restoration of the good will so rapidly shattered by Stalin and Molotov in the last four years, probably prevailed. William Hayter keeps writing me letters from Moscow saying that he and Chip would really see to it that I had an interesting time if I came to Moscow this summer, and I dare say I should be in a better position to answer your questions if I could go, but alas, I probably cannot, so I continue in my benighted ignorance: I have not read the piece in the 12 February issue of *The Economist*,[3] but that, I should think, might have been inspired by Deutscher, and if so was certainly worthless. Far more surprising was the piece in the London *Times*[4] which claimed Malenkov's self-denigration as an obviously sincere and almost noble piece of public integrity – an example to other statesmen. But leaving these aberrations aside, let me return to the central thesis: I do not believe that one can distinguish between a personal struggle for power and economic issues; by which I mean that I think that, as in other organisations, men are identified

1 Karl Berngardovich Radek (1885–c.1939), né Sobelsohn, prominent Polish-Jewish revolutionary; imprisoned for treason in 1937 during Stalin's Great Purges.
2 Evgeny Alekseevich Preobrazhensky (1886–1937), leading Bolshevik, shot during the purges.
3 'The Fall of Malenkov', *The Economist*, 12 February 1955, 511–13.
4 Presumably the editorial 'The Change', *The Times*, 9 February 1955, 9.

with policies; but there is no doubt that Khrushchev[1] always stood for maximum toughness, repression and the bullying of the population, especially Ukrainian; that the failure of any given policy is obviously fraught with danger to those who advocated it most strongly, unless they are the dictator himself; that the relative failure of K's policy of the *agrogorod*[2] did put him in a queer position of either having to retreat himself or having to consolidate his position to such effect that he could successfully put the blame for the failure, at least officially, on other shoulders – which appears to be exactly what he has done. Again, I have the impression, for which I cannot give you evidence, that the fall of Malenkov was precipitated by an economic crisis and not simply by a struggle for power independent of what was going on socially or economically; I cannot believe that it is possible for a man of the calibre of Malenkov to be ousted just because enough members of the Politburo don't like him or wish to down his particular set, out of a blue sky, without a sufficient sense of crisis and urgency which itself can only be stimulated by some real fire – and fire can be bellowed up, but there must be enough of it to produce the required volume of smoke. The fire in this case was probably some sort of aggravation in the agricultural crisis which in one form or another has, after all, lasted since 1945, and that plus the failure to prevent German rearmament, the relative impotence to affect political decisions of the Communist parties of the West, and I should think quite genuine worries about war in Asia, and a certain degree of intractability on the part of the Chinese, and insufficient affability on the part of potential Middle Eastern allies, could be worked up into a very menacing picture, needing a strong hand at the helm. It was odd that Malenkov, with all his experience of party management behind him, allowed himself to be outmanoeuvred as he obviously must have done, but in the very fluid state of alliances at present prevailing, with nobody quite certain of who comes next and what alignment of power is likely to occur, it may all be a matter of touch and go, and a sufficiently strong party boss, which K has always been, particularly if he gets the benevolent support of, say, the Army chiefs (who are, I am sure, of no weight independently but can contribute to the overall weight of a particular power grouping), can manage to assert himself, at least for a while. Anyway, I should like to stick to my old opinion of Soviet policy as proceeding by a bogus dialectic, namely an artificial zigzag – by which we have alternating periods of both 'soft' and 'hard' policies – which (a) keeps people on their toes, and (b) allows them that degree of elasticity in policy which in democratic countries is secured by the general interplay of free forces. Only

1 Nikita Sergeevich Khrushchev (1894–1971), First Secretary, Communist Party of the Ukraine, 1938–49; Secretary of the Central Committee of the Communist Party of the Soviet Union 1949–53, First Secretary 1953–64; Chairman of Council of Ministers (Prime Minister) of the Soviet Union 1958–64; the rising star of the Soviet Communist Party at this time.

2 'Farm town', an amalgamated group of collective farms; such amalgamations had been one of Khrushchev's main agricultural policies from 1949 but had suffered from Malenkov's disapproval.

in Stalin's day it was Stalin himself who managed the dialectical machine, and zigged and zagged as and when he wished and displayed an extraordinary sense of timing; after his death it seems to me that the zigzag became more uncontrolled, that there really were various pressure groups in favour of various types of tactic, and that what we shall get is still a zigzag – 'soft' and 'hard', consumers' goods and capital goods, united fronts and fierce Communist conspiracy, co-existence and denunciation – only every time the zig changes into a zag and vice versa more persons may lose their heads than used to in the past, not by orders from above but by sheer defeat of their projects in the sovereign body. I see no reason why physical elimination need be so frequent – once a principle can be established that eminent leaders apologise in public and then are not executed, this is, on the whole, a more convenient method of proceeding and distresses all foreign comrades less. And after all, it could be argued that Stalin had to eliminate his rivals, partly for personal temperament and habits, but partly also because there was more ideology in the air in general, more liability to conspiracy, the monolithic nature of the regime had not been grasped properly yet by the old Bolshevik guard, and there were people for them to plot with, or at least hold subversive conversations with; whereas now the ideological level is so low that there simply aren't enough dissident ideologies about the place to constitute any possible nuclei for at least ideological disaffection – other forms of disaffection can be dealt with by quite different methods; by suppression and elimination at a much lower level than some national leader. So my general impression is that there is an economic crisis and there is a personal struggle for power, and one, in fact, cannot be disentangled from the other; that given the condition of complete or semi-cold war, for which the Russians probably genuinely don't hold themselves responsible, and of which they regard themselves as the inevitable victims – no doubt made inevitably so by the 'logic of history', but still victims – the tough policy will always win in the end and all such concessions as more consumer goods or gentle words to foreign powers, or other forms of new mildness or 'liberalism', will always lose to the perpetual necessity for straining every muscle against the forthcoming struggle. I have also the impression that, if his physical health holds, K is in for quite a long time, or others like him – dead-panned, tough suppressers of a competent managerial type, with heavy industrial experience, rather than party specialists or propagandists, or other distinguished ideologists. Having said this, I now confidently expect to see that K has been eliminated tomorrow morning, for that is what happens to most of my prophecies. But there it all is for what it is worth. I am sorry it is so confused and doesn't build up to a lucid and coherent pattern, but these are my casual thoughts at the moment – remember that I have been out of commission now for three months. [. . .]

Yours ever,

The news of IB's engagement started to spread round Oxford. Jenifer Hart
in particular recalled 'this terrible moment in the quad at All Souls after the
Encaenia lunch when – I think it was Stuart Hampshire [...] – came up to us
and said, "Hey, have you heard the latest news? Isaiah is getting married." He'd
tried to get hold of me to tell me; I hadn't seen him for a little time [...] I didn't
know he was really interested in her.'[1] And despite the need for discretion, IB
could not long remain totally silent to his American friends.

TO JOSEPHINE SINGER

9 August 1955

All Souls College

Dear Jo,

[...] It is wonderful news that you are going to be in Europe for over a
year. How much you will enjoy living in France I do not know. I admire the
French, am delighted to be in their country; I think every face is intelligent,
full of life, individual, exactly what human beings are intended to be – in
fact that they are more like human beings as described both in works of
philosophy and of fiction than anyone else, and yet to live among them I find
absolutely impossible. They are too unspontaneous, too buttoned up, and
ladle out their emotions by the thimbleful. [...]

A very great deal has happened to me, in all kinds of ways, since we last
communicated – and about that I propose to tell you when I see you. [...]
I am trying to write reviews, trying to write a book, trying to recover from
having examined in the Final School of PPE, but all this is nothing in comparison with the long conversation which I propose to have with you. I really
have something to tell at last, at some length, so prepare your thoughts both
for a period of relative silence (as if this was something new) while I tell my
extraordinary saga. [...]

Yours ever,

Isaiah

TO T. S. ELIOT

9 August 1955

All Souls

Dear Eliot,

Thank you very much for sending me *The Literature of Politics*,[2] by which
I was greatly interested and instructed. I am sure you are right (by which
I may perhaps only mean that I agree with you) in thinking that the 'pre-

1 Tape MI B6.
2 *The Literature of Politics* (London, 1955), the published version of Eliot's lecture to a Conservative
Party literary lunch in April 1955. The copy Eliot gave to IB has not been found.

political era' alone is that in which lasting effects are achieved by human thought about political or social matters. As for your kind reference to me on page 11, and your description of it on the fly leaf, I was delighted by it, as one always is when one is given more than one's due. This is surely preferable to strict justice, but if torrents feel as I do when I speak in public or over the wireless, I feel sorry for them, for their state of mind must be anything but agreeable. 'Torrential?' I ask myself. It must be that you must have been reading *Romola*, where, in the third chapter, the Greek stranger chooses to interpret the barber's quotation from Juvenal[1] – who was ironical about the Greeks – as a compliment; and quotes the full passage, which ends with the words 'sermo promptus, et Isaeo torrentior'. I feel quite sure that, for all your disclaimers, your erudition, as well as your wisdom, are far profounder than mine will ever be. Not that it would take much to be that; but it is all that I can offer, sincerely, in return, and I do offer it to you in all humility and admiration.

Yours sincerely,
Isaiah Berlin.

Eliot replied on 7 September:

Dear Berlin,
I have just returned from abroad to find your letter of 9 August, which has given me much pleasure. I was already convinced that you are my superior in learning, profundity and eloquence. I am now of the opinion that you far surpass me in the art of flattery.

With reciprocal humility,
Yours ever,
T. S. Eliot

IB admitted defeat: 'I have received a funny letter from T. S. Eliot, in which there is an ironical reference to me which he maintains [...] is a compliment. I do not know how to reply and therefore he wins.'[2]

TO ALICE JAMES
12 August 1955 [*manuscript*]

49 Hollycroft Avenue

Dearest Alice,
I *must* write you, yet I cannot: for much has happened in my life which I

---

1 'Ingenium velox, audacia perdita, sermo / promptus, et Isaeo torrentior' ('[The Greeks are] quick-witted, shamelessly impudent, and always ready to hold forth – more torrentially than Isaeus'). Juvenal, Satire 3, lines 73–4; quoted in George Eliot's novel (Leipzig, 1863), vol. 1, 42. Isaeus was an Assyrian rhetorician.
2 9 August 1955 to Alexander Gerschenkron.

dare not entrust to a cold page of paper, not even to such {a} dear, under-standing, wise, good, best possible friends like you & Billy: I do not know if you have heard rumours: there appear to have been many: but I am hoping, next year, to be married. To Mrs Halban who you met. I have loved her long & very silently for fear of upsetting what seemed to me a household – a construction – a life – not necessarily very happy but still a life: with which surely one has no right to interfere in the least degree. Then all kinds of things happened: her marriage to her husband began to crack: still I hung back: tormented but unable to believe that I had a right to advance even though the breach was not of my making: then my father died: I said too much: events occurred (nothing but words: but as Henry James pointed out so finally – & for the first time – words count more – & are more violent than deeds: or can be). No 'deeds' occurred: but a divorce in Paris (they are both French)[1] is in train: peacefully: in France it is as in U.S. & no co-respondents or desertion or squalor occurs. She is to come to U.S. in December: I am naturally in a state of enormous bliss: & think myself fantastically lucky: & cannot conceive how such happiness can have come my way after eating my heart out now for years (I first saw *her* in 1941) nor does Dr Halban seem to mind much *now*: but I'll tell you all when I see you. My mother seems pleased: so does Aline's (her father is dead). I've told something to Olivia [Constable] who kindly came to see my mother who has broken her foot & lies in plaster of Paris, well but frustrated, accumulating energy like a *battery*.

I go to Rome to a Historic Congress on the 22[d]: am back Sept. 20: sail for N.Y. on Nov 3: go straight to Chicago via Mt. Holyoke without even a day in New York: return to N.Y. on Dec. 16 or 17: & stay 3 weeks in the course of which I shall *of course* come to Cambridge to see you: Oh, I cannot go on: officially nothing is supposed to be known: I cannot describe to you what I felt at a dinner for 64 of the Aldrich's[2] when Cynthia Jebb[3] in her highest coloratura began to cry: "oh what wonderful news! may I congratulate ..." "Sh sh sh" I hissed: "why?" said she crestfallen "is it *off*?". I do hope Billy is *well*: I am worried by what you say. Love to him & I'll write again & the news is still *secret* (Olivia knows: & I told Rowland when he stayed with Mrs H – had to) – I am bewitched – terribly happy – & send you my love.

Isaiah

1 Though born Austrian, Hans Halban had been granted French nationality during the war.
2 Winthrop Aldrich and his wife, the former Harriet Crocker Alexander (1888–1972).
3 Cynthia Jebb (1898–1990), née Noble, wife of Gladwyn Jebb; Lady Gladwyn 1960 (when her husband became Baron Gladwyn).

TO VICTOR GOLLANCZ

20 August 1955 [*carbon*]

All Souls

Dear Victor,

I wish I knew my mind about capital punishment.[1] I am more against it than for it, and if it were abolished I should, I think, feel relief. Although, at the same time, I do not feel strongly enough to wish to identify myself with a movement of the completely converted. I am in the queer, paradoxical position of being prepared to make a contribution without wishing to join the Committee. I do not feel indignant when brutal murderers are executed, although I would rather they were not. While I am in this condition I think I had better not join. But thank you very much for thinking of me.

Yours ever,

IB joined Aline in Bordeaux on 23 August; they then drove through the South of France, calling on friends and relatives, before continuing to Italy on their way to Rome.

TO SAM BEHRMAN

[29 August 1955, *manuscript*]

Excelsior Palace & Kursaal, Rapallo

My dear Sam

But I dare not call on Max Beerbohm. And I leave to-day. I am not absolutely alone: but how can I tell you? no doubt George & Evie [Backer] (to whom I, under several oaths, breathed not a word) have told you all. And I counted, as a result of relying on the Weisgal Information Service (quantity rather than quality: true facts, false facts, the point is the quantity & the variety) on finding you here & telling you in tedious detail about my plans for the future & the long & secret period of anxiety which preceded the present, not least happy moment in my troubled life. I cannot speak of being engaged – while one of the two parties is still married there is a grammatical solecism involved; which, I hope, time and action will obliterate; but at the moment I can only indulge in enormous Jamesish circumlocutions, not at all like the lively brisk style I associate with you & Dr Whitehill.[2] Where are you [when]? after Rome (& Weisgal – & 2000 historians, but they are an irrelevance) I return to London on Sept 20 & to Chicago on Nov. 15 – & you? & you? [. . .]

Isaiah

1 Gollancz chaired the newly-formed National Campaign for the Abolition of Capital Punishment, and had asked IB to join its Committee of Honour.
2 Possibly Walter Muir Whitehill (1905–78), historian; Director and Librarian, Boston Athenaeum, 1946–73; Peabody Museum of Archaeology and Ethnology, Harvard, 1951–72 (Allston Burr Senior Tutor, Lowell House, 1952–6).

TO MARIE BERLIN

2 September 1955 [*manuscript*]

Rome

Dear Mama

Your two letters were most welcome & delightful – I am most grateful. The whole French & Italian journeys were *pure* delight – enchantment. Aline is very well & happy – so you can assume I am too, despite the charming chastoushka.[1] I lunched with Weisgal today whom Aline found charming – les extrèmes se touchent[2] – I *must* telephone Chain[3] – The Congress[4] has begun & I am wearing a small medal like the other Congressisti[5] – really there is nothing to say except that I am extremely happy & well & everything is going beautifully – [...] Italy is such a divine land – & my life is so marvellously transformed – when I remember the discomforts & *imperfect* uncomplete nervous неуютность[6] of my earlier holidays here – with Sir Bowra[7] or Hampshire – I *am* lucky & so beautifully balanced & harmonious again – I thank my stars & will go to Synagogue somewhere on ראש השנה[8] to thank the Lord. Aline is calling – I must go to her – warmest best love – You are behaving so understandingly & well – darling –

Isaiah

As the Congress drew to its close, IB and Aline moved on to Naples and Amalfi, then spent Rosh Hashanah in Milan before returning to England.

TO SHIELA SOKOLOV GRANT

21 September 1955

All Souls

Dear Shiela,

[...] You spoke confidently about the opening of the new Anglo-Russian relations. I have just been to Rome, which was attended by no fewer than

---

1 A short Russian ditty, often humorous: presumably Marie had enclosed one with her letter.
2 'Extremes meet.'
3 Ernst Boris Chain (1906–79), German-born biochemist; Max Beloff's brother-in-law; an active Zionist, well known to IB's parents; shared Nobel Prize for Physiology / Medicine 1945 with Sir Alexander Fleming and Sir Howard Florey for their work on penicillin; Scientific Director of International Research Centre for Chemical Microbiology, Istituto Superiore di Sanità, Rome, 1948–64; later (1961–73) Professor of Biochemistry, London (Imperial).
4 The 10th International Congress of Historical Sciences, held in Rome 4–11 September 1955. Presumably IB here refers to pre-Conference gatherings.
5 'Participants in the Congress'.
6 'Neuyutnost'' ('uncosiness').
7 A family joke deriving from Marie Berlin's imperfect grasp of English?
8 'Rosh Hashanah', the two-day Jewish New Year, at the beginning of the month of Tishrei, which usually falls in September – in 1955, on 17–18 September.

twenty-five Soviet historians.[1] Butter would not melt in their mouths. That the whole thing is merely a tactic I haven't the slightest doubt. That no genuine change of spirit is intended I am sure. Nevertheless, even though the Russians may think they are playing a game it is possible that its consequences will, in fact, lead to a decrease of tension, whether they intend it or not; there is perhaps such a thing as the cunning of history. So I too am not unhopeful. What I feel sure of is what an old Italian radical said to me in Italy, namely that the bomb has saved us. That it is very much not to be desired that there should be an agreement about it, for if there is an agreement it will be broken and somebody will blow us up, whereas if there is no agreement there will be mutual apprehension, extreme nervousness on all sides, tension and peace. Better remain sceptical and alive than idealistic and full of faith and many wars and frightful destruction.[2]

I hear Goronwy was refused a visa to Moscow.[3] Is this true? And if so why? Do you believe that Guy Burgess was a Soviet spy[4] for twenty years? I do. And tremble at the thought. ⟨I cd not have uttered a word to him, ever, if I even dimly suspected this. Did anyone ever tell him anything confidential? Incredible.⟩ I have an absolute sense of horror about the whole thing now, which I had not before somehow. How can someone so like a human being behave with such systematic duplicity? But then was anyone ever insane enough to tell him anything important? But I suppose he saw a lot of Foreign Office telegrams. But I must stop these speculations and go to bed for I am very tired after a long journey through Europe. France, as usual, sent far the most intelligent persons to the Congress, and the least sympathetic ones, the Slavs the nicest and the silliest. When are you coming to Oxford?

Yours

Shaya

---

1 Described by IB as 'anxious to agree with everyone everywhere, all the time, about everything, dominated by a monstrous hatchet of a woman called Professor Pankratova, who, as you know, writes all the Soviet textbooks – and before her, cowering, timid but disarming and sweet, a group of frightened Russian scholars, genuinely knowledgeable, blinking in the light, delighted to be in Rome, terrified of opening their mouths and terrified of keeping them shut too long, lest they be accused of letting down the side and letting the bourgeois historians have it all their own way' (23 September to Donald Treadgold); and 'sad relics of an old intelligentsia, who somehow managed to make semi-coherent speeches when they were not reading mechanically dictated papers' (23 September to Philip Mosely). IB had been the interpreter at a 'Very gay' formal meeting between the Russian and British delegations (11 September to Marie Berlin): 'The goodwill is *tremendous* & very comical; in a sense they *are* relieved to be able to be nice to us; in another sense they enjoy acting a new part: that of kindly allies – all is forgiven & forgotten.'
2 IB had earlier stated his position on the Cold War to Henry Brandon: 'I think I am still a pro-containment man, in fact a Kennanite.' Letter of 2 May 1955.
3 At the time Rees was apparently writing a book on Guy Burgess – which never materialised.
4 On 19 September 1955 the *People* published the revelation by Vladimir Mikhailovich Petrov, a former Soviet agent who had changed sides in Australia, that Guy Burgess and Donald Maclean had been long-term Soviet agents recruited at Cambridge University.

TO GIORGIO DE SANTILLANA

21 September 1955 [*carbon*]

All Souls

Dear Giorgio,

But I do contemplate coming to America. I shall be in Chicago between 15 November and 15 December and New York thereafter for three weeks or so, where everything will be much easier and correspondence much more effective, powerful, fertile, and worthy of immortality. I am beginning to get worried. As you suggest, White's book is not a model for you at all,[1] nor any book, since the Renaissance is on its own, as it were, and I must break the news to you, painful as it is, and a betrayal of all my own principles, that I have completed my dreary eighteenth-century volume, and it is in New York in the hands of those extraordinary people. Damned dull it is too – and it is nothing but hack passages out of Locke, Hume, Berkeley, with a very

The front cover of the first edition of IB's The Age of Enlightenment, *1956, designed by Hans Erni*

1 De Santillana was working on *The Age of Adventure: The Renaissance Philosophers* (New York, 1956) for the same series as Morton White's *The Age of Analysis* and IB's *The Age of Enlightenment*.

little garniture[1] from Voltaire etc. to spice it; the cover design shows a figure vaguely resembling Voltaire, and at the back some pompous ass in a periwig, who may or may not be like and might indeed be anybody. It is hideous. The whole thing is a nightmare.[2] [...]

Your list is splendid, and snippets, I am sure, is right. Why should a particular view of the Renaissance be as such? I should have thought the more fanatical the better. And damn balance and let there be a single coherent fanatical pattern. What a lot of irritating fumisme[3] Southern Italy seems to have produced! Bruno,[4] Campanella,[5] Pico[6] (the best), Croce (the worst) etc. If people like Paracelsus,[7] Pico and Bruno are to come in, a very great deal of interpretative 'tissue' will have to be woven in. For as they stand these gentlemen will make little sense to a reader, and you rightly don't wish to make the whole thing an elementary textbook for sophomores fresh from Ohio. Mind you, the Renaissance is simply a procession by Benozzo Gozzoli[8] or an enormous choral dance like the *Paradise* by Tintoretto. But I really have no concrete ideas until you shove something at me, then I won't look at it for weeks, and in the end come out with grotesque suggestions. These may have the effect of making you think that your original ideas, which appeared dubious to you at first, are inspired and infallible in comparison with my idiotic suggestions. So much the better. [...]

Yours ever,

TO THE EDITOR OF THE *NEW STATESMAN AND NATION*[9]

Rome

Sir,

Mr Hobsbawm[10] is indignant because Mr Trevor-Roper (in your issue of

1 'Decoration'.
2 The series was none the less a success. By 14 May 1956 Victor Weybright was able to report 'your book is selling at the rate of fiction on the racks in the Walgreen drugstore at the Port of New York Authority Bus Terminal, largely to New Jersey commuters. This is eloquent testimony to the conceptual approach which you inspired and personally demonstrated.'
3 An iconoclastic attitude to society and art, characterised by practical jokes and satire, prevalent in the period 1880–1900.
4 Giordano (né Filippo) Bruno (1548–1600), Italian philosopher and cosmologist, burned at the stake for heresy, especially his belief in a plurality of worlds.
5 Tommaso (né Giovanni Domenico) Campanella (1568–1639), Italian philosopher, theologian and astrologer, imprisoned for much of his life for his bizarre and unorthodox views.
6 Giovanni Pico della Mirandola (1463–94), Italian philosopher of eclectic sympathies, who rejected astrology as being incompatible with human free will.
7 Paracelsus, the name adopted by Philippus Theophrastus Aureolus Bombastus von Hohenheim (1493–1541), Swiss physician, alchemist and astrologer who introduced the medical skills of the Middle East to Western Europe.
8 Benozzo Gozzoli (c.1421–97), painter of the Florentine Renaissance mainly famed for a vibrant, detailed series of murals depicting contemporary personalities in procession under the guise of *The Journey of the Magi to Bethlehem*.
9 'Marx as Historian', *New Statesman and Nation*, 24 September 1955, 366.
10 Eric John Ernest Hobsbawm (b. 1917), Marxist historian; Fellow, King's Cambridge, 1949–55;

20 August) said that Jacob Burckhardt[1] was a better historian and a more accurate prophet than Karl Marx. But his own argument seems to me to establish nothing at all. No educated person today would seek to deny the paramount influence, for good or ill (or both) of Marxism on all forms of historical writing; least of all Mr Trevor-Roper. But this does not alter the fact that Burckhardt's masterpiece on the Italian Renaissance profoundly affected the methods of study of European civilisation in the last millennium; and has acted as a powerful antidote to one-sided interpretations of the facts by the bigoted followers of many a fanatical creed. Mr Trevor-Roper points out quite correctly that, whereas Burckhardt's predictions were of a startling originality and accuracy, Marx's were largely falsified by events. To this Mr Hobsbawm can find nothing better to say than that Heine, too, had successfully seen into the future. So, for that matter, had more than one member of the opposite camp – Maistre and Dostoevsky, for example. Yet none of these claims to be scientific. Marx and Engels did. One of the tests of a true science is capacity for correct prediction. In this, as Mr Trevor-Roper was concerned to point out, Marx (in company with the other builders of vast historical cosmologies during the last hundred years) had notoriously failed. As for the *Eighteenth Brumaire*,[2] does even Mr Hobsbawm believe that this interesting *pièce d'occasion*[3] would have survived on its own unaided merits – if its author had not been Karl Marx? Little service is rendered to the memory of one man of genius by wantonly representing his minor writings as incomparably superior to the major achievement of another.

Isaiah Berlin

TO MORTON WHITE

17 October 1955

All Souls

Dear Morton,

You ask my views about Burton Dreben.[4] His merits seem to me of a really remarkable order; he has a sharp mind, his ideas are clear, orderly and

---

Lecturer in History, Birkbeck, London, 1947–59, Reader 1959–70; later (1970–82) Professor of Economic and Social History, London (Birkbeck). In a letter to the *New Statesman* ('Marx as Historian', 20 August 1955, 217), he had commented on Trevor-Roper's review ('The Faustian Historian', *New Statesman*, 4 August 1955, 164–5) of *The Letters of Jacob Burckhardt*, trans. and ed. Alexander Dru (London and New York, 1955).

1 Jacob Burckhardt (1818–97), Swiss cultural and artistic historian, known particularly for his *The Civilisation of the Renaissance in Italy* (1860).

2 Marx's *The Eighteenth Brumaire of Louis Napoleon*, written in 1851–2 during the rise to power of the future Emperor Napoleon III.

3 'Occasional piece'.

4 On 7 October MW had requested 'a strong testimonial in behalf of Burton Dreben', whom he hoped Harvard could 'rescue [...] from Chicago'.

coherent, and he possesses a disinterested love of the truth greater than in almost any human being I have ever met.

In addition to these qualities he has a very acute eye for what is important and what is trivial in both the writings and the spoken words of philosophers; and, when he came to Oxford some years ago, although the University and its philosophers must have seemed very strange and peculiar to him, he appraised the scene perfectly correctly within a very few weeks. At first the Oxford philosophers could not make out how much there was behind his obvious passion and sincerity; it was not clear whether he was a remarkably lucid expositor or whether he had something original of his own to say as well. Presently it became plain that he lived for his subject, and was capable of discussing it at almost any level with great intellectual stimulation and profit to his interlocutors. In consequence our leading philosophers, e.g. Professors Ryle and Austin as well as the younger men – Hampshire, Warnock,[1] Pears[2] and others – became devoted to him personally and intellectually. Students, both graduate and undergraduate, also clustered round him, attracted perhaps as much by the warmth and integrity of his personality as by the fact that he invariably had something to say – [since he] could always be relied upon to deliver the goods. He seems to me a dedicated philosopher and a born teacher, certainly any college here could well employ him as a tutor; he seems to be well above the level of the majority of our philosophers, and that at a period when philosophy is flourishing as never before in this university; and while I should not go so far as to say that he possessed anything like philosophical genius, it seems to me that he has a capacity for assimilating and understanding what is most original and important in the philosophy of his own time ⟨⟨more particularly logic and the relevant mathematics⟩⟩, which, from the point of view of teaching and creating an atmosphere in which philosophy flourishes, is almost more important. I cannot think of any philosophical community which his presence would not both morally and intellectually benefit. You have not told me what post it is that is being discussed in connection with him; but if it is a teaching position I can recommend him more wholeheartedly than I have ever recommended any pupil of my own. ⟨And of course, as we both know, he is a very, very good human being and loyal and generous colleague.⟩

Yours sincerely,
Isaiah Berlin

---

1 Geoffrey James Warnock (1923–95), Fellow and Lecturer in Philosophy, Brasenose, 1950–2; Fellow and Tutor in Philosophy, Magdalen, 1952–71; later (1971–88) Principal, Hertford, and (1981–5) Vice-Chancellor, Oxford University.

2 David Francis Pears (1921–2009), Fellow and Tutor in Philosophy, CCC, 1950–60.

1955–1956

CHICAGO AND NEW YORK

To live on a perpetual rising wave of very strong very calm very real emotion is a luxury not known to me before.[1]

How warm hearted, nice, welcoming, sincere & sweet all these people are, & how impossible it is to live among them![2]

1 To Marie Berlin, 16 November 1955.
2 ibid.

On 3 November IB once again sailed to the US on the Queen Elizabeth, *bound this time, via Mount Holyoke, for the University of Chicago, where he was to spend five weeks as Alexander White Visiting Professor.*

TO MARIE BERLIN

11 a.m. [3? November 1955, *manuscript card*]

Southampton

You looked *too* sad when I left the house – it is a terrible *bore* that I should go away now – & a nuisance – but not tragic. And I do think you should, as soon as you walk quite freely, take a holiday – in Paris – in Rapallo (*not* San Remo) in December. When I think of what state I was in last November 3 – in Oxford – very nervous, uncertain of everything – trying to fill my life with Barclay & Selzer news[1] – pessimistic about my own future – emotionally still connected unsuitably – I must say, 1955 is the most triumphant year of my life. [...]
love
    Isaiah   [...]

TO MARIE BERLIN

Monday, Midnight & Tuesday morning [8 November 1955, New York postmark, *manuscript*]

RMS *Queen Elizabeth*

Dearest Mama,
    The journey was delicious. One slightly rough day but I felt nothing. Who did I know on board? some wartime colleagues: Milstein[2] the violinist with whom I shared a table at his request: to whom I talked Russian & with whom I sang a good deal. He comes from Odessa and plays extremely well. Like all virtuosi very self-centred but in response to my Russian flirtation, melted. We are now friends. The Baroness[3] very gracious. Thinks she knows me much better – & wished me to tell Aline that she is very much "for" – more & more with every day – she is under the spell of her Norwegian maid who is however nice, & does not exploit her position. Madame de Gunzbourg is like those widowed queens – Queen Anne[4] or Anna Ioannovna,[5] who are

1 Clifford Henry Barclay (1907–92), businessman, accountant and educational benefactor, gave financial advice on Mendel Berlin's estate to IB and his mother; Maurice (Maishel) Selzer (1913–90) appears to have succeeded his father Schaie, who died in 1944, as Mendel's partner in his bristle business.
2 Nathan Mironovich Milstein (1903–92), Ukrainian-born violinist.
3 Aline Halban's mother, Baronne Yvonne de Gunzbourg (1882–1969), née Deutsch de la Meurthe, widow of Baron Pierre de Gunzbourg.
4 Queen Anne (1665–1714) reigned 1702–14, and was influenced for many years (long before being widowed in 1708) by Sarah Churchill, Duchess of Marlborough, and then by Abigail Hill, later Baroness Masham.
5 Anna Ioannovna (1693–1740), Tsarina of Russia 1730–40, daughter of Tsar Ivan V and niece of

shrewd, ignorant, kind & frightened of the world & liable to fall under the influence of favourites. Our relations are very good. Aline telephoned twice to the boat as she will probably tell you. I've worked quite well, but never enough: one or two intellectual American ladies discovered my presence & invited me to dinner: earnest, boring, kind & exhausting. The baroness attracted various rich semi-Jewish Europeans to all of whom she "told the news". She is disarmingly indiscreet. [...]

Warmest love
    Isaiah

We have stopped in New York harbour. I shall post this in New York in an hour.

TO MARIE BERLIN

16 November 1955 [*manuscript*]

Chicago

Dearest Mama,

Thank you for your letters. I am glad that Elath wrote – he *is* a very nice man. As for the cultivation of my future belle-mère[1] on the ship, she was perfectly sweet & all went well. Here life is perfectly peaceful & dull. The hotel is comfortable, the food excellent: the city I consider hideously ugly. I have an absolutely regular day with no complications. For once I have managed to avoid social life; nobody knows me here: by the time they "discover" me and start inviting I shall be gone. I am, as always, a little nervous about my lectures:[2] not that it matters terribly: but unless I fuss they do not come out 'right' – still I am much much better than I used to be. My health is *excellent*: I am a little bored. I have absolutely nothing to write. Aline sends me wonderful letters, on these I feed. Tonight I shall go to the opera, which is magnificent:[3] tomorrow to a concert (before my lecture – so I *must* be less nervous than I was) the hotel is full of rich Jewish ladies who are not very different from either Lady Joseph[4] or the friends of Clifford Barclay: the line travels up & up & reaches the baroness Ginzburg in the end: I *could* not live here: plenty of Yiddish is to be heard: "Mogen Dovid" wine[5] is boldly adver-

Peter the Great, widowed in 1711 soon after her marriage, became an autocratic ruler surrounded by German favourites, notably Ernst Johann von Biron, who may have been her lover.

1 'Mother-in-law'.

2 On 'The Romantic Revolution in Philosophy'. If there was a text, it does not survive.

3 The Lyric Theatre of Chicago (renamed as Lyric Opera of Chicago in 1956) had been founded in 1954; its policy of employing European (especially Italian) singers under-used by the other major US opera companies achieved immediate success. Maria Callas was one of the stars of the 1954 and 1955 seasons.

4 Presumably Lady (Hellen Louise) Joseph (1930–2003), née Guggenheimer, the American first wife of Conservative politician Sir Keith Joseph.

5 The Yiddish pronunciation of 'Mogen David' ('Star of David'), a brand of sweet kosher wine.

tised in all the elevated railway stations: & still & yet it is a frightful culture: provincial, gross, terribly "prost"[1] – everything I cannot bear: *everyone* looks like Mr Gordon *père* or Mr Gordon *fils*,[2] no air for me to breathe. So I shall be glad to escape to New York & Washington which I much prefer. But why am I writing all this rubbish to you? even Israel affairs don't grip me as much as they should – for I am happily in love. It is an astonishing sensation – quite different not only from the long Patricia involvement – which was exalté but wretched & hysterical – but also the one with J. which was harmonious but could lead nowhere & therefore full of anxiety & a sense of pointlessness. To live on a perpetual rising wave of very strong very calm very real emotion is a luxury not known to me before: pourvu que ça dure[3] – but I am sure, I know it will. So all these anxieties about lectures, solitudes etc. are obliterated by a pervading sense of happiness – a miraculous state which no one who has not had it can imagine. Philippe[4] now says *he* wants to be a witness at the marriage: but he may be in America. I am very happy about your foot – I am sure that it will not only heal beautifully but the *massage* & diathermic rays will make the other one better too. Now I *must* stop, since a typist has arrived and I must, as always, dictate answers to the Universities of Wisconsin, Iowa, Ohio, and Michigan to say that I either cannot – or can – visit them next week. How warm hearted, nice, welcoming, sincere & sweet all these people are, & how impossible it is to live among them! Au revoir – I'll write again very soon.

fondest love

Isaiah

TO MARIE BERLIN

Sunday 20 November 1955 [*manuscript*]

Chicago

Dearest Ma.

I am in a gay mood. Today is Sunday (I haven't written to you for a day or two, because too busy) – I am not socially too busy – *that* is the only thing which really exhausts one – not work – that + lectures which are themselves a kind of social occupation. My first lecture, last Thursday was tremendously well attended – instead of 125 expected 400 appeared – I hate shouting – but still I suppose if one is a tenor one likes an audience. The lecture itself was I think only so-so; but the next one will be better. I was much entertained by

---

1 'Uncultured'.

2 Friends of the Berlin family.

3 'Provided that it lasts'. Perhaps IB was thinking of the occurrence of this phrase that he quoted in a much later essay on the fall of Communism: 'as Madame Bonaparte said when congratulated on the historically unique distinction of being mother to an emperor, three kings and a queen, "Oui, pourvu que ça dure."' 'The Survival of the Russian Intelligentsia', SM 166.

4 Aline Halban's brother, Baron Philippe de Gunzbourg (1904–86), a hero of the French Resistance.

a jolly Jew called Goddard Lieberson:[1] stammt aus Dvinsk:[2] this only came out *very* late in the day; he was very kind, took me to the Opera etc. – the Italian singers here, Chicago being very rich, are splendid: Tebaldi,[3] Callas etc. – Callas had to *flee* because someone was claiming 8000 dollars from her & she didn't want to pay – *after* the performance in the dressing room some legal officials ("acting on behalf of lawyers Berelson, Levy, Washington Cohen (that's good!) etc".) tried to intercept her but she flew off to Canada quickly and was gone.[4] Tonight I dine & stay the night with Adlai Stevenson (don't tell people: a) envy b) someone will tell further, & it will appear in the Evening Standard & that would be *terrible*) because he is a friend of Trees & Schlesinger & they wrote him about me. Oovidim.[5] Nice man, I am sure, gentleman etc. but v nashikh delakh[6] a bit à la Eden. Still, we'll see. I am sure I shall have an agreeable evening. No sign of Shneyerson;[7] as I do not know where *he* is, I can do nothing. Telephone call from Washington (elaborate programme of entertainment December 16–20) & Boston (Mrs Constable, rightly, thinks Aline & I had better stay in a *hotel*: then nobody will be offended, & more freedom) – I don't like Chicago as such – & the clever Jews in the university are too smart & "prost" for me – but I *think* I've concealed this successfully so far – but I've found two nice serious ones: I don't like potential Bundists[8] if you know what I mean: Jews with colossal noses, who hate Zionism, make jolly Jewish jokes, but ultimately *are* ashamed and aggressive: Roosevelt liked them – Foster likes them – Laski was such a one – & I cannot stand them & father disliked them too – it is all a matter of 'touch' – hence my liking for David Cecil, love for Aline etc. – it is all part of the same Drang nach schöne[n] Seelen[9] & away from "*Poshlost'*" (пошлость).[10] A charming note

1 Goddard Lieberson (1911–77), President of Columbia Records 1956–71, 1973–5; composer and influential music executive, prominent in introducing the long-playing record and original-cast recordings of musicals, and in fostering the recording of classical music, including the complete operas of leading operatic composers; born in England.
2 'Originates from Dvinsk' (now Daugavpils in Latvia).
3 Renata Ersilia Clotilde Tebaldi (1922–2004), Italian operatic soprano, at this time based in the US. IB arrived in Chicago too late to attend her performances at the Lyric Theatre in 1955.
4 On 17 November 1955, as Callas left the stage of the Lyric Theatre after her final performance in *Madama Butterfly*, a US Marshal served her with a subpoena in relation to Eddy Bargozy's claim to be her agent, entitled to a percentage of her earnings; Callas's furious reaction received worldwide publicity.
5 'We'll see.'
6 'In our affairs', i.e. on Jewish matters.
7 Presumably Menachem Mendel Schneerson (1902–94), 7th Lubavitcher (517/4) Rebbe (leader of the Chabad sect of Hasidic Judaism), to whom IB was distantly related, and who was based in New York from 1941.
8 Members of the Bund ('Federation' or 'Union'; at its founding in 1897 the General Jewish Labour Union of Lithuania, Poland and Russia), a socialist, anti-Zionist political party; after the war, more significant in the US than in Europe.
9 'Attraction to elegant spirits'.
10 'Vulgarity'. The prime after the Cyrillic form is redundant.

from Rev. I Levy[1] offering to marry us. Aline's last letter still talks about the Synagogue – I am not clear whether the Chupah[2] is to be in Dennington Park Road[3] or Hollycroft! does not matter anyhow. Now I have to take a bath (yes, yes!) shower, dress, & go to lunch with a Professor. Breakfast in bed makes an *enormous* difference to one's physical state: I don't feel tired at all. [...]

Much love
    Isaiah

TO ALICE JAMES

Wednesday before Thanksgiving [23 November 1955, *manuscript*]

Chicago

Dear Alice,

Here I am in this extraordinary town: the vast distances, the sharp social contrasts between wealth and poverty, the tough, exhilarating, fascinating, slightly brutal & at the same time warm hearted atmosphere are all very different from the East Coast – I see what is meant by regarding Boston & even New York as tainted with Europe. The University is going through a crisis: abandoned by the impetuous & fascinating & perverse but remarkable Hutchins,[4] it is like a lady deserted by a demon lover: slightly dazed & wondering what next. The students at my classes are very interested & lively & delightful: & my colleagues are all charming to me: as so often in this country I dislike no one: not even the fabulous monsters among the professors whom other professors solemnly warn me against.[5] I like them all, even the sinister McKeon,[6] professor of philosophy, object of horror to the Harvard philosophers: last night I dined with a man of great charm – von Simson,[7] an art historian; I seldom like Germans: but he and his wife detest Wagner and are very sympathetic. I have been to the Opera where Mme Callas made a violent scene[8] about being nearly arrested for not paying some real or imaginary debt – like Comic Opera in itself – & have met Mr Adlai Stevenson. So, you see, I have "done" the sights: & am much more at peace than ever I was at Cambridge, partly no doubt for

1 Isaac ('Harry') Levy (1910–2005), British army chaplain (involved in the liberation of Bergen-Belsen); committed Zionist; minister of Hampstead Synagogue 1946–65.
2 The open-sided canopy under which a Jewish wedding is solemnised.
3 The address of Hampstead Synagogue.
4 Robert Hutchins had resigned in 1951, after 22 controversial years as President of the University of Chicago, to become an Associate Director of the Ford Foundation.
5 'This is quite an interesting place, intellectually. And Morty's [Morton White's] fears that I have fallen among bandits are on the whole groundless. The sinister monsters turn out to be quite gentle and civilised and interesting people, and the students are splendid.' To Chadbourne Gilpatric, 23 November 1955.
6 Richard Peter McKeon (1900–85), Charles F. Grey Distinguished Service Professor of Greek and Philosophy, Chicago, 1947–74.
7 Otto Georg von Simson (1912–93), German art historian who taught at University of Chicago 1945–57 (Professor 1951–7).
8 IB cannot have attended this particular performance as he was lecturing at the time.

personal "inner" reasons: I am deeply in love, miss Aline most terribly, write
to her daily, & cannot wait for her to come. The divorce won't be through till
the end of January, so till then, we must go on waiting patiently. Olivia wrote
& very kindly offered to "give us" a party: & I gratefully accepted. My plan is
to stay here till the 12th: by this time Aline arrives in N.Y. to her mother [...] We
are not to be too long together – life is full of frustrations – for she must go to
her children at Mégève, in the Alps, (they haven't been told about my future
rôle: oh dear, how *will* they take it, the little ones?) while I return to Oxford.
Will you be in Cambridge on Dec. 27–29? I don't allow the possibility that you
will not even to cross my mind. I have kept myself very free of specific engagements – I don't know for which day Olivia plans her party – I shall ask her to
ask all the people who otherwise I would have to pay separate visits to – I mean
professors & graduate students – apart from those she would wish to invite
anyway. I must be up & go & hold a class – I do tremble about my lectures anew
each time – it is silly but I do – my love to Billy – it *is* so curious to be happy and
suffer pangs of parting at the same time – I'll have an enormous amount to
tell you when I see you alone – which I am most determined to do – however
late, however early
    love from
      Isaiah

A correspondence in the Spectator[1] *about the power of the British Establishment led to a complaint from an old friend.*[2]

1 After the revelation by the former KGB agent Vladimir Petrov that Guy Burgess and Donald
   Maclean had been long-term Soviet agents, the British Government responded by publishing (on
   23 September) their own (much-criticised) report on the defection of the two diplomats. But in
   the meantime Henry Fairlie (511/1) had used this opportunity to expound his own theories of
   the influence of what he termed 'the Establishment' – 'the whole matrix of official and social
   relations within which power is exercised' (*Spectator*, 23 September 1955, 380). Citing Lady Violet
   Bonham Carter as one of the 'divinities' of the Establishment and the Foreign Office as its power-
   base, Fairlie implied that VBC had influenced the press in favour of Burgess and Maclean. The
   next week (30 September) the *Spectator*'s letter-columns rang with cries of protest: VBC pointed
   out that her letter to *The Times* of 21 July 1952 had dealt solely with press harassment of Maclean's
   family and misrepresentation of Foreign Office comments; John Sparrow defended the Foreign
   Office's recruitment procedures, in which he had taken part. Fairlie stood his ground, and on
   7 October VBC further proclaimed her innocence of his (unspecified) accusations, and other
   correspondents joined the fray, David Astor and Randolph Churchill broadly supporting VBC,
   while Robert Boothby steered the debate into turbulent new waters: 'I am not surprised that
   Warden Sparrow has weighed in with an offensive letter about Mr Fairlie's article [...]. All Souls
   was the headquarters of the Establishment during the decade immediately preceding the Second
   World War; and it would be difficult to overestimate the damage then done to this country at
   that disastrous dinner table.' Boothby later expanded on this, concluding: 'The Fellows of All
   Souls included Dr Lang, Lord Halifax, Mr Geoffrey Dawson, Sir John Simon, Mr Lionel Curtis,
   Sir Donald Somervell and Mr R. H. Brand – all recognised members of "the Establishment". I
   cannot say, because I do not know, which side each of them took on the great controversial issues
   of the day; but it is not difficult to imagine the desperate and losing post-prandial actions that
   must have been conducted by Mr Amery' (*Spectator*, 21 October 1955, 528).
2 'I have had a silly letter from Violet Bonham Carter – following one in which she congratulates
   me on you – & said she loved me more than anyone outside her children – not wholly false

TO VIOLET BONHAM CARTER

26 November 1955 [*manuscript*]

Chicago

Dearest Violet,

First things first. Let me thank you with all my heart for your letter to me about my impending marriage: it was a long & agonised business about which I shall tell you – if you will not refuse to listen to a long & terribly personal saga – when I return in January: everything has to be kept hideously secret till late this year, then it "leaked" in Paris via my future wife's mother – baronne De Gunzbourg – who told some relative who told Diana Cooper who told . . . you can imagine for yourself. At any rate I've told Mark a good deal: I am excited, happy, & long to tell you. I am truly devoted to you & would have told you all myself if I could bring myself to mention it casually when we saw each other – but the whole thing is so odd & has transformed my life to such a fantastic degree, that I should like a peaceful & private context in which I could describe it all – I am deeply deeply grateful to you for your wonderfully written (as all that you do is – however direct & personal & spontaneous) and moving letter; I really love you very much.

Now as to Boothby etc. I am a little wounded – save that your first letter stanched the blood – by the fact that you could ever have conceived me guilty of giving aid and comfort to your detractors. *Of course* I abhor Fairlie (who once attacked me too)[1] Muggeridge,[2] Colm Brogan[3] et *hoc genus omne*,[4] utterly: & hope never to be in the same room with any of them. I have never seen them, & don't wish [*illegible*]: the whole "campaign" was utterly *vile*. For Bob I have a warm spot, as you have, & as John Sparrow too has (who is an intimate friend of his) – he is a loveable *scamp*. I met him at lunch at Ava Waverley's house: there too was my colleague John Foster. I said (to the best of my recollection: Bob's is *shocking*, mine is, I hope, much better) "I suppose I ought not to shake hands with you' & then told him what indeed I think to be true – that some of the authors of Munich – Halifax, Simon, Dawson,[5]

---

possibly – she is a queer inhuman distinguished clever cerebral monster – I appeal to ladies over 60 it seems – & blamed me for telling Bob Boothby that All Souls was pro-Munich, or something – & contradicting something *she* had said in the *Spectator*.' To Aline Halban [28 November 1955].

1　Henry Jones Fairlie (1924–90), journalist and author; political leader-writer, *The Times*, 1950–4; political columnist, *Spectator*, 1954–6; settled in the US in 1965. See 471/8 for his review of HI.

2　(Thomas) Malcolm Muggeridge (1903–90), journalist and author; deputy editor, *Daily Telegraph*, 1950–2; editor, *Punch*, 1953–7; impugned VBC's intelligence in a fiercely anti-Establishment letter (*Spectator* 1955, 496).

3　Colm Brogan (1902–77), journalist; agreed with Fairlie and accused VBC of 'a self-assurance too solid and too unconscious to be called merely smug' (*Spectator*, 14 October 1955, 498), but the following week admitted to factual errors in his argument.

4　'And all their kind'.

5　Geoffrey Dawson (1874–1944), né Robinson, historian; Fellow of All Souls, 1898–1906, 1911–44; editor, *The Times*, 1912–19, 1923–41.

Lang[1] etc. were indeed all at All Souls & one used to hear them – & their guests of similar opinions – talk in a Munichois manner in the thirties – that he was *wrong* in thinking the pitched battles were fought by the anti-Munich Amery & them – that while Amery *was* against Munich, *I* never heard him thunder at the Munichois at All Souls – & that one understood how Munich came about when one heard this group of Fellows talking – that in this sense All Souls was a club at which they met – & that annoyance *had* been caused by his letter, particularly to Brand whom he mentioned – Bob said he had hoped that Brand would *not* have seen his letter. That was all. Nothing about doves or dovecotes – it is not a phrase I've ever used in my life – nor, *of course*, about how salutary for All Souls his letter had been. John Foster, Ava, Nancy Mitford, Malcolm [sc. Alan?] Bullock, Clarissa Eden, & possibly others were there – they are my witnesses. John F. will remember best, as I involved him – as a fellow – Fellow – in my jolly exchanges with Bob – certainly his version is what is called "gravely misleading" & you can tell him so if occasion should arise – let me repeat: I may well have corroborated that All Souls in the thirties *was* a centre of some powerful Munichois – of course not *qua* All Souls – but I implied no possible approval of his attack on John Sparrow & All Souls – which John didn't much mind – indeed he invited Bob, I think, to visit (indeed chided him for associating with Muggeridge) "the All Souls Establishment" which Bob prudently refused. So that is that. I think you did nobly in the *Spectator*: so did John Sparrow: & am glad to hear that Bob had the decency to grovel to you, however unconvincingly! I like him: but his letter, as I told John Sp. was evoked by hatred of Simon – who he blamed for his own political ruin in 1940[2] – intelligible but not very excusable:

  love

   yrs

     Isaiah

P.S. All Bob is trying to do is to rescue himself by muddling me – of whom he knows you to be a friend – into the story. But I am truly innocent: I am getting angry at being alleged to speak of fluttering dovecotes when the relevant doves are dead & gone – & All Souls was always full of violent anti-Nazi feeling.

---

1 Cosmo Gordon Lang (1864–1945), 1st Baron Lang 1942; Fellow of All Souls 1889–93, 1897–1928; Archbishop of Canterbury 1928–42.
2 In 1941 Boothby, a rising political star, had been forced to resign from his post as Parliamentary Secretary at the Ministry of Food when a parliamentary inquiry found him guilty of improper financial conduct.

TO MARIE BERLIN

28 November 1955 [*manuscript*]

Chicago

Dearest Mama,

The days are passing, thank God, for although I am well and quite busy, I am bored. Not terribly, but it is somehow a *pure* waste of time: I have met some new people, but I still make no permanent friends here: & so much the better, I have enough – too many. The lectures are going quite well: people seem not dissatisfied.[1] Two nights ago, I don't know why, I visited a friend of Fred Rau whom I last met in New York in 1941: lower middle class Chicago Jews. Warm hearted, vulgar, noisy, half Yiddish speaking – Zionist, anti-British, pro-Russian, ignorant, hideous to look at – the *grossness* is too great. I am sorry to say I *could* not take it. I behaved well: but they were embarrassed by me – I was too grand – & were by turn obsequious & aggressive. They are excellent people – generous, natural etc. but like an over-rich Kosher meal – I get nauseated. Never mind. The next night I went to hear Oistrakh[2] play (in *Time Magazine* he jokes about his name being = ой страх!)[3] he was *marvellous*. First of all it is nice that he looks like a solid Russian Jew. Secondly he plays with freshness, appetite, sweetness of tone, ease, & a simple uncomplicated attitude of a bootmaker making boots. No nonsense. Much better than either Heifetz or Menuhin,[4] even than Stern.[5] No Goyim could be seen in the audience. I went with a Zionist philosopher[6] & we enjoyed ourselves greatly. Apart from weighing 200 lb. I have no troubles. Aline writes very nice letters every day & so do I. I shall be glad to see her, to say the least. I have replied to Levy, & had a nice letter from Barclay (in answer to mine) not telling me much. Arrangements are being made to entertain "us" in Washington & Boston whither we go like visiting celebrities: Mrs James & Olivia Constable in Boston (both of whom send you their love in their letters to me) in Washington by Frankfurter – Alsop – Lady Harcourt etc. I am very well: content: not overworked: well fed: bored: no more to say. Aline wants to be married in synagogue: very well. I feel lucky, happy, arrived at a destination. Au revoir – I'll write to you soon again –

Love

Isaiah   [. . .]

---

1 To Aline he was more outspoken: 'I have just lectured: it was a colossal success, I have to admit. I was warned that the original 300 wd melt – two concerts & a public meeting was occurring – 450 came & were turned away from the largest hall in the place – it is shameful virtuosity' (letter of 21 November 1955).

2 David Fedorovich Oistrakh (1908–74), Russian Jewish violinist, born in Odessa (Ukraine).

3 'He half humorously traces his name to the Yiddish exclamation *oi* and the Russian word *strakh*, which means fear' (*Time*, 28 November 1955, 42).

4 Yehudi Menuhin (1916–99), later (1993) Baron Menuhin, US violinist of Russian Jewish descent; IB's fourth cousin.

5 Isaac Stern (1920–2001), US violinist (born in Ukraine to Russian Jewish parents).

6 Burton Dreben.

TO ALICE JAMES

30 November 1955 [*manuscript*]

Chicago

Dear Alice,

Thank you ever so much for your very sweet good letter. I am delighted to hear that Billy is so much better – is it really necessary to take "wonder" drugs – I know that my dear father suffered tortures as a result of strepto-mycin – still he *did* recover in 1952 – & his later, fatal, illness had *nothing* to do with the earlier one. I do hope Billy is not too gloomy & won't think it necessary to rise & welcome us when we come – I'll come & call on him with Aline – I know he likes her – separately & specially & at length – & we'll have our talk while they speak of painters [...] – oh it is a queer sensa-tion, & an astonishing & very radiant one to be so deeply & so happily in love after 46 years of – well perhaps this is exaggeration – one is scarcely a bachelor at the age of 2 – after say 27 years of taken for granted solitude! I am glad Maurice approves – Aline likes him v. much. I really am pining for her now – I am not exactly bored here – I worry about my lectures too much – but it is a strange place, left in a state of emotional exhaustion after its long & turbulent rule by Hutchins – they don't know how their future is to be – but there is plenty of *life* here & the students most responsive & the whole thing fascinating. I'll tell you when I see you – & now I must proceed to my lonely visit to the Opera[1] – not long alone I hope. My fondest love to you & Billy – you mean so much, really so much to me – & Aline loves you so well – I never can answer Billy's marvellous letters – the standard is too high – I feel one cannot just scribble –

love

Isaiah

TO JOHN SPARROW

2 December 1955

Chicago

My dear John,

[...] You will have learned from my earlier letter, I attended a dinner and a lecture by our old friend.[2] I think he made quite a good impression during an earlier visit when he addressed the experts in English history of the Middle West. However, the lecture on the Elizabethan Age[3] was a trifle misconceived. He spoke before an academic audience in a huge theatre in

1 To see Donizetti's *L'elisir d'amore*.
2 A. L. Rowse.
3 Rowse frequently lectured in the US, mainly on Elizabethan England at this time; he had pub-lished *The England of Elizabeth*, the first of three related books, in 1950.

front of a velvet curtain, was introduced in a courteous and amusing speech by the chief local historian, then proceeded to give such a lecture as must have given pleasure to the ladies' luncheon clubs in Cheltenham and Bath, and perhaps their equivalents here too. The colleagues who were sitting on either side of me began to simmer with indignation quite early and proceeded to rise to boiling point long before he was done.

He was arch, coy, facetious, made little jokes about the appeal of jewellery to ladies and the terrible inroads this must make into their husbands' purses, both now and then in the Elizabethan Age, took us for a tour of a country house or two, and made some flattering references to one or two local professors and one or two efforts intended [for] me, who was sitting virtually in the front row glaring at him. I was referred to as one of the most eminent institutions of the great College from which he had the honour to visit us, and also as one of the most distinguished inhabitants of a building which was once described by some American visitors as a collection of ruins. He imitated the imaginary accent of a Middlewestern lady – 'Say, are these ruins inhabited?' – in the middle of the lecture. (I could have died of embarrassment.)

Afterwards he seized me by the arm and said, 'I must admit to you, my dear, that this was gamma, definitely gamma.' It was a great deal worse and I had difficulty to defend this before the angry local faculty. What an extraordinary man he is. He called on me the next morning to ask me why the intellectuals hate him so much.

He is making a tour of the Southern Universities and although his books are probably quite good – and have obtained glowing reviews in the New York press – he is likely to do us little good. When I see you, I shall give you an even more vivid impression, if I can, of what it is like to sit there, in the first row, with some perfectly decent American professors, unable to look or listen. (He has written to this university, soliciting a post. It is really *too* awful.)

'How did you like it?' he asked me. Insincerely, and quite truthfully, I said, 'I could have gone on listening for ever', for the sheer monstrosity of it. Toward the end I did lose my embarrassment and wondered what you would have done. It was not boring; in the sense in which Grand Guignol is not boring. [...]

Yours ever,

  Isaiah

IB had missed Aline desperately during his time in Chicago. On 10 December she joined him. But they were not to have much time alone. IB's American friends had arranged a full programme of social events so that they could meet his bride.

TO MARIE BERLIN

10 December 1955 [*cablegram*]

Chicago

WE ARE EXTREMELY HAPPY FONDEST LOVE ISAIALINE

TO MARIE BERLIN

21 December 1955 [*manuscript*]

New York

Dearest Mama

I apologise *deeply* for not writing for a week: I am of course *extremely* well and very very happy. Last Friday, after a few delightful days in New York (Mme de Gunzburg likes me *very* much) we went to Washington: triumphal tour. First evening quiet with *Harcourts*: met at station by 2 Vissons (назой-ливый еврей!)[1] while I was trying to explain how to get a porter to a Russian orthodox bishop: fantastic spectacle. Then life in a suite, expensive but at least intimate, in the Mayflower Hotel. Lunch with Felix: both are delighted with Aline. Marion permanently on her back with arthritis: perhaps she *could* get up, but obviously doesn't *want* to: wants to remain alone in a room forever like Heine: Felix very warm & doesn't understand why I took *so* long to woo my bride: *he* would have done it quicker (he says) – he showed me a most charming letter from Bowra really *very* warm & sweet, about me & my happiness. Even if he knew it might be shown to people, he need not have written. Tea with an 83 year old hostess – tout Washington[2] – unaltered from 1942 – snobbish & to me agreeably ancien régime. Dinner – enormous – Joe Alsop: very gay & friendly: Cabot Lodge,[3] Mrs Longworth, Mrs Alsop (mère) Stuart Alsop & wife,[4] Grahams (I am officially "reconciled" to him),[5] Felix, Johnny Walkers etc. etc. Sunday breakfast Eban: lunch American officials: Allen Dulles & his staff: later Francis Biddle & wife: dinner, a hostess called Mrs Bliss[6] (what Nabokov calls Blissukha)[7] followed by a concert: Monday visit to say good bye to Mrs Frankfurter, lunch with Henry Brandon (né

1 'Nazoilivyi evrei!' ('the importunate Jew!').
2 'All Washington' (sc. was in attendance).
3 Henry Cabot Lodge, Jr (1902–85), Republican Senator for Massachusetts 1947–53; US Ambassador to UN 1953–60; Richard Nixon's running-mate in his unsuccessful 1960 bid for the Presidency.
4 Stewart Johonnot Oliver Alsop (1914–74), newspaper columnist and editor; younger brother of Joe, with whom he wrote the syndicated 'Matter of Fact' column 1945–58. His English wife was the former Patricia Barnard ('Tish') Hankey (b. 1926).
5 IB and Phil Graham had been estranged since a 'terrible row' in March 1952: 'he was v. rude to me at his own table & I've never spoken to him since. He wrote a letter of apology which I didn't answer.' 23 November 1955 to Aline Halban.
6 Mildred Bliss (1875–1969), née Barnes, one of the leading Washington hostesses, wife of the diplomat and fellow art-collector Robert Woods Bliss; the Blisses gave their house, Dumbarton Oaks, to Harvard University in 1949.
7 'That Bliss woman', roughly: the suffix '-ukha' is pejorative.

Brandeis) of *our* Sunday Times[1] with more American officials, my lecture[2] –
Lippmann & Felix at opposite ends – oh I forgot, Sunday 6 p.m. visit to Sir R.
Makins – we could not lunch with him Monday, so he came to my lecture –
really *very* friendly – with Indian & Irish Ambassadors! lecture great success –
then dinner with *all* our friends – grand finale – & off on Tuesday morning.
Not forgetting 12 p.m. meeting with Dr Lattmann[3] – Heifetz friend – who
played Chassidic records & told me my lecture was like a *Rebbe's* allocution.
I go to Yahrzeit to Lubavitch Minyan![4]

    Love
       Isaiah

TO MARIE BERLIN

   1 January 1956 [*cablegram*]

New York

ARRIVING QUEEN MARY NINTH APOLOGISE NOT WRITTEN LIFE TOO
FULL EXTREMELY HAPPY FONDEST LOVE ISAIAH

TO MARION FRANKFURTER

   4 January 1956 [*manuscript*]

The Carlyle Hotel, New York

Dearest Marion

   I have delayed writing till the boat is nearly gone – it sails in ½ an hour –
& the condition for writing is not propitious. Why such tardiness? because
despite the great recent reforms, my life is still {is} a melancholy chaos, I
see people I don't wish to see in increasing quantities, which maddens Aline
and humiliates me; & cannot see those whom I wish to see through lazi-
ness, shyness (oddly enough: such as being unable to telephone the Hands)[5]

1 (Oscar) Henry Brandon (1916–93), né Brandeis in what soon became Czechoslovakia; correspondent, *Sunday Times*, 1939–83 (in Washington from 1949).
2 IB lectured on 'Contemporary Philosophical Revolution' on 19 December, probably at the
Institute of Contemporary Arts in Washington.
3 Isidore Lattman (*sic*) (1894–1971), Russian-born radiologist, Children's Hospital, Columbia,
1932–63 (also in private practice until 1954); a passionate music-lover with an interest in history
and philosophy, and a fund of Toscanini anecdotes. IB wrote to him on 11 August 1955: 'I now
consider myself to have recovered in the sense that I refuse to go and have any further cardio-
grams from anybody, and shall indeed not do so until I see you [...] Ever since you looked after
me in 1945 I have had no faith in anyone else.'
4 The Yahrzeit (anniversary in Jewish lunar months) of Mendel Berlin's death on 13 December 1953
fell on 24 December in 1955. Minyan ('number') signifies communal prayers, for which a quorum
of 10 is necessary. The small town of Lubavitch (between Vitebsk and Smolensk) was the base of
the Chabad sect for over a century. The sect combines a distinctive attitude to human knowledge
of the divine, and scholarly respect for the sacred texts, with the emotional fervour in prayer and
religious observance introduced by the original Hasidim. IB was normally wary of contact with
his distant cousin, the Lubavitcher Rebbe, and his followers.
5 Judge Learned Hand and his wife, the former Frances Amelia Fincke (1876–1963).

& fatalism about social life & the possibility of obtaining more than very little from "human contacts" – far less than I used to think possible before; perhaps far less also in fact. The phrase was used by a Chinese logician to me last year: "how many human contacts do you make in 1 day?" he asked: next time I come I shall not course about so madly (I say to myself as if I did not know myself) and sit quiet. I am glad you liked Aline. She liked Washington a great deal, Cambridge Mass not much, Mrs W[hitehead] not much. I called on Mr Burlingham,[1] unwisely, & it was a colossal failure. He rightly suspected that I was interested in his *age*, & resented this, & said so with some fire: said he did not wish to be stared at like a monster. Oh Lord, I must go & catch the ship. The culminating absurdity of my life wd be to miss it. Maurice's letter[2] was marvellous I thought – you are right to be violently with & for him: it is easier from here: but justified everywhere. I liked (in New York – human contacts) Miss Marianne Moore,[3] Auden, and Sam Behrman. Edmund Wilson seemed happy & much calmer & sweeter: marriage does widen the neck of the flask & soothe (at least his) savage breasts. He *adored* Israel – every one in it – I think mainly because I said he wouldn't. My new relations, French, Italian, Russian, are amiable enough, but a thin lot: & goggle at me as Mr Burlingham supposed I did at him: I shall be glad to be back in dreary old Oxford. Why do all splendid Americans – C. C. Burlingham – Hand – etc. *adore* Goodhart? Somewhere there *is* an absence of discrimination, & a public standard of values which surely won't do. I shall, I hope, return in a year's time, married, with wife & kids, & report to you on one year of marriage. Goodness me: I don't feel enormously real: I *suppose* it is all in order: I *suppose* it *is* right to embark on such critical courses with no sense of drama, like opening a window: anyway I'll soon know: or will I not?

Love

Isaiah

---

1 Charles Culp Burlingham (1858–1959), lawyer and civic reformer, influential in key judicial appointments and a major force in combating political corruption in New York in the 1930s.
2 See 516.
3 Marianne Moore (1887–1972), US poet and critic.

1956–1957

MARRIAGE AND RECOGNITION

[...] that unheard of wonder – the rarest of all things – the most wonderful luck & coincidence – the knowledge that one has arrived where one has always wanted to be.[1]

[...] there really is such a thing as shame before undeserved rewards [...][2]

1 To Aline Halban, 10 August 1955.
2 To Charles Webster, 7 July 1957.

TO MARIE BERLIN

30 January 1956 [*manuscript*]

All Souls

Dearest Mama,

[...] Your letter re the "children"[1] is a document of moral genius and I am *deeply* grateful for it. You are *quite* right: & it will alter my life & conduct. I have wired Ida. I have spoken to Elath: he will come to Hollycroft at 2.45 p.m. 7*th*, & *take* us to the Synagogue for the wedding at 3 p.m. sharp. The Evening Standard *keeps* telephoning: so far I have revealed *nothing*. And you know nothing of course. Levy comes to us Monday 6*th* at 5.30 p.m.

Love love love

IB and Aline Halban were married at Hampstead Synagogue on 7 February.

TO WILLIAM AND ALICE JAMES

8 February 1956 [*telegram*]

Oxford

SAFELY MARRIED ISAIAH ALINE

A similar message was sent a further 21 times to other friends.

TO ROWLAND BURDON-MULLER

13 February 1956 [*manuscript card*]

Headington House

Dearest Rowland

I cannot forebear from writing to you from this strange – in a sense – new address: I am indubitably happier than I've ever been before & the concept of happiness has been vastly widened. Not but what I am in bed with a cold inevitable after so much strain – delightful, but still, exhausting. I see, it does not do to be married too frequently. The wedding was *very* 'quiet' as the *Times* said.[2] There were present only the Rev. Mr Levy; my mother; my aunt, her sister; my witness – the Israel Ambassador; Aline's witness – Victor Rothschild; her son Michel[3] who expressed a strong desire to be present in defiance of all that Freud etc. might say (I don't know *what* Marietta would say to that) & an old lady, friend to my mama who could not be kept out. Nobody else. The *Hampstead & Highgate News*[4] published a

---

1 Not found.
2 *The Times*, 8 February 1956, 10 ('The marriage took place quietly yesterday [...]').
3 Michel Jules Strauss (b. 1936), son of Aline Halban and her first husband André Strauss. See further 792 under Halban, Aline.
4 The front-page article referred to 'a very hush-hush wedding' conducted in great secrecy, quoted

headline about "Hush-hush wedding" & the *Evening Standard* had an innocuous gossip item,[1] having been prudently "squared" by me via intermediaries
beforehand. Otherwise nothing save the formal announcement in the *Times*.
We stayed two nights at the Ritz & came here & all goes well, touch wood.[2]
The stepchildren seem very affable, though little Peter tactfully suppresses
his sighs for his father. Write to us.

love

    Isaiah.

*IB had been on the Board of the Royal Opera House (and of the Sadler's Wells
Trust) since late 1954, with responsibilities covering both of the ROH's resident
companies, the long-established Sadler's Wells Ballet and the Covent Garden
Opera Company, formed in 1946. His extensive knowledge of opera made him
an influential adviser.*

TO DAVID WEBSTER[3]

2 March 1956

                                                        Headington House

Dear Webster,

I was exceedingly sorry not to be able to attend the last meeting of the
Directors, especially as I feel somewhat worried about our policy with regard
to opera in 1957/8.[4] I was glad to see that *Boris* will probably be substituted
for *Tristan*; since it seems to me that with *The Ring* and *The Master-Singers*

IB on the circumstances of their meeting 'in the middle of the Atlantic in 1941', mentioned
Aline's prowess in golf and described her outfit: 'a mink coat over a navy costume, black skull
hat with veil and black court shoes diamanté buckled'. 'The wedding that was kept secret',
Hampstead and Highgate Express, 10 February 1956, 1.

1 In 'The Londoner's Diary', 6 February, 4, describing IB as 'a brilliant conversationalist; he is an
excellent story-teller, with an almost legendary talent for mimicry'.

2 A few days later, IB reported to Arthur Schlesinger 'a condition of besotted bliss': 21 February
1956. In a letter of 15 March 1956, Maurice Bowra wrote to Alice James 'The young Berlins have
settled in to their charming house on Headington, and are doing it up from top to toe to suit
Isaiah's tastes and remove memories. They are very happy together, and it is delightful to see
them. The trouble now is that Isaiah hardly ever comes down the hill into Oxford and is even
more invisible than before.'

3 David Lumsden Webster (1903–71), General Administrator, Royal Opera House, 1946–70.

4 The (not previously mentioned) operas and composers IB goes on to discuss are (with dates of
first performance): *Boris Godunov* (1874; Modest Mussorgsky); *Tristan und Isolde* (1865), the four-
part Ring Cycle (*Der Ring des Nibelungen*, 'The Nibelung's Ring'; 1876, composed 1854–74) and *Die
Meistersinger von Nürnberg* ('The Master-Singers of Nuremberg', 1868), all by Richard Wagner;
Oberon (1826; Carl Maria von Weber); *Les Troyens* ('The Trojans'; 1863–90) and *The Damnation
of Faust* (1846) by Hector Berlioz; *Wozzeck* (1925; Alban Berg); *Les Huguenots* (1836; Giacomo
Meyerbeer); *Lady Macbeth of the Mtsensk District* (1934; Dmitry Shostakovich); the orchestral can-
tata *Atlántida* ('Atlantis', 1962, composed 1927–46; Manuel de Falla); *The Magic Flute* (1791) and
The Marriage of Figaro (1786) by Mozart; *Norma* (1831; Vincenzo Bellini); and *Lucia di Lammermoor*
(1835; Gaetano Donizetti).

the overweight of Wagner and German opera over Italian is a little too great. However this is no doubt a matter of straight musical prejudice. What worries me more are the proposals for *Oberon* and *Les Troyens*. I have seen both these works twice, as it happens. The former (which I saw conducted by Walter[1] at Salzburg before the war) needs a very lavish and expensive production – it has the usual fantastic Weber libretto as you know, and, I should have thought, has not quite enough musical merit to be worth so much money and so much trouble, despite the fact that it was specially written for Covent Garden. Shall we really be able to secure a singer to do justice to 'Ozean, Du Ungeheurer'?[2] The Parisians, who have now gone in for show at the expense of music, were naturally attracted by it – but it seems to me contrary to our tradition both financially and artistically. As for *The Trojans*, I saw it both in Glasgow and Oxford. I am a fanatical Berliozian, and there are marvellous things in these two operas, and the sets would not be too costly – they are static pseudo-classical works – but even if they are conflated as they were at Oxford, the dramatic action is still almost nil; there are *tremendous* longueurs;[3] apart from the love duet and the sailor's song the arias are tedious; and I strongly doubt whether a succession of *tableaux vivants* could possibly be a popular success, and therefore whether, in our present straitened circumstances, this is the moment to mount something musically so ambitious. I am all for Berlioz, and wonder whether *The Damnation of Faust* – which can be done as an opera – could not suit us better. We have a duty to produce works of genius – e.g. *Wozzeck* – even if they are not popular: but if so I should suggest *Armide* (Gluck's I mean), which is a work of sustained beauty and nobility – at least as good as *Iphigenia in Tauris* – although it, too, requires imaginative and, I fear, expensive sets, and beautiful voices. I should myself be delighted if we could stoop to Meyerbeer[4] which would, I believe, exhilarate the public. Certainly *Les Huguenots*, performed as *Gli Ughenotti* in about 1926 at Covent Garden, with (I seem to recollect) Beecham, was a great success. *The Times* would probably be as severe about Meyerbeer as about Bellini: but no matter. Indeed I believe we would thrive more on lively opposition than faint praise. There is, I suppose, no hope of getting the full scores of Shostakovich's *Lady Macbeth of Mtsensk* or Falla's unpublished *Atlántida*?

As the result of seeing *The Magic Flute*, & with Glyndebourne and possibly the Viennese fresh in people's memories, I have certain unworthy doubts about the advisability of *Figaro*, but that I do not press. I thought *The Magic Flute* inadequate: the Queen of the Night and Sarastro were too poor, and

---

1 Bruno Walter (1876–1962), né Bruno Walter Schlesinger, German-born conductor and composer.
2 'Ocean, you Mighty Monster', the aria for soprano for which *Oberon* is best known.
3 'Tedious passages'.
4 Giacomo Meyerbeer (1791–1864), né Jacob Liebmann Beer, German-born composer of (often melodramatic and spectacular) operas.

nobody so splendid as to outweigh this. The Metropolitan seem to have failed with their *Magic Flute* too, but this is no comfort to us.

I am not a member of the Opera Sub-Committee and do not wish to waste the time of the full body of directors with a protracted discussion about the advisability of specific operas; but I should greatly value an opportunity of talking about this to yourself and Mr Kubelik[1] some time. ⟨Perhaps I could induce you to come to lunch with me at Brooks's say on the 22ᵈ or 23ᵈ March? I'd be delighted if you could then, or on some other day.⟩

I am sorry that Callas does not wish to sing in *Norma*, and I ardently hope that we have the sets of *Lucia*. If this is not possible, is it out of the question to put on something by Rossini or Bellini? Is Callas not too queenly for *Traviata*?

Yours ever,

Isaiah Berlin

At the end of March IB and Aline travelled to Israel for what was effectively their honeymoon. It was Aline's first visit and IB was anxious to see what had changed since 1951. After a few days staying with Vera Weizmann at Rehovot, they toured the country, ending in Jerusalem, where IB delivered 'two lectures on entirely abstract subjects utterly unrelated to any possible present situation in Jerusalem'.[2] Family and friends took up much of their time, but IB also took the opportunity to put his political views to those in power.[3]

TO VERA WEIZMANN

16 April 1956 [*manuscript*]

Pensione Bencistá, Florence

Dearest Mrs Weizmann

I have no idea what Aline has written – she won't let me read it – but I am sure it is all true, and in her usual manner, understated. It was a most moving and unforgettably genuine honeymoon for us. I cannot help looking at Israel and at your house in particular "зачарованными глазами"[4] – the whole thing is, in spite of the very grim and dangerous reality,[5] a vivid dream

1 Rafael Jeroným Kubelík (1914–96), Czech conductor; Musical Director, Czech Philharmonic Orchestra 1941–8, Chicago Symphony Orchestra 1950–3, Covent Garden Opera Company 1955–8.

2 IB to Teddy Kollek, 13 March 1956. These were the Orde Wingate Memorial Lectures for 1956 (which IB had offered on his withdrawal as the previous year's lecturer), given on 10 and 11 April 1956 at the Hebrew University's Faculty of Law, and entitled 'Two Concepts of Political Thought'.

3 'I have one or two concrete suggestions to make to yourself or Moshe [Dayan]. I have talked to one or two persons of considerable importance and would like to be allowed to discuss this with yourself and others, to B.G. himself I hardly aspire. But if he would like to see me I should of course be delighted. The situation here is extremely confused and seems to me very malleable.' ibid.

4 'Zacharovannymi glazami' ('with spellbound eyes').

5 Israel was suffering persistent attacks along its borders by Egyptian-backed fedayeen (Palestinian guerrillas). In 1955 Colonel Nasser had committed Egypt, now strengthened by arms imports

to me: I live at two levels: on the one hand I try to understand the political and social facts, to realize the tensions, danger of war & even annihilation, the Arab question within & without (it is at least nice to substitute the Arab problem for the Jewish problem) etc. but I cannot help at the same time being unbelievably fascinated, even intoxicated, by the new Jewish Society which has come into being. To assimilate with it I cannot – I have often wished I could: I am like a Catholisant[1] who somehow cannot quite enter the Church but is willing to defend it all his life & even baptise his children into it. The best days were in Rehovot – best morally and physically. Jerusalem was spoilt by worrying about the lectures – needlessly, for it does not make them any better. The University – at least its Germano-Galician section – seems to me what Ahad Haam[2] called Slavery in the midst of Freedom: the symbiosis of German pedantry with the Talmud is not attractive:

The German Gelehrte[3] – the Sharon Hotel – and the pensions of Haifa are extraterritorial – outside Israel – bewildered, echt-Deutsch[4] and slightly resentful – Немецкая Слобода[5] – useful, civilized but a ghetto. Tel-Aviv is chaotic but free. Rehavia is nostalgic for Zurich, Stuttgart, Fürth. The whole thing makes me more pro-Ostjüdisch[6] than ever. I wish I thought Mr Hammarskjöld[7] thought so too: I am afraid his neat, tidy, cool, Swedish soul will not warm to the marvellous life which Israel has created. I try to forget that I am a Jew, a Zionist, etc. I still think that it is morally the best society in existence. I have written a long unwanted essay on Israel when all I wanted to do was to tell you that we love you – thank you fervently – & wish to see you in summer.

love

Isaiah

My warmest wishes to M. Gilbert[8] – I like & admire him *very* much.

---

from the Soviet bloc, to the destruction of Israel. During IB's visit artillery attacks had been launched against Israel from the Egyptian-occupied Gaza Strip. IB commented to his mother that the Israelis 'are not neurotic or panicky [...] but grim and dignified. They pin their hopes to the French & ultimately Americans, & have written off England as blind and incapable of leading anyone.' Postcard from Florence, 15 April 1956.

1 'Person with Catholic leanings'.
2 Ahad Ha'am, pseudonym of Ascher Hirsch Ginsberg (1856–1927), Ukrainian-born writer and leading Zionist thinker; in an 1891 essay he described the lives of emancipated Jews in post-Revolutionary France as *'spiritual slavery under the veil of outward freedom'*. 'Slavery in Freedom', in Ahad Haam, *Selected Essays*, trans. Leon Simon (Philadelphia, 1912), 171–194, at 177.
3 'Scholars'.
4 'Genuinely German'.
5 'Nemetskaya Sloboda' ('the German Quarter').
6 'In favour of Eastern European Jewishness'.
7 Dag Hjalmar Agne Carl Hammarskjöld (1905–61), Secretary-General, United Nations, 1953–61; at the time on a visit to the Middle East to check on compliance with the armistice agreements then in force.
8 Pierre-Étienne Gilbert, (openly pro-Israeli) French Ambassador to Israel 1953–9.

In February 1956, at a Press Conference in Moscow, Guy Burgess and Donald Maclean admitted having spied for the Soviet Union. Soon afterwards IB and many of his friends were shocked by a series of articles in the People *newspaper[1] under the overall title 'Burgess stripped bare'. The anonymous author, who admitted to being Burgess's closest friend, claimed to reveal the truth about the traitor's decadent lifestyle and long career as a spy. Sensationalist in style, and clearly based on an account written by Goronwy Rees (though denuded of his normally elegant prose style), the articles were thick with allegations about the incompetence of the security services, the blindness of those who had appointed Burgess to positions of trust, the risk that his homosexual friends might be blackmailed by Soviet agents, and the certainty that other spies were still active. One alleged Comintern agent, named only as 'X' (in the second article), was readily identified by IB and his friends as Anthony Blunt. Victor Rothschild was among others mentioned by name as associates of Burgess.*

The third article described, inaccurately, the journey to the US that IB and Burgess had made in 1940. After alleging that Burgess had been recruited into an organisation run by Sir Joseph Ball,[2] the article went on:

He enlisted at least one friend – one of the most brilliant Oxford historians of his time. He certainly had no idea that Guy was a Russian agent. [...] they were sent out together on a secret mission in 1940. Together they travelled to America. The friend was due to go on to Moscow. Guy was ordered to remain in Washington. But before their mission could get really going, they received a wire from the War Office. 'Burgess will return to London,' it said. 'Your assistant may do as he likes.'[3]

IB wrote to Rees, apparently to protest; Rees replied in two letters,[4] first justifying his actions and then asking for confirmation that some of his published allegations about the circumstances of the 1940 trip to the US were correct.

TO GORONWY REES

27 April 1956 [*carbon*]

[Headington House]

Dear Goronwy,

Believe me, you are mistaken. I had never seen the name of Sir Joseph

---

1 'GUY BURGESS stripped bare!' (11 March 1956, 3); 'He kept BLACKMAIL LETTERS in his room' (18 March 1956, 3); 'He kept his sex book in Ernest Bevin's safe' (25 March 1956, 3); 'HIS FAREWELL PARTY ENDED IN A BOTTLE FIGHT' (1 April 1956, 3); and 'THE UNHOLY BOND' (8 April 1956, 10).

2 Sir (George) Joseph Ball (1885–1961), intelligence officer, Conservative Party administrator and businessman; Deputy Chairman, Home Defence (Security) Executive, 1940–2.

3 For a more accurate account of these events see L1 311–35.

4 Dated 19 March (IB did not reply) and 24 April 1956.

Ball, as far as I know, before I came across it in your articles in the *People*, and I am therefore absolutely certain that I cannot have told you anything about whether or not Guy B. was or was not working for him at any time. I have no idea even now who he is or was.

You said in your article that I was supposed to be 'recruited' by Guy into Sir J. Ball's organisation. I can assure you that I was not, and had never heard of him, nor became a member of any organisation Guy was working for. Nor have I ever been sent on any secret mission anywhere by anyone; nor was I Guy's assistant; nor was such a telegram as the article quoted ever sent – the telegrams about Guy and about me were separate. I do not know what source his came from; mine was sent by the Foreign Office, which was supposed to be employing me, and did not refer to him; nor of course so far as I know (but here I no longer speak from direct personal knowledge) did he get into any intelligence organisation as a result of the abortive American journey, but on the contrary, so far as I know, the result of it was that he was sacked from whatever office he was in, and was then put by someone into the BBC and rendered presumably less dangerous than before. However, I lost touch with him after July 1940,[1] and this last point is based on general hearsay, I do not understand even now, and even on your premises, what the point of that story was. However, I only wanted to answer your letter and say that so far as I was concerned it was very inaccurate. As for the general issue, I agree with Sylvester.[2]

Yours,

TO MORTON WHITE

8 May 1956

Headington House

Dear Morton,

It is a terrible thing that nothing quickens the blood so much as praise, whether deserved or undeserved; and I hasten to answer to you more rapidly (introspection reveals this shameful but alas indubitable fact) than if you had consulted me on some purely objective point of abstract theory.

First, as to *Historical Inevitability*, you really do praise me too much.[3] While I admit that we are both splendid – that our combination of analyti-

1 Only temporarily. IB later recalled several lunches with Burgess after the war including some 'quite sharp encounters' with him and Anthony Blunt in the Reform Club in 1947–8 when they argued about Zionism. MI Tape 7.
2 Rees received a number of angry letters from those who had previously been his friends and now dropped him. IB particularly objected to the portrayal of the Foreign Office as a den of homosexuals and Communist sympathisers, and feared that Victor Rothschild might suffer guilt by association.
3 In his review of HI, MW described the lecture as 'brilliant and provocative', despite his disagreement with IB on certain points. Morton White, *Perspectives USA* No 16 (Summer 1956), 191–6, at 196.

cal dryness and interest in interesting questions is pretty unique (if Moore passed that expression) and we deserve each other's warm and benevolent feelings, yet I wonder whether it is not too much to say that I was a genuinely *influential* figure in the Oxford analytical movement, among the people who had memorised *Principia*.[1] Perhaps you ought to say rather that I was their friend and ally, although I had always occupied a more or less independent position of my own and regarded the extremer forms of positivism with permanent scepticism. Still, if it is difficult to change the text, let it stand. Some hideously unfair attack upon me by someone else somewhere else (e.g. by E. H. Carr in last week's *Times Literary Supplement*)[2] will offset the excess of undeserved praise in your splendid piece. And I wonder whether my Russian origins had much to do with my 'versatility' – interest in the philosophy of history – possibly so, you would see better than I. [...]

Much love from my wife and myself,

Yours ever,

Isaiah

P.S. I am reading (as the result of wanting to read you) the article by Meyer on Freud and Leonardo.[3] It is splendid and somehow incurably comic too. The point at which he suddenly says that Sir Eric Maclagan[4] pointed out that what had been taken by Freud to mean vulture in fact means kite is very funny. He treats it all with such severity and one takes the whole thing with such faith and partisan fashion, he is intellectually so energetic and consistent and pure, and so contemptuous of common sense, that the mixture of admiration and amusement with which one sees all he does is somehow heightened here. I do not really believe a word of those kind of articles. Perhaps that is merely a reflection of my own philistinism. In the interests of science, let us hope so; in the interests of our collaboration, let us hope not.

1 G. E. Moore's *Principia Ethica* (Cambridge, 1903).

2 In his review of *Continuity and Change in Russian and Soviet Thought*, ed. Ernest J. Simmons (Cambridge, Massachusetts, 1955), Carr described IB's contribution, 'Herzen and Bakunin on Individual Liberty', as 'the best written, if not the most convincing, article in the book' and took issue with IB's portrayal of Alexander Herzen. E. H. Carr, 'Continuity in Russia', *TLS*, 20 April 1956, 229.

3 Meyer Schapiro's 'Leonardo and Freud: An Art-Historical Study', in *Journal of the History of Ideas* 17 (1956), 147–78.

4 Sir Eric Robert Dalrymple Maclagan (1879–1971), Directory and Secretary, Victoria and Albert Museum, 1924–45.

TO IRVING KRISTOL[1]

15 May 1956

Headington House

Dear Mr Kristol,

You are quite right. My indignation was exaggerated – greater than the 'crime' deserved[2] – though my distress, as you rightly guess, was acute. All your facts are perfectly correct, my manuscript only contained a general title, and subtitles do, no doubt, help. I have no recollection of the first two subtitles and probably was just as blind to it [sc. them] as I was to this one when it arrived in proof (I was deeply shaken when this fact was pointed out to me by Stephen – it is extraordinary to me even now that one can look at proofs and not see prominently displayed words – I shall always remember this as evidence of the untrustworthiness of the most violently asseverated personal recollections by otherwise reliable witnesses). Still, I wish you had underlined it or done something to attract attention to it in the first place – I do not accuse you of negligence, indeed anything at all by now, I only lament the event.

As for Cold-War propaganda – you must not be hurt. My point was that my article on Herzen is of course in a sense permeated by anti-totalitarian, and in particular anti-Communist, feeling – and I find that I constantly quote passages from Herzen which illustrate this particular aspect of his own thought, perhaps with too exaggerated emphasis; I cannot help that, for it gives me too much pleasure constantly to find echoes of this in Herzen's own writings, but of course it infuriates people like E. H. Carr etc. and this does not disturb me deeply either, as you may imagine. Still, if I were accused of looking on Herzen consciously as a prototype of anti-Communism, and a general arsenal of intellectual weapons, I do not think I could deny it. 'The Grand Inquisitors' did suggest to me, not just spiritual and intellectual orthodoxy, so much as torturers with ideologies – but I think this is what it suggests to the ordinary English reader today. Consequently, the use of this subtitle seemed to me to underline and emphasise what is indeed in the article, but for that very reason seemed to me undesirable to advertise as the main purpose of it, which indeed it was not, hence my annoyance. I still think that the subtitle suggests just that, but on that I daresay there is room for more than one plausible interpretation. But if you feel that this is unjust, that I have placed you in some category to which you do not feel that you belong,

1 Irving Kristol (b. 1920), managing editor, *Commentary*, 1947–52; (with Stephen Spender) co-founder and editor, *Encounter*, 1953–8; editor, *Reporter*, 1959–60.

2 When publishing IB's Northcliffe Lectures (as 'A Marvellous Decade'), *Encounter* had added subtitles to the individual articles; that for the final article was 'Herzen and the Grand Inquisitors' – see *Encounter* 6 No 5 (May 1956), 20–34. IB apparently wrote to Kristol in angry protest. Unabashed, Kristol pointed out (letter of 9 May 1956) that IB had not altered the subtitle when reading the proofs, and vigorously denied IB's allegation that the subtitle was an attempt to turn the article into Cold-War propaganda.

and that I accused you of addiction to propaganda when in fact you feel innocent of any such charge, then I withdraw any implication you may have felt and minded unreservedly. I have a great liking and respect for everything you write, and if I have hurt your feelings I am exceedingly sorry. Whenever I look at the cover of *Encounter* and see 'and the Grand Inquisitors' I still feel a twinge, and do indeed feel that there is a Cold-War implication about the words. You think that fantastic. Perhaps it is – in that case you must take my remarks as purely autobiographical and no more. I shall continue to suffer, but so far as I can see through no fault of my own. [...]

Yours ever,

Isaiah Berlin

Lewis Namier's letter of thanks to IB for a copy of Historical Inevitability *was, to Namier's embarrassment, publicly misconstrued.*[1]

TO LEWIS NAMIER

25 May 1956

Headington House

Dear Lewis,

I was most deeply touched by your letter: and no less affected by your action in writing to the *Sunday Times*. I assure you that I took no offence in the first place, and that the whole thing has grown in transmission in the lurid and I fear unkind imagination of our friend E. H. Carr and your friend Stanley Morison.[2] When first I received your letter in acknowledgement of my little tract, I thought your phrase about being clever enough to understand what I wrote very delightful: I was not sure, I admit, how

---

1 In his letter of 10 February 1955 Namier observed: 'how intelligent you must be to understand all you write'. Over a year later, the Atticus column in the *Sunday Times* (6 May 1956, 3, item entitled 'Oxford Acid') reported pleasure that Namier's honorary degree from Oxford had 'not blunted the cutting edge of his pen. Recently an Oxford don of massive erudition sent Sir Lewis a copy of his latest work. "How clever you must be", Sir Lewis replied, "to understand the sort of books you write."' Namier wrote to IB on 8 May: 'I was really upset to see last Sunday Atticus's note [...] some time ago I heard from Stanley Morison that you had shown my letter to Ted Carr and that you were annoyed by my remark. [...] Obviously you did not believe me sincere: which I was. [...] Why will people not believe me when I admit my limitations? I am no good at abstract thought. [...] You did me injustice in treating as ill-mannered irony, and circulating as such, a remark which expressed sincere admiration.' Namier enclosed his letter to the *Sunday Times* (published 13 May, 2), which denied 'misplaced and ill-mannered irony' and explained: 'A friend sent me an essay of a philosophical character. Philosophy is beyond my reach. Never before had I got farther than the second page of a philosophical treatise. But as I admire my friend's mind, and he had the courtesy to send me his essay, I plodded through it. I saw that it was a fine piece of work although I could not always follow him in the realm of abstract thought. I wrote in perfect simplicity – "how clever you must be to understand what you write" – a sincere remark seriously meant in a letter to a friend I value.'

2 Stanley Arthur Morison (1889–1967), typographer, historian of the press and bibliographer; *The Times* 1930–60; editor, *TLS*, 1945–7; James P. R. Lyell Reader in Bibliography, Oxford, 1956–7.

ironical you meant it to be, or whether you meant it to be an irony at all. But even if you did, it seemed to me well within the bounds of friendship, and I certainly did not complain to Carr, or to anyone else, although I repeated it to one or two persons (and may indeed have shown the letter to Carr, who came to visit me on the afternoon on which I received it) as an example of your formidable idiom. I was amused and pleased and replied to you, as you will remember, in the same spirit, begging you not to waste your time on metaphysical subtleties when you had real work of such magnificence to do. This was represented to you as a wounded reaction on my part; and then appeared in a garbled and idiotic form in the *Sunday Times* (I have no idea through whose kind offices). I would not have seen it had you not written to me, for I did not see a copy of the *Sunday Times* on the relevant weekend, having just come back from Jerusalem and Florence and having a mass of correspondence to get through. What you did and what you wrote was most generous and moved me greatly. I am sorry that any distress, even the most minor *gêne*,[1] should have been caused to you, but I am glad at the same time to have been both the occasion and the object of such a letter to me ⟨from yourself. I was truly delighted to receive it.⟩ [...]

Yours ever,
Isaiah

Irritated at the lack of a proper response from David Webster, IB wondered whether to leave the Board of the Royal Opera House.

TO GARRETT MOORE[2]

1 June 1956

Headington House

Dear Garrett,

About Covent Garden: I feel, perhaps unreasonably, frustrated and totally ineffective as a member of the Board and am meditating resignation, at any rate after the Russian ballet,[3] the last bright and promising event I can think of. I really think I had better do that soon, and make way for someone better capable of 'putting his personality across' in resisting what seems to me Webster's vested interest in mediocrity. As it is I feel a broken reed to you and everyone. I observe with delight that you are now Chairman of the Opera

---

1 'Discomfort, embarrassment'.
2 (Charles) Garrett Ponsonby Moore (1910–89), 11th Earl of Drogheda 1957; Managing Director, *Financial Times*, 1945–70; Secretary to the Board, ROH, 1951–8, Chairman 1958–74; notorious for the notes (dubbed Droghedagrams) with which he bombarded employees, colleagues and critics. His wife was the former Joan Eleanor Carr (1903–89).
3 The Russian Theatre Ballet was due to perform at the Royal Opera House for several weeks during October 1956; despite crises, the visit proved a great success.

Sub-Committee. Are *The Trojans* and *Jenufa*[1] inevitable? The latter is harmless and Kubelik has to have a sop, but as to the former, I feel unregenerate, it has much beautiful music, but the lack of action is such that it cannot help to redress our balance of payments, nor will Piper's[2] gloomy décor, reminiscent of the worst depression of the 30s, reduce our deficit further. Believe me, a gaily done production of a Rossini opera (whatever anyone may tell you, do not believe that there are no adequate voices – *The Italian [Girl] in Algiers*[3] which I saw in Amsterdam last year was beautifully sung, it is much the most difficult of them all), with décor by Messel,[4] would cost no more & do us and the arts in England far more good. So would a revival of an opera by Vivaldi which would rivet international attention in a way in which *The Trojans* will not. However, I am sure you have gone over that with Webster and Robbins[5] etc., and all my suggestions were probably impracticable and foolish. So I will say no more, miss the monthly meetings peacefully, and in due course be painlessly dropped. I feel that there must have been something to be said for poor Steuart Wilson's[6] point of view after all, though at the time I thought it quite mad. Do not imitate Ava and show this letter to anyone, but destroy it.

When are you and Joan coming to see us here? Sundays in our garden can be very heavenly, and you could even play croquet. What about 23 or 24 June, or 8 July or thereabouts? We shall be most delighted.

Yours ever,
    Isaiah

TO GARRETT MOORE
    12 June 1956 [*manuscript*]

Headington House

Dear Garrett,

I am deeply grateful to you for your letter and feel ashamed of having put you to the trouble of writing it. One ought to cope oneself with crises of this type, particularly when they are of such moderate dimensions. I have brooded on your wise words and think you have formulated the issues beautifully: a) the compatibility of an adequate standard in opera with insistence on English, and b) the practicality of forming a resident company capable of performing without outside aid. I agree with all that you say about the degree of interference with the administrators by the directors: especially those who

1 Leoš Janáček's 1904 opera.
2 John Egerton Christmas Piper (1903–92), painter, writer and designer for opera and ballet.
3 Rossini's *L'italiana in Algeri*, first performed in 1813.
4 Oliver Hilary Sambourne Messel (1904–78), artist and leading designer for the stage and films.
5 Lionel Robbins was a Director of the Royal Opera House 1955–81.
6 Sir (James) Steuart Wilson (1889–1966), singer and music administrator; Deputy General Administrator, ROH, 1950–5.

21 With Stuart Hampshire at All Souls

22 Delivering one of the two Orde Wingate Memorial Lectures on 'Two Concepts of Political Thought' at the Hebrew University of Jerusalem, April 1956. The chairman is Nathan Rotenstreich, Dean of the Faculty of Humanities. In the front row, counting from the right, are (1) Zalman Shazar, (3) Nathan Feinberg, (6, *hand raised*) Moshe Pearlman.

23 Violet Bonham Carter and
Tom Driberg, 1956

24 Teddy Kollek, 1956

25 David Cecil, 1957

26 John Sparrow

27 Crossing the Channel with Aline, 3 January 1957

28 Headington House

29 Morton White, *c.*1951

30 S. N. (Sam) Behrman, 1952

31 Hamilton Fish Armstrong, 1953

32 Arthur Schlesinger, Jr, in the Widener
Library, Harvard, 1957

33 Charles E. ('Chip') Bohlen, 1960

34 Diana Cooper, 1958

35 Rowland Burdon-Muller, 1965

36 Felix Frankfurter, 1958

37 *The Reunion* by Leonid Pasternak, given to IB in 1958: Vera Lebedeva (*in shadow*), Ekaterina Breshkovskaya, Prince Petr Kropotkin, Nikolay Chaikovsky, Vladimir Burtsev, Nikolay Morozov

38 Boris Pasternak on the front cover of *Time*, 15 December 1958

39 In the Great Quadrangle, All Souls, 1959, 'taken by the now famous Mr Armstrong-Jones […] when I was not looking – I realised it only too late. It is not particularly flattering but very true' (IB to Elizabeth Jennings, 29 February 1959)

40 Enlightening an audience at the Bath Festival, 4 June 1959: Yehudi Menuhin, Nicolas Nabokov, IB, William Glock

41 With Avraham Harman after receiving honorary degrees at the Jewish Theological
Seminary of America, New York, 20 December 1959

42 Aline Berlin with her children, Philippe Halban, Peter Halban and Michel Strauss
(with his first wife, Margery), Headington House, Christmas 1959

live 60 miles away and are liable to journeys abroad & who should therefore
be pleased to be there at all. Having emerged from the gloomy state of mind
in which I fired off my rather neurotic letter at your innocent head, I now,
more sanely & more modestly, think that perhaps I am mistaken: perhaps a
resident troupe *is* possible: perhaps opera in English, though it is demanded
by fewer than is commonly supposed, is not ruinous *per se*; & that perhaps
my suggestions about the *Trojans* etc. are not infallible, since there is a hope,
in the present musical mood, that Berlioz will provoke sufficient enthusiasm.
I do not really believe all this, but I don't feel enough moral assurance to
assert the opposite dogmatically. And anyway, being relatively new, I ought
to await for at least a year, say, before deciding that I am quite useless and
can contribute nothing, which is the only proper ground for resignation, it
seems to me. I think that the moral of your admirable letter is the need for
humility: & I accept it. What really irritated me, I think, is that my letter to
Webster (*not* the ½ page of impromptu suggestions, which I expect were
useless) fell on such very deaf ears or blind eyes: & that he fobbed me off
a little too easily. My views may have been absurd or importunate: but it
would have been more civil to answer them orally or in writing. So that I
really wished to resign out of pure pique, & that would be silly.

So for the moment I propose to attend meetings, and hope for the best:
contain my feelings & not harry you or anyone else. I've asked Webster to
lunch (alone) & don't expect him to reply. I wish that, like Lord Halifax or a
saint, I were unsnubbable. But I am not.

I must now go off to our Auden–Cocteau Festival for which *Time* Magazine
has sent down a battery of photographers. Cocteau's gown is said to have
been made by Balmain,[1] his sword, as you know, by Cartier.[2] I don't know
what this ancient university is coming to.

Bob Brand has rightly refused to assist at these *louche* celebrations. Halifax,
on the other hand, has decided that it is all great fun & is to pose for a picture
with Cocteau.

We are both very sorry that you cannot come on either of the suggested
Sundays: would some other day in July suit you? Thank you again for your
letter, & my love to Joan.

Yours ever,
    Isaiah.

*Within days Garrett Moore provided IB with an outlet for his views by making
him a member of the Opera Sub-Committee.*

---

1 Pierre Alexandre Claudius Balmain (1914–82), French fashion designer.
2 Firm of exclusive jewellers and watchmakers based in Paris, London and New York.

TO SHIELA SOKOLOV GRANT

21 June 1956

Headington House

Dear Shiela,

I am very sorry about the condition of the telephone boxes, nevertheless your story is a terrible truth to life. I have no further news about Goronwy, except that someone – I think Osbert Lancaster[1] – told me that he intended to publish those articles[2] in book form with a preface by Cyril Connolly; this sounds too bad to be true even in these circumstances. His conduct, despite hysteria, terror etc., still puzzles me, although I suppose it is true to say that his articles have had relatively little effect except upon his own fortunes[3] – neither doing the good which he maintains he was aiming at – which could not conceivably have been done – nor the harm which terrified me. Meanwhile what about all this about Adam? David Astor's letter[4] is certainly gravely misleading ⟨but the article in the Evening Standard[5] – did you read it? – was *monstrous* & horrible.⟩, but it is impossible to say what one believes to be true without appalling bad taste – [w]e will [not] die as bravely as Adam did, the truth about him has to be told only for the purpose of exonerating people unjustly accused – and as all David Astor's accusations are delivered ominously at unmentioned persons (among whom I vaguely, but very vaguely, count myself), we must let it be, I think. It is very well to argue that Adam had to write bogus reports in order to keep in with the Nazis and conceal his own true activities, but his report in fact seems to me pretty accurate. Anyway, let it be. Let him be sent to history as a pure-hearted democrat and man of rigid principle, and not an ambitious, fascinating, self-romanticising, personally delightful and politically ambivalent figure with a passion for very high-level intrigue. The question is whether good looks, charm, patriotism, and courage are enough; I think you almost used to think they were, do you still?

Alas, we shall not be here on Friday the 29th, but at Glyndebourne, and the 30th and the 1st also – not so much at Glyndebourne as at Brighton I suppose. The chances of our being in London are very slim. We shall go to a party on the 6th, we may be in London on the evening of the 5th,

---

1 Osbert Lancaster (1908–86), cartoonist, theatrical designer and author.

2 See 526/1.

3 As well as being ostracised by many of his friends, Rees was facing a campaign to remove him as Principal of the University College of Wales, Aberystwyth; it eventually succeeded when he was forced to resign in March 1957.

4 The publication in May 1956 of an official report to the German Government by Adam von Trott about his visit to England in 1939 strengthened suspicions that he had been a Nazi spy. His close friend David Astor publicly rejected this view in his article 'Von Trott's Mission: The Story of an Anti-Nazi', *Manchester Guardian*, 4 June 1956, 6.

5 Robert J. Edwards, 'The Spy at Cliveden . . .', *Evening Standard*, 19 June 1956, 5, which argued that von Trott had been a Nazi spy.

perhaps you would telephone at about 10.30 a.m. or so on the 6th either at my mother's house or the Ritz – kindly repress the natural exclamation which the last word would normally evoke from you – my wife is a director of that establishment and we obtain a large discount. So there. I long to see you and introduce my wife to you. I have only just discovered your note explaining away another note – the second one lay in London unopened and unattended for some months and I have just received it from my mother. It was very nice of you to write it.

    Yours ever, with much love
      Shaya

TO JOSEPH ALSOP
    27 July 1956

                                  Headington House

Dearest Joe,

Forgive me if I do not write to you now, for we leave for Moscow tomorrow,[1] and you can imagine the chaos our house and general arrangements are in at the moment. [...] I understand perfectly what you mean about the Israeli moral climate.[2] You can well imagine that idealising as I do the Russian nineteenth-century intellectuals who talked about this kind of thing wistfully, when I did come across it in Israel, I was, quite apart from other obvious causes and reasons, knocked over. There are many vices which you were too generous to mention: and their attitude towards their own Arab minority and towards the Arab refugees is both blind and immoral. Nevertheless I accept Eban's point of view as reported to me by Phil D.[3] that the important thing is to save face – that is by giving enough arms to Israel, to make it possible for Nasser[4] to say that he cannot afford to attack; and for B.G. to say there is no need to have preventive war as they will be just as strong tomorrow. [...] I wonder if you are right about the effect of Dulles turning down the Dam project[5] – Nasser may, of course, be forced to go to the Russians, but he and his friends realise the consequences of that

1 This letter must have been dictated before Nasser's nationalisation of the Suez Canal on 26 July, of which IB makes no mention; but IB and Aline did not leave for Moscow (via Copenhagen, Helsinki and Leningrad) until 29 July.
2 Alsop had sent IB a pre-publication copy of an article he had written on the sense of purpose inspiring Israelis: 'Why Israel Will Survive', *Saturday Evening Post*, 8 September 1956, 38–9, 60, 64, 69.
3 Unidentified (unless the typist misheard a reference to 'Phil G[raham]').
4 Gamel Abdel Nasser (1918–70), Prime Minister of Egypt 1954–6, President 1956–8; President of the United Arab Republic 1958–70 (and Prime Minister 1967–70); an Arab nationalist, socialist and anti-colonialist who led the 1952 coup during which King Farouk was deposed. In 1955 he had threatened to destroy Israel and had begun importing arms from Czechoslovakia.
5 Negotiations were well advanced for substantial loans from the US and British Governments and the World Bank for the building of the Aswan High Dam on the Nile when on 20 July the US abruptly withdrew its offer because of Egypt's growing links with the Soviet bloc; the UK then

HEADINGTON HOUSE,

OLD HIGH STREET, HEADINGTON,

OXFORD.
—2—
TEL. OXFORD 61005.

blind and immoral. Nevertheless I accept Eban's point of
view reported to me by Phil D. that the important thing
is to save face -   that is by giving enough ~~assurance~~ arms
& [naval, ~~marine~~] to make it possible for Nasser to say that he
cannot afford to attack; and for B.G. to say there is no
need to have preventive war as they will be just as
strong tomorrow. I cannot see whith [I]ong with that argument,
nor with Hudsonx's argument either. I believe that
B[a]ro[a]de whom I don't know, was taken for a ride by Nasser
— so probably too was Trevelyan. If you like, why not say?

I wonder if you are right about Dulles limiting down x
the Dam project - Nasser may of course, be forced to
~~withdrawn~~ go to the Russians, ~~marion~~ but he & his friends
~~satisfaction~~ realise the consequences of that themselves — & will be v. reluctant. If they do
I should have thought they will soon fall from power: chaos by
follows, but that
I must say I view without alarm. I never believe in a secret Chinese
silhouette unless   You speak of "Pat and Top " and also cutting
there is Nasser down to size - I am not sure that I believe that
an actual people like Nasser can be cut down to size, any more
have. But than Moussadeq could be. I should have thought the only
you may sensible policy was to continue to give x limited aid
be right: to both Arabs and Jews and ignore bloodcurdling threats;
yet I Evelyn Shuckburgh who is suppose to be responsible for
can't help our Middle Eastern policy has become so discouraged
thinking that he has decided to ask for a year's leave. It is now
that too to be run by a combination of my old pupil Archie Ross
pro-Nasserite - a wellmeaning and very wooden Wykhamist who puts both
in line feet into his own and any other mouth that may be gaping
Sir J. open - and our Pat old friend Beeley, a man of considerable
Simon charm and ~~xxxxx~~ fanaticism on this particular subject.
than he So my anticipations are at least as gloomy as yours.
found in 1935 I shan't betray you to Pam. I shall tell you what I
think of the 'Encounter' piece when I emerge from Moscow
found in 1935 that Mussolini's fall so lead to 'communism & worse' in
Italy. So what as in Persia now? is this totally impossible?

A page from the letter to Joseph Alsop of 27 July 1956

themselves – and will be very reluctant. If they do I should have thought they will soon fall from power: 'chaos' may follow, but I must say I view that without alarm. ⟨I cannot believe in a second Chinese situation unless there is an actual war. But you may be right: yet I can't help thinking that the pro-Nasserites are like Sir J. Simon when he feared in 1935 that Mussolini's fall wd lead to 'Communism and worse' in Italy. Why not as in Persia now?[1] Is this totally impossible?⟩

You speak of 'Pat and tap' and also cutting Nasser down to size – I am not sure that I believe that people like Nasser can be cut down to size, any more than Mossadeq[2] could be. I should have thought the only sensible policy was to continue to give limited aid to both Arabs and Jews and ignore bloodcurdling threats; Evelyn Shuckburgh[3] who is supposed to be responsible for our Middle Eastern policy has become so discouraged that he has decided to ask for a year's leave. It is now to be run by a combination of my old pupil Archie Ross[4] – a well-meaning and very wooden Wykehamist who puts both feet into his own and any other mouth that may be gaping open – and our old friend Beeley, a man of considerable charm and total fanaticism on this particular subject. So my anticipations are at least as gloomy as yours. [. . .]

Yours ever,
Isaiah

The death of Stalin and the emergence of Khrushchev as leader of the Soviet Union had led to signs of the relaxation of internal Soviet controls. In February 1956 Khrushchev had savaged Stalin's reputation and in April paid his first visit to Britain (including New College, where IB had met him). With Chip Bohlen as the US Ambassador in Moscow and William Hayter as his British counterpart, it was a propitious moment for IB to assess for himself whether the Soviet Union had really changed, and for Aline to get to know the land of her ancestors. At the end of July they flew to Copenhagen and Helsinki, then continued by train to Leningrad and Moscow, staying initially with the Hayters at the British Embassy.

---

did the same and the World Bank loan proposal also collapsed. Nasser then nationalised the Suez Canal to provide alternative funding for the dam project.

1 The Shah of Iran remained in power and friendly to the Western powers until 1979.
2 Mohammed Mossadeq (1882–1967), anti-colonialist Prime Minister of Iran 1951–3, a supporter of the nationalisation of the Iranian oil industry developed by the British; his fall from power resulted largely from covert CIA action.
3 (Charles Arthur) Evelyn Shuckburgh (1909–94), diplomat; Assistant Under-Secretary of State, FO, 1954–6.
4 Archibald David Manisty Ross (1911–96), New College classics 1930–4, then a diplomat; Assistant Under-Secretary of State, FO, 1956–60.

TO MARIE BERLIN

Postmark 13 August [1956, *manuscript*]

British Embassy, Moscow

Dearest Mama

All wonderful: Leningrad – much to tell: I won't go into it now – I met someone who knew me when I was 7 – here I've seen the kind Hayters – tonight Avidar[1] (Israel Minister) I met Shepilov[2] at an Indian reception – things have changed here (for the better, mostly) since 11 years ago. I shall try to telephone you one morning at 10–11 a.m. our time (8–9 a.m. your time). Aline is excited happy & a wonderfully acute observer of people & things. Very bad Carmen[3] by a Perm´ company (Пермская)[4] may be better Chaikovsky this week by singers from Saratov.[5] Plenty of my American students here from Harvard etc. – Bohlens charming – don't know yet when we leave – shall write again very soon indeed – so far no news of anybody & expect none – have met fewer, many fewer people than in 1945 & am making no great efforts – this is really to say that we are both *very* well – the caviare & bliny and bitki v. smetane[6] are ideal for me & nearly so for Aline –

Much love –

Isaiah

At the reception in the Indian Embassy IB had encountered Stalin's notorious henchman Kaganovich:[7]

A great big, tough, bull-necked, coarse-faced Jewish gangster or American trade union leader, a teamster – you know, the Teamsters Union – powerful, sort of fleshy face with huge neck and Soviet uniform, you can imagine, a sort of tunic and all the rest of it. And he said to me, 'What are you?'

I said, 'I teach philosophy.'

'Idealist or materialist?'

I said, 'These distinctions become rather blurred in the West.'

'Now, now! Не убегайте! Don't run away!' – this kind of thing. 'Materialist or Idealist?'

1 Yosef Avidar (1905–95), Israeli Ambassador to the Soviet Union 1955–8.
2 The recently appointed Soviet Foreign Minister, Dmitry Trofimovich Shepilov (1905–95), propagandist and Communist theoretician; Director, Propaganda and Agitation Department, Central Committee, Communist Party, 1948–9; editor-in-chief, *Pravda*, 1952–6; Foreign Minister 1956–7; formerly a protégé of Andrey Zhdanov, he was at this time an ally of Khrushchev and largely responsible for the Soviet Union's growing links with Egypt.
3 Bizet's 1875 opera.
4 The name of the company, 'Permskaya [opera]' ('Perm´ Opera'). Perm´ is a city at the foot of the Ural mountains (since 1995 twinned with Oxford).
5 A port on the Volga.
6 *Bitki v smetane* are meatballs in sour cream.
7 Lazar Moiseevich Kaganovich (1893–1991), Jewish-Ukrainian politician and administrator, one of Stalin's most loyal and ruthless adherents, whose influence waned after Stalin's death; First Vice-Premier of the Soviet Council of Ministries (and member of the Politburo) 1952–7.

I said, 'Well . . .'.

He interrupted me and he said, 'What do they read in your University? Kant?'

'Yes.'

'Idealist.'

'Gegel?'

I said, 'Not much.'

'Idealist. What else?'

I said, 'Hume.'

'He was not a philosopher, he was a historian. What else?'

God knows what I said. 'Mill.'

'Stuart Mill? He was not a philosopher, he was an economist. I know what you are, you're a creeping empiricist – ползающий эмпирист.'

That was the phrase used in *Kommunist*, which was a party journal, about logical positivism, that very month, that's where he got it from – ползающий эмпирист.

I said, 'Well, I expect I am.'

IB declined, with difficulty, Kaganovich's offer to round up large numbers of Soviet philosophers for him to confront in debate, 'a sort of medieval disputation'.[1]

TO MARIE BERLIN

17 August 1956 [*manuscript*]

British Embassy, Moscow

Dearest Ma,

We are having a *wonderful* time. Aline has gone to see Vladimir & Suzdal'[2] while I remained because I can see a poet[3] to-morrow & I prefer people to architecture. The visit to the Leningrad Synagogue & to Yasnaya Polyana[4] were very memorable. Do you remember a man called Eppel from Andreapol?[5] I have seen & communicated with *no* relations: but I know

---

1 MI Tape 25. The Russian phrases are 'Ne ubegaite' and 'polzayushchii empirist [properly 'empirik']'.

2 Vladimir, a historic city some 120 miles east of Moscow, was one of the medieval capitals of Russia. The nearby town of Suzdal' is famous for its picturesque setting and architectural riches, particularly its numerous churches.

3 This was presumably the visit to Boris Pasternak in Peredelkino described by IB in 'Meetings with Russian Writers' (Pl2 227–31), during which Pasternak entrusted IB with a manuscript of *Dr Zhivago*. William Hayter remembered the effect on IB: 'Isaiah had read it all through, sat up all night reading it, he was in tears by the end of it [. . .] It obviously made a deep impression on him.' MI Tape B7.

4 Yasnaya Polyana ('Clear Glade'), the home of Lev Tolstoy, 100 miles south of Moscow, where he was born, lived and is buried. IB had presumably visited the memorial museum at Tolstoy's estate, restored after wartime damage.

5 Andreapol' is a logging town upriver from Riga where IB and his parents had lived in 1915–16.

that L. died over a year ago, quite normally,[1] I know nothing about Zhen.[2] or Lyom.[3] only that their brother M.[4] does *not* wish to see me. Ephraim Halevy[5] is here & may see Z.[6] More when I talk to you. I plan to leave with the American Ambassadress Avis Bohlen & her daughter[7] on the 31st by train via Berlin or Vienna, we don't yet know which: I'll telephone you as soon as we reach "The West". The impressions crowd in: life *is* easier. I talked to Shepilov & Kaganovich. The latter looks like any member of Mapai.[8] The Israel Minister[9] is charming. My chief reason for staying so long is that I've discovered marvellous books in the big library[10] & since who knows when I shall be here again, I want to make hay while the sun shines (it is in fact raining kak iz vedra)[11] & read what I can. The Hayters are sweet: he is gone with Aline to Vladimir, she has stayed behind with me. Never mind – I cannot go on writing – all much better when we speak. I will arrive in Portofino on about the 2d September & shall talk to you in London & after the 4th at the Park Hotel Lugano. I am very well: & seeing life.

Love
    Isaiah

IB did manage to see one of his relatives while in Moscow. In the early hours
of one morning he and Efraim Halevy, who had slipped away from his 'tail',
succeeded in meeting IB's aunt Zelma Zhmudsky. The Soviet authorities appear
not to have discovered this; but the future head of the Mossad was harassed

1 IB later elaborated: 'Leiba [Leo Berlin] died 2 years ago – his name appeared in an official place in the Vechernyaya Moskva [the 'Moscow Evening' newspaper] so he must have been politically all right – but I have a feeling that *during* the last years of Stalin's reign there *was* some trouble: otherwise they could have seen me.' [6 September] 1956 to Marie. See also 357/2.
2 Evgenia ('Jenny') Landoberg (c.1890–1954), née Berlin, IB's aunt; the former wife of Yitzhak Sadeh (né Isaac Landoberg).
3 Solomon Berlin (1893–1978), engineer, one of IB's two surviving uncles.
4 Samuel ('Mulya') Berlin (1897–1988), engineer, twin brother of Leo.
5 Efraim Halevy (b. 1934), son of Elazar and Rivka Halevy, hence a distant relative of IB's; born and educated in London; moved to Israel in 1948 and studied law; editor and author of *Monthly Survey* (an educational journal for the Israeli armed forces) 1957–61; then joined the Mossad (Director 1998–2002). As Secretary-General of the National Union of Israeli Students, he was in Moscow ostensibly to assist in planning for an international youth festival to be held in Moscow the following year, but his main intention was to make contact (normally impossible) with young Russian Jews.
6 IB's aunt Zelma Zhmudsky (1888–1978), née Volshonok, who lived in Moscow; sister of Marie Berlin and Ida Samunov.
7 Either Avis Thayer Bohlen (b. 1940), later an arms-control expert and diplomat, or her sister Celestine Ellen Bohlen (b. 1950), later a journalist. For the final part of their visit the Berlins were the guests of the Bohlen family at the US Embassy.
8 Mapai (Hebrew acronym of Mifleget Poalei Eretz Yisrael, 'Workers' Party of Eretz Israel') was the dominant political party in Israel from the country's foundation until the 1960s, and the ancestor of the Israeli Labour Party.
9 Yosef Avidar.
10 The V. I. Lenin State Library of the USSR (from 1992 the Russian State Library).
11 'As from a bucket'.

and delayed on his way out of the Soviet Union for the 'crime' of escaping from surveillance.

Once IB and Aline had left the Soviet Union for their Italian holiday (in Portofino and the nearby village of Paraggi), IB felt able to comment more freely on what he had seen:

At a certain level there is a thaw – possibility of contacts etc – but not at mine, alas. For instance it was forbidden to see Mme A.[1] – & others – one can see only the approved. [...] If one stays in the U.S.S.R. more than two weeks one's perspective & values are fatally transformed: to leave it is like waking from a dream: there is no bridge with reality. There is *no* real change: only legalization of a previously "proizvolnaya' situation.[2]

And as for the Soviet leadership:[3]

The governing body of the U.S.S.R. is the most terrifying body of toughs I've ever seen. They are about as moderate & reasonable as the R. Church in the 16th & 17th century, it will take time to make them tolerant of humane and civilized people: the gap between governors and governed is enormous.[4]

The slow pace of emancipation in the Soviet Union posed one immediate problem. Against IB's anxiety to ensure the publication of Dr Zhivago *had to be set the danger that Pasternak would suffer from incautious enthusiasm outside the Soviet Union.*

TO HAMISH HAMILTON

5 October 1956 [*carbon*]

[Paris]

Dear Jamie,

When I saw our old friend Moura at lunch in the British Embassy in Paris the other day I told her a story which I thought might be of interest to you, namely that the great Russian poet, Pasternak, has written a novel which he regards as a work of genius, and on the whole thinks it unlikely that he will be able to publish it in Russia. He is a man of great, and perhaps excessive, seriousness, and having written it feels that he would rather have the novel published than anything else in the world, and would be prepared to lose possessions, liberty etc. rather than let it be buried. Naturally, his family

---

1 Anna Akhmatova had informed IB, through Pasternak, that she did not want to meet him in case her son Lev Gumilev, newly released from prison camp, should suffer, but they spoke once on the telephone.
2 Postcard to Anna Kallin from Portofino, September 1956; 'proizvol´naya' means 'arbitrary'.
3 IB had encountered most of the Politburo at a reception in the Indonesian Embassy.
4 Postcard to Rowland Burdon-Muller from Portofino, 7 September 1956. For a fuller account by IB of his impressions see 'Four Weeks in the Soviet Union', in SM.

think all this very unwise, but he goes on about it at great length and feels most passionately that it is the greatest thing he has ever done. I have not read it[1] and cannot myself tell. Meanwhile, an Italian representative of the Milan firm of Feltrinelli[2] called on him in Moscow, it seems, to secure a copy of the Russian manuscript, which he carried off with him to Milan. There was a fearful fuss in Moscow, efforts were made to get him to recover it, but this he stubbornly and triumphantly refused to do. So Feltrinelli presumably has it, plus the rights not only of the Italian translation but of translation into other languages – under the terms of the sort of contract by which he pays 50 per cent to the poet and keeps the rest himself, or perhaps those are not the terms, but at any rate he has the rights.

Shortly after telling Moura the story and asking her to communicate it to you, because she will be in England before me (I am dictating this in Paris), I received an enquiry from Mark Bonham Carter about this very matter, and have now, by the same post, written him a letter on the subject too, adding that Moura would probably be telling you all about it. The whole problem of publishing this novel, should it prove feasible – when it is unlikely to be published in Russia itself – is a ticklish one. The only people really worth consulting – morally entitled to it, I mean – are the two sisters of the poet,[3] who live in Oxford, who perhaps would be able to pronounce upon it. I may have a text of it myself – the Russian text I mean – though I am not sure about this. Myself, I should think that it would be better to wait for a little while – it is possible we may be able to confer an honorary degree on the poet and get him to England first, before announcing the publication of the novel, which may cook his goose completely with the authorities. However, all this had better be talked about than written. I feel sure that the publication of this novel in English, whether by yourself or by Mark or by anyone else, would cause a great flutter, as his name is in any case well known and it is a great thing to publish a novel which is plainly out of tune with the views of the regime, and very different from anything else that has come out of the Soviet Union in the last thirty years. I have no personal interest in the matter – I would not undertake to translate it, for it is a gigantic task – but since Feltrinelli has a copy of the novel, I do not think it is damaging for these facts about the poet to be known, otherwise, especially since my last visit to Russia, despite all the alleged new freedom, I feel more than ever that one

1 But see 539/3.
2 Sergio d'Angelo (b. 1922), Italian Communist journalist, at the time working with Radio Moscow and as talent-scout for Giangiacomo Feltrinelli (1926–72), Communist founder (in 1954) of the Milan publishing firm Giangiacomo Feltrinelli Editore, had in May 1956 persuaded Pasternak to release a copy of Dr Zhivago for publication outside the Soviet Union, as no Soviet publishers had yet accepted it.
3 Josephine (Zhozefina) Leonidovna Pasternak (1900–93), philosopher (married to her second cousin Frederick Pasternak); and Lydia Elisabeth Leonidovna Pasternak Slater (1902–89; former wife of Eliot Slater), biochemist and translator of her brother's poetry.

can compromise the dwellers in that region only too easily by displaying too great an interest in their doings in a manner not approved of by the regime. If you write to Feltrinelli he will probably be able to give you details. If he is cagey do let me know again, as I think I could probably procure the manuscript somewhere, some time, but I cannot guarantee this of course. Do not tell anyone else about it at the moment, except Mark, of course.

Yours ever

Isaiah Berlin p.p.

[...]

TO PETER STEIN[1]

5 October 1956 [carbon][2]

[Paris]

Dear Professor Stein,

I hope you will excuse my extreme lateness in answering, but your letter pursued me all over Italy and has only caught up with me in Paris now. I shall be in England in three or four days and hope to be able to answer you more fully then. I have not seen the printed version of my own lecture on Montesquieu[3] – for I have been abroad for the last two months and it must have appeared during that period. So I don't know what occurred on page 292, but what I meant to say – and perhaps said obscurely and unsuccessfully – was, so far as I remember, that there were indeed two lines of thought each of which is to be found in Montesquieu, unreconciled – and connected mainly by the desire to protect the liberty of individuals against arbitrary interference. The first is, as you say, the pragmatic development of law, both conservative and radical, the second is indeed the tradition of written, codified legislation, which so far from being able to adapt it to specific circumstances in the light of tradition or his own sense of equity, or any other relevant factor, judges are expected to translate into practice with the most rigorous deductive fidelity, i.e. apply clearly articulated, formulated laws to specific situations in accordance with rules over which they have no control – this presumably in order to avoid tampering with the law in a corrupt or intricate or capricious manner. The notion of judges as being required to make their tasks as mechanical and impersonal as possible seems to me at obvious variance with the pragmatic conception of justice, and more closely related to, for example, the physiocratic notion, whereby laws are simply

1 Peter Gonville Stein (b. 1926), Professor of Jurisprudence, Aberdeen, 1956–68; later (1968–93) Regius Professor of Civil Law, Cambridge. He had written to IB on 11 September seeking clarification on a point in IB's Montesquieu lecture (note 3 below).
2 Almost certainly dictated on 1 October in Paris and typed for signature in Oxford on 5 October.
3 Charles-Louis de Secondat, baron de La Brède et de Montesquieu (1689–1755), French political thinker. IB's lecture on him to the British Academy on 19 October 1955 had been published as 'Montesquieu', *Proceedings of the British Academy* 41 (1955), 267–96. The matter at 292 appears at AC 156–7.

the transcription into words of objective necessities discovered in nature, than the relativistic and flexible conception of law inherited by the school of Holmes and his disciples. It is clear that laws at once cannot be regarded as rigid mechanisms to be either fully carried out or abrogated and at the same time as a kind of lead piping fitting circumstances and responsive to variances in culture and environment. This seems to me a genuine contradiction which, as often happens, is concealed by the overmastering motive of both – namely prevention of arbitrary authority, despotism, dogmatic faith, prejudice, superstition, and abuse of authority, in the interests of individuals, sections, etc. etc. But the contradiction remains.

Without my text I do not know whether I said this or not, but it is certainly what I meant. I hope this gives you what you wished me to answer. If not please do not hesitate to let me know again.

Yours sincerely,

Isaiah Berlin

Following Egypt's nationalisation of the Suez Canal on 26 July, an international conference in August had produced proposals for a system of international management of the Canal to resolve the crisis; these were rejected by Nasser in early September. Britain, France and the US nevertheless pressed on with setting up a Suez Canal Users' Association. In private the British and French Governments were preparing for possible military action. The key development was the series of meetings at Sèvres near Paris on 22–4 October at which the governments of Britain, France and Israel (who wanted to restore access from Eilat to the sea) reached a secret agreement, not made public until much later, that Israel should start military action against the Egyptian army in Sinai and that Britain and France should then intervene, ostensibly in defence of the Canal; the dual objectives of the campaign would be to recover the Canal and remove Nasser from power. Dubbed Operation Musketeer, the plan was launched a few days later.

The following letter was written in several different stages during the unfolding of the Suez Crisis. Chronologically unravelled, it illustrates IB's changing responses (though he remained unaware of the collusion behind the military action). For ease of reading, the letter has been split into its two main sections.

TO ARTHUR SCHLESINGER

⟨dictated 1st⟩ 5 October 1956 ⟨~~sent off~~ mislaid 19·10·56.⟩[1]

All Souls

Dear Arthur

I ought to have written to you long ago on emerging out of the Soviet Onion, but what with sitting idly on the beaches of Italy with the Bohlen family and Tommy Thompson[2] and visits from Nabokov, and then really ferocious hard work in Paris for once – you know, I am sure, for you are like me in that respect, what it is like after a long spell of pleasure and idleness to settle down to work, stimulated by guilt and hideous shame – here in Paris ⟨here in Paris is good⟩.

To get rid of all my trivial enquiries first – Is it true that dear Mary – or is it Marietta? – has been jettisoned by Adlai,[3] as gossips here – not among the kindest of mankind – are maintaining? Ronnie dined with us last night but, naturally enough, I did not like to ask him. Is it true that Adlai really has a chance of winning, as I think he has? Do you still maintain your view of him? What do you and the ⟨(I wonder whom I meant)⟩[4] think ought to be done about Suez? Chip is very Dullesish about it all,[5] while I have to restrain my natural anti-Egyptian impulses and say firmly to myself that war against Egypt might end anywhere and is not very advisable but that the idea of 'cutting Nasser down to size' is an absurd Utopia – and unless he is in some way eliminated we shall have a lot of trouble. I have had to reprove Rowland[6] for saying the Jews of Israel are a violent, ungrateful, aggressive lot, who have occupied their country as a result of the betrayal of the Arabs and are a barbarous collection, very unlike 'the normal Jews we know', and must have embittered Dr Weizmann's last years. Without going into Joe's raptures on the subject, I'd rather spend an evening with Ben-Gurion than Madame

1 The chronology of this letter appears to be: (i) the first section was dictated on 1 October in Paris for expected signature on 5 October when IB returned to Oxford (IB has written '1st' over the typist's '5th'); (ii) on 19 October a few manuscript additions were made to this section, which was then mislaid; (iii) the remainder of the letter (553–9) was dictated early–mid November after rediscovery of the first part; and (iv) final manuscript comments to the whole letter were added shortly afterwards on signature.

2 Llewellyn E. ('Tommy') Thompson (1904–72), US diplomat; Ambassador to Austria 1955–7, to the Soviet Union 1957–62, 1966–9.

3 On the contrary: the political connection between Marietta Tree and Adlai Stevenson, at its height during the 1956 presidential election campaign, was soon to develop into a love affair.

4 Perhaps 'the Justice', i.e. Felix Frankfurter.

5 Dulles, whose change of tack over funding for the Aswan Dam had done much to bring about the whole crisis, was now backing the Suez Canal Users' Association and opposing the idea of using force.

6 'Suez *is* very disturbing: & *very* mishandled: but Nasser is a stupid Mussolini not just an inflamed nationalist (like, say, Krishna Menon: or Ben Gurion who is behaving, surely, quite well at the moment!) – as for the Israelis, [. . .] I think them, by & large, the most calm, morally decent, well mannered, unaggressive body of Jews I know.' Postcard of 7 September 1956 to Rowland Burdon-Muller.

de Becker any night ⟨very much written on Oct. 5: on Nov 5 I was much readier to condemn Israel & assassinate Ben G. than be cross with Eden.⟩, but you needn't tell Rowland. I'm sure Marian [*sic*] will agree. Meanwhile, I cannot say that my Prime Minister has behaved with great brilliance, or the Russians with great stupidity.[1] I still think that the absurdity of the Middle East situation is not the common hatred of Israel, real though that is – just as hatred of Hungary was real enough in the Little Entente[2] before the war but was not itself a fatal factor – but in the fact that these oil producing kingdoms are rich and have no way of spending their money productively, while the Arab populations, by and large, are poor and angry and politically liable to be led in any direction by exasperated men. Some sort of socialism in the Middle East – or at any rate huge New Deal-like amalgamation – still seems to me the only possible solution. It may be too late for this now, but all other courses seem to be merely preventive and impermanent. So if Nasser were assassinated it would probably do more good than harm. But he will not be. No bad men ever are, only harmless Kings of Portugal or Mayors of Chicago.[3]

After these Joe-like cosmic reflections, let me turn to the Soviet Union. I hear that Jakobson came back in a very glowing state, and indeed if you come as an official guest or a member of a delegation you do meet people who do talk to you with apparent freedom, and in order to emphasise the difference between the new, better time and the old terrorist time, tell you risqué stories, talk with open horror about the victims of the past, tell you that there are a great many things they can now tell you which they would not have been able to say in 1945 or 1950, and all this is true, and yet artificial too. The Society for Cultural Relations with the Western World sent a circular round to all the Russian Academics saying that those who knew some foreign languages had better brush them up for contacts were about to be established and it was desirable to talk to foreigners. I met several people who had received these instructions and told me confidentially about them. But these people, although they do seek out foreigners, are quite clearly expected to write little reports about them afterwards. They need not be intelligence reports, or particularly vicious, but reports they remain, and this leads to a certain artificiality of relationship. I visited the Academy of Philosophy and never did I meet a body of men more obviously bored with their own tedious subjects. They practised it, as theology was probably practised in the Middle Ages, [as] a compulsory course for everyone, learned by rote and accepted

1 The Soviet Union, while broadly supporting Egypt, had nevertheless taken part in the international efforts to find a solution to the crisis.
2 An anti-Hungarian alliance between Czechoslovakia, Romania and Yugoslavia (supported by France) during the 1920s.
3 Carlos Fernando Luís Maria Victor Miguel Rafael Gabriel Gonzaga Xavier Francisco de Assis José Simão de Bragança (1863–1908), King Carlos I of Portugal (1889–1908), was assassinated, as was Anton (Tony) Joseph Cermak (1873–1933), Democratic mayor of Chicago 1931–3.

as serious by no one, with some people practising with greater virtuosity than others, but to which no one attached genuine importance except a few fanatics and fools. There is no living Marxism in the Soviet Union, despite the removal of the ban and freedom not to mention Stalin. The physicists and natural scientists generally, who seem to be paid even higher salaries than ballerinas, treat it with open contempt. So does everyone else who can afford to, and those who cannot quietly sabotage it.[1]

[continued on 553 below]

On 29 October Israeli forces launched an invasion of Sinai and headed towards the Suez Canal. The next day Britain and France issued an ultimatum to Israel and Egypt demanding withdrawal within 12 hours from the Canal area to allow temporary Anglo-French occupation. Egypt rejected the ultimatum. On 31 October Britain and France commenced military action by bombing Egyptian airfields and sinking an Egyptian ship. The announcement that Britain had embarked on an armed conflict against Egypt led to uproar in the House of Commons, international condemnation, and deep division across Britain.

TO CLARISSA EDEN

1 November 1956 [*manuscript*]

Headington House

Dearest Clarissa,

This is only to say that at this moment when undergraduates are demonstrating in the High Street against the government, and dons are going about speechless with indignation, and the *Manchester Guardian*[2] has declared that our moral credit has gone virtually forever, and the *Observer* is surely going to preach with the peculiar mixture of sanctimoniousness & hysteria which is more nauseating than even the *New Statesman* – I should like to offer the Prime Minister all my admiration and sympathy. His action seems to me very brave very patriotic and – I shd have thought – absolutely just. I am prejudiced, I suppose, in favour of Israel, who have undoubtedly committed what is, at any rate technically, an act of aggression. No doubt provoked & over provoked: & done in genuine self defence, but still, against the official rules. It would have been easier to mark time, see which way various cats jumped, and evade responsibility and compromise with one's conscience and wriggle out of looking at the agonizing dilemma on the ground that one must be patient, sensible, march in step with public opinion here & abroad, & do nothing the consequences of which cannot be clearly calculated. At

---

1 This point is developed at length in 'Four Weeks in the Soviet Union' and 'Soviet Russian Culture' (both in SM).

2 Its editorial on 1 November 1956, 8, described the attack on Egypt as 'a disaster of the first magnitude. It is wrong on every count – moral, military and political.'

the risk of sounding terribly pompous (why shd my views be of the slightest interest to anyone?) I wish to say that I really have tried to put aside all my own predilections & prejudices: & it seems to me that Anthony (if I may call him that) has behaved with great moral splendour: whatever the outcome he has risked his own reputation for what he thinks to be a vital national interest. I think his policy is in essentials absolutely right. But whatever view may be taken of his judgment, his courage, honesty, and strength of will, in circumstances which put these qualities to a most appalling test, have been such that he will, I believe, turn out to have saved England. You must forgive me for all this outpouring: I have never in my life written in such terms before to you or to anybody: but I feel passionately – & a pretty lonely figure I am in this wishy washy town – dear good people but with enormous reluctance to look at facts rather than rules of conduct – & I really could not refrain from writing to you to say that I send you all my affection & devotion and good will and everything else that you may feel in need of – pride and spirit & happiness you have in sufficient measure already.

    With fondest love
        Isaiah

P.S. Gaitskell was awful.[1] Even the Americans will not like his last speech. I am glad I am not a socialist & torn with conflicting loyalty & contempt. Very wet he fundamentally is. If we must have Wykehamists I prefer Kenneth Younger.[2] He may be mistaken but he follows principles & doesn't tergiversate (forgive this last word – remember I am a don after all).

P.P.S. Don't answer –

A fierce ground action by British and French paratroops to retake the Canal area began on 5 November and was successfully completed the following day, coinciding with the re-election of President Eisenhower. But the US Government's earlier disinclination to support the use of force over Suez, the lack of prior consultation with the US by Britain and France, the Soviet invasion of Hungary[3] on 4 November (an armed intervention in another

1 In the House of Commons on 31 October the Leader of the Opposition had scathingly condemned the Government's action as 'disastrous folly', promised all possible constitutional opposition to it and tabled a motion of censure (*The Times*, 1 November, 1956, 10).
2 Kenneth Gilmour Younger (1908–76), Labour MP 1945–59; Parliamentary Secretary, Home Office, 1947–50, Minister of State 1950–1; Vice-Chairman, RIIA, 1953–5, 1958–9, Director 1959–71.
3 Student demonstrations in Hungary in late October 1956 led to widespread violence and the fall of the Soviet-dominated Communist government. The new government under Imre Nagy promised reform and the violence subsided. The Soviet Union at first decided not to intervene, but reversed this decision on 31 October after Hungary's proclamation of neutrality and its withdrawal from the Warsaw Pact. On 4 November Soviet troops attacked Budapest with ground troops, tanks, artillery and air power. The fighting lasted until 10 November, by which time Soviet control had been re-established.

country which the US strongly condemned), and the possibility of Soviet
intervention on Egypt's behalf combined to deny Britain the American support
Eden had expected. The US Government applied political and financial pressure
which forced the British Government to agree to a ceasefire, effective from
midnight on 6 November. A UN contingent was then to replace the Anglo-French
forces.

TO MICHEL STRAUSS

8 November 1956

Headington House

Dear Michel,

I am glad that you are doing Russian literature;[1] your mother is studying
Russian with Mrs Pasternak; I seem to have given a strong Russian twist to
the entire family. [...]

But the world is a very confusing place at the moment. I wish I knew what
to think. That the British Government has committed a blunder cannot seriously be doubted. At the same time I am not prepared to sign letters, signed
by 350 dons and 2000 undergraduates, complaining of this. I cannot feel
morally indignant. I see that they really were faced with a terrible dilemma.
Once Israel had attacked – and however great the provocation, and it was
very great, an attack is an attack and provoked aggression is still aggression,
and I wonder if they will have to pay for it – ⟨although I suppose you cd
argue that if country X keeps saying it is at war with country Y & is resolved
to exterminate it utterly, country X is not breaking the peace if it attacks it –
still –⟩ what were they to do? There is a great deal in what Eden said about
the inefficiency of the United Nations. But if what the British wanted was
to get Nasser down, he certainly would have fallen much more obviously
if Israel had won on its own, than as the result of the attack by two greater
powers, which makes him look like a martyr and a hero – a kind of Emperor
of Abyssinia.[2] I see in a way that given that Arabian oil is a vital necessity, and
given the attitude of Nasser towards England and France, Eden could not
put himself in a position where he came to the aid of Nasser, even though
technically he was the aggressed party, against the Israeli aggressor. If he had
simply tamely voted at the United Nations to check aggression and help the
victim he would have found himself opposed to both Egypt and Israel at the
same time, which would have been even more absurd than what happened.
He bears no great love for Israel certainly, a State which came into being

---

1 MS had recently started studying Russian literature and the history of art as an undergraduate at
   Harvard.
2 Haile Selassie I (1892–1975), né Tafari Makonnen, Emperor of Ethiopia (Abyssinia) 1930–74, was
   forced into exile 1936–41 by the Italian occupation of his country. His appeal to the League of
   Nations in 1936 brought him international sympathy (but no practical help).

very much against his wishes, for remember that he was after all originally the founder of the Arab League, a section of which at any rate has bitten his hand so sharply. Nevertheless he obviously looks on Nasser as being a kind of Arab Mussolini, who unless checked could easily become the aggressive leader of a vast Moslem empire stretching from Morocco to the Persian Gulf, bitterly hostile to all Europeans and a very fertile soil for Russian infiltration. Having learned his lesson over Hitler and Mussolini he wanted to prevent even the beginnings of this from happening, and felt convinced that the Americans, whether from jealousy of the British, or a sentimental regard for ex-colonial peoples whom they believe to be virtuous simply because they had been originally exploited or oppressed, did not see and therefore would not help against. No doubt there was much else in it – pique with the Arabs, dislike for Dulles, desire to show himself a man to the original Suezite clique which has taunted him with weakness before, pressure on the part of the French who look to Israel as their sole ally against Nasser, whom they regard, justly, as the source of weapons and dynamism to the [insurgents?] in Morocco, Algiers etc., but the fundamental motive was to nip something in the bud, not to let the power of Nasser develop in the atmosphere of impotence created by the endless talk in the United Nations, with America morally indignant but unable or unwilling to act, very much as England was morally indignant but did relatively nothing to stop Hitler or Mussolini in the thirties. I think the vividest memory to him is of the reoccupation of the Rhineland by the Germans in 1936, when if the French had decided to march against the Germans, a similar cry of anguish would have come from England about the flouting of the constitution of the League and 'taking the law into one's own hands'. Nevertheless if what he wanted was the downfall of Nasser – an end devoutly to be desired, he might have acted very differently. To begin with he could have issued his ultimatum not for 12 hours but say for 72; in which case the Israelis would have, almost certainly, achieved their victories against the Egyptians, though at greater cost to themselves – which would have had the effect of humiliating the Egyptians ever so much more than one won by the French and English. (Have I said all this before? I keep repeating myself terribly, I apologise.) Secondly, if he had done that, he could have told the United Nations that they must act for themselves; that if they would not or could not, then he would act, but not until they had shown their impotence quite clearly. To do what he did behind America's back, behind the Empire's back, was childish folly, and I quite understand America's rage. It is difficult to defend the acts of the Government on legal grounds; on moral grounds or political ones it is defensible only if one thinks that the Israeli war, unchecked at least for some time – while the United States mustered its weapons – would have set the whole Middle East on fire & offered opportunity for sabotage on so great a scale as to create economic chaos in Europe, or at any rate England, and given the Russians an indefinite opportunity of making permanent and growing trouble. One of the parallels is that of the Far Eastern situation, where because the Chinese civil war and the Japanese–Chinese war were allowed to go on comparatively uncontrolled by other powers, the ground was made fertile for the ultimate invasion of an aggressively anti-Western Communism. Well, all this is rather like a Lippmann article, and I won't go on.

Here the mood is odd. Whereas in France everybody, with the exception of one or two journalists and the friends of Mendès France are rallied round the acts of the Government and extremely pro-Israel, here the majority of the nation is probably against what Eden has done. Indeed the latest Gallup Poll says about 48% is against what the Government has done, 40% for, and the rest are undecided. Tremendous campaigning is going on through the press – on one side Maurice Bowra, the Warden of New College, the Wardens of some other colleges and all socialists, liberals and idealistic persons you can think of, all our friends etc. etc., on the other side, Sparrow, Harrod, Gilbert Murray, the Master of Balliol,[1] the Master of University,[2] and one or two other similar persons.

I have kept very silent and signed no letters or counter-letters, appeared on no platforms or counter-platforms, since I feel [I] might not be unbiased on the matter.

Meanwhile Ben-Gurion has thunderously proclaimed that he will allow no foreign troops, however described, to appear anywhere his troops are. I am afraid he will have to pay for this. ⟨*Stop Press*: Thank God he has changed his mind.⟩[3] He is a very obstinate, fiery, self-dramatising man, whose heroes are Tito and Winston, and he believes in defiance for the sake of defiance, and in standing alone against all the Goliaths: he won splendid victories, the first against the embattled Arab States, the second against the Egyptians now (of fantastic speed and dimensions), and having conquered territory twice the size of his own, he is not disposed to compromise. On the other hand, I feel that both America and England will not accept this, will try to be 'impartial' and will try and put him back by force, which he is bound to resist. The Russians moreover now look upon him virtually as enemy No 1, a small but frightful little nuisance in the Middle East to be eliminated at all costs. Hated by our Foreign Office, he has, because supported by the French, become a kind of unwanted representative of England and France in the Middle East, without being loved by them, but hated by Arabs and Russians. An unenviable situation to be in. I wish I knew how it was going to end.

He is an attractive, romantic, fiery, passionate, blind, self-intoxicated sort of man who would rather die in a fury of martyrdom and heroism, than

1 Sir David Keir.
2 Arthur Goodhart.
3 On 8 November Israel undertook to withdraw its forces from Sinai once United Nations troops occupied the Canal zone.

survive to govern a peaceful country in a mild and moderate way. That is why I feel pessimistic. On the other hand I am a terrible defeatist and perhaps none of this will come to pass and everything will shake down nicely and Ben-Gurion be enabled to reach some sort of direct agreement with the Egyptians and gradually fit the Middle East picture. But I doubt it.

Meanwhile Hungary occupies all minds, and your friends the Rankins, or rather one Rankin,[1] following in the wake of Oakeshott of Balliol,[2] has been through with some medical supplies to Hungary and back and is now appropriately gated by Christ Church. Hungary is a very romantic cause; all sorts of young men want to go there and die for liberty, although plainly they cannot be of any use now that the Russians have crushed the resistance. But they very properly feel that something must be done, that awful things are happening, that one cannot be supine, and that unless someone does something mad and heroic, vile things will be tolerated. The instinct is very good, it is rather like what was felt during the Spanish civil war, in 'my' time. What do they feel about that at Harvard?

To return to the Middle Eastern problem for a second (I do feel this is more and more becoming a solid political lecture): the great fallacy, particularly in America, is to suppose that people, because they are poor, unwashed, have been oppressed and exploited, are peasants and need missionary help, are therefore good people, and their cause is a good cause, and that they are incapable of producing oppressors and Fascists of their own. There is something inherently wrong about taking the side of one people against another on the ground that [that] people are by nature better, more virtuous, more noble. Until and unless (I say solemnly) people are able, with a cool calculation of human happiness, to arrange affairs in such a way that claims of national rights and national glory and traditional aspirations and historic rights and all the rest of it do not interfere with the satisfaction of basic human desires for life and liberty and food and shelter and security and freedom of speech etc., until that happens, awful things will go on. But I must go away – your mother is pressing me to stop talking next door, for she wishes to sleep and she says that she is about to have a headache unless I stop instantly. [...]

You will be amused to hear that both Jacob[3] and David Pryce-Jones[4] had thoughts of leaving as volunteers for Hungary and that I lectured them both

1 Ian Niall Rankin (b. 1932), Christ Church PPE 1953–7. His account of the situation in Hungary, 'Students Led Hungarian Revolt', appeared in the *Observer*, 4 November 1956, 7. His brother was Alick Michael Rankin (1935–99), Christ Church PPE 1955–6. Both became businessmen.
2 Robert Noel Waddington Oakeshott (b. 1933), son of Walter Oakeshott, then Rector of Lincoln College; Balliol classics 1953–7; *Financial Times* 1957–63; journalist, author and specialist on workers' cooperatives.
3 (Nathaniel Charles) Jacob Rothschild (b. 1936), 4th Baron Rothschild 1990; banker.
4 David Eugene Henry Pryce-Jones (b. 1936), son of Alan Pryce-Jones; journalist and author; literary editor, *Financial Times*, 1959–61.

on the fact that one must not take oneself so seriously, that undergraduates are undergraduates, that one must not ask oneself at every turn whether one is fulfilling one's purposes here or should be somewhere else, and one must just carry on with whatever one is doing without feeling that the safety and happiness of the world depends upon one's position, or that one has some special calling or mission. [...]

    Love

      Yours ever,

        Isaiah

TO ARTHUR SCHLESINGER

    [early/mid-November 1956; *continued from 547 above*]

At this point my letter seems to have broken off, and many things have happened both public and private. I returned to England, found my papers and books in chaos, an enormous amount of work to do, and general ⟨confusion and new duties⟩ of my 'new' life. As you can see from the date on top of this letter,[1] I was about to finish the letter with a few affectionate manuscript scribblings, but characteristically lost the sheet of paper and have only just recovered it. After losing it I went to bed for over a fortnight, had to cancel my projected visit to India as a British delegate to [a] UNESCO Conference[2] in company with three of the most charming men in the world – Sir David Eccles, Sir Kenneth Clark and Sir Charles Darwin[3] – on the ground that I was too ill to be inoculated (this was true), but no sooner had I, full of guilt and shame, resigned, than I recovered rapidly, which indicates a strongly psychosomatic origin of my disease. Then the political crisis broke in all its horror.

    I wish I knew what I thought. This University, as you know, has been upheaved to the highest degree. 350 of my colleagues ⟨e.g. Maurice, Hampshire, etc.⟩ have written violently protesting against the Government, and about another 30 have supported it, led by Sparrow, Beloff and Goodhart (the latter in very moderate and Lippmanlike tones). To my horror I discovered that one knows very little about oneself. When somebody telephoned to me from London to say that the Israelis had crossed the border, I was really filled with the direst forebodings and fearful consternation. I have a sneaking liking for Ben-Gurion, but he is a dervish of the most unbridled kind whose central image is England in 1940, who prefers desperate situations in which he is with his back to the wall, defying all the storms of the world, dying in an agony of glory and violent resistance to everything and everybody, thus

---

1 19 October 1956.

2 IB had agreed to form part of the UK delegation to the General Conference of UNESCO starting in New Delhi on 5 November 1956.

3 Sir Charles Galton Darwin (1887–1962), physicist; Director of the National Physical Laboratory 1938–49.

cancelling many centuries of humiliating Jewish history etc. Not a very good set of attributes in a constructive democratic statesman of a New Dealish State. Indeed, when I was in Israel in the spring, something of this had been whispered to me by the one-eyed (in every sense) Chief of Staff,[1] an amateur archaeologist as they all are, who said they wanted a small victory in Sinai, promised not to move to Cairo, which would surely knock down Nasser, which everybody must want. I argued in vain against this notion of a 'small fresh gay little war' on the Moltke model,[2] on the chance that if nothing else, whatever they might gain on the field, they would certainly lose at the conference table, where the whole United Nations would be bitterly and virtuously opposed to this act of aggression. Surely, they said, if you have a neighbouring State which utters bloodcurdling threats all the time, says it is at war with you, sends armed men to kill your citizens, and swears that it will exterminate every man, woman and child, it is difficult to say that one is at peace with such people, or that an attack upon them is an act of war rather than an act of self-defence in a war already in existence? I found that I was about 49% on their side, but 51% against. War is war and provoked aggression is still aggression etc. And this I still feel. However, when I heard the news I was as I say plunged in gloom. I must say I never conceived it possible that our Government would in fact have done what it [did]. At the same time I did not experience *any* moral shock, unlike all my colleagues. I must either be very cynical, or else so heavily biased in favour of the Israelis that I reacted differently from other good and virtuous men, with whom I long wistfully to be associated. I merely made a utilitarian calculation of the consequences: it seemed to me that to have let Israel do the job alone, even if it suffered heavier casualties and was attacked by other Arab States, would have had the desired consequence, namely the elimination of Nasser – whereas our intervention, by making him a martyr and an Emperor of Abyssinia, could not possibly have that effect. It seemed to me lunatic not to consult either the Empire or the USA. On the other side I could see that if we did nothing and simply behaved respectably, complained to the United Nations, argued about who was the aggressor and to what extent, then, whether the Israelis won or lost, the British would no longer be in a commanding position in the Middle East at the end of the episode, would lose not merely the canal but the oil, on which, I think, Eden correctly says our lifeline genuinely depends. Gladwyn Jebb, whom I saw the week before, said to me that if we were faced with an Israeli or an Egyptian aggression, we would have the prospect of being simultaneously hostile to Egypt and to Israel, which seemed difficult.

---

1 Moshe Dayan (1915–81), Israeli soldier and politician; Chief of Staff, Israeli Defense Forces, 1955–8 (in personal command of the forces in Sinai in 1956); wore an eye-patch after losing an eye during the Second World War.
2 Helmuth Karl Bernhard von Moltke (1800–91), Graf von Moltke, Prussian (later German) Field Marshal and leading military theorist, who saw war as a necessary feature of human life.

Why did Eden do what he did? Why did Salisbury and Macmillan[1] and other members of the Cabinet (other, that is, one is told, than Monckton[2] and Butler)[3] decide to do what they did? Historically speaking the facts I think are these. There are always certain formative years in the lives of emotionally affectable politicians, which set the pattern for their future thought. In Eden's and Salisbury's lives, this was certainly the middle and late 1930s, and the spectre of Mussolini, even more than Hitler, broods over them all. It is clear that Eden thought that if Mussolini had been stopped, however much in defiance of the League of Nations, say at the time of the Abyssinian war, or if Hitler had been stopped in the Rhineland, whatever the League might have said, it would have saved the peace, and it was craven and stupid not to have done so. The same applies to Salisbury, who more or less said so. And I daresay Macmillan too. Moreover Eden is genuinely vain, felt that the Arab League was something he had brought into being, that Nasser had bit the hand that fed him – his feelings were not unlike those of Chamberlain when he came back and said about Hitler, 'He lied to *me*' – he had promised the Conservatives over a year ago that our Mediterranean policy rested on the secure foundation of Nasser's friendship given in exchange for the evacuation of Suez,[4] and felt dreadfully humiliated by the failure of his prophecies, felt too long taunted by the gibes of his right-wing supporters, and wished to show himself a man – all this is true, and yet of course he need not have done what he did. He should I suppose immediately have consulted both the Empire and the United States. True, Dulles would probably have told him to do nothing, but to go behind the back of America, like a child which is afraid that the governess will tell him not to do something, was childish and on the whole very ruinous. He could have blackmailed by threatening to do something immediately in order to stop a war which it was genuinely believed might have spread over the Middle East and drawn the Russians in. This might have had bad consequences but not as bad as those which this independent act is bound to have, at any rate on Anglo-American and Anglo-world relations. He might have argued at UNO about who was the aggressor, he might even have vetoed, or at least acquiesced in a veto by France of, punitive action against Israel if this had been automatically decided (as it well might have been) – again this would have led to trouble but not as much as was in fact created.

1 (Maurice) Harold Macmillan (1894–1986), 1st Earl of Stockton 1984, publisher and Conservative politician; Foreign Secretary 1955; Chancellor of the Exchequer 1955–7; Prime Minister 1957–63.

2 Walter Turner Monckton (1891–1965), 1st Viscount Monckton of Brenchley 1957, barrister and Conservative politician; Minister of Labour and National Service 1951–5; Minister of Defence 1955 to October 1956; Paymaster-General, October 1956 to 1957 (a change of roles resulting from his opposition to the invasion).

3 Richard Austen ('Rab') Butler (1902–82), Baron Butler of Saffron Walden 1965, Conservative politician; Chancellor of the Exchequer 1951–5; Lord Privy Seal 1955–9; Leader of the House of Commons 1955–61; Home Secretary 1957–62.

4 British troops previously based in Egypt were evacuated during 1954–5.

In short, he ought to have waited. Even if he had given his ultimatum 72 hours instead of 12, this would have been far, far better. On the other hand, simply to have reported a breach of the peace to UNO, and then have gone through the official machinery in a middle-class manner, ⟨carefully pondered Nehru's[1] or Pakistani feeling as Attlee wld have done,⟩ would have created a kind of Spanish War situation in the Middle East, which the Russians plainly intended, which would have ended badly, or rather worse, I think, than even the present situation. I can understand the moral shock of my colleagues; the British in general are in anything but a cynically buccaneering mood: they hate not behaving decently and well, they hate breaking the laws brazenly, they hate being divided from the respectable statesmen of the Empire (although I think they do not really mind much about the coloured subjects of Her Majesty). The awful thing is that this touched me very little – was it just Israeli bias? Possibly. Or was it some hideous opportunism of nature? When I felt that Eden really had sacrificed American goodwill, had broken too many links, had deceived too many people, had upset too many good men, had broken his own undertakings to the United Nations etc., this simply went into one end of the scale: on the other were the relevant advantages – the foiling of certain Russian plans, ⟨the mere fact of intervention which is pleasing when one remembers what "non-intervention' meant in Spain;⟩ the frustration of Nasser, the brutal awakening of opinion to the crude political issues involved; the undoubted courage balanced by the undoubted unwisdom etc., I apologise for giving you this story in such very introspective terms: I think the act was immature, unwise, precipitate, dangerous etc., that there are wounds – we may have lost more than we gained etc. – but I cannot help seeing the whole situation in terms of a utilitarian balance and not as a moral issue. The moral issue (to me) is the general balance of happiness over misery or security versus danger in the lives of nations or people in general and not living according to rules or the sacredness of treaties and undertakings. As such I felt no moral shock, I feel no moral shock now. I was pressed to sign both the documents condemning the Government and documents containing the commendation. For the first time I found that what Walter Lippmann had said[2] made sense. I cannot recognise myself. I wish you would tell me what you think – do you simply regard this as a straight crime against international morality with no saving circumstances – or just a blunder, the immorality of which merely consists in the general lowering of international solidarity, but not a wicked, shameful act? Or none or all of these? Our undergraduates are on the whole apathetic and uninterested; the people who fuss are the dons of whom the vast majority is violently against the Government. People even like Marcus Dick who are Conservatives and

---

1 Shri Jawaharlal Nehru (1889–1964), Prime Minister and Minister for External Affairs, India, 1947–64.
2 Lippmann was less critical of the Anglo-French action than many of his compatriots.

members of the Conservative Party are dreadfully upset and cannot eat or drink, and find themselves unable to teach and are all in a condition of moral torpor and go about with a hang-dog look and think the whole thing worse than Munich and the day when it happened as literally the worst day of their lives. I do not *begin* to think all this, whereas of course I felt it about Munich, and when my friend Lady Violet Bonham Carter writes letters to *The Times*[1] saying that she has to bow her head in grief, shame and humiliation and that we cannot speak about Hungary in the manner in which we should because we ourselves have committed a sin against the Holy Ghost – personified by the United Nations – I cannot but feel that she is at best self-deceived and this represents some form of objective humbug, that even if we have been morally pure – as pure as the United States (which I must own behaved perfectly well) – our violent protests about Hungary would have made no difference. That the whole nineteenth century is filled with noble protests about martyred Poland or martyred Hungary or martyred Italy, and that the comfort from these things to the martyrs themselves was less than nothing. There is a rumour that the United States would, but for Suez, have sent arms or men to Hungary. Unless they are prepared for genuine war against the Soviet Union, this would certainly not have helped. Clearly the Russians would have sent enough to crush the Hungarians whatever the resistance.

As for Israel, I do not begrudge them their triumph,[2] but I must say I was enormously relieved when Ben-Gurion agreed to withdraw from Egypt for the benefit of the United Nations. If she had not done that she would have been set upon with great enthusiasm by everybody, and the result would again have been difficult to calculate. As it is, I suppose the Russians will pump arms into Syria etc., and men too, with the absurdity from their point of view of letting all these arms be captured. They might as well send them to Israel direct straight away, and then when there are enough your Government will threaten the Russians and we shall have a temporary stalemate again, and so we shall jog on. I still do not, unlike the Swiss, believe in the imminence of the Third World War. The Russians are no doubt in a hideous mood – furious about the ceasefire, enraged by the feebleness of Arab military prowess, but determined to do all they can to stir up a holy war. It really is time that people ceased to be pro-Arab or pro-Israel. Cold calculation, power politics, balances of power, I am beginning to sound like Peter Viereck – all these are preferable to the mechanical application of principles, however good. Chip must be furious. Burdon-Muller must be talking a lot. ⟨Lady Pamela [Berry] must be a lonely gallant figure. Joe is delighted?⟩

But do give me your news and do tell me whether I ought to morally boil.

---

1 *The Times*, 6 November 1956, 11.

2 IB's views had hardened by 27 November: 'I cannot understand why nobody agrees with me that Israel did wrong to attack. […] I thought that the Israelis had committed a crime far greater than any Eden could be accused of.' To Herbert Hart.

If you tell me to perhaps I shall begin to do so. I ask myself what I should have felt if Israel had not been involved, if, say, this quarrel had broken out between two other powers or groups of powers in which I have no emotional involvement. I simply don't know: I felt no indignation about American action in Guatemala, and none about Formosa.[1] I really am anti-Wilson and pro-Salisbury – the old Prime Minister rather than his now passionately militant grandson.[2] When asked when one is justified in going to war he said it is like asking oneself whether [one] should take an umbrella: one could not tell what the weather was going to be, but one had to make up one's mind and decide, and either take one or not. I look upon the breach in international solidarity as just one enormous factor, but still only one factor among many. That is to say I view the faith and the indignation of the betrayed believers in UNO, whether here or in America, from outside, as something which statesmen have to take into account in formulating policies calculated to promote happiness, justice, liberty etc., but not as something which I feel myself. If all this jars deeply on you, and you altogether disagree, do tell me. And tell me anyway what you think.

As for the American election, surely you cannot have expected anything else.[3] I forbear from comment for fear of making remarks in well-known bad taste about the candidate. I believe you would have done better with Kefauver[4] or Harriman. This may sound mad, but I really do believe it. Further evidence of my derangement and political and moral blindness. [...].

How typical of George Kennan to accuse America of all recent misdeeds,[5] as such. A. J. P. Taylor is said to be preparing a blistering review of his last and obviously excellent book.[6] How strange too the difference between us and France – where with the exception of the Communists, and a very few

1 In 1954 a CIA covert operation had secured the ousting of the democratically elected Guatemalan President Jacobo Arbenz Gúzman, who was suspected of Communist sympathies, and whose land-reform programme was seen as a threat to US interests in both Guatemala and neighbouring countries; decades of civil war followed. Early in 1955 the US had threatened to use nuclear weapons against the People's Republic of China if necessary to defend Formosa and the islands between it and mainland China.

2 (Thomas) Woodrow Wilson (1856–1924), Democratic US President 1913–21, argued for US intervention in world affairs in pursuance of liberal and democratic ideals; in contrast Robert Arthur Talbot Gascoyne-Cecil (1830–1903), 3rd Marquess of Salisbury, Conservative Prime Minister 1885–6, 1886–92, 1895–1902, favoured detachment from the European system of competitive alliances and, in particular, preservation of the existing balance of power.

3 Eisenhower's victory over Stevenson on 6 November had been convincing.

4 (Carey) Estes Kefauver (1903–63), Democratic Senator for Tennessee 1949–63; a leading contender for the Democratic candidature in the 1952 and 1956 presidential elections, losing to Adlai Stevenson both times; Stevenson's running-mate in 1956.

5 On 3 November a letter from Kennan appeared in the *Washington Post* strongly criticising the UN resolution tabled by the US against the action by Israel, Britain and France, and deploring the recent handling of US foreign policy. Although he did not approve of the Tripartite action, he argued that the US should bear its fair share of responsibility for the present situation and not abandon its allies, least of all by aligning itself with the Soviet Union and Nasser.

6 Kennan's book was *Soviet-American Relations, 1917–1920*, vol. 1, *Russia Leaves the War* (Princeton, 1956); in his review, 'The Cold Shoulder', *New Statesman and Nation*, 8 December 1956, 762–3,

Mendès France neutralists, everybody is madly for the Suez intervention, 100% pro-Israel, delighted by the snub to the United States, and united as never before. Nothing is less true of this country, where old friendships are broken and people cannot speak to their friends. I have just signed a violent document about Hungary,[1] which will deprive me of a Soviet visa for ever and put an end to my scholarly career. Do write. ⟨And our love to Marion [*sic*]. I've only glanced at this terrible long letter. Forgive me if it is boring, silly, or dotty.⟩

Yours ever,

Isaiah

TO TEDDY KOLLEK

6 December 1956

Headington House

My dear Teddy,

I was very sorry that we were not able to see each other for a greater length of time when you were in London. Meanwhile events are marching. I have a curious feeling that perhaps my acute pessimism as expressed to Dayan when I was in Israel in the spring may not be so groundless after all. Although I sincerely hope that it is. Do you not think that when, as is inevitable, the Western Powers do get together at least for the purposes of formulating a common policy, whatever the degree of genuine trust, in order to show the world, the United Nations and the Arabs that they are in fact impartial; that aggression does not pay; and that compromise is always best – the 1948 frontiers of Israel, which our Prime Minister is still, I am pretty sure, fixed on (remember that he is an acutely obstinate and not very far-sighted man) will be presented as being at once the voice of objective justice as uttered by the United Nations, impartial, in the days when all the Powers were still friends, and at the same time as representing a compromise between the maximum demands of the Arabs (i.e., the total extermination of Israel, which cannot be allowed) and its expansionist policy (which cannot be allowed either). In return for this dismemberment the frontiers will doubtless be guaranteed as in the case of Czechoslovakia in 1938. I do not know why I have a feeling about this, but even if it is not literally implemented, I do not know what else the empty formulae about guaranteeing of frontier mutually agreed by both sides which Ike seems to be mouthing can possibly mean. So do not let us be too sanguine. And let your people guard against this particular danger. On the other hand, let me press upon you with the greatest warmth the

Taylor criticised Kennan's rigidly anti-Bolshevik position while praising his scholarship and literary style.

1 Perhaps the declaration condemning the Soviet action organised by undergraduates of Lincoln College, who had canvassed throughout the University for signatures.

following consideration: now and now only is the moment for a grand and generous gesture by Israel. Why cannot B.G. announce that he is willing to pay for the resettlement of the Gaza refugees? That he has not the money, but that he will attempt to raise it somehow? And also offer to take in, say 40 or 50,000 of them, which really cannot make a difference to the fifth column in the land. I know that Horowitz[1] and others come here and talk to leaders of the Labour Party whose influence, despite all that you hear, is still very low. They may come into office, but by the time they do that, even if they do it at all, which seems in spite of everything somewhat dubious, it will be too late. If we (i.e. Israel) are to make concessions of this type – and it is certainly desirable that we should – the effect upon world opinion, which after all Israel can ignore less now than ever before, would be immense – then for God's sake let it be done now, spontaneously, and not under obvious pressure by Americans or socialists or other friends or under the stress of events when it will seem too little and too late. One cannot exaggerate what effect this kind of gesture, if made with sufficient publicity and drama, would have at a time when everyone appears to be behaving in a suspicious, resentful, troubled, ashamed and shaming manner. It would not matter even if Egypt rejected it with scorn, or the other Arab States as well. It would be there for the record and the difference it would make would be gigantic. Do press this upon the 'Old Man'.[2] Let him not revert to the thoughts that the outside world will not help Israel anyway, that it is alone in the world, and that what it loses it loses for ever without obtaining a moral return. Any plots which may be meditated against its frontiers or other possessions will be far more effectively frustrated by a spontaneous gesture on its part of this type than by concessions extorted from it at the obvious pistol point of some great power. Do not, I beg you again, be unduly optimistic about the help likely to be given to Israel just because of rage felt against Egypt by us or against England by Ike or Dulles. Eban is always too optimistic and the desire not to give the Arabs an excuse for falling into the Soviet orbit is still very great. You must remember that the Americans are treating the English precisely as the English treated the French in 1944–5 – nice people who unfortunately have behaved so abominably to the Arabs that they have become an embarrassing nuisance. One almost begins to believe in Marxism and the contradictions of capitalist society, when one thinks that the same tactics will inevitably be employed by the Soviet Union vis-à-vis America in ten to fifteen years' time, if things go on as they do at present.

I have heard from Joe Alsop that he intends to leave Washington and become a roaming correspondent in Europe and will be going to Russia for six weeks. I hope he visits you as well. But let me repeat again and again and

1 Presumably David Horowitz (1899–1979), economist; Director-General, (Israeli) Ministry of Finance; founding Governor, Bank of Israel 1954–71.
2 Ben-Gurion.

again, now is the moment to make a gesture and a large one. In the most crudely materialistic utilitarian sense of the word, believe me that it will more than repay for itself in the most concrete terms, and again that it is no good simply relying upon the conversations of Israeli socialists and London socialists. A lot of good that has done at the Congress in Copenhagen.[1] If the gesture is to be made, don't enquire of other people how they will react, neither the Americans nor the English, let it be done genuinely and unilaterally without consultation as a spontaneous large-scale offer. Never did the Germans do themselves so much good as by similar treatment of Israel. Forgive me for this vehemence, but I have never felt so strongly about anything before in my life.

Yours ever,

ישעיהו[2]

Kollek replied on 23 January 1957: 'I accept your pessimistic analysis of the situation without the slightest reservation' but 'the kind of gesture that you suggest would be taken by the general public as a further withdrawal and further concession which will weaken us and which will be quickly exploited by the Arabs'.

TO WERNER PHILIPP[3]

6 December 1956 [*typescript draft heavily corrected in manuscript*]

Headington House

Dear Professor Philipp,

I am writing this in a state of the greatest possible regret and contrition and feel both frustrated and ashamed. But I fear I shall not be able to come to Berlin at the end of January[4] after all. [. . .] I am most acutely disappointed: although, as I told you, I do not enjoy lecturing, I should have done so out of an obscure sense of having to function as best one can, if called upon to do so, within one's own *Fach*.[5] But I am very much in favour of the projected Institute; but have grave fears, that unless some counter-influence is brought to bear, it may be founded upon the assumption that dialectical materialism really means a good deal to its practitioners in the Soviet Union. If there is one thing of which I became convinced during my recent visit to Moscow,

1 The Council of the Socialist International, meeting in Copenhagen, had been hostile to the Anglo-French invasion of Egypt, which caused the French delegation to walk out on 2 December.
2 'Isaiah'.
3 Werner Philipp (1908–96), from 1952 Professor in the Osteuropa-Institut of the Freie Universität, Berlin (Director 1970–2).
4 IB had agreed to give a lecture on Plekhanov at an international conference to be held in Berlin in early 1957 to discuss ways of setting up an Institute, funded by the Rockefeller Foundation, for the study of Marxism and Leninism and the production of scholarly material to aid researchers.
5 'Field of activity'.

it is that (at any rate since about 1930, before which philosophical discussion was both genuine within its own severe limitations, and in a state of direct interplay with economic and political activities) today philosophy in Russia is not only a direct instrument of political and social policy (which in a Marxist State it cannot in any sense help being), but not much else: it is used cynically, to mark changes in political, economic or social policy, which themselves have nothing to do with any philosophical thought, and are conceived and ordered by persons with a crude and openly contemptuous attitude towards philosophy, which they, in practice, conceive of as so much nonsensical chatter. For this reason, the attempt to extract some sort of philosophical sense out of recent philosophical literature in the Soviet Union, whether by way of intrinsic meaning (i.e. as embodying the genuine thoughts of genuine thinkers, however crude, primitive, perverse, mistaken, uneducated etc.) or as an attempt to give ideological justification of a serious kind to policies adopted on some other ground (i.e. an attempt to believe that what is being done is in some sense a form of orthodox Marxism, with the corollary, however artificial and self-induced, that those who disagree are in some genuine sense heretical or treacherous), is beside the mark. The only real importance of ideological discussions within the Soviet Union (I do not think this extends to the satellites, where I think genuine thought may be occurring) is as a symptom, in the deeply despised field of philosophy, of political or social developments in some other sphere. So, for example, when there was an order during the war to look on Hegel as a German Fascist, to disregard his influence, and to look for Russian roots for Lenin, this was merely a symptom of what the proper attitude towards Germany or foreign countries was to be, and not an attempt, however tortured, actually to alter philosophical thinking, which in any case had been suppressed many years before. Similarly an elaborate essay in a recent copy of *Kommunist* of 1956,[1] about the Hegelian law of the negation of the negation, is largely meaningless, until it reaches the concrete purpose of the article – to indicate that the rejection of all Western science, mathematics etc. as non-Marxist rubbish is dangerous to the security of the Soviet Union and is a form of cultural 'nihilism' which may have been practised during the period of the 'cult of personality', but must now be rejected if Soviet science is to help to build up a proper economic (and I suppose war) potential. For this reason, attempts to analyse the recent developments, let us say of Soviet ethics or Soviet theory of knowledge, except in a diagnostic way, as an atheist might analyse theology, or [a] psychoanalyst dreams, namely as symptoms of some political or social development – seem to me a waste of time and energy. (This does not apply to non-mathematical formal logic, which is left in rela-

---

1 I. Khlyabich, 'K voprosu ob otsenke filosofskogo nasledstva Gegela' ('On a Question about Hegel's Philosophical Legacy'), *Kommunist* (the main journal of the Soviet Communist Party), 1956 No 17, 115–22.

tive freedom. But it is totally uninteresting at present, being a rudimentary form of Western formal logic.) The philosophers I talked to in Moscow when I was there did not pretend that their philosophy was of interest even to themselves, and still less to others. One of them said that nobody took them or their subject seriously, neither teachers nor taught. If one was not so prominent or secure, one said nothing. It seemed exactly like the attitude of the Russian intelligentsia towards the compulsory teaching of [the] scriptures in Russian schools before the Revolution – it was felt to be idle to blame the poor priests who were compelled to do this, but neither they nor the pupils were expected to take them seriously. On the other hand, as an esoteric symbolism indicating which way the regime is going in its social and political policies, philosophical pronouncements are of considerable importance. The directions given to (or adopted by) historians, economists, philosophers, literary & art critics, and even biologists & logicians and still more their execution of such orders, are of first rate importance as indications of where the regime is proposing to go: & of fascinating interest to students of Soviet society, if not to those of history, philosophy, biology etc. In this sense it is an artificially created 'superstructure' invented & designed deliberately to reflect the political reality. On these grounds, and because the history of Marxism is of crucial importance for understanding the present, in the satellite countries, especially Poland & Hungary, there really may exist *genuine* & effective belief in and adherence to various doctrines, as there certainly is in Western countries and Asia. I am sure the Foundation Institute is very well justified. I wish I could have come and put forward this point of view personally, and lectured, as you kindly suggested, on the transformation of Marxism as a philosophy from the flourishing days of Plekhanov to the open cynicism and sabotage of the Soviet present. But, alas, I cannot. If one was an important person, say an atomic physicist, whose work was really valuable for the State, one was allowed to express open contempt for all this. I should be grateful if you would convey my regrets to Mosely, Robinson[1] and anyone else whom I know who may be there; and of course first and foremost please accept them yourself. I really am bitterly disappointed. [. . .]

    Yours sincerely,
    Isaiah Berlin

---

1 Geroid Tanquary Robinson (1892–1971), historian of Russia; Director of Russian Institute, Columbia University, 1946–51, Seth Low Professor of History 1950–71.

TO FRANCO VENTURI

10 December 1956

Headington House

Dear Venturi,

Thank you very much for your letter which, as you may well suppose, gave me the greatest possible delight. I really am in love with Herzen, I think, and any praise of him I take, rather vainly, as praise of myself. You could not give me greater pleasure than by saying what you did. Do look into his Italian journey – to Florence, towards the end of his life – as well as the sojourn in the 'Sardinian Kingdom', in which all the tragedies occurred. His remarks about the officials of Savoy and Piedmont are moderately interesting too. He adored Italians, as you know, more than anyone after the Russians. And rightly so. It is [a view] I believe all Russians to share in, and for these purposes I am doubly so. The project of the Paris journey is still 'aktuell',[1] but if, that is, there is even a minimum of heating to be found at 21 Avenue Foch.[2] Do you think the fact that it is next door to the Egyptian Embassy increases or decreases the chances of that?

I am about to deliver a broadcast on Plekhanov,[3] whose centenary – the centenary of whose birth – it is. The old man is almost completely forgotten, I feel, and yet without him things would not have happened, both good and bad. Personally I like the thought of this 'Zloy Professor'[4] very much – I think he is the last of the progeny of Herzen – a left-wing 'Barin',[5] the most attractive of all types of humanity, now alas almost extinct because of the double disappearance both of 'Bare' and of anything authentically left-wing. Or is this groundless pessimism, and is a new light to come from Poland and Hungary? I feel we are in at the end of Marxism and that something new, exciting and menacing is about to take its place alongside Thomism, Positivism, Conservatism, Liberalism etc. The mutiny against Communism by something still wilder and more destructive is described with a certain horrible prescience by Herzen in *From the Other Shore*. I have a feeling that we shall not have lived out our lives without something of the kind occurring. Or is this just romantic Russian talk?

Yours ever,

Isaiah Berlin

[. . .]

---

1 'Current'.

2 The home of Alix de Rothschild.

3 'The Father of Russian Marxism: G. V. Plekhanov (1856–1918)', BBC Third Programme, 11 December 1956; published as 'The Father of Russian Marxism', *Listener*, 27 December 1956, 1063–4, 1077, and in POI.

4 'Malicious Professor'. Presumably one of Plekhanov's opponents had so described him.

5 Landowner, nobleman ('bare' is the plural).

TO VIOLET BONHAM CARTER

10 January 1957 [*manuscript postcard*]

Hotel Weisskreuz, Klosters, Switzerland

While my wife & stepchildren are furiously, and no doubt, enjoyably whizzing down snowy slopes and generally taking ardent part in the (almost entirely English) vie sportive[1] of this hamlet, I have acquired a convenient cold and huddle indoors. I shall call upon you as soon as possible – and answer all your questions to the very best of my ability [...]; what Russia was like – the Politbureau really do look horrifying – like a collection of tough & cunning College porters – with a leer & a wink and a knowledge of how much each don or undergraduate or visitor is worth – at once smooth and brutal, class conscious and corrupt, hideously jovial and with an easy gangsterish flow of sentimental reminiscence – I met Driberg[2] there – but I'll tell you all, if you would like it, when we meet. Also about the mad Prime Minister; I certainly thought & think the 'intervention' lunatic in the form it took; & being very pro-Israel, thought worse of their attack than anyone else I met (I told Evelyn Shuckburgh it wd happen) I think our old disreputable friend Boothby was right: that we ought to have waited 4–5 days & then issued our ultimatum to U.N. & was glad to find Mark agreed. I am not as sound as you, but sound. [...]

Isaiah.

TO ROWLAND BURDON-MULLER

10 January 1957 [*manuscript postcard*]

Hotel Weisskreuz, Klosters, Switzerland

While Aline and the children are indulging in bracing 'Winter Sports', I am peacefully in bed with a slight but convenient sinusitis, which keeps me warm and frees me from having to dine with Mr Irwin Shaw[3] the American novelist this evening. I am not at all sorry. Do tell Michel to listen to Gaitskell.[4] He is no great shakes: a decent, intelligent, nice, weak, British civil servant, conventional, amiable, easily dazzled by 'upper class douceur de vivre',[5] fond of ladies, & of Sir M. Bowra, with a powerful Jewish wife[6] who is three times

1 'Sporting life'.
2 Thomas Edward Neil Driberg (1905–76), Baron Bradwell 1975, journalist, lecturer, broadcaster; former Communist (and possibly a Soviet agent); left-wing Labour MP 1945–55, 1959–74; notorious for his promiscuous homosexuality. IB had met Driberg (in Moscow to interview Guy Burgess) at the Indonesian Embassy reception.
3 Irwin Shaw (1913–84), né Irwin Gilbert Shamforoff, US playwright, screenwriter, novelist and short-story writer; at this time living in Europe after being placed on the Hollywood blacklist as a suspected Communist in 1950.
4 Gaitskell was to undergo questioning on *Face the Nation*, a US television programme on current affairs, on 13 January.
5 'Sweetness of living'.
6 (Anna) Dora Gaitskell (1901–89), née Creditor, formerly Frost, Baroness Gaitskell 1963; born in

the man – & the socialist – he is; in fact more like Eden, Stevenson, Acheson, etc. – dull & well meaning Porcellian[1] figures – nice and liable to be rattled easily – than real leaders like Roosevelt, Truman, Churchill, & even Spaak, all of whom are basically very sane and libertarian. [...]

Love
    Isaiah

On his return IB had to finalise his application for the Chichele Chair of Social and Political Theory, which was to become vacant on G. D. H. Cole's imminent retirement. He saw the choice of referees as crucial.

TO CHARLES WEBSTER[2]

28 January 1957 [*manuscript*]

Headington House

Dear Charles

I am, of course, most deeply grateful to you for your letter. Weighty as your arguments are for making a choice of a specialist in political theory as a sponsor, they are defeated by my very great feeling of pride & pleasure in having you as a referee – simply as an end in itself, so to speak. So pray allow me to nominate you, whatever the effect upon the electors. These are: the Vice Chancellor (now J. C. Masterman), the Warden of All Souls (John Sparrow), (Prof.) Habakkuk,[3] Wheare, Sir G. N. Clark,[4] (Prof.) Austin, & (Prof) H. L. A. Hart (now prof. of Jurisprudence). Of these Hart is likely to be in America but will perhaps write a letter; Sparrow, Austin, & probably Wheare know me well enough in one way & another to reach their conclusions independently of much new evidence. I don't know about Habakkuk who, I shd think, will think his own thoughts but may take his cue from G.N.C. – him you know (and probably like) better than I do – he may or may not favour the very worthy and decent candidature of his own Oriel product Plamenatz more than my (to his eye) less orthodox claims. Masterman will incline with the bien pensants & have little view of his own. You are of course quite right to wonder why I shd have chosen three historians. I shd have asked yourself & Pares anyhow, out of admiration – I say quite sincerely, & as an obviously good judger of academic quality. And I don't

Riga to Russian Jewish parents who soon moved to London; former medical student; Labour Party activist and Zionist.

1 An exclusive Harvard dining club.
2 Sir Charles Kingsley Webster (1886–1961), Stevenson Professor of International History, London (LSE), 1932–53; a wartime colleague of IB's in the US.
3 (Hrothgar) John Habakkuk (1915–2002), Chichele Professor of Economic History, Oxford, 1950–67.
4 Sir George Norman Clark (1890–1979), Balliol 1908–12; Chichele Professor of Economic History, Oxford, and Fellow of All Souls 1931–43; Provost of Oriel 1947–57.

wish to alter Pares's (who wrote to me much as you yourself did, accepting but saying he was not weighty in this field) any more than your own name, in sending my list of referees. Ensor[1] (who also offered to be replaced) I could perhaps replace with someone more relevant: I thought of all the specialists in Political theory: – I *could* not appeal to Mabbott, or Wel{l}don, or McCallum,[2] or Oakeshott, or Brogan, or even Popper whom I respect but who is so chancy: & I don't know Ernest Barker.[3] The point is that Political Theory (or Philosophy) is moribund in England, otherwise there would be some good professors & many more candidates for this particular Chair. Sir David Ross[4] is not especially a friend of mine – our relations are remote if quite cordial, & he is bound to prefer Plamenatz who is the voice & method of his old Oriel tutor applied to political theory – indeed that is his major virtue & his principal defect in one – Ross's techniques applied to politics clear up a lot of waffle & nonsense, & yield clear, honest, shallow, platitudinous results. I had thought of Charles Wilson,[5] who might have been the likeliest to get this Chair if he were still here – but I don't know what he thinks of me: I shd think he wd be tepidly courteous. As to Robbins I had no idea he thought anything of me & am delighted & flattered by your report: do you think he wd be better than Ensor? he is, after all, an historian & critic of economic ideas, whereas Ensor used to be an elector to the Chair himself, & might be thought to understand local needs. But if you tell me to ask Robbins in place of Ensor, I shall follow your advice, since Ensor, sadly reduced by Parkinsons Disease, more or less declares himself unfit to do much anyway: and I could tell him that I felt the need of someone closer to political theory. But I think his judgement is respected. I shd be grateful for your guidance. You are profoundly right about the strange field of force that an Oxford electoral committee is liable to be: but I do not somehow think that this one will be divided by bitter cross-currents of feeling as the one that appointed Woodward's[6] successor[7] to Worcester must have been. Heaven knows whom Macmillan will give us as Regius Professor: I have a feeling that Alan Taylor, despite all his real ability, has somehow gone too far astray: despite his health Pares wd probably give deeper satisfaction to the

1 Sir Robert Charles Kirkwood Ensor (1877–1958), journalist and historian; Fellow, Corpus Christi, 1937–46; Faculty Fellow, Nuffield, 1938–46.
2 Ronald Buchanan McCallum (1898–1973), historian; Master, Pembroke, 1955–67.
3 Sir Ernest Barker (1874–1960), Professor of Political Science, Cambridge, 1928–39, Cologne 1947–8.
4 Sir (William) David Ross (1877–1971), philosopher; Provost, Oriel, 1929–47.
5 Charles Haynes Wilson (1909–2002), Fellow and Tutor in History, Corpus Christi, 1939–52; Principal, Leicester, 1952–7 (Vice-Chancellor 1957–61).
6 Sir (Ernest) Llewellyn Woodward (1890–1971), Montague Burton Professor of International Relations, Oxford, and Fellow of Balliol 1944–7; Professor of Modern History, Oxford, and Fellow of Worcester 1947–51; Professor, Institute for Advanced Study, Princeton, 1951–62.
7 Richard Bruce Wernham (1906–99) succeeded Woodward in the Chair of Modern History and the associated Fellowship at Worcester in 1951; Namier, A. J. P. Taylor and Trevor-Roper were rivals for the post.

greatest number of good & clever men: & if he does not hold it long, there is always the tough & heartless but genuinely scholarly & professorabile Trevor Roper. But this is all off my beat. I enclose both my list of publications etc. and the draft of my actual application. If you think there is something amiss in either, I should be most deeply beholden to you if you cd say so, for I am much embarrassed about the whole thing, & don't want to appear either too scattered or too immodest, & hope that I am not, in fact. I am giving you much too much trouble: & only hope you will not mind too much: I shd like the job: but may well not be worthy of it.

 yrs ever
  Isaiah B.

TO CHARLES WEBSTER

 2 February 1957 [*manuscript*]

Headington House

Dear Charles,

 Thank you ever so much for your most helpful and generous letter. I have altered my application accordingly: & propose to send it in on Tuesday. After lengthy reflection I decided to replace Ensor with Gilbert Ryle, one of our three professors of philosophy. Not that he takes the faintest interest in political ideas: but Richard Pares said to me, wisely as I thought, that after all these years as a professional philosopher I ought to get some eminent member of that profession to testify to the fact (assuming it to be such) that I had not taken to political thought merely because I had fizzled out as a "pure" thinker. I thought this sound, and as Ryle knows me pretty well after 25 years acquaintance, & does not, I believe, think too ill of me, & is in a position to comment on my pre-war activities, I asked him. He replied most warmly, so my list is complete. Ryle writes pretty tactless testimonials – in which he summarises his subject in some explosive epigram & then proceeds to insult the electors or the Chair itself. However, I think he will rein himself in this time (when recommending Herbert Hart as Prof. of Jurisprudence, he said it was high time that a man of integrity & intelligence were to occupy a chair hitherto held by fools, knaves etc. As two previous holders[1] were, as it happens among the electors (I shall reveal the names to you only if you really want to know – it is not a secret) this caused pained reactions and my poor friend almost went down in the ensuing indignation. Still, one cannot have everything & Ryle it must be for me. After sending in the document amended in accordance with all your suggestions,[2] I shall cease thinking

---

1 Only Sir Carleton Kemp Allen (1887–1966) had been (1929–31) Professor of Jurisprudence, but Frederick Henry Lawson (1897–1983) was Professor of Comparative Law 1948–64 and Harold Greville Hanbury (1898–1993) Vinerian Professor of English Law 1949–64.
2 IB's application for the Chichele Chair, submitted on 5 February, consisted of a letter (see IBVL)

about the subject. Meanwhile the chair which is really exciting people is the Regius one of history. Taylor, McFarlane,[1] Southern,[2] Trevor Roper, Rowse, are all in a great frenzy. The patronage secretary has been down, & saw x & y & z, but not a or b or c – all this leads to speculation and comment & is like a succession of scenes in Trollope. I asked Richard Pares, whether if offered it, he would accept: he said he would not (for reasons, which as you may imagine do him nothing but the greatest honour, & are of a Sumner-like scruple and integrity) even though he realized that an offer to him would cause less pain, on the whole, than the nomination of almost anybody else. So we go on [...].

yrs
    Isaiah.

After several bouts of ill health, Alice James suffered a severe cerebral haemorrhage in January 1957.

TO WILLIAM JAMES

2 February 1957 [*manuscript*]

Headington House

Dear Bill,

We were all extremely distressed by your news [...]. I wish one knew why the good are punished and the bad and indifferent receive rewards: I would much rather believe in pure chance and a godless world (in fact – I think I do) than in a capricious deity or an unfathomable mystery: a random world at least makes it unnecessary to torment oneself with unanswerable questions, and leaves things as they are. I will not believe (contradicting the above instantly!) that all that goodness and vitality and courage and generosity and love are destined to flow in some narrowed or stunted channel. Alice, dear Alice, will surely, like Winston, recover through sheer innocence and confidence and love of life (like Winston).[3] [...] I can well imagine what you have been going through – it is surely harder for you than even for Alice – to support, to decide, to imagine, to be talked at by clumsy friends – but then the thought that she may wish to say something, which physically she cannot articulate, that is very very tough. [...] I am so sorry to be saying all this so inadequately – my fondest love and I feel *sure* she

---

summarising his academic career to date and his plans for the future, and a list of his publications. Both were littered with minor inaccuracies and his statement of progress on current projects was wildly exaggerated.

1 Kenneth Bruce McFarlane (1903–66), Fellow and Tutor in History, Magdalen, 1928–66.
2 Richard William Southern (1912–2001), Fellow and Tutor in History, Balliol, 1937–61; Chichele Professor of Modern History, Oxford, 1961–9.
3 Churchill had survived the series of strokes which had led to his resignation in April 1955.

will – in her strength & goodness – triumph over it all and still be happy & make you happy too.

Yours

Isaiah   [. . .]

Despite the trials that Hamilton Fish Armstrong had endured in extracting
'Generalissimo Stalin and the Art of Government' from IB (or rather from his
alter ego, O. Utis), Armstrong wrote on 18 January 1957 to 'O. Utis, Esq., care
Isaiah Berlin, Esq.', recalling with admiration the 'subtle and accurate analyis'
of the earlier article and suggesting that Mr Utis should produce a further piece
to relate his thesis to developments in the Soviet Union since Stalin's death.
Mr Utis agreed to produce something by the summer; Armstrong stressed the
importance of the deadline of the first week of August.

TO HAMILTON FISH ARMSTRONG

6 February 1957

Headington House

Dear Mr Armstrong,

My friend Mr Utis is, as you know, a poor correspondent and liable to be distracted by too many small and mostly worthless preoccupations. Your praise acted upon him as a heady wine, but his moods are changeable, and although, as his only dependable friend, I am trying to act as his moral backbone – an element which he conspicuously lacks – it is difficult to make any promises on his behalf, and the prospect of a decision by him on the subject of which you wrote, especially by the first week in August, is by no means certain. It would therefore be a *far far* safer thing not to anticipate its arrival *too* confidently. I will bring what pressure I can upon my poor friend, but I need not tell you, who have had so many dealings with him in the past, that his temperament and performance are unsteady and a source of exasperation and disappointment to those few who put any faith in him. I shall report to you, naturally, of what progress there may be – there is, alas, no hope of a permanent improvement in his character. Utis is under the queer illusion that his very unreliability is in itself a disarming and even amiable characteristic. Nothing could be further from the truth, but he is too old to learn, and if it were not for the many years of association with him which I have had to suffer, I should have given up this tiresome figure long ago. Nor could I, or anyone, blame you if you resolved to do this; there is no room for such behaviour in a serious world, without something more to show for it than poor Utis has thus far been able to achieve. You are too kind to him; and he, impenitently, takes it all too much for granted.

Yours ever,

An old friend.

TO TEDDY KOLLEK
   Received 5 March 1957

Headington House

My dear Teddy,
   Thank you very much for your letter[1] about the general situation – I did
not really expect B.G. to write – nor is there much point in his doing so now
as the situation has altered to such a degree that all those mild measures of
propitiation which might have been timely long ago would now certainly be
pointless and perhaps even politically misunderstood and harmful. So I withdraw all that. The rallying of British opinion to Israel since then has been
very remarkable, but who would have dreamt that Senators Knowland[2] and
Styles Bridges[3] would emerge as its champions! I feel sure that the central
nub of the whole thing ⟨more even than oil & USSR,⟩ is the fact that Ike has
been teased too much about American policy always in the end coming down
on the Jewish side for various disreputable reasons – this is obviously the
point which Arab after Arab has rubbed into him – and that he is determined
(as he genuinely thinks for patriotic and even objectively moral reasons) to
show himself 'strong' – rather like Eden vis-à-vis Nasser – so that if his face
can be saved about this, everything else can be settled relatively easily. ⟨The
literal repetition of British policy of the thirties vis-à-vis Arabs by the U.S.
for the same old reasons – bribery after it is too late – attempts to buy off
various potential Rashid Alis[4] – is very gloomy. I'll talk to Joe A. if and when
I see him. Chip B. will, I am sure, disagree with me about this, and defend
Ike's policy[5] very ably, sincerely and mistakenly.⟩ This is my usual tendency
to reduce politics to personal issues, and may be insufficiently objective. I
shall always believe it to be true. Anyway things look a little brighter this
morning, but I have a notion that Shepilov's change of office[6] is useful, since
he was personally much involved with Nasser. ⟨(But there is little in this).⟩ I
won't go on thinking aloud in this manner.
   Let me now come to more concrete and entertaining matters. About your

1 Dated 23 January 1957.
2 William Fife Knowland (1908–74), newspaperman; Republican Senator for California 1945–59;
   Senate majority leader 1953–5, minority leader 1955–9. A strong anti-Communist who had previously argued for greater support of the Nationalist Chinese government based in Formosa,
   Knowland publicly opposed Eisenhower's threat of sanctions against Israel unless it withdrew its
   forces from Egyptian territory, as no such action had been taken over the Soviet Union's crushing
   of the Hungarian uprising.
3 Henry Styles Bridges (1898–1961), influential right-wing Republican Senator for New Hampshire
   1937–61; Senate Minority Leader 1952–3; President Pro Tempore of the Senate 1953–5; Chairman,
   Republican Policy Committee, 1954–61; opposed sanctions against Israel.
4 Rashid Ali al-Gaylani, (1892–1965), anti-British (and pro-Axis) Arab Nationalist; Prime Minister of
   Iraq three times between 1933 and 1941.
5 Under the Eisenhower Doctrine, announced on 5 January 1957, the US would be willing to
   offer military and financial assistance, on request, to Middle Eastern countries opposed to
   Communism.
6 Shepilov had recently been replaced as Soviet Foreign Minister by Andrey Gromyko.

coming visitors. 1) Lady Bonham Carter. I hope she is given proper VIP treatment and that if she wants to go on to Jordan it will not be resented too much. She is a splendid public speaker, a great friend of both Winston and Macmillan, and not without influence in America. She was pro-Zionist in the early days, was almost turned into the opposite by the hanging of the sergeants,[1] wrote a letter to Dr Weizmann appealing to his moral sense and got a rather dusty answer with a not very convincing quotation from Goethe, which shocked her and left her in an ambivalent state. She is full of feeling, very clear-headed, and although stranded on a shoal as a Liberal without a party, a public personality of some size. She is a great friend of mine and asks for advice about Israel. I do not know what to tell her except that I hope she will have a good and serious time – statesmen are her line and the pure principles of anti-socialist liberalism her beliefs. She was out-raged by Eden on Suez and shakes her head over my shilly-shallying in this connection. If treated with insufficient respect or excessive familiarity she could have a Summerskill reaction.[2] One must never forget that she was the great Asquith's daughter and knew all the greatest men of her time, etc. ⟨Professors and politicians – her line.⟩

Your other visitors are very different. I managed to persuade Diana Cooper not to go, for she likes cosiness with a touch of tarnish and café society, which Israel does not provide in the right quality or quantity. So you will get Loelia, Duchess of Westminster, plus Lady Pamela Berry; the former is a good-time girl, extremely intelligent and her future connection with Israel cancer research is something we had better not dwell on too long, although it may work out. She and Lady P. Berry, particularly the latter who is now the central political hostess of the post-Eden Conservatives (her husband, a very old friend of mine who owns the *Daily Telegraph*, is very nervous about the whole expedition) should meet not elderly professors (more suitable for Lady V.) but dashing young Generals, preferably good-looking. Yigal Allon,[3] and above all Dayan are absolutely *de rigueur* for both the noble ladies, not Walter [Eytan]. ⟨Yadin[4] too, but less good.⟩ If you have some brave romantic soldiers, they, in combination with Mr Bejarano,[5] are what you must lay on, but of course you must see them yourself. I told them I would write to you. Lady P. is a great friend of ours and we are constantly meeting eminent

1 See 30–1.
2 Dr Edith Clara Summerskill (1901–80), Baroness Summerskill 1961, Labour MP 1938–61 (junior ministerial posts 1945–51); Chairman of Labour Party 1954–5. A fact-finding visit to Israel and Jordan in early 1955 had left her deeply affected by the Arab plight.
3 Yigal Allon (1918–80), Commander of the Palmach 1945–8; Lieutenant-General, Israel Defense Forces, 1948–50; Mapai member of the Knesset 1955–79; later (1967–74) Deputy Prime Minister of Israel.
4 Yigael Yadin (1917–84), né Yigal Sukenik, active in the Haganah when young; Chief of Staff, Israeli Defense Force, 1949–52; thereafter an archaeologist.
5 Moses 'Moshe' Bejarano (1901?–57), Israeli industrialist (cigarette-making and canning); trade attaché in Moscow 1948–9, with continuing government connections.

statesmen at her salon. She was the greatest single opposing factor in the anti-Eden campaign, having no love for Lady E., and is an intimate friend of the entire new Cabinet, particularly Butler and Macmillan, less so of Sandys[1] and Selwyn Lloyd.[2] There is no harm in persons like Moish[3] and Agron[4] seeing them (I had to write down all these names on the back of a menu card for them), but what they like is dash, heroism, fun, romantic colour – the Duchess has of course already visited the Lebanon with Bustani[5] and is full of guilt but likes to be paid for. Lady P. is free of such associations. I shall say all these thing to Meyer, but you must certainly know them.

I regret that they will all have to see B.G. – he must not refuse to see them, it will do more good than seeing many of his visitors. Lady P. will doubtless want to see finance ⟨& other⟩ ministers etc. as well, but should be kept from socialist intellectuals of a doctrinaire kind. Her tastes but not her temperament are very unlike those of Crossman.

About Bill Deakin of St Antony's, who is coming to see you in April, I need not tell you. His ex-students, Allon etc., should prove capable of looking after him. He likes lapsing back into his Intelligence Officer Winstonian days and will I am sure want to go to Gaza, Aqaba etc., nothing that is Balkan is alien to him. He is a very nice man and justly popular in London and knows Walter and likes him and will delight you all.

They all groan slightly at the prospect of having to spend time with Mrs Weizmann, but they know they have to do it, and Lady V. is made for it. Do waste a little of your time on all these people, however tense the international situation; it really will be worth it. Alas, Aline and I will not be coming this year.

Much love,
    Yours ever,
        ישעיהו[6]

The election of the next Chichele Professor of Social and Political Theory took place on 12 March.

1 Duncan Edwin Sandys (1908–87), Baron Duncan-Sandys 1974, Conservative politician; Minister of Supply 1951–4, Housing and Local Government 1954–7, Defence 1957–9, Aviation 1959–60.
2 (John) Selwyn Brooke Lloyd (1904–78), Baron Selwyn-Lloyd 1976, Conservative politician; Minister of Supply 1954–5, Defence 1955; Foreign Secretary 1955–60; Chancellor of the Exchequer 1960–2.
3 Perhaps Moshe Sharett.
4 Gershon Agron (1894–1959), né Agronsky in the Ukraine; newspaper correspondent and editor; founder in 1932 of the *Palestine Post* (renamed the *Jerusalem Post* 1950); Mayor of Jerusalem 1955–9.
5 Emile Murshid Bustani (1907–63), Lebanese businessman, philanthropist and politician.
6 'Isaiah'.

TO CHARLES WEBSTER

14 March 1957 [*manuscript*]

Headington House

Dear Charles,

It is all over – was indeed on Tuesday – & I am a little dazed at being appointed Cole's successor. Admittedly the "field" was pretty miserable – though I am the last person who should say so – since Plamenatz, for example, who probably deserved the Chair better than anyone, did not put in, I've no idea why [...]. I know (very properly, I am afraid) almost nothing of what occurred, save that Sir G. Clark favoured Gough[1] and (nothing new or surprising – this) thought pretty poorly of me. [...] Now that it is all over, I feel nervous and wonder if I am really the man to revive what {it} is indubitably a moribund subject in Oxford at present: still there's no use repining now – I am in this hard & dangerous looking saddle, & must try to ride. Moreover I've asked for it myself: & must seek to justify myself. I really *shall* produce the delayed book: I arrive late but I arrive. So I hope you will have no cause to feel too deeply ashamed of me. And in the meanwhile I do want to say again how deeply grateful I am.

yrs ever
    Isaiah.   [...]

Letters of congratulation flooded in.

TO ALAN PRYCE-JONES

15 March 1957 [*manuscript*]

Headington House

Dearest Alan,

[...] Thank you ever so much. Of course when I learnt that I was to be appointed, I fell into the blackest depression because

1) Why should one run into the nearest noose just because it is there? & if a set of rusty chains is seen slipping to the ground why should one automatically put them on? why should I believe blindly a lonely crowd?[2]

2) It is a very difficult subject. I shall be a target of much justified & unjustified criticism & abuse & sneering, & I am not a tough character & hate responsibility & either answering back or not answering back.

3) The same two points in a worse form. Maurice telephoned to express his sentiments: he was most kind: but I think he thinks I am not exuding

---

1 John Wiedhofft Gough (1900–76), Fellow, Oriel, 1931–67; historian and political philosopher, specialising in 17th-century Britain.
2 Transcription and meaning of this sentence uncertain. Possibly a reference to David Riesman, *The Lonely Crowd: A Study of the Changing American Character* (London and New Haven, 1950).

enough sweat blood or tears to get a professorship: & I can imagine that sincere as his congratulations were, his condolences, had I failed, wd have been sincerer still: he wd have comforted me with great sympathy & skill. I cd reproduce the words.

4) On the other hand if I *had* failed, I should have been even more depressed. It is a situation of which one hates both alternatives & necessarily regrets the unrealised one. [...]

love

Isaiah

TO HUGH TREVOR-ROPER

15 March 1957 [*manuscript*]

Headington House

Dear Hugh,

Thank you for your letter. I cannot deny that I feel relief that the tension is over [...] There is a whole generation of pre-1914 Balliol worthies – G. N. Clark – Sumner, Toynbee, actual & assimilated Wykehamists – who include Woodward & Sumner's Epigoni, Christopher Hill, Hancock,[1] & other non-conformist fanatics, who find me instinctively distasteful: They dominated Oxford in the thirties, and are now on the way out: timid right wing labour or piously atheistical persons solemn, self conscious, inferiority-ridden, and deeply resentful of almost all forms of spontaneity & life. I cd not bear them: the mixture of secularised protestant sentimentality, tame public school 'leftism', and appalling priggishness created an air in which I suffocated much more quickly than the wildest excesses of Conservatism or Communism: on the whole it was Asquith worshipping, naturally more at home in Germany than in France, pro-Arab & conscientiously anti-anti-semitic, excited by pseudo-*révolté*[2] figures like Rowse or Crossman, and deeply craven and empty inside. [...]

Isaiah

TO PATRICK GARDINER[3]

22 March 1957 [*manuscript*]

Headington House

Dear Patrick

Thank you very much. I think that Herbert Hart in a letter to Jenifer

1 Sir (William) Keith Hancock (1898–1988), Australian, Balliol history 1922–3; Chichele Professor of Economic History, Oxford, and Fellow of All Souls 1944–9; Director, Institute of Commonwealth Studies, and Professor of British Commonwealth Affairs, London, 1949–56; Director, Research School of Social Sciences, Australian National University, 1957–61.

2 sc. pseudo-*révolté*, 'pseudo-rebellious'.

3 Patrick Lancaster Gardiner (1922–97), Fellow, St Antony's, 1952–8; Fellow and Tutor in Philosophy,

probably put the matter best – though not, perhaps, most tactfully when he decided that I was probably "the best of a despicable collection". Alas, I'll settle for that: my rivals having been: Gough; Harrison;[1] Warrender;[2] Professor Catlin.[3] Where were Bowle,[4] Cranston,[5] Fairlie?[6] Plamenatz explained that his reasons were neither modesty nor the identity of his potential rivals: but desire to go on at Lechlade.[7] I wonder. I am now depressed & think it all an error. The fact that if I had been passed over I should have felt more depressed, does not help somehow. I must brace myself to all those pairs of brown African Asian eyes with the light of Laski shining from them. Do you remember Wittgenstein's "I hope to God I will be a jolly decent Prof:"? But seriously, I was greatly touched by you & Susan's writing at all.

  Yrs ever
  Isaiah

En route to a holiday in Sicily, IB and Aline stopped briefly in Rome.

TO VIOLET BONHAM CARTER

  31 March 1956 [sc. 1957; *manuscript postcard*]

Hotel de la Ville, Rome

I cannot say that in most respects this city is superior to Jerusalem: it certainly does not weigh one down with concentrated tension and hatred and violent sense of wrongs unrighted & perhaps unrighteable, so much: tho' perhaps in the 19th century when all liberals were outraged by it, this was true here too. I am very glad you found Israel impressive: such passion to assert national identity and live a new and un-ghetto-ish life, surely had to have found vent sometime, & if blocked too long would have exploded more disastrously than – even counting all Arab wrongs real *and* imaginary – it did [...].

  Love
  Isaiah   [...]

Magdalen, 1958–89; married (Kathleen) Susan Booth (1934–2006) in 1955.
1 Wilfrid Harrison (1909–80), Fellow, Queen's, 1939–57; editor, *Political Studies*, 1952–63; Professor of Political Theory and Institutions, Liverpool, 1957–64.
2 (James) Howard Warrender (1922–85), Head of Department of Political Science, Glasgow, 1946–59, Queen's Belfast, 1959–72; specialist on Thomas Hobbes.
3 George Edward Gordon Catlin (1896–1979), Bronfman Professor of Political Science, McGill, 1956–60; strong proponent of the Atlantic alliance who worked mainly in the US and Canada; married to author Vera Brittain, father of politician Shirley Williams.
4 John Edward Bowle (1905–85), Professor of Political Theory, College of Europe, Bruges, 1950–67.
5 Maurice William Cranston (1920–93), Lecturer in Social Philosophy, London, 1950–9; later (1969–85) Professor of Political Science, London (LSE).
6 Henry Fairlie.
7 The town about 20 miles west of Oxford where Plamenatz and his wife then lived.

TO ROWLAND BURDON-MULLER

13 April 1957 [*manuscript*]

As from Villa Igiea, Palermo

Dear Rowland

Thank you ever so much for your two delightful and most informative & interesting letters. We are at peace here – Taormina we thought appalling – despite the *Reichtum*[1] extracted out of *Schönheit*[2] – with the most unattractive imaginable Germans thickly everywhere. One should, I am sure, fight against one's own prejudices: I feel about the Germans what many worthy persons must feel about Jews: that although there are no doubt some very noble & good ones – Goethe etc. – & some of my friends etc. – yet this makes no difference to my reaction to loud German confidently, even insolently, spoken, in public places. From this one's feeling spreads to all emitters of the hated sounds – particularly when accompanied by the peculiar looks, at once defensive & aggressive, which Germans abroad often have. Even when one meets a nice German, the harmless Dieckmann,[3] or the German ambassador to London, "Johnny" von Herwarth,[4] one feels (I mean I feel) that they are nice *although* German: this is exactly what reputable & decent antisemites feel vis-à-vis reputable Jews: it is a disreputable feeling & I am sorry to have it, but it does help one to understand how prejudice works – Edmund Wilson has it acutely vis a vis all the English – Sir M. Bowra (and much more secretly, Lord Salisbury) has it vis a vis all Americans, I feel it also towards Poles, Balts, Hungarians, & feel correspondingly well disposed to all Italians, Dutchmen, Americans (& feel astonished when they turn out to be awful). [...] I still think they were unwise – and wrong – to march in October, but not wicked: given that dear Nasser & all the other Arabs kept dedicating themselves publicly & every evening to their total extermination, & given that extermination was a pretty fresh memory to most of the new immigrants, & not just a rhetorical flourish, they cannot be blamed much except for existing: that is their crime; & when I *pleaded* against bellicose policies in the spring of last year, when Aline & I visited Israel, my chief argument was that weak states, born against their parents wishes, & like a foundling, nurtured with unloving irritation by Foreign Offices which had much rather the creature had been strangled at birth – that power such as that, had better lie low & practise virtue beyond the normal standard: but this, not very surprisingly, was not the view of Gen. Dayan, born in Israel, & a Middle Eastern uninhibited warrior, tough, gay, handsome, a native leader,

---

1 'Riches'.
2 'Beauty'.
3 Herbert Dieckmann (1906–86), German-born Associate Professor of French, Harvard, 1950–2, Professor 1952–7, Smith Professor of French and Spanish Languages 1957–65.
4 Hans Heinrich Herwarth ('Johnnie') von Bittenfeld (1904–99), anti-Nazi German diplomat; first post-war Ambassador in London 1955–61.

as un-Jewish as most of them, by now, are. But I prefer Israelis to Jews: they are not riddled with ghastly psychological *malaises*. [...]

I was *terribly* sorry about Alice.[1] She did spread light & kindness & warmth wherever she moved. All her faults were venial, & all her virtues great & massive, like her figure. I was very very fond of her, & I think she had warm feelings for me, as for so many others: she will be genuinely & widely missed, & her death leaves her world colder: I had a very nice letter about it all from Hester Pickman: but how *is* Bill? I *must* write to him, but it is so difficult to know what to say to him: he does feel about every word & comma, almost like Uncle Henry. [...]

Much love
Isaiah

TO W. G. CONSTABLE[2]

25 April 1957 [*manuscript*]

Paris

Dear W.G.

It was very good of you to write. Whether it is a matter of congratulation or condolence to be made a Professor, I am not quite sure. I have, like a Soviet Economist, calculated that I have 800 lectures to deliver: after that ga ga & pension. I do envy you – you have reached that most desirable condition with all your excellent powers unimpaired, & a large, pleasant peaceful prospect, like a Dutch landscape, generously stretching before you. I must now gird *my* loins & write an inaugural lecture, opening with an éloge of Cole, which I shall find it aesthetically but not morally difficult to compose: for he is a very nice, very honest, prodigiously learned, touchingly sincere human being: & touchingly vain and boyishly noble too. And I must write to Bill James too – I was terribly sorry to hear that Mrs James had died: she was so genuinely kind & good & all her foibles were delightful & comical and she created lives for people, & gave inner cosiness & warmth to the whole place – how will Bill take it all? will he be lost and absolutely comfortless? or will he begin a strange new life of his own? My love to Olivia (to whom I shall write as soon as I get back to Oxford) & to John[3] & Giles[4] – when will you all come to see us – for I don't know (now that I am a university

---

1 Alice James had died on 30 March.
2 William George Constable (1887–1976), British-born Curator of Paintings, Boston Museum of Fine Arts, 1938–57.
3 John Davidson Constable (b. 1927) became a plastic surgeon and tissue conservationist (Associate Clinical Professor, Harvard Medical School) particularly committed to helping Vietnamese burns victims.
4 Giles Constable (b. 1929), at this time a PhD student at Harvard; later a historian of medieval religious and intellectual history (Associate Professor, Harvard, 1958–66); later Lea Professor of Medieval History, Harvard, 1966–77, and Professor, Institute of Advanced Study, Princeton, 1985–2003.

bureaucrat) when I shall ever come to Boston again. I met Francis H. Taylor[1] in Rome: terrifying I thought.

Yrs ever
    Isaiah

TO ARTHUR SCHLESINGER
7 May 1957

Headington House

Dear Arthur

Thank you for your letter of April 16 – I hate the sound of 'Professor Berlin' – if ever I write anything the reviewer can always give 'Professor' a mocking sound to which it seems peculiarly liable – one can no longer support highbrow causes without an acute sense of being thought one has a vested interest in such things of an obvious kind – of having forfeited some kind of vague freelance status – and ceased to be a gentleman and become a player. Talking of gentlemen, have you read Lord Halifax's Memoirs?[2] He really does belong to the class of persons to whom the Russian proverb about 'those who can emerge out of the water dry' seems singularly to hold. He manages to tell one nothing at all except occasional little digs at Winston, but not so dreary or ill-intentioned as Bryant's[3] edition of Alanbrooke's Memoirs. That has done neither Alanbrooke nor Bryant any good, I am glad to think. Someone ought to make an anthology one day of the resentful things said in a polite tone about great men by the exasperated mediocrities who have fought to serve them and who are reluctant to recognise their genius, while at the same time complaining endlessly about their interferences, tiresomenesses, etc. [. . .]

Yours ever,
    Isaiah

---

1 Francis Henry Taylor (1903–57), Director, Metropolitan Museum of Art, New York, 1940–55; Director, Worcester Art Museum, 1955–7. IB and Aline apparently met him at a dinner given by the Director of the American Academy in Rome, Laurance P. Roberts, and his wife Isabel.

2 *Fulness of Days* (London, 1957).

3 Sir Arthur Bryant (1899–1985), writer on history; his *The Turn of the Tide, 1939–1943* (London, 1957) was based on the war diaries of Alan Francis Brooke (1883–1963), 1st Viscount Alanbrooke 1946, Chief of Imperial General Staff 1941–6, Field Marshal 1944.

*On 7 May, only five weeks after Alice James's death, IB heard that James de
Rothschild had also died. IB wrote at once to his widow, and eventually to
William James.*

TO DOLLIE DE ROTHSCHILD[1]

8 May 1957 [*manuscript*]

Headington House

Dearest Dollie

I know that it cannot have been unexpected, and that you must at times
have tried to imagine what it would be like, and yet that when it came it was
not like that at all, and not bearable, and goes on being insoluble, and little
does any good, and nothing is the same, and words are no good at all. I learnt
of it by chance, from Rosemary d'Avigdor, who was told by Harry,[2] & then
learnt from Worden[3] that it was sudden and peaceful and as one would not
mind ending oneself. I could not go on with my day in London and had to
take the train and return to Oxford. I loved and admired him more, I think,
than he cd have realised: more than anyone not of his own family, I feel
sure, towards the end of his life. I adored absolutely *everything* about him:
his appearance, his tone of voice, his gestures, his eccentricities, above all the
pride, the splendour of the inner and outer style, the vitality, the humour,
the irresistible charm, but above all the enormous generous scale on which
he was built, and the marvellous moral strength and dignity – which so often
goes with simplicity and even stupidity of a monumental kind, but which
in his case was allied to an acute, uncompromising insight into everything
and everybody, and which made him invulnerable as a human being and as
a Jew – rarest of things! – unsnubbable, a natural *grand seigneur* and morally
undeceivable, before whom all that was false, cowardly, protected itself from
the truth behind *alibis*, [all] that was bogus or pompous or not quite genuine
fled from him or cowered uncomfortably. You cannot imagine how much
the thought of what he would think or *say* – the mere image of him – influenced me (and perhaps others too) in all sorts of awkward situations and
saved one from cowardice or unworthy evasions. You cannot (or perhaps you
can more than anybody) imagine what an enormous relief, what a luxurious
experience it was to find this ideal champion of all that one believed and
wanted to believe – who contained so much life, wit, gallantry, honour, taste,
irrepressible sense of the comedy of life, with the most delicate and sensitive human perceptions, acute Jewish humour, and the most natural, deep,
unconcealed concern for everything that touched the Jews, with a – to me –

1 Dorothy Mathilde ('Dollie') de Rothschild (1895–1988), née Pinto, wife of James de Rothschild;
   like him a Jewish (and Zionist) activist and philanthropist.
2 Sir Henry d'Avigdor-Goldsmid.
3 Possibly Arthur Warden, one of James de Rothschild's staff, mentioned in his will.

heavenly contempt for those who evaded or betrayed or behaved in a servile or even faintly squalid fashion. I admired Dr Weizmann because he was proud, unbroken, and faced the truth, but he was also, perhaps inevitably, ruthless, cynical and terribly tough. Jimmy filled one with no less pride and his back was just as straight, but he also filled one with gaiety and delight and possessed that kind of moral quality which would be bound to know what is right and behave superbly in any crisis – and goodness me how wonderful it was to know that his heart was always, *always* in the right place, that he would always react painfully responsibly to any complexities that put one in a quandary, and always with absolute courage and fortitude and unswerving uprightness.

You must forgive me for pouring all this out at a moment that is so dark for you – but he meant so much to me – so much more than he could possibly have known – that I feel, perhaps arrogantly, that I have a kind of right to impose all this on you. Please forgive me. You always were more patient than he. His very impatience went with all those enchanting thoroughbred characteristics. I shall never cease to bless John Foster for taking me to see [him] in Waddesdon[1] in 1932. I have never in my life enjoyed a friendship so much – or looked forward more to any visit – there was nothing one could not talk about, nothing that was not made exhilarating, nothing about which there was not a degree of moral sympathy which I found nowhere – literally nowhere – else before or after. I really did idolise him, & with reason: both as a public figure and as the man I was best pleased and proudest to know in all my life. It seems a most terrible presumption but I think I know what you must feel: at least I try to guess and if it would be at all tolerable for you, I should like to come to see you: whenever you like, and when you think you could bear to be impinged upon. The most painful experience I have ever had was my father's death, & then I wanted to see no one – not even the people I was fondest of – only to lick my wound in total solitude. It may seem odd to speak of this now, but if you came to stay with us here, you would find it very quiet and not, I think, irritating or abrading in any way. We should both adore it and do nothing to clutter you up. Of course, you must not answer this ever – I wish words weren't sticks and so utterly incapable of expressing anything real – only, at most, that one wants badly to say things and cannot. If there is anything I could do, please say. I cannot say how much I feel[2] –

Isaiah

1 Waddesdon Manor in Buckinghamshire (a Victorian reproduction of a French Renaissance chateau), the home of James de Rothschild, bequeathed by him to the National Trust.
2 A lively supplementary obituary by IB and Miriam Rothschild (Lane) paid tribute to 'a brilliant conversationalist, a formidable opponent in controversy, a cultivated, generous and modest gentleman'. 'Mr James de Rothschild: "Grand Seigneur"', *The Times*, 13 May 1957, 15.

TO WILLIAM JAMES

11 May 1957 [*manuscript*]

Headington House

Dear Bill,

I know that, of course, you must often have thought about what it would be like, and visualised it or attempted to – as I did in the case of my father. But when it happens it is quite different and very little is of help. Only, then, the steady hands and competent help of old friends. And of that, I know, you can have had no want. Words help least of all: and yet I cannot – and you will forgive me I hope and pray – not say what love and admiration I had for Alice. She created an immense amount of life round her by sheer generous expenditure of her own person, and gave what she gave with such love, such uncalculating prodigality, to so many, with such unbelievable faith and hope and charity, with such allowance for every kind of human frailty, that no one was frozen or ashamed to tell her whatever it was that they most wanted to say: & a great many corners of the prodigiously inhibited & contorted Anglo Saxon hearts, congealed by circumstances or by other, chillier human beings, must have opened & thawed and resumed their life as a result of contact with her enormous humanity. She really was a great bringer to life and maintainer of persons & the texture of friendship, and my life in Harvard, when I look back on it, has her & you as its centre – however cluttered up & wasted in worthless activities it often was, it seemed to acquire both firmness & dignity in my own eyes – & I am terribly liable to self-contempt even if not self-pity – when I reflected, or simply was aware of, my relationship to both of you which I valued above any other in my Harvard Life & then, as you know, far outside & beyond it. It seemed to me that although her heart seemed to have no limits – & the shrewdness, which only people of exceptional human sympathies ever have, seemed to embrace all human frailties – yet that I received an exceptionally rich gift{s}, an undeserved & marvellously large share of it. I was very deeply delighted by this and still am, & most grateful and cannot begin to convey what a difference it made.[1] I learnt from Rowland that the end was not painful – & indeed I should not mind ending so myself. But those who are gone, are gone: and one's feelings are for the living: and so I should like to ask, if it is not too impertinent, how are you? will you not come to stay with us here? it wd be a change, & our lives are quiet and lie in the pleasant surroundings that you have seen: you like the Tiepolos and the other pictures upon the walls already: Aline wd be delighted, I shd be delighted, you wd find it all not thrilling indeed, but peaceful, beautiful, and good for the nerves. How can I tempt you further? we shall be here all July & half August, & again in October: now that I am an official (knell-like word)

---

1 William James replied: 'of all the men of different ages and countries and backgrounds that Alice was fond of I believe you stood nearest to her' (letter of 3 June 1957).

professor, I am tied to Oxford more than before, & shall not travel far: please won't you come. Aline wants me to say how much there is that she too has to convey: but never will, for unlike me, she has a deep, reticent, fastidious, not too articulate nature – when she does speak out, it is marvellous. I hope that you are as you always were: better than that there is no need to be, for anybody, ever.

Yours
    Isaiah.

TO TEDDY KOLLEK

21 May 1957

Headington House

Dear Teddy,

Lady Pamela has had tremendous second thoughts.[1] [. . .] She said that she had liked everything in Israel, some things more than others, but everything a great deal. She liked Yadin, Dayan, yourself, Meltzer[2] (him the Duchess also adored quite genuinely), and several other people whose names I forget, quite extraordinarily. And it must be admitted that her *constant* appearances at Zionist functions in London, to women of remote districts of North London, and lectures apparently stressing the beauties and sublimities of everything in Israel over and over again do bear out that at any rate she wishes to give the impression of being a staunch and passionate friend. Nevertheless obviously her first impressions were what in fact she felt, and her second impressions are what she has now persuaded herself that it is right and proper to feel. Do not let us look gift horses in the mouth, and let us give her the benefit of every doubt and the due for all the true services which she at present is performing. [. . .]

The Herbert Agars have returned absolutely lyrical about Israel. Herbert Agar was always an opponent, but has now completely reversed his position and they are bubbling over with absolutely genuine passion and tell everyone about it and they are extremely loyal and eloquent friends, and Mrs A. has written me a long enthusiastic letter saying that she never expected to find anything so inspiring in her life and she will be a friend to Israel for ever and ever and ever etc. So on the whole you are not doing too badly, I must say, in purely social terms at any rate. This is really only to ask you how you are and to tell you that all your recent visitors – Lady Violet, even the Duchess (the

---

1 IB had reported her initial reaction to Kollek on 8 April 1957: 'She liked you, Yadin, & on the whole nobody else. She says she is an ally of Israel politically: but that everyone she talked to (with the above exceptions) were violently anglophobe. She saw why this was so, but naturally (I suppose) was not too pleased.'

2 Julian Louis Meltzer (1904–77), journalist, writer and translator; Executive Vice-Chairman for Public Affairs, Weizmann Institute, 1946–72; later (1966–75) Director, Weizmann Archives.

most doubtful) are to be counted as allies. Lady Pamela wants to be thought *very* friendly, wants to come back again, and is, as I said, *furiously* angry with me for suggesting that there was anything at all that she dislikes. Do convey this wherever necessary.

Yours ever,

ישעיהו[1]

TO ARTHUR SCHLESINGER

27 May 1957

Headington House

Dear Arthur

I must report to you that A.E.S. came and made a profound impression. His lecture,[2] in a sense, pleased everybody. It was very sincere, very moving, the jokes at the beginning about Oxford being the home of lost causes – with himself as the most conspicuous contemporary lost cause in the world – were very funny. The content of what he said was entirely reasonable, not unexpected, against sin, and made everyone like him very very much indeed. *The Times* did not report him at all well[3] – too briefly and too stupidly – but I must admit that the intellectual content was really rather low. He is an egghead morally and politically rather than intellectually: dear Harry [Truman] would have had more to say and said it a good deal more trenchantly. The lack of political oomph in A.E.S. seems to me enormous. I sat next to him at dinner or rather at dessert in All Souls afterwards and found him [a] most charming, sweet, honest nice man – but curiously nervous, timid, not at all because of anything in Oxford, I thought, in need of perpetual encouragement and comfort, whether from pretty ladies or affectionate friends, or whoever it might be, and lacking the toughness and water-displacing quality (as opposed to ambition which he may not have) which leaders of large countries, I fear, require. I do not budge from my original opinion: he is really much too nice, sensitive, too nervous, with a touch of real neurosis somewhere in his system – to be a great success as an elected leader of anything. I am sure he would make an excellent Secretary of State. [...]

Yours ever,

Isaiah   [...]

On 13 June the Birthday Honours List announced the award of a knighthood

1 'Isaiah'.
2 After receiving an honorary degree of Doctor of Civil Law at Oxford on 24 May, Adlai Stevenson lectured on 'The Common Task of the United States and the Commonwealth'.
3 'Mr Adlai Stevenson Criticizes "Crumbling Alliance" Talk', *The Times*, 25 May 1957, 4.

to IB. A further round of congratulations followed, some more generous than others.[1]

TO ROWLAND BURDON-MULLER

20 June 1957 [*manuscript*]

Headington House

Dear Rowland

Thank you for your cable. Aline is pleased by it too. Too kind. To you at least I can say how *ridiculous* I feel: some suits don't go with some figures: & when the P.M. decided to make an eccentric gesture just to show how different he was to his predecessor, I was embarrassed: deeply. But then my mama burst into tears at the mere suggestion that I shd refuse: that was that: I consulted my clergyman – dear Stuart. He told me that my poor mother's pleasure outweighed my embarrassment at making a fool of myself: & I agreed that I minded being laughed at less than most. So I accepted & tried to think no more of it (& consoled myself with the reflection that after all if I had, as I felt (& feel) inclined to refuse, I shd insult all the other dear academic knights – Sir A. Blunt, Sir W. Coldstream,[2] & indeed Sir M. Bowra himself, by a desire to be chic & superior. But now it has occurred I am in a painful state of gêne.[3] I expect it will wear off. Adlai was very dull & sweet: *can* you *like* the Sword of the Spirit – Barbara Ward? she seems to me to me like a walking cliché – *looks* like a cliché even – virtuóus, kind, but intolerably girlish & coy: I cannot speak to her. I had a sweet letter from Bill James. And have bought 30 letters from Turgenev to Aline's grandfather[4] in Russian.

love

Isaiah

TO ROY HARROD

22 June 1957 [*manuscript*]

Headington House

Dear Roy

I was much moved by your very kind and good letter. I feel embarrassed by

1 The absence of a citation prompted Lady Patricia Hornak to suggest that the title had been awarded for 'brilliant conversation' (undated letter). Herbert Hart wrote from Harvard to his wife Jenifer, 'How awful about Isaiah: really horrid [...]. What was it said to be for? Not attacking govt. during Suez? Conversation? Solving problem of Free Will? [...] There's much mockery here.' Nicola Lacey, *A Life of H. L. A. Hart: The Nightmare and the Noble Dream* (Oxford 2004), 206.
2 Sir William Menzies Coldstream (1908–87), Slade Professor of Fine Art, London (UCL) 1949–75; knighted 1956.
3 'Discomfort, embarrassment'.
4 Baron Horace (Naphtali Herz) de Gunzburg (1833–1909), Russian Jewish financier, State councillor to the Russian Government, promoter of the interests of Russian Jews, philanthropist and patron of the arts and sciences.

these honours, and ashamed: not out of false modesty, but because I have a feeling that some hats do not fit some heads, & I feel it all most inappropriate and too unearned, too much altogether. I am all for getting more than one's due – it is gayer than strict justice: the whimsical prodigality of our rulers in an irresponsible mood does not, I suppose, do any harm: & variegates life. Still there are limits, which, I am not sure in this case, are not overstepped. I did think of refusing: but I was deterred by very personal reasons; and by thinking that one must not make too much ado about so little: merely because it made one a trifle (I *hope* only a trifle) ridiculous: I don't, I suppose, mind being made ridiculous as much as other people: so I subsided. And still it is awkward to be given gratuities when others are deprived of much larger just rewards. But again one should not fuss. So that is that.

I am glad to be reminded of a quarter of a century ago: you did not care for logical positivism then, neither did I, and who shall say that, historically speaking, we turned out to be mistaken? only yesterday I heard Freddie Ayer say in a television performance that L[ogical] P[ositivism] was now 'officially dead'.[1] No other philosophical movement was ever 'officially' declared deceased, by its own followers: it is a great disgrace. I keep writing a book on political thought in 1760–1840, but all the words become like sticks, & all the sentences seem pompous platitudes: I have little intellectual (or any other) self confidence: every criticism of me ever made I have thought just. It is very nice of you to wish me to write. I shall. But I shall disappoint you,

Yours ever,

Shaya

TO CHARLES WEBSTER

7 July 1957 [*manuscript*]

Headington House

Dear Charles

Thank you very much for your charming & generous letter which I am much too late in acknowledging: & generosity is, alas, needed, for well do I know that I have, this year received far more than any conceivable due: & I fear others must realise this too. I have no notion who engineered this last "elevation": there really is such a thing as shame before undeserved rewards [. . .]. On the same day[2] arrived a notice saying that unless I was blackballed (in effect) I should be elected a Fellow of the British Academy.[3] I feel like Polycrates[4] & don't know what ring to throw into what sea. I feel so

---

1 Ayer used these words in the episode of the BBC television discussion programme *The Brains Trust* broadcast on 23 June 1957 [transcript at BBC Written Archives Centre].
2 As his acceptance.
3 IB was indeed elected a Fellow of the British Academy on 10 July 1957.
4 Polycrates, tyrant of Samos in the 6th century BC, threw his most precious possession, a ring,

embarrassed about the "Sir" that I have asked them to omit it on the Oxford lecture list; it is like a tie a friend gives one, that one admires, appreciates but thinks too showy: I propose to cover it with the long luxuriant beard of the Professorship. Prof. Berlin will conceal Sir Isaiah. [. . .]

yrs
Isaiah

Despite the respect in which the BBC's Third Programme was held, its audience was limited, and in 1957 it became a target for cost-cutting. After a determined campaign by its listeners, the separate identity of the Third Programme was preserved, but its weekly broadcasts were to be cut by almost half. Opposition to this proposal led to meetings – including one in Oxford, chaired by Alan Bullock, on 17 July – between BBC representatives and concerned parties. As a known devotee of the Third Programme, IB was a natural defender of its interests.

TO GEORGE BARNES[1]

18 July 1957

Headington House

Dear George

I memorised your letter before I burnt it and did my best to say these things to the eminent persons who arrived. The Vice-Chancellor[2] was not present and Veale said not a word, but on the whole agreed with every word that Ian Jacob[3] said. Bullock was forthright, but on the whole represents the interests of the Home Service with decent respect for the Third. I took the brunt of the latter, and made myself appear somewhat unpopular by expressing shock and horror at the policy. They were very nice and extremely embarrassed, and I had the impression that they had no idea that what they had done would stir up so much opposition in so many quarters. They were much impressed by the point about the fact that Frogs, even if prodded, and even if the job was a put-up job, could not be got to praise any other British institution; and on the whole took the line that there was no reason to judge quality by quantity, and that a three-hour programme would be all that we possibly could desire, that they were simply cutting out superfluous fat. They did say, and begged that this would be secret, that if at the end of six months they found that what was happening was not adequate they would reconsider and lengthen the programme again; at the moment they seem

into the sea to avert any possible reversal of his previous good fortune (the ring returned to him inside a fish which had swallowed it).

1 Sir George Reginald Barnes (1904–60), BBC (founding Head, Third Programme, 1946–8; Director, Spoken Word, 1948–50; Director of Television, 1950–6); Principal, University College of North Staffordshire (later Keele University), 1956–60.

2 J. C. Masterman.

3 Sir (Edward) Ian Claud Jacob (1899–1993), Director-General, BBC, 1952–60.

in a contrite mood and want to use any opportunity for broadcasting long operas and otherwise make the three hours seem like five. I said that under the circumstances I should recommend anyone I knew not to do any talks on the BBC as this would be taking away indispensable time from music; and that any talks on the Third Programme now were a deprivation of the public and that if I saw Bertrand Russell, E. M. Forster, or the like, I would urgently plead with them, despite the demands of self-interest, to sacrifice themselves for the common cause, and refuse to talk until and unless the programme was revised. I have never known myself so militant and was somewhat ashamed of it afterwards. However we had lunch together and nobody could have been happier. Wellington[1] and Morris[2] kept assuring me that it hurt them more than it hurt me and that they only did it with tears in their eyes. I think they are genuinely rattled, but whether anything will come of it I do not know. Meanwhile having never spoken up in a committee before in my life, I am grateful to you for having provided me with a brief. I did my best but I may have ruined the cause (that too is a sort of megalomania I suppose).

Forgive me for all this – I thought the person who displayed the least degree of either shame or good will towards the Third Programme was of all people H. Grisewood. I wonder why. Guilt perhaps. I asked them (it is becoming intolerable, this boasting of one's smart points) what they would say if *The Times*, being hard-pressed financially, were to cut *The Times Literary Supplement* to four pages. Although nobody thinks this is an organ of genius, the general effect on educated opinion would not be fortunate. This for some reason went home. That is to say it was thought specious, ingenious, unfair, but made a sort of mark. I had a feeling that there was a soft under-belly somewhere and that if anyone could be made to lunge at it it would produce results. So mobilise (funny that I should say this to you) anyone you can and I think there may be results. I have honestly done all I could.

Yours ever,
    Isaiah

PS [...] For the first (and I daresay for the last) time I felt glad to be a Sir: it seemed to carry more authority. Terrible, but it seemed so.

Minor changes were made to the proposed cuts, but the battle was effectively lost. In October 1957 the Third Programme was reduced to 24 hours a week.

1 (Reginald Everard) Lindsay Wellington (1901–85), Director of Sound Broadcasting, BBC, 1952–63.
2 (Charles) John Morris (1895–1980), Controller, Third Programme, BBC, 1952–8.

TO MORTON WHITE

19 July 1957

Headington House

Dear Morton,

I was happy and relieved to get your letter. I feel the kind of guilt about the knighthood which you can only too well imagine. On the whole it is an embarrassment to me. [...]

You are quite right, people like the Harts and my predecessor Cole and others do think of me as having 'sold out' to some vague establishment. Cole indeed wrote me a severe little note saying that he was shocked to see that I had allowed myself to visit the Palace inhabited by 'That Woman', and afterwards when speaking to me explained that although he thought that Attlee had rendered considerable services to the Labour movement, he, Cole, was forced to break off relations with him, virtually, after he had allowed himself to be compromised by 'That Woman'. This is sufficiently old-fashioned to be pure and touching and I rather like him for it.

A. J. P. Taylor, who is furious at not being made Regius Professor, has attacked Namier, whom he regards as responsible, in the *New Statesman* and made a side-swipe at me by implying that the Prime Minister was dispensing patronage to people who entertain or amuse him in one fashion or another.[1] Which may indeed be true, for the reason for this 'elevation' is genuinely obscure to me, as to others. On the whole it embarrasses me, every time I see the word on an envelope – still worse when it is spoken, I wince deeply. It gives me no pleasure at all. I ask myself why I should have accepted it and the answer, on the whole, is (*a*) because I could never have concealed the fact that it had been offered to me, being myself; (*b*) that it gives my mother the most enormous pleasure and will send her, unhappy as she is, far far happier along whatever years remain to her[2] – this seems a sentimental not to say a banal reason, but it is perfectly true. When I suggested to her that I might refuse, she virtually burst into tears. I then took a utilitarian line with myself, saying that on the whole the whole thing did not matter and that to make her miserable for the sake of so little was in fact wrong. And now I have my doubts – she has undoubtedly been made [happy]; but it seems to me that I mind too much. (*c*) Also I try to argue with myself that it is a good thing that Governments should give these things to the intelligentsia,

1 'Mr Macmillan sees himself as Henry Pelham, if not as the supposedly great Sir Robert Walpole, though I doubt whether he will last as long. This explains why he has taken Sir Lewis Namier as his adviser on practically everything. [...] Honours and appointments go to Mr Macmillan's relatives or to those who entertain him by talking amusingly at lunch.' A. J. P. Taylor, 'London Diary', *New Statesman*, 6 July 1957, 6. The (mid-18th-century) periods of office as Prime Minister of Walpole and Pelham were marked by their use of patronage as a political tool.

2 The entry for 14 August 1957 in Marie's diary confirms that IB's Professorship and knighthood brought her 'a long chain of happiness. Nobody, nobody could mar it. Just inner joy deep in my being, without compromise.'

however harmless (e.g. myself), and that I should have refused had I been genuinely egalitarian, but that in fact I did not at all dislike the Honours system, thought these things were harmless baubles and on the whole rather liked it when other people got them. I had no idea I should mind so much myself. I mind only because it seems to me that it sets me off as a pompous person, not so easily addressed in familiar terms by people with whom I like to associate on inconspicuous and unselfconscious terms. This does not obviously apply to friends, but it does to undergraduates, graduate students, colleagues etc. etc. I also feel faintly like a poacher turned gamekeeper, but only faintly: I always was a gamekeeper at heart I daresay.

The ceremony at the Palace[1] when I was 'dubbed' was inexpressibly tedious – enormous boredom marked by slight terror at grotesquely appearing on the stage accompanied by courtiers. I have had a wonderful series of letters from various persons – the three Professors of Philosophy each behaving most characteristically. Austin quite straightforwardly expressed his pleasure. Price wrote me a letter about the Order of Knights, pointing out that the first knight was none other than Totila the Hun,[2] and went off into an elaborate historical excursus on the subject, saying that the duty of knights in those days was to fight for a semi-Roman civilisation against barbarism, and that he supposed that I was doing that already, etc. And finally Gilbert [Ryle], who said 'Felicitations (I suppose).' All highly typical.

[...] Herbert is back,[3] and tells me that Harvard is full of my enemies – Friedrich,[4] and Bill Elliott (as I expected) mainly on ideological but partly also he thought on personal grounds. That is not discreditable. Also Aiken (more surprising) and Marshall Cohen[5] (whom I hardly know and do not mind about). Why is Henry hostile? But perhaps he is not. Anyway one can't mind everything everywhere all the time.

I am not at all despairing about our book, in fact I fully intend to make everything possible to let it materialise. A queer expression: all I mean is that I should like to write it with you. Please send me your lectures. My whole reason for wanting to be Professor is to be sucked more into the general

---

1 On 16 July.
2 Totila (or Baduila), last king of the Ostrogoths 541–52, who fought the Byzantine Empire for control of Italy. He died in the battle near Targinae which lost the Ostrogoths their territorial gains. Price wrote 'Totila the Ostrogoth' (letter of 13 June): IB confuses him with Attila the Hun (406–53).
3 Hart had spent the academic year 1956–7 as Visiting Professor at Harvard.
4 Carl Joachim Friedrich (1901–84), German-born political scientist and specialist on totalitarianism; Professor of Government, Harvard, 1936–55, Eaton Professor of the Science of Government 1955–71.
5 (Stephen) Marshall Cohen (b. 1929), philosopher (mainly legal, political, moral and aesthetic); Junior (Society of Fellows) Fellow in Philosophy, Harvard, 1955–8, Assistant Professor, General Education and Philosophy, 1958–62; taught later at Chicago (1962–6) and Rockefeller (1967–70) Universities, CUNY (from 1970) and University of Southern California (from 1983); founding editor of Philosophy and Public Affairs 1971–98. He later attacked Berlin in 'Berlin and the Liberal Tradition', Philosophical Quarterly 10 (1960), 216–27.

routine of academic life, to write books and to lecture, and to think about that instead of the fiddling round the edges which went on before.

Herbert likes you very much indeed and I shall certainly not repeat a word. But he says exactly that about you which you say about him: about being doctrinaire etc. Yes, he is very rigid: he seems very indignant with Russell about his attack on Strawson in *Mind*.[1] I rather enjoyed it, without asking myself too much how far he was being unfair. I have written a long queer article about aspects of Marxism in Russia which I propose to send to *Foreign Affairs*.[2] The main thesis is that, historically speaking, a curious thing has happened, that all the Marxist categories such as 'exploitation' or 'surplus value' or 'lackeys of the bourgeoisie' or 'base and superstructure' etc. etc., which fit the West with difficulty, and may be illuminating but certainly are not infallible categories fitting into pre-established grooves so far as the West is concerned, seem to fit the Soviet system like a glove. And that this is due to the fact that when Lenin and Trotsky were establishing the Russian Government they believed that they had to make it go through certain stages which the Western world, according to Marx, had already traversed; these stages were described in the works of Marx and Engels, were none too true about the West, though of course extremely brilliant and suggestive, and were turned from being a description, as intended in the works of Marx, into something normative by Lenin and Trotsky. In short that the Bolsheviks forced Russian society to go through stages which they had supposed, not altogether correctly, on the basis of studying books and not reality, to have been experienced by the West. Not unlike what happened about the American constitution as the result of Montesquieu's misinterpretation of the British constitution,[3] only more so. I wonder if this is merely an amusing paradox or has something in it. At least to me it illuminates quite a lot of what in fact happened in Russia and seems further evidence in support of the thesis that ruthless men in a 'flexible' or chaotic situation are capable of giving the life of a nation a violent and unexpected and irrational twist not really predictable by sober students of social history. Anyway I will send you the article or some text or other on the subject. [...]

Yours ever,
Isaiah   [...]

---

1 Bertrand Russell, 'Mr Strawson on Referring', *Mind* 66 (1957), 385–9.
2 593/1.
3 'His most famous doctrine, that of the separation of powers, an enthusiastic but mistaken tribute to the system that he had so falsely imagined to prevail in England, [...] had been much too faithfully adopted in the United States, with results not altogether fortunate.' 'Montesquieu' (543/3), 268 (AC 131).

TO EDMUND WILSON

27 August 1957 [*manuscript*]

As from Headington House

Dear Edmund

[...] I did indeed lunch with the Queen.[1] It is really very good of the American press of the more respectable kind to take such interest in the life of our dear Queen: and to offer such balanced and judicious views: I fear it overestimates my own humble part in broadening the mind of our monarch: on the occasion to which I've referred, ignoring the frowns of the somewhat puritan members of the left wing of the labour party amongst whom I was incongruously included, I pressed the merits of the works of Genet,[2] *Memoirs of Hecate County*,[3] and *Lolita*[4] upon Her Majesty; these titles were duly written down by a courtier; I was severely reproved for this later by the Home Secretary[5] who presented me for my honour and acts as unofficial censor in this country; but the damage, I hope, was done. The Queen was quite jolly: denounced tyrants, in particular Peron,[6] the effects of President Eisenhower's digestion on the American economy[7] and the Trooping the Colour. She asked me if I read much – & said that her father once informed his luncheon guests that he had been reading a *most* interesting book – the Bible – & had any of them read it, & if so, what did they think of it. You cannot tell me that I shd have had a gayer time at the White House or the Elysee. The Queen inquired after my views of the works of Louise de Vilmorin – I asked hers regarding Cocteau. I think perhaps you had better *not* disillusion the benevolent U.S. press with their view of this grave, dull, limited, horsey young early Victorian prig. The food was very indifferent. No real footmen. No pomp. No formal dress. All very Scandinavian. [...]

Yrs

Isaiah.

1 Wilson had apparently sent IB a copy of an article by Peregrine Worsthorne ('Elizabeth II can't be Elizabeth I', *New York Times*, 18 August 1957, SM6), which mentioned that IB had lunched with the Queen (on 11 June, among other eminent guests). IB wrote to Arthur Schlesinger that the accompanying 'v. gay' letter from Wilson (received 24 August) expressed 'pleasure & relief that I am doing my bit to counteract the Queen's isolation so appropriately pointed out by Lord Altrincham' (letter of 24 August). An article by Lord Altrincham (605/1) on 'The Monarchy Today', published in his low-circulation monthly *The National and English Review* in August, had attracted worldwide attention (much of it hostile) for its mild criticisms of the monarch and her court, and its suggestions for reform. Worsthorne's response was measured, but the Duke of Argyll suggested hanging, drawing and quartering, and an irate monarchist hit Altrincham in the face.
2 Jean Genet (1910–86), French novelist and playwright, many of whose works were banned in the US for their celebration of homosexuality and crime.
3 Wilson's 1946 work was banned in the US for many years for its sexual explicitness.
4 Vladimir Nabokov's novel *Lolita* had been published in Paris in 1955 but then banned for obscenity in the UK and France.
5 'Rab' Butler.
6 Juan Domingo Perón (1895–1974), President of Argentina 1946–55, 1973–4.
7 In June 1956 Eisenhower had undergone surgery for inflammation of the small intestine.

IB finally produced an article[1] *for* Foreign Affairs, *sending it to Hamilton Fish Armstrong on 16 August with the suggestion that, as the seventh and final section was more autobiographical than the rest, it should be printed separately under the pseudonym he had used in 1952, 'O. Utis'; the main body of the article could appear in IB's name. On 28 August Armstrong wrote accepting this suggestion: the final section would appear in the same edition as a separate piece, entitled 'The Soviet Child-Man' and attributed to O. Utis. IB (on holiday in Italy) cabled, then wrote, objecting to the title and changing his mind about re-using the pseudonym. By then the articles were being printed, and the cost of stopping the presses was considerable. In partial compensation, Armstrong withheld IB's honorarium for the second article.*

TO HAMILTON FISH ARMSTRONG

13 September 1957 [*manuscript*]

Paraggi, Italy

Dear Ham,

You see now what an appalling client you have entangled yourself with. Surely, surely you will not again let kindness, friendship, generous feeling trap you into asking me to contribute, when the price you have to pay is so huge & undeserved? I should have warned you, or Aline should, about how awful I can be. But I should not like you to believe that my behaviour was gratuitous. I made that terrible fuss (the thought of it makes me hot to think of – yet I could no other) because I am consumed with feelings of responsibility towards the poor people I talked to in Russia, who really did talk freely to me, some of them, – since I penetrated into politically "unsatisfactory" circles which the authorities discourage all contact with, not merely in the case of foreigners, but their own people as well; and I am bound to wish to protect them to the maximum degree. "Utis" is now no good because George Kennan publicly identified him,[2] very gratuitously, it seems to me. It is not, as you know, that one hopes seriously to disguise one's identity from Soviet agents: one does, but one takes the obvious risk of its being penetrated. The point, rather, is that if one goes through the farce of wearing a black domino, the Soviet authorities do not *need* to take official notice, denounce, thunder & above all punish alleged friends & allies of the culprit. So I had to kill "Utis", & "N"[3] will do very well as the initial of the

---

1 IB's draft, then entitled 'Notes on Soviet Culture' (included in SM as 'Soviet Russian Culture'), was split into two articles published in *Foreign Affairs* 36 (1957) as 'The Silence in Russian Culture' and 'The Soviet Intelligentsia', in the latter case under the pseudonym 'L.'; the articles were separated by other pieces to throw readers further off the scent.

2 Possibly during a talk given at the Overseas Press Club, New York, on 7 May, though there is no mention of IB in Kennan's surviving notes, or in a summary published as 'A Fresh Look at Russia' in *Foreign Policy Bulletin*, 15 June 1957, 145.

3 IB's mistake; Armstrong had told him the article would be credited to 'L.'

English equivalent. The same applies to the title: I own I did not enormously take to it anyway: & as you once wisely dissuaded me from using a vulgar quotation at the head of the Utis article – for which I am now very grateful, so I allowed myself the luxury of giving in to the fullest degree to my initial reaction to the title; but still, after your letter about costs & difficulties, I should, normally, have swallowed my misgivings if it weren't for the probable consequences to my exposed Soviet ci-devant intellectuals. Once that comes into play, I can't, alas, compromise. So forgive me: Aline can tell you what agonies I went through: & of course you must pay "N" nothing. Nemini nihil debetur.[1] Captain Nemo[2] cannot be owed to. But I shd still beg you to send me the 50 offprints which you think can be made – free allowance. Or fewer if this is easier: of both articles. When your wire came a stone rolled off my chest – & I only hope not on to yours. Again I beg you to forgive me: Mr E. M. Forster somewhere speaks of the atmosphere of "tears, telegrams, anger".[3] And expense, too, I must add. And if you were disposed to cancel my other fee as well, I really should not think that too unjust. But when I recall the actual *faces* & expressions of the dwindling Soviet Bloomsbury, a frivolous formula for a most tragic, & to those who haven't seen them face to face, unimaginable group of saints & martyrs, I can't hesitate.[4] Believe me this is not hysterical self-justification. I shan't, alas, see you at Xmas. If you can bear to see me again, will you not come to Oxford next year? Aline sends love, & I to Christa.

Love
　　Isaiah

TO IRVING KRISTOL

28 September 1957

Headington House

Dear Irving,

Forgive me for not replying to both your letters – of the 18th and 20th – sooner, but I have only just seen them, for I only returned a few hours ago.

Let me take them in chronological order.

1. I would love to review a book for *Encounter* one day – but I cannot do

---

1 'To nobody nothing is owed' ('nemini' is the dative of 'nemo').
2 Captain Nemo ('Nobody') is a character in Jules Verne's novels *Twenty Thousand Leagues under the Sea* (1870) and *The Mysterious Island* (1874), among IB's childhood favourites.
3 'The truth is that there is a great outer life that you and I have never touched – a life in which telegrams and anger count. Personal relations, that we think supreme, are not supreme there.' E. M. Forster, *Howard's End*, chapter 4.
4 IB continued protecting the identity of 'L.': 'Poor "L."! After his incautious utterance a dreadful fate overtook him – the minions of the Great Eastern despotism liquidated him and not a trace remains of what once looked like a promising career. [...] He will never arise again, it will be only idle antiquaries who will spend their time on identifying idiosyncrasies of style that will establish his identity.' To Armstrong, 13 November 1957.

anything for the next four or five months, for I am in a state of hysteria about
my coming lectures as Professor here, not one of which I have written, and
am therefore unable to think about anything else, or indeed to think at all, so
long as this hideous situation persists. [...]

2. Now as to Pasternak. That is a very complicated story. There is a complete manuscript of the novel in Italy in the hands of the publisher Feltrinelli,
who is supposed to be producing an Italian version of it. The first rumour
was that as he was a Stalinist he was going to suppress it: the second rumour
that he has broken with Stalinists under the influence of Reale[1] and will
now produce a translation. Gallimard[2] are certainly hurrying on with their
translation of a version, since they have four translators on the job, according to Souvarine, who knows them all. In England the only people who have
any intention of doing anything about it are Collins (Mark Bonham Carter).
I have read most of the novel, and it is a masterpiece, though whether this
will be thought by persons differently conditioned, I do not know. If one has
any Russian background the nostalgia and profound emotional perturbation
which it causes are quite unique. Professeur Pascal[3] in Paris, for example,
does not think it so marvellous. Katkov in Oxford is wildly excited, and so
are Pasternak's two sisters, who are terrified of its appearing and doing their
brother damage, since of course it has been forbidden in the Soviet Union
(again Nabokov says that it is now likely to appear in 'a shortened version'
in the Soviet Union – that is the latest rumour). And so it goes on [...] – it is
by no means easy, the bits, let us say, which describe Siberian witches laying
spells on cows for the purpose of producing milk are not written in very
translatable Russian: there is a tremendous amount of heavily wrought,
complicated, both regional and typically Pasternakian language which does
not lend itself easily even to normal understanding, let alone translation.
Still, worse tasks have been overcome. The whole thing is semi-secret,
nobody knows who is translating how much of what, there are two tendencies at work – the desire to produce this masterpiece in order to confute
the Reds (which it would do: although it is not anti-Communist literally,
the effect is devastating – much more so than Koestler or any of the other
cheapjacks); and the desire not to expose the poet himself to any reprisals. As
a result the two sisters in Oxford, who secretly have the manuscript, sit over
it like two Cerberuses and will not let people see it, and nobody knows what
they are allowed to know, and what not. Consequently if you do get hold of
Mark Bonham Carter or Mrs Harari,[4] best not say you have all this from me,
but simply that you have heard that Feltrinelli and Gallimard are publishing

1 Eugenio Reale (1905–86), leading member of the Italian Communist Party, but left it after the
  invasion of Hungary.
2 Major French publisher.
3 Pierre Pascal (1890–1983), Professor of Slavic Languages and Literature at the Sorbonne from
  1950, had lived in Russia 1916–33.
4 Manya Harari (1905–69), née Benenson, born in Baku, sister of Flora Solomon; publisher and

translations in Italian and French respectively, and that I had told you that they were the English publishers most interested in the thing.

Yours ever,
Isaiah Berlin

translator; in 1946 co-founded, with Marjorie Villiers, the Harvill Press (from 1954 a subsidiary of Collins), publishers in 1958 of the translation of Dr Zhivago by herself and Max Hayward.

1957–1960

THE CHICHELE CHAIR

I have the impression that the level of seriousness has gone up & the level of ability, originality, & optimistic faith in human action, down in Oxford (& perhaps the world).[1]

[...] did I produce anything worth while, ever?[2]

1 To Jenifer Hart, summer 1958.
2 To Miriam Lane, 1 January 1959.

TO ROWLAND BURDON-MULLER

13 December 1957

Headington House

Dear Rowland,

Aline is gone,[1] and it seems odd to be writing to you when she will tell you about everything so much more clearly and in so much greater detail.

I have had a fantastically busy term, but an extremely enjoyable one in a way. I knew I was putting my head in a noose when I applied for the Professorship which ultimately I was granted, but it turned out that, noose as it is, it does not suit me too badly. I have to prepare every lecture like an undergraduate preparing his essay for his tutor; but to have regular hours, something to do, and an enormous amount of work and no time to go up to London and indulge either in social distractions or the million duties which crop up in any unordered life, has done me nothing but good. My health is far better, and although doctors maintain that there is some irregularity about my electrocardiograms, which no one seems able to explain, and I have been told to grow less fat (which I have done), to cultivate serenity, which does not come easily to me, but which nevertheless I try and attain, and to live quietly and regularly, which I do far more than ever before, I feel moderately well. Even the trembling of my eyelid which, trivial as it is, made me miserable for eight months, and really interfered with every pleasure and made life, at times, [sic] seems gone. I wear my knighthood still with difficulty; cannot say it on the telephone; describe myself with relief as Professor Berlin, and cause footmen to announce us as Professor and Lady Berlin, for fear of hearing the dreaded monosyllable. Perhaps I shall get over this, it is not rational, I have no objection to it, all the arguments I used to you and you to me to reassure me are still valid. But these feelings are difficult to overcome.

Intellectual excitement has been great here this term; Wind has lectured[2] in a most splendid manner, eclipsing everyone else. [...]

Douglas's own lectures,[3] as Aline will also tell you, were not as lectures very brilliant – though for God's sake do not say that to anybody, for you know what it is like to utter the faintest breath of criticism in that direction, and how terrible vengeance can be when the great barbarian king of the Pont du Gard begins a campaign and marches into battle. I think that he thought that universities were places in which one had to be terribly accurate about facts and very academic; with the result that he only began getting

1 To New York and Boston.

2 Edgar Wind had since 1955 been the first Professor of the History of Art at Oxford. The Playhouse Theatre was used for his lectures because of their popularity, and even there the queues for entry became legendary.

3 (Arthur William) Douglas Cooper (1911–84), art historian and collector, at whose home, the Château de Castille near the Pont du Gard in the south of France, IB and Aline had encountered Picasso and Cocteau (485). As the 1957–8 Slade Professor of Fine Art at Oxford, Cooper lectured on 'Revolutions in Art'.

into his proper form with his last lecture, on Gauguin. Next term, when he will be in his own home country of Cubism etc., I am sure it will be marvellous. Even as it was, it was interesting enough, but nothing like as fascinating as the Cagliostro-like[1] performances of the great magician Wind.

So poor Moore is to be transferred to Finland – unless it is Berne. I do not know if that has been decided yet. He won't dislike Finland as such – he so liked the Germans, and the Finns are not unlike the Germans, but the perpetual arrivals of Ambassadors and diplomats from Moscow for a breathing-spell in civilised Finland from the terrible deprivations of Moscow, and the assumptions that the local British Legation can put them up and do everything for them, will drive poor Moore off his head. He is not by nature undiscriminatingly hospitable like you or I, and he will make his impatience and rage felt. Even Switzerland does not seem to be too good a place for him in that connection. Anyway, all this is supposed to be dead secret, and members of the Foreign Office are very astonished that I should know; that is enjoyable too. You are getting in place of Moore my old friend Harold Beeley. He has a tic, and is the greatest pro-Arab in the Foreign Office, having got into it after this war; he is amusing, cynical, quite civilised, and has divorced his poor first wife[2] – who was a genuine daughter of the people, happier in the kitchen than in the drawing-room, unable to face any of his colleagues, but quite a nice woman whom he has not treated altogether well – I have just got her a job in a local library.[3] But you may like him. Brian [Urquhart] quite rightly (au fond) doesn't. Brian's tastes are ultimately governed by moral considerations and by whether he thinks people are noble, good, right-minded, and not merely by whether they are amusing or good company. From that point of view Beeley leaves much to be desired. His advice to the Foreign Office on Jews and Arabs has been quite sincere and honest and always systematically wrong. Even poor Mr Bevin would not have made the mistakes he did if he had not been so consistently and fanatically misled. I remember long walks which I used to take with Beeley on Hampstead Heath in the later 1940s, in which he used to give me brilliant and at the time convincing accounts of exactly how various countries would behave and how various votes at the United Nations would be cast, all of which was always unerringly and wholly upset by events. Anyway he is very different from Moore – no dowagers, no *bas-fonds*[4] – much more a certain lower middle-class bohemianism and liability to be taken in by very second- and third-rate glitter. However, you will doubtless meet him and judge for yourself. I shall be fascinated to know what you think. I have always rather liked him because

---

1 Count Alessandro di Cagliostro (1743–95), probably an alias for Giuseppe Balsamo; occultist, Freemason, alleged magnetic healer, and (apparently) skilful charlatan.
2 Millicent Mary Beeley (1910–2003), née Chinn; divorced 1953.
3 In fact the Codrington Library at All Souls.
4 'Low-lifes'.

he wasn't a stuffy official, but a don, and because of the irony, malice and ultimate frivolity which underlay all his fanaticism and wrong-headedness. Two eminent Arabs called on me yesterday, with whom I had a very peaceful talk about Suez. What upset them most of all was that so many upper-class persons were pro-Suez, and so many lower-class ones against – the last thing that any Arab wants is support from the Labour Party, they are all snobs and terribly upset by the thought that Lord Salisbury should have gone wrong, and that the bulk of their support came from intellectuals and socialists. My two visitors saw the Arab world as the last haven of style and gracious living, to be allied with all great positive forces of the world, the Roman Church, the American millionaires, British peers etc., against Russia, mobs, workers and Jewish journalists. I saw how their world-picture was formed, but could give them little comfort in this regard.

Thank you very much for sending me Edmund Wilson's article on Turgenev.[1] Curiously enough I found it, for the first time, disappointing. [...] He will be here soon – I must write and thank him (for he also sent me a copy). Yet I do not know [how] to say it. I am reduced to the expedient of saying nothing. When the *Sunday Times* this year, as it always does, asked me to take part in a symposium of opinions on the best books of the year, just as last year I was silent because I could not sufficiently praise David Cecil's last book,[2] but did not wish to offend him by praising somebody else; so this year I have found myself in the same awkward situation vis-à-vis Sir Maurice's last book,[3] which is a great deal better than his previous works, and has been praised frantically and lyrically by all kinds of people – by Paddy Leigh Fermor,[4] by Trevor-Roper (you must ask Aline about his lecture), by Arnold Toynbee etc., but which I find ultimately rather philistine and uninteresting. I do not go so far as Sparrow, who describes him as 'a noisy bore', but I agree with him that his style is that of the kind of Palladian used by modern English banks –

I have seldom enjoyed an event more than Trevor-Roper's inaugural lecture,[5] it was amusing in itself – I must send you a copy – but what was funny were the preliminaries: he had hoped for a large incursion of smart persons from London and deputed Lord Furneaux[6] and Chips Channon's

1 Edmund Wilson, 'Turgenev and the Life-Giving Drop', *New Yorker*, 19 October 1957, 150–200.
2 Presumably either *Lord M.* (1954) or the combination of this with Cecil's earlier *The Young Melbourne* (1939) to produce *Melbourne* (1955).
3 *The Greek Experience* (London, 1957).
4 Patrick Michael Leigh Fermor (b. 1915), travel writer, who fought with the wartime Cretan Resistance and has spent much of his life in Greece; the publicity for *The Greek Experience* quoted his comment that 'One has the compelling impression, on closing the book, of having finished a masterpiece.'
5 'History: Professional and Lay', delivered on 12 November. 'Never within living memory had so many people attended an inaugural lecture, occupying every square foot of the Examination Schools' (Philip Mansel's obituary of Trevor-Roper – by then Lord Dacre – *Independent*, 27 January 2003, 14).
6 Frederick William Robin Smith (1936–85), Viscount Furneaux, 3rd Earl of Birkenhead 1975; later wrote under the pen-name Robin Furneaux.

son[1] – he wrote them that he gathered that they were socially-minded and would know the faces of Cabinet Ministers and Ambassadors – to act as ushers. He caused four rows of the School to be kept empty for him for the 'quality', it was terrible to see aged dons and white-haired ladies rudely pushed away from these empty places which were waiting to be filled by elegant persons from London. In the end, apart from the Duke of Wellington[2] and about eight members of the Astor family and his own wife[3] and her sister Doria,[4] nobody came and the seats were filled by plebeians in the end. We went with Elizabeth Bowen and watched the whole proceeding with mounting delight. The best moment was when Nancy Lancaster[5] – Ronnie Tree's first wife – who had previously already had it remarked to her that Xandra Trevor-Roper looked like a very young and very sprightly eighty – marvellously fresh and vigorous for her advancing years – when we were all bidden to dinner rushed up to Lady Alexandra, clasped her hands and said, 'Oh, oh, the bride's mother!' There was a deathly silence, but poor Xandra smiled wanly and we sat down to dinner.

Well, I must not go on gossiping, particularly as it is one o'clock in the morning and I must cultivate peace, rest, serenity, good habits etc. But I am very sorry not to be in Boston with Aline – I hope that she will have done her duties towards the Perkinses[6] etc. without too much waste of effort, and look forward greatly to seeing you in the spring – for rumour has it that you really are coming. That will be very delightful.

Yours ever, with *much* love

Isaiah

TO SAM BEHRMAN

17 December 1957

Headington House

Dear Sam,

I ought to have written to you weeks ago in answer to your first letter and apologise for not doing so. But my life has suddenly sunk into the exquisite

1 (Henry) Paul Guinness Channon (1935–2007), Baron Kelvedon 1997, Christ Church PPE 1956–8; Conservative MP 1959–97. His father (whose constituency he took over after abandoning his degree course) was Sir Henry ('Chips') Channon (1897–1958), US-born Conservative MP 1935–58 and diarist.
2 Gerald Wellesley (1885–1972), 7th Duke of Wellington, Lord Lieutenant of Hampshire 1949–60; Chancellor, University of Southampton, 1951–62; Governor, Isle of Wight, 1956–65.
3 In 1954 Trevor-Roper had married Lady Alexandra Henrietta Louisa ('Xandra') Howard-Johnston (1907–97), daughter of 1st Earl Haig.
4 Lady Victoria (Montague-Douglas-)Scott (157/6).
5 Nancy Keene Lancaster (1897–1994), née Perkins, married to Henry Field, Ronnie Tree and finally Claude Lancaster; US-born interior designer who settled in England and took over the firm of Colefax & Fowler.
6 Elliott and Mary Perkins.

routine of a decent old hack, a nice old provincial Prof. running smoothly between lecture and lecture, interviewing graduate students, and occasionally with much excitement taking the train to London for the purpose of delivering a lecture to a learned society, carefully prepared beforehand, too long, read through at breathless and breakneck pace to a small and elderly audience of learned persons, all of whom, or nearly all, do this themselves. The only gap in this terrible and peaceful routine were my two appearances in London – one for a great many Jews[1] – ostensibly members of the Jewish Historical Society – to whom I read in a thunderous voice extracts from a book written by a man called Moses Hess[2] in the nineteenth century, who was both a Zionist and a Communist – more or less simultaneously. This was to honour a man called Lucien Wolf,[3] whose chief hatreds were Zionism and Communism. The irony did not altogether pass unnoticed. Fortunately Lord Halifax, who was to have presided, caught a cold. Hess's chief emphasis lay on the wickedness of changing names and abandoning old habits. In 1861 he denounced the German Jews for changing their names, adopting a thin cheap imitation of Christianity called Reformed Judaism, and told them that what the Germans disliked about them was not their religion but their race, their noses, their curly hair, their swarthy complexions. That is why they were apt to conceal their race rather than their religion. He pointed out that Meyerbeer[4] gained nothing by avoiding Biblical libretti in his operas. As my audience consisted almost entirely of dark, small, curly-haired persons who changed their names and who used very few Biblical libretti in the course of business, the effect may be imagined. It was all sound anti-Semitic stuff by a very nice man who married a prostitute in the 1850s 'in order to redress the injustice done by society', and then lived happily and peacefully with her till the end of quite a long life. Also rather unsuitable for the more respectable parts of my audience. In the same week I delivered a lecture on Dr Weizmann,[5] which summed him up in, you will altogether be surprised to learn, a favourable manner. However, the main result of that was a letter from a very disgruntled old gentleman[6] who says he worked with Weizmann from 1903 till 1933, and did not recognise the man he knew in my flattering

1 On 11 December 1957 IB delivered the Lucien Wolf Memorial Lecture in Friends House, London, on 'From Communism to Zionism: The Life and Opinions of Moses Hess', published as *The Life and Opinions of Moses Hess* (Cambridge, 1959), reprinted in AC.

2 Moses Hess (1812–75), German Jewish writer, socialist and, eventually, an early Zionist. IB's references are to Hess's most significant work, *Rom und Jerusalem: die letzte Nationalitätsfrage, Briefe und Noten* (Leipzig, 1862).

3 Lucien Wolf (1857–1930), journalist, historian, and defender of Jewish interests; founding President of the Jewish Historical Society of England.

4 Meyerbeer suffered persistent and vitriolic anti-Semitic attacks from Richard Wagner, which damaged his later popularity.

5 On 19 November IB gave the second Herbert Samuel Lecture, published as *Chaim Weizmann* (London, 1958), reprinted in PI.

6 Israel Cohen (1879–1961), active Zionist, author and journalist.

portrait. The only characteristic he recognised was my attribution to him of a habit of discarding anyone for whom he had no further use: that was a characteristic he was very familiar with. Poor man. I saw what happened to him and also exactly how and why it happened. Our friend did not suffer fools gladly and about this particular man he said that he was a horse made up to look like a horse. I daresay that did not go down too well.

My final thing was when I had to celebrate the obsequies of my old friend Gaetano Salvemini at the Italian Institute. Salvemini really did say some rather sharp things in his life, indeed the last thing he said to me, when I asked him how he intended to vote, was 'I have told the Communists that if they shoot the Pope I shall vote for them. If not, not.' This I did not quote. The audience was elderly, the Chairman was Professor Gooch,[1] aged 85, a telegram was read from B.B., aged 92, I quoted from a judgement in the Supreme Court,[2] quoting Salvemini, delivered by Felix Frankfurter, aged 75. And, prodded on by Arthur Waley,[3] who has a schoolboy humour and does not care about the consequences to his friends, I told them that the last thing Salvemini said to me was 'Mussolini is dead. Croce is dead. Why then am I not more happy?' As there was a large portrait of Croce facing me, flanked by Garibaldi – the two patron saints, with Dante, of all Italians everywhere, this produced an agonised laugh from those members of the audience to whom this remark was violently surprising, though not necessarily pleasing or in good taste. I cannot think why I do these things: in my own estimation I am a mild peaceful character anxious to please even the least considered of men, and yet when, nervous and trembling, I appear before an audience, something possesses me to say these terrible things, which give me the reputation of a Clemenceau,[4] to which I then fail over and over again and most miserably to live up. That is no doubt the picture that Mr Todd has of me: it differs greatly from Aline's.

David Cecil is coming to tea this afternoon – was there something I was to tell him? I cannot recollect. I have no notion how far his work has advanced.[5] Meanwhile Edmund Wilson kindly sent me his long piece on Turgenev in the New Yorker and, but don't tell him this, it seems to me on the whole one of the least good things he has done. I do not know why this should be so. As always he says some telling and interesting things – particularly about Turgenev being virtually the only Russian writer in the nineteenth

1 George Peabody Gooch (1873–1968), historian (highly respected but not a Professor).
2 In Baumgartner v. US, 322 US 665 (1944), Felix Frankfurter, delivering the Court's opinion on a withdrawal of citizenship by the Government, quoted in a footnote Salvemini's comments on his own naturalisation.
3 Arthur David Waley (1889–1966), né Schloss, sinologist and translator of much Chinese and Japanese literature.
4 Georges Benjamin Clemenceau (1841–1929), Prime Minister of France 1906–9, 1917–20; nick-named 'The Tiger' for his radical views and forceful debating style.
5 On Cecil's biography of Max Beerbohm.

century to tell the unvarnished truth and not the dramatic exaggerations and egomaniacal versions of things which both Dostoevsky and Tolstoy perpetrated; and also he attributes his hatred of the serfs and general liberalism to his abominable mother and her treatment of him. All this is all right. But as for the rest he seems to be telling the plots of Turgenev's novels 'in his own words', as one used to be told to do at school – perhaps he is very poor and it is simply a matter of words on a page. But this is perhaps a too malicious suggestion even for me, and I half withdraw it. But somehow the whole article was uninteresting, did not bring out what was fascinating; the book he was reviewing is a very inferior one and he would not recognise that because the English reviewer had said so, the name of the author is Russian Jewish and Wilson therefore feels it necessary to defend him against the English snobs. I do not know what to say – I ought to write to him and tell him how well I think of it etc., but he is a clever enough man to see through hollow praise. So I am silent and embarrassed, he will think that I am silent because I took offence at a very amusing and gay little cutting that he sent me from I think the *New York Times* reporting that I had been to lunch with the Queen, and commenting that he was glad to see that some of the unsatisfactory arrangements denounced by Lord Altrincham[1] were at last being satisfactorily remedied. Let him think that if he wishes, if you see him give him my love, and give yourself a great deal of it – Aline is in New York at the Carlyle Hotel. I wish you would ring her up if you get this in time. She may be too shy to do so. She loves you but, as I learnt from experience, there are many human beings in the world who stress their feelings more frequently and eagerly than she. So do ring her up – have you met her mother? You should if you haven't, very different from mine, though they get on surprisingly. She is very shy, wholly uncorrupted by her possessions, and perfectly at ease with me – which proves what I have always maintained, that I lack personality and my presence or absence from the room cannot and never has made any difference to anyone anywhere.

On this sad, peaceful, typically self-flattering note, I end my deeply masochistic letter.

Yours ever,

Isaiah

⟨Who knows what is in this letter? I dictate, but cannot – for reasons which S. Freud might have known – re-read: the stream may be that of my typist's – Miss Townshend's[2] – a clergyman's daughter's consciousness ...⟩

1 John Edward Poynder Grigg (1924–2001), 2nd Baron Altrincham 1955–63 (title disclaimed); author, journalist and broadcaster; owner and editor, *The National and English Review*, 1954–60.
2 Violet Frances Victoria Townshend (1894–1985), daughter of the Revd Edward Mansel Townshend (1860–1947), Rector of Llanvapley, Monmouthshire, 1898–1947. She was IB's typist for several years after his marriage, and later did secretarial work for Aline, cycling to Headington House from her nearby home with her dog in her bicycle basket.

TO PHILIP TOYNBEE

24 January 1958

Headington House

Dear Philip,

Thank you very much for your tract.[1] I was moved by it, feel great respect for your views, understand well (or think that I understand) your reasons for holding them, and disagree wholly.[2] I have read it through only once, but shall set down my views as briefly as I can, in the form in which they come to me. After all, this is a private letter and you do not intend to do anything with – publish – or do anything else with – what I say. So if the form is chaotic, forgive me.

Supposing I begin with asking you a question: if I ask you whether it would have been worth while, in your view, to have allowed and encouraged or aided the French in reoccupying the Rhineland whenever the problem came up – 1936 I think – even though the Germans might have resisted and there might have been so[me?] bloodshed. Apart from hindsight, many people (including myself) believed that it was worth while, in the sense that it was likely to prevent the far worse things which happened later, and which even then, although not in any detail, could be foreseen by persons of very moderate intelligence and political knowledge. Let me assume, then, that you would have said that the death of whatever Nazi troops might have occurred would have been a price worth paying for averting war, or Nazi domination of large sections of Europe. And now let me ask what you think of those plans which were mooted in the late 1940s and early 1950s (before the Russians had built up their present weapons) of dropping bombs on them – in short, engaging in a preventive war which would doubtless have cost very many innocent lives. I seem to remember that Bertrand Russell at that period was in favour of dropping bombs, on the ground that it might avert a far worse future. Perhaps he was right. ⟨I don't in fact begin to think so.⟩ Yet I remember that I myself was against it, not merely on the purely utilitarian ground that a victory over the Russians, while it might kill the Communist system, would breed such hatred not merely among them, but in the whole of Asia, as to make almost inevitable a war of revenge say 25 years later, which would nullify any possible benefit of the defeat of the Russians, but on the far simpler and more instinctive moral ground that if you are going to commit a major crime – or at least inflict a vast degree of suffering upon the innocent – to avert a hypothetically worse situation, the hypothetical situation must be very probable and the certain evil that you are about to commit at once must not be such as to outweigh the future evil

---

1 In December 1957 Toynbee had written an essay on nuclear policy and sent it to some 75 people for comment. He published the essay, a selection of the comments (not including IB's), and his replies as *The Fearful Choice: A Debate on Nuclear Policy Conducted by Philip Toynbee with [...]* (London, 1958).

2 Toynbee's 10 February response opens with similar wording.

and its probability. Perhaps I am not making myself clear. What I mean is that although I am not at all a pacifist, and believe that some wars are fully justified, not merely wars of defence – i.e., after aggression has been committed by the other side – but even preventive wars (such as the 1936 one might have been), where the probability of aggression from the other side is very high, or where the political system inflicts a very great deal of suffering upon a very great many persons, yet if you ask me how much suffering upon how many people, or how high the probability has to be, how can I possibly answer? These things are settled in one's mind on ultimately the same principles, frivolous as this may sound, as those which Lord Salisbury once said were involved when one asked oneself if one should carry an umbrella if one saw a cloudy sky. This sounds frivolous, and yet the principle is accurate: you weigh up the factors as best you can, you rely upon all the knowledge at your disposal, scientific, your own experience, your general sense of what is likely to occur, what human beings are like, what the world is like. You discount your own capacity for error, you listen to persons you think wise, in the end you decide as you decide, and you are responsible for what you have done, and if what you have done is foolish, then no matter how pure your motives, you have committed a crime. All you can say – all you can ever say – is that you have done your best to behave well in accordance with such moral values and such facts as you possess.

Very well then: you want to know whether unilateral disarmament on our part (and I note that Kennan does not advocate this) is not morally right because if we don't disarm and let other people arm, then even though America and Russia may hold each other in check like two gladiators (to borrow Hobbes's image)[1] with their spears aimed at each other – or like two gangsters 'covering' each other with their guns – yet the probability of a misunderstood order or a sudden act of lunacy, folly, irresponsibility is such that with these terrible weapons knocking about there is too high a chance of the extermination of all or of large sections of humanity. I grant that this is possible. All I can say is that:

1. The probability of the Russians genuinely disarming in the sense of ceasing to manufacture or possess H-bombs etc. seems to me too low to be worth calculating; whatever may happen, whether the Americans disarm or not, the Russians mean to advance (do not ask me how I know this: I do not, but I believe it as strongly as any empirical proposition that I know about anybody's political intentions). If they are resisted they will try and accumulate a striking power greater than their enemies'; if they are not resisted, they will write them down for fools and capture them without effort.

2. I think the probability of the Russians acting so is not merely higher but

1 '[K]ings and persons of sovereign authority, because of their independency, are in continual jealousies, and in the state and posture of gladiators, having their weapons pointing, and their eyes fixed on one another.' Thomas Hobbes, *Leviathan* (1651), chapter 13.

much higher than the probability of some trigger-happy fool, madman etc. loosing off something that destroys the world.

3. I do not think that a weapon once invented can be de-invented, that is to say forgotten. Poison gas may not have been used in the last war, but the possibility of it still exists. The risks of the world being destroyed by the new weapons will always hover over us, whatever happens.

4. The probability of the Russians being deterred by the possession of sufficient striking power by the West, from using their own, seems to me very high.

5. There is a certain point (this is where we shall disagree most profoundly, I suspect) at which you are allowed to defend your way of living, whatever the odds, and whatever the results to anybody, even to people other than yourself. If your whole mode of living is threatened with extermination – if you yourself would rather be dead than suffer a certain kind of regime, and live among people whom you believe (on the whole) to share some such point of view to a high degree – how high cannot be precisely determined – if your own beliefs are not isolated but are held as part of a general attitude which is not too uncommon among your neighbours, in virtue of which you are said to form one society at all – when such a situation arises, you are allowed to defend yourself, *coûte que coûte*.[1] When the Czechs were threatened by the Germans in 1938, they should have fought. The argument which no doubt was very earnestly held by some of them, that by yielding they may have averted a general war, seems to me merely a rationalisation of a general desire to yield. (the same holds of the excellent, rational, humane but (as we all rightly felt at the time) contemptible reasoning which the French used to prove that it was their *duty* to yield to Hitler & make the best terms they could in 1940.) The strength of one's views, loyalties, attachments, beliefs, ethical principles, is ultimately measured by how much one is prepared to pay for them. And if you then argue that it is not only you, but others who must pay for it as well, the answer must be that no man is responsible for the whole world, that in democracies governments must accept responsibility for populations, and do what they can and leave others to do what they can. If the Russians come to us and say you must yield, otherwise we destroy the universe, I see no reason for yielding. Unless there is some point at which you are prepared to fight against whatever odds, and whatever the threat may be, not merely to yourself but to anybody, all principles become flexible, all codes melt, and all ends-in-themselves for which we live disappear before the sole duty of making a utilitarian calculation of how much happiness to the world in general will be produced by one course and how much misery by other courses, and stake all on that alone – this is a calculation not only difficult (scarcely possible) to make, but largely unreal the larger the

---

1 'Cost what it may'.

number of persons involved, the remoter they are from you, and the darker the future. But I would go further than this.

6. I need not have used this last argument at all, although in fact I believe it. I need only say that it seems to me that mere survival is too high a price for political enormities. For if we accept that, then no tyranny may be resisted if rebellion involves the possible deaths of innocent persons. Like you I think Communism as practised in the Soviet Union is not much better, if at all, than Fascism. If that is so, and if the danger of extermination is not made *certain* by resistance (if it is, even I would quail before the consequences, and try and promote arrangements by which only those who would rather be dead than live under Communism – like me – should in fact have the opportunity of perishing), there is no case for not doing everything possible to deter the enemies to our forms of life, where they are as dangerous and as odious as these are. In short, I think that the risks of universal extermination involved in acquiring and possessing the H-bombs (and the doubtless even more powerful weapons that are to come) is sufficiently less great than the probability of Soviet conquest of the world, and the infliction of ghastly humiliations and cruelties by it if unresisted, to make the possession of them the lesser evil – the one that one chooses when one chooses between evils. You, in effect, argue that the evil of H-bombs being loosed off, multiplied by the probability of this event if we should not disarm, makes a bigger sum, or at least a sum not smaller than, the evil of Soviet domination multiplied by the probability of its occurrence. I think the opposite. I think (a) that the chances of deterring the Russians and of not being blown up by a madman or a fool or a knave are high enough to make NATO etc. worth keeping; and (b) that in certain situations one cannot calculate too far – if one is oneself prepared to die rather than suffer a given fate one is allowed to resist it by whatever means there are to hand. When I say if one is prepared to die, I do not mean in a purely personal capacity of course, but as a member of some social whole with which one feels solidarity and about whose attitudes one is reasonably convinced – that is the only and I think true principle which makes it possible for democracies to go to war without cynicism, without the supposition that the vast mass of people led to war are thrust into it in some bemused or fraudulent fashion – just butchered by stupid or wicked leaders.

I am sorry this is all so muddled, but I daresay the general point emerges. For God's sake, having read it tear it up, and come and see me whenever you feel inclined. I do not see you nearly enough and am very sorry this is so, and have regretted this for a very long time.

Yours ever,
    Isaiah

⟨Sorry this has lain in my pocket for so long.⟩

TO RICHARD WOLLHEIM

24 January 1958

Headington House

Dear Richard,

[...] Now as to your review,[1] and quite independently of the *TLS*, on which I have no influence and which I am sure will print the whole thing in full. I enjoyed it very much and agreed with much of it, but where I disagreed, I disagreed sharply. If nothing but your references to Prof. Oakeshott[2] survived, the world would, you must agree, get a very exaggerated impression both of the depths of his thought, the quality of his personality, and his immense influence. However, if you admire him, you admire him. I, who have just for the first time read his introduction to Hobbes[3] after (instead of before) reading the *Leviathan*, cannot agree. I wrote to Utley in that connection and said that I placed him somewhat below Jouvenel.[4] Stuart wildly overpraised the latter. I hear you think his book[5] unintelligible. I think it perfectly intelligible but of no great importance. Stuart's review of it in the *Sunday Times*[6] really did frighten me into supposing that it might have to be taken seriously. In a way I am disappointed that it need not. What has there appeared in political philosophy that demands to be taken seriously? Nothing at all, it seems to me. And this brings me to my first point (and the last in your exposition). You produce a list of names which should have been mentioned in any anthology of political thought in the mid-twentieth century. Freud, Schumpeter,[7] Popper, the American jurists, the French existentialists, yes. Keynes, Kelsen,[8] possibly. But why on earth Aron? He has written nothing of the slightest interest on any theoretical issue. His two books[9] on history and sociology are third-rate rather than second-, I have

---

1 'Thinking about Politics', review of T. E. Utley and J. Stuart Maclure (611/10) (eds), *Documents of Modern Political Thought* (Cambridge, 1957) (DMPT in further notes to this letter), *TLS*, 28 February 1958, 109–10.
2 Wollheim acknowledged (on 16 January) Oakeshott's 'sensibility' and 'high intelligence', and admired his achievement in producing *The Social and Political Doctrines of Contemporary Europe* (Cambridge, 1939).
3 Oakeshott's 1946 edition of Thomas Hobbes's *Leviathan* included an Introduction, reprinted in *Hobbes on Civil Association* (Oxford, 1975).
4 Bertrand de Jouvenel, the original for the hero of the novel *Chéri* by Colette (Jouvenel's stepmother, with whom he had an affair as a teenager).
5 Bertrand de Jouvenel, *De la souveraineté: à la recherche du bien politique* (Paris, [1955]), trans. J. F. Huntington as *Sovereignty: An Inquiry into the Political Good* (Cambridge, 1957).
6 'Democratic Doubt', *Sunday Times*, 6 October 1957, 6.
7 Joseph Alois Schumpeter (1883–1950), Moravian economist and political scientist (working in the US from 1932).
8 Hans Kelsen was a legal positivist with particular interests in constitutional and international law.
9 Presumably *La Sociologie allemande contemporaine* (Paris, 1935), trans. Mary and Thomas Bottomore as *German Sociology* (London, 1957), and *Introduction à la philosophie de l'histoire: essai sur les limites de l'objectivité historique* (Paris, 1938), trans. George J. Irwin as *Introduction to the Philosophy of History: An Essay on the Limits of Historical Objectivity* (London, 1961).

read them both and regretted the time wasted upon them. As for *The Opium of the Intellectuals*,[1] it is quite sprightly and makes some points, but it is on the whole not as good as Lippmann, whom I despise quite sufficiently. Even Charles Beard[2] or Dewey[3] and the other characters whom Morton White admires would do better.

2. About the Conservative extracts you are more than right. Hailsham,[4] the *Times* editorial,[5] Winston[6] etc. are disgraceful. But Fascism was not merely a piece of pathological paranoia, Mussolini was a competent journalist and his exposition of Fascism is a theoretical statement of a position. It is not very high-grade and would not have been very interesting but for our recent history. As for Auschwitz, you might as well argue that Communism was not worth considering because of the mountains of Stalin's victims. There is – you would surely be the last to deny this – a tradition of irrationalist European thought beginning with Rousseau or the counter-revolutionary reactionaries or in some such region that includes Carlyle, Nietzsche, Sorel,[7] of which Fascism is no more a travesty than Leninism is of Marx. Anyone wanting to know what people believed in the mid-twentieth century – what, for example, Ezra Pound was imprisoned for or what is meant by calling T. S. Eliot a Fascist – the question of whether this is fair or unfair etc., must have something to read. I do not recommend Hitler, nor even Rosenberg,[8] but Gentile,[9] Mussolini himself, and some of his hacks have their place. Alas. But I do not see how this can be denied. And if Maclure[10] likes to say that Fascism is directly against rationalism, cosmopolitanism, liberalism etc., I think this is not necessarily misleading. Stuart made the same point in his review: he wanted the authors, presumably, to express execration of these views, and not (as you point out) be ironical about Stalin instead. I agree that there is an inconsistency and a nasty one: I should have no objection if they spoke in

1 Aron's *L'Opium des intellectuels* (Paris, 1955), trans. Terence Kilmartin as *The Opium of the Intellectuals* (London, 1957).

2 Charles Austin Beard (1874–1948), US historian who stressed the the importance of economic motivation and favoured US isolationism.

3 John Dewey (1859–1952), US philosopher, psychologist and educationalist; an early and influential Pragmatist.

4 Quintin McGarel Hogg (1907–2001), 2nd Viscount Hailsham 1950 (title disclaimed 1963), Baron Hailsham 1970; Fellow of All Souls 1931–8, 1961–2001; barrister; Conservative MP 1938–50, 1963–70; First Lord of the Admiralty 1956–7; Minister of Education 1957; Lord Privy Seal 1959–60; later (1970–4, 1979–87) Lord Chancellor; the piece in question, 'The Conservative Case (1)', DMPT 73–5, was from his *The Case for Conservatism* (West Drayton, 1947), chapter 10, 62–4.

5 'Majority Rule', *The Times*, 2 February 1953, 9 ('The Democratic Case Analysed', DMPT 33–5).

6 The passage was from his speech to the Conservative Party Conference, Brighton, 4 October 1947 ('The Conservative Case (2): The Basic Minimum', DMPT 75–6).

7 Georges Eugène Sorel (1847–1922), French philosopher, whose thinking combined elements of Marxism and Fascism; see IB's later essay on him in AC.

8 Alfred Rosenberg (1893–1946), Nazi ideologue and racial theorist; executed as a war criminal.

9 Giovanni Gentile (1875–1944), Idealist Italian philosopher, known as 'the philosopher of Fascism'.

10 (John) Stuart Maclure (b. 1926), *Times Educational Supplement* 1951–89 (editor 1969–89).

dispassionate accents about both or alternatively were nasty about both. But
I do not think that what they say is strictly false. You speak of psychosis. In
Hitler's case this was no doubt so. But Mussolini was perfectly sane and his
cynicism had a perfectly definite system and method about it – when Pareto
accepted Fascism formally – or when the Sitwells or various French intellectuals in 1940 began to toy with it, the motive may have been psychotic, but
the theses, however disgusting, were intelligibly and sometimes ably argued
(as by Maurras or even, at times, Goebbels).[1]

3. I profoundly disagree that the section on Communism in this book is
at all good. You seem to me to be as far [wide of the mark] – I do not quite
understand why – in praising this as in condemning the rest. To begin with
I do not understand why Communism should be so rigidly – for ideological
purposes – discriminated from socialism. I see no objection to all the hack
bits from Lenin and Stalin, but it is time that someone noticed that *The State
and Revolution*[2] is the only work of Lenin with no bearing whatever upon
practice, and was a purely Utopian little work to which he never makes a
return in any of his later writings, and which is not anticipated much in
the earlier ones, although as a coherent doctrine it is useful to anthologists,
although inconsistent with much else that he said. If anyone really wants to
know what socialism and Communism asserted in the twentieth century,
there must be texts other than Tawney for them to read? Nobody wanting to
know what the issues were in 1917 in Russia could discover it from this book,
not [so much] because of the overweight of Conservative and Catholic quotations as because of the complete absence of socialist ones, e.g. my friend
Plekhanov, who might at least have illuminated what orthodox Marxists
were thinking in 1910 – even Kautsky[3] or Bernstein[4] would not be altogether
irrelevant. Why is Trotsky omitted or Rosa Luxemburg?[5] Or any of the ideas
upon which Western socialism or in part the American New Deal grew up?
Even poor old Tito and his henchmen, even Silone[6] or the Rossellis[7] – and
certainly Salvemini – throw more light upon what left-wing intellectuals
were thinking – what were the issues raised, say, by the Spanish war – than
anything in the anthology by the orthodox Communist leaders. I would be

1 (Paul) Joseph Goebbels (1897–1945), Minister for Public Enlightenment and Propaganda under
  Hitler.
2 Published in 1918.
3 Karl Kautsky (1854–1938), born in Prague, active mainly in Germany; Marxist theoretician and
  editor.
4 Edouard Bernstein (1850–32), German political thinker and social-democratic activist; proponent
  of reformism (evolutionary socialism).
5 Rosalia ('Rosa') Luxemburg (c.1870–1919), Polish-born Marxist theoretician and activist; co-
  founder (with Karl Liebknecht) of what became the German Communist Party.
6 Ignazio Silone (1900–78), Italian socialist politician and writer.
7 Carlo Rosselli (1899–1937), Italian anti-Fascist political activist, as was his brother Sabatino
  ('Nello') Rosselli (1900–37); author, editor and advocate of 'liberal socialism', inspired by the
  British Labour Party.

prepared to admit at a considerable price, of even Kenneth J. Arrow,[1] if you allowed me a little bit of Jaurès[2] and the Dreyfusards[3] and radicals from 1900 onwards. They have not played a trivial part in human affairs – they have influenced present ideals in the West, America – even Latin America – in the whole of Europe – even Eastern Europe – more than Marx or the Pope. Of this there is no recognition.

But I agree that the book is not good, that it is a kind of party pamphlet: and that [it is] its acute anti-liberalism and in a sense anti-socialism which makes him give so much space to the dreariest and most orthodox pronouncements of the Marxists as representing after all some kind of conservatism and 'realism' as opposed to the 'silly radicalism' of the left – and this I violently object to, but if Alan asks me anything I shall do exactly as you say.[4] [...]

Our loves,

Yours ever,

Isaiah

⟨Not read, only dictated.⟩

TO TEDDY KOLLEK

7 February 1958

Headington House

Dear Teddy,

[...] there are due to arrive in Israel for about four weeks, Sir John and Lady Beazley[5] of this University, they are very different from each other and both very notable. He is the world's greatest living authority on Greek vase paintings, is the only authentic man of genius in this University (now alas aged over 70 and deaf), a man of marvellous originality, imagination and distinction, who created a subject all by himself, a most original and poetical figure and certainly 10 or 20 years ago, and even now, the possessor of the most strikingly beautiful head I have ever seen. All classical scholars in the world bow down before him. No German claims to be superior to him; in his youth he was the friend of various exotic poets and perhaps it was his love of exoticism that made him marry his wife. He is her second husband, she is a

---

1 Kenneth Joseph Arrow (b. 1921), influential US economist (Nobel Prize-winner 1972), whose *Social Choice and Individual Values* (New York, 1951) had a major impact on social choice theory.
2 (Auguste Marie Joseph) Jean Léon Jaurès (1859–1914), anti-militaristic French socialist politician.
3 The (generally left-wing) supporters of Alfred Dreyfus.
4 Wollheim had asked IB, whose advice Alan Pryce-Jones might seek, to defend his review against cuts (letter of 16 January 1958).
5 Lady (Marie) Beazley (c.1881–1967), née Blumenfeld, widow of David Ezra (1885–1918); photographer who acted as her second husband's assistant; IB described her as 'an acquired taste which I have long ago acquired' (16 May 1958 to Kollek).

Romanian Jewess, used to be married to a man called Ezra, who I think was killed in the war, and at whom she used to throw soup plates, perhaps death was a better alternative. She then firmly married Beazley; she is a highly eccentric, Oriental and powerful lady, passionate, and in her own way brilliant, who knows that she is married to a man of genius, and, arrogant to everyone else, worships him. She is by nature a terrorist and is constantly asking me for means of sending help to Israelis who are prepared to exterminate the maximum number of Arabs. You see the implacable nature of her temperament. She has no small talk, always talks about important things in an earnest manner and is therefore somewhat exhausting, and has known some of the most interesting people of her day. Altogether a formidable pair. No doubt they will need the most important archaeologists but I feel they need something more, a burning patriot to show them round, preferably with a sense of humour, who will realise what an interesting couple they are. I am just warning you, but I may give her a letter to you. Then you will be put through the process which we have all gone through here – I do not see why not, equality must be among your professed ideals, as it is among mine, it is only the practice which is so punishing.

Yours ever,
Isaiah   [. . .]

In March IB was to attend a meeting in Israel about Chaim Weizmann's papers.
A prestigious invitation produced the following rare example of a letter written
by IB entirely in (imperfect) Hebrew.

TO RABBI ISAAC HERZOG[1]
11 March 1958

All Souls

לאדמור הרב הכללי והראשי לישראל
הרב יצחק הלוי הרצוג, ברגש ידידות וכבוד גדול מאוד.

רב הראשי המכובד!

באמת אנו – אני ואשתי מקוים להיות בארץ ישראל לחג הפסח והיינו מאושרים מאוד לקבל
את הזמנת כב׳ ולהיות עם כב׳ ועם אשתו המכובדה בליל פסח. אבל כבר הבטחתי למר מאיר
וייסגל – (שהזמין אותי עם אחרים, כדי לסדר את ה Nachlass שעזב חיים וייצמן, לרחובות)
שאהיה אצלו בליל הסדר. ואף על פי שהייתי באמת מאושר מאוד מאוד לעבור את הלילה הזה
בבית היותר מכובדה (ועם מותר לאמר זאת) הקדושה בכל הארץ, בכל זאת אינני רוצה לשפוך דם
איש בפומבית, ולעזוב את שולחן וייסגל כדי לקבל כבוד יותר גדול. ומקווה אני שיהיה אפשר

---

1 Yitzhak (Isaac) Halevi Herzog (1889–1959), born in Poland, educated in Leeds, Paris and London; Rabbi of Belfast 1916–19, Dublin 1919–22; Chief Rabbi, Irish Free State, 1922–36; Chief Rabbi, British Mandate of Palestine 1937–48, Israel 1948–59. His wife was the former Sarah Hillman (1898–1979).

All Souls College,
Oxford.

11.3.58.

IB's Hebrew letter to Rabbi Isaac Herzog, 11 March 1958

לראות את כבודו ואת גברת הרצוג כאשר נהיה בירושלים למוצאי יום א׳ דפסח ומקוה אני גם כן
שכב׳ אינו חושב שקל היה בשבילי להחליט את משהחלטתי. ויסלח לי בעד הלשון – העברית –
הנוראה שלי. השפה לא שגורה היא לא בפי ולא בעטי. ואפילו עם האנגלית שלי הייתה יותר
ברורה, לא יכולתי להכריח את עצמי לכתוב בה לכבודו.
בידידות ויקר וכבוד גדל
ישעיהו ברלין

[To the Admor[1] the General and Chief Rabbi of Israel, Rabbi Isaac Halevi
Herzog, with a feeling of friendship, and with very great respect.

Honoured Chief Rabbi!

We – I and my wife – really hope to be in the land of Israel for the Passover
holiday, and would be most happy to accept His Honour's invitation and be
with His Honour and his honoured wife on Passover Eve. But I have already
promised Mr Meyer Weisgal (who invited me along with others to Rehovot,
for the purpose of bringing some order to the *Nachlass* of Chaim Weizmann)
that I should be with him on the night of the Seder. And even though I
should truly be very very happy to pass this night at the most respected and
(if it is allowed to say so) holy home in the entire land, still I should not want
to spill a man's blood in public[2] and forsake Weisgal's table for the sake of
receiving a higher honour.

I hope that it will be possible to see His Honour and Mrs Herzog when
we shall be in Jerusalem on the night after the first day of Passover. And I
hope also that His Honour does not think that it was easy for me to make the
decision that I have made. And please forgive me for the terrible quality of
my Hebrew. The language does not fall naturally from my lips or from my
pen. But even if my English were clearer, I could not force myself to write
in it to His Honour.

In friendship, honour and great respect
    Isaiah Berlin][3]

*IB travelled to Israel via Italy, spending a night at I Tatti to visit Bernard
Berenson.*

1 Acronym for 'Our Master, Guide and Teacher', a standard form of address used mostly by
  Hasidim for their Rebbe.
2 A Hebrew expression meaning to cause embarrassment or humiliation.
3 This translation, made by Edna Ullmann-Margalit and Leon Wieseltier, does not attempt to
  reflect the many mistakes in IB's Hebrew.

TO BERNARD BERENSON

11 p.m., 11 April 1958 [*manuscript*]

As from S.S. Theodor Herzl of the *Zim* Line[1]

Straits of Messina en route to Marseilles

Dear B.B.

I must begin (as I shall probably also end – for it is the thought upper-most in my mind at this moment) by saying how grateful I am to have been allowed to spend an afternoon, evening and a morning with you. Too many of your visitors must have testified to the same noble experience: for you this must be monotonous: as it was for Goethe, who was equally generous with his friends. But to those who came it was always unique. I cannot tell you what a thing it is to come away so much better off than one arrived: with new capital to spend – recharged, humiliated by the thinness of one's daily life, excited, delighted, ashamed of one's own flibbertyjibbettiness, determined (a little pompously and self consciously) to sift the chaff from the grain in the future, not to waste so much, and wondering if it is not too late.[2] I went on reflecting agreeably on our morning's conversation while being talked to by my neighbour (in the Pullman car which Nicky had so kindly provided) – the head of the U.S. information office in Florence,[3] & his friend La Pira[4] who had recently visited Ben Gurion in Jerusalem and found in him another 'charismatic' politician, half boss half religious inspirer. In Naples the sea was calm but the boat from Israel, late. I wandered till 9 p.m. & then went to the pier. I was told by the Master of the Deposito of luggage to go & get my passport stamped. The passport room, designed for about 50 persons, had 350 milling Jews in it, mostly American. The Italian officials took their time. After an hour or so, babies were crying, women threatening to faint, and all these affluent Yiddish speaking first class passengers from Brooklyn or the suburbs of Chicago became a mob of helpless, desperate refugees, human flotsam from some concentration camp, jostling, screaming, with no vestige of self-control, shaming & horrible, for no reason at all, except that they were tired & were not being allowed on to the boat fast enough. The officials remained calm and contemptuous: the porters threw the luggage on board, into the hold, & disappeared. It was horrible but fascinating: the Israelis stood out among the American pilgrims – there are no tourists to Israel, only pilgrims, like civilised, self-controlled, unhysterical "goyim": it

1 The SS *Theodor Herzl* and its sister ship the SS *Jerusalem*, both launched in 1957, were the newest additions to the passenger fleet of the ZIM Israel Navigation Company, servicing the route between Haifa, Naples/Genoa and Marseilles.

2 This will strike many who did so as an apt description of spending time with IB.

3 Perhaps the US Consul in Florence, William Dale Fisher (1919–61).

4 Giorgio la Pira (1904–77), Italian Christian Democratic politician; Mayor of Florence 1950–6, 1960–4; active internationally in the search for peace, including peace between Israel and her Arab neighbours; lay member of the Dominican Order, now (2008) undergoing beatification by the Catholic Church.

was the wealthy Americans who lapsed back into the helpless, unsightly victims of the ghettos of their fathers & grand fathers – very sickening sight – until three or four hours later, they poured into the S.S. Jerusalem & were given cold meat & tea. They then calmed down. I went to recover my luggage from the *Deposito*. No porters. I asked the head of the luggage room what I was to do with my bags. 'Quest e la democrazia'[1] he said, & then with real venom 'eccola! eccola!'[2] & seeing my sad state, piled the bags on to a trolley, wheeled it to my cabin, waving away customs inspectors who obeyed him. He then shook hands with me, refused a tip, said something like 'Viva la democrazia' & departed. I shall never, so long as I live, forget those terrible milling Jews – the first class passengers, the S.S. Yerushalaim, who suddenly lost all sense of human worth, just because the Neapolitan authorities were inefficient, slow and unfriendly. The Israelis alone did not speak Yiddish & remained calm. Zionism really *has* turned them into decent emancipated human beings. It was the best advertisement for it I ever saw. In the boat I sat in the dining room beside Captain Freudenberg[3] (a German socialist turned Israeli by antisemitism within the German left socialist party in Königsberg) and Mar[4] Dan Avni,[5] member of the Israel foreign office, born Signor Segre of Turin, a good looking young man whose father was an Italian general, his wife a converted Italian Catholic. He was very civilised & charming & explained that the three centres of untarnished idealism in Israel were: the army: the Kibbutzim: the University + the Haifa Technion. He turned out quite right. The army is *extraordinary*: it melts the Yemenites, the Irakis, the Tunisians, the Germans, the Poles, the South Africans, the Bulgarians into one coherent, attractive, simple, unsophisticated, "natural" human type, with a rapidity which has to be seen. The communal settlements too are still delightful to visit. They are not self-consciously virtuous: they do not preach: they do not all eat at the same table: Aline who arrived after me, was surprised (she naturally was ready to discount my enthusiasm very heavily) & charmed. As for Namier, he was walking on air. He had last visited Palestine in 1936, and assured me that he was ready to weep & repent his long cynical life. With all his formidable apparatus, his marvellous &

---

1 sc. *Quest'è*, 'This is democracy.'
2 'Look at it!' (literally 'Here it is!').
3 Presumably Captain Avner Freudenberg (b. *c*.1911), later commander of the ill-fated luxury liner *Shalom*, which in 1964 sliced through a Norwegian tanker in fog off New York.
4 A Hebrew term of respect.
5 Vittorio Dan Segre (b. 1922), né Vittorio Emilio Giuseppe Segre, adopted the name Dan Avni on emigrating from Italy to Palestine in 1939; sometimes known as Dan Vittorio Avni-Segre; married to Rosetta Bauducco; fought for the British Army and in the Israeli War of Independence; became an Israeli diplomat in 1949; from 1967 an academic (in the US, at Oxford and Haifa, then back in Italy), author and journalist. His father was Arturo Segre, assimilated Jewish landowner in Piedmont, local mayor, officer in the Italian Army in the First World War, senior Fascist official between the wars.

sophisticated intellect, his academic terribilitá,[1] there is something childlike
& helpless about him, & he leans trustfully upon his (to me) inscrutable
Russian wife.[2] He was in a state of unspeakable admiration: loved everybody
& everything: & when I complained that Tel-Aviv was hideously ugly, tawdry,
noisy, tense, that Jewish Jerusalem was like the Princeton Institute – self
conscious, pedantic, sad, pretentious and snobbish in a petit bourgeois way,
he waved all this aside furiously, & said that the people *he* met were simple,
dignified, brave, constructive and life enhancing, & were also kind, generous
and unbroken as human beings, & he was sorry to be seventy & not to be
able to emigrate. He concealed his baptism most sedulously, & I did nothing
to expose him. I asked him if there were not too many Rabbis for him. At
this point he did react a little, & said he wanted them *all* dead. When I went
to Jerusalem with him (where he seems to have delivered a most solemn and
émotionné[3] address to some university seminar) every time he saw an old
Chassid with a fur hat & side curls and long black coat, he gnashed his teeth
and clenched his fists & uttered threatening sounds. And it *is* odd: nobody,
not even the rich Jews, or the Arabs did so much to destroy Zionism as the
rabbis: they preached, they cursed, they incited the European governments
against Herzl,[4] Weizmann & their allies. Yet once Israel came into being,
they asserted themselves: they do not dominate life there as much as the
priests in Italy or South Germany – let alone Ireland or Spain – they are
regularly humiliated by Ben Gurion, but they interfere. *I must stop.*

(13·4·58. 7 a.m. in sight of Marseilles) A paper factory could not function
because they said that if the machines worked on the Sabbath, no prayer
books wd be printed on the factory's paper. The boat on which I am now
writing this cannot give us (Catholic priests from Athens included) bread
while the Passover is on, & nobody smokes on the Sabbath. Yet it is a losing
cause.[5] Their hold over the young is feeble. In the army only the Oriental
Jews are dévot,[6] & the bigots who throw stones at passing cars on the Sabbath
are disliked & despised. Certainly it is the only country in which the Jews are
losing their best known diaspora characteristics: they are perfectly natural:
they are not clever, not financially gifted, not addicted to political casuistry

1 sc. *terribilità*, 'awesome power'.
2 Namier had married Iulia (Julia) Michaelovna de Beausobre (1893–1977), née Kazarin, Russian-
   born (and devoutly Orthodox) author, in 1947.
3 'Emotional'.
4 Theodor (Binyamin Ze'ev) Herzl (1860–1904), Austro-Hungarian Jewish journalist whose 1896
   pamphlet *The Jewish State* led to the setting up of the Zionist Organization (later the World
   Zionist Organization).
5 IB later remembered evidence against this: 'in Athens, at 6.45 p.m., while the sun was setting, &
   our S.S. *Theodor Herzl* was about to take off, a small lion bearded man marched up to the Bridge
   & loudly told the captain that if the ship did not go within 7 minutes, the seventh day of the
   Passover having recommenced, the ship wd be *obliged*, on his Supreme authority, to stay in port
   for 48 hours. We sailed within six minutes. I must admit I felt as violently about this as the poor,
   bullied, indignant, humiliated Captain Hans Axell aus Prag.' Postcard of 17 April to Berenson.
6 'Devout'.

or theories of theories, or chess or central European *neuroses* of a Koestlerish kind; they are, in short, becoming crude, happy, like Goyim: & the sentimental pilgrims from New York, Buenos Aires, Leeds, Paris, feel uncosy among them: they wd like cantors wrapped in talliths to intone heart-rending songs their mothers taught them, & they find the unsentimental natives of some Mediterranean shore – Cypriots or Maltese, uninterested in their ancestors' pains and aches and self pity and the endless tales of the life of slaves & the subterfuges & the cruel lash of their masters. Hence they do not feel at home here, & go back admiring but frozen. There are corners of Tel-Aviv where they find some kindred spirits: the Seder service Aline & I went to was full of American & British milch cows, milked, or about to be milked for the benefit of this or that institution. The State of Israel, as a unit, is to other nations what individual Jews used to be: an unpopular problem-state: a schnorrer & a very arrogant & blackmailing one at that. But *within* that is not the feeling: they are normal & without complexes: all but the German professors who wd still rather be at Breslau or Freiburg im Breisgau. But then this applies to them in Oxford and Harvard too. Learned monsters, they remain unassimilable and resentful. Live in Israel I could not: it is too stuffy & provincial. But those who do live there are healed by that very parochialism & regionalism & absence of cosmopolitan *Angst*. I have never anywhere seen happier & healthier children: & life in Kibbutzim seems to me more satisfactory – both more productive and freer & happier than anywhere else on earth. Enough, surely. In short I am for them. They haven't a friend in the world & they are good people, living & letting live. In private homes in the Kibbutzim, bread is eaten on Passover & the Day of Atonement is not enforced. To speak of theocracy (as Koestler did) or of rabbinical tyranny (as the Communists do) seems to me deliberate falsification. The pleasantest spot outside Tiberias or the groves of Jezreel is the Weizmann scientific institute: the scientists are charming & happy: the worst is the centre of Tel-Aviv – like Los Angeles. We land in 10 minutes. I think of *I Tatti* with great πόθος.[1]

My love to Nicky & to Willie-M-O.[2]

Yrs ever

Isaiah.

I did have a Namier moment of my own: the ancient cemetery of Beth Shearim[3] near Haifa, with inscriptions marking the son of Rabban Gamaliel

---

1 'Desire'.

2 William ('Willy') Mostyn-Owen (b. 1929), art historian, whose bibliography of Berenson's works had been published in 1955.

3 The excavation of the recently rediscovered ancient Jewish city and underground cemetery of Beth She'arim started during 1936–9 and continued in 1953–8. Beth She'arim had been one of the sites of the Great Sanhedrin, the Jewish supreme court, after the destruction of the Temple, and many Jewish notables were brought for burial in its necropolis, where there are richly decorated

or daughter of Rabban Simeon, President of the Sanhedrin, caused even me
a moment of recuiellement.[1]

None of the following letters mentions the sad background to the Berlins'
domestic life after they returned from Israel. Aline's brother Philippe brought his
family to Headington House while his wife had medical treatment in Oxford;
the day before they were due to leave, their five-year-old daughter suffered
a playground accident which endangered her life and caused serious brain
damage, from which she never recovered. Other family members arrived from
France and for months the house was full of worried relatives.[2]

TO DAVID ASTOR

[19 April 1958, *manuscript*]

Headington House

Dear Mr Astor, (I follow your usage)[3]

Thank you for your kind proposal that I write on Israel for the *Observer*.
I am sorry to have been away, among other places in Israel (where I had to
go to attend a meeting on the future of Weizmann's letters and papers) and
so not to have replied before. I could not, in any case have taken this on. I
am not unbiassed about Israel: I like them all, or nearly all, too well, & think
that despite their faults and crimes they have developed a form of life – in
the Kibbutzim, in the University, & in the Army – which is morally more
attractive than any that I've seen elsewhere, because it is egalitarian without
being priggish or oppressive, and just without being stiff or unspontaneous.
Aesthetically – but that is another matter. At any rate I love them: & feel
partial: & therefore wholly unfit to testify about them in public. For this
reason I have steadily declined to write about them for anyone – the N.Y.
Times, the Sunday Times, etc. which occasionally ask me. Nor would I wish
to pillory their faults & crimes in public: their Arab policy is foolish and
blind, & Suez was, I persist in thinking, a greater crime on their part, since
small countries depend on the purity of their public character, than on Sir
A. Eden's: indeed I do not think – but this will take me too far. So I should, I
fear, have declined to write in any case, and to this I adhere. The only thing
that might have shaken me was your decision to invite Deutscher to do it, if
I refused. Fortunately it is all too late to involve me in the agony of decision.
Deutscher, whatever he may say tomorrow, (I shall look at it with the worst
anticipations) hates Israel. It is a living refutation of all that this still most
fanatical of Marxists believes. When I dared, in the worst of our very brief

(probably third-century) tombs bearing inscriptions thought to refer to Rabban Gamaliel III,
President of the Sanhedrin, and his brother Simeon.
1 sc. *recuiellement*, 'stillness'.
2 'Life really *is* a little grim', IB wrote to Shirley Anglesey on 23 May.
3 'Dear Sir Isaiah'.

acquaintance, say to him that I thought Marx & Trotsky victims of a false historical theory, he changed colour, could not continue {his} in his chair, & then, shortly after, abused me, as he had every right to do, in the *Observer*. In Israel even the most left wing socialists of those I met – the friends of Aneurin Bevan & Barbara Castle[1] – expressed deep personal aversion to him as an embittered Leninist who had not deviated a millimetre from what he believed in 1930. He told them that they were a foolish temporary expedient to save the Jews from Hitler's wrath: that it was sad that Jews in the 19th century became identified with the merchant & capitalist class – no fault of theirs – but history was cruel but just – & their destruction as part of the condemned capitalist world was inevitable and just. It was [a] pity that six millions perished as they did: but history will not be cheated, & they were on the wrong side, & deserved ("objectively") to be exterminated. He feared the same was in store for the Jews of Israel & advised them to make their peace with the Soviet Union before it was too late. The Israel Communists (who are few) & the fellow travellers were delighted by all this. The Bevanites very dismayed. He left as an avowed enemy of this "petty agrarian" utopia. You can imagine, then, with what curiosity I shall look at the *Observer* to-morrow: to see, if nothing else, how much of this bubbling hatred this incurable hater, who really does abominate the West, manages to conceal under those slow, cool & smooth sounding sentences that used to please *The Economist* so. And still, I shall not (even if you were kind enough to urge me to) want to answer him. I cannot stomach *real* inhuman, 100% Communists (even non-Stalinite), & cannot communicate with them. And my pro-Israel bias is too clear to me to make possible the required degree of dispassionate pursuit of truth. I envy Geoffrey Hudson[2] his marvellous detachment and capacity for stating the truth. I too am glad about Elath: his government complain that nice & honourable & popular as he is, he has made no dif-ference to the Foreign Office: & that Beeley is more influential than before. That is true. But Ambassadors cannot alter interests, or the collective politi-cal habits of an entire establishment; I travelled home with Knox Helm, the rather tough first British Ambassador to Tel-Aviv. He was in great despair about our Middle Eastern policy: and he thought the misunderstanding of Arabs & what they were & wanted was incurable. If he thinks this (but will *never* say it publicly), what can poor Elath do? he is very very frustrated. You must forgive me for this gratuitous outpouring. Term is not yet, & I am free.

    Yrs sincerely

      Isaiah Berlin

1 Barbara Anne Castle (1910–2002), née Betts, Baroness Castle 1990, left-wing Labour MP 1945–79; held several Cabinet posts during the 1960s and 1970s.

2 Geoffrey Francis Hudson (1903–74), orientalist; Fellow of All Souls 1926–54; Fellow and Director of Far Eastern Studies, St Antony's; in 1938 he wrote articles on Palestine for the *Spectator* (see L1 290).

TO MORTON WHITE
   21 April 1958

                                                  Headington House

Dear Morton,

    [...] I have been trying to read Hegel. Friedrich's edition[1] of him is exceedingly dishonest, and his text consciously unintelligible, I think. There is 'something there' – but it is all theology and cosmic feeling – something about people not liking to be cut off from the group and wanting to get back into it and re-establish solidarity. Certainly that is all that the Paris Hegelians are talking about – the whole of history is seen as the story of the Fall, in which something was broken and the rest of history is spent in trying to piece the fragments together again. It is all to do with discomfort caused either by abominable solitude or being misfitted. A perfectly genuine subject, I am not sure how far philosophical. But when I try to sit down and read Hegel in the text of whatever language it seems absolute gibberish to me. How can it not have done so to everyone else? I simply cannot tune in. All I hear is atmospherics. Does Henry Aiken really pretend to have grasped the inner essence? If he does, tell him he is a charlatan.

    I have now lectured on the entire history of political philosophy from the Flood till approximately Rousseau, in order to learn about it primarily. There are three great crises – (1) Between Aristotle and the Stoics, (2) Machiavelli, (3) the eighteenth-century Germans.[2] Each time something totally new did happen. Hegel says new things only happen in the realm of thought, that nature merely perpetually repeats herself – a boring round of finite combinations. If technology, bombs etc. are part of the realm of thought there is no doubt something in this. Oh dear, we have a great deal to talk about. I wish you would come here this summer.

    Yours ever,
      Isaiah

TO DAVID ASTOR
   14 May 1958

                                                  Headington House

Dear David,

    Thank you for your letter, which it was very good of you to write. I have genuinely no wish to go on about poor old Deutscher, who at any rate writes well if a little like a cat treading warily on hot bricks. But I cannot resist saying that his piece on Israel[3] did, despite all his careful qualifications, deeply

---

1 *The Philosophy of Hegel*, a selection edited by Carl J. Friedrich (New York, [1954]).
2 cf. IB's 1962 Storrs Lectures at Yale, 'Three Turning-Points in the History of Political Thought'.
3 Isaac Deutscher, 'A Birthday Hope for Israel', *Observer*, 11 May 1958, 12.

irritate me. You say that he is a man of courage, integrity and independ-ence; you know him and I have only met him casually, and you do speak from long experience. His courage I do not question. But as for integrity and independence – can one speak of such qualities in the case of real, con-vinced, incurable believers in a total creed? Beneath his appearance of cool judgement and the temperate tone there is, I am sure, an icy fanaticism. He is a complete bolshevik of Lenin's time. He has a quarrel with Stalin, and he is a *rigid* heretic. It was brave of him to resist Beaverbrook about the Russian honeymoon,[1] certainly; and, no doubt, he compels himself to be 'realistic' about Germans or Americans or others whom he may emotionally dislike. Trotsky, too, was full of bitter feelings, personal emotion, resentments, loves and hates, but he kept himself going by applying to everything a rigorous Marxist scale of values – the more (in terms of factual truth or personal inclinations) it cost him to do it, the more serious and true to his principles he (and other Marxists – e.g. Christopher Hill or Prof. Levy,[2] or other party members who sacrificed their private feelings) felt himself to be. In such cases 'integrity' is not a relevant term, surely. If you mean D. is not venal, not opportunist, not personally ambitious, yes, of course; nor are other pervert-ers of truth who squeeze the facts into iron frameworks of doctrine, against all that their hearts or consciences tell them. But they do destroy themselves and us. There is no need to read Koestler to realise this. No wonder that D. thinks that Koestler, Borkenau and other 'renegades' behaved *indecently* in attacking their old gods. For he may have a quarrel within the party: but he totally rejects the Western world. You speak of independence: of Western values, yes. But he is not independent of Marxist ones. There is not an idea in D.'s articles in the last four or five years – since Stalin's death – that a Russian communist could radically dissent from. I met him only twice – on both occasions he told me that he thought Marx the greatest *philosopher* of the Western world – not merely the only economist and social thinker who was wholly right, but a greater scientist than Darwin, philosopher than Kant etc. etc. Someone, at a meeting in Balliol – a Pole called Pelczynski[3] – asked him why Marxists in the USSR used such awful jargon. D. literally rose to his feet, glared round him, and said something like: 'If Einstein and Freud can use scientific terminology not readily intelligible to men in the street, why not the Marxists?' When the same questioner said, 'Oh, but the justification

---

1 In his letter of 7 May Astor had defended Deutscher partly because 'In the early days of the Anglo-Russian wartime alliance he persisted in writing on Soviet affairs with such critical detachment that he was sacked from the *Evening Standard*. At that time [...] the honeymoon atmosphere was so strong in this country that it required considerable moral courage to write of Russia in unsentimental terms.'

2 Hyman Levy (1889–1975), Professor of Mathematics, London (Imperial), 1923–54; expelled from the British Communist Party in 1958 because of his criticism of the treatment of Jews in the Soviet Union.

3 Zbigniew Andrzej Pełczyński (b. 1925), Lecturer in Politics, Trinity 1953–5, Balliol and Merton 1955–7, Pembroke 1957–61, Merton 1957–80; Fellow and Tutor in Politics, Pembroke, 1961–93.

of mathematical or psychological technical terms is that they lead to predictions verified in practice.' D. said in his quiet, measured tone: 'I should have thought that a creed that stretches from Malaya to the Adriatic is also verified in practice', or something like this. I said that he surely would not defend *all* that had been believed in the middle ages, by counting the heads stuffed with all such beliefs? From that moment he decided quite correctly that I was on the wrong side and to be vigorously condemned. I did not feel that he was very human: I have met his like only among Spanish Jesuits. They too are independent – but only of the secular world and its human and humane values. I think him a wicked man: I wish your letter had altered my view: as it is I feel as Froude about Freeman[1] 'that I do not wish to enter any relations with him, not even those of hostility'. What D. said about Israel was said by some Soviet foreign office official to the Israel ambassador in Moscow. The latter asked what it was that the USSR really had against Israel. The Soviet official said that there was nothing Israel could do. They had, fatally for themselves, attached themselves to the West. The new ex-colonial States and the Soviet Union were on the march against imperialism, and the West, willy-nilly, would succumb. The USSR recognised its error in assisting Israel to come into existence, for from its very nature it was out of tune with, and could scarcely integrate itself into, the rising communist world. This is in effect very like Deutscher's thesis: he first tries to account for what, according to the Marxist scheme, should never have happened – the birth of Israel – by saying that it was born of despair (not very true: Weizmann, Ben Gurion etc. were not filled with a bleak and violent neurosis: and the Jewish State could well have come into existence in 1936, before the Nazi slaughter) and when the Arabs had no friends (on the contrary: Mr Bevin was very friendly to them: they did not lack arms or encouragement) as a result of a small minority movement among the Eastern Jews (this is a plain and easily demonstrable falsehood) – i.e., it was a queer historical accident, which history will probably soon iron out. He tells the Jews not to underestimate the technological progress of the (presumably in this respect mainly Soviet-aided) Arabs – and that they cannot survive in a hostile sea – as if they were not themselves most painfully and constantly aware of this, as if the 'tragic folly' of Suez were not an effort – mistaken perhaps – to protect themselves against neighbours who made it plain that what they wanted was not *bon voisinage*[2] but the elimination of the Jews as a State. I was, myself, in a tiny minority in this country (as Philip Toynbee can tell you) who thought the Israeli attack not necessarily a tactical error – which it may or may not prove to be – but morally wrong. Deutscher has no truck with such obsolete concepts: realism – the direction of the historical current, is all that matters

1 See 71/3.
2 'Good-neighbourliness'.

to him or to E. H. Carr – and this is what saves him from moral qualms, and gives him the illusion that he is being coldly scientific about Jews, Germans, Russians, Arabs etc. – nothing that he says is out of tune for a single moment with the central Marxist iron curtain line. If you want to read someone not rendered morally dead by such 'realism', do read, if you haven't, the piece by Kołakowski,[1] a Pole of *Nowa Kultura*[2] (recently exorcised by Gomulka),[3] in *East Europe*: called, I think, 'History and Responsibility'. Philip T[oynbee] really would be moved by this, and so would you, – it is a very noble plea for human values by a man who calls himself a Marxist (in fact, obviously a most honourable democratic socialist and a genuinely brave and independent and free man). D. tells the Jews to make friends with the Arabs: how? By giving up the Negev or half Galilee? In Jerusalem they say this might please Nuri,[4] but Nasser needs only denounce this – if it is the final solution – as a shameful betrayal of Arab claims to all Palestine, under Western pressure, to outbid the 'moderates', and stultify this act of appeasement. They are told to trust the UN, but the UN did nothing for them in 1948 – why should they now? Some say rich Jews can pay the Arabs off and should get together in London or New York to arrange this; but the time for that is long past (Weizmann was always wanting to do that, naively – but he was naive in many ways). But I do apologise for writing much too much again – old age and garrulity are upon me – don't, I beg you, feel you must ever answer any of this: but if the spirit should ever move you to come to Oxford, please let me know, and we could have a talk about this and that, which would give me the greatest pleasure.

　　Yours,

　　　　Isaiah Berlin

1 Leszek Kołakowski (b. 1927), Polish philosopher; taught at Warsaw University 1950–9, Professor of History of Philosophy 1959–68 (expelled for his pro-democracy political views); later taught in the US and became (1970–95) a Fellow of All Souls. At the time of this letter he had moved from orthodox Marxism to Marxist humanism and had been forced to leave the editorial board of *Nowa Kultura* (next note) because of his fierce attacks on Soviet Communism, 'Responsibility and History', *Nowa Kultura* Nos 35–8 (1, 8, 15 and 22 September 1957); reprinted in *East Europe*, 6 No 12 (December 1957) and 7 Nos 2, 3 and 5 (February, March and May 1958), and in his *Marxism and Beyond*, trans. Jane Zielonko Peel (London, 1969).

2 Polish literary journal published weekly in Warsaw; the organ of the State-controlled Association of Polish Writers.

3 Władysław Gomułka (1905–82), Polish Communist leader, Deputy Prime Minister 1945–7; expelled from the central committee of the Communist Party 1949, arrested 1951 for Titoist deviationism, released 1955, rehabilitated 1956; First Secretary, Polish United Workers' Party, 1956–70; a liberalising influence in 1956, he gradually reverted to a harder pro-Soviet line.

4 Nuri es-Said (1888–1958), pro-British Prime Minister of Iraq 1930–40, 1941–58 (executed in a coup).

TO K. R. JOHNSTONE[1]

14 May 1958 [carbon]

[Headington House]

Dear Mr Johnstone,

Thank you for your letter of May 12.[2] I am much interested by the proposal which you have outlined of a visit by a small group of economists, philosophers and historians to the Soviet Union, and should be ready to discuss the possibility of joining such a group, at any rate in principle. I should not be able to go in November, but should I think be able to go in December.

I have some experience of such discussions since on my last visit to the Soviet Union in the summer of 1956 I visited the Soviet Academy of Philosophy and spent some two hours in a discussion with some of its members. I think that if such a delegation as you contemplate is to be a success, certain conditions would have to be imposed at our end; as I think that Professor Ayer would corroborate, the formal pronouncements of Soviet philosophers (and this holds for historians too, whom I heard in Rome some years ago, I do not know about the economists) read from bits of papers on platforms are quite worthless. They do not express anything that their authors may in fact be thinking, but are plainly written for or by them by mechanical expounders of the official doctrine. The first condition to be insisted on, therefore, is that each of the experts in the British delegation be permitted to meet with Soviet experts either face to face (although I think that this will hardly be permitted – they are too terrified of meeting foreigners alone – there have to be at least two persons in the room) or in groups of not more than four or five. All formal conferences, speeches, and even banquets (though these may be an unavoidable evil) must be ruled out. Unlike Poles or even Czechs and Romanians, Soviet 'humanists' seldom permit themselves to say what they actually think, but confine themselves to wooden formulae, which they repeat over and over again, whatever may be said to them. They know perfectly well that this does not make a good impression, but it is a measure of self-protection which they evidently place above the need to impress foreign visitors. On the other hand an opportunity for informal chat in a room, even though informers may be present who will report every word to the authorities, does make it possible for them more easily to convey what they are really thinking – without necessarily saying it – than do formal occasions; moreover they can on such informal occasions absorb what we have to offer them – and they are very avid for information

1 Kenneth Roy Johnstone (1902–78), Deputy Director-General, British Council, 1953–62.
2 The British Council had discussed with Bill Deakin and Christopher Mayhew (Under-Secretary of State at the Foreign Office) Hugh Gaitskell's suggestion of informal Anglo-Russian talks on current topics. Johnstone had invited IB to participate in the proposed visit and in a preliminary meeting.

about intellectual movements in Europe – without having formally to react. Unless this condition really can be promised, a visit of this type will certainly prove very frustrating to our delegation. My conversations with Soviet intellectuals, when I could get them by themselves or in twos, were of a totally different type from my official exchanges with them in a lecture-room of the Academy. But all this can perhaps be discussed if such a meeting as you adumbrate takes place. At any rate I should like to thank you for thinking of me in this connection and to say that I am interested.

Yours sincerely,

The Berlins helped Boris Pasternak's sisters mount a memorial exhibition to their father, the artist Leonid Pasternak,[1] who had spent his last years in Oxford. IB was particularly attracted to a 1917 work entitled The Reunion, *depicting a group of anti-Bolshevik Russian revolutionaries,[2] and asked Josephine Pasternak whether he could buy it from the family. She presented it to him as a gift.*

TO JOSEPHINE PASTERNAK
15 May 1958 [*manuscript*]

Headington House

Dear Josephine,

I write from London (more accurately the train to a suburb) – despite the address – where I have just heard of your immense generosity. I am grateful, delighted, terribly moved and terribly embarrassed. Of course I should have *known* that if I expressed a desire for this picture, there was a grave risk that you would immediately give it to me: if I had supposed this for an instant, I should have said nothing: and so inevitably and sadly lost a very great source of pleasure – & more than pleasure – you cannot imagine with what a mixture of devotion, nostalgia, irony, affection and, above all, consuming personal self-identification (probably founded on a total or partial illusion)

1 Leonid Osipovich Pasternak (1862–1945), Russian Jewish painter born in Odessa, self-proclaimed Impressionist, who moved to Berlin in 1921 and England in 1938.
2 Plate 37. Those pictured are (i) Vera Dmitrievna Lebedeva (1846–1919), née Dubenskaya, in whose Moscow apartment the reunion occurred, friend of many of the Narodnaya Volya ('The People's Will') revolutionaries; (ii) Ekaterina Konstantinovna Breshko-Breshkovskaya (1844–1934), Russian revolutionary, follower of Bakunin; known as the Babushka ('Grandmother') of the Revolution; exiled to Siberia 1878–96 (with hard labour) and 1910–17; helped found the Socialist Revolutionary Party 1901; member of the Provisional Government 1917; fled Russia after the Bolsheviks took power; (iii) Prince Petr Alekseevich Kropotkin (1842–1921), Russian soldier, geographer, supporter of anarchist communism and anti-Bolshevik revolutionary; (iv) Nikolay Vasil´evich Chaikovsky (1851–1926), Russian anti-Bolshevik revolutionary; head of the White Russian Government during the Civil War 1918–19; (v) Vladimir L´vovich Burtsev (1862–1942), Russian revolutionary activist, publisher and editor, opposed in turn to Tsarist, Bolshevik and Fascist totalitarianism; and (vi) Nikolay Aleksandrovich Morozov (1855–1946), Russian revolutionary, scientist and poet; imprisoned 1882–1905.

I look on everything to do with Russia in the 19th century which extends exactly to 1918. I have a weak and conventional visual sensibility: I am, on the whole, ashamed of my taste in painting & sculpture: I am left too unmoved by Gothic, by Poussin, by the Bellinis; unless there are non-'malerisch'[1] associations, I do not feel or see enough. But this particular pastel is so deeply penetrated by the feeling of 1917 – that pathetic, noble, comical, terribly touching & pure moment in the revolution – before Lenin contemptuously crushed and kicked the whole of this structure into the gutter – that I kept remembering and lingering over it. And, perhaps wrongly and arrogantly, I wondered who, besides your family, really understood what it was all about, and responded to the unique incarnation of this particular moment and the marvellous concentration of feeling with which it is expressed. (*Zhivago* is not irrelevant to this too). But, goodness me, if I had suspected that this would cause you to *give* it to me – me who very respectably & honestly wanted to make you an offer for it which you could have rejected – an attitude I should have more than understood – I should not, I could never have written! I did *nothing* to deserve it: if anyone helped it was Aline alone. I merely felt ashamed I could not do more. And now this: oh dear: it is for me to thank *you*: everything to do with your family, your brother, Moscow which in 1945 I therefore saw with quite different eyes, has enriched my life very greatly. But I am expressing myself, as usual, abominably: I wish to say that I am terribly grateful, do not know, as they say, how to thank you, think you too generous, should like to do something splendid and memorable to celebrate this, & don't know how. Thank you very very very much. Blessings upon all your heads.

Isaiah.

TO JOHANNA LAMBERT

20 May 1958 [*carbon*]

[Headington House]

Dear Hansi,

Good gracious me! When I sent you that stern message by Alix, I did not mean it to be taken too seriously – Alix did say that you had come back passionately pro-Arab, and I, having just visited Israel, and being passionately pro-Israel, how could I but send you a ringing challenge? But if we are to be serious, let me say that there is nothing in your letter – except the final recommendations[2] – with which I can possibly disagree. First of all I entirely agree about the Egyptians – whom I only saw for 24 hours in 1934 and whom I thought the greasiest, most contemptible, most awful people I had ever seen.

1 'Painterly'.
2 That IB should play a role in arranging a meeting between Ben-Gurion and Nasser.

Whereas the Arabs of the (then) Palestine, Jordan, Syria, and even Lebanon were greatly superior. I did not care for the Syrians much. I thought they were humourless fanatics, grim, provincial, violent and, if not so barbarous as the Iraquis, more fanatical and more permanently bitter by temperament. However, one must not generalise, and I agree that they were certainly passionate and proud, which the Egyptians were not. The Palestinian and Jordanian Arabs I loved, they were nationalistic and difficult, but gay, full of temper, full of spirit, and with a charm to which I quite understood why the English in particular were only too ready to succumb, whereas the Jews were charmless, heterosexual, terribly provincial also, shrill, thin-skinned, resentful, and impossible. So the story of Palestine in the 1930s is not very difficult to grasp, if you understand the English public schools and whom Englishmen fall in love with and why.

Now as to the present, you say that the Jews and Arabs are indispensable to one another. I wish I could agree. I do not think that Jews are indispensable to the Arabs at all, indeed I am sure the Arabs would be obviously much happier without them. Furthermore, I must admit that anyone who says that the arrival of the Jews could only do the Arabs good is guilty of considerable hypocrisy. Zionists have been liable to say that – they did talk about raising the cultural and economic standards of the Arabs – and of course they have done that – but this is no reason, by itself, for coming. If I live in an untidy room, in hideously primitive and disgusting surroundings, and wish to go on living like that, your arrival with sanitary implements, telephones and telegraphs and television sets, assuring me that you will make my life much more blissful on only one small condition – that you will live with me in this room yourself for ever – would naturally not satisfy me, and I would do my best to kick you out. That Arab rights have been trodden on – that a wrong to them has been committed – it seems to be morally shameful to deny. If you then ask me why I am pro-Zionist, it is because I think that where right clashes with right – or rather misery with misery – one must not think about rights, which always exist – whether those of the French and Germans or the Russians and Americans – but of some calm utilitarian solution which produces on the whole the best or happiest solution in the end. In human affairs I am prepared to adopt a Catholic standpoint, accept original sin, and agree that men are imperfect, and that whatever we do someone will suffer and no solution can be lasting. That being said, the reason for admitting the Jews to Palestine was that their misery has been too long and too great; that the only way to cure people of that particular form of distortion is by creating the possibility of normal existence for them, of normal virtues and vices, of private life, as it were, not too much overlooked by others, instead of dinning into their ears that they must try and behave like other people under their perpetual observation, so that if one of them commits a wrong, the whole lot are punished for it. These harsh words being said, it seemed to me that the wrong done to the Arabs – who had no Palestinian nationalism in 1918, and who had had vast tracts of land to expand over, was smaller than the wrong which would have been done to the Jews had they been left to welter. But this is about the past, and although I am prepared to defend this position, you may not wish to go into this at all, and discuss more painfully but profitably the future.

Changes of population do not seem to me to be the most terrible solution possible – when the Greeks and the Turks exchanged populations,[1] under much more brutal conditions than anything [which] occurred in Palestine, an appalling series of bloody conflicts were in fact averted. The entrance of a million Jews to displace the 800,000 Arabs (if that is the right number), although not an ideal arrangement, does not in itself seem to me to cry out to Heaven. What does is the condition of the Arab refugees. Although I think the Arabs are principally responsible, both for the exodus of the Arabs (the Jews certainly did not expel them by force in most cases – they fled because they did not wish to be involved in a civil war and were promised to come back together with the victorious Arab armies. I, like everybody else at the time, also believed that the Arabs were bound to win that war – the Jewish victory surprised every single political observer – so that what happened was that they betted quite naturally and intelligibly on their own horse. This is tragic, but not entirely the Jews' fault), and their actual condition now. The Arabs may be responsible – the Arab Governments may exploit the refugees to keep the wound running – but still the Jews should have shown more imagination than they did. They should have offered money for resettlement on a large scale, however they might have raised it. No doubt the Arabs would have refused and thrown the money in their faces, but still it would have been the required gesture, and at least not the somewhat blind – or at any rate short-sighted – complacency with which at present they regard the whole outside world, being concentrated, not altogether surprisingly, but still dangerously, on their own internal problems. This is the single largest problem, it seems to me, and not that of the frontiers. I see that the Arabs might easily tremble at the thought of another three million Jews being stuffed into Israel, which certainly would create an attempt to burst out on the part even of people who at present contemplate no such thing. But who speaks of another three millions? Where are they to come from? Not unless the Russians let out their Jews (and even then how many of them would go? not three millions!). Is this in the least feasible? The only thing which would make it so would be a violent upsurge of anti-Semitism in the world. So far from weakening the Jews, as you think, it would, in a horrible way, strengthen them. The entire economic

---

[1] In 1923, under the Treaty of Lausanne, over two million people moved between Greek and Turkish territory.

and technical strength of the Jews in Israel in the 1930s came from Hitler's persecutions; if it were not for that, all those rich, able, competent and effective Jews upon whom the whole economic and bureaucratic life of Israel rests would never have dreamt of coming. Even as it is they seem a little bewildered, but the Germans gave them no choice. But the fear of another three million Jews does seem to me to be an absurd nightmare, it is like the statements which the Arabs are constantly making in the United Nations that the Jews have in their parliament a great inscription (this is solemnly reported to me by my friend Burdon-Muller, coming from some New York source) saying that the 'natural' frontiers of Israel are from the Euphrates to the Nile. This is pure invention and not one which anyone who knows the facts genuinely believes, even in Syria, even in Jordan. Although I grant that the Arabs are children and are capable of believing anything, that is part of their charm and their dangerousness. There are at present about two million inhabitants in Israel. Every single British report on Palestine from 1921 onwards maintained that it was physically and economically impossible under any conceivable conditions that more than say 40 per cent of this number could ever conceivably begin to live human lives in that country. So the prophecies of external demographers I am somewhat inclined to dismiss, as it seems to me that the number of inhabitants in a country depends on factors other than those which are usually taken into account. Japan is much more thickly settled than ever Israel will be, even if five million persons ever settled in the present frontiers of Israel (which I admit is not thinkable, and I can assure you will never occur).[1] What of course has to be done is to allay Arab fears in this respect, and there is nothing the Israelis desire more than to have their present frontiers guaranteed by the Powers, so that no matter what tribulations and other troubles they may have, the slightest infringement of the frontiers will immediately be punished by United Nations or other sanctions. The United Nations may be laughable in their relations with the Great Powers, but there is nothing they enjoy so much as disciplining the weak – as indeed it turned out at the time of Suez. Consequently I think that if the frontiers were guaranteed by the Powers, the first Jew who crossed it would be obliterated with the greatest good will by the guarantors, and if they did show bellicose and imperialist tendencies they could be stopped with the greatest ease. Appeasement of the weak has not been an attribute of any Great Power lately: unless some Great Power aligns itself with the Jews, they cannot possibly move, and what Great Power would? And if a Great Power did, that would be the signal for a general war and the relatively unimportant issue between Jews and Arabs would be obliterated in a general holocaust. So I think that a guarantee of the frontiers is the key to the whole

---

1 In April 2007 the population of Israel (a larger country than in 1958 because of the 1967 territorial gains) stood at over seven million, of whom 76 per cent were Jewish.

situation, it would allay Arab fears, and allow the Jews to get on with developing their own State. You say that Ben-Gurion must make the first move. But of what kind? The Foreign Offices of America, England and the Soviet Union are agreed upon one thing – the Jews must move back to the frontiers of 1947; this seems to me a most fatal solution and one which cannot possibly last. Quite apart from the question that a country which loses a third of its territory suddenly is too economically and militarily weakened and demoralised ever to recover properly, if all it has is ten years of previous independence, what would the good of this be? It would enable Nuri, the hope of the West, to maintain that by peaceful means he had got more for the Arabs than ever Nasser had. All that Nasser need do then is to say that this is a shameful betrayal of the Arab cause, a piece of monstrous appeasement, the recognition of the right of a truncated Israel to go on existing, the denial of the eternal Arab claim to the whole of Palestine, and he can turn out or assassinate Nuri with the greatest ease and turn this very event into a lever which would give him the other Arab peoples. If one is to appease, one must see to it that the meat shown to the tiger really does satisfy him – the bits of Palestine which Ben Gurion can offer, if at all considerable, may continue the flow of oil for six months, nine months perhaps. After that the tiger, much refreshed, must pounce again. The example of Czechoslovakia is fresh to everyone's memory. No official in America or England to whom I have spoken seriously maintains that the yielding up of territory will satisfy the Arabs in any serious way. They only want Israel to do it because they feel terrified of the sudden stoppage of the oil (quite naturally and intelligibly – this seems to be a perfectly valid point) and realise that the only price which the Arabs would accept for going on is the Jews. And as the Jewish State was created in the teeth of the Powers, and they bear no love for it, they see no reason for not forcing some such policy on it. How can the Israelis be expected to listen to such advice? The questions of local frontier adjustments are quite reasonable and they are prepared to discuss them. The question of raising money to repatriate or at any rate re-settle Arab refugees – yes, I think they are short-sighted about that and should do something spontaneous, even if, as I said, this is flung back in their teeth. But they certainly cannot give up bits of their soil in any considerable quantity, and nobody who wants them to survive in any form, on reflection, is prepared to tell them to do that. They know very well that the Russian menace to them is graver than to the Arabs; the Russians hate them, among other things, because while they think they can manage peasants – and could crack Nasser like a nut if it came to the point and if they were not afraid of Western reactions – the Jews, though few, would have to be exterminated or transplanted bodily, since they are so very unadjustable to the Soviet system, and are the only nation in the Middle East which is genuinely anti-Communist, not because they are paid to be, but out of conviction. This is conceded even by their enemies here. I do not go so far as Randolph Churchill in maintaining that England should drop the Arabs as a bad bet, relegate them to the Russians and simply ally herself with Israel and the Turks as the only reliable anti-Soviet bulwarks in the Middle East – though they are that. I see that the oil is needed, and that a more cautious policy is inevitable. And I agree with you profoundly that unless the Jews come to an understanding with the Arabs, they are done for. Yet every day and in every way feelers are put out by the Jews even towards Nasser to see on what conditions a compromise could be arranged. The Arabs, encouraged by all the Great Powers, but especially by Russia and to a large degree by the local English and Americans, see no profit to be gained from that, they do not trust the Jews, as you rightly say, they fear them, they do look on them as the Austrians looked on the Prussians, and they have a hope that with enough energy and patience the Jews can be pushed into the sea and exterminated. After all, the Christian kingdoms were in the end obliterated, the Jews are foreign invaders like the Crusaders, and like them they will leave nothing but a vague historical memory. That is certainly their hope. The Lebanese Christians don't quite agree with all this, but they daren't speak out for fear of having their throats cut by their Muslim cousins. (I well remember having a conversation with Charles Malik,[1] in San Francisco, which he would strenuously deny today, in which he bitterly regretted English action in expelling the French from the Lebanon as relegating the Lebanese Christians to the tender mercies of the Muslims who had persecuted them for centuries. He daren't say this now. But I have yet to meet a Lebanese Christian who does not to some degree feel it.) So what is to be done? Your analogy with Stresemann and Briand[2] is not alas one that awakens the highest hopes. Stresemann quietly re-armed, Briand died, and we know what happened. Certainly you are right: unless the Jews integrate themselves somehow into the Arab world, they are doomed. How are they to do it? What price will the Arabs want? The repatriation of the Arab refugees on to their old lands in Israel will merely create an enormous minority problem of a kind which used to drive the peoples of Europe quite mad. The creation of a corridor – the yielding of a neck of land between Egypt and Jordan – will merely terrify Jordan. You are quite right in saying that the Arabs are afraid of the Jews, the West and the Russians. Moreover their hatred of Israel is perfectly genuine, and if I were an Arab I

1 Charles Habib Malik (1906–87), Lebanese philosopher, diplomat and Greek Orthodox theologian; Ambassador to US and UN 1945–55; member of Lebanese Cabinet 1956–8; President of UN General Assembly 1958–9.
2 IB had written to Teddy Kollek: 'Now I must write a letter to a Baroness in Brussels explaining why it is not right to expect me to make peace between B[en]-G[urion] and Nasser on the lines of Stresemann and Briand, not that that led to such splendid consequences!' (16 May 1958). Gustav Stresemann (1878–1929; Chancellor of Germany 1923, Foreign Secretary 1923–9) and Aristide Briand (1862–1932; six times Prime Minister of France between 1909 and 1929) were jointly awarded the Nobel Peace Prize in 1926 for their work towards Franco-German reconciliation, embodied in the 1925 Locarno Treaties.

would hate Israel too. It is most painful and unfortunate that the Jews, who, had they been left to stew in their original miseries, would certainly have driven the rest of the world mad, can only obtain a minimumly decent national existence in the land to which alone they were prepared to go for non-economic, disinterested or spiritual reasons, and that this land should have contained 400,000 Arabs. Still, more terrible historical messes have been ironed out. The real difficulty is that the Arabs hope somehow to exterminate the Jews or that the Jews will somehow lift like a nightmare and be no more. What can the Jews do to convince them of the opposite? The Sinai campaign did something, but obviously not enough. An international port at Haifa? Economic and social facilities of an indefinite kind? For all this the Israelis are perfectly prepared. I agree that from the present quarrels nobody derives any benefit except the Russians. The only hope the Jews have – and they are terribly aware of their danger, but since they can do nothing they shut their eyes and live in a kind of conscious fool's paradise, trying to engage in their artificial internal economy – lies in integrating their economy with that of the Arabs. How on earth are they to do it? The only man who was prepared to help them to do that was the late Emir Abdullah, who really did foresee some kind of Arab–Jewish federation, or something like it, but was assassinated for his pains. Those leaders of the Arab Legion who write autobiographies and speak about 'the outpourings of the scum of the ghettos' naturally do not make the Arabs feel that anyone among their friends really want them to take the Jews seriously in that sense. I think that Gurion, tough and not entirely amiable as he is, sometimes wonders if his son will live in an independent Jewish State. Anyone who can induce the Arabs to recognise for ever the continued existence of Israel would save the West and the world – otherwise I think the dangers are really terrible.

What can the Jews hope for now? Only that the Russians will not openly state their support for the 1947 frontiers, for fear that some Arab will take them seriously, and start a war against the Jews which they know they cannot win by themselves on the assumption of the support by Russian 'volunteers'. Whilst these 'volunteers' come, there will be 'volunteers' from the other side too, and so a kind of Korea will begin, and where that will end who can tell? The Jews hope that even the Russians, even in their most anti-Semitic moments, will not quite want to be responsible for unleashing that, but it is a slender hope. On the whole I cannot deny to you that the life of some of the Israelis – in the Communist settlements, in the Army, among the University students – seems to me to be more satisfactory than that lived by anyone else that I have seen. I am much too old and sophisticated and unadjustable to be able to lead it properly myself, but I am sorry that I am all this. Israel is the only country where there are no 'angry young men'. Even in Russia there is plenty of cynicism, ennui, lack of ideals, total apathy or ignorance of why one goes on doing whatever one is doing. In Israel they all seem to be possessed by some kind of purpose, which is not militaristic in character. It is rather depressing to anyone who wants a gentle form of *far niente*,[1] as I do, emotionally moving, but a kind of moral reproach to one for one's over-civilised tastes. But I have no doubt that if they are exterminated – and this could easily happen – it will be the destruction of the most hopeful form of social life, inasmuch as it isn't an untidy combination of socialism and capitalism – adjusted to human needs and the vagaries of human temperament, instead of some hideous mechanical imposition of ruthless doctrinal dictates as in Communist countries – that the world at present affords. Of course this has been done at the expense of the Arabs. Of course they mind. Of course they are right to mind. The Red Indians were right too, and the East Indians, and the Italians in the eighteenth century, and the Slovaks who groaned under the Hungarians, and everyone in history who has ever had to give up something they want to somebody who in their eyes had no right to it and came down like a wolf on the fold without rhyme or reason, a scourge of God not to be endured patiently by men of courage, patriotism, pride. All this I understand very well, and if one looks for solutions, one cannot look for the best, only for what will work, given fallible human nature: the problem is how to preserve the splendid, moving, and truly noble values of Israel – the total transformation of a people from cripples of the ghetto into farmers and soldiers and coarse, tough, non-intellectual exploiters of nature, with their chess-players, bankers, tough intellectuals, cynics and sceptics and every form of decadence that we love but cannot be allowed to promote too far – and yet allow for a natural expansion of the violent nationalism which quite intelligibly is at present stirring the Arabs. I feel no hatred or indignation against Nasser. After long humiliation, too much, too many tears, blood always follows. Mussolini was the result of too much contempt for Italy, and Hitler of too much hatred for Germany. Considering what the Jews have been through, it is in a way surprising that they are not more horrifying than they are. But I agree: sooner or later, Arab–Jewish talks, independently of everyone, will have to occur – mediation by outsiders will help no one – but for that one must wait for passions to cool, and that simply means that the Jews have to sit tight.

Oh dear, I have gone on too long. My language is too passionate. Yet I long to see you. When are you coming to stay with Stephen? When will I introduce my wife to you at last? When shall we have a talk about you, your beloved Syrians, I, my beloved Israelis? Israel has the same effect on me as Churchill's speeches in 1940. The Arabs perhaps seem to you ancient, dispossessed aristocrats. Do let us talk about it. I do long to see you.

Yours,

---

1 'Doing nothing'.

The Berlins were hosts to Dmitry Shostakovich when he came to Oxford to be made an honorary Doctor of Music at the Encaenia ceremony on 26 June. Francis Poulenc, similarly honoured, stayed with the Trevor-Ropers, whose house was to be the venue for a joint musical gathering.

TO ROWLAND BURDON-MULLER

28 June 1958

Headington House

Dear Rowland,

[...] Poulenc and Shostakovich have come and gone. Goodness, but it was a business. First a great fuss about the British Council which had arranged elaborately for a musical party for S. on Monday night (we were to entertain him on Tuesday and he was to get his honorary degree with Macmillan and Gaitskell on Wednesday), but the Soviet Embassy appears to be engaged in some kind of warfare with the British Council and more or less forbade him to have anything to do with them. The result was that the party was held without him, much bad blood, general indignation, telegrams, anger, tears. He finally materialised on Tuesday, and it was a wonderful business. First there arrived in our drawing room a very stiff and upright, rather handsome young Soviet official, who said: 'I wish to introduce myself. My name is Loginov.[1] The composer D. D. Shostakovich is in car outside. We were told you were expecting him at 4.00. It is now 3.00. Do you wish him to remain in car, or what?' We explained that we were expecting him at 3.00, and it would be perfectly permissible for him to enter straight away. Whereupon the car was ceremonially driven in, another Soviet official leapt out, and finally the composer himself appeared, small, shy, like a chemist from Canada (Western States), terribly nervous, with a twitch playing in his face almost perpetually – I have never seen anyone so frightened and crushed in all my life – he re-introduced the two Soviet officials as 'my friends, my great friends', but after he had been with us for a bit, and the Soviet officials were got out of the way, he never referred to them as that again, but only as 'the diplomats'. Every time he mentioned them a curious expression of angst appeared on his face, rather like the expression which sometimes enters Aline's face – indeed on the last morning of all when he was waiting for the two officials to appear and was in a state of utter panic and despair, I said in English (which he does not understand) to Aline, who was also looking rather distraught, that the expression of their faces was identical. Anyway the problem was how to get Shostakovich to stay to dinner and go on to the musical party given in the Trevor-Ropers' house for him and Poulenc, and how to get rid of the two Soviet officials, who would cast a terrible frost on the occasion. In the end, I

1 Y. Loginov, 3rd Secretary at the Soviet Embassy in London.

announced firmly to them that the University had a strict set of rules which it obeyed: under these a University official would appear in half an hour, and take them off to dinner in New College, after which they would be allowed to see a play (by David Pryce-Jones), while for Shostakovich an entirely different arrangement had been made. This they took calmly – after glancing at one another to see if it was all right – and bowed their heads submissively. The University official duly called, some unfortunate Fellow at New College was suborned to look after the two 'diplomats', and Shostakovich was left with us. His manner brightened. But throughout the visit he looked like a man who had passed most of his life in some dark forbidding place under the supervision of jailers of some sort, and whenever the slightest reference was made to contemporary events or contemporary personalities, the old painful spasm would pass over his face, and his face would assume a haunted, even persecuted expression and he would fall into a kind of terrified silence. It was depressing and very harrowing, and made one like him and pity him a great deal. In due course the other guests appeared, Poulenc, Cecile,[1] the Cecils, Jimmy Smith,[2] the Trevor-Ropers etc., Poulenc was charming to S., and he visibly thawed under the benign influence. We dined, and went on to the Trevor-Ropers' drawing room. There S. immediately made for the nearest corner and sat there, contracted like a hedgehog, occasionally smiling wanly if I made a particularly bold boutade.[3] His cello sonata was played by a young and very handsome cellist from Ceylon,[4] he listened to it calmly, said to me that the cellist was good, and the pianist very bad (which was perfectly true), and complained to the cellist that he had played two passages incorrectly. The cellist flushed, produced the score, and S. saw that the score bore out the cellist. He could not think how this could be, suddenly realised that it had been edited [by] Piatigorsky, who had of course altered the score arbitrarily to please himself; this was the moment at which he came nearest to real rage, took out a pencil and violently crossed out Piatigorsky's forgeries, and substituted his own original version. After that his brow cleared, and he returned to his little corner. Songs by Poulenc were then sung by Miss Margaret Ritchie,[5] absurdly, in the ludicrous Victorian English fashion, Shostakovich writhed a little, but Poulenc, very polite, very mondain,[6] congratulated her and made grimaces to others behind her back. After this a movement of Poulenc's cello sonata was played, to placate him, and then there was a silence, and I said to S. that everyone would be delighted if he too played a little. Without a word he went to the piano and played a prelude

---

1 Baroness Cécile de Rothschild (1913–95), sister of Elie de Rothschild and a close friend of Aline's.
2 James Frederick Arthur ('Jimmy') Smith (1906–80), Chairman, Sadler's Wells Trust, 1948–61; Director, ROH, 1950–61.
3 'Sally'.
4 (Frank) Rohan de Saram (b. 1939), then starting his distinguished international career.
5 Margaret Ritchie, stage-name of Mabel Willard Ritchie (1902–69), soprano.
6 'Worldly'.

and fugue – one of the twenty-four he has composed like Bach – with such magnificence, such depth and passion, the work itself was so marvellous, so serious and so original and unforgettable, that everything by Poulenc flew through the window and could not be recaptured. Poulenc did play something from *Les Biches*,[1] and something else, but his music could not be listened to any more, the decadence of the Western world had alas become all too apparent. While playing, S's face really had become transformed, the shyness and the terror had gone, and a look of tremendous intensity and indeed inspiration appeared; I imagine that is how nineteenth-century composers may have looked like when they played. But I do not think it has been seen much in the Western world in the twentieth. After that he ceased playing and various people wished to be presented. He showed the first violin[2] of the Philharmonia Orchestra how to play the second and third movements of his concerto; he told Desmond Shawe-Taylor[3] about his future plans; he gave autographs, he ate and drank. Poulenc, although looked after nicely, felt somewhat relegated, rather like Cocteau when Picasso is about. Everyone felt that this was a remarkable occasion, unique and moving, and although he spoke no English, everyone except the thickest-skinned and most philistine (like for example Mr Hodson, the editor of the *Sunday Times*, superfluously invited by the Ropers)[4] felt moved, and said so in various ways afterwards. It really was an occasion and an experience. After this, at home, he did talk a little, complained about no piano, discoursed on his musical taste, and went to bed almost happy I think. Meanwhile his two guardians went to an undergraduate party at New College, then to the Exeter Ball, had a tremendous time, exchanged insults and pleasantries with undergraduates and dons, and obviously enjoyed themselves. Very nice they turned out to be – they may have had their hands dripping with Hungarian blood, but personally they were innocent, rather wooden peasants, who obviously at an order from above would have had no compunction in shooting one dead, but at the same time had a certain charm.

On the next day the nervous tic began in S. again, he went through the horrors of the degree ceremony, was terribly embarrassed at meeting various people who spoke Russian at the All Souls luncheon, was always

---

1 'The Hinds', Poulenc's 1924 ballet, which he later revised as an orchestral suite.

2 Presumably Manoug Parikian (1920–87), Leader, Philharmonia Orchestra, 1949–57, thereafter soloist; he had performed Shostakovich's violin concerto and spoke Russian.

3 Desmond Christopher Shawe-Taylor (1907–95), chief music critic, *Sunday Times*, 1958–83.

4 Hugh Trevor-Roper recounted to Bernard Berenson that IB had taken offence at Harry Hodson's publishing in the *Sunday Times* (as 'Philosopher on TV', in the 'Atticus' column, *Sunday Times*, 8 June 1958, 5) an item describing IB's 'huge liquid voice' as 'like a melting Russian river in spring', had threatened to boycott the gathering (of which he was the joint host) if Hodson attended, and was finally placated only by complicated arrangements ensuring that they never met (*Letters from Oxford*, 253–4). The item in question, heralding IB's first and only appearance on *The Brains Trust* (on that same day), also mentioned IB's 'bulky figure' and his dislike of the countryside, and suggested that he had sought Khrushchev's help in obtaining a visa for his 1956 visit to Moscow.

taking cover with me, who after all was an accredited representative of the University registered by the Soviet Embassy as such. People asked him intolerable questions such as 'What has happened to your second, third and fourth symphonies?' – admirable works condemned by the regime. He would answer lamely, 'They were not a very great success', which was literally true, but he suffered as he spoke. An absurd incident occurred when Lord Beveridge,[1] aged 84, tried to present him with a bunch of flowers – too large for a buttonhole, too small for a proper bouquet, which he had been charged to give him by some dim Welsh composer, and chose the middle of lunch to do so. Poor S. got up, mumbled, Beveridge, who was out of his mind, also mumbled, and they were taken apart with difficulty. Various White Russians tried to engage him in conversation, naturally enough, and he managed to disengage himself with enormous effort and agony. Finally we took him home, dressed him in a white tie and sent him to dine at Christ Church with the other recipients of honorary degrees, such as the Prime Minister, Gaitskell etc. He came home more dead than alive, but got up early the next morning and presented us with scores of three works with suitable inscriptions, and even talked a little about his wife and children. At 10.00 a.m. the guardians were to call for him, but they were late. He got into a state of appalling nervous panic, made me ring the Mitre Hotel three times, began to wring his hands, wondered what would happen if he arrived late at the Embassy, how he would explain it, wondered whether his guardians had somehow abandoned him, or some mistake had been made for which he would be blamed, and got into an appalling neurotic state. However, they appeared, explained they were late because they had been buying guides to Oxfordshire at Blackwells, and took him off. I was invited to lunch with him in the Soviet Embassy next day, but refused. S. had seen enough of me, and knew enough about me to realise that I understood his position too well, and that I thought that it would be better for him to meet all the British musicians etc., whom he would meet in London through interpreters, and without being self-conscious about an observer understanding his reactions a little too well. So out of a kind of delicacy – I think you will agree it was not inappropriate – I refused, and that was that.

The whole thing has left me with a curious sensation of what it is to live in an artificial nineteenth century – for that is what Shostakovich does – and what an extraordinary effect censorship and prison has on creative genius. It limits it, but deepens it.

I must stop and go down to lunch with Peter and his school friends assembled round the table, but S's face will always haunt me somewhat, it is terrible to see a man of genius victimised by a regime, crushed by it into accepting

1 William Henry Beveridge (1879–1963), 1st Baron Beveridge 1946, economist and social reformer; Director, LSE, 1919–37; Master, Univ., 1937–45; Chairman of the Committee which in 1942 recommended the introduction of the Welfare State.

his fate as something normal, terrified almost of being plunged into some other life, with all powers of indignation, resistance, protest removed like a sting from a bee, thinking that unhappiness is happiness and torture is normal life. On this sombre note I must stop and go down to lunch. [...]

Yours ever, with much love,

Isaiah

PS I have had no time to write to you about Callas[1] – really like a nineteenth-century prima donna of a sinister kind, pale face, huge eyes, dominating, nasty, hypnotic, romantic, like Turgenev's mistress.[2]

TO OLIVER FRANKS

11 July 1958 [*carbon*]

[Headington House]

Dear Oliver,

[...] About Covent Garden. I think I ought to tell you about a meeting of the Opera Sub-Committee which was held yesterday, as I shall unfortunately not be able to be present on the 15th at the Board. The question of the Musical Director was much discussed, and Tom Armstrong[3] pressed the claims of Benjamin Britten. I was Chairman, and was perhaps rather weak: Jack Donaldson[4] and I (Tom Armstrong was the only other member of the Sub-Committee present besides the officials) were against it, he fairly vehemently and I more feebly. It is difficult to think of arguments against him, and he would certainly be a 'prestige' appointment and satisfy a section of the critics and the musicians; what I have against him is that he is part of the same gang as Webster and, not to put too fine a point upon it, opera is an essentially heterosexual art, and those who do not feel affinity with this tend to employ feeble voices, effeminate producers etc., which is a very large factor in our present misfortunes. [...] Here is Britten, a composer of immense talent – whose music I do not greatly enjoy, though I admire it and am prepared to concede that he is a composer of genuine genius – who has at Aldeburgh created a kind of sweetly arty-crafty little Festival to which all the members of his 'persuasion' flock, and it has its own quality no doubt, but it would be hateful to see Covent Garden going that way – indeed it is

1 Presumably a reference to Callas's appearance at the Centenary Gala of the Royal Opera House on 10 June, in a scene from Bellini's *I puritani*.

2 Pauline Viardot (1821–1910), née García, Spanish-born operatic mezzo-soprano, based mainly in France; though she lacked beauty, her personality, musical technique and passionate performances brought her a succession of male admirers, and the devotion of Turgenev, who came to live with the Viardot family.

3 Sir Thomas Henry Wait Armstrong (1898–1994), Principal, Royal Academy of Music, 1955–68; Director, ROH, 1958–69.

4 John George Stuart ('Jack') Donaldson (1907–1998), Baron Donaldson 1967, farmer; Director, ROH, 1958–74; later (1976–9) Minister for the Arts.

far too much that way already. I wish I did not sound so much like Maxwell Fyfe.[1] No doubt it will be thought unrespectable to oppose Britten, and yet I think it would be a genuine disaster. Garrett D[rogheda] certainly feels that way about it, but he is not a man of great strength of character and could yield to sufficient pressure. All I feel is that we are better off without any musical director at all than with the triumph of this particular faction; 'dixi salvavi' etc. etc.[2]

But even if I am wrong about all this, surely deferment in the absence of the Chairman can do no harm.

Yours ever,

TO JOHN PLAMENATZ
15 July 1958 [carbon]

[Headington House]

[. . .] I think I know the novel you mean[3] – though I do not know the title – there was a previous one in which I was supposed to figure as the central detective and the author, not at all a nice man, was very scared that I might sue for libel. No doubt I had excellent grounds, but as you can imagine I did not pursue the matter and let it go. To appear in a novel of this kind is rather like appearing in other people's dreams: and one cannot exactly avoid doing so, nor is one responsible for the shape one takes, and yet the results inevitably offend one. I wish people left one alone – that is a concept of freedom to which I adhere, but as I have now been reading a certain amount of Hegel and other similar writers my ideas are now in a whirl and, like you, I have become aware of the extreme narrowness and blindness of our education here, and of the fact that many things said about us abroad, which used to strike one as simply the unfair observations of half-journalists, half-charlatans, have a great deal of horrible truth in them. Even Stuart is, I think, reading Hegel. I wonder what it will all lead to.

At the end of July IB and Aline left Oxford for their holiday in France, Monaco and Italy; Aline's children joined them at Paraggi in late August. IB's main task on holiday was to prepare his Inaugural Lecture.[4] Dictation started on 29 August and the first draft was rapidly completed.

1 Sir David Patrick Maxwell Fyfe (1900–67), Viscount Kilmuir 1954, 1st Earl of Kilmuir 1962; barrister and Conservative MP; Lord Chancellor 1954–62.
2 See 48/3.
3 Plamenatz had apparently been given a copy of *The Naked Villainy* (London and New York, 1958), the second in a series of detective stories by Jocelyn Davey in which the central character, Ambrose Usher, was based on IB; the first book had appeared in 1956, as *The Undoubted Deed* in London and as *A Capitol Offense* in New York. 'Jocelyn Davey' was a pen-name of Chaim Raphael (1908–84), né Hyman Isaac Rabinovitch (British Information Services, New York, 1942–57; Information Division, Treasury, 1957–9, Head 1959–68), who also wrote under his own name on Jewish history.
4 Not entirely from scratch. IB had lectured on positive and negative freedom a number of times

TO MARIE BERLIN

Saturday. שבת שלום.[1] [30 August 1958?, *manuscript postcard*]

Hotel Argentina, Paraggi

Have just completed dictating into my machine a text of my Inaugural Lecture.[2] To read aloud it would take 4 hours or so. I doubt if my Oxford audience will like that much. So I must cut – at least for delivery if not for printing. But it is, pour le moment,[3] off my shoulders. I am said to look young, well, brown. I feel wonderful. Even the eye trembles no more![4]

IB

TO GLADWYN JEBB

1 September 1958 [*typed transcript of untraced manuscript original*]

Paraggi

Dear Gladwyn,

[...] I see the difficulties about *Dr Zhivago*.[5] The poet's efforts to get his characters into a plot and on to the stage are too clumsy and confused: the who's who unfollowable: and the incidents jerky and inconsequent. The book only really gets going when it becomes obviously autobiographical, i.e. with the 1914 war. I feel personally responsible for inflicting this on you and propose to persist: I have now piled Pelion on Ossa by ordering you the *English* translation, which is furnished with a list of characters, their relationships, etc. What can I do but utter encouraging cries? Obstinately cite the experience of other swimmers in those, at first, overgrown and overstocked waters, who, after an initial struggle, enter the great splendid lagoon – or real fleuve[6] – which begins after 1914? The marvellous pages (soaked, I admit, in Tolstoy, who brooded over Pasternak's childhood since his father was T's great and adored friend) are the Siberian ones – the civil war there, and the romance with a lady called Lara, who, some say, is a symbol of Russia, but who certainly exists in her own (unsymbolic) right. You need not bother *at all* about who is related to whom, and how – the plot, as in Tolstoy, is relatively unimportant – but the quality of Russia 1917–21, as felt by a civilised and Westernised figure, has never been described anywhere at all. And the 'metaphysical' excursions – Christianity and all – seem to me wonderful. Still, you may think it too boring to persist with, as some do with Henry James,

before, for example at Bryn Mawr and Yale, and in Jerusalem.
1 'Shabbat shalom' ('a peaceful Sabbath'), the conventional Sabbath greeting.
2 This first draft of the lecture survives on Dictabelts, which have been transcribed.
3 'For the moment'.
4 IB had been suffering from a trembling eyelid since early 1957.
5 The large cast of characters in *Dr Zhivago* initially hindered Jebb's enjoyment (of the French version). The English translation by Max Hayward and Manya Harari (London and New York, 1958) was published on 5 September 1958.
6 'River'.

Elizabeth Bowen, for example. And the first 100 pages or so *are* bad: like Virginia Woolf herself trying, with blind and ignorant aversion, to describe sexual relationships, like an outraged governess. But do try just once more. If *that* doesn't work (in the clumsy but faithful English rendering) I'll stop pestering you. We are here till the 12th: the Venice (philosophical) congress:[1] the confluence of philosophers, modern music amateurs and the usual Venetian congregation of mid-September will, I hope, be agreeably bizarre. We should be in Paris round about the 22nd or 23rd for a day or two before the gloomy return to Oxford where I have to deliver an 'Inaugural' lecture to celebrate my accession to a Chair which I've already held for better or worse for a year, under the Chairmanship of Vice-Chancellor Boase; my subject is Liberty, on which, I feel, rather too much has already been said during the last 300 years or so; my inspiration Benjamin Constant, a much underrated political writer, abler and more original as a theorist than anybody in his time: the only Liberal thinker of the first water, miles better than Mill, and even Tocqueville. But there, I must not go on: I must say it all to the boys in Oxford, a nice, mild, respectful captive audience who make all lecturers seem to themselves far more impressive than they really are. The undergraduates are *very* respectful in Oxford now: only the dons snarl and bite. I'll telephone you in Paris if I may.

Isaiah

TO RICHARD PIPES[2]

20 September 1958[3]

Headington House

Dear Pipes,

What an excellent idea – the notion of a book on the Russian intelligent-sia.[4] You are quite right about my views – nor am I in a condition to contribute anything to anyone just at present, being, as usual, overloaded. But the question of what the intelligentsia was, whether it exists, what the concept involves, whether it is co-terminous with liberal intellectuals in general or has a special meaning in countries like Russia or Spain, etc., should, I think, be ventilated. You ask about names and subjects. First about names. I have a feeling that one should be genuinely careful: Karpovitch is, of course an

1 The 12th International Congress of Philosophy, held (mainly) in Venice 12–18 September 1958.
2 Richard Edgar Pipes (b. 1923), Polish-born US historian, specialist on the Soviet Union; taught at Harvard from 1950; Frank B. Baird Jr Professor of History, Harvard, 1958–96 (Director, Russian Research Center, Harvard, 1968–73).
3 The date is almost certainly that of typing: IB appears to have dictated the letter in mid-September in Venice and sent the Dictabelt back to Oxford for typing on pre-signed paper. He did not return to Oxford until 23 or 24 September.
4 On 5 September Pipes had invited IB to contribute to a volume he was editing, eventually published as *The Russian Intelligentsia* in 1961.

excellent idea, the best possible – but he was not exactly a central figure of the intelligentsia type ever, I should have thought; in spite of all his left-wing antecedents. He is a little too respectful to established authority, has too much natural piety, so to speak, for that. Of course he does belong to it and understands it. Nevertheless, the real members of the intelligentsia – as I need not tell you – are the high-minded, liberal, anti-clerical, pro-Western, constantly indignant, old-fashioned radicals: to whom Weidle,[1] for example, most emphatically never belonged, and towards whom his attitude is courteously hostile. He was and is an aesthete (a very different thing) and a very nice, sensitive and honourable man and good writer. But if the line of division is one where writers like Tolstoy, Dostoevsky and even Chekhov fall on one side – not intelligentsia – with only say Turgenev among the great writers, and people like Ivanov-Razumnik,[2] his friends and heroes on the other, then Weidle and suchlike do not belong, whereas, let us say, Jakobson most emphatically does. I do not say that people who are not themselves members of a movement cannot describe it well, but where the issues are so hotly felt still I think you will find that on the 'right wing' there will be a tendency to discourage the radical intelligentsia. No doubt they were often foolish, pompous, madly irritating, etc., and generated a quite phenomenal quantity of platitudes, one way or another. Nevertheless, if they are to be taken seriously at all, I think perhaps a chance ought to be given to the real survivors. [...]

Perhaps Edmund Wilson ought to write something about the intelligentsia in general – what they are and where, in various countries – or Dwight Macdonald,[3] or both. These two are more like the old Russian intelligentsia than any American-born persons can ever have been. Or you might think of Meyer Schapiro, the art historian of Columbia University, who is a living incarnation of what this attitude and way of life are, and a very noble and distinguished one. Enough, enough.

As for me, I am painfully struggling with the material for an Inaugural Lecture on *Liberty* – as if the subject had not been sufficiently discussed in the last three hundred years or so – with an article for an Encyclopaedia on Karl Marx's views;[4] with a huge essay on Vico,[5] which I have just completed – I

1 Wladimir Ivanovich Weidle, sometimes 'Weidlé' (1895–1979), Russian-born art and literary critic and historian; taught at the Russian Theological Institute, Paris, 1924–52.

2 Razumnik Vasil´evich Ivanov-Razumnik (1878–1946), real surname Ivanov, influential literary critic, friend of Aleksandr Blok; linked to the Socialist Revolutionaries; recorded his frequent experiences of political imprisonment 1901–43.

3 Dwight Macdonald (1906–82), US political writer, cultural critic and editor; politically volatile former Marxist turned fierce anti-Communist; left *Partisan Review* to found and edit *Politics* 1944–9; long-term contributor to the *New Yorker*.

4 'Marx', in J. O. Urmson (ed.), *Concise Encyclopedia of Western Philosophy and Philosophers* (London, 1960); reprinted as 'The Philosophy of Karl Marx' in POI.

5 Giambattista Vico (1668–1744), Italian philosopher, jurist and professor of rhetoric, the subject of IB's 'The Philosophical Ideas of Giambattista Vico', in *Art and Ideas in Eighteenth-Century Italy*

do not know where it will be published – I think in the proceedings of the Italian Institute in London, of all places – with an old essay on Maistre which the *Partisan Review* have asked for[1] – it is certainly too long for anyone in England – but which is perhaps more suitable for the *Journal of the History of Ideas*; with Venturi's book, for which I promised to write an introduction,[2] and everything, in short, which keeps me from writing a proper book of dignified depth and size, such as you write. [...] Have you read Pasternak's novel yet? People here seem to disagree. I am clear that it is a work of genius. The first hundred pages are clumsy and awkward, he is obviously bored with having to get his people on to the stage, but the rest is magnificent. Is he a member of the intelligentsia, old or new? Not quite: too odd, too religious, too remote from the ideals of scientific enlightenment, political democracy etc. etc. But his father was. There really was a gap in 1910 between inspired symbolist poets on the one hand and bearded liberal professors and their followers on the other, and they did not belong to the same camp, though for political purposes they could unite. But there I go and must not start again. Do write to me again when you have leisure.

Yours ever,

Isaiah Berlin

IB's stay in Venice coincided with a visit by Igor Stravinsky, who was to conduct the première of his new work, Threni,[3] *on 23 September as part of the Venice Biennale. On 19 September Stravinsky, whom IB had met briefly in 1956, conducted his opera* Oedipus Rex *and his ballet* The Rite of Spring *at a concert in the Fenice Theatre: IB was overwhelmed.*

TO IGOR STRAVINSKY

21 September 1958 [*manuscript*]

Hotel Europa e Britannia, Venice

Milii[4] Igor Fedorovich,

This is only to say how greatly moved and delighted I was by being allowed to hear the Sacre[5] and Oedipus last Friday, and the rehearsals of them which you conducted, and indeed by being permitted to meet you – all of which

---

(Rome, 1960); reprinted in revised form in TCE. IB regarded him as 'one of the boldest innovators in the history of human thought' (POI 53).

1 This essay, which IB had worked on intermittently for many years, was not in the end published by the *Partisan Review*, or in the *Journal of the History of Ideas* (which wanted cuts and revisions), but eventually appeared in 1990 in CTH as 'Joseph de Maistre and the Origins of Fascism'.

2 Introduction to Franco Venturi, *Roots of Revolution* (London, 1960); reprinted as 'Russian Populism' in RT.

3 Stravinsky's setting of the Lamentations of Jeremiah for soloists, four-part chorus and large orchestra was his first entirely 12-tone composition.

4 'Dear'.

5 *Le Sacre du printemps* ('The Rite of Spring').

I owe to Nicholai N[abokov] – to whom I shall be eternally grateful. It is an impertinence on my part to inflict yet another fan letter upon you, but you will, I hope believe me, if I say that I am writing it – with embarrassment, since who am I to offer judgments on music, and still less, on his own work to a master of genius? – only because I cannot believe that you will too much dislike the expression of a feeling which is too strong and unique to be indefinitely repressed. I thought that the Sacre and Oedipus glowed with marvellous original colour and form, like the paintings of Carpaccio,[1] which time has done nothing to dim; that, despite the faithful but too Sachlich[2] German player, and in this fearfully corrupt and decadent town – worse than late Puccini, more *pourri*[3] than Alban Berg[4] – something so firm, so splendid, so marvellously made and untouchable by change in fashion and feeling, can still dominate everybody and everything, and stand up, and remain beautiful and elusively strong and faultless, in the crumbling of so much else – especially politics and philosophy with which I deal. It will sound sentimental and perhaps even rhetorical – but the experience has been, for me, transforming. How can I not attempt to say it, however badly? I write in English because although it is a luxury and a deep pleasure to me to talk Russian, I cannot write it: all the words become sticks. The gondola is bobbing up and down in the canal, and I must go to catch the train. This is the first, and probably the last fan letter which I shall ever have written.

I apologize for going on in this fashion – and only hope that you will allow me to see you again somewhere – perhaps you will, after all, come to old Oxford to collect a doctorate, not honoris but genii, causa[5] – what other way is there of expressing proper homage, how else can universities show that they are not philistine and sunk in their own lives? oh dear: I cannot write: all this is not what I should be saying: mes hommages[6] to Mme Stravinsky[7]

yrs with deep admiration,
    Isaiah Berlin

1 Vittore Carpaccio (*c*.1460–*c*.1526), né Scarpazza, Venetian painter.
2 'Mechanical'.
3 'Rotten'.
4 Alban Maria Johannes Berg (1885–1935), Viennese composer (influenced by Schoenberg, as was Stravinsky).
5 'For genius rather than as an honour'.
6 'My respects'.
7 Vera Stravinsky (1888–1982), née de Bosset, dancer, costume designer and painter; Stravinsky's long-time mistress, then second wife (he was her fourth husband).

TO ROBERT CRAFT[1]

5.50 p.m., 21 September 1958 [*manuscript postcard*]

Ferrovia, Venice

[...] I wrote a fan letter to S.: it is an absurdly pompous document which I regretted immediately [...] but I both wished to say that I had had a most moving & bouleversant[2] experience, *and* am too anglicized to be able to do it simply & convincingly. So do defend me if he mentions it: tell him I meant well & did what I could.[3] I shd *never* have left before Threni if it weren't for illness[4] & my stepchildren. More demanding than real children. And I much enjoyed our few brief conversations.

yrs
    Isaiah B.

Heat. Hurry. Lost Tempers. Glad to leave this Sodom.

TO ANNA KALLIN

25 September 1958

Headington House

Dearest N.,

My wound still smarts as you have so heartlessly refused to apply any balm to it. *How* can you deny that I was the victim of a *most* unprovoked act of *gratuitous aggression*?[5] However that may be, let me now reply to the message I received via Nabokov about my Inaugural Lecture. I am in my usual state of despair on the subject which will not be unfamiliar to you. This time from far graver intellectual causes than before – i.e., that I no longer know the truth and think that I shall utter not platitudes but confusions and falsehoods. In any case I would rather not have it recorded –

(*a*) because that would be (rightly) ill-viewed here – the thing appears in print almost immediately after – if of course I can get the MS out which is dubious enough. But the actual delivering must be *urbi* and not *orbi*.[6] About this I think local taste is quite right, and Auden had a genuine case.[7]

(*b*) Because I genuinely am determined to be faithful to my vow, made at

1 Robert Lawson Craft (b. 1923), US conductor and writer on music, whose close friendship with Stravinsky developed into an artistic partnership.
2 'Overwhelming'.
3 Robert Craft reported on 26 September that Stravinsky had been very touched to receive IB's letter – which, according to Craft's memoirs, *An Improbable Life* (Nashville, 2002), 220 note 2, Nicolas Nabokov purloined from Stravinsky's room in the Hotel Bauer Grünwald; Craft adds that Nabokov returned it to IB, but it is now among Nabokov's papers.
4 Miss Lee, the family's nanny, was suffering from phlebitis.
5 IB appears to have heard rumours that AK had referred to him disparagingly.
6 'To the city and not to the world'; see 118/4.
7 Auden had delivered his Inaugural Lecture as Professor of Poetry in 1956.

the time of the truncation of the Third Programme, that talks of an hour's length should be declined as occupying too great a proportion of the little time left for music etc. So long as the Third Programme is the mutilated fragment that it is, any plan to extrude music in favour of lectures on abstract subjects on that scale seems to me wickedness.

(c) I have forgotten (c). [...]

Yours,

Isaiah

TO DONALD FANGER[1]

1 October 1958 [*Dictabelt; inaudible matter conjecturally restored*]

[Headington House]

Dear Mr Fanger,

I envy you greatly. There is nothing I should like to do more than to spend some time in Moscow now, and indeed to see Pasternak. I'm sure you're quite right to take all possible reviews of *Dr Zhivago* to him, as no author can fail to be interested in the fate of his work, and Pasternak will be, if only [he is allowed to?], passionately eager to see you. I really do not know what advice to give you. I am not clear about what change in his circumstances has occurred since I last saw him in 1956 – he's clearly even more badly viewed than he was then, but whether a visit by you would compromise him it is difficult to say. The Soviet authorities are not at all surprised by the desire on the part of foreigners to see him – particularly now. Consequently from that point of view no great harm can come to him, as you are not, I imagine, a particularly marked man, else you would not have got a visa to stay so long.

It would be the greatest of kindnesses on your part if you could stop over in London, if only for the purpose of seeing his sisters, who live in Oxford, and whom Mimi Berlin[2] contrived to see. They would certainly fill you up with messages and it would be a most noble and disinterested act on your part. [...]

Everyone of course has praised it madly – but not very intelligently. The *Daily Express* (of all papers) is serialising it, and bits are being read in Russian on the Russian Service of the BBC, beamed to the Soviet Union – a rather dubious proceeding, I feel, but perhaps it will do him no harm. As for books

---

1 Donald Lee Fanger (b. 1929), at the time a PhD student at Harvard; later (1968–98) Professor of Slavic and Comparative Literature, Harvard. This letter arrived only after his (re-arranged) departure for Moscow as an exchange student.

2 Miriam ('Mimi') Berlin (1926), née Haskell; taught at Harvard 1951–6 (affiliated to Russian Research Center from 1956); Assistant Professor in Russian, European and Middle Eastern History, Wellesley College, 1958–75. In 1957 she had visited Pasternak at Peredelkino and reported his determination that *Dr Zhivago* should be published outside the Soviet Union, at whatever cost to himself: 'It does not matter what might happen to me. My life is finished. This book is my last word to the civilised world.' Miriam H. Berlin, 'A Visit to Pasternak', *American Scholar* 53 No 3 (Summer 1983), 327–35, at 333.

and periodicals, I do not know what to advise; there is no telling but what he might like *Lolita* – though I should strongly doubt it. It is a terrible reflection that nothing has been produced in the Western world in the last three, four, five years, or even longer, which seems worthy of him or likely to engage his interest. I think that if you simply took a selection of contemporary periodicals of the more literary kind, both English and American, of the last year or two, as well as French ones, particularly Sartre's – the numbers in which Kołakowski wrote his articles (*Temps modernes*, May–June and July 1958)[1] – that would fascinate him. I doubt whether he realises that his name is as world-famous today as it is. [...]

Yours sincerely,   [...]

TO LYDIA PASTERNAK SLATER

1 October 1958 [*Dictabelt*]

[Headington House]

Dear Lydia Leonidovna,

I am back – or rather you are – and I am in a state of hysteria about a forth-coming inaugural lecture, which is too long, unwritten (if you can imagine how these contradictories combine), and full of contemptible nonsense. I feel too tired and too depressed to do much about this now, but work day and night in order simply to write it all down, all for an hour's mockery by my colleagues. However, if it must be, it must be. Until 31 October I shall scarcely breathe. I wish I could retire.

I enclose a collection of American reviews of *Zhivago* sent to me by a friend. Everyone is full of praise, but the number of perceptive persons is very small. The only ones I thought were even tolerable were Chiaromonte in *Partisan Review*[2] (which I haven't got, alas), Crankshaw in the *Observer*[3] – who felt something – and a forthcoming piece by Stuart Hampshire in *Encounter*.[4] I saw with pleasure that one of your poems was used in the book itself,[5] and one in the *Times Literary Supplement*.[6] So the barriers have been lifted. Perhaps it was my absence abroad. But you really did me a grave injustice[7]

1 'Responsibility and History' (626/1), trans. into French by Anna Posner as 'Responsabilité et Histoire', *Les Temps modernes* (of which Jean-Paul Sartre was a founder, and at the time chief editor) Nos 147–8 (May–June 1958), 2049–93, and 149 (July 1958), 264–97.

2 'Pasternak's Message', *Partisan Review*, 25 No 1 (Winter 1958), 127–34, by Nicola Chiaromonte (1905–72), Italian writer and left-wing political activist (anti-Fascist and anti-Communist), who with Ignazio Silone founded and edited the liberal cultural-political journal *Tempo presente* 1956–68.

3 Edward Crankshaw, 'A Russian Masterpiece', *Observer*, 7 September 1958, 16.

4 'Dr Zhivago', *Encounter*, November 1958, 3–5.

5 'Fairy-Tale', LPS's translation of one of the poems in *Dr Zhivago*.

6 L. Slater, 'Translation from Pasternak' (first line 'It is not seemly to be famous'), *TLS*, 25 September 1958, 546.

7 For the past year LPS had been trying to secure publication of her translations of her brother's poems. Stephen Spender had rejected them for *Encounter* and LPS suspected IB (who regarded

in the entire matter – why, I cannot conceive; or rather I can, but would rather not formulate it even to myself.

And now I must collect some thoughts for the opening of the exhibition of your father's pictures in London, which I so rashly promised to open. Would you or your sister tell me what to say? You know that I am blind or nearly so about the visual arts, although I know something about music. Perhaps you would telephone one of these days and we could make an appointment to meet.

I heard works by Stravinsky this summer in Venice and I must admit that beside him everyone else – even my beloved Shostakovich – is nothing at all. He has been king of music now for fifty years, not without reason. I see nothing much to look forward to in any of the arts – *Zhivago* is the greatest possible reminder of how poor the West has become.

Yours ever,   [. . .]

TO EDGAR WIND

4 October 1959 [sc. 1958; *manuscript postcard*]

[Headington House?]

Thank you *ever* so much for your book.[1] I wish I could sit down & read it immediately instead of worrying about the mediaeval mysteries in a welfare state which is our academic life to a large & superfluous degree. I long to retire: and live in open idleness like one or two heads of Colleges that we know – there are enough ideas: they do nothing but get into people's heads, & as Heine said,[2] arm barbarians with just what they need to destroy us. Sorry about the apocalyptic tone of this. It is due to the 2000 "philosophers" of Venice.

Isaiah.

On 23 October Boris Pasternak was awarded the Nobel Prize for Literature 'for his notable achievement in both contemporary poetry and the field of the great Russian narrative tradition'.[3] He accepted by telegram – 'IMMENSELY THANKFUL TOUCHED PROUD ASTONISHED ABASHED PASTERNAK'[4] *– prompting an intense and vituperative Soviet press campaign against him.*

the originals as virtually untranslatable, but had suggested possible publishers for the translations) of conspiring against her; although she liked and admired IB, she had complained that his
'present power over literature, in fact over everything in every field, is at times almost disastrous,
I do not know how he contrives to hold everybody in such constant awe and fear of his casual
judgment' (LPS to Spender, 18 June 1958; transcript sent to IB by Spender [MSB 283/31–2, at 31]).
1 *Pagan Mysteries in the Renaissance* (London, 1958).
2 Heinrich Heine, *Zur Geschichte der Religion und Philosophie in Deutschland* (1834); translated by John
  Snodgrass as *Religion and Philosophy in Germany* (1882), book 3, 106 and 158–61; and see L 167 and
  POI ix, note 1.
3 *Les Prix Nobel en 1958* (Stockholm, 1959), 37.
4 Telegram of 25 October to Anders Österling [Swedish Academy].

Pasternak was expelled from the Union of Soviet Writers on 27 October and on the same day he renounced the award in a second telegram.[1]

TO DAVID ASTOR

27 October 1958 [*carbon*]

[Headington House]

Dear David,

As you can imagine, the position about Pasternak is very complicated. The only thing which deterred me in the past, and still does, from saying anything in public about him is that as I am (though this may be megalomania on my part) a fairly marked person from the Soviet point of view, this might do some harm. He tells all the foreigners he sees that he does not mind publicity for all the facts about himself, and is obviously in a genuinely exalted mood and prepared for martyrdom. Still I do not [believe] this gives us a right to press the martyr's crown upon his brow. When the BBC began broadcasting bits of the novel in Russian over their Russian service I thought that wicked irresponsibility, and I was very sorry to see the account of the Swedish article about him in *The Times* last week.[2] Every little thing may help to destroy him. Nevertheless I now see no reason why a profile should not appear, provided it suppresses some of the truth and omits his obviously anti-Soviet attitude. I should be very ready to help Crankshaw – although by now he must know as much as I do – but would rather not write anything myself, if only because the *Manchester Guardian* asked me to do something similar for them and I said I might if they did not print my name, and then after the fuss about the Nobel Prize I said I would rather wait. I do not know if I shall write anything for them, but if I do I think they will have to have priority as they asked me first and I have three-quarters said I would. But do tell Crankshaw to come and see me. I scarcely ever go to London now and should prefer to see him in Oxford.

If something awful happens to Pasternak, I do not want to feel that anything I did could have even remotely contributed to it. I tried in my time to persuade him to postpone the publication of the novel in Italy; he was very disdainful of this and chose open-eyed to do what he did, fully realising the danger to himself and his family. I was scolded severely for trying to save him from himself. Nevertheless I cannot bring myself to 'accept his sacrifice', as

---

1 'EN VUE DU SENSE QUE CETTE DISTINCTION SUBIT DANS LA SOCIETE QUE JE PARTAGE JE DOIS RENONCER AU PRIX IMMERITE QUI MA ETE ATTRIBUE NE PRENEZ PAS EN OFFENSE MON REFUS VOLONTAIRE' ('Because of the significance this honour has assumed in the society I belong to, I must decline the undeserved prize that has been bestowed on me; do not be offended by my refusal, which was not forced on me'). A facsimile of this telegram appears in Gerd Ruge, *Pasternak: A Pictorial Biography* (London, 1959), 122.

2 'Nobel Prize for Mr Pasternak?', *The Times*, 23 October 1958, 12.

the BBC said to his distraught sisters they were glad to do. I am sure you will understand and appreciate the moral complications of this whole issue, but to help Crankshaw cannot be wrong, so do tell him to talk to me whenever he likes – his piece on the subject is far and away the best that has appeared anywhere, just as his review of the book was the only one truly worthy of its subject (with perhaps Stuart Hampshire's) to appear so far.

Yours,

IB delivered his Inaugural Lecture on 'Two Concepts of Liberty' at 5 p.m. in the South School of Oxford's Examination Schools on what he called 'Black Friday',[1] *31 October. Beforehand, his self-confidence was low: 'the Inaugural Lecture is hell, pretty bad, long, empty, involved. Herbert Hart, who alone has seen it, rightly thinks poorly of it, it is like a piece of [a]tonal music in which the same row of notes repeats itself endlessly in a finite number of combinations.'*[2] *The occasion attracted a record audience from Oxford and beyond; those arriving too late for a place in the South School were accommodated in the North School, to which the lecture was relayed. By ruthlessly cutting his original text IB managed to keep close to the allotted hour. He improved his audibility by careful attention to diction, although not all those present immediately grasped his full meaning:*

He spoke for an hour and ten minutes, slowly for him, and it was a triumph. [...] I shall read [the text] myself, at least twice, as it was the tightest lecture I ever heard, and it would be hypocritical to pretend that I didn't miss a lot. I am so badly educated and I never heard of Fichte before, let alone understand his relationship to Hegel.[3]

Not all academics were so impressed:

secretly, I thought it disappointing. It was crammed with matter [...] but less general and also less original and less gay than I had hoped. In fact, it was almost a conventional piece of liberal school-philosophy, within rather narrow limits. I'm afraid Isaiah's genius is not really adapted to a formal lecture: like a natural, swollen, unharnessed torrent, its greatness depends upon its spontaneous overflow. He should talk, not write. [...] I think he took enormous trouble over his elocution: but that also reduced its spontaneity.[4]

The Oxford Mail *offered a balanced verdict:*

Though reading a prepared text, he made it sound spontaneous, and even argumentative. [...] The philosophy of his address was a fairly conventional

---

1 Letter to Anna Kallin, 24 October 1958.
2 Letter to Richard Wollheim, 13 October 1958.
3 *To Marietta from Paris* (37/2), 331; Susan Mary Patten had accompanied Lady Pamela Berry to the lecture.
4 Hugh Trevor-Roper, *Letters from Oxford*, 261.

liberalism [...] not a new version, but rather a rediscovery of a familiar one – like the cleaning of an old master whose details have long been obscured by time and neglect.[1]

TO STEPHEN SPENDER

18 November 1958

Headington House

Dear Stephen,

Thank you for your letter[2] about my lecture, it did appear after the proofs had gone, nevertheless I read it with the greatest interest and anxiety, as anything you say always affects me more directly than what is said by other people. I think you will find in the printed version, of which a 'compressed' (if such a thing can be applied to anything I do) version was spoken by me, things which answer your points. I did say that the idea of freedom which I discussed was primarily the child of a capitalist system,[3] and that where there was no private property and no desire to keep other people off, it was meaningless;[4] and you will find in the printed version something about the proposition 'freedom is a very different thing for an Oxford don than for an Egyptian peasant',[5] and about people who say that they don't want to have freedom if their brothers wallow in the mud (Belinsky[6] etc.), feel shame about hideous inequalities and about buying their freedom at the expense of that of the masses, which is as deep and as absolute a value as that of freedom but is not identical with it.[7] To feed and clothe people may be more important than to liberate them, and to talk about freedom to the naked and starving may be frivolous and heartless, but this doesn't seem to me to alter the fact that freedom, at least in one of its political senses, is freedom from interference; and the fact that other values may be more important, and incompatible with this – say love or equality or fraternity or friendly co-operation, or all the things that people like Rousseau and G. D. H. Cole[8]

---

1 'Oxford Diary', *Oxford Mail*, 1 November 1958, 4.
2 Spender wrote on 5 November suggesting that in his lecture IB had ignored physical and economic realities and that the 'unfreedom of whole populations' damaged others' enjoyment of their own freedom.
3 See L 217.
4 See L 171.
5 ibid.
6 'What is it to me that genius on earth should live in heaven, while the common herd rolls in the mud? What is it to me if *I* apprehend [. . .] the essence of art or religion or history, if I cannot share this with all those who should be my human brothers [...]?' Letter to V. P. Botkin, 8 September 1841, in V. G. Belinsky, *Polnoe sobranie sochinenii* (Moscow, 1953–9), vol. 12, 69; cf. RT2 194, L 172.
7 See L 172.
8 Cole received the published version (Oxford, 1958) shortly before his death and responded with enthusiastic praise of 'the best contribution by a living writer to social theory that I have ever read. [...] You have made me all the more pleased to have so vastly satisfying a successor.' Letter dated 11 January 1959, transcribed and sent to IB by Cole's family after his death on 14 January.

1. [14?]

TWO CONCEPTS OF LIBERTY.

Mr.Vice-Chancellor,

If men never disagreed about the ends of life, if our an-

cestors had remained undisturbed in the Garden of Eden, the studies

to which the Chichele Chair of Social and Political Theory is dedi-

cated, could scarcely have been conceived. For political studies

spring from, and thrive on, discord. This might be questioned. It

might be said, that even in a society of saintly anarchists, where

no conflicts about ultimate purposes can take place, political

problems - for instance constitutional or legislative issues -

might still arise. But this objection rests on a mistake. Where

ends are agreed, the only questions left, are those of means,

and these are not political but technical, that is to say, they

are capable of being settled by scientific experts , like argu-

ments between engineers or doctors; or perhaps by machines. That

is why those, who put their faith in some immense, world-trans-

forming, phenomenen, like the universal triumph of reason, or the

First page of the delivery text of IB's Inaugural Lecture, Two Concepts of Liberty, *1958*

believe in (for all their talk about liberty they prefer these warm-hearted and cosy things to liberty, which is not particularly warm and not at all cosy) – does not make liberty identical with them. 'Freedom for the pike is death to the minnows' – freedom for the English is oppression for the Irish, the Indians etc. – that is the great source of guilt in the nineteenth century. The proposition that freedom for the pike is compatible with freedom for the minnows is at the very least questionable; if it is not, leftists are of course faced with the dilemma, do we preserve the pike – because he is what Mill likes: original, enterprising, full of spirit, capable of creating much more interesting things than the dull minnows – or do we for decency's sake suppress the pike and make life tolerable for the minnows, although aesthetically this is going to be very depressing (e.g. the Soviet Union or Israel)? The one answer which seems to me to be a piece of straight hypocrisy is that the freedom of the pike *must be* compatible – always compatible – nay, almost inconceivable without – the freedom of the minnows. It is more plausible to say – more like life – that freedom for the pike means death to the minnows, and enough freedom for enough minnows death for the pike. The importance of freedom – at least one of the reasons for its importance – is that it is involved in the necessity for these hideous choices, the making of which liberals should certainly regard as an end in itself; the proposition that I cannot be happy unless everyone else is happy too, or cannot tolerate being free unless everyone else is free too, is to reject freedom ultimately in the face of equality, or else to assume that these things can be married to each other, when no one has any reasons for supposing this to be true. Oh dear, I am being even more obscure than in my lecture, but I will send you the text and you shall judge for yourself. ⟨Of course the notion of freedom depends on the 'concrete' social situation. But this situation hasn't in essentials altered all that much since the Middle Ages.⟩

What have you been saying about Pasternak? I cannot help thinking that the less said the better. But particularly by anyone in England or America, don't you? *Time Magazine* is to print a cover piece.[1] Hell. [...]

Yours ever, with much love

Isaiah

---

1 IB apparently asked his friend Raimund von Hofmannsthal, who worked for *Time* in London, to forward to his superiors in New York his assessment (included as an Appendix, 761–2) of the likely political consequences, and threat to Pasternak, of the proposed cover (Plate 38). His views were clearly ignored, as the cover and the related article, 'The Passion of Yurii Zhivago' (*Time*, 15 December 1958, 55–8), went ahead.

TO JAMES JOLL

25 November 1958 [*carbon*]

Headington House

My dear James,

What am I to tell you about the events of the term? It started off in a splendid manner by the denunciation of certain types of practice by one of the Professors of Theology, the Rev. Kilpatrick,[1] a man entirely unknown to me, who denounced immorality between older men and announced that the undergraduates were in grave danger. This was answered by a splendid letter[2] by the Warden of Wadham, who said that he knew that certain types of romantic friendship occasionally occurred, both in older and younger persons, but these things never led to anything further, that he knew far more about the subject than the Professor, and that the allegations were totally untrue and completely fantastic. The letter was an absolute master-piece and much enjoyed by all. Mr Hale[3] wrote some blush-making awful things about this in the magazine and Dr Creed[4] was with difficulty per-suaded by Nicholas and others not to send in a passionate letter saying that as a medical man of 30 years' standing he wished most powerfully to support the Professor of Theology and say there was indeed a grave danger and that these things must not be treated in a flippant way in which the *Oxford Magazine* treated them, but with the utmost gravity as a national issue on the eve of the Wolfenden debate.[5] The poor man is obviously off his head, which has been suspected for some time. This was followed by various local developments of the Pasternak case, which is an altogether graver issue. I have had a virtual rupture of relations with Dr Katkov as the result of his avowed activities in forcing the BBC to broadcast the text of the novel in Russian over their Russian service in instalments – the text was officially stolen[6] as the publishers stoutly denied giving it, although Mrs Harari doubt-

---

1 Reverend George Dunbar Kilpatrick (1910–89), Dean Ireland's Professor of Exegesis of Holy Scripture, Oxford, 1949–77.

2 No letter has been found, but Bowra's comments on the sermon as quoted in *The Times*, 14 October 1958, 13, and elsewhere match IB's description.

3 John Rigby Hale (1923–99), Fellow and Tutor in History, Jesus, 1949–64; editor, *Oxford Magazine*, 1958–9; later Professor of History, Warwick, 1964–9, Professor of Italian History, London (UCL), 1981–3, of Italian 1985–8.

4 Richard Stephen Creed (1898–1964), Fellow and Tutor in Physiology, New College, 1925–60; Chairman, Management Committee, Warneford Hospital, 1947–60.

5 The Committee on Homosexual Offences and Prostitution, established by the Home Secretary and chaired by Sir John Wolfenden, had in 1957 recommended the decriminalisation of most homosexual activity; the House of Commons debated the Report on 26 November 1958.

6 Allegations were made then and later that the CIA, with British help, had arranged an emergency stop of an aircraft in Malta in order to remove the manuscript from a passenger's baggage and photocopy it for clandestine publication in Russian, thus enabling *Dr Zhivago* to be taken into consideration by the Nobel Prize Committee (which required publication in a work's original language), and embarrassing the Soviet Union. See, for example, Peter Finn, 'The Plot Thickens', *Washington Post*, 27 January 2007, C1.

less knew all about it. I took the, for me, rather severe line that the danger to the poet was great and the advantage, even from the most extreme Cold-War point of view, not very great, and that playing about with lives in this way was a hideous immorality. Dr K. said that he had spent three sleepless nights pondering over it, but finally decided that Pasternak, particularly as he obviously wished to be a martyr, had to be sacrificed to the 'cause'. For once I find myself cosily ensconced with the Left. I have scattered letters in all directions complaining about this, caused the sisters to complain to Sir Ian Jacob and to write personal pleas to Mr Henry Luce asking him not to have a cover issue of the poet, and generally busied myself with what Silone calls the 'defence of the moral rights of Pasternak', for which he proposes to found a special society to protect him against Dr Katkov, *Time Magazine* etc. The BBC broadcasts were in fact the first move in a general succession which brought about the Nobel Prize scandal. If the Nobel awarders – and I do not really believe this was politically inspired – had only postponed their award for about a year, I think the poet would not have suffered quite so much. Of course he knew there was going to be a scandal and he did not really mind – he was obviously determined to speak across the heads of his jailers to the free world and succeeded – a unique event in our time – nevertheless just because someone is prepared for a martyr's crown, that doesn't give one the right to press it on his brow. The whole thing really is revolting. Stuart goes about complaining that major works of art should not be used for propaganda purposes – I agree but think that the personal safety of the poet is an even more important issue and that preaching aesthetic values to Dr Katkov or Mr Luce or the BBC does little good. The BBC sent a special man[1] to see me in order to explain their policy, but he obviously didn't believe a word he was saying himself, was extremely embarrassed, told me he thought I was on the whole right, but that he was paid to say the opposite.

What more can I tell you? I did deliver my Inaugural Lecture and carefully stowed away my non-academic visitors in such a way that they were not prominently displayed in the front rows à la Trevor-Roper. However the Chancellor insisted on coming and there was some problem as to whether I could address myself to the Vice-Chancellor. However I did so. There did appear to be a number of persons present, but in my usual way I could not look at anyone and was glad when the whole thing was over. The contents

---

1 James Monahan (1912–85), arts administrator, ballet critic and poet; BBC, Head of Western European Services 1946–52, Controller of European Services 1952–71, Director of Programmes, External Services, 1971–2; as 'James Kennedy', ballet critic (and film critic until 1963), *Guardian*, from 1945; later (1971–7) Director, Royal Ballet School. To Anna Kallin IB gave a slightly different account of the meeting: 'We were both clear at the end of the interview – he was perfectly courteous – that his explanation had had no effect upon me, I told him that I thought the act was immoral, he shook his head sadly and said that he estimated the risk as smaller than I did. I said that there was no excuse for fine calculations involving a man's security in situations which did not require any calculation at all. There we left it' (letter of 13 October 1958).

of my lecture were strongly approved of by Hart and disapproved by Stuart. Sparrow (I am afraid) thought quite well of it, whereas Dr Wind was I am sure more dubious. Richard thought it all true but not original, which is about right. Anyway it is all over and thank God. I hated doing it more than almost anything in my life.

Should Sparrow become Vice-Chancellor?[1] As he totally lacks public spirit, one would have said not. He certainly is most reluctant to do it himself. On the other hand, All Souls would be extremely displeased, and the University will finally relegate him into darkness – which he won't like – and ignore him even beyond the extent to which he chooses to be ignored by his own will. On the other hand if he does become Vice-Chancellor, he will certainly denounce women, Indians etc., and cause major scandals in the national press. On balance I suppose it is better that he should not be. He will be very ill-thought for it, but that I suppose was bound to happen in any case. We are all being consulted day and night as you can well imagine.

Maurice has been very ill – first flu and bronchitis and then pneumonia and the Acland Home. He is back in Wadham and very feeble and very conscious of who did or did not write to him, visit him, telephone, send champagne etc. Sparrow who sent champagne after all of us was judged to be very slow off the mark.

TO ROWLAND BURDON-MULLER

17 December 1958

Headington House

My dear Rowland,

You ask me about Nixon[2] and the Prime Minister. You must forgive me if this letter sounds rather exhausted, but I am just back from a peculiarly tiring meeting of the Covent Garden Directors in London, where stormy debates occurred about what operas to do and who shall do them. My colleagues have become rather turbulent, and as I am their operatic expert at the moment, I am covered in scars – honourable wounds of battle, but annoying nevertheless. Nothing makes a body of men more fierce with each other than aesthetic questions on which everybody, rightly I suppose, regards themselves as an ultimate authority and on which it is impossible to criticise views without appearing to insult other people's tastes. However that may be, let me get on to the subject of your fundamental enquiry.

We were very surprised to receive the Prime Minister's invitation. We are

---

1 The rotating Vice-Chancellorship of Oxford University was due to fall on All Souls in 1959; Sparrow agonised about whether to accept the post, consulted widely, and eventually turned it down.

2 Nixon was in England mainly to attend the dedication of an American Memorial Chapel in St Paul's Cathedral on 26 November.

not on visiting terms with him, and as I bear a peculiar hatred of Nixon – I do not know how deserved even now – and sympathise with all those in America who refer to him as a white-collar McCarthy, I was at first disinclined to accept. Aline however pointed out that it would be agreeable, once in one's life, to go to a formal banquet at 10 Downing Street, that we liked the Prime Minister and his wife particularly, and that meeting Nixon was no more degrading, if anything, less, than all those Soviet Russian worthies upon whom we lavished so much attention. How far I was convinced by this argument I am not sure, but I agreed that I liked the Prime Minister, liked his wife particularly, and accepted. I was aware that in some circles this might be criticised (dear Stuart, for example), but since I am adventurous in my social life, and intensely touristic, and since I had to admit that Nixon was certainly no worse than the bloodstained Russians, and his views not (morally) so very much worse than those of the Soviet Third Secretary or Mr Malik,[1] whom one would obviously be prepared to meet, perhaps there was not much in the moral argument. So after suppressing some qualms – Sparrow particularly enjoyed Stuart's indignation – we went. Macmillan was charming; firstly I like his face, secondly I like the fact that he enjoys his position so much and governs the country with such aplomb and success, and is not embarrassing like Eden (of whom later), and is a good deal less priggish than Gaitskell and not in any definable sense reactionary or hypocritical or Dulles-like in any way. His Balliol 1912 Christianity is not quite sympathetic to me – but one cannot have everything.[2] He was always very nice to me at the Beefsteak Club and places like that, and I cannot have it positively *against* him that he should have offered me a knighthood, and after all it was not his fault if I accepted it. His wife is genuinely sweet, and her private life fascinating to a degree[3] – I must not go on about this in a letter, for even now the facts are not all that discussible. Anyway we accepted. It was a curious dinner party: we were ushered into a handsome room in Downing Street, where we met Lord and Lady Baillieu[4] – a somewhat decayed industrial king whom I remembered in Washington – Canadian or Australian, I think, and his wife – with corresponding qualities. Behind them entered Sir William and Lady Rootes,[5] the motor magnate – he exactly as you would imagine, his wife

---

1 Jacob Malik, then Soviet Ambassador in London.

2 Cf. 'I am not at all surprised at Macmillan's rise to favour: he has *some* Rooseveltian properties – he is tough, very clever & *enjoys* power (such as it is), & is not full of hesitations & nervous wonder about means and ends like Gaitskell, who is like Stevenson.' Postcard to Arthur Schlesinger, 1 September 1958.

3 Lady Dorothy Evelyn Macmillan (1900–66), née Cavendish, daughter of the 9th Duke of Devonshire, had an affair lasting over 30 years with Macmillan's (bisexual) friend and political colleague Bob Boothby.

4 Clive Latham Baillieu (1889–1967), 1st Baron Baillieu 1953, Australian-born industrialist, and his wife, the former Ruby Florence Evelyn Clark (1892–1962).

5 Sir William Edward Rootes (1894–1964), 1st Baron Rootes 1959, motor manufacturer, who had married as his second wife (Ruby Joy) Ann Peek (1909–68), previously Mappin, née Duff.

unspeakable. Then appeared the Lord Chancellor and his wife,[1] the Foreign Secretary (his wife not there because she ran away with somebody some time ago – nor do I blame her);[2] our friends the Wheeler-Bennetts,[3] Sir Frank and Lady Soskice[4] (he was Solicitor-General in the Labour Government and is a very very high-minded man indeed, who taught me Latin for about a fortnight in 1921); Mr Willis, Chairman of the Trades Union Congress[5] (with whom Aline got on particularly well); Lady Brabourne;[6] and then entered the Americans – the Vice-President and Mrs Pat,[7] Senator Jackson of Washington,[8] Representative Canfield of New Jersey,[9] and two or three private secretaries, Parliamentary private secretaries etc., attached to the Prime Minister. This rather motley group wandered about in the drawing room, not quite knowing what to do, and I really did not feel happy until I saw my friend Julian Amery and his wife (Macmillan's daughter),[10] who admitted they were asked at the last moment because obviously various persons had refused. I enquired later as to who had refused and learnt that as Gaitskell had already seen him at the Pilgrims' Dinner[11] the night before and would see him at lunch the next day, and dinner again at the American Embassy, he did not, I must say, understandably, want to see him again so soon and so much. I have a notion that R. A. Butler also declined.

There he was – Nixon – looking rather louche, very vulgar; I was over-come with horror at his appearance and scarcely shook hands with him, certainly I uttered no words, nor did he, and for the rest of the evening I cannot tell you much about him, for I avoided him most studiously and saw

1 Viscount and Viscountess Kilmuir. She was the former Sylvia Margaret Harrison (1903–92), sister of the actor Rex Harrison, and after Lord Kilmuir's death married the 9th Earl de la Warr; Vice-Chairman, Conservative Party, 1951–4.
2 In 1957 Selwyn Lloyd became the first Cabinet Minister to remain in office after divorcing his wife (his former secretary, some 20 years his junior, who admitted adultery).
3 John Wheeler Wheeler-Bennett (1902–75), historian; Lecturer in International Politics, New College, 1946–50; Fellow, St Antony's, 1950–7; from 1958 helped set up the Ditchley Foundation, of which he was Founding Chairman 1961–3; a wartime colleague of IB's in the US. His American wife was the former Ruth Harrison Risher (1900–91).
4 Sir Frank Soskice (1902–79), Baron Stow Hill 1966, son of a Russian Jewish Menshevik journalist; barrister and Labour MP; Solicitor-General 1945–51, Attorney-General 1951; later (1964–5) Home Secretary. Lady Soskice was the former Doreen Isabel Cloudsley ('Susan') Hunter (1909–95).
5 Robert ('Bob') Willis (1904–82), printer and trades unionist; General Secretary of the London Society of Compositors 1945–55 and of its successor the London Typographical Society 1955–63; General Council of Trades Union Congress 1947–65 (President 1958–9).
6 Doreen (Geraldine), Lady Brabourne (1896–1979), née Browne, daughter of the 6th Marquess of Sligo, widow of the 5th Baron Brabourne; later killed in Ireland by the same terrorist bomb as Lord Mountbatten (662/3).
7 Thelma Catherine ('Patricia'/'Pat') Nixon (1912–93), née Ryan.
8 Henry Martin ('Scoop') Jackson (1912–83), Democratic Senator for Washington State 1941–83.
9 Gordon Canfield (1898–1972), Republican Representative from New Jersey 1941–61.
10 (Harold) Julian Amery (1919–96), Baron Amery of Lustleigh 1992, son of Leo Amery; Conservative MP 1950–66, 1969–92; junior ministerial posts in War Office 1957–8, Colonial Office 1958–60. His wife was Catherine (1926–91), daughter of Harold and Dorothy Macmillan.
11 Nixon had been the guest of honour at a lunch given by the Pilgrims of Great Britain in the Savoy Hotel on 25 November (the day of the dinner).

him towards the end of the evening, when the party occurred (of which
later), swaying I thought drunkenly in a corner, but about this I may be mistaken. Do not quote me, pray, for this is sueable. Presently we sat down to
table, and I found myself between Mrs Wheeler-Bennett whom I know well
here in Oxford, and the Principal Private Secretary,[1] whom I cross-examined
on the method of awarding honours to people, and how far they look into
private lives of people, and what is done about cases like Sir John Gielgud,[2]
which frightened them for good and all, since he was fined £5 in a park too
soon after getting his knighthood (and now an honorary degree). All this
was gay enough, while Aline was getting away with Mr Willis of the TUC
on one side, and less well with Mr Canfield of New Jersey. There was to
be a reception afterwards and so the dinner was brought to a fairly rapid
close. The Prime Minister delivered a short and perfectly decent little speech,
welcoming the Vice-President as Vice-President. The Vice-President replied
in a dreary political performance, which every one else thought quite well
of, but I thought poor. There is really nothing to report to you about dinner,
which was exactly like a dinner of dons or club-men almost anywhere – I
might have been dining at Christ Church as the guest of some professor, for
all the brilliance and gaiety that my neighbours or for that matter I myself
displayed. After dinner I was approached by the Prime Minister, who said
something about deciding not to invite the 'usual' people but something
'more amusing'. I was not sure that this was the highest of compliments, but
decided to take it as such and chatted amiably to him about persons of our
common acquaintance. The food was not too good – somewhat like a private
Christ Church dinner of a middling kind, the partridge was very tough but
not bad – the rest I fear contemptible. As for the wines I am no judge, but
Aline said it was tepid hock and very indifferent claret. Crème de menthe
was carried round later. The doors then opened and we were hurled into the
general reception which was far grander than the dinner itself. Enormous
numbers of persons in white ties and decorations, the entire Establishment,
in fact – the Treasury, the Foreign Office, Mountbatten,[3] Cabinet Ministers
who had not been at dinner, and the whole pride and glory of England. I met
all my old friends from Washington, all beribboned and bedecked with brilliant stars and enormous blue sashes stretching across their stiff shirt-fronts,
and introduced them all to Aline, who presently became bewildered by the
lists of names and titles. What was curious, however, was the absence of the
genuine aristocracy. No Salisburys, no Cavendishes, nobody much from the
House of Lords except Cabinet Ministers, no Mayfair, no society, save the

1 Frederick Arthur Bishop (1915–2005), Principal Private Secretary to the Prime Minister 1956–9.
2 The actor (Arthur) John Gielgud was knighted in June 1953 but fined £10 for homosexual impor-
  tuning in Chelsea a few months later.
3 Louis Francis Albert Victor Nicholas Mountbatten (1900–79), 1st Earl Mountbatten of Burma
  1947; Governor-General of India 1947–8; First Sea Lord 1955–9; Admiral of the Fleet 1956.

newspaper world (Lady Pamela Berry and the like), unsmart essentially but functional and important.

Nixon did not seem to me to move through this body too easily; considering that the day before[1] he had made so splendid an impression on the leaders of the Labour Party – I am told that Gaitskell and Aneurin Bevan cannot speak too highly of his intelligence and accessibility – and that on the next day when he came to Oxford[2] (though we were not here then, and indeed not asked) he made a most favourable impression on the hotly democratic and left-wing body of American Rhodes Scholars and Fulbright Fellows – considering in short that his visit was a triumphal success more with the left than with the right, that he answered all questions, it seems candidly and truthfully – made excellent jokes and delighted all our most anti-American and critical persons who had sworn to hate him and stayed to bless – considering all this, he cut a very poor figure at my dinner party. Nobody seemed anxious to speak to him; he was constantly left alone and the poor private secretaries had to march up reluctant figures saying loudly 'I am sure the Vice-President will be delighted to speak to Mr X', whereupon Mr X would uncomfortably stay for a few moments, desperately looking round for some opportunity to slip away or introduce someone to relieve him. I thought he was appallingly common and his wife worse. The American Ambassador[3] (I forgot to say he was present at the dinner too, as well as the British Ambassador in Washington)[4] obviously was not a great friend – and Nixon seemed to me to make every effort not to be identified with him, and indeed was obviously playing the part of a son of the people, a barefoot boy from Wall Street, terribly anxious not to be identified with the rich and the smart, and playing boldly and successfully to the gallery – our gallery as well as to yours. I am sure he would find it as easy to be a Socialist or a Democratic candidate as he does to be a Republican; that, I fear, is what found such favour in English left-wing eyes, so that not a word of criticism of him was uttered even in our left-wing press. Indeed David Astor, who kindly invited us to meet Stravinsky in London, to whom I spoke about him, spoke with furious indignation about the monstrous campaign against him conducted by the American left, which had fortunately not deceived the English, who had realised what a sterling true good man he was. Dear me. Why is it that I do go entirely on appearances? It seemed to me that he was a most shifty, vulgar, dishonest and repellent human being, with whom I should not care to have any relations at all. Am I mistaken? Is this unjust? On the whole, at the end of the dinner I approached Soskice, who I

---

1 In fact on 27 November, two days later.
2 On 28 November Nixon addressed 400 American and British undergraduates at Rhodes House, Oxford, and was enthusiastically received.
3 John Hay ('Jock') Whitney (1904–82), US Ambassador to Britain 1957–61.
4 Sir Harold Anthony Caccia (1905–90), Baron Caccia 1965, diplomat; Ambassador to Austria 1951–4, to US 1956–61.

thought might be sympathetic, and said that I felt some embarrassment at being present at this dinner at all, and that doing honour to Nixon was not something I ever thought I should be doing. He looked at me very sharply and said 'I do not understand this at all: I should understand it if you said that about those horrible Russians who come here, real thugs and murderers. But this seems a very nice sort of man.' One should remember of course that Sir Frank Soskice's father – unbeknown to most people but known to me – was Kerensky's private secretary,[1] and that he is in fact the son of a Russian revolutionary who obviously hated the Bolsheviks. But this seemed to be the general line taken by the left.

Dear Agnes Mongan lunched with us on the next day, together with the Winds, and had the full impact of our impressions. I do not think that I denounced Nixon quite as violently as I have to you, since I do not know her well enough to know how far I dare go. So far as I can see I was the only person in the British Isles who continues to hate Nixon. Everyone else is charmed. Very different was the impression made by his fellow Californian, Igor Stravinsky, whom we had seen in Venice, and who came to lunch with us here last Friday, or rather the week before. He was absolutely charming. He is far tinier than anyone supposes, and his face has a kind of ceaseless mobility which makes it fascinating to look at as well as to listen to. He appeared with his amiable, blowsy wife, whom he married in Boston in 1940, and talked delightfully about all kinds of things. We took him to the Ashmolean, and Sparrow gave a little party for him, or rather we gave a party in Sparrow's drawing-room for him, and dear Stuart came despite our sin in shaking hands with Nixon. John Bryson[2] talked nicely to Madame S., which was right, efforts were made to persuade him to attend a performance of his own opera, *Oedipus*, which the undergraduates were performing that evening, but he stubbornly refused. The thing in Oxford that made the deepest impression on him in previous years was Gerald Berners's house[3] – he could not forget the painted pigeons which walked about on the lawn – do you remember them? And Madame S. said she brought special saffron with which to dye some of the birds – and he remembered too those extraordinary masks of dogs with which Gerald used to cover the faces of the busts of his ancestors in the hallway – that world has gone and bitterly does he regret it. He is a staunch American patriot and a stout-hearted Republican, like Nixon (are you not a registered Republican too?). I do now remember a

1 David Vladimirovich Soskice (1866–1941), né Soskis, Russian-born journalist and revolutionary campaigner, who settled in Britain, returned to Russia in 1917 and briefly formed part of the secretariat of Alexander Fedorovich Kerensky (1881–1970), Prime Minister of the Provisional Government of Russia July–November 1917.

2 John Norman Bryson (1896–1976), Fellow of Balliol 1940–63, Tutor in English and Librarian 1949–61; a connoisseur of art, music and the theatre.

3 Faringdon House, Berkshire, where the fantail pigeons were often dyed to match their owner's mood.

conversation with the American Congressman from New Jersey, whom I asked when I sat next to him after dinner whether he hated Roosevelt. He said he hated no one. He said that during Democratic landslides he was always elected by large votes in New Jersey, because everyone knew that he was secretly for all constructive measures, whether they were Roosevelt's or not. I asked him what he felt about the future of the administration. He was not sanguine. He did not think the Republicans would be re-elected, and showed no great love for Nixon, and not much respect for Eisenhower. Despite all this he was pretty stupid. He was like the man in those little drawings by Gluyas Williams,[1] if you remember them – the average little American Babbitt, with a kind heart and no intelligence whatever, steadily voting for the stupidest and dullest party on principle. However, he was in some sense sweet, which his party leader was not. I cannot help feeling that Nixon is a kind of Poujade[2] (that is what I got into trouble with David Astor for), and my hatred for him is increased rather than decreased by seeing him plain. I really must not go on. I daresay your Mr Kennedy[3] is just as bad. Who are you going to elect as President? I asked Stravinsky that, but he did not seem very interested and thought poorly of all the candidates. I was able to tell him when later we dined with him in London after one of his concerts that I had in between met a delegation of Soviet students here who said that the things which had most shocked them in England were (*a*) the inferior quality of lectures on logic at the University of Liverpool – I was able to do little to reassure them on that point, knowing nothing of the University of Liverpool – and (*b*) the terrible goings-on in the University of Bangor in North Wales, to which I myself was proceeding in two or three days' time to deliver some lectures. I pressed the leader of the students' delegation about Bangor and she said that they were of course expecting rock and roll, but that what they saw in Bangor at a students' dance was far far worse. Not only kissing, not only embracing, but ... she was unable to go on. At this point she called for the support of three of her fellow students (as is always the case with Soviet students, persons of between 30 and 40, mature schoolmistresses with good party records) and they all expressed horror at the unspeakable orgies which they were forced to witness at a student dance at Bangor. I did not know what to say. We were surrounded by students, both English and Russian, and I felt that I had to make some kind of statement. 'I see you do not believe in personal liberty' said I feebly. 'That you, a Professor, into whose care young people are entrusted,' said Madame Titova, 'you, who have had so much rich experience of students and other young people, that

1 Gluyas Williams (1888–1982), US cartoonist.
2 Pierre Poujade (1920–2003), French politician who during the 1950s launched a movement of small businessmen against government tax regimes and the impact of social and economic change.
3 John Fitzgerald Kennedy (1917–63), Democratic Senator for Massachusetts 1953–61, who narrowly defeated Nixon in the 1960 election to become US President 1961–3.

you should make a remark of this type is perhaps the most horrifying thing that we have heard in this country yet!' 'But surely these young people were not doing any harm?' said I. 'Not doing any harm? They were spreading vice. Do you call that doing no harm?' At this point I felt that some stronger measures were required, so I delivered a sharp lecture on how people always reacted against their parents, how the Russians were puritanical because the Whites were so loose and promiscuous, whereas German Communists were themselves given to loose living because their parents were strait-laced Junkers. This did not seem very convincing, as I was told they knew nothing about the Germans and the Germans were disgusting anyway. I then moved up some heavier armour, and I said that the behaviour of Soviet troops in Central Europe had been pretty shocking to some people. I was interrupted and told about the horrors which the Germans had perpetrated in Russia. I said I knew all about that and they had not behaved themselves too well in Holland or France either, but that we fully realised that the behaviour of Soviet troops was due to the way they were brought up, the particular standard of culture, and to the kind of forces against which they were reacting, and did not condemn them too much for it. Surely they could show the same degree of understanding and toleration for the poor unhappy students of Bangor? On this our first encounter ended. Stravinsky said that far the most horrifying thing which had happened was obviously the total lack of humour on the part of these sad Soviet visitors, who obviously were very unlike the Russians of his day. On the next day I showed my Russians – thirty in all – round All Souls. They enquired as to whether the portrait of Lord Halifax in the hall was a portrait of the 'terrible Foreign Minister of 1939', and I was unable to deny that this was in fact the case. I then led them into the Codrington Library, where they suddenly fanned out, ran round the place and began to interfere with the readers in the sense of looking behind their backs, seeing what they were writing, creeping up behind them, standing up and looking at the shelves, and otherwise making a nuisance of themselves. I apologised to the librarian and finally managed to shepherd them out in fairly good order. One of the young women came up to me with blazing eyes and said that not only had she discovered in Birmingham that her birthplace, Murmansk, was described in some Birmingham geographical lectures as a frozen desert – whereas it was covered with factories, shops and other delightful forms of human activity – but she had seen a volume of history dealing with world history in 1940 which had not even mentioned the German invasion of the Soviet Union. I pointed out as calmly as I could that it was difficult for books dealing with the events of 1940 to describe the events of 1941, but waiving that, I said I did not think it credible, though I did not doubt her veracity, that English history books dealing with 1941 should omit the invasion of the Soviet Union, and demanded to see the offending text. She took me to the centre of the library and there before the bemused eyes of the readers she pulled out triumphantly a volume of the *Journal of Modern History* for 1941 and said that in the index[1] the Soviet Union was not mentioned. It took me a long time to explain to her that a volume of a journal printed in 1941 would not necessarily be dealing with the events of 1941, but on the contrary with those of the thirteenth and seventeenth centuries, as it happened. In the end I did convince her and she apologised. But, throughout, my Soviet delegation, though sweet, as they always are, were singularly truculent and in the end observed that England was a decadent country, that our undergraduates did not know what to do with their lives, that the proportion of workers' and peasants' children in Oxford seemed not at all high (there are no English peasants, I said sourly; 'you know what we mean,' they said, and I was forced to admit that I did), and in general that they were shocked and surprised by the decadence, the lack of masculine vigour, the feeble courtesies of life here. They were singularly shocked by the existence of scouts.[2] Someone asked some of them whether there were no batmen in the Russian Army. This they denied. It took them about half an hour's argument to convince them that everyone who had ever served anywhere near the Soviet Army was perfectly aware that even the lowest rank of Soviet officer had batmen, and that all Russians above a certain station had domestic servants in any number. [...]

  Yours with deep affection
     Isaiah   [...]

TO EDMUND WILSON

23 December 1958 [*manuscript*]

                                                        As from Headington House

Dear Edmund

  I only received the cutting from the *New Yorker* – & the entire magazine at the same time – 10 days ago. My first instinct on reading your article on *Zhivago*[3] was to send you a deeply "*прочувственную*"[4] cable, saying that this is the best piece on it which has been, will be, could have been, could be, written on it by anyone anywhere: then I remembered that you had accused me of a tendency to hero worship, and this charge, true enough, inhibited me from so naked a display of cult of (your) personality. But the facts which moved me, persist. In the welter of what has been said and written about *Doctor Z.* your essay alone is worthy of being put beside the novel. The last paragraph moved me literally to tears – & when I read & re-read the essay, produced the

---

1 sc. list of contents.
2 Domestic staff in Oxford colleges.
3 'Doctor Life and His Guardian Angel', *New Yorker*, 15 November 1958, 201–26, in which Wilson concluded that *Dr Zhivago* would 'come to stand as one of the great events in man's literary and moral history [...] a great act of faith in art and in the human spirit'.
4 'Prochuvstvennuyu' ('heartfelt').

same effect. This, you could rightly remark, is merely a fact about me and not about your critical gift or *Dr. Z.* Possibly. But, living as I mostly do in the pre-1917 world, I would rather not suppress it. If you had not written as you did, then in spite of the perfectly sincere & touching response of Pritchett,[1] Crankshaw, Chiaromonte & even the old racketeer J. B. Priestley, the reception of *Dr. Z.* in the West would have remained inadequate. As it is, all is much better than we could have hoped for. There is no need to feel shame vis a vis Boris Leonidovich. *He*, if he has (as surely he must have) read your notice, must be satisfied that someone has seen the full point. As you know, he is terribly concerned with the proper understanding of his *aveu*.[2] He is probably the last Russian *pisatel'*[3] standing in a public place & testifying to the truth. What you have written is no less true & absolutely wonderful: & will stand up for years and years in its own right as an independent masterpiece, morally and as literature. If this is hero worship, *пусть* так и будет.[4] The sisters in Oxford are dreadfully worried about the whole thing, especially about the use of it (shameful it is too) made by the B.B.C. which broadcast Z. in Russian, serially, on its Russian service. That, & P.'s appearance on the cover of *Time* will do him some harm. Or perhaps he is beyond it all. He seems like Tolstoy in 1903 or so, when all the disseminators of his gospel were punished by the government, but the old man himself was too eminent & odd to be touched by the police. Or like Chaadaev[5] who was, you remember, declared a lunatic in 1835 (I *think*) for libelling his country's culture, & denounced in terms which, *ceteris paribus*, are very similar to the attacks on P. – a doctor was sent to examine Chaadaev weekly – the same seems to have been done to P. – he was a public enemy too dotty to be touched officially – & pilgrimages by foreigners to his house in Moscow were very similar to the endless stream of foreigners & Russian students who are trying to see the poet. Both enjoyed it. Your piece is very like the accolade given Chaadaev by Herzen (but you don't share my boundless admiration for H. I seem to remember). The sisters declare that their brother was entirely untouched by Russian orthodox theology before 1936: & I saw no traces of it in 1945. All *that* is a late accretion. He is a Jew on both sides, his father painted Zionist worthies in the twenties & thirties & *Gordon*[6] is a plain effort to canalize all this off & remove the curse which B.L. obviously thinks a bore & a nuisance. Merry Xmas: Lehithraoth:[7]

    Yrs devotedly
      Isaiah B.

1 Victor Sawdon Pritchett (1900–97), writer and critic, who reviewed *Dr Zhivago* in 'In the Great Tradition', *New Statesman*, 13 September 1958, 354–5.
2 'Avowal'.
3 'Writer'.
4 '*Pust'* tak i budet' ('*Let* it be so').
5 Petr Yakovlevich Chaadaev (1794–1856), Russian philosopher certified insane for his criticisms of Russia in his *Philosophical Letters* (first published in French in 1829).
6 Zhivago's friend Misha Gordon is the main Jewish character in the novel.
7 'Goodbye'.

TO MIRIAM LANE

1 January 1959 [*manuscript*]

[Gare de Lyon, Paris]

My dear Toth,[1]

I have hunted high & low for a young man for you:[2] but I am not one to ask: I see few young men of a possible kind: I live at home and (believe me – Aline is at last a witness – nobody ever knew before) work. Unprofitably. I tear up everything; but I do. I work slowly, painfully, unsuccessfully, self-destructively, you say anti-semitically. I take little pleasure in it. I do it because of lack of imagination: set on this course, I continue. I do not find work boring, at least not ¾ of the time, only difficult. I like little that I read by others, if it is serious: then it seems to me inadequate: especially profound works praised heavily by humourless critics (Eliot, Philip Toynbee (probably) Alix, even dear Stuart – [destroy this!])[3] only frivolous ones do I really like, even if not very good: Diana Cooper,[4] Rachel,[5] Roy Jenkins,[6] gossipy memoirs, light novels, intellectually unexacting things. I fear things are getting very serious. I am felt to be somewhat ironical & not quite filled with solidarity for their work by my more respectable colleagues: they cannot quite put a finger on it: outwardly all seems conventional enough: I lecture: undergraduates come like sheep: they too vaguely feel that what I give them is not quite right for their studies, but they are less dogmatic & watchful. In the end nobody – if ever it comes into their heads to ask themselves the question – will quite know what to say about me: did I produce *anything* worth while, ever? was I ever worth anything to anybody (serious)? it won't be ruled *out*: but neither will it be indisputably *in*. Like John Foster, rather, in its own way. Not in the central stream of anybody, & not an individual little stream of a classifiable kind either. But I am not really very concerned, else I should, out of ambition, find a leader (I couldn't *lead*) & be counted. [...] A few more hours in Paris & I am off to London which I *much* prefer: Italians, Russians, Englishmen, Americans, anything but frogs. *Why* did the Rothschild family set up its centre in *Paris*? It does not really suit the genius of our race: too dry, calculable, inhuman, self centred. [...]

love

Isaiah

---

1 IB's nickname for ML (who spelt it 'Thoth'), based on her supposed facial resemblance to one of the four Egyptian Pharaohs called T(h)othmes (probably Thothmes III).
2 ML was looking for a tutor for her son.
3 IB's brackets.
4 Who had recently published the first volume of her reminiscences, *The Rainbow Comes and Goes* (London, 1958).
5 Rachel Cecil had written a novel, *Theresa's Choice* (London, 1958).
6 Roy Harris Jenkins (1920–2003), Baron Jenkins of Hillhead 1987, politician and biographer; Labour MP 1948–76 (Home Secretary 1965–7, 1974–6, Chancellor of the Exchequer 1967–70); later, founding member of Social Democratic Party 1981, Chancellor, Oxford University, 1987–2003. IB presumably refers to Jenkins's biography *Sir Charles Dilke: A Victorian Tragedy* (London, 1958).

TO A. J. AYER

9 January 1959

Headington House

Dear Freddie,

Yes, of course. I am sorry I shall not be able to come to your lecture at the British Academy,[1] but I have had to agree to stay here to attend a Committee which proposes to transform PPE in a very disastrous way. I have sent off a spiffing testimonial[2] – all that I could say I said. I should be extremely pleased if anyone said a tenth part about me in any connection. On the other hand, I don't think they will respect my views in this matter in the very least. Still it does not matter what anyone writes, you are far too well known. My main point was that you would transform the scene here and possess prestige mondial[3] of [an] unprecedented kind, and that it was immodest of me to praise your intellectual properties, which anyway they knew far too well and admired far too much for me to enlarge upon them. However it does say what an excellent lecturer, teacher and organiser you are, and how immortal your writings are bound to be.

Yours ever,

Isaiah

⟨*I* think you may well be elected: I shall be *very* pleased & think it merely *just*.⟩

In late 1958 IB had been one of over 50 distinguished Jews around the world to be handed a poisoned chalice by David Ben-Gurion. Responding to a consultation about one specific matter, how Israel should treat the offspring of certain mixed marriages, meant confronting the whole question of whether Israel should be a secular or a religious state. IB discussed the matter with Sir Leon Simon,[4] another of those consulted; both were unenthusiastic about the task they had been set.

1 On 'Privacy', delivered 14 January 1959, *Proceedings of the British Academy* 45 (1959), 43–65.
2 Enclosed with a letter of 9 January 1959 to the Registrar, Oxford University. IB comments: 'If he is not an innovator of genius, in the sense that Moore, Russell or Wittgenstein could be so described, his intellectual power is great, and his gift for lucid and elegant exposition is unique in his generation – not inferior, it seems to me, to that of Hume or Mill or Russell; and as in their case it amounts to a high philosophical talent in itself. [...] Mr Ayer is a born teacher, with the power of stimulating pupils second to none. [...] Polemical and competitive by temperament, he has not, I think, found opponents fully worthy of his steel in London, and it is probably this, more than any other factor, that has led to a certain monotonous, and unexpectedly staid, quality in his latest productions. [...] whatever impression he may have left on those who saw him only as the *enfant terrible* of Oxford philosophy in the 1930s, he is today a kind and responsive human being, and a most conscientious and intellectually responsible colleague. [...] He would, I feel sure, make an admirable, and perhaps memorable, Wykeham Professor of Logic.'
3 'Worldwide influence'.
4 Sir Leon Simon (1881–1965), former UK Civil Servant (GPO); Chairman, Executive Council, Hebrew University of Jerusalem, 1946–9, Board of Governors 1949–50; President, Israel Post Office Bank, 1950–3.

TO DAVID BEN-GURION

23 January 1959

Headington House

Dear Mr Prime Minister,

I must begin with a number of apologies. The first for delaying for so many weeks in answering your enquiry[1] (which I received towards the end of last year, about a month after the letter was dated), with regard to the definition of Jews in Israel, and with special regard to the problem of the children of a certain type of mixed marriage. I must apologise also for not replying to you in Hebrew, a language which I love so much more deeply than I know it that it may be that I have not perfectly understood the sense of your letter, and for this too I must ask to be forgiven; and finally, for the observations that I am about to make.

I was naturally greatly honoured by the fact that you should have considered me worthy of being consulted on a matter of such importance; and it is not only because of the intrinsic interest and urgency of the matter, but, far more, because of the deep respect (as you must know) and admiration which I feel towards yourself and the principles for which you stand, that I have done my best to produce an answer. At the same time I should not be wholly candid if I did not add that your letter placed me in a somewhat embarrassing, not to say false, position: for I do not believe that much good can be done by consulting anyone outside the frontiers of the State of Israel on a matter which is not only ultimately, but immediately, the administrative responsibility of the Israeli Government itself, and can be settled only by it and the Knesset. You speak, unanswerably, of the bonds that unite the Jews of Israel with the Jewish community in the rest of the world: nevertheless a minute examination of these bonds is bound to bring up issues concerning which there may be profound disagreement, not merely between Israel and the Diaspora, but within Israel itself, and the Diaspora itself. In so far as Israel is a sovereign State, founded to give full political and social expression to the Jewish nation, it must (and does), whenever critical issues present themselves, act on its own responsibility as a sovereign State, and on behalf of what it conceives to be the interests of the nation of which it is the political expression, without responsibility to, and without being obliged to seek the advice of, Jews beyond its borders. It cannot (and would not wish to) escape the judgement of public opinion among the Jews of the world, any more than a British Government could escape the judgement of many men of British race in other parts of the world. But it cannot be guided by such

---

1 Ben-Gurion's Hebrew letter, dated 27 October 1958, described administrative difficulties concerning the registration of the offspring of a Jewish father and a non-Jewish mother who had not converted to Judaism, listed the considerations of principle to be taken into account in deciding who should be granted Israeli citizenship, and sought advice on the appropriate legal provisions.

opinion directly. If, of course, the Jews are to be conceived as principally a *religious* establishment – a kind of Church – then nothing is more natural than to seek the expression of the views of the members of the Church before an important decision by the leaders of the Church is made. But I cannot believe that you hold this view. It appears to me, and I am sure you will agree, that the status of the Jews is unique and anomalous, composed of national, cultural, religious strands, inextricably intertwined. To attempt either to affirm their indissolubility, or to attempt the separation of these strands, must inevitably lead to much deep and bitter disagreement. It seems to me that unless and until it becomes imperative, as it may one day, to face Jews with so crucial an issue, little advantage is to be gained from doing so. It does not seem to me that the case concerning which you have formulated your enquiry is crucial in this extreme sense, and that therefore little good and perhaps some harm could result from forcing an alignment on it, i.e. by getting various individual Jews to state their cut-and-dried opinion on the subject, declare themselves, and fly a flag.

If, of course, you think that a *Kulturkampf* [1] is, in any case, inevitable, that the civil status of the State of Israel must be sharply and definitively divided from Judaism as an established religion (a point of view with which I have some sympathy), and that this is the moment to establish once and for all the principle that a modern liberal State is, and must be, secular in character, and that the religion of its citizens is, in so far as it is a State and nothing else, indifferent to it, then you may be right to issue such a questionnaire. I myself feel qualms before adding even my own minute drop of fuel to what is not yet a major conflagration. I was much tempted to follow the example of my illustrious friend Justice Felix Frankfurter, and refrain from giving a definite reply to your questions. But I have not his protection of judicial neutrality in political matters; and I therefore do append an answer (which does not satisfy me, but is the best that I can produce) because my regard for your person is greater than my wish to preserve myself from error by refusing to commit myself, where factors are so precariously balanced and in a field where I am (and am known to be) an ignoramus, and the issue so dubious. This is my only reason for sending a reply. I have shown it to Sir Leon Simon, and find that while I share some of his views, I do not share others. I am neither a rabbi, nor a lawyer, nor a specialist in Jewish history or sociology: my opinion is not, you must believe me, worth much: but I cannot bear to be so self-regarding or self-important as to decline to give it because it is not weighty enough, or may expose me to justified (or unjustified) criticisms.

I hope profoundly that it will not be necessary to advertise the results of this great enquiry in any way – not only that individual replies will be

1 'Culture struggle'; a term applied to the policies adopted by the Prussian Chancellor, Otto von Bismarck, during the 1870s to reduce the power of the Roman Catholic Church and strengthen moves towards secularisation.

treated as confidential;[1] and that when the Government finally acts it will do so without too much regard for, and too much open debate with, its outside advisers. I hope you will forgive me for all this gratuitous advice in your uniquely responsible and historic predicament. It is not meant to be officious or immodest.

I should like to say once more how deeply I appreciate the fact that you have done me the honour of asking for my views.

Yours sincerely,
Isaiah Berlin

TO MORTON WHITE
6 February 1959

Headington House

Dear Morton,

I long to write you a long letter but have really nothing much to write about. Arthur and Marian have been here and very delightful it was to see them. It is rather sweet and rather touching to hear Arthur talking in a romantic way about how he likes ladies to wear jewellery and use foundation cream and be elegant and rich-looking and wonderful and glamorous: it is all marvellously innocent and sweet, and he really has a very nice, uncomplicated, generous, pure nature. Marian looked almost too soignée – I was sorry not to see more of them, they came on a weekend when there were too many people wanting to see them, American students (they seem to batten indifferently upon Democrats and Republicans, Arthur and Nixon). [...]

[...] Koestler's book[2] is extraordinary: I have only browsed about in it but it is plain that he identifies Galileo with Communists or fellow-travellers and consequently stoutly takes the side of the Roman Church, loves Kepler,[3] with whom he identifies himself (partly because of the similarity of their names?) because he is a man both of faith and of science, whereas Galileo stands for nothing but horrible, naked, arrogant reason, and compromised the cause of mankind by tactlessly pushing forward his rational wares when a little more 'insight' and modesty and humanity would have prevented the terrible breach between science and faith into which the Church was forced

---

1 IB's reply, printed below (763–7) as an Appendix, was in fact included (in its original English form) in two mimeographed pamphlets: the first of these (untitled) was produced by the Prime Minister's Office in Jerusalem in 1959, and not continuously paginated; the second appeared in 1969 under the title *Miqra'a be-inyan 'Mi Yehudi': Qovets teshuvot shel hakhmei Yisrael ve-nispahim* ['A Reader on "Who Is a Jew?": A Collection of Answers by Jewish Intellectuals, with Appendices'] (IB's letter at 78–82). It has also been published in Eliezer Ben Rafael (ed.), *Jewish Identities: Fifty Intellectuals Answer Ben Gurion* (Leiden/Boston, 2002), 168–76.

2 *The Sleepwalkers* (London, 1959), a study of the history of astronomy and cosmology.

3 Johannes Kepler (1571–1630), German astronomer, who combined religious and scientific theories in his works.

by Galileo and from which we have been suffering ever since. This, as Stuart pointed out in a review, is exactly what has been said about Pasternak by the fellow-travellers here – *just* when things were getting better in Russia, this 'idiot' insisted on writing and publishing his idiotic upsetting book, and a lot of horrible Westerners thereupon shied away from the Soviet Union, and the breach was widened; and the liberal tendencies in Russia, just about matur- ing, were inevitably extinguished. I see that Koestler has done this to the seventeenth century, and that this perhaps is a trend of the times. Although I have greater respect for Niebuhr than you have, if that is what we are to face, I cannot doubt which side of the barricades I am on: I dislike almost equally (as you would if you were here) the new Marxism preached by sincere and muddleheaded people here: an attempt to produce a kind of amalgam out of Hegel, the young Hegelians, the early ('humanistic') Marx with a lot of talk about alienation and the teleology deduced from a correct perception of the true 'nature' of man into which then are also heaped the concept of the lonely crowd, escape from freedom, Riesman,[1] Fromm,[2] Merleau-Ponty,[3] Sartre, Miss Arendt and all.

It is idle no doubt for me to point out that alienation in Hegel is something very odd – God is alienated from the universe by self-individuation, whatever that may mean – and this cannot be quite the same as a lot of gloomy Jews in Chicago who do not feel integrated properly into their society or their time, and one begins to understand at last what the climate was like in 1840, and how wonderful it was to be a follower even of Comte, let alone Mill. Talking of whom, I expect by now you have received my lecture.[4] I should love to know what you think of it, but since I read but little myself I cannot expect you to plough through those 56 pages, let alone write me a letter.

Thank you very much for your book,[5] which Arthur brought and which I have read with admiration and agreement – I understand what you say better than anybody's words or thoughts, and I still wish we could write that book together – but perhaps you had better write it alone, or perhaps you could write an entire book and I could write a treatise on it, and you could write a treatise on that and we could publish it as a volume like one of Mortimer Adler's latest works?[6] I do not mean this entirely frivolously: if you

1 David Riesman (1909–2002), US lawyer and sociologist, famous for his 1950 study of US society, *The Lonely Crowd*; Professor of Social Sciences, Chicago, 1949–58; Henry Ford II Professor of Social Sciences, Harvard, 1958–80.
2 Erich Pinchas Fromm (1900–80), German-born psychoanalyst and philosopher; taught at National Autonomous University of Mexico 1951–65; Professor of Psychology, Michigan, 1957–61. His first major work, in 1941, was *Escape from Freedom* (*Fear of Freedom* in the UK).
3 Maurice Merleau-Ponty (1908–61), French phenomenologist; Professor of Philosophy, Collège de France, 1952–61.
4 *John Stuart Mill and the Ends of Life*, Robert Waley Cohen Memorial Lecture (London, 1959), reprinted in *Four Essays on Liberty* (168/2) and L.
5 A collection of essays, *Religion, Politics and the Higher Learning* (Cambridge, Mass., 1959).
6 Adler's *The Idea of Freedom: A Dialectical Examination of the Conceptions of Freedom* (New York,

do send me a typescript on the philosophy of history I genuinely do promise to respond and at length.

Meanwhile attacks on my thesis on Inevitability continue, I see – I saw a rather fierce one by Passmore,[1] whose book on philosophy in the last hundred years seemed to me rather good – I must stop myself from thinking it less good as a result of his article which praises Popper in order to damn me – one of his points may I think be sound and a valid objection to things I say, the rest seemed to me rhetorical, arrogant and fallacious. It all appeared in the Cornell philosophical periodical – which is so much better than *Mind*, I now think. Talking of *Mind*, we have as you know elected Freddie.[2] Let me tell you the secret gossip: a frightful row broke out among the electors at the election, mainly about procedure: Ryle affects to find Freddie's election quite all right, although he himself I suspect voted for Kneale,[3] as did Mabbott, an obscure respectable philosopher whom you may not even remember. The Master (Austin) voted, I think, for Strawson. Consequently Freddie was elected by the votes of Wisdom, Quinton and the two non-philosophical voters, the Vice-Chancellor[4] and the Warden of New College,[5] which has I suspect infuriated both Ryle and Austin. They now wish to change the entire electoral system, have resigned from all their various electoral boards etc. etc. All this officially I do not know: it is all a dead secret and it would be terrible if it was known that I had told you these things, so for God's sake burn this letter and destroy your memory of it as soon as may be. I was one of Freddie's testimonial writers and am pleased by the outcome. Austin quite obviously is not. With all his excellent merits the presence of someone who is likely to give him rather too much trouble at philosophical societies is not to him an entrancing prospect. His followers, even the undergraduates (the anti-Freddie propaganda is real *odium philosophicum*)[6] go about saying it is a mere nuisance to have someone who will always be asking 'Is this a logical or a causal must?' However I think it is an excellent thing and will raise the tone, inject new vitality into philosophy and prevent the fearful smugness and self-satisfaction which appears to me to be entering our sacred precincts.[7] [...]

1958) resulted from a five-year collaborative effort by over 20 contributors.

1 John Arthur Passmore (1914–2004), Australian philosopher and historian of ideas; Professor of Philosophy, Otago, New Zealand, 1950–5; Reader in Philosophy, Australian National University, 1956–9, Professor 1959–79; author of *A Hundred Years of Philosophy* (London, 1957). His article was 'History, the Individual, and Inevitability', *Philosophical Review* 68 No 1 (January 1959), 93–102.

2 Ayer's election to the Wykeham Professorship of Logic at Oxford from 1 October was announced in *The Times* on 29 January 1959, 12.

3 William Calvert Kneale (1906–90), Fellow and Lecturer in Philosophy, Exeter College, 1933–60; later (1960–6) White's Professor of Moral Philosophy, Oxford.

4 Tom Boase.

5 William Hayter.

6 'Philosophers' hatred'.

7 IB commented on the whole saga 'it is such things that make academic life like all other [...] life, and so far from making it seem trivial and petty, make it – to me at least – seem full of humour and point and reality'. Letter of 25 February 1959 to Miriam Lane.

Have you read Strawson's book?[1] Is it any good? Would I be able to tell? It looks to me a decent, but ultimately provincial, performance. That is my view of him in general but I am told that I am deeply mistaken and that I might have thought the same about Kant. But I stick to my view: it may just be his face, his manner, his general behaviour, but I cannot help it, I take the view of the romantic philosophers that personality and philosophical capacity and outlook are not totally dissociable, logic and mathematics are one thing and philosophy another, and what is provincial about any personality remains provincial about all manifestations.

As for Grice,[2] he obviously enjoyed Cambridge very much indeed: the mere thought of him in a room together with Burdon-Muller makes me laugh. I really think you ought to meet him – make the Schlesingers invite you together. You must look upon him objectively rather than subjectively as the most perfect exquisitely preserved survival of the culture whom the more exquisite Edwardian novelists write about – all the men who would not really have enjoyed meeting Harry Levin. [...]

How is dear Meyer? I have actually bought a work by Halbwachs![3] What about Miss Arendt? The *New Statesman* sent me a book for review,[4] but I returned it, for I found it absolutely unreadable, and all the rot about the Greeks not liking work and the Jews liking it and men being alienated first from God and the Renaissance and now from Mother Earth herself – the desire to go to the moon being a deep metaphysical anxiety for flight from one's roots and origins – that is in the first forty pages – I found absolutely awful. Is there something in her after all? Can Mary McCarthy, Dwight Macdonald, Philip Toynbee etc. etc. all be wrong? Do tell me about that too. If you tell me to read her I will. Alternatively you must up and rout her. I do not see why *Partisan Review* should be allowed to get away with nonsense just [because] it has printed you or me or Arthur in the past. This sacred duty I lay upon you.

Do write again, your letters are a source of infinite pleasure to me.

Yours,

Isaiah

---

1 *Individuals: An Essay in Descriptive Metaphysics* (London, 1959).

2 (Herbert) Paul Grice (1913–88), Fellow and Tutor in Philosophy, St John's, Oxford, 1939–67; later (1967–79) Professor of Philosophy, California (Berkeley); a man of 'formidable intellectual gifts, enormous energy, brooding temperament, [...] fiercely competitive spirit[, ...] strong appetites and impressive girth' who thrived on intellectual debate and was content to work in conditions of disorganised squalor. Barry Stroud and G. J. Warnock, ODNB.

3 An unidentified work by Maurice Halbwachs (1877–1945), French philosopher and sociologist.

4 *The Human Condition* (Chicago, 1958). In 1958 IB had written a relentlessly negative report for Faber and Faber, who were considering publishing the book in the UK. The opening lines summarise his views: 'I could recommend no publisher to buy the UK rights of this book. There are two objections to it: it will not sell, and it is no good.' A separate UK edition has never appeared.

TO ARCADI NEBOLSINE[1]

23 February 1959 [carbon]

Headington House

Dear Arcadi,

[...] What about *Zhivago*? I think it is a marvellous book and agree with every line of Edmund Wilson's essay in the *New Yorker*; he is still working on it and I get letters from him occasionally discovering new cryptograms or mysterious symbolic allusions, references to saints or things in the New Testament etc., all of which are typically Pasternak. Who speaks of the connection between Pasternak and Samarin?[2] This is interesting for I worked out for myself that it is full of Slavophil feeling and of course as Peredelkino, where Pasternak lives, is on the original land of the Samarins and he constantly thinks of this and knew Samarin's son, and refers to him in a poem[3] etc., all this connects. Do let me know. [...]

What about *Lolita*? I signed a letter to *The Times*[4] demanding that it should be published in England, but found it dreadfully tedious, over-wrought, and rather intolerable, deeply anti-American, extremely amusing in places, conveying the horror of motels etc., and a certain type of American life with appalling vividness, but too contrived, dead, and somehow White Guardish for me. It is said that he is coming to England soon, on the day of the publication of the novel here when his publisher will probably go to jail and we shall all send him food parcels in honour of freedom of speech. [...]

I hope you notice the curious attitude to the Jews in *Zhivago* – Pasternak obviously dislikes being one and has ladled all of his characteristics as one (and they are exceedingly prominent) into a character called Gordon so as to cleanse Zhivago himself of them. It is not a very successful move and his sisters in Oxford feel embarrassed about the result. His relationship to the Orthodox Church is very like that of Chaadaev to the Church of Rome; his attitude to Russia is that passionate love which people of incompletely

---

1 Arcadi Nebolsine (b. 1932), Christ Church history 1952–5, then graduate student at Columbia; later a specialist in Russian and European culture.

2 Yury Fedorovich Samarin (1819–76), Russian government official, philosopher and leading Slavophil. His great-nephew Dmitry Fedorovich Samarin had been a close friend of Pasternak's from their youth; he died from typhus in the early 1920s and may have partly inspired the character of Yuri Zhivago.

3 'Legends have aged the park. / Napoleon camped here, / And Samarin the Slavophil / Served and was buried near.' From 'The Old Park', in Boris Pasternak, *Selected Poems*, trans. Jon Stallworthy and Peter France (London, 1983), 119–20, at 120.

4 'Lolita', *The Times*, 23 January 1959, 11; the other signatories were J. R. Ackerley, Walter Allen, A. Alvarez, C. M. Bowra, Storm Jameson, Frank Kermode, Allen Lane, Margaret Lane, Rosamond Lehmann, Compton Mackenzie, Iris Murdoch, William Plomer, V. S. Pritchett, Alan Pryce-Jones, Peter Quennell, Herbert Read, Stephen Spender, Philip Toynbee, Bernard Wall and Angus Wilson. The letter provoked a hostile response from (John) Douglas Woodruff (1897–1978), historian and journalist, editor 1936–67 of *The Tablet*, a weekly London-based Roman Catholic newspaper, who argued that literary merit should not overrule 'the claims of public decency' (ibid., 28 January 1959, 9).

Russian origin – like Herzen or George Kennan (not a Russian at all I mean) – feel towards countries which they view with infatuation precisely because they come from its edges and are incompletely assimilated to them – like Napoleon about France and the foreign-born members of the editorial staff of *Time* and *Life* about America. It is sincere, sometimes profound, and often moving, but it is not what it pretends to be, i.e. the natural attitude of sons to their country, it is a kind of unhappy love affair, where love grows deeper and more desperate the more obviously it is unrequited. [...]

Yours,

When IB was asked whether he favoured the endowment of a Chair in Diplomacy at the Hebrew University, to be occupied initially by Eliahu Elath, the outgoing Israeli Ambassador in London, he suggested that it would be better to establish an independent Institute for International Affairs in Israel. This could produce works of permanent historical and political worth and, even more important, provide unbiased information about the social, political and economic situation in Israel. As Israel's future was so dependent on world opinion, an impartial and objective source of facts about the State, which could command international respect, would be of great value.

TO ALEC LERNER[1]

2 March 1959 [*carbon*]

[Headington House]

Dear Alec,

Enclosed the Memorandum which I promised you.[2] I feel absolutely sure that the creation of a kind of Israel Chatham House is more important than ten chairs at the University. Everyone speaks of the necessity of creating or raising standards – moral, intellectual, social etc. – in Israel, and a centre of moral and intellectual authority, which would produce publications likely to win the esteem of people outside – whether annual surveys of political and social affairs or the history of the rise of the State of Israel, or the books and speeches and works of Dr Weizmann (I think that the Weizmann publication scheme could certainly be connected with such an Institute), or whatever it may be – would be useful in many ways: both in training journalists and historians and diplomats in Israel itself and in giving a proper background to ideas about Israel to the editor of *The Times* in London or Walter Lippmann in America or government officials in other countries, or indeed all the

---

1 Alec Lerner (1913–99), Canadian doctor; his first wife (1941) was Hannah, daughter of Simon Marks; joined Board of Marks & Spencer 1954 (Assistant Managing Director 1963–9, after which he settled in Israel); active in Jewish and Zionist causes.

2 One version of the memorandum is posted at http://berlin.wolf.ox.ac.uk/lists/nachlass/1959memorandum.pdf.

serious opinion-forming groups of individuals whose views matter so very greatly in our affairs. I think that the value of this kind of high-up publicity is underestimated in Israel itself, where it is said that personal contact and straight propaganda and being nice to visitors and so on is enough. It is quite a lot, but by no means enough. Small and precarious countries like Israel need both to be and to seem virtuous to the world – their public virtue is a far greater asset to them than to larger and more powerful countries. But I need not labour the point.

One more idea: I think that Eliahu [Elath] would be an ideal head for such an Institute. I need not enumerate his virtues to you: he has the admiration of almost all the persons who matter in the outside world to make the thing a success, he has organising capacity, wisdom, tact, wit, integrity, intellectual capacity and good will. He would do far more good in such a position than as President of the University or Professor or in any other high post that I can think of. [...]

Do tell me what you think of all this.

Yours,

TO ARTHUR SCHLESINGER

4 March 1959

Headington House

Dear Arthur

Indeed it was a terrible business about Ryle, Ayer etc. I had nothing formally to do with it except that I wrote Ayer's testimonial and that he got the Chair. What occurred is not clear – the only reliable version is that both Austin and Ryle were furious with the Vice-Chancellor for getting the whole thing over within twenty minutes – a post for twenty years should not be settled in twenty minutes, Austin said bitterly – and against the wishes of the professors concerned. Their formal complaint was that they were not even made to vote, but that after they had expressed their views, expecting a long and serious discussion, with deep deference paid to the more important members of the Board, the Vice-Chancellor (Boase) briskly said, 'Well, that's that, I am for Ayer, four-three, I declare him elected.' I fear that although they have a case – the thing was rather hustled – it was a case of abraded vanity. It is the right of every member of the Board to ask for an adjournment and two members of the Board can compel it. Had they secured this adjournment, they could no doubt have twisted the arm of one of the electors to obtain some other result; but it did not occur to them to do so, and now they blame both themselves and others for this oversight. Poor Freddie, who has thought of Ryle as his greatest friend for twenty-five years, will be upset when he learns of it, as indeed he must already have done, although I have told him nothing. I think it an excellent election myself, and so you will find

with people at Harvard, especially Quine and Morton White. For God's sake
don't repeat this verbatim to either of them, or rather, if you do, represent
it as having been gleaned from general gossip and not as coming from me,
as I deeply don't want to be embroiled in this sad situation – at least sad only
because it will annoy Freddie and lead to a great deal of fuss here about
altering the constitution of electoral boards, eliminating college representatives as uninstructed laymen, forcing all meetings to settle posts to come up
at least more than once to allow for maximum opportunity for intrigue and
intimidation etc., all of which I regard with horror. So don't have heard from
me, just let it have seeped into your mind in some anonymous way. Maurice
could have told you even more than I did, so by now could anyone else. [...]
    Love to Marian and from Aline,
    Yours ever,
        Isaiah

Karl Popper wrote on 17 February to thank IB for his complimentary copy of
Two Concepts of Liberty *and to comment on it:*

I have hardly ever read anything on the philosophy of politics with which I
agreed so completely on all important issues – and the issues are very important
indeed. I am delighted by your clear distinction between what you call negative
and positive freedom; in your own confession of faith – even though it is
only implicit, it is no less open and forceful – for negative freedom; by your
exposition of the dangers of the ideology of positive freedom; your stand [...]
against moral historism and historicism; your warnings against the assumption
that social problems must be soluble in principle, and that all ('real') goods must
be compatible, and in harmony; and above all, your declaration on absolute
human rights [...]. On all these things, there is perfect agreement between us;
and I believe that the way in which you have discussed and presented these ideas
is admirable.
    Nevertheless I have some criticisms – in fact, a long list.

However, Popper devoted the rest of his letter to just two points from his list.

TO KARL POPPER

    16 March 1959 [*manuscript*]

                                        As from Headington House
Dear Karl,
    [...] I am glad & relieved that you agree with the main theses of my
lecture. But I long to know what your "long list of criticisms' contains. I
have little confidence in the validity of my own intellectual processes: rather
more in their veridicity: but not enough in either not to welcome criticism.
Particularly yours, as well you know. As to the two points you speak of:

1. Of course I do not suppose that you could ever have subscribed to any of the propositions listed on p. 39:[1] but I do think that the classical rationalists – from Plato & Aristotle to Descartes, Spinoza, Leibniz etc. could scarcely have denied them. What would Socrates have had against them?[2] could he really have denied that all genuine questions had one true answer & one only, & that all rational men must, pro tanto, be capable of reaching perfect agreement on these answers? I think that Hume may have asked too much of rationality: but did Descartes or Aristotle ask less? I think they were genuinely mistaken about what being rational was: if my text implied that the alternative is rejection of reason in favour of some kind of Rousseau-ish état d'âme,[3] I have failed to convey my meaning. I feel at least as hostile to Rousseau as you do: I realise his vast influence, but dislike his very prose – or bad poetry – so deeply, that I feel I cannot do justice even to the original psychological aperçus which it occasionally contains. The last thing that I want to do is to hold open the door for romanticism and blind faith – what socialists in the nineteenth century used to call "fidéisme".[4] But unless the pretensions of "rationalistic" reason are seen in correct perspective, will the disappointment in which they end not always tend to bring grist to the irrationalist mill? will the effort to be "scientific" where this does not fit – by Russell, or Marxists, or various kinds of positivists – not inevitably drive the victims & their sympathisers into the arms of sceptics, cynics, Hegelians and other Charlatans? I think that you believe me liable to discredit too much – in my zeal to refute metaphysical rationalism, to cast suspicion on reason as such. Perhaps this is just. It is always more difficult to be positive & defend the good than negative & attack wickedness.

Of course I have nothing against *sapere aude*.[5] Kant's essay on the notion of Enlightenment is moving and unforgettable. But in the days of Socrates *sapere* had not yet accumulated the association it acquired from being used as a weapon – *the* weapon – by every authoritarian and monopolistic doctrine that ever slaughtered people on its altars. By Kant's time it was surely not enough to ask only for *sapere* – only for satisfaction of intellectual curiosity – or even *knowledge* in its widest sense. Kant himself has won immortal

---

1 '[F]irst, that all men have one true purpose, [...] that of rational self-direction; second, that the ends of all rational beings must of necessity fit into a single universal, harmonious pattern [...]; third, that all conflict [...] is due solely to the clash of reason with the irrational [...] and that such clashes are, in principle, avoidable [...]; finally, that when all men have been made rational, they will obey the rational laws of their own natures, which are one and the same in them all, and so be at once wholly law-abiding and wholly free.' L 200.

2 Popper had written: 'I am far from convinced that Socrates would have accepted your four basic assumptions, although I agree that Hume would have rejected them.'

3 'State of mind'.

4 'Fideism', a system of belief whereby reason is either opposed or irrelevant to religious faith.

5 'Sapere aude! ["Dare to know!"] Have the courage to use your *own* understanding! is therefore the motto of Enlightenment.' Immanuel Kant, 'An Answer to the Question: What is Enlightenment?' (1784).

glory by stressing the very fact that a man might know & know & still be a villain. The whole of my lecture, in a sense, is an attempt at a brief study – or prolegomenon to the study – of the way in which innocent or virtuous or truly liberating ideas (γνῶθι σεαυτόν[1] or sapere aude or the man who is free although he is a slave, in prison etc.) tend (not inevitably!) to become authoritarian & despotic and lead to enslavement and slaughter when they are isolated & driven ahead by themselves. With what you say about the idea of rational activity[2] I agree most passionately. All I say – & the quotation from Schumpeter at the end[3] – is meant to support this. But I believe (with Hayek, I suppose; although he goes much too far in his application of his principles, too far for me, that is) that there exists a scientistic obscurantism no less oppressive than that of historicism: & in our day, more menacing: & that although the former may be a perversion of scientific method & scientific temper, as the latter is of the historical, yet scientists *are* liable to this distortion as strongly as historians to theirs: to every age its own vices, its own dangers: but I daresay that what you imply (but out of wisdom & courtesy do not say) is true: namely that in castigating vice (an easier & gayer task) I do not take sufficient care to draw a precise frontier between it & the cognate virtue to which it is closely & curiously related. And because of this it might look as if I were offering comfort to anti-rationalism, which is a dreadful thought. You have a right to complain since it is from your writings that people like me have drawn so much – as indeed all the (relevant) world knows. Thank you very much for writing to me: & please forgive this scrawl –

Yours,

Isaiah B.

TO IDA SAMUNOV

16 March 1959 [*carbon*]

Headington House

Dearest Ida,

[. . .] As for *Dr Zhivago*, I think it is a work of genius. True, the author is not at all anxious to be a Jew, and has to pour off all the Jewish characteristics into a character called Gordon so as to remove the curse from himself and identify

---

1 'Gnōthi seauton' ('know yourself').
2 '"[R]ationality" means, for me, the readiness to pay attention to criticism and argument – to other people's criticism of what one thinks and says, and to be highly critical of one's own views and predilections' (Popper's letter of 17 February).
3 'To realise the relative validity of one's convictions and yet stand for them unflinchingly is what distinguishes a civilised man from a barbarian.' Quoted at L 217 from Schumpeter's *Capitalism, Socialism, and Democracy* (London, 1943), 243. In the first (dictated) draft of the lecture IB adds: 'That appears to me to be the best statement that has ever been made about the character of our ultimate convictions.'

himself wholly with the very Russian figure of the Doctor himself. What he says about Jews, nationalism etc. is ordinary routine liberal assimilationist talk of about 1910, and why B.G. should have fired off that rocket against him[1] I do not really understand. Of course it is all rubbish – a great many of the philosophical, theological discussions in the book are a confused kind of semi-Christianity – he is not exactly a Christian (he was never baptised), but he is a kind of fellow-traveller of the Russian Orthodox Church, which a good many spiritually confused Jews were becoming [in] 1914 – the thing to remember is that he became intellectually arrested as it were in about 1914 and has written the whole novel in an old-fashioned pre-1914 style, which is what makes it so attractive and intelligible to us. The descriptions of the Revolution, of love, of human relations and of art seem to be unequalled in our day. Never mind about the Jews, the novel is not about that. I thought it absolutely marvellous and if I can will send you a Russian copy.

Yours,   [. . .]

When the Foreign Office needed to demonstrate the paucity of English literature on sale in the Soviet Union, IB was an obvious source of advice.

TO THOMAS BRIMELOW[2]

31 March 1959 [*carbon*]

[Headington House]

Dear Brimelow,

This is a wonderful opportunity (I refer to your last letter to me)[3] to call our old friend's bluff. I do not believe that it would serve any useful purpose to invite them to peruse the works of Evelyn Waugh or George Orwell[4] or even Aldous Huxley – nor will these provide them with that corrective to Dickens which we are supposedly anxious to direct their attention towards. Hence I should suggest the following authors[5] (on the assumption that social

---

1 Ben-Gurion had described *Dr Zhivago* as 'one of the most despicable books about Jews ever to be written by a man of Jewish origin' (*Jewish Chronicle*, 20 February 1959, 36), in response to the assimilationist and pro-Christian views expressed in particular by Misha Gordon.

2 Thomas Brimelow (1915–95), Baron Brimelow 1976, diplomat; Head of Northern Department, FO, 1956–60; later (1973–5) Permanent Under-Secretary of State, FCO, and Head of the Diplomatic Service.

3 'In a recent conversation with the Soviet Ambassador in London, Sir Anthony Rumbold (one of our Assistant Under-Secretaries) remarked on the limited range of English literature which was published in the Soviet Union. Mr Malik challenged him on this and invited Sir Anthony to name twenty books, by which I gather he meant mainly novels, which ought to be published in the Soviet Union to give a fair representation of conditions in this country.' Letter of 20 March 1959 from Sir Thomas Brimelow.

4 The pen-name of Eric Arthur Blair (1903–50), novelist, essayist, critic and journalist.

5 Those not previously annotated are (Enoch) Arnold Bennett (1867–1931); Joseph Conrad (1857–1924; né Józef Teodor Konrad Korzeniowski in Poland); (Edward Montague) Compton Mackenzie (1883–1972); Anthony Dymoke Powell (1905–2000); Siegfried Loraine Sassoon

realism is what they understand and that their cultural climate is much more like that of late Victorians or Edwardians than like our own):

Arnold Bennett
Joseph Conrad
Compton Mackenzie
Hugh Walpole
E. M. Forster
Anthony Powell
Elizabeth Bowen
Kingsley Amis
Siegfried Sassoon
John Wain
Angus Wilson (?)
Anthony Trollope (the political novels) and – why not? – Disraeli
Kingsley's *Alton Locke*
Maurice Baring
P. G. Wodehouse
Sir Charles Snow, and, although they can scarcely be called descriptions of English life, yet because works of genius make their own impact,
Virginia Woolf
Joyce Cary

This is all that occurs to me at the moment, but if they accepted even a quarter of these it would I think justify the approach.

I was much against the expedition to Moscow[1] of the four dons originally promoted by the British Council, as you may have gathered, perhaps; but I think that if other 'cultural contacts' are to be officially promoted, this idea might be revived for next Christmas. Ayer and MacDougall[2] would certainly be ready to go, I think, and so should I. Alternatively, if pomp and circumstance are to be preferred (as they so often are in dealing with the Russians), perhaps the Academy of Sciences could be stimulated to extend an invitation to the British Academy, of which Ayer and I are members, and from which

---

(1886–1967; poet and autobiographical novelist); John Barrington Wain (1925–94; also a poet and critic); Angus Frank Johnstone Wilson (1913–91); Benjamin Disraeli (1804–81; 1st Earl of Beaconsfield; also Conservative politician, twice Prime Minister); Charles Kingsley (1819–75; his novel about social injustice, *Alton Locke*, was published in 1850); Maurice Baring (1874–1945; also playwright, poet, travel writer, essayist, translator and war correspondent); P(elham) G(renville) Wodehouse (1881–1975; playwright and lyricist as well as comic novelist); C(harles) P(ercy) Snow (1905–80; Baron Snow 1964; physicist, public servant and novelist); and the Irish-born writer (Arthur) Joyce Lunel Cary (1888–1957).

1 See 627/2 . The trip planned for December 1958 had been postponed; IB had become increasingly disillusioned about the usefulness of the proposed arrangements.

2 Sir (George) Donald Alastair MacDougall (1912–2004), economist; Fellow of Nuffield, 1950–64; later (1969–73) Head of Government Economic Service and Chief Economic Adviser to the Treasury.

a small but moderately effective and ice-cutting delegation could be carved. [. . .]

Yours sincerely,

IB then remembered that he had been asked to suggest specific novels.

TO THOMAS BRIMELOW

3 April 1959 [*carbon*]

[Headington House]

Dear Brimelow,

[. . .]

PS 8 April [. . .] I agree with you about the need not to treat the Russians with too much British squalor, at the same time if we carefully suppress such titles they will realise all too well why we do, and publish them with a certain perversity. I am in favour I must admit of offering such things to them rather than not, including even Miss Doris Lessing.[1]

The list I would propose would be:[2]

Arnold Bennett (something about the Five Towns, *Clayhanger* etc., and some of the gayer ones, as *The Card, Lord Raingo, Grand Babylon Hotel* etc.)

Joseph Conrad (*Lord Jim* or *Typhoon*)

Compton Mackenzie (*Sinister Street* (why not?) or any of the Greek novels. But I do not read him much.)

Hugh Walpole (*Mr Perrin and Mr Traill*, or *Jeremy*)

E. M. Forster (*The Longest Journey* – but we cannot conceal the existence of *A Passage to India*)

Elizabeth Bowen (*The Heat of the Day*)

Kingsley Amis (*Lucky Jim* – not too squalid surely – I hate him myself)

Siegfried Sassoon (*Memoirs of a Fox-Hunting Man* – the whole trilogy in one)

John Wain – I detest him but perhaps it is right to have him.

Angus Wilson (*Anglo-Saxon Attitudes*)

Anthony Trollope (*The Prime Minister, Phineas Finn, Phineas Redux* etc.)

Charles Kingsley (*Alton Locke*)

Virginia Woolf (*The Lighthouse* and perhaps *Night and Day*)

---

1 Doris May Lessing (b. 1919), née Tayler, novelist and short-story writer.
2 Dates of first publication (in book form) not already given are: *Clayhanger* 1900; *The Card* 1911; *Lord Raingo* 1926; *The Grand Babylon Hotel* 1902; *Lord Jim* 1900; *Typhoon* 1903; *Sinister Street* 1913; *Mr Perrin and Mr Traill* 1911; *Jeremy* 1919; *The Longest Journey* 1907; *A Passage to India* 1924; *The Heat of the Day* 1949; *Memoirs of a Fox-Hunting Man* 1928 (re-published in 1937 with its sequels *Memoirs of an Infantry Officer* and *Sherston's Progress* as *The Complete Memoirs of George Sherston*); *Anglo-Saxon Attitudes* 1956; *The Prime Minister* 1876; *Phineas Finn* 1869; *Phineas Redux* 1874; *To the Lighthouse* 1927; *Night and Day* 1919; *The Horse's Mouth* 1944.

Joyce Cary (*The Horse's Mouth*)

P. G. Wodehouse (not the ones about Jeeves but the ones about Lord Emsworth, and they can make the worst of it)

Phyllis Bentley[1] (something about Yorkshire)

Perhaps something by R. H. Mottram[2] – our 'regional' literature should be done very well.

TO TEDDY KOLLEK

17 April 1959

Headington House

Dear Teddy,

[...] Did you get my letter? And what did you think of it? I have not spoken to Elath yet about this, but no doubt soon will. Let me complain about your office: the Prime Minister writes me a long and elaborate enquiry in a language I but imperfectly read, and I sweat drops of blood and produce a long, and I daresay useless, answer about the children of anti-clerical Zionist Gentile wives, etc. etc., and not even an acknowledgement. I do not mind my letter being consigned to some dusty archives, but I should like to be sure that it has arrived. I do not even ask for it to be read.

On the other matter, which I regard as of considerably more importance, I really should like to have a talk to you: I gather from Marks and Spencer that one of the chief objectors to an independent Institute is ~~Mazar~~ (the Univ. of Jerusalem),[3] which does not surprise me; every day the University seems to me to grow more and more like some Western American State University, with greater attention to buildings and benefactors than to students or professors, with 'empire building', extra non-academic considerations of every kind, political cross-currents etc. etc. Perhaps I am being unjust (and disloyal too for am I not a Governor of this institution?) and yet I cannot bring myself to feel enough *moral* respect for those who run its policies. There is a kind of spiritual rot which Magnes originally injected into it, which seems to have infected everything except the natural sciences, which are mysteriously free from this kind of corruption. Anyway I wish you would come and talk to me about all that: Israel seems to me to have far more to lose or gain externally (as well as internally) by its cultural life than larger and stronger and older countries. No doubt deeds speak loudest: but the alliances which Israel seeks cannot be obtained among black and yellow-skinned men alone: the white world is quite strong still: and there, funnily enough, ideas are the

---

1 Phyllis Bentley (1894–1977), whose novels almost all depict Yorkshire life.

2 Ralph Hale Mottram (1883–1971), whose home town of Norwich appears in many of his novels.

3 IB dictated 'Mazar', but amended this as shown. Benjamin Mazar (1906–95), né Maisler, Polish-born archaeologist and historian; Professor of Biblical History and Archaeology of Palestine, Hebrew University of Jerusalem, 1951–77, Rector 1952–61, President 1953–61.

only weapons with which Israelis can operate. So do take a little time off and come and see me soon – I really do not exaggerate what I regard as the importance of this.

Yours ever,

Isaiah [. . .]

IB's idea of an Israeli Chatham House did not please Vera Weizmann, who saw the scheme as a rival to her own plans for Rehovot. On 14 April she wrote to IB that a meeting was soon to be held to 'announce the purpose of the Weizmann Archives and the formation of the Weizmann House Institute for International Affairs (or Foreign Affairs)'. She continued:

The success of such Institute can be assured if you graciously accept to be the Chairman of it. [. . .] Isaiah dear, you will remember that on the passing away of my husband you wrote me an unforgettable letter in which you said 'I long to do anything you may wish me to do. Is there anything? I feel dearly privileged even to be able to ask this.'[1] The moment has come and I feel confident you will 'honour' your pledge.

IB's first response was to profess bemusement at her proposals and to question the availability of funds but Vera Weizmann was undaunted: steps were already being taken towards the eventual establishment of an Israeli Chatham House at Rehovot. The assets of the Weizmann Archive were many, but the first amongst them was 'You, my dear Isaiah'. As for funds:

If we could say that you will write Weizmann's biography, Meyer [Weisgal] undertakes to have one hundred thousand dollars within two weeks. [. . .] You, my dear friend, and no one else can do it. Your background, your 100% Jewishness, your friendship with Chief, your approach so unusual to Chaim's personality, qualify *you* and no one else to do it. You have been chosen for the work by fate.[2]

IB's initial reaction to this pressure appears to have been a long and robust explanation of how his proposal had originated and why he did not consider the Weizmann Archives the right home for the proposed Institute of Contemporary Affairs. But the letter he dictated was never sent. In its place he substituted the following more emollient reply.

1 This letter has not been found.
2 Letter from Vera Weizmann, 30 April 1959.

TO VERA WEIZMANN

4 May 1959 [*manuscript*]

As from Headington House

Dearest Mrs Weizmann,

Thank you for your last letter. I see that I have acted hastily, & for this I apologize. I have tried to sort out my ideas, and I now think that there is room, and indeed need, for two quite distinct institutions [...]. Whether this is so or not – & whether I am right or wrong about my distinction between the two institutions, the mere fact that you think as you do is sufficient and more than sufficient reason for me to withdraw my participation from the Chatham House (non-Rehovot) scheme. [...] I propose to tell all concerned that my loyalty to Rehovot comes first: that I cannot take an active interest in any scheme which even threatens to overlap with it in minor respects. My first duty is to say so to *Eliahu Elath* whom I hope to see in a week or two: then, & not before (he will think ill of me for this, but it cannot be helped. I acted in haste & must bear the consequences) I will write formally to you [...] & whoever else is concerned. [...] I am *very* sorry if I have caused you the slightest annoyance. My first loyalty is to Rehovot & to yourself, & this I shall make clear. In the meanwhile I beg you to wait for my "formal" letter, which will be (I say this to relieve you!) typewritten. The whole thing has been upsetting & I shall "liquidate" it as rapidly as I can.

As for the biography – dearest Mrs Weizmann – I hope not to die before writing something else about Dr Weizmann – a book I hope. But it wd be very dishonourable of me to break all my engagements now & devote myself to it as I should. I am a *painfully* slow worker – I am behindhand with *everything* – I am in terrible intellectual debt to Oxford & to publishers – I cannot begin on a new task, however sacred – until I feel a free man. At least relatively free – not guilt-stricken as at present I am.

Much love and devotion

Yours for ever

　　Isaiah

IB duly withdrew from any connection with the scheme he had discussed with Alec Lerner, even though explaining his volte-face to Eliahu Elath was 'an embarrassing and painful thing to do [...] an agonising experience'.[1] Although IB continued to support the Chatham House proposal in private, in public he remained silent, reflecting that 'I seem to have upset everybody and in future shall confine my resolutions – good, bad and indifferent – to myself.'[2]

1 Letter of 11 May 1959 to Vera Weizmann.
2 Letter of 29 May 1959 to Vera Weizmann.

*On 4 June IB joined Yehudi Menuhin, Nicolas Nabokov and William Glock[1] on
a platform at the Bath Festival.*

TO WILLIAM CLARK

8 June 1959

Headington House

Dear William,

[...] I have not seen the *Jewish Chronicle* myself, although I cannot deny
that my mother did tell me something had appeared.[2] I shall procure and
read it – what more can one ask for than that if one is mentioned at all
(which I sincerely detest – I am sure you know that I am all too sincere – I
loathe the appearance of my name in print however kindly the mention) it
should be 'flattering but true'. The mention of me in the last issue of your
worthy journal, which I did see, was I thought neither – I weakly succumbed
to Menuhin's saintly pleadings, and agreed to be a kind of Chairman at a
musical discussion in Bath; the *Daily Express* complained that there was no
Chairman; your Miss Gray(?)[3] noted that I was put in my place by the moral
superiority of Menuhin, the nobler eloquence of Nabokov and the quiet
authority of Glock. Perhaps I am mistaken and what your journal said was
unflattering but true. *The Observer* teaches one the unwisdom of performing
unthinking favours even to the best and purest of men.

In spite of which, it would be very nice to meet again.

Yours,

Isaiah

TO MARGOT FONTEYN

19 June 1959 [*carbon*]

[Headington House]

Dear Dr (to be) Fonteyn,

May I say how very delighted I am that my ancient University should have

---

1 William Frederick Glock (1908–2000), music critic and musical administrator; editor, *Score*, 1949–
   61; Director, Summer School of Music, Dartington Hall, 1953–79; music critic, *New Statesman*,
   1958–9. The four men are pictured together in Plate 40.

2 The *Jewish Chronicle* published an admiring profile of IB to mark his 50th birthday: anon., 'Sir
   Isaiah Berlin' ('Silhouette' feature), *Jewish Chronicle*, 5 June 1959, 77.

3 Patience Gray (1917–2005), the name adopted by Patience Jean Stanham (later Mommens),
   cookery writer, who ran the *Observer* women's page 1958–62 and introduced cultural items despite
   lack of enthusiasm from above. Her article 'A Festival in the Menuhin Manner', *Observer*, 7 June
   1959, 21, described the discussion as 'a stimulating experience' which revealed 'Menuhin as a
   natural leader [...] His mind is clear cut [...] This shone out through the turbulent conversational
   brilliance of Nabokov, the verbal fusillades detonated by Sir Isaiah, and the quieter but telling
   sallies of William Glock.' IB ('philosopher friend of Stravinsky') 'whose solo performances are
   celebrated, had his thunder stolen by Nabokov's tirades and Menuhin's marvellous composure'.

taken off the frosted spectacles of scholarship and at last recognised true merit and genius where it lies, and done what it should have done long ago, but not too late for those whom it wishes to honour to enjoy it.

We are heartbroken at not being able to be present at Encaenia – when the sun shines it can be delightful. The lunch at All Souls is brief, quite agreeable, and wholly painless. The Warden of All Souls is a balletomane and a true and deep admirer of your genius. If we could only be here, instead of in Paris, I should beg you as an honour and a favour to use my rooms to rest in, at any rate between the luncheon and the Garden Party at Magdalen, at which I expect you will be expected to appear by the gaping mobs. The Vice-Chancellor asked us to dinner with you the night before, but alas we leave today.

Long may you enjoy the delicious gown provided. The composer Shostakovich could not be parted from his, despite the glares and frowns of the Soviet Embassy officials who thought that he was almost too delighted by this bourgeois honour.

And you must forgive me too for being unable to speak to the ballerinas. My appearance at the Bath Festival with Menuhin and others was a fiasco of the first order. I speak in a low rapid voice at my boots, am just audible enough to make people think that if they strain their ears a little more there might be something worth hearing, and inaudible enough to make this exercise quite fruitless. Believe me, you are well out of me: I am a miserable public speaker, though if my good will towards the Ballet were equal to my capacity to say what I feel in public, it would be a prodigious performance. Ava Waverley will, you will be sorry to hear, not be there, for she says she does not feel well enough, but Lady Eden and Lady Pamela Berry, who are not on speaking terms, will both be present, so we shall have missed something.

I do hope you have a day of uninterrupted enjoyment.

Yours very sincerely,

TO MARTIN BRAUN[1]

7 July 1959

Headington House

Dear Mr Braun,

I enjoyed your talk[2] on Cavour and Garibaldi very much indeed. No, you have not misinterpreted me, I do admire Cavour and empiricism; I am terribly reluctant to think of Garibaldi as a kind of charismatic personality. He was the forerunner of the monsters from whom we have suffered

---

1 Martin Braun (c.1903–75), historian.
2 MB had sent IB a script of his recent talk on 'Cavour and Garibaldi 1859–1959', broadcast by the Italian section of the BBC.

in our own day, but you may be right. I don't know upon what principles one can abhor Wilhelm II,[1] Hitler, Mussolini, Stalin, Lenin, even the now much-sympathised-with Trotsky, and accept de Gaulle, de Valera,[2] Nehru etc. because they are personally less unattractive. Except I suppose that any over-stern embracing of principles, even selecting the right kind of political leaders for approval, would itself lead to some kind of dogma and in the end nonsense. However that may be I should like to talk to you about it one day. [...]

Yours sincerely,
Isaiah Berlin

TO ROWLAND BURDON-MULLER
7 July 1959

Headington House

Dear Rowland,

There is very little to tell you about our dinner[3] with Miss Callas and the Queen Mother. They were like two prima donnas, one emitting white and [the] other black magic. Each tried to engage the attention of the table, Miss Callas crudely and violently, the Queen Mother with infinite gracefulness and charm of a slightly watery and impersonal kind. I have been known to compare her to your friend Barbara Ward, but upon all sides I am told this is very unfair to the QM – even Stuart, whose feelings for royalty are as you can imagine not terribly warm, is a very strong anti-BW partisan; I am not, but I do think her of a commonplaceness not to be equalled, good as her manners are. However, on that point I daresay we disagree. The dinner party consisted of the QM, the diva, Lady Fermoy[4] (in waiting), Lady Rosebery,[5] Mr Anthony Gishford[6] (late of Boosey & Hawkes, who used to edit *Isis* when I was an undergraduate, slightly disreputable and quite nice), Mr David Webster, and the Harewoods. I sat between the QM and Lady Rosebery and enjoyed myself. Aline sat next to (I forgot to add him) Arthur Penn[7] – she got

---

1 Wilhelm II (1859–1941), né Prince Friedrich Wilhelm Albert Viktor of Prussia, Emperor of Germany and King of Prussia 1888–1918.

2 Éamon (né Edward George) de Valera (1882–1975), Irish politician who took part in the 1916 Easter Rising, became leader of Sinn Féin, and was three times Prime Minister; President of Ireland 1959–73 (he took office a few days before this letter was written).

3 Probably on 30 June, under which IB noted 'dinner Harewood' in his pocket engagement diary.

4 Ruth Sylvia Roche (1908–93), née Gill, widow of 4th Baron Fermoy, Extra Woman of the Bedchamber to the Queen Mother 1956–60 (Woman of the Bedchamber 1960–93); music patron and gifted musician; later maternal grandmother of Diana, Princess of Wales.

5 Eva Isabel Marion Primrose (1892–1987), née Bruce, daughter of 2nd Baron Aberdare, by her second marriage the second wife of the 6th Earl of Rosebery (692/3).

6 Anthony Joseph Gishford (1908–75), writer on music; editor, *Tempo*, 1947–58; Director, Boosey & Hawkes, 1951–7; Honorary Secretary, The Pilgrims of Great Britain, 1952–64.

7 Sir Arthur Horace Penn (1886–1960), businessman and long-time royal servant; Treasurer to the Queen Mother 1946–60.

on beautifully with him as indeed with the Marshal of the Diplomatic Corps,
General Salisbury Jones,[1] who has sent her a dedicated book on General de
Lattre de Tassigny. She is rather ashamed of getting on as well as she does
with courtiers and court officials, but she undoubtedly does. Arthur Penn
was very lyrical in her praises; I daresay such persons meet very few well-
mannered ladies nowadays, particularly of Aline's age. My neighbour Lady
Rosebery was very talkative and agreeable. She told me a tale about Philip
[sc. Cyril?] Connolly which I cannot forbear to repeat to you. He arrived in
Edinburgh shortly after the war to deliver a lecture at the Edinburgh Festival
at which Lady Rosebery presides, and approaching her said, 'We have never
met but I am told at White's that your husband keeps the best cellar north
of the Tweed. If I had known that I should have tried to invite myself to stay
with you. As it is I am fixed up with Christopher Glen[2] and cannot get out
of it. It is quite maddening. I am afraid that's where I shall have to go.' Lord
Rosebery,[3] when this conversation was reported to him, is alleged to have
blown up and said he would not have the fellow in the house or have him
darken his doorway under any conditions whatever. I well understand that.
I have never heard a more characteristically [catty?] remark – it is a sad thing
that gifted literary men are eaten by snobbery to a degree which makes them
produce artificial sentences in artificial voices about White's, cellars, north
of the Tweed, Christopher Glen etc., but I found it an enjoyable story. The
QM, on the other hand, discussed the subject of courage and ventured the
proposition that wholly fearless men are often boring. I pounced on that and
produced a list of men distinguished in public life – such as General Freyburg[4]
and other VCs – whom we then duly found boring. It was such a conversation as might have occurred in about 1903 with the then still young Princess
May.[5] I enjoyed it in an artificial sort of way and thought the QM not indeed
particularly intelligent nor even terribly nice, but a very strong personality –
much more stronger than I thought her – and filled with the possibility of

1 Major-General Sir (Arthur) Guy Salisbury-Jones (1896–1985), Head of British Military Mission to
France and Military Attaché, Paris, 1946–9; Marshal of the Diplomatic Corps 1950–61; his biography of Jean Joseph Marie Gabriel de Lattre de Tassigny (1889–1952), the French general who
played a major part in the liberation of France and the defeat of Germany in the Second World
War, was *So Full a Glory* (London, 1954).
2 Christopher Grey Tennant (1899–1983), 2nd Baron Glenconner, whose home was in the Scottish
Borders.
3 (Albert Edward) Harry Meyer Archibald Primrose (1882–1974), 6th Earl of Rosebery; Lord
Lieutenant of Midlothian 1929–64; Chairman, Royal Fine Art Commission for Scotland 1952–7,
Scottish Tourist Board 1955–65.
4 Bernard Freyburg (1889–1963), 1st Baron Freyburg 1951, VC 1916, General Officer Commanding
New Zealand Forces 1939–45; Governor-General of New Zealand 1946–52; Lieutenant-Governor,
Windsor Castle, 1953–63.
5 The name used by Princess Victoria Mary Augusta Louise Olga Pauline Claudine Agnes of Teck
(1867–1953), before her marriage in 1893 to the future King George V, when she became Duchess
of York; made Princess of Wales in 1901 and became Queen Mary on her husband's accession in
1910; remembered for her rectitude and sense of duty.

unexpected answers, in this respect differing from Barbara Ward. In short I enjoyed my evening a good deal. Callas on the other hand was simply splendid: she violently attacked the other prima donna – Cossotto[1] – who sang beautifully, so far as beauty of voice very superior to Callas, as being noisy, vulgar, loud, untrained, ill-rehearsed, beastly, inartistic and embarrassing. Exactly what you would expect a prima donna to do. But she looked most magnificent: I see that she is the strongest musical personality on the opera stage since Chaliapin.[2] [...]

I am delighted to think that I shall see you at Christmas.

Yours, with much love

Isaiah

TO LEONARD WOOLF

8 July 1959

Headington House

Dear Mr Woolf,

I would rather not review *The American Science of Politics* for anyone if you will forgive me. I am in bed with a sprained sacroiliac joint, and as soon as this is over shall go to Italy, and would rather not read books for review, especially by Mr Crick,[3] whom I have met and thought not over-intelligent. I may well be wrong about this, but I do not feel anxious to test my view by this degree of exhaustion. I should love to review something for you at a later date if you can think of something suitable – for the moment I should like to be allowed to go off on holiday with only a half-dozen reviews that I have had hanging over me for the last two years to do.

Thank you for your kind words about *Two Concepts of Liberty*. As to the question of individual liberty as a political ideal in the ancient world and Pericles' speech,[4] I am not sure. At the time when I wrote this lecture I felt

1 Fiorenza Cossotto (b. 1935), Italian mezzo-soprano, made her Covent Garden début in late June 1959 as Neris in *Medea* (the Italian version of Cherubini's 1797 opera), alongside Callas in the title-role.

2 Fedor Ivanovich Shalyapin (usually 'Chaliapin' in English; 1873–1938), Russian operatic bass renowned for his powerful stage presence; IB remembered hearing him sing the title role in *Boris Godunov* in St Petersburg in 1917.

3 Bernard Crick (1929–2008), political theorist; taught at Harvard 1952–4, McGill 1954–5, LSE 1957–65; Visiting Fellow, Berkeley, 1955–6; later Professor of Political Theory and Institutions, Sheffield, 1965–71, and Professor of Politics, London (Birkbeck), 1971–84. *The American Science of Politics* (London and Berkeley, 1959) was his first major work.

4 In his *History of the Peloponnesian War* the Greek historian Thucydides (c.460–c.399 BC) allegedly reproduces the funeral oration for those fallen in battle given by the Athenian leader Pericles (c.495–429 BC), a speech which details the characteristics of Athenian democracy, including an individual's rights to self-determination: 'we live as free citizens, both in our public life and in our attitude to one another in the affairs of daily life; we are not angry with our neighbour if he behaves as he pleases, we do not cast sour looks at him, which if they can do no harm nevertheless can cause pain' (2. 37). For a fuller treatment of the issue broached here by IB see his 'The

pretty certain that individual liberty – and especially privacy – were not ideals which anyone had thought of in the ancient world, either Greek or Hebrew. I have read and re-read the relevant passage and I cannot persuade myself that Thucydides means much more than that there are tough States like Sparta and States of a looser texture; that in Athens people are much more easy-going and nobody gives black looks at other people simply for doing what they want to do, and that there is a good deal of individual liberty in existence. But this is a very different thing, it seems to me (that is a point on which I should like to secure your agreement), from saying that there is a con-ception of the *right* to individual activity, or a *right* not to be interfered with, or something intrinsic, something the violation of which is a violation of some ultimate principle. It seems to me that among the Greeks the polis gives and the polis takes away: it is the sole source of authority, or no doubt is itself obliged to live under some kind of unwritten eternal laws which Antigone talks about,[1] [and] which the priests or legislators or immemorial custom protect. The City can no doubt let you do what you want, and that is more civilised and more agreeable and a matter of pride to the Athenians, but if it chooses to take these liberties away, whether because there is a genuine crisis or because severer men are in charge, the individual surely has no concep-tion – in the ancient world – of the violation of his rights as an individual, of some walled-off area within which external authority has no right of entrance. That was my point, and despite Pericles' remarks I think it still stands.

As for the Romans etc., the name that made the strongest impression on me was a Strasbourg Professor of Law called Villey,[2] who, in a book I quoted in a footnote in the lecture, seemed to me to have proved that the Romans talked about Law and about Right, but that the notion of individual rights as inhering in individuals or corporations, as inhering at all (a metaphysical enough idea but important in modern political development), is medieval in character and not to be met with before Occam. I was very surprised by this, as I had always assumed that there was a lot about private rights in Roman Law – and that is, I think, what most of the Roman lawyers probably still think. But Villey's arguments seem to me very good. I may be wrong: but I cannot help thinking that there is a gap between the idea that in good and secure times individuals, like children, are allowed to play by a kind and tolerant State, and the idea that all men possess certain delimited areas within which no other agency is permitted to enter at all – by an absolute rule – or else he is permitted to enter only under highly exceptional and crit-

Birth of Greek Individualism: A Turning-Point in the History of Political Thought', in L: this passage is discussed at 300; cf. L 33.
1 She says to King Creon: 'I did not think your proclamations had sufficient power to enable you, a mortal, to transgress the gods' unwritten, immutable laws.' Sophocles, *Antigone*, 453–5.
2 Michel Villey (1914–88), at this time Professor of Law in Strasbourg (later in Paris). In his lecture (L 176, note 1) IB refers approvingly to Villey's *Leçons d'histoire de la philosophie du droit* (Paris, 1957).

ical circumstances. The conflict in the *Antigone* is between reasons of State and natural law – but the further proposition that every man [has?] such a right to dispose himself in certain ways as he pleases, as part of the natural law, seems to me much much later. However, I may be hopelessly mistaken about this. The Professor of Greek History in this University – Andrewes – quoting another Professor of Greek History – Gomme[1] – agrees with you. I am shaken, but still obdurate.

Yours,

Isaiah Berlin

TO KAY GRAHAM

18 July 1959 [*manuscript*]

Headington House

Dearest Kay

I was very very sorry to read that your father[2] had died. No doubt you were, in some sense, expecting this for some time: at least it was not *totally* surprising, & yet when it happens it is not what one expects. I had the self same experience in 1953: I knew my father was dying of leukaemia – it is a most awful thing – & in your case I hope fervently that it was sudden, painless, swift. But in one's own case the oldest root in one's life goes, & nothing is ever quite the same. Not that anyone can ever quite know anyone else's feeling: but I have a notion (perhaps this is presumption) that I do somehow know. I admired your father greatly. I liked & respected the stout hearted firm texture – the strong & simple moral foundation of his beliefs & life – he seemed to me totally free from fear & feelings of shame – nothing scared him, he had nothing to be ashamed of – goodness how enviable; you once remarked with some sharpness of insight about me (you won't even remember) that I seemed to make for solid rooted characters whatever their other attributes – e.g. Rumbolds, Joe (he is *rooted* enough) Chip Bohlen, etc. & away from sensitive cosmopolitans. Your father possessed a head, a heart, a steady sense of reality, colossal dependability – it could *never* have occurred to anyone not to trust him – firm values & an affectionate nature. He was, it seemed to me who wobble & am never sure that what I do, think etc. is right – never – that he was always on top of *his* subjects, his activities: a brave, public spirited, very good man. [...]

My fondest love & Aline's

Isaiah

---

1 Arnold Wycombe Gomme (1886–1959), Professor of Greek, Glasgow, 1946–57.

2 KG's father, Eugene Isaac Meyer (1875–1959), owner of the *Washington Post* 1933–59 (publisher 1933–46, editor 1940–6), had died on 17 July.

IB and Aline spent the summer at the Villa Cipressina, 'a house in Portofino which we should like to buy if only its owner were prepared to sell, overlooking the piazza and the port'.[1] As IB's back recovered, days 'acquired a fixed rhythm: in the morning sea & sand; lunch; rest; work; dinner; conversation',[2] interrupted only by visits to Aix-en-Provence and Verona for opera performances. In late August Aline's children and a fluctuating population of other visitors joined them. Plans were made for the wedding of Michel Strauss and his Australian fiancée[3] in October, IB prepared for his new role as Chairman of the Opera Sub-Committee at Covent Garden, and the demands of academic life remained inescapable: 'What gets me down is that nothing is ever a holiday: one worries, dictates into [a] machine, takes notes of dull but indispensable writers, prepares lectures, reviews, articles continuously & no moment is genuinely free.'[4]

TO DAVID FREUDENTHAL[5]

14 August 1959 [*carbon*]

Villa Cipressina, Portofino

Dear David,

Thank you for your letter of July 23. In this terrestrial paradise where I am it is indeed difficult to think of anything serious, but I shall attempt it. He was indeed a man of contradictory traits. Weizmann, I mean – or rather a mixture of attractive and unattractive characteristics – not, I think, contradictory in any way. It seemed to me, on the contrary, that he was very harmonious and monolithic, and although his ruthlessness, lack of scruple where great political ends were concerned, total disregard of personalities, vast appetite for life and experience, which certainly precluded the more saintly and private virtues – while all this might have been repellent to some, contradicted nothing else in his nature. I should like to know what you found self-contradictory in him, for others have said similar things to me and I was never clear about what exactly was meant. As for Brandeis, the conflict was partly a direct one of dominant personalities, for in his gentle, high-minded, infinitely scrupulous way, Brandeis wanted to play second fiddle to no one, and regarded himself, rightly, as first among American Zionists, the first man of any stature to break with conformity and respectability in this regard and

1 Letter of 23 February to Arcadi Nebolsine.
2 Postcard of 2 August to Marie Berlin.
3 Margery Tongway (b. 1932).
4 Postcard of 11 September to Jack Donaldson.
5 David Martin Freudenthal (1895–1977), US businessman who, as special assistant to the Economic Cooperation Administration [Marshall Plan] Mission in Rome 1948–9 (and afterwards), contributed to the post-war revival of Italian economic and cultural life; a Director of Farrar, Straus and Cudahy, the US publishers of IB's Herbert Samuel Lecture on Weizmann, about which he had written to IB with congratulations and comments.

to move in an ideologically very bold direction, which frightened a great many respectable Jews in its time – and therefore wanted at least equality of status with Weizmann, quite naturally. This Weizmann was prepared to grant to no one – like Churchill, he either dominated or retreated. He was not prepared to co-operate in any serious way; and this was one of the vices of his unique virtues. The real issue over which they quarrelled was, I think, genuine and not personal – objective I mean. Brandeis did want to develop Palestine on rational, businesslike lines, like the enlightened European country in its attitude to a colony which is to be a future dominion, and ultimately independent. This is a very rational and sensible approach, but not one which corresponded to or could be blended with the character or aspirations of the Eastern European masses whom Weizmann not merely represented but regarded (rightly, I think) as ultimately the only people whose attitude, rate of immigration etc. would make an ultimate difference to the country. This is what he meant by his 'democratic' as opposed to Brandeis's 'technocratic' approach. I think that ultimately he was right. To turn Palestine into a model country of immigration managed by pure, disinterested, enlightened experts, for the benefit of their less fortunate and less enlightened and technically untrained brothers was, in the conditions of the 1920s and 1930s, Utopian, quite apart from such natural moral reactions as would have occurred among the potential immigrants towards their remote benefactors, however devoted. This is what got Weizmann into trouble with various representatives of the Warburgs in America[1] and of similar millionaires in England operating in Palestine itself. In these regards he saw himself as the representative of the crude masses and his strength and success lay precisely in that. Brandeis behaved too much like a Westerner, whereas Palestine was built up not only out of Eastern human beings but their atmosphere and attitudes as well, which, however open to criticism, was all there was to operate with. That at least is my reading of what happened. I have never got Felix Frankfurter to agree.

As to the remark on page 40,[2] I do indeed think that when a man enters public life, then to retreat because he cannot bear to compromise his own integrity in any degree – because he is anxious about his own moral condition beyond that of the utilitarian considerations – the lives and happiness of the people who have come to depend on him – is in the end a kind of very, very noble, grand, morally moving, infinitely to be sympathised with spiritual pride. I do not think that Woodrow Wilson's tragedy[3] is quite of this

---

1 Felix Moritz Warburg (1871–1937), banker and philanthropist from the German banking dynasty, had become one of the leaders of US Jewry; though an active suppporter of Jewish activities in Palestine, he was not a Zionist and often clashed with Weizmann.

2 'He did not disguise his lack of respect for purists of this type. [...] it is a point of view that seems to me superior to its opposite.' PI2 54.

3 Little of Wilson's 14-point idealistic plan for world affairs after the First World War came into effect; in particular he failed to achieve US membership of the League of Nations.

sort – he was genuinely politically blinded by his own moral idealism and was not prepared to compromise the future of the world in a direction which he thought immoral, either by promising less than he did in Europe or by playing along with American public opinion at the cost of his own ultimate convictions. This is simply to make a mistake about what public life is and what kind of material people are made of, and it is tragic when it happens to a man in a powerful position, for it involves terrible suffering for others, but it isn't quite the contrast I wanted to draw between Weizmann's position and that of people who were shocked by his behaviour. These people ultimately wanted to keep themselves pure from the contamination of public life altogether, because it involved too much 'flexibility' of principles. They preferred a tranquil conscience to doing good if these two things came into conflict. If they do come into conflict, it is a terrible moral *naïveté* which leads to terrible trouble to think all good things are compatible and that if only one is honest enough and strong-willed enough, one will do more good than if one understands the material one is moulding. This Weizmann did not believe, and although one respects people who prefer private virtues – indeed I feel morally far more comfortable among them myself – I do not really like the company of great men who are necessarily too brutal and contemptuous of individuals for my taste – yet if there is to be public life it cannot be conducted by such as us (I include you confidently, I hope you do not mind).

I should love to hear your reactions to all this – I do not know when I shall be in America again. It was very nice hearing from you.

Yours ever,

TO WILLIAM JAMES

14 August 1959 [*carbon*]

Villa Cipressina

Dear Bill,

Despite the Vespas, the monotony of the food, the tourists, the Germans, the French, the English, the Americans, the Swiss, the Swedes, this is an earthly paradise. We wish you were here – you would like it better than even Tucson, although the light is so clear, the colours are so primary, life seems so natural and intelligible that it does not dispose to metaphysical or any other speculation. But perhaps better so. About Killian,[1] Whitehead and

---

1 James Rhyne Killian (1904–88), President, MIT, 1948–59; Special Assistant (to President Eisenhower) for Science and Technology 1957–9. WJ had written on 5 March 1959: 'I asked Killian if it was true that atomic physicists now agree that the observer and the observed may no longer be divorced. He answered yes. So, I now ask you why this does not end the dualism of subjective and objective, – and put the old positivists out of the window. Why doesn't someone write the implications of this? If I understand Whitehead, he was already there.'

the observer and the observed. Certainly, once one leaves common sense (as in philosophy perhaps one shouldn't) the hard lumps of our past have dissolved into something that in ordinary language neither makes nor is meant to make any sense at all. The physical properties of the observer are certainly now intermixed with those of the object he observes. I am not sure whether philosophically this really does make as much difference as many – since Whitehead and Eddington[1] – have maintained, for the philosophical observer was seldom the body in space which was conceived as a disembodied observer whose body was part of the object rather than the observing subject. On the other hand, if one were to maintain, as some very intelligent people have, that it makes no sense to speak of disembodied observers who observe at or from no particular place and at no particular date or instant, then we are indeed in trouble. Ever since I have left logic and theory of knowledge and metaphysics for the wilder (this is not a misprint for wider) delights of political thought, I have mere amateur status as a philosopher and am looked at with kindly but patronising affection by my ex-colleagues, like Austin and Hampshire (I do not remember if you met him while you were in Oxford – I think you did – a very good-looking and elegant, and sweet and noble young philosopher, whose book,[2] just appeared, I am sending you). But never mind, I shall go struggling on. In political philosophy the observer certainly cannot be divorced from what he observes, and nobody has ever tried to maintain that he could. My subject has fallen on evil days. In the days of the great bearded sages of Balliol and the German universities, political philosophy was regarded as the peak towards which all other forms of thought were climbing. This was certainly absurd – but I am not sure that the reaction has not gone too far, whereby these problems, which after all dominate people's lives, divide the world and cause dreadful troubles, are intellectually all that contemptible.

We are expecting a visit from the Marchesa Origo, whom I expect you know. I am not sure that Aline wants to see anyone just now – surrounded by her children she gives herself to the forces of nature, which seem to me glad enough to accept her. I repeat: I wish you were here. While one is in Italy one cannot conceive of any motive for being anywhere else. It is a terrible thought that all the references, so contemptuous, to Italians in the nineteenth century as unworthy descendants of the glorious Romans, which you will find in all English novels, guide books, journals etc., have ceased, not as the result of deeper insight or better manners, but because of Fascism and the respect that it extorted. Upon this sad reflection upon human frailty I end. We may be in America at Christmas. If so I shall certainly let you know

---

1 Sir Arthur Stanley Eddington (1882–1944), astrophysicist who contributed to the theories of relativity.
2 *Thought and Action* (London, 1959).

at once – alternatively, we may go to Moscow. We only go to the centres of power.

Yours ever,

TO PATRICK SWIFT[1]

14 August 1959

Villa Cipressina

Dear Mr Swift,

I am most grateful to you for your letter of July 31 – it is a great compliment to me that you should think me qualified to write about the Romantic tradition, but really I am not: I have very little visual sensibility and it would be sheer impertinence for me to write about criticism connected with the visual arts, even though writers like Byron, Stendhal, Delacroix etc. are of the deepest interest to me. I must, therefore, decline your very kind offer, simply on the ground of incompetence – believe me, this is not false modesty, but the plain truth. On the other hand, I am delighted that a serious periodical of the kind you describe is about to appear, and wish it every possible success.

I have a piece which may be of interest to you, in my drawer, on the reactionary Catholic apologist, Joseph de Maistre.[2] It is somewhat long – I should think about twelve thousand words[3] – and it would need a little revision before it was printed – it has no direct relationship to the kind of Romanticism about which you speak, save that of course he was a writer of that age, was deeply anti-revolutionary and anti-liberal, said some of the most crushing things ever said about enlightenment, many of which were unfair and brutal, but all of which possessed a certain depth of brilliance which none of the Fascists who followed him (he has some right to be considered as a genuine predecessor if not the father of Fascism) ever showed. If you think that this might be suitable for you I should be delighted to let you have it some time in October or November. There is a sense in which Maistre, although he regarded himself as a classical author, imbued with Latin genius, Thomas Aquinas etc., was the typical Romantic of the 'black' Nietzschian type. My essay is really nothing other than an attempt to give his due to a thinker relatively neglected in England, thought of as a mere bitter reactionary – a kind of throw-back to an earlier period, a medieval

---

1 Patrick Swift (1927–83), Irish-born painter; founding editor (with the poet David Wright) of *X*, a quarterly literary and artistic review, 1959–62. His letter of 31 July to IB had sought, for the magazine's first issue, comments on the Romantic Exhibition then running in London, and identified the 'prophetic nature of the vision of the major writers' of the Romantic age as 'an active and disturbing element in the psychology of an artist or thinker of today'.

2 See 646/1. PS expressed interest but IB then remembered that he had promised the piece to the (US) *Partisan Review*; publication in both magazines was considered but proved impractical (and the piece was far too long for either). In the end neither published it.

3 A characteristic underestimate. The text published in CTH runs to over 25,000 words.

schoolman born too late: whereas in fact I think he was an anticipator of much of the anti-rationalism that is most horrifying in the present, and said a great deal that is romantically violent, disagreeable but extremely true, and which liberals lose by averting their faces from it. I shall be here until mid-September, but if you write to All Souls the letter will be forwarded to me.

Yours sincerely,

Igor Stravinsky had concert and recording engagements in London during November; IB drew on Aline's links with the Ritz Hotel to arrange his accommodation.

TO ROBERT CRAFT

28 September 1959

Headington House

Dear Robert,

I was delighted to receive your letter. All that I could do about the Ritz I have done. [...] The rooms in the Ritz are solid, bathrooms enormous, the service moderately good, old-fashioned but dependable, the porters excellent (one has just written his memoirs,[1] mainly about the Aga Khan), the manager an idiot (Schwenter[2] is the name), the restaurant large, quiet and restful to the nerves, but the food dull and uninspiring to a degree – the owner of the Ritz,[3] an old dog-racing specialist known to my wife, does not want it to be smart, efficient, or attract too much custom. Hence the restaurant is discouraged from tempting its clients and the food is kept deliberately British and tedious. Unless you countermand the order I shall go and inspect the Stravinskys' apartments next Tuesday and shall try and secure for them one large bedroom and adhering to it one smaller one (that is the normal pattern), since two large inter-communicating bedrooms do not I think exist unless there is a drawing-room in between in which case the whole thing becomes a suite and costs a good deal more. My telegram about quiet versus space is due to the fact that the handsome tall rooms are in Piccadilly, the views agreeable and lively but the noise is considerable, and one has to put wax boules in one's ears if one is to sleep at all soundly; alternatively one can probably secure a room looking over the Green Park, quieter (not as quiet as Claridge's) but smaller, less solidly built etc. I shall try and balance all these factors as best I can and persuade the manager that the honour to him is so great that he must climb out of his skin to please. But I am convinced that

---

1 George Criticos, *The Life Story of George of the Ritz as Told to Richard Viner* (London, 1959).

2 Edward Francis Schwenter (1897–1976), General Manager of the Ritz Hotel for many years.

3 Sir Bracewell Smith (1884–1966), 1st Baronet 1947, property investor and Conservative politician; Chairman, Arsenal Football Club, 1948–61. In his speech as Company Chairman to the AGM of The Ritz Hotel (London) Limited on 30 April 1954 he undertook that the hotel's 'cuisine must be of the highest possible standard'. 'Ritz Hotel', *The Times*, 3 May 1954, 12.

he will think the whole thing is a practical joke, as he has never heard of music, composers, or anything but the name of the proprietor of the hotel and some racing peers and one or two quiet Americans. I shall do my best.

We shall do our best to go to all possible concerts: whether this will be possible will depend a little on my academic duties. I am a tremulous and unexpectedly conscientious Professor and if I have a lecture on the next morning I find it very difficult to go out on the night before.[1] But I shall do everything that is possible, naturally enough: 2 November (a Monday?) will suit us very well, if that is when you all want to come. We shall be delighted, not have a formal reception as last time, but ask one or two people who are likely to give pleasure, for example, Prof. Ayer, whom you ask for, who by that time will be living here, I think; on the other hand, Harold Nicolson and Vita (Victoria) Sackville-West[2] are remote from Oxford and might be lured to London – he is always there, she comes if pressed. She is very unamusing, though gifted, and has strong saps of the earth running powerfully through her veins, and is interested in flowers and land, and is like a figure of earth. I admire her, but do not find her sympathetic or gay. When you say Forster, you mean E. M.? He is a gentle old creature who speaks in a low, low voice, giggles like a schoolgirl, and likes flattening subjects to the lowest level to which they can naturally attain if unsupported, in this respect rather like T. S. Eliot. I do not know him well – I must have met him two or three times in my life – he is very clever, charming, and deliberately provincial: his outlook is that of, let us say, the city of Guildford, where he comes from. He is very fond of Wagner, and is the most English of all English phenomena, somewhat self-consciously and deliberately so. Stephen could ask him easily, but if the evening or afternoon is not to end in a series of gentle whimpers, someone with a little vitality would have to be imported to keep him going, unless you or the Stravinskys are prepared to prod him into constant life. His principal interests in the world are what Mr Kolodin, in his notorious review of Spoleto,[3] so disagreeably refers to as the third sex. Whenever a book by one of its inhabitants is unfavourably reviewed by anyone known to

1 To Nancy Lancaster IB admitted 'I hate going to lectures myself, I don't think I have ever heard anyone who kept my attention for an hour. Hugh's Inaugural did because of all the barbs – and the person I most detest listening to is myself. I would willingly stop lecturing if it were permitted, and if I were not so ashamed of seeming to do no work; I have no conscience in the matter, only fear of the opinion of others, I think.' Letter of 19 October 1959.
2 Victoria Mary ('Vita') Sackville-West (1892–1962), daughter of 3rd Baron Sackville, wife of Harold Nicolson and mother of IB's friend Ben Nicolson; poet, novelist, short-story writer and biographer; during the 1930s she created, with her husband, a world-famous garden at Sissinghurst, Kent, and wrote a weekly gardening column for the Observer 1946–61 (of which Vera Stravinsky was a reader; her husband had read all Sackville-West's works, according to Craft).
3 Irving Kolodin (1908–88), influential music critic of the Saturday Review 1947–82. His unenthusiastic review of the 1959 Festival dei Due Mondi at Spoleto described it as 'involving what might be called the three sexes' and deplored 'the preciosity and the prejudices' that the homosexual coterie brought to opera. 'Menotti, and Some Other Opera Composers', Saturday Review, 25 July 1959, 41.

Forster, he despatches a small postcard saying 'How could you have brought yourself, in these days, to have written . . .?' etc. Isherwood's devotion to him rests entirely on this. Still, he is the best living English novelist without a doubt. If you have tea with him it is exactly like having one with an excellent character-actor who pretends to be a distraught old aunt: 'Oh dear, oh dear, where have I put my spectacles? – what a lot of jam we have all eaten! Electric torches are much more practical than candles, I never know how to ask for the right kind of batteries' etc. I should love to see him and Nicolas Nabokov in a room together, it would be a clash of cultures such as has never been. [. . .]

Yours,

Isaiah

One of the many responses to Two Concepts of Liberty *was from an undergraduate who claimed the largely uncritical acceptance in Oxford of IB's arguments as evidence of the deplorable state of education in the University and throughout the country.*

TO THE EDITOR OF THE *NEW STATESMAN*[1]

Oxford

Sir,

In an article entitled 'An Oxford Manifesto'[2] which appeared in your issue of 10 October, Mr J. Ungoed-Thomas[3] expressed his surprise and concern at the fact that certain views which, according to him, I had stated in a recent published lecture had not met with sharper criticism.

These views are summed up by him as (1) that 'the desire to participate in governing the community to which one belongs ought to be repressed, for it can lead to tyranny'; and (2) something less definite which might lead us to 'shrug our shoulders and worry only about ourselves, as Berlin seems to advocate'. The fact that no voices were raised against such sentiments does, on the face of it, seem surprising, and indeed disturbing, and is regarded by your contributor as a symptom of the decadence of Oxford in particular and England in general.

The explanation is, however, a good deal more simple. These views are not to be found in my lecture. I did not express, nor do I support, either

---

1 'An Oxford Manifesto', *New Statesman*, 17 October 1959, 511.

2 Jasper Ungoed-Thomas, 'An Oxford Manifesto', *New Statesman*, 10 October 1959, 463–4, which concludes with a call for 'workers' controls and comprehensive schools' and the construction of a 'self-reliant society' free of 'all class systems whether based on wealth, birth or intellect'.

3 Jasper Rhodri Ungoed-Thomas (b. 1937), educated at Eton, Magdalen history 1957–60; later (1975–92) an HM Inspector of Schools and author of *Moral Education in the Secondary School* (1972) and *The Moral Situation of Children* (1978).

of these opinions or attitudes. I do not advocate quietism, or anarchism, or withdrawal from public activity or social responsibility, since I believe in the duty of political commitment no less than in individual rights. I have no idea what could have possessed Mr Ungoed-Thomas to impute to me opinions which I do not hold, as well as other absurdities with which he chooses to saddle me. If it is a misunderstanding, it is so profound as to be unique. I have no strong objection to acting as a peg on which your contributor hangs his somewhat censorious sermon on the shortcomings of his contemporaries; and I have complete sympathy with his plea for democratic, self-reliant humanism. But (to borrow your contributor's own tone) he should remember that ferocious misrepresentation, whatever its cause, does not make for an increase in human solidarity, and that the first and highest value of humanism has always been regard for the truth.

Isaiah Berlin

IB's young critic returned to the attack, but, faced with continuing misrepresentation of his arguments, IB brought the correspondence to an end.[1]

Bernard Berenson died on 6 October 1959, after two years of declining health.

TO NICKY MARIANO

19 October 1959 [*carbon*]

Headington House

Dearest Nicky,

If ever I ought to write by hand, it is now. But I decided that you would have enough to do as it is without the gratuitous imposition of having to read my wretched illegible Colefax-like hand.[2]

Of course you anticipated it for a long time and in some sense you must have been ready (was B.B.? He was so passionately fond of life and fought for it so well) and you must have been snowed under with letters and telegrams and messages, so I thought I would wait a little. Although you must have expected it, yet when it comes it is always different and more painful, and to answer all the letters and messages can be a very deadening task and merely physically exhausting (you mustn't dream of even acknowledging this one at least as such, there are nevertheless one or two questions I should like to put). I was very sorry to have met him so late in life, but I absolutely adored him, particularly when he said things with which I didn't agree. He looked on me, as you know, as someone who, having come from Eastern Europe and

---

1 The further instalments of the correspondence in the *New Statesman*, both headed 'An Oxford Manifesto', were Jasper Ungoed-Thomas's second letter, 24 October 1959, 545, and IB's reply, 31 October 1959, 582.
2 Sibyl Colefax's writing was notoriously illegible.

settled in the West, was able to understand the particular synthesis which he represented, and it is true in a sense. I was and am. On the last two occasions that I saw him he talked, when we were alone, at immense length about the Jews and his attitude towards them, about the persecution he underwent in their hands in the 1880s in New York – at the hands of the German ones – and how his life in some sense was inspired by a desire to avenge himself upon them by rising above and beyond, and compelling an admiration from them which he despised. This is not in the books, and I shall not tell Sylvia S.,[1] but it was a very rare glimpse, and I was terribly grateful to have been vouchsafed it. In other respects I find that I can only repeat about him what other people have said better, about his unbelievable charm, the universality of his gifts, his ruthless sense of quality, his lifelong service to the cause of the only thing which stands up in the chaos of this or any period – the works of human hands, art and thought. I thought that K. Clark's piece in the *Sunday Times*[2] was wonderfully good, both in substance and in content, although I have not told him so yet. What I myself thought quite extraordinary was his unflagging determination and capacity always *vom Leben abgewinnen*,[3] always to get whatever could be got from life and experience, from men and objects, the notion that it was shameful to give in to natural brute forces, that one must triumph over them and build something and understand everything, and mould everything, and realise all that is in one to the highest and freest possible degree. It is not a very religious ideal – I was fascinated to see in the otherwise dreary *Times* obituary[4] that he had been converted to Rome early in life – but it is a noble humanistic one, and nobody in our day has borne that flag so high and with such right. I also thought that his sense of truth and reality were greater than that of any man I had ever met – that he knew what was what by instinct which could not be deceived, that he was both very clever and very wise, and that this was due to some mysterious capacity that he had of living with and not against nature, that he was not in the usual sense *déraciné* or, as it is fashionable to say now, 'alienated' from his roots – he was not an insulated intellectual or expert or even not a genius cut off from his proper environment and milieu who had made the best of his solitude in the world and created as he did out of the wound which this had inflicted. This was true of a great many of his friends and contemporaries,

---

1 Sylvia Sprigge (1903–66), née Saunders, journalist, author, biographer, translator; Italian correspondent of the *Manchester Guardian* 1928–31 (succeeding her future husband) and 1943–53. When her biography *Berenson* (London, 1960) appeared, IB commented: 'I have only read one chapter, in which I found no fewer than thirty-seven errors, seven howlers, and a great many inaccuracies [...]. She was devoted to BB in her way, but is not a very fastidious or penetrating or perceptive writer.' Letter to Myron Gilmore, 18 March 1960.
2 Sir Kenneth Clark, 'The Sage of Art', *Sunday Times*, 11 October 1959, 15.
3 Correctly 'dem Leben etwas abzugewinnen' ('to get something out of life').
4 'Mr Bernard Berenson', *The Times*, 8 October 1959, 17.

Proust or Rilke[1] or Namier or Klemperer[2] (poor Klemperer is now so ill with a new illness – at present kept secret – pericarditis). I thought on the contrary that he was harmonious and integrated, and that his marvellous vitality and insight and economy of means and hatred of chaos and waste came from being in place. But then the noble tranquillity of I Tatti was surely as much due to yourself. I never knew Mrs Berenson,[3] but I cannot believe that it was anyone but you who could have given him – in the years when I knew him – the love, the devotion, the dignity and peace and sensibility and intelligence without which he could not have breathed.

I won't go on. The question I was going to put was only this. Now that Harvard is about to enter[4] and the new life begins, *aus den Ruinen*,[5] won't you come to England and stay with us? Or at least visit us? We would be so very genuinely pleased. I was due to come and visit you this summer from Portofino and would have made the suggestion then for some indefinite future, but then I thought that BB was well one day, and feeble the next, that I might be de trop, and did not do anything. Iris Origo came to see us and said that visitors did not improve things, in August. I do sincerely hope that his end was painless. He complained, as you know far better than I, of not having achieved this or that in his life, but it seems to me that his life was most enviable. I only hope that Harvard will understand how to preserve a memorial worthy of him. Somebody ought to write the truth about him one day, for it is marvellously worth telling – his attitude to Americans, to Italy, to his origins, to himself. It is uniquely fascinating. The only contribution I have made was to refuse to write an article for Max Ascoli on the subject of the kind that his readers would, in his view, have savoured. I do not think that BB would have disapproved of my act.

Do come and see us, and do forgive this most inadequate letter. Words are like sticks when it comes to talking about serious things. I would tear all this up except that I cannot not write, and nothing that I write would be any good.

With much love,
        Yours ever,

1 Rainer Maria Rilke (1875–1926), né René Karl Wilhelm Johann Josef Maria Rilke, German poet.

2 Otto Klemperer (1885–1973), German-born conductor, had suffered a succession of major health problems, including partial paralysis after removal of a brain tumour, a severe fall, and scalding.

3 Mary Berenson (1864–1945), née Smith, sister of Logan Pearsall Smith and of Bertrand Russell's first wife Alys; formerly married to Frank Costelloe; like her husband, an art historian, who contributed to his books; grandmother of IB's friend Barbara Halpern, née Strachey. Kenneth Clark contrasted her 'Giottoesque bulk' with Berenson's diminutive figure, while admitting that 'Mrs Berenson gave her volatile husband some of the ballast he lacked': op. cit. (705/2).

4 Berenson bequeathed I Tatti (together with its library, archives and works of art) to Harvard University, which established the Harvard University Center for Italian Renaissance Studies there.

5 'From the ruins'.

TO SIMON MARKS

23 October 1959 [*carbon*]

[Headington House]

Dear Simon,

I have been asked by an old friend of mine – and a man whom I admire and like very much indeed – called Alan Bullock, who is the head of St Catherine's College here, to introduce him to you. He is the head of a new College[1] to be constructed by a Danish architect[2] (much criticism, but the designs are far more splendid than anything offered by any British architect that I know) which is to do a lot for scientists at Oxford, who are at present miserably provided for – it will not consist exclusively of scientists but half and half of scientists and 'humanists'. I cannot disguise from you the fact that his purpose in seeking you out is probably to ask for some help with this project – he has received a good deal already both from individuals and firms, particularly Wolfson[3] (who has been very generous), Woolworth's etc. You will be thinking that I really have embarked upon a career as a schnorrer – I wish I had – I suspect it of being an amusing, agreeable and repaying one, full of the most delightful variety and wonderful moments – but alas, it is not in my timid temperament.

Alan Bullock is a very forthright northcountryman, with great warmth of heart, and one of the very best academic administrators in this country. I have a feeling that he will not ultimately remain here, but is bound to ascend to the top as head of the BBC, or editor of the *Manchester Guardian* or President of the British Republic or something of that kind. His book on Hitler[4] was a masterpiece (he rather resembles him – which only shows that appearance is not everything). At present he is engaged on a book about Bevin[5] – do not let that deter you – he is a just, good, honourable and very very sympathetic person. You will in fact enjoy meeting him – this is often said but seldom with such predictable truth.

I wish we met more often. Your last visit to Oxford incognito was a most shameful thing (I mean the not coming to see us). When will you? Any day or any hour. I really mean this – and Aline just as much.

I fear you will get a request for an interview from Alan Bullock – that honest Yorkshire Baptist face and the personality that sticks right out are

1 Alan Bullock was energetically raising funds to build St Catherine's College, as St Catherine's Society was to become. (He later raised the initial funds for the project of which the present volume is part.)

2 Arne Jacobsen (1902–71); his controversial design for St Catherine's College was later listed Grade I.

3 Isaac Wolfson (1897–1991), businessman. The Wolfson Foundation donated £75,000 for the library of St Catherine's College (and later funded the buildings for Wolfson College).

4 *Hitler: A Study in Tyranny* (London, 1952).

5 *The Life and Times of Ernest Bevin* (London, 1960, 1967, 1983), later condensed by Brian Brivati into one volume as *Ernest Bevin: A Biography* (London, 2002).

alone worth meeting – you may have watched him on television on which he constantly appears. But I must stop.

Yours,

TO DAN DAVIN

11 November 1959

Headington House

Dear Davin,

Thank you for your letter of 5 November.[1] I fully understand your difficulties with regard to the Oxford History of Modern Europe and am grateful for the very frank way in which you have put your enquiry to me. It has compelled me to think out my position in this matter, which I shall try to put to you with equal frankness.

When the idea of writing a *History of Ideas in Europe, 1789–1848* was first broached to me,[2] I explained to Dr Lane Poole,[3] with whom I discussed this, that since I had committed myself to two other books I could not begin to think of this one until the early 1960s. I hope I conveyed the same impression to the editors of the series[4] – certainly I intended to do so. For this reason I said that I could not be bound by date, and would try and compose a volume if and when I could. In the meanwhile I have other priorities on my list: the first is a book on political thought in the romantic age, arising out of the Bryn Mawr Lectures which I delivered some years ago, which are, according to my contract with them, to be published by the Oxford Press, certainly in America and I should hope here. After that comes a volume on Russian intellectual history, which certainly cannot take less than two years of continuous research to produce. Under these circumstances I cannot make any concrete promise about the volume in the Oxford History of Modern Europe.

I must also add that the idea in general, now that I have come to closer quarters with what its realisation must mean, daunts me. I should do my best to cope with the political, social and intellectual currents of the time; but perhaps the greatest and most influential factor of this period was the advance of the natural sciences. To write about that without some expert knowledge seems to me possibly fraudulent, certainly superficial; to omit it is unthinkable. Somewhat similar considerations apply to the history of the arts, particularly the visual arts, and of economic history, on which I am insufficiently expert. All this has been borne in upon me as the result

---

1 In which Davin enquired when IB was likely to finish the volume expected from him, and requested a specimen chapter as a 'help and encouragement' to OUP.
2 In 1948.
3 Austin Lane Poole (1889–1963), historian; President, St John's, Oxford, 1947–57; Delegate of OUP 1944–63.
4 Alan Bullock (Censor of St Catherine's) and Bill Deakin (Warden of St Antony's).

of my studies in the social and political history of the time, as well as the history of ideas; I am now inclined to think that no book on this general subject could in principle be of value, unless carried out by a man of near omniscience – or at any rate much broader knowledge in many fields than my own. But even if I am mistaken about this, I feel quite sure that this is not a task which I could promise to carry out. I feel less badly than I might about this prospect, since it seems to me that the purely narrative volumes in the Oxford History cannot in any case afford to leave out social and intellectual factors, and do not need such an auxiliary volume as was proposed to me in order to perform their own tasks.

Nevertheless I must own to having been at fault, if only because I had not thought all this out sufficiently when I too rashly said that I would attempt to write this volume. I have not given up hope of doing so. Arising out of the earlier volume more narrowly confined to social and political thought there will, I think, be other cognate issues in the same period with which I should like to try to deal. But it would be to deceive both the editors and yourself – as well as myself – if I were to say that I could make a concrete promise now.

I should therefore like to be released from this obligation. If I do produce such a volume, and it is unsuitable for the Oxford History, I shall understand this only too well and attempt to secure publication for it by some other means.

As for a specimen chapter – I have never been asked to do this before by any publisher, and although I fully understand your motive in doing so, I do not think I could bring myself to do so with regard to any book I am ever likely to publish.

I fear I have been too presumptuous and overestimated my own capacities, and so led the editors and yourself into error [in] that regard. I think it would be in your best interests, as well as mine, if my obligation in this matter were regarded as null and void. If, of course, you feel that I have in some way infringed some legal undertaking that I have made, I should like to be told what steps I can take to remedy this.

I sincerely hope that this makes matters clear between us, and apologise for not having offered these reflections spontaneously to you before you, quite understandably, decided to write me your letter.

I have sent a copy of this letter to the Warden of St Antony's and the Censor of St Catherine's.

Yours sincerely,
    Isaiah Berlin

Davin suggested on 24 November that the status quo should remain undisturbed: OUP would continue to wait until IB had time to write his volume. IB immediately accepted, admitting with relief that 'the whole thing is a great load off my conscience, which I hope you will believe me exists, and even gives trouble from time to time'.[1] *The book was never written.*

TO NORMAN CHESTER

5 December 1959 [*carbon*]

[Headington House]

Dear Norman,

[...] There are certainly no 'young political theorists' about, good or bad, who come to my mind. Interest in ideas is visibly declining not only in Oxford but in England generally, not only in political ideas but ideas about most other things as well; I don't wish to be unduly pessimistic about this, but I am; London University has a perfectly good Readership in the History of Political Ideas and there is no one to fill it. Three American universities have written to me asking whether there are any young Englishmen interested in contemporary problems, with theoretical equipment to analyse them, of a top-notch kind. I know of no one: neither, it seems, do they. Queer. Meanwhile the young left-wing undergraduates are looking for a father figure.

Yours,

TO THE EDITOR OF THE *JEWISH OBSERVER AND MIDDLE EAST REVIEW*[2]

Headington House

Sir,

In the course of your most interesting and, if I may say so, very generous review of my lecture on Moses Hess in your issue of 4 December[3] (which I deeply appreciate), you attribute to me at least one opinion which I do not hold. You say that Hess believed (although he did not state this directly) that even after the creation of the Jewish State all Jews must accept Jewish nationality if the Jewish problem was to be solved. And you add that few Zionists believe this today and that 'Sir Isaiah shares Moses Hess's conclusions that there is no eluding these requirements.'

I do not myself believe that Hess thought it necessary for all Jews to become nationals of the Jewish State after it had been created. Indeed I think that he considered that once a Jewish State was in existence, those who chose to dissociate themselves from it would then have a better moral right to do so, than to disown their persecuted brothers so long as they suffered the

---

1 Letter of 25 November 1959.
2 'Isaiah Berlin and Moses Hess', *Jewish Observer and Middle East Review*, 18 December 1959, 17.
3 Jon Kimche, 'Moses Hess or Isaiah Berlin', *Jewish Observer and Middle East Review*, 4 December 1959, 14–5, which described the published version of IB's 1957 lecture (603/1) as 'the outstanding Zionist book of the year, probably of many years'.

miseries of the Diaspora. But on this point your opinion is as valid as mine, and it may well be that I am mistaken.

But even if I am in error about Hess's views, I can hardly be so about my own, and if I gave you the impression that the view you attribute to Hess is also mine, then I have misled you and perhaps others. I did not set out to give my views on the problems that troubled Hess, although of course I may have conveyed them unintentionally; at any rate the view that there is a moral obligation upon all Jews to become members of the Jewish State is a view which I do not hold; indeed I am specifically opposed to it. I have tried to give my reasons for this elsewhere, and will not burden your pages with them. I cannot think how I could have come to convey the opposite impression; in any case I am grateful for this opportunity of clearing up a misunderstanding.

As for Marx's anti-Semitism, there is, I suspect, a genuine difference of opinion between us. Marx attacks Christianity as a historically conditioned illusion unavoidable in its own time, whose hour has struck at last. He attacks Judaism as a parasitic growth upon society, neither race nor religion but an economic junction identical with money-lending and exploitation, which is the language of an anti-Semite. If you need further evidence for his attitude there are some apposite quotations in Mr E. H. Carr's biography of Marx,[1] in which Marx refers to Lassalle's[2] 'Jewish whine', speculates about the negroid shape of his head, etc., which seems to me the very language of 'vulgar anti-Semites' from which you wish to defend him. It is part of the nobility of Hess's character to have ignored these weaknesses, and remained loyal to the end to a man in whose genius, whether rightly or wrongly, he believed to his dying day.

Isaiah Berlin

TO NORMAN BIRNBAUM[3]

8 December 1959 [carbon]

[Headington House]

Dear Birnbaum,

You really must write an essay on the adventures of the idea of alienation. That in any case. As to what you rightly call the 'boom' in the word, it is not

1 *Karl Marx: A Study in Fanaticism* (London, 1934).
2 Ferdinand Lassalle (1825–64), German Jewish lawyer, political thinker and active socialist (who died after a duel with a rival in love).
3 Norman Birnbaum (b. 1926), US sociologist; taught at LSE 1953–9; Fellow of Nuffield 1959–66; later Mellon Professor of Humanities, Georgetown, 1979–81, University Professor 1981–2001. In his letter of 5 December NB discussed the popularity and value of 'alienation' as a concept, thanked IB for encouraging him to move to Oxford and reflected: 'how starved, and how blind the young! [...] What can one say about a great university in which all the bright young men spend most of their time attacking one of their most distinguished teachers, namely yourself, for views which he patently does not hold?'

really a good thing. You say the intellectuals need a metaphysical beginning-point for their search for a way out of the present discontents. I agree. There are at least two things very wrong with making 'alienation' this base. Firstly, it is a genuinely obscure notion. It may tie Marxism with Freud, but since the concept of alienation is not a very empirically solid one, either in Marx or in Freud, the combination of the two merely leads to a typical Central European amalgam against which sooner or later there will be a violent reaction with excessively deflationary consequences (as happened with the case of logical positivism). Metaphysical foundations are needed all right, but alienation seems to me not so much metaphysical as historical and theo-logical and precisely the kind of thing against which Marx in the 1840s and Freud in the 1890s reacted in a very iconoclastic and tough-minded manner. In short I think it is a piece of foggy obfuscating woolly old-fashioned ideal-ism in the worst sense. If cleaned up, no doubt it could be of use, but this would have to be done first. This is conspicuously not the case either in Paris or Oxford.

Secondly, more important is the fact that, as preached at present, it is part and parcel of a doctrine which presupposes the possibility of some kind of terrestrial paradise – an ideal state of affairs which is the solution of all problems and the harmonisation of all values. Freud certainly lends no plausibility to such a notion and Hegel not much: it derives partly from eighteenth-century rationalism, partly from Christianity, both of which are based upon the idea that a final solution for all human ills is possible once and for all. I cannot deny that I do believe the opposite of all this, and if the young men attack me for that, they attack me rightly. (I wonder who the brightest young men really are: mostly they are philosophers here at present and they certainly have no truck with alienation. The ones that do are non-philosophers who hanker after ideas. What is true is that in the non-philosophical departments of Oxford the absence of ideas and fear of them is acute and dangerous. Among the philosophers the ideas may be inadequate or false but at least they are ideas. Hence again I think Gellner[1] has shot at the wrong target; I think his own fate, if he goes on like this, will be very like that of Poujade – namely to be forgotten. He is an able man and in a way quite nice, but this was a very unworthy performance. Still he could, if he became serious, and got on with the positive side of his job, do a great deal of good. I wish this didn't sound so governessy, but I have a feeling about his book that it was a piece of private self-indulgence and not a disinterested piece of rescue work.

1 Ernest André Gellner (1925–95), of Czech descent, philosopher and (later) anthropologist; taught at LSE 1949–62 (Professor 1962–84); later (1984–93) William Wyse Professor of Social Anthropology, Cambridge. His first book, *Words and Things* (London, 1959), an attack on the lin-guistic philosophy of the time (and its mainly Oxford-based practitioners), brought him instant fame. Gilbert Ryle's refusal to have the book reviewed in *Mind* provoked a long correspondence in *The Times* during November 1959.

At the base of Chuck Taylor's[1] beliefs is (a) teleology – the notion that there is a spiritual direction of human affairs as stated by the Roman Catholic faith; (b) the notion of the perfect state or ideal condition in which everything is harmonised. I believe in neither of these things and think, like some old-fashioned rationalist – Raphael[2] or Moore – that beliefs founded on falsehoods should not be propagated, don't you agree? I see that in 1840 secularised religion was a natural bridge to secularism, but why should we – you and I – be going through this now? And because there is a natural reaction against the dry bones of atheistical positivism at its shallowest and dreariest, should one not take care not to take part in a [word(s) missing] boom, in which everything will appear as something else and in which the later deflators will rightly mock at the ghastly piece of confused spiritual self-indulgence?

Do write to me to the Carlyle Hotel, Madison Avenue, New York, if you have a moment. I will certainly give your love to Messrs White, Hughes, and Schlesinger.

Yours,

In mid-December IB returned to America. The main purpose of the trip was to read a paper[3] to over 3,000 members of the American Historical Association on 28 December in Chicago, in 'the biggest ballroom in the biggest hotel in the world',[4] but most of IB's stay was in New York, where he received an honorary degree from the Jewish Theological Seminary of America[5] and where his mother-in-law was a permanent resident of the Carlyle Hotel. He returned to Oxford in early January 1960.

1 Charles Margrave ('Chuck') Taylor (b. 1931), Canadian philosopher (and Roman Catholic); Balliol PPE 1952–5; Fellow of All Souls 1956–61; taught at McGill 1961–76 (Professor of Philosophy 1973–6); IB's successor but one as Chichele Professor of Social and Political Theory, Oxford, 1976–81; Professor of Political Science and Philosophy, McGill, 1982–98.
2 David Daiches Raphael (b. 1916), Lecturer in Moral Philosophy, Glasgow, 1949–51, Senior Lecturer 1951–60; later (1973–83) Professor of Philosophy, London (Imperial).
3 'On the Notion of Scientific History', the short version – theoretically 35 minutes long – of what was published as 'History and Theory: The Concept of Scientific History' in *History and Theory* 1 (1960), 1–31. IB went through his usual agonies as he prepared the lecture, fearing that 'the paper that I am to read is too long, too obscure, too foggy, ill-shaped, dough-like, and probably too dogmatic, obscurantist and rhetorical' (letter to Myron Gilmore, 25 September 1959), but Gilmore thought it 'wonderful' (letter of 4 January 1960), and when IB repeated the lecture soon afterwards in Oxford the future journalist Paul Foot described it enthusiastically to his godfather (who passed the praise on to IB): 'a glorious talk by Sir Isaiah on the philosophy of history in which he took by the throat the theory that History is a natural science "like biology", shook it to pieces with his enormous intellect and threw it out of existence. What a wonderful man he is! It is in brief periods like that that I realise the true glory of education – the confronting of a superb mind, coupled with supreme articulacy and irrepressible enthusiasm.' Undated letter (May? 1960) from Stewart Perowne.
4 Letter of 16 May 1960 replying to Perowne (see previous note).
5 IB was made an honorary Doctor of Laws there on 20 December (Plate 41).

"OXFORD" PANTS
FOR KNOWLEDGE

"Liberty" 7/6d.
"Unilateral"   "Airstrip'   "Papyrus"   "Hoplite"   "Parson's Pleasure"   "Stricken Deer"
£3 15s. 6d.   1½d.   15/-   3 dr.   £47 10s. 0d.

Drawing by David Hawkins in the Oxford undergraduate magazine Mesopotamia,
*early 1960: A. J. P. Taylor (a supporter of unilateral nuclear disarmament), A. J. Ayer, IB,
E. R. Dodds (Regius Professor of Greek), the ancient historian Russell Meiggs (a hoplite is a
heavily armed ancient Greek foot soldier; the price is given in Greek drachmas), generic figure
('Parson's Pleasure' was a nude male bathing area on the river Cherwell), David Cecil (whose
1929 life of Cowper is entitled* The Stricken Deer*)*

TO NICHOLAS SEKERS[1]

15 January 1960 [*carbon*]

Headington House

Dear Mr Sekers,

Thank you for your most delightful letter. I too feel our bond to be a
source of pride and pleasure to me.

Also of immense relief. No doctor has ever finally pronounced about
my poor heart. It was 'discovered' quite unnecessarily by a London doctor,[2]
who decided to take an electrocardiogram simply because he had installed

---

1 Nicholas Thomas ('Miki') Sekers (1910–72), né Szekeres in Hungary; textile manufacturer and
   energetic patron of the arts. Responding to a request from IB for details of his heart condition, he
   described (letter of 14 December 1959) the pessimistic prognoses offered by doctors in Hungary
   and England and the more reassuring diagnosis by Dr Goldman that his system was coping well
   with a congenital condition. However, within a decade NS needed major heart surgery and died
   suddenly two years afterwards.
2 Dr Jacob Snowman; see 468/2.

a new apparatus in his office and wished to test [it] on someone. I was its first victim. Upon looking at my cardiogram he whistled (this was about five years ago) and attributed a hideous heart condition to me. I was taken from heart specialist to heart specialist, all of whom shook their heads and made gestures of despair over the cardiogram, which, they had declared, appeared to them unlike any that had ever been seen. One of them decided to send it to a medical journal. I have no idea whether he in fact did so or not. I too developed mild pains, which caused a Paris doctor[1] to diagnose me as a victim of ischaemia, while the London doctors used other words. In the end it was agreed that my only complaint was cardiographic. Dr Goldman[2] merely confirmed what everyone else had said – namely that I might be prey to some mysterious ailment, but that neither the symptoms nor the remedies could possibly be normal, and therefore I was to ignore, forget, disinterest myself in my peculiar condition. I too bubble and boil far more than is necessary: certainly far more than the normal inhabitants of this not over-energetic island. My condition induces a certain natural hypochondria in me, which I find comforting and socially infinitely useful. My pains have disappeared. I take no pills. But when things are too much, and both objects and persons begin accumulating in menacing quantities round one, my 'condition' gives me a respectable excuse for retirement. If, like me, one suffers too easily from guilt, justification is constantly needed. I suspect this is Nature's way of supplying a permanent alibi.

I am delighted to think of your tireless energy and its splendid results. I tire more easily, and the results, I am sure, are correspondingly less abiding. But we must keep each other informed of our general state, and derive reciprocal encouragement from each other's achievements. What can be better than to profit oneself from one's benevolent interest in one's brother's condition?

I send you my wishes for your continued energy and happiness, with self-interested sincerity. I hope we may meet again soon.

Yours sincerely,

---

1 Camille Dreyfus (1897–1966), doctor interested professionally in haematology and personally in Judaism, food and the arts; originally from Alsace, he spent the war years in Boston and New York.

2 Carl Heinz Goldman (1904–92), German-born society doctor with a practice in Upper Wimpole Street; in IB's view 'a German charlatan with a beautiful bedside manner who seems to be very clever and good and also a charlatan if you see what I mean, one can separate off the charlatanism from the genuineness as one removes fat from the top of the soup'. To Ida Samunov, 16 March 1959.

IB's new role as Chairman of the Opera Sub-Committee at Covent Garden
brought him into close contact with the many problems facing the still-young
opera company.

TO BURNET PAVITT[1]

22 January 1960 [*carbon*]

Headington House

Dear Burnet,

I ought to have written to you long ago to thank you for your most informative and in every way delightful letter. Since then the skies have clouded again: after gadding about in the Metropolitan – they have more money, better singers, more room to expand in, general sense of luxe in the choice of artists etc., than we have, it really is most enviable – after hearing a good *Figaro*, a strange *Tristan* (with Nilsson,[2] who has just been discovered in New York and acclaimed as nobody has been since Flagstad), I returned to London to find *Traviata* a real fiasco – we have come a tremendous cropper, and nobody denies it. Sutherland[3] didn't know her part, and the conductor[4] was apparently very bad, the whole thing was taken at funereal pace – Cimmerian[5] effects – *Traviata* was already beat and down and out at the beginning of the first act – all the critics either ironical or quietly abusive, particularly Andrew Porter[6] – and a difficult mood prevailing. The post mortem occurred yesterday. Harewood with a very stiff upper lip took the blame for Santi. The difficult bit to get over was why the 'musical staff' allowed Sutherland to go on singing badly and not remember her lines until the point of no return; not much was said about that. The A.D.,[7] now Sir A.D. (Joan[8] prefers Slippery Sam, I am not sure) blamed Sutherland herself for behaving very badly etc., Eddy [Sackville-West] wanted Garrett [Drogheda] to stop her singing *Traviata* altogether, and I was instructed to tell Harewood to tell her to do so or Garrett to do it himself. I managed with some difficulty (though I say it myself) to smooth this out, and it was agreed that it was not right to run out on her at the first sign of failure for she would

1 Burnet Percy Pavitt (1908–2002), businessman; Managing Director, Hoffmann-La Roche UK, 1956–71; Director, ROH, 1957–80; IB had a high regard for his penetrating and unbiased opinions.
2 Birgit Nilsson (1918–2005), the stage name of Birgit Märta Svensson, Swedish operatic soprano.
3 Joan Sutherland (b. 1926), Australian operatic soprano, since 1952 based at Covent Garden, where she achieved international fame in Donizetti's *Lucia di Lammermoor* in February 1959.
4 Nello Santi (b. 1931), Italian conductor.
5 'Dark; gloomy'; in the *Odyssey*, Homer describes the Cimmerians as living in a sunless place near the entrance to Hades.
6 Andrew Brian Porter (b. 1928), music critic, *Financial Times*, 1952–72; a particular thorn in Covent Garden's side as his twin sister worked in their press office and Lord Drogheda was his employer.
7 IB clearly means David Webster, the General Administrator, who had just been awarded a knighthood; the initials are likely to stand for Artistic (or Acting) Director, as Webster was at the time covering the vacant post of Musical Director.
8 Lady Drogheda (with whom Pavitt played piano duets).

undoubtedly improve later, sing beautifully, bear us a grudge and leave us at the first convenient moment (she may do that anyway, but at least our record will be kept straight). So again in a highly British manner we stand by her, we tell her she is a good girl, but must work harder and never never do this again. There is no doubt that the administration slipped up badly in a way which could never have happened at the Metropolitan, where Bing lives in the Opera – I have never seen a man who was there so much – I went to five or six rehearsals and he was never not there; true, he is an absolute dictator, the committee have nothing to say, and his taste is not impeccable, but he is a genuine intendant, and looks after everything, more than can be said for our lot.

Walter[1] is not at all in favour of Solti,[2] I don't know why, and must try to persuade Garrett that we must have a succession of conductors for two months each on approval. I think this will probably drive the administration mad, at any rate I was not consulted and Garrett turned it down out of hand (I think rightly). A man who longs to come to us is I think Leinsdorf,[3] a very competent Met. conductor, who seems to me, however, uninspired. Never above and never below a very high second-rate, totally competent, absolutely reliable, somewhat mechanical performance. His arms shoot out like precise snakes, and the result is always dependable, always efficient, the singers sing well, the orchestra plays decently, and there is never a moment of inspiration, always a certain incurable pedestrianism. [...]

You and I have always maintained that Sutherland was not made by God to be a courtesan: but I suppose she had to be allowed to do this part and if someone had taken her in hand – anyone – the disaster might have been averted. Perhaps the administration have learnt their lesson. I wonder.

[...] It is 2.00 a.m. and I must stop. Now Meyer[4] won't sing in *The Trojans*, oh dear, it is always the same.

Yours ever,

---

1 (Harry) Walter Legge (1906–79), record producer, music journalist and impresario; founder of the Philharmonia orchestra and chorus; Director of ROH 1958–63; IB regarded him as 'a valuable gadfly' at Covent Garden (to Garrett Drogheda, 13 June 1960).

2 Georg Solti (1912–97), né György Stern in Hungary, conductor and pianist; Musical Director, Bavarian State Opera 1946–52, Frankfurt Opera 1952–61, Covent Garden 1961–71; later (1969–91) Music Director, Chicago Symphony Orchestra. Solti had conducted *Der Rosenkavalier* at Covent Garden in December 1959 and soon afterwards agreed to take over as Musical Director there in September 1961.

3 Erich Leinsdorf (1912–93), né Landauer in Austria; conducted at the Metropolitan Opera, New York, 1957–62; later (1962–9) Music Director, Boston Symphony Orchestra.

4 Kerstin Margareta Meyer (b. 1928), Swedish mezzo-soprano, who did in the end make her Covent Garden début as Dido in *The Trojans* on 29 April 1960.

On his return to Oxford, IB had received shocking news.

TO MORTON WHITE

27 January 1960

Headington House

Dear Morton,

I have an immense amount of frustration after our too brief interview in New York. You didn't say enough to me, I didn't say enough to you. It is necessary to talk at greater length more freely in less hectic surroundings. I came back to Oxford and found all kinds of distresses, miseries: one of my nicest colleagues at All Souls being terribly ill;[1] my second stepson in tears of nostalgia at his new public school, and what is far worse – but I really must not tell you for it is a secret, especially from his children who know nothing – our friend J.L.A.[2] dying slowly of an incurable disease. I cannot recover from this at all. I have been to see him and he knows roughly what is wrong with him, but I think has no idea of how little time the doctors anticipate for him. His children know nothing, and his wife[3] cannot be looked at. She has no face on her: for her it is worse than for anyone comparable. The whole thing is a dead secret, except from half-a-dozen people, in case his children should get to hear it – moreover, what the doctors say in such cases is never reliable, and people last on in surprising ways. But I am pessimistic. He is marvellously cheerful and stoical and is behaving much too well, stiff upper lip – too much so – I go to see him once a week – I am really terribly fond of him, and he has certainly taught me more philosophy than anyone has, and I think on the whole that he is the cleverest man I have ever known – in curious ways also the nicest, perhaps not *the* nicest, but wonderfully benevolent, kind, good and just, in spite of all his little vanities, etc. His strange behaviour this year, of which I told you, must now be attributed, at least in part, to the fact that he has had this terrible thing for far longer than he or anyone else suspected. He was misdiagnosed in the first place, although whether anything could have been done if an idiotic mistake had not been made is not clear. The fate of his wife, whom he married as an undergraduate (I mean *she* was), and who has had no life apart from him at all – 'I took his cue for everything' she said to me – is difficult to think of. He talks of *Sense and Sensibilia*[4] (the title of his lectures), about everything still, and the whole thing is very like the end of Hume. I wish I were an Adam Smith[5] and could describe things for posterity properly.

1 See 847.
2 John Langshaw Austin.
3 Jean Austin (b. 1918), née Coutts, philosopher; later (1964–86) Fellow of St Hilda's.
4 A reconstruction by Geoffrey Warnock of Austin's lecture notes was later published under this title (Oxford, 1962).
5 Adam Smith (1723–90), Scottish philosopher and economist, described David Hume's last days in a letter to William Stra(c)han on 9 November 1776.

What a strange country England is: a letter suddenly appeared in *The Times Literary Supplement* apropos of a very stupid review of Strawson[1] by Sir Edward Boyle,[2] who I think is Financial Secretary to the Treasury or something of the kind, and who did History at Oxford (in which he got a Third Class although he is quite an intelligent man), to say that attacks on linguistic philosophy are monstrous, that it is very important to know what words mean, that Austin's work in this respect has been invaluable and has made a great deal of difference to people's thinking, and that philistine attacks upon Oxford Philosophy, e.g. like the one he was writing about in *The Times Literary Supplement* against Strawson's book, should not be permitted, etc. That a Conservative Minister, whatever his motive, can strike a blow for reason of this kind is, I suppose, encouraging. The mere fact that some 25 letters about Gellner's book should have appeared in *The Times* is remarkable in itself. I really think you had better come and spend a year here.

Now as to our arrangements. I have this difficulty: I want to write a book about the crisis in moral and political thought created by the Romantic Movement in the eighteenth century, about which I have lectured incompetently on and off at Bryn Mawr, in Chicago, on the BBC etc. now for years. The thing is vaguely festering inside me and I think I must get it out before anything else. I feel too badly about not producing a book about anything since 1938. To write this book I shall have to read and read, particularly in the, to me, ghastly and semi-unintelligible German romantic writings, for weeks and months. However I am determined to do it and unless I do this I shall fall into a state of self-contempt which I am sure you would understand well. For this reason I propose to spend next term and the summer vacation in preparing myself for this ghastly task, for I can never write without reading and reading and reading, far too much, far too widely, and not altogether very intelligently. Secondly, I am most anxious to write the book on the philosophy of history with you. [...] The serious summer we must spend together is in 1961 and we must go on into the winter as we planned. Could you shift your arrangements accordingly? It is a great deal to ask, I know. My only difficulty is that I know that I cannot postpone the other thing because it will go on eating at me – it has been now for about two years – I keep on reading books and making notes and the notes get lost and I can't continue, and the whole thing is driving me into a neurotic state, which can only be

1 E. W. F. Tomlin, 'The Latent Structure of Thought', *TLS*, 15 January 1960, 38.
2 Sir Edward Charles Gurney Boyle (1923–81), Baron Boyle 1970, Conservative MP 1950–70; Financial Secretary to the Treasury 1959–62; later Minister of Education 1962–4, Minister of State, Department of Education and Science, 1964–70. His letter was 'Individuals', *TLS*, 22 January 1960, 49; IB wrote on 5 February to congratulate him on his 'very shrewd blow for reason [...] on behalf of the Oxford philosophers. They have their faults: but they are immensely superior to their philistine detractors, especially those in the *Literary Supplement*, which seems to me to have sunk to a very dismal level of reviewing in general. I have reached the point when I feel ashamed of the favourable notices they occasionally give to what I myself write. To say "ashamed" is perhaps exaggerated and even hypocritical: perhaps I should say "made to feel uneasy".'

healed by giving birth to something however misbegotten and disappointing (I expect anything I write to be that and always have). [...]

I went to a class held here by Ryle and Hempel on historical explanation ⟨– here the machine broke down. What *can* I have said? Only that the class is worse than useless. That they are talking about deductive models which they do not pretend has relevance to history. Ryle asks whether to say that 'I know X's left eye is blue; therefore I predict his right eye will be blue too' is an explanation & if not why not: this, as⟩ everyone in the class knows, will have no application to historical thinking. Hempel has been riding on the same patch of ground many times in the same battered little Carnap model, and is simply repeating himself with great sincerity and freshness, without thinking at all, and writes down things on the blackboard of the most naive and truistic kind. Ryle is just plain bored. The boys contribute nothing useful. The whole thing is at a low level, a large number of people attend since they feel that it is not difficult to follow, and that *any* statement will be greeted without too much disrespect. [...]

Yours ever,

Isaiah

P.S. Not a word about J.L.A. (I don't think anyone in America knows) [...]

TO MORTON WHITE

12 February 1960

Headington House

Dear Morton,

Austin died two days ago,[1] being I gather in no great pain since he was heavily drugged. He had been wandering in his mind for some time before that, although there were lucid intervals in which he talked coherently to his wife. I enclose the *Times* obituary,[2] which was certainly written by Ryle and which, though it brings out certain things, does not bring out (*a*) that he was probably the most influential philosopher, at the time of his death, in the English-speaking world: and (*b*) his humanity, his charm and general sweetness of character, and the devotion which he inspired in you, in me, in Burton [Dreben], and all the graduate students up and down America. Also the fact that the vivid examples he used in his lectures were sometimes carried away by a pupil who had only heard him lecture once and then went on using them endlessly in their own lectures on this and that, and this applied to physicists as well as philosophers. I have tried to stimulate

1 On 8 February 1960.
2 *The Times*, 10 February 1960, 13. A further tribute by C.H.R. (Colin Henderson Roberts, Secretary to the Delegates, OUP) was the only other piece about Austin to appear in *The Times* (11 February 1960, 15).

Herbert Hart to add to the obituary in *The Times*, and also Marcus Dick will write on what it was like to be his pupil. Perhaps that will be enough so far as Oxford is concerned; but if you and/or Burton both wrote little letters to *The Times* of the form 'Professor X of Harvard writes', or 'a friend writes', or 'M.G.W. writes', it would I am sure give his wife pleasure and also to all his friends. So do do it if you feel inclined; it will not be too late if you write when you receive this. The funeral is tomorrow and will be attended by no more than a dozen intimate friends; there will be a memorial service later no doubt. There is really nothing to say: we know each other's feelings for him. I think that someone will have to write a notice about him for the British Academy,[1] perhaps George Paul; if it appears I will endeavour to send it to you. I wonder how long it will take for the edifice that he built more or less unaided in Oxford to crumble: will the epigoni – Warnock, Urmson and the others – be able to carry on? I doubt it somehow. I wonder what next. Not Ryle, not Quine, something more romantic, possibly more woolly, but also closer to answers to problems which people are oppressed by. I think that an inflationary spiral is due, with mathematical logicians going their way, while the others will talk in less ~~permanent~~[2] and more humanistic language. I am not sure that this is a good thing ⟨(in fact I think, on the whole, very much *not*)⟩, but I have a feeling that it is what will happen. [...]

We are all fairly in order – my American trip (the recent one) really was a pleasurable experience, marred only by meeting dear Harry [Levin] in Cambridge, and by losing an absolutely unique object, a German letter written by Pasternak to his publishers in Germany, containing (apparently valuable) aesthetic doctrine about which Edmund Wilson was going to write an entire article or something more; he lent it to me, and I have not seen it from the moment that he lent it to me ever again; perhaps overborne by the horrors of my night in Cambridge – the vigil in the snow[3] outside Mrs Whitehead's house – the ghastly conversations with her on the telephone – the difficulties of getting to the airport in the early morning, the stormy flight, and other nightmare experiences, I lost it or left it somewhere. At any rate I feel like Mill about Carlyle.[4] I have written a *mea culpa* letter to

---

1 G. J. Warnock, 'John Langshaw Austin, 1911–1960', *Proceedings of the British Academy* 49 (1963), 345–63; this revealed that 'Professor Berlin had at one time, on his mantelpiece in New College, a large card, roughly two feet by six inches, obtained presumably from some car-dealer and bearing the legend AUSTIN; he kept it "as a reminder that there are acute critics at work"' (352, note 1).

2 IB has crossed the word out, but not supplied a substitute.

3 Hoping to see Evelyn Whitehead without having to do the complete Harvard social circuit, IB had travelled clandestinely from Chicago to Cambridge; he called on Edmund and Elena Wilson, then tried to visit Mrs Whitehead after midnight, too late for her to admit anyone. Annoyed at his late arrival, she refused to receive him the next morning too, so he flew to New York without having seen her, which she later regretted.

4 In 1835 Thomas Carlyle lent J. S. Mill the only copy of the first volume of his history of the French Revolution; Mill then had to confess to him that a maid had mistakenly burnt it.

Edmund[1] and feel terrible about the whole thing. I shall try and extract another copy of this letter from the German publisher,[2] in case he is able to give me one – I do not know what it is about, and there must be hundreds of letters of which it might possibly be the copy. Indeed it has been a black two days for me, what with Austin's death, Edmund's reproachful letter, and general self-contempt and distress about the decay of one's intellectual faculties, and the belief that if only I had written something at the age of thirty or forty it might have been worth reading, but now . . . – I daresay I shall recover from this mood some time.

Do write me.

Yours ever,

Isaiah

PS This is a, for me, rather neurotic letter. But I feel rather less gloomy than it implies. The local election of the Chancellor of Oxford – a purely decorative office – seems to preoccupy everyone: Franks – Macmillan – Salisbury, they are the candidates. I cannot develop any interest in the matter. [. . .]

TO FELIX FRANKFURTER

29 February 1960 [*carbon*]

Headington House

Dearest F.F.,

Let me tell you all: the position about the Warden of Wadham is relatively simple. He disliked Oliver fairly strongly and steadily for about twenty years, and indeed longer, and whenever I said the faintest word in praise of him I was, as they say in the United States, slapped down smartly and told that Oliver was a cold nasty prig, inhuman, disapproving etc. etc., an enemy to all pleasure and life. Then he met him on the Hellenic cruise at which Maurice lectured and Oliver Franks (who is an excellent listener) asked questions and generally made himself amiable – and conceived a passion for him. This happens to our old friend fairly frequently and sometimes he pays for it and sometimes he does not, but it is a symptom of his truly generous, spontaneous, and sometimes miraculously uncalculating nature. In fact there is a lot of old Lear about him and the Regans and Gonerils abound – [. . .] they make

---

1 In which he admitted that this was not his first offence: 'In June 1940 I was unable to think about the German capture of Paris because I had lost 142 logic scripts done by undergraduates here for their final examination. [. . .] I recovered the scripts. I hope to recover the letter.' To Edmund Wilson, 12 February 1960.

2 The letter of 19 February from 'Professor Sir Isaiah Berlin, CBE, FBA, Professor of Social and Political Theory in the University of Oxford' to Gottfried Bermann-Fischer requesting a copy of Pasternak's letter makes no mention of IB's negligence, and promises to 'treat as wholly confidential' the document which 'looked so interesting that I could not refrain from seeking to see it again, as Mr Edmund Wilson did not wish his copy to leave America'.

up to him, he likes them, he appoints them to jobs, they bite, he conceives a violent hatred for them and feels a woman scorned. I do not think this is likely to happen with Oliver: but I must admit that Oliver in his relations with reference to Maurice, to me in the past, although cautious was as you might say reserved;[1] one felt that he liked, say, Miss Sutherland,[2] or other serious and grim-faced persons, rather better. At any rate shortly before time I received a telephone call from our old friend who said in effect, 'To hell with Salisbury, to hell with the Tories, I don't mind Macmillan but he is no good to us, I am looking for a candidate, what about Franks?' I said, 'But will he not be King Stork, will he not interfere, will he not seek to run the University, for he despises democratic bodies and councils most of all which he does not conceal?' To which our old friend replied, 'If he gives pain to Vice-Chancellor Turpin,'[3] or whoever it was, it may have been some other name, 'I could not care less.' Or words to that effect. All this will strike you I am sure as being as authentic as in fact it was. He then called together a meeting of the heads of houses, which subsequently was thought to be a disgraceful caucus but in which there was intrinsically nothing wrong – to invite all the MAs in the world would have produced an intolerable bear garden, or so I was informed even by the supporters of Macmillan – and in this secret meeting he proceeded to shoot down Salisbury, shoot down Bridges, eliminate Monckton, and even the candidate of the Master of University[4] – I need hardly tell you who this was – the Duke of Edinburgh[5] of course – he stuck to him loyally through all the votes, it appears, but in the end yielded to the majority. The majority were informed that the Chancellor would have to cope with Government and big business, that Edward[6] had been good in all these ways (devoted to him as I was I fear I must reveal to you that he never lifted a finger, as Chancellor, nor was expected to, the office has hitherto been considered as a purely decorative one [...]). At any rate having shot down all our pretenders Maurice jumped for Franks and took no fewer than 17 heads of houses – observing this landslide or bandwagon the rest followed suit – not all the rest of course, but some six or seven of them, among them our old friend Professor Goodhart; there remained uncommitted Sparrow (who wanted Salisbury and suspected that what had been said about him was not exactly verifiably true), Masterman, Keir (who was

---

1 This clumsy passage, possibly a product of bad dictation and/or secretarial mangling, perhaps means: 'I must admit that Oliver, judging by what he related to me (though with some caution) about Maurice in the past, was as you might say reserved towards him.'

2 Lucy Stuart Sutherland (1903–80), Australian-born historian brought up in South Africa; Principal, LMH, 1945–71.

3 A mistake. Kenneth Charles Turpin (1915–2005), Provost of Oriel 1957–80, was not Vice-Chancellor until 1966–9.

4 Arthur Goodhart.

5 Prince Philip (Mountbatten; b. 1921), husband of Queen Elizabeth II.

6 Lord Halifax, the previous Chancellor, who died on 23 December 1959.

in Africa), Boase (the Vice-Chancellor, who was in hospital), Norrington[1]
(the coming Vice-Chancellor, who was also in hospital), and all the other
heads of houses who had been Vice-Chancellors and were therefore dead, or
broken, or otherwise crushed by their office – Maurice alone standing like
an unbowed tree in the midst of this devastation. Thereupon Trevor-Roper,
who loves a fight, likes intrigue, conflict, destruction, rose with a banner
for Macmillan. Sparrow, who wanted Salisbury, was, as you may imagine,
slow, finicky, gentlemanly, and began an elaborate exchange of letters whose
literary merit is very high but relevance to action negative; poor Salisbury
was therefore of no further account, because of the speed and ruthlessness
with which Macmillan's supporters proceeded: he had made it plain that he
would not stand against his party leader; privately his feelings were doubtless
very different; but he is now a peaceful Macmillan supporter and that is the
end of his cause. I was telephoned to almost immediately by all three party
leaders. To Maurice I was compelled to say that I had certain doubts about
wishing to be governed by an enlightened despot, beneficent but icy, whom I
knew well, and he was indeed a friend of mine, but whose understanding of
persons and individual issues was limited. To Trevor-Roper I explained that
the supporters of Franks maintained that the Prime Minister as an active
politician could not do the University good precisely because of his loftiness
and impartiality (at least the necessity for its appearance) whereas when he
was in the Opposition he was merely a goad to the Labour Government to
anti-Oxford excesses and what did he have to say to that? In fact I used the
arguments of each party to the other for pure pleasure, I settled myself comfortably on the fence, a nice wide roomy structure upon which two thirds of
the University, together with myself at present, cosily repose. The campaign
is nothing but pure pleasure. [...] Aline wishes me to vote for Macmillan on
the ground that Oliver, whom she knows well, and to whom indeed she sold
her old house, is too ordinary – that it is not right that one should see the
Chancellor of Oxford on platform 1 every morning, that a certain magical
distance is indispensable to symbolic offices (for it is at present, as you know,
no more than that) and that she finds Macmillan gay and friendly, beneficial.
[...] Here is Franks, a ruthless, high-minded, cold fish, who will certainly
bring us money and cow the civil servants; here is Macmillan, civilised, gay,
sentimental, every inch an alumnus of Balliol, who will never lift a finger
for the University and would not expect to be asked to and will come down
year after year looking like a tired and faithful hound and tell long stories,
tell them well and amusingly, but over and over and over again. [...] If the
votes were left to the University only, Franks should certainly get in, the
dislike for the Tory grandees or even publishers is very great. The left wing

---

1 Arthur Lionel Pugh Norrington (1899–1982), President of Trinity 1954–70, Vice-Chancellor,
Oxford, 1960–2.

is dissatisfied with both sides and would have preferred Attlee. The ballot
is secret but Maurice is the officer in charge. I have told Trevor-Roper that
nothing would induce me to vote for his candidate and the same to Maurice;
there is no excitement but much pleasure. [...]

Yours,

TO MAURICE BOWRA

4 March 1960 [*manuscript*]

All Souls

Dear Maurice,

When you asked me yesterday whether I had voted, I told you truthfully
that I had. I voted for Macmillan: I meant to tell you this and didn't, I daresay
out of cowardice: for fear of a scolding from you. However I can't bear not
to tell you (I've told scarcely anyone else, nor did I put my name down for M.
because I cd not bear to give Trevor Roper pleasure) otherwise it would ruin
my relationship with you, which means an immense amount to me, as you
know, and rests on absolute candour (& always has: & always will). Why did
I do it? I sat on the fence for days, feeling (a) that it did not much matter how
I voted (b) wondering what I thought right. I went into the Divinity School
literally undecided what to do, & when a horrible man from the *D. Telegraph*
+ Sir E. Boyle asked me how I would vote, said just this, & was reported
by the *D. Telegraph*, quite accurately, as an undecided or floating voter,[1] an
absurd condition. In the end I thought that Macmillan was civilised, a human
being, and rather nice. I met him by pure accident a few days ago & he was
very jolly & gay & nice about you (and I admit to me too) & about (oddly
enough) Mure[2] who was in his "election" at Eton, & spoke of you v. sweetly
as an old friend, & said he respected your motives & did not mind terribly
about the outcome but thought it pompous to decline the contest. I thought
he was shrewd, fond of Oxford, and wd leave us alone. Oliver, on the other
hand was not quite human, nor really fond of people, I remembered how
Waverleyish he is on all the Committees on which I have sat & sit with him,
& that it is the soul that delivers the goods. I wondered if it wd be uncomfortable to go on meeting him after voting against him, whether or not he got
in, & thought it would be: & that it was too weak to evade the issue (e.g. not
vote at all) because of this. I thought that he really wd perhaps defend the
university well, but be too crushing & unscrupulous about it – so in I went
& voted. I was immediately, of course, seized with guilt. Perhaps Franks is,
politically, the man for us. Also I saw the ghastly line of Tory M.P.s lined up

---

1 'Even on the threshold, Sir Isaiah confessed that he had not made up his mind which way to
vote – probably the most imprecise statement ever uttered by this distinguished philosopher.'
'London Day by Day', *Daily Telegraph*, 4 March 1960, 12.

2 Geoffrey Reginald Gilchrist Mure (1893–1979), philosopher; Warden of Merton 1947–63.

& felt ashamed to be on their side, despite the left wing pro-M. vote which
was very visible too (Balogh, Leys,[1] Corbett[2] etc.). Above all, and slightly
perhaps to my own surprise, I felt Zaehner-like feelings: that I shd not have
voted against your wishes on any university issue, quite apart from my own
views, for the sake of love & friendship. I therefore went about in a state of
misery all day, & would not tell anyone how I had voted, so as not to give
comfort to the Macmillanites who are repulsive on the whole, even though
their candidate is more liberal than Oliver (e.g. on S. Africa) & anyway, mine.
I wd have rung you up, but it is *now* too late (1 a.m.). I tried to *before* voting,
but you were away – your telephone didn't answer at all, & tomorrow you
will be early in the D. School, & we are off for the week-end. You are probably right about what the university needs, & I may have made a mistake.
But the image of F. fills me with the gloom it used to fill you [with] years
ago. Anyhow I must tell you what I did (just as I shall have to tell Franks too,
I expect) in case you assume the opposite (I began pro-Franks, of course,
but he really is too cold for me: and terrible on human issues) – which I shd
find unbearable. Do not be cross with me: do not denounce me even in your
heart: it may be frivolous not to be able to vote for mechanical men – he is
actually embarrassingly half human & genuinely heartless – but I cannot do
it. The only thing I regret is that I did not tell you before: you might have
convinced me of the opposite, & I shd not now wonder whether I did right.
But all that really matters to me is that you shd not mind: or regard it as an
act of disloyalty to yourself. When you dedicated a book to me, it was the
greatest single moment of exaltation in my life. What I felt then, I feel now.
I bitterly regret not seeing you more often: my debt to you, my love for you
are very deep: but living in Headington *is* insulating: we see (given my old
undiscriminating gregariousness) astonishingly few people: nobody wanders
in, I don't wander into anyone's room either. Forgive me: don't write me
off or put me in some contemptuous category: even if you do, my feelings
won't alter although my growing sense of isolation will increase. To have
voted with Xman[3] & Roy is punishment enough. Please don't condemn me
to people: you may think I deserve it: but friendship is different from justice.
I still expect you to dine on Sunday week, or if you prefer it, on the following
Friday. And whatever you do or think, remember that I've never loved anyone
more constantly, or been pleased to have lived by anyone's side more than
by yours. You really have no time off from university affairs, so don't answer
this: you have a very large & generous nature: in this I trust. I honestly can't
say more. I am a terrible fool: & lack wisdom, courage & self-confidence to
a fearful degree. Even if you agree with this (why not?) don't, I beg you, say

1 Colin Temple Leys (b. 1931), Fellow of Balliol 1953–60, Tutor in Politics 1956–60.
2 John Patrick Corbett (1916–99), Fellow and Tutor in Philosophy, Balliol, 1945–61.
3 Richard Crossman.

so now: for I am in a low state. And forgive this long, tedious, and not at all relief-affording outpouring: but I really cd not bear not to do it.

Yrs with much love
Isaiah

Saturday. 9 a.m.

I rose this morning in a slightly saner state of mind: I realise that I am suffering from a "latent hatred" of O.F. – very like Price vis a vis Waismann: & that this is not an adequate reason in public action: though not all that inadequate either. I forgot to add that perturbed by my own motives – like any character in Tolstoy – I persuaded the vacillating Lord Harcourt (who expects preferment from M.) to vote for Franks (on Thursday) on the ground that bankers shd stick together. I failed over Lord Birkenhead,[1] however, who hates both, but will vote for "Harold". Really I think I am quite mad. I shall have recovered by Monday at the latest. If I don't hear, I'll assume that you'll dine on Sunday: if you prefer the Friday after, wd you signify.

I have not read through all this. Couldn't. I apologise for length, turgid repetition etc. – as you have often remarked, writing is not my thing.

TO ELIZABETH JENNINGS[2]

8 March 1960

Headington House

Dear Miss Jennings,

Very well: I only say that I hope the book may be called: *Three Critics of the Enlightenment*,[3] and will consist of three studies.[4] The first on the seventeenth-century Italian thinker, Giambattista Vico, an attempt to deal with a thinker of genius, unrecognised in his own day and then forgotten and rediscovered at regular intervals, until our own time, to which he has more to say than to his own age. The second study is concerned with the far better-known Johann Gottfried Herder, the founder of modern nationalism (this has not even been begun!). The third study deals with the opinions of

---

1 Frederick Winston Furneaux Smith (1907–75), 2nd Earl of Birkenhead, brother of Lady Pamela Berry.

2 Elizabeth Joan Jennings (1926–2001), poet; publishers' reader, Chatto & Windus (of which the Hogarth Press then formed part), 1958–60. She had asked IB for a description of his allegedly forthcoming book for the Hogarth Press catalogue.

3 In the event, no book of this name was published until 2000, and even then the contents differed from IB's original proposal: *The Magus of the North* (about Johann Georg Hamann) replaced the essay on Maistre, which had by then appeared in CTH. See the Preface to TCE for the tortuous history of this publishing venture.

4 IB recognised that working on shorter pieces was an escape route for him: 'I really ought to be writing a solid book – I know what it is to be about, the material in some sense is in my head, but I seek for every possible avenue of escape, and all these articles, introductions etc. are so many straws at which I clutch in order not to be drowned in real writing. Every time I promise to do one of these smaller things I feel shame and relief.' 11 March 1960 to Peter Calvocoressi.

Joseph de Maistre, a Savoyard Count, the most gifted of all the reactionary publicists of the early nineteenth century. My thesis is that what unites
these three writers is their antipathy to the fundamental ideas of the French
Enlightenment, and the depth and permanent force of their critical reflections on them. Herder's ideas contributed more to the counter-revolution
against positivism and rationalism than those of any other thinker. As for
Vico and de Maistre, the originality and truth of their ideas have been vin-
dicated, both for better and for worse, by the history of our own time to
an extent, and in a hair-raising fashion which their contemporaries did not
begin to foresee. The issue between the advocates of the Enlightenment and
these critics is today at least as crucial as it was in its beginnings, and the
fashion in which the rival theses were stated in their original form is clearer,
simpler and bolder than at any subsequent time. Vico's conception of history,
culture and society, Herder's contrast between scientific rationalism and the
properties that create civilisations and make them intelligible, and Maistre's
terrifying analysis of irrational and unconscious elements in men and their
part in the life of individuals and societies seem more realistic and relevant
to the central issues of our time than the generally accepted doctrines which
form the main stream of European thought. [. . .]

Yours sincerely,
      Isaiah Berlin

*At Anna Kallin's request, IB had reluctantly agreed to let the BBC film him
apparently recording part of his 1955 broadcasts of 'A Marvellous Decade'.
The short extracts were for inclusion in a promotional film,* This Is the BBC,
*a montage of a wide range of the BBC's activities: the film's long list of credits
concluded '. . . Cliff Michelmore, Cy Grant, Sir Isaiah Berlin, Michael Aldridge,
The George Mitchell Singers, The Television Toppers, Janie Marden'. In March
1960, by which time the film had already been shown over 300 times at venues
across the country, the Controller of the Third Programme went to Oxford
to seek IB's agreement to a new contract which would allow the showing of
the film on British television. However, IB had been alarmed by reports of
the premiere at the Odeon, Leicester Square, which he had refused to attend,
and formed the impression that his appearance was somewhat comic and had
provoked laughter. His initial reaction was that the four clips[1] (totalling 11
seconds) in which he was mentioned or appeared should be cut, even when
assured that this was technically impossible; but he undertook to consider the
matter further.*

---

1 The longest one can be seen in the IBVL: see http://berlin.wolf.ox.ac.uk/lists/broadcasts/, item
19.

TO P. H. NEWBY[1]

18 March 1960 [*carbon*]

Headington House

Dear Newby,

I have had a word with my wife as I promised. I am quite clear that I cannot bring myself to face the prospect of appearing in a piece of montage on television, for the reasons that you know. This would humiliate me, and be degrading to my profession, and on these grounds I cannot agree to alter the original contract or make a new one which would allow this to take place. I cannot myself see why it should be particularly impossible to insert a new sequence in place of that excised to eliminate my appearance – but that is not for me to say. As you know I acceded to your request to 'appear' in the studio with the greatest reluctance, and should certainly never have dreamt of doing so had I not been assured that the film would not be shown in the United Kingdom to critics and other public commentators. I think there is a limit to the extent to which dons should be allowed to appear as clowns for the benefit of the public. I think if I were to accede to your request I should be overstepping it.

Yours sincerely,

The BBC remade the offending part of the film for television at considerable expense, replacing IB with John Lehmann.

In late March IB went to Italy; a week in Rome was followed by visits to Portofino, Zurich and Milan, academic commitments being interspersed with social and musical activities.

TO IRIS ORIGO

29 March 1960 [*manuscript*]

As from Hotel de la Ville. [Rome]

You must forgive me if I write to thank you at much smaller length than I shd like: but it is 3 a.m. – we leave at (what I think of as) crack of dawn, i.e. 9 a.m. & there is still some packing to do: this is all due to disorderly habits and not doing things when they should be done, & doing them only when they needn't – which, I daresay, is due to my Russian origins (though B.B. was so very different). Which brings me to the subject. I do admire all that you write, as you know, greatly and continuously: if we had never met I should feel the same pleasure and respect (and a kind of mild envy – but I am really very unambitious) whenever I read you. I did so indeed long before we met. Your sketch of B.B.,[2] as indeed Nicky said in the car going home, makes up

1 (Percy) Howard Newby (1918–97), Controller of BBC Third Programme 1958–69.
2 Iris Origo, 'The Long Pilgrimage: One Aspect of Bernard Berenson', *Cornhill Magazine* No 1023 (Spring 1960), 139–55.

somewhat for Mrs. Sprigge's enormities. It is a wonderful piece, not merely as such, as a sketch for a portrait, and a piece of literature with independent value, but because it answers the questions of the sceptical (he was a wonderful talker, doubtless, but is this enough? what about his snobbery, pettiness, malice, waste of his life in social gossip, desire to be confessor to young women, failure to write one abiding work of major scholarship like Burckhardt or Mommsen, etc. etc.) and creates a clear, noble, permanent image: graver, solid and marvellously authentic. The question of how he was unique, why doubters fell under his charm – and more, perceived, as you so excellently convey, the integrity and service of truth & independence (rarest of qualities) through all the devices & the deviousnesses & the coquettishness & the obvious ruses – this is answered. There is nothing so luxurious as to find a precise, unexaggerated, unimprovable upon description of an experience one has had oneself: the articulation of something true, familiar, interesting, personal, and unexpressed; in a manner which fits exactly, which completes the pattern, which gives one the delicious sense of harmony and completeness which only truth and the uninflated use of words can give. It really *is* very late: even by my flexible standards: but I really do want to say somehow (I am not a precise writer, alas, and have to circumnavigate a subject & not pierce its heart once & for all) that I think that what you have written is very, very good. That the shades of our old friend have been avenged, whatever is now written: that out of the *culte* & the nonsense and the chitter chatter the fine, serene, features emerge: he probably was the last humanist in Europe, or the world, as you said. [...]

Yours sincerely
　　Isaiah B.

TO ROWLAND BURDON-MULLER

19 April 1960 [*manuscript*]

Grand Hotel Continental, Milan

Dearest Rowland

In half an hour my train goes: my mother & I must be off, while Aline returns independently from her (to me detestable) Davos mountains where the snow still lies high. Rome was marvellous: We met a charming grand-daughter of Tolstoy, called Mme Albertini,[1] with whom I have to negotiate about the Tolstoy fiesta in Venice in late June[2] [...] – I lectured in Italian[3] – unintelligible (virtually) to me, but translated beautifully by a

---

1 Tatiana ('Tania') Albertini (b. 1905), née Soukhotine.

2 A conference, organised largely by Nicolas Nabokov, to be held at the Fondazione Giorgio Cini, on the Isola San Giorgio in Venice, from 29 June to 3 July 1960, to mark the 50th anniversary of Tolstoy's death on 20 November 1910.

3 At the invitation of Professors Federico Chabod and Alberto Maria Ghisalberti of Rome University IB gave two lectures (the first on 24 March, the second a day or two later); the first

Barone Aquilecchia[1] in London – the *noisier* chatterers among my audience (they talk, as during opera) were *prevented* from attending my second lecture, as the Chairman thought the British Ambassador[2] was *shocked* by the noise made during the first lecture which he kindly attended. He gave us lunch and played waltzes on the piano to us afterwards – very nice man – married, as you know, to Evangeline Bruce's sister – there are mauvaises langues[3] who say they are separating when he retires – this year – but this may be malicious invention. I am glad about Gladwyn's peerage & his excellent title:[4] his signature won't alter. Very sensible. Trevor Roper had lectured before me – he was full, so Nicky Mariano said, of the election of the Chancellor at Oxford which he stage managed for Macmillan. I *could* not get up enough interest in this hollow honour: & wd not tell T-R. how I wd vote – & was canvassed busily by Maurice B. (Franks's leader) & T-R & maddened them by saying I was very comfortable on my fence & might never get off it, as the issue was social & trivial. In the end I voted for Macm. who will be conventional & decorative (fairly) as opp[o]s[ed] to my old friend & colleague Sir O. F[ranks] whom I respect & (quite) like – since he is a planner, a puritan & over energetic: I prefer liberty to efficiency & loose textures to fanatical tidiness, & always will. I had to make peace with Sir Maurice & the Centre-Left (Franks) – the *very* left abstained; Sparrow wanted Lord Salisbury, but owing to dilatoriness missed the bus: T-R got in his man first & canvassed like a maniac, & S. could not stand against his kinsman, premier, leader & expeller-from-the-cabinet – Harold M. I met Macm. while all this went on at Lady Cholmondeley's[5] – he said "I am told I have much to lose & little to gain by being a candidate. But as at fox hunting, one does not *want* to kill the fox particularly, but it is fun: others ride: one rides oneself: I don't mind a contest: I'll take it on." Whether or not one likes the simile, he has a certain gaiety of spirit, lacking in the other Conservatives. Anyway it is a matter of no moment. [...] In Zurich I heard ¹⁄₁₀ part of a concert by the ex-Nazi Schwarzkopf,[6] which I had to listen to since her fascinating scamp of a husband is my colleague on Cv. Garden,

lecture (and probably the second as a continuation) was 'La rivoluzione romantica: una crisi nella storia del pensiero moderno', later published in IB, *Tra la filosofia e la storia delle idee: intervista autobiografica*, ed. Steven Lukes (Florence, 1994), and in its original English version as 'The Romantic Revolution: A Crisis in the History of Modern Thought' in SR.

1 Giovanni ('Gianni') Aquilecchia (1923–2001), Reader in Italian, London (UCL), 1959–61; later (1970–89) Professor of Italian, London; his family was of noble descent.

2 Sir (Henry) Ashley Clarke (1903–94), UK Ambassador to Italy 1953–62; three months after this letter he obtained a decree nisi against his wife Virginia (b. 1917), née Bell, later Craig, then Surtees, author and literary editor, sister of Evangeline Bruce.

3 'Mischief-makers'.

4 Gladwyn Jebb had been made 1st Baron Gladwyn of Bramfield.

5 Sybil Rachel Betty Cecile Cholmondeley (*sic*) (1894–1989), née Sassoon, wife of the 5th Marquess of Cholmondeley.

6 Elisabeth Friederike Marie Olga Schwarzkopf (1915–2006), operatic soprano, German by birth, Austrian by adopted citizenship, then British by marriage (in 1953) to Walter Legge; she joined the Nazi Party in 1940.

& saw the excellent Bührle collection[1] which I am sure you know. In Milan a decent Carmen & a splendid Aida with Nilsson. The Italian critics were, of course, hostile: said she was not Verdian etc. etc. – but she is a magnificent singer & never to be missed. [...] Oh dear, it looks like Kennedy v. Nixon[2] & nowhere for an honest man to turn! And South Africa![3] From bad to worse as you (& Joe A.) have always said!

Much love
from Isaiah

TO ALAN BULLOCK

22 April 1960 [*carbon*]

[Headington House]

Dear Alan,

[...] I am very glad about the universal acclaim of *Bevin*, which I am sure is just. I do not as you know ever read anything, but when your second volume appears I shall read the whole thing at one gulp. My only memory of Bevin was in Moscow in 1945, when he was colossally rude on my being introduced as a despatch writer from Washington. I said nothing at all; he said 'Your despatches were not very useful, the newspapers arrived earlier and told much more', and more in the same jolly style. He felt he had gone a little too far and asked me to sit next to him at dinner afterwards, when he denounced British colonial administration everywhere at all times. Clark Kerr, the Ambassador, flattered him up hill and down dale more crudely than I can describe, with a kind of terrible wink to all of us – the staff, whom he had warned of this previously. But he got what he wanted, namely appointment as Ambassador at Washington, when he was over age, against the wishes of the Foreign Office; he was a disaster there, but that could not have been foretold. On the other hand, Bevin's dealings with Byrnes and the Russians were very masterly and I could tell you about that too some day if you wanted to know, also his remarks about Crossman and why he had put him on the Palestine Commission etc.

Yours,

1 Emil Georg Bührle (1890–1956), Swiss industrialist, amassed an outstanding collection of mainly 19th- and 20th-century art, some of which was put on public view in Zurich in 1960.
2 John Kennedy and Richard Nixon were indeed adopted as the Democratic and Republican candidates in the 1960 presidential election in July that year.
3 On 21 March some 69 people had been shot dead by the South African police at Sharpeville during a demonstration against aspects of the Government's apartheid policies; on 30 March, as part of a major crackdown against opposition, the South African Government declared a state of emergency. IB soon became 'a leader of the anti-apartheid movement in Oxford, raised on the shields of my followers, exposed to splendid contumely by reactionary colleagues'. 22 May 1960 to Richard Wollheim.

The music critic Eddy Sackville-West was one of IB's colleagues on the Opera
Sub-Committee at Covent Garden; an infrequent attender at meetings, he was
unhappy about recent decisions.

TO EDWARD SACKVILLE-WEST

30 May 1960

Headington House

Dear Eddy,

You do sound cross.[1] You must know that I have the deepest veneration
for your views, and always have had, so if you really think that things are
going badly I shall be alarmed and distressed. I shall do my best to answer all
your points and give you a general account of what has been happening, and
why. If at the end of that you still feel indignant, you must come and say so,
and have it out with David Webster and the new Musical Director and all. A
new leaf is being turned over – heaven knows what it will reveal; and Solti,
although much beloved by David and Garrett at the moment, seems to me
not untricky, but he is gifted, has a larger horizon than poor Kubelík,[2] and
in the present state of flux all kinds of things can be done: this is certainly
the moment to strike, the iron may not be hot but it is pretty warm, so let
me adjure you to act as you think right. But before you do so, hear or rather
read me out.

I hope I am not one of the overbearing and over-garrulous members of
the Committee who talk you down: even if I am, let me offer you at least
some crumbs of comfort, and, I think, solider fare. With much of what
you say I am in profound agreement, it is only your pessimistic conclusions
which do not seem to me to emerge. Let us begin then.

1. *Mozart*. No doubt *Figaro* has been too often heard and people know it
far too well everywhere in the world, I should think, by now. On the other
hand, surely all major opera houses must have a solid base of repertory from
among the canonical pieces. Walter Legge was always urging this upon us,
and, for once, I think he is right. We must have capital – the basic works
of Mozart, Verdi, perhaps even Puccini, Wagner, Strauss, not only to fall
back on when imagination falters or other things fall through, but as a

---

1 ES-W had written at great length on 25 May 1960, disagreeing with decisions about the choice
of operas for performance in the immediate future and questioning the policy on designers and
producers. He opposed the operas of Mozart (apart from *Don Giovanni*) as too well known, and,
on musical grounds, Alban Berg's *Lulu* (1937) and Verdi's *La forza del destino* (1862); but he argued
that Schoenberg's *Moses and Aaron* (composed 1930–2, first performed 1957) merited an earlier
production than planned. His letter concluded: 'the supreme self-confidence and garrulity of
some members of the committee so often leave me with little to say on the spot'.
2 Sir Thomas Beecham's public criticism of the appointment of foreigners to run a national opera
company influenced Kubelík's decision to leave.

kind of general backbone of continuous operatic life. This we have not got.
[...]

I am by no means sold on *Lulu* – I have never heard it on the stage – it was
only mentioned because Solti was so keen on it, having just scored a huge
success with it in Paris, but this is very much subject to review, and if it is
really ghastly on the stage, don't let's have it. You must represent your own
views *strongly* when you come – never mind the fact that the talk goes to the
talkative – and if you do not come I will [speak] for you as best I can. If we
are overborne it will at least be not for lack of plain speaking.

Now as to *Moses and Aaron*. Believe me I am as keen on this as you and,
so far as I know, in fact no one (except Legge) is against it. And the fact that
Legge is against it automatically stimulates his antagonists to press for it (e.g.
Burnet [Pavitt], Sir T[homas] Armstrong etc. How indiscreet I am being).
[...]

[...] (How I agree with you about the awful habit of putting on jolly
amateur performances and praising the effort put in, instead of finished professional ones – I shall never forget Lord Waverley saying to Ava when she
criticised some dancer, 'Don't *crab* her, Ava. She is doing her *best*.' But if you
have any suggestions, do send them in, for now is the time to strike, and Solti
is very receptive and David Webster not too bad.

[...] Our new acquisition, Mr Keeffe,[1] has the idea of getting some of
our singers to perform for relatively low salaries in provincial continental
opera houses so as to gain experience – say Frankfurt, with which Solti may
still retain a connection, or wherever else we can get them in, and perhaps
exchange singers with them on a two or three year basis or something of
that kind; this might also be done with producers. Our difficulty, obviously,
is that there are no minor opera houses in England, hence no class of operatic producers as such can be expected to come into being, and the ones we
borrow from the straight stage – Peter Brook,[2] Gielgud etc. – really do not
do well. The same problem, in a modified form, applies to designers. If we
could only acquire someone like some very gifted person from Visconti's[3]
atelier, or even someone like Schuh,[4] or the excellent Hamburg people, that
would send standards shooting up, and perhaps stimulate native genius; but
that I suppose is too much to hope for. But you are right to complain. Still, I
agree with Desmond: beautiful singing is the thing; and yet what a fantastic

1 Bernard Francis Keeffe (b. 1925), conductor, broadcaster and writer; producer and conductor,
  BBC Music Department, 1955–60 (Head of Radio Opera 1959); Controller of Opera Planning,
  ROH, 1960–2.
2 Peter Paul Stephen Brook (b. 1925), theatre producer; Director of Productions, ROH, 1947–50.
3 Luchino Visconti di Modrone, Count of Lonate Pozzolo (1906–76), Italian theatre and cinema
  director, who had designed and produced Verdi's *Don Carlos* at Covent Garden in 1958.
4 Oscar Fritz Schuh (1904–84), German opera producer and theatre director, who in 1963 produced
  Le nozze di Figaro at Covent Garden.

difference the production of *Cav* and *Pag*[1] made! When I go to *Puritani*,[2] who am I to believe – Cairns,[3] who says it is worth many *Lucias*, or Heyworth,[4] who says it has about five minutes of true music? All criticisms no doubt have a right to be subjective, but our critics abuse the privilege.

[...] Garrett seems to me to look on Legge much as Macmillan looks on Khrushchev – and on me as a shock-absorber, which indeed, ex officio, I suppose I have to be. Have I answered all your points? I answered them not for the sake of answering them, believe me, but because I think that you really do not possess information which because of your enforced absences you could not have obtained: but do come to the meetings if you possibly can – it makes an enormous difference as you well know. Mr Keeffe is new blood, he has not been trained in the old school of ignoring the wishes of the Committee, and would take serious notice, and with Solti coming so will D. Webster: he knows perfectly well that he cannot run the place without musical advice and authority. [...] Meanwhile Coke[5] and Armstrong want us to do *Idomeneo*.[6] How *can* we, with *Orfeo*[7] and perhaps *Iphigenia*?[8] – we shall sink under the weight of these noble static masterpieces and then Klemperer will die, Giulini[9] will be bought by the Met, Legge will leave us in a fury and call off his conscript singers, Solti will have rows with Garrett or Webster and Joan Sutherland, Vickers[10] and Evans[11] will disappear to Vienna or Milan leaving us with Miss Shacklock[12] and Jess Walters.[13] There is no reason why any or all of these things should not happen. In the end we shall accede to Jimmie Smith's wishes and put Robert Boothby on to the Board, which will automatically cut off our Treasury grant, and the Board will be reconstituted under Dame Irene Ward.[14] In this dark mood I end, envying you your Irish

---

1 The new production at Covent Garden in December 1959, by Franco Zeffirelli, of Pietro Mascagni's *Cavalleria rusticana* (1890) and Ruggero Leoncavallo's *Pagliacci* (1892) had been a great success.

2 *I Puritani*, Vincenzo Bellini's 1835 opera.

3 David Adam Cairns (b. 1926), music critic, *Evening Standard* and *Spectator*, 1958–62; later Berlioz's biographer.

4 Peter Lawrence Frederick Heyworth (1921–91), chief music critic, *Observer*, 1955–87.

5 Gerald Edward Coke (1907–90), merchant banker and patron of the arts; Chairman, Glyndebourne Arts Trust, 1955–75; Director, ROH, 1958–64.

6 Mozart's 1781 opera.

7 Gluck's *Orfeo ed Euridice* (1762).

8 *Iphigénie en Tauride* (139/1).

9 Carlo Maria Giulini (1914–2005), Italian conductor who had made his Covent Garden début in 1958 conducting Verdi's *Don Carlos*.

10 Jonathan Stewart ('Jon') Vickers (b. 1926), Canadian operatic tenor who sang at Covent Garden from 1957.

11 Geraint Llewellyn Evans (1922–92), principal baritone, ROH, 1948–84.

12 Constance Bertha Shacklock (1913–99), principal mezzo-soprano, ROH, 1946–56; later appeared as Mother Abbess in *The Sound of Music* 1961–6 and became a stalwart of the Last Night of the Proms.

13 Jess Walters (1908–2000), né Jesse Wolk, US-born baritone; sang at the ROH 1947–59.

14 Dame Irene Mary Bewick Ward (1895–1980), Baroness Ward 1974, Conservative MP; member of the Trust which helped to finance the Carl Rosa Opera Company.

remoteness and the dependable joys of pianos, gramophones, scores, and a splendid and inexhaustible memory.

Yours ever,
Isaiah   [...]

TO GARRETT DROGHEDA
    15 June 1960

Headington House

Dear Garrett,

Thank you for your delicious letter. I wrote sentimentally to Walter [Legge], but received a rather sharp telegram from Vienna in reply in which my letter to him was described as a manifesto – he does not seem to have appreciated its sublimer points. I am not so sure that he will not get off the Board if we aren't fairly careful with him. I do not believe at all, I must confess to you, in the meeting between him and David [Webster], they both hate each other absolutely, and although prepared for a short-term collabor-ation on their Soviet–Nazi Pact principles for limited objectives, cannot be got to co-operate in a public-school manner. I should therefore warmly urge upon you to deal with them separately and act as a shock absorber if need be (as I more or less do). [...]

I think the combination Solti–Walter has to be tried out, but not Walter and David.

Bolena[1] and Giulini is a wonderful idea – it will be condemned by *The Times*, the *Observer*, the *Spectator* etc., nevertheless we ought to do it. I quite agree with you that 'the whole thing is mad' – the relations of members of the Board I mean – but I am sure you ought to continue to steer the craft, not by splendid team-spirit as Jack [Donaldson] would like it, but by allowing the rival geniuses of Walter and David to discharge their feelings at lofty and disinterested spirits like ours rather than at each other. This won't go on for ever and there will I expect be a general show-down some time. But much can be done before then. Further hope I do not put out: qualified pessimism I am sure is our right mood, rather like Mr Macmillan, whose current state of mind I am sure this is. [...]

Yours,
    Isaiah

When Boris Pasternak died on 30 May, IB had written: 'how much exploitation of the corpse is going to occur I cannot bear to think. I am determined to preserve silence as long as possible and not dishonour his memory by writing

---

1 *Anna Bolena*, Donizetti's 1830 opera about Anne Boleyn.

for newspapers, supplying information about him etc.'[1] *But no such embargo was needed in the case of Tolstoy, who had died 50 years before, and IB had let himself be persuaded by Tania Albertini to deliver an address to the congress held – in Venice, incongruously – to mark the anniversary.*[2] *The whole event proved unexpectedly enjoyable.*

During a brief return home, as IB prepared for his annual trip to Italy for the summer, Felix Frankfurter's memoirs reminded him of what life had been like in Oxford before the war.

TO FELIX FRANKFURTER

15 July 1960 [*carbon*]

Headington House

Dearest F.F.,

I received your book[3] on the eve of going to Venice to 'celebrate', if that is the phrase, the fiftieth anniversary of the death of Tolstoy – and left it behind for fear of losing it on journeys, as I lose almost everything that I value. I came back for a day and looked at it with the most immense pleasure, but have not read more than about ten pages, and shall read it on the way back to Portofino, where we propose to spend the next six weeks. I [gaze?] at it continuously, having meals over it etc., I may contrive to reserve [sc. review?] it. I know from Maurice that he has sent you a list of addenda and corrigenda, so that I shall not trouble to do that. This is only to say that something comes through even in the first pages, certain turns of phrase and types of word order, which convey a personality with extreme vividness – I turned immediately to our term in Oxford, and read with the greatest possible pleasure your account of that splendid evening[4] in Eastwood House with Sylvester and Freddie – you do not mention the extraordinary behaviour of Mrs A.[5] – just as well perhaps – and the bit about 'Whereof one cannot

1 To Margot de Gunzbourg, 1 June 1960.

2 See 730/2. On 1 July IB opened a session on 'Tolstoy and the social and political ideas of his time' with a talk on 'Tolstoy on the Relation of Educated Men to the Masses', which he subsequently expanded into 'Tolstoy and Enlightenment', the PEN Hermon Ould Memorial Lecture for 1960, *Encounter* 16 No 2 (February 1961), reprinted in RT.

3 *Felix Frankfurter Reminisces* (New York, 1960). Privately IB was horrified: 'really people must not let out books which misspell all names. [...] the vulgarity of the whole thing is exceedingly depressing. [...] the book has given me nothing but acute embarrassment, although it is quite nice about me'. 16 September 1960 to Rowland Burdon-Muller.

4 In the summer of 1934 Felix and Marion Frankfurter gave a memorable dinner party at Eastman House (the official residence of George Eastman Visiting Professors, at that time 18 Norham Gardens) for guests including IB, Sylvester Gates, A. J. Ayer and his then wife Renée (next note), Maurice Bowra, Goronwy Rees and (IB thought) Guy Burgess; Sylvester Gates won a bet with Ayer (and IB) about how often Wittgenstein states 'Whereof one cannot speak, thereof one must be silent' in his *Tractatus Logico-Philosophicus* (it occurs in the Preface and at the end of the main text: see 360/2 and PI2 117–18).

5 (Grace Isabel) Renée Ayer (1909–80), née Lees, wife of A. J. Ayer 1932–42; later (1961) married Stuart Hampshire, the co-respondent in her divorce.

speak, thereof one must be silent' etc. I remember the evening, I remember the walk to, and the walk from, your house, I remember the order in which we sat round the table, and everything else, with the utmost clarity – at least I think I do (that is the kind of phrase that I was taught to use by Sumner and Mynors[1] and all the people of that time and age and temper) – surely we were very pleased and very happy then? Although Salter the other day reminded me of Marion's strictures about Oxford, which were apparently very stern at that season. [...]

Maurice seems to me in excellent state: the wounds of the Chancellorial election are not quite healed, but nearly; Macmillan is a trifle stiff with him – or was at the Encaenia – but not too stiff; and he had a delicious conversation with Lady Dorothy; having got me into grave trouble with the American Ambassador[2] by causing me to repeat his, Maurice's, complaints about the American Ambassador's alleged meanness to Oxford in making no contribution to the Oxford Buildings (it turned out that he had contributed £10,000 anonymously via Franks), he then was personally crowned by the American Ambassador, who gave a special party for him in order to elevate him to some immense American status – the Academy of Arts and Letters, I think,[3] of which he had become a member. I was invited, but did not have the effrontery to go.

You speak in your book (which I haven't read – I read no books as you know) of the effect upon you of Bryan's speech[4] – I wish I'd ever heard [a really brilliant?] political orator in the flesh – Winston over the wireless is the nearest to it – by nature I am a hero-worshipper who has found insufficient heroes in his life, at whose feet I could continuously sit. Nothing could be a more humiliating confession, and yet about me it is I fear perfectly true. Always the nearly great or always too remote or in other centuries. Whom am I to respect as a political leader in England now, for example? With the death of Aneurin Bevan, the last human being seems to have disappeared from British politics – if you had seen the Encaenia lunch party on the lawn – as you have seen it more than once in your life – like a Conservative fête, strewn with minor Conservative politicians and hostesses, it really would have struck you as being the end, rather than the beginning, of some long political development, 'the end of a long period of political elaboration' as Yeats[5] describes his own time,[6] and as I am sure every generation, when

1 Roger Aubrey Baskerville Mynors (1903–89), Corpus Christi Professor of Latin Language and Literature, Oxford, 1953–70.
2 John Hay Whitney.
3 He was indeed made an Honorary Member of the American Academy of Arts and Letters.
4 William Jennings Bryan (1860–1925), US lawyer and Democratic politician; Secretary of State 1913–15; one of FF's early heroes for his political idealism and oratorical fluency: 'the golden voice of the Middle West beginning to feel that Eastern capitalism was exploiting it' – op. cit. (737/3), 6.
5 William Butler Yeats (1865–1939), Irish poet and politician.
6 This does not appear to be a quotation from Yeats's published work.

in a melancholy state, conceives its own condition. The liveliest, gayest, youngest, most optimistic man I have ever yet met is Elias Lowe,[1] who is still dashing about the world with extraordinary speed and effectiveness and denounced Jack Kennedy to me in ringing terms. Is there anybody whom you really want to become President of the United States? I know, Johnson,[2] but really? Is there anyone I want to be Prime Minister of England? Dear Gaitskell is a very nice man, even Macmillan is really rather a nice man, or is it only that one has been robbed of the magic of distance and that when one was young and pure and obscure and remote, the feet of clay were merely invisible? But I must stop from these very inferior meditations, not merely platitudinous, but somewhat false, I think, and tell you that far the funniest thing that happened at the Venice Congress on Tolstoy – Venice, a town that Tolstoy cordially loathed, regarded as a home of vice and luxury and never visited – was a remark by George Kennan, who, rising solemnly to his feet after three days of agony in preparing an address, [. . .] declared that Tolstoy in the nineteenth century had been wracked and tortured by sex; but that we had solved this problem in the twentieth century by means of the sense of humour. David Cecil[3] immediately sent me a little scribbled note, saying that this gave him an entirely new view of Mrs Kennan.[4] It really was wonderfully comical. You can imagine what George Kennan looked like when he was saying it, that grey fanatical passionate Presbyterian appearance, with a total lack of spark anywhere, and the bleak, solemn, sweet, serious, Ibsenite look on the face of his wife. (For goodness sake don't circulate this letter or read it to anybody, destroy, destroy it, were it never safe enough!) [. . .]

Then there was the Russian delegation, which went on at some length, as you may imagine, about the exact steps being taken by the Soviet Government about celebrating Tolstoy's memory, which towns were producing which plays, which Central Asiatic editions were producing how many copies of which of Tolstoy's works, and how many formats etc. Curiously enough, they sent me two bottles of vodka and two tins of caviar – which made me dreadfully self-conscious. I appeared to be one of only two persons at this Conference who had received a similar gift, can it be that I am regarded as the weakest link in the capitalist chain? Am I? It certainly made me much more affable to them, as they no doubt intended. [. . .]

1 Elias Avery Lowe (1879–1969), né Loew in Lithuania, US palaeographer. Reader in Palaeography, Oxford, 1927–48; Professor in Palaeography, Institute for Advanced Study, Princeton, 1936–46.
2 Lyndon Baines Johnson (1908–73), Democratic Senator for Texas, 1949–61; Majority Leader 1955–61; John F. Kennedy's running-mate in the 1960 election; Vice-President 1961–3; President 1963–9.
3 One of the British representatives, with Salvador de Madariaga and Iris Murdoch.
4 Annelise Kennan (b. 1910), née Sorensen, Norwegian by birth. Elsewhere IB attributes the comment to Nicolas Nabokov (letter of 16 September 1960 to Rowland Burdon-Muller).

There was a rather moving address by the abbé Pierre,[1] who talked about love and explained that according to Tolstoy freedom was not an end in itself, but that its value depended upon the purposes with which it was used – this, as you may imagine, was vigorously taken up by the Soviet delegation, which found itself as usual in a clerical alliance against the last surviving defenders of individual liberty – you and me (and Maurice). [...]

I must stop, I must stop, the train is going to London, and from London I must go straight to Portofino. Is one not allowed to hope that one day we shall all meet again, you and I and Marion, and Freddie and Sylvester, and even Mrs. A., and Maurice, and Aline too, and celebrate the events of August 30 years ago? I am sure it could happen. I am sure it should.

Yours,   [...]

---

1 The name adopted by Henri Antoine Grouès (1912–2007), Roman Catholic priest, former member of the French Resistance, political and social activist; founder of the Emmaus movement for the poor and homeless.

APPENDICES

The transpopulation of the long memoranda to appendices is, I am convinced, a very great improvement: it lightens the text and gives the whole added balance, momentum and coherence.

IB to Winston Churchill, 14 February 1948

THE ANGLO-AMERICAN PREDICAMENT

A GREAT DEAL was being said in England a few weeks ago about American dissatisfaction with Britain and her economy. British observers in the United States and elsewhere reported 'mounting waves of discontent', 'rising dissatisfaction', 'a chorus of hostile comment' etc., intending thereby to convey that Anglo-American relations were deteriorating fast and steeply, and that evil influences not unlike such traditional bogeys as Anglophobia, isolationism, 'the Big Stick' etc. were once more abroad menacing British interests and ideals.

We were told that the United States' charges were flying thick and fast from every conceivable quarter, that the Government and people of Britain were being accused of idleness, fecklessness, inefficiency, economic blindness, embittered nationalism, and above all a hopeless and obstinate infatuation with an unrealisable or undesirable socialist ideal; and we were even told that there is a danger that Americans of great influence and power were seriously threatening to withdraw all help if this kind of thing continued in the British Isles. There are, of course, some people who said and still say all this, but it is not the terrific business it is represented as being, and the *Manchester Guardian* has almost alone in this country performed the valuable service of placing this grotesquely overrated campaign in its proper perspective.

But even allowing for much exaggeration, both of the extent and importance of such criticism, there is obviously enough here to cause anxiety; anxiety to those who, whether or not they feel any favourable sentiment towards America, have grasped the fact that British fortunes are today indissolubly tied to those of the United States. But the interesting thing is that this particular cloud seems to possess a lining which seems silver to some, and darker than the cloud itself to others; in either case it deserves attention.

Let me say something about the history of this situation. Ten, or even seven, years ago anti-British feeling in the United States, which was really very strong, came from individuals and groups who, because of their disapproval of or dislike for Britain, desired to have as little as possible to do with her; or else if they were compelled to deal with her at all, demanded that various forms of pressure be brought to bear on her to deter her from the graver misdeeds of which they declared her to be guilty. The basic assumption that underlay this was that the United States could afford either to conduct no foreign policy at all, or else one largely independent of Britain's, or even unfriendly to it; and not merely could do this, but should.

The purpose of the traditional anti-British outcry was to liberate the United States from what were conceived to be the tentacles with which the sinister British octopus had all but enveloped an all too trustful American democracy; tentacles which, if not cut rapidly and brutally, might drag America, all innocence, and quite insensible of the terrible danger, into a watery grave. Defenders of Britain, consequently, concentrated on proving either that this image was mythical and that no tentacles, unless perhaps those of the Fascist powers, were reaching out towards the sacred flame of American democracy; or, alternatively, that what had been described as the antennae of a greedy monster were in reality the sacred ties of sentiment and interest, which very properly connected the two great English-speaking democracies. But the central problem was whether or not the United States could or should deliberately ignore, or even oppose, the policies of Britain and her Empire.

Today the picture is infinitely altered. The problem of America is not whether or not to cut adrift but how, since no one save a negligible minority assumes that America can proceed alone, this pas de deux with Great Britain is to continue, without too much stumbling and misunderstanding and bad blood. Today the problem is not whether or not to accept alliance with Britain and Western Europe in general, but how, given that such alliance is inescapable, to avoid paying the maximum price for an arrangement so novel, so unfamiliar, and indeed maddening in a hundred ways.

And the volume of protest alleged to be 'mounting', 'swelling', 'bursting' etc. in the United States, so far as it exists, does not, at least in responsible quarters, spring from a desire to liquidate so awkward an arrangement as the Marshall Plan and European aid; such a step, whether good or bad, is not considered to be realisable by serious persons whose opinion counts in America; on the contrary, they anxiously ask themselves how to persuade or, if need be, bully, or even force so obstinate an institution as Britain – obstinate with all the force of age, tradition, pride, insensitiveness to world opinion, and now, it is thought, political doctrine ('ideology') as well – in short, how to get this ancient and powerful organisation to fit into the political and economic pattern which governs the thinking of the policy-makers of the State Department or the Senate or the White House; a pattern which, many among them hold, can alone save the world, if not for untrammelled private enterprise, at any rate for civil liberties and freedom from the arbitrary use of force, and will alone make possible a minimum standard of economic security, and of political and social equality.

The American conceptions of what is freedom from tyranny, and what is equality, may differ by a whole world from those prevalent in England or France or Italy, but the ideals themselves are very powerful and deep-seated, and emotional attachment to them is very great, and their effects on action very powerful, and unless their influence is allowed for at least as much as that of the more obvious and somewhat less idealistic interests of Standard

Oil or General Motors or the bankers whom Mr Snyder[1] is held to represent, grave mistakes of interpretation and of action will be made (as they have been) by European negotiators and their advisers.

Furthermore, it is important to grasp that the stereotyped mythological image of Britain used to be that of a great unredeemed imperialist oppressor, and it is this image that has become altered in America; and this alone has made a radical difference to American thinking and action. Here, one must understand the role of immigrants in American thinking about foreign nations. America is, after all, largely populated by immigrants or the descendants of immigrants; some of whom had escaped from some kind of political and economic yoke – whether real or imaginary makes little difference. They pooled their grievances many years ago, with the result that Czechs and Lithuanians out of sheer fellow feeling were prepared to disapprove of Britain, and the Irish were prepared to display a corresponding hostility to Austria–Hungary or Russia. But since the flood of immigrants subsided, many years have passed: and by, let us say, 1920 the other great historic oppressors of the old world had either crumbled into ruin or contrived to wash themselves of their sins. Austria–Hungary had disappeared; the Turkish Empire collapsed; Imperial Russia, whatever was thought of the Soviet Union, was at any rate something quite different from the ancient persecutor of Poles or Finns or Jews. France and Belgium, Holland and Portugal did indeed continue to rule other peoples, but few native inhabitants of their colonial empires raised their voice in the United States. Britain almost alone remained as the great unregenerate landlord nation, ruling the waves with all her ancient, careless, eighteenth-century confidence.

The picture is utterly different today. The stumbling blocks are largely gone. The latter-day British sins against which all American history was interpreted as being so much living testimony – India, Palestine, even Ireland, despite the agitation carried on by the government of Eire – are today virtually dead or dying issues so far as the majority of Americans is concerned. The business world may proclaim its fear of socialism, but even so it does not seriously fear the early arrival of it on American shores; and for America's New Deal and Fair Deal and Welfare State even Colonel McCormick[2] can scarcely blame Britain – and, strangely enough, scarcely does.

There is a new assumption in existence today which seems to me to lie embedded more deeply in American thinking than in British; and it seems to me largely valid, perhaps because the Americans, as a still new and rising power, see somewhat further, and in larger, if often in cruder, terms, than older peoples. It is this – and it is the cloud's new lining, whether silver or black – that abandonment of Britain, economically and politically, is literally

1 John Wesley Snyder (1895–1985), US Secretary of the Treasury 1946–53.
2 Robert Rutherford McCormick (1880-1955), editor and publisher of the *Chicago Tribune*: opponent of the New Deal and fervent isolationist.

unthinkable if a preponderance of power against the Soviet Union as well as a tolerable life in the Western world is to be maintained. It is this oppressive sense of the unbreakable permanence of the ties with Great Britain that irritates more Americans, whether benevolently disposed or not, than the actual misdeeds of Britain herself. For Americans bitterly realise more clearly than we do the automatic power to cajole, and if need be to bully, possessed by a debtor who cannot be allowed to go bankrupt by his creditors. Nothing is more maddening to a prosperous captain of industry than the thought of an older and poorer partner with a passion for independence of action, a partner with a firm intention of realising ideas upon which the richer partner has always looked with genuine horror – ideas and tastes which he feels powerless to ignore, because the dissolution of the firm will clearly spell ruin to both sides.

The celebrated marriage between Britain and America for which Mr Churchill has sighed so often, and which seemed so desirable and unattainable a goal in the England of 1940–1, has almost come about. It is a marriage from which, in the view of one of the partners at least – the American – there is no hope, or fear, of ultimate divorce. The marriage may at times be unhappy, but it cannot be annulled without destroying both partners equally. This does something to explain the irritation of those Americans who on the whole believe in the virtues of this marriage, or at least think it unavoidable, but who at times feel exceedingly frustrated by what seems to them unreasonable behaviour on the part of the British, and long to use strong language, but are inhibited by the thought that they must never do anything so violent as to cause an irreparable breach.

American irritation is further increased by the dim realisation that the British do not regard the marriage – or near-marriage – as so utterly irrevocable and permanent, or perhaps do not conceive of themselves as married at all. For the British, when annoyed, speak of breaking loose, of running away as it were from this rich but confining environment, of running away and not coming back. And when they speak in this fashion and make meaningful references to European union or an 'Eastern' orientation, many Americans on the whole consider that these are not realistic policies, that the runaway would be compelled to return in the end; but the very assumption of total economic independence by Britain grates upon them since they believe that they have made great sacrifices precisely because it is impracticable. Yet they know they should restrain their tempers to prevent a fatal break, and this further annoys them, and leads to outbreaks of intemperate language and even action, all of which, sooner or later, has, of course, afterwards to be retracted and apologised for, but which leaves inevitable scars upon the flesh of both.

It is the heavy burden of this new relationship, with the realisation that it probably can never be unmade, that so exasperates both those Americans who realise, with mounting gloom, what a thing it is to have to keep in permanent step – to run a three-legged race – with a semi-foreign power, and help it over stiles and prop its faltering frame; and equally infuriates those Englishmen who fear the despotic American monster in the guise provided for it by its European detractors. In Britain many worthy persons both on the right and on the left go on hoping against hope that the dreadful union forced upon them by the exigencies of the war will not last for ever, that one day they will again breathe freely, liberated from the fear of plutocracy and materialism, and political witch-hunts, and racial intolerance, and the death of individual life and art, and the dissolution of all style and taste and feeling in an ocean of American vulgarity.

There is a reality reflected and distorted in both nightmares, but the British fear seems to be the more exaggerated. American complaints about the difficulties arising from this inevitable partnership may often be unjustified, but they are almost always intelligible. The friction may be inevitable, as it is certainly profoundly annoying; but at least the more far-sighted and enlightened among the ruling groups in America, even in the business world, realise that this is the price of a changed world situation. The point I wish to make is that the notion of ever closer collaboration with Britain is today something more deeply taken for granted by Americans than even the average enlightened American may himself consciously realise; and I say this because I think there is little doubt that if American policy, rather than statements about it even by its makers, is studied, it becomes clear that Britain has become part of the natural sphere of United Sates policy to a far greater extent than, for example, France or Italy, which theoretically are just as intrinsic to the overall strategic plan of the West. But these countries are to Americans psychologically remoter, and the thought of them tends to be less irritating in proportion as their presence is not so acutely felt in day-to-day American proceedings.

To anyone lately returned from the United States it seems that British irritation with America – as opposed to resistance to American plans, which is often most amply justified – goes beyond the norm to be expected even of a people as naturally reluctant to recognise a shift in world balance as we obviously are; goes beyond the degree to be expected of a people deeply irked by the need to receive benefits at all, even if only temporary, and even though (as is so tirelessly if unanswerably repeated) these benefits are but a small return for the heroism and suffering which Britain showed when she saved humanity by her example. It is an irritation which arises partly from a lack of historical imagination, which is a faculty born of the buffetings of fortune from which this once happy island has so long been mercifully preserved; and it leads to a desire to close one's eyes to the kind of close relationship which must be maintained with the great American giant if we are to preserve not merely an adequate standard of living, but life and liberty itself. For what other avenues are there? A Western European Union, desirable as it may be in itself, is a very rickety structure unless integrated with the economies of both America and the British Empire; an Eastern orientation is scarcely compatible with the preservation of civil liberties. An adjustment to a new level is inevitable, and this is always a painful thing for nations no less than individuals.

It is particularly difficult to acknowledge the fact that the old paths to survival and recovery are gone; and this truth, which American statesmen discern, often in a very dim and stumbling fashion, and articulate in crude and at times needlessly provocative language, is nevertheless a truth; a truth which some of our own leaders have tried to circumnavigate with much subtlety and intelligence and a desperate reluctance to realise that things are what they are and that their consequences will be what they will be.

In vain. For it cannot be helped, the union grows more real every day. Whether it will in the short, as well as the long, run be a source of strength and a better life, or of much unnecessary friction and mutual frustration, will in the end be determined by the genius of both peoples, and not least by the historical insight of their chosen leaders, today and tomorrow.

First broadcast on the BBC Third Programme, 21 September 1949; published in the Listener, *29 September 1949, 518–19, 538; see also letters to the editor, 20 October 1949, 681, 10 November 1949, 813, 815*

THE INTELLECTUAL LIFE OF AMERICAN
UNIVERSITIES

HAVING RECENTLY returned from an extended visit to the oldest and most distinguished of American universities, I found myself making inevitable comparisons between it and our own ancient foundations; not in general terms, because the differences are not so much of degree as of kind, too wide and pervasive to make a parallel suggestive, but in terms of my own personal experience, in terms of the particular group of graduate students whom I met; and them I tried to set beside the abler among the undergraduates with a sprinkling of postgraduates who, in my own university today, roughly correspond to one of the graduate schools of America.

The differences, which are striking, seem to me symptomatic of the deeper differences between our two countries or even continents. There is still something, noticed by all Europeans whether with pleasure or distaste, of that disarming innocence which belongs to the America equally of Chateaubriand and Henry James (and so strenuously denied by some American critics; but the very fire of their indignation tends to support the validity of this thesis).

The American students seemed to me more intellectually curious, more responsive to every influence, more deeply and immediately charmed by everything new, or even true, and above all endowed with a quality of moral vitality unlike any I had found anywhere else, although I suspected its existence, even now, not very far beneath the surface, in the Soviet Union. The American students seemed intellectually less parochial and provincial than even the most intelligent and gifted among our own undergraduates – thus, for example, they assumed that they might be required to seek for first-hand information in books or periodicals written in languages other than English or even French; and again, however isolationist or xenophobic their political outlook might be, they took the unity of the intellectual world more for granted than the young men in our universities and probably in those of France and Italy, too. They were, for the most part, almost entirely lacking in irony or malice, naively earnest and naively cynical and quite astonishingly open-minded. Every idea which was placed before them was seized upon with an extraordinary eagerness, nothing seemed too bizarre or too obvious to be denied some degree of serious consideration.

They seemed (and this could at times be very exhausting) almost incapable of boredom, or of more than a very surface scepticism. The majority, no matter how hardboiled or rough they might appear, turned out, as a rule, to be touchingly honest and idealistic; and wished to fit into their lives such revelation as they hoped to find in books or in the teachers provided by the university; even the most frivolous among them were inwardly deeply Victorian; and looked out upon the world with earnest, energetic, optimistic eyes. The abler among them were very able indeed; and their freedom from academic, and indeed many other present-day European, conventions, and their fresh and often childlike eye invested them with a quality of pure-hearted curiosity and originality which could not fail to attract any practitioner genuinely devoted to his subject; particularly one who, despite all the weight of intellectual conviction, is yet, at times, made to feel doubt about its value in the ruthlessly deflationary atmosphere prevalent in the centres of European civilisation today.

So far all seems pure gain: moral seriousness, generous enthusiasms, energy, good will, capacity for genuine intellectual passion – no one could (or should) look down upon so rich a cluster of virtues, and they were truly present among the people of whom I speak. On the other side it must be remarked that many of these excellent young people could not, as a general rule, either read or write, as these activities are understood in our best universities. That is to say, their thoughts came higgledy-piggledy out of the big, buzzing, booming confusion of their minds, too many pouring out chaotically in the same instant, and the task of sorting them into orderly sentences – or thoughts – was sometimes more than many of their owners could achieve. They had a great deal to say, perhaps more than corresponding Europeans, but their means for saying it were altogether inadequate. Somewhere in their early education there was a failure to order, to connect and to discriminate.

Nor had they in many cases learnt how to read intelligently; and consequently they tended to look to their professors to tell them not merely what books to read but sometimes what chapters and what pages; on being told, the more serious among them would throw themselves upon the recommended pabulum and would try to absorb it in a very frenzied fashion. They read rapidly, desperately and far too much. And because they tended to believe that all facts (and only facts) were important and, what is more, equally important, the result was often a fearful intellectual congestion from which many of them will probably suffer for the rest of their lives.

It is true that our students are better trained, have a better natural sense of the quality – or at least of the value for themselves personally – of books and lectures and persons, and are endowed with the inestimably precious gifts of scepticism and irony, which act as a powerful preservative from the frantic mill-race of the industrious American student.

On the other hand, they are a good deal narrower and less imaginative; their vision is more limited and far more convention-ridden; their general outlook is – perhaps because of the obvious social and economic ills of our time – more obviously utilitarian. They are more easily disheartened, their curiosity is less strong and even less disinterested, although, of course, much less moralistic; they care less acutely about truth or aesthetic satisfaction, or improving the world, or their own state, or whatever other goal their activity is intended to attain. Consequently, all but the best are at times less interesting to teach even while they profit far more by what they get, intellectually, and in the short run; but not morally, or in the long run intellectually either; since in the end what they accumulate often peters out, or becomes stabilised at a level of irredeemable mediocrity, unless kept alive by an energy incapable of surviving in an atmosphere of too much civilised distaste for excess.

The passionate concern for the truth which lives in the morally uncomplicated and fervently serious American student (how well and sympathetically and yet with what irony Tolstoy could have described it, and indeed Turgenev, too) is virtually unknown in the older seats of British learning. The added quality of open-mindedness and the romantic view of themselves as pioneers in all spheres of life and experience, however exasperating to European visitors with longer historical memories, does make it easier for Americans to perceive unobvious connections between their own subjects and adjacent or remote disciplines. Often, of course, these connections are largely illusory or invented and the result is a mass of woolly, confused and sometimes dishonest patter which plagues such modern fields of study (or at least of discussion) as the various branches of 'social science' as it is understood in America today. In this now fashionable domain so much is spoken, so little said, still less demonstrated or rendered plausible, so many old, trite truths come masquerading as new discoveries (for all the world like ordinary persons who insist on visiting each other's houses grotesquely clad in divers' suits for which there is no apparent need, harmless but queer), that fastidious Europeans with severe intellectual standards, trained minds and easily wounded aesthetic sensibilities are at first puzzled and in the end irritated and maddened.

Despite, however, all such mystification, crudeness, nonsense and even charlatanism, the American method of entering new fields of knowledge, although it raises unnecessary dust, yet achieves a good deal; indeed at its bulldozing best it opens new avenues which Europeans can conceive but by the very virtues of their education are sometimes prevented from bringing into existence. British students tend to recoil from all this noise and clatter, not because of any natural blindness or shallowness or timidity, so much as from lack of appetite – because of more civilised and scrupulous, but sometimes incurably unenterprising, intellectual habits and a tendency to the routine production of familiar, carefully tested results, within the cosy, solid framework of a more dependable, but smaller-scale, academic tradition.

Some of the English students who came over armed with fellowships to my American university, unless their subject was, say, the ancient world, where their own standards were far higher than those they found, were a little bewildered, but presently exhilarated, by the peculiar new intellectual atmosphere into which they were plunged, and in one or two cases flew to the opposite extreme and decried their English education as having been too absurdly confining and dull, not realising how well it had equipped them to cope with whatever came their way without losing equilibrium, or feeling puzzled, frustrated, inadequate and vaguely indignant, which is at times the fate of some of the ablest, most serious and fiercely energetic American students in England and in France.

This lopsided excess of earnestness upholstered by little sense of the past – or indeed of any historical proportions – this conspicuous lack of that tranquil intellectual self-confidence which Oxford and Cambridge and the École Normale, for example, are so good at providing, is, of course, the stock object of caricature from Dickens and Trollope to Max Beerbohm, Waugh and Wodehouse; this often ludicrous lack of natural balance accompanied by acute self-consciousness which all foreigners remark in Americans, while it may be an irreplaceable asset in a life dedicated to unremitting action, carries its own terrible dangers, since it exposes its victims to a degree of unnecessary moral guilt which often, in the end, corrodes their lives.

II

The intellectual life of American universities is faced by at least three enemies, all formidable, but one of them comparatively new and more sinister than the others. Two of them are old and familiar enough. The first is the businessman or politician who often dominates the alumni associations and corporations which financially and administratively control American universities; this figure notoriously disapproves of anything not obviously economically useful or politically conformist; this is the prototype of Babbitt, Elmer Gantry and all the other bad characters systematically exposed by all American defenders of minorities from the great specialist, Mr Sinclair Lewis, to the latest avant-garde novelist or poet; and on the whole the older and more distinguished American universities have held this particular enemy at bay with reasonable success.

The struggle against barbarians and their allies – quacks, knaves and those well-intentioned but muddle-headed uplift-mongers who are so frequently found embedded in the great American educational trusts – has almost the advantage of communicating a certain quality of austere heroism to the embattled defenders of academic liberties, intellectual standards, disinterested learning and the life of reason in general; which in its turn satisfies the desire to do what is right (most obviously so when it involves swimming against the current), very strong in most Americans and particularly in the inhabitants of New England. The danger is doubtless genuine enough and at times serious, but on the whole it is fended off with courage and relatively few casualties.

The second enemy is the state of mind of academic persons themselves whom war service or some other sharp new experience has made painfully aware of the social and economic miseries of their society. Like the youthful Kropotkin and many noble young men and women before and after him, a student or professor in this condition wonders whether it can be right for him to continue to absorb himself in the study of, let us say, the early Greek epic at Harvard, while the poor of south Boston go hungry and unshod, and Negroes are denied fundamental rights in the Deep South. This honour-able predicament is, of course, the precise opposite of the earlier menace – militant philistinism – and is indeed an impulse which has created heroes and martyrs and saints; in universities it leads those who are caught in it to wish to abandon their studies or at least do something of greater and more immediate social usefulness.

It is clear that this tendency, enlightened as it is, would, if it became too widespread, mean a rapid end of all the liberal arts and sciences. Against it, however, it is at least possible to argue. It is possible to urge that while only the stoniest heart would deny the claims of social welfare as being valid and important and indeed urgent, yet they must not be allowed to absorb the whole of life; that even if the Boston poor were adequately clothed and fed, and the Negroes in the South enjoyed their full human and civic rights, there would still require to be something for them to do. One can offer the obvious, but apparently not too obvious, truth that people must be taught to be sufficiently discriminating to know what things would most satisfactorily fulfil their intellectual and moral needs, and that this cannot be achieved if everyone is engaged solely, or even for the most part, in the circular opera-tion of providing the material means towards improving the lives of others.

The circle is not vicious, but it is a denial of the ends of life. In such a world A is busily engaged in helping B to train C to help A – to help him towards what goal? Only to make him more useful to B and C; useful in what respect? To make A, B and C in general more helpful to one another; helpful in doing or being what? This remains unanswered and, in a world dedicated to social service as its main activity, unanswerable. Means displace ends and nothing is now worth doing or being for its own sake. This is no doubt less morally repulsive than the wicked world against which it is directed, but it is infinitely more futile; in the latter there are at least some ends – power or wealth or heartless enjoyment – which, however ethically disreputable, function as motives of action and provide the content of thought or feeling, of science and art; without these it is difficult to conceive of the possibility of mental or emotional life as we know it.

It is one thing to be secretly bored by, or even hate, one's subject, and to accept a new public career offered by a great social cataclysm – the New Deal or the outbreak of war – as a release from an unloved occupation; and this doubtless did liberate many consciously or unconsciously unhappy academic persons in many countries during the last decade. It is a very different thing, however, to be genuinely devoted and absorbed by some 'pure' subject, let us say, medieval art, and to be ridden by the guilty feeling that in a world so full of disease, poverty and injustice, it is a wicked self-indulgence to devote one's abilities to a pursuit likely to provide direct comfort to so few of one's less fortunate fellow-citizens.

The American Puritan conscience here enters into a dreadful collaboration with the idealistic materialism present in the average American (for idealistic he undoubtedly is), and whatever causal hypothesis be made about non-conscious roots of human behaviour – by Marxists or Freudians or neo-Buddhists or followers of Nietzsche or Dr Toynbee – yet the conscious spring and motive behind many of his acts is as often a naive but genuine and sincere – and troubled – desire to improve the human lot as any crude desire for personal gain or fame or power which is attributed to him so unconditionally by outraged, and occasionally envious, foreigners. This form of moral guilt turns out to be the most dangerous and destructive of all, for so long as the scholars and the intellectuals themselves believe in their own form of life, there is a hope that unless the forces of the external enemy prove overwhelming, they will find themselves able to repel his onslaughts as they have done so often in the past, indeed throughout the history of civilised institutions. But once the defenders themselves begin to doubt the rightness of their cause, the Trojan Horse has penetrated the walls; a fifth column begins to operate within the fortress and the cause of reason is in jeopardy.

It is not that his subject has grown any less attractive to its now unhappy practitioner. He loves it, we will assume, more ardently than ever, but he now feels that with society in a state of misery or injustice, his occupation is a luxury which it should not be able to afford; and from this flows the feeling that if only he can devote some – perhaps the greater part – of his time to some activity more obviously useful to society, work for a government department, or journalism, or administration and organisation of some kind, and so forth, he might still with this pay for the right to pursue his proper subject (now rapidly, in his own eyes, acquiring the status of a private hobby), and it turns into something for which he is required to pay a moral price in the form of some 'useful' activity for which he may not be specially fitted and which he may well, even if he executes it competently, find profoundly irksome and distasteful.

Once this step has been taken, the game is up, the enemy is within the gates. The ends for the sake of which one does what one does, the pursuit of activities or forms of life solely because they are what they are, and are worth living, and at times dying, for – the whole structure of civilised life is utterly compromised, the means have destroyed the end. Those who have ceased to believe in the paramount value of the subject to which they have been devoted in the past find themselves no longer able to pursue it fruitfully, and discover that they are in what is called a false position; once this has happened the level of culture, intellectual, moral, artistic and ultimately technical and physical, too, must sharply decline. Unless people do what they do because to some degree they like doing it, the results of their work are sterile. Once a community automatically begins to consider disinterested curiosity as being something idle, time-wasting, self-indulgent and, therefore, immoral, it is in a very bad way.

It may be safely asserted that whatever the role of environmental or social or economic factors, few great works of art, or great discoveries of science, have ever been made by men with one eye on the social consequences of their activity. I can think of no exception to this rule, but I hesitate to affirm it without adequate knowledge. Yet if there are exceptions they will, I believe, be found to prove the rule – i.e. such social consciousness, whatever its other merits, will be found to have interfered to some extent with the excellence of the act of creation or discovery itself. I feel sure that neither Michelangelo nor Mozart, neither Newton nor Hume nor Gauss nor Einstein, gave a conscious thought to beneficial or deleterious social consequences while they were engaged on their labours; and when Tolstoy did so he became as unreadable as he, being Tolstoy, could be.

Darwin, one feels convinced, would not have been deterred from putting forward his theories, whatever view he might have taken of its effects upon human happiness; he left that to Huxley, who was an expositor of great skill and imagination rather than a great discoverer; and yet neither of these eminent Victorians can be accused of lack of moral sentiment, and Huxley fervently wished to improve the world. But they considered that the truth, like goodness, or any other absolute end, was socially and in every other respect valuable enough in itself for its pursuit to need no further justification: it was something which justified other things and did not itself require – did not in principle, whatever its consequences, social or individual, need – justification by something outside itself. As for Michelangelo or Mozart or Keats, they might have been satisfied well enough, perhaps, by the truth that works of genuine art, in Mr Forster's phrase, 'stand up' when other things collapse or wither away; and there is little surely to add to that.

The canker I speak of is not so widespread in American universities as to have created a catastrophic situation; nevertheless, men of great intellectual distinction occasionally fall conspicuous victims to it: gifted researchers become indifferent half-time bureaucrats and infect their friends and colleagues with their own uneasy conscience. The general crisis of faith in the value of their own lives and work has spread to all professions in America – for little else will explain the sensational growth of psychoanalytic and other therapeutic practices with their promise of relief from mental stress, which are today threatening to become the universal drug of the entire American upper and middle class, very much as the growing addiction to Eastern mystery religions reflected the anxieties and disorientation of Roman society in decay.

Nor is our own country as free from this kind of confused sense of the moral need for self-immolation as its English civilisation might seem to guarantee. When the unhappy and sterile and frustrated seek to blame their own shortcomings (often with justice) upon the dislocations of society and preach and practise 'social work' as a means of salvation, as a means of drowning their private miseries in a great impersonal sea, that is intelligible if often disastrous. But when gifted, fruitful, articulate scholars and artists, men with capacity and opportunity for rich and effective self-expression fall victim to such prevalent forms of morally and intellectually wasting disease, the situation grows alarming.

When I tried to suggest to my more socially conscious American students that intellectual curiosity was not necessarily a form of sin or even frivolity and that a possible valid reason for pursuing this or that branch of knowledge was merely that they were interested in it, that they liked such activity and nothing more, I could see that I was thought, I do not say by all, but certainly by many, to be expounding what is vaguely thought of as the 'European' point of view – at best something like an audacious, ruthless, pagan individualism, a violent, brazenly anti-social Nietzschean egoism, to the falsity of which the American way of life was the great living witness. It was made clear that unless one's activity specifically added to the sum of social welfare it stood in desperate need of justification.

This naive, sincere and touching morality, according to which (as I said before) the primary duty of everyone is to help others – and so on, and so on – with no indication of what it is that everyone is to help others to be or do, is itself a symptom of a larger attitude, which seems to me the peculiar, and frightening, contribution of the twentieth century to the sum of human ideals. It is an attitude which so far as I know has no parallel in any previous condition of society, at any rate since the darkest portion of the Dark Ages. This is the last and most destructive enemy. And if its peculiar nature has not been more often noticed, that is perhaps because it has crept in upon us very gradually, and has in consequence been taken altogether too much for granted.

III

In the past, the primary aim of education was so to train people that they were able to solve the problems considered to be important more successfully than if they were left to their own devices. Opinions, doubtless, differed at various times and in different cultures as to what these problems were. And they differed, of course, about the best techniques for their solution. The history of these differences is a familiar and at times tragic story: while some looked for the answer in sacred books and others to the inspired teachings of priests or divinely appointed leaders, still others insisted that observation of natural phenomena, or scientific experiment, or the inner light, or metaphysical speculation, or what one's nurse used to say, were the sole sources of reliable truth. So crucially important were these differences of method felt to be that, ostensibly at least, wars were fought and blood was shed over little else during long periods of human history.

But while these disagreements about the proper way to the discovery of the truth were wide and often sharp and irreconcilable, there was a considerable degree of general agreement, at any rate in the Western world, about what were the great problems to the solution of any one of which a man might worthily devote his whole life. Such questions as the nature of laws governing the external world, its origins, its history, its purpose, and the more alarming question whether it could be said to have a purpose at all; the proper ends of human life; the existence and attributes of God, and again whether anything at all is meant by even asserting his existence, and if so what; the best ways of making or judging beautiful or remarkable objects; the laws which govern the mental life of individuals or of societies, and the ways in which they should govern themselves or one another, and the reasons for this; all these were regarded as issues worthy of the most serious and sustained effort which could be applied to their study.

There were doubtless persons at all times who suggested less or more openly that no final answers to such questions could in principle ever be obtained; because such answers differed for persons or societies in differing conditions, or depended upon such variable factors as geography or climate or methods of obtaining sustenance, or the condition of the questioner's glands or brain cells, or his early upbringing or his mood and whether he was poor or rich, or satisfied or hungry, or well or sick or crossed in love. Such relativity-minded persons were usually considered irritating and sometimes dangerous sceptics and at moments of social crisis they were liable to extreme persecution. But even they did not doubt that the questions asked were themselves both universal and important. They differed from the majority of their society about the kinds of answers obtainable: they did not question the genuineness of the need for answers of some kind. From the pressure of such puzzles, whether articulated in words or expressed in behaviour which indicated perplexity and a quest for ways out of it, sprang the sciences and the arts, the progress of which constitutes the history of human culture.

It has been left to the twentieth century to do something undreamed of in previous ages: instead of seeking to answer these questions, an attempt is being made to suppress, or rather eliminate, the questions themselves. For that is what the widespread modern preoccupation with maladjustments and neuroses amounts to. It was found that of the questions human beings asked themselves, some did not seem immediately answerable by the methods in ordinary use; that the remorseless pressure of such unanswered questions tended to lead to a condition sometimes amounting to self-torture and great mental misery. In the past this painful experience ended sometimes in sterile frustration; at others in discoveries, inventions and works of art of varying degrees of genius. But now, in our own century, all misery or evil began to be considered as a bad state, a species of psychological malaise, needing, in the first place, a remedy. Since *ex hypothesi* no obvious answers could be found to the tormenting problems, the best method of putting an end to intellectual and moral discomfort was by curing people of the very desire to ask such trouble-giving questions. Many techniques appeared simultaneously in answer to the demand of the new Zeitgeist, which sought, above all, 'adjustment', harmony, peace of mind.

In philosophy this took the form of the comparatively cautious and, to a limited degree, very useful maxim that any problem the path to the solution of which could not even in principle be so much as indicated was probably not a genuine problem at all, but a mere verbal muddle to be cleared up: from this process there might emerge genuine problems to be treated appropriately. This did at least concede the need for the untying of genuine – as opposed to bogus – knots; but a further and more fatal step was taken when the powerful weapon of psychoanalysis was introduced to cure the patient, not merely of the genuine mental disease with which he was afflicted, but of the discomforts and discontent occasioned by the presence of problems felt to be at once too urgent to be ignored and too obscure to point to any obvious type of rational or artistic solution.

Difficult problems, cruces, tormenting puzzles, dilemmas of behaviour all cause anxiety. Anxiety is a disease and must be cured. This can be done by so treating the patient that the problem no longer troubles him: and this is best achieved by removing it – like an aching tooth. Instead of unravelling you cut. Instead of answering the question you remove it from the questioner's consciousness.

Fascist and Communist dictatorships, obedient to the *Zeitgeist*, have tended as much and more than the most intolerant theocracies of the past to circumscribe the intellectual horizon of their subjects so as to suppress insistent questions and preoccupations likely to disturb the rigid social adjustment on which such systems of government necessarily rest. Fascism did this openly: Communism, theoretically wedded to a kind of rationalism, began with misgivings which, however, it managed quickly to forget. Disciplines sprang up and found their ways into universities the purpose of which was not the discovery and dissemination of knowledge, nor the promotion of beautiful or interesting objects or experiences, nor training calculated to improve human powers of creation or understanding or enjoyment or communication; but they were designed primarily to provide individuals or societies with techniques of more successful adjustment with their fellows, a direct attempt to 'get at' them in some non-rational fashion, in order to impose upon them a shape likely to fit the desired social pattern more smoothly, with less friction, less frustration: in short, to promote contentment, stability and an unworried condition of social and individual peace.

No doubt our age, like every other, is a time of crisis, and anything which diminishes unnecessary maladjustments within and between human beings is to be welcomed. But the price paid for this, particularly in the United States, seems extravagantly and, indeed, fatally high; the premium at present placed upon all sciences and pseudo-sciences which promise to reduce tension among individuals or societies operates directly to discredit disinterested curiosity if it is too troublesome, the pursuit of knowledge if it is too disturbing, or the development of talents and faculties for their own sakes, as being somehow an evasion of responsibility to society; when the ends of society itself must ultimately consist in goals of this kind.

The picture has indeed been transformed since a century or two ago; in the eighteenth century, where the Church sought to soothe and suppress, Voltaire boldly questioned. Ibsen protested and exposed, and, of course, the timid and the *bien-pensant* averted their gaze: the lines were clearly drawn between obscurantism and the search for truth. But today the tendency to conciliate, smooth away, treat vital problems as symptoms of a morbid condition – with no disgrace attached since we are all equally liable to it, and so on – comes itself decked out in the uniform of science and of reason. The enemy is within the rationalist camp: the case for reason is lost before it has been pleaded. This is a change indeed.

Because there has been too much callousness in the past towards mental suffering, and the healing of mental disorders is no less important than of those of the body; and because psychiatrists are and always have been genuinely needed and have discovered remarkable new techniques, and their activities are more adequately appreciated today than they were in the past, it still does not follow that their function is literally of transcendent value, that there is little that is higher, better, more important, for the reason that everyone is in some degree diseased and, therefore, to cure or be cured is the primary purpose of the inhabitants of the earth.

The view of the world presupposed by the activities of a large section of the intelligentsia of America and increasingly of Europe is that of an enormous hospital of which all men are inmates, with the obligation of acting as nurses and physicians to one another to the limit of their abilities. The substitution for spontaneity and mental energy of characteristics likely to secure the maximum degree of frictionless contentment does not merely atrophy the creative impulse (save, I suppose, in the promotion of the therapeutic arts) but will in the end lead to a violent anti-humanitarian, anti-utilitarian, anti-scientific reaction conceived in the kind of mood in which Trotsky used to speak of 'Kantian-Liberal-Quaker-Vegetarian nonsense', beside which the extravagances of Fascism and other forms of anti-rationalist aggressive self-assertion will seem relatively tame and orderly and traditionalist.

Perhaps I am exaggerating both the extent of this phenomenon and its danger. But in what other period of human existence has so much effort been devoted, not to the painfully difficult task of looking for light, but to the protection – and deterring – of individuals from the intellectual and moral burden of facing problems that may be too deep or complex to be dealt with by any patented method, with a clear guarantee of success? And if this process continues (although, of course, in the end, like all compounds of false sciences and bogus faiths, it will break down), and if what can be done (but may scarcely be worth the effort) gradually replaces what can perhaps not be done (but is worth any amount of effort), what is to become of us?

'Notes on the Way' column, Time and Tide, *12, 19 and 26 November 1949*

ZHIVAGO

IB's arguments against putting Boris Pasternak on the cover of Time *magazine (see 656/1)*

1. So long as *Dr Zhivago*, after it had been published abroad, continued to be suppressed in the USSR, this was a grave source of embarrassment to the Soviet authorities. It was acclaimed as a work of genius in Italy, France, England, and its anti-Marxist passages were (rightly) not regarded as central. Surkov and other old Stalinists in the Writers' Union found it increasingly difficult to explain why a possible masterpiece had been suppressed: they played down the issue; and the 'floating vote' in the Cold War – liberals, neutralists, opinion-forming groups in uncommitted countries, in Asia as well as Europe – took an increasingly indignant and anti-Soviet line. This seems to have been welcomed by disaffected artists behind the Iron Curtain, who used it as a weapon against the Commissars: very *openly in Poland*; cautiously in Russia, Hungary etc. The Commissars were on the defensive: and there was no question of penalising Pasternak himself. The appearance of the novel was mildly criticised: but weathercocks like Ehrenburg, or the Minister of Culture, Mikhailov, referred to Pasternak with nervous respect as a poet of genius etc. The 'scandal' of publication was a literary event of the first magnitude and undoubtedly a pure asset for the West.

2. This began to alter when journalists – especially the A[ssociated] P[ress], and reviewers in the USA, and the *Daily Express* in England – began to extract the few anti-Marxist passages and highlighted them. Then the BBC broadcast a serialised version of *Dr Zhivago* in Russian over their Russian service. This made a very bad impression on some of those who heard about this in England, not only because the use of a novel of genius as an official propaganda instrument endangered Pasternak's safety, but also because it seemed likely to rebound against the users, by stimulating a patriotic anti-Western reaction among the Russian writers – even the critics of the regime. The fact that the Nobel award was interpreted in some Western circles as a political step strengthened this. The Russian oppositional writers – so the Polish writers (who are unanimously pro-Pasternak) report – began to feel that if Pasternak's novel was to be looked on as a Cold-War, anti-Soviet weapon in the West, their own position would be impossibly compromised. They wondered if the publication of *Zhivago* would not destroy them, as an act of terrorism by one of their members breaks a moderate opposition: awakes fear and hatred and unchains reprisals against them, which crushes them out of

existence; kills all hope of reform, still less resistance. Pasternak's 'retraction' is certainly, so the Poles say, a *sincere* reaction against crude Western efforts to use *Zhivago* as a propaganda weapon: somewhat like the bitter indignation of the Hungarian freedom-fighters with the use made of them by anti-Soviet radio stations in Munich.

3. *Time* and *Life* are regarded as the spearhead of the Cold-War party in the West. For them to play up Pasternak's heroism and martyrdom, even in its [*sic*] literary section, is to align him with the enemies of the Soviet Union so openly as not only to expose him to further dangers, but also to produce a violently anti-American reaction among the uncommitted Asians, European liberals etc., who may be anti-Communist, but don't wish to feel allied to the bugbears of 'Wall Street imperialists' and other reactionaries. Just as the use of, say, Laski's attacks on British institutions in the 1930s by isolationists, Anglophobes and fellow-travellers in America infuriated most Englishmen who heard about this, and increased their nationalism and their anti-American and blimpish feelings; just as support for the Polish rising in 1863 by the French and English press turned the majority of Russian liberals and even revolutionaries into supporters of Tsar and Church against the West, which was held to be using the Polish issue to dismember the Russian Empire; so support for, or playing up of, Pasternak's cause by openly anti-Soviet organs may compromise him finally – lead him sincerely and desperately to disavow such alliances – cause the wobblers and the uncommitted and the anti-Communist left to think that perhaps the Soviet Writers' Union *had* to pillory *Zhivago* openly, if it was to be exploited by the 'imperialist[s]' for their own wicked ends. This could happen a hundredfold in the USSR where a patriotic reaction might easily be sparked off; and where it will be rubbed into Pasternak that he had, whether or not he desired this, been turned into a major ally of capitalism (which he genuinely abhors) – of the enemies not merely of the Soviet system but of Russia herself. This makes Pasternak's letter to Khrushchev absolutely sincere.

4. This is why so passionate an anti-Communist as Ignazio Silone and his friends want to found a 'committee for the protection of the moral rights of Pasternak', i.e. against his shameless exploitation for political or just sensational purposes; why Lord Russell, T. S. Eliot, Rebecca West and the others who sent an open letter to Khrushchev were so careful to insist on *Zhivago* as personal testimony and not a political piece; and why prominence in *Time* or *Life* may well cause a setback to the very cause of human liberty which they are anxious to promote.

WHO IS A JEW?

This is IB's formal response (sent on 23 January 1959; see 671–3) to a letter from David Ben-Gurion to over 50 eminent Jews, seeking advice on how Israel should treat the offspring of certain mixed marriages.

MEMORANDUM TO THE PRIME MINISTER OF ISRAEL

1. I assume that the main problem before the State of Israel is of the attitude that it should take towards the children of Jewish fathers and non-Jewish mothers, where the mother has not been converted to Judaism, and both parents desire the child to be registered as a Jew in Israel. There is also the related question created by whether or not the religious authorities can accept as Jews persons who for their own reasons do not desire to belong to any religious denomination, or avail themselves of facilities provided by religious bodies. The two classes may of course overlap.

2. Should children of such mixed marriages be regarded and registered as Jews in Israel? Should persons who declare themselves atheists or belong to some religion other than Jewish, but who nevertheless claim to be Jews by nationality, be permitted to register as (say) atheists or Christians by religion, and Jews by nationality? What would this latter category connote, and what privileges and rights would it carry or forfeit?

3. In connection with this it seems to me not a merely academic fact that most words in common use are susceptible to at least two types of definitions: (*a*) a precise and clear but somewhat artificial definition necessitated by legal or theological or scientific requirements; and (*b*) the loose definition entailed by the use of words in everyday speech. The word 'Jew' has, so far as I can tell, this narrower or tighter meaning as defined by Halacha – namely the son of a Jewess or a convert to Judaism – but equally it has a looser connotation in common speech. A Jew in this looser sense is anyone whom a normal person, acquainted with the customary use of the term, would, without too much reflection, describe as a Jew (just as a table is what most people agree to be a table, even though, e.g. for certain commercial or legal purposes, the meaning of the word 'table' may have to be artificially tightened up). In this normal sense we can speak of 'atheistic Jews' without any sense of contradiction; for we should take a man to be a Jew if he were in most respects identified with a Jewish community, despite the fact that his mother may be an unconverted non-Jewess, and that the rabbis may

therefore quite correctly reject his claims to be a Jew in the religious – narrower – sense of the word.

4. The practice of the State of Israel, inasmuch as it involves the ascription to Jews of certain rights and duties which may not necessarily also be ascribed to non-Jews, creates the need for a legally precise definition of the term 'Jew'. How should it be defined?

5. It seems clear to me that, inasmuch as the State of Israel claims to be (as I think it does – and with justice) a liberal State and not a theocracy, it cannot define the status of its citizens or even of its residents in purely religious terms. If Israel is not to be a theocracy, or impose religious tests of civil rights, it cannot withhold such rights as marriage, divorce, burial etc. from persons who proclaim themselves avowed atheists, or from those who do not profess a religion recognised as such by the State, simply on those grounds alone. If there is to be no religious coercion, as your letter so properly states, it must be possible for any resident of Israel to be married and divorced without recourse to a religious ceremony of any kind. If this is at present not politically feasible, owing to the strength of Israeli or Jewish opinion against it, this makes for some, if not a very high degree of, religious discrimination, and the problem of how to guarantee the civil liberties of the entire Israeli population, as civil freedom is understood in modern States today, seems to me, so long as this persists in principle, not soluble. This may, in view of the small number of persons affected by the absence of the civil institutions of marriage, divorce etc., not be an urgent problem at present. But the existence of this situation is nevertheless a blemish; and grave though the moral and spiritual problems its solution may pose, nothing is gained by denying its existence.

6. If Israel is to be, in the full sense, a modern liberal State, the question of religious affiliation should make no difference to its laws of citizenship, or the civil and political rights enjoyed by its inhabitants. On the other hand, it is clear that there would have come into being no State of Israel if Judaism were merely a religion, and not, in some sense, a nationality as well. I assume that, for reasons of security, if none other, the inhabitants of Israel may, at any rate for some time, be required to register as either Jews or non-Jews of various categories. Should persons who are recognised (by members of their society, Jewish or non-Jewish) as Jews in the common sense of the word, but are not recognised as Jews by the rabbis interpreting the Halacha in the traditionally accepted manner, be regarded as politically and legally Jews or not? There can be no clear-cut or ready-made solution to this problem. If we are to rule out religious coercion even of the mildest kind – by the pressure of custom and public opinion – as being incompatible with the minimum

requirements of individual liberty (and I cannot see how Israel can morally fail to do so – it was not denial of religious liberties that created Zionism), then there must exist a category of persons who will be entitled to register themselves as Jews by nationality, but not by religion. What criterion can be used in determining who these persons are? I must admit that the common-sense criterion, according to which anyone is a Jew who is taken to be a Jew, particularly by his Gentile neighbours in the countries of the Dispersion, seems to me near the mark, but somewhat fluid and vague. We can invent one, e.g. the criterion already proposed by some in Israel, including, I believe, yourself, of a declaration that one belongs to no other religion and therefore desires to be a Jew. Against that, some may argue that this definition is too wide – it could include persons not normally thought of as Jews by anyone (say an ex-Nazi pagan) – and too narrow, for it should in principle be possible – however few persons will follow this in practice, or however anomalous this may seem – for a man to be nationally a Jew and by religion a Christian, a Muslim or whatever he pleases. To say that the national categories of Jew, Arab, Armenian etc. may be retained, but that, if a man is a Christian, he is automatically deprived of some political rights, does seem to me – even if it is politically unavoidable and demanded by Jewish public opinion – to be a form of religious discrimination. You may call this academic, since it is not, at present, an important practical issue, since the number of eccentrics who desire to live as Jews in Israel, and yet practise some non-Jewish religion, does not at present seem likely to become at all significant. Nevertheless, the issue of principle is there, and might one day (if, for example, Christian missions succeed in making converts) become important. Perhaps, therefore, the best solution to this problem, so long as the Law of Return operates, is to determine the nationality of such queer borderline cases (and it is only about them that this issue revolves) by means of ad hoc machinery: to establish a Commission, whether as part of an existing Ministry, or as a special institution consisting of qualified experts, to determine with regard to potential immigrants, and to those already resident in Israel, both children and adults, who should and who should not be qualified to register as (politically) a Jew. No clear directives could, in the nature of the case, be given to this body. They will have to be guided by the light of reason and common sense and public opinion. I should have thought that (a) someone who has lived the life of a Jew outside Israel, e.g. by being identified with the Jewish community in some clear sense, even though his mother may be a non-Jewess, would be cruelly punished if he were excluded from Jewish nationality – and not only from the Jewish religious community – on religious grounds. Such persons may of course choose to go through the rite of formal conversion (as, for example, I am told that the late Lord Melchett in England did), but even if they do not, to exclude them from the (politically) Jewish community unless they do so seems to me gratuitous and harsh; (b) similarly, children of mixed marriages whose Jewish fathers desire them to be brought up as Jews should in my view be allowed to be registered as Jews, in the expectation that the mere process of being brought up with other Jews in Israel will surely do its work of adequate assimilation. This is how I should be inclined to decide if I were a member of such a Registration Commission. But if they decide differently, let it be so.

7. Since the rabbinical authorities will of necessity, and quite properly, not regard such classes of persons as Jews, there will be a certain inevitable social pressure upon them, whatever steps may be taken to prevent this from becoming a form of coercion, to leap over the final fence which stands between them and full membership of the Jewish community everywhere, i.e. accept actual conversion to the Jewish religion. It may well be that most such persons will have little objection to accepting and practising the Jewish religion, at any rate the minimum required by Halacha. But some may choose not to do so, and they may, when they leave Israel, find themselves debarred from being accepted as members of Jewish communities in lands outside Israel. This is a necessary consequence of the structure of any organised religion, which rightly makes certain minimum demands of its members, and cannot relax them for political or legal or moral or any non-religious reasons. But the number of such persons is likely to be exceedingly small, nor, it seems to me, will the bonds which unite Israel to the Diaspora be likely to be snapped or even strained by the existence of such persons, and by their necessarily anomalous status. To repeat my earlier point again, I see no way of finally determining the status of these persons except by means of a Commission which judges each particular case, whether or not he or she satisfies a sufficient number of the clearly felt, but often indefinable, conditions of being a member of the (politically) Jewish community in Israel.

8. If it is felt that public opinion in Israel is not yet ripe for such a solution, and may indeed be outraged by it, that it may lead to a ferocious *Kulturkampf* within Israel, and indeed to a schism between Israel and the Jewish community beyond its borders, then, if it is desired to avoid an early head-on crash with painful consequences, I think that some kind of interim status could be created for these problematical cases. The children of unconverted non-Jewesses, the unconverted wives of Jews in Israel (who desire to play their full part in the Jewish community) and similar persons could be registered not as 'Jews' politically, but as 'of Jewish origin; father a Jew' or 'wife of a Jew', 'paternal grandfather and maternal grandfather Jews', or the like, simply recording the facts; and a special status would then have to be created for such cases in anticipation that this will itself lead to crystallisation of the issue, that the persons placed in this no man's land would either ultimately become assimilated wholly into the Jewish community, or drop out of it; or

at worst continue indefinitely as borderline cases until such time as a more liberal legislation is politically feasible and they can be freely absorbed into the Jewish texture without too much protest by anyone. This is not a satisfactory solution but, in the circumstances assumed above, the most painless that I can think of. This situation must on no account be allowed to be more than temporary; nothing would be more iniquitous or ruinous than to permit the emergence of a permanent category of citizens of inferior status – half-Jews, with incomplete civil and political rights; an abominable inverted caricature of anti-Semitic persecution in other countries. If religious resistance to the free integration of such persons is really too slow to be overcome by the authority of the State at present, it would be better not to allow such persons to immigrate than to expose them to the horrors of minority status.

9. I must admit that I find it hard to believe that the acceptance into the Jewish community of persons who would normally be regarded as Jews (at any rate by those who, for whatever reasons, are interested in such matters – persons conscious of what it is to be a Jew), even if they do not fully qualify under the rules of rigorously applied Halacha, would cause a deep rift either within Israel or between Israel and the Jews of the outside world. But about this I may well be mistaken; on this issue I should not like to volunteer a view. Historically, the Jewish religion, the Jewish race, and all the factors which combine into Jewish culture, have combined into a single, persistent entity, incapable of being neatly fitted into the political pattern of a modern State of a Western type. The rise of the State of Israel can 'normalise' the Jewish population only by allowing – not necessarily encouraging – each of these factors to pursue a separate career. This seems to be neither avoidable nor necessarily undesirable: one must hope that it will upset as few Jewish convictions and loyalties as possible; but I doubt whether it is realistic to hope that it will offend against none. I feel this the more strongly, since I am not happy about this 'solution' myself.

Isaiah Berlin

CHRONOLOGY

The only sound basis for the publication of papers, whether private or public, is, I feel absolutely sure, chronology and nothing else. One can add notes, interpretations, but the chronological skeleton is indispensable, and without it scholars cannot do their work, and suspect all selection, however noble the aim, of having some artificial and probably propagandist purpose [...]

To Boris Guriel, 1 January 1957

7 April **1946** (aged **36**)	Sailed back to England from New York on the *Queen Mary,* returning to his role as Lecturer and Tutor in Philosophy at New College, Oxford, and to a hectic social life
May	First discussions about translating Turgenev's *First Love*
27 June (**37**)	Spoke at Royal Institute of International Affairs (Chatham House) on 'Why the Soviet Union Chooses to Insulate Itself'
Early August	To Paris for two or three days, then on to Geneva to visit Elliott Felkin; stayed in a pension to work on lectures
Early September	Joined parents in Switzerland
Mid-September	Stayed for 10 days at the British Embassy, Paris, on the way home
1 October	Appointed University Lecturer in Philosophy
Michaelmas Term (October–December)	Lectured on 'European Political and Social Thought in the Early Nineteenth Century' and gave a graduate class with J. L. Austin on 'Things'
17 December	Broadcast of IB's first talk for the BBC Third Programme (on Lassalle)
January **1947**	Sounded out (to no effect) about a position in the Jewish Agency in charge of the newly established European section of its Political Department
Hilary Term (January–March)	Lectured on 'Berkeley's Theory of the External World'
March	Further (unavailing) approach from the Jewish Agency at a higher level (a telegram from Ben-Gurion and Shertok) inviting IB to join their Political Department
April	Holiday in Italy, including Florence and Siena
May–June	Gave four classes on 'Radical Intelligentsia 1825–1881: Western Ideas'
Late June to July (**38**)	Travelled with Mendel to Palestine, sailing via Genoa,

Athens (where they spent two socially active days with
friends at the British Embassy) and Cyprus; disembarked
at Haifa; IB stayed with the Weizmanns at Rehovot, met
army officers and civil servants, visited friends and relations
in Jerusalem and Tel Aviv, gathered inside information on
UNSCOP, went on a two-day tour of northern Palestine
with his father and aunt, and had a clandestine meeting in
the back of a Tel Aviv café with his father's cousin Yitzhak
Sadeh

Late July	Flew to Geneva and thence via Paris back to Oxford to deliver three lectures to the Summer School for Foreign Students
Early August	Personal phone call from Moshe Shertok to offer IB a senior position (in charge of Eastern and Central Europe) in the Jewish Agency; he declined
Mid-August	Approached by Sir Oliver Franks to join the British team forming part of the Committee of European Economic Cooperation set up to establish the workings of the Marshall Plan; IB's main role would be to write the Report
18 August	Travelled at very short notice to Paris to live in the Hotel Crillon and work in demanding conditions in the Grand Palais
Early September	After three weeks of intensive effort handed over the final revision of the Report to Otto Clarke and left for his holiday in Italy
9–21 September	In Amalfi with Bowra and the Guy Chilvers
Late September	A few days in Rome (hoping to meet Patricia de Bendern); on Yom Kippur (25 September) attended the Sephardi Synagogue there; returned via Lausanne and Paris (where he saw Weizmann) to London in early October
Late November?	Gave a lecture on the Russian Revolution of 1905, probably as part of a series of lectures on 'Crises in European History, 1867–1914'
Early December	Ill with tonsillitis
Hilary Term **1948** (January–March)	Lectured on 'Problems in the Theory of Knowledge'
Trinity Term (April–June)	Lectured on 'Moral and Political Ideas in the Nineteenth Century' and gave a graduate class with Friedrich Waismann (see 62/2)
July (39)	Suffering from two duodenal ulcers
Late July	Nominally Director of philosophical section of Summer School for Foreign Students, but because of illness did not play a major part
Mid-August	To Salzburg, then on to Venice and various other places in

	Italy; saw the Weizmanns (on 15 September); joined parents in Aix-les-Bains
October	Moved into new rooms in New College
Michaelmas Term (October–December)	Gave a graduate class with Alan Bullock on 'Concepts and Categories in History'
16 October	Shirley Morgan's wedding to Henry Paget, Marquess of Anglesey
1 January 1949	Sailed from Southampton on the *Queen Mary* for New York; other passengers included around 20 friends and acquaintances; through a severe gale en route to Cherbourg, where more passengers, including Aline Halban, joined the ship; the gale drove the ship on to a sandbank in Cherbourg harbour and damaged the keel
2 January	The *Queen Mary* limped back to the Isle of Wight, where it was inspected for damage, then re-docked in Southampton for repairs; Aline Halban took IB back to Oxford until the ship was ready to leave again on 5 January
10 January	Went on from New York to Harvard to take up appointment as Visiting Lecturer on Regional Studies and Research Associate in the Russian Research Center
Mid-January	Spent a week in Washington renewing friendships made during the war; on return to Harvard, settled into Lowell House and a routine of solid work in the Widener Library during the week, with weekend visits to friends elsewhere
Late January	Mendel Berlin came to the US on a business trip until 19 February; he and IB met several times in New York and Harvard
8 February	Start of IB's Harvard lecture-classes on 'The Development of Revolutionary Ideas in Russia'
March	Social and speaking invitations started building up
19 March	Speech to the Signet Society
21 March	Took part in discussion on 'England in a Two-Power World' for broadcast on 22 March
Late March	Offered a teaching post at Harvard
4 May	Indictment of Ed Prichard for ballot-stuffing
Mid-May	End of lecture-classes; start of examining and sciatica
Late June	Spent a weekend at the home of Joe Alsop's parents before going on to Mount Holyoke
28 June (40)	Speech on 'Democracy, Communism and the Individual' at the Mount Holyoke College Institute on the United Nations; a brief discussion with a journalist led to a report in the City edition of the *New York Times* the next day that seemed to IB to portray him as an apologist for

	Communism; IB sent letters in all directions in an attempt to avoid FBI suspicion
*c.*29 June	Flew to Cincinnati to dine with Ed Prichard a few days before his trial on 5 July
Early–mid-July	A round of goodbye visits in Harvard and Washington, then to New York
13 July	Arrived in New York, where a pickpocket on a bus stole his passport and sailing documents
14 July	At the British Consulate pleading his urgent need of replacement documents; after initial caution IB's stock gradually rose and all was well
15 July	Sailed from New York on the *Queen Elizabeth*; persuaded a helpful fellow passenger to disembark with the bulk of IB's luggage and deliver it to London so that IB could go direct to France
20 July	Disembarked at Cherbourg, then went on to Paris before taking an overnight train to Marseilles on 22 July
23 July–2 August	At the Aix-en-Provence Music Festival, staying at the Hotel Roi René as a guest of Rowland Burdon-Muller; the highlight was a performance of *Don Giovanni*; also there were Patricia de Bendern and her lover Jacques Abreu
2 August	Night train-journey from Marseilles to Geneva, where he stayed with Elliott Felkin and listened to *Fidelio* on the radio
4 August	Lunch with the Israeli delegation to the Lausanne Conference, then to Palace Hotel, Bürgenstock, near Lucerne, to visit the Weizmanns
9 August	Having delayed his return home at Weizmann's request, took the opportunity to attend a rehearsal and concert at the Lucerne Music Festival
12 August	Back in London
Late August	To Oxford and a final visit to Ditchley before the Trees sold it
30 August	Recorded for the Third Programme a review of *Don Giovanni* (tape inadvertently destroyed before transmission); a talk on 'The Anglo-American Predicament' was recorded at about the same time
2 September	Confined to bed for several weeks on medical advice because of sciatica; while immobile, wrote an article on the intellectual life of American universities for *Time and Tide*
19 September	Publication in US, in *Atlantic Monthly*, of article on Churchill
21 September	Broadcast of 'The Anglo-American Predicament' (published in the *Listener* of 29 September, provoking correspondence)

5 October	*Evening Standard* attack on 'Mr Berlin'
12, 19 and 26 November	Publication in *Time and Tide*, in three parts, of article on American universities
12 December	Précis of *Time and Tide* articles published in *Time* magazine
Hilary Term **1950** (January–March)	Lectured on 'Berkeley's Theory of Meaning'
26 January	Re-recording, in an Outside Broadcast van in Oxford, of IB's review of 'Don Giovanni at Aix-en-Provence', broadcast that evening
18–20 March	In Paris, catching up with old friends; then overnight train to Marseilles
21–6 March	Sailing from Marseilles to Haifa, then on to Rehovot to stay with the Weizmanns
March/April	Publication in *Foreign Affairs* of IB's article on 'Political Ideas in the Twentieth Century'
Late March– early April	An intensive round of meetings in Israel with friends, relatives, politicians and civil servants
Mid-April	A week in Paris staying with Avis Bohlen, before returning home
May	Publication of IB's translation of Turgenev's *First Love*
24 May	Lectured on Joseph de Maistre for G. D. H. Cole's series 'Some Social and Political Thinkers'
June–July (41)	Busy examining and suffering from various minor ailments; started a secret affair with Jenifer Hart
1 July	Appointed, for five years in the first instance, to a Robertson Research Fellowship at All Souls (but for the time being continued to live in New College, where he was appointed Lecturer in Philosophy)
Mid-July	Visit of Felix and Marion Frankfurter to Oxford
29 July–2 August	Staying with the Hayters in Paris
2–20 August	With his parents in Vevey, Switzerland, for a holiday
20–7 August	In Berne, visiting the Weizmanns; at a Herbert von Karajan concert in Lucerne on 23 August
25 August	Heard of death of his uncle Yitzhak Samunov
27–9 August	In Geneva for rest, reading and a visit to aged Russian revolutionary friends
29 August	To Milan; dinner with Arthur and Marian Schlesinger
30 August	In Santa Margherita Ligure with Raimund and Liz von Hofmannsthal
1 September	To the Fortezza della Brunella, Aulla, for a holiday with Maurice Bowra, Marcus Dick, James Joll and David Pears; while there worked on his essay on Maistre

20 September	Via Siena to Florence for a Yom Kippur service; back to Siena the next day
22 September	After hearing some of the music performed at the Siena Musical Week, travelled to Vallombrosa, where Bernard Berenson and Nicky Mariano spent the summer; returned the following day to Aulla
26 September	Set off for Oxford (to attend an examiners' meeting) by way of Chambéry and Paris (where he saw the Weizmanns briefly)
Michaelmas Term (October–December)	Gave a graduate class with Friedrich Waismann on 'Verifiability'
25 November	Article by Robert Kee on 'Eternal Oxford' in *Picture Post*
Early December	A visit from David Ben-Gurion in Oxford
End December	Staying with the Angleseys at Plas Newydd
Hilary Term 1951 (January–March)	Gave a graduate class with G. D. H. Cole on 'Political Theories of Hegel and Marx'
22 March	Set off on annual trip to Israel, flying on 25 March from Rome to Israel (mainly based at the Sharon Hotel, Herzlia); gave several lectures to trainee diplomats, including one to the Political Department (the future Mossad)
10 April	Sailed from Israel with his aunt Ida Samunov to join his parents on holiday in Nice
18 April	Back in London (to Oxford on 23 April)
Trinity Term (April–June)	Lectured on 'Social and Political Ideas in the Early Nineteenth Century'
25 April	Death of Humphrey Sumner (Warden of All Souls)
29 April	Overnight stay at Simon Marks's 'farm' in Berkshire
Early May	Became a candidate for the Wardenship of All Souls
c.19 May	First official exploratory meeting in Wardenship election; IB remained a candidate but Edward Bridges looked likely to be elected
25 May	Defection of Burgess and Maclean (Goronwy Rees alerted security services c.27 May, but the disappearance of the two diplomats was not made public until 7 June)
29 May	Lady Pamela Berry's dinner party: IB, Anthony Blunt, John Betjeman and Lady Elizabeth Cavendish attended; Guy Burgess failed to appear
End May	Bridges withdrew candidature; Rowse proposed Eric Beckett as an alternative
2 June	Beckett achieved majority of votes at second exploratory meeting but IB's supporters fought on
Early June (42)	IB visited by Rowse who suggested he withdraw his candidature in favour of Beckett

9 June	Intensive discussions in Wardenship election; stalemate between Beckett and IB
10 June	Withdrawal of IB from Wardenship election; election of Hubert Henderson as Warden
20 June	Henderson suffered heart attack during Encaenia
12 July	Gave (over-long) talk on Maistre at Anglo-American Conference of Historians
Mid-July	Finally moved from New College into rooms at All Souls
August	Started trying to lose weight
28 August (evening)	Sailed on *Mauretania*, arriving 4 September in New York, where he spent the night
5–17 September	Staying with Rowland Burdon-Muller in Maine
18 September	At Lowell House, Harvard, as Visiting Professor until December, lecturing on 'The Development of Social and Political Ideas in Russia 1825–1920'
24 December	To New York and Washington for 10 days of catching up with friends, interrupted by a visit to Bryn Mawr to read a philosophy paper ('Synthetic A Priori Propositions') at the American Philosophical Association (Eastern Division) meeting, held 27–9 December
4 January **1952**	Back to Harvard
Mid-January	Resignation of Hubert Henderson; a further Wardenship election at All Souls
Late January	Stayed for a week with Edgar and Margaret Wind in Northampton, Mass., working on his Bryn Mawr lectures
Early February	Moved from Harvard to Bryn Mawr, where he was to deliver the Mary Flexner Lectures on 'The Rise of Modern Political Ideas in the Romantic Age: 1760–1830'
11 February	1st Mary Flexner Lecture ('Nature and the Science of Politics: Helvétius and Holbach')
18 February	2nd Flexner Lecture ('Political Liberty and the Ethical Imperative: Kant and Rousseau')
25 February	3rd Flexner Lecture ('Liberalism and Romanticism: Fichte and the Rights of Man')
1 March	Formal announcement of John Sparrow's election as the next Warden of All Souls
3 March	4th Flexner Lecture ('Individual Freedom and the March of History: Herder and Hegel')
10 March	5th Flexner Lecture ('The Organisation of Society and the Golden Age: Saint-Simon and his Disciples')
11–14 March	A visit to Princeton
17 March	Final (6th) Flexner Lecture ('The Counter-Revolution: Maistre and the Beginnings of Fascism')

18 March	Left Bryn Mawr for New York; then gave two more lectures (at a Jewish Temple in Syracuse and at the University of Rochester)
22–6 March	In Cambridge, Mass., saying his farewells
26 March–1 April	Back in New York, at the Madison Hotel
29 March	Attended a Toscanini concert instead of catching the *Queen Mary*
1/2 April	Flew to Paris
6 April	Heard that his parents' health problems would prevent their planned holiday in Nice and Italy
7 April	Attempted to fly to London but had to abandon the plane when it burst into flames on the runway; caught a later flight
Late April	An interrupted tryst with Jenifer Hart at his parents' house in Hampstead
Trinity Term (May–June)	Lectured on 'Western Political Ideas, 1750–1850'
29 May	Success in IB's campaign to have a telephone (Oxford 3625) installed in his All Souls rooms
11–13 June (43)	In Brussels for a Slavonic Conference
June–August	Mendel Berlin had a sequence of operations
19–20 July	En route to Aix-en-Provence with stops in Paris and Valence: Aline Halban was his driver
21 July	The start of a week staying at the Hotel Roi René in Aix-en-Provence for the Music Festival; his companions were Alix de Rothschild and Aline Halban; significant emotional developments
August/September	Recorded for the BBC six talks based on his Mary Flexner Lectures
29 September/ 1 October	Toscanini concerts in the Festival Hall (IB attended the second and a rehearsal)
Michaelmas Term (October–December)	A graduate class with G. D. H. Cole on 'Utopian Socialists 1789–1870'; lectured on Saint-Simon for J. P. Plamenatz's series 'The Development of Sociological Thought in France'
29 October– 3 December	The Third Programme broadcast IB's six pre-recorded weekly talks on 'Freedom and its Betrayal', provoking widespread interest, a deluge of letters and a *Times* leader (on 6 December)
9 November	Death of Weizmann
Hilary Term **1953** (January–March)	Gave a graduate class with Stuart Hampshire on 'Moral Presuppositions of Liberalism (Condorcet, Kant, Mill, Moore)'

20 March		To Paris, then on to Monte Carlo and Nice for a holiday with his parents
Early April		Continued (without his parents) to Italy, travelling via Florence (visiting Berenson) to join Maurice Bowra in Rome
Early May		Attended (with other luminaries) a conference in London under the auspices of the Fund for the Advancement of Education, initiated by Robert Hutchins of the Ford Foundation, to discuss 'the problems of education in relation to the philosophical diversity of our times'
12 May		Delivered the first Auguste Comte Lecture at the LSE, on 'History as an Alibi'
2 June		Watched the Coronation of HM Queen Elizabeth II from the *Daily Telegraph* window in Piccadilly, with Michael Berry
June	(44)	Told by his mother that his father was probably suffering from incurable, and inevitably fatal, leukaemia
Mid-July		At the Metropole Hotel, Brighton, with his parents
2 August		Delivered a lecture on 'The Beginnings of Russian Music' to the International Summer School held at Dartington Hall, Devon; a conversation with Michael Straight led to an article in the *New Republic* about Anna Akhmatova which enraged IB
10 September		Sailed to the US (with the Trees and Giles Constable) on the *Queen Elizabeth*, initially to take up a post as Visiting Lecturer at Harvard (on 'The Development of Social and Political Ideas in Russia, 1825–1925')
1 October		Nominal start of a further five-year term as a University Lecturer at Oxford
9 October		Gave an Elizabeth Cutter Morrow Lecture on 'The Sense of Reality' at Smith College, Northampton, Mass.
Early November		Received a proposal from Nuffield College that he should stand for (certain) election as Warden; the start of a long process of consultation and agonising
Mid-November		Organised a week of activities connected with a visit by Lady Violet Bonham Carter; on 16 November co-hosted with Raymond Bonham Carter a large party in her honour in Cambridge, Mass.
November		Publication of *The Hedgehog and the Fox*
12 December		On receiving sudden bad news about Mendel's health, cancelled plans to return (temporarily) on the *Queen Mary* on 23 December and flew home overnight from Boston to London
13–14 December		Two days visiting his father in hospital
15 December		Mendel Berlin died in his sleep from leukaemia

Late December	After the seven-day Jewish mourning period, IB faced an avalanche of condolence letters and the financial implications of his father's death
26 January **1954**	Finally declined Nuffield's offer of the Wardenship
February–March	Weekly trips to London to look after his mother and sort out his father's business affairs; after one of them IB told Aline Halban of his feelings for her; they began meeting clandestinely
Mid-March	Backed out of arrangements to return to the US to deliver a lecture for Columbia's Bicentenary
12–25 April	On holiday with his mother in Geneva and Nice; a long phone conversation between IB in Geneva and Aline in Paris was overheard by Hans Halban, who demanded that their meetings cease; on reaching Nice, IB found a letter from Aline ending their relationship; shattered, he retreated to bed for two days
25 April	Flew home, angry at Aline's abandonment of him; his mother went on to visit her sister Ida in Jerusalem
Trinity Term (April–June)	Lectured on 'Historicism'
c. 1 May	The Halbans attended a pre-arranged drinks party given by IB; soon afterwards IB and Aline started meeting again
8–9 May	Visited Paris immediately after the French defeat at Dien Bien Phu, in the frustrated hope of seeing the Moscow Ballet
May/June	The Headington House summit, at which IB confronted Hans Halban on the psychology of freedom and won his agreement to weekly meetings with Aline
1 June	Attended the opening night of *The Frog* at the Scala Theatre, London, with Alix de Rothschild
10 June	**(45)** Sat with Margot Fonteyn, Cecil Beaton and Alan Pryce-Jones to watch the Trooping of the Colour ceremony
23 June	IB's guests for Encaenia included Alice and Billy James, the Halbans, the Cecils, Elizabeth Bowen and Felicity Rumbold
12–15 August	A weekend staying with Guy and Alix de Rothschild at their stud-farm (le Haras de Reux) in Normandy; IB met the Halbans, who were staying in Deauville, at the Casino
15 August	Aline drove IB to Paris, where they lunched with her mother; after dinner with Chip Bohlen, IB took an overnight train to Milan and continued to Perugia for an open-air performance of *Rigoletto*
18 August	Arrived in Cortona to join Stuart Hampshire, Marcus and Cecilia Dick, David Pears and Patrick Nowell-Smith; IB worked while the others went sightseeing

25 August	To Urbino and Ravenna with David Pears
28 August	On to Venice, where he met John Sparrow; worked hard on his Northcliffe Lectures
7 September	Home after a weekend with Raphael and Adriana Salem in Aix-en-Provence
Michaelmas Term (October–December)	Class with E. H. Carr on 'Some Precursors of the Russian Revolution since 1830'
October	Invited to become a Director of the Sadler's Wells Trust
18 October	Delivered first of four Lord Northcliffe Lectures in Literature at UCL, on 'A Marvellous Decade: Literature and Social Criticism in Russia 1838–48'
25 October	Second Northcliffe Lecture
1 November	Third Northcliffe Lecture
8 November	Fourth and final Northcliffe Lecture
Late November	Confined to bed in Hampstead for 10 days suffering from bronchitis; publication of *Historical Inevitability*
Early December	Visited in Oxford by Mike Todd, who was planning to film *War and Peace*
Mid-December	Aline Halban went on a family skiing holiday in Mégève as her marriage approached breaking-point; IB's health suffered from the tension; heart problems were suspected
16 December	Re-recorded two of the Northcliffe Lectures for the BBC, with impromptu additions
Late December	Appointed a Director of the Royal Opera House
January 1955	IB's continuing illnesses and possible pericarditis kept him mainly in Hampstead, under the care of his mother, with weekly visits to Oxford to fulfil his minimum teaching requirements
Hilary Term (January–March)	Continuation of class with E. H. Carr
Late January	Aline and Hans Halban agreed to separate (though Hans Halban did not leave Headington House until March)
18 February	Engagement of IB and Aline Halban
February–March	Despite medical orders to take a complete rest, IB gradually resumed normal activities as his mood and physical condition improved
29 March–22 April	With Aline in Nice, Grasse and Avignon (met Picasso and Cocteau at Douglas Cooper's home, the Château de Castille); returned via Lyon and Paris
1 July (46)	Re-election to a Robertson Research Fellowship at All Souls took effect (until 1960)
July	Photographic session with Cecil Beaton

22 August	To Paris, then by train to join Aline in Bordeaux (23 August); lunch with her brother and his wife the next day en route by car to Aix-en-Provence, to stay with Raphael and Adriana Salem (24–6 August); visited St Tropez (meeting Aline's ex-sister-in-law) and San Remo, Rapallo (27–8 August; dinner with Arthur Schlesinger), Lerici (29–30 August) and Siena (31 August) before arriving in Rome on 1 September
4–10 September	Attended the 10th International Congress of 'Scienze Storiche' in Rome, after which IB and Aline continued to Naples (10–13 September), Amalfi (13–16 September) and Milan (for Rosh Hashanah on 17–18 September); back in England on 21 September
1 October	Resigned University Lectureship because teaching had fallen below minimum of six hours a week
19 October	Lectured on 'Montesquieu' at the British Academy
3 November	Sailed on the *Queen Elizabeth* for New York (arriving 8 November); Aline Halban's mother was a fellow passenger
9–10 November	Lectured twice at Mount Holyoke, then on to Chicago (as Alexander White Visiting Professor, living in the Hotel Windermere East)
November–December	Delivered four Alexander White Lectures at the University of Chicago on 'The Romantic Revolution in Philosophy' (and held classes on 15, 22 and 29 November and 6 December); for relaxation enjoyed the excellent opera programme at the Lyric Theatre of Chicago, including *Rigoletto* (12 November), *Il tabarro* (19 November; paired with a Monteverdi masque), *L'elisir d'amore* (30 November) and *Un ballo in maschera* (3 December), and attended a concert by David Oistrakh (28 November)
17 November	First Alexander White Lecture
20 November	An overnight visit to the home of Adlai Stevenson
21 November	Second Alexander White Lecture
23 November	Endured, in acute embarrassment, a badly judged lecture by A. L. Rowse
24 November	Spent Thanksgiving with Burton Dreben and his wife Raya
1 December	Third Alexander White Lecture
2/3 December	At Iowa University to read a 'quasi-paper' on Herzen and Russian radicalism
8 December	Final Alexander White Lecture
9 December	Lectured on 'The Nature of Political Judgement' at North Western University (in Evanston, an hour and a half from Chicago)
10 December	Joined by Aline

Mid–late December	A hectic round of social commitments: 12–16 December in New York (where IB and Aline saw Renata Tebaldi in *Tosca* on 13 December); 16–20 December in Washington (IB lectured on 'The Contemporary Philosophical Revolution' at the Institute of Contemporary Arts on 19 December); 20–7 December in New York again; 27–9 December in Cambridge, Mass., before returning to New York
4 January **1956**	IB and Aline due to sail from New York on the *Queen Mary*; departure delayed by fog, but they still reached England on 9 January
Hilary Term (January–March)	Gave a graduate class with Patrick Gardiner on 'Concepts of History'
7 February	Married Aline Elisabeth Yvonne Halban, daughter of Baron Pierre de Gunzbourg of Paris, at Hampstead Synagogue; they spent two days in the Ritz Hotel, London, then IB moved into Headington House
2 April	IB and Aline flew to Tel Aviv to spend a few days with Vera Weizmann at Rehovot and to visit friends, relatives and political contacts while allowing Aline to experience Israeli life and landscape
9 April	To Jerusalem (the King David Hotel)
10 and 11 April	Gave two Orde Wingate Memorial Lectures at the Hebrew University of Jerusalem on 'Two Concepts of Political Thought'
12 April	The Berlins flew to Rome, then spent a few days in Florence, where they visited Bernard Berenson; then to Paris (arriving 19 April)
21 April	On his return to Oxford, IB met Khrushchev and Bulganin during their visit to New College
Late June **(47)**	Appointed to the Opera Sub-Committee at Covent Garden
29 July	IB and Aline flew London–Copenhagen, then on by rail to Helsinki (30 July), and from there to Leningrad (31 July)
4 August	They continued, by train, to Moscow
5–22 August	Staying with William and Iris Hayter at the British Embassy; IB called at the Academy of Philosophy, encountered Shepilov and Kaganovich at an Indian Embassy reception, and visited Tolstoy's home, 100 miles south of Moscow; while Aline was visiting historic towns outside Moscow, IB saw Boris Pasternak at Peredelkino (18 August); he returned to the Embassy with a copy of *Dr Zhivago*, which he read through the night; at their next meeting a few days later, Pasternak insisted on going ahead with publication whatever the risks and gave IB news of Anna Akhmatova (whom IB then telephoned)
22–*c*.31 August	IB and Aline moved to the US Embassy as guests of the

	Bohlens; during their stay IB attended (as did the Politburo) a reception in the Indonesian Embassy, and spoke to Khrushchev again; IB made use of the resources of the State Library; one night he and Efraim Halevy succeeded in meeting IB's aunt Zelma in secret
2 September	On holiday with the Bohlens and others at the Hotel Splendido, Portofino
9 September	The Berlin and Bohlen families moved to the Pensione Argentina, Paraggi; IB attended synagogue in Genoa for Yom Kippur (15 September), then, while the rest of the family returned home, went on to Lugano (17 September), where Marie was on holiday
19 September	To Paris, staying in Aline's flat, for a fortnight of hard work
Early October	Back in Oxford
Late October	Ill in bed for a fortnight; cancelled a planned trip to India as British delegate to UNESCO conference
Late October–early November	Bewildered by his own reactions to the Suez Crisis, but standing fast against condemnation of the British Government
Mid-January **1957**	Family holiday in Klosters, Switzerland
Hilary Term (January–March)	Gave a graduate class with G. D. H. Cole on 'The Political Thought of Hegel and Marx'
16 March	Formal announcement that IB was to be the next Chichele Professor of Social and Political Theory (already known in Oxford); for much of the rest of the year (and beyond) he was afflicted by a trembling eyelid
End March	Via Amsterdam, Paris and Rome for three weeks' holiday with Aline in Sicily
End April	Returned to Oxford via Naples and Paris
Trinity Term (April–June)	Gave a graduate class with Patrick Nowell-Smith on 'Historical and Political Judgement'
11 June (48)	Attended a luncheon-party at Buckingham Palace
13 June	Received a knighthood in the Birthday Honours List
10 July	Elected a Fellow of the British Academy
16 July	Created Knight Bachelor in a ceremony at Buckingham Palace attended by Aline, Marie Berlin and Peter Halban
17 July	Defended the interests of the Third Programme in an Oxford meeting between academics and BBC officials
20–30 August	Staying with friends in Scotland
2–18 September	Family holiday at Pensione Argentina, Paraggi, Italy; Stuart Hampshire joined them; a few days in Paris on the way home

1 October	Took up his new duties as Chichele Professor of Social and Political Theory
Michaelmas Term (October–December)	Lectured on 'Types of European Political Theory'
12 November	Attended Hugh Trevor-Roper's Inaugural Lecture
19 November	Gave the second Herbert Samuel Lecture, on Chaim Weizmann (under the auspices of the British Friends of the Hebrew University in Jerusalem)
11 December	Delivered the Lucien Wolf Memorial Lecture, 'From Communism to Zionism: The Life and Opinions of Moses Hess', to the Jewish Historical Society of England in Friends House, London
12 December	One of the speakers at the Italian Institute in London commemorating the life of Gaetano Salvemini
Hilary Term 1958 (January–March)	Lectured on 'Types of Political Theory since Machiavelli'
20 March	To Italy
21 March	Visited Bernard Berenson at I Tatti, embarking on the *Jerusalem* in Naples the next day
25 March	Arrived in Haifa and taken straight to Rehovot
26 March–1 April	The usual round of meetings with friends, relatives and political contacts (including Ben-Gurion) in Rehovot, Tel Aviv and Jerusalem; discussions (30–1 March) at Rehovot about Weizmann's papers
2 April	Joined by Aline
4 April	Moved to the King David Hotel, Jerusalem
8 April	Sailed from Haifa on the *Theodor Herzl* (arriving in Marseilles on 13 April); home via Paris
Mid-April	Tragic accident to Aline's niece while her family were staying at Headington House
Trinity Term (April–June)	Took a graduate class with Charles Taylor on 'The Political Philosophy of Hegel and Marx'
25–7 June **(49)**	Visit of Dmitry Shostakovich to receive honorary degree at Encaenia on 26 June; dinner and music (on 25 June) *chez* Hugh and Xandra Trevor-Roper (where Francis Poulenc was staying)
Late July	Joined Aline in Aix-en-Provence, then continued to Monte Carlo (31 July–13 August), Verona and Lake Garda
20 August	IB, Aline and Aline's children all arrived at Pensione Argentina, Paraggi, for their family holiday (until 12 September)
29–30 August	Dictated first draft of his Inaugural Lecture

5 September	Publication of English translation of Boris Pasternak's *Dr Zhivago*
12–21 September	In Venice for International Congress of Philosophy; Aline arrived 15 September
19 September	Heard Stravinsky conduct a concert of his work at La Fenice
21 September	Left for home via Paris and London
Michaelmas Term (October–December)	Lectured on 'European Political Thought in the Romantic Age'
7 October	Opened an exhibition of Leonid Pasternak's works at the Pushkin Club, London
23 October	Boris Pasternak awarded the Nobel Prize for Literature; press campaign against him from 25 October; Pasternak, expelled from the Union of Soviet Writers, refused the Nobel Prize (27 October); IB continued to be active in (largely unsuccessful) campaign to protect Pasternak from misguided or politically inspired Western propaganda (e.g. broadcasts of extracts from *Dr Zhivago* on the BBC Russian Service and a cover feature on Pasternak in *Time* magazine)
31 October	Delivered his Inaugural Lecture on 'Two Concepts of Liberty' to a large audience in the Examination Schools; the longer printed version was officially published the same year, but in fact appeared in January 1959
25 November	Attended, with Aline, a dinner and reception at 10 Downing Street in honour of Vice-President Richard Nixon
5 December	Entertained Stravinsky and his wife to lunch at Headington House
7–10 December	Stayed with Lord and Lady Anglesey when delivering two lectures at the University of Bangor; decadent activities there had recently been described to IB (to his amusement) by a shocked visiting delegation of Soviet students
10 December	Dined with Stravinsky after his concert in the Royal Festival Hall
15 December	Boris Pasternak appeared on the cover of *Time* magazine
21 December	To Paris for a week, then a few days in Italy
1 January **1959**	In Paris, on the way home
Hilary Term (January–March)	Lectured on 'Russian Political Thought and the West'
Trinity Term (April–June)	Took a graduate class with Patrick Gardiner on 'Central Concepts of History'
4 June	Chaired a musical discussion between Yehudi Menuhin, Nicolas Nabokov and William Glock at the Bath Festival
June (50)	Sprained his sacroiliac joint

30? June	Attended a dinner where fellow guests included the Queen Mother and Maria Callas
Late July	To Portofino (Villa Cipressina) for the summer; opera-going trips to Aix-en-Provence (end of July) and Verona (mid-August) with Aline before the arrival (21 August) of her children and a succession of guests (including Stuart Hampshire, Julian Ayer and his girlfriend, David Cecil and family, and Garrett Drogheda)
Late September	Back home
2 October	Wedding of Aline Berlin's eldest son, Michel Strauss
Michaelmas Term (October–December)	Lectured on 'Political Thought: Machiavelli to Rousseau'
Mid-December	Sailed to New York, where he stayed at the Carlyle Hotel
20 December	Received an honorary degree of Doctor of Laws at the Jewish Theological Seminary of America, New York
27 December	To Chicago
28 December	Gave a talk 'On the Notion of Scientific History' at the meeting in Evanston, Illinois, of the American Historical Association; returned via Cambridge, Mass., where he visited Edmund and Elena Wilson (encountering Harry Levin), failed to see Evelyn Whitehead (his main reason for going there), and spent one very short night in the Commander Hotel before flying back to New York; en route he lost an important letter by Boris Pasternak, which Edmund Wilson had reluctantly lent him
Early January 1960	Returned home after visiting friends in Washington
Hilary Term (January–March)	Lectured on 'The Social Thinkers of the Enlightenment and Their Critics'
20 March	To Rome to deliver two lectures on 'The Romantic Revolution: A Crisis in the History of Modern Thought'; saw Iris Origo and Nicky Mariano, and met Tolstoy's granddaughter, Tania Albertini
30 March	A week in Portofino, then to Zurich to meet Marie and on to Milan for the opera; home (via Paris) in late April
Trinity Term (April–June)	Took a graduate class on 'The Political Ideas of Hegel, Marx and Lenin'
29 June–3 July (51)	Attended a conference on the 50th anniversary of the death of Tolstoy at Fondazione Giorgio Cini, Isola San Giorgio, Venice; gave (on 1 July) an early version of the lecture that became 'Tolstoy and Enlightenment'
Early July	Returned briefly to Oxford before leaving to spend the summer in Portofino

SELECT BIOGRAPHICAL GLOSSARY

These notes on some important and/or frequently mentioned dramatis personae include rather more information than is appropriate in a footnote. The existence of these supplementary notes is flagged by asterisks attached to the relevant surnames on their first occurrence in a footnote, and in the index, thus: Isaiah *Berlin. As in the footnotes, coverage concentrates mainly on the period covered by the present volume.

Alsop, Joseph Wright ('Joe') (1910–89), Connecticut patrician whose mother was Eleanor Roosevelt's cousin; after war service in the Far East, returned to his career as a syndicated political columnist; from 1946, jointly with his younger brother Stewart, wrote the influential thrice-weekly 'Matter of Fact' column syndicated by the *New York Herald Tribune* (continuing alone, after Stewart's departure in 1958, until 1974 for the *Los Angeles Times* syndicate). Stewart remained US-based, while Joe concentrated on foreign affairs and hence travelled widely; Joe in particular became strongly anti-Communist and prophesied disaster if Soviet expansion was not resisted. A closet homosexual, Alsop survived (with the help of Chip Bohlen) an attempt at blackmail by the KGB in 1957 during his only visit to the Soviet Union. Married 1961–78 to Susan Mary Patten (1918–2004), whose late husband Bill had been a close friend of Alsop's. See also L1 703.

Ayer, Alfred Jules ('Freddie') (1910–89), Fellow of Wadham 1944–6, Grote Professor of the Philosophy of Mind and Logic, London, 1946–59, Wykeham Professor of Logic and Fellow of New College, Oxford, 1959–78. His first marriage (1932–42) was to (Grace Isabel) Renée Lees (1909–80), who later married Stuart Hampshire; his second, in 1960, was (like his fourth and final marriage) to Alberta Constance ('Dee') Wells (1925–2003), née Chapman. Works include *Philosophical Essays* (1954), *The Problem of Knowledge* (1956). See also L1 703.

Behrman, Samuel Nathan (1893–1973), US-born, Harvard-educated son of Lithuanian Jewish immigrants; prolific playwright (particularly noted for sophisticated drawing-room comedies of emotional depth and psychological insight), screenwriter and author with a wide range of contacts in US and European artistic and intellectual circles; married 1936 Elza Stone (1905–98), sister of the violinist Jascha Heifetz. Mary McCarthy described him as 'pure Hollywood style vulgarian' and 'a funny man – bald, heavy, white-faced yet somehow mottled [...] His two favorite people [...] are [William] Shawn and Isaiah [Berlin]. He thinks Isaiah a terrific brain, which made me suddenly realize that I didn't.'[1] As well as plays, Behrman's works include *Duveen* (biography, 1952), *The Worcester Account* (autobiographical essays, 1954), *Portrait of Max: An Intimate Memoir of Sir Max Beerbohm* (1960).

Bendern, Lady Patricia Sybil de (1918–91), née Douglas, daughter of the 11th

---

1 To Bowden Broadwater, 5 May 1957, quoted by Carol Brightman, *Writing Dangerously* (New York, 1992), 391.

Marquess of Queensberry; married 1938–50 to Count John Gerard de Bendern (1907–97), during which time she had affairs with (at least) Jacques Abreu, A. J. Ayer, Alastair Forbes and Herman ('Marno') Hornak (1912–97), to whom she was married 1952–60. IB met her in 1942 and soon fell in love with her. The infatuation lasted until 1949, although he remained well aware of the unreliability of this notorious femme fatale:

> She was small, thin, had an exquisite face and strong personality and natural aesthetic taste, greater than anyone I've ever met. She wasn't at all tutored; she was an extreme liar, total, I mean a mythomaniac of the first order. Not a word was true, I mean she invented right and left. [...] She was very intelligent to talk to. [...] she was very candid in stating her views, she was highly critical and totally independent. She wasn't a society girl in the ordinary sense at all. [...] she had violent passions, and they were quite genuine. She read books, and was extremely perceptive and interesting about them; she was perceptive about pictures; she was perceptive about music; she liked best Bach unaccompanied cello sonatas, about which she talked very well. She was unusual, in other words.[1]

Alastair Forbes's obituary, with its startling account of her love-life, is recommended.[2]

Berenson, Bernard (1865–1959), Harvard-educated art historian whose family emigrated from Lithuania to the US during his childhood. He settled in Italy, became an authority on the Italian Renaissance, and wealthy as a result of his collaboration with art dealer Joseph Duveen: Berenson's authentication of a painting as genuine increased its market value. He bought I Tatti, a villa near Florence (gradually building up there an outstanding art collection and library) and married (1900) Mary Costelloe (1864–1945), sister of Logan Pearsall Smith and of Bernard Russell's first wife, Alys. He was Jewish by birth, but a Roman Catholic for much of his life. After his wife's death their devoted companion Nicky Mariano acted as the chatelaine of I Tatti. IB regarded Berenson as 'in some ways rather a rogue' but 'a brilliant and fascinating man'.[3]

Berlin, Isaiah (1909–97), born in Riga; St Paul's School, London, 1922–8; CCC classics 1928–31, PPE 1931–2; Prize Fellow, All Souls, 1932–8; Lecturer in Philosophy, New College, 1932–8, Fellow 1938–50; war service with Ministry of Information in New York 1941–2, at British Embassy in Washington 1942–6, at British Embassy, Moscow, September 1945 to January 1946. Research Fellow, All Souls, 1950–7, Chichele Professor of Social and Political Theory (and Fellow of All Souls) 1957–67. Broadcast for the BBC Third Programme from 1946. Visiting Professorships: Harvard 1949, 1951, 1953, Bryn Mawr 1952, Chicago 1955; Northcliffe Lecturer, UCL, 1954. Director, ROH, 1954–65, Sadler's Wells Trust 1954–60. Knighted 1957; Fellow of the British Academy from 1957 (Vice-President 1959–61, President 1974–8). Married 1956 Aline Halban (q.v.). Works include a translation of Turgenev's *First Love* (1950), *The Hedgehog and the Fox* (1953), *Historical Inevitability* (1954), *The Age of Enlightenment* (1956), *Two*

---

1 MI Tape 14.
2 *Sunday Telegraph*, 27 January 1991, 20.
3 To Henry Hardy, 25 October 1993.

Concepts of Liberty (1958), *The Life and Opinions of Moses Hess* (1959), *John Stuart Mill and the Ends of Life* (1959).

Berlin, (Mussa) Marie (*c.*1880–1974), née Volshonok ('Wolfson'), IB's mother, first cousin of her husband Mendel; after her death IB remembered her as 'a genuine fighter for what she believed in' and commented 'I quarrelled with her incessantly, but I loved and admired her equally continuously.'[1] See also L1 704.

Berlin, Mendel (1884–1953), timber and bristle trader, IB's father. He deflated IB's enthusiasm for high society with gentle mockery: 'Lady Cunard, Lady Colefax, all these ladies I used to go to dinner with – and he would say to me, "How has your evening been tonight? Did you see Bip? Puff? Muff? Dip?" He invented a lot of nicknames for all these terrible ladies – many of them did have those sort of names. "How was Nip?"'[2] IB described his 'very candid, spontaneous & in some way childlike nature':[3] 'I always felt that he was something like a younger brother whom I had to take out to the theatre, give a good time to, teach about life etc. & who reproached me, when he did, from some peculiarly unworldly standpoint of his own. [...] my father was very like the Russian liberal Cadet merchant milieu in which he had lived'.[4] See also L1 704–5.

Bohlen, Avis Howard (1912–81), née Thayer, from an East Coast patrician family, who met Chip Bohlen (q.v.) in 1934 while visiting her diplomat brother at the US Embassy in Moscow; they married a year later. IB liked and admired her greatly, reflecting during her last illness: 'why should we believe, as she believes, in a God in Heaven who allows this to happen to His most faithful, noble, saintly servant?'[5]

Bohlen, Charles Eustis ('Chip') (1904–74), US diplomat and Soviet specialist; fluent in Russian, presidential interpreter at the Teheran, Yalta and Potsdam conferences; minister at US Embassy, Paris, 1949–51; US Ambassador to Soviet Union 1953–7 (surviving an attack by Senator McCarthy on his appointment to succeed George Kennan), the Philippines 1957–9, France 1962–8. With his friend George Kennan (though not always in agreement with him), one of the most influential advisers on US policy towards the Soviet Union. William Hayter, his British opposite number in Moscow, regarded him as 'one of the best Ambassadors I've ever encountered, very strong personality. Splendid man to work with [...] a lovely sort of hearty figure'[6] with a passionate and all-consuming interest in the Soviet Union. At his death IB recalled that 'with all those achievements, grandeur of status, all that required discretion and official duties, he remained so wonderfully unpompous (with *everybody*), unstuffy, with such a sense of fun, of the ridiculous, with such a capacity for life, affection, pleasure, friendship, [...] his heart remained so pure & untouched by influence and diplomatic life'.[7]

Bonham Carter, Lady (Helen) Violet (1887–1969), Baroness Asquith of Yarnbury

---

1 To Efraim Halevy, 1 April 1974.
2 MI Tape 22.
3 To Christopher Cox, 1 January 1954.
4 To Anna Kallin, 13 January 1954.
5 To Joe Alsop, 2 February 1981.
6 MI Tape B7.
7 To Avis Bohlen, 3 January 1974.

1964, daughter of Herbert Asquith (Prime Minister 1908–16 and from 1925 1st Earl of Oxford and Asquith); wife of Sir Maurice Bonham Carter (1880–1960); mother of Cressida Ridley; Governor, BBC, 1941–6; Governor, Old Vic, 1945–69; Liberal Party Parliamentary candidate 1945, 1951; President, Liberal Party Organisation, 1945–7; Vice-Chairman, United Europe Movement, 1947; Royal Commission on the Press 1947–9. The *grande dame* of the Liberal Party, with whom IB enjoyed a long and close friendship. She claimed to love him like a son, and expected reciprocal devotion, but did not refrain from criticism of him, to IB's occasional irritation.

Bowra, (Cecil) Maurice (1898–1971), classicist; Warden, Wadham, 1938–70; Professor of Poetry (1946–51) and Vice-Chancellor (1951–4), Oxford. Fellow of the British Academy from 1938 (Vice-President 1953–4, President 1958–62). Knighted 1951. Works include *The Creative Experiment* (1949), *The Romantic Imagination* (1950), *Heroic Poetry* (1952), *Problems in Greek Poetry* (1954), *Inspiration and Poetry* (1955), *The Greek Experience* (1957). See also L1 705–6; subject of a study in PI.

Burdon-Muller, Rowland (1891–1980), connoisseur of the arts; educated at Eton and Oxford (Oriel, English literature, then French), but left Oxford on health grounds before taking a degree; moved to the US in 1924 and became well known as an interior designer; soon met Charles Bain Hoyt, with whom he lived (until Hoyt's death in 1949) in Boston, a country house in Maine, and a house and large garden at Utenberg near Lucerne, Switzerland (which they donated to the Canton after the war); both men made significant art donations to museums. He moved to Lausanne in 1970. Elegant, dapper, fastidious, generous, sometimes acerbic, Edwardian in his approach to life, gastronome, great raconteur and master letter-writer, he demanded high standards from his correspondents and was the recipient of many of IB's most entertaining letters. In person, IB enjoyed his company in small doses: 'he tends to talk a very great deal, and enunciates extremely radical political sentiments in a piercing high voice'.[1]

Cecil, Lord (Edward Christian) David (Gascoyne) (1902–86), Fellow of Wadham 1924–30, New College 1939–69; Goldsmiths' Professor of English Literature, Oxford, 1948–69. Married 1932 Rachel Mary Veronica MacCarthy (1909–82), daughter of literary critic Desmond MacCarthy. IB's long-standing friendship with him suffered from their difference of opinion over the candidates for an English fellowship at New College in 1949–50; in literary criticism Cecil favoured 'a purely aesthetic approach, which ultimately [...] means some kind of delicate tracing of the actual creative, literary process'.[2] Works include *Two Quiet Lives* (1948), *Poets and Story-Tellers* (1949), *Reading as One of the Fine Arts* (1949), *Lord M.* (1954), *Walter Pater* (1955), *The Fine Art of Reading and other literary studies* (1957), *Modern Verse in English 1900–1950* (1958). See also L1 706; subject of a study in PI2.

Churchill, (Anne) Clarissa (b. 1920), daughter of Winston Churchill's younger brother John ('Jack') Spencer-Churchill; brought up as a Catholic (her mother's religion). Took philosophy lessons in Oxford with IB and others 1939–40 then

1 To John Carter, 27 October 1953.
2 MI Tape 15.

worked for Chatham House, the FO (interrupted by illness) and the Ministry of Information during the war, and after it for *Vogue*, London Film Productions (Alexander Korda's company) and *Contact* (a literary and political periodical set up by George Weidenfeld). Married 1952 Anthony Eden, the (divorced) Foreign Secretary (Prime Minister 1955–7). Became Lady Eden on her husband's knighthood (1954) and the Countess of Avon on his ennoblement (1961).

Cooper, Lady Diana Olivia Winifred Maud (1893–1986), née Manners; officially the daughter of the 8th Duke of Rutland but probably fathered by Henry Cust; a famous beauty when young; achieved international fame as an actress (on stage in Max Reinhardt's production of *The Miracle* and in silent films) and socialite; her 1919 marriage to Duff Cooper (q.v.) produced deep mutual devotion despite his constant infidelities; a notable hostess at the British Embassy in Paris while her husband was Ambassador, and at their chateau near Chantilly after his retirement; the original for Lady Leone in Nancy Mitford's novel *Don't Tell Alfred* (London, 1960). Refused to change her name when her husband became Viscount Norwich in 1952. IB (who had first met her in an air-raid shelter during the war) liked and admired her:

> She was extraordinary. Her guts were something unbelievable – sheer guts, capacity for going on. She was extremely handsome, and very witty, and very non-sexy. [...] She was like a very clever schoolboy who was top of the form and could do crossword puzzles – quick, clever, amusing, sharp. By the time I came to know her she was rather like an ageing actress – no *savoir-vivre*, she didn't know how to behave, she didn't quite know how to treat people, made mistakes. But she was extremely witty and amusing, and her vitality was unbelievable, and she was very good company. Her stories were wonderful, her language was extraordinary.[1]

Memoirs: *The Rainbow Comes and Goes* (1958), *The Light of Common Day* (1959), *Trumpets from the Steep* (1960).

Cooper, (Alfred) Duff (1890–1954), 1st Viscount Norwich 1952; Conservative politician, diplomat and writer; MP 1924–9, 1931–45; held various ministerial posts, including Secretary of State for War 1935–7 and First Lord of the Admiralty 1937–8, which he resigned in protest at the Munich Agreement; recalled to Churchill's wartime coalition government as Minister of Information 1940–1, Chancellor of the Duchy of Lancaster 1941–3; liaised with the French Committee of National Liberation, then appointed Ambassador to France 1944–7. Noted for his attachment to women and drink, sound political judgement, violent rages and considerable ability as historian and author. IB was not close to him: 'Duff Cooper [...] I never liked. Rather frightened of him: he was too choleric, too easily stirred to rage, too red-faced and drunken, too Guard's Officer for my taste. We got on officially perfectly well, but fundamentally not.'[2] Works include *Sergeant Shakespeare* (1949), *Operation Heartbreak* (1950) and his autobiography *Old Men Forget* (1953).

Felkin, (Arthur) Elliott (1892–1968), international civil servant who spent most

---

1 MI Tape 22.
2 ibid.

of his career in Geneva; Secretariat, League of Nations, 1923–38; Secretary, Permanent Central Opium Board, 1938–53 (after which he retired to Grasse in the South of France); married 1920 (Sybil) Joyce Chapman (divorced during the war). In his professional career 'Unpretentious, Felkin carried on dutifully through bureaucratic upset, world war, and personal illness brought on by overwork. Prudence personified, he represents the epitome of diplomatic discretion.'[1] Personally, he valued friendship, conversation and the pleasures of the senses; his many literary friends included Thomas Hardy and Goldsworthy Lowes Dickinson. Jenifer Hart, whose first lover he was, described him as 'an unabashed hedonist'[2] and reported the Bloomsbury-influenced (and far from prudent) sexual ethos of Felkin's circle in pre-war Geneva who 'did not subscribe to conventional morality in connection with sexual relations. They were not indiscriminately promiscuous, but they saw no harm in the natural consummation of loving relationships. Indeed they went further and positively advocated this kind of behaviour unless it would cause pain to others.'[3]

Frankfurter, Felix (1882–1965), born in Vienna, Byrne Professor of Administrative Law, Harvard, 1914–39, George Eastman Visiting Professor, Oxford, 1933–4 (when his friendship with IB started), Associate Justice of the US Supreme Court, 1939–62. See also L1 708–9; subject of a memoir in PI.

Frankfurter, Marion A. (1890–1975), née Denman, daughter of a Presbyterian minister. Married Felix Frankfurter (q.v.) 1919. Co-edited *The Letters of Sacco and Vanzetti* (1928), and edited her husband's non-juridical writings after his death. She suffered periodic bouts of depression, and psychological factors may have combined with arthritis to confine her to bed for the last 20 years of her life. See also L1 709.

Franks, Oliver Shewell (1905–92), Baron Franks of Headington 1962, Professor of Moral Philosophy, Glasgow, 1937–45; Permanent Secretary, Ministry of Supply, 1945–6; Provost of Queen's College, Oxford, 1946–8; Chairman (and leader of British delegation), Committee of European Economic Cooperation (formulating the European input to the Marshall Plan), 1947; Ambassador to Washington 1948–52; Director, Lloyds Bank, 1953–75 (Chairman 1954–62). Married 1931 Barbara Tanner (1907–87). According to IB 'a v. high minded & ruthless man, very like England to-day: exactly the right mixture of non-party austerity with a formidable Quaker wife made of very hard stone'.[4]

Gilmore, Myron Piper (1910–78), Renaissance scholar; taught history at Harvard 1937–74 (Associate Professor 1942–54, Professor 1954–74); Director, Harvard University Center for Italian Renaissance Studies, Villa I Tatti, Florence, 1964–73. Married 1938 Sheila Dehn (1917–95), A. N. Whitehead's English step-granddaughter. Works include *The World of Humanism* (1952).

Graham, Katharine ('Kay') (1917–2001), daughter of Eugene Meyer; wrote for the *Washington Post* 1939–45; married 1940 Phil Graham (q.v.); after his death in 1963 she took control of the Washington Post Company previously run by her

---

1 William B. McAllister, *Drug Diplomacy in the Twentieth Century* (London, 2000), 129.
2 *Ask Me No More* (London, 1998), 35.
3 ibid., 38.
4 Late January/early February 1948 to Philip Graham.

father and husband; officially publisher of the *Washington Post* 1969–79 (though in practice from 1963), Chairman of the Board and Chief Executive 1973–91.

Graham, Philip Leslie ('Phil') (1915–63), lawyer (former pupil of Felix Frankfurter), journalist and publisher; from 1946 publisher of the *Washington Post* in succession to his father-in-law, Eugene Meyer. IB had known him in Washington during the war and had an increasingly edgy friendship with him, with a break 1952–5 when IB refused to forgive Graham for insulting him. Committed suicide after several years of manic depression.

Halban, Aline Elisabeth Yvonne (b. 1915), daughter of Russian-born Baron Pierre de Gunzbourg (a banker who had settled in Paris) and the former Yvonne Deutsch de la Meurthe, daughter of a French Jewish industrialist; granddaughter of Baron Horace de Gunzburg, banker (in St Petersburg), philanthropist and Russian Jewish community leader. French women's golf champion 1934. Married:

(i) 1934 André Strauss (1903–39), son of art collector Jules Strauss; one son, Michel Jules Strauss (b. 1936), Director, Impressionist and Modern Art Department, Sotheby's, 1961–2000, married first (1959) Margery Tongway (b. 1932)

(ii) 1943 (divorced 1955) Hans Halban (q.v.); two sons, Peter Francis Halban (b. 1946), publisher, and Philippe Alexandre Halban (b. 1950), cell biologist, specialising in diabetes (Professor of Medicine, Geneva)

(iii) 1956 Isaiah Berlin (q.v.).

Halban, Hans Heinrich (1908–64), né von Halban, Austrian-born (naturalised French) nuclear physicist; of part-Jewish descent; educated in Germany and Switzerland; played a major role in the discovery and development of nuclear fission, working at the Collège de France, Paris, 1937–40, the Cavendish Laboratory, Cambridge, 1940–3, in the British-Canadian Atomic Laboratory (a research venture linked to the US Manhattan Project) in Montreal 1943–5, at the Clarendon Laboratory, Oxford, 1946–55, and the Laboratoire de l'Accélérateur Linéaire, Paris, 1955–61. Fellow of St Antony's, 1950–6 (Professor 1954–6); Professor, Sorbonne, 1956–61. Married to: (i) 1933–42 Els Fanny Andriesse (b. c.1912; one daughter, Catherine Maulde Halban, 1939–93), who later married the physicist George Placzek; (ii) 1943–55 Aline de Gunzbourg (see Halban, Aline); (iii) from 1959 Micheline Lazare-Vernier (1929–88).

Hampshire, Stuart Newton (1914–2004), Balliol classics 1933–6, philosopher, Fellow of All Souls 1936–40, philosophy lecturer, Queen's, 1936–9, military intelligence 1940–5; posts in FO and Ministry of Food, 1945–7; Lecturer in Philosophy, University College, London (1947–59), Grote Professor of Mind and Logic, London (1960–3), Professor of Philosophy, Princeton (1963–70), Warden, Wadham (1970–84). Co-respondent in the 1942 divorce of A. J. Ayer (q.v.) from his wife Renée, with whom Hampshire had two children (the elder brought up as Ayer's son) before their marriage in 1961. When Hampshire was to visit Israel in 1959, IB described his closest friend to Teddy Kollek:

Hampshire has been a philosopher here for many years, is a socialist and a friend of Gaitskell, and has been known to sit in on committees of the Labour Party's drafting programmes. He is a person of some sophistication and great charm as well as exceptional looks. He likes parties, is a most intimate friend of Victor Rothschild, should think kibbutzim marvellous, but being a sophisticated person may not – there is never any telling – and fancies himself as a realist and one who understands trade unions, real poverty, real remedies for it, and not just intellectual intelligentsia idealism. Nevertheless he is in fact a gentle, feminine, exceedingly sensitive, very, very nice and distinguished person. [...] the students are bound to like him [...] He respects doctors, scientists, musicians, left-wing politicians, and practical men. He is none of these things himself. And I think I probably like him best of anyone in England; so do be nice to him.[1]

Works include *Spinoza* (1951), *The Age of Reason: The Seventeenth-Century Philosophers* (1956), *Thought and Action* (1959).

Hart, Herbert Lionel Adolphus (1907–92), New College classics 1926–9, Chancery Bar 1932–40, War Office 1940–5; married Jenifer Williams (see Hart, Jenifer) 1941; Fellow and Tutor in Philosophy, New College, 1945–52; Professor of Jurisprudence, Oxford, 1952–68; Principal, Brasenose, 1973–8. IB admitted that as a result of his affair with Hart's wife Jenifer 'my relations with him suffered a certain change [...] which has remained, [although] we're still great friends'.[2] See Nicola Lacey's revealing biography, *The Nightmare and the Noble Dream* (Oxford, 2004). Works include *Definition and Theory in Jurisprudence* (1953; Hart's inaugural lecture as Professor), *Causation in the Law* (1959).

Hart, Jenifer Margaret (1914–2005), née Williams; educated partly in Paris (in the same class as Aline de Gunzbourg); Somerville history 1932–5; Civil Service 1936–47; Fellow and Tutor in History, St Anne's, 1952–81. Close and lifelong friend of IB from their first meeting in 1934; married Herbert Hart 1941 but had many lovers thereafter, including IB from 1950. Works include *The British Police* (1951), *The County and Borough Police Act, 1856* (1956) and her autobiography *Ask Me No More* (1998). See also L1 722.

Hofmannsthal, Lady Elizabeth Hester Mary von (1916–80), née Paget, second daughter of the 6th Marquess of Anglesey, niece of Lady Diana Cooper, sister of Lady Caroline Paget and of Henry Paget, the 7th Marquess (who married Shirley Morgan); married 1939 Raimund von Hofmannsthal (q.v.). A great beauty, much admired by the couple's friend A . J. Ayer among others, she was described by Duff Cooper as 'good and wise with a lovely sense of humour and ready laughter'.[3]

Hofmannsthal, Raimund von (1906–74), son of the Austrian poet, playwright and librettist Hugo von Hofmannsthal (1874–1929); for many years London correspondent of *Time*; naturalised US citizen who lived mainly in England and at his castle at Zell am See, Austria. Married: (i) 1933 Ava Astor (1902–56); (ii) 1939 Lady Elizabeth Paget (see Hofmannsthal, Lady Elizabeth von). One of Lady Diana Cooper's lifelong admirers. IB, who met him first in the US, described

---

1 To Teddy Kollek, 20 April 1959.
2 MI Tape 14.
3 *The Duff Cooper Diaries*, ed. John Julius Norwich (London, 2005), 240.

him as 'amusing, Austrian, full of charm and a wonderful flatterer. In his presence you felt better dressed, you felt you talked better, you were better looking, you were everything possible'[1] and commented on his romantic view of the world: 'he saw human beings in aesthetic and emotional terms – Society, the great world, was, to him, a stage, a pageant, a dream or a nightmare, but seldom a realistic spectacle of humdrum, every day life'.[2]

James, Alice Rutherford (*c.*1887–1957), née Runnells, from a wealthy Chicago railroad family; tall and energetic but suffered regular ill-health; married 1912 William ('Billy') James (q.v.) and was a favourite with the James family, particularly Henry the novelist; became a Cambridge hostess, meeting and befriending IB in 1949. Amused by her bossiness and snobbery, IB regarded her and Billy as 'a most blameless, touchingly good couple'.[3] Her portrait, painted by John Singer Sargent in 1921, hangs in the Boston Museum of Fine Arts.

James, William ('Billy') (1882–1961), painter; critic of painting (1913–25) and Acting Director (1930–7), Boston School of Music and Fine Arts. Son of the philosopher William James, nephew of the novelist Henry James; described by IB as 'of great superiority of character; [...] a wonderfully hesitant, scrupulous, frail, and touchingly sensitive representative of that remarkable family'.[4] Married: (i) 1912 Alice Rutherford Runnells (see James, Alice); (ii) 1959 Mary Brush Pierce (1898–1974). His marriage to Alice nearly foundered during the 1940s, partly because of his sexual frustration. Morton White remembered Billy with Alice: 'He had a pronounced stutter that became worse when he was nervous, and he would introduce himself at cocktail parties by pointing to his chest and saying "J-j-james". Often he would have in tow his large wife and, according to some wit, would nudge her along as if he were a tugboat and she a large liner.'[5]

Kallin, Anna ('Niouta') (1896–1984), born in Moscow to a wealthy Russian Jewish merchant family; educated partly in Germany before coming to England in 1921 and working as freelance reviewer, translator and publisher's reader; various posts in the BBC (mainly European Service) 1940–6; appointed Producer, Home Talks, 1946, and spent the rest of her career (to 1964) bringing highly intellectual talks (including the Reith Lectures and in 1952 IB's *Freedom and Its Betrayal*) to the newly created Third Programme, whose uncompromisingly highbrow character she did much to create; shared a house with IB's friend Salome Halpern after the death of the latter's husband Alexander, constantly taking issue with Salome's pro-Soviet sympathies. IB described her as 'a typical Moscow intellectual, high-grade, highbrow, [...] a brilliant and interesting woman';[6] according to her obituary, 'Fiercely individual, having intense convictions, and intolerant of all sloppiness, whether in thinking or in execution', with deep, discriminating friendships, 'a very human companion, an eager listener, a passionate talker, an earnest persuader, all without false pride or arrogance'.[7]

1 MI Tape 22.
2 *The Times*, 26 April 1974, 20.
3 To Arthur Schlesinger, 19 February 1957.
4 To John Carter, 27 October 1953.
5 *A Philosopher's Story* (230/1), 153.
6 MI Tape 25.
7 *The Times*, 16 October 1984, 18.

Kennan, George Frost (1904–2005), US diplomat, historian and Soviet expert; Foreign Service 1926–53, specialising in the Soviet Union from the outset; minister-counsellor, US Embassy, Moscow, 1944–6 (in March 1946 sending the 8000-word 'Long Telegram'); Director of Policy Planning, State Department, 1947–9; Counsellor, State Department, 1949–50 (continuing to advise Secretary of State Dean Acheson until 1952); US Ambassador in Moscow May–October 1952 (expelled as *persona non grata*); Professor of Historical Studies, Institute of Advanced Study, Princeton, 1956–74; George Eastman Visiting Professor, Oxford, 1957–8; Ambassador to Yugoslavia 1961–3. Influential in the determining of US policy towards the Soviet Union in the immediate post-war period, but from the early 1950s increasingly in disagreement with US foreign policy and dismayed by the misapplication of the policy of containment of the Soviet Union that he had expounded in an article, signed 'X', on 'The Sources of Soviet Conduct', published in *Foreign Affairs* in July 1947. On leaving Oxford in 1958 he wrote to IB:

> You have unquestionably the greatest critical mind of this generation – warmed with a charity that might well be the envy of 99 out of 100 Christians, and enriched with an ordering power so extraordinary that its mere operation is itself a creative act, affecting that which it touches & even changing it – just as scientific experimentation is said to alter, by its own action, the substance it is supposed to illuminate. You have taught numbers of us – including even those who have no idea how to show it – to see these things in a much more useful way & to find meaning where we would never ourselves have found it; & those of us who are conscious of this are immensely grateful.[1]

Kollek, Theodor ('Teddy') (1911–2007), born in Hungary to a Zionist family, grew up in Vienna, emigrated to Palestine 1935; worked in a kibbutz, rescuing European Jews and procuring arms for Haganah, and (1940–47) for the Jewish Agency in Europe (mainly on intelligence work); fund-raising and arms-procurement mission in the US for Haganah 1947–9; Head of US Division, Israeli Ministry of Foreign Affairs, 1950–1; Minister Plenipotentiary, Washington, 1951–2; Director-General, Prime Minister's office, 1952–65; Chair, Government Tourist Corporation, 1958–65; Mayor of Jerusalem 1965–93; renowned for his energy, pragmatism, religious toleration, cultural enthusiasm, short temper, hands-on approach and prodigious fund-raising skills.

Morgan, (Elizabeth) Shirley Vaughan (b. 1924), daughter of the novelists Charles Morgan and Hilda Vaughan; helped IB to prepare the translation of *First Love* for publication. Became Marchioness of Anglesey after her marriage in October 1948 to Henry Paget, 7th Marquess of Anglesey (b. 1922); IB often visited the couple at Plas Newydd, their home on Anglesey.

Nabokov, Nicolas (1903–78), né Nikolay Dmitrievich, composer, teacher, writer and cultural administrator; cousin of the novelist Vladimir Nabokov. After the Russian Revolution, lived in the Crimea, Stuttgart, Berlin and Paris before settling in the US in 1933 (naturalised 1939). Professor of Composition, Peabody Conservatory of Music, Baltimore, 1943–5 and 1947–51; civilian

1 Letter of 16 June 1958.

cultural adviser, American Military Government, Berlin, 1945–7, helped set up the Russian Broadcast Unit of the Voice of America 1947; Director of Music, American Academy, Rome, 1950–1; Secretary-General of the (covertly CIA-funded) Congress for Cultural Freedom, based mainly in Paris and New York, 1951–63; later a cultural adviser in Berlin; organised many major cultural conferences and music festivals. Married to: (i) 1927–39 Princess (Knyazhna) Natalia Alexevna Shakhovskoya (1903–88); (ii) 1939–46 Constance Holladay (1917–2001); (iii) 1948–52 Patricia Page Blake (b. 1925); (iv) 1953–70 Marie-Claire Paulette Joséphine Brot (b. 1921); (v) from 1970 Dominique Cibiel (b. *c.*1945); all five wives attended his funeral. Close friend of Chip Bohlen and of IB, whom he met in 1943. In an obituary IB described him as 'Large-hearted, affectionate, honourable, gifted with sharp moral and political insight, and a well developed sense of the ridiculous, an irresistible source of torrential wit and fancy, immensely sociable, [...] one of the last and most attractive representatives of the pre-Revolutionary Russian liberal intelligentsia';[1] for another friend he was 'blessed by the gods with all the possible gifts but that of moderation'.[2] Works include *Old Friends and New Music* (memoirs, 1951) and the opera *Rasputin's End* (1959; libretto by Stephen Spender).

Newsome, Shiela (1913–2004), née Grant Duff, later Sokolov Grant; LMH PPE 1931–4; then foreign correspondent in Germany and Czechoslovakia; FRPS 1939–41, BBC Foreign Service 1941–4; married 1942–52 to Noel Francis Newsome (1906–76) and from 1952 to Micheal Sokolov (1923–98; changed his name to Sokolov Grant before the marriage), with whom she farmed in Cumberland, then in Ireland.

Pasternak, Boris Leonidovich (1890–1960), Russian poet, translator and novelist; eldest of the four children of the painter Leonid Pasternak and his wife Rosa, a concert pianist (who with their two daughters moved to Germany in 1921 and eventually settled in England); studied musical composition and philosophy before settling on poetry; turned to translation, particularly of Shakespeare, to escape the Soviet demand for realism in art; started his only major novel, *Dr Zhivago*, after the war and, failing to find a Soviet publisher, delivered it to Giangiacomo Feltrinelli's publishing firm, which published an Italian translation in 1957, an English version following a year later (although a Russian edition appeared in the West, it was banned in the Soviet Union until 1988); awarded the 1958 Nobel Prize for Literature but declined it after pressure from the Soviet Government and his expulsion from the Union of Soviet Writers. Lived in Moscow and in the writers' village at Peredelkino. Married: (i) 1922 Evgeniya Vladimirovna Lur´e; (ii) 1934 Zinaida Nikolaevna Neigauz; the character of Lara in *Dr Zhivago* is thought to be based on his mistress Olga Ivinskaya. IB met Pasternak several times in 1945 and was given an early version of part of *Dr Zhivago* (see also L1 593); he was entrusted with a complete text during his 1956 visit and read it overnight. IB admired Pasternak's literary genius but not his rejection of his Jewish heritage: 'Pasternak loathed being a Jew, he loathed it to a pathological degree. [...] I didn't respect him for that. I could see he

1 *The Times*, 15 April 1978, 16.
2 Alain Daniélou, *The Way to the Labyrinth*, trans. Marie-Claire Cournand (New York, 1987), 240.

just wanted to be a Russian hero; he'd be a blond [...] Sadko, a merchant of Novgorod – that's what he wanted to be.'[1]

Prichard ('Prich'), Ed(ward) Fretwell, Jr (1915–84), educated at Harvard, brilliant New Deal lawyer of huge girth; briefly shared a house with IB in Washington during the summer of 1943 while working for FDR on the US wartime economy (where he incurred the enmity of J. Edgar Hoover); on returning to Kentucky in 1945 he set up a successful legal practice and was widely seen as a future Governor of Kentucky. Accused (justly, as Prichard later admitted) in May 1949 of stuffing 254 ballots in a Senatorial election in Bourbon County, Kentucky, in November 1948, he was tried and found guilty in July 1949 but released on bail pending an appeal (the cost of which required substantial contributions from Prichard's friends); this appeal and others failed, so in July 1950 Prichard started a two-year prison sentence in the Federal Correctional Institution, Ashland, Kentucky, commuted to time served by the outgoing President Truman in December that year. Released, but with his legal and political career in ruins, Prichard struggled financially but gradually redeemed his reputation through public service, becoming a notable champion of higher education. Married 1947 Lucy Marshall Elliott (1919–2006).

Rowse, (Alfred) Leslie (1903–97), historian and poet, from a poor Cornish background, homosexual; Fellow of All Souls 1925–74; after failing to become Warden in 1952 he spent an increasingly large part of each year researching in the Huntington Library, California, and lecturing at US universities. A socialist when young, later conservative; notorious for his extraordinary egoism and the forceful expression of his numerous dislikes. Rowse appears to have had a (relatively) soft spot for IB – despite despising IB's lack of productivity – without realising that IB regarded him as a dangerous monomaniac. His many works include *The Use of History* (1946), *The England of Elizabeth* (1950), *The Expansion of Elizabethan England* (1955), *The Early Churchills* (1956), *The Later Churchills* (1958), *The Elizabethans and America* (1959), *All Souls and Appeasement* (1961).

Schapiro, Meyer (1904–96), art historian, artist, polymath and inspirational teacher, with particular interests in Romanesque sculpture and the art of the late nineteenth century and the early twentieth; born in Lithuania and emigrated to the US as a child; taught art history at Columbia University from 1928 (Associate Professor 1946–52, Professor 1952–65, University Professor 1965–73); married 1928 the paediatrician Dr Lillian Milgram (1902–2006). Works include *Vincent Van Gogh* (1951), *Paul Cézanne* (1952). See also L1 715–16.

Schlesinger, Arthur Meier, Jr (1917–2007), US historian and liberal political activist; son of the Harvard Professor of History Arthur Meier Schlesinger (whose name he adopted by replacing his original second name of Bancroft); Associate Professor of History, Harvard, 1946–54, Professor 1954–62 (taking leave of absence to support Adlai Stevenson's presidential candidacy in 1952 and 1956); Special Assistant to the President 1961–4; Albert Schweitzer Professor of the Humanities, City University of New York, 1966–95. Married 1940–70 to Marian Cannon (b. 1912) and from 1971 to Alexandra Temple Allan (b. c.1936), née Emmet. One of IB's closest friends:

1 MI Tape 31.

I met him in Washington in 1943. I liked him very much. I know exactly what's said against him. It's true that he's rather superficial, it's true that he's ambitious politically, in love with the Kennedys, [...] anti-Communist to a fanatical degree. Fundamentally he's an extremely nice man; the point is, he has a kind heart and is perfectly decent, upright and honest. What he is, is dazzled [...] by brilliance, by charm, by a court, by beautiful women, by wonderful dinner parties, by marvellous White House goings-on. Not by power. [...] He is simple, rather naive [...]. I remember he was married to a wife, a rather strong character, she was his first wife, [...] and he said to me, 'You know, I've got an awful house. When I come home, the ice cubes have melted, there's nothing in the fridge much, she's out, when she comes she's tired, God knows what I get to eat.' What he dreamt about was [...] luxury, exquisite meals served by a very beautiful wife, delightful, witty friends making agreeable conversation, cigars, a glass of wine, a very simple idea of gracious living.'[1]

Works include *The Vital Center* (1949), *The Age of Roosevelt* (three volumes, 1957–1960).

Sparrow, John Hanbury Angus (1906–92), classicist, barrister, prolific reviewer, bibliophile, homosexual; Fellow of All Souls 1929–52, then (1952–77) Warden; War Office 1941–50. As Warden, Sparrow did little for the academic standing of All Souls and his clashes with some of the Fellows produced an uneasy atmosphere; nevertheless IB remembered him in his prime as 'the best company in the world, extremely intelligent, able, amusing, independent, fearless, comically reactionary but delightful'.[2] Works include *Great Poetry* (1960). See also L1 716–17.

Tree, Mary Endicott ('Marietta'; 1917–91), née Peabody, daughter of an Episcopalian minister in New England; socialite and liberal political activist. Married first (1939–47) to Desmond Fitzgerald (1910–67); after her 1947 marriage to Ronald Tree (q.v.), moved to England to become chatelaine of Ditchley Park, a role created by her husband's first wife, Nancy. Returned to New York in 1949 after the sale of Ditchley, and became involved in Democratic Party politics, especially during the presidential elections unsuccessfully fought by her husband's friend Adlai Stevenson in 1952 and 1956 (her close political friendship with him later developed into an affair). Commission of Inter-Group Relations of New York City 1959–61; US representative on UN Human Rights Commission 1961–4, on UN Trusteeship Council 1964–5; member of U Thant's staff, UN Secretariat, 1966–7.

Tree, (Arthur) Ronald Lambert Field (1897–1976), Anglo-American; Conservative MP 1933–45. The mansion at Ditchley Park, near Oxford, which he and his first wife restored was frequently used as a venue for social and political gatherings, and as a country retreat for Churchill during the war (Chequers being considered vulnerable to bombing); Tree sold Ditchley in 1949 (after tax changes cut his income) and thereafter divided his time between properties in New York and (increasingly) Barbados. A bisexual, married first (1920–47) to Nancy Perkins

---

1 MI Tape 23.
2 To Joe Alsop, 30 September 1981.

Field (1897–1994; later Lancaster), then from 1947 to Marietta Fitzgerald (see Tree, Mary).

Weizmann, Chaim (1874–1952), chemist and statesman; born near Pinsk (now in Belarus) but naturalised British in 1910; a Zionist from his student days who played a major role in securing the Balfour Declaration in 1917; President, Zionist Organization (and from 1929 of the Jewish Agency for Palestine) 1921–1931, 1935–46; played a major role in the founding of the Hebrew University in Jerusalem in 1925 and in its later governance; founded the Daniel Sieff Research Institute (later the Weizmann Institute of Science) at Rehovot, Palestine, 1934; President of the Provisional Council of the State of Israel 1948–9; first President of Israel from 1949. For IB 'the greatest man I ever knew very well'.[1] Married 1906 Vera Chatzman (see Weizmann, Vera). See also L1 721; subject of a study in PI.

Weizmann, Vera (1881–1966), née Chatzman, Russian-born paediatrician, married 1906 Chaim Weizmann (q.v.), naturalised British 1910; co-founder 1920 with Rebecca Sieff and others of the Women's International Zionist Organization (WIZO) and active in Palestinian/Israeli charitable causes, even though her main priority was the support of her husband. In widowhood a leading force in the work of the Weizmann Archive at Rehovot. Her enjoyment of IB's company was not fully reciprocated:

> The point about her was she was not interested in Jews in general. [...] she fell in love with him physically, as a man; she took no interest in Zionism as such. [...] the Zionists didn't like her. It was clear that she looked down on them. [...] what she liked was upper-class English persons whom the political efforts of Weizmann brought her in touch with. They admired him but couldn't bear her; in fact she was not a success, but she didn't know that. [...] She was a very artificial, rather false lady – false character in many ways – snobbish, and wanted to show off, and not very sincere – and she was very much disliked in Israel to begin with, until he died. Then she became Lenin's widow, then she became grand and so on, and everyone looked up to her. [...] She was like a Russian Colonel's lady in Paris, with a little dog and a new book from the lending library every week.[2]

White, Morton Gabriel (b. 1917), philosopher and historian of ideas. Assistant Professor of Philosophy, Pennsylvania, 1946–8; Assistant Professor of Philosophy, Harvard, 1948–50, Associate Professor 1950–3, Professor 1953–70. Married 1940 Lucia Perry (1909–96). Works include *Social Thought in America* (1949), *The Age of Analysis* (1955), *Toward Reunion in Philosophy* (1956), *Religion, Politics and the Higher Learning* (1959). A long-planned joint work with IB on the philosophy of history never materialised (mainly because of IB's non-availability).

Wilson, Edmund (1895–1972), journalist and influential critic of literature in several languages. IB remembered meeting in 1946 'a thickset, red-faced, pot-bellied figure' who spoke 'as if ideas jostled and thrashed about inside him, getting in each other's way as they struggled to emerge, which made for short bursts,

1 To Alice James, 9 December 1952.
2 MI Tape 19.

emitted staccato, interspersed with gentle, low-voiced, legato passages'.
Wilson's fascinating conversation, wide cultural knowledge, admirable moral
outlook and sensitive understanding of Russian literature appealed to IB, who
commented after Wilson's death: 'His judgements were often erratic, and he
was prey to delusions, but his humanity and integrity were total.'[1] A heavy
drinker and notorious womaniser, he was married to: (i) 1923–30 Mary Blair
(c. 1896–1947); (ii) 1930–2 Margaret Canby (1895–1932), née Waterman; (iii)
1938–46 the novelist and critic Mary Therese McCarthy (1912–89); (iv) from
1946 Helene-Marthe ('Elena') Thornton (1906–79), née Mumm. Works include
Memoirs of Hecate County (1946), *Europe without Baedeker* (1947), *Classics and
Commercials* (1950), *The Shores of Light* (1953), *The Scrolls from the Dead Sea*
(1955), *Red, Black, Blond and Olive* (1956), *A Piece of My Mind* (1956), *The American
Earthquake* (1958), *Apologies to the Iroquois* (1960).

1 'Edmund Wilson at Oxford', PI2 172, 182.

INDEX OF CORRESPONDENTS
AND SOURCES

The source of a correspondent's letters is given in square brackets after his or her name; or, when only one letter is in question, after the page reference for that letter. Where letters for a given correspondent come from more than one source, the main source is given after the name (unless it is the Isaiah Berlin Papers in the Bodleian Library in Oxford), and the subsidiary source after the relevant page reference(s). Where no source is given, (a copy of) the letter was supplied by the correspondent in question.

Where the top copy and a carbon of a letter are both available, the source of the top copy is given but not that of the carbon. Where we have had to rely on a carbon copy, we insert '[carbon]' in the text after the date of the letter, and the relevant reference is given here. Information on the whereabouts of originals of which we have seen only carbon copies would be gratefully received. Note that in some cases top copies are in the Bodleian: for example, letters from IB to his parents came into his possession after his mother's death, and letters to some correspondents who predeceased him (for instance, Rowland Burdon-Muller and Anna Kallin) were returned to him on their deaths.

Specific archival references for individual items (which are in any case subject to alteration when recataloguing occurs) are not given except for items in the Isaiah Berlin Papers (but see under NA below) and when the archive required this to be done: when the omitted references are not available online (though they increasingly are), they can usually be readily ascertained from the archive in question.

Page references for letters *to* IB are in italics. References are provided *in situ* where letters between other correspondents, or other archival documents, are quoted in the notes; here, too, lack of a source after a quotation from a letter indicates that the recipient provided the letter.

Abbreviations used in this index

[123/4]	Oxford, Bodleian Library, MS. Berlin (by shelfmark/folio)
BBC	BBC Written Archives, Caversham
BL	British Library
Beinecke	Beinecke Library, Yale
Bodleian	Oxford, Bodleian Library
CT	connective tissue (editorial commentary)
Dictabelt	Dictabelt (Dictaphone) recording made by IB for a typist
Houghton	Houghton Library, Harvard
Hoover	Hoover Institution, Stanford University, California
King's	King's College, Cambridge
LOC	Library of Congress
NA	National Archives, Kew, London (followed by the reference under which the cited document is catalogued, e.g. FO 953/144)
NYPL	New York Public Library
OUA	Oxford University Archives
OUP	Oxford University Press

1 By permission of the Master and Fellows of St John's College, Cambridge.

GENERAL INDEX

References in italics are to pages where a note provides basic biographical information on a person. An asterisk preceding a name indicates an entry in the Glossary. Works by IB appear under their titles, works by others under their authors' names. The Chronology is not indexed.

This print (artist unkown), published by Charles Magnus in 1885, was one of many produced in anticipation of the erection (in 1886), on Bedloe's Island in New York Harbour, of Frédéric Auguste Bartholdi's Statue of Liberty, officially known as 'Liberty Enlightening the World' – a serendipitously Berlinian title

SUPPLEMENTARY NOTE

The information given here came to our attention too late for it to be included in its proper place.

p. 718 Almost certainly Donald Bradley Somervell (1889–1960), Baron Somervell of Harrow 1954, barrister and Conservative politician; Attorney-General 1936–45; Lord Justice of Appeal 1964–54; Lord of Appeal in Ordinary 1954–60. Elected a Fellow of All Souls in 1912, he was at the time of this letter dying of cancer.